Fodor's

Spain

The complete guide, thoroughly up-to-date

Packed with details that will make your trip

The must-see sights, off and on the beaten path

What to see, what to skip

Mix-and-match vacation itineraries

City strolls, countryside adventures

Smart lodging and dining options

Essential local do's and taboos

Transportation tips, distances and directions

Key contacts, savvy travel tips

When to go, what to pack

Clear, accurate, easy-to-use maps

Books to read, films to watch, background essays

Fodor's Travel Publications, Inc.
New York • Toronto • London • Sydney • Auckland
www.fodors.com

Fodor's Spain

EDITOR: Christine Cipriani

Editorial Contributors: David Brown, Mark Little, Helayne Schiff, M. T. Schwartzman (Gold Guide editor), George Semler, Katherine Semler, Annie Ward

Editorial Production: Melissa Klurman

Maps: David Lindroth, *cartographer*; Steven Amsterdam, *map editor*

Design: Fabrizio La Rocca, *creative director*; Guido Caroti, *associate art director*; Jolie Novak, *photo editor*

Production/Manufacturing: Mike Costa

Cover Photograph: Harry Gruyaert/Magnum

Copyright

Special Sales

Fodor's Travel Publications are available at special discounts for bulk purchases for sales promotions or premiums. Special editions, including personalized covers, excerpts of existing guides, and corporate imprints, can be created in large quantities for special needs. For more information, contact your local bookseller or write to Special Markets, Fodor's Travel Publications, 201 East 50th Street, New York, NY 10022. Inquiries from Canada should be directed to your local Canadian bookseller or sent to Random House of Canada, Ltd., Marketing Department, 2775 Matheson Boulevard East, Mississauga, Ontario L4W 4P7. Inquiries from the United Kingdom should be sent to Fodor's Travel Publications, 20 Vauxhall Bridge Road, London SW1V 2SA, England.

PRINTED IN THE UNITED STATES OF AMERICA

10 9 8 7 6 5 4 3 2 1

CONTENTS

ON THE ROAD WITH FODOR'S

WHEN I PLAN A VACATION, the first thing I do is cast around among my friends and colleagues to find someone who's just been where I'm going. That's because there's no substitute for a recommendation from a good friend who knows your tastes, your budget, and your circumstances, someone who's just been there. Unfortunately, such friends are few and far between. So it's nice to know that there's *Fodor's Spain '99*.

In the first place, this book won't stay home when you hit the road. It will accompany you every step of the way, steering you away from wrong turns and wrong choices and never expecting a thing in return. It includes a wonderful, full-color map from Rand McNally, the world's largest commercial mapmaker. Most important of all, it's written and assiduously updated by the kind of people you *would* hit up for travel tips if you knew them. They're as choosy as your pickiest friend, except they've probably seen a lot more of Spain. In these pages, they don't send you chasing down every town and sight in Spain but have instead selected the best ones, the ones that are worthy of your time and money. To make it easy for you to put it all together in the time you have, they've created short, medium, and long itineraries and, in cities, neighborhood walks that you can mix and match in a snap. Just tear out the map at the perforation, and join us on the road in Spain. Will this be the vacation of your dreams? We hope so.

About Our Writers

Our success in helping to make your trip the best of all possible vacations is a credit to the hard work of our extraordinary writers and editors.

Mark Little was born in New York, but he has lived in southern Spain since age 10. For 15 years he was editor of *Lookout* magazine, an English-language glossy aimed at Spain's large expatriate community. He is now a freelance writer, specializing in Spanish travel, food, and wine. Little lives in Mijas with his Spanish wife and their three children.

Californian journalist **Deborah Luhrman** has visited many parts of the globe both as a travel writer and as press attaché for the Madrid-based World Tourism Organization, where she helps other journalists write about tourism and assists tourism ministries in dealing with the media. She has called Spain home for the past nine years and loves it, but still finds time for adventures in the likes of Egypt, China, and Germany.

Born and educated in the United States, writer, journalist, and translator **George Semler** has lived in Spain for the last 25 years. During that time he has published works on Spain, Catalonia, the Pyrenees, France, North Africa, and the Mediterranean region for the *International Herald Tribune,* the *Los Angeles Times, Forbes,* and *Saveur,* among other publications. When not hiking, skiing, playing hockey, or fly-fishing in the streams of the Pyrenees, he finds time to contribute to Fodor's guides, write poetry, and work on a magnum opus about the Pyrenees. He is also the author of books on Madrid and Barcelona.

Raised in Madrid, San Sebastián, and Barcelona, **Katherine Semler** attended preschool in Euskera (the Basque language), kindergarten in Spanish, elementary school in French, and secondary school in the United States in English. She went on to earn a B.A. in French and Russian literature at Vassar and an M.A. in French and Catalan literature at Dartmouth. (We are not making this up.) Married to singer-songwriter Sam Lardner, she now lives in Barcelona.

A native of Kansas City, **Annie Ward** holds a B.A. in English literature from the University of California–Los Angeles and an M.F.A. in screenwriting from the American Film Institute. Her first short film, *Strange Habit,* was the grand jury's selection for Best Film at the 1996 Aspen Film Festival. She lived in Spain for several years, where she taught screenwriting at the American Center of Barcelona, and now lives in Sofia, Bulgaria, where she is a reporter for the Bulgarian English-language newspaper *The Sofia Independent*. She has edited English translations of Bulgarian children's books, and is completing a novel set in both Spain and Bulgaria.

We'd also like to thank Pilar Vico and Natalia Zapatero at the Tourist Office of Spain, New York, for their kind assistance.

New This Year

Morocco now has a chapter of its own, complete with 3-, 5-, and 10-day driving tours of the country's highlights. We've doubled our coverage of this fascinating country, adding Ouarzazate, Zagora, Essaouira, Volubilis, the Merzouga dunes, and several other towns and sights. A Close-Up on Frank Gehry's new Guggenheim Museum explores the renaissance taking place in Bilbao; and wine lovers will appreciate our new section on La Rioja, Spain's wine country.

Connections

We're pleased that the American Society of Travel Agents continues to endorse Fodor's as its guidebook of choice. ASTA is the world's largest and most influential travel trade association, operating in more than 170 countries, with 27,000 members pledged to adhere to a strict code of ethics reflecting the Society's motto, "Integrity in Travel." ASTA shares Fodor's devotion to providing smart, honest travel information and advice to travelers, and we've long recommended that our readers—even those who have guidebooks and traveling friends—consult ASTA member agents for the experience and professionalism they bring to your vacation planning.

On Fodor's Web site (www.fodors.com), check out the new Resource Center, an online companion to the Gold Guide chapter of this book, complete with useful hot links to related sites. In our forums, you can also get lively advice from other travelers and more great tips from Fodor's experts worldwide.

How to Use This Book

Organization

Up front is the **Gold Guide,** an easy-to-use section arranged alphabetically by topic. Under each listing you'll find tips and information that will help you accomplish what you need to in Spain. You'll also find addresses and telephone numbers of organizations and companies that offer destination-related services and detailed information and publications.

The first chapter in the guide, Destination: Spain helps get you in the mood for your trip. New and Noteworthy cues you in on trends and happenings, What's Where gets you oriented, Pleasures and Pastimes describes the activities and sights that make Spain unique, Great Itineraries lays out a selection of complete trips, Fodor's Choice showcases our top picks, and Festivals and Seasonal Events alerts you to special events you'll want to seek out.

Chapters in *Fodor's Spain '99* are arranged by city or region, including two island chapters and one on Morocco. Each city chapter begins with Exploring information, which is divided into neighborhood sections; each recommends a walking or driving tour and lists sights in alphabetical order. Each regional chapter is divided by geographical area; within each area, towns are covered in logical geographical order, and attractive stretches of road and minor points of interest between them are indicated by the designation *En Route*. And within town sections, all restaurants and lodgings are grouped.

To help you decide what to visit in the time you have, all chapters begin with our recommended itineraries. The A to Z section that ends all chapters covers getting there and getting around. It also provides helpful contacts and resources.

At the end of the book you'll find Portraits of Spain—an exposé on the cultural divide between Madrid and Barcelona, and an appetizing profile of Spanish food and wine—followed by suggestions for pretrip research, from recommended reading and audiotapes to films that use Spain as a backdrop.

Icons and Symbols

★ Our special recommendations
✕ Restaurant
🏠 Lodging establishment
✕🏠 Lodging establishment whose restaurant warrants a special trip
🐤 Good for kids (rubber duck)
☞ Sends you to another section of the guide for more information
✉ Address
☎ Telephone number
🕐 Opening and closing times

Admission prices (those we give apply to adults; substantially reduced fees are almost always available for children, students, and senior citizens)

Numbers in white and black circles ③ ❸ that appear on the maps, in the margins, and within the tours correspond to one another.

Dining and Lodging

The restaurants and lodgings we list are the cream of the crop in each price range. Price charts appear in the Pleasures and Pastimes section that follows each chapter introduction.

Hotel Facilities

We always list the facilities that are available—but we don't specify whether you'll be charged extra to use them: When pricing accommodations, always ask what's included. In addition, assume that all rooms have private baths unless noted otherwise. In addition, when you book a room, be sure to mention if you have a disability or are traveling with children, if you prefer a private bath or a certain type of bed, or if you have specific dietary needs or other concerns.

Assume that hotels operate on the **European Plan** (EP, with no meals) unless we specify that they use the **Continental Plan** (CP, with a Continental breakfast daily), **Modified American Plan** (MAP, with breakfast and dinner daily), or the **Full American Plan** (FAP, with all meals).

Restaurant Reservations and Dress Codes

Reservations are always a good idea; we mention them only when they're essential or are not accepted. Book as far ahead as you can, and reconfirm as soon as you arrive. Unless otherwise noted, the restaurants listed are open daily for lunch and dinner. We mention dress only when men are required to wear a jacket or a jacket and tie. Look for an overview of local dining-out habits in the Gold Guide and in the Pleasures and Pastimes section that follows each chapter introduction.

Credit Cards

The following abbreviations are used: **AE**, American Express; **DC**, Diners Club; **MC**, MasterCard; and **V**, Visa.

Don't Forget to Write

You can use this book in the confidence that all prices and opening times are based on information supplied to us at press time; Fodor's cannot accept responsibility for any errors. Time inevitably brings changes, so always confirm information when it matters—especially if you're making a detour to visit a specific place.

Were the restaurants we recommended as described? Did our hotel picks exceed your expectations? Did you find a museum we recommended a waste of time? Keeping a travel guide fresh and up-to-date is a big job, and we welcome your feedback, positive *and* negative. If you have complaints, we'll look into them and revise our entries when the facts warrant it. If you've discovered a special place that we haven't included, we'll pass the information along to our correspondents and have them check it out. So send us your thoughts via e-mail at editors@fodors.com (specifying the name of the book on the subject line) or on paper in care of the Spain editor at Fodor's, 201 East 50th Street, New York, New York 10022. In the meantime, have a wonderful trip!

Karen Cure
Editorial Director

Spain

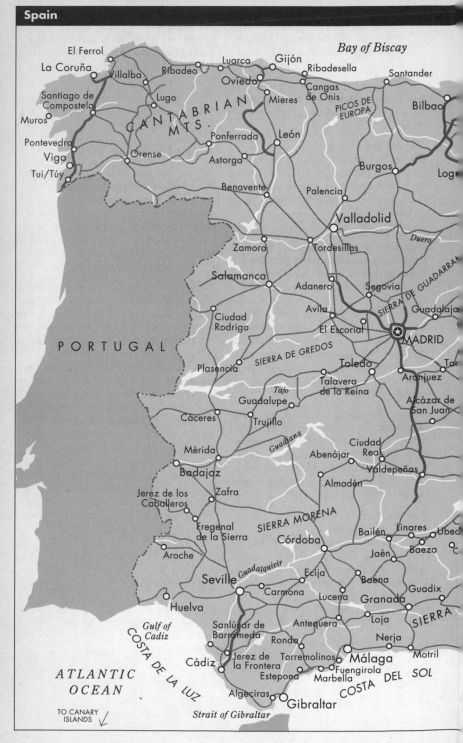

Bay of Biscay

El Ferrol
La Coruña
Villalba
Ribadeo
Luarca
Gijón
Ribadesella
Santander
Oviedo
Cangas de Onis
PICOS DE EUROPA
Bilbao
Santiago de Compostela
Lugo
Mieres
CANTABRIAN MTS.
Muros
Ponferrada
León
Burgos
Log
Pontevedra
Orense
Astorga
Vigo
Tui/Túy
Benavente
Palencia
Valladolid
Duero
Zamora
Tordesillas
Salamanca
Adanero
Segovia
SIERRA DE GUADARRA
Ciudad Rodrigo
Avila
Guadalaja
El Escorial
MADRID
PORTUGAL
SIERRA DE GREDOS
Toledo
Tar
Plasencia
Talavera de la Reina
Aranjuez
Tajo
Guadalupe
Alcázar de San Juan
Cáceres
Trujillo
Mérida
Guadiana
Ciudad Real
Badajoz
Abenójar
Valdepeñas
Jerez de los Caballeros
Zafra
Almadén
Fregenal de la Sierra
SIERRA MORENA
Córdoba
Bailén
Linares
Ubed
Aroche
Jaén
Baeza
C.
Seville
Guadalquivir
Ecija
Baena
Guadix
Carmona
Lucena
Granada
Huelva
Antequera
Loja
SIERRA
Gulf of Cadiz
Sanlúcar de Barrameda
Ronda
Nerja
COSTA DE LA LUZ
Cádiz
Jerez de la Frontera
Torremolinos
Málaga
Motril
ATLANTIC OCEAN
Estepona
Fuengirola
Marbella
COSTA DEL SOL
Algeciras
Gibraltar
TO CANARY ISLANDS
Strait of Gibraltar

Autonomous Regions and Provinces

Bay of Biscay

La Coruña
Gijón
Oviedo
Santander
VIZCAYA

LA CORUÑA
LUGO
ASTURIAS
CANTABRIA

Santiago de
Compostela
Lugo
Bilbao

Lugo

GALICIA
León
BURGOS

Pontevedra
LEON
Burgos
LA

PONTEVEDRA
PALENCIA
Palencia

Orense
ORENSE
ZAMORA
Valladolid

Zamora
VALLADOLID
Duero

CASTILLA -Y LEON

Salamanca
SEGOVIA

SALAMANCA
Segovia
GU

AVILA
Guadalajara

Avila
MADRID

P O R T U G A L
MADRID

Toledo
Aranjuez

CACERES
Tajo
TOLEDO

Cáceres
Trujillo
CASTILLA - LA MAN

EXTREMADURA
Alcázar

Mérida
Guadiana
CIUDAD REAL

Badajoz
Ciudad
Real
Valdepeñas

BADAJOZ

CORDOBA
JAEN

Córdoba
Jaén

HUELVA
Guadalquivir
ANDALUCIA

SEVILLA
Granada

Huelva
Seville
GRANADA

Jerez
Antequera

Cádiz
MALAGA
Málaga

*ATLANTIC
OCEAN*
CADIZ
COSTA DEL SOL

Gibraltar

COSTA DE LA LUZ

SMART TRAVEL TIPS A TO Z

Basic Information on Traveling in Spain, Savvy Tips to Make Your Trip a Breeze, and Companies and Organizations to Contact

AIR TRAVEL

MAJOR AIRLINE OR LOW-COST CARRIER?

Most people choose a flight based on price, although there are other issues to consider. Major airlines offer the greatest number of departures; smaller airlines—including regional, low-cost, and no-frill airlines—usually have a more limited number of flights daily. Major airlines have frequent-flyer partners, which allow you to credit mileage earned on one airline to your account with another. Low-cost airlines offer a definite price advantage and fewer restrictions, such as advance-purchase requirements. Safety-wise, low-cost carriers as a group have a good history, but **check the safety record before booking** any low-cost carrier; call the Federal Aviation Administration's Consumer Hotline (☞ Airline Complaints, *below*).

American, US Airways, and Air Europa travel to Madrid; Continental, Delta, Iberia, and TWA travel to Madrid and Barcelona. For flights from New York to the Canary Islands, *see* Chapter 15.

➤ NONSTOP FROM NORTH AMERICA: AeroMexico (☎ 800/237–6639). **Air Europa** (☎ 888/238–7672). **American** (☎ 800/433–7300). **Continental** (☎ 800/231–0856). **Delta** (☎ 800/221–1212). **Iberia** (☎ 800/772–4642). **Spanair** (☎ 888/545–5757). **TWA** (☎ 800/892–4141). **US Airways** (☎ 800/428–4322).

➤ FROM THE U.K.: **British Airways** (☎ 0345/222–111). **Iberia** (☎ 0171/830–0011).

GET THE LOWEST FARE

The least-expensive airfares to Spain are priced for round-trip travel. Major airlines usually require that you **book far in advance and stay at least 7 days** and no more than 30 to get the lowest fares. Ask about "ultrasaver" fares, which are the cheapest; they must be booked 90 days in advance and are nonrefundable. A little more expensive are "supersaver" fares, which require only a 30-day advance purchase. Remember that penalties for refunds or scheduling changes are stiffer for international tickets, usually about $150. International flights are also sensitive to the season: **plan to fly in the off season** for the cheapest fares. If your destination or home city has more than one gateway, **compare prices to and from different airports.** Also price flights scheduled for off-peak hours, which may be significantly less expensive.

To save money on flights from the United Kingdom and back, **look into an APEX or Super-PEX ticket.** APEX tickets must be booked in advance and have certain restrictions. Super-PEX tickets can be purchased at the airport on the day of departure—subject to availability.

DISCOUNT PASSES

If you buy a round-trip transatlantic ticket on **Iberia** (☞ *above*), you might want to purchase a Visit Spain pass, good for four domestic flights during your trip. It must be purchased before you arrive in Spain, all flights must be booked in advance, and the cost is $260, or $350 if you want to include flights to the Canary Islands (prices are $20 to $50 less if you travel during the low season, between October 1 and June 14).

On certain days of the week, Iberia also offers minifares, which can save you 40% on domestic flights. Tickets must be purchased in advance, and you must stay over Saturday night (☞ Discounts, *below*).

DON'T STOP UNLESS YOU MUST

When you book, **look for nonstop flights** and **remember that "direct" flights stop at least once.** International flights on a country's flag carrier are almost always nonstop; U.S. airlines often fly direct. Try to **avoid connecting flights,** which require a change of plane. Two airlines may jointly operate a connecting flight, so ask if your airline operates every segment—you may find that your preferred carrier flies you only part of the way.

USE AN AGENT

Travel agents, especially those who specialize in finding the lowest fares (☞ Discounts & Deals, *below*), can be especially helpful when booking a plane ticket. When you're quoted a price, **ask your agent if the price is likely to get any lower.** Good agents know the seasonal fluctuations of airfares and can usually anticipate a sale or fare war. However, waiting can be risky: the fare might go *up* as seats become scarce, and you may wait so long that your preferred flight sells out. A wait-and-see strategy works best if your plans are flexible, but if you must arrive and depart on certain dates, don't delay.

CHECK WITH CONSOLIDATORS

Consolidators buy tickets for scheduled flights at reduced rates from the airlines, then sell them at prices that beat the best fare available directly from the airlines, usually without advance restrictions. Sometimes you can even get your money back if you need to return the ticket. Carefully read the fine print detailing penalties for changes and cancellations, and **confirm your consolidator reservation with the airline.**

➤ CHARTERS: **Air Comet** (☎ 615/373–7904 or 800/234–1700). **Air Europa** (contact Spanish Heritage, ☎ 718/244–6017, 718/544–2752, or 800/221–2580). **Oasis International** (Club Vacations, ☎ 615/373–7904 or 800/234–1700). **Toto Tours International** (☎ 718/237–2312 or 800/676–7843).

➤ CONSOLIDATORS: **United States Air Consolidators Association** (✉ 925 L St., Suite 220, Sacramento, CA 95814, ☎ 916/441–4166, FAX 916/441–3520).

COMPLAIN IF NECESSARY

If your baggage goes astray or your flight goes awry, complain right away. Most carriers require that you file a claim immediately.

➤ AIRLINE COMPLAINTS: **U.S. Department of Transportation, Aviation Consumer Protection Division** (✉ C-75, Washington, DC 20590, ☎ 202/366–2220). **Federal Aviation Administration (FAA) Consumer Hotline** (☎ 800/322–7873).

WITHIN SPAIN

Iberia and its sister carrier, Aviaco, are the main airlines offering domestic service. Two independent airlines, Air Europa and Spanair, offer a number of domestic routes at lower prices.

➤ CARRIERS: **Iberia** (☎ 91/329–4353). **Aviaco** (☎ 91/554–3600). **Air Europa** (☎ 91/540–6000 or 91/305–8159). **Spanair** (☎ 91/393–6740).

AIRPORTS

All transatlantic flights arriving in Spain from the United States and Canada pass through Madrid's Barajas airport. The country's other major gateway is Barcelona's El Prat de Llobregat.

Flying time is seven hours from New York and 14½ hours from Los Angeles.

➤ AIRPORT INFORMATION: Madrid: **Barajas airport** (☎ 91/305–8343). Barcelona:**El Prat de Llobregat** (☎ 93/298–3838).

BUS TRAVEL

An array of private companies operate Spain's buses, providing service that ranges from knee-crunchingly basic to luxurious. Some buses have televisions and free drinks, and many offer tours (easily arranged through your hotel) in English. Fares are lower than the corresponding train fares. If you want to reach a town not served by train, you can be sure a bus will go there. Spanish towns don't usually have a central bus depot, so ask at the tourist office where to pick up a bus to your destination. There

THE GOLD GUIDE / SMART TRAVEL TIPS

are depots in Madrid, but some of the companies are expected to move to a new terminal. Call ahead.

➤ FROM THE U.K.: **Eurolines/National Express** (☎ 0171/730–0202).

➤ TOURS WITHIN SPAIN: **Julià Tours** (✉ Gran Vía 68, Madrid, ☎ 91/571–5300). **Pullmantur** (✉ Plaza de Oriente 8, Madrid, ☎ 91/541–1805). **Marsans** (✉ Gran Vía 59, Madrid, ☎ 91/547–7300).

➤ COMMUTER BUS SERVICE WITHIN SPAIN: **Enatcar** (✉ C/ Canarias 17, Madrid, ☎ 91/527–9927. **Autored** (✉ C/ Fernandez Shaw 1, Madrid, ☎ 91/551–7200. **Continental Auto** (✉ C/ Alenza 20, Madrid, ☎ 91/533–0400. **Sepulvedana** (✉ C/ Palos de la Frontera 16, Madrid, ☎ 91/530–4800).

BUSINESS HOURS

Banks are generally open weekdays 8:30–2, Saturday 8:30–1, but in the summer most banks close at 1 PM weekdays and do not open on Saturday. Currency exchanges at airports and train stations stay open later. Traveler's checks can also be cashed at El Corte Inglés department stores until 9 PM.

Most museums are open from 9:30 to 2 and from 4 to 7 and are closed one day a week, usually Monday; but opening hours vary widely, so check before you set off. A few large museums, such as Madrid's Prado and Reina Sofía and Barcelona's Picasso Museum, stay open all day.

When planning a shopping day in Spain, **keep in mind that almost all shops close at midday** for at least three hours, except for the department-store chain El Corte Inglés. Stores are generally open from 10 to 1:30 and from 5 to 8. Shops are closed all day Sunday, and in Madrid and several other places they are also closed Saturday afternoon.

CAMPING

Camping in Spain is not a wilderness experience. There are more than 500 campgrounds, and many of them have excellent facilities, including hot showers, restaurants, swimming pools, tennis courts, and even night-clubs. But in summer, especially in August, be aware that **the best campgrounds are filled with Spanish families who move in with their entire households:** pets, grandparents, even the kitchen sink and stove! You can pick up an official listing of all Spanish campgrounds at the tourist office, or at the main post office in Madrid.

CAR RENTAL

Rates in Madrid begin at $38 a day and $132 a week for an economy car with air conditioning, a manual transmission, and unlimited mileage. This does not include the tax on car rentals, which is 16%.

➤ MAJOR AGENCIES: **Budget** (☎ 800/527–0700; 0800/181181 in the U.K.). **Dollar** (☎ 800/800–4000; 0990/565656 in the U.K., where it's known as Eurodollar). **Hertz** (☎ 800/654–3001; 800/263–0600 in Canada; 0345/555888 in the U.K.). **National InterRent** (Europcar InterRent, ☎ 800/227–3876; 0345/222525 in the U.K.).

➤ LOCAL AGENCIES: **ATESA** (✉ Infante Mercedes 90, Madrid, ☎ 91/571–1931; ✉ Plaza Carmen Benítez 7, Seville, ☎ 95/441–9712).

NEED INSURANCE?

When driving a rented car you are generally responsible for any damage to or loss of the vehicle. Before you rent, **see what coverage you already have** under the terms of your personal auto-insurance policy and credit cards.

Collision policies that car-rental companies sell for European rentals typically do not cover stolen vehicles. Before you buy additional coverage for theft, find out if your credit card or personal auto insurance will cover the loss.

BEWARE SURCHARGES

Before you pick up a car in one city and leave it in another, **ask about drop-off charges or one-way service fees,** which can be substantial. Note, too, that some rental agencies charge extra if you return the car before the time specified on your contract. To avoid a hefty refueling fee, **fill the tank just before you turn in the car,** but be aware that gas stations near the rental outlet may overcharge.

MEET THE REQUIREMENTS

Your own driver's license is valid in Spain, but you may want to get an International Driver's Permit for extra assurance; it's available from the American or Canadian automobile association, or, in the United Kingdom, from the Automobile Association or Royal Automobile Club.

CAR TRAVEL

Driving is the best way to see rural areas and get off the beaten track. Roads are classified as follows: A for *autopista* (toll road or *peaje*); N for *nacional* (main roads that are either divided highways or two lanes); and C for *comarcal* (local roads that crisscross the countryside).

Spain's highway system now includes some 6,000 km (3,600 mi) of superhighways. Still, you'll find some stretches of major national highways that are two lanes wide, where traffic often backs up behind heavy trucks. Autopista tolls are steep.

Most Spanish cities have notoriously long morning and evening rush hours that can try any driver's patience. Traffic jams (*atascos*) are especially bad in and around Barcelona and Madrid. If possible, it's best to **avoid the morning rush hour, which can last until noon, and the evening rush hour, which runs from 7 PM to 9 PM.**

Driving is on the right, and horns are banned in cities, but that doesn't keep Spaniards from blasting away. Children under 10 may not ride in the front seat, and seat belts are compulsory everywhere. Speed limits are 60 kph (37 mph) in cities, 100 kph (62 mph) on N roads, 120 kph (74 mph) on the autopista, and 90 kph (56 mph) unless otherwise signposted on other roads.

Gas stations are plentiful. Prices, decontrolled in 1993, were 112 ptas. a liter for *normal* (regular; 92 octane) and 117 ptas. a liter for *super* (97 octane) at press time. Some small-town service stations do not sell unleaded gas. Credit cards are widely accepted, especially along main routes.

The large car-rental companies, Hertz and Avis, have 24-hour breakdown service. If you belong to an automobile club (AAA, CAA, or AA), you can get help from the Spanish auto club, RACE.

➤ AUTO CLUBS: In the United States: **American Automobile Association** (☎ 800/564–6222). In the United Kingdom: **Automobile Association** (AA, ☎ 0990/500–600), **Royal Automobile Club** (RAC, ☎ 0990/722–722 membership; 0345/121–345 insurance). In Spain: **RACE** (✉ José Abascal 10, Madrid, ☎ 91/447–3200; 91/593–3333 for emergency assistance).

CHILDREN & TRAVEL

CHILDREN IN SPAIN

Spaniards love children. You'll see children accompanying their parents everywhere, including bars and restaurants, so bringing yours along on your trip should not be a problem. Shopkeepers will shower your child with *caramelos* (sweets), and even the coldest waiters tend to be friendlier when you have a youngster with you. But although you won't be shunted into a remote corner when you bring kids into a Spanish restaurant, **you won't find high chairs or special children's menus.** Children are expected to eat what their parents do, and it is perfectly acceptable to ask for an extra plate and share your food. Museum admissions and bus and metro rides are generally free for children up to age five. Be prepared for late bedtimes—especially in summer; it's surprisingly common to see under-fives playing cheerfully outdoors until midnight. Disposable diapers (*pañales*), formula (*papillas*), and bottled baby foods are readily available at supermarkets and pharmacies.

FLYING

As a general rule, infants under age two not occupying a seat fly at greatly reduced fares and occasionally for free. If your child is two or older, **ask about children's airfares.**

The adult baggage allowance generally applies to children paying half or more of the adult fare. When booking, **ask about carry-on allowances**

THE GOLD GUIDE / SMART TRAVEL TIPS

for those traveling with infants. In general, for babies charged 10% of the adult fare you are allowed one carry-on bag and a collapsible stroller, which may have to be checked; you may be limited to less if the flight is full.

The FAA recommends using safety seats aloft for children weighing less than 40 pounds. Airlines, however, can set their own policies: U.S. carriers allow FAA-approved models but usually require that you buy a ticket, even if your child would otherwise ride free, since the safety seats must be strapped into regular seats. Airline rules vary regarding their use, so it's important to **check your airline's policy about using safety seats during takeoff and landing.** Safety seats cannot obstruct any of the other passengers in the row, so get an appropriate seat assignment as early as possible.

When making your reservation, **request children's meals or a free-standing bassinet** if you need them; the latter are available only to those seated at the bulkhead, where there's enough legroom. Remember, however, that bulkhead seats may not have their own overhead bins, and there's no storage space in front of you—a major inconvenience.

CONSUMER PROTECTION TIPS

Whenever possible, **pay with a major credit card** so you can cancel payment if there's a problem, as long as you can provide documentation. This is a good practice whether you're buying travel arrangements before your trip or shopping in your destination.

➤ LOCAL BBBs: **Council of Better Business Bureaus** (✉ 4200 Wilson Blvd., Suite 800, Arlington, VA 22203, ☎ 703/276–0100, FAX 703/525–8277).

CUSTOMS & DUTIES

When shopping, **keep receipts** for all of your purchases. Upon reentering the country, **be ready to show customs officials what you've bought.** If you feel a duty is incorrect, appeal the assessment. If you object to the way your clearance was handled, get the inspector's badge number. In either case, first ask to see a supervisor, then write to the port director at the address listed on your receipt. Send a copy of the receipt and other appropriate documentation. If you still don't get satisfaction you can take your case to customs headquarters in Washington.

ENTERING SPAIN

From countries that are not part of the European Union, visitors age 15 and over are permitted to bring into Spain up to 200 cigarettes or 50 cigars, up to one liter of alcohol over 22 proof, and up to two liters of wine. Dogs and cats are admitted, as long as they have up-to-date vaccination records from their home country.

BACK IN THE U.S.

You may bring home $400 worth of foreign goods duty-free if you've been out of the country for at least 48 hours and haven't already used the $400 allowance or any part of it in the past 30 days.

Travelers 21 and older may bring back one liter of alcohol duty-free. In addition, regardless of your age, you are allowed 200 cigarettes and 100 non-Cuban cigars. (At press time, a federal rule restricting tobacco access to persons 18 years and older did not apply to importation.) Antiques, which the U.S. Customs Service defines as objects more than 100 years old, enter duty-free, as do original works of art done entirely by hand, including paintings, drawings, and sculptures.

You may also send packages home duty-free: up to $200 worth of goods for personal use, with a limit of one parcel per addressee per day (and no alcohol or tobacco products or perfume worth more than $5); label the package PERSONAL USE, and attach a list of its contents and their retail value. Do not label the package UNSOLICITED GIFT, or your duty-free exemption will drop to $100. Mailed items do not affect your duty-free allowance on your return.

➤ INFORMATION: **U.S. Customs Service** (Inquiries: ✉ Box 7407, Washington, DC 20044, ☎ 202/927–6724; complaints: ✉ Commissioner's

Office, 1301 Constitution Ave. NW, Washington, DC 20229; registration of equipment, ✉ Resource Management, 1301 Constitution Ave. NW, Washington, DC, 20229, ☎ 202/927–0540).

BACK IN CANADA

If you've been out of Canada for at least seven days you may bring in C$500 worth of goods duty-free. If you've been away for fewer than seven days but more than 48 hours, the duty-free allowance drops to C$200; if your trip lasts 24–48 hours, the allowance is C$50. You may not pool allowances with family members. Goods claimed under the C$500 exemption may follow you by mail; those claimed under the lesser exemptions must accompany you.

Alcohol and tobacco products may be included in the seven-day and 48-hour exemptions but not in the 24-hour exemption. If you meet the age requirements of the province or territory through which you reenter Canada you may bring in, duty-free, 1.14 liters (40 imperial ounces) of wine or liquor *or* 24 12-ounce cans or bottles of beer or ale. If you are 16 or older you may bring in, duty-free, 200 cigarettes and 50 cigars; these items must accompany you.

You may send an unlimited number of gifts worth up to C$60 each duty-free to Canada. Label the package UNSOLICITED GIFT—VALUE UNDER $60. Alcohol and tobacco are excluded.

➤ INFORMATION: **Revenue Canada** (✉ 2265 St. Laurent Blvd. S, Ottawa, Ontario K1G 4K3, ☎ 613/993–0534; 800/461–9999 in Canada).

BACK IN THE U.K.

If your journey was wholly within EU countries you needn't pass through customs when you return to the United Kingdom. If you plan to bring back large quantities of alcohol or tobacco, check on EU limits beforehand.

➤ INFORMATION: **HM Customs and Excise** (✉ Dorset House, Stamford St., London SE1 9NG, ☎ 0171/202–4227).

ACCESS IN SPAIN

Unfortunately, Spain has done little to make traveling easy for visitors with disabilities; however, most public buildings built within the last five years are accessible, so **it's advisable to stay in newer lodgings.** Only the Prado and newer museums, such as the Reina Sofía and the Thyssen-Bornemisza museum in Madrid, have wheelchair-accessible entrances or elevators. Most of the churches, castles, and monasteries on a tourist's itinerary involve quite a bit of walking, often on uneven terrain.

TIPS & HINTS

When discussing accessibility with an operator or reservationist, **ask hard questions.** Are there any stairs, inside *or* out? Are there grab bars next to the toilet *and* in the shower/tub? How wide is the doorway to the room? To the bathroom? For the most extensive facilities meeting the latest legal specifications, **opt for newer accommodations,** which are more likely to have been designed with access in mind. Older buildings or ships may have more limited facilities. Be sure to **discuss your needs before booking.**

➤ COMPLAINTS: **Disability Rights Section** (✉ U.S. Dept. of Justice, Box 66738, Washington, DC 20035-6738, ☎ 202/514–0301 or 800/514–0301, TTY 202/514–0383 or 800/514–0383; FAX 202/307–1198). **Aviation Consumer Protection Division** (☞ Air Travel, *above*) for airline-related problems. **Civil Rights Office** (✉ U.S. Dept. of Transportation, Departmental Office of Civil Rights, S-30, 400 7th St. SW, Room 10215, Washington, DC 20590, ☎ 202/366–4648) for problems with surface transportation.

TRAVEL AGENCIES & TOUR OPERATORS

The Americans with Disabilities Act requires that travel firms serve the needs of all travelers. That said, you should note that some agencies and operators specialize in making travel arrangements for individuals and groups with disabilities.

THE GOLD GUIDE / SMART TRAVEL TIPS

➤ TRAVELERS WITH MOBILITY PROBLEMS: **Access Adventures** (⊠ 206 Chestnut Ridge Rd., Rochester, NY 14624, ☎ 716/889–9096). **Flying Wheels Travel** (⊠ 143 W. Bridge St., Box 382, Owatonna, MN 55060, ☎ 507/451–5005 or 800/535–6790) for European cruises and tours. **Hinsdale Travel Service** (⊠ 201 E. Ogden Ave., Suite 100, Hinsdale, IL 60521, ☎ 630/325–1335). **Wheelchair Journeys** (⊠ 16979 Redmond Way, Redmond, WA 98052, ☎ 206/885–2210 or 800/313–4751).

DISCOUNTS & DEALS

Be a smart shopper—**compare all your options before making a choice.** A plane ticket bought with a promotional coupon may not be cheaper than the least expensive fare from a discount ticket agency. For high-price travel purchases, such as packages or tours, keep in mind that what you get for the money is just as important as what you save. Just because something is cheap doesn't mean it's a bargain.

LOOK IN YOUR WALLET

When you use your credit card to make travel purchases, you may get free travel-accident insurance, collision-damage insurance, and medical or legal assistance, depending on the card and the bank that issued it. American Express, MasterCard, and Visa provide one or more of these services, so **get a copy of your credit card's travel-benefits policy.** If you belong to the American Automobile Association (AAA) or an oil company–sponsored road-assistance plan, always **ask hotel or car-rental reservationists about auto-club discounts.** Some clubs offer additional discounts on tours, cruises, or admission to attractions. And don't forget that auto-club membership entitles you to free maps and trip-planning services.

DIAL FOR DOLLARS

To save money, **look into "1-800" discount reservations services,** which use their buying power to get better prices on hotels, airline tickets, and even car rentals. When reserving a room, always **call the hotel's local toll-free number** (if one is available) rather than the central reservations

number—you'll often get a better price. Always ask about special packages or, if applicable, corporate rates.

When shopping for the best deals on hotels and car rentals **look for guaranteed exchange rates,** which protect you against a falling dollar. With your rate locked in you won't pay more even if the price goes up in the local currency.

➤ AIRLINE TICKETS: 800/FLY–4–LESS.

➤ HOTEL ROOMS: **Hotels Plus** (☎ 800/235–0909). **International Marketing & Travel Concepts** (☎ 800/790–4682).

SAVE ON COMBOS

Packages and guided tours can both save you money, but don't confuse the two. When you buy a package your travel remains independent, just as though you had planned and booked the trip yourself. Fly-drive packages, which combine airfare and car rental, are often a good deal. If you **buy a rail/drive pass** you'll save on train tickets and car rentals. All Eurail- and Europass holders get a discount on Eurostar fares through the Channel Tunnel.

ELECTRICITY

To use your U.S.-purchased electric-powered equipment, **bring a converter and adapter.** The electrical current in Spain is 220 volts, 50 cycles alternating current (AC); wall outlets take Continental-type plugs, with two round prongs.

If your appliances are dual-voltage, you'll need only an adapter. Don't use 110-volt outlets, marked FOR SHAVERS ONLY, for high-wattage appliances such as blow-dryers. Most laptops operate equally well on 110 and 220 volts, so they require only an adapter.

FERRY TRAVEL

➤ FROM THE U.K.: **Brittany Ferries** (☎ 0752/221–321). **Hover-Speed** (☎ 0171/554–7061). **P&O European Ferries** (☎ 0181/575–8555). **Sealink** (☎ 0223/47047). **SNCF** (☎ 0171/409–3518 for Motorail).

GAY & LESBIAN TRAVEL

Since the end of Franco's dictatorship, the situation for gays and lesbians in Spain has improved dramatically: the paragraph in the Spanish civil code that made homosexuality a crime was repealed in 1978. Violence against gays does exist, but it is generally restricted to the rougher areas of very large cities.

In the summer, the beaches of the Balearics (especially Ibiza), the Costa del Sol (Torremolinos and Benidorm), and the Costa Brava (Sitges and Lloret del Mar) are gay and lesbian hot spots; Playa del Inglés and Maspaloma, in the Canary Islands, are popular in winter.

➤ LOCAL RESOURCES: **Gai Inform** (✉ C. Carretas 12, 3-2a, 28012 Madrid, ☎ 91/523–0070). **Teléfono Rosa** (✉ C. Carolinas 13, 08012 Barcelona, ☎ 93/234–7070).

➤ TOUR OPERATORS: **Olivia** (✉ 4400 Market St., Oakland, CA 94608, ☎ 510/655–0364 or 800/631–6277).

➤ GAY- AND LESBIAN-FRIENDLY TRAVEL AGENCIES: **Advance Damron** (✉ 1 Greenway Plaza, Suite 800, Houston, TX 77046, ☎ 713/682–2002 or 800/695–0880, FAX 713/888–1010). **Club Travel** (✉ 8739 Santa Monica Blvd., West Hollywood, CA 90069, ☎ 310/358–2200 or 800/429–8747, FAX 310/358–2222). **Islanders/Kennedy Travel** (✉ 183 W. 10th St., New York, NY 10014, ☎ 212/242–3222 or 800/988–1181, FAX 212/929–8530). **Now Voyager** (✉ 4406 18th St., San Francisco, CA 94114, ☎ 415/626–1169 or 800/255–6951, FAX 415/626–8626). **Yellowbrick Road** (✉ 1500 W. Balmoral Ave., Chicago, IL 60640, ☎ 773/561–1800 or 800/642–2488, FAX 773/561–4497). **Skylink Women's Travel** (✉ 3577 Moorland Ave., Santa Rosa, CA 95407, ☎ 707/585–8355 or 800/225–5759, FAX 707/584–5637), serving lesbian travelers.

HEALTH

Two problems frequently encountered during Spanish summers are sunburn and sunstroke. On hot, sunny days, even people who are not normally bothered by strong sun should cover themselves with a long-sleeve shirt, a hat, and long pants or a beach wrap. These are essential for a day at the beach, but they're also advisable for a long day of touring. Carry sunblock lotion for your nose, ears, and other sensitive areas, such as eyelids or ankles. Be sure to drink enough liquids. Above all, limit your sun time for the first few days until you become accustomed to the heat.

Spain has recently had the highest number of AIDS cases in Europe. Those applying for work permits will be asked for proof of HIV-negative status.

MEDICAL PLANS

No one plans to get sick while traveling, but it happens, so **consider signing up with a medical-assistance company.** Members get doctor referrals, emergency evacuation or repatriation, 24-hour telephone hot lines for medical consultation, cash for emergencies, and other personal and legal assistance. Coverage varies by plan, so **review the benefits carefully.**

➤ MEDICAL-ASSISTANCE COMPANIES: **International SOS Assistance** (✉ Box 11568, Philadelphia, PA 19116, ☎ 215/244–1500 or 800/523–8930; ✉ Box 466, pl. Bonaventure, Montréal, Québec H5A 1C1, ☎ 514/874–7674 or 800/363–0263; ✉ 7 Old Lodge Pl., St. Margarets, Twickenham TW1 1RQ, England, ☎ 0181/744–0033). **MEDEX Assistance Corporation** (✉ Box 5375, Timonium, MD 21094, ☎ 410/453–6300 or 800/537–2029). **Traveler's Emergency Network** (✉ 3100 Tower Blvd., Suite 1000B, Durham, NC 27707, ☎ 919/490–6055 or 800/275–4836, FAX 919/493–8262). **TravMed** (✉ Box 5375, Timonium, MD 21094, ☎ 410/453–6380 or 800/732–5309). **Worldwide Assistance Services** (✉ 1133 15th St. NW, Suite 400, Washington, DC 20005, ☎ 202/331–1609 or 800/821–2828, FAX 202/828–5896).

HOLIDAYS

In 1999, Spain's national holidays include: January 1, January 6 (Epiphany), March 19 (St. Joseph), April 2 (Good Friday), April 5 (Easter Monday), May 1 (May Day), August 15 (Assumption), October 12 (National Day), November 1 (All Saints), December 6 (Constitution), December 8 (Immaculate Conception), December 25, and December 26 (Boxing Day).

In addition, each city and town has its own holidays honoring political events and patron saints. Madrid holidays include May 2 (Madrid Day), May 15 (St. Isidro), and November 9 (Almudena). Barcelona celebrates April 23 (St. George), September 11 (Catalonia Day), and September 24 (Merced). Valencia's community day is October 9.

If a public holiday falls on a Tuesday or Thursday, **remember that many businesses also close on the nearest Monday or Friday** for a long weekend called a *puente* (bridge).

INSURANCE

Travel insurance is the best way to **protect yourself against financial loss.** The most useful policies are trip-cancellation-and-interruption, default, medical, and comprehensive insurance.

Without insurance you will lose all or most of your money if you cancel your trip, regardless of the reason. It's essential that you **buy trip-cancellation-and-interruption insurance,** particularly if your airline ticket, cruise, or package tour is nonrefundable and cannot be changed. When considering how much coverage you need, look for a policy that will cover the cost of your trip plus the nondiscounted price of a one-way airline ticket, should you need to return home early. Also **consider default or bankruptcy insurance,** which protects you against a supplier's failure to deliver.

Medicare generally does not cover health-care costs outside the United States, nor do many privately issued policies. If your own policy does not cover you outside the United States, **consider buying supplemental medical coverage.** Remember that travel health insurance is different from a medical-assistance plan (☞ Health, *above*).

Citizens of the United Kingdom can buy an annual travel-insurance policy valid for most vacations during the year in which it's purchased. Make sure you're covered if you're pregnant or have a preexisting medical condition.

If you've purchased an expensive vacation, comprehensive insurance is a must. It's important to **look for comprehensive policies that include trip-delay insurance,** which will protect you in the event that weather problems cause you to miss your flight, tour, or cruise. A few insurers sell waivers for preexisting medical conditions. Companies that offer both features include Access America, Carefree Travel, Travel Guard, and Travel Insured International (☞ *below*).

Always **buy travel insurance directly from the insurance company.** If you buy it from a travel agency or tour operator that goes out of business, you will probably not be covered for the agency or operator's default, a major risk. Before you make any purchase, **review your existing health and home-owner's policies** to see whether they cover expenses incurred while traveling.

➤ TRAVEL INSURERS: In the United States: **Access America** (✉ 6600 W. Broad St., Richmond, VA 23230, ☎ 804/285–3300 or 800/284–8300). **Carefree Travel Insurance** (✉ Box 9366, 100 Garden City Plaza, Garden City, NY 11530, ☎ 516/294–0220 or 800/323–3149). **Near Travel Services** (✉ Box 1339, Calumet City, IL 60409, ☎ 708/868–6700 or 800/654–6700). **Travel Guard International** (✉ 1145 Clark St., Stevens Point, WI 54481, ☎ 715/345–0505 or 800/826–1300). **Travel Insured International** (✉ Box 280568, East Hartford, CT 06128-0568, ☎ 860/528–7663 or 800/243–3174). **Travelex Insurance Services** (✉ 11717 Burt St., Suite 202, Omaha, NE 68154-1500, ☎ 402/445–8637 or 800/228–9792, FAX 800/867–9531). **Wallach & Company** (✉ 107 W. Federal St., Box 480, Middleburg, VA 20118, ☎ 540/687–3166 or 800/237–6615). In Canada: **Mutual of Omaha** (✉ Travel Division, 500 University Ave., Toronto, Ontario M5G 1V8, ☎ 416/598–4083; 800/268–8825 in Canada). In the United Kingdom: **Association of British Insurers** (✉ 51 Gresham St., London EC2V 7HQ, ☎ 0171/600–3333).

LANGUAGE

Although Spaniards exported their language to all Central and South

America, you may be surprised to find that Spanish is not the principal language in all of Spain. The Basques speak Euskera; in Catalonia, you'll hear Catalan and in Galicia, Gallego. While almost everyone in these regions also speaks and understands Spanish, **expect local radio and television stations to broadcast in these languages and road signs to be printed or spray-painted over with the preferred regional language.** Spanish is referred to as Castellano, or Castilian.

Fortunately, Spanish is fairly easy to pick up, and your efforts to speak the local tongue will be graciously received. Learn at least the following basic phrases: *buenos días* (hello—until 2 PM), *buenas tardes* (good afternoon—until 8 PM), *buenas noches* (hello—after dark), *por favor* (please), *gracias* (thank you), *adiós* (good-bye), *sí* (yes), *no* (no), *los servicios* (the toilets), *la cuenta* (bill/check), *habla inglés?* (do you speak English?), *no comprendo* (I don't understand). See the Spanish Vocabulary *in* Chapter 17 or, better yet, pick up a copy of *Fodor's Spanish for Travelers* for more helpful expressions.

If your Spanish breaks down, you should have no trouble finding people who speak English in major cities and coastal resorts, but you won't necessarily be able to count on the bus driver or the passerby on the street. Those who do speak English may speak the British variety, so don't be surprised if you're told to queue (line up) or take the lift (elevator) to the loo (toilet). Many guided tours offered at museums and historic sites are in Spanish; ask about the language that will be spoken before signing up.

LODGING

The Spanish government has spent decades buying up old castles and historic buildings and converting them into outstanding lodgings for its parador hotel chain. The rest of Spain's hotels tend to be relatively new high-rises, although there is a growing trend toward the restoration of historic buildings. By law, prices must be posted at the reception desk

and should indicate whether tax is included. Breakfast is not usually included in the room price.

For information on hotel consolidators, *see* Discounts, *above.*

APARTMENT & VILLA RENTALS

If you want a home base that's roomy enough for a family and comes with cooking facilities, **consider a furnished rental.** These can save you money, although some are luxury properties, economical only when your party is large. Home-exchange directories list rentals (often second homes owned by prospective house swappers), and some services search for a house or apartment for you (even a castle if that's your fancy) and handle the paperwork. Some send an illustrated catalog; others send photographs only of specific properties, sometimes for a fee. Up-front registration fees may apply.

➤ RENTAL AGENTS: **At Home Abroad** (⊠ 405 E. 56th St., Suite 6H, New York, NY 10022, ☎ 212/421–9165, FAX 212/752–1591). **Europa-Let/Tropical Inn-Let** (⊠ 92 N. Main St., Ashland, OR 97520, ☎ 541/482–5806 or 800/462–4486, FAX 541/482–0660). **Hometours International** (⊠ Box 11503, Knoxville, TN 37939, ☎ 423/690–8484 or 800/367–4668). **Interhome** (⊠ 124 Little Falls Rd., Fairfield, NJ 07004, ☎ 201/882–6864, FAX 201/808–1742). **Property Rentals International** (⊠ 1008 Mansfield Crossing Rd., Richmond, VA 23236, ☎ 804/378–6054 or 800/220–3332, FAX 804/379–2073). **Rental Directories International** (⊠ 2044 Rittenhouse Sq., Philadelphia, PA 19103, ☎ 215/985–4001, FAX 215/985–0323). **Rent-a-Home International** (⊠ 7200 34th Ave. NW, Seattle, WA 98117, ☎ 206/789–9377 or 800/488–7368, FAX 206/789–9379). **Villas and Apartments Abroad** (⊠ 420 Madison Ave., Suite 1003, New York, NY 10017, ☎ 212/759–1025 or 800/433–3020, FAX 212/755–8316). **Villas International** (⊠ 605 Market St., Suite 510, San Francisco, CA 94105, ☎ 415/281–0910 or 800/221–2260, FAX 415/281–0919). **Hideaways International** (⊠ 767 Islington St., Portsmouth, NH 03801, ☎ 603/430–4433 or

800/843–4433, FAX 603/430–4444); for $99 a year members arrange rentals among themselves.

HOME EXCHANGES

If you would like to exchange your home for someone else's, **join a home-exchange organization** (for about $83 a year), which will send you its updated listings of available exchanges for a year and will include your own listing in at least one of them. Making the arrangements is up to you.

➤ EXCHANGE CLUBS: **HomeLink International** (⊠ Box 650, Key West, FL 33041, ☎ 305/294–7766 or 800/638–3841, FAX 305/294–1148).

HOTELS

Hotels are rated by the government with one to five stars. While quality is a factor, **the rating is technically only an indication of how many facilities the hotel offers.** For example, you may find a three-star hotel just as comfortable as a four-star hotel, but lacking a swimming pool.

The major, private hotel groups in Spain include the upscale Meliá chain and the moderately priced Tryp and Sol chains. Dozens of reasonably priced beachside high-rises along the coast cater to package tours.

High-season rates prevail not only in summer but also during Holy Week and local fiestas.

Estancias de España is an association of 20 independently owned hotels in restored palaces, monasteries, mills, and post houses, generally in rural Spain; a free directory is available.

➤ SMALL HOTELS: **Estancias de España** (⊠ Menéndez Pidal 31-bajo izq., 28036 Madrid, ☎ 91/345–4141, FAX 91/345–5174).

PARADORS

There are about 100 paradors in Spain. Some are in castles on a hill with sweeping views; others are in historic monasteries or convents filled with art treasures; still others are in modern buildings on Spain's choicest beachfront property. Prices are reasonable, considering that most paradors are four- and five-star hotels. Paradors are immaculate and tastefully furnished, often with an-

tiques or reproductions. All have restaurants that serve some regional specialties, and you can stop in for a meal or a drink without spending the night. Breakfast, however, is an expensive buffet; you'll do better to go down the street for a cup of coffee and a roll.

Because paradors are extremely popular with foreigners and Spaniards alike, **make reservations well in advance.**

➤ INFORMATION: In Spain: **Paradores de España** (⊠ Central de Reservas, Requena 3, Madrid 28013, ☎ 91/516–6666, FAX 91/516–6657). In the United States: **Marketing Ahead** (⊠ 433 5th Ave., New York, NY 10016, ☎ 212/686–9213 or 800/223–1356). In the United Kingdom: **Keytel International** (⊠ 402 Edgeware Rd., London W2 1ED, ☎ 0171/402–8182).

MAIL

RATES

Airmail letters to the United States and Canada cost 94 ptas. up to 15 grams. Letters to the United Kingdom and other EU countries cost 65 ptas. up to 20 grams. Letters within Spain are 32 ptas. Postcards are charged the same rate as letters. Letters and postcards mailed within the same city are 21 ptas. You can buy stamps at post offices and at government-run tobacco shops.

RECEIVING MAIL

Because mail delivery in Spain can often be slow and unreliable, it's best to have your mail sent to American Express. An alternative is to have mail held at a Spanish post office; have it addressed to **Lista de Correos** (general delivery) in a town you'll be visiting. Postal addresses should include the name of the province in parentheses, e.g., Marbella (Málaga).

You can pick up mail at **American Express** (☎ 800/528–4800 for a list of foreign American Express offices).

MONEY

The peseta (pta.) is Spain's unit of currency. Bills are 10,000, 5,000, 2,000, and 1,000 ptas. Coins are 500, 200, 100, 50, 25, 10, 5, and 1 pta. Be careful not to confuse the 100- and 500-pta. coins—they're the same color and almost the same size. Five-pta. coins are called *duros*. At press time European currency markets were highly unstable, with exchange rates of 145 ptas. to the U.S. dollar, 106 ptas. per Canadian dollar, and 232 ptas. to the pound sterling.

ATMS

Before leaving home, **make sure that your credit cards have been programmed for ATM use in Spain.** Note that Discover is accepted mainly in the United States. Local bank cards often do not work overseas or may access only your checking account; **ask your bank about a MasterCard/ Cirrus or Visa debit card,** which works like a bank card but can be used at any ATM displaying a MasterCard/Cirrus or Visa logo. These cards, too, may tap only your checking account; check with your bank about their policy.

➤ ATM LOCATIONS: **Cirrus** (☎ 800/ 424–7787).

COSTS

Coffee in a bar: 125 ptas. (standing), 150 ptas. (seated). Beer in a bar: 125 ptas. (standing), 150 ptas. (seated). Small glass of wine in a bar: 100 ptas. Soft drink: 150–200 ptas. a bottle. Ham-and-cheese sandwich: 300–450 ptas. One-mile taxi ride: 400 ptas., but the meter keeps ticking in traffic jams. Local bus or subway ride: 125– 150 ptas. Movie ticket: 500–600 ptas. Foreign newspaper: 225 ptas.

CURRENCY EXCHANGE

For the most favorable rates, **change money at banks.** Although fees charged for ATM transactions may be higher abroad than at home, Cirrus and Plus exchange rates are excellent because they're based on wholesale rates offered only by major banks. You won't do as well at exchange booths in airports or rail and bus stations, in hotels, in restaurants, or in stores, although you may find their hours more convenient. To avoid lines at airport exchange booths, **get some Spanish currency before you leave home.**

➤ EXCHANGE SERVICES: **International Currency Express** (☎ 888/842–0880 on the East Coast; 888/278–6628 on the West Coast for telephone orders). **Thomas Cook Currency Services** (☎ 800/287–7362 for telephone orders and retail locations).

TRAVELER'S CHECKS

Whether or not you'll need traveler's checks depends on where you are headed. **Take cash if your trip includes rural areas** and small towns; take traveler's checks to cities. If your checks are lost or stolen, they can usually be replaced within 24 hours. To ensure a speedy refund, buy your checks yourself (don't ask someone else to make the purchase). When making a claim for stolen or lost checks, the person who bought the checks should make the call.

PACKING FOR SPAIN

Pack light. Although baggage carts are free and plentiful in most Spanish airports, they're rare in train and bus stations.

On the whole, Spaniards dress up more than Americans or the British. What you bring should depend on the season. Summer will be hot nearly everywhere, but **don't forget a rain-coat or an umbrella.** Visits in winter, fall, and spring call for warm clothing and boots.

It's sensible to wear casual, comfortable clothing and shoes when sightseeing, but you'll want to **dress up a bit when visiting the cities, especially if you'll be going to fine restaurants and nightclubs.** American tourists are easily spotted in Spain because they're the ones wearing sneakers—if you want to blend in, wear leather shoes.

On the beach, anything goes; it's common to see females of all ages wearing only bikini bottoms, and many of the more remote beaches allow nude sunbathing. Regardless of your style, **bring a cover-up** to wear over your bathing suit when you leave the beach.

Bring an extra pair of eyeglasses or contact lenses in your carry-on luggage. If you have a health problem, **pack enough medication** to last the

THE GOLD GUIDE / SMART TRAVEL TIPS

THE GOLD GUIDE / SMART TRAVEL TIPS

entire trip or have your doctor write you a prescription using the drug's generic name, as brand names vary from country to country. It's important that you **don't put prescription drugs or valuables in luggage to be checked:** it might go astray. To avoid problems with customs officials, carry medications in the original packaging. And don't forget to pack the addresses of offices that handle refunds of lost traveler's checks.

PASSPORTS & VISAS

Once your travel plans are confirmed, **check the expiration date of your passport.** It's also a good idea to **make photocopies of the data page;** leave one copy with someone at home and keep another with you, separated from your passport. If you lose your passport, promptly call the nearest embassy or consulate and the local police. Having a copy of the data page can speed replacement.

U.S. CITIZENS

All U.S. citizens, including infants, need only a valid passport to enter Spain for stays of up to 90 days.

➤ INFORMATION: **Office of Passport Services** (☎ 202/647–0518).

CANADIANS

You need only a valid passport to enter Spain for stays of up to 90 days.

➤ INFORMATION: **Passport Office** (☎ 819/994–3500 or 800/567–6868).

U.K. CITIZENS

As members of the European Union, citizens of the United Kingdom need only valid identification to enter Spain.

➤ INFORMATION: **London Passport Office** (☎ 0990/21010).

SENIOR-CITIZEN TRAVEL

While there are few early-bird specials or movie discounts, senior citizens generally enjoy discounts at museums in Spain. Spanish social life encompasses all ages—it's very common to see senior citizens having coffee next to young couples or families at late-night cafés.

To qualify for age-related discounts, **mention your senior-citizen status up front** when booking hotel reservations (not when checking out) and before you're seated in restaurants (not when paying the bill). Note that discounts may be limited to certain menus, days, or hours. When renting a car, **ask about promotional car-rental discounts,** which can be cheaper than senior-citizen rates.

➤ EDUCATIONAL TRAVEL PROGRAMS: **Elderhostel** (✉ 75 Federal St., 3rd floor, Boston, MA 02110, ☎ 617/426–7788). **Interhostel** (✉ University of New Hampshire, 6 Garrison Ave., Durham, NH 03824, ☎ 603/862–1147 or 800/733–9753, FAX 603/862–1113).

SPORTS

Spain's sports-specific agencies can provide listings to help you choose your court, course, mooring, and more. The local tourist offices (☞ Visitor Information, *below*) can also be very helpful.

➤ BOATING CHARTERS: **Federación Española de Motonautica** (✉ Spanish Motorboat Federation, Avda. de América 33, 4-B, 28002 Madrid, ☎ 91/415–3769).

➤ BOATING MARINAS: **Federación Española de Vela** (✉ Spanish Sailing Federation, Luís de Salazar 12, 28002, Madrid, ☎ 91/519–5008). **Federación de Actividades Subacuáticas** (✉ Spanish Underwater Activities Federation, Santaló 15, 08021 Barcelona, ☎ 93/200–6769). **Federación Española de Esquí Nautico** (✉ Spanish Waterskiing Federation, Sabiano Aran 30, 08028 Barcelona, ☎ 93/330–8903).

➤ CYCLING TOURS: **Bicibus** (✉ Puerta del Sol 14, 2nd floor, Madrid, ☎ 91/522–4501).

➤ EQUESTRIAN: **Federación Española de Polo** (✉ Spanish Polo Federation, Comandante Zorita 13, 28020 Madrid, ☎ 91/533–7569). **Federación Hípica Española** (✉ Spanish Horseracing Federation, Monte Esquinza 8, 28010 Madrid, ☎ 91/319–0233).

➤ FISHING PERMITS: **ICONA** (✉ Environmental Institute, Princesa 3, Madrid, ☎ 91/580–1653). Federación Española de Pesca (✉ Navas de Tolosa 3, 28013 Madrid, ☎ 91/532–8353).

➤ FLYING INFORMATION: **Federación Nacional de Deporte Aéreo** (✉ Spanish Flying Federation, Ferraz 16, 28008 Madrid, ☎ 91/547–5922).

➤ GOLF: **Real Federación Española de Golf** (✉ Capitán Haya 9, 28020 Madrid, ☎ 91/555–2757).

➤ HIKING: **Federación Española de Montañismo** (✉ Alberto Aguilera 3, 28015 Madrid, ☎ 91/445–1382).

➤ SKIING INFORMATION: **Federación Española de Deportes de Invierno** (✉ Infanta María Teresa 14, 28016 Madrid, ☎ 91/344–0944). **Tourism and Ski-run Information Line** (☎ 91/359–1557).

➤ SPA: **La Asociación Nacional de Estaciones Termales** (✉ National Health Spa Association, Rodrígues San Pedro 56-3, 28015 Madrid, ☎ 91/549–0300).

➤ TENNIS: **Real Federación Española de Tenis** (✉ Spanish Tennis Federation, Diagonal 618, 01028 Barcelona, ☎ 93/201–0844).

STUDENTS

➤ STUDENT IDS AND SERVICES: In the United States: **Council on International Educational Exchange** (✉ CIEE, 205 E. 42nd St., 14th floor, New York, NY 10017, ☎ 212/822–2600 or 888/268–6245, FAX 212/822–2699), for mail orders only. In Canada: **Travel Cuts** (✉ 187 College St., Toronto, Ontario M5T 1P7, ☎ 416/979–2406 or 800/667–2887).

➤ HOSTELING: **Hostelling International—American Youth Hostels** (✉ 733 15th St. NW, Suite 840, Washington, DC 20005, ☎ 202/783–6161, FAX 202/783–6171). **Hostelling International—Canada** (✉ 400-205 Catherine St., Ottawa, Ontario K2P 1C3, ☎ 613/237–7884, FAX 613/237–7868). **Youth Hostel Association of England and Wales** (✉ Trevelyan House, 8 St. Stephen's Hill, St. Albans, Hertfordshire AL1 2DY, ☎ 01727/855215 or 01727/845047, FAX 01727/844126). Membership in the United States, $25; in Canada, C$26.75; in the United Kingdom, £9.30.

➤ STUDENT TOURS: **Contiki Holidays** (✉ 300 Plaza Alicante, Suite 900, Garden Grove, CA 92840, ☎ 714/740–0808 or 800/266–8454, FAX 714/740–0818). **AESU Travel** (✉ 2 Hamill Rd., Suite 248, Baltimore, MD 21210-1807, ☎ 410/323–4416 or 800/638–7640, FAX 410/323–4498).

TAXES

VALUE-ADDED TAX (VAT)

Value-added tax (or sales tax) is called IVA in Spain. It is levied on services, such as hotels and restaurants, and on many categories of consumer products. When in doubt about whether tax is included, ask, *Está incluido el IVA* (ee-vah)?

The IVA rate (7%) is the same for all categories of hotels and restaurants, regardless of their number of stars or forks. A special tax law for the Canary Islands allows all hotels and restaurants there to charge 4% IVA. Menus will generally say at the bottom whether tax is included (*IVA incluido*) or not (*más 7% IVA*).

A number of shops, particularly large stores and boutiques in holiday resorts, offer a refund of 16% IVA sales tax on purchases of more than 15,000 ptas. You **show your passport and fill out a form, and the store mails the refund to your home.** The receipt must detail the purchase and IVA paid, be signed by vendor and customer, and be sealed.

You can also **present your original receipt in the VAT office at the airport** (the airports in both Barcelona and Madrid have IVA booths near their duty free shops). Customs signs the original and gives it back to the customer, who mails it to the vendor. The vendor then mails the refund to the customer.

TELEPHONES

The country code for Spain is 34.

All provincial codes begin with a 9. To call within Spain—even locally—dial the area code first. Large cities such as Madrid (91), Barcelona (93), Bilbao (94), Sevilla (95), and Valencia (96) have a two-digit area code followed by a seven-digit local number; less populous regions have a three-

THE GOLD GUIDE / SMART TRAVEL TIPS

digit area code followed by a six-digit local number.

CALLING HOME

International calls are awkward from public pay phones because of the enormous number of coins needed, and they can be expensive from hotels, which often add a surcharge. The best way to phone home is to go to the local telephone office. Every town has one, and major cities have several. When the call is connected, you'll be sent to a quiet cubicle, and charged according to the meter. If the price is 500 ptas. or more, you can pay with Visa or MasterCard.

To make an international call yourself, dial 07 and wait for a loud tone. Then dial the country code (1 for the United States, 01 for Canada, 44 for the United Kingdom), followed by the area code and number.

In Madrid the main telephone office is at Gran Vía 28. There is another at the main post office, and a third at Paseo Recoletos 43, just off Plaza Colón. In Barcelona you can phone overseas from the office at Carrer de Fontanella 4, off Plaça de Catalunya.

Before you go, **find out the local long-distance access codes** for your destinations. AT&T, MCI, and Sprint long-distance services make calling home relatively convenient, but you may find the local access code blocked in many hotel rooms. First ask the hotel operator to connect you. If the hotel operator balks, ask for an international operator, or dial the international operator yourself. One way to improve your odds of getting connected to your long-distance carrier is to travel with more than one company's calling card (a hotel may block Sprint, for example, but not MCI). If all else fails, **call your phone company collect in the United States** or call from a pay phone in the hotel lobby.

➤ To Obtain Access Codes: **AT&T USADirect** (☎ 800/874–4000). **MCI Call USA** (☎ 800/444–4444). **Sprint Express** (☎ 800/793–1153).

OPERATORS & INFORMATION

For general information in Spain, dial 003. The operator for international information and assistance is at 025 (some operators speak English).

PAY PHONES

There are three types of pay phones in Spain, all of them bright green or dull blue. The most common kind has a digital readout, so you can see your money ticking away. You need at least 25 ptas. for a local call, 75 ptas. to call another province. Simply insert coins and wait for a dial tone. (At older models, you line coins up in a groove on top of the dial, and they drop down as needed.)

Newer pay phones work on special phone cards, which you can buy at any tobacco shop for 1,000 or 2,000 ptas.

TIPPING

Pride keeps Spaniards from acknowledging tips, but waiters and other service people are poorly paid, and you can be sure that your contribution will be appreciated. On the other hand, if you run into some bad or surly service, don't feel obligated to leave a tip.

Restaurant checks may or may not include service, but **do not tip more than 10% of the bill in any case,** and leave less if you eat tapas or sandwiches at a bar—just enough to round out the bill to the nearest 100. Tip cocktail servers 50–75 ptas. a drink, depending on the bar.

Tip taxi drivers about 10% of the total fare, but more for long rides or extra help with luggage. Note, though, that there is an official surcharge for airport runs and baggage.

Tip hotel porters 50–100 ptas. a bag, and the bearer of room service 50–100 ptas. A doorman who calls a taxi for you gets 100 ptas. If you stay in a hotel for more than two nights, tip the maid about 100 ptas. per night. A concierge should receive a tip for any additional help he or she provides.

Tour guides should be tipped about 300 ptas., ushers in theaters or at bullfights 25–50 ptas., barbers 100 ptas., and ladies' hairdressers at least 200 ptas. for a wash and style. Restroom attendants are tipped 10–25 ptas.

TOUR OPERATORS

Buying a package tour or independent vacation can make your trip to Spain less expensive and more hassle-free. Because everything is prearranged, you'll spend less time planning.

Operators that handle several hundred thousand travelers per year can use their purchasing power to give you a good price. Their high volume may also indicate financial stability. But some small companies provide more personalized service, and because they tend to specialize, they may also be more knowledgeable about a given area.

A GOOD DEAL?

The more your package or tour includes, the better you can predict the ultimate cost of your vacation. Make sure you know exactly what's covered, and **beware of hidden costs.** Are taxes, tips, and service charges included? Transfers and baggage handling? Entertainment and excursions? These can add up.

If the price of the package or tour you're considering is lower than in your wildest dreams, **be skeptical.** Also, **make sure your travel agent knows the accommodations** and other services. Ask about the hotel's location, room size, beds, and whether it has a pool, room service, or programs for children, if you care about these. Has your agent been there in person or sent others you can contact?

BUYER BEWARE

Each year consumers are stranded or lose their money when tour operators—even very large ones with excellent reputations—go out of business. So check out the operator. Find out how long the company has been in business, and ask several agents about its reputation. Unless the firm has a consumer-protection program, **don't book through it.**

Members of the National Tour Association and United States Tour Operators Association are required to set aside funds to cover your payments and travel arrangements in case the company defaults. Nonmembers may carry insurance instead. Look for the details, and for the name of an underwriter with a solid reputation, in the operator's brochure. Note: when it comes to tour operators, **don't trust escrow accounts.** Although there are laws governing charter-flight operators, no governmental body prevents tour operators from raiding the till. For more information, *see* Consumer Protection, *above.*

➤ TOUR-OPERATOR RECOMMENDATIONS: **National Tour Association** (✉ NTA, 546 E. Main St., Lexington, KY 40508, ☎ 606/226–4444 or 800/755–8687). **United States Tour Operators Association** (✉ USTOA, 342 Madison Ave., Suite 1522, New York, NY 10173, ☎ 212/599–6599, FAX 212/599–6744).

USING AN AGENT

Travel agents are excellent resources. When shopping for an agent, however, you should **collect brochures from several sources;** some agents' suggestions may be skewed by promotional relationships with tour and package firms that reward them for volume sales. If you have a special interest, **find an agent with expertise in that area** (☞ Travel Agents, *below*). Don't rely solely on your agent, who may be unaware of niche operators. Note that some special-interest travel companies only sell directly to the public, and that some large operators only accept bookings made through travel agents.

SINGLE TRAVELERS

Prices for packages and tours are usually quoted per person, based on two sharing a room. If you're traveling solo, you may be required to pay the full double-occupancy rate. Some operators eliminate this surcharge if you agree to be matched with a roommate of the same sex, even if one is not found by departure time.

GROUP TOURS

Among companies that sell tours to Spain, the following are nationally known, have a proven reputation, and offer plenty of options. The classifications used below represent different price categories, and you'll probably encounter these terms when talking to a travel agent or tour operator. The key difference is usually in accommodations, which run from budget to better, and better yet to best.

➤ SUPER-DELUXE: **Abercrombie & Kent** (✉ 1520 Kensington Rd., Oak Brook, IL 60521-2141, ☎ 630/954–2944 or 800/323–7308, FAX 630/954–3324). **Travcoa** (✉ Box 2630, 2350 S.E. Bristol St., Newport Beach, CA 92660, ☎ 714/476–2800 or 800/992–2003, FAX 714/476–2538).

➤ DELUXE: **Central Holidays** (✉ 206 Central Ave., Jersey City, NJ 07307, ☎ 201/798–5777 or 800/935–5000). **Globus** (✉ 5301 S. Federal Circle, Littleton, CO 80123-2980, ☎ 303/797–2800 or 800/221–0090, FAX 303/347–2080). **Tauck Tours** (✉ Box 5027, 276 Post Rd. W, Westport, CT 06881-5027, ☎ 203/226–6911 or 800/468–2825, FAX 203/221–6866).

➤ FIRST CLASS: **Brendan Tours** (✉ 15137 Califa St., Van Nuys, CA 91411, ☎ 818/785–9696 or 800/421–8446, FAX 818/902–9876). **Caravan Tours** (✉ 401 N. Michigan Ave., Chicago, IL 60611, ☎ 312/321–9800 or 800/227–2826, FAX 312/321–9845). **Collette Tours** (✉ 162 Middle St., Pawtucket, RI 02860, ☎ 401/728–3805 or 800/340–5158, FAX 401/728–4745). **Delta Vacations** (☎ 800/872–7786). **DER Tours** (✉ 9501 W. Devon St., Rosemont, IL 60018, ☎ 800/937–1235, FAX 847/692–4141 or 800/282–7474, 800/860–9944 for brochures). **Odysseys Adventures** (✉ 537 Chestnut St., BOX 305, Cedarhurst, NY 11516-2223, ☎ 516/569–2812 or 800/344–0013, FAX 516/569–2998). **Spain Tours and Beyond** (✉ 261 W. 70th St., New York, NY 10023, ☎ 212/595–2400, FAX 212/580–8935). **Trafalgar Tours** (✉ 11 E. 26th St., New York, NY 10010, ☎ 212/689–8977 or 800/854–0103, FAX 800/457–6644). **TWA Getaway Vacations** (☎ 800/438–2929). **Viajes Corte Inglés** (✉ 500 5th Ave., Suite 1044, New York, NY 10110, ☎ 212/944–9400 or 800/333–2469).

➤ BUDGET: **Cosmos** (☞ Globus, *above*).

PACKAGES

Like group tours, independent vacation packages are available from major tour operators and airlines. The companies listed below offer vacation packages in a broad price range.

➤ AIR/HOTEL: **Continental Vacations** (☎ 800/634–5555). **Delta Vacations** (☎ 800/872–7786). **DER Tours** (☞ Group Tours, above). **4th Dimension Tours** (✉ 7101 S.W. 99th Ave., No. 105, Miami, FL 33173, ☎ 305/279–0014 or 800/644–0438, FAX 305/273–9777). **Odysseys Adventures** (☞ Group Tours, *above*). **Spain Tours and Beyond** (☞ Group Tours, *above*). **TWA Getaway Vacations** (☎ 800/438–2929). **VE Tours** (✉ 7270 N.W. 12th St., Suite 210, Miami, FL 33126, ☎ 305/477–5161 or 800/222–8383). **US Airways Vacations** (☎ 800/455–0123). **Viajes Corte Inglés** (☞ Group Tours, *above*).

➤ FLY/DRIVE: **Delta Vacations** (☎ 800/872–7786).

➤ FROM THE U.K.: **British Airways Holidays** (✉ Astral Towers, Betts Way, London Rd., Crawley, West Sussex RH10 2XA, ☎ 01293/722–727, FAX 01293/722–624). **Mundi Color** (✉ 276 Vauxhall Bridge Rd., London SW1V 1BE, ☎ 0171/828–6021). **Page & Moy Ltd.** (✉ 136–140 London Rd., Leicester LE2 1EN, ☎ 0116/250–7676). **Magic of Spain** (✉ 227 Shepherds Bush Rd., London W6 7AS, ☎ 0181/748–4220).

THEME TRIPS

➤ ADVENTURE: **Himalayan Travel** (✉110 Prospect St., Stamford, CT 06901, ☎ 203/359–3711 or 800/225–2380, FAX 203/359–3669). **Mountain Travel-Sobek** (✉ 6420 Fairmount Ave., El Cerrito, CA 94530, ☎ 510/527–8100 or 888/687–6235, FAX 510/525–7710).

➤ ARCHAEOLOGY: **Earthwatch** (✉ Box 9104, 680 Mount Auburn St., Watertown, MA 02272, ☎ 617/926–8200 or 800/776–0188, FAX 617/926–8532).

➤ ART AND ARCHITECTURE: **4th Dimension Tours** (☞ Packages, *above*).

➤ BICYCLING: **Backroads** (✉ 801 Cedar St., Berkeley, CA 94710-1800, ☎ 510/527–1555 or 800/462–2848, FAX 510-527–1444). **Bike Riders** (✉ Box 254, Boston, MA 02113, ☎ 617/

723–2354 or 800/473–7040, FAX 617/723–2355). **Butterfield & Robinson** (✉ 70 Bond St., Toronto, Ontario, Canada M5B 1X3, ☎ 416/864–1354 or 800/678–1147, FAX 416/864–0541). **Camino Tours** (✉ 7044 18th Ave. NE, Seattle, WA 98115, ☎ 206/523–1764 or 800/938–9311). **Easy Rider Tours** (✉ Box 228, Newburyport, MA 01950, ☎ 978/463–6955 or 800/488–8332, FAX 978/463–6988). **Euro-Bike Tours** (✉ Box 990, De Kalb, IL 60115, ☎ 800/321–6060, FAX 815/758–8851). **Progressive Travels** (✉ 224 W. Galer Ave., Suite C, Seattle, WA 98119, ☎ 206/285–1987 or 800/245–2229, FAX 206/285–1988). **Vermont Bicycle Touring** (✉ Box 711, Bristol, VT, 05443-0711, ☎ 800/245–3868 or 802/453–4811, FAX 802/453–4806).

➤ FOOD AND WINE: **Odysseys Adventures** (☞ Group Tours, *above*).

➤ GOLF: **Golf International** (✉ 275 Madison Ave., New York, NY 10016, ☎ 212/986–9176 or 800/833–1389, FAX 212/986–3720). **ITC Golf Tours** (✉ 4134 Atlantic Ave., No. 205, Long Beach, CA 90807, ☎ 310/595–6905 or 800/257–4981). **Odysseys Adventures** (☞ Group Tours, *above*).

➤ HORSEBACK RIDING: **Equitour FITS Equestrian** (✉ Box 807, Dubois, WY 82513, ☎ 307/455–3363 or 800/545–0019, FAX 307/455–2354).

➤ JEWISH HERITAGE: **Kesher Tours** (✉ 370 Lexington Ave., New York, NY 10017, ☎ 212/949–9580 or 800/847–0700, FAX 212/599–6086). **Odysseys Adventures** (☞ Group Tours, *above*).

➤ LEARNING: **Smithsonian Study Tours and Seminars** (✉ 1100 Jefferson Dr. SW, Room 3045, MRC 702, Washington, DC 20560, ☎ 202/357–4700, FAX 202/633–9250). **Victor Emanuel Nature Tours** (✉ Box 33008, Austin, TX 78764, ☎ 512/328–5221 or 800/328–8368, FAX 512/328–2919).

➤ MOTORCYCLING: **Edelweiss Bike Travel** (✉ Hartford Holidays Travel, 129 Hillside Ave., Williston Park, NY 11596, ☎ 516/746–6761 or 800/877–2784, FAX 516/746–6690).

➤ SPAS: **Spa-Finders** (✉ 91 5th Ave., No. 301, New York, NY 10003-

3039, ☎ 212/924–6800 or 800/255–7727).

➤ WALKING/HIKING: **Abercrombie & Kent** (☞ Group Tours, *above*). **Adventure Center** (✉ 1311 63rd St., No. 200, Emeryville, CA 94608, ☎ 510/654–1879 or 800/227–8747, FAX 510/654–4200). **Butterfield & Robinson** (☞ Bicycling, *above*). **Camino Tours** (☞ Bicycling, *above*). **Country Walkers** (✉ Box 180, Waterbury, VT 05676-0180, ☎ 802/244–1387 or 800/464–9255, FAX 802/244–5661). **Himalayan Travel** (☞ Adventure, *above*). **Mountain Travel-Sobek** (✉ 6420 Fairmount Ave., El Cerrito, CA 94530, ☎ 510/527–8100 or 800/227–2384, FAX 510/525–7710). **Uniquely Europe** (✉ 2819 1st Ave., Ste. 280, Seattle, WA 98121-1113, ☎ 206/441–8682 or 800/426–3615, FAX 206/441–8862). **Wilderness Travel** (✉ 1102 Ninth St., Berkeley, CA 94710, ☎ 510/558–2488 or 800/368–2794).

➤ YACHT CHARTERS: **Huntley Yacht Vacations** (✉ 210 Preston Rd., Wernersville, PA 19565, ☎ 610/678–2628 or 800/322–9224, FAX 610/670–1767). **Lynn Jachney Charters** (✉ Box 302, Marblehead, MA 01945, ☎ 617/639–0787 or 800/223–2050, FAX 617/639–0216). **The Moorings** (✉ 19345 U.S. Hwy. 19 N, 4th floor, Clearwater, FL 34624-3193, ☎ 813/530–5424 or 800/535–7289, FAX 813/530–9474). **Ocean Voyages** (✉ 1709 Bridgeway, Sausalito, CA 94965, ☎ 415/332–4681 or 800/299–4444, FAX 415/332–7460).

TRAIN TRAVEL

International overnight trains run from Madrid to Lisbon and Barcelona to Paris (both 11½ hours). A daytime trip runs from Barcelona to Grenoble and Geneva (10 hours).

If you purchase a same-day round-trip ticket while in Spain, a 20% discount applies; if you purchase a different-day round-trip ticket, you will get a 10% discount.

Spain's high-speed train, the AVE, travels between Madrid and Seville in less than three hours. However, the rest of the government-run railroad, RENFE, remains below par by European standards. Train travel can be

THE GOLD GUIDE / SMART TRAVEL TIPS

tediously slow, and most long-distance trips run at night. While overnight trains have comfortable sleeper cars, first-class fares that include a sleeping compartment are comparable to airfares.

For most journeys, however, trains are the most economical way to go. First- and second-class seats are reasonably priced, and you can get a bunk in a compartment with five other people for a supplement of about $25. The most comfortable train, TALGO, has a special inverted suspension system designed to give a faster and smoother ride on winding rails. Food in the dining cars and bars is overpriced and uninspired.

Most Spaniards buy train tickets in advance by standing in long lines at the station. The overworked clerks rarely speak English, however, so if you don't speak Spanish, you're better off going to a travel agency that displays the blue-and-yellow RENFE sign. The price is the same.

To save money, **look into rail passes,** but be aware that unless you plan to cover many miles, you may come out ahead by sticking to individual tickets.

DISCOUNT PASSES

If Spain is your only destination in Europe, **consider purchasing a Spain Flexipass.** Prices begin at $144 for three days of second-class travel within a two-month period and $180 for first class. Other passes cover more days and longer periods.

Spain is one of 17 countries in which you can **use EurailPasses,** which provide unlimited first-class rail travel in all of the participating countries, for the duration of the pass. If you plan to rack up the miles, get a standard pass. These are available for 15 days ($522), 21 days ($678), one month ($838), two months ($1,148), and three months ($1,468). If your plans call for only limited train travel, **look into a Europass,** which costs less money than a EurailPass but allows a limited number of travel days, in a limited number of countries, during a specified time period. For example, a two-month pass ($316) allows between 5 and 15 days of rail travel but costs $200 less than the least expensive EurailPass. Keep in mind, however, that the Europass is good only in France, Germany, Italy, Spain, and Switzerland, and the number of countries you can visit is further limited by the type of pass you buy. For example, the basic two-month pass allows you to visit only three of the five participating countries.

In addition to standard EurailPasses, **ask about special rail-pass plans.** Among these are the Eurail Youthpass (for those under age 26), the Eurail Saverpass (which gives a discount for two or more people traveling together), a Eurail Flexipass (which allows a certain number of travel days within a set period), the Euraildrive Pass and the Europass Drive (which combines travel by train and rental car). Whichever pass you choose, remember that you must **purchase your pass before you leave** for Europe.

Many travelers assume that rail passes guarantee them seats on the trains they wish to ride. Not so: you need to **reserve seats in advance even if you're using a rail pass.** Seat reservations are required on some European trains, particularly high-speed trains, and are a good idea on trains that may be crowded—particularly in summer on popular routes. You'll also need a reservation if you purchase sleeping accommodations.

➤ INFORMATION AND PASSES: **Rail Europe** (⊠ 226–230 Westchester Ave., White Plains, NY 10604, ☎ 914/682–5172 or 800/438–7245; ⊠ 2087 Dundas E, Suite 105, Mississauga, Ontario L4X 1M2, ☎ 416/602–4195). **DER Tours** (⊠ Box 1606, Des Plaines, IL 60017, ☎ 800/782–2424, FAX 800/282–7474). **CIT Tours Corp.** (⊠ 342 Madison Ave., Suite 207, New York, NY 10173, ☎ 212/697–2100 or 800/248–8687; 800/248–7245 in western U.S.).

FROM THE U.K.

Train services to Spain are not as frequent, fast, or inexpensive as airplane travel. To reach Spain from Britain, you have to change trains (and rail stations) in Paris. It's worth paying extra for a Talgo express or for the Puerta del Sol express to avoid having to change trains again at the Spanish border. Journey time to Paris is around six hours; from Paris to Madrid, an additional 13 hours. Allow at least two hours in Paris for changing trains. If you're under 26 years old, Eurotrain has excellent deals.

➤ FROM THE U.K.: **British Rail Travel Centers** (☎ 0171/834–2345). **Eurotrain** (✉ 52 Grosvenor Gardens, London SW1W OAG, ☎ 0171/730–3402). **Transalpino** (✉ 71–75 Buckingham Palace Rd., London SW1W ORE, ☎ 0171/834–9656).

LUXURY TRAIN

The luxurious turn-of-the-century *Al Andalus Express* makes five-day trips in Andalusia for sightseeing in Córdoba, Granada, and Seville; the cost is about $2,600 per person.

➤ RESERVATIONS: **Marketing Ahead** (✉ 433 5th Ave., New York, NY 10016, ☎ 212/686–9213 or 800/223–1356) or **DER Tours** (✉ Box 1606, Des Plaines, IL 60017, ☎ 800/782–2424, FAX 800/282–7474).

TRANSPORTATION

Most towns are connected by railway. Occasionally, however, you'll have to resort to buses, which are usually faster and more expensive than trains for short distances but slower and much cheaper for longer distances.

TRAVEL AGENCIES

A good travel agent puts your needs first. It's important to **look for an agency that specializes in your destination, has been in business at least five years, and emphasizes customer service.** If you're looking for an agency-organized package or tour, your best bet is an agency that's a member of the National Tour Association or the United States Tour Operator's Association (☞ Tour Operators, *above*).

➤ LOCAL AGENT REFERRALS: **American Society of Travel Agents** (✉ ASTA, 1101 King St., Suite 200, Alexandria, VA 22314, ☎ 703/739–2782, FAX 703/684–8319). **Alliance of Canadian Travel Associations** (✉ 1729 Bank St., Suite 201, Ottawa, Ontario K1V 7Z5, ☎ 613/521–

0474, FAX 613/521–0805). **Association of British Travel Agents** (✉ 55–57 Newman St., London W1P 4AH, ☎ 0171/637–2444, FAX 0171/637–0713).

U.S. GOVERNMENT

The U.S. government can be an excellent source of inexpensive travel information. When planning your trip, **find out what government materials are available.**

➤ ADVISORIES: **U.S. Department of State American Citizens Services Office** (✉ Room 4811; Washington, DC 20520), enclose a self-addressed, stamped envelope. **Interactive hotline** (☎ 202/647–5225, FAX 202/647–3000). **Computer bulletin board** (☎ 202/647–9225).

➤ PAMPHLETS: **Consumer Information Center** (✉ Consumer Information Catalogue, Pueblo, CO 81009, ☎ 719/948–3334).

VISITOR INFORMATION

For general information, contact the tourism offices below. If calling the brochure line in the United Kingdom, remember it costs 50p per minute peak rate, 45p per minute cheap rate.

➤ TOURIST OFFICE OF SPAIN: U.S. Nationwide (✉ 666 5th Ave., 35th floor, New York, NY 10103, ☎ 212/265–8822, FAX 212/265–8864). Chicago (✉ 845 N. Michigan Ave., Chicago, IL 60611, ☎ 312/642–1992, FAX 312/642–9817). Los Angeles (✉ 8383 Wilshire Blvd., Suite 960, Beverly Hills, CA 90211, ☎ 213/658–7188, FAX 213/658–1061). Miami (✉ 1221 Brickell Ave., Suite 1850, Miami, FL 33131, ☎ 305/358–1992, FAX 305/358–8223). Canada (✉ 2 Bloor St. W, 34th floor, Toronto, Ontario M4W 3E2, ☎ 416/961–3131, FAX 416/961–1992). United Kingdom (✉ 57–58 St. James's St., London SW1A 1LD, ☎ 0171/499–0901; 0891/669–920 for brochures; FAX 0171/629–4257).

WEB SITES

Do **check out the World Wide Web** when you're planning. You'll find everything from up-to-date weather forecasts to virtual tours of famous cities. Fodor's Web site, www.

fodors.com, is a great place to start your online travels. For more information specifically on Spain, visit www.okspain.org and www.tourspain.es.

WHEN TO GO

May and October, when the weather is generally warm and dry, are considered the best months for touring Spain. May gives you more hours of daylight for sightseeing, while October offers a chance to enjoy the harvest season, which is especially colorful in Spain's many wine regions.

In April you can glimpse some of Spain's most spectacular fiestas, in honor of Semana Santa (Holy Week). Weather in southern Spain warms up enough by April to make sightseeing comfortable.

Spain is the number-one destination for European tourists, so **if you want to avoid crowds, don't go in June, July, August, or September.** It's crowded and more expensive then, especially along the coasts. However, most people find the waters of the Mediterranean too cold for swimming the rest of the year, and beach season on the Atlantic coast is slightly shorter. Spaniards themselves vacation in August, and their annual migration to the beaches cause huge traffic jams on August 1 and 31. Major cities are delightfully relaxed and empty for the duration; small shops and some restaurants shut down for the entire month, but museums remain open.

Summers in Spain are hot; temperatures frequently hit 100°F (38°C), and air conditioning is not widespread. Try to **limit your touring to the morning hours and take a siesta in the afternoon.** Warm summer nights are among Spain's most pleasant experiences.

Winters in Spain are mild and rainy along the coasts, especially in Galicia. Elsewhere winter blows bitterly cold. Snow is infrequent except in the mountains, where skiing is possible from December to March in the Pyrenees and other resorts near Granada, Madrid, and Burgos.

CLIMATE

➤ FORECASTS: **Weather Channel Connection** (☎ 900/932–8437), 95¢ per minute from a Touch-Tone phone.

The following are average daily maximum and minimum temperatures for major cities in Spain.

Climate in Spain

MADRID

Jan.	48F	9C	May	70F	21C	Sept.	77F	25C
	36	2		50	10		57	14
Feb.	52F	11C	June	81F	27C	Oct.	66F	19C
	36	2		59	15		50	10
Mar.	59F	15C	July	88F	31C	Nov.	55F	13C
	41	5		63	17		41	5
Apr.	64F	18C	Aug.	86F	30C	Dec.	48F	9C
	45	7		63	17		36	2

BARCELONA

Jan.	55F	13C	May	70F	21C	Sept.	77F	25C
	43	6		57	14		66	19
Feb.	57F	14C	June	77F	25C	Oct.	70F	21C
	45	7		64	18		59	15
Mar.	61F	16C	July	82F	28C	Nov.	61F	16C
	48	9		70	21		52	11
Apr.	64F	18C	Aug.	82F	28C	Dec.	55F	13C
	52	11		70	21		46	8

SEVILLE

Jan.	59F	15C	May	81F	27C	Sept.	90F	32C
	43	6		55	13		64	18
Feb.	63F	17C	June	90F	32C	Oct.	79F	26C
	45	7		63	17		57	14
Mar.	68F	20C	July	97F	36C	Nov.	68F	20C
	48	9		68	20		50	10
Apr.	75F	24C	Aug.	97F	36C	Dec.	61F	16C
	52	11		68	20		45	7

CÓRDOBA

Jan.	55F	13C	May	79F	26C	Sept.	88F	31C
	41	5		55	13		63	17
Feb.	61F	16C	June	90F	32C	Oct.	77F	25C
	43	6		63	17		55	13
Mar.	66F	19C	July	99F	37C	Nov.	66F	19C
	46	8		68	20		48	9
Apr.	73F	23C	Aug.	97F	36C	Dec.	57F	14C
	50	10		68	20		41	5

GRANADA

Jan.	54F	12C	May	73F	23C	Sept.	84F	29C
	36	2		50	10		59	15
Feb.	57F	14C	June	86F	30C	Oct.	73F	23C
	37	3		59	15		50	10
Mar.	63F	17C	July	93F	34C	Nov.	63F	17C
	41	5		63	17		43	6
Apr.	68F	20C	Aug.	91F	33C	Dec.	54F	12C
	45	7		63	17		37	3

THE GOLD GUIDE / SMART TRAVEL TIPS

1 Destination: Spain

SPAIN'S SECOND GOLDEN AGE

THE SENSE OF EXCITEMENT in Spain today is contagious. The first thing that's bound to strike the traveler is this palpable exhilaration, a feeling that seems to electrify Spain from remote mountain villages to the poshest avenues of Madrid and Barcelona. Naturally, there are dark spots in the picture—beggars in the streets, Basque terrorism, huge economic adjustments required by the country's 1986 entry into the European Union—and yet it's difficult not to be infected by the overall optimism. You can see it in the general sprucing up of recent years. You can feel it, especially in the bars and restaurants. Life is loved and celebrated here; few peoples seem to have such a capacity for enjoyment. In many ways, the Spanish have always been like this—Richard Wright, visiting in the 1950s, called it "pagan Spain"—but for 36 years of the 20th century, they lived and labored under a repressive, ultraconservative regime that ended only with the death of Francisco Franco in 1975. The renaissance that followed has been not just political but also creative and economic.

In imagining the Spanish landscape, you may picture the scorched, orange plains of La Mancha, where Don Quixote tilted, or the softly rolling hills of Andalusia, or even the overdeveloped beaches of the Costa del Sol. But after Switzerland, Spain is the most mountainous country in Europe, and also one of the most geographically diverse, ranging from the soggy northwest (wetter than Ireland) to the haunting plains of the central *meseta*, from the cascading trout streams of the Pyrenees to the marshes and dunes of Doñana National Park, on the Costa de la Luz. There are deep caves, lonely coves, rock canyons, mountain meadows, coastal rice paddies, volcanic island peaks . . . and, of course, the great, snowy wall of the Pyrenees, which has always isolated Spain from France and northern Europe as well as separated the different Pyrenean peoples and cultures.

More than almost any other country its size—it's the second largest in Europe, after France—Spain is characterized by the distinctness of its many parts and peoples. The Galicians of the northwest are descended from the same Celtic tribes that colonized the British Isles. Bagpipes are a local instrument, and kilts not unknown; and the local language, Gallego, is a mixture of Spanish and Portuguese. The Basque Country, whose eastern end abuts the French border, also has its own language, Euskera, a tongue so mysterious that linguists have never agreed where it began. Local pride is fierce here; the Basque language and culture are purposefully celebrated, and independentist sentiment is strong. Outright separatism is embodied in the terrorist group ETA (Euskadi Ta Askatasuna), which has killed almost 900 Spaniards over the past three decades. (The violence is extremely unlikely to affect travelers.) The Catalans, who populate northeastern Spain around Barcelona, speak the country's most substantial regional language, Catalan, which is closer to Provençal French than to Castilian (Spanish); residents of the province of Valencia and the Balearic islands speak and study in their own local versions of Catalan. All of these areas suffered systematic cultural and linguistic repression under the totalitarian centralist pressure of the Franco regime.

The Iberian Peninsula's early peoples included Basques, Celts, Iberians, Greeks, Romans, and Visigoths. But Christians in the centuries after Christ widely intermarried with Jewish and Moorish minorities. Most Spaniards today see themselves as purely Catholic, but almost all have Jewish and/or Muslim ancestors.

Most of Spain transformed itself from an agrarian and largely feudal economy to a modern, capitalist one in remarkably little time, over the first half of the 20th century. Now, a lively economy and optimistic outlook are giving modern Spain an anything-is-possible air, despite a high unemployment rate and the continuing scourge of terrorism. The 1992 Olympic Games, the Guggenheim Museum Bilbao, new freeways, high-speed trains, and state-of-the-art technology have replaced a country that was often described 25 years ago as borderline third-world.

Modernity has come at a price. For generations, Spain was the travel destination of choice for the penniless artist, the adventurer willing to forego comfort for rugged romance. All that has changed. After years of inflation, and a value-added tax imposed as a condition of entry into the European Union, Spain's cost of living compares to that of partners like France. The festivities of 1992—the Summer Olympics, in Barcelona, and the Universal Exposition, in Seville—further inflated hotel and restaurant prices in those cities. The rate of price increases has slowed in the late 1990s, however, and Americans in particular can now enjoy the benefits of a relatively strong dollar.

SPAIN HAS AN extraordinary heritage of history, art, and architecture. It begins with the ancient caves at Altamira, in which people wearing skins for warmth painted delicate animals on a rock ceiling. During the Age of Exploration, robust adventurers left hardscrabble Extremadura, Spain's poorest province, to probe the New World, and some returned to build great stone palaces on Extremadura's stark, scrubby landscape. Stretched across northern Spain are the Romanesque churches of the Camino de Santiago (Way of St. James), which was Europe's most famous Christian pilgrimage in the Middle Ages; the journey culminated at the soaring cathedral of Santiago de Compostela. Cave churches of the Visigoths (early Christians) are scattered across the north as a sort of graphic counterpoint. Seville, the pastel-color city of Don Juan, still spreads elegantly along the banks of the Guadalquivir. More than ten thousand castles are sprinkled across the Iberian Peninsula, some merely ruins, others in extraordinarily good shape. Villages of whitewashed buildings, harbors stuffed with brightly painted fishing boats, and majestic towns welded to craggy mountaintops are easy to find. Still washed by that subtle light that inspired Velázquez, the Spanish countryside remains mercifully unchanged.

The story of this land, a romance-tinged tale of counts, caliphs, crusaders, and kings, begins long before written history. The Basques were among the first here, huddling in the cold mountain valleys of the north. The Iberians came next, apparently crossing the Mediterranean from North Africa around 3,000 BC. The Celts arrived from the north about a thousand years later. The seafaring Phoenicians founded Gadir (now Cádiz) and several coastal cities in the south. The parade continued with the Greeks, who settled parts of the east coast, and then the Carthaginians, who founded Cartagena around 225 BC—and who dubbed the then-wild, forested country Spania.

Modern civilization really began with the Romans, who expelled the Carthaginians and turned the peninsula into three imperial provinces. It took the Romans 200 years to subdue the fiercely resisting Celts, Iberians, and Basques—ending shortly before the birth of Christ—but their influence was lasting. Evidence of the Roman epoch is left today in the great ruins at Mérida, Segovia, Tarragona, and other cities; in the peninsula's legal system; and in the Latin base of its three Romance languages. In the early 5th century, various invading barbarians crossed the Pyrenees to attack the weakening Roman empire. The Visigoths became the dominant force in northern Spain by 419, establishing their kingdom at Toledo and eventually adopting Christianity.

But they, too, were to fall before a wave of invaders, this time that of the Moors, a Berber-led Arab force that crossed the Strait of Gibraltar from North Africa. The Moors swept through Spain in an astonishingly short time, meeting only token resistance and launching almost eight centuries of Muslim rule—a period that in many respects was the pinnacle of Spanish civilization. Unlike the semibarbaric Visigoths, the Moors were extremely cultured. Arabs, Jews, and Christians lived together in peace during their reign, although many Christians did convert to Islam. The Moors also brought with them citrus fruits, rice, cotton, sugar, palm trees, glassmaking, and the complex irrigation system still used around Valencia. Their influence is evident in modern Spanish, where most words beginning with "al" are Arabic in origin, such as *albóndig* (meatball), *alcalde* (mayor), *almohada* (pillow), and *alcázar* (fortress). To the traveler, Moorish culture is most spectacularly evident in modern-day Andalusia, the kingdom the Moors called al-Andalus. The grand, fairy-tale Alhambra palace, which still crowns the beautiful city of Granada, embodies both the ambition and the delicacy of the Moorish aesthetic.

The Moors never managed to subdue northwestern Galicia and Asturias, and it was in the latter that a minor Christian king, Pelayo, began the long crusade that came to be known as the *Reconquista* (Reconquest). By 1085, Alfonso VI of Castile had captured Toledo, giving the Christians a firm grip on the north. In the 13th century, Valencia, Seville, and finally Córdoba—the capital of the Muslim caliphate in Spain—fell to Christian forces, leaving only Granada in Moorish hands. Two hundred years later, two Catholic monarchs, Ferdinand of Aragon and Isabella of Castile, were joined in a marriage that would change the world.

THE YEAR 1492 is a watershed in Spanish history, the beginning of the nation's political golden age and the moment of some of its worst excesses of intolerance. That year, the 23rd of Ferdinand and Isabella's marriage, Christian forces conquered Granada and unified all of current-day Spain as a single kingdom. Jews and Muslims who did not convert to Christianity were expelled from the country en masse. Christopher Columbus, under the sponsorship of Isabella, landed in the Americas, initiating the Age of Exploration; but the departure of educated Muslims and Jews was a blow to the nation's economy from which it would never recover. The Inquisition, which had been established in 1478, further persecuted those who chose to stay. The colonies of the New World greatly enriched Spain at first, but massive shipments of Peruvian and Mexican gold later produced terrible inflation. The so-called Catholic Monarchs and their centralizing successors maintained Spain's unity, but they sacrificed the spirit of international free trade that was beginning to bring capitalist prosperity to other parts of Europe.

Ferdinand and Isabella were succeeded by their grandson Carlos, who became the first Spanish Habsburg and one of the most powerful rulers in history. Cortés reached Mexico and Pizarro conquered Peru under his rule. Carlos also inherited Austria and the Netherlands and in 1519, three years into his reign, was elected Holy Roman Emperor (as Charles V), wasting little time in annexing Naples and Milan. He championed the Counter-Reformation and saw the Jesuit order created to help defend Catholicism against European Protestantism. But Charles cost the nation with his penchant for waging war, particularly against the Ottomans and German Lutherans. His son, Philip II, followed in the same, expensive path, ultimately defeating the Turks and ordering the construction of the somber Escorial monastery, outside Madrid. It was here that Philip died, 10 years after losing the Spanish Armada in an attack on Protestant England.

The War of the Spanish Succession was ignited by the death, without issue, in 1700 of Charles II, the last Spanish Habsburg. Philip of Anjou was crowned Philip V and inaugurated the Bourbon line in Spain (a representative of which sits on the throne today). The Bourbons of that era, a Frenchified lot, copied many of the attitudes and fashions of their northern neighbors, but the infatuation ended with Napoleon's 1808 installation of his brother, José Bonaparte. Mocked bitterly as "Pepe Botella" for his fondness for drink (*botella* means "bottle"), Bonaparte was widely despised, and an 1808 uprising against him in Madrid—chronicled harrowingly by the great painter Francisco de Goya y Lucientes (1746–1828)—began the War of Independence, known to foreigners as the Peninsular War. Britain, siding with Spain, sent the Duke of Wellington to the rescue. With the aid of Spanish guerillas, the French were finally expelled, but not before they had looted Spain's major churches and cathedrals. Most of Spain's American colonies took advantage of the war to claim their independence.

The rest of the century was not a happy one for Spain, as conservative regimes grappled with civil wars and revolts inspired by the currents of European republicanism. The final blow came with the loss of Cuba, Puerto Rico, and the Philippines in 1898, a military disaster that ironically sparked a remarkable literary renaissance—the so-called Generation of '98, whose members included writers Miguel de Unamuno and Pío Baroja and poet Antonio Machado. In 1902 Alfonso XIII came to the throne, but rising civil strife got the better of him and ended in his self-imposed exile in 1931. A fledgling republic followed, to the delight of most

Spaniards, but the 1936 election of a left-wing Popular Front government ignited bitter opposition from the right. In the end, a young general named Francisco Franco used the assassination of a monarchist leader as an excuse for a military revolt.

The Spanish civil war (1936–39) was the single most tragic episode in Spanish history. More than half a million people died in the conflict. Intellectuals and leftists the world over sympathized with the elected government, and the International Brigades, with many American, British, and Canadian volunteers, took part in some of the worst fighting, including the storied defense of Madrid. But Franco, backed by the Catholic Church, got far more help from Nazi Germany, whose Condor legions destroyed the Basque town of Guernica (in a horror made infamous by Picasso's monumental painting), and from Fascist Italy. For three years, European governments stood quietly by as Franco's armies vanquished Barcelona, Madrid, and the last capital of the Republic, Valencia.

Officially neutral during World War II but sympathetic to the Axis powers, Spain was largely shunned by the world until, in a 1953 agreement, the United States provided aid in exchange for the building of NATO bases. Gradually, the shattered economy began to pick up, especially with the surge of tourism that gathered steam in the late 1960s. But when Franco announced in 1969 that his successor would be Juan Carlos, the grandson of Alfonso XIII and a prince whose militaristic education had been strictly overseen by the aging general, the hopes of a nation longing for freedom sagged. Imagine the Spaniards' surprise when, six years later, Franco died and the young monarch revealed himself to be a closet democrat. Under his nurturing, a new constitution restoring civil liberties and freedom of expression was adopted in 1978. On February 23, 1981, the king proved his mettle once and for all, when a nostalgic Civil Guard colonel with visions of a return to Franco's authoritarian regime, along with a unit of would-be rebels, held the Spanish parliament—then center-right—captive for some 24 hours. Only the heroism of King Juan Carlos, who personally called military commanders across the country to ensure their loyalty to the elected government, quelled the coup attempt. The Socialists ruled Spain from 1982 until early 1996, when conservative José María Aznar was elected prime minister.

In the arts, Spain seems to have picked up where it left off when the civil war and the ensuing 40-year cultural silence of the Franco regime intervened. Whereas the first third of the century produced such towering figures as poet Federico García Lorca, filmmaker Luis Buñuel, and painters Pablo Picasso, Joan Miró, and Salvador Dalí, the final quarter (since Franco's death in 1975) will be known for novelist Camilo José Cela's 1989 Nobel Prize (for *The Family of Pascual Duarte*), filmmaker Pedro Almodóvar's postmodern Spanish films, Basque sculptor Eduardo Chillida's blocky forms, and the conceptually challenging works of Catalan painter Antoni Tapiès.

Dip into the Portraits of Spain (☞ Chapter 17) before you leave home. When you get here, take the country as the Spanish do, piece by piece. Spain at the end of the 20th century is a patchwork of cultures and nationalities: Andalusia and Catalonia are as different as France and England, maybe more so. The miracle is that a common language and a central government have managed to bring these "Autonomous Communities" as close together as they are. Castilians, Basques, Galicians, Asturians, Catalans, and Andalusians all contribute separately and equally to a Spain that approaches the millennium as one of the most vibrant nations in Europe.

NEW AND NOTEWORTHY

A general travel trend throughout Spain is to depart from the usual full-service lodging and spend the night in a more rustic and romantic setting, such as a farmhouse, manor house, or restored noble home.

Madrid

With Madrid increasingly recognized as one of Europe's great cultural centers, Madrileños are prouder than ever of their beautiful and historic buildings, ancient landmarks, and urban showpieces. The city is constantly investing in renovations, restorations, and beautification projects, most recently that of the opera house, legendary for its disastrous history of fire, bombs, and structural problems. Overhauled at a staggering expense of $150 million, the gilded and gleaming Teatro Real reopened to much fanfare in October 1997.

Bilbao

The highly publicized and universally acclaimed Guggenheim Museum Bilbao, designed by American architect Frank Gehry and opened in October 1997, is putting Bilbao on travelers' maps. Holy Week 1998 was a complete sellout for hotels and transport alike; make reservations early, and prepare to be impressed. While you're in town, take a ride on Bilbao's designer subway, designed by British architect Norman Foster, and have a careful look through the excellent Museum of Fine Arts.

Galicia

The newest attraction in Galicia is the Casa del Hombre, or Domus, in La Coruña. This must-see interactive museum is devoted to the study of mankind, from the evolution of one person to man's relationship with society. Among the exhibits is the *Giaconda Sapiens,* a reproduction of the *Mona Lisa* (*La Gioconda*) made of a composite of photos of more than 10,000 faces from 110 countries, illustrating the incredible diversity and unity of the human race.

Barcelona

Barcelona will be more musical than ever when its fabled Liceu Opera House reopens, in early 1999. Check out the new, computerized Catalonian tourist office in the Palau Robert (at Passeig de Gràcia and Diagonal) and the Espai Gaudí, the best Gaudí composite ever assembled, atop La Pedrera. Meanwhile, FC (Futbol Club) Barcelona will be playing in the European Champions League in early 1999, possibly sending the city into a soccer frenzy.

Andalusia

Thanks to a new network of four-lane highways that connects all eight Andalusian capitals, driving in southern Spain is faster and safer; travelers can spend more time in their destinations and less behind the steering wheel. New trains shoot from Madrid to Seville in 2½ hours, to Málaga in less than four. But southern Spain's greatest pleasure is exploring the great

landscapes and unspoiled *pueblos* (villages) on relatively traffic-free secondary roads—or, if you really want a civilized pace, on the *Al-Andalus Express,* a luxury train composed of five exquisitely restored, vintage 1920s coaches that wind their way through the dramatic scenery in six- and seven-day journeys.

The Canary Islands

A new conference and convention center at Tenerife's Playa de las Américas has brought the area several large, new hotels. Puerto de la Cruz is showing the results of a downtown beautification program whereby traffic through the business district has been rerouted, trees planted, and storefronts refurbished. An island "dignification" campaign has had a positive effect on Gran Canaria's image: the desert-dune beach at Maspalomas was chosen as the sight of the 1997 WOMAD (World of Music, Arts, and Dance) festival, which drew talent and audiences from all over the world for three days of celebrating global culture.

WHAT'S WHERE

Madrid

Madrid, smack in the middle of Spain, is one of Europe's most vibrant cities. Madrileños are a vigorous, joyful lot, famous for their apparent ability to defy the need for sleep; they embrace their city's cultural offerings and make enthusiastic use of its cafés and bars. If you can match this energy, you'll take in Madrid's museum mile, with more masterpieces per yard than anywhere else in the world; the palaces and boutiques of regal Madrid; the dark, narrow lanes of medieval Madrid; and Madrid post-midnight, where today's action is.

Around Madrid

Castilla (Castile), the area surrounding Madrid, is a vast, windswept plateau with clear skies and endless vistas. An outstanding Roman aqueduct and a fairy-tale castle and cathedral make Segovia one of the most popular excursions from Madrid. The walled city of Ávila was the home of St. Teresa, Spain's female patron saint, and the university town of Salamanca is a flourish of golden sandstone. Aranjuez tempts with the French-style elegance of a Bourbon palace, while enigmatic Toledo is dramatic and austere, with rich legacies from three religions.

León, Galicia, and Asturias

In Spain's dense, green, and stormy northwest, the Celtic-flavored provinces León, Galicia, and Asturias mix breathtaking mountains, medieval villages, and quiet beaches. Follow the pilgrimage route of St. James; take refuge in the awesome cathedral at Santiago de Compostela; sip hard cider in Villaviciosa; stand peacefully on a shore so perilous that it's been called the Coast of Death, at La Coruña; and feast everywhere on fresh seafood.

Burgos, Santander, and the Basque Country

Burgos, home of the 11th-century military hero El Cid, is a somber city in a parched landscape of stone villages; Santander is a beach resort flanked by the Cantabrian mountains; and the Basque country, with its own language, moist green hills, and rugged coast, has a population devoted to gastronomy, sports, and rural culture and a small but determined minority that wants independence from Spain. La Rioja, at the southern edge of Basque country, produces Spain's finest wines.

The Pyrenees

The Pyrenees, snowcapped mountains that have historically sealed off the Iberian Peninsula from the rest of Western Europe, have long been a source of fascination, legend, and superstition. Pyrenean meadows and valleys have protected the last vestiges of several ancient cultures. To explore any one of these valleys thoroughly—flora, fauna, architecture, remote glacial ponds and streams, and the Romanesque art hidden in a thousand chapels and hermitages—could take a lifetime.

Barcelona

Barcelona is one of Europe's most dynamic and artistic cities. From the medieval atmosphere of the Gothic Quarter's narrow alleys to the elegance of the Moderniste Eixample or the action-packed modern Olympic Village, Barcelona is on the move. Picasso, Miró, and Dalí have links to this vibrant city with its ever-stronger Catalan identity. After 40 years of repression through post–civil-war Franco dictatorship, Catalan language and culture have

flourished since home rule was granted in 1975. Now this ancient romance language is heard in every street and is, along with Castilian Spanish, Barcelona's co-official language.

Southern Catalonia and the Levante

Southern Catalonia's Tarragona province and the Valencia region—known as the Levante because the sun rises (*se levanta*) out of the Mediterranean here—are a landscape of grayish, arid mountains backing a lush coast of sandy beaches, many marred by modern tourist developments. Inland, the rugged landscape is dotted with small fortified towns that were strategically important in medieval times. Tarragona bursts with Roman antiquities, and Valencia, Spain's third-largest city, is rich in art and architecture.

The Southeast

Spain's southeastern corner has a flat, fertile coastal plain characterized by orange groves, rice paddies, and mountains that give rise to the strange, almost lunar desert landscape of Almería. Most travelers come to the Southeast for its beautiful beaches, but the region's inland vistas are just as attractive. Both the province and the coast are dappled with striking white architecture, a legacy of long Moorish occupation.

The Balearic Islands

The Balearics' strategic position—off the eastern coast of Spain, halfway between France and Africa—has historically placed the archipelago in the middle of Mediterranean territorial disputes. Although Menorca and Formentera remain largely unspoiled, great stretches of the coasts of Majorca and Ibiza have been marred by developments catering to tourists on package vacations. Still, Majorca's northwestern coast remains nearly as rough and remote as it was when George Sand and Frédéric Chopin spent a winter among its rugged mountains a century and a half ago.

The Costa del Sol

Most of the Costa del Sol—the central Andalusian coast—is an overdeveloped package-tour magnet for northern European sunseekers and a retirement haven for Britons and Americans. Marbella's luxury hotels attract the most glamorous crowd, Torremolinos the wildest; but just a few miles inland from either are breathtaking scenery and mountain villages, cultural light-years away from the hedonistic carnival raging on the coast. The tiny British colony of Gibraltar has its own English atmosphere.

Granada, Córdoba, and Eastern Andalusia

Eastern Andalusia is a region of lively cities with a deep sense of history; rolling plains whose ordered ranks of olive trees stretch into the distance; mountainous vistas; and whitewashed villages clinging to parched hillsides. Here you'll find two of Spain's most famous monuments, Granada's magical Alhambra palace and Córdoba's great mosque; the Sierra Nevada; and the source of the mighty Guadalquivir River.

Seville and Western Andalusia

The flat expanse of fertile pastures, muddy marshlands, chalky vineyards, and sandy beaches in western Andalusia contrasts vividly with the mountainous provinces to the east. Enjoy the history and romance of Seville; trace the career of Christopher Columbus; sample the famous sherries of Jerez; and visit the region's famous tapas bars.

Extremadura

Extremadura is Spain's Wild West. One of the least-explored regions in the nation, Extremadura is a desert wilderness that quietly inspired several renowned writers (Cervantes, Cela, de Vega). In the quiet villages of Cáceres and Trujillo, medieval quarters and conquistadors' palaces stand perfectly preserved; in Mérida, Roman ruins bake in the sun; and out in the country, a deep blue sky stretches over flora, fauna, lakes, and stark plains. Here you'll find hearty, friendly people; colorful ceramics; and a local cuisine to please any carnivore.

The Canary Islands

Closer to North Africa than to Spain, the ruggedly exotic Canary Islands pack multicultural cities as well as Spanish villages, parched sand dunes as well as seaside resorts. Each of the seven islands in this volcanic archipelago has its own personality. Explore caves once inhabited by ancient tribes; hike to snow-covered peaks; savor a meal grilled over the heat from a volcanic crater. With water sports, wine-tasting opportunities, and year-round sun

and nightlife, the Canary Islands have long been Europe's favorite winter retreat.

PLEASURES AND PASTIMES

Bullfighting

Bullfighting is a form of ritualized slaughter: The bull never wins, and gorings are unusual. Those who can conceive of the bull as a symbol rather than as an animal, who can remain undisturbed by the blood, and who can appreciate the drama and the fanfare will get the most out of a bullfight. For Spaniards, it's an art form and a national passion.

Bullfights start with a procession of banderilleros, picadors, and matadors. First, the matador waves capes to encourage the bull's charges. Then a picador, on horseback, stabs the bull's neck and shoulder area. Next, banderilleros plant darts in the bull's back. After more cape taunting, the matador kills the bull with a sword: He or she (some matadors are female) may receive the bull's ears and/or tail for a job well done. Six bulls are killed per day, by several different matadors.

Corridas (bullfights), are normally held around 5 PM on Sundays, from April to early November. Hemingway made famous **Pamplona**'s running of the bulls and bullfighting during the feast of San Fermín, in the second week of July, but nowhere is bullfighting better than at **Madrid**'s Las Ventas, where three weeks of daily *corridas* in May mark the festival of San Isidro. **Seville** is the home of Spain's most hallowed bullring; during the April Fair, daily *corridas* here feature Spain's leading *toreros*. **Valencia** hosts the best bullfighters on July 25 and during the Fallas, in March. **Ronda**'s picturesque bullring is rarely used for taurine events except during festivals in May and September.

Dining

Seafood and roast meats are Spain's national specialties. Foods are lightly seasoned, although garlic is considered a basic ingredient. Salads are delicious and fundamental, especially in the heat of summer. *Ensalada mixta* includes canned tuna, asparagus, olives, tomatoes, onions, and egg. *Ensalada verde* is simpler, usually limited to lettuce, tomato, and onion.

Breakfast in Spain is usually coffee and a roll; in Madrid, it might be *churros* (strips of fried dough) and *chocolate* (thick, hot cocoa). Spanish coffee is strong espresso taken straight (*café solo*) or with hot milk (*café con leche*). If you prefer weaker coffee, ask for *café américano*.

Spaniards generally eat paella, the delicious seafood and saffron-spiced rice dish, at midday, preferably at a beachside restaurant or around a campfire at a country picnic.

Lunch usually consists of a first plate, which is a salad, soup, vegetable, or smoked fish or cured meat; a second plate, almost always meat or fish; and dessert, which can be ice cream, yogurt, or flan but is more often a piece of fresh fruit, which natives peel deftly with a knife and fork. All this is accompanied by bread (no butter) and washed down with a bottle of wine. In big cities, some workers now grab a quick sandwich instead of stopping for the traditional three-course lunch.

Restaurants are required by law to offer for lunch a *menú del día,* which includes all the above for 80% of what the courses would cost à la carte. Restaurants that specialize in a *menú del día* post it at the door; in others, you have to inquire, and the *menú del día* may be only a couple of unappetizing choices designed to get you to order from the regular menu.

Supper is three courses, sometimes with lighter fare replacing the meat course. Some restaurants may offer a *menú del día,* but it's usually leftover lunch.

Shopping

Clothing is expensive in Spain; World-famous Spanish **leather** jackets and shoes are beautiful, if pricey. Madrid has the best selection of leather clothing, purses, and shoes; shoes are generally made in Alicante and the Balearic Islands. Distinctive, country-style **ceramics** are in ready supply throughout the country; most are made in Talavera, Puente del Arzobispo (Toledo), and Seville.

In any **stationery** shop you'll find unusual pen and pencil boxes.

Other shopping in Spain will probably have something to do with **alcohol.** Each region produces its own wine, with the sherries of Jerez, the Riojas of the north, and the sparkling wines (*cavas*) of Catalonia famous around the world.

Sports

Sailing, boating, and other **water sports** are popular along the Mediterranean coast and in the Balearic Islands. Mountain streams in the Pyrenees and other ranges offer excellent **fishing.** The **golf** course at El Saler, south of Valencia, is considered one of the best in Continental Europe. Marbella has 14 excellent courses, and the Costa Brava and Costa Blanca also have commendable courses. The Valderrama Golf Club on the Costa del Sol hosted the prestigious Ryder Cup in September 1997. **Hiking** is excellent in the Canary Islands, the interior of Spain, and the numerous national parks, from the marshy Doñana to the mountainous Picos de Europa. The Pyrenees and the Sierra de Gredos are also popular. Spain has excellent **skiing and winter sports** facilities, with major resorts including Baqueira-Beret, Port del Compte, Llessui, and Formigal, in the Pyrenees; Sierra Nevada, near Granada; and Navacerrada, Valcoto, and Valdesqui, near Madrid. Spain is renowned for its horses: **polo** is played at the magnificent Puerta de Hierro Country Club, in Madrid, and the Royal Polo Club, in Barcelona. Thousands of pedal-pushers turn out in early summer, when the roads are closed off for Madrid's annual bicycle day. Otherwise, **bicycling** is impossible in crowded cities, but many coastal resorts rent bikes.

GREAT ITINERARIES

Essential Spain for First-Time Visitors

The best of both historic and modern Spain lies in this basic itinerary: experience the sophistication of Madrid and Barcelona, the medieval luster of Toledo and Segovia, the Moorish splendor of Granada and Córdoba, and end up in romantic Seville.

DURATION➤ 14 days

GETTING AROUND➤ You can take this tour by car (on divided highways), train, bus, or plane. A one-hour plane trip will save a day's travel time between Barcelona and Madrid. Driving between Granada,

Córdoba, and Seville allows you to see more of the Andalusian countryside and is still faster than the train, which tends to stop in every village. For the trip home, the ultramodern, high-speed AVE train can return you from Seville to Madrid in 2½ hours.

THE MAIN ROUTE➤ **Day 1: Barcelona.** Stay near the city center. Visit the cathedral and stroll through the Gothic Quarter. Promenade along the Ramblas and duck into the Bouquería market. Visit the Renaissance palace that houses the Picasso Museum, and stop into the nearby church of Santa María del Mar. Sample paella or seafood at an outdoor restaurant on the Barceloneta waterfront.

Day 2: Barcelona. Visit the fantastical Sagrada Familia church, designed by Antoni Gaudí and still under construction. Walk by Gaudí's buildings on the Passeig de Gràcia, the Casa Milà and the Casa Batlló; hop up to Parc Güell for a look over Barcelona from Gaudí's extraordinary park.

Day 3: Barcelona–Madrid. If you drive, stop outside Barcelona at the mountaintop monastery of Montserrat.

Day 4: Madrid. Visit the Royal Palace, and then stroll through old Madrid. Stop at one of the bars on the Plaza Mayor.

Day 5: Segovia. Using Madrid as your base, make a day trip to Segovia to see the Roman aqueduct, cathedral, and turreted castle. Have a grand Segovian lunch of roast suckling pig or venture out to the huge, gray monastery at El Escorial.

Day 6: Madrid. Stroll the leafy Paseo del Prado, visit the Prado Museum, and then recover with a stop at Retiro Park.

Day 7: Toledo. Toledo is the spiritual center of Spain. You can see it as a day trip from Madrid or, for those traveling by car, as your first stop on the way down to Granada. Soak up Spanish history in its cobbled alleyways, explore the cathedral, visit the synagogue, and imagine daily life in medieval Spain at the re-created house of El Greco.

Day 8: Madrid–Granada. En route, detour to the sleepy town of Consuegra, in La Mancha, to see Don Quixote's windmills.

Day 9: Granada. Explore the lush Moorish palace and gardens of the Alhambra. Poke into the Royal Chapel, adjoining the cathedral, where Ferdinand and Isabella are buried, and dine in the hillside Arab quarter, the Albaicín.

Day 10: Granada–Córdoba. In Córdoba, once the headquarters of the Moorish caliphate in Spain, visit the incredible mosque, with its red-and-white-striped arches and sparkling mosaics.

Day 11: Córdoba–Seville. Stop in Carmona, one of the oldest villages in Spain. Once in Seville, stroll along the Guadalquivir River and lose yourself among the winding streets and patios of the romantic Barrio Santa Cruz.

Day 12: Seville. Visit the splendid Moorish palace of the Alcázar, climb the Giralda, relax in the sweet-smelling orange-blossom patio by the cathedral, and ride a horse-drawn carriage to the tile-encrusted Plaza de España.

Day 13: Jerez de la Frontera and Arcos de la Frontera. Visit a sherry winery in Jerez; then make your way to the white hilltop town of Arcos in time for sunset.

Day 14: Seville–Madrid. Return by car, plane, or the AVE train.

Art and Architecture

This unique north–south tour avoids the big cities, concentrating solely on Spain's rich architectural history. You'll see superb examples of every major building style from the Romans on.

DURATION➤ 12 days

GETTING AROUND➤ A car is essential for this route, which sometimes winds over steep back roads and through narrow gates into walled cities.

THE MAIN ROUTE➤ **Day 1: Oviedo.** The capital of the province of Asturias, Oviedo has Europe's best examples of pre-Romanesque art. Visit the primitive yet graceful 9th-century chapels of Santa María del Naranco and San Miguel de Lillo, on a hill overlooking the city. Don't miss the treasures of Oviedo's Gothic cathedral, which include Visigoth-style jeweled crosses that commemorate the first Christian victory over the Moors, in 718.

Day 2: Oviedo–León. Cross the Pajares pass and descend to the high plains of Castile. In León, stay at the Parador San Marcos, a sumptuous Renaissance monastery that once headquartered the Knights of St.

James. Visit the basilica of San Isidro, with its primitive, medieval frescoes; linger in the 13th-century Gothic cathedral, which glitters with stained glass; and visit the arcaded Plaza Mayor, with its half-timbered houses.

Day 3: León–Segovia. Follow the back roads and stop at the imposing castles of Peñafiel and Coca, two of Spain's best.

Day 4: Segovia. Visit the Roman aqueduct, the cathedral, and the turreted castle, and wander the charming streets. From here you can make excursions to the French-inspired palace of La Granja or the medieval stone village of La Pedraza.

Day 5: Segovia–Ávila–Salamanca. In Ávila, walk the ramparts of the medieval city walls, the best-preserved in Spain. A detour through the Puerto del Pico pass, in the Sierra de Gredos, takes you over a still-intact Roman road, the likes of which once crisscrossed this countryside.

Day 6: Salamanca. The arcaded Plaza Mayor, the plateresque buildings of the university, and the soaring cathedrals make the entire city of Salamanca an architectural treasure.

Day 7: Salamanca–Cáceres. In Cáceres, stay in the unspoiled old town, whose stone palaces and plazas served as backdrops for Ridley Scott's film on the life of Columbus.

Day 8: Cáceres–Mérida. Explore Mérida's exquisite Roman theater (24 BC), and later take a break on the seats of the cruder amphitheater, where you can easily imagine the bloody battles of the gladiator days.

Day 9: Mérida–Seville. Travel day.

Day 10: Seville. Visit the splendid Moorish palace of the Alcázar, climb the Giralda, a 12th-century minaret; and tour the immense cathedral—the largest in Spain. Stroll under flowered Andalusian balconies in the Barrio Santa Cruz and ride a horse-drawn carriage to the tile-encrusted Plaza de España. Have a look at some of Spain's most modern architecture, including two soaring suspension bridges, on the island of La Cartuja, site of the 1992 Universal Expo.

Day 11: Seville–Córdoba. In Córdoba, once the headquarters of the Moorish caliphate in Spain, visit the incredible mosque, with its red-and-white-striped arches and sparkling mosaics. Stroll the narrow streets of the Judería and peer into the flowering Andalusian patios.

Day 12: Córdoba–Granada. End your trip with a stop at the grand palaces and gardens of the Alhambra, the last Moorish outpost in Europe. Explore the old Arab quarter, the Albaicín, with its unforgettable views of the Alhambra.

Castles

The Spanish countryside is packed with castles. This tour takes you to some of the best and allows you to spend the night in medieval splendor. The route fans out from Madrid and zigzags through Spain's center, where castles of Castile and La Mancha once served as the front line of defense between Christian and Muslim Spain. Children will enjoy this tour, and any of the days described can also stand on its own as an excursion from the capital.

DURATION➤ 7 days

GETTING AROUND➤ A car is essential for this tour, which goes through some fairly hilly, rugged territory. Rent in Madrid.

THE MAIN ROUTE➤ **Day 1: Madrid–Alarcón.** En route, stop at the Royal Palace of Aranjuez. Crossing the narrow bridge into the walled city and castle of Alarcón will take you back to the Middle Ages. The castle is a parador; try to book a room in the tower.

Day 2: Alarcón–Sigüenza. The ruined castle of Jadraque is worth a stop en route to Sigüenza, where a crenellated 14th-century castle lords over the village. Sigüenza's castle is one of Spain's most popular paradors. Ask to see the chapel.

Day 3: Sigüenza–Manzanares El Real–Segovia. Crossing back through Madrid, head for the charming foothill village of Manzanares El Real, whose picture-perfect square castle is one of Spain's best examples of double-walled fortification.

Day 4: Segovia. The turreted castle of Segovia, though scorned by purists because of its massive reconstruction, is one of Spain's most famous landmarks. Unlike most other Spanish castles, which are empty inside, this one has a fine collection of armor and furnishings from the period of the Catholic Monarchs.

Day 5: Segovia–Castillo de Coca. Using Segovia as a base, make an excursion into the Castilian countryside. The brick fortress of Coca was built in the 15th century but shows unmistakable Moorish influence.

Day 6: Segovia–Ávila. While Ávila does not have a castle as such, its thick city walls turn the entire town into a fortress. Walk the ramparts, and be sure to see the walls lit up at night (the best viewpoint is at Cuatro Postes, below the city). The parador is built right into the walls.

Day 7: Ávila–Madrid. Return to Madrid through the Sierra de Gredos and over the Puerto del Pico, with its Roman road. Below the pass, visit the romantic castle of Mombeltran, built in the 14th century by the Duke of Albuquerque.

Camino de Santiago (Way of St. James)

Pilgrims have made the lengthy and dangerous journey to the shrine of St. James, in Santiago de Compostela, for more than a thousand years and have left in their wake a wealth of Romanesque buildings and art treasures. A number of books and brochures describe the route and its attractions. If you can't make the whole trip, you can pick up the road in León and still see a good representation of the *camino*'s history.

DURATION➤ 6 days

GETTING AROUND➤ The whole trail is signposted. It's possible to walk the entire distance, but the less doughty can make their pilgrimage by car.

THE MAIN ROUTE➤ **Day 1: Roncesvalles–Estella.** This Pyrenean pass was the traditional entry point for pilgrims arriving from France. Visit the chapel. In Estella, see the 12th-century palace of the dukes of Granada and the early churches.

Day 2: Estella–Burgos. Visit the church of Santiago in Logroño, the cathedral in Santo Domingo de la Calzada, the many monasteries along the way, and the arcaded square in Belorado. In Burgos, see the massive cathedral.

Day 3: Burgos–León. Explore León's half-timbered medieval section, and wander the cathedral, decorated with 125 stained-glass windows.

Day 4: León–Villafranca del Bierzo. Stop at the pilgrims' museum in Astorga, housed in a palace designed by Antoni Gaudí. Explore the Knights Templar castle in Ponferrada. In Villafranca, see the church of Santiago.

Day 5: Villafranca–Santiago de Compostela. Examine round, primitive Celtic houses in the medieval ghost town of O Cebreiro. In Santiago, the cathedral and the Hotel of the Catholic Monarchs are masterpieces of stone carving.

Day 6: Santiago. Wander through the town on narrow streets covered by arched stone ceilings—built to protect Galicians from the stormy climate—and take a short scenic trip to the nearby town of Padrón.

FODOR'S CHOICE

No two people agree on what makes a perfect trip, but it can be helpful to know what others have experienced. For more details on these suggestions, see their individual entries in the relevant chapters.

Castles and Palaces

★ **Alarcón, Cuenca.** Crossing the narrow bridge into the walled city and castle of Alarcón—a parador with a memorable restaurant—will catapult you into medieval times. Throw open the shutters of the turret's bedroom window and cry, "The legions are approaching!"

★ **Alhambra, Granada.** One of Spain's most popular attractions, this citadel is an endlessly intricate fantasy of lavishly carved and colored patios, arches, and cupolas.

★ **Castle, Sigüenza.** At the very top of the beautiful town of Sigüenza, this mighty, crenellated parador has hosted royalty over the centuries, from Ferdinand and Isabella to Juan Carlos.

★ **Palacio Real, Aranjuez.** Surrounded by extensive gardens and woods, this palace reflects a French grandeur. The high point of the sumptuous interior is a room covered entirely with porcelain.

★ **Palacio Real, La Granja.** The gardens are the draw: terraces, lakes, classical statuary, woods, and elaborate fountains encourage aimless ambling. In summer, the fountains are turned on one by one for an exciting spectacle.

Churches, Monasteries, and Mosques

★ **Capilla Real, Granada.** A masterpiece of the ornate Gothic style known in Spain as Isabelline, the Royal Chapel is the resting place of the Catholic Monarchs.

★ **Cathedral, Léon.** The flying buttresses of Léon's soaring Gothic cathedral, begun in 1205, support walls that contain more glass than stone. The ethereal feel of the lofty interior is enhanced by a kaleidoscope of stunning colors from the 125 stained-glass windows and three giant rose windows.

★ **Cathedral, Santiago de Compostela.** Destination of pilgrims for almost a millennium, this enormous, opulent building houses the relics of the apostle St. James; Romanesque sculpture; a gold and silver high altar; and a dazzling array of decoration and drapery.

★ **El Escorial, Madrid.** This great, granite monastery holds the bodies of many a Spanish king as well as priceless tapestries, paintings by Velázquez and El Greco, a lavish library with rare works, and a basilica with a Titian fresco.

★ **Mezquita, Córdoba.** Built between the 8th and 9th centuries, the Mezquita (mosque) is a breathtaking example of Spanish Muslim architecture. Some 850 columns create a forest of onyx, jasper, marble, and granite, all topped with stunning, red-and-white-striped horseshoe arches and surrounded by delicate mosaics and plasterwork.

★ **Temple Expiatori de la Sagrada Família, Barcelona.** Unfinished at the time of Antoni Gaudí's death in 1926, this surreal cathedral has been amended by other architects, who have themselves not shied away from controversy. Take an elevator to one of the spires for a magnificent view of the city.

★ **Monasterio de Guadalupe, Puebla de Guadalupe.** Christopher Columbus came here before and after his famous voyage to pay respects to the Virgin in this wondrous, art-filled, 14th-century Gothic and Moorish hybrid monastery, nestled in the Altamira mountains of Extremadura, land of the Conquistadors. One of the most important spiritual centers for both Spain and the New World, Guadalupe was declared a World Heritage Site in 1993 by UNESCO.

Museums

★ **Archbishop's Palace, Astorga.** No expense was spared in Gaudí's fairy-tale, neo-

Gothic building, which houses the Museum of the Way of St. James.

★ **Museu Picasso, Barcelona.** You rather expect to see Juliet leaning over the courtyard balcony of this 15th-century palace, which houses Picasso's childhood sketches and paintings from his Rose and Blue periods. The surrounding cobblestone streets are full of shops and tapas bars.

★ **National Museum of Sculpture, Valladolid.** Set in a masterpiece of the Isabelline plateresque style, this museum superbly displays an excellent collection of different styles of sculpture, from the highly polished and decorative to the severely plain.

★ **Prado, Madrid.** One of the world's greatest museums, the Prado has masterpieces by Italian and Flemish painters, but its jewels are the works of Spaniards: Goya, Velázquez, and El Greco.

Other Sights

★ **Roman ruins in Mérida, Segovia, and Tarragona.** Mérida has Spain's largest concentration of Roman monuments, including a 64-arch bridge, a fortress, and a Roman ampitheater that once drew crowds of more than 14,000 to grizzly duels between gladiators and wild beasts. The enchanting city of Segovia, near Madrid, has a nearly 3,000-ft aqueduct that dates from the 1st century AD; and Tarragona, near Barcelona, has many classical remains, the highlight of which is an amphitheater near the sea.

★ **Pasajes de San Juan.** Near San Sebastián, this charming, tiny settlement of 18th- and 19th-century buildings along the straits (*pasajes*) leading into the port of Renteria is famous for its fine restaurants.

★ **Ronda, Málaga.** Built on a rock, the town of Ronda has spectacular views, a dramatic ravine, an old Moorish section, and a picturesque bullring with a bullfighting museum

★ **University, Salamanca.** Founded in 1220, Salamanca's university is one of the most prestigious in Europe. The architectural highlight is the Escuelas Mayores, whose ornate eyeful of a frontispiece is surrounded by graceful quadrangles and greens.

FESTIVALS AND SEASONAL EVENTS

From solemn Holy Week processions to hilarious wine and tomato battles, Spain has a fiesta for every occasion. The most famous is probably Pamplona's feast of San Fermín, with its legendary running of the bulls—immortalized by Ernest Hemingway in *The Sun Also Rises*. Valencia's Fallas (end-of-winter celebrations) and Seville's Semana Santa (Holy Week) and April Fair also top the list. All require hotel reservations far in advance.

WINTER

➤ DEC.: **New Year's Eve** ticks away at Madrid's Puerta del Sol, where crowds gather to eat 12 grapes, one on each stroke of midnight, to guarantee good fortune in the coming year.

➤ JAN.: **Epiphany,** on the 6th, is a Spanish child's Christmas. Youngsters leave their shoes on the doorstep to be filled with gifts from the Three Kings. In towns throughout Spain, the Wise Men arrive by boat, camel, or car and are featured in a parade on the night of January 5.

➤ FEB.: **Carnival** dances through Spain as a final fiesta before Lent. The most flamboyant parades take place in Santa Cruz de Tenerife, Cádiz, and Sitges (Barcelona).

SPRING

➤ MAR.: Papier-mâché figures up to 30 ft tall are torched for the **Fallas,** lighting up the sky of Valencia.

➤ APR.: Seville's **April Fair** brings out the best of Andalusian hospitality. Parades on horseback and women in ruffled skirts make this one of Spain's most picturesque fiestas. **Semana Santa** (Holy Week; March 28–April 4 in 1999), Spain's most spectacular fiesta; the most famous processions take place in Seville, Valladolid, Toledo, Murcia, Lorca, and Cuenca.

➤ MAY: The **Jerez Horse Fair** (second week of May) presents a pageant of equestrian events, bull-fighting, flamenco music, and dance. The smells of rosemary and thyme fill Barcelona on **Sant Ponç** (May 11), when farmers come into the city to sell their products (honey, cheeses, herbs, sausages, wooden utensils, artisanal oils). **San Isidro** (May 15) begins two weeks of the best bullfighting in Spain in honor of the patron saint of Madrid. The **Romería del Rocío** pilgrimage (May 21–23) rolls across the dusty fields and marshes of Doñana (Huelva) to converge on the Shrine of El Rocío.

SUMMER

➤ JUNE: Beginning in mid-month, Granada's **International Festival of Music and Dance** brings symphony orchestras, opera companies, and ballet corps from around the world to perform on the grounds of the Alhambra through mid-July. The **Classical Theater Festival** uses the beautifully preserved 1st-century BC Roman theater in Mérida to present Greek and Roman dramas in Spanish from mid-June through mid-August. **Corpus Christi** (June 3) is celebrated with processions throughout Spain, but the most magnificent are in Toledo and Sitges (Barcelona). The **Wine War** in Haro (La Rioja, June 29) wastes thousands of gallons of delicious Rioja wine and proves that a *bota* bag makes a better squirt gun than a canteen.

➤ JULY: **Veranos de la Villa** cools off Madrid's summer nights with a series of outdoor films as well as concerts of everything from flamenco to rock-and-roll all summer long. The **Fiesta de San Fermín** and the accompanying **running of the bulls** (July 6–13) through the streets of Pamplona (Navarra) unleash wine, bravado, and general merriment. Valencia's **Moors and Christians**

Festival, at the end of the month, finds locals in medieval costumes reenacting battles of long ago (a delicious rice-and-beans meal is called *Moros y Christianos*).

➤ AUG.: For four weeks in August, the **International Music and Ballet Festival** brings world-class performances to the popular beach resort of Santander. **El Misteri** of Elche (Alicante, August 11–15) is Europe's oldest Christian mystery play. Also in mid-month, the upper-crust resort of San Sebastián lets down its hair for **Big Week,** with parades, fireworks, sporting events, and cardboard-bull running. **Tomato Battle**

(August 25) turns the entire town of Buñol (Valencia) red. The end of the month is tinged another color for the **Saffron Rose Festival** in Consuegra (near Toledo), the world's saffron capital. Participants celebrate the harvest of the world's most expensive spice with three days of music, dance, and regional folklore exhibits.

AUTUMN

➤ SEPT.: For the last two weeks of September and first two weeks of Octo

ber, the sherry town of Jerez celebrates the harvest season with the **Fiestas de Otoño** (Autumn Festivals). **La Merch** is celebrated in Barcelona on September 24 with concerts, fireworks, and parades in which people wear giant papier-mâché heads.

➤ OCT.: On the 12th, **El Pilar** gives the children of Zaragoza a chance to dress up in regional costumes for parades and *jota* dance contests.

2 Madrid

Madrid is one of Europe's most vibrant cities. Madrileños are a vigorous, joyful lot, famous for their apparent ability to defy the need for sleep; they embrace their city's cultural offerings and make enthusiastic use of its cafés and bars. If you can match this energy, you'll take in Madrid's museum mile, with more masterpieces per square foot than anywhere else in the world; the palaces and boutiques of regal Madrid; the dark, narrow lanes of medieval Madrid; and Madrid post-midnight, where today's action is.

By Mark Potok
and Deborah
Luhrman

Updated by
Annie Ward

LIFE IN MADRID is lived in the crowded streets and in the
noisy cafés, where talking, toasting, and tapa-tasting
last long into the night. Many find the city's endless
energy hard to resist, and its social lifestyle makes it especially easy for
travelers to get involved.

Madrid's other chief attraction is its unsurpassed collection of paint-
ings by some of the world's great artists, among them Goya, El Greco,
Velázquez, Picasso, and Dalí. Nowhere else will you find such a con-
centration of masterpieces as in the three museums—the Prado, the Reina
Sofía, and the Thyssen-Bornemisza—that make up Madrid's so-called
Golden Triangle of Art.

The bright blue sky, as immortalized in Velázquez's paintings, is probably the first thing you'll notice about Madrid. Despite 20th-century
pollution, that sky is still much in evidence thanks to breezes that sweep
down from the Guadarrama mountains, blowing away the urban smog.

The skyline has its share of skyscrapers, but these are far outnumbered
by the more typical Madrid towers of red brick crowned by gray slate
roofs and spires. Built in the 16th and 17th centuries by the occupying Habsburgs, who made Madrid the capital of the Iberian realm, this
architecture gives parts of Madrid a timeless, Old World feel. Monumental neoclassical structures, like the Prado Museum, the Royal
Palace, and the Puerta de Alcalá arch—the sights most visited by travelers—make up Madrid's other historic face. Most of these were built
in the 18th century, during the reign of Bourbon monarch Charles III;
inspired by the enlightened ideas of the age, Charles also created Retiro Park and the broad, leafy boulevard Paseo del Prado.

Modern-day Madrid sprawls northward in block after block of dreary,
high-rise brick apartment and office buildings. The swelling population of 3.2 million is also moving into surrounding villages and new
suburbs, creating traffic problems in and around the city. Although these
new quarters and many of Madrid's crumbling old residential neighborhoods may seem uninviting, don't be put off by first impressions.
Much of the city's appeal comes from its vivacious people and the elec-
tricity they generate, whether at play in the bars and clubs or at work
in Spain's advertising, television, and film industries, all headquartered
here.

Poised on a plateau 2,120 ft above sea level, Madrid is the highest capital in Europe. It can be one of the world's hottest cities in summer,
and freezing cold in winter. Spring and summer are the most delightful times to visit, when balmy evenings have virtually everyone in
town lingering at outdoor cafés, but each season has its own charms;
in winter, steamy café windows beckon, and the famous blue skies are
especially crisp and bright. That's when Madrid, as the local bumper
stickers will tell you, is the next best place to heaven.

The city's sophistication stands in vivid contrast to the ancient ways
of the historic villages nearby. Less than an hour away from the downtown skyscrapers are villages where farm fields are still plowed by mules.
Like urbanites the world over, Madrileños like to escape to the countryside. Getaways to the dozens of Castilian hamlets nearby and to
Toledo, El Escorial, and Segovia are cherished by both locals and
travelers.

Pleasures and Pastimes

Art Museums

Madrid's greatest attractions are its three world-class art museums, the Prado, the Reina Sofía, and the Thyssen-Bornemisza, all within 1 km (½ mi) of each other along the leafy Paseo del Prado, sometimes called the Golden Triangle of Art. The Prado houses Spain's old masters, with the world's foremost collections of Goya, El Greco, and Velázquez along with hundreds of other 17th-, 18th-, and 19th-century masterpieces. The Reina Sofía focuses on modern art, especially Dalí, Miró and Picasso, whose famous *Guernica* hangs here; it also shows modern Spanish sculptors, such as Eduardo Chillida, and hosts excellent temporary exhibits. The Thyssen-Bornemisza attempts to trace the entire history of Western art and includes good collections of impressionist and German expressionist works.

Dining

Unlike most other regions of Spain, Madrid does not really have a native cuisine. But as capital of the realm and home of the king, Madrid has attracted generations of courtiers, foreign diplomats, politicians, and tradesmen, all of whom have brought their own culinary styles and tastes, both from other regions of Spain and from abroad.

The roast meats of Castile and the seafoods of the Cantabrian coast are just as at home in Madrid as they are in their native lands. Madrid's best restaurants specialize in Basque cooking, Spain's haute cuisine, and seafood houses take advantage of the capital's abundant supply of fish and shellfish, trucked in nightly from the coast. Spaniards quip that Madrid is Spain's biggest seaport.

The only truly local dishes are *cocido a la Madrileño* (garbanzo-bean stew) and *callos a la Madrileño* (stewed tripe). Given half a chance, Madrileños will wax lyrically over the mouthwatering merits of both. The *cocido* is a delicious and hearty winter meal consisting of garbanzo beans, vegetables, potatoes, sausages, and pork. The best cocidos are slowly simmered in earthenware crocks over open fires and served as a complete meal in several courses: first the broth, which comes with angel-hair pasta, then the beans and vegetables, and finally the meat. You can order cocido in the most elegant restaurants, such as Lhardy and at the Ritz hotel, as well as at the humblest holes-in-the-wall, and it's usually offered as a midday selection on Monday or Wednesday. The *callos* is a much simpler concoction of veal tripe stewed with tomatoes, onions, and garlic. *Jamon serrano* (cured ham) a specialty from the livestock lands of Extremadura and Andalusia, has become a beloved staple in Madrid; travelers can hardly walk a city block without coming upon a *museo del jamon* (ham museum), where endless legs of the dried delicacy dangle in the windows, inviting passersby in for a taste. Busy Madrileños grab a *bocadillo* (sandwich) from a stand for a quick bite; a *bocadillo de calamares* (calamari sandwich), often served with mayonnaise, is a tasty favorite and a meal in itself.

Although the countryside near the capital produces some wines, they are less than exceptional. The house wine in nearly all Madrid restaurants is a sturdy, uncomplicated *Valdepeñas* from La Mancha. A traditional, anise-flavored liqueur called *Anís* is manufactured just outside the village of Chinchón.

CATEGORY	COST*
$$$$	over 6,000 ptas.
$$$	4,000–6,000 ptas.
$$	1,800–4,000 ptas.
$	under 1,800 ptas.

per person for three-course meal, excluding drinks, service, and tax

Lodging

Hotel prices in Madrid have come down significantly since the glory days of the early '90s, especially in the upper price brackets. The Ritz and the Villamagna both once charged upwards of $600 a night, but each now offers a room rate comparable to that in other world capitals—$250 to $300 a night. If that's still too steep, try bargaining— surveys show that only 15% of Madrid's hotel guests pay the posted room rate. As most hotels cater to business travelers, special weekend rates are widely available; you can generally save 50% on a Friday, Saturday, or Sunday night, and many hotels throw in extras, like meals or museum admissions. Business customers can ask for a business or professional discount, which can amount to up to 40% off.

If you're willing to hunt a bit, you can also find *hostels* for 4,000 pesetas or even less. Most of these very cheap rooms are on the upper floors of apartment buildings and have shared baths. They are frequently full, however, and don't take reservations, so we don't list them here; you simply have to go door-to-door and trust your luck. Many such places are concentrated in the old city between the Prado Museum and the Puerta del Sol; start by looking around the Plaza Santa Ana.

CATEGORY	COST*
$$$$	over 25,000 ptas.
$$$	14,000–25,000 ptas.
$$	10,000–14,000 ptas.
$	under 10,000 ptas.

All prices are for a standard double room, excluding tax.

Tapas Bars

Madrid has some of the best tapas bars in Spain. A *tapa* is a bit of food that usually comes free with a drink; it might be a few olives, a mussel in vinaigrette, a sardine, or spicy potatoes. You can also order a larger plate of the same sort of food, called a *ración,* meant to be eaten with toothpicks and shared among friends. Tapas bars are sprinkled throughout the city, but the best place to start a tapa tour is near the Plaza Santa Ana or at the *mésones* built into the wall beneath the Plaza Mayor, along Cava San Miguel. These are some of the oldest buildings in the city, and each bar specializes in a different tapa—for example, potato-and-egg tortillas (a Spanish tortilla is an omelet of sorts, not to be confused with the Mexican tortilla), garlicky mushrooms, or a small wedge of *empañada de atún,* a rich, fried pastry stuffed with tuna, egg, and onions.

EXPLORING MADRID

Madrid is a compact city, and most of the things visitors want to see are concentrated in a downtown area barely a mile across, stretching between the Royal Palace and Retiro Park. Broad *avenidas,* twisting medieval alleys, grand museums, stately gardens, and tiny, tiled taverns are all jumbled together in an area easily covered on foot.

The texture of Madrid is so rich that walking is really the only way to experience those special moments—peeking in on a guitar maker at work or watching a child dip sweet *churros* into a steamy cup of hot chocolate—whose images linger long after the photos have faded.

Numbers in the text correspond to numbers in the margin and on the Madrid, Madrid Excursions, and El Escorial maps.

Great Itineraries

IF YOU HAVE 2 DAYS

On a brief stay, you should limit yourself to only one or two museums, leaving the remainder of your time to soak up the rest of the city. See the works of Spain's great masters at the **Museo del Prado** ⑦; then visit the **Palacio Real** ② for a regal display of art, architecture, and history. The palace tour includes admission to the Royal Library and Royal Armory, both sights in their own right. Stroll along the Paseo de la Castellana to see the fountains **Fuente de la Cibeles** ⑨ and **Fuente de Neptuno** ⑥. Visit the **Puerta del Sol** ⑤, and then relax at an outdoor café on the **Plaza Mayor** ④. Try some of the historic tapas bars along the **Cava de San Miguel** ㉚.

IF YOU HAVE 4 DAYS

Four days will give you time to uncover historic Madrid, visit more museums, and take an excursion outside the city.

Visit the **Centro de Arte Reina Sofía** ⑳ and the **Museo Thyssen-Bornemisza** ⑧. Don't miss the 16th-century **Convento de las Descalzas Reales** ㉒, with a beautiful frescoed staircase, paintings by Zurbarán and Titian, and a hall of sumptuous tapestries. Explore medieval Madrid, beginning on Calle Mayor toward the **Plaza de la Villa** ㉙, to see Spain's Mudéjar architecture and flamboyant plateresque decoration. Turn onto Calle Segovia, a main medieval drag, and make your way to the **Plaza de Paja** ㉛ and the Museo de San Isidro, named for Madrid's patron saint and the site of his most famous miracle. Take an excursion outside of Madrid to **El Escorial** ㊳ and the **Real Monasterio de San Lorenzo de El Escorial,** 50 km (31 mi) from Madrid in the Guadarrama mountains. Here, in the Royal Pantheon, are the bodies of most of Spain's kings since Carlos I. A few miles away is Franco's tomb, **Valle de los Caídos** ㊴, built with the forced labor of Republican prisoners after the civil war.

Central Madrid

Central Madrid stretches between the Royal Palace, to the west, and Retiro Park, to the east—a distance of about 3 km (2 mi) that's loaded with most of the city's museums, monuments, and historic buildings.

A Good Walk

A leisurely walk across town will help you get your bearings while locating many of the major sights. Begin at the **Plaza de Oriente** ①. From your position in the round plaza, you'll see the majestic **Palacio Real** (Royal Palace) ②, a glimpse of the impressive **Catedral de la Almudena** ㉔, on Calle Bailén, the Palacio's **Jardines Sabatini** ㉕, and **Campo del Moro** ㉖. Just east of the Plaza de Oriente is the newly restored **Teatro Real** ③. Walk south on Calle Bailén, then east on Calle Mayor toward the **Plaza Mayor** ④. On the way, walk through the narrow San Ginés passageway, which runs along the 14th-century church of **San Ginés,** one of the oldest in the city; wooden stalls selling used books and prints of old Madrid are built into the church wall. This is one of Madrid's most picturesque corners. Where the passageway jogs to the right is the Chocolatería San Ginés, known for its chocolate and churros, and the final stop on many a wee-hours bar crawl. Leaving the Plaza Mayor, wend your way east among the crowds to the **Puerta del Sol** ⑤.

A little detour to the northwest, on Calle de Arenal, will bring you to the **Convento de las Descalzas Reales** ㉒ and the **Convento de la Encarnación** ㉓. Backtrack to Puerta del Sol and wander along Carrera San Jerónimo, a jumble of shops and cafés. Turn south on Calle de la Cruz for a quick peek into the delicatessen at Lhardy, one of Madrid's oldest and most traditional restaurants. Shoppers stop in here on cold winter mornings for steamy cups of *caldo* (chicken broth). Be sure to look up at the buildings' beautifully tiled and decorated upper floors, especially at the corner of Calle Sevilla. The big, white-granite building on the left with the lions out in front is the Congress, the lower house of Spain's parliament.

You'll reach the wide Paseo del Prado right across from the renowned **Museo del Prado** ⑦, with the **Fuente de Neptuno** ⑥ right in front of you. A left turn will take you past the **Museo Thyssen-Bornemisza** ⑧ and the elegant Ritz Hotel to the plaza with the **Fuente de la Cibeles** ⑨, beautifully framed by the **Palacio de Comunicaciones** ⑩, now the post office; **Banco de España** ⑪; and **Casa de las Américas** ⑫. The grand yellow mansion near the post office (now the Banco Argentaria) was once the home of the Marquis of Salamanca, who at the turn of the 20th century built the exclusive shopping and residential neighborhood that bears his name. Go right at Calle Alcalá and you'll see Madrid's symbol, the **Puerta de Alcalá** ⑬, and the Retiro. Detour north for the **Museo Arqueológico** ⑭ and **Plaza Colón** ⑮.

Back at the Fuente de Neptuno: heading due east, you'll find the **Museo del Ejército** ⑯, the **Casón del Buen Retiro** ⑰, and the **Parque del Retiro** ⑱. Heading south on Paseo del Prado, you'll come to the **Jardín Botánico** ⑲ and eventually the **Atocha** train station, spruced up in 1992. The high-speed train (AVE) to Córdoba and Seville leaves from here, as do regular trains to other points south and local trains to Toledo and Segovia. Across the traffic circle, the immense pile of painted tiles and winged statues houses the Ministerio de Agricultura (Agriculture Ministry). The **Centro de Arte Reina Sofía** ⑳, home to Picasso's *Guernica,* is in the building with the glass elevators on the front.

If you choose to do this walk in reverse, you can head from the **Royal Palace** ② to the **Parque del Oeste** (West Park; stop first for coffee at the Café de Oriente) to explore the Egyptian **Templo de Debod.** Then visit the **Convento de la Encarnación** ㉓, **Convento de la Descalzas Reales** ㉒, and **Academia de Bellas Artes de San Fernando** ㉑ on your way east.

TIMING
This walk covers about 3 km (2 mi) and, depending on how often you stop, can be covered in two to three hours.

Set aside an entire morning or afternoon for return visits to each of Madrid's main sights: the Royal Palace, the Prado, the Reina Sofía, and the Thyssen-Bornemisza.

Sights to See

㉑ **Academia de Bellas Artes de San Fernando** (St. Fernando Academy of Fine Arts). Designed by Churriguera in the waning baroque years of the early 18th century, this little-visited museum is a showcase of painting and the other plastic arts. The same building houses the **Instituto de Calcografía** (Prints Institute), which sells limited-edition prints from original plates engraved by Spanish artists, including Goya. ✉ *Alcalá 13,* ☎ *91/522–1491.* 💲 *300 ptas.* 🕐 *Tues.–Fri. 9–7, Sat.– Mon. 9–2.*

⑪ **Banco de España.** Spain's equivalent of the U.S. Federal Reserve, the massive 1884 building takes up an entire city block. It's said that the nation's gold reserves are held in great vaults that stretch under the Plaza de Cibeles traffic circle all the way to the fountain. The bank is not open to visitors, but if you want to risk dodging traffic to reach the median strip in front of it, you can take a fine photo of the fountain and the palaces with the monumental Puerta de Alcalá arch in the background.

22

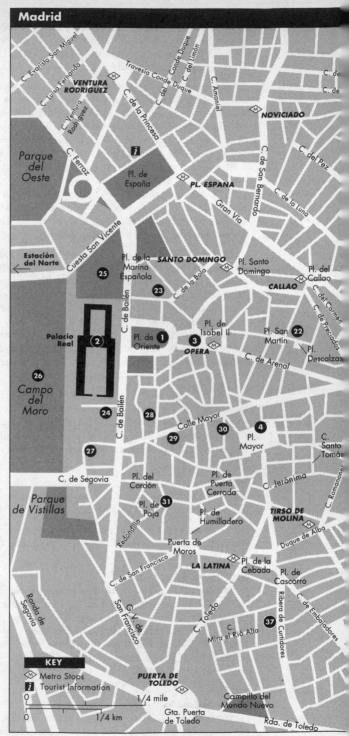

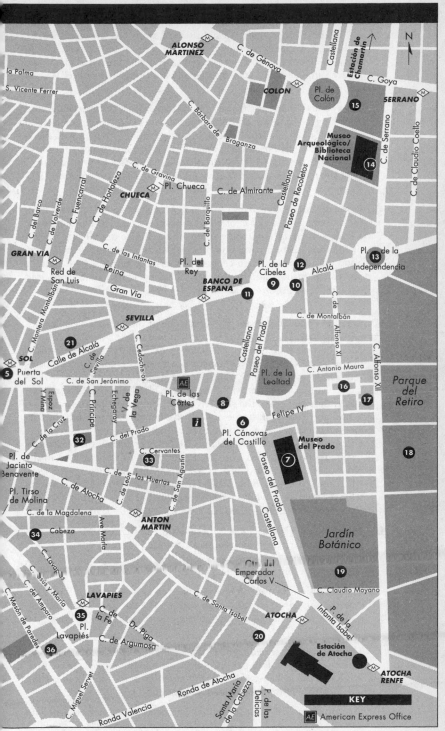

㉖ **Campo del Moro** (Moors' Field). Below the Sabatini Gardens, but accessible only by walking around to an entrance on the far side, is the Campo del Moro. This park's clusters of shady trees, winding paths, and long lawn leading up to the Royal Palace make for strategically beautiful photographs. Even without considering the riches inside, the palace's immense size (twice as large as Buckingham Palace) is awe-inspiring.

⑫ **Casa de las Américas** (House of the Americas). A cultural center and art gallery focusing on Latin America, the Casa de las Américas is housed in the allegedly haunted Palacio de Linares, built by a man who made his fortune in the New World and returned to a life of incestuous love and strange deaths. ⊠ *Paseo Recoletos 2,* ☎ *91/595–4800.* 🎫 *Palace tour 300 ptas., art gallery free.* ⊘ *Palace tour Tues.–Fri. 9:30–11:30, weekends 10–1:30; art gallery Tues.–Sat. 11–7, Sun. 11–2.*

⑰ **Casón del Buen Retiro.** This Prado annex is just a five-minute walk from the museum and can be entered on the same ticket. The building, once a ballroom, and the formal gardens in the Retiro are all that remain of Madrid's second royal complex, which filled the entire neighborhood until the early 19th century. On display here are 19th-century Spanish paintings and sculpture, including works by Sorolla and Rusiñol. ⊠ *C. Alfonso XII s/n,* ☎ *91/330–2867.* ⊘ *Tues.–Sat. 9–7, Sun. 9–2.*

㉔ **Catedral de la Almudena.** The first stone of the cathedral (which adjoins the Royal Palace to the south) was laid in 1883 by King Alfonso XII; the whole was consecrated by Pope John Paul II in 1993. The building was intended to be Gothic-style, with needles and spires, but as time ran long and money ran short, the design was simplified by Fernando Chueca Goltia into the more austere, classical form you see today. The cathedral houses the remains of Madrid's male patron saint, St. Isidro, and a wooden statue of Madrid's female patron saint, the Virgin of Almudena, which is said to have been discovered following the Christian reconquest of Madrid in 1085. Legend has it that a divinely inspired woman named María led authorities to a secret spot in the old wall of the Alcázar (which in Arabic can also be called *almudeyna*), where the statue was found framed by two lighted candles inside a grain storage vault. That wall is part of the cathedral's foundation. ⊠ *C. de Bailén s/n,* ☎ *91/542–2200.* 🎫 *Free.* ⊘ *Daily 10–1:30 and 6–7:45.*

★ ⑳ **Centro de Arte Reina Sofía** (Queen Sofia Art Center). Madrid's museum of modern art is housed in a converted hospital whose classic, granite austerity is somewhat relieved (or ruined, depending on your point of view) by the two glass elevator shafts on the facade.

The collection focuses on Spain's three great modern masters: Pablo Picasso, Salvador Dalí, and Joan Miró. Take the elevator to the second floor to see the permanent collections; the other floors house visiting exhibits.

The first rooms are dedicated to the beginnings of Spain's modern-art movement and contain paintings from around the turn of the century. The focal point is Picasso's 1901 *Woman in Blue*—hardly beautiful, but surprisingly representational compared to his later works.

Moving on to the **Cubist collection,** which includes nine works by Juan Gris, be sure to see Dalí's splintered, blue-gray *Self-Portrait,* in which the artist painted his favorite things—a morning newspaper and a pack of cigarettes. The other highlight here is Picasso's *Musical Instruments on a Table,* one of many variations on this theme.

The museum's showpiece is Picasso's famous *Guernica,* which occupies the center hall and is surrounded by dozens of studies for individual figures within it. The huge painting depicts the horror of the Nazi Condor Legion's bombing of the ancient Basque town of Guernica, in 1937, an act that brought Spanish dictator Francisco Franco to power. The work—in many ways a 20th-century version of Goya's *The 3rd of May*—is something of a national shrine, as evidenced by the solemnity of Spaniards viewing it. The painting was not brought into Spain until 1981; Picasso, an ardent antifascist, refused to allow it to enter the country while Franco was alive.

The room in front of *Guernica* contains a collection of **surrealist works,** including six canvases by Miró, known for his childlike graphicism. Opposite *Guernica* is a hall dedicated to the surrealist Salvador Dalí, with paintings bequeathed to the government in the artist's will. Although Dalí is perhaps best known for works of a somewhat whimsical nature, many of these canvases are dark and haunting and bursting with symbolism. Among the best known are *The Great Masturbator* (1929) and *The Enigma of Hitler* (1939), with its broken, dripping telephone.

The rest of the museum is devoted to more recent art, including the massive, gravity-defying sculpture *Toki Egin,* by Eduardo Chillida, considered Spain's greatest living sculptor, and five textural paintings by Barcelona artist Antoní Tàpies, who incorporates materials such as wrinkled sheets and straw into his works. ⊠ *Santa Isabel 52,* ☎ *91/467–5062.* ▦ *400 ptas.; free Sat. 2:30–9 and Sun.* ⊘ *Mon. and Wed.–Sat. 10–9, Sun. 10–2:30.*

㉓ **Convento de la Encarnación** (Convent of the Incarnation). Once connected to the Royal Palace by an underground passageway, this Augustinian convent was founded in 1611 by the wife of Felipe III. It has many artistic treasures, but the convent's biggest attraction is the reliquary, which holds among the sacred bones a vial containing the dried blood of St. Pantaleón, which is said to liquify every year on July 27. You can enter Encarnación on the same ticket as the Convent of Descalzas Reales. ⊠ *Plaza de la Encarnación 1,* ☎ *91/547–0510.* ▦ *400 ptas.* ⊘ *Wed. and Sat. 10:30–1 and 4–5:30, Sun. 11–1:30.*

㉒ **Convento de las Descalzas Reales** (Convent of the Royal Barefoot Nuns). This 16th-century building was restricted for 200 years to women of royal blood. Its plain, brick-and-stone facade hides a treasure trove, including paintings by Zurbarán, Titian, and Breughel the Elder, as well as a hall of sumptuous tapestries crafted from drawings by Rubens. The convent was founded in 1559 by Juana of Austria, whose daughter shut herself up here rather than endure marriage to Felipe II. A handful of nuns (not necessarily royal) still live here, cultivating their own vegetables in the convent's garden. You must visit as part of a guided tour, conducted once a day in English, the rest of the day in Spanish. ⊠ *Plaza de las Descalzas Reales 3,* ☎ *91/542–0059.* ▦ *650 ptas.* ⊘ *Tues.–Thurs. and Sat. 10:30–12:30 and 4–5:30, Fri. 10:30–12:30, Sun. 11–1:30.*

⑨ **Fuente de la Cibeles** (Fountain of Sybil). A landscaped walkway runs down the center of the Paseo del Prado to the Plaza de la Cibeles, where this famous fountain depicts Sybil, the wife of Saturn, driving a chariot drawn by lions. Even more than the officially designated bear and strawberry tree, this monument, beautifully lighted at night, has come to symbolize Madrid—so much so that during the civil war, patriotic Madrileños risked life and limb to sandbag it as Nationalist aircraft bombed the city.

⑥ **Fuente de Neptuno** (Neptune's Fountain). Just outside the Palace Hotel and the boutiques-filled Galerias del Prado shopping center, on the Plaza Canovas del Castillo, this fountain is at the hub of Madrid's so-called Golden Triangle of Art, made up of the redbrick Prado Museum spreading out along the east side of the boulevard, the Thyssen-Bornemisza Museum across the plaza, and, five blocks to the south, the Reina Sofía art center.

⑲ **Jardín Botánico** (Botanical Gardens). Just south of the Prado Museum, the gardens provide a pleasant place to stroll or sit under the trees. True to the wishes of King Carlos III, they hold an array of plants, flowers, and cacti from around the world. ⊠ *Plaza de Murillo 2,* ☎ *91/585–4700.* ⌨ *200 ptas.* ☉ *Summer, daily 10–9; winter, daily 10–6.*

㉕ **Jardines Sabatini** (Sabatini Gardens). The formal gardens to the north of the Royal Palace are crawling with stray cats, but they're a pleasant place to rest or watch the sun set.

⑭ **Museo Arqueológico** (Museum of Archaeology). The museum shares its neoclassical building with the **Biblioteca Nacional** (National Library). The biggest attraction here is a replica of the prehistoric cave paintings in Altamira, Cantabria, located underground in the garden. (Only scholars are allowed to see the real thing.) Inside the museum, look for the *Dama de Elche,* a bust of a wealthy, 4th-century Iberian woman, and notice how her headgear is a rough precursor to the mantillas and hair combs still associated with traditional Spanish dress. Be sure to see the ancient Visigothic votive crowns, discovered in 1859 near Toledo and believed to date back to the 8th century. ⊠ *C. Serrano 13,* ☎ *91/577–7912.* ⌨ *500 ptas.; free Sat. afternoon and Sun. morning.* ☉ *Tues.–Sat. 9:30–8:30, Sun. 9:30–2:30.*

⑯ **Museo del Ejército** (Army Museum). A real treat for arms-and-armor buffs, this museum is right on the museum mile. Among the 27,000 items on view are a sword which allegedly belonged to the Spanish hero El Cid; suits of armor; bizarre-looking pistols with barrels capable of holding scores of bullets; Moorish tents; and a cross carried by Christopher Columbus. It's an unusually entertaining collection. ⊠ *Mendez Nuñez 1,* ☎ *91/522–8977.* ⌨ *100 ptas.* ☉ *Tues.–Sun. 10–2.*

★ ⑦ **Museo del Prado** (Prado Museum). When the Prado was commissioned by King Carlos III, in 1785, it was meant to be a natural-science museum. The king, popularly remembered as "Madrid's best mayor," wanted the museum, the adjoining botanical gardens, and the elegant Paseo del Prado to serve as a center of scientific enlightenment for his subjects. By the time the building was completed in 1819, its purpose had changed to exhibiting the vast collection of art gathered by Spanish royalty since the time of Ferdinand and Isabella.

Painting is one of Spain's greatest contributions to world culture, and the Prado's jewels are works by the nation's three great masters: Francisco Goya, Diego Velázquez, and El Greco. The museum also contains masterpieces of Flemish and Italian artists, collected when their lands were part of the Spanish Empire. The museum benefited greatly from the anticlerical laws of 1836, which forced monasteries, convents, and churches to turn over much of their art treasures so that the general public could enjoy them.

A visit to the Prado begins on the upper floor (*primera planta*), where you enter through a series of halls dedicated to **Renaissance painters**. Many people hurry through these rooms to get to the Spanish canvases, but it's worth stopping for Titian's *Portrait of Emperor Charles V* and Raphael's exquisite *Portrait of a Cardinal.*

Next comes a hall filled with the passionately spiritual works of **El Greco** (Doménikos Theotokópoulos, 1541–1614), the Greek-born artist who lived and worked in Toledo. El Greco is known for his mystical, elongated faces. His style was quite shocking to a public accustomed to strict, representational realism; and because he wanted his art to provoke emotion, El Greco is sometimes called the world's first "modern" painter. *The Resurrection* and *The Adoration of the Shepherds,* considered two of his greatest paintings, are on view here.

You can see the meticulous brushwork of **Velázquez** (1599–1660) in his numerous portraits of kings and queens. Be sure to look for the magnificent *Las Hilanderas* (*The Spinners*), evidence of the artist's talent for painting light. One hall is reserved exclusively for the Prado's most famous canvas, Velázquez's *Las Meninas* (*The Maids of Honor*), which combines a self-portrait of the artist at work with a mirror reflection of the king and queen in a revolutionary interplay of space and perspectives. Picasso was obsessed with this work and painted several copies of it in his own abstract style, now on display in the Picasso Museum in Barcelona.

The south end of the first floor is reserved for **Goya** (1746–1828), whose works span a staggering range of tone, from bucolic to horrific. Among his early masterpieces are portraits of the family of King Carlos IV, for whom he was court painter—one glance at their unflattering and imbecilic expressions, especially in the painting *The Family of Carlos IV,* reveals the loathing Goya developed for these self-indulgent and reactionary rulers. His famous side-by-side canvases, *The Clothed Maja* and *The Nude Maja,* may represent the young duchess of Alba, whom Goya adored and frequently painted. No one knows whether she ever returned his affection. The adjacent rooms house a series of bucolic scenes of Spaniards at play, painted as designs for tapestries.

Goya's paintings take on political purpose starting in 1808, when the population of Madrid rose up against occupying French troops. *The 2nd of May* portrays the insurrection at the Puerta del Sol, and its even more terrifying companion piece, *The 3rd of May,* depicts the nighttime executions of patriots who had rebelled the day before. The garish light effects in this work typify the romantic style, which favors drama over detail, and make it one of the most powerful indictments of violence ever committed to canvas.

Downstairs you'll find Goya's "black paintings"—dark, disturbing works, completed late in his life, that reflect his inner turmoil after losing his hearing, and his deep embitterment over the bloody War of Independence. The rest of the ground floor is taken up with Flemish paintings, including the bizarre masterpiece *Garden of Earthly Delights,* by Hieronymous Bosch. ⊠ *Paseo del Prado s/n,* ☎ *91/330–2800.* ☞ *500 ptas.; free Sat. afternoon and Sun. morning.* ☉ *Tues.–Sat. 9–7, Sun. 9–2.*

NEED A
BREAK? **La Dolores** (⊠ Plaza de Jesús 4) is one of Madrid's most atmospheric old tiled bars, the perfect place for a beer or glass of wine and a plate of olives. It's a great alternative to the Prado's so-so basement cafeteria and is just across the Paseo, then one block up on Calle Lope de Vega to the tiny plaza.

8 Museo Thyssen-Bornemisza. Madrid's third and newest art center, elegantly renovated to create lots of space and natural light, opened in 1992 in the Villahermosa Palace. This ambitious collection of 800 paintings traces the history of Western art with examples from all the important movements, beginning with 13th-century Italy.

The artworks were gathered over the past 70 years by industrialist Baron Hans Heinrich Thyssen-Bornemisza and his father. At the urging of his Spanish wife (a former Miss Spain), the baron agreed to donate the collection to Spain. Critics have described the collection as the minor works of major artists and the major works of minor artists, but the museum itself is beautiful, and its impressionist paintings are the only ones on display in the country.

Among the museum's gems are Hans Holbein's *Portrait of Henry VIII* (purchased from the late Princess Diana's grandfather, who used the money to buy a new Bugatti sports car). American artists are also well represented; look for the Gilbert Stuart portrait of George Washington's cook, and note how closely the composition and rendering resembles the artist's famous painting of the Founding Father himself. Two halls are devoted to the impressionists and post-impressionists, including many works by Pissarro and a few each by Renoir, Monet, Degas, Van Gogh, and Cézanne.

Within 20th-century art, the baron shows a proclivity for terror-filled (albeit dynamic and colorful) German expressionism, but there are also some soothing works by Georgia O'Keeffe and Andrew Wyeth. ✉ *Paseo del Prado 8,* ☎ *91/369–0151.* 💰 *600 ptas.* 🕐 *Tues.–Sun. 10–7.*

⑩ **Palacio de Comunicaciones.** This ornate building on the southeast side of Plaza de Cibeles is otherwise known as the main post office. 🕐 *Stamps weekdays 9 AM–10 PM, Sat. 9–8, Sun. 10–1; phone, telex, telegrams, and fax weekdays 8 AM–midnight, weekends 8 AM–10 PM.*

★ ❷ **Palacio Real** (Royal Palace). The Royal Palace was commissioned in the early 1700s by the first of Spain's Bourbon rulers, Felipe V, on the same strategic spot where Madrid's first Alcázar (Moorish fortress) was built in the 9th century.

Before entering, take time to walk around the graceful **Patio de Armas** and admire the classical French architecture. King Felipe was obviously inspired by his childhood days with his grandfather Louis XIV at Versailles. Look for the stone statues of Inca prince Atahualpa and Aztec king Montezuma, perhaps the only tributes in Spain to these pre-Columbian American rulers. Notice how the steep bluff drops westward to the Manzanares River; on a clear day, this vantage point also commands a good view of the mountain passes leading into Madrid from Old Castile, and it becomes obvious why the Moors picked this particular spot for a fortress.

Inside, the palace's 2,800 rooms compete with each other for over-the-top opulence. A nearly two-hour guided tour in English winds a mile-long path through the palace. Highlights include the **Salón de Gasparini,** King Carlos III's private apartments—a riot of rococo decoration, with swirling, inlaid floors and curlicued, ceramic wall and ceiling decoration, all glistening in the light of a 2-ton crystal chandelier; the **Salón del Trono,** an exceedingly grand throne room with the royal seats of King Juan Carlos and Queen Sofía; and the **banquet hall,** the palace's largest room, which seats up to 140 people for state dinners. No monarch has lived here since 1931, when Alfonso XIII was hounded out of the country by a populace fed up with centuries of royal oppression. The current king and queen live in the far simpler Zarzuela Palace, on the outskirts of Madrid, using this Royal Palace only for state functions and official occasions, such as the first Middle East peace talks, in 1991.

Within the palace, you can also visit the **Biblioteca Real** (Royal Library), which has a first edition of Cervantes's *Don Quixote;* the **Museo de Música** (Music Museum), where five stringed instruments by Stradivarius form the world's largest collection; the **Armería Real** (Royal Armory), with its vast array of historic suits of armor and some frightening medieval torture implements; and the **Real Oficina de Farmacía** (Royal Pharmacy), with an assortment of vials and flasks that were used to mix the king's medicines. ✉ *C. Bailén s/n,* ☎ *91/559–7404.* 🎫 *850 ptas.* ⊙ *Mon.–Sat. 9:30–6, Sun. 9–3; Closed during official receptions.*

★ ⊙ ⑱ **Parque del Retiro** (literally, The Retreat). Once the private playground of royalty, the park is a vast expanse of green that includes formal gardens, fountains, lakes (complete with rowboats for rent), exhibition halls, children's play areas, and a **Puppet Theater,** featuring slapstick routines that even non–Spanish speakers will enjoy. Shows take place on Saturday at 1 and on Sunday at 1, 6, and 7; admission is free. The park is especially lively on weekends, when it fills with street musicians, jugglers, clowns, gypsy fortune-tellers, and sidewalk painters along with hundreds of Spanish families out for a walk. The park hosts a month-long book fair in May and often flamenco concerts in summer.

From the entrance at the Puerta de Alcalá, head straight toward the center of Retiro and you'll find the **Estanque** (lake), presided over by a grandiose equestrian statue of King Alfonso XII, erected by his mother. Just behind the lake, north of the statue, is one of the best of the many cafés within the park. If you're feeling energetic, you can rent a boat and work up an appetite just rowing around the lake.

The 19th-century **Palacio de Cristal** (Crystal Palace), southeast of the Estanque, was built to house a collection of exotic plants from the Philippines, a Spanish possession at the time. This airy marvel of steel and glass sits on a base of decorative tile. Next door is a small lake with ducks and swans. At the south end of the park, along the Paseo del Uruguay, is the **Rosaleda** (rose garden), an English garden bursting with color and heavy with floral scents for most of the summer. West of the Rosaleda, look for a statue called the **Ángel Caído** (Fallen Angel), which Madrileños claim is the only one in the world depicting the prince of darkness before—during, actually—his fall from grace.

⑮ **Plaza Colón.** The modern plaza is named for Christopher Columbus. A statue of the explorer (identical to one in Barcelona's port) looks west from a high tower in the middle of the square. The airport bus leaves from the station beneath here every 15 minutes. Behind Plaza Colón is **Calle Serrano,** the city's number one shopping street (think Gucci, Prada, and Loewe). Take a stroll in either direction on Serrano for some window-shopping.

NEED A BREAK? Decorated in the style of Belle Epoque Paris, **El Espejo** is the ideal place to rest your feet and sip a cup of coffee or a beer. You can pull up a chair on the shady terrace or inside the air-conditioned, stained-glass bar. It's right in the center of the *paseo,* at Plaza Colón. ✉ *Paseo Recoletos 31,* ☎ *91/308-2347.* ⊙ *Daily 10 AM–2 AM.*

❶ **Plaza de Oriente.** The stately plaza in front of the Royal Palace is surrounded by massive stone statues of all the Spanish kings from Ataulfo to Fernando VI. These sculptures were meant to be mounted on the railing on top of the palace (where there are now stone urns), but Queen Isabel of Farnesio, one of the first royals to live in the palace, had them taken off because she was afraid their enormous weight would bring the roof down. At least that's what she *said* . . . palace insiders said the queen wanted the statues removed because her own likeness had not been placed front and center.

The statue of King Felipe IV in the center of the plaza was the first equestrian bronze ever to be cast with a horse rearing. The action pose comes from a Velázquez painting of the king with which the monarch was so smitten that in 1641 he commissioned an Italian artist, Pietro de Tacca, to turn it into a sculpture. De Tacca enlisted Galileo's help in configuring the statue's weight so that it wouldn't topple over.

In the minds of most Madrileños, the Plaza de Oriente is forever linked with Francisco Franco. The *generalísimo* liked to make speeches from the roof of the Royal Palace to his thousands of followers, crammed into the plaza below. Even now, on the November anniversary of Franco's death, the plaza fills with supporters, most of whom are old-timers, though lately the occasion has also drawn Nazi flag–waving skinheads from other European countries in a chilling fascist tribute.

4 **Plaza Mayor.** Austere, grand, and surprisingly quiet compared to the rest of the city, this arcaded square has seen it all: autos-da-fé (trials of faith, that is, public burnings of heretics); the canonization of saints; criminal executions; royal marriages, such as that of Princess María and the King of Hungary in 1629; bullfights (until 1847); masked balls; fireworks; and all manner of events and celebrations. It still hosts fairs, bazaars, and performances.

Measuring 360 by 300 ft, Madrid's Plaza Mayor is one of the largest and grandest public squares in Europe. It was designed by Juan de Herrera, the architect to Felipe II and designer of the forbidding El Escorial monastery, outside Madrid. Construction of the plaza lasted just two years and was finished in 1620 under Felipe III, whose **equestrian statue** stands in the center. The inauguration ceremonies included the canonization of four Spanish saints: Teresa of Ávila, Ignatius of Loyola, Isidro (Madrid's male patron saint), and Francis Xavier.

Prior to becoming the Plaza Mayor, this space was occupied by a city market, and many of the surrounding streets retain the names of the trades and foodstuffs once headquartered there. Nearby are Calle de Cuchilleros (Knifemakers' Street), Calle de Lechuga (Lettuce Street), Calle de Fresa (Strawberry Street), and Calle de Botoneros (Buttonmakers' Street). The plaza's oldest building is the one with the brightly painted murals and the gray spires, Casa de la Panadería (the bakery) in honor of the bread shop on top of which it was built. Opposite it is the Casa de la Carnicería (the butcher shop), now a police station.

The plaza is closed to motorized traffic, making it a pleasant place to sit in the sun or to while away a warm summer evening at one of the sidewalk cafés, watching alfresco artists, street musicians, and Madrileños from all walks of life. At Christmas the plaza fills with stalls selling trees, ornaments, and nativity scenes, as well as all types of practical jokes and tricks for December 28, *Día de los Inocentes,* a Spanish version of April Fool's Day.

13 **Puerta de Alcalá.** Marking the spot of the ancient city gates, this triumphal arch was built by Carlos III in 1778. You can still see the bomb damage inflicted on the arch during the civil war.

5 **Puerta del Sol.** Always crowded with both people and exhaust fumes, Sol is the nerve center of Madrid's traffic. The city's main subway interchange is below, and buses fan out through the city from here. A brass plaque in the sidewalk on the south side of the plaza marks Kilometer 0, the spot from which all distances in Spain are measured. The restored 1756 French neoclassical building near the marker now houses government offices, but during the Franco period it was used as a political prison and is still known as the Casa de los Gritos (House of Screams). Across the square is a bronze statue of Madrid's official symbol, a bear and a *madroño* (strawberry tree).

③ Teatro Real (Royal Theater). This neoclassical theater was built in 1850 and was long a cultural center for Madrileño society. Plagued by disasters more recently, including fires, a bombing, and profound structural problems, the house went dark in 1988. Closed for almost a decade for an indulgent restoration, it reopened to worldwide fanfare in October 1997. Now replete with golden balconies, plush seats, and state-of-the-art stage equipment for operas and ballets, the theater is a modern showpiece with its vintage appeal intact. ⊠ *Plaza Isabell II.* ☎ *91/516–0606.*

⟲ Telefèrico (cable car). Children love this cable car, which takes you from just above the Rosaleda gardens in the Parque del Oeste to the center of Casa de Campo. Be warned, however, that the walk from where the cable car drops you off to the zoo and the amusement park is at least 2 km (1 mi), and you'll have to ask directions. ⊠ *Estación Terminal Telefèrico, Jardines Rosaleda,* ☎ *91/541–7440.* 🎫 *490 ptas.* ⊙ *Apr.– Sept., daily noon–sundown; Oct.–Mar., weekends noon–sundown.*

Templo de Debod (Debod Temple). This authentic 4th-century BC Egyptian temple was donated to Spain in gratitude for its technical assistance with the construction of the Aswan Dam. It's near the site of the former Montaña barracks, where Madrileños bloodily crushed the beginnings of a Francoist uprising in 1936. ⊠ *Hill in Parque de la Montaña, near Estación del Norte train station,* ☎ *91/409–6165.* 🎫 *300 ptas.* ⊙ *Tues.–Fri. 10–1 and 4–7, weekends 10–1.*

Medieval Madrid

The narrow streets of medieval Madrid wind back through the city's history to its beginnings as an Arab fortress. Madrid's historic quarters are not so readily apparent as the ancient neighborhoods of Toledo and Segovia, nor are they so grand. But the traveler who takes time to explore their quiet, winding alleys gets an impression of the city that is light-years away from today's traffic-clogged avenues.

A Good Walk

The walk begins near the Royal Palace, at the 8th-century **Arab Wall** ㉗ on Cuesta de la Vega street. Traveling east on Calle Mayor to **Plaza de la Villa** ㉙, you'll find Spanish Mudéjar architecture and old family crests carved above doorways. Off Calle Mayor to the left is the church of **San Nicolás de Servitas** ㉘, whose tower is one of the oldest structures in Madrid. Below the Plaza Mayor on **Cava de San Miguel** ㉚ are Madrid's oldest tapas bars, taverns, and restaurants.

From the Puerta Cerrada, Calle Segovia guides you to ramped alleyways that lead to the **Plaza de Paja** ㉛, the heart of the old city, where peasants would deposit their crops as tithes to the church in the Middle Ages. Here you can visit the **Museo de San Isidro,** the site where Madrid's patron saint performed his most famous miracle.

Walk west from the Plaza de Paja on Calle de la Redondilla for one block to the **Plaza Morería,** which is really no more than a wide spot in the street. This neighborhood once housed Moors who chose to stay in Madrid after the Christian Reconquest. Although most of the buildings date from the 18th and 19th centuries, the steep, narrow streets and twisting alleyways recall the much older *medina* (old quarter).

Climb the stairway and cross Calle Bailén near the **Viaduct,** a metal bridge that spans a ravine 100 ft above Calle Segovia. The viaduct has grisly fame as Madrid's preferred spot for suicides.

Across the street on Calle Bailén is the neighborhood **Las Vistillas,** named for the pleasant park on the bluffs overlooking Madrid's western edge.

It's a great place to watch the sun go down or catch a cool breeze on a hot summer night; find an outdoor table and order a drink.

TIMING

This three-hour walk covers 2½ km (1½ mi) and requires some short uphill climbs through the winding streets. Give yourself ample time for stops to absorb the Old World charm (especially in summer, when heat will be a factor).

Sights to See

㉗ Arab Wall. The city of Madrid was founded on Calle Cuesta de la Vega at the ruins of this wall, which protected a fortress built here in the 8th century by Emir Mohammed I. In addition to being an excellent defensive position, the site had plentiful water and was called *Mayrit,* which is Arabic for "water source" and the likely origin of the city's name. All that remains of the *medina*—the old Arab city that formed within the walls of the fortress—is the neighborhood's crazy quilt of streets and plazas, which probably follow the same layout they followed more than 1,100 years ago. The park **Emir Mohammed I** (⊠ Cuesta de la Vega s/n), alongside the wall, hosts summertime concerts and plays.

★ ㉚ **Cava de San Miguel.** The narrow, picturesque streets behind the Plaza de la Villa are well worth exploring. From Calle Mayor, turn onto the Plaza de San Miguel and continue down Cava de San Miguel. With the Plaza Mayor on your left and the glass-and-iron San Miguel market on your right, walk downhill past the row of **ancient tapas bars** built right into the retaining wall of the plaza above. Each one specializes in something different: Mesón de Champiñones has mushrooms; Mesón de Boquerones serves anchovies; Mesón de Tortilla cooks up excellent Spanish omelets; and so on. Madrileños and tourists alike flock here each evening to sample the food and sing along with raucous musicians, who delight in playing foreign tunes for tourists.

Costanilla de San Andrés. This ramped street leads to the heart of the old city. To find it, follow Calle Segovia from the Plaza Puerta Cerrada until you reach Plaza Cruz Verde; then turn left up the ramped street. Halfway up the hill, look left down the narrow Calle Principe Anglona for a good view of the Mudéjar tower on the church of **San Pedro el Viejo,** (St. Peter the Elder), one of the city's oldest. The brick tower is believed to have been built in 1354 following the Christian reconquest of Algeciras, in southern Spain. Notice the tiny defensive slits, designed to accommodate crossbows.

Cuevas de Luis Candelas. The oldest of Madrid's taverns, about halfway down Cava San Miguel, is named for a 19th-century Madrid version of Robin Hood who was famous for his ingenious ways of tricking the rich out of their money and jewels. As Cava San Miguel becomes Calle Cuchilleros, you'll see **Casa Botín** (☞ Dining, *below*) on the left, Madrid's oldest restaurant and a favorite haunt of Ernest Hemingway. The curving Cuchilleros was once a moat just outside the city walls. The plaza with the bright murals at the intersection of Calle Segovia is called the **Puerta Cerrada** (⊠ Cava San Miguel and Calle Cuchilleros), or Closed Gate, named for the entrance to the city that once stood here.

Museo de San Isidro. Just behind the church of San Andrés is the site of St. Isidro's most famous miracle, and the new museum houses the original *pozo milagroso* (miracle well). It is said that when Isidro's infant son Illán fell into the well one day, Isidro raised the water level so that his son floated up to the top and could be pulled out. ⊠ *Plaza San Isidro s/n,* ☎ *91/522–5732.* 🎫 *Free.* 🕙 *Aug.–June, Tues.–Sun. 10–2.*

Palacio de la Nunciatura (Palace of the Nunciat). This mansion once housed the Pope's ambassadors to Spain and is now the official residence of the Archbishop of Madrid. It's near the Plaza Puerta Cerrada off Calle Segovia, one of the main streets of Madrid during the Middle Ages. Although it's not open to the public, you can peek inside the Renaissance garden. ⊠ *Costanilla del Nuncio s/n.*

NEED A
BREAK?
The **Café del Nuncio** (⊠ Costanilla del Nuncio s/n), on the corner of Calle Segovia, is a relaxing Old World spot for a coffee or beer. Classical music plays in the background.

㉙ Plaza de la Villa. Madrid's town council has met here since the Middle Ages. A medieval-looking complex, the Plaza is now Madrid's city hall. It's just two blocks west of the Plaza Mayor on Calle Mayor and was once called the Plaza de San Salvador for a church that used to stand here. The **Casa de los Lujanes** is the oldest building in the Plaza—it's the one with the Mudéjar tower, on the plaza's east side. Built as a family home in the late 15th century, it carries the Lujanes crest over the main doorway. On the east side of the Plaza is the brick-and-stone **Casa de la Villa,** built in 1629, a classic example of Madrid design with its clean lines and spire-topped corner towers. Connected by an overhead walkway, the **Casa de Cisneros** was commissioned in 1537 by the nephew of Cardinal Cisneros. It's one of Madrid's rare examples of the flamboyant plateresque style, which has been likened to splashing water—liquid exuberance wrought in stone. ⊠ *C. Mayor.* ⊙ *Guided tour in Spanish Mon. at 5.*

㉛ Plaza de Paja. At the top of the hill, on Costanillo San Andrés, this is medieval Madrid's most important square. Although a few upscale restaurants have moved in, the small plaza retains its own atmosphere. The jewel is the **Capilla del Obispo** (Bishop's Chapel), built between 1520 and 1530; this was where peasants deposited their tithes, called *diezmas*—literally, one-tenth of their crop. The stacks of wheat on the chapel's ceramic tiles refer to this tradition. Architecturally, the chapel marks a transition from the blockish Gothic period (which gave this structure its basic shape) to the Renaissance (which provided the decorations). Try to get inside to see the intricately carved polychrome altarpiece by Francisco Giralta, featuring scenes from the life of Christ. Opening hours are erratic; the best time to visit is during mass or on feast days.

The chapel forms part of the complex of the church of **San Andrés,** whose dome was raised to house the remains of Madrid's male patron saint, San Isidro Labrador. Isidro was a peasant who worked fields belonging to the Vargas family. The 16th-century **Vargas palace** (⊠ Plaza de Paja s/n) forms the eastern side of the Plaza de Paja. According to legend, St. Isidro actually worked little but had the best-tended fields thanks to many hours of prayer. When Señor Vargas came out to investigate the phenomenon, Isidro made a spring of sweet water spurt from the ground to quench his master's thirst. Because St. Isidro's power had to do with water, his remains were paraded through the city in times of drought in the hope that he would bring rain, even as recently as the turn of the 20th century.

㉘ San Nicolás de las Servitas (Church of St. Nicholas of the Servitas). The church tower is one of the oldest buildings in Madrid, and there's some debate over whether it once formed part of an Arab mosque. More likely, it was built after the Christian reconquest of Madrid in 1085, but the brickwork and the horseshoe arches are clear evidence that it was crafted by either Moorish workers (Mudéjars) or Spaniards well versed in the style. Inside the church, exhibits detail the Islamic history of early Madrid. ✉ *Near the Plaza de San Nicolás,* ☎ *91/559–4064.* 💵 *100 ptas.* ⏲ *Tues.–Sun. 6:30 AM–8:30 PM or by appointment.*

Castizo Madrid

A Good Walk

The Spanish word *castizo* means "authentic." There are few "sights" in the usual sense on this tour; instead, we wander through some of Madrid's most traditional and lively neighborhoods.

Begin at the **Plaza Santa Ana** ㉜, which was the hub of the theater district in the 17th century and is now known for its lively nightlife. Around the plaza are many noteworthy sights, such as the **Teatro Español** and the tile facade of the **Casa de Guadalajara,** one of the most beautiful buildings in Madrid. Walk east two blocks on Calle del Prado; then turn right on Calle León, named for a lion kept here long ago by a resident Moor. One block on this street brings you to the corner of **Calle Cervantes,** where the author of *Don Quixote* lived in what is now called the **Casa de Cervantes** ㉝.

Continuing down Calle León one block, turn left on Calle de las Huertas, the premier street of bars in bar-speckled Madrid. One block down Huertas turn right onto **Calle Amor de Dios,** the center of the city's flamenco community. Look for the music shops and guitar makers.

Follow Calle Amor de Dios until it ends at the busy Calle Atocha. Across the street you'll see the church of **San Nicolás.** Next door is the **Pasaje Doré,** home to a colorful assortment of market stalls typical of most Madrid neighborhoods.

Cross the street and walk down Calle Isabel until it bisects Calle de la Rosa. Veer right and follow Calle de la Rosa until it jogs to the left and turns into Calle de la Cabeza; at this point, follow the narrow street south. This is the beginning of the **Barrio Lavapiés**—the old *Judería* (Jewish Quarter). Today, Lavapiés remains one of Madrid's most *castizo* working-class neighborhoods, although gentrification is beginning to creep in. Don't be surprised to see graffiti reading "Yuppies No!" The older buildings are currently being reinforced, and heavy construction has torn up some of the most charming alleyways and marred the most picturesque views. Explore side streets off Calle Lavapiés to escape the sound of jackhammers, but continue winding west—passing the Cárcel de la Inquisición ㉞—and south until you reach the heart of the neighborhood, **Plaza Lavapiés** ㉟.

Leave the plaza heading southwest on Calle Sombrerete. After two blocks you'll reach the intersection of Calle Mesón de Paredes; on the corner, you'll see a lovingly preserved example of a popular Madrid architecture, called the **Corrala building** ㊱. Life in this type of balconied apartment building is lived very publicly, with laundry flapping in the breeze, babies crying, and old women dressed in black gossiping over the railings. In the past, neighbors shared common kitchen and bathroom facilities in the patio.

Work your way west, crossing Calle de Embajadores into the neighborhood known as **El Rastro** ㊲. This is a shopper's paradise, with streets of small family shops selling furniture, antiques, and a cornucopia of used junk (some of it highly overpriced). On Sunday, El Rastro becomes a flea market, and Calle de Ribera de Curtidores, the main drag, is closed to traffic, jammed with outdoor booths and shoppers.

TIMING

One of this walk's main attractions is simply the atmosphere. Plan to spend at least three hours. A good time to visit is on a weekday morning, when the markets are bustling.

Plaza Santa Ana is interesting at night as well, with some of Madrid's best tapas bars and nightspots lining its side streets. El Rastro can be saved for a Sunday morning if you decide to brave the crowds at the flea market.

Sights to See

Barrio Lavapiés. The Barrio Lavapiés is the old *Judería* (Jewish Quarter). Like Moors, Jews were forced to live outside the city walls after the Christian reconquest hit Madrid in 1085; this was one of the suburbs they founded.

㉞ Cárcel de la Inquisición (Inquisition Jail). For a chilling reminder of the depth of the Catholic Monarchs' intolerance, stop at the southeast corner of Calle Cabeza and Calle Lavapiés. Unmarked by any historical plaque, the former jail is now a lumber warehouse. Here Jews, Moors, and others designated unrepentant heathens or sinners suffered the many tortures devised by the merciless inquisitors.

㉝ Casa de Cervantes. A plaque marks the house where the author of *Don Quixote* lived and died. Miguel de Cervantes's 1605 epic story of the man with the impossible dream is said to be the world's most widely translated and read book in the world after the Bible. ⊠ *C. Cervantes and C. León.*

Casa de Lope de Vega. The home of Lope de Vega, a contemporary of Cervantes, has been turned into a museum that shows how a typical home of the period was furnished. Considered the Shakespeare of Spanish literature, Lope de Vega (1562–1635) wrote some 1,800 plays and enjoyed huge success during his lifetime. ⊠ *C. Cervantes 11,* ☎ *91/429–9216.* ⊠ *200 ptas.* ☉ *Weekdays 9:30–3, Sat. 10–2.*

NEED A
BREAK?

Taberna de Antonio Sánchez. Drop in at Madrid's oldest bar for a glass of wine and some tapas, or just a peek inside. The dark walls (lined with bullfighting paintings), zinc bar, and pulley system used to lift casks of wine from the cellar look much the same as they did when the place was first opened, in 1830. Meals are also served in a dining room in the back. Specialties include *rabo de buey* (bull's-tail stew) and *morcillo al horno* (a beef stew). ⊠ *Mesón de Paredes 13.*

Cine Doré. A rare example of Art Nouveau architecture in Madrid, the Cine Doré shows movies from the Spanish National Film Archives and eclectic foreign films, usually in the original language. Show times are listed in newspapers under FILMOTECA. ⊠ *C. Santa Isabel 3,* ☎ *91/369–1125.* ☉ *Tues.–Sun.; hrs vary depending on show times.*

㊱ Corrala building. This building is not unlike the *corrales* that were used as the city's early theater venues; there is even a plaque here to remind visitors that the setting for the famous 19th-century *zarzuela* (light opera) *La Revoltosa* was a *corrala* like this one. City-sponsored musical-theater events are occasionally held here in summer. The ruins across the street were once the Escalopíos de San Fernando, one of several churches and parochial schools that fell victim to anti-Catholic sentiments in this neighborhood during the civil war. ⊠ *C. Mesón de Paredes and C. Sombrerete.*

㊲ El Rastro. Filled with tiny shops selling antiques and all manner of used stuff (some of it junk), the *rastro* becomes an overcrowded flea market on Sunday morning from 10 to 2. The best time to explore is any other morning, when a little browsing and bargaining are likely to turn up such treasures as old iron grillwork, marble tabletops, or gilt picture frames. The main street of the *rastro* is Ribera de Curtidores; the best streets for shopping are the ones to the west.

㉟ Plaza Lavapiés. This is the heart of the historic Jewish *barrio*. To the left is the Calle de la Fe (Street of Faith), which was called Calle Sinagoga until the expulsion of the Jews in 1492. The church of **San Pedro el Real** (Royal St. Peter) was built on the site of the razed synagogue. Legend has it that Jews and Moors who chose baptism over exile were forced to walk up this street barefoot to be baptized as a demonstration of the sincerity of their new faith. ⊠ *Top of C. de la Fe.*

㉜ Plaza Santa Ana. This plaza was the heart of the theater district in the 17th century—the golden age of Spanish literature—and is now the center of Madrid's thriving nightlife. In the plaza is a statue of 15th-century playwright Pedro Calderón de la Barca delivering one of his own lines. Barca's likeness faces the **Teatro Español,** which is adorned with the names of Spain's greatest playwrights. The theater, rebuilt in 1980 following a fire, stands in the same spot where plays were performed as early as the 16th century, at that time in a rowdy outdoor setting called a *corrala.* These makeshift theaters were usually installed in a vacant lot between two apartment buildings, and families with balconies overlooking the action rented out seats to wealthy patrons of the arts. The **Casa de Guadalajara,** with a ceramic-tile facade, is one of the most beautiful buildings in Madrid and currently a popular nightspot. It faces the Teatro Español across the Plaza Santa Ana. The recently refurbished **Hotel Victoria,** on the Plaza Santa Ana, is now an upscale establishment but was once a rundown residence frequented by famous and not-so-famous bullfighters, including Manolete.

To the side of the hotel is the diminutive **Plaza del Ángel,** home of one of Madrid's best jazz clubs, the Café Central. Back on the Plaza Santa Ana is one of Madrid's most famous cafés, the **Cervecería Alemana,** another Hemingway haunt. It still attracts struggling writers, poets, and beer drinkers.

San Nicolás. The predecessor of this plain, modern church was burned in 1936, a story vividly described by writer Arturo Barea in his autobiographical *The Forge.* Little of the original structure remains. Like many other churches during that turbulent period, the original church of St. Nicholas fell to the wrath of working-class crowds who felt that they were the victims of centuries of clerical oppression. ⊠ *C. Atocha and Plaza Anton Martín.*

DINING

Madrileños tend to eat their meals even later than other Spaniards—and that's saying something. Restaurants generally open for lunch at 1:30 and fill up by 3. Dinnertime begins at 9, but reservations for 11 are common. A meal in Madrid is usually a lengthy (up to three hours) and rather formal affair, even at inexpensive places. Restaurants are at their best at midday, when most places offer a *menú del día* (daily special), containing a main course, dessert, wine, and coffee.

Dinner, on the other hand, can present a problem if you don't want to eat such a big meal so late. One solution is to take your evening meal at one of Madrid's many foreign restaurants; good-quality Italian, Mexican, Russian, Argentine, and American places abound and on the whole tend to open earlier and to be less formal. It's worth trying to defy your body clock for at least one evening, though; a late dinner is a far more authentic experience.

What to Wear

Dress in most Madrid restaurants and tapas bars is stylish but casual. The more expensive places tend to be a bit more formal; men generally wear jackets and ties, and women wear skirts.

$$$$ ✕ **Horcher.** Housed in a luxurious mansion at the edge of Retiro, this
★ classic restaurant is renowned for hearty but elegant fare served with impeccable style. Specialties include the types of game dishes traditionally favored by Spanish aristocracy; try the wild boar, venison, or roast wild duck with almond croquettes. The star appetizer is lobster salad with truffles. Dishes like stroganoff with mustard, pork chops with sauerkraut, and *baumkuchen* (a chocolate-covered fruit and cake dessert) reflect the restaurant's Germanic roots. (The Horcher family operated a restaurant in Berlin at the turn of the century.) The intimate dining room is decorated with rust-colored brocade and antique Austrian porcelain. A wide selection of French and German wines rounds out the menu. ⊠ *Alfonso XII 6,* ☎ *91/522–0731. Reservations essential. AE, DC, MC, V. Closed Sun. No lunch Sat.*

$$$$ ✕ **Lhardy.** Serving Madrid specialties in the same central location for more than 150 years, Lhardy looks pretty much the same as it must have on day one, with its dark-wood paneling, brass chandeliers, and red-velvet chairs. The menu offers international fare, but most diners come for the traditional *cocido a la Madrileño* and *callos a la Madrileño.* Sea bass in champagne sauce, game, and dessert soufflés are also finely prepared. The dining rooms are upstairs; the ground-floor entry doubles as a delicatessen and stand-up coffee bar that on chilly winter mornings fills with shivering souls sipping steaming-hot *caldo* (chicken broth) from silver urns. ⊠ *Carrera de San Jerónimo 8,* ☎ *91/522–2207. AE, DC, MC, V. No dinner Sun.*

$$$$ ✕ **Viridiana.** The trendiest of Madrid's gourmet restaurants, Viridiana has a relaxed bistro atmosphere and black-and-white decor punctuated by prints from Luis Buñuel's classic, anticlerical film (for which the place is named). Iconoclast chef Abraham Garcia says "market-based" is too narrow a description for his creative menu, though the list does change every two weeks depending on what's locally available. Offerings include such varied fare as red onions stuffed with *morcilla* (black pudding); soft flour tortillas wrapped around marinated fresh tuna; and filet mignon in white truffle sauce. If it's available, try the superb duck pâté drizzled with sherry and served with Tokay wine. The tangy grapefruit sherbet is a marvel. ⊠ *Juan de Mena 14,* ☎ *91/531–5222. Reservations essential. No credit cards. Closed Sun., Holy Wk, and Aug.*

$$$$ ✕ **Zalacaín.** A deep-apricot color scheme, set off by dark wood and gleaming silver, makes this restaurant look like an exclusive villa. Zalacaín introduced nouvelle cuisine to Spain and continues to set the pace after 20 years at the top. Splurge on such dishes as prawn salad in avocado vinaigrette, scallops and leeks in Albariño wine, and roast pheasant with truffles; a prix-fixe tasting menu allows you to sample the restaurant's best for about 6,500 pesetas. Service staff is somewhat stuffy. ⊠ *Alvarez de Baena 4,* ☎ *91/561–5935. Reservations essential. AE, DC, V. Closed Sun., Aug., and Holy Wk. No lunch Sat.*

$$$ ✕ **Ciao.** Always noisy and packed with happy diners, Ciao is Madrid's best Italian restaurant. Homemade pastas, like tagliatelle with wild mushrooms or *panzerotti* stuffed with spinach and ricotta, are popular as inexpensive main courses; but the kitchen also turns out credible versions of osso buco and veal scallopini, accompanied by a good selection of Italian wines. The decor—mirrored walls and sleek black furniture—convincingly evokes fashionable Milan. A second location (⊠ Apodaca 20, ☎ 91/447–0036), run by the owner's sons and

38

Madrid Dining

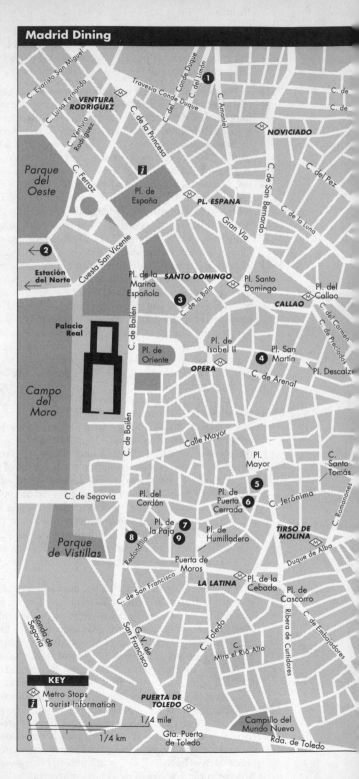

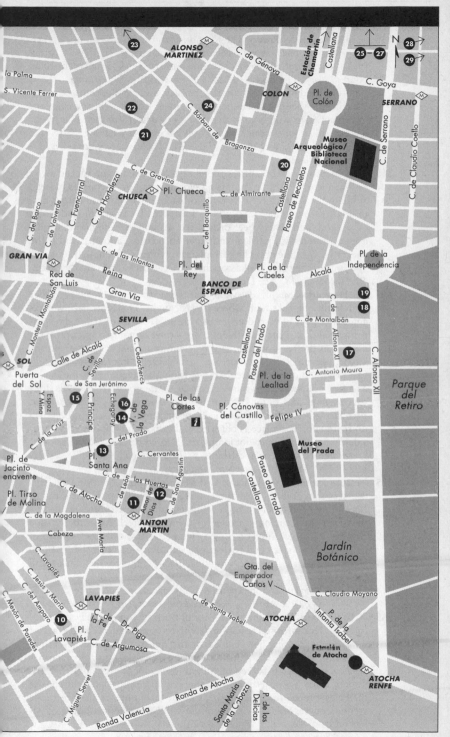

daughter, also serves pizza. ⊠ *Argensola 7,* ☎ *91/308–2519. Reservations essential. AE, DC, MC, V. Closed Sun. No lunch Sat.*

$$$ ✕ **El Cenador del Prado.** The Cenador's innovative menu has French
★   and Asian touches, as well as exotic Spanish dishes that you'll rarely find in restaurants. Dine in a baroque salon or a less formal plant-filled conservatory. The house specialty is *patatas a la importancia* (sliced potatoes fried in a sauce of garlic, parsley, and clams); other possibilities include shellfish consommé with ginger ravioli, veal and eggplant in béchamel, or wild boar with prunes. For dessert try the *cañas fritas,* a cream-filled pastry once served only at Spanish weddings. ⊠ *C. del Prado 4,* ☎ *91/429–1561. AE, DC, MC, V. Closed Sun. and Aug. 1– 15. No lunch Sat.*

$$$ ✕ **El Cosaco.** This romantic, candlelit Russian restaurant, tucked away
★   on the ancient Plaza de Paja, is a favorite with young couples in love. While some diners have eyes only for each other, the food here is definitely worth a look—savory blini stuffed with caviar, smoked trout, or salmon, and hearty beef dishes like stroganoff. The dining rooms are decorated with paisley wallpaper and dark-red linens, and if the cheery glow of the crackling fireplace in winter isn't enough to warm you, one of the eight vodkas ought to do the trick. ⊠ *Plaza de Paja 2,* ☎ *91/365–3548. AE, DC.*

$$$ ✕ **El Pescador.** Spaniards swear that the seafood in Madrid is fresher
★   than in the coastal towns where it was caught. That's probably an exaggeration, but El Pescador, one of Madrid's best-loved seafood restaurants, makes it seem plausible. Before sitting down to dinner, stop for a drink at the bar and take in the delicious aromas wafting from the kitchen, where skilled chefs dressed in fishermen's smocks prepare shellfish just behind the counter. Among the tapas available at the bar or as a first course of your meal, the *salpicón de mariscos* (mussels, lobster, shrimp, and onions in vinaigrette) is incredible. The *lenguado Evaristo* (grilled sole), named for the restaurant's owner, is the best dish on the menu. The place is cheerful and noisy, and the decor is dockside-rustic, with lobster-pot lamps, red-and-white-checked tablecloths, and rough-hewn posts and beams. ⊠ *José Ortega y Gasset 75,* ☎ *91/ 402–1290. MC, V. Closed Sun. and Aug.*

$$$ ✕ **Gure-Etxea.** In the heart of Old Madrid, on the Plaza de Paja, this is one of the capital's most authentic Basque restaurants. The ground-floor dining room is airy, high-ceilinged, and elegant; brick walls line the lower level, giving it a country-farmhouse feel. As in the Basque country, you are waited on only by women. Classic dishes include *bacalao al pil-pil* (spicy cod fried in garlic and oil—making the "pil-pil" sound), *rape en salsa verde* (monkfish in garlic-and-parsley sauce), and for dessert *leche frita* (fried custard). On weekdays, the lunch menu includes a hearty and inexpensive daily special. ⊠ *Plaza de Paja 12,* ☎ *91/365–6149. AE, DC, V. Closed Sun. and Aug. No lunch Mon.*

$$$ ✕ **La Trainera.** La Trainera is all about fresh seafood—the best money can buy. This informal restaurant, with its nautical decor and maze of little dining rooms, has reigned as the queen of Madrid's seafood houses for decades. Crab, lobster, shrimp, mussels, and a dozen other types of shellfish are served by weight in *raciones* (large portions). Although many Spanish diners share several plates of these delicacies as their entire meal, the grilled hake, sole, or turbot makes an unbeatable second course. Skip the listless house wine and go for a bottle of Albariño from the cellar. ⊠ *Lagasca 60,* ☎ *91/576–8035. AE, MC, V. Closed Sun. and Aug.*

$$$ ✕ **Mentidero de la Villa.** The decor of this intimate eatery is a bewitching blend of pastel colors, pale wood, and candlelight, with fanciful, rough-hewn sculptures of rocking horses. The French and Spanish menu is adventuresome—even the chef's salad mixes fresh kelp and lettuce. Spe-

cialties include breast of squab in cherry vinegar, pheasant and chestnuts in wine, and halibut in a black-olive sauce. Apropos of the restaurant's name (which means "gossip shop"), service is informal and chatty. ⊠ *Santo Tomé 6,* ☎ *91/308–1285. AE, MC, V. Closed Sun. and Aug. No lunch Sat.*

$$ ✕ **Brasserie de Lista.** For a gourmet meal in a comfortable, informal setting, this bistro-style spot amid designer boutiques can't be beat. A long, marble bar, lots of brass, and frosted glass create a turn-of-the-century ambience. Waiters in long white aprons serve Spanish specialties with nouvelle touches, such as grilled monkfish with toasted garlic and steak with *cabrales* (blue cheese sauce). The varied menu also includes international fare such as chicken-and-avocado salad with chutney, and beef carpaccio. The weekday lunch special is a good value. ⊠ *José Ortega y Gasset 6,* ☎ *91/435–2818. AE, MC, V.*

$$ ✕ **Botín.** The *Guinness Book of Records* calls this the world's oldest
★ restaurant (1725), and Hemingway called it the best. The latter claim may be a touch over the top, but the restaurant *is* excellent and extremely charming, despite the hordes of tourists. There are four floors of tiled and wood-beamed dining rooms, and ovens dating back several centuries, which you'll pass if you're seated upstairs. Traditionally garbed musical groups called *tunas* often drop in. Essential specialties are *cochinillo asado* (roast suckling pig) and *cordero asado* (roast lamb). It is said that Francesco Goya was a dishwasher here before he made it as a painter. ⊠ *Cuchilleros 17, off Plaza Mayor,* ☎ *91/366–4217. AE, DC, MC, V.*

$$ ✕ **Café Balear.** Sophisticated yet informal, Café Balear draws creative types from the fashion and advertising worlds and serves them some of the best paella in Madrid. Art prints and potted palms are the only nods to decoration in the stark, white dining room. Specialties include paella *centolla* (with crab) and *arroz negro* (rice with squid in its ink). The perfectly prepared paella *mixta* combines seafood, pork, and vegetables. ⊠ *Sagunto 18,* ☎ *91/447–9115. AE, V. No dinner Sun.–Mon.*

$$ ✕ **Cañas y Barro.** Hidden away on an unspoiled plaza that was the center of Madrid's university in the 19th century, this Valencian restaurant specializes in rice dishes with flair. The most popular is *arroz a la banda* (rice with peeled shrimp cooked in seafood broth). Another good choice is the paella Valenciana, made with chicken, rabbit, and vegetables. The service is friendly and unpretentious, and white-plaster friezes lend the pink dining room a touch of elegance. ⊠ *Amaniel 23,* ☎ *91/542–4798. AE, DC, MC, V. Closed Mon. and Aug. No dinner Sun.*

$$ ✕ **Casa Paco.** This popular Castilian tavern wouldn't have looked out
★ of place two or three centuries ago. Squeeze your way past the old, zinc-topped bar, always crowded with Madrileños downing shots of red wine, and into the tiled dining rooms. People come here to feast on thick slabs of red meat, served sizzling on plates so hot that the meat continues to cook at your table. The beef is superb, and the Spanish consider overcooking a sin—so if you ask for your meat well done, be prepared for nasty glares. You order the meat by weight, so remember that a *medio kilo* is more than a pound. Try the *pisto manchego* (the La Mancha version of ratatouille) to start. ⊠ *Puerta Cerrada 11,* ☎ *91/366–3166. DC, V. Closed Sun. and Aug.*

$$ ✕ **Casa Vallejo.** With its homey dining room, friendly staff, creative menu, and reasonable prices, Casa Vallejo is the well-kept secret of Madrid's budget gourmets. Try the tomato, zucchini, and cheese tart or artichokes and clams to start; then follow up with duck breast in prune sauce or meatballs made with lamb, almonds, and pine nuts. The fudge-and-raspberry pie alone makes it worth the trip. ⊠ *San Lorenzo 9,* ☎ *91/308–6158. Reservations essential. MC, V. No dinner Sun.–Mon.*

$$ ✕ **Cornucopia en Descalzas.** Owned by two Americans, a Frenchman, and a Spaniard, this young and friendly restaurant on the first floor of an old mansion (just off the historic Plaza de las Descalzas Reales) serves what it calls Euro-American cuisine. The menu changes with the season; possibilities include grilled entrecote marinated in bourbon and honey, bream on a dill compote, and stewed rabbit with tomatoes, onion, and thyme. In winter, the restaurant becomes a tea room, Saturday and Sunday from 5 to 8. ✉ *Flora 1,* ☎ *91/547–6465. AE, MC, V. Closed Mon. and1 wk in Aug.*.

$$ ✕ **La Bola.** First opened as a *botellería* (wine shop) in 1802, La Bola
★ developed slowly into a tapas bar and eventually into a full-fledged restaurant. Tradition is the main draw; blood-red paneling outside beckons you into the original bar and cozy dining nooks decorated with polished wood, Spanish tile, and lace curtains. The restaurant still belongs to the founding family, with the seventh generation currently in training to take over. Dinner is served, but the house specialty is that quintessential Madrid meal *cocido Madrileño,* served only at lunch and accompanied by crusty bread and a hearty red wine. ✉ *Bola 5,* ☎ *91/547–6930. No credit cards. No dinner Sun.*

$$ ✕ **La Cacharrería.** The name of this restaurant means "junkyard," and it's reflected in the funky decor—a mix of dusty calico, old lace, and gilt mirrors, all tucked into the medieval quarter. The cooking, however, is decidedly upscale, with a market-based menu that changes daily and an excellent selection of wines. Venison stew and fresh tuna steaks with *cava* (champagne) and leeks were among the recent specialties. Whatever else you order, save room for the homemade lemon tart. ✉ *Moreiria 9,* ☎ *91/365–3930. AE, DC, MC, V. Closed Sun.*

$$ ✕ **La Gamella.** American-born chef Dick Stephens has created a new,
★ reasonably priced menu at this perennially popular dinner spot. The sophisticated rust-red dining room, batik tablecloths, oversize plates, and attentive service remain the same, but much of the nouvelle cuisine has been replaced by more traditional fare, such as chicken in garlic, beef bourguignonne, and steak tartare à la Jack Daniels. A few of the old favorite signature dishes, like sausage-and-red-pepper quiche and bittersweet chocolate pâté, remain. The lunchtime *menú del día* is a great value at 1,700 pesetas. ✉ *Alfonso XII 4,* ☎ *91/532–4509. AE, DC, MC, V. Closed Sun. and Aug. 15–30. No lunch Sat.*

★ ۞ **$$** ✕ **La Pampa de Lavapiés.** This excellent Argentine restaurant is secluded on a side street in Lavapiés. As you enter there's a small eating area to the left, but most people prefer to sit in the rustic dining room to the right. The massive and delicious *bife La Pampa* is the house specialty (enough steak, fried eggs, peas, and tomatoes for two light eaters) and contains enough protein for a week. The pasta dishes, such as cannelloni Rossini, are also good. If you feel like dancing off your dinner, you can tango here on weekends. Sundays—when kids get free pasta—are equally boisterous. ✉ *Amparo 61,* ☎ *91/528–0449. AE, DC, MC, V. Closed Mon.*

$$ ✕ **Nabucco.** Had enough Spanish food for the moment? With pastel-washed walls and subtle lighting from gigantic, wrought-iron candelabras, this pizzeria and trattoria is a trendy but elegant haven in gritty Chueca. Fresh bread sticks and garlic olive oil show up within minutes of your arrival. The spinach, ricotta, and walnut ravioli is heavenly, and this may be the only Italian restaurant in Madrid where you can order (California-style?) barbecued-chicken pizza. Considering the ambience and quality, the bill is a pleasant surprise. ✉ *Hortaleza 108,* ☎ *91/310–0611. AE, MC, V.*

$$ ✕ **Sí Señor.** One of Madrid's new crop of entertaining restaurants, Sí Señor specializes in Mexican food and tequila slammers. The big bar in the entryway serves Mexican-style tapas (quesadillas or chips with guacamole). The huge, noisy dining hall is lined with oversize paintings, artfully executed in a unique Mexican pop-art style. The drinks here are far better than the food, but do try the beef enchiladas or *pollo pibil*, a spicy Yucatán-style chicken dish. ⊠ *Paseo de la Castellana 128,* ☎ *91/564–0604. AE, DC, MC, V.*

$ ✗ **Casa Mingo.** Resembling an Asturian cider tavern, Casa Mingo is
★ built into a stone wall beneath the Estación del Norte train station, across the street from the hermitage of San Antonio de la Florida. It's a bustling place; you share long plank tables with other diners, and the only things on the menu are succulent roast chicken, salad, and sausages, all to be washed down with numerous bottles of *sidra* (hard cider). Small tables are set up on the sidewalk in summer. Try to get here early (1 for lunch, 8:30 for dinner) to avoid the wait. ⊠ *Paseo de la Florida 2,* ☎ *91/547–7918. Reservations not accepted. No credit cards.*

$ ✗ **Inti de Oro.** This Peruvian restaurant on one of Madrid's premier restaurant rows is a big hit, thanks largely to the care the owners put into their native traditional specialties. Try the *ceviche de camarones* (shrimp in lime juice), *conejo con maní* (rabbit in peanut sauce), or *seco de cabrito* (goat-meat stew). The dining room is light, and the walls are adorned with handicrafts. ⊠ *Ventura de la Vega 12,* ☎ *91/429–6703. AE, DC, V.*

$ ✗ **La Biotika.** A vegetarian's dream in the heart of the bar district just east of Plaza Santa Ana, this small, cozy restaurant serves macrobiotic vegetarian cuisine every day of the week. Enormous salads, hearty soups, fresh bread, and creative tofu dishes make the meal flavorful as well as healthy. A small market at the entrance sells macrobiotic groceries. ⊠ *Amor de Dios 3,* ☎ *91/429–0780. No credit cards.*

$ ✗ **Puebla.** Puebla is always crowded with bankers and congressmen from the nearby Cortés. Although the decor lacks charm (the fake wood beams fool no one), you'd be hard pressed to find better-prepared food at such affordable prices anywhere else in Madrid. There are two price ranges for the *menú del día,* each covering more than a dozen choices. The selection changes frequently, but be sure to try the *berenjenas a la romana* (batter-fried eggplant) if it's offered. The soups are always great; other dishes include roast lamb, trout, and calamari. ⊠ *Ventura de la Vega 12,* ☎ *91/429–6713. AE, DC, MC, V. Closed Sun.*

$ ✗ **Sanabresa.** You can tell by the clientele what a find this place is. Professionals who demand quality but don't want to spend too much money come here daily, as does an international assortment of students from the nearby flamenco school. The menu is classic Spanish fare— hearty, wholesome meals like *pechuga villaroy* (breaded and fried chicken breast in béchamel) and paella (for lunch Thursday and Sunday only). The functional, green-tiled dining room is always crowded, so be sure to arrive by 1:30 for lunch or 8:30 for dinner. ⊠ *Amor de Dios 12,* ☎ *no phone. Reservations not accepted. No credit cards. Closed Aug. No dinner Sun.*

LODGING

There are booking services at the airport and the Chamartín and Atocha train stations. You can also contact the **La Brujula** agency (⊠ Torre de Madrid, 6th floor, Plaza de España, ☎ 91/559–9705); the fee is a modest 250 pesetas. The staff speaks English and can book rooms and tours all over Spain. Unless otherwise indicated, all rooms have private baths.

$$$$ **Palace.** Built in 1912, this enormous, Belle Epoque grand hotel is
★ a creation of Alfonso XIII. At less than two-thirds the price of the nearby

44

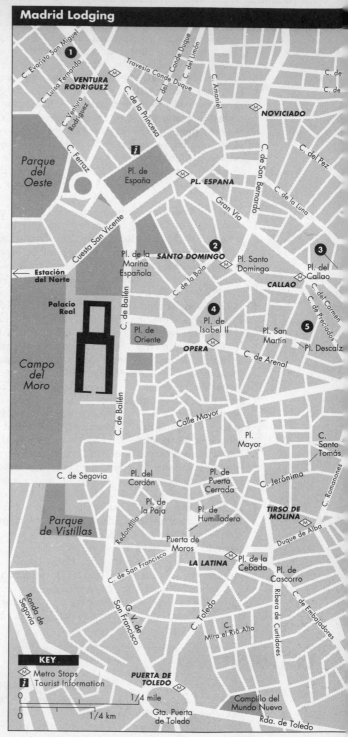

Madrid Lodging

KEY
Ⓜ Metro Stops
ⓘ Tourist Information

0   1/4 mile
0   1/4 km

45

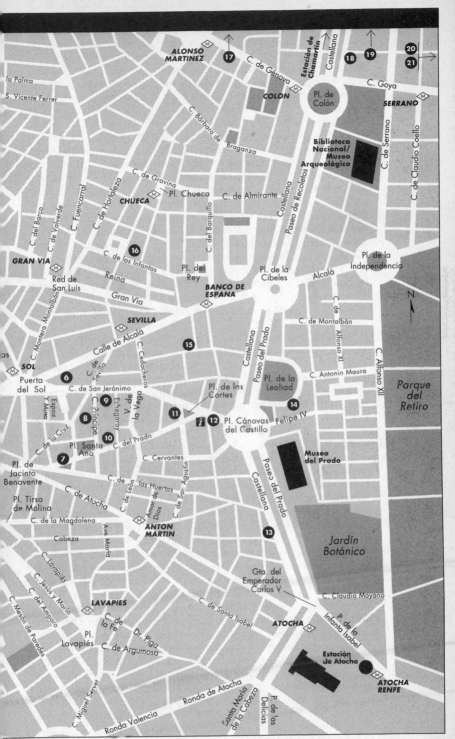

Ritz, the Palace is a pleasure, though its attractions are concentrated in the opulent public areas, including a large cupola with a stained-glass ceiling. The rooms aren't impressive for a hotel of this caliber—they're plain and most are small, with a pronounced 1960s American flavor. Bathrooms are spacious, however, with double sinks, tubs, separate shower stalls, and other welcome touches such as bathrobes and magnifying mirrors. In 1997, *Condé Nast Traveler* readers placed the Palace among the top 25 hotels in Europe. ⊠ *Plaza de las Cortes 7, 28014,* ☎ *91/429–7551,* FAX *91/429–8266. 436 rooms, 20 suites. Restaurant, bar, beauty salon, parking. AE, DC, MC, V.*

$$$$ ⊞ **Ritz.** When Alfonso XIII was preparing for his marriage to Queen
★ Victoria's granddaughter, he realized to his dismay that Madrid did not have a single hotel up to the exacting standards of his royal guests. Thus was born the Ritz. Opened in 1910 by the king himself, who had personally overseen its construction, the Ritz is a monument to the Belle Epoque, furnished with rare antiques in every public room, hand-embroidered linens from Robinson and Cleaver of London, and all manner of other luxurious details. Guest rooms are carpeted, hung with chandeliers, and decorated in pastels; many have good views of the Prado or the Castellana. The Ritz was named one of Europe's top five hotels by *Condé Nast Traveler* readers in 1997; visit the garden terrace even if you don't stay here. ⊠ *Plaza de Lealtad 5, 28014,* ☎ *91/521–2857,* FAX *91/532–8776. 158 rooms. Restaurant, bar, beauty salon, health club, parking. AE, DC, MC, V.*

$$$$ ⊞ **Santo Mauro.** Once the Canadian embassy, this turn-of-the-century mansion was reopened in 1992 as an intimate luxury hotel. The neoclassical architecture is accented by contemporary furniture (such as suede armchairs) in such hues as mustard, teal, and eggplant. Twelve of the rooms are in the main building, which also houses a popular gourmet restaurant; the other rooms are in a new annex and are split-level, with stereos and VCRs. ⊠ *Zurbano 36, 28010,* ☎ *91/319–6900,* FAX *91/308–5477. 37 rooms. Restaurant, bar, parking. AE, DC, MC, V.*

$$$$ ⊞ **Villa Real.** If you fancy a luxury hotel that combines elegance, modern amenities, *and* a great location, this is the ticket. A simulated 19th-century facade gives way to lobbies garnished with potted palms. Each room has a character of its own, albeit with an overall French feel; some suites have both saunas and whirlpool baths. The hotel faces the Cortés and is convenient to almost everything. The staff is very friendly. ⊠ *Plaza de las Cortés 10, 28014,* ☎ *91/420–3767,* FAX *91/420–2547. 94 rooms, 20 suites. Restaurant, bar. AE, DC, MC, V.*

$$$$ ⊞ **Villamagna.** Renowned in the early '90s as the favorite of visiting financiers and reclusive rock stars, the Villamagna has been humbled by competition, and its reputation for ultra exclusivity has faded with the decor of its green-and-white lobby. Still, it's one of Madrid's top luxury hotels, its modern facade belying an exquisite interior furnished with 18th-century antiques. It's somewhat overpriced but does have some finishing touches hard to find elsewhere; a pianist provides soothing music in the lounge at lunchtime and during cocktail hour, and rooms all have desks with plenty of working space as well as hidden TVs, VCRs, and plants in the bathrooms. The restaurant, Berceo, has cozy walnut paneling and the feel of an English library; its garden terrace is open for dinner in warm weather. ⊠ *Paseo de la Castellana 22, 28046,* ☎ *91/576–7500,* FAX *91/575–9504. 164 rooms, 18 suites. Restaurant, bar, beauty salon, exercise room, parking. AE, DC, MC, V.*

$$$ ⊞ **El Prado.** Wedged in between the classic buildings of *castizo* Madrid, this skinny, new hotel is within stumbling distance of the city's best bars and nightclubs and is priced accordingly. Rooms are basic but spacious and virtually immune to street noise thanks to double-paned windows. Decorative touches include pastel floral prints and gleaming marble baths. ✉ *C. Prado 11, 28014,* ☎ *91/429–0234,* FAX *91/429–2829. 47 rooms. Cafeteria, parking. AE, DC, MC, V.*

$$$ 🏨 **Fenix.** A magnificent marble lobby greets your arrival at this Madrid institution, overlooking Plaza de Colón on the Castellana. The hotel is also just a few steps from the posh shopping street Serrano. Its spacious rooms, decorated in beiges and golds, are carpeted and amply furnished. Flowers abound. ✉ *Hermosilla 2, 28001,* ☎ *91/431–6700,* FAX *91/576–0661. 204 rooms, 12 suites. Bar, café, beauty salon. AE, DC, MC, V.*

$$$ 🏨 **Hotel Santo Domingo.** An intimate hotel that artfully blends the best of classical and modern design, the five-year-old Santo Domingo is about 10 minutes' walk from the Puerta del Sol, just off Gran Vía. Rooms are decorated in soft tones of peach and ocher, and all feature telephones with voice mail and double-paned windows for soundproofing. An especially friendly and well-trained staff gives the place a personal feel. ✉ *Plaza Santo Domingo 13, 28013,* ☎ *91/547–9800,* FAX *91/547–5995. 120 rooms. Restaurant, bar, parking. AE, DC, MC, V.*

$$$ 🏨 **Lagasca.** In the heart of the elegant Salamanca neighborhood, this newish hotel combines large, brightly decorated rooms with an unbeatable location two blocks from Madrid's main shopping street, Calle Serrano. The marble lobbies border on the coldly functional, but they're fine as a meeting place. ✉ *Lagasca 64, 28001,* ☎ *91/575–4606,* FAX *91/575–1694. 100 rooms. Restaurant, bar, parking. AE, DC, MC, V.*

$$$ 🏨 **Reina Victoria.** The Tryp chain recently bought and extensively ren-
★   ovated this grande dame, one of Madrid's most historic and beloved hotels. Now, besides the attractive exterior and great location on one of Madrid's most charming squares, the Victoria draws a far more upscale clientele than its former down-at-the-heels bullfighters and American writers, such as Ernest Hemingway (it now gets well-heeled bullfighters). Beyond the fairly charmless lobby and public rooms, the hotel is quite attractive, with handsome details and an overall stately effect in the hallways and the big, bright, airy guest rooms. The best rooms overlook the Plaza Santa Ana. Reservations are increasingly necessary. ✉ *Plaza del Ángel 7, 28014,* ☎ *91/531–4500,* FAX *91/522–0307. 201 rooms. Restaurant, bar, parking. AE, DC, MC, V.*

$$$ 🏨 **Suecia.** The chief attraction of the Suecia is its location, right next to the superchic Círculo de Bellas Artes (an arts society/café/film/theater complex). Though recently remodeled, its lobby is still somewhat soulless. The rooms are trendy, with modern art on the walls and futuristic light fixtures. ✉ *Marqués de Riera 4, 28014,* ☎ *91/531–6900,* FAX *91/521–7141. 119 rooms, 9 suites. 2 restaurants, bar. AE, DC, MC, V.*

$$$ 🏨 **Tryp Ambassador.** Ideally located on an old street between Gran Vía
★   and the Royal Palace, this hotel occupies the renovated 19th-century palace of the Dukes of Granada. A magnificent front door and a graceful three-story staircase are legacies of the building's aristocratic past; the rest has been transformed into elegant lodgings favored by executives. Bedrooms are large, with separate sitting areas, and have mahogany furnishings, floral drapes, and bedspreads. The greenhouse bar, filled with plants and songbirds, is especially pleasant on cold days. ✉ *Cuesta Santo Domingo 5 and 7, 28013,* ☎ *91/541–6700,* FAX *91/ 559–1040. 181 rooms. Restaurant, bar, parking. AE, DC, MC, V.*

$$ 🏨 **Atlántico.** Don't be put off by the location, on a noisy stretch of Gran Vía, or by the rather shabby third-floor lobby. The Atlántico delivers bright, clean accommodations at good prices. Rooms are small but comfortable, with fabric wall coverings and new furniture. All have tile baths. A member of the Best Western chain, this hotel is a favorite with British travelers and is almost always full, so it's wise to book well in advance. ✉ *Gran Vía 38, 28013,* ☎ *91/522–6480,* FAX *91/531–0210. 80 rooms. Snack bar. AE, MC, V.*

$$ ⊞ **Carlos V.** If you like to be in the center of things, hang your hat at this classic hotel on a pedestrian street: it's just a few steps away from the Puerta del Sol, Plaza Mayor, and Descalzas Reales convent, and the price is right. A suit of armor decorates the tiny lobby, while crystal chandeliers add elegance to the second-floor guest lounge. All rooms are bright and carpeted. ⊠ *Maestro Victoria 5, 28013,* ☎ *91/531–4100,* FAX *91/531–3761. 67 rooms, 41 with bath. AE, DC, MC, V.*

$$ ⊞ **Inglés.** Virginia Woolf was one of the first luminaries to discover this hotel, which is smack in the middle of the old city's bar-and-restaurant district. Since Woolf's time, the Inglés has attracted more than its share of less-celebrated artists and writers. Rather deteriorated and drab now, it's best for those looking for location and value rather than luxury. (Run-down suites cost what you'd normally pay for a standard double.) The balconies overlooking Calle Echegaray give you an unusual view of the medieval quarter from the air, all red Mediterranean tiles and ramshackle gables. ⊠ *C. Echegaray 8, 28014,* ☎ *91/429–6551,* FAX *91/420–2423. 58 rooms. Bar, cafeteria, exercise room, parking. AE, DC, MC, V.*

$$ ⊞ **Muralto.** Though uninspiring from the outside, the Muralto offers apartments with full kitchens at a price comparable to ordinary doubles in nearby hotels. It's convenient to much of western Madrid—the Royal Palace, Plaza de España, El Corte Ingles department store, and Estación de Norte are all within walking distance. The arrangement buys you convenience and independence to compensate for the drab facade and colorless decor. ⊠ *Calle Tutor 37, 28008,* ☎ *91/542–4400. 68 rooms. Restaurant, bar, parking (free). AE, DC, MC, V.*

$$ ⊞ **Paris.** You can't get more central than this; for a remarkably fair
★   price, the Paris offers delightful Old World charm right at the corner of the Puerta del Sol and Calle de Alcalá. The odd-shape rooms are clean, spacious, and decorated with orange bedspreads and curtains. The lobby is dark, woody, and somehow redolent of times long past. There's no bar, but three meals are served in the bright second-floor restaurant. All in all, the Paris is an unusual deal. ⊠ *Alcalá 2, 28014,* ☎ *91/521–6496,* FAX *91/531–0188. 114 rooms. Restaurant. MC, V.*

$ ⊞ **Monaco.** Just a few steps from the tiny Plaza de Chueca, the Monaco is an eccentric delight. The lobby is resplendent with red-carpeted stairs, potted plants, brass rails, and mirrors—and the rooms are similar, with Louis XIV–style furniture and mirrored walls. The Portuguese owner is very gracious. The location is lively but marginal, hence the bargain rates; be aware when coming and going. Bar- and club-heavy Chueca is known for drug traffic and pickpockets. ⊠ *Barbieri 5, 28004,* ☎ *91/522–4630,* FAX *91/521–1601. 33 rooms. Restaurant, bar, cafeteria. AE, MC, V.*

$ ⊞ **Mora.** Directly across the Paseo del Prado from the Botanical Gar-
★   dens, the Mora welcomes weary travelers with a sparkling, faux-marble lobby and bright, carpeted hallways. The guest rooms are modestly decorated but large and comfortable; those on the street side have great views of the gardens and the Prado. Double-paned windows keep them fairly quiet. ⊠ *Paseo del Prado 32, 28014,* ☎ *91/420–1569,* FAX *91/420–0564. 61 rooms. AE, DC, MC, V.*

$ ⊞ **Ramón de la Cruz.** If you don't mind a longish metro ride from the city center, this medium-size hotel is a find. The rooms are large, with modern bathrooms, and the stone-floor lobby is spacious. For Madrid, it's a bargain. ⊠ *Don Ramón de la Cruz 94, 28006,* ☎ *91/401–7200,* FAX *91/402–2126. 103 rooms. Cafeteria. MC, V.*

$ ⊞ **Villar.** All of these rooms are pleasant, clean, and tastefully furnished, with antique beds and armoires, but the real attractions are the eight rooms with balconies. Laden with flowers, the balconies overlook lively Calle Príncipe and have corner views of the Plaza Santa Ana, in-

cluding the well-heeled crowds arriving at the Teatro Español. The best
bargain in the area, Villar is on the second floor of a beautiful old building with a marble foyer and winding staircase. ⊠ *Calle Príncipe 18,
28014,* ☎ *91/531–6600,* ☎ *91/521–5073. 34 rooms, 18 with bath.
AE, DC, MC, V.*

NIGHTLIFE AND THE ARTS

The Arts

Madrid's cultural scene is so lively that it's hard to follow. As the city's
reputation as a vibrant and contemporary arts center has grown, artists
and performers of all stripes have arrived in droves. The best way to
stay abreast of events is through the weekly *Guía de Ocio* (published
Monday) or daily listings in the leading newspaper, *El País.* Both
sources are relatively easy to comprehend even if you don't read Spanish. Tickets to performances are usually best purchased at the hall itself; in the case of major popular concerts, the Corte Inglés department
stores have **Discoplay** outlets for advance sales.

The city throws major arts festivals in each of the four seasons. The
most comprehensive is the Festival de Otoño (Autumn Festival), from
late September to late November, which blankets the entire city with
poetry readings, pop concerts, flamenco, and performances by world-
renowned ballet and theater companies. Other annual events include
world-class jazz, salsa, African music, and rock; art exhibits; film festivals; and more—all at very reasonable prices. More often than not,
the events take place outdoors, in city parks and amphitheaters.

Concerts/Ballet

Opened in 1988, the modern **Auditorio Nacional de Música** (⊠ Príncipe
de Vergara 136, ☎ 91/337–0100) is Madrid's main hall for classical
music and regularly hosts major orchestras from around the world. The
newly reopened **Teatro Real** (⊠ Plaza de Isabell II, ☎ 91/516–0606)
is the center for ballet and opera.

Film

Nearly a dozen theaters regularly show undubbed foreign films, the
majority of them in English. These are listed in newspapers and in the
Guía de Ocio under "V.O."—meaning original version. Leading V.O.
theaters include the **Alphaville** (⊠ Martín de los Héroes 14, ☎ 91/559–
3836) and **Renoir** (⊠ Martín de los Héroes 12, ☎ 91/559–5760), both
just off the Plaza de España. Excellent, classic V.O. films change daily
at the **Filmoteca Cine Doré** (⊠ Santa Isabel 3, ☎ 91/369–1125).

Theater

English-speaking performances are a rarity, and when they do come
to town, they play on any of a dozen Madrid stages; check local news-
papers.One theater you won't need Spanish for is the **Teatro de la
Zarzuela** (⊠ Jovellanos 4, ☎ 91/524–5400), which puts on the traditional Spanish operettas known as *zarzuela,* a kind of bawdy comedy. The **Teatro Español** (⊠ Príncipe 25, ☎ 91/429–6297) specializes
in 17th-century Spanish classics.

Nightlife

Nightlife—or *la marcha,* as the Spanish fondly call it—reaches legendary
heights in Spain's capital. It's been said that Madrileños rarely sleep,
and that's largely because they spend so much time in bars—not drunk,
but socializing in the easy, sophisticated way that is unique to this city.
This is true of old as well as young, and it's not uncommon for chil-

dren to play on the sidewalks past midnight while multigenerational families and friends convene over coffee or cocktails at an outdoor café. The streets most famous for their social scenes, however, do tend to attract a younger clientele; these include Huertas, Moratín, Segovia, Victoria, and the areas around the Plaza Santa Ana and the Plaza de Anton Martín. Adventuresome travelers may want to explore the scruffier bar district around the Plaza Dos de Mayo, in the Malasaña area, where trendy, smoke-filled hangouts line both sides of Calle San Vicente Ferrer. Equally brave souls can venture a few blocks east to the notorious haunts of neighboring Chueca, where tattoo studios and street-chic boutiques break up the endless alleys of techno discos and after-hours clubs.

Bars

There are countless bars in Madrid, and while almost all serve food, many are known more for their atmosphere. Some recommendations:

Cafe Gijón (⊠ Paseo de Recoletos 24, ☏ 91/521–5425) may be Madrid's most famous café-bar. It has hosted the city's most high-falutin *tertulias* (discussion groups that meet regularly to hash out the issues of the day) for more than a century.

Cervantes (⊠ León 8, ☏ 91/429–6093) is a bright, tiled bar where you can also get a pizza or pasta in a small dining room at the back. It caters to a young neighborhood crowd.

Chicote (⊠ Gran Vía 12, ☏ 91/532–6737) was immortalized in several of Hemingway's short stories about the Spanish civil war and still makes an interesting stop.

Hard Rock Cafe (⊠ Paseo Castellana 2, ☏ 91/435–0200) is wildly popular with young Spaniards. Madrid's version of this U.S. classic opened in 1994 and serves up the usual drinks, burgers, and salads with a heavy dose of loud music.

Hermanos Muñiz (⊠ Huertas 29, ☏ 91/429–5452) is the quintessential Spanish neighborhood bar, neither trendy nor touristy. The tapas here are uniformly excellent, and the men who serve them are both friendly and superbly professional.

La Champañería Gala (⊠ Moratín 24, ☏ 91/429–2562) is one of the city's better-known champagne bars, offering especially good Catalan *cavas* (Spanish champagnes).

Los Gabrieles (⊠ Echegaray 17, ☏ 91/429–6261) is featured in most of Madrid's tourist literature for its remarkable tile walls, but the clientele is, actually, mostly fashionable Spaniards.

Oliver (⊠ Almirante 12, ☏ 91/521–7379) is two bars in one. It's open afternoons and evenings for relaxing live piano music in the upstairs lounge; after midnight, the downstairs becomes a full-fledged Chueca disco.

Palacio de Gaviria (⊠ Arenal 9, ☏ 91/526–8089) is an impeccably restored, 19th-century baroque palace hidden away on the upper floors of a tawdry commercial street between Puerta del Sol and the Royal Palace. Allegedly built to house one of Queen Isabel II's lovers, the palace now serves drinks in an elegant setting, with live jazz late at night.

Soho (⊠ Jorge Juan 50, ☎ 91/577–8973) is something of a slice of New York in the Salamanca district. Filled with rap and reggae fans, it has an eclectic menu that includes exotic island drinks as well as Spanish variants of Tex-Mex cuisine.

Taberna de Antonio Sanchez (⊠ Mesón de Paredes 13, ☎ 91/539–7826) is reputed to be the oldest bar in Madrid—the proprietors claim it's been around since 1830. Order wine and tapas at the old zinc bar in front; head to the back to order a full meal.

Viva Madrid (⊠ Manuel Fernández y González 7, ☎ 91/429–3640) is an extremely popular bar with a Brassai motif and serious personality. Packed with both Spaniards and foreigners, it has become something of a singles scene. There are tables and a small selection of bar food in the rear.

Cabaret

Berlin Cabaret (⊠ Costanilla de San Pedro 11, ☎ 91/366–2034) professes to provide authentic cabaret as it was performed in Berlin in the '30s. (These days the audience is *much* different.) Combining magic, chorus girls, and ribald comedy, it draws an eccentric crowd for vintage café theater. On weekends, the absurd fun lasts until daybreak.

Discos

Madrid's hippest new club is a three-story bar, disco, and cabaret called **Bagelus** (⊠ María de Molina 25, ☎ 91/561–6100). **Joy Eslava** (⊠ Arenal 11, ☎ 91/366–3733), a downtown disco in a converted theater, is an old standby. **Pacha** (⊠ Barceló 11, ☎ 91/466–0137), one of Spain's infamous chain discos, is always energetic. The well-heeled crowd likes **Archy's** (⊠ Marqués de Riscal 11, ☎ 91/308–3162). **Space of Sound** (⊠ Plz. Estación de Chamartin [in the train station] , ☎ 91/733–3505) almost fails to qualify as a nightclub: it's open Saturday and Sunday mornings from dawn until noon, full of drag queens and club kids who refuse to let the night end. Salsa has become a fixture in Madrid; check out the most spectacular moves at **Azucar** (Sugar; ⊠ Paseo Reina Cristina 7, ☎ 91/501–6107).

Flamenco

Madrid is not a great city for flamenco, but if you won't be traveling south, here are a few possibilities:

Café de Chinitas (⊠ Torija 7, ☎ 91/559–5135) puts on the city's best-known show, and its patrons have included such diplomatic guests as former Nicaraguan president Daniel Ortega. It's expensive, but the dancing is the best in Madrid. Try to reserve in advance; it often sells out.

Casa Pulus (⊠ Canizares 10, ☎ 91/369–0496) is one of Madrid's main flamenco spaces. Along with tapas, it offers good, if a little touristy, performances. The prices are more reasonable than elsewhere.

Corral de la Moreria (⊠ Morería 17, ☎ 91/365–8446) serves dinner à la carte and invites well-known flamenco stars to perform with the resident group. Since Morería opened its doors in 1956, visiting celebrities such as Frank Sinatra and Ava Gardner have left their autographed photos for the walls.

Nightclubs

Jazz, rock, flamenco, and classical music are all popular in Madrid's many small clubs. A few of the more interesting:

Amadis (✉ Covarrubias 42, underneath the Luchana Cinema, ☎ 91/446–0036) has telephones on every table, encouraging people to call each other with invitations to dance. The scene is sophisticated; you must be over 25 to enter.

Café Central (✉ Plaza de Ángel 10, ☎ 91/369–4143), the city's best-known jazz venue, is chic and well run, and the musicians are often very good. Performances generally begin at 10 PM.

Cafe del Foro (✉ San Andrés 38, ☎ 91/448–9464) is a funky, friendly club on the edge of Malasaña, with live music every night starting at 11:30.

Café Jazz Populart (✉ Huertas 22, ☎ 91/429–8407) features blues, Brazilian music, reggae, and salsa, starting at 11 PM.

Clamores (✉ Albuquerque 14, ☎ 91/445–7938), another famous jazz club, serves a wide selection of French and Spanish champagnes.

Maravillas (✉ San Vicente Ferrer 35, ☎ no phone) draws an indie crowd for live alternative music in a laid-back, inexpensive dive bar.

Siroco (✉ San Dimas 3, ☎ 91/593–3070) offers two different kinds of music Tuesday through Saturday: live Spanish pop downstairs, '70s disco and acid jazz on the second-story dance floor.

Torero (✉ Cruz 26, ☎ 91/523–1129), a thoroughly modern club despite its name, is for the beautiful people—quite literally: a bouncer allows only those judged *gente guapa* (beautiful people) to enter. It's one of Madrid's most stylin' spots.

Tapas Bars

The practice of spending one's evening going from bar to bar and eating tapas is so popular that the Spanish have a verb to describe it: *tapear.* The selection is endless; the best-known tapas bars are the *cuevas* clustered around Cava de San Miguel (☞ Medieval Madrid, *above*). Here are a few more suggestions:

Bocaíto (✉ Libertad 6, ☎ 91/532–1219) is said by some to serve the best tapas in Madrid—a heady claim. You can have a full meal here or just dip into a few tapas before heading on to the many other fine places in the immediate vicinity.

El Rey de Pimiento (✉ Plaza Puerta Cerrada, ☎ no phone) serves some 40 different kinds of tapas, including, in keeping with its name (The Pepper King), roasted red pimientos as well as the intermittently hot pimientos *de padrón.*

El Rincon de la Alpujara (✉ Puerto Rico 35, ☎ 91/359–9000) is one of the few tapas bars in Madrid with an outdoor terrace in summer. If you order from the excellent, international wine selection, the first tapa offered will probably be a wedge of *queso manchego,* a sharp regional cheese.

El Ventorrillo (✉ Bailén 14, ☎ 91/366–3578) is a place to go between May and October, when tables are set up in the shady park of Las Vistillas overlooking the city's western edge. Specialties include croquettes and mushrooms. This is Madrid's premier place to watch the sun go down.

La Chuleta (✉ Echegaray 20, ☎ 91/429–3729) is a cheery corner bar hung with bullfight memorabilia and stocked with a colorful selection of tapas on the bar. Seating is available.

La Dolores (✉ Plaza de Jesús 4, ☎ 91/429–2243) is a crowded, noisy, and wonderful place that's rightly reputed to serve the best draft beer in Madrid. Located just behind the Palace Hotel, it has a very few tables in back.

La Trucha (✉ Manuel Fernández y González 3, ☎ 91/532–0890) is hung with hams and garlic and feels like a medieval inn. It's also a restaurant, but the wonderful tapas that line the aging bar are far better.

Las Bravas (✉ Alvarez Gato 3, ☎ 91/532–2620), hidden away in an alley off the Plaza Santa Ana, isn't much to look at, but it's here that *patatas bravas* (potatoes in a spicy tomato sauce) were invented. They're now classic Spanish tapas.

Mesón Gallego (✉ León 4, ☎ 91/429–8997) is a hole-in-the-wall that serves wonderfully hearty Galician potato soup (a famous cure for those who've drunk too much) called *caldo gallego*. Not for everyone is the *Ribeiro*, the somewhat acidic white wine made with grapes from Galician riverbanks.

Museo del Jamon (Ham Museum; ✉ Carrera de San Jeronimo 6, ☎ 91/458–0163) is a Madrid chain of tapas bars that has become an institution. Look for the window full of dangling hams with hoofs. The best tapas here are, of course, the selection of hams from around the country. Don't be daunted by the variety; try the *serrano* or the *iberico* to start.

The Reporter (✉ Fúcar 6, ☎ 91/429–3922), true to its English name, is hung with great Spanish and world news photos. Its other great attraction is a garden terrace shaded by a grapevine trellis. The *raciones* (entrée-size portions of tapas, intended for sharing) are very good, and the pâté plate is terrific.

Taberna de Cien Vinos (✉ Nuncio 17, ☎ 91/365–4704) is the latest addition to Madrid's tapas circuit. It's tucked into a charming old house with wooden shutters and stone columns. You can order by the glass from a wide selection of Spanish wines, and the *raciones* border on the gourmet.

OUTDOOR ACTIVITIES AND SPORTS

Participant Sports

Horseback Riding
On the other side of Casa de Campo, **Club El Trébol** (☎ 91/518–1066) rents both animals and equipment at reasonable prices.

Jogging
Your best bet is **Retiro Park,** where one path circles the entire park and numerous others weave their way under trees and through formal gardens. **Casa de Campo** is crisscrossed by numerous, less-shady trails.

Swimming
Madrid has the perfect antidote to the dry, sometimes intense heat of the summer months—a superb system of clean, popular, and well-run municipal swimming pools (admission about 350 pesetas; there are several reduced-price, multiple-ticket options). Most neighborhoods have pools, but the biggest and best—fitted with a comfortable, tree-shaded restaurant—is in the **Casa de Campo** (take the metro to Lago and walk

up the hill a few yards; ☎ 91/463–0050). Another good choice in the city center is the ☺ **Piscina Canal Isabel II** (✉ Plaza Juan Zorrila, entrance off Avda. de Filipinas, ☎ no phone), with diving boards and a wading pool for kids.

Tennis

Club de Tenis Chamartín (✉ Federico Salmon 2, ☎ 91/345–2500), with 28 courts, is open to the public. There are also public courts in the **Casa de Campo** and on the Avenida de Vírgen del Puerto, behind the Palacio Real. (Ask for details at the tourist office.)

Spectator Sports

Bullfighting

For better or for worse, bullfighting is a spectacle, not a sport. For those not turned off by the death of six bulls every Sunday afternoon from April to early November, it offers all the excitement of any major stadium event. Nowhere in the world is bullfighting better than at Madrid's **Las Ventas** (✉ C. Alcalá 231, ☎ 91/356–2200; Metro Las Ventas), formally called the Plaza de Toros Monumental. The sophisticated audience, which follows the sport intensely, is more critical in Madrid than anywhere else, and you'll be amazed at how confusing their reactions to the fights are to the uninitiated. Cheers and hoots are difficult at first to distinguish, and it may take years to understand what prompts the wrath of this most difficult-to-please crowd. For a traveler, the bullfight audience can be the most entertaining part of the experience. Tickets may be purchased at the ring or, for a 20% surcharge, at the agencies on Calle Victoria, just off the Puerta del Sol. Most fights start in the late afternoon, and the best of all—the world's top display of bullfighting—come during the three weeks of consecutive daily fights that mark the feast of San Isidro, in May. Tickets can be tough to get through normal channels, but they're always available from scalpers in the Calle Victoria and at the stadium. You can bargain, but even Spaniards pay prices of perhaps 10 times the face value—up to 10,000 pesetas or even more.

Soccer

Spain's number-one sport is soccer, known locally as *fútbol*. Madrid has two teams, Real Madrid and Atletico Madrid, both among Europe's best, and two stadiums to match. The enormous **Santiago Bernabeu Stadium** (✉ Paseo de la Castellana 140, ☎ 91/315–0046), capacity 130,000 is home to the more popular Real Madrid, while the **Vicente Calderón Stadium** (✉ Paseo de Melancólicos s/n, ☎ 91/366–4704), on the outskirts of town, is where Atlético Madrid defends. You'll generally have to stand in line at the stadium to get tickets, but tickets for many major games are available at agencies inside Corte Inglés department stores (☞ Shopping, *below*).

SHOPPING

Beyond the popular Lladró porcelain and bullfighting posters, Madrid has a great selection of gift items and unique souvenirs. In recent years Spain has been recognized as one of the world's top design centers. You'll have no trouble finding traditional crafts in Madrid, such as ceramics, guitars, and leather goods (albeit not at traditional, countryside prices), but don't stop there. Madrid is now more like Rodeo Drive than the bargain bin that it was just a decade ago. Famous for contemporary furniture and decorator items as well as chic clothing, shoes, and jewelry, Spain's capital is stiff competition for Barcelona, a city that now considers itself the fashion capital of Europe. Most shops accept most major credit cards.

Department Stores

El Corte Inglés. The largest of Spain's chain department stores carries the best selection of everything, from auto parts to groceries to designer fashions. ✉ *Goya 76,* ☎ *91/577–7171;* ✉ *Goya 87,* ☎ *91/432–9300;* ✉ *Preciados 3,* ☎ *91/379–8000;* ✉ *Princesa 42,* ☎ *91/542–4800;* ✉ *Serrano 47,* ☎ *432–5490;* ✉ *La Vaguada Mall,* ☎ *91/387–4000;* ✉ *Parquesur Mall,* ☎ *91/558–4400;* ✉ *Raimundo Fernández Villaverde 79,* ☎ *91/556–2300.*

Marks & Spencer. British chain "Marks & Sparks" is best known for its woolens and underwear, but most shoppers head straight for the gourmet-food shop in the basement. ✉ *Serrano 52,* ☎ *91/520–0000.*

Zara. For those with young tastes and slim pocketbooks (picture hip clothes that you'll throw away in about six months), Zara has the latest looks for men, women, and children. ✉ *Carretas 10,* ☎ *91/522–6945;* ✉ *Gran Vía 32,* ☎ *91/522–9727;* ✉ *Narvaez 20,* ☎ *91/575–0424;* ✉ *Preciados 20,* ☎ *91/532–2014;* ✉ *Princesa 45,* ☎ *91/543–2415;* ✉ *Conde de Peñalver 4,* ☎ *91/435–4135.*

Flea Market

El Rastro (☞ *Castizo Madrid, above*). On Sunday, Calle de Ribera de Curtidores, the Rastro market's main thoroughfare, is closed to traffic and jammed with outdoor booths selling everything under the sun. The Sunday crowds grow so thick that it takes a while just to advance a few feet amid the hawkers and the gawkers. A word of warning: hang on to your purse and wallet, and be especially careful if you choose to bring a camera—pickpockets abound. The flea market sprawls into most of the surrounding streets, with certain areas specializing in particular products. Many of the goods sold here are wildly overpriced.

But what goods! You'll find everything from antique furniture to exotic parrots and cuddly puppies; from pirated cassette tapes of flamenco music to key chains emblazoned with symbols of the CNT, Spain's old anarchist trade union. Practice your Spanish by bargaining with the vendors over paintings, colorful Gypsy oxen yokes, heraldic iron gates, new and used clothes, and even hashish pipes. They may not lower their prices, but sometimes they'll throw in a handmade bracelet or a stack of postcards to sweeten the deal.

Off the Ribera are two *galerías,* courtyards where small shops offer higher-quality, higher-priced antiques and other goods. The whole spectacle shuts down around 2 PM.

Shopping Districts

Madrid has two main centers for shopping. The first is in the center of town, around the **Puerta del Sol,** and includes the major department stores (El Corte Inglés, the French music-and-book chain Fnac, etc.) and a large number of midline shops in the streets nearby. The second area, far more elegant and expensive, is in the northwestern **Salamanca** district, bounded roughly by Serrano, Goya, and Conde de Peñalver. These streets, just off the Plaza de Colón (particularly Calle Serrano), have the widest selection of smart boutiques and designer fashions—think Prada, Armani, and Donna Karan New York, as well as renowned Spanish designers such as Sybilla and Josep Font-Luz Diaz. If you're in the market for clothes, you may find that Spaniards, like Italians, favor browns and oranges; cool palettes don't prevail, though of course black is readily available.

South of the city center, an old factory building has been turned into the **Mercado Puerta de Toledo** (✉ Ronda de Toledo 1), an ultraslick, government-subsidized mall full of upscale shops charging upscale prices. **Galerías del Prado** (✉ Plaza de las Cortes 7) is another attractive mall, tucked under the Palace Hotel on the Paseo del Prado; shop here for fine books, gourmet foods, clothing, leather goods, art, and more. The newest of them all is a four-decker mall in the beautifully renovated, 19th-century **Centro Comercial ABC** (✉ Paseo de la Castellana 34), named for the daily newspaper that started there. The building is a Madrid landmark with an ornate tile facade; inside, a large café is surrounded by shops of all kinds, including leather stores and hairdressers. The fourth-floor coffee shop has a rooftop terrace with scenic urban views. For street-chic shopping closer to medieval Madrid, check out the playful window displays at the **Madrid Fusion Centro de Moda** (✉ Plaza Tirso de Molina 15, ☎ 91/369–0018), where up-and-coming Spanish design houses such as Instinto, Kika, and Extart fill five floors with faux furs, funky jewelry, and Madrid's most eccentric collection of shoes.

Specialty Stores

Ceramics

Antigua Casa Talavera (✉ Isabel la Católica 2, ☎ 91/547–3417) is the best of Madrid's numerous ceramics shops. Despite the name, the finest ware sold here is from Manises, near Valencia, but the blue-and-yellow Talavera ceramics are also excellent.

Cerámica El Alfar (✉ Claudio Coello 112, ☎ 91/411–3587) is laden with pottery from all corners of Spain.

Sagardelos (✉ Zurbano 46, ☎ 91/310–4830) specializes in distinctive, modern Spanish ceramics from Galicia and has excellent selections of breakfast sets, coffee pots, and objets d'art.

Clothing

Adolfo Domínguez (✉ Serrano 96, ☎ 91/576–7053; ✉ Serrano 18, ☎ 91/577–8280) is one of many fashion studios in the Salamanca district. Domínguez is one of Spain's best-known designers, with lines for both men and women.

Del Valle (✉ Conde Xiqueno 2, ☎ 91/531–1587; ✉ Princesa 47, ☎ 91/547–1216; ✉ Orense 6, ☎ 91/556–2735; ✉ Serrano 88, ☎ 91/577–6149) is an upscale women's boutique with a tasteful collection of evening and casual wear and an emphasis on leather.

Seseña (✉ De la Cruz 23, ☎ 91/531–6840) has outfitted Hollywood stars (and Hillary Rodham Clinton) and famous painters since the turn of the century, with capes in wool or velvet, some lined with red satin.

Sybilla (✉ Jorge Juan 12, ☎ 91/578–1322) is the studio of Spain's best-known woman designer. Her fluid dresses and hand-knit sweaters, which have made her a favorite with supermodel Helena Christensen, come in natural colors and fabrics.

Crafts

Artespaña (✉ Hermosilla 14, ☎ 91/435–0221) used to be run by the government to encourage Spanish craftsmanship. The store stylishly displays the best decorative crafts, such as furniture, lamps, and rugs.

El Arco (✉ Plaza Mayor 9, ☎ 91/365–2680) has a good selection of contemporary handicrafts from all over Spain, including modern ceramics, handblown glassware, jewelry, and leather items as well as a whimsical collection of pendulum clocks.

Fans

Casa Jimenez (✉ Preciados 42, ☎ 91/431–6592) gets a nod from locals as the best place to buy an authentic Spanish fan. The selection ranges from handpainted works of art to cheaper souvenirs. Open since the 1950s, this homey shop is still family-run.

Guitars

Conde Hermanos (✉ Felipe II 2, ☎ 91/547–0612) is a workshop where three generations of the same family have been building and selling professional guitars since 1917.

José Ramirez (✉ Concepción Jerónimo 2, ☎ 91/369–2211) was founded in 1882 and has been exporting guitars to the rest of the world ever since. Prices start at 15,000 pesetas. The shop includes a museum of antique instruments.

Hats

Casa Yustas (✉ Plaza Mayor 30, ☎ 91/366–5084) is a century-old shop featuring every type of headgear, from the old three-cornered, patent-leather hats of the Guardia Civil to the berets worn by the Guardia's frequent enemy, the Basques. These berets are much wider than those worn by the French and make excellent gifts.

Leather Goods

Caligae (✉ Augusto Figueroa 27, ☎ 91/531–5343) is on a street full of bargain shoe stores (*muestrarios*) and is probably the best of the bunch, offering close-out prices on the avant-garde designs of Parisian Stephane Kélian.

Duna (✉ Lagasca 7, ☎ 91/435–2061) has the best prices in town on fine Spanish leather clothing and shoes, but the selection is somewhat limited.

Loewe (✉ Serrano 26, ☎ 91/577–6056; ✉ Gran Vía 8, ☎ 91/522–6815; ✉ Palace Hotel, ☎ 91/429–8530) features ultra-high-quality designer purses, accessories, and clothing made of buttery-soft leather in dyed, jewellike colors. Prices often hit the stratosphere.

Tenorio (✉ Plaza de la Provincia 6, ☎ no phone) is where you'll find those fine old boots of Spanish leather, made to order with workmanship that should last a lifetime.

SIDE TRIPS

El Escorial

⓳ *50 km (31 mi) northwest of Madrid.*

Felipe II was one of history's most deeply religious and forbidding monarchs—not to mention one of its most powerful—and the great granite monastery that he had constructed in a remarkable 21 years (1563–84) is an enduring testimony to his austere character. Severe, rectilinear, and unforgiving, the Real Monasterio de San Lorenzo de El Escorial (El Escorial Monastery) is 50 km (31 mi) outside Madrid on the slopes of the Guadarrama Mountains and is one of the most massive yet simple architectural monuments on the Iberian Peninsula.

Felipe built the monastery in the village of San Lorenzo de El Escorial to commemorate Spain's crushing victory over the French at Saint-Quentin on August 10, 1557, and as a final resting place for his all-powerful father, the emperor Carlos V. The vast rectangle it traces, encompassing 16 courts, is modeled on the red-hot grille upon which San Lorenzo was martyred—appropriate enough, since August 10 was

Side Trips from Madrid

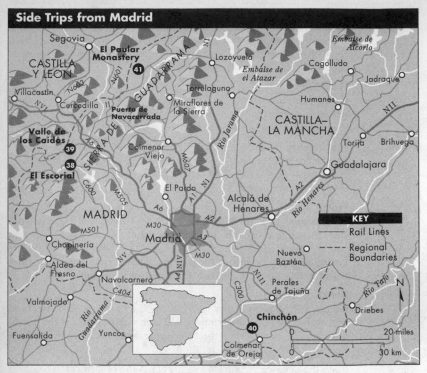

that saint's day. (It's also said that Felipe's troops accidentally destroyed a church dedicated to San Lorenzo during the battle, and he sought to make amends.) A Spanish psychohistorian recently theorized that the building is shaped like a prone woman and is thus an unintended emblem of Felipe's sexual repression. Lo and behold, this thesis provoked several newspaper articles and a rash of other commentary.

El Escorial is easily reached by car, train, bus, or organized tour; simply inquire at a travel agency or the appropriate station. Although the building and its adjuncts—a palace, museum, church, and more—can take hours or even days to tour, you should be able to include a day trip to the Valley of the Fallen, an underground basilica where General Franco is buried. Be prepared for the mobs of tourists who visit El Escorial daily, especially during the summer.

The monastery was begun by Juan Bautista de Toledo but finished in 1584 by Juan de Herrera, who would eventually give his name to a major Spanish architectural school. It was completed just in time for Felipe to die here—gangrenous and tortured by the gout that had plagued him for years—in the tiny, sparsely furnished bedroom that resembled a monk's cell more than the resting place of a great monarch. It is in this bedroom—which looks out, through a private entrance, into the royal chapel—that one most appreciates the man's spartan nature. Spain's later, Bourbon kings, such as Carlos III and Carlos IV, had clearly different tastes, and their apartments, connected to Felipe's by the Hall of Battles, are far more luxurious.

Perhaps the most interesting place in the entire Escorial is the **Royal Pantheon**, which contains the body of every king since Carlos I save three—Felipe V (buried at La Granja), Ferdinand VI (in Madrid), and Amadeus of Savoy (in Italy). The body of Alfonso XIII, who died in

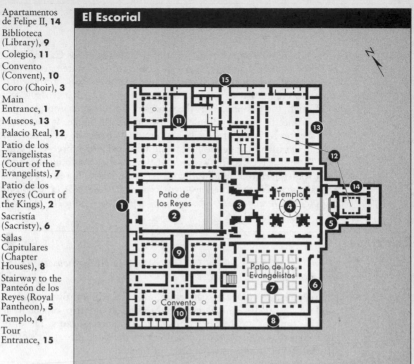

El Escorial

Rome in 1941, was brought to El Escorial in January 1980. The rulers' bodies lie in 26 sumptuous marble and bronze sarcophagi that line the walls (three of which are empty, awaiting future rulers). Only those queens who bore sons later crowned lie in the same crypt; the others, along with royal sons and daughters who never ruled, lie nearby, in the **Pantheon of the Infants.** Many of the royal children are in a single, circular tomb made of Carrara marble.

Another highlight is the monastery's uncharacteristically lavish and beautiful **library,** with 50,000 rare manuscripts, codices, and ancient books, including the diary of St. Teresa of Ávila and the gold-lettered, illuminated *Codex Aureus.* Tapestries, woven from cartoons by Goya, Rubens, and El Greco, cover almost every inch of wall space in huge sections of the building, and extraordinary canvases by Velázquez, El Greco, David, Ribera, Tintoretto, Rubens, and other masters have been collected from around the monastery and are now displayed in the New Museums. In the **basilica,** don't miss the fresco above the choir, depicting heaven, or Titian's fresco, *The Martyrdom of St. Lawrence,* which shows the saint being roasted alive. ⊠ *San Lorenzo de El Escorial,* ☎ *91/890–5905.* ▣ *800 ptas.* ◷ *Apr.–Sept., Tues.–Sun. 10–6; Oct.–Mar., Tues.–Sun. 10–5.*

NEED A BREAK?

Many Madrileños consider El Escorial the perfect place for an enormous weekend lunch. Topping the list of favorite eating spots is the outdoor terrace of **Charoles** (⊠ Floridablanca 24, ☎ 91/890–5975), where imaginative seasonal specialties round out a menu of Spanish favorites, such as *bacalao al pil-pil* (a fried, salted cod, served still sizzling) and grilled *chuletón* (steak).

Valle de los Caídos (Valley of the Fallen)

39 *13 km (8 mi) north of El Escorial on the C600.*

Just a few minutes north of El Escorial is the Valle de los Caídos (Valley of the Fallen). You drive through a pine-studded state park to this massive basilica, which is carved out inside a hill of solid granite and commands magnificent views to the east. Topped with a cross nearly 500 ft high, the basilica holds the tombs of both Franco and José Antonio Primo de Rivera, founder of the Spanish Falange. It was built with the forced labor of Republican prisoners after the civil war and dedicated, rather disingenuously, to all who died in the three-year conflict. The inside recalls *The Wizard of Oz* more than anything else, with every footstep resounding loudly off its stone walls. Tapestries of the Apocalypse add to the generally terrifying air. ☎ 91/890–5611. ✉ *Basilica 600 ptas., funicular 300 ptas.* ☉ *Apr.–Sept., Tues.–Sun. 10–7; Oct.–Mar., Tues.–Sun. 10–6.*

Chinchón

40 *54 km (28 mi) southeast of Madrid, off the N III highway to Valencia on the C300 local road.*

The picturesque village of Chinchón, a true Castilian town, seems a good four centuries removed. It makes an ideal day trip, especially if you take time for lunch at one of its many rustic restaurants. The only problem is that swarms of Madrileños have the same idea, so it's often difficult to get a table at lunchtime on weekends.

The high point of Chinchón is its charming Plaza Mayor, an uneven circle of ancient three- and four-story houses embellished with wooden balconies resting on granite columns. It's something like an open-air Elizabethan theater, but with a Spanish flavor. In fact, the entire plaza is converted to a bullring from time to time, with temporary bleachers erected in the center and seats on the privately owned balconies rented out for splendid views of the festivities. (These fights are rare and tickets hard to come by, as they're snatched up by Spanish tourists as soon as they go on sale.) The commanding **Iglesia de la Asunción** (Church of the Assumption) overlooks the plaza; it's known for its Goya mural, *The Assumption of the Virgin.*

NEED A
BREAK?

Two of the best and most popular restaurants on Chinchón's arcaded plaza are **Mesón de la Virreina** (✉ Plaza Mayor 21, ☎ 91/894–0015) and **Café de la Iberia** (✉ Plaza Mayor 17, ☎ 91/894–0998).

Both have balconies for outdoor dining; it's wise to reserve in advance for an outdoor table. The food in each is hearty Castilian fare, such as roast lamb and suckling pig or thick steaks. Be sure to try the locally made *anís* (anise), a licorice-flavored spirit—Chinchón is so famous for its anís that Spaniards converge here every April for the annual Fiesta del Anís y del Vino (Anise and Wine Festival).

On the way back to Madrid, where C300 joins the main highway, you'll pass through the Jarama Valley. This was the scene of one of the bloodiest battles in which the Abraham Lincoln Brigade (American volunteers fighting with the Republicans against Franco in the Spanish civil war) played a major role. The fight was immortalized by folk singer Pete Seeger, who sang, "There's a valley in Spain called Jarama . . .". Until just a few years ago, you could find bones and rusty military hardware in the fields here; today, there are still a number of clearly discernible trenches.

El Paular Monastery and the Lozoya Valley

❹ *100 km (62 mi) north of Madrid.*

Behind the great *meseta* on which Madrid sits, the Sierra de Guadarrama rises like a dark, jagged shield separating Old and New Castile. Snowcapped for much of the year, the mountains are indeed rough-hewn in many spots, particularly on their northern face, but there is a dramatic exception—the Lozoya Valley.

About 100 km (62 mi) north of the capital, this valley of pines, poplars, and babbling brooks is a cool, green retreat from the often searing heat of the plain. Madrileños often repair here for a picnic or a simple drive, rarely joined by foreign travelers, to whom the area is virtually unknown.

You'll need a car to make this trip, and the drive is a pleasant one. Take the A6 motorway northwest from the city and exit at signs for the Navacerrada Pass on the N601. As you climb toward the 6,100-ft mountain pass, you'll come to a road bearing off to the left toward Cercedilla. This little village is also accessible by train from Madrid; it's a popular base for hikes. Just above Cercedilla, an old Roman road leads up to the ridge of the Guadarrama, where an ancient fountain, known as Fuenfría, long provided the spring water that fed the Roman aqueduct of Segovia (☞ Chapter 3). The path traced by this cobble road is very close to the route Hemingway had his hero Robert Jordan take in *For Whom the Bell Tolls*; eventually it takes you near the bridge that Jordan blew up in the novel.

If you continue past the Cercedilla road, you'll come to a ski resort at the highest point of the Navacerrada Pass. Take a right here on the C604 and you'll follow the ridge of the mountains for a few miles before descending into the Lozoya Valley.

The monastery of **El Paular** (☎ 91/869–1425) will loom on your left as you approach the valley floor. This was the first Carthusian monastery in Castile, built by King Juan I in 1390, but it has been badly neglected since the Disentailment of 1836, when religious organizations gave their artistic treasures to the state. Fewer than a dozen Benedictine monks still live here, eating and praying exactly as their predecessors did centuries ago. One of them gives daily tours—and perhaps advice on the state of your soul—at noon, 1, and 5.

The monastery is physically attached to the hotel **Santa María del Paular** (☎ 91/869–1011, ⅀ 91/869–1006), most of whose rooms were tastefully refurbished in 1996. The hotel is charming but not as grand as similarly priced paradors.

The valley is filled with picnic spots along the Lozoya River, including several campgrounds. Afterward, take the C604 north a few kilometers to Rascafria, and then turn right on a smaller road marked for Miraflores de la Sierra. In that town you'll turn right again, following signs for Colmenar Viejo, and then pick up a short expressway back to Madrid.

MADRID A TO Z

Arriving and Departing

By Bus

Madrid has no central bus station; buses are generally less popular than trains (though they can be faster). Most of southern Spain is served by the **Estación del Sur** (⌧ Canarias 17, ☎ 91/468–4200), while buses for much of the rest of the peninsula, including Cuenca, Extremadura,

Salamanca, and Valencia, depart from the **Auto Res Station** (⊠ Plaza Conde de Casal 6, ☏ 91/551–7200).There are several other, smaller stations, however, so inquire at travel agencies for the one serving your destination.

Bus companies of interest include **La Sepulvedana** (⊠ Paseo de la Florida 11, near Estación de Norte, ☏ 91/530–4800), serving Segovia, Ávila, and La Granja; **Herranz** (departures from Fernández de los Ríos s/n, ☏ 91/543–8167; Metro Moncloa), for El Escorial and the Valley of the Fallen; **Continental Auto** (⊠ Alenza 20, ☏ 91/533–0400; Metro Ríos Rosas), serving Cantabria and the Basque region; and **La Veloz** (⊠ Mediterraneo 49, ☏ 91/409–7602; Metro Conde de Casal), with service to Chinchón.

By Car

Felipe II made Madrid the capital of Spain because it was at the geographic center of his peninsular domains, and today many of the nation's highways radiate from Madrid like the spokes of a wheel. Originating at Kilometer 0 (marked by a brass plaque on the sidewalk of the Puerta del Sol), these highways include A6 (Segovia, Salamanca, Galicia); A1 (Burgos and the Basque Country); the N II (Guadalajara, Barcelona, France); the N III (Cuenca, Valencia, the Mediterranean coast); the A4 (Aranjuez, La Mancha, Granada, Seville); N401 (Toledo); and the N V (Talavera de la Reina, Portugal). The city is surrounded by M30 (the inner ring road) and M40 (the outer ring road), from which most of these highways are easily picked up.

By Plane

Madrid is served by **Barajas Airport,** 12 km (7 mi) east of the city. It's a rather grim-looking facility, and the national terminal is still undergoing renovations. Major carriers, including American, Delta, TWA, US Airways, Iberia, and United, provide regular service to the United States. Most connections go through New York, Washington, or Miami, but American has daily direct flights to and from Dallas–Fort Worth, and US Airways flies into Philadelphia (reserve well in advance). Many carriers serve London and other European capitals daily, but if you shop around at Madrid travel agencies, you'll probably find better deals than those available abroad (especially to and from Great Britain). For more information on flying to Madrid, *see* Air Travel *in* The Gold Guide. For general information and information on flight delays, call the airport (☏ 91/305–8343, 91/305–8344, or 91/305–8345).

BETWEEN THE AIRPORT AND DOWNTOWN
For a mere 450 pesetas there's a convenient **bus** to the central Plaza Colón, where taxis can take you to your hotel. The buses leave every 15 minutes between 5:40 AM and 2 AM (albeit slightly less often very early or late in the day). Be sure to watch your belongings, as the underground Plaza Colón bus station is a favorite haunt of purse snatchers and con artists. **Taxis** are normally waiting outside the airport terminal near the clearly marked bus stop; expect to pay up to 2,000 pesetas, more in heavy traffic, plus small holiday, late-night, and/or luggage surcharges. Make sure the driver works on the meter; off-the-meter "deals" almost always cost more.

By Train

Madrid has three train stations: Chamartín, Atocha, and Norte. Generally speaking, **Chamartín,** near the northern tip of the Paseo Castellana, serves trains heading for points north and west, including Barcelona, San Sebastián, Burgos, León, Oviedo, La Coruña, Segovia, Salamanca, as well as France and Portugal. **Atocha,** at the southern end of the Paseo del Prado, was spiffily renovated for the inauguration of

AVE (high-speed) train service in 1992 and serves points south and east, including Seville, Málaga, Córdoba, Valencia, Castellón, and Toledo. The Estación de **Norte** station is primarily for local trains serving Madrid's western suburbs, including El Escorial. For schedules and reservations call RENFE (☎ 91/563–0202), or go to the information counter in any of the train stations. You can make reservations by phone, charge your tickets to a credit card, and even have them delivered to your hotel. Most major travel agencies can also provide information and tickets.

Getting Around

Madrid has a distinctly different feel depending on the neighborhood. You'll probably want to start out in the old city, where the majority of attractions are clustered, but the spirit of adventure is bound to call you to other parts of town.

By Bus

Red city buses run between 6 AM and midnight and cost 130 pesetas per ride. Signs listing stops by street name are located at every stop, but they're hard to comprehend if you don't know the city well. Pick up a free route map from EMT kiosks on the Plaza de Cibeles or the Puerta del Sol, where you can also buy a 10-ride ticket (*bonobus*, 645 pesetas). If you speak Spanish, you can call for information (☎ 91/401–9900).

Drivers will make change for you, generally up to a 2,000-peseta note. If you've bought a 10-ride ticket, step up just behind the driver and insert it in the ticket-punching machine until the mechanism makes a "ding."

By Car

Driving in Madrid is best avoided by all but the bravest souls. Parking is nightmarish, traffic is extremely heavy almost all the time, and the city's daredevil drivers can be frightening. August may be an exception; the streets are then largely emptied by the mass exodus of Madrileños on vacation.

By Metro

The metro is quick, frequent, and, at 130 pesetas no matter how far you travel, cheap. Even cheaper is the 10-ride *billete de diez,* which costs 645 pesetas and has the added advantage of being accepted by automatic turnstiles (lines at ticket booths can be long). The system is open from 6 AM to 1:30 AM, though a few entrances close earlier. There are 10 metro lines, and system maps in every station detail their routes. Note the end station of the line you need, and just follow the signs to the correct corridor. Exits are marked SALIDA. Crime is rare.

By Motorbike

You can rent motorbikes, scooters, and motorcycles by the day or week at **Moto Alquiler** (✉ Conde Duque 13, ☎ 91/542–0657) If you're up to battling Madrid's traffic, this is a fast and pleasant way to see the city. You'll need your passport, your driver's license, and either a cash deposit or a credit card.

By Taxi

Taxis are one of Madrid's few truly good deals. Meters start at 170 pesetas and add 70 pesetas per kilometer (½ mile) thereafter. Numerous supplemental charges, however, mean that your total cost often bears little resemblance to what you see on the meter. There's a 150-peseta supplement on Sundays and holidays and between 11 PM and 6 AM; 150 pesetas to sports stadiums or the bullring; and 350 pesetas to or from the airport, plus 150 pesetas per suitcase.

Madrid Metro

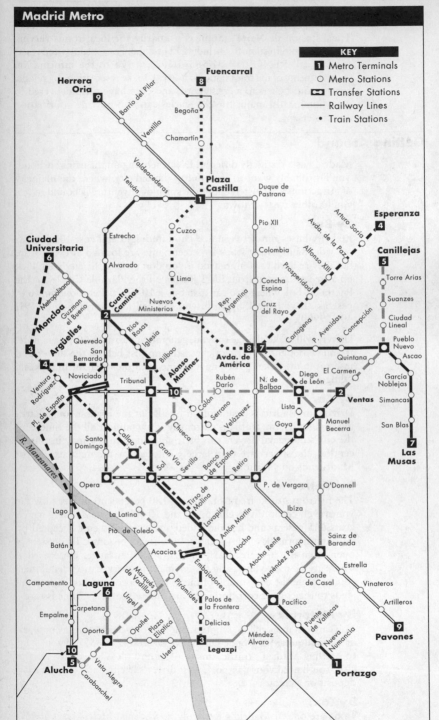

KEY

1 Metro Terminals
○ Metro Stations
🚇 Transfer Stations
— Railway Lines
• Train Stations

Herrera Oria
9

Fuencarral
8

Barrio del Pilar
Begoña
Ventilla
Chamartín
Valdeacederas
Tetuán
Plaza Castilla
1
Duque de Pastrana

Ciudad Universitaria
6

Estrecho
Cuzco
Pio XII

Alvarado
Lima
Colombia

Esperanza
4

Metropolitano
Guzman el Bueno
Moncloa
Cuatro Caminos
2
Nuevos Ministerios
Rep. Argentina
Concha Espina
Prosperidad
Avda. de la Paz
Arturo Soria
Alfonso XIII
Cruz del Rayo

Canillejas
5
Torre Arias
Suanzes
Ciudad Lineal

Argüelles
3
Quevedo
San Bernardo
4
Rios Rosas
Iglesia
Bilbao
Cartagena
P. Avenidas
B. Concepción
Pueblo Nuevo
Ascao

Noviciado
Ventura Rodríguez
Pl. de España
Tribunal
Alonso Martínez
10
Rubén Darío
Avda. de América
8 7
N. de Balboa
Diego de León
El Carmen
Quintana
García Noblejas
Simancas

Santo Domingo
Callao
Chueca
Colón
Serrano
Velázquez
Lista
Goya
Manuel Becerra
2
Ventas
San Blas
7
Las Musas

Opera
Gran Via
Sol
Sevilla
Banco de España
Retiro
P. de Vergara
O'Donnell

Lago
La Latina
Tirso de Molina
Lavapiés
Anton Martin
Ibíza
Sainz de Baranda

Batán
Pta. de Toledo
Acacias
Atocha
Atocha Renfe
Menéndez Pelayo
Estrella
Vinateros

Campamento
Laguna
6
Marqués de Vadillo
Pirámides
Embajadores
Palos de la Frontera
Conde de Casal
Artilleros

Empalme
Carpetana
Urgel
Opañel
Delicias
Pacífico
Puente de Vallecas
Nueva Numancia
9
Pavones

Oporto
Plaza Elíptica
Usera
Méndez Alvaro
Legazpi
3

10
5
Aluche
Vista Alegre
Carabanchel

R. Manzanares

1
Portazgo

Taxi stands are numerous, and taxis are easily hailed in the street—except when it rains, at which point they're exceedingly hard to come by. Available cabs display a LIBRE sign during the day, a green light at night. Generally, a tip of about 25 pesetas is right for shorter rides; you may want to go as high as 10% for a trip to the airport. You can call a cab through **Tele-Taxi** (☎ 91/445–9008 or 91/448–4259), **Radio-teléfono Taxi** (☎ 91/547–8200), or **Radio Taxi Gremial** (☎ 91/447–5180).

Contacts and Resources

Embassies

United States (✉ Serrano 75, ☎ 91/577–4000), **Canada** (✉ Nuñez de Balboa 35, ☎ 91/431–4300), and **United Kingdom** (✉ Fernando el Santo 16, ☎ 91/319–0200).

Emergencies

Police (☎ 091). **Ambulance** (☎ 061 or 91/522–2222). English-speaking doctors (✉ Conde de Aranda 7, ☎ 91/435–1823). Major **hospitals** include **La Paz** (☎ 91/358–2600), **Ramon y Cajal** (☎ 91/336–8000), and **12 de Octubre** (☎ 91/390–8000).

English-Language Bookstores

Turner's English Bookshop (✉ Génova 3, ☎ 91/319–0926) has a substantial collection of English-language books and throws in a useful bulletin-board exchange. **Booksellers** (✉ José Abascal 48, ☎ 91/442–8104) also has a large selection of books in English.

Guided Tours

ORIENTATION

Your hotel can arrange standard city tours in either English or Spanish; most offer **Madrid Artístico** (including the Royal Palace and the Prado), **Madrid Panorámico** (a half-day tour for first-time visitors), **Madrid de Noche** (combinations include a flamenco or a nightclub show), and **Panorámico y Toros** (on Sunday, a brief city overview followed by a bullfight). **Trapsatur** (✉ San Bernardo 23, ☎ 91/302–6039) runs the *Madridvision* tourist bus, which makes a 1½-hour sightseeing circuit of the city with recorded commentary in English. No advance reservation is needed. Buses leave from the front of the Prado Museum every 1½ hours beginning at 12:30 Monday–Saturday, 10:30 on Sunday. A round-trip ticket costs 1,500 pesetas; a day pass, which allows you to get on and off at various attractions, is 2,000 pesetas.

PERSONAL GUIDES

Contact the **Asociación Profesional de Informadores** (✉ Ferraz 82, ☎ 91/542–1214 or 91/541–1221) to hire a personal guide.

Late-Night Pharmacies

Emergency pharmacies are required by law to be open 24 hours a day on a rotating basis. All major daily newspapers publish the list of pharmacies open round-the-clock on any given day.

Travel Agencies

Travel agencies are scattered throughout Madrid and are generally the best way to get deals, tickets, and information without hassles. Some major agencies: **American Express,** next door to the Cortés (parliament building) on Génova (✉ Plaza de las Cortés 2, ☎ 91/322–5445); **Carlson Wagons-Lits** (✉ Paseo de la Castellana 96, ☎ 91/563–1202); and **Pullmantur,** across the street from the Royal Palace (✉ Plaza de Oriente 8, ☎ 91/541–1807).

Visitor Information

There are four provincial tourist offices in Madrid, but the best is on the ground floor of the Torre Madrid building, on the **Plaza España** (✉ Princesa 1, ☎ 91/541–2325. ⊙ open weekdays 9–7, Saturday 9:30–1:30). Others are at **Barajas Airport** (☎ 91/305–8656), ⊙ open weekdays 8–8, Saturday 9–1; the **Chamartín** train station (☎ 91/315–9976), ⊙ open weekdays 8–8, Saturday 9–1; and **Duque de Medinaceli** (☎ 91/429–4951), ⊙ open weekdays 9–7, Saturday 9–1. The city tourism office on the **Plaza Mayor** (☎ 91/366–5477), ⊙ open weekdays 10–8 and Saturday 10–2, is good for little save a few pamphlets.

3 Around Madrid

Castilla (Castile), the area surrounding Madrid, is a vast, windswept plateau with clear skies and endless vistas. An outstanding Roman aqueduct and a fairy-tale castle and cathedral make Segovia one of the most popular excursions from Madrid. The walled city of Ávila was the home of St. Teresa, Spain's female patron saint, and the university town of Salamanca is a flourish of golden sandstone. Aranjuez tempts with the French-style elegance of a Bourbon palace, while enigmatic Toledo is dramatic and austere, with rich legacies from three religions.

By Michael
Jacobs

Updated by
Katherine
Semler

FOR ALL THE VARIETY in the towns and countryside outside Madrid, there is an underlying unity. Castile is essentially an endless plain—gray, bronze, green, and severe. Over the centuries, poets and others have characterized it as austere and melancholy, most notably Antonio Machado, whose experiences at Soria in the early 20th century inspired his memorable and haunting *Campos de Castilla* (*Fields of Castile*).

Stone is a dominant element in the Castilian countryside, and it plays a large part in the region's character. Gaunt mountain ranges frame the horizons; gorges and rocky outcrops break up flat expanses; and the fields around Ávila and Segovia are littered with giant boulders. The villages are built predominantly of granite, and their solid, formidable look contrasts markedly with the whitewashed walls of most of southern Spain. The presence of so much stone may help to explain the region's rich tradition of sculpture—Castile has one of Europe's most significant stashes of sculptural treasures, many on display in the unrivaled National Museum of Sculpture, in Valladolid.

Castile is more accurately labeled Old and New Castile, the former north of Madrid, the latter south—known as "New" because it was captured from the Moors at a slightly later date. Whereas southern Spaniards are traditionally passive and peace-loving, Castilians have been a race of soldiers. The very name of the region (in effect, *la región castilla,* the region of castles) refers to the great line of castles and fortified towns built in the 12th century between Salamanca, in the west, and Soria, in the east. Segovia's Alcázar, Ávila's fully intact city walls, and countless other military installations are among Castile's greatest monuments, and some of them—the castles at Sigüenza and Ciudad Rodrigo, for instance—are also splendid hotels.

Faced with the austerity of the Castilian environment, many have taken refuge in the worlds of the spirit and the imagination. Ávila is closely associated with two of Europe's most renowned mystics, St. Teresa and her disciple St. John of the Cross, and Toledo was the main home of one of the most spiritual of all western painters, El Greco. As for escape into fantasy, this is best illustrated by Cervantes' hero Don Quixote, in whose formidable imagination even the dreary expanse of La Mancha—one of the bleakest parts of Spain—became something magical. Many of the region's architects were similarly fanciful: Castile in the 15th and 16th centuries was the center of the plateresque, an ornamental style of extraordinary intricacy and fantasy, suggestive of silverwork. Developed in Toledo and Valladolid, it reached its exuberant climax in the university town of Salamanca.

Pleasures and Pastimes

Dining

The classic dishes of Castile are *cordero* (lamb) and *cochinillo* (suckling pig), the latter roasted in a wood oven. These are specialties of Segovia, widely regarded as Castile's gastronomic capital thanks largely to such long-established restaurants as the Mesón de Cándido and the Mesón Duque. In the Segovian village of Pedraza, superb roast lamb is served with hearty red wine.

The mountainous districts of Salamanca, particularly the villages of Guijuelo and Candelario, are renowned for their hams and sausages. Bean dishes are a specialty of the villages El Barco (Ávila) and La Granja (Segovia), while *trucha* (trout) and *cangrejos de río* (river crab) are common to Guadalajara. Game is abundant throughout Castile, two famous dishes being *perdiz en escabeche* (the marinated partridge of Soria) and *perdiz estofada a la Toledana* (the stewed partridge of Toledo). The most exotic and complex cuisine in Castile is perhaps that of Cuenca, with two outstanding restaurants, Figon de Pedro and Los Claveles. Here a Moorish influence appears in such dishes as *gazpacho pastor* (a hot terrine made with a variety of game, topped with grapes).

Among the region's sweets are the *yemas* (sugared egg yolks) of Ávila, *almendras garrapiñadas* (candied almonds) of Alcalá de Henares, *mazapán* (marzipans) of Toledo, and *ponche Segovia* (egg toddy) of Segovia. La Mancha is the main area for cheese, while Aranjuez is famous for its strawberries and asparagus.

Much of Spain's cheap wine comes from La Mancha, south of Toledo. Far better in quality, and indeed among the most superior Spanish wines, are those from the Duero Valley, around Valladolid. Look for the Marqués de Riscal whites from Rueda and the Vega Sicilia reds from Valbuena; Peñafiel is the most common of the Duero wines. An excellent, if extremely sweet, Castilian liqueur is Cuenca's *resolí*, made from aquavit, coffee, vanilla, orange peel, and sugar and often sold in bottles in the shape of Cuenca's Casas Colgadas (Hanging Houses).

CATEGORY	COST*
$$$$	over 6,500 ptas.
$$$	4,000–6,500 ptas.
$$	2,500–4,000 ptas.
$	under 2,500 ptas.

*per person for a three-course meal, including wine, excluding tax and tip

Lodging

Spain's most stylish hotels are usually the paradors. This holds true in Castile, but the region's oldest and most attractive paradors are generally found in the lesser towns, such as Ciudad Real and Sigüenza, rather than the major tourist centers. The paradors in Salamanca, Toledo, Segovia, and Soria are all in ugly or nondescript modern buildings, albeit with magnificent views. Fortunately, the region has many pleasant alternatives to paradors, such as Segovia's centrally situated Los Linajes, Ávila's Palacio de Valderrábanos (a 15th-century palace next to the cathedral), and Cuenca's Posada San José (a 16th-century convent).

CATEGORY	COST*
$$$$	over 14,000 ptas.
$$$	8,000–14,000 ptas.
$$	4,000–8,000 ptas.
$	under 4,000 ptas.

*All prices are for a standard double room, excluding tax.

Exploring Around Madrid

Two main regions surround Madrid—Castile and León to the north and west, and Castile–La Mancha to the south and east. From Segovia south to Toledo, there's plenty to see.

Numbers in the text correspond to numbers in the margin and on the Around Madrid, Segovia, Salamanca, and Toledo maps.

Great Itineraries

You can visit Aranjuez, Ávila, Segovia, and Toledo on day trips from Madrid. Salamanca and other major towns can also be day trips from the capital, but you might find yourself spending more time traveling than actually being there. Ideally, especially if you have a car, take at least a four-day trip around the area, staying in Toledo, Segovia, and Salamanca and passing through Ávila. Both Toledo and Segovia have an extra charm at night, not only because their monuments are so beautifully illuminated, but also because they are free of the crowds of tourists that congest them by day. To visit all of the region's main sights would require at least another three to six days, with overnight stays in Zamora, Soria, Sigüenza, and Cuenca.

IF YOU HAVE 3 DAYS

▣ **Toledo** ⑤⓪–⑥⑤, which was for many years Spain's intellectual and spiritual capital, is a must-see. Spend a night and visit El Greco's former stomping grounds before moving on to **Aranjuez** ㊾, the summer retreat of the Bourbon monarchy. Next, head north of Madrid to **Segovia** ①–⑬, with its Roman aqueduct, countless Romanesque churches, and inviting side streets. On your last day, try to catch the incredible fountain display in the gardens of **El Palacio de La Granja** ⑭ before heading back to Madrid.

IF YOU HAVE 4 DAYS

Visit **El Palacio de La Granja** ⑭ on the way to ▣ **Segovia** ①–⑬. After viewing the Roman aqueduct and other attractions, visit the famous medieval **Castillo de Coca** ⑰. From there go to ▣ **Salamanca** ㉒–㉝ to soak up the university atmosphere and some of Spain's architectural treasures. The following day, spend some time in **Ávila** ⑱, famous for its intact medieval walls and the legacy of St. Teresa, Spain's female patron saint, who lived most of her life here. Finally, wander austere ▣ **Toledo** ⑤⓪–⑥⑤, once the home of El Greco and full of tiny, hilly, winding lanes.

When to Tour Around Madrid

The best time to tour Madrid's environs is between May and October, when the weather is sunny. Many restaurants and cafés have sidewalk terraces where you can relax and people-watch. Be warned, however, that July and August can be brutally hot at times, especially south of Madrid. If possible, arrange to spend at least one weekend night in Salamanca, where the social atmosphere is something to behold. November through February can be rather cold, especially in the Sierra Guadarrama, north and west of Madrid; if you don't mind touring in a winter coat, however, the Christmas holidays can be a good time to visit, with the streets enlivened by decorative lights and colorful processions. Nota bene: many museums in all of these areas are closed on Monday, so you may want to spend that day in places where museums will not be your main focus.

SEGOVIA AND ITS PROVINCE

Segovia, El Palacio de la Granja, Pedraza, Sepúlveda, and Castillo de Coca

The area north of Madrid is dotted with rich and varied history, from the Roman aqueduct in exquisite Segovia to the small 16th-century village of Pedraza. Either town makes a pleasant place to spend the night. Other towns worth a visit include Sepúlveda and Castillo de Coca, for their medieval monuments, and La Granja, where the impressive gardens become even more spectacular when the fountains are turned on, creating an effect to rival that of Versailles.

Segovia

★ ❶ *87 km (54 mi) west of Madrid.*

Segovia's breathtaking location—on a ridge in the middle of a gorgeously stark, undulating plain—is only enhanced by its outstanding Roman and medieval monuments, its excellent cuisine, its embroideries and textiles, and its general personality. An important military town in Roman times, Segovia was later established by the Arabs as a major textile center. Captured by the Christians in 1085, it was enriched by a royal residence, and in 1474 the half sister of Henry IV, Isabella the Catholic (Isabel la Católica, of Castile, married to Ferdinand of Aragon), was crowned queen of Castile here. By that time Segovia was a bustling city of about 60,000 (there are 54,000 today), but its importance soon diminished as a result of its taking the (losing) side of the Comuneros in the popular revolt against the emperor Charles V. Though the construction in the 18th century of a royal palace in nearby La Granja helped revive the town's fortunes somewhat, it never recovered its former vitality. Early in the 20th century, Segovia's sleepy charm came to be appreciated by numerous artists and writers, among them painter Ignacio Zuloaga and poet Antonio Machado. Today it swarms with tourists and day-trippers from Madrid, and you may want to avoid it in the summer, especially on weekends or public holidays. On weekdays in the winter, you can fully appreciate its haunting peace.

When you approach Segovia driving west from Madrid along N603, the first building you see is the cathedral, which seems to rise directly from the fields. Between you and Segovia lies, in fact, a steep and narrow valley, which shields the old town from view. Only when you descend into the valley do you begin to see the old town's spectacular position, rising on top of a narrow rock ledge shaped like a ship. As soon as you reach the modern outskirts, turn left onto the Paseo E. González and follow the road marked **"Ruta Panorámica"**; you'll soon find yourself descending on the narrow and winding Cuesta de los Hoyos, which takes you to the bottom of the wooded valley that dips to the south of the old town. Above, you can see the Romanesque church of San Martín to the right; the cathedral in the middle; and, on the far left, where the rock ledge tapers, the turrets, spires, and battlements of Segovia's castle, known as the Alcázar.

A Good Walk

Driving and parking are problems on the narrow streets of old Segovia, so it's best to leave the car and explore on foot. In short, start in front of the Roman aqueduct in the Plaza de la Artillería, and then walk northwest to the Plaza Mayor on Calle Cervantes, ending your excursion at the Alcázar.

Beginning at the church of **San Millán** ②, go up Avenida de Fernández Ladreda until you come to the **Acueducto Romano** ③. Pass under the arches to the Plaza del Azoguejo, which was once the marketplace and center of the town's activity. Head up Calle Cervantes and look to the left—in the distance is the Sierra de Guadarrama.

Continue up the same pedestrian shopping street, now called Calle de Juan Bravo, and veer off to the right onto Herrería for a look at the late-Gothic **Palacio de los Condes de Alpuente** ④, covered with *esgrafiado* plasterwork. Back on Calle Juan Bravo, and further ahead, you'll come to the small, delightful Plaza Martín, on which rises another Romanesque church, **San Martín** ⑤.

Off to the left of Juan Bravo, across from the Plaza Martín, is the refreshing **Paseo de Salón,** a small promenade at the foot of the town's

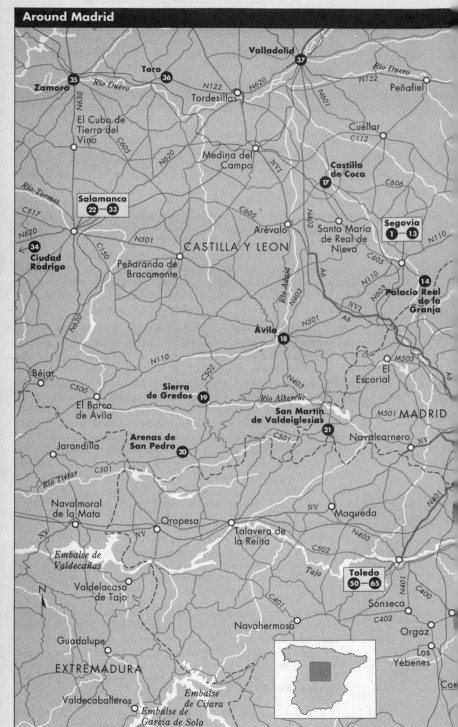

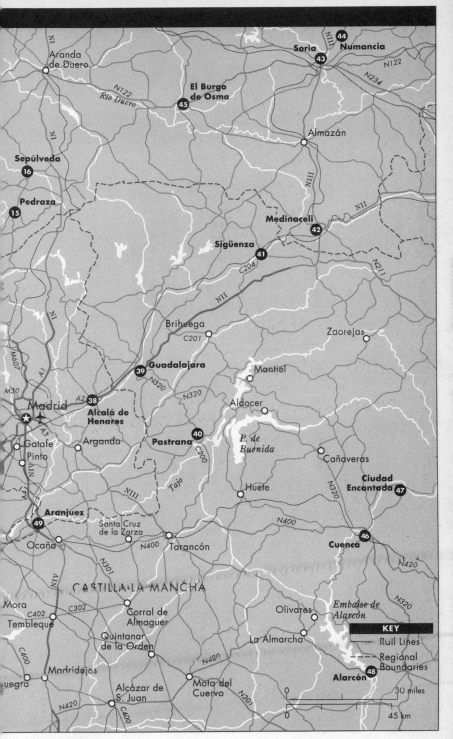

74

Segovia

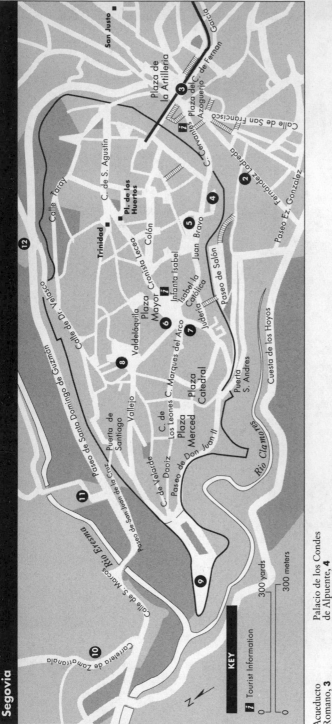

KEY

i Tourist Information

0   300 yards

0   300 meters

Acueducto
Romano, **3**
Alcázar, **9**
Ayuntamiento, **6**
Casa de la
Moneda, **11**
Cathedral, **7**
Convento de la
Santa Cruz, **12**

Palacio de los Condes
de Alpuente, **4**
San Estéban, **8**
San Martín, **5**
San Millán, **2**
Vera Cruz, **10**

southern walls. This walk was very popular with Spain's 19th-century queen, Isabel II; it offers good views over the wooded valley to the south and toward the Sierra de Guadarrama.

At the Plaza del Corpus, where Juan Bravo splits into Calle de La Judería Vieja and Isabel la Católica, head left up Calle de La Judería Vieja into the former Jewish Quarter, where Segovia's Jews lived as early as the 13th century. At Calle de San Frutos, turn right and step into the lively Plaza Mayor. The plaza is lined with bars and terraces, making it an ideal place for a lunch break or early-evening drink. Along the *paseo* of the arcaded main square stand the 17th-century **ayuntamiento** ⑥ and the **cathedral** ⑦. From the *paseo* pick up Calle de Valdeláguila to **San Estéban** ⑧.Calle de Los Leones, lined with tourist shops, slopes gently down from the cathedral toward the western extremity of the old town's ridge. From the partially shaded Plaza del Alcázar, you have excellent views to the north and south. At the western end of the square is the famous **Alcázar** ⑨.

From the Alcázar, you can see the church of **Vera Cruz** ⑩ and the **Casa de la Moneda** (former Mint) ⑪. A walk along the city's peripheral road, Paseo de Santo Domingo de Guzmán, leads to the **Convento de la Santa Cruz** ⑫.

TIMING
This walk can be covered in a few hours, depending on how long you stop at each sight.

Sights to See

③ **Acueducto Romano** (Roman aqueduct). Segovia's leading monument, the aqueduct ranks with the Pont du Gard in France as one of the greatest surviving examples of Roman engineering. Spanning the dip that stretches from the walls of the old town to the lower slopes of the Sierra de Guadarrama, it is about 2,952 ft long, and rises in two tiers—above the Plaza del Azoguejo—to a height of 115 ft. The raised section of stonework in the center originally carried an inscription, of which only the holes for the bronze letters remain. The massive, granite blocks are held together by neither mortar nor clamps, but the aqueduct has been standing since the end of the first century AD. The only damage it has suffered is the demolition of 35 of its arches by the Moors, and these were later replaced on the orders of Ferdinand and Isabella. Steps at the side of the aqueduct lead up to the walls of the old town, offering at the top an amazing side view of the structure. ⊠ *Plaza de Azoguerjo ("highest point" of Aqueduct).*

⑨ **Alcázar.** Possibly dating from Roman times, this castle was considerably expanded in the 14th century, remodeled in the 15th, altered again toward the end of the 16th century, and completely redone after being gutted by a fire in 1862, when it was used as an artillery school. The exterior, especially when seen from the Ruta Panorámica, is certainly imposing, but the castle is little more than a medieval sham, with the exception of the keep through which you enter, the last remnant of the original structure. Crowned by crenellated towers that seem to have been carved out of icing, the keep can be climbed for superb views. The rest of the interior is a bit disappointing. ☎ *921/460759.* ☜ *375 ptas.* ☉ *May–Sept., daily 10–7; Oct.–Apr., daily 10–6.*

⑥ **Ayuntamiento.** The 17th-century town hall stands on the active **Plaza Mayor.** It's closed to the public, but it's a great place to sit and watch the world go by. ⊠ *Plaza Mayor.*

⑪ **Casa de la Moneda** (Mint). All Spanish coinage was struck here from 1455 to 1730. The building is closed for reconstruction, but it's worth a look. ⊠ *C. de la Moneda s/n, just south of River Eresma.*

❽ **Cathedral.** Begun in 1525 and completed 65 years later, the cathedral was intended to replace an earlier one near the Alcázar, destroyed during the revolt of the Comuneros against Charles V. It's one of the most harmonious in Spain, and one of the country's last great examples of the Gothic style. The designs were drawn up by the leading late-Gothicist Juan Gil de Hontañon but executed by his son Rodrigo, in whose work can be seen a transition from the Gothic to the Renaissance style. The tall proportions and buttressing are pure Gothic, but much of the detailing—on the crossing tower, for instance—is classical. The golden interior, illuminated by 16th-century Flemish windows, is remarkably light and uncluttered, the one distracting detail being the wooden, neoclassical choir. You enter through the north transept, which is marked MUSEO; turn right, and the first chapel on your right has a lamentation group in wood by the baroque sculptor Gregorio Fernández.

Across from the entrance, on the southern transept, is a door opening into the late-Gothic cloister; this and the elaborate door leading into it were transported from the old cathedral and are the work of Juan Guas, architect of the church of San Juan de Los Reyes, in Toledo. Under the pavement immediately inside the cloisters are the tombs of Juan and Rodrigo Gil de Hontañón; that these two lie in a space designed by Guas is appropriate, for the three men together dominated the last phase of the Gothic style in Spain. Off the cloister, a small museum of religious art, installed partly in the first-floor chapter house, is worth a visit for its 17th-century white-and-gold ceiling, a late and splendid example of Mudéjar *artesonado* work. ☎ *921/435325.* 🖼 *Museum 250 ptas.* ☉ *June–Sept., daily 9–7; Oct.–May, daily 9–6.*

⑫ **Convento de la Santa Cruz.** This 13th-century church was established by St. Dominick of Guzmán, the founder of the Dominican order, and rebuilt in the 15th century by Ferdinand and Isabella. In 1996 it was turned into a private university, La Universidad Sec. During the academic year, you can catch a view of the attractive interior, Gothic with plateresque and Renaissance touches. ✉ *C. Cardenal Zúñiga s/n,* ☎ *921/471997.*

❹ **Palacio de los Condes de Alpuente** (Palace of the Counts of Alpuente). This late-Gothic palace is covered with a type of plasterwork known as *esgrafiado,* incised with regular patterns; the style was most likely introduced by the Moors and is characteristic of Segovian architecture. The building is now used for city administrative offices and is no longer open to the public. ✉ *Plaza del Platero Oquendo s/n,* ☎ *no phone.*

❽ **San Estéban.** This porticoed church is the third of Segovia's major Romanesque monuments. Though the interior has a baroque facing, the exterior has kept some splendid capitals, as well as an exceptionally tall and elegant tower. Due east of the attractive square on which the church stands is the **Capilla de San Juan de Dios,** next to which is the former pension where the poet Antonio Machado spent his last years in Spain. The family who looked after Machado still owns the building and will show you on request the poet's room, with its paraffin stove, iron bed, and round table. The church is open for mass only. ✉ *Plaza de San Esteban s/n.* ☉ *Mass daily 8–10 AM and 7–9 PM.*

❺ **San Martín.** This Romanesque church stands in an attractive little plaza by the same name. ✉ *Plaza San Martín s/n,* ☎ *921/443402.* ☉ *Open for mass only.*

❷ **San Millán.** This 12th-century church is a perfect example of the Segovian Romanesque and is perhaps the finest church in town apart from the cathedral. The exterior is notable for its arcaded porch, where church meetings were once held. The virtually untouched Romanesque interior is dominated by massive columns, whose capitals carry such carved scenes as the Flight into Egypt and the Adoration of the Magi. The vaulting on the crossing shows the Moorish influence on Spanish medieval architecture. ⊠ *Avda. Fernández Ladreda 26, 5-min walk outside town walls.* ☉ *Open for mass only, daily 8–10* AM *and 7–9* PM.

❿ Vera Cruz. This isolated Romanesque church, made of the warm orange stone of the area, was built in 1208 for the Knights Templar. Like other buildings associated with this order, it is round, inspired by the Church of the Holy Sepulchre, in Jerusalem. Your trip here pays off in full when you climb the bell tower and see all of Segovia profiled against the Sierra de Guadarrama, which is capped with snow in winter. ⊠ *Carretera de Zamarramala s/n, on northern outskirts of town, off Cuesta de los Hoyos,* ☎ *921/431475.* ▭ *150 ptas.* ☉ *May–Sept., Tues.–Sun. 10:30–1:30 and 3:30–7; Oct.–Apr., Tues.–Sun. 10:30–1:30 and 3:30–6. Closed Nov. .*

Dining and Lodging

$$$ ✕ **Casa Duque.** Founded by Dionisio Duque in 1895 and still in the family, Casa Duque is the second-most-famous restaurant in town. The intimate interior, with its homey wood-beam decoration and plethora of fascinating *objets,* is similar to that of Cándido (☞ *below*); but Casa Duque is smaller, and benefits greatly from the charismatic presence of owner Julian Duque. Never still for a moment, Duque attends to all his clients with eccentric charm. Roasts are the specialty, but you should also try the *judiones de La Granja Duque*—the excellent kidney beans from nearby La Granja, served with sausages. ⊠ *Cervantes 12,* ☎ *921/430537. Reservations essential. AE, DC, MC, V.*

$$$ ✕ **Mesón de Cándido.** More than a restaurant, Cándido was declared
★ a national monument in 1941. Tucked cozily under the aqueduct, comprising a quaint medley of small, irregular dining rooms covered with memorabilia, it has served as an inn since at least the 18th century. Señor Cándido took it over in 1931 and, with his energy and flair for publicity, managed to make it the Spanish restaurant best known abroad: amid the dark-wood beams and Castilian knickknacks hang photos of the many celebrities who have dined here, from Ernest Hemingway to Princess Grace of Monaco. Cándido passed away several years ago, and the place is now run by his son. First-time visitors are virtually obliged to eat the *cochinillo,* the delicacy of which used to be attested to by Cándido's slicing it with the edge of a plate. The trout here is also renowned. ⊠ *Plaza de Azoguejo 5,* ☎ *921/425911. Reservations essential. AE, DC, MC, V.*

$$$ ✕ **Mesón de José María.** In this case, the exceptionally lively bar,
★ which you must pass to reach the restaurant, augurs well for the rest of the establishment. Though relatively new in Segovian terms, the Mesón de José María has already surpassed its formidable rivals culinarily and deserves to be considered one of Spain's finest restaurants. The hospitable and passionately dedicated owner is devoted to maintaining traditional Castilian specialties while concocting Innovations of his own. The emphasis is on freshness and quality of produce, and the menu changes constantly. The large, old-style, brightly lit dining room is often packed, and the waiters are uncommonly friendly. Although it's a bit touristy, with a set menu in English, this *mesón* is also a favorite of the locals. ⊠ *Cronista Lecea 11,* ☎ *921/461111. AE, DC, MC, V.*

$$$$ ✕▥ **Parador Nacional de Segovia.** Architecturally one of the most interesting and handsome of the modern paradors, this low building is spaciously arranged amid greenery on a hillside. The rooms are light, with generous amounts of glass. The panorama of Segovia and its aqueduct is unbeatable, but there are disadvantages in staying so far from the town center. The restaurant serves traditional Segovian and international dishes, such as *lomo de merluza al aroma de estragón* (hake fillet with tarragon and shrimp). ⊠ *Carretera de Valladolid s/n, 40003,* ☎ *921/443737,* ₣ᴬˣ *921/437362. 113 rooms. Restaurant, pool, meeting room. AE, DC, MC, V.*

$$$ ✕🏨 **Los Arcos.** The comfortable lodgings at this modern hotel, a 5- to 10-minute walk from the Roman aqueduct, are a favorite with business travelers. The staff is friendly and always willing to assist in whatever way it can. The rooms are brightly decorated, and many include a small sitting area. The restaurant is attractive, with hardwood floors and arched redbrick doorways. Specialties include *cochinillo* and *lechazo* (baby lamb). ⊠ *Paseo Ezequiel González 26, 40002,* ☎ *921/ 437462,* ₣ᴬˣ *921/428161. 59 rooms. Restaurant, bar. AE, DC, MC, V.*

$$$ 🏨 **Infanta Isabel.** This small hotel is in a recently restored building with
★ a Victorian feel. It's right on the Plaza Mayor—with an entrance on the charming, if congested, pedestrian shopping street Infanta Isabel— and has great views of Segovia's cathedral. The rooms are spacious, feminine, and light, with painted white furnishings. ⊠ *Plaza Mayor s/n, 40001,* ☎ *921/ 461300,* ₣ᴬˣ *921/ 462217 . 29 rooms. Coffee shop. AE, DC, MC, V.*

Shopping

After Toledo, the province of Segovia is Castile's most important for crafts. **Glass** and **crystal** are specialties of La Granja, while **ironwork, lace,** and **embroidery** are famous in Segovia itself. In search of the old, authentic article, go to San Martín 4 (⊠ Plaza San Martín 4), an excellent **antiques** shop. You can buy good **lace** from the Gypsies in Segovia's Plaza del Alcázar, but be prepared for some strenuous bargaining, and never offer more than half the opening price.

Palacio Real (Royal Palace) de la Granja

⑭ *11 km (7 mi) southeast of Segovia on the N601.*

The major attraction in Segovia's immediate vicinity, the palace of La Granja stands in the town of San Ildefonso de la Granja, on the northern slopes of the Guadarrama range. Its site was once occupied by a hunting lodge and a shrine to San Ildefonso, administered by Hieronymite monks from the Segovian monastery of El Parral. Commissioned by the Bourbon king Philip V in 1719, the palace has sometimes been described as the first great building of the Spanish Bourbon dynasty. The 19th-century English writer Richard Ford likened it to "a theatrical French château, the antithesis of the proud, gloomy Escorial, on which it turns its back." The architects who brought it to completion in 1739 and gave it such distinction were, in fact, not French but Italian—Juvarra and Sachetti. They were responsible for the imposing garden facade, a late-baroque masterpiece anchored throughout its length by a giant order of columns. The interior has been badly gutted by fire, and the few undamaged rooms are heavy and monotonous; the highlight of the interior is the collection of 15th- to 18th-century tapestries, gathered together in a special museum. It is the **gardens of La Granja** that you come to see—here, terraces, ornamental ponds, lakes, classical statuary, woods, and late-baroque fountains dot the slopes of the Guadarrama. On Wednesday, Saturday, and Sunday evenings in the summer (6–7 PM, May–Sept.), the fountains are turned on, one by one, creating one of the most exciting spectacles in Europe. The starting time has been known to change on a whim; call to check the time. ☎ *921/470020.* 🎫 *Palace 650 ptas., gardens free.*

⊘ *Palace Oct.–May, Tues.–Sat. 10–1:30 and 3–5, Sun. 10–2 (10–6 Apr. and May); June–Sept., Tues.–Sun. 10–6. Garden daily 10–sunset.*

Pedraza

⑮ *30 km (19 mi) northeast of Segovia.*

Though it's been commercialized and overprettified in recent years, Pedraza is still a striking 16th-century village. Crowning a rocky outcrop and completely encircled by its walls, it is perfectly preserved, with wonderful views of the Sierra de Guadarrama. Farther up, at the very top of the tiny village, is a Renaissance castle that was bought as a private residence by the painter Ignacio Zuloaga early in the 20th century. Two sons of the French king Francis I were held hostage here after the Battle of Pavia, together with their majordomo, the father of the Renaissance poet Pierre de Ronsard. In the center of the village is the attractive, irregularly shaped main square, lined with rustic wooden porticoes and dominated by a Romanesque bell tower.

Dining and Lodging

$$–$$$ ✕ **El Yantar de Pedraza.** This traditional restaurant, with wooden tables and beamed ceilings, is famous for roast meats. Right on Pedraza's main square, it's the place to come for that most celebrated of the town's specialties—*corderito lechal en horno de leña* (baby lamb roasted in a wood oven). ⊠ *Plaza Mayor,* ☎ *921/509842. AE, DC, MC, V. Closed Mon. No dinner Sept. 15–July 15.*

$$$ ▥ **La Posada de Don Mariano.** This hotel was originally a farmer's home. Each room in the picturesque old building is decorated differently, but all have rustic furniture and antiques. The atmosphere is intimate, though prices are grand. The restaurant, Enebro, serves a good selection of red meat. ⊠ *Plaza Mayor, 40172,* ☎ FAX *921/509886. 18 rooms. Restaurant, bar. AE, DC, MC, V.*

Sepúlveda

⑯ *24 km (15 mi) north of Pedraza, 60 km (37 mi) northeast of Segovia.*

A walled village with a commanding position, Sepúlveda has a charming main square, but its main attraction is the **11th-century Church of El Salvador,** the highest monument within the walled perimeter. Older than any other Romanesque church in the province of Segovia, it has a crude but amusing example of the porches found in later Segovia buildings: the carvings on its oversize capitals, probably the work of a Moorish convert, are fantastical and have little to do with Christianity.

Castillo de Coca

⑰ *52 km (32 mi) northwest of Segovia.*

Perhaps the most famous medieval sight near Segovia, worth a detour between Segovia and Ávila or Valladolid, is the Castillo de Coca. Built in the 15th century for Archbishop Alonso de Fonseca I, the castle is a turreted structure, in plaster and red brick, surrounded by a deep moat. It looks like a stage set for a fairy tale, and indeed, it was intended not as a defense but as a place for the notoriously pleasure-loving Archbishop Fonseca to hold riotous parties. The interior, now occupied by a forestry school, has been modernized, with only fragments of the original decoration preserved.

ÁVILA AND THE SIERRA DE GREDOS

Ávila, Sierra de Gredos, Arenas de San Pedro, San Martín de Valdeiglesias

From the spectacular medieval walls of Ávila to the mountains of the Sierra de Gredos, this area yields more than just spectacular views. In Ávila, you can trace the history of St. Teresa, who lived much of her life here. If you're looking for outdoor diversion, the Sierra de Gredos makes for ideal hiking and skiing. Other sights include the small, attractive villages near Arenas de San Pedro and the ancient stone bulls of San Martín de Valdeiglesias.

Ávila

18 *107 km (66 mi) northwest of Madrid.*

In the middle of a windy plateau littered with giant boulders, Ávila can look wild and sinister. Modern development on the outskirts of town partially obscures Ávila's intact surrounding **walls,** which, restored in parts, look exactly as they did in the Middle Ages. Begun in 1090, shortly after the town was reclaimed from the Moors, the walls were completed in only nine years—a feat accomplished by the daily employment of an estimated 1,900 men. Featuring nine gates and 88 cylindrical towers bunched together, they are unique to Spain in form, unlike the Moorish defense architecture that the Christians adapted elsewhere. They're most striking when viewed from outside the town; for the most extensive view on foot, cross the Adaja River, take a right on the Carretera de Salamanca, and walk uphill about 250 yards to a monument consisting of four pilasters surrounding a cross. And when you ultimately leave Ávila, look back on your way out.

The walls clearly reflect Ávila's importance during the Middle Ages. Populated by Alfonso VI mainly with Christians from Asturias, the town came to be known as Ávila of the Knights, on account of the high proportion of nobles. Decline set in at the beginning of the 15th century, with the gradual departure of the nobility to the court of Charles V in Toledo. Ávila's fame later on was due largely to St. Teresa, Spain's female patron saint (St. James the Apostle is her male counterpart). Born here in 1515 to a noble family of Jewish origin, Teresa spent much of her life in Ávila, leaving a legacy of various convents and the ubiquitous *yemas* (candied egg yolks), originally distributed free to the poor but now sold for high prices to tourists. Ávila today is well preserved but with a sad, austere, and slightly desolate atmosphere.

The battlement apse of the **cathedral** forms the most impressive part of the walls. The apse was built mainly in the late 12th century, but the construction of the rest of the cathedral continued until the 18th century. Entering the town gate to the right of the apse, you'll reach the sculpted north portal (originally the west portal, until it was moved in 1455 by the architect Juan Guas) by turning left and walking a few steps. The present west portal, flanked by 18th-century towers, is notable for the crude carvings of hairy male figures on each side; known as "wild men," these figures appear in many Castilian palaces of this period, but their significance is disputed.

The Transitional Gothic interior, with its granite nave, is heavy and severe. The Lisbon earthquake of 1755 deprived the building of its Flemish stained glass, so the main note of color appears in the beautiful mottled stone in the apse, tinted yellow and red. Elaborate, plateresque choir stalls built in 1547 complement the powerful high altar of circa 1504 by painters Juan de Borgoña and Pedro Berruguete. On the wall of the ambulatory, look for the early 16th-century marble sepulchre of Bishop Alonso de Madrigal, a remarkably lifelike representation of the bishop seated at his writing table. Known as "El Tostado" for his swarthy complexion, the bishop was a tiny man of enormous intellect, the author of 54 books. When on one occasion Pope Eugenius IV ordered him to stand—mistakenly thinking him to be still on his knees—the bishop indicated the space between his eyebrows and hairline, retorting, "A man's stature is to be measured from here to here!" ☎ 920/211641. ▣ 250 ptas. ◷ Daily 10–1:30 and 3:30–6:30 .

The 15th-century **Casa de Deanes** (Deans' House) is now a cheerful provincial museum of local archaeology and folklore. It's just a few minutes' walk to the east of the cathedral apse. ☎ 920/211003. ▣ 200 ptas., weekends free. ◷ Tues.–Sat. 10:30–2 and 5–7:30, Sun. 11–2.

The museum in the **Convento de San José** (or de Las Madres), east of the cathedral, displays the musical instruments used by St. Teresa and her nuns at Christmas. Teresa herself specialized in percussion. ☎ 920/222127. ▣ 50 ptas. ◷ Spring–fall, daily 10–1:30 and 3–6; summer, daily 9:30–1 and 4–7 .

North of Ávila's cathedral, on Plaza de San Vincente, is the much-venerated Romanesque **Basílica de San Vicente** (Basilica of St. Vincent), founded on the supposed site where St. Vincent was martyred in 303, together with his sisters Sts. Sabina and Cristeta. The west front, shielded by a narthex, has damaged but expressive Romanesque carvings depicting the death of Lazarus and the parable of the rich man's table. The sarcophagus of St. Vincent, surrounded with delicate carvings from this period, forms the centerpiece of the basilica's Romanesque interior; the extraordinary, Asian-looking canopy that rises over the sarcophagus is a 15th-century addition paid for by the Knights of Ávila. ☎ 920/255230. ▣ 100 ptas. ◷ Daily 10–2 and 4–7:30.

On Calle de Lopez Nuñez, the elegant chapel of **Mosen Rubi** (circa 1516) is illuminated by Renaissance stained glass by Nicolás de Holanda. Try to persuade the nuns in the adjoining convent to let you inside.

At the bottom of the town's surrounding walls, just above the river, is the small, Romanesque **Ermita de San Segundo** (Hermitage of St. Secundus). This is an enchanting farmyard, nearly hidden by poplars. Founded on the site where the remains of St. Secundus (a follower of St. Peter) were reputedly discovered, the hermitage houses a realistic marble monument to the saint, carved by Juan de Juni. ▣ Tip caretaker in adjoining house, where you may have to ask for key. ◷ Spring–fall, daily 4:30–6; summer, daily 4–6.

Inside the south wall on Calle Dama, the **Convento de Santa Teresa** was founded in the 17th century on the site of the saint's birthplace. Her famous written account of an ecstatic vision she had, in which an angel pierced her heart, would influence many baroque artists, most famously the Italian sculptor Giovanni Bernini. The convent has a small museum, with relics including one of Teresa's fingers, and you can also see the small and rather gloomy garden where she played as a child. ☎ 920/211030. ▣ Free. ◷ Daily 9:30–1:30 and 3:30–7:30.

The **Convento de la Encarnación** is where St. Teresa first took orders and was then based for more than 30 years. Its museum has an interesting drawing of the crucifixion by her disciple St. John of the Cross, as well as a reconstruction of the cell she used when she was a prioress here. The convent is outside the walls in the north part of town, on the Paseo de la Encarnación. ☎ 920/211212. ⌨ *150 ptas.* ☉ *May–Sept., daily 9:30–1 and 4–7; Oct.–Apr., daily 9:30–1:30 and 3:30–6.*

The most interesting architectural monument on Ávila's outskirts is the **Monasterio de Santo Tomás.** A good 10-minute walk from the walls among blackened housing projects, it's not where you would expect to find one of the most important religious institutions in Castile. The monastery was founded by Ferdinand and Isabella with the financial assistance of the notorious Inquisitor-General Tomás de Torquemada, who is buried in the sacristy. Further funds were provided by the confiscated property of converted Jews who ran afoul of the Inquisition. Three decorated cloisters lead to the church; inside, a masterly high altar (circa 1506) by Pedro Berruguete overlooks a serene marble tomb by the Italian artist Domenico Fancelli. This influential work, one of the earliest examples of the Italian Renaissance style in Spain, was built for Prince Juan, the only son of Ferdinand and Isabella, who died at 19 while a student at Salamanca University. After Juan's burial here, his heartbroken parents found themselves unable to return to the institution they had founded. In happier times, they had frequently attended mass here, seated in the upper choir behind a balustrade exquisitely carved with their coats of arms; you can reach the choir from the upper part of the Kings' Cloister. The Museum of Eastern Art contains works collected from Dominican missions in Vietnam. ☎ 920/220400. ⌨ *Cloister 150 ptas., Museum 100 ptas.* ☉ *Cloister daily 10–1 and 4–7, museum daily 11–1 and 4–6 .*

Dining and Lodging

$$ ✕ **El Fogón de Santa Teresa.** Despite its English-language menu, this newly decorated restaurant is less touristy than most others in Ávila. It offers a traditional array of meats and fish. Try the house specialty, *truchas al fogón* (fried trout with ham). ⌨ *Alemania 7,* ☎ *no phone. AE, DC, MC, V.*

$$ ✕ **El Molino de la Losa.** Few restaurants could have a better or more
★ distinctive situation than this one. Standing in the middle of the River Adaja, with one of the best views of the town walls, it occupies a 15th-century mill, the working mechanism of which has been well preserved and provides much distraction for those seated in the animated bar. Lamb is roasted in a medieval wood oven, and fish comes straight from the river; this is also a good place to try the beans from nearby El Barco (*judías de El Barco*). In the refreshing garden outside is a small playground for children. ⌨ *Bajada de la Losa 12,* ☎ *920/211101 or 920/211102. AE, MC, V. Closed Mon. in winter.*

$$ ✕ **Mesón del Rastro.** This restaurant occupies a wing of the medieval Abrantes Palace and has an attractive Castilian interior with exposed stone walls and beams, low lighting, and dark-wood furniture. Once again, try the lamb and the El Barco beans; also worthwhile is the *caldereta de cabrito* (goat stew). The place suffers somewhat from its popularity with tour buses, and service is sometimes slow and impersonal. ⌨ *Plaza Rastro 1,* ☎ *920/211218. AE, DC, MC, V.*

$$$$ 🏨 **Meliá Palacio de los Velada.** Ávila's top hotel opened in April 1995
★ in a beautifully restored 16th-century palace. In the heart of the city, right beside the cathedral, the Meliá is the perfect spot to relax between sightseeing jaunts. The lovely courtyard has become a popular meeting place. Rooms are modern and comfortable. ⌨ *Plaza de la Catedral 10, 05001,* ☎ *920/255100,* 🏧 *920/254900. 85 rooms. 2 restaurants, bar, meeting rooms. AE, DC, MC, V.*

$$$ 🏨 **Parador Nacional Raimundo de Borgoña.** A largely rebuilt medieval castle attached to the town walls, Ávila's parador has the advantage of a garden, from which you can sometimes climb up onto the

ramparts. The decor throughout is warm and finely executed, mostly in tawny tones, and the public rooms are convivial. Guest rooms have terra-cotta tile floors and leather chairs, and their bathrooms are spacious, gleamingly modern, and fashionably designed. ⊠ *Marqués de Canales de Chozas 2, 05001,* ☎ *920/211340,* ℻ *920/226166. 61 rooms. Restaurant, bar, café, meeting room. AE, DC, MC, V.*

$$ 🖾 **Hostal Alcántara.** This small hostel has modest, clean rooms and is just a two-minute walk from the cathedral. ⊠ *Esteban Domingo 11, 05001,* ☎ *920/225003 or 920/223804. 9 rooms. MC, V.*

Sierra de Gredos

⑲ *79 km (50 mi) southwest of Ávila.*

The small C502 route from Ávila follows a road dating from Roman times, when it was used for the transport of oil and flour from Ávila in exchange for potatoes and wood. In winter, the Sierra de Gredos, Castile's most dramatic mountain range, gives the region a majestic, snowy backdrop. You can enjoy extensive views from the **Puerto del Pico** (4,435 ft); soon after descending, you'll see below you a perfectly preserved stretch of the Roman road, zigzagging down into the valley and crossing the modern road every now and then. Today it is used by hikers, as well as by shepherds transporting their flocks to lower pastures in early December.

Lodging

$$$ 🖾 **Parador Nacional de Gredos.** Built in 1926 on a site chosen by Alfonso XIII, this was the first parador in Spain. It was enlarged in 1941 and again in 1975. Though modern, the stone architecture has a sturdy, traditional look and blends well with the magnificent surroundings. The rooms are standard parador, with heavy, dark furniture and light walls, and over half have excellent views of the Sierra. The parador is the ideal base for a hiking or climbing jaunt. ⊠ *Carretera Barraco-Béjar, 05132,* ☎ *920/348048,* ℻ *920/348205. 77 rooms. Restaurant, meeting room. AE, DC, MC, V.*

Outdoor Activities and Sports

HIKING AND MOUNTAINEERING

Castile's best area for both hiking and mountaineering is the **Sierra de Gredos.** You can base yourself at the Parador Nacional de Gredos (☞ *above*); the range also has six mountain huts with limited accommodations and facilities. For information on huts and on mountaineering in general, contact the Federación Española de Montañismo (Spanish Mountaineering Federation, ☎ 93/426–4267, in Barcelona).

SKIING

Skiing is popular in the Sierra de Gredos and in the Guadarrama resorts of La Pinilla (Segovia), Navacerrada (Madrid), Valdesqui (Madrid), and Valcotos (Madrid). You can get information on ski conditions from **ATUDEM** (☎ 91/350–2020), but it's better to call the slope you're considering. General information is available from **Federación Madrileña de Deportes de Invierno** (Madrid Federation of Winter Sports, ☎ 91/547–0101) .

Arenas de San Pedro

⑳ *143 km (89 mi) west of Madrid.*

This medieval town is surrounded by pretty villages such as Mombeltrán, Guisando, and Candeleda, where wooden balconies are decorated with flowers. A colorful sight in Candeleda are wicker baskets filled with pimientos for sale. Guisando, incidentally, has nothing to do with the famous stone bulls of that name, 60 km (37 mi) to the east.

San Martín de Valdeiglesias

㉑ *73 km (45 mi) west of Madrid.*

The **Toros de Guisando** are stone bulls dating from the 6th century BC, thought to have been used as land markers on the frontier of a Celto-Iberian tribe. Just three of many such bulls once scattered around the Castilian countryside, they take their name from the nearby Cerro Guisando (Guisando Hill) and are now a symbol of the Spanish Tourist Board. To see these taurine effigies, head back east from Arenas on the C501 to this town; it's a pleasant drive through countryside bordered to the north by the Gredos range. Just 6 km (4 mi) before San Martín, on the right side of the road, is a stone inscription in front of a hedge; this marks the site where, in 1468, Isabella the Catholic was acknowledged by the assembled Castilian nobility as rightful successor to Henry IV. On the other side of the hedge stand the forlorn stone bulls, whose rustic setting gives them an undeniable pathos and power.

SALAMANCA AND ITS PROVINCE

Salamanca and Ciudad Rodrigo

Salamanca's radiant sandstone buildings and immense Plaza Mayor make it one of the most attractive cities in Spain. Today, as it did centuries ago, the university predominates and creates a stimulating atmosphere. About an hour from here are the preserved medieval walls of Ciudad Rodrigo, an interesting town with fewer tourists.

Salamanca

★ **㉒** *205 km (125 mi) northwest of Madrid.*

If you approach from Madrid or Ávila, you'll first see Salamanca rising on the northern banks of the wide and murky River Tormes. In the foreground is its sturdy 15-arch Roman bridge; above this, dominating the view, soars the bulk of the old and new cathedrals. Piercing the skyline to the right is the Renaissance monastery and church of San Esteban, the city's second most prominent ecclesiastical structure. Behind San Esteban and the cathedrals, and largely out of sight from the river, extends a stunning series of palaces, convents, and university buildings that culminates in the Plaza Mayor, one of the most elegant squares in Spain. Despite considerable damage over the centuries, Salamanca remains one of Spain's greatest cities architecturally, a showpiece of the Spanish Renaissance. It is the golden sandstone, which seems to glow throughout the city, that you will remember above all things after leaving.

Already an important settlement in Iberian times, Salamanca was captured by Hannibal in 217 BC and later flourished as a major Roman station on the road between Mérida and Astorga. Converted to Christianity by at least the end of the 6th century, it later passed back and forth between Christians and Moors and began to experience prolonged stability only after the Reconquest of Toledo in 1085. The town's later importance was due largely to its university, which grew out of a college founded around 1220 by Alfonso IV of León.

Salamanca thrived in the 15th and early 16th centuries, and the number of students at its university rose to almost 10,000. Its greatest royal benefactor was Isabella, who generously financed both the magnificent New Cathedral and the rebuilding of the university. A dual portrait of Isabella and Ferdinand is incorporated into the facade of the main university building to commemorate her patronage.

Nearly all of Salamanca's other outstanding Renaissance buildings bear the five-star crest of the all-powerful and ostentatious Fonseca family. The most famous Fonseca, Alonso de Fonseca I, was the archbishop of Santiago and then of Seville; he was also a notorious womanizer and one of the patrons of the Spanish Renaissance.

Both Salamanca and its university began to decline in the early 17th century, corrupted by ultraclericalism and devastated by a flood in 1626. Some of the town's former glory was recovered in the 18th century, with the construction of the Plaza Mayor by the native Churrigueras, who were among the most influential architects of the Spanish baroque. The town suffered in the Peninsular War of the early 19th century and was damaged by ugly, modern development initiated by Franco after the civil war; but the university has revived in recent years and is again one of the most prestigious in Europe.

A Good Walk

A good walk in Salamanca starts at the Puente Romano, goes north to the Plaza Mayor, and finishes at the church of San Estebán.

In terms of both chronology and available parking space, the well-preserved **Puente Romano** ㉓ makes a good starting point for your tour. This is a quiet, evocatively decayed part of town, with a strong rural character. After crossing the bridge, head up the sloping, cobblestone Puerta del Rio and make your way up to the old and new **cathedrals** ㉔, built side by side. Across the Plaza Anaya is the neoclassic Colegio de Anaya, which now houses the university's philosophy department. If you face the New Cathedral from the Plaza, the back of the main building of the **universidad** ㉕ is ahead and to your right, facing the cathedral's west facade. Walk between the two down Calle Cardenal Pla y Deniel, turn right on Calle de Calderón de la Barca, then right again on Calle de Los Libreros, and you'll come into the enchanting quadrangle known as the Patio de Las Escuelas. The main university building (Escuelas Mayores) is to your right, while surrounding the square is the Escuelas Menores, built in the early 16th century as a secondary school preparing candidates for the university proper. In the middle of the square is a modern statue of the 16th-century poet and philosopher Fay Luis de León, one of the greatest teachers in the history of the university. On the far side of the Patio is the entrance to the **Museo de Salamanca.**

If you walk north from the Patio de Las Escuelas on Calle de Los Libreros, then bear right onto Rua Antigua, you can't miss the **Casa de Las Conchas** ㉖. Turn left at Calle de Compañía toward the **Palacio de Monterrey** ㉗. Off to the left of the palace, follow Calle de Ramón y Cajal to the **Colegio Mayor Arzobispo Fonseca** ㉘. Walk back east through the Campo de San Francisco. On the corner of Calle Las Ursulas and Calle Bordadores is the **Convento de Las Ursulas** ㉙. Farther ahead on Calle Bordadores is the bizarre **Casa de Las Muertes** ㉚.

Walk east along Calle del Prior to the **Plaza Mayor** ㉛, the center of town. South of the plaza, on Calle de San Pablo, is the Torre del Clavero, a late-15th-century tower topped by fantastic battlements built for the *clavero* (key warden) of the order of Alcántara. Farther down, the Palacio de La Salina is another Fonseca palace designed by Rodrigo Gil de Hontañón. Try to pop inside for a glimpse of the courtyard, where a projecting gallery is supported by wooden consoles carved with expressive nudes and other dynamic forms.

Walking south on Calle de San Pablo and bearing left, you'll circle the Dominican **Convento de las Dueñas** ㉜. Facing the Dueñas, up a monumental flight of steps, is the **Convento de San Estéban** ㉝.

Salamanca

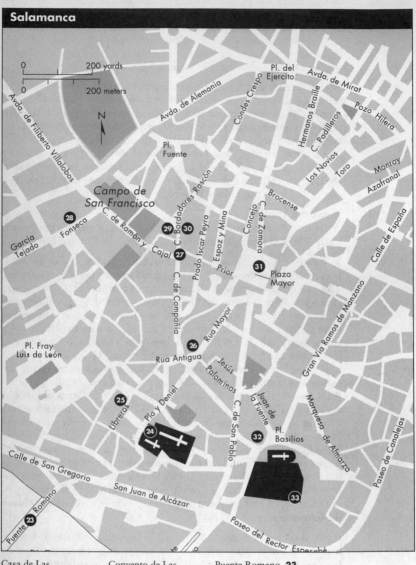

Casa de Las Conchas, **26**

Casa de Las Muertes, **30**

Cathedrals, **24**

Colegio Mayor Arzobispo Fonseca/ Colegio de los Irlandeses, **28**

Convento de Las Dueñas, **32**

Convento de Las Ursulas, **29**

Palacio de Monterrey, **27**

Plaza Mayor, **31**

Puente Romano, **23**

San Estéban, **33**

Universidad, **25**

TIMING

The length of this walk depends on how much time you spend at each sight, but you'll want to allow at least half a day.

Sights to See

㉖ Casa de Las Conchas (House of Shells). This house was built around 1500 for Dr. Rodrigo Maldonado de Talavera, a professor of medicine at the university and a doctor at the court of Isabella. The scallop motif was a reference to Talavera's status as chancellor of the Order of Santiago, whose symbol is the shell. Among the playful plateresque details are the lions over the main entrance, engaged in a fearful tug-of-war with the Talavera crest. The interior has been converted into a public library. Duck into the charming courtyard, which has an upper balustrade carved with virtuoso intricacy in imitation of basketwork. ⊠ *C. Compañia 2,* ☎ *923/269317.* 🎟 *Free.* ⊙ *Weekdays 9–9, weekends 10–2 and 4–7.*

㉚ Casa de Las Muertes (House of the Dead). Built in about 1513 for the majordomo of Alonso de Fonseca II, the house received its name on account of the four tiny skulls that adorn its top two windows. Alonso de Fonseca II commissioned them to commemorate his deceased uncle, the licentious archbishop who lies in the Convento de Las Ursulas, across the street (☞ *below*). For the same reason, the facade also bears the archbishop's portrait. The small square in front of the house was a favorite haunt of the poet, philosopher, and university rector Miguel de Unamuno, whose statue stands here. At the outbreak of the Civil War, Unamuno supported the Nationalists under Franco, but he later turned against them. Placed under virtual house arrest, Unamuno died in the house next door in 1938. During the Franco period, students often daubed his statue red to suggest that his heart still bled for Spain.

㉔ Cathedrals. For a complete tour of the old and new buildings' exterior (an arduous 10-minute walk), circle the complex counterclockwise. Near st the river stands the **Catedral Vieja** (Old Cathedral), built in the late 12th century, one of the most interesting examples of the Spanish Romanesque. Because the dome of the crossing tower features strange, plumelike ribbing, it is known as the Torre del Gallo (the rooster's tower). The much larger **Catedral Nueva** (New Cathedral) dates mainly from the 16th century, though some parts, including the dome over the crossing and the bell tower attached to the west facade, had to be rebuilt after the Lisbon earthquake of 1755. Work began in 1513 under the direction of the distinguished late-Gothic architect Juan Gil de Hontañón; as at Segovia's cathedral, Juan's son Rodrigo took over the work after his father's death in 1526. Of the many outstanding architects in 16th-century Salamanca, Rodrigo Gil de Hontañón left the greatest mark, as one of the leading exponents of the classical plateresque. The New Cathedral's north facade (where the main entrance is) is ornamental enough, but the west facade is dazzling in its sculptural complexity. Try to come here in the late afternoon, when the sun shines directly on it.

The interior of the New Cathedral is as light and harmonious as that of Segovia's cathedral, but larger. Here you are treated to a triumphant baroque conception designed by the Churrigueras. The wooden choir seems almost alive with anxiously active cherubim and saints. From a door in the south aisle, steps descend into the Old Cathedral, where boldly carved capitals supporting the vaulting feature a range of foliage, strange animals, and touches of pure fantasy. Then comes the dome, which seems to owe much to Byzantine architecture; it's a remarkably light structure raised on two tiers of arcaded openings. Not the least of the Old Cathedral's attractions are its furnishings, including sepulchres from the 12th and 13th centuries and a magnificent, curved high altar comprising 53 colorful and delicate scenes by the mid-15th-century artist Nicolás Florentino. In the apse above, Florentino painted an astonishingly fresh Last Judgment fresco.

From the south transept of the Old Cathedral, a door leads into the cloister, begun in 1177. From about 1230 until the construction of the main university building in the early 15th century, the chapels around the cloister served as classrooms for the university students. In the chapel of St. Barbara, on the eastern side, theology students answered the grueling questions meted out by their doctoral examiners. The chair in which they sat is still there, in front of a recumbent effigy of Bishop Juan Lucero, on whose head the students would place their feet for inspiration. Also attached to the cloister is a small cathedral museum with a 15th-century triptych of St. Catherine by Salamanca's greatest native artist, Fernando Gallego. ☎ 923/217476. ⊠ *New Cathedral free, Old Cathedral 300 ptas.* ⊙ *New Cathedral daily 10–1 and 4–6, Old Cathedral daily 10–12:30 and 4–5:30.*

㉘ **Colegio Mayor Arzobispo Fonseca/Colegio de Los Irlandeses.** (Irish College). This small college was founded by Alonso de Fonseca II in 1521 to train young Irish priests. Today it is a residence hall for guest lecturers at the university. The surroundings are not attractive; this part of town was the most severely damaged during the Peninsular War of the early 19th century, and still has a slightly derelict character. The interior of the building, however, is a treat. Immediately inside to the right is an elegant and spacious late-Gothic chapel, while beyond is one of the most classical and genuinely Italianate of Salamanca's many beautiful courtyards. The architect may have been Diego de Siloe, Spain's answer to Michelangelo. ⊠ *C. Fonseca 4,* ☎ *923/294570.* 🖅 *100 ptas.* ⊙ *Daily 10–2 and 4–6.*

㉜ **Convento de Las Dueñas** (Convent of the Dames). Founded in 1419, this convent contains a 16th-century cloister that is the most fantastically decorated in Salamanca, if not in the whole of Spain. The capitals of its two superimposed Salamantine arcades are crowded with a baffling profusion of grotesques that could absorb you for hours. There's another good reason to come here: the nuns make and sell excellent sweets and pastries. ⊠ *C. Plaza Concilio de Trento s/n,* ☎ *923/215442.* 🖅 *200 ptas.* ⊙ *Daily 10:30–1 and 4:30–7.*

㉙ **Convento de Las Ursulas** (Convent of the Ursulines). Archbishop Alonso de Fonseca I lies here, in a splendid marble tomb created by Diego de Siloe during the first half of the 16th century. ⊠ *C. Las Ursulas 2,* ☎ *923/219877.* 🖅 *100 ptas.* ⊙ *Daily 10–1 and 4:30–7.*

Museo Art Nouveau y Art Deco. Opened to the public in 1995, the museum is housed in the Casa Lis, a modernist building from the end of the 19th century. On display are 19th-century paintings and glass, as well as French and German china dolls, Viennese bronze statues, furniture, jewelry, enamels, and jars. Note: here and at the university you can buy a 500-pta. *conjunto* (joint ticket) for admission to this museum, the university, the Museum of Salamanca, and the Irish College. ⊠ *C. Gibraltar 14,* ☎ *923/121425.* ⊙ *Tues.–Fri. 11–2 and 4–7, weekends 11–8.*

Museo de Salamanca (also Museo de Bellas Artes). Consisting mainly of minor 17th- and 18th-century paintings, this museum is also interesting for its 15th-century building, which belonged to Isabella's physician, Alvárez Abarca. ⊠ *Patio de Escuelas Menores s/n,* ☎ *923/212235.* 🖅 *200 ptas.* ⊙ *Tues.–Fri. 9:30–2 and 5 –8, Sat. 10–2 and 4:30–7:30, Sun. 10–2.*

㉗ **Palacio de Monterrey** (Palace of Monterrey). Built after 1538 by Rodrigo Gil de Hontañón, this palace was meant for an illegitimate son of Alonso de Fonseca I. Only one of its four wings was completed, but this one alone makes the palace one of the most imposing in Salamanca. As in Rodrigo's other local palaces, the building is flanked on each side by towers and has an open arcaded gallery running the whole length of the upper level. Such galleries—which in Italy you would expect to see on the ground floor—are common in Spanish Renaissance palaces and were intended as areas where the women of the house could exercise unseen and undisturbed. They also helped to cool the floor below during the summer months. The palace is privately owned and not open to visitors, but you can stroll around the exterior. ⊠ *C. de Comañía s/n.*

㉛ **Plaza Mayor.** Built in the 1730s by Alberto and Nicolás Churriguera, Salamanca's Plaza Mayor is one of the largest squares in Spain, and many find it the most beautiful. Its northern side is dominated by the grandly elegant, pinkish **ayuntamiento** (town hall). The square and its arcades are popular gathering spots for most of Salamancan society, and indeed, the many surrounding cafés make this the perfect spot for a coffee break.

㉓ **Puente Romano** (Roman Bridge). Next to the bridge is an Iberian stone bull, and opposite the bull is a statue commemorating Lazarillo de Tormes, the young hero of the eponymous (and anonymous) 16th-century work that is one of the masterpieces of Spanish literature.

㉝ **Convento de San Esteban**(Convent of St. Stephen). The vast size of this building is a measure of its importance in Salamanca's history: its monks, among the most enlightened teachers at the university, were the first to take Columbus's ideas seriously and helped him gain his introduction to Isabella (hence his statue in the nearby Plaza de Colón, back toward Calle de San Pablo). The complex was designed by one of San Esteban's monks, Juan de Alava. The door to the right of the west facade leads you into a gloomy cloister with Gothic arcading, interrupted by tall, spindly columns adorned with classical motifs. From the cloister, you enter the church at its eastern end. The interior is unified and uncluttered, but also dark and severe. The one note of color is provided by the sumptuously ornate and gilded high altar of 1692, a baroque masterpiece by José Churriguera. The most exciting feature of San Esteban, though, is the massive west facade, a thrilling plateresque work in which sculpted figures and ornamentation are piled up to a height of more than 98 ft. ⊠ *Plaza de San Esteban s/n,* ☎ *923/215000* 🔳 *200 ptas.* ⏱ *Daily 9–1 and 4–7.*

㉕ **Universidad** (University). The university's walls, like those of the cathedral and other structures in Salamanca, are covered with large, ocher lettering recording the names of famous university graduates. The earliest names are said to have been written in the blood of the bulls killed to celebrate the successful completion of a doctorate.

The **Escuelas Mayores** (Major Schools) dates to 1415, but it was not until more than 100 years later that an unknown architect provided the building with its gloriously elaborate frontispiece, generally acknowledged as one of the finest works of the classical plateresque. Immediately above the main door is the famous double portrait of Isabella and Ferdinand, surrounded by ornamentation that plays on the yoke-and-arrow heraldic motifs of the two monarchs. The double-eagle crest of Charles V, flanked by portraits of the emperor and empress in classical guise, dominates the middle layer of the frontispiece. On the highest layer is a panel recently identified as representing Pope Mar-

tin V (one of the university's greatest benefactors), accompanied by cardinals and university rectors. The whole is crowned by a characteristically elaborate plateresque balustrade.

The interior of the Escuelas Mayores, which has been drastically restored in parts, comes as a slight disappointment after the splendor of
the facade. But the *aula* (lecture hall) of Fray Luis de León, where Cervantes, Calderón de la Barca, and numerous other luminaries of Spain's
golden age once sat, is of particular interest. Here Fray Luis, returning after five years' imprisonment for having translated the *Song of
Solomon* into Spanish, began his lecture, "As I was saying yester-
day . . ."

Your ticket to visit the Escuelas Mayores permits entrance to the
nearby **Escuelas Menores** (Minor Schools), built in the early 16th century as a secondary school preparing candidates for the university
proper. Passing through a gate crowned with the double-eagle crest of
Charles V, you'll come to a green, on the other side of which is a modern building housing a fascinating ceiling fresco of the zodiac, originally in the library of the main university building. This painting, a
fragment of a much larger whole, is generally attributed to Fernando
Gallego. Note: at the university and the Museum of Art Nouveau and
Art Deco, you can buy a 500-pta. *conjunto* (joint ticket) for admission to the university, the Museum of Art Nouveau and Art Deco, the
Museum of Salamanca, and the Irish College. ☎ 923/294400, ext. 1150.
🖼 300 ptas. ⊘ Weekdays 9:30–1:30 and 4–7:30, Sat. 9:30–1:30 and
4–7, Sun. 10–1 .

Dining and Lodging

$$$ ✕ **Chez Victor.** If you're tired of traditional Castilian cuisine, try this
chic restaurant. Owner and cook Victoriano Salvador learned his trade
in France and adapts French food to Spanish taste, with whimsical
touches all his own. Try *patatas rellenas de bacalao* (potatoes stuffed
with salt cod) and ravioli *rellenos de marisco* (stuffed with shellfish).
Desserts are outstanding, especially the chocolate ones. ⊠ *Espoz y Mina
26,* ☎ *923/213123. AE, DC, MC, V. Closed Sun. July and Aug.*

$$ ✕ **La Aldaba.** This new restaurant is tastefully decorated in a country
style, with stone walls, a skylight, and a wood-beamed ceiling. Friendly
owners, good food, and a cozy ambience make for a special meal, often
centering around the meat from local Cabracho cows. The *carne de
Cabracho* is served as *chuletón* (flank steak), *solomillo* (loin), or *carpaccio* (thinly sliced, uncooked, marinated meat). The *alcachofas rellenas*
(stuffed artichokes) are also excellent. ⊠ *Felipe Espino 6, 37001,* ☎
923/212779. AE, MC, V.

$$–$$$ ✕ **Río de la Plata.** This tiny basement restaurant, just off Calle de San
Pablo, has been in business since 1958 and retains an old-fashioned
character. The elegant, gilded decor is a pleasant change of scenery, and
the fireplace and local crowd provide warmth. The food is simple but
carefully prepared, with good-quality fish and meat. ⊠ *Plaza Peso 1,*
☎ *923/219005. AE, MC, V. Closed Mon. and July.*

$$$$ 🏨 **Gran Hotel.** The grande dame of Salamanca's hotels offers stylishly
baroque lounges and refurbished yet old-fashioned oversize rooms, just
steps from the Plaza Mayor. ⊠ *Plaza Poeta Iglesias 3, 37001,* ☎ *923/
213500,* FAX *923/213501. 140 rooms. Restaurant, bar. AE, DC, MC, V.*

$$$$ 🏨 **Palacio del Castellanos.** Opened in 1992 in an immaculately restored
15th-century palace, this hotel is a much-needed alternative to Salamanca's parador (probably the ugliest in the chain). There's an exquisite
interior patio and an equally beautiful restaurant, as well as a lovely
terrace overlooking San Esteban. ⊠ *San Pablo 58,* ☎ *923/261818,* FAX
923/261819. 69 rooms. Restaurant. AE, DC, MC, V.

$$$$ ⚑ **Rector.** This beautiful hotel is a true European experience, from the elegant front gate to the high-ceilinged rooms. The sitting areas, hallways, and breakfast room are all spotless, spacious, and warm, yet even more remarkable is the service: the owners, clerks, and porters are all incredibly friendly and will devote themselves to your every whim. Take advantage of their willingness to tell you all about Salamanca. You'll feel like you're staying with family—in high places. ⊠ *Rector Esperabé 10,* ☏ *923/218482,* ℻ *923/214008. 14 rooms. Bar, breakfast room, in-room faxes. AE, DC, MC, V.*

$$ ⚑ **Hostal Plaza Mayor.** You can't beat the location of this great little hostel, just steps from the Plaza Mayor. Completely renovated in 1994, it offers small but modern rooms. Reservations are advisable, as rooms fill up fast. ⊠ *Plaza del Corrillo 20, 37008,* ☏ *923/262020,* ℻ *923/217548. 19 rooms. Restaurant. MC, V.*

Nightlife

The main area for nightclubs is around Calle Bermejeros, but for a fashionable bar-discotheque, try **Camelot,** on Calle Bordadores, or **Abadia,** on Rua Mayor.

Shopping

Salamanca has a reputation for fine **leatherwork**; the most traditional shop in town is **Salón Campero** (⊠ Plaza Corrillo 5).

Ciudad Rodrigo

③④ *88 km (54 mi) west of Salamanca.*

Apart from Salamanca itself, Ciudad Rodrigo is the most interesting destination in Salamanca's province. Surveying the fertile valley of the River Agueda, this small town has numerous well-preserved palaces and churches and makes an excellent overnight stop on the way from Spain to Portugal.

The **cathedral** combines the Romanesque and Transitional Gothic styles, and holds a great deal of fine sculpture. Take a close look at the early 16th-century choir stalls, elaborately carved with entertaining grotesques by Rodrigo Alemán. The cloister has carved capitals, and the cypresses in its center lend tranquility. The cathedral's outer walls are still scarred by cannonballs fired during the Peninsular War. ▣ *Cathedral free, museum 250 ptas.* ☉ *Daily 10–1 and 4–6.*

The town's other chief monument is its fortified medieval **castle,** part of which has been turned into a parador. From here you can climb onto the town's battlements.

Dining and Lodging

$–$$ ✕ **Mayton.** This restaurant has a most engaging interior, backed with wood beams and bursting with a wonderfully eccentric collection of antiques ranging from mortars and pestles to Portuguese yokes and old typewriters. In contrast to the decor, the cooking is simple; the specialties are fish, seafood, goat, and lamb. ⊠ *La Colada 9,* ☏ *923/460720. AE, DC, MC, V.*

$$$–$$$$ ⚑ **Parador Nacional Enrique II.** Occupying part of the magnificent castle built by Enrique II of Trastamara to guard over the Agueda Valley, this parador is a series of small, white rooms along the building's sturdy and gently sloping outer walls. Ask for Room 10 if you want one with original vaulting. A special feature throughout the hotel is the under-floor heating in the bathrooms. Some rooms, as well as the restaurant, overlook a beautiful garden that runs down to the River Agueda; beyond the river, the view surveys fertile plains. ⊠ *Plaza Castillo 1, 37500,* ☏ *923/460150,* ℻ *923/460404. 27 rooms. Restaurant, bar, meeting room. AE, DC, MC, V.*

PROVINCE OF ZAMORA AND CITY OF VALLADOLID

Zamora, Toro, and Valladolid

Zamora is a densely fertile province divided by the River Duero into two distinct zones: the "land of bread," to the north, and the "land of wine," to the south. The area is most interesting for its Romanesque churches, the finest of which are concentrated in the towns of Zamora and Toro. The city of Valladolid, by contrast, is one of the flattest and dreariest spots in the Castilian countryside, but it has the National Museum of Sculpture and plenty of interesting history.

Zamora

③⑤ *248 km (154 mi) northwest of Madrid.*

Zamora, on a bluff above the Duero, is not conventionally beautiful, as its many interesting monuments are isolated from one another by ramshackle 19th- and 20th-century development. It does have lively, old-fashioned character, making it a pleasant stop for a night or two.

In the medieval center of town, on the south side of the Plaza Mayor, is the Romanesque church of **San Juan** (open for mass only), remarkable for its elaborate rose window. North of the Plaza Mayor, at the end of Calle Reina, is one of the town's surviving medieval gates; near here is the Romanesque church of **Santa María.**

Zamora is famous for its Holy Week celebrations. The **Museo de Semana Santa** (Museum of Holy Week) houses the processional sculptures paraded around the streets during that time. Of relatively recent date, these works have an appealing provincial quality; you'll find, for instance, a Crucifixion group filled with what appears to be the contents of a hardware store, including bales of rope, a saw, a spade, and numerous nails. The museum is located in a hideous modern building next to the church of Santa María. ⊠ *300 ptas.* ⊘ *Mon.–Sat. 10–2 and 4–7 (4–8 in summer), Sun. and holidays 10–2 .*

Zamora's **cathedral** is in a hauntingly attractive square, situated at the highest and westernmost point of old Zamora. The bulk of the cathedral is Romanesque, and the most remarkable feature of the exterior is its dome, which is flanked by turrets, articulated by spiny ribs, and covered in overlapping stones, like scales. The dark interior is notable for its early 16th-century choir stalls. The austere, late-16th-century cloister has a small museum upstairs, with an intricate *custodia* (monstrance, or receptacle for the Host) by Juan de Arce and some badly displayed but intriguing Flemish tapestries from the 15th and 16th centuries. ⊠ *300 ptas.* ⊘ *Mon. 4–6, Tues.–Sat. 11–2 and 4–7 (5–8 in summer), Sun. 11–2.*

Surrounding Zamora's cathedral to the north is an attractive park incorporating the town's heavily restored **castle.** Calle Trascastillo, descending south from the cathedral to the river, affords views of the fertile countryside to the south and the town's **old Roman bridge.**

Lodging

$$$$ ⊞ **Parador Nacional Condes de Alba y Aliste.** This restored Renaissance palace is central yet quiet, in an historic building with a distinctive patio adorned with classical medallions of mythological and historical personages. The views are excellent, and the staff is friendly and resourceful. ⊠ *Plaza Viriato 5, 49001,* ☎ *980/514497,* ꜰꜰꜳꝪ *980/530063. 52 rooms. Restaurant, bar, pool. AE, DC, MC, V.*

Toro

③⑥ *33 km (20 mi) east of Zamora, 272 km (169 mi) northwest of Madrid.*

Standing above a loop of the River Duero and commanding extensive views over the vast plain to the south, Toro was also a provincial capital at one time. In 1833, however, it was absorbed into Zamora's province in a loss of status that worked in some ways to its advantage. Zamora developed into a thriving modern town, but Toro slumbered and preserved its old appearance.The town is crowded with Romanesque churches, of which the most important is the **Colegiata,** begun in 1160. The protected west portal, or Portico de La Gloria, has a colorfully painted, perfectly preserved statuary from the early 13th century. The Serbian-Byzantine dome is also prominent. In the sacristy is an anonymous 15th-century painting of the Virgin; this touching work, in the so-called Hispano-Flemish style, is titled *The Virgin of the Fly* because of the fly painted on the Virgin's robe, a rather unusual detail. ⌘ *Free.* ☉ *Summer, Tues.–Sun. 11–1:30 and 5–7:30; winter, Tues.–Sun. 11:30–1:15 and 7:30–8:30; Mon. open for mass only.*

Valladolid

③⑦ *96 km (60 mi) east of Zamora, 193 km (120 mi) northwest of Madrid.*

Modern Valladolid is a large, dirty, and singularly ugly modern city in the middle of one of Castile's dullest stretches. It has one outstanding
★ attraction, however—the **Museo Nacional de Escultura** (National Museum of Sculpture)—and many other interesting sights. It is also one of the most important cities in Spain's history. Ferdinand and Isabella were married here, Philip II was born and baptized here, and Philip III made Valladolid the capital of Spain for six years.

To cope with the chaos, take a taxi—from the bus station, train station, or wherever you parked your car—and head for the National Museum of Sculpture, at the northernmost point of the old town. The late-15th-century Colegio de San Gregorio, in which the museum is housed, is a masterpiece of the so-called Isabelline or Gothic plateresque, an ornamental style of exceptional intricacy featuring playful, naturalistic detail. The facade is especially fantastic, with ribs in the form of pollarded trees, sprouting branches, and—to punctuate the forest motif—a row of wild men bearing mighty clubs.

The museum is arranged in rooms off an elaborate, arcaded courtyard. Its collections do for Spanish sculpture what those in the Prado do for Spanish painting; the only difference is that most people have heard of Velázquez, El Greco, Goya, and Murillo, whereas few are familiar with Alonso de Berruguete, Juan de Juni, and Gregorio Fernández, the three great names represented here.

Attendants and directional cues encourage you to tour the museum in chronological order. Begin on the ground floor, with Alonso de Berruguete's remarkable sculptures from the dismantled high altar in the Valladolid church of San Benito (1532). Berruguete, who trained in Italy under Michelangelo, is the most widely appreciated of Spain's postmedieval sculptors. He strove for pathos rather than realism, and his works have an extraordinarily expressive quality. The San Benito altar was the most important commission of his life, and the fragments here allow you to scrutinize his powerfully emotional art. In the museum's elegant chapel (which you normally see at the end of the tour) is a Berruguete retable from 1526, his first known work; on either side kneel gilded bronze figures by the Italian-born Pompeo Leoni, whose polished and highly decorative art is diametrically opposed to that of Berruguete.

Many critics of Spanish sculpture feel that decline set in with the late-16th-century artist Juan de Juni, who used glass for eyes and pearls for tears. Juni's many admirers, however, find his works intensely exciting, and they are in any case the highlights of the museum's upper floor. Many of the 16th-, 17th-, and 18th-century sculptures on this floor were originally paraded around the streets during Valladolid's celebrated Easter processions; should you ever attend one of these thrilling pageants, the power of Spanish baroque sculpture will be instantly clear.

Dominating Castilian sculpture of the 17th century was the Galician-born Gregorio Fernández, in whose works the dividing line between sculpture and theater becomes tenuous. Respect for Fernández has been diminished by the number of vulgar imitators that his work has spawned, even up to the present day, but at Valladolid you can see his art at its best. The enormous, dramatic, and moving sculptural groups that have been assembled in the museum's last series of rooms (on the ground floor near the entrance) form a suitably spectacular climax to this fine collection. ⊠ *C. Cadenas San Gregorio 1,* ☎ *983/250375.* ☜ *400 ptas., free Sat. afternoon and Sun.* ☉ *Tues.–Sat. 10–2 and 4–6, Sun. 10–2.*

Philip II's birthplace is a brick mansion on the Plaza de San Pablo, at the corner of Calle Angustias. The late-15th-century church of **San Pablo** has another overwhelmingly elaborate facade.The city's **cathedral,** however, is disappointing. Though its foundations were laid in late-Gothic times, the building owes much of its appearance to designs executed in the late 16th century by Juan de Herrera, the architect of the Escorial. Further work was carried out by Alberto de Churriguera in the early 18th century, but the building is still only a fraction of its intended size. The Juni altarpiece is the one bit of color and life in an otherwise visually chilly place. ☎ *983/304362.* ☜ *Cathedral free, museum 250 ptas.* ☉ *Tues.–Fri. 10–1:30 and 4:30–7, weekends 10–2.*

The main **university** building sits opposite the green space just south of the cathedral. The exuberant and dynamic late-baroque frontispiece is by Narciso Tomé, creator of the remarkable *Transparente* in Toledo's cathedral. Calle Librería leads south from the main university building to the magnificent **Colegio de Santa Cruz,** a large university college begun in 1487 in the Gothic style and completed in 1491 by Lorenzo Vázquez in a tentative and pioneering Renaissance mode. Inside is a harmonious courtyard.

The house where Columbus died, in 1506, has been extensively rebuilt and is open to visitors; inside, the excellent **Museo de Colón** (Columbus Museum) has a well-arranged collection of objects, models, and informational panels illuminating the life and times of the explorer. ⊠ *C. Colón,* ☎ *983/291353.* ☜ *Free.* ☉ *Tues.–Sat. 10–2 and 4–6 (5–7 in summer), Sun. 10:30–2.*

A more interesting remnant of Spain's golden age is the tiny house where the writer Miguel de Cervantes lived from 1603 to 1606. A haven of peace set back from a noisy thoroughfare, **Casa de Cervantes** (Cervantes' House) is best reached by taxi. Furnished in the early 20th century in a pseudo-Renaissance style by the Marquis of Valle-Inclan—the creator of the El Greco Museum in Toledo—it has a cozy atmosphere. ⊠ *C. Rastro s/n,* ☎ *983/308810.* ☜ *400 ptas., free on Sun.* ☉ *Tues.–Sat. 10–3:30, Sun. 10–3.*

Dining and Lodging

$$$ ✕ **La Fragua.** In a modern building with a traditional Castilian interior of white walls and wood-beamed ceilings, Valladolid's most famous and stylish restaurant counts members of the Spanish royal family among its guests. Specialties include meat roasted in a wood oven

and such imaginative dishes as *rape Castellano Gran Mesón* (breaded monkfish with clams and peppers) and *lengua empiñonada* (tongue coated in pine nuts). ✉ *Paseo Zorrilla 10,* ☎ *983/337102. AE, DC, MC, V. No dinner Sun. Closed Aug.*

$$$$ ⊞ **Valladolid Meliá.** Despite being in the middle of one of Valladolid's oldest and most attractive districts, this hotel sits on a modern block. The building was erected in the early 1970s and completely redecorated in 1994, with blond-wood furniture and new baths. The ground and first floors have a pristine, marbled elegance. ✉ *Plaza de San Miguel 10, 47003,* ☎ *983/357200,* FAX *983/336828. 211 rooms. Restaurant, bar, cafeteria, meeting room. AE, DC, MC, V.*

Nightlife

Valladolid has a wide range of nightspots. The Zona Francisco Suarez and the Zona Iglesia La Antigua are two districts popular with students. Livelier and more fashionable are the Zona Cantarranas (in particular, the **Atomium**) and the area around the Plaza Mayor.

NORTHEAST OF MADRID

Alcalá de Henares, Guadalajara, Pastrana, Sigüenza, Medinaceli, and Soria, Numancia, El Burgo de Osma

They're off the main tourist tracks, but the provinces of Guadalajara and Soria have a lot to offer and are—for a change—easily accessible by train. The line from Madrid to Zaragoza passes through all of the towns named above, allowing a manageable and interesting excursion of two to three days. If you have a car, you can extend this trip by detouring into beautiful, unspoiled countryside.

Alcalá de Henares

38 *30 km (19 mi) east of Madrid.*

Alcalá's past fame was due largely to its university, founded in 1498 by Cardinal Cisneros. In 1836 the university was moved to Madrid, and Alcalá's decline was hastened. The Civil War destroyed much of the town's artistic and architectural heritage, and in recent years Alcalá has emerged as a dormer town for Madrid. Nevertheless, enough survives of old Alcalá to give a good impression of what it must have been like during its golden age.

The town's main monument is its enormous **Universidad Complutense,** built between 1537 and 1553 by the great Rodrigo Gil de Hontañón. (Complutum was Alcalá's Roman name.) Though this is one of Spain's earliest and most important Italian Renaissance buildings, most Italian architects of the time would probably have shrieked in terror at its principal facade. The use of the classical order is all wrong; the main block is out of line with the two that flank it; and the whole is crowned by a heavy and elaborate gallery. All this is typically Spanish, as is the prominence given to the massive crest of Cardinal Cisneros and to the ironwork, both of which form integral parts of the powerful overall design. Inside are three patios, of which the most impressive is the first, comprising three superimposed arcades. A guided tour of the interior takes you to a delightfully decorated room where exams were once held, and to the chapel of San Ildefonso, with its richly sculpted Renaissance mausoleum of Cardinal Cisneros. ✉ *Plaza San Diego s/n.* ▣ *250 ptas.* ☉ *Tues.–Fri. 11:30–1:30 and 5–6, weekends 11–2 and 4–7.*

On one side of the university square is the **Convento de San Diego,** where Clarissan nuns make and sell *almendras garrapiñadas* (candy-coated almonds), a town specialty. The other side adjoins the large and arcaded **Plaza de Cervantes,** Alcalá's animated center. Off the plaza runs the arcaded Calle Mayor, which still looks much as it did in the 16th and 17th centuries.

Miguel de Cervantes was born in a house on this street in 1547; a charming replica, **Casa de Cervantes,** built in 1955, contains a small **Cervantes museum.** ⊠ *Calle Mayor 48,* ☎ *91/889–9654.* 🖼 *Free.* ⊙ *Weekdays 10–2 and 4–7, weekends 10–2.*

Dining

$$ ✕ **Hostería del Estudiante.** In one of the first buildings acquired by Spain's parador chain, this restaurant is magnificently set around a 15th-century cloister and features wood-beamed ceilings, a large and splendid fireplace, and glass-and-tin lanterns. Appropriate to the traditional setting is the good and simple Castilian food, with roast lamb a particular specialty. ⊠ *Los Colegios 3,* ☎ *91/888–0330. AE, DC, MC, V.*

Guadalajara

③⑨ *17 km (10 mi) east of Alcalá, 55 km (34 mi) northeast of Madrid.*

This provincial capital was severely damaged in the Civil War, but its **Palacio del Infantado** (Palace of the Prince's Territory) still stands and is one of the most important Spanish palaces of its period. Built between 1461 and 1492 by Juan Guas, it's a bizarre and potent mix of Gothic, classical, and Mudéjar influences. The main facade is rich; the lower floors are studded with diamond shapes; and the whole is crowned by a complex Gothic gallery supported on a frieze pitted with intricate Moorish cellular work (the honeycomb motif). Inside is a fanciful and exciting courtyard, though little else; the magnificent Renaissance frescoes that once covered the palace's rooms were largely obliterated in the Civil War. On the ground floor is a modest provincial art gallery. ⊠ *Plaza de los Caídos 1.* 🖼 *200 ptas.* ⊙ *Tues.–Sat. 10:30–2 and 4:15–7, Sun. 10:30–2.*

En Route East of Guadalajara extends the Alcarria, an area of high plateau crossed by rivers forming verdant valleys. It was made famous in the 1950s by one of the great classics of Spanish travel literature, Camilo José Cela's *Journey to the Alcarria,* in which Cela evoked the backwardness and remoteness of an area barely an hour from Madrid. Even today you can feel far removed here from the modern world.

Pastrana

④⓪ *42 km (26 mi) southeast of Guadalajara.*

High on a hill, Pastrana's narrow lanes merge into the landscape. This is a pretty village of Roman origin, once the capital of a small duchy. The tiny **museum** attached to Pastrana's **Colegiata** (collegiate church) displays a glorious series of Gothic tapestries. 🖼 *125 ptas.* ⊙ *Weekends 1–3 and 4–6.*

Sigüenza

④① *86 km (54 mi) northeast of Guadalajara.*

Sigüenza, the next major stop on the journey east from Madrid, is one of the most beautiful towns in Castile. Begun around 1150 and not completed until the early 16th century, Sigüenza's remarkable **cathedral** is an anthology of Spanish architecture from the Romanesque period to the Renaissance. The sturdy western front has a forbidding, fortresslike appearance but contains an inviting wealth of ornamental and artistic masterpieces. Go directly to the sacristan (the sacristy is at the north end of the ambulatory) for an informative guided tour. The sacristy is an outstanding Renaissance structure, covered in a barrel vault designed by the great Alonso de Covarrubias; its coffering is studded with hundreds of sculpted heads, which stare at you disarmingly. The tour then takes you into the late-Gothic cloister, off which is a room lined with 17th-century Flemish tapestries. You will also have illuminated for you (in the north transept) the ornate, late-15th-century sepulchre of Dom Fadrique of Portugal, an early example of the classical plateresque. The cathedral's high point is the Chapel of the Doncel (to the right of the sanctuary), in which you'll see Spain's most celebrated funerary monument, the tomb of Don Martín Vázquez de Arca, commissioned by Isabella, to whom Don Martín served as *doncel* (page) before dying young at the gates of Granada in 1486. The reclining Don Martín is lifelike, an open book in his hands and a wistful melancholy in his eyes. More than a memorial to an individual, this tomb, with its surrounding late-Gothic foliage and tiny mourners, is like an epitaph of the Age of Chivalry, a final flowering of the Gothic spirit. ⊞ *300 ptas.* ⊙ *Daily 11–1 and 4–6 (until 7 in summer).*

In a refurbished early-19th-century house, next to the cathedral's west facade, the **Museo Diocesano de Arte Sacro** (Diocesan Museum of Sacred Art) contains a prehistoric section and much religious art from the 12th to 18th centuries. ⊞ *200 ptas.* ⊙ *Tues.–Sun. 11–2 and 4:30–6:30 (4:30–7:30 in summer).*

The south side of the cathedral overlooks the arcaded **Plaza Mayor,** a harmonious Renaissance square commissioned by Cardinal Mendoza. The small palaces and cobbled alleys in the area mark the virtually intact Old Quarter. Along Calle Mayor you'll find the palace that belonged to the *doncel*'s family. The enchanting **castle** at the top of the street, overlooking wild, hilly countryside from above Sigüenza, is now a parador (☞ Lodging, *below*). Founded by the Romans but rebuilt at various later periods, most of the present structure was put up in the 14th century, when it was transformed into a residence for the queen of Castile, Doña Blanca de Borbón, who was banished here by her husband, Peter the Cruel.

Lodging

$$$–$$$$
★ ⌂ **Parador Nacional Castillo de Sigüenza.** Of the many castles in the parador chain, this is one of the most impressive and historically significant. At the very top of the town, this mighty, crenellated structure has hosted royalty over the centuries, from Ferdinand and Isabella right up to the present king, Juan Carlos. Some of the rooms have four-poster beds and balconies overlooking the wild landscape. ⊠ *Plaza del Castillo s/n, 19250,* ☎ *949/390100,* ⠵ *949/391364. 81 rooms. Restaurant, meeting room, parking. AE, DC, MC, V.*

Medinaceli

㊷ *32 km (20 mi) northeast of Sigüenza.*

The preserved village of Medinaceli commands an exhilarating position on the top of a long, steep ridge. Dominating the skyline is a Roman triumphal arch from the 2nd or 3rd century AD, the only surviving triple archway of this period in Spain. (The arch's silhouette is now featured in signposts to national monuments throughout the country.) The surrounding village, once the seat of one of Spain's most powerful dukes, had virtually been abandoned by its inhabitants by the end of the 19th century, and if you come here during the week you'll find yourself in a near ghost town. Many Madrileños have weekend houses here, and various Americans are also in part-time residence. The place is undeniably beautiful, with extensive views, picturesquely overgrown houses, and unpaved lanes leading directly into wild countryside. The former palace of the dukes of Medinaceli is currently undergoing restoration, and Roman excavations are also being carried out in one of the squares.

Soria

43 *74 km (46 mi) north of Medinaceli, 234 km (145 mi) northeast of Madrid.*

This provincial capital, which has prospered for centuries as a center of sheep farming, has been spoiled by modern development and is frequently beset by cold, biting winds. Yet its situation in the wooded valley of the Duero is splendid, and it has a number of fascinating Romanesque buildings.

Soria has strong connections with Antonio Machado, Spain's most popular 20th-century poet after García Lorca. The Seville-born poet lived a bohemian life in Paris for many years , but he eventually returned to Spain and taught French in Soria from 1909 to 1911. A large bronze head of Machado is displayed outside the **school** where he taught; and his former classroom (now called the Aula Machado) contains a tiny collection of memorabilia. It was in Soria that Machado fell in love with and married the 16-year-old daughter of his landlady, and when she died only two years later, he felt he could no longer stay in a town so full of her memories. He moved on to Baeza, in his native Andalucía, and then went to Segovia, where he spent his last years in Spain (he died early in the civil war, shortly after escaping to France). His most successful work, the *Campos de Castilla,* was greatly inspired by Soria and by his dead wife, Leonor; the town and the woman both haunted him until his death.

The main roads to Soria converge onto the wide, modern promenade El Espolón, where you'll find the **Museo Numantino** (Museum of Numancia). Founded in 1919, the museum contains a collection of local archaeological finds. Few other museums in Spain are laid out quite as well or as spaciously; the collections are rich in prehistoric and Iberian finds, and one section—on the top floor—is dedicated to the important Iberian-Roman settlement at nearby Numancia (☞ *below*). ⊠ C. Polón 8, ☎ 975/221397. ⊠ *200 ptas.* ☉ *May–Sept., Tues.–Sat. 9–2 and 5–9, Sun. 9–2; Oct.–Apr., Tues.–Sat. 9–8:30, Sun. 10–2.*

At the top of **Calle Aduana Vieja** is the late-12th-century church of **San Domingo,** with its richly carved, Romanesque west facade. The imposing, 16th-century palace of the counts of Gomara (now a law court) is on Calle Estudios. Dominating the hill just south of the River Dueron is the Antonio Machado parador (☞ Dining and Lodging, *below*), which shares a park with the ruins of the town's castle. Machado loved the views of the town and valley from this hill. Calle de Santiago, which leads to the parador, passes the church and cemetery of El Espino, where Machado's wife, Leonor, is buried. Just before the river is the **cathedral,** a late-Gothic hall church attached to a large Romanesque cloister.

Across the River Dueron from Soria, in a wooded setting overlooking the river, is the deconsecrated church of **San Juan de Duero,** once the property of the Knights Hospitalers. Outside the church are the curious ruins of a Romanesque cloister, featuring a rare Spanish example of interlaced arching. The church itself, now looked after by the Museo

Numantino, is a small, didactic museum of Romanesque art and architecture. ⌧ *100 ptas.* ⊘ *Winter, Tues.–Sat. 10–2 and 4–6, Sun. 10–2; summer, Tues.–Sat. 10–2 and 5–9, Sun. 10–2.*

Take an evocative, half-hour walk along the Duero River to the **Ermita (Hermitage) de San Saturio**; you'll follow a path (accessible by car) lined by poplars. The hermitage was built in the 18th century above a cave where the Anchorite St. Saturio fasted and prayed. You can climb up to the building through the cave. ⌧ *Free.* ⊘ *Winter, daily 10:30–2 and 4–6; summer, daily 10:30–2 and 5–9.*

Dining and Lodging

$$ ✕ **Mesón Castellano.** The most traditional restaurant in town, this cozy establishment has a large, open fire over which succulent *chuletón de ternera* (veal chops) are cooked. Another house specialty is *migas pastoriles* (soaked bread crumbs fried with peppers and bacon), a local dish. ✉ *Plaza Mayor 2,* ☎ *975/213045. AE, DC, MC, V.*

$$$ ▥ **Parador Nacional Antonio Machado.** This modern building has a superb hilltop setting, surrounded by trees and parkland, and excellent views of the hilly Duero Valley. The poet came often to this site for inspiration. ✉ *Parque del Castillo, 42005,* ☎ *975/213445,* ⟪FAX⟫ *975/212849. 34 rooms. Restaurant, bar. AE, DC, MC, V.*

Numancia

④④ *7 km (4 mi) north of Soria.*

The bleak hilltop ruins of Numancia, an important Iberian settlement, are just a few minutes from Soria and accessible only by car. Viciously besieged by the Romans in 135–134 BC, Numancia's inhabitants chose death rather than surrender. Most of the foundations that have been unearthed date from the time of the Roman occupation. ⌧ *100 ptas.* ⊘ *Winter, Tues.–Sat. 10–2 and 4–6, Sun. 10–2; summer, Tues.–Sat. 10–2 and 5–9, Sun. 10–2.*

El Burgo de Osma

④⑤ *56 km (35 mi) west of Soria.*

El Burgo de Osma is an attractive medieval and Renaissance town dominated by a Gothic cathedral and a baroque bell tower.

Dining and Lodging

$$ ✕ **Virrey Palafox.** One of Castile's best-known restaurants, this is a family-run enterprise set in a modern building. Inside, the decor is traditional Castilian, complete with white walls and a wood-beamed ceiling. The long dining room, adorned with old furnishings, is divided into smoking and nonsmoking sections. The emphasis is on fresh, seasonal produce; vegetables are home-grown; and there is excellent local game throughout the year. The house specialty is fish, in particular *merluza Virrey* (hake stuffed with eels and salmon). On February and March weekends a pig is slaughtered, and a marvelous and very popular banquet is held; admission is about 5,000 ptas. ✉ *Universidad 7,* ☎ *975/340222. AE, DC, MC, V. Closed Sun. and Dec. 22–Jan. 10.*

$$$ ▥ **Virrey II.** A few hundred yards from the restaurant, and under the same management, the Virrey II offers pleasant accommodations. Situated on the village's main square, it adjoins the 16th-century Convent of San Agustín and appears to form part of it. Though the hotel was only built in 1990, it was made with traditional materials and has an Old-World look. The rooms, most of which overlook the square,

have marble floors, stone walls, and tastefully simple decoration. ⊠
C. Mayor 2, 42300, ☎ *975/341311,* FAX *975/340855. 52 rooms. Dining room, meeting room. AE, DC, MC, V.*

SOUTHEAST OF MADRID
Cuenca, Ciudad Encantada, Alarcón

Dramatic landscapes are the main attraction here. The rocky countryside
and magnificent gorges of the rivers Huécar and Júcar make for spectacular views. Cuenca offers a museum devoted to abstract art, impressive
for both its content and its setting. Nearby towns like Ciudad Encan-
tada, with its rock formations, and Alarcón, home to a medieval castle, make pleasant excursions.

Cuenca

46 *167 km (104 mi) southeast of Madrid.*

Built onto a wild and rocky countryside cut with dramatic gorges, Cuenca
has a haunting atmosphere and outstanding cuisine. On the north side
of the River Huécar, the old town rises steeply, hugging a spine of rock
thrust up between the gorges of the Huécar and the Júcar and bordered
on two sides by sheer precipices, over which soars the odd hawk or
eagle. The lower half of the old town is a maze of tiny streets, any of
which will take you up to the Plaza del Carmen. From here the town
narrows, and a single street, Calle Alfonso VIII, continues the ascent
up to the Plaza Mayor, which you reach after passing under the arch
of the town hall.

Just off Calle San Pedro, clinging to the western edge of Cuenca, is the
tiny **Plaza San Nicolás,** a picturesquely dilapidated square. Nearby, the
unpaved Ronda del Júcar hovers over the Júcar gorge and commands
remarkable views over the mountainous landscape. The best views of
the mountains are from the square in front of the **castle,** at the very
top of Cuenca, where the town tapers out to the narrowest of ledges.
Gorges are on either side of you, while directly in front, old houses
sweep down toward a distant plateau. The castle itself, which served
as the town prison for many years, is now a parador.

The **Museo Diocesano de Arte Sacro** (Diocesan Museum of Sacred Art)
is housed in what were once the cellars of the Bishop's Palace. The beautifully clear display features a jewel-encrusted, Byzantine diptych of the
13th century; a Crucifixion by the 15th-century Flemish artist Gerard
David; and two small El Grecos. From the Plaza Mayor, take Calle
Obispo Valero and follow signs pointing toward the Casas Colgadas.
☎ *969/212011.* 🖾 *200 ptas.* ☉ *Tues.–Fri. 11–2 and 4–6, Sat. 11–
2 and 4–8, Sun. 11–2.*

★   Cuenca's most famous buildings, the **Casas Colgadas** (Hanging Houses),
form one of the finest and most curious of Spain's museums. This joined
group of houses, literally projecting over the town's eastern precipice,
originally formed a 15th-century palace; later they served as a town
hall before falling into disuse and decay in the 19th century. During
the restoration campaign of 1927, the cantilevered balconies that had
once hung over the gorge were rebuilt, and finally, in 1966, the painter
Fernando Zóbel decided to create inside them the world's first museum
devoted exclusively to abstract art. The works he gathered are almost
all by the remarkable generation of Spanish artists who grew up in the
1950s and were essentially forced to live abroad during the Franco
regime: the major names include Carlos Saura, Eduardo Chillida,

Muñoz, Millares, Antoni Tàpies, and Zóbel. Even if you don't think abstract art is your thing, this museum is likely to win you over with its honeycomb of dazzlingly white rooms and its vistas of sky and gorge. ☞ *500 ptas.* ◷ *Tues.–Fri. 11–2 and 4–6, Sat. 11–2 and 4–8, Sun. 11–2 .*

An iron footbridge over the Huécar gorge, the **Puente de San Pablo** was built in 1903 for the convenience of the Dominican monks of San Pablo, who live on the other side. If you've no fear of heights, cross the narrow bridge to take in the vertiginous view of the river below and the equally thrilling panorama of the Casas Colgadas. A path from the bridge descends to the bottom of the gorge, landing you by the bridge that you crossed to enter the old town.

Dining and Lodging

$$$ ✕ **El Figón de Pedro.** This restaurant's owner, Pedro Torres Pacheco,
★ is one of Spain's most famous restaurateurs and has done much to promote the excellence of Cuenca's cuisine. In this pleasantly low-key spot in the lively heart of the modern town, you can try such local specialties as *gazpacho pastor, ajo arriero* (a paste made with pounded salt cod and served with toasted bread), and *alaju* (a Moorish sweet made with honey, bread crumbs, almonds, and orange water). Wash down your meal with *resolí,* Cuenca's liqueur. ✉ *Cervantes 13,* ☎ 969/ 226821. *AE, DC, MC, V. Closed Feb. No dinner Sun.*

$$$ ✕ **Mesón Casas Colgadas.** Run by the same management as El Figón de Pedro (☞ *above*), this *mesón* offers much the same fare, but more pretentiously. The dining room is ultramodern and white and sits next to the Museum of Abstract Art in the spectacularly situated Casas Colgadas. ✉ *Canónigos s/n,* ☎ 969/223509. *Reservations essential. AE, DC, MC, V. No dinner Tues.*

$$ ✕ **Las Brasas.** Meats cooked over wood coals and hearty bean con-
★ coctions characterize this fairly typical Spanish restaurant. Both the cooking and the fire, visible from the bar, make a meal here comforting and festive. The owners use vegetables from their own garden to make a delicious *pucherete* (white bean soup). The decor is Castilian, with wood floors and dark wood furniture. ✉ *Alfonso VIII 105,* ☎ 969/213821. *MC, V. Closed Wed. and July.*

$$$$ ▥ **Parador de Cuenca.** Spain's newest parador (b. 1993) is in an exquisitely restored 16th-century monastery in the gorge beneath the Casas Colgadas. The guest rooms are furnished in a lighter and more luxurious style than you'd normally find in Castilian houses of this vintage. ✉ *Paseo Hoz de Huécar s/n, 16001,* ☎ 969/232320, ℻ 969/ 232534. 63 rooms. Restaurant, bar, pool, tennis court. AE, DC, MC, V.*

$$$ ▥ **Cueva del Fraile.** This luxurious hotel, 7 km (4½ mi) out of town on the Buenache road, occupies a 16th-century building in dramatic surroundings. The white rooms have reproduction traditional furniture, stone floors, and in some cases wood ceilings. ✉ *Ctra. Cuenca-Buenache, 16001,* ☎ 969/211571, ℻ 969/256047. 62 rooms. Pool, tennis court, meeting room. AE, MC, V. Closed Jan.–Feb.*

$$–$$$ ▥ **Posada San José.** This is still the only hotel in the Old Town, and
★ it's just as good as—if somewhat more modest than—the nearby parador. Tastefully installed in a 16th-century convent, the *posada* clings to the top of the Huécar gorge, which most of its rooms overlook. The furnishings are traditional, in the spirit of the building. The atmosphere is friendly and intimate. Reservations are essential and should be made well in advance. ✉ *Julián Romero 4, 16001,* ☎ 969/211300. 29 rooms, 21 with bath. Bar, cafeteria. AE, DC, MC, V.*

Ciudad Encantada

④⑦ *35 km (21 mi) north of Cuenca.*

The "Enchanted City" comprises a series of large and fantastic rock formations erupting in a landscape of pines. If you like to explore on foot, this town is well worth a visit; a footpath can guide you through striking outcrops with names like "El Tobagón" (The Toboggan) and "Mar de Piedras" (Sea of Stones).

Alarcón

④⑧ *69 km (43 mi) south of Cuenca.*

This fortified village on the edge of the great plains of La Mancha stands impressively on a high spur of land encircled almost entirely by a bend of the River Júcar. Its **castle** dates to Visigothic times; in the 14th century it came into the hands of the infante Don Juan Manuel, who wrote a collection of moral tales that rank among the great treasures of medieval Spanish literature. Today the castle is one of Spain's finest paradors (☞ Dining and Lodging, *below*).

Dining and Lodging

$$$$ ✕🏠 **Parador Nacional Marqués de Villena.** As a place to indulge in medieval fantasies, this parador, in a 12th-century castle perched above a gorge, can't be beat. There are only 13 rooms here, 12 of them quite small (the turret room is large). Some rooms are in the corner towers and have as windows the narrow slots once used to shoot arrows from; others have window niches where the women of the household sat to do needlework. Dinner is served in a high-arched baronial hall adorned with shields, armor, and a gigantic fireplace recalling medieval banquets. The nearest train connection to Alarcón is Cuenca, 69 km (43 mi) away; a bus to Motilla will leave you a short taxi ride away (call ☎ 969/331797 for a cab). ✉ *Avda. Amigos de los Castillos 3, 16213,* ☎ *969/330315,* ☎ *969/330303. 13 rooms. Restaurant. AE, DC, MC, V.*

SOUTH OF MADRID

Aranjuez and Toledo

The small town of Aranjuez is home to the Palacio Real, a sumptuously decorated French-style palace. Nearby Toledo, on the other hand, is a study in austerity, its introverted, gold-toned houses daring you to know them better. Here you can explore the mighty Gothic cathedral and the Tránsito Synagogue; contemplate El Greco's most famous painting, *The Burial of Count Orgaz*; or just roam the winding lanes.

Aranjuez

④⑨ *47 km (29 mi) south of Madrid.*

Once the site of a Habsburg hunting lodge on the banks of the Tajo, Aranjuez became a favorite summer residence of the Bourbons in the 18th century; they built a large palace and other buildings, designed extensive gardens, and planted woods. In the 19th century, Aranjuez developed into a popular retreat for Madrileños. Today, the spaciously and neatly laid-out town that grew up in the vicinity of the palace retains a faded elegance.

Aranjuez's **Palacio Real** (Royal Palace) reflects French grandeur. The high point of the sumptuous interior is a room covered entirely with porcelain; there are also numerous elaborate clocks and a good museum of costumes. Shaded riverside gardens full of statuary and fountains allow pleasant relaxation after the palace tour. ☎ *91/891–1344.* ⌧ *Palace 500 ptas., gardens free.* ⊘ *Palace May–Sept., Tues.–Sun. 10–6:15; Oct.–Apr., Tues.–Sun. 10–5:15. Gardens May–Sept., daily 8–6:30; Oct.–Apr., daily 8 AM–8:30 PM.*

The charming **Casa del Labrador** (Farmer's Cottage), a small, intimate palace at the eastern end of Aranjuez, was built by Carlos IV in 1804 and has a jewel-like interior bursting with color and crowded with delicate objects. Between the Royal Palace and the Casa del Labrador is the **Casa de Marinos** (Sailors' House), where you'll see a gondola that belonged to Philip V and other decorated pleasure boats that once plied the river. ⌧ *Casa del Labrador 425 ptas., Casa de Marinos 325 ptas.* ⊘ *May–Sept., Tues.–Sun. 10–6:30; Oct.–Apr., Tues.–Sun. 10–5:30.*

Toledo

★ ➄ *35 km (22 mi) southwest of Aranjuez, 71 km (44 mi) southwest of Madrid.*

The contrast between Aranjuez and nearby Toledo could hardly be more marked. From the sensuous surroundings and French-style elegance of the former, you move to a place of drama and austerity, tinged with mysticism, that was long the spiritual and intellectual capital of Spain. No matter which route you take from Madrid, your first glimpse of Toledo will take in its northern gates and battlements rising up on a massive granite escarpment. The flat countryside comes to an end, and a steep range of ocher-colored hills rises on each side of the city.

The rock on which Toledo stands was inhabited in prehistoric times, and there was already an important Iberian settlement here when the Romans came in 192 BC. On the highest point of the rock —on which now stands the Alcázar, the dominant building in Toledo's skyline— the Romans built a large fort; this was later remodeled by the Visigoths, who transformed the town into their capital by the middle of the 6th century AD. In the early 8th century, the Moors arrived.

During their occupation of Toledo, the Moors furthered its reputation as a great center of learning and religion. Unusual tolerance was extended to those who continued to practice Christianity (the so-called Mozarabs), as well as to the town's exceptionally large Jewish population. Today the Moorish legacy is evident in Toledo's strong crafts tradition, in the mazelike arrangement of the streets, and in the predominance of brick rather than stone. To the Moors, beauty was a quality to be savored within rather than displayed on the surface, and it is significant that even Toledo's cathedral—one of the most richly endowed in Spain—is difficult to see from the outside, largely obscured by the warren of houses that surrounds it. Long after the departure of the Moors, Toledo remained secretive, its life and treasures hidden behind closed doors and forbidding facades.

Alfonso VI, aided by El Cid, captured Toledo in 1085 and styled himself Emperor of Toledo. Under the Christians, the town's strong intellectual life was maintained, and Toledo became famous for its school of translators who spread to the West a knowledge of Arab medicine, law, culture, and philosophy. Religious tolerance continued, and during the rule of Peter the Cruel (so named because he allegedly had members of his own family murdered to advance himself), a Jewish banker, Samuel Levi, became the royal treasurer and one of the wealthiest and most important men in town. By the early 15th century, however, hostility toward both Jews and Arabs had grown as Toledo developed more and more into a bastion of the Catholic Church.

As Florence had the Medici and Rome the papacy, so Toledo had its long and distinguished line of cardinals, most notably Mendoza, Tavera, and Cisneros. Under these great patrons of the arts, Renaissance Toledo emerged as a center of humanism. Economically and politically, however, Toledo had already begun to decline in the 16th century. The expulsion of the Jews from Spain in 1492 had particularly serious economic consequences for Toledo; the decision in 1561 to make Madrid the permanent center of the Spanish court led to the town's loss of political importance; and the expulsion from Spain of the converted Arabs (Moriscos) in 1601 resulted in the departure of most of Toledo's celebrated artisan community. The years the painter El Greco spent in Toledo—from 1572 to his death in 1614—were those of the town's decline. Its transformation into a major tourist center began in the late 19th century, when the works of El Greco came to be widely appreciated after years of neglect. Today, Toledo is prosperous and conservative, expensive, silent at night, and closed in atmosphere. Yet Spain has no other town of this size with such a concentration of monuments and works of art.

A Good Walk

The eastern end of the gorge, along Calle de Circunvalación, has a panoramic view of Toledo. Here you can park your car (except in the middle of the day, when buses line up) and look down over almost all of Toledo's main monuments.

Start at the **Puente de Alcántara** ⑤. If you choose to go north, skirting the city walls, you'll come to the **Hospital de Tavera** ㉒. If you enter the city wall, travel west and pass the **Plaza de Zocodover** ㉓, the **Museo de la Santa Cruz** ㉔, and the **Capilla del Cristo de la Luz** ㉕. From opposite the southwestern corner of the **Alcázar** ㉖, a series of alleys descends to the east end of the **cathedral** ㉗, affording good views of the cathedral tower. Make your way around the southern side of the building, passing the mid-15th-century Puerta de los Leones, with detailed and realistic carvings by artists of northern descent. Emerging into the small square in front of the cathedral's west facade, you will see to your right the elegant *ayuntamiento,* begun by the young Juan de Herrera and completed by El Greco's son, Jorge Manuel Theotokópoulos.

Near the Museo de los Concilios, on Calle de San Clemente, take in the richly sculpted portal by Covarrubias on the Convento de San Clemente; across the street is the church of **San Román** ㉘. Almost every wall in this quiet part of town belongs to a convent, and the empty streets make for contemplative walks. This was a district loved by the Romantic poet Gustavo Adolfo Bécquer, author of *Rimas (Rhymes),* the most popular collection of Spanish verse before García Lorca's *Romancero Gitano.* Bécquer's favorite corner was the tiny square in front of the 16th-century convent church of **Santo Domingo** ㉙, a few minutes' walk north of San Román, below the Plazuela de Padilla.

Backtrack following Calle de San Clemente through the Plaza de Valdecaleros to Calle de Santo Tomé to get to the church of **Santo Tomé** ㉖⓪. Down the hill from Santo Tomé, off Calle de San Juan de Díos, is the **Casa de El Greco** ㉖①. Next door to the Casa de El Greco is the 14th-century **Sinagoga del Tránsito** ㉖②, financed by Samuel Levi, and the accompanying **Museo Sefardi.** Come out of the synagogue and turn right up Calle de Reyes Católicos. A few steps past the town's other synagogue, **Santa María la Blanca** ㉖③, is the late-15th-century church of **San Juan de los Reyes** ㉖④, the most prominent monument in western Toledo. The walk finishes at the city's western extremity, the **Puente de San Martín** ㉖⑤.

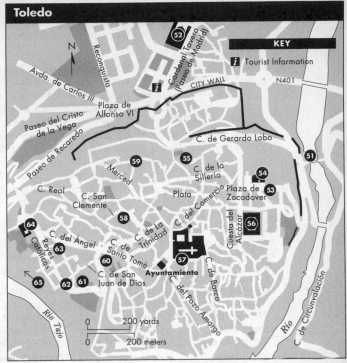

Toledo

KEY

i Tourist Information

TIMING

Toledo's winding streets and steep hills can be exasperating at times, especially when you're looking for a specific sight; but one of the main attractions of this walk is simply enjoying the medieval atmosphere. Plan to spend the whole day.

Sights to See

56 Alcázar. Early birds, take note: this is the sight with the earliest opening time. The south facade, the most severe, is the work of Juan de Herrera, of Escorial fame; the east facade gives a good idea of the building's medieval appearance, incorporating a large section of battlements. The finest facade is undoubtedly the northern, one of many Toledan works by Alonso de Covarrubias, who did more than any other architect to introduce the Renaissance style here.

Within the building are a military headquarters and a large military museum—one of Spain's few remaining homages to Francoism, hung with tributes from various right-wing military groups and figures from around the world. The Alcázar's architectural highlight is Covarrubias's harmonious Italianate courtyard, which, like most other parts of the building, was largely rebuilt after the Civil War, when the Alcázar was besieged by the Republicans. Though the Nationalists' ranks were depleted, they managed to hold on to the building. Franco later turned the Alcázar into a monument to Nationalist bravery; the office of the Nationalist general who defended the building, General Moscardó, has been left exactly as it was after the war, complete with peeling ceiling paper and mortar holes. The gloomy tour can continue with a visit to the dark cellars, which evoke living conditions at the time of the siege.

More cheerful is a ground-floor room full of beautifully crafted swords, a Toledan specialty introduced by Moorish silversmiths. At the top of the grand staircase, which apparently made even Carlos V "feel like an emperor," are rooms displaying a vast collection of toy soldiers. ☎ *925/223038.* ✆ *125 ptas.* ☉ *Tues.–Sun. 10–1:30 and 4–5:30 (4–6:30 in summer).*

55   **Capilla del Cristo de la Luz** (Chapel of Christ of the Light). This chapel lies behind railings in a small park above the town's northern ramparts. The gardener will open the gate for you and show you around; if he's not there, inquire at the house opposite. The exposed chapel was originally a tiny Visigothic church, transformed into a mosque during the Moorish occupation; the arches and vaulting of the mosque survive, making this the most important relic of Moorish Toledo. The chapel got its name when the horse of Alfonso VI, who was riding in triumph into Toledo in 1085, knelt in front of the building; it was then discovered that behind the masonry was a candle that had burned continuously throughout the time that the so-called Infidels had been in power. The first Mass of the Reconquest was said here, and later a Mudéjar apse was added (now shielded by glass). After you've looked at the chapel, the gardener will take you across the ramparts to climb to the top of the Puerta del Sol, a 12th-century Mudéjar gatehouse. ✆ *Tip to gardener.* ☉ *Any reasonable hr.*

61   **Casa de El Greco** (El Greco's House). This tourist magnet is on the property that belonged to Peter the Cruel's Jewish treasurer, Samuel Levi. The artist once lived in a house owned by this man, but it's pure conjecture that he lived in this particular one. The interior, done up in the late 19th century to resemble a "typical" house of El Greco's time, is a pure fake, albeit a pleasant one. The once-drab museum next door is currently being restored and remodeled; one of the few El Grecos currently on display is a large panorama of Toledo, with the Hospital of Tavera in the foreground. ✉ *C. Samuel Levi 3,* ☎ *925/224046.* ✆ *200 ptas.* ☉ *Tues.–Sat. 10–2 and 4–6, Sun. 10–2.*

57   **Cathedral.** Jorge Manuel Theotokópoulos was responsible for the cathedral's Mozarabic chapel, the elongated dome of which crowns the right-hand side of the west facade. The rest of this facade is mainly early-15th-century and features a depiction of the Virgin presenting her robe to Toledo's patron saint, the Visigothic Ildefonsus.

Enter the cathedral from the 14th-century cloisters to the left of the west facade. The primarily 13th-century architecture was inspired by the great Gothic cathedrals of France, such as Chartres; the squat proportions, however, give it a Spanish feel, as do the wealth and weight of the furnishings and the location of the elaborate choir in the center of the nave. Immediately to your right as you enter the building is a beautifully carved plateresque doorway by Covarrubias, marking the entrance to the Treasury. The latter houses a small Crucifixion by the Italian painter Cimabue and an extraordinarily intricate late-15th-century monstrance by Juan del Arfe, a silversmith of German descent; the ceiling is an excellent example of Mudéjar workmanship.

From here, walk around to the ambulatory, off the right side of which is a chapter house featuring a strange and quintessentially Spanish mixture of Italianate frescoes by Juan de Borgoña. In the middle of the ambulatory is a dazzling and famous example of baroque illusionism by Narciso Tomé, known as the *Transparente*, a blend of painting, stucco, and sculpture.

Finally, off the northern end of the ambulatory, you'll come to the sacristy, where you'll find a number of El Grecos, most notably the work known as *El Espolio* (Christ Being Stripped of his Raiment). One of

El Greco's earliest works in Toledo, it fell afoul of the Inquisition, which accused the artist of putting Christ on a lower level than some of the onlookers. El Greco was thrown into prison, and there his career might have ended had he not by this stage formed friendships with some of Toledo's more moderate clergy. Before leaving the sacristy, look up at the colorful and spirited late-baroque ceiling painting by the Italian Luca Giordano. ⌨ *500 ptas.* ☉ *Mon.–Sat. 10:30–1 and 3:30–6 (3:30–7 in summer), Sun. 10:30–1:30 and 4–6 (4–7 in summer).*

㊾ Hospital de Tavera. You'll find this hospital, Covarrubias's last work, outside the walls beyond Covarrubia's imposing Puerta de Bisagra, Toledo's main northern gate. Unlike the former Hospital of Santa Cruz, this complex is unfinished and slightly dilapidated, but it is nonetheless full of character and has an evocatively ramshackle museum in its southern wing, looked after by two exceptionally friendly and eccentric women. The most important work in the museum's miscellaneous collection is a painting by the 17th-century artist José Ribera. In the hospital's monumental chapel are El Greco's *Baptism of Christ* and the exquisitely carved marble tomb of Cardinal Tavera, the last work of Alonso de Berruguete. Descend into the crypt to experience some bizarre acoustical effects. ☎ *925/220451.* ⌨ *500 ptas.* ☉ *Daily 10–1:30 and 3:30–6.*

㊴ Museo de la Santa Cruz. One of the joys of this museum is its location in a beautiful Renaissance hospital with a stunning classical-plateresque facade. Unlike Toledo's other monuments, the museum is open all day without a break and is delightfully quiet in the early afternoon. The light and elegant interior has changed little since the 16th century, the main difference being that works of art have replaced the hospital beds; among the displays is El Greco's *Assumption* of 1613, the artist's last known work. A small **Museo de Arqueología** (Museum of Archaeology) has been arranged in and around the hospital's delightful cloister, off which you'll also find a beautifully decorated staircase by Alonso de Covarrubias. ✉ *C. de Cervantes 3,* ☎ *925/221036.* ⌨ *200 ptas.* ☉ *Mon. 10–2 and 4–6:30, Tues.–Sat. 10–6:30, Sun. 10–2.*

㊳ Plaza de Zocodover. The town's main square was built in the early 17th century as part of an unsuccessful attempt to impose a rigid geometry on the chaotic Moorish ground plan. Nearby, you'll find **Calle del Comercio,** the town's narrow and lively pedestrian thoroughfare, lined with bars and shops and shaded in the summer months by awnings suspended from the roofs of tall houses.

㊱ Puente de Alcántara. Here is the town's oldest bridge, Roman in origin. Next to the bridge is a heavily restored castle built after the Christian capture of 1085, and above this a vast and depressingly severe military academy, a typical example of Fascist architecture under Franco. The bridge is off the city's eastern peripheral road, just north of the New Bridge.

㊺ Puente de San Martín. A pedestrian bridge on the western edge of the town, the Puente de San Martín dates from 1203 and features splendid horseshoe arches.

㊽ San Juan de los Reyes. This convent church in western Toledo was erected by Ferdinand and Isabella to commemorate their victory at the battle of Toro in 1476 and was intended to be their burial place. The building is largely the work of Juan Guas, who considered it his masterpiece and asked to be buried here himself. Guas, one of the greatest exponents of the Gothic, or Isabelline, was an architect of prolific imagination and great decorative exuberance. In true plateresque fashion, the white interior is covered with inscriptions and heraldic motifs. ☎ *925/223802.* ▣ *150 ptas.* ☼ *Daily 10–1:45 and 3:30–5:45 (until 6:45 in summer).*

⑤⑧ San Román. In a virtually unspoiled part of Toledo is this early 13th-century Mudéjar church, with extensive remains of frescoes inside. It has been deconsecrated and now serves as the **Museo de los Concilios y de la Cultura Visigoda** (Museum of Visigothic Art), featuring statuary, manuscript illustrations, and delicate jewelry. ▣ *C. de San Clemente s/n,* ☎ *925/227872.* ▣ *100 ptas.* ☼ *Tues.–Sat. 10–2 and 4–6:30, Sun. 10–2.*

⑥③ Santa María la Blanca. Founded in 1203, Toledo's second synagogue is nearly two centuries older than the Tránsito Synagogue. The white interior features a forest of columns supporting capitals of the most enchanting filigree workmanship. Stormed in the early 15th century by a Christian mob led by St. Vincent Ferrer, the synagogue was later put to a variety of uses—as a carpenter's workshop, a store, a barracks, and a refuge for reformed prostitutes. ▣ *Calle Reyes Católicos 2,* ☎ *925/227257.* ▣ *150 ptas.* ☼ *Daily 10–1:45 and 3:30–5:45 (3:30–7 in summer).*

⑤⑨ Santo Domingo. A few minutes' walk north of San Román is this 16th-century convent church where you'll find the earliest of El Greco's Toledo paintings as well as the crypt where the artist is believed to be buried. The friendly nuns at the convent will show you around an odd little museum that includes documents bearing El Greco's signature. ▣ *Plaza Santo Domingo el Antiguo s/n,* ☎ *925/222930.* ▣ *150 ptas.* ☼ *Mon.–Sat. 11–1:30 and 4–7, Sun. 4–7 (weekends only in winter).*

⑥⓪ Santo Tomé. This is the home of El Greco's most famous painting, *The Burial of Count Orgaz.* If possible, arrive as soon as the building opens, as you may have to wait in line to get inside later on in the day, especially in summer. Adorned by an elegant Mudéjar tower, the chapel was specially built for its current purpose. The painting—the only El Greco to have been consistently admired over the centuries—portrays the benefactor of the church being buried with the posthumous assistance of St. Augustine and St. Stephen, who have miraculously appeared at the funeral to thank him for all the money he gave to religious institutions named after them. Though the count's burial took place in the 14th century, El Greco painted the onlookers in contemporary costumes and included people he knew; the boy in the foreground is one of El Greco's sons, and the sixth figure on the left is said to be the artist himself. ▣ *Plaza del Conde 1,* ☎ *925/210209.* ▣ *150 ptas.* ☼ *Daily 10–1:45 and 3:30–5:45 (3:30–6:45 in summer).*

⑥② Sinagoga del Tránsito (Tránsito Synagogue). Financed by Samuel Levi, this 14th-century rectangular structure is plain on the outside, but the inside walls are sumptuously covered with intricate Mudéjar decoration, as well as Hebraic inscriptions glorifying God, Peter the Cruel, and Levi himself. It is said that Levi imported cedars from Lebanon for the building's construction as did Solomon when he built the Temple in Jerusalem. Adjoining the main hall is the **Museo Sefardí** (Sephardic Museum), a small museum of Jewish culture in Spain. ▣ *C. Samuel Levi s/n,* ☎ *925/223665.* ▣ *400 ptas., free Sun.* ☼ *Tues.–Sat. 10–1:45 and 4–5:45, Sun. 10–1:45.*

Dining and Lodging

$$$ ✕ **Asador Adolfo.** Only a few steps from the cathedral, but discreetly
 ★   hidden away and making no attempt to attract the tourist trade, this is unquestionably the best and most dignified restaurant in town. The

modern main entrance shields an old and intimate interior featuring in its principal dining room a wood-beam ceiling with extensive painted decoration from the 14th century. The emphasis is on freshness of produce and traditional Toledan dishes, but there is also much innovation. Especially tasty to start is the *tempura de flor de calabacín* (zucchini blossom tempura in a saffron sauce); a flavorful entrée is the *solomillo de cerdo* (pork loin with wild mushrooms and black truffles). Finish with a Toledan specialty, *delicias de mazapán* (marzipan), which is cooked here in a wooden oven and is the finest and lightest in the whole town. ⊠ *Granada 6 and Hombre de Palo 7*, ☎ *925/227321. Reservations essential. AE, DC, MC, V. No dinner Sun.*

$$ ✕ **Hierbabuena.** Here you can dine on an enclosed Moorish patio with plenty of natural light, at tables covered with crocheted tablecloths. The food is just as inviting as the setting, and the prices are surprisingly reasonable. The menu changes with the season; possibilities include artichokes stuffed with seafood and steak with blue-cheese sauce. ⊠ *Cristo de la Luz 9*, ☎ *925/223463. AE, DC, MC, V. No dinner Sun. Closed Mon.*

$–$$ ✕ **La Ria.** Down a tiny alley in front of Santo Tomé (☞ *above*), this little tapas bar serves generous helpings of fresh seafood. English is not spoken, but the linguistic effort is worth it. ⊠ *Callejón Bodegones 9*, ☎ *925/252532. No credit cards.*

$–$$ ✕ **Restaurant Maravilla.** With a quaint atmosphere and modestly priced menus, Maravilla is a great choice. Specialties include Toledan preparations of partridge or quail and a variety of seafood dishes. ⊠ *Plaza Barrio Rey 7*, ☎ *925/228582 or 925/228317. AE, DC, MC, V.*

$$–$$$ ✕🏠 **Hostal del Cardenal.** Built in the 18th century as a summer palace for Cardinal Lorenzana, this is a quiet and beautiful hotel whose light-colored rooms are decorated with old furniture. Some rooms overlook the hotel's enchanting wooded garden, which lies at the foot of the town's walls. From here it's hard to believe that the main road to Madrid is not far off. The restaurant has a longstanding reputation and is very popular with tourists; the setting is beautiful, and both the food and service are good. The dishes are mainly local, and in season you'll find delicious asparagus and strawberries from Aranjuez. ⊠ *Paseo Recaredo 24, 45004*, ☎ *925/224900*, 🖷 *925/222991. 27 rooms. Restaurant. AE, DC, MC, V.*

$$$ ✕🏠 **Hotel Alfonso VI.** Smack in the middle of the historic district, this hotel offers great views of the city from its summer terrace. The rooms are modern, clean, and inviting; the restaurant is decorated in the ubiquitous Mudéjar style and serves delicious food. ⊠ *General Moscardo 2, 45001*, ☎ *925/222600*, 🖷 *925/214458. 85 rooms. Restaurant. AE, MC, V.*

$$$$ 🏠 **Parador Nacional Conde de Orgaz.** This modern building on Toledo's outskirts blends well with its rural surroundings and has an unbeatable panorama of the town. The architecture and furnishings, emphasizing brick and wood, nod to the traditional Toledan style. ⊠ *Paseo Emperador s/n, 45001*, ☎ *925/221850*, 🖷 *925/225166. 77 rooms. Pool. AE, DC, MC, V.*

$$$ 🏠 **Hotel Pintor El Greco.** Next door to the famous painter's house-museum, this friendly hotel occupies what was once a 17th-century bakery. Extensive renovation has resulted in a light and modern interior with some antique touches, such as exposed brick vaulting. ⊠ *Alamillos del Transito 13, 45002*, ☎ *925/214250*, 🖷 *925/215819. 33 rooms. AE, DC, MC, V.*

Shopping

Toledo's province is the most renowned crafts center in Castile, if not all of Spain. Here, the Moors established **silverwork, damascene** (metalwork inlaid with gold or silver), **embroidery,** and **pottery** traditions that are still very much alive. Next to Toledo's church of San Juan de los Reyes is a turn-of-the-century art school that teaches these various crafts and helps to maintain standards. For cheaper pottery, you're better off stopping at the large roadside emporia on the outskirts of town, on the main road to Madrid. Better still, go to **Talavera la Reina,** 76 km (47 mi) west of Toledo, where most of this pottery is made. The finest embroidery in the province comes from **Oropesa** and **Lagartera.**

AROUND MADRID A TO Z

Arriving and Departing

By Plane

The only international airport in either Old or New Castile is Madrid's Barajas. Valladolid Airport has flights to Barcelona. For information on airlines serving Madrid, *see* Madrid A to Z *in* Chapter 2.

Getting Around

By Bus

Bus connections between Madrid and Castile are excellent. Two of the most popular services go to Toledo (1 hour) and Segovia (1½ hours); buses to the former leave every half hour from the **Estación del Sur** (✉ C. Canaría 17, ☎ 91/468–4200), to the latter every hour from **La Sepulvedana** (✉ Paseo de la Florida 11, ☎ 91/527–9537). Buses to Soria (3 hours) and Burgo de Osma (2½ hours) leave from **Continental Auto** (✉ C. Alenza 20, ☎ 91/533–0400), while **Auto Res** (✉ Plaza Conde de Casal 6, ☎ 91/551–7200) runs services to Cuenca (2 hours, 50 minutes) and Salamanca (3 hours). Services between the provincial towns are not as good as those to and from Madrid; if you're traveling between, say, Cuenca and Toledo, you will find it quicker to return to Madrid and make your way from there. Reservations are rarely necessary; if demand arises, additional buses are usually called into service.

By Car

A series of major roads with extensive stretches of divided highway—the N I, II, III, IV, and V—radiate from Madrid in every direction and make transport to the outlying towns easy. If possible, however, avoid returning to Madrid on these roads at the end of a weekend or on a public holiday. The side roads vary in quality and are rarely of the high standard that you find in, say, provincial France, but they constitute one of the great pleasures of traveling around the Castilian countryside by car—you are constantly coming across unexpected architectural delights and wild and spectacular vistas. Above all, you rarely come across other tourists.

By Train

All the main towns covered in this section are accessible by train from Madrid, and it's quite possible to visit each in separate day trips. There are commuter trains from Madrid to Segovia (2 hours), Alcalá de Henares (45 minutes), Guadalajara (1 hour), and Toledo (1½ hours). Train travel in Spain has improved in recent years, but it's still often faster to reach your destination by bus. Trains to Toledo depart from Madrid's **Atocha** station; trains to Salamanca depart from **Chamartín** station; and both stations serve Ávila, Segovia, El Escorial, and Siguenza, although Chamartín may offer more frequent service to some. The one important town that can be reached only by train is Sigüenza. Check with **RENFE** for details (☎ 91/328–9020).

Contacts and Resources

Car Rental

It's often cheaper to rent cars in advance, while still at home, through international firms such as Hertz and Avis (☞ Car Rental *in* the Gold Guide). Spain's leading car-rental agency is **Atesa** (⊠ Infanta Mercedes 90, Madrid, ☎ 91/571–2145).

Fishing

The most common fish in Castile's rivers are trout, pike, black bass, and blue carp; among the main trout rivers are the Eresma, Alto Duero, Júcar, Jarama, Manzanares, Tajo, and Tormes. Madrid's **provincial office** (⊠ Princesa 3, ☎ 91/580–1653) has more information.

Golf

There are golf courses at Alcalá de Henares, Salamanca, and numerous smaller places immediately surrounding Madrid. For further information, contact the **Real Federación Española de Golf** (⊠ Capitán Haya 9, Madrid, 28020, ☎ 91/555–2682).

Guided Tours

Current information on city tours can be obtained from the local tourist offices, where you can also ask about hiring guides. You should be especially wary of local guides in Ávila and Toledo; they can be quite ruthless in trying to impose their services. If you join one, do not buy goods in the shops he takes you to; the prices are probably inflated, and the guide gets a kickback.

For a special art tour of Castile, including Salamanca, contact **Prospect Music & Art Tours Ltd.** (⊠ 10 Barley Mow Passage, Chiswick, London W4 4PH, ☎ 0181/995–2163). At the same address is by far the best of Great Britain's cultural-tour specialists, **Martin Randall Travel** (☎ 0181/994–6477), which offers an excellent five-day trip that includes Madrid and Toledo.

Visitor Information

The main provincial tourist office in **Madrid** is on the Plaza de España (⊠ Princesa 1, ☎ 91/541–2325). Useful information and excellent town plans can be obtained from the following local offices:

Alcalá de Henares (⊠ Callejón de Santa María, ☎ 91/889–2694), **Aranjuez** (⊠ Plaza San Antonio 9, ☎ 91/891–0427), **Ávila** (⊠ Plaza de la Catedral 4, ☎ 920/211387), **Ciudad Real** (⊠ Avda. Alarcos 21, ☎ 926/212925), **Ciudad Rodrigo** (⊠ Puerta de Amayuelas 5, ☎ 923/460561), **Cuenca** (⊠ Glorieta González Valencia 2, ☎ 969/178800), **Guadalajara** (⊠ Plaza Mayor 7, ☎ 949/211626), **Salamanca** (⊠ Casa de las Conchas, Rúa Mor s/n, ☎ 923/268571), **Segovia** (⊠ Plaza Mayor 10, ☎ 921/460334), **Sigüenza** (⊠ Plaza Mayor 1, ☎ 949/393251), **Soria** (⊠ Plaza Ramón y Cajal s/n, ☎ 975/212052), **Toledo** (⊠ Puerta de Bisagra s/n, ☎ 925/220843), **Valladolid** (⊠ Plaza de Zorrilla s/n, ☎ 983/351801), and **Zamora** (⊠ C. Santa Clara 20, ☎ 980/531845).

4 León, Galicia, and Asturias

In Spain's dense, green, and stormy northwest, the Celtic-flavored provinces of León, Galicia, and Asturias mix medieval villages with breathtaking mountains and quiet beaches. Follow the pilgrimage route of St. James; take refuge in the awesome cathedral at Santiago de Compostela; sip hard cider in Villaviciosa; stand peacefully on a shore so perilous that it's been called the Coast of Death, at La Coruña; and feast everywhere on fresh seafood.

DIVERSE AND FAR-FLUNG, Spain's most Atlantic region contains the country's wildest mountain scenery, in the Picos de Europa, and most pristine beaches, in the coves of the Lugo coast. Stretching from Galicia's ramshackle countryside to Castile's lonesome plains, near León, it incorporates both verdant wilds and heavy industry.

By Deborah Luhrman

Updated by Annie Ward

Northwestern Spain is all about green, rainy landscapes, stretching from your feet to the horizon. Ancient granite buildings wear a blanket of moss, and even the *horreos* (granaries) are built on stilts above the damp ground. Swirling fog and heavy mist help maintain local folk tales of the supernatural. The *gaita* (bagpipe) replace the guitar, evidence of an ancient Celtic legacy, and a local folk dance, the *muñeira*, resembles a combination highland fling and Irish jig.

Though Galicia, Asturias, and León are off the beaten track for many foreigners, they are not undiscovered: Spanish families flock to the cool northern beaches and mountains each summer. The city of Santiago de Compostela, whose cathedral is said to house the remains of the apostle St. James, has drawn pilgrims and travelers for more than 900 years. Today's route to Santiago is the same one detailed in the first guidebook ever published, the Calixtus Codex of 1130. Because so many medieval pilgrims made this journey to Santiago, the northwest is dotted with churches, shrines, and hospitals. Indeed, most man-made sights in León and Galicia owe their existence to the pilgrimage route.

Asturias, north of the main pilgrim trail, has always maintained a slightly separate identity, isolated from the rest of the country by a ring of high mountains. This is the only part of Spain never conquered by the Moors, so there is little Arab influence in the architecture. It was from their mountain base at Covadonga that the Christians won their first decisive battle against the Moors and launched the Reconquest of Spain, which, though it took some 700 years, made Spain one of the world's most uniformly Catholic countries, a legacy that remains.

Note that in the Gallego (Galician) dialect, the Castilian *plaza* (town square) is *praza*, and the Castilian *playa* (beach) is *praya*. Gallego is actually an offshoot of Portuguese, and sounds very different from Spanish.

Pleasures and Pastimes

Beaches

After allowing unbridled development to tarnish the Costa del Sol, the Spanish government is now promoting the attractions of northern beaches. The weather in this region is not reliable, but if the sun comes out, try one of the following beaches: Llanes, Ribadesella, Cudillero, Santa Ana at Cadavedo, Luarca, Tapia de Casariego, Muros, Noya, El Grove, Islas Cies, Boa, and Testal. Not recommended because of industrial pollution are San Lorenzo, in Gijón; the beaches near Avilés; and the beaches of the Rías Bajas. There are more than enough pristine beaches in the area, however, to accommodate the growing interest in scuba diving.

Canoes and Kayaking

Ribadesella, in Asturias, is the white-water capital of Spain. The season highlight is an international race, in August, which starts at Arriondas and finishes in Ribadesella. There are several other navigable waterways; the tourist office can help you plan a route.

Dining

Galicia and Asturias are famous throughout Spain for their seafood. The quality of the fish is so high that chefs frown on drowning inherent flavors in heavy sauces or overly pungent seasonings; expect simplicity rather than spice. Specialties include *merluza a la Gallega* (steamed hake in Galician paprika sauce) and *merluza a la sidra* (steamed hake in a tangy Asturian cider sauce). *Vieira* (scallops), the symbol of the pilgrimage to Santiago, are popular in Galicia, where it's also common to find entire bars serving nothing but wine and *pulpo a feira* (boiled and broiled octopus) or *berberechos* (cockles). Ham lovers should try *lacón con grelos* (baked shoulder of pork served with sautéed turnip tops). Cheeses are delicious all over the region; try the fragrant *queso de Cabrales* (blue cheese from Asturias) and the Galician *queso de tetilla* (a creamy, semisoft cheese in the form of a woman's breast), delicious with *membrillo* (a fruit spread made from quince) for dessert. In Asturias, salmon and trout from local rivers are a treat. The region is rightly famous for hearty stews; in Asturias try *fabada* (butter beans and sausage), and in Galicia sample *caldo Gallego* (stew of potatoes, cabbage, chickpeas, and meat broth). Savory fish or meat pies called *empanadas* are native to Galicia and can be eaten out of the hand like a sandwich. In Asturias, try *entrecote con queso cabrales* (a hearty combination of steak topped by a sauce made with the principality's famed blue cheese). The province of León specializes in *cordero asado* (roast lamb), *afumados* (assorted smoked meats), *morcillas* (varieties of sausages), and *lechón* (suckling pig) and produces a sparkling rosé wine called Bierzo, similar to the acidic Galician Ribeiro, which is often served in a ceramic bowl rather than a glass. The best Galician wine is the smooth, crisp, white Albariño, while Asturias is famous for its *sidra* (hard cider), served either carbonated or still. Brandy aficionados should try Galicia's *queimada* (which superstitious Galicians claim is a witches' brew), made of potent, grappa-like *orujo* mixed with lemon peel and sugar in an earthenware bowl, then set aflame and stirred until the desired amount of alcohol is burned off. Although much of this region is rural and remote, restaurant prices are not substantially lower than those in the rest of the country, especially in Asturias and Santiago.

CATEGORY	COST*
$$$$	over 6,500 ptas.
$$$	4,500–6,500 ptas.
$$	3,000–4,500 ptas.
$	under 3,000 ptas.

per person for a three-course meal, excluding drinks, service, and tax

Fiestas

JANUARY

Visitors to Tordesillas can see the ritual rooster sacrifice during the feast of St. Vincent the Martyr. The Festa do Chourizo en Sant Anton de Abedes (St. Anthony of Abedes Sausage Festival), held January 17 in Verin (Orense), includes a parade and sausage festival in honor of the local patron saint. The Procesión dos Fachos (Procession of the Scarecrows, January 20), in Castro Caldelas (Orense), has a torchlight procession commemorating the village's survival of a cholera outbreak in 1753.

MARCH

The Fiesta del Queso (Cheese Festival), in Aruza (La Coruña) the first week of March, celebrates folklore and food, and includes a cheese contest.

APRIL

During the last week in April, in the cloister at León's San Isidoro, the town councilors and ecclesiastical authorities bow to each other ceremoniously. To the delight of all present, this is a reminder of an ancient dispute over the distribution of power between the clergy and the civil authorities.

MAY

During San Isidoro Labrador, May 15, in Cacabelos (León), villagers parade through town on foot and in decorated horse-drawn carriages, carrying flower garlands in honor of the workers' saint.

JULY

In Pontevedra, there's the Rapa das Bestas (Taming of the Beasts—the breaking of wild horses) on July 7–8. An apple-scented cider festival is held mid-July in Nava. July 25 brings a shepherds' festival to both Cangas de Onís and Covadonga National Park, with regional dances and bagpipe music. Día de Santiago (St. James Day) is celebrated on July 25 in Santiago; fireworks light the festivities, and mass is celebrated with the *botafumeiro* incense burner.

AUGUST

The Albariño Wine Festival takes place in Cambados the first Sunday in August.

SEPTEMBER

The Procesión de las Mortajas (Procession of the Shrouded), in Pobra do Carmiñal (La Coruña), takes place on the third Sunday in September. Following a tradition that dates from the 15th century, those who have been cured of ailments, bad luck, or bad loves prepare open coffins, lie in them, and are carried in a procession around the village.

OCTOBER

At the Festa do Marisco (Seafood Festival), the second week in October, the town of O Grove celebrates the bounty of shellfish and seafood. Eat lobster, mussels, clams, *percebes* (goose barnacles that look like tiny elephant feet but are, in fact, sugar-sweet), spiny *néora* crabs, shrimp, and more.

OTHER FIESTAS

During Carnival, León and nearby La Bañeza are popular for Castilian pre-Lenten partying. During Semana Santa (Holy Week), in Viveiro, you can watch a barefoot procession of flagellants illuminated by hundreds of candles held by spectators and participants.

Lodging

The state-run parador hotels have cornered the market on charming places to stay in this region. Galicia has nine paradors, three in elegant manor houses and two in old fortresses. León has one of the finest, in a stunning converted convent. Check descriptions before choosing a parador; some are in modern buildings. Most quality hotels are high-rises geared toward business travelers or tour groups; some rooms, even in fine hotels, can be suffocatingly small. Reservations are important in high season, May–October, but not essential the rest of the year. Another possibility is to stay in a monastery; many provide simple lodgings at very reasonable prices in some more rural areas. Contact the nearest Tourist Office of Spain for a list.

CATEGORY	COST*
$$$$	over 16,500 ptas.
$$$	12,500–16,500 ptas.
$$	8,500–12,500 ptas.
$	under 8,500 ptas.

All prices are for a standard double room, excluding tax and breakfast.

Skiing

The three small ski areas in this region cater mostly to families and residents. The largest is San Isidoro, in the Cantabrian Mountains, with one chairlift and 12 slopes. Just east of there is Valgrande Pajares, with two chairlifts and eight slopes. West of Orense, in Galicia, Manzaneda has one chairlift and seven slopes. Valgrande Pajares and Manzaneda also have cross-country skiing.

Exploring León, Galicia, and Asturias

Begin your visit in classically Castilian León, with its austere architecture and Gothic stained-glass cathedral. Leaving the city, modern-day defenders (or admirers) of the faith can head west toward Galicia and pick up the pilgrims' trail along the ancient Camino de Santiago (Way of St. James), ticking off the well-marked stops along the way: Astorga; the isolated, thatched-roof hamlet of O Cebreiro; Samos; and Sarria. Follow the *camino* to Santiago de Compostela, and then travel west to the beach resort of Muros, with arcaded streets, and south to Pontevedra and the fishing towns of the Rías Bajas. Venture north again to the thriving port of La Coruña before moving east to Oviedo, capital of emerald-green Asturias, with its apple orchards, cider bars, and some of Spain's most jagged mountains, the Picos de Europa.

Numbers in the text correspond to numbers in the margin and on the León, Galicia, and Asturias and Santiago de Compostela maps.

Great Itineraries

The best way to explore the north is by car. It takes only a few days for this part of Spain to cast its spell; five days would be enough to get the flavor of each of the three regions. Seven days would allow for more leisurely explorations of the main towns and cities combined with stops in smaller villages. Ten days would allow relaxed landloping through scenic countryside and villages where time appears to have stopped.

No matter how many days you spend here, be prepared to fall in love with this magical region. In the Galician dialect they call the feeling *morriña,* an indescribable longing for a person or place just out of reach.

IF YOU HAVE 5 DAYS

⛨ **León** ① makes a good starting point. This elegant Castilian capital combines the buzz of a modern-day city with the flavor of centuries past. On day two, follow the Camino de Santiago pilgrims' route toward Santiago. Head for **Astorga** ②, whose Archbishop's Palace was designed by Gaudí; then step back into the 17th century in the nearby stone village of **Castrillo de los Polvazares** ③. Wend your way through the hilly countryside past **Ponferrada** ④, stopping to admire the 13th-century Castillo de los Templarios (Templar's Castle) on the edge of town, and continue to ⛨ **Villafranca del Bierzo** ⑤, a medieval village in León's wine country. Day three will take you through lovely small towns along the pilgrims' route to ⛨ **Santiago de Compostela** - ⑩–⑰; spend the night there, and on day four, explore the soaring Romanesque cathedral, plazas, and old town. Then drive north to ⛨ **La Coruña** ㉑, one of Spain's busiest ports. Admire the windowed, wooden balconies along the waterfront of this Ciudad de Cristal (City of Glass), and visit the Torre de Hercules, the world's oldest functioning Roman lighthouse. The next day, head north for the coast and some of the country's loveliest beaches (and, unfortunately, slowest roads), stopping for a stroll around the ancient walled town of **Viveiro** ㉔. Continue on to Asturias, stopping in **Luarca** ㉞, a cozy village in a cove, and the lively coastal city of **Gijón** ㊱. End your tour by driving south to 🏨 **Oviedo** ㉟, the provincial capital.

IF YOU HAVE 7 DAYS

Spend day one exploring 🏨 **León** ①. Next morning, take off for the Camino de Santiago. On your way, admire the 13th-century Orbigo Bridge where Quiñones made his last stand. Set your compass for **Astorga** ②, with recently unearthed Roman ruins and Gaudí's fantastic Archbishop's Palace; the nearby ex-muleteer town of **Castrillo de los Polvazares** ③; and medieval 🏨 **Villafranca del Bierzo** ⑤, once home to Grand Inquisitor Torquemada. On day three, continue west through towns dear to pilgrims: the medieval ghost town of **O Cebreiro** ⑥, with its round thatched-roof huts; Samos; Sarria; **Portomarín** ⑦; **Vilar de Donas** ⑧; **Leboreiro** ⑨; and on to 🏨 **Santiago de Compostela** ⑩–⑰. A UNESCO World Heritage Site, Santiago will be your base for the next two nights. The next day, visit the impressive cathedral, wander through the old town and visit a museum or two, and make an excursion to nearby **Padrón** ⑲, the birthplace of poet Rosalía de Castro, one of Galicia's literary heroines. On day five, drive north about 45 minutes to 🏨 **La Coruña** ㉑; on the way, visit **Pazo de Oca** ⑱, a restored manor house, and see how wealthy Galicians lived. La Coruña is a lively, medium-size port city with a small-town atmosphere; see the sights and feast on shellfish. The next day head up to the coast, driving through picturesque **Betanzos** ⑳ and **Mondoñedo** ㉓, one of the capitals of ancient Galicia. Along the coast, you'll come to 🏨 **Ribadeo** ㉕, one of the smallest and most beautiful towns around and the medieval seat of the local aristocracy; it has a charming parador and exceptional views of the surrounding cliffs. Day seven brings you to the Asturian seaside towns of **Luarca** ㉞, Avilés, and **Gijón** ㊱, then inland to 🏨 **Oviedo** ㉟, capital of the principality and the onetime capital of Christian Spain. From there, head to nearby **Cangas de Onís** ㊴ and the famous 8th-century shrine of **Covadonga** ㊵, considered the birthplace of Spain.

When to Tour León, Galicia, and Asturias

The most popular and significant festivals take place during the pre-Lenten revels of Carnival (dates vary but generally fall in the end of February or beginning of March) and Easter's Semana Santa (Holy Week). But one town or another will be having a fair or festival just about any week of the year (☞ Fiestas *in* Pleasures and Pastimes, *above*).

Summer is best for swimming and enjoying water sports. Many consider spring and fall the ideal time to explore, since winters can be bitterly cold (León), or rainy (Galicia and Asturias) to the point of saturation—not for nothing is this region called Green Spain.

The northwest is still relatively unknown to most American travelers. This can be exhilarating or disconcerting, depending on your sense of adventure.

THE CAMINO DE SANTIAGO

In the Middle Ages, Santiago de Compostela, where the apostle St. James is said to be buried, was considered the third-most-important shrine in the Christian world, after Jerusalem and Rome. Making the difficult pilgrimage here all but ensured the faithful a spot in heaven. At peak periods in the 12th century, as many as 2 million people a year traveled to Santiago from all over Europe. The route was crowded with highway thieves; gallant knights, who swore to protect the pilgrims; and innkeepers, who grew wealthy in the pilgrim trade. There were even souvenir hawkers back then, providing the scallop shells that pilgrims wore as a symbol of St. James, a fisherman.

The main pilgrimage route traverses the Pyrenees at Roncesvalles and crosses northern Spain to Santiago. Picking up the Way of St. James in León and following it to Santiago will give you plenty to see.

León

❶ *333 km (207 mi) northwest of Madrid, 334 km (208 mi) east of La Coruña, 277 km (172 mi) east of Santiago de Compostela.*

Old, cultural León, capital of the province of Castilla y León (Castile and León), sits on the banks of the Benesga River in the high plains of Old Castile. Historians say that the name of the city, which was founded as a permanent camp for the Roman legions in AD 70, has nothing to do with the proud lion that has been its emblem for centuries but is instead a corruption of the Roman word *legio* (legion).

The capital of Christian Spain was moved south to León from Oviedo in 914 as the Reconquest spread, launching the city's richest era. Walls went up around the old Roman town, and you can still see parts of the 6-ft-thick ramparts in the middle of the modern city.

Today, León is a wealthy provincial capital and prestigious university town with a cosmopolitan flavor. The wide avenues of western León are lined with modern boutiques, while the twisting alleys of the half-timbered old town hide the bars, bookstores, and *chocolaterías* most popular with students.

★ León is proudest of its soaring Gothic **cathedral,** on the Plaza de Regla, whose flying buttresses are built with more windows than stone. The front of the cathedral is decorated with three weather-worn, arched doorways, the middle one adorned with slender statues of the apostles.

Begun in 1205, the cathedral contains 125 stained-glass windows plus three giant rose windows. The glass casts bejeweled shafts of light throughout the lofty interior; a clear glass door on the choir gives an unobstructed view of the altar and the apse windows. You'll see little 13th-century faces looking at you amid a kaleidoscope of colors from the lower-level windows. The cathedral also contains the sculpted tomb of King Ordoño II, who moved the capital of Christian Spain to León. In the **museum,** look for the carved-wood Mudéjar archives, with a letter of the alphabet above each door. It's one of the world's oldest file cabinets. ⊠ *Plaza de Regla,* ☎ *987/230060.* 🎫 *Museum 450 ptas.* ☉ *Weekdays 9:30–1 and 4–6, Sat. 10–1.*

The 19th-century **Farmacia Marino,** opened in 1827, offers a glimpse into a Spanish drugstore of yore. The ceiling is richly carved, as are the walls, which include a niche for each apothecary jar. Only the medicines have changed since the place opened. It's down the street from the cathedral, on Avenida Generalísimo Franco.

The arcaded **Plaza Mayor** in the heart of León's old town is surrounded by simple, half-timbered houses. On Wednesday and Saturday, the plaza bustles with farmers selling produce and cheeses. Look at their feet; many still wear wooden shoes called *madreñas,* which are raised on three heels, two in the front and one in the back.

As you're wandering the old town, look down occasionally and you just might notice small **brass scallop shells** set into the street. These were installed by the town government to mark the path for modern-day pilgrims on their way to Santiago.

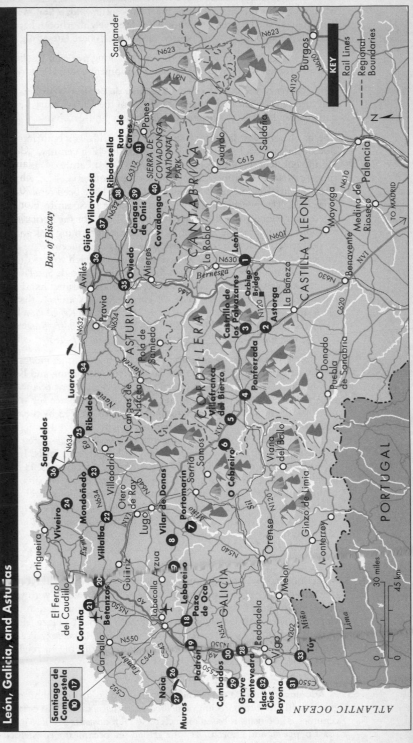

León, Galicia, and Asturias

Santiago de Compostela
10 — 17

KEY
Rail Lines
Regional Boundaries

Most of León's tapas bars are in the 12th-century **Plaza San Martín.** This area is called the Barrio Húmedo, or Wet Neighborhood, because of the large amount of wine poured (and spilled) here late at night.

☺ If you're traveling with children, León has a long **park** on the banks of the Bernesga River, with playground equipment every 100 ft or so.

In the center of the modern city is the **Casa de Botines,** a multigabled and turreted behemoth designed at the end of the 19th century by that controversial Catalan, Antonio Gaudí. It now houses a bank.

★ The basilica of **San Isidoro el Real,** on Calle Cid, was built into the side of the city wall in 1063 and rebuilt in the 12th century. Adjoining the basilica, the **Panteón de los Reyes** (Royal Pantheon) is sometimes called the Sistine Chapel of Romanesque art. The vibrant 12th-century frescoes on the pillars and ceiling have been remarkably preserved. The pantheon was the first building in Spain to be decorated with scenes from the New Testament. Look for the agricultural calendar painted on one archway, showing which farming task should be performed each month. Twenty-three kings and queens were once buried here, but their tombs were destroyed by French troops during the Napoleonic Wars. Treasures in the adjacent **Museo de San Isidoro** include a jewel-encrusted agate chalice, a richly illustrated handwritten Bible, and a huge collection of polychrome wood statues of the Virgin Mary. ⊠ *Plaza de San Isidoro,* ☎ *987/229608.* ▣ *Royal Pantheon 350 ptas.* ☉ *July–Aug., Mon.–Sat. 10–1:30 and 3–8:30, Sun. 9–2; Sept.–June, Tues.–Sat. 10–1:30 and 4–6:30, Sun. 10–1:30.*

The sumptuous **Antiguo Monasterio de San Marcos,** a former monastery, is now a five-star hotel, the **Hostal San Marcos** (☞ Dining and Lodging, *below*). Originally a home for knights of the Order of Santiago, who patrolled the Way of St. James, and a stopping place for weary pilgrims, the monastery you see today was begun in 1513 by the head of the order, King Ferdinand, who felt that knights deserved something better. Finished at the height of the Renaissance, the building's plateresque facade is a sea of small sculptures, many of knights and lords. Inside is an elegant staircase and a cloister full of medieval statues. Have a drink in the bar; the tiny windows are the original defensive slits. The building also houses the **Museo Arqueológico** (Museum of Archaeology), famous for its 11th-century ivory Carrizo crucifix. ⊠ *Plaza de San Marcos,* ☎ *987/245061 or 987/236405.* ▣ *Museum 200 ptas.* ☉ *May–Sept., Tues.–Sat. 10–2 and 5–8:30, Sun. 10–2; Oct.–Apr., Tues.–Sat. 10–2 and 4:30–8, Sun. 10–2.*

Bars and Cafés

Most of León's liveliest hangouts are clustered in the **Plaza Mayor** and the 12th-century **Plaza San Martín.** The streets are packed with tapas bars; in the Plaza Mayor, you might want to start your taste tour at Universal, Mesón de Don Quijote, Casa Benito, or Bar La Plaza Mayor. In the Plaza San Martín, have a *pinchito* (tidbit) at the cozy Prada a Tope bar, which serves the region's Bierzo wine out of a big barrel; Rancho Chico; Nuevo Racimo de Oro; or La Bicha.

Dining and Lodging

$$ ✕ **Adonias.** Enter on the ground-floor bar and go up one flight to the green, softly lit dining room, furnished with rustic tables and colorful ceramics. The cuisine is based on such regional foodstuffs as cured hams, roast peppers, and chorizo. Try the grilled sea bream, the roast suckling pig, and the homemade banana pudding with chocolate sauce. ⊠ *Santa Nonia 16,* ☎ *987/206768. AE, DC, MC, V. Closed last 2 wks of July.*

$$ ✕ **Casa Pozo.** This longtime favorite is across from city hall on the historic Plaza de San Marcelo. Past the noisy bar, the bright dining rooms are furnished with heavy Castilian furniture. Owner Gabriel del Pozo Alvarez, called Pin, supervises the busy kitchen and attentive waitstaff. Specialties include fresh peas with ham, roast lamb, and deep-fried hake. ⊠ *Plaza de San Marcelo 15,* ☎ *987/237103. AE, DC, V.*

$$ ✕ **Nuevo Racimo de Oro.** On the second floor of a ramshackle, 12th-century tavern in the heart of the old town, this restaurant specializes in roast suckling lamb cooked in a wood-fired clay oven. Try the spicy *sopa de ajo* (Castilian garlic soup), served in a wooden bowl with a wooden spoon, or the medieval-style spinach with raisins and pine nuts. ⊠ *Plaza San Martín 8,* ☎ *987/214767. MC, V. Closed Tues. No dinner Sun.*

$$$$ ✕⌂ **Hotel San Marcos.** This magnificent parador occupies a restored
★   16th-century monastery built by King Ferdinand to shelter pilgrims walking the *camino*. The plateresque facade is longer than a football field—the building also houses a church and an archaeology museum. Rooms have antiques and high-quality reproductions. One wing is modern, with a pool; if you want medieval luxury, ask for a room in the old section. The elegant dining room, overlooking the Bernesga River, serves braised baby lamb chops, sole with raisin and pine-nut sauce, *congrío con patatas al arriero* (river eel stewed with potatoes), and *cecina* (smoked beef). Top off the meal with *leche quemada* (a light egg custard topped with caramelized sugar) or *arroz con leche* (rice pudding). ⊠ *Plaza de San Marcos 7, 24001,* ☎ *987/237300,* ℻ *987/233458. 230 rooms. 2 restaurants, bar, beauty salon, parking. AE, DC, MC, V.*

$ ✕⌂ **Hotel Riosol.** This modern high-rise is across the river from town, not far from the train station. The comfortable, carpeted rooms, decorated with black-lacquer furniture and gold wallpaper, are popular with business travelers. ⊠ *Avda. de Palencia 3, 24009,* ☎ *987/216850,* ℻ *987/216997. 137 rooms. Restaurant. AE, DC, MC, V.*

Shopping

ARTS AND CRAFTS

In Villar de Mazarife, 22 km (15 mi) west of León on the way to Astorga, **Monseñor** (⊠ Camino de León 21, ☎ 987/300338) paints adaptations of Roman archaeological finds and makes ceramic-tile reproductions of the frescoes in the Royal Pantheon. For fine yet funky gifts, visit **Tricosis** (⊠ Calle Mulhacín 3, ☎ 987/202953), a gallery opened by art students from the universities of Leon and Gijón, where colorful papier-mâché and experimental media form outstanding lamps, candleholders, vases, and frames.

FOOD

Tasty regional treats on which to blow your pesetas include roasted red peppers, potent brandy-soaked cherries, and candied chestnuts. You can buy these in food shops all over the city, or shop while "doing" tapas at **Prada a Tope** (⊠ Plaza San Martín 1), where they're packaged by the house.

En Route   Leaving León, follow signs to the N120 and head southwest. Stop to admire the 13th-century Orbigo Bridge, 23 km (14 mi) outside the city, where the knight Quiñones made his stand. Legend has it that Quiñones was the toughest *hombre* on the Way of St. James; in 1434, he staked out his turf on this bridge and for a month challenged every other knight who policed the route. You are now on the Camino de Santiago itself, marked with large signs for drivers and small signs for those who make the journey on foot.

Astorga

❷ *46 km (29 mi) southwest of León.*

Astorga, where the pilgrimage roads from France and Portugal merge, once boasted 22 **hospitals** to lodge and care for travelers. The only one left today is next to the cathedral. The **cathedral** itself is a huge 15th-century building with baroque decorations and four statues of St. James.

★ Astorga's drabness is relieved by the fairy-tale, neo-Gothic **Palacio Episcopal** (Archbishop's Palace), designed for a Catalan cleric by Gaudí just before the turn of the century. No expense was spared in creating this fanciful building, which houses the **Museo del Camino** (Museum of the Way). The eclectic collection has folk items, such as the standard pilgrim costume—heavy black cloak, staff hung with gourds, and wide-brimmed hat bedecked with scallop shells—as well as outstanding contemporary Spanish art. ⊠ *Adjacent to cathedral,* ☎ 987/ 618882. ▨ *400 ptas.* ☼ *Apr.–Sept., daily 10–2 and 4–8; Oct.–Mar., Tues.–Sun. 11–2 and 3:30–6:30.*

Castillo de los Polvazares

❸ *51 km (32 mi) west of León, 5 km (3 mi) west of Astorga.*

A short walk or 15-minute drive from Astorga is Castillo de los Polvazares, a 17th-century village built on the site of a fortified Roman settlement. The city's 30-odd residents live in stone houses emblazoned with crests above their green doorways. Walk down the stone streets—there are no sidewalks and no asphalt—and look for storks' nests on top of the village church. Telephone wires are the only evidence of modernity.

Castillo de los Polvazares is in León's Maragatería region, whose people are believed to be a mixture of the ancient Celts and Phoenicians. This doughty group of traders resisted the Roman invasion of the Iberian Peninsula and reached the height of their prowess as muleteers in the 18th and 19th centuries (hence the wide doorways around town), transporting gold from the Americas to the royal court in Madrid.

Ponferrada

❹ *115 km (71 mi) west of León, 64 km (40 mi) west of Astorga; follow the Madrid–La Coruña highway, N VI, west.*

Ponferrada, nestled in a hilly region with beautiful, fertile valleys, is a mining and industrial center that gets its name from an iron toll bridge built by a local bishop in the 1100s. The tall, slim turrets of the 13th-century **Castillo de los Templarios** (Templars' Castle) on the western edge of town command sweeping views of the countryside and may once have been used by the knights of the Order of St. James to police the route. ⊠ *Florez Osorio 4,* ☎ *no phone.* ▨ *Free.* ☼ *Apr.–Sept., Wed.–Mon. 9–1 and 4–7; Oct.–Mar., Wed.–Mon. 9–1 and 3–6.*

Villafranca del Bierzo

❺ *135 km (84 mi) west of León, 20 km (12 mi) west of Ponferrada.*

After crossing the grape-growing region of León, where the slightly acidic Bierzo wine is produced, you'll arrive in Villafranca del Bierzo. This medieval village is dominated by a massive and still-inhabited feudal fortress. Villafranca was a destination in itself for Santiago's pilgrims;

visit the Romanesque church of **Santiago** and see the Door of Pardon, a sort of spiritual consolation prize for exhausted pilgrims who couldn't make it over the mountains. Stroll the streets, look for the crests on the old manor houses, and seek out the onetime **home of the infamous Grand Inquisitor Torquemada.** On the way out, you can buy some wine at the **Cooperativo Villafranquina,** on the highway.

Dining and Lodging

$–$$ ✕⌂ **Parador de Villafranca del Bierzo.** This modern, two-story hotel sits on a hilltop overlooking the Bierzo valley. The ample rooms have heavy wood furniture, shuttered windows, and large baths. The brick and wrought-iron dining room serves fresh Bierzo trout, *chanfaina barciana* (fried liver and bread crumbs), and chorizo *con alubias* (a hearty dish of white beans and sausage). Try the local Bierzo wine. ✉ *Calvo Sotelo s/n, 24500,* ☎ *987/540175,* ⅎ *987/540001. 40 rooms. Restaurant, bar. AE, DC, MC, V.*

En Route The Way of St. James veers left, to the south, from the N VI at the pass of Pedrafita. Climb the steep, narrow road and you'll arrive at one of the most unusual hamlets in Spain, O Cebreiro.

O Cebreiro

⑥ *32 km (20 mi) northwest of Villafranca del Bierzo.*

Deserted and haunting outside the tourist season, O Cebreiro is a stark settlement built around a 9th-century church. Known for its round, thatched-roof stone huts, called *pallozas,* the town has been perfectly preserved and is now an open-air museum that provides a glimpse into the way folks in these windswept mountains lived in the Middle Ages—indeed, lived up until a few decades ago. One hut is now a **museum** of the region's Celtic heritage. High up, at 3,648 ft, the village also contains a rustic **sanctuary** from the 9th century.

En Route Continue along the mountain road to the town of Samos, with a Benedictine monastery. From Samos head to Sarria, a medieval village with a pilgrims' hospital, La Magdalena.

Portomarín

⑦ *40 km (25 mi) south of Lugo.*

In Portomarín, on the Miño River, the **Romanesque church** was moved, stone by stone, before a new dam flooded the town.

Vilar de Donas

⑧ *32 km (19 mi) northwest of Portomarín.*

Beyond Portomarín, stop at the church in Vilar de Donas to pay tribute to the knights of St. James, whose tombs line the inside walls. Portraits of the two medieval noblewomen who built the church are mixed with those of the apostles in the 15th-century frescoes on the apse.

Leboreiro

⑨ *38 km (23 mi) west of Vilar de Donas.*

From Vilar de Donas, the countryside flattens out. Leboreiro, a village with simple medieval stone houses surrounding a Romanesque church, makes a pleasant stop. A stretch of the ancient road, paved with granite boulders, is still surprisingly intact.

Santiago de Compostela

⑩ *277 km (172 mi) west of León, 650 km (403 mi) northwest of Madrid.*

Once the western limit of the known world, this corner of Galicia was called *finis terrae* (end of the lands). Appropriately, Santiago de Compostela was built to impress and has exuded a sense of the mystical for ages. Imagine pilgrims walking across Spain for 30 days and finally arriving at the foot of the great cathedral: the sheer size of the opulent building is awe-inspiring, its main entrance raised two stories above the spacious Plaza del Obradoiro. Its twin towers give a sense of harmony, and a benign St. James, dressed in pilgrim's costume, smiles down from his perch.

One starry night in the year 813, a hermit was directed by a divine light to a field just outside present-day Santiago. He set a dig in motion, and religious leaders unearthed a sarcophagus said to contain the remains of St. James. The name Compostela is believed to have come from the Latin *campus stellae* (field of the stars). How the apostle's remains got to Galicia is something of a mystery. One legend says that after St. James was beheaded by King Herod in Jerusalem, his headless body was smuggled to Spain, where it lay hidden for centuries.

The discovery came at a time when the Moors ruled most of the country and only a fragment of the Christian army remained. Those Christian soldiers said that St. James, armed with a great sword and riding a white charger, led them to their first victory against the Moors, in Clavijo in 844. James earned himself the nickname Santiago Matamoros (St. James the Moorslayer) and became the patron saint of Spain. Carrying his banner throughout the Reconquest, the Christians went on to expel the Moors from Spain and conquer much of the Americas.

⑪ Climb the two flights of steps to the main doorway of the **cathedral,** and inside you'll see the one of the finest Romanesque sculptures in the world, the 12th-century **Pórtico de la Gloria.** Completed in 1188 by Maestro Mateo, this is the cathedral's original entrance. Its three arches are carved with biblical figures from the Last Judgment and Purgatory. In the center, Christ is flanked by his apostles and the 24 Elders of the Apocalypse, playing celestial instruments. Just below Christ is a serene St. James, poised on a carved column that includes the humble face of Maestro Mateo at the bottom. Look carefully at this pillar and you'll see five indentations, made over the centuries by the millions of pilgrims who have placed their hands here as they leaned forward to touch foreheads with Maestro Mateo in tribute to his genius.

Dressed in a sumptuous jeweled cloak, St. James presides over the gold and silver **high altar.** Climb the stairs behind the altar and you'll be standing at the cathedral's focal point, surrounded by a dazzling array of decorations, sculptures, and drapery. At this point, pilgrims kiss the cloak of St. James in the grand finale of their spiritual journey. Beneath the altar in the crypt are the alleged remains of St. James and two of his disciples, St. Theodore and St. Athanasius.

Pilgrims' masses are sung in the cathedral every day at noon. On special occasions, a huge incense burner is attached to the thick ropes hanging from the ceiling and anchored against the wall. Eight strong priests swing the *botafumeiro* (large incense burner) in wide arcs over the congregation. In earlier centuries, this was an air freshener; by the time pilgrims reached Santiago, many smelled, shall we say, ripe. National television broadcasts this ceremony live on St. James's Day, July 25.

You can see a *botafumeiro* and the rest of the cathedral's treasures in the **museums,** downstairs. ⊠ *Plaza del Obradoiro,* ☎ *981/561527.* ▥

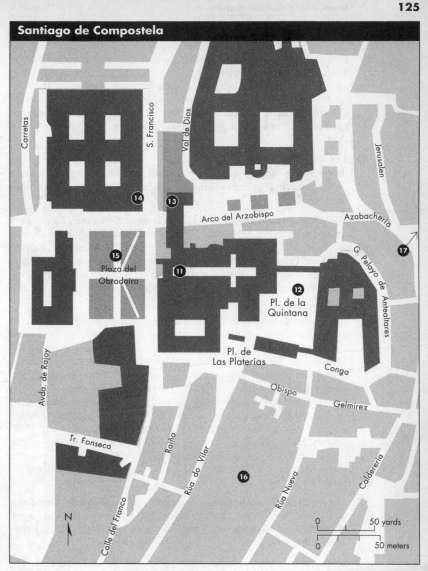

Santiago de Compostela

Carretas
S. Francisco
Val de Dios
Jerusalen
Arco del Arzobispo
Azabacheria
G. Pelayo de Antealtares
Plaza del Obradoiro
Pl. de la Quintana
Pl. de Las Platerías
Conga
Obispo
Gelmirez
Avda. de Rajoy
Tr. Fonseca
Raiña
Rúa do Vilar
Rúa Nueva
Caldereria
Calle del Franco

N

0   50 yards
0   50 meters

Cathedral, **11**

Centro Gallego
de Arte
Contemporánea, **17**

Hostal de los Reyes
Católicos, **14**

Old town, **16**

Palacio Xelmírez, **13**

Plaza de la
Quintana, **12**

Plaza del
Obradoiro, **15**

400 ptas. ☉ *July–Oct., Mon.–Sat. 10–1:30 and 4–7:30, Sun. 10–1:30
and 4–7; Nov.–June, Mon.–Sat. 11–1 and 4–6, Sun. 10–1:30.*

Exit through the **Puerta de las Platerías,** on the right side of the nave.
The so-called silversmith's door is named for the plateresque carving—
resembling silverwork—that completely covers the entryway. The double doorway is the only purely Romanesque part of the exterior; it opens
onto the **Plaza de las Platerías** (named for the silversmiths' shops that
used to line the square), whose graceful fountain is a favorite photo
spot.

⑫ The wide **Plaza de la Quintana,** on the other side of the cathedral, is
the haunt of young travelers and musicians in summer. The **Puerta Santa**
on this square is opened only those years in which St. James's Day falls
on a Sunday.

The surrounding complex of buildings is a handsome one. As you pass
under the Arco del Arzobispo (Archbishop's Arch) and arrive back at
⑬ the Plaza del Obradoiro, stop into the rich 12th-century **Palacio
Xelmírez** (Palace of Archbishop Xelmírez), with its Baroque apartments
and a lavish 30-yard-long meeting room crowned by a carved ceiling
depicting the marriage of King Alfonso IX. ☎ *981/572300.* 🖃 *200
ptas.* ☉ *Tues.–Sun. 10–1:30 and 4:30–7:30.*

⑭ The **Hostal de los Reyes Católicos** (Hostel of the Catholic Monarchs)
is Santiago's other eye-catching building, built in 1499 by Ferdinand
and Isabella in gratitude to Santiago for having finally expelled the
Moors. The oldest refuge in the world, it's been fortifying travelers for
nearly five hundred years. Now a parador (☞ Dining and Lodging,
below), the building was originally a hospital for those who fell ill along
the road, and it remained a hospital until 1953, when it was converted
to a luxury lodging. The four arcaded patios enclose fountains and are
adorned with gargoyle rainspouts said to be caricatures of the 16th-
century townsfolk. You can pay a visit in the company of an official
city guide; looky-loos without room keys risk being unceremoniously
asked to leave. ⊠ *Plaza del Obradoiro,* ☎ *981/582200.* 🖃 *Free.* ☉
Daily 10–1 and 4–6.

⑮ The building directly opposite the cathedral in the **Plaza del Obradoiro**
is the **Palacio de Rajoy** (Rajoy Palace), now the city hall. The fourth
side of the square is enclosed by the **Colegio de San Jerónimo** (San Jerónimo College).

Santiago de Compostela has many old manor houses, convents, and
churches that in most towns would receive headline attention. But the
⑯ best way to spend your remaining time here is to walk around the **old
town,** losing yourself in the maze of plazas and narrow streets. Santiago's most beautiful streets are the arcaded Rúa do Vilar, Calle del
Franco, and Rúa Nova. You'll notice that a remarkable number of the
streets are covered by arched ceilings, built into the surrounding buildings and supported by pillars, in response to the stormy climate. You
can almost traverse the entire town without stepping out from under
the stone canopy; nevertheless, the people of Santiago rarely leave
home without an umbrella.

This incredible city has long been open to all byways and cultures. It's
⑰ now connected to present-day creativity in the relatively new **Centro
Gallego de Arte Contemporánea** (Galician Center of Contemporary Art),
with works by regional, national, and international artists. It's on the
north side of town, just off the Porta de Camino. ⊠ *Rúa de Valle In-
clán s/n,* ☎ *981/546629.* 🖃 *Free.* ☉ *Tues.–Sat. 11–8, Sun. 11–2.*

⑱ Twenty-seven km (17 mi) southeast of Santiago is **Pazo de Oca,** a Galician-style country manor house. The feudal barons who controlled Galicia's peasant society lived in homes like this one, known as *pazos,* which were once sprinkled throughout the region. Walk through the gardens to the lily pond and lake, where a stone boat stays miraculously afloat. ☎ *981/570761.* 🖾 *175 ptas.* ⊙ *Apr.–Sept., daily 9–1 and 4–8; Oct.– Mar., daily 10–1 and 3–6.*

Dining and Lodging

$$$ ✕ **Anexo Vilas.** Owner Moncho Vilas likes to mingle with his happy
★ customers and loves to promote Galician cuisine. His cooking has won acclaim from Spanish gourmets; he even prepared a banquet for Pope John Paul II when the pontiff visited Santiago in 1989. Specialties include salmon with clams, hake *a la Gallega* (with paprika sauce) or *a la Vasca* (in a green sauce), and a tender steak with garlicky potatoes. ⊠ *Avda. Villagarcia 21,* ☎ *981/598387. AE, DC, MC, V.*

$$$ ✕ **O Papa Upa.** For traditional Galician food in a lively, contemporary setting, it doesn't get much better than this. Come here with an appetite: In addition to a decadent assortment of shellfish, the house specialty is the entrecôte Papa Upa, a massive T-bone steak. Wash down your meal as the locals do—partake in the "rite of burning firewater" by ordering the *queimada,* a potent, flaming drink served with a flourish in a ceramic bowl. ⊠ *Calle Raiña 18,* ☎ *981/566598. AE, MC, V. Closed Sun.*

$$ ✕ **San Clemente.** On a tiny square off the Plaza del Obradoiro, this restaurant serves high-quality seafood at just about any time of day or night. Walk past the long bar to the large dining room and feast on scallops, shrimp, sole, hake, perccbes, or Galicia's famous *pulpo a feira* (boiled and broiled octopus). ⊠ *San Clemente 6,* ☎ *981/565426. AE, DC, MC, V.*

$$$$ ✕🏨 **Hostal de los Reyes Católicos.** A converted 15th-century hospi-
★ tal, this is one of Santiago's main tourist attractions (☞ *above*). Behind a two-story plateresque facade are four interior patios with formal gardens, fountains, and carved-stone arcades. The large rooms are furnished with antiques that span five centuries and include regal canopy beds. The luxurious, high-ceilinged dining room serves regional specialties; try the *lubina con setas y gambas* (sea bass with mushrooms and shrimp) or *lacón con grelos y cachelos* (fresh ham with chard and boiled potatoes). For dessert, try the Galician treat *filloas* (apple pancakes) with whipped cream. ⊠ *Plaza del Obradoiro 1, 15705,* ☎ *981/582200,* 🖹 *981/563094. 136 rooms. 2 restaurants, bas beauty salon. AE, DC, MC, V.*

$$$$ 🏨 **Araguaney.** This glass-and-chrome palace was built by an Arab who came to Santiago as a medical student and fell in love with the daughter of a wealthy Galician family. The rooms are spacious. The dance club, built underneath the glass-bottom pool, is one of the trendiest nightspots in town. ⊠ *Alfredo Brañas 5, 15701,* ☎ *981/595900,* 🖹 *981/590287. 72 rooms. Restaurant, bar, pool, sauna, dance club, parking (free). AE, DC, MC, V.*

$$ 🏨 **Universal.** Considering its location—adjacent to both the old and new quarters—this hotel and residence is a bargain. You're steps away from the Plaza Galicia and the tapas district. The lobby and exterior are a bit on the shabby side, but the spare, comfortable, antiques-furnished rooms have the same ageless charm as the city. The jovial innkeeper will prepare a meal if you order in advance. ⊠ *Plaza de Galicia 2, 15706,* ☎ *981/585800,* 🖹 *981/585790. 54 rooms. Breakfast room. AE, DC, MC, V.*

Nightlife and the Arts

Bars line the streets of the old town; the **Calles del Franco, Raiña,** and **Vilar,** near the cathedral, are full of places with good tapas and lots of *ambiente* (atmosphere). The most popular club is **Casting,** in the Araguaney Hotel (☞ Dining and Lodging, *above*), but you must be dressed to the hilt and prepared to pay a subjective cover charge. For less flash and cash, imported beer, sangria, tapas, and live music make **Retablo Concerto** (⊠ Rúa Nova 13, ☎ 981/585907), a cozy yet cool alternative.

The **Auditorio de Galicia** hosts concerts by internationally known orchestras and soloists. The tourist office has a schedule of programs.

The **Hostal de los Reyes Católicos** (☞ above) holds a classical-music course from July 20 to August 10 each summer. Some 150 musicians from several countries participate, and free concerts are given in the hotel's beautiful performance hall every night.

Shopping

ARTS AND CRAFTS

Galicia is famous throughout Spain for its distinctive blue-and-white ceramics with bold modern designs, made in Sargadelos and O Castro. Peruse a wide selection at **Sargadelos** (⊠ Rúa Nueva 16, ☎ 981/581905).

Look for beautifully crafted gold, silver, and black stone jewelry, called *azabache* (jet), at **Antonio Uzal Vázquez** (⊠ Abril Ares 8, ☎ 981/583483).

The women of the fishing town of Camariñas fashion exquisite handmade lace collars and scarves as well as table linens. The best place to buy their work here is **Vainica** (⊠ Rúa do Vilar 58, ☎ 981/566722).

FOOD

Personal-size Santiago almond cakes are sold at **Confitería Vilas** (⊠ Rosalía de Castro 70, Santiago, ☎ 981/596858)—the same ones served at Anexo Vilas (☞ Dining and Lodging, *above*).

THE NORTHERN GALICIAN COAST

Santiago, Padrón, Pazo de Oca, Betanzos, La Coruña, Villalba, Mondoñedo, Ribadeo

Galicia's gusty and rainy northern coast has inspired local poets to wax lyrical about raindrops falling continuously on one's head. The sun does shine here, though, suffusing town and country with a golden glow. Either way, prepare to be enthralled by the seaside activity of cosmopolitan La Coruña and the quieter beauty of the ancient kingdom of Mondoñedo. Man-made scenery takes such forms as the many-paned *miradores* (glass galleries) lining the waterfront of the *Costa del Muerte* (Coast of Death), the charming gazebo in the center of Betanzos, and the tiny castle hotel in Villalba.

Padrón

❿ *18 km (11 mi) south of Santiago.*

Padrón grew up beside the Roman port of Iria Flavia and is the birthplace of one of Galicia's heroines, the 19th-century poet Rosalía de Castro. But the town is probably best known for its delicious *pimientos de Padrón* (tiny green peppers fried and sprinkled with sea salt). The fun in eating these is that one in five or so is spicy-hot.

Betanzos

㉠ *65 km (40 mi) northeast of Santiago, 25 km (15 mi) east of La Coruña.*

You enter the medieval town of Betanzos through one of its old gateways; parts of the old walls still stand. The 12th-century church of **San Francisco** contains the remains of Fernán Perez de Andrade, one of Galicia's feudal nobles. The 15th-century church of **Santa María de Azogue** was built by the mariners' guild, while the tailors' guild put up the Gothic-style church of **Santiago,** which includes a Door of Glory inspired by the one in Santiago's cathedral.

Shopping
Throughout Galicia, you'll hear the haunting tones of the bagpipe, a fond token of the area's Celtic past. In Betanzos, outside La Coruña, you can visit a bagpipe workshop and buy the real thing at **Sellas y Gaitas** (⊠ Cerca s/n), open weekdays 10–1 and 5–8.

La Coruña

㉑ *57 km (26 mi) north of Santiago.*

One of Spain's busiest ports, La Coruña prides itself on being the most progressive city in the region. The weather here can be fierce, wet, and windy, giving this stretch of the Galician seaboard its nickname, the Coast of Death; climate also explains the enclosed, wood balconies, called *miradores,* on the tall harbor houses. Small panes of glass keep the gales at bay and capture the warmth of the sun, when it shines.

La Coruña sits on a narrow strip of land jutting out to sea. On the tip of the peninsula is the **Torre de Hercules** lighthouse. It was originally built during the reign of Trajan, the Roman emperor born in Spain in AD 98, and then rebuilt in the 18th century; all that remains from Roman times are inscribed foundation stones. Scale the 242 steps for superb views of the city and coastline—and if you're here on a Friday or Saturday, come back at midnight, when nocturnal tower tours let you soak in a night view of lights along the Atlantic. Imagine the scene on July 11, 1544, when Spain's Prince Philip set sail with a fleet of 78 vessels for his wedding to Mary Tudor, the daughter of Henry VIII and Catherine of Aragon. In June 1588, King Felipe II assembled another fleet at La Coruña, and the "invincible" Spanish Armada sailed from here to conquer England. This might have succeeded if not for the ferocious storm that scattered the fleet; the surviving ships limped back into La Coruña a month later. Spain's spirit was badly shaken, and to make matters worse, England's notorious Sir Francis Drake sacked La Coruña the following year. The damage done by the English would have been much worse if not for a local housewife, María Pita; she saw Drake's men climb the hill into the old town and, at great risk, fired a cannon to warn the natives.

The small **Museo de la Torre de Hercules** (Tower of Hercules Museum) is an open-air museum with items dug up during the restoration of the lighthouse and the surrounding area. ⊠ *Carretera de la Torre s/n,* ☎ *981/221054.* ▩ *400 ptas.* ☉ *Mon.–Sun. 10–6.*

At the northeastern tip of the old town is the **Castillo de San Antón** (St. Anthony's Castle), a 16th-century fort. It now houses the **Museum of Archaeology,** where you can see remnants of the prehistoric Celtic culture that once thrived in these parts. The collection includes silver artifacts as well as pieces of the Celtic stone forts called *castros.* ☎ *981/ 205994.* ▩ *400 ptas.* ☉ *June–Sept., daily 10–2 and 4:30–7:30; Oct.– May, daily 10–2 and 4:30–7.*

The **Museo de Bellas Artes** (Museum of Fine Art), in two lovely old mansions on the edge of the old town, features French, Spanish, and Italian paintings and a curious collection of etchings by Goya. ⊠ *Plaza del Pintor Sotomayor,* ☎ *981/223723.* ☑ *400 ptas.* ⊘ *Tues. 10–3, Wed.–Fri. 10–8, Sat. 10–2 and 4:30–8, Sun. 10–2.*

Up on a hill is the **Casa de las Ciencias** (Science Museum), a hands-on museum where children can learn the principles of physics and technology. ⊠ *Parque Santa Margarita,* ☎ *981/274107.* ☑ *Museum 225 ptas., planetarium 400 ptas.* ⊘ *Tues.–Sat. 10–7, Sun. 11–2:30.*

On the other side of town, just off the Playa das Amorosas and near the Torre de Hercules, is Coruña's newest museum, the **Domus/Casa del Hombre.** This extraordinary museum is dedicated to the interdisciplinary study of mankind; exhibits range from the evolution of a single individual to the study of man's relationship to society. Displays are interactive and involve the senses, allowing you to become part of the action. ⊠ *Parque de Santa Teresa,* ☎ *981/228947.* ☑ *400 ptas.* ⊘ *June–Sept., Tues.–Sat. 11–9, Sun. 11–2:30; Oct.–May, Tues.–Sat. 10–7, Sun. 11–2:30.*

Dining and Lodging

$$–$$$ ✕ **Casa Pardo.** This chic eatery near the port is an elegant study in soft ocher tones, with perfectly matched wood furniture and cool lighting. Try the *merluza a la cazuela* (bay leaf–scented hake and potatoes drizzled with oil and sprinkled with paprika, baked in a clay casserole). For dessert, indulge in almond cake or chocolate mousse. ⊠ *Novoa Santos 15,* ☎ *981/287178. AE, MC, V. Closed Sun.*

$$–$$$ ✕ **El Coral.** The front window is a high altar of shellfish, with varieties
★ of mollusks and crustaceans you've probably never seen before. Inside, wood-paneled walls, crystal chandeliers, and 12 white-clad tables provide the setting for an intimate, elegant yet casual meal. Specialties include regional dishes such as *turbante de mariscos* (a platter—literally, a "turban"—of steamed and boiled shellfish). ⊠ *Avda. Marina Callejón de la Estacada 9,* ☎ *981/221082. Reservations essential. AE, DC, MC, V. Closed Sun.*

$–$$ ✕ **La Marina.** One of the classic *coruñés* restaurants is on a busy street
★ near the port in a large, converted private home. The elegant and intimate dining rooms are decorated in a rustic style; lots of warm pastels and floral chintz radiate an elegant country charm. Try the regional dishes: empanadas with meat or tuna filling, *lacón* (fresh country ham), or one of the house specialties, *croquetas de mariscos* (seafood croquettes). Top it all off with a light dessert of *natillas* (cream custard). ⊠ *Avda. de la Marina 14,* ☎ *981/223914. AE, MC, V.*

$$$$ 🏨 **Finisterre.** This superbly located high-rise, where the old town joins the bay, has its own sports complex and four pools. Long a favorite with businesspeople and families, Finisterre has large, carpeted rooms with modern wood furnishings and brightly colored upholstery. Ask for one of the many rooms overlooking the bay. ⊠ *Paseo del Parrote 22, 15001,* ☎ *981/205400,* 🏢 *981/208462. 127 rooms. Restaurant, bar, 4 pools, sauna, beauty salon, 2 tennis courts, health club, playground. AE, DC, MC, V.*

$$$ 🏨 **Melia Confort Coruña.** As the name suggests, this is a comfortable and upscale lodging convenient to the bus and train stations as well as the port. With all the amenities, and a shopping gallery next door, it's a less expensive but comparable alternative to the Finisterre. ⊠ *Ramón y Cajal 53, 15001,* ☎ *981/242711,* 🏢 *981/236728. 181 rooms. Restaurant, bar, sauna, exercise room. AE, DC, MC, V.*

Nightlife and the Arts

Begin the evening at the **Praza de María Pita** square—*cervecerías,* coffee houses, and tapas bars dominate the area off its northwest corner and farther inland. Wander along **Calle Estrella, Calle de los Olmos,** and **La Galera** for *pinchitos* and local Ribeiro wine served in bowls. Serious night owls head for the posh and pricey clubs around **Praya del Orzán** (Orzán Beach), particularly along **Calle Juan Canalejo.** For lower-key entertainment, the **streets of old town** have lots of cozy taverns where you can grab a nightcap even as the new day dawns.

If you feel like gambling, head for the **Casino del Atlántico** (✉ Jardines de Médez Nuñez, ☎ 981/221600).

Shopping

ARTS AND CRAFTS

You'll find the famous blue-and-white pottery at the factory, museum, and showroom in nearby Cervo, on the Lugo coast, at **Cerámica de Sargadelos** (✉ Carretera Paraña s/n, ☎ 982/557841 or 982/557600), open weekdays 8:30–1 and 4:30–6. A wide selection is also on sale in nearby Sada, at the factory and museum **Cerámicas del Castro** (✉ Carretera Sada–La Coruña s/n, ☎ 981/620225).

Glazed terra-cotta ceramics from Buño, 40 km (25 mi) west of La Coruña on C552, are prized by aficionados. Stop by **Alfaería y Cerámica de Buño** (✉ C. Barreiros s/n, Buño, ☎ 981/711251) for a selection of vases, plates, and wine jugs based on traditional designs.

One of the best places to buy the famous **Camariñas lace** is at **Carmina Touriña** (✉ Panaderas 19, La Coruña, ☎ 981/206290).

CLOTHING

Galicia is home to some of Spain's top fashion designers, notably **Adolfo Domínguez** (✉ Finisterre 3, ☎ 981/251539).

For berets, the traditional male headgear of the region (and the country), try **Luis Tomé Pérez Fábrica de Gorras y Boinas** (✉ Linares Rivas 52, ☎ 981/232014), in Coruña, an old-world hat and cap emporium.

Pilgrim *sombreros* and hand-painted wooden shoes (still worn in some villages) make great gifts and souvenirs. For truly authentic Galician *zapatos* (shoes), trek 15 minutes south to the neighboring village of **Carballo,** where you'll find the workshop of **José López Rama** (✉ Rúa do Muiño 7, ☎ 981/701068). For hats and other Galician folk clothing in La Coruña, stop by **Sastrería Iglesias** (✉ Rego do Auga 14, ☎ 981/221634), where artisan José Luis Iglesias Rodrígues sells his tortilas.

FOOD

Want to take home some Galician delicacies? Hit the *supermercado* (supermarket) floor of **El Corte Inglés** department stores for vacuum-packed food items that customs will not need to remove from your luggage (✉ Ramón y Cajal 57–59, ☎ 981/290011).

SPORTING GOODS

In Xubia, along the Calle de Castilla road between Coruña and El Ferrol, **Armería Domingo** (✉ C. de Castilla 982, ☎ 981/302018) is an old-fashioned sporting-goods store (rumored to have been one of Franco's favorite places to browse), with fishing rods, all-weather gear, and camping knives for roadside picnics.

Villalba

㉒ *70 km (43 mi) east of La Coruña.*

This part of Galicia is called *Terra Cha* (Flat Land). Known as the Galician Mesopotamia, it's the source of several rivers, most notably the

Miño, which flows down into Portugal (where it's known as the Minho). The countryside is pretty, with gentle hills and knolls adding texture to the plain. The largest city in this area is Villalba, which has a tiny parador in a castle associated with the Andrade family, who wielded considerable power here in the Middle Ages.

Dining and Lodging

$$$ ✕ 🏨 **Parador Condes de Villalba.** This tiny parador is in a 15th-century tower that was once a fortress belonging to the powerful, local Andrade family. A drawbridge leads to the two-story lobby, which is hung with medieval-style tapestries. The rooms—three large, octagonal chambers in the massive tower, three in a lower building—have beamed ceilings and hardwood floors, hand-carved Spanish-style furniture, and wood chandeliers. The restaurant's specialty is empanadas (try the empanada *de Rax*, made of beef loin, or the traditional empanada *de atún*, with tuna); for dessert, sample the region's renowned *San Simón* (cone-shape, birch-smoked cheese with apples or pears). ✉ *Valeriano Valdesuso s/n, 27800,* ☎ *982/510011,* 🖷 *982/510090. 6 rooms. Restaurant, bar. AE, DC, MC, V.*

Mondoñedo

㉓ *122 km (76 mi) northeast of La Coruña, 52 km (32 mi) northeast of Villalba.*

This dignified town, founded in AD 1156, was one of the seven original capitals of the kingdom of Galicia from the 16th to early 19th century. The most impressive building here is the **cathedral,** consecrated in 1248. The surrounding peaceful streets and squares are filled with old buildings, monasteries, churches, and an old Jewish quarter.

En Route Instead of stopping in Mondoñedo, you could continue along a winding 81-km (50-mi) road past Villalba on N634 and return to the coast. Spain's cleanest and least-crowded beaches are north of here.

Viveiro

㉔ *184 km (114 mi) northeast of La Coruña, 81 km (50 mi) northeast of Villalba.*

Stroll the narrow streets of this ancient town whose once-turreted walls are still partially intact. During Semana Santa, you can see penitents following religious processions on bloodied knees.

OFF THE BEATEN PATH   **CERVO** – If the weather is nice, you may want to visit some beaches or, in the town of Cervo, 10 km (6 mi) east of Vivero, visit the Sargadelos factory and store, where Spain's most distinctive blue-, white-, and red-glazed modern-design ceramics are made.

Ribadeo

㉕ *25 km (16 mi) east of Cervo, 81 km (50 mi) northeast of Villalba, 113 km (70 mi) northwest of Mondoñedo.*

Ribadeo, on the broad *ría* (estuary) of the same name, is the last coastal town before Asturias. The view of Castropol, on the other side of the *ría,* is marvelous. Walk out to the **estuary lighthouse,** where you can watch waves crash against the rocks and fishermen haul in their catch. Upriver is a favorite haunt for salmon and trout fishermen.

Just 2 km (1 mi) outside Ribadeo is the **Santa Cruz hill,** with more sweeping views and a monument to the bagpipe, the most common folk instrument in both Galicia and Asturias.

Dining and Lodging

$$ ✕ **O Xardin.** This garden restaurant is old-fashioned and charming. Specialties include mint-scented vegetable pudding, casserole of monkfish and scallops, and sole with wild mushroom and Albariño wine sauce. ⊠ *Reinante 20,* ☎ *982/128222. Reservations not accepted. AE, DC, MC, V. Closed Mon. winter–spring.*

$$ ✕⌂ **Parador de Ribadeo.** This whitewashed modern parador is on the banks of the Eo River, with good views across to Asturias. Gleaming hardwood floors and hefty rafters create a feeling of warmth. Rooms have Castilian-style furniture, artisan rugs, and large baths. The estuary provides a cornucopia of shellfish for the dining room, including cockles, clams, and oysters. Try the chocolate mousse for dessert. ⊠ *Amador Fernández s/n, 27700,* ☎ *982/100825,* ℻ *982/100346. 47 rooms. Restaurant. AE, DC, MC, V.*

SOUTHWESTERN GALICIA AND THE ATLANTIC COAST

Noia, Muros, Pontevedra, O Grove, Bayona, Túy

If you love beaches—and who doesn't?—head due west from Santiago along scenic C543 toward the coast, sliced by a series of wide estuaries called the Rías Altas (High Estuaries) and Rías Bajas (Low Estuaries). The hilly drive takes you through countryside dotted with tiny farms and *horreos* (granaries). Even the vineyards are staked with granite posts. You are likely to see stout, black-clad peasant women carrying heavy loads on their heads.

Noia

㉖ *36 km (22 mi) west of Santiago.*

A 45-minute drive from Santiago along the curving, scenic C543 brings you to Noia, a historic town with the Gothic **church of San Martín** facing resolutely out to sea, and mysterious Celtic inscriptions on the gravestones in the medieval cemetery. The best places to swim and sun are the Testal and Boa beaches.

En Route Cross the narrow neck of the Tambre River and head up the other side of the *ría* to Muros.

Muros

㉗ *30 km (19 mi) west of Noia, 65 km (40 mi) southwest of Santiago, 75 km (47 mi) southwest of La Coruña.*

The cheerful harbor town of Muros is a popular summer resort with lovely, Gothic-arched, arcaded streets and good beaches nearby on Point Louro. Try Praia de San Francisco or Praia de Area. The bay is dotted with mussel-breeding platforms.

Pontevedra

㉘ *55 km (34 mi) southeast of Noia, 59 km (37 mi) south of Santiago, 28 km (17 mi) south of Padrón, 120 km (75 mi) south of La Coruña.*

Down toward Portugal, Pontevedra is the next-largest city on the western coast after La Coruña. You've probably noticed that road signs are difficult to read in Galicia because most have been spray-painted over with place names in Gallego. Situated at the juncture of three rivers—the Lerez, the Toeza and the Alba—Pontevedra is charming, well preserved, and, unlike Santiago, largely undiscovered.

On the edge of the maze of granite-block streets and plazas is the seafarers' 16th-century church of **Santa María Mayor,** which has a beautifully carved facade in the intricate plateresque style.

The **Museo Provincial** (Provincial Museum) is in two 18th-century mansions. Its medieval statues were taken from the Door of Glory on Santiago's cathedral when the new facade was built. ⊠ *Sarmiento 51,* ☎ *986/851455.* 🖾 *275 ptas.* ⊙ *Daily 11–1:30 and 5–8.*

Dining and Lodging

$$ ✕ **Casa Solla.** Owner Pepe Solla makes the most of the bountiful har-
★   vest from local coasts and vineyards at his terraced garden restaurant, 2 km (1 mi) outside town on the highway to O Grove. Try the sole in Albariño wine sauce, filet mignon in red wine, and, in summer, fresh figs with Cabrales cheese. ⊠ *Avda. Sireiro 7, O Grove, Km 2,* ☎ *986/ 872884. AE, DC, MC, V. Closed Thurs. and mid-Dec.–mid-Jan. No dinner Sun.*

$$$ ✕🖾 **Casa del Barón.** A 16th-century manor house (built over the foundations of an ancient Roman villa) in the heart of Pontevedra, this parador has a baronial stone stairway winding into the front lobby. The rooms have antique reproductions and face a rose garden. The dining room is full of antique mirrors, candelabras, portraits of people who look vaguely familiar, and a kitchen that prepares tasty seafood, shellfish, and meat dishes. Try the grilled squid with garlic and parsley. ⊠ *Barón 19, 36002,* ☎ *986/855800,* 📠 *986/852195. 47 rooms. Restaurant, bar, café, library. AE, DC, MC, V.*

En Route   Driving west on C550 from Pontevedra, you'll see the Albariño vineyards, which produce the region's best and rarest wine. Some connoisseurs think it beats the revered Rioja.

O Grove

㉙   *20 km (12 mi) west of Pontevedra, 75 km (47 mi) south of Santiago, 138 km (86 mi) south of La Coruña.*

The gourmet paradise of O Grove, on the peninsula, throws a shellfish festival the second week of October, but you can enjoy the day's catch in taverns and restaurants year-round. From here you can cross a bridge to the island of La Toja, famous for its spas (*see below*).

Dining

$$ ✕ **Posada del Mar.** Overlooking the channel that separates O Grove from La Toja, this dining room is decorated with a collection of ceramics from all over Spain. Expertly prepared seafood is king here: Try the monkfish in garlic butter or the fish soup, thick with chunks of sugar-sweet turbot. ⊠ *Rúa de Castelao 202,* ☎ *986/730106. AE, MC, V. Closed mid-Dec.–Feb.*

Cambados

㉚   *34 km (21 mi) north of Pontevedra, 53 km (33 mi) south of Santiago.*

The town of Cambados has colorfully painted houses in its old town and the imposing 17th-century Fefiñanes palace covering almost half of the main square. Cambados is also convenient to the wooded **island of La Toja,** with a luxury spa hotel and golf course (☞ Dining and Lodging, *below*). Legend has it that a man abandoned an ailing donkey here and, upon his return, found it up on all fours and rejuvenated. The waters are still said to have peculiar healing properties.

Dining and Lodging

$$$$ ✕⌧ **Gran Hotel de la Toja.** Extravagant and exorbitant (for the region), this sybaritic Spanish version of Belle Epoque elegance is surrounded by the pine forest that blankets the land between O Grove and Cambados. Rooms are simple and have a slightly faded charm compared to the grandiose formality of the public salons and foyers. Dining areas have expansive sea views, and special diet menus are available. ⌧ *Isla de la Toja, 36991,* ☎ *986/730025,* FAX *986/730026 or 986/731201. 198 rooms. Restaurant, pool, spa, 9-hole golf course, tennis court, health club, horseback riding, beach, casino, dance club. AE, DC, MC, V.*

$$$ ✕⌧ **Parador El Albariño.** Built in 1966 in the style of an old manor house, this parador faces the Atlantic. The lobby has heavy, leather furniture and beamed ceilings. Rooms are simply furnished with wrought-iron lamps, handmade rugs, and ceiling-high wood shutters over small-paned windows. The dining room serves such Galician dishes as *lacón con grelos* (baled shoulder of pork served with sautéed turnip tops). Be sure to order a bottle of the local Albariño wine. ⌧ *Paseo de Cervantes s/n, 36630, Cambados,* ☎ *986/542250,* FAX *986/542068. 63 rooms. Restaurant, bar, pool, tennis court. AE, DC, MC, V.*

Nightlife and the Arts

If you get itchy out here, try **Casino La Toja** (⌧ La Toja, ☎ 986/731000).

Bayona

③ *30 km (19 mi) south of Pontevedra, 128 km (80 mi) south of Santiago, 160 km (100 mi) south of La Coruña.*

The A9 expressway takes you from Pontevedra to the industrial center of Vigo in about half an hour. Bayona is on the southern bank of the Río Vigo, on the cape. When Columbus's *Pinta* landed here in 1492, Bayona became the first town to receive the news of the discovery of the New World. Once a fortified hilltop castle, **Monte Real** is now one of Spain's most popular paradors. Walk around the battlements for superb views. On your way into or out of town, check out the graceful Roman bridge.

Dining and Lodging

$$$$ ✕⌧ **Parador Conde de Gondomar.** This modern hotel was built inside
★ the walls of a medieval castle, on a hilltop fortified since 200 BC. Rooms are furnished with period reproductions; some have balconies with ocean views. The dining room serves regional specialties; try *entremeses variados* (mixed appetizers) for a sampler of typical seafood, and perhaps the *robalo con navallas* (sea bass with razor clams) as an entrée. ⌧ *Carretera de Bayona at Montereal, 36300,* ☎ *986/355000,* FAX *986/355076. 66 rooms. Restaurant, bar, pool, tennis court, health club, beach, playground. AE, DC, MC, V.*

Shopping

There is a branch of the department store **El Corte Inglés** in nearby Vigo (⌧ Avda. Gran Vía 25–27, ☎ 986/415111). While in Vigo, peek in at the **Universidade Popular de Vigo** (⌧ Avda. García Barbón 5, ☎ 986/228088), where traditional musical instruments such as the bagpipe are studied, displayed, and sold.

Islas Cies

③② *35 km (21 mi) out from Vigo in Atlantic Ocean.*

The Islas Cies, or Cies Islands, are one of the last unspoiled refuges on the Spanish coast. From July to September, about eight boats a day leave from Vigo harbor and return later in the day; the round-trip fare is about $32. The 45-minute ride brings you to fine white-sand beaches. This is a nature reserve: birds abound, and the only land transportation are your own two feet. It takes about an hour to hike across the main island. For camping reservations (required), call **Camping Islas Cies** (☎ 986/438358).

Túy

③③ *14 km (9 mi) south of Bayona, 50 km (31 mi) south of Pontevedra, 200 km (124 mi) south of La Coruña.*

If you have ample time, leave Vigo on the scenic coastal route C555, which takes you up the banks of the Miño River, along the Portuguese border. If time is short, jump on the inland A55. Both routes will deliver you directly into the town of Túy. During the medieval wars between Castile and Portugal, Tuy was in a strategic position—which explains why the 13th-century **cathedral** looks like a fortress. The steep, narrow streets are rich with ancient, crested mansions, evidence of Túy's past life as one of the seven capitals of the Galician kingdom. Today it is an important border town, and you can see the mountains of Portugal from the cathedral.

Dining and Lodging

$$ ✕⌑ **Parador San Telmo.** This granite-and-chestnut hotel stands on the bluffs overlooking the Miño. Rural antiques and paintings by local artists decorate the lobbies. Rooms are furnished with convincing reproductions. Good views of the surrounding woods grace the dining room, where the specialties include river salmon, lamprey eel, and trout. For dessert, try the almond *pececitos* (almond cookie–like pastries made by local convent nuns). ✉ *Avda. del Portugal s/n, 36700, Túy,* ☎ *986/ 600309,* ℻ *986/602163. 30 rooms. Restaurant, bar, pool, tennis courts, parking. AE, DC, MC, V.*

OVIEDO AND THE PRINCIPALITY OF ASTURIAS

Luarca, Cudillero, Gijón, Villaviciosa, Cangas de Onís, Cavadonga, Ribadesella

As you cross the border into the Principality of Asturias, Galicia's intense green countryside continues, belying the fact that this is a major mining region. (Ancient Roman conquerors coveted the iron- and gold-rich earth.) Spaniards call the two regions *primos hermanos* (cousins) because the geographical resemblance is so strong. But Asturias is more mountainous, bordered on the south by the imposing, snowcapped Picos de Europa; the Cantabrian Sea and its enviable long and wide beaches to the north; the Deva River to the east; and the Eo River to the west. Listen closely and, as in Galicia, you might just hear the mournful notes of the bagpipe, souvenir of the Celts.

Luarca

③④ *75 km (47 mi) east of Ribadeo, 92 km (57 mi) northeast of Oviedo, 95 km (59 mi) west of Gijón.*

The N634 wanders through the far-western reaches of Asturias into Oviedo. On the way, stop at the village of Luarca, tucked into a cove with a sparkling bay and a fishing port. It's a maze of cobblestone streets, stone stairways, and whitewashed houses, with painted flowerpots decorating the edge of the harbor. The smells wafting from the many bars and restaurants will tempt you to stay a while and sample the freshly caught seafood.

Dining and Lodging

$$ ✕ **Leonés.** The large iron chandeliers and rural antiques that line these walls inspire medieval thoughts. Try peppers stuffed with shellfish or *fabada* and, for dessert, apple sherbet. If you can pay in cash, you can order from a cheaper menu. ⊠ *Paseo Alfonso X el Sabio,* ☎ *98/ 5640995. Reservations not accepted. AE, DC, MC, V.*

$$ ✕▦ **Gayoso.** This comfortable, old, and charming hotel has been run by the same family for more than 120 years. It has spacious rooms and wooden balconies with views of the Black River. Five of the hotel's 60 rooms have been upgraded to three-star status and cost almost twice as much as the others. ⊠ *Paseo de Gómez 4, 33700,* ☎ *98/5640054,* FAX *98/5470271. Bar. AE, DC, MC, V.*

En Route   The coast road leads to Cudillero, a town 35 km (22 mi) east of Luarca, which rises up an incline from a tiny port. On a sunny day, the emerald green of the surrounding hills, the bright blue of the sparkling water, the white of the houses, and the smell of the sea might make you want to give it all up and buy a boat here.

Oviedo

③⑤ *92 km (57 mi) southeast of Luarca, 50 km (31 mi) southeast of Cudillero, 30 km (19 mi) south of Gijón.*

As you move inland, you'll notice that the countryside begins to look a bit more prosperous. Wooden, thatched-roof *horreos* strung with golden bundles of drying corn replace the stark, granite sheds of Galicia. Drive through the rolling hills and industrialized valleys and soon you'll arrive in Oviedo, the Asturian capital. Though primarily an industrial city, Oviedo has three of the most famous churches in Spain and a large university, giving it an ancient charm and a youthful zest lacking in most business centers.

★   Start your visit to Oviedo just outside the city on the slopes of Mt. Naranco, with its two exquisite 9th-century chapels. The church of **Santa María del Naranco,** with its superb views, and its plainer sister, **San Miguel de Lillo,** 300 yards uphill, are the jewels of an early architectural style called Asturian Pre-Romanesque, which was centuries ahead of its time. The carved hunting scenes and ceiling vaulting reveal art and architecture that didn't show up in the rest of Europe for another 200 years. These masterpieces were commissioned as part of a summer palace by King Ramiro I when Oviedo was the capital of Christian Spain. They have survived more than 1,000 years, and you can still enjoy them in the same natural setting for which they were designed. From the arched porches of Santa María, the valley of Oviedo spreads out at your feet. On a clear day the mighty, snowcapped Picos de Europa gleam in the distance. ⊠ *Carretera de los Monumentos, 2 km (1 mi) outside town,* ☎ *98/529–6755.* ▦ *200 ptas.; free Mon.* ☉ *Apr.–*

Sept., Mon.–Sat. 10–1 and 3–7, Sun. 10–1; Oct.–Mar., Mon.–Sat. 10–1 and 3–5, Sun. 10–1.

The tallest building in the skyline is the Gothic **cathedral,** built from the 14th to the 16th century around Oviedo's most cherished monument, the **Cámara Santa** (Holy Chamber). King Ramiro's predecessor, Alfonso the Chaste (792–842), built this chamber to hide the treasures of Christian Spain during the long struggle with the Moors. It was heavily damaged during the Spanish civil war but has since been rebuilt. Inside is the gold-leaf **Cross of the Angels,** encrusted with pearls and jewels. It was commissioned by Alfonso the Chaste in 808 and is inscribed with the warning: "May anyone who dares to remove me from the place I have been willingly donated be struck down by a bolt of divine lightning." On the left is the more elegant **Victory Cross,** actually a jeweled sheath crafted in AD 908 to cover the oak cross used by Pelayo in the battle of Covadonga (☞ Covadonga, *below*). Despite the warning, the crosses and other treasures were stolen from the cathedral in 1977 but were recovered relatively intact as thieves tried to spirit them out of Europe through Portugal. ⊠ *Plaza Alfonso II El Casto,* ☎ *98/5221033.* 🎫 *300 ptas.* ◯ *May–Oct., Mon.–Sat. 10–1 and 4–7; Nov.–Apr., Mon.–Sat. 10–1 and 4–6.*

Look directly across the Plaza Alfonso from the cathedral for the 15th-century **Palacio de la Rúa;** it is the oldest palace in town and is still inhabited. The beautifully cleaned 16th-century **Antigua Universidad de Oviedo** is across from the Palacio de la Rúa.

Behind the cathedral, the **Museo Arqueológico** (Museum of Archaeology), housed in the splendid Monastery of San Vicente, contains fragments of pre-Romanesque buildings. ⊠ *San Vicente 3,* ☎ *98/5125405.* 🎫 *Free.* ◯ *Tues.–Sat. 10–1:30 and 4–6, Sun. 11–1.*

If you've got a taste for Asturian art, visit the **Santullano Church,** which was built in the 9th century. ⊠ *Plaza Santullano.* 🎫 *Free.* ◯ *May–Oct., Tues.–Sun. 11–1 and 4:30–6; Nov.–Apr., Tues.–Sun. noon–1 and 4–5.*

If you are a fan of exquisite hotels, take a peek at the **Hotel de la Reconquista** (☞ Dining and Lodging, *below*), a former 18th-century hospice with an imposing Baroque shield on the front. The Spanish crown prince, who carries the title Prince of Asturias, presents an award for world achievement each year from the ornate hotel chapel.

Dining and Lodging

$$$ ✕ **Casa Fermín.** This sophisticated pink-and-granite restaurant, com-
★ plete with plants and skylights, has an air of modernity that belies more than 50 years of experience in the kitchen. Founder Luis Gil has introduced traditional Asturian cuisine to seminars around the world. The wine cellar is extensive. Specialties include *fabada,* wild game in season, hake in cider, and a tortilla *de angulas*(spaghetti-thin baby eels), a pricey delicacy adored by lovers of Spanish haute cuisine. ⊠ *San Francisco 8,* ☎ *98/5216452. AE, DC, MC, V. No dinner Sun. except in May and Sept.*

$$$ ✕ **La Boca Mar.** Award-winning nouvelle-Spanish cuisine is presented
★ with flair at this unusual restaurant. Tucked into a vine-covered building in the plaza that houses Oviedo's fish market, La Boca Mar is a jumble of cozy wooden booths. Try fried prawns, filet mignon with sweet mustard, or *angulas* (eels). ⊠ *Plaza Trascorrales 14,* ☎ *98/ 5204126. AE, DC, MC, V. Closed Sun.*

$$ ✕ **El Raitan.** Owned by the same family as La Boca Mar (☞ *above*), and just across the plaza, El Raitan is perfect for big appetites. The restaurant is styled like an old-fashioned kitchen, with an antique stove in the entrance. At lunch, there's no menu; everyone is served the same nine dishes, all Asturian specialties: seafood soup, crab bisque, vegetable and bean stew, *fabada*, potatoes stuffed with meat, onions filled with tomatoes, rice pudding, crepes, and nut pastries. ⊠ *Plaza Trascorrales 6, ☎ 98/5214218. AE, DC, MC, V. No dinner Sun.*

$ ✕ **La Máquina.** For the best *fabada* in Asturias, head 6 km (4 mi) outside Oviedo on the road to Avilés. Stop when you see the farmhouse with the miniature locomotive out front. The L-shape, whitewashed dining room has been attracting customers from all over Spain for 50 years, some of whom think nothing of making a weekend trip solely for the purpose of eating here. The memorable rice pudding is topped with a crisp layer of hot caramel. ⊠ *Avda. de Santa Bárbara 59, ☎ 98/5260019. AE, MC. Closed Sun. No dinner.*

$$$$ ▥ **Hotel de la Reconquista.** Housed in an 18th-century hospice emblazoned with a huge stone coat of arms, the Reconquista is run by the Spanish Occidental chain. It's ultraluxurious, and costs nearly twice as much as the region's other fine hotels. The wide lobby is circled by a balcony and has 18th-century paintings and velvet upholstery. A pianist entertains nightly. Rooms are large and modern, with comfortable beds and big armchairs. ⊠ *Gil de Jaz 16, 33004, ☎ 98/5241100,* 𝖥𝖠𝖷 *98/5241166. 142 rooms. Restaurant, bar, coffee shop, beauty salon. AE, DC, MC, V.*

$$ ✕▥ **Hotel Principado.** If you prize friendliness over flash, try the Principado, between the old town and park. The lobby resembles a comfortable living room. ⊠ *San Francisco 6, 33003, ☎ 98/5217792,* 𝖥𝖠𝖷 *98/5213946. 70 rooms. Restaurant, bar. AE, MC, V.*

Nightlife and the Arts

A rather rowdy town after dark, Oviedo has a lot to offer if you like loud, live music. **Calle Carta Puebla** is packed with pubs, many of them Irish owing to the region's Celtic heritage. You can get a nightcap at the plant-filled **Sidrería Venicia** (⊠ Doctor Casal 13) or enjoy loud rock at the brass-and-glass **La Loggia,** across the street from the cathedral. For dance action, the busiest club district in the old town is **Calle Canóniga,** shooting away from the cathedral. If you're still awake when the old town goes to sleep, try the new town's **Sir Lawrance** (⊠ Eugenio Tamayo 3), where you're likely to dance out into daylight.

Plays and concerts are presented at the Municipal Theater in Oviedo; check newspapers for schedules.

Shopping

ARTS AND CRAFTS

Look for Asturias' distinctive black pottery at **Esacanda** (⊠ Jovellanos 5, ☎ no phone).

FOOD

If you like *fabada*, take home a do-it-yourself kit—beans and meat conserved in a vacuum pack—from **Casa Veneranda** (⊠ Melquiades Alvarez 23, ☎ 98/5212454).

JEWELRY

Throughout the city shops carry beautiful jewelry made of *azabache* (jet).

Gijón

㊱ *30 km (19 mi) north of Oviedo, 95 km (59 mi) east of Luarca, 50 km (31 mi) east of Cudillero.*

Gijón (pronounced "he-*hone*") can seem overwhelming at first, presenting the traveler with factories, warehouses, and heavy industry. Ask most Spaniards for their favorite city in Asturias, however, and they're likely to answer "Gijón" with great fondness. Full of hidden hot spots and friendly people, this lively city is part fishing port, part summer resort, and part university town, packed with inviting cafés and excellent restaurants. The promenade along **Praya San Lorenzo** extends from one end of town to the other; summer swimming is sometimes prohibited due to pollution. Across the narrow peninsula is the harbor, where the fishing fleet comes in with the day's catch; on the hill at the tip is the old fishermen's quarter, **Cimadevilla,** now the hub of the city's nightlife. The **Roman Baths** (⊠ Campo Valdez), dating back to the time of Emperor Augustus, are closed for excavations. The **Parque Isabel la Católica,** at the eastern edge of town, is home to the **Museo de la Gaita** (Bagpipe Museum), which has a collection of bagpipes from all over the world as well as crafts workshops. ⊠ *Bagpipe Museum,* ☎ *98/5332244.* 🎦 *Free.* ☉ *Sept.–June, Tues.–Sat. 10–1 and 5–8, Sun. 11–1; July–Aug., Tues.–Sat. 11–1:30 and 5–9.*

Dining and Lodging

$$ ✕ **Casa Victor.** Owner Victor Bango runs an inventive seafood restaurant that modernizes traditional Asturian dishes. The bright and noisy dining room is always packed; service is friendly. Try the hake in leek sauce, clams with asparagus, or the house variation of *caldereta* (fish stew). ⊠ *Carmen 11,* ☎ *98/5350093. AE, DC, MC, V. Closed Thurs. and Nov. No dinner Sun.*

$$ ✕🏠 **Parador Gijón.** The only parador in Asturias is one of the simplest and friendliest in Spain. The modern rooms are small, with bleached-wood floors and thick pine shutters. Most have wonderful views, over the adjacent lake or the city park. The dining room and garden cider bar are popular with locals. Try the *tigres* (spicy stuffed mussels), *pimientos de piquillos rellenos de champiñones* (green peppers stuffed with squid, mushrooms, and rice), or the *oricios* (sea urchins), raw or served steamed with lemon juice or a spicy sauce. For dessert, try fresh figs (in season) with *cabrales* (regional blue cheese). ⊠ *Parque Isabel la Católica s/n, 33203,* ☎ *98/5370511,* ℻ *98/ 5370233. 40 rooms. Restaurant, cafeteria. AE, DC, MC, V.*

En Route   Eastward from Gijón on N632 is apple-orchard country, the source of Asturias' famous hard cider. Rolling hills, cows, and white chalets make it look more like Switzerland than Spain.

Villaviciosa

③⑦ *32 km (20 mi) east of Gijón, 45 km (28 mi) northeast of Oviedo, 125 km (78 mi) east of Luarca.*

Cider capital Villaviciosa has a big dairy and several cider-bottling plants, as well as a picturesque old quarter. Emperor Charles V first set foot in Spain just down the road from here.

Shopping

You'll find beautiful *azabache* jewelry at **Adolfo Cayado Alonso** (⊠ C. Vedriñana) and at **José Ordieres Rodríguez** (⊠ C. Arguero).

Ribadesella

③⑧ *38 km (24 mi) east of Gijón, 48 km (30 mi) northeast of Oviedo, 128 km (80 mi) east of Luarca.*

This fishing village and beach resort is famous for international canoe races held on the Sella River the first Saturday of August; plentiful, fresh seafood; and the **Cueva Tito Bustillo.** The cave was discovered in 1968 by Señor Bustillo; its 20,000-year-old paintings are on par with those in Lascaux, France, and Altamira. Giant horses and deer prance about the walls. To protect the paintings, no more than 400 visitors a day are allowed inside. Guided tours are given in Spanish. ☎ 98/5861118 or 98/5861120. ✑ 400 ptas.; free Tues. ⊘ Sept.–June, daily 10–1 and 3:30–5:15; July–Aug., Mon.–Sat. 10–1 and 3:30–5:15.

OFF THE BEATEN PATH	**LLANES** – Llanes is a pretty town on the Costa Verde (Green Coast), 40 km (25 mi) east of Ribadesella on the way to Santander. Stretch your legs and go for an invigorating cliffside stroll along the seaside. Llanes is home to one of the most immaculate and secluded beaches in the area, **Playa Balota,** 1 km (½ mi) to the east. Balota has private coves for picnicking and the only stretch of nudist sand in Asturias.

Dining

$ ✕ **El Repollu.** This small, homey grill specializes in fish dishes. Try the fresh-grilled turbot and the house Cabrales cheese, or sugar-sweet grilled *gambas* (shrimp). ⊠ *Santa Marina 2,* ☎ *98/5860734. Reservations not accepted. AE, DC, MC, V. Closed Oct.*

Cangas de Onís

39 *25 km (16 mi) south of Ribadesella, 70 km (43 mi) east of Oviedo.*

Cangas de Onís lies in the narrow valley carved by the Sella River. This town was the first capital of Christian Spain and has the feel of a bracing mountain village. The hump-backed, ivy-covered **Roman bridge** that spans the Sella River gorge is a favorite spot for photos.

En Route To the east of Cangas de Onís, on the C6312 road, is the turnoff for the imposing **Peña Santa peak** (8,488 ft). At the end of the winding road is Covadonga's famous shrine.

Covadonga

40 *84 km (52 mi) from Oviedo.*

★ Covadonga's **shrine** is considered the birthplace of Spain. Here, in AD 718, a handful of sturdy Asturian Christians, led by Don Pelayo, took refuge in the Cave of St. Mary, about halfway up a cliff, where they prayed to the Virgin Mary to give them strength to turn back the Moors. Pelayo and his followers resisted the superior Moorish forces and set up a Christian kingdom that eventually led to the Reconquest. Covadonga itself has a basilica in a magnificent mountain setting and a shrine in the legendary cave, which includes an 18th-century statue of the Virgin and Don Pelayo's grave. The museum displays the treasures donated to the Virgin of the Cave, including a crown studded with more than 1,000 diamonds. ☎ 98/5846077 or 98/5241412. ✑ *Suggested admission 200 ptas.* ⊘ *Mar.–June, daily 11–2 and 4–6; July–Sept., daily 10:30–2 and 4–7:30; Oct., daily 11:30–2 and 4–6; Nov.–Feb., weekends 11:30–2 and 4–6.*

Covadonga is connected to the **Sierra de Covadonga National Park** by a narrow lane. Don't miss the two alpine lakes at the top of the road, Lake Enol and Lake Ercina. Wild horses graze nearby. Pope John Paul II was brought here to picnic during his 1989 tour of Galicia and Asturias. Head uphill for a spectacular view all the way to the ocean from the **Mirador de la Reina** (The Queen's Lookout).

Ruta de Cares (Cares Route)

⟨41⟩ *Between Cangas de Onís and Panes.*

Wind back toward Cangas de Onís, but when you reach C6312, turn east toward Panes. This 55-km (34-mi) drive between Cangas de Onís and Panes, called the Ruta de Cares, is the most beautiful in Asturias. The road passes through the towns of Benia and Carreña, with their crested houses, to arrive in **Arenas de Cabrales.** This is the area where the popular Cabrales blue cheese is made. From here, a branch of the road heads into the mountains, and you can follow the Cares River toward the toothlike **Naranjo de Bulnes** (8,264 ft). Hiking trails begin here for treks to the villages of Carmarmeña and Bulnes and the spectacular Cares Gorge. From the town of Arenas, follow the road east to Panes, and from there you can head for the coast.

Dining and Lodging

$$ ✕⌑ **La Tiendona.** This restored roadhouse is strategically located halfway between the mountains of Cangas de Onís and the beaches of Ribadesella. Rooms have country-style furnishings. The dining room emphasizes regional specialties, such as smoked salmon, fabada, and cider. ✉ *Ctra. Nacional Arriondas-Ribadesella,* ☎ *98/5840474,* 𝔽𝔸𝕏 *98/ 5841316. 18 rooms. Restaurant, bar. DC, V.*

$$ ⌑ **La Posada de Babel.** In the small village of Llanes, this exquisite, family-run inn provides roaring fires in the public rooms and plenty of personal attention. One of the bedrooms is in a converted granary. ✉ *Los Pasucos y La Pereda, 33509,* ☎ *98/5402525. 8 rooms. Restaurant, bar, horseback riding, bicycles, library. AE, DC, MC, V.*

LEÓN, GALICIA, AND ASTURIAS A TO Z

Arriving and Departing

By Bus

ALSA runs daily buses to Galicia and Asturias from Madrid and has weekly service from Paris, Brussels, Zurich, Nîmes, Toulouse, and Lyon. Several other companies connect the region with major Spanish cities. Contact the bus stations for information in **León** (✉ Cardenal Lorenzana s/n, ☎ 987/211000), **Oviedo** (✉ Plaza Primo de Rivera 1, ☎ 98/5281200), and **Santiago** (✉ San Cayetano, ☎ 981/587700).

By Car

The N VI, also called La Coruña Highway, links Spain's northwestern region with Madrid. Although it's a four-lane expressway for the first 90 km (56 mi) out of the capital, the rest of the road is two or three lanes. Be warned that it is heavily traveled by slow-moving trucks. Distance between Madrid and La Coruña is 609 km (378 mi), between Madrid and León (via the N VI highway to Benavente, where you pick up the N630) 333 km (207 mi). Good highways connect Santiago and La Coruña, Ferrol and Vigo, Caraballo and La Coruña, and Vigo and Túy (on the border with Portugal).

Although distances are great and traffic slow due to the winding, mountainous roads, driving is really the best way to appreciate the countryside in Galicia and Asturias.

By Plane

Galicia is served by an international airport 12 km (7 mi) east of **Santiago de Compostela** at Labacolla (☎ 981/547500 or 981/597400), with daily flights on Iberia to London, Paris, Zurich, Geneva, and Frankfurt. Regular domestic flights connect Santiago with the rest of Spain, including daily service to Madrid and Barcelona. The region's other two domestic airports are in **La Coruña** (☎ 981/187200) and in Asturias, near **San Estéban de Pravia,** 47 km (29 mi) north of Oviedo (☎ 98/5127500).

Iberia has ticket offices in Gijón (✉ Alfredo Truán 8, ☎ 98/5351790), **La Coruña** (✉ Plaza de Galicia 6, ☎ 981/228730), **Oviedo** (✉ Uria 21, ☎ 98/5240250), and **Santiago de Compostela** (✉ Calvo Sotelo 25, ☎ 981/590551).

Airport buses leave from in front of the Iberia office and the bus station (☞ *above*) in **Santiago.** The Asturias airport can be reached by buses that leave from the Iberia office in **Gijón** and the Iberia terminal in **Oviedo** (✉ Marqués de Pidal 20).

By Train
RENFE runs several trains a day from Madrid to León (4 hours), Oviedo (7 hours), and Gijón (8 hours), while a separate RENFE line serves Galicia (11 hours to Santiago). Daytime first-class and second-class cars are available, as is an overnight train with sleeping compartments. RENFE ticket windows are at the stations in **Gijón** (☎ 98/5170202), **La Coruña** (☎ 981/150202), **León** (☎ 987/270202), **Oviedo** (☎ 98/5250202), and **Santiago de Compostela** (☎ 981/520202).

Getting Around

By Bus
For information on the numerous local bus routes, contact the tourist offices or bus stations (☞ Arriving and Departing, *above*).

By Car
A four-lane, divided highway links León with Oviedo and Gijón and is the fastest way to cross the Cantabrian Mountains. A north–south Galician expressway was completed in 1992, shortening the travel time between La Coruña, Santiago, Pontevedra, and Vigo. Elsewhere, roads wind along the coast or climb over hills, always slow and seldom direct. Allow more time than you think it will take.

By Train
Local trains connect all the small towns with the major cities of Galicia and Asturias, but be prepared for dozens of stops.

Narrow-gauge **FEVE trains** clatter across northern Spain, connecting Galicia and Asturias with Santander, Bilbao, and Irún, on the French border. Tickets can be purchased at the train stations or the main office in Oviedo (✉ Avda. Santander s/n, ☎ 98/5290104).

Contacts and Resources

Car Rentals
Hertz has a main reservation office at the airport in Madrid (☎ 91/3058457). Other offices include León (✉ C. Santiro 20, ☎ 987/231999), Santiago (✉ Airport, ☎ 981/598893), La Coruña (✉ Vítor López Seoane, 2, ☎ 981/245424), and Oviedo (✉ C. Ventura Rodríguez 4, ☎ 98/5270824).

Budget has a main reservation office in Madrid (✉ Alcántara 59 , ☎ 91/3295048). Other offices are in La Coruña (✉ C. Doctor Fleming 16-Bajo, ☎ 981/151112) and Oviedo (✉ C. Arquitecto Regueira 5, ☎ 98/5244943).

Avis has an office in Madrid at the airport (☎ 91/3058532 or 91/305-4273). Other offices are in León (✉ Paseo de la Condesa s/n, ☎ 987/270075), Santiago (✉ Airport , ☎ 981/596101), La Coruña (✉ Plaza de Vigo 5, ☎ 981/121201), and Oviedo (✉ Airport, ☎ 98/5562111).

Golf
Asturias has two good golf courses, the **Club de Golf de Castiello** in Gijón (☎ 98/5366313) and **La Barganiza** in Siero (☎ 98/5742468). León's **Club de Golf León** (✉ San Miguel del Camino , ☎ 987/303400) is 15 km (9 mi) from the city. Galician courses include **Monte la Zapateira** (✉ C. Zapateira s/n, 15310 La Coruña, ☎ 981/285200), 11 km (7 mi) from the city; **Domaio** (✉ Domaio, Pontevedra, ☎ 986/330386); **La Toja** (✉ Isla La Toja, Pontevedra, ☎ 986/730818); and **Padrón** (✉ Padrón, La Coruña, ☎ 981/598891). Santiago's links are near the airport, at **Campo de Golf del Aero Club Labacolla** (☎ 981/888406). Call the club a day in advance to reserve equipment.

Guided Tours
The **Transcantábrico narrow-gauge train tour** offered by FEVE is an eight-day, 1,000-km (600-mi) journey through Basque country, Galicia, and Asturias, with English-speaking guides and a private bus that takes the group from train stations to regional artistic and natural attractions. Passengers sleep on the train and dine on local specialties. Trains run from June through September; the cost is about $1,575 per person, all-inclusive. Contact Transcantábrico (✉ General Rodrígo 6, 28003 Madrid, ☎ 91/5537656), **E.C. Tours** (✉ 10153½ Riverside Dr., Toluca Lake, CA 91602 , ☎ 213/874–3848 or 800/388–0877), **Conference Travel Int'l.** (✉ 157 Glen Head Rd., Glen Head, NY 11545, ☎ 516/671–5298 or 800/527–4852), or **Marsans** (✉ 66 Whitmore St., London W1H 9LG , ☎ 0171/224–0504).

Trastur, in Oviedo (✉ Muñalen, 33873 Tineo, ☎ 98/5806036), offers wilderness trips on horseback through the remote valleys of western Asturias. The 5- to 10-day trips are designed for both beginners and experienced cowboys; mountain cabins provide shelter along the trail. Tours begin and end in Oviedo and cost about $100 a day, all-inclusive. In the Ourense area, contact the active folks at **Galiciaventura** (✉ (Manuel Pereira 10, lower level, 32003, ☎ 988/241810, FAX 988/235374) for guided rafting, spelunking, scuba diving, and trekking excursions. The **Centro Hípico de Turismo Ecuestre y de Aventuras "Granjo O Castelo"** in Galicia (✉ Rúa Urzaiz 91-5A, 36201 Vigo, ☎ 986/425937) conducts horseback-riding excursions along the pilgrimage routes to Santiago from Pedrafita do Cebreiro and from Braga (in Portugal). **Reatur** (✉ Rúa Castelao 11-1, 3266 Allariz, Orense, ☎ 988/442066) offers guided historical and cultural walks, some of which include hiking, horseback riding, mountain biking, and canoeing in the surrounding areas. In Pontedvedra, you can rent mountain bikes at **Turnauga** (✉ Avda. Ponteares 31/3, 36680, ☎ 986/571604, FAX 986/571604).

In Santiago, walking tours with multilingual guides are organized by the **tourist office** (✉ Rúa do Vilar 43, ☎ 981/584081) during peak travel periods. The three-hour tour covers all the major monuments and costs about $12.

Hiking and Climbing
With so much rugged wilderness, northwestern Spain has become the country's premier outdoor-adventure region. The active traveler can choose from a huge variety of sports. **Nortrek,** in La Coruña, (✉ Inés de Castro 7 bajo- APDO 626, 15080, ☎ 981/151674) is a one-stop source for information and equipment for hiking, rock climbing, skiing, and bungee-jumping.

The Picos de Europa and the Covadonga National Park are excellent trekking areas. One of the most popular walks is the **Cares Gorge.** The tourist offices in Oviedo and Cangas de Onís can help you organize your trek, but for more technical climbing contact **Servicio de Guías**

de Montaña (⊠ Cangas de Onís, ☏ 98/5848916). **Mazaneda Estación de Montaña** in Orense (⊠ 31875 Pobra de Trives, ☏ 988/308767) is a full-service resort with mountaineering, biking, and skiing programs.

Skiing

The three small ski areas in this region cater mostly to families and local residents. The largest is **San Isidoro** (☏ 987/731115 or 987/721118), in the Cantabrian Mountains, with one chairlift and 12 slopes. Just east of there is **Valgrande Pajares** (☏ 98/5496123), with two chairlifts and eight slopes. West of Orense, in Galicia, **Manzaneda** (☏ 988/310875) has one chairlift and seven slopes. Valgrande Pajares and Manzaneda also have cross-country skiing.

Water Sports

In Santiago de Compostela, contact diving experts **Turisnorte** (⊠ Rosalía de Castro 16-2-1A; ☏ 981/530009, ℻ 981/522810), for information on scuba lessons, equipment rental, and guided dives. They can also hook you up for windsurfing and parasailing. For courageous and experienced sailors, yachting is a spectacular way to discover the hidden gems of the coast. At La Coruña's port, **Yatesport Coruña,** (⊠ Avda. del Puerto 28, 15160, ☏ 981/623351, ℻ 981/624208) rents private yachts and can arrange sailing lessons.

Visitor Information

Tourist offices are usually open 9–2 or 3 and 5–7. For information about the city and province of **León,** contact the **Oficina de Turismo de León** (⊠ Plaza de Regla 3, 24003 León, ☏ 987/237082); for information about **Galicia** and the city of **Santiago de Compostela,** contact the **Oficina de Turismo** (⊠ Rúa do Vilar 43, 15705 Santiago de Compostela, ☏ 981/584081), and about the principality of **Asturias,** contact the **Oficina de Turismo** (⊠ Plaza de la Catedral 6, 33007 Oviedo, ☏ 98/5213385).

Other tourist offices in towns covered in this chapter are **Astorga** (⊠ Plaza de España, ☏ 987/616838), **Cangas de Onís** (⊠ Emilio Laria 2, ☏ 98/5848005), **El Grove** (⊠ Plaza Corgo, ☏ 986/730975), **Gijón** (⊠ Marqués de San Estéban 1, ☏ 98/5346046), **La Coruña** (⊠ Dársena de la Marina, ☏ 981/221822), **Ponferrada** (⊠ Next to castle, ☏ 987/424236), **Pontevedra** (⊠ General Mola 2, ☏ 986/850814), **Ribadeo** (⊠ Plaza de España, ☏ 982/110689), **Ribadesella** (⊠ Carretera Piconera, ☏ 98/5860038), **Túy** (⊠ Puente Tripes, ☏ 986/601785), and **Vigo** (⊠ Jardines de las Avenidas, ☏ 986/430577).

5 Burgos, Santander, the Basque Country, and La Rioja

Burgos, home of the 11th-century military hero El Cid, is a somber city in a parched landscape of stone villages; Santander is a beach resort flanked by the Cantabrian mountains. The Basque country, with its own language, moist green hills, and rugged coast, has long celebrated gastronomy, sports, and rural culture, yet is drawing new crowds thanks to the Guggenheim Museum Bilbao. La Rioja, at the southern edge of Basque country, produces Spain's finest wines.

By George
Semler

THIS CHAPTER EXPLORES FOUR very different regions of northern Spain. Burgos, at the edge of the central *meseta* (plain), is one of the most Castilian cities; Santander (also known as Cantabria), once the main seaport for Old Castile on the Bay of Biscay, is a beach resort and mountainous zone wedged between the Basque country, to the east, and Asturias, to the west. The semi-autonomous Basque country (whose natives speak Euskadi, a mysterious, non–Indo-European tongue), with its moist, green hills and rugged coastline, is a distinct national and cultural entity within the Spanish state. La Rioja, between the Sierra de la Demanda and the Ebro River, is wine country.

Burgos was the 11th-century capital of Castile and the native city of El Cid ("Lord Conqueror"), Spain's legendary hero of the Christian Reconquest of the Iberian Peninsula from Moorish domination. Franco's wartime headquarters were established at Burgos during the Spanish civil war (1936–39), possibly as much for symbolic as for strategic reasons. Even today the army and the clergy seem to set the tone in this somber city, which sprawls in the shadow of one of Europe's finest Gothic cathedrals.

Santander and the Cantabrian region are traditionally a Castilian stronghold with sandy beaches, the Cantabrian mountains, tiny highland towns, and colorful fishing villages.

The Basque region is more a country within a country, or a nation within a state (the semantics are much debated, even today), with a language of its own: Euskera. In contrast to the traditionally individualistic and passionate Latin peoples who have been their neighbors, the Basques have often been regarded as more collective-minded and practical. They are also known to love competition—it has been said that Basques will bet on anything that has numbers on it and moves. Such traditional rural sports as chopping mammoth tree trunks, lifting boulders, and scything grass reflect the Basques' traditional attachment to the land and to farm life as well as an ingrained enthusiasm for feats of strength and endurance. Even poetry and gastronomy become contests in Euskadi, as *bertsolaris* (amateur poets) improvise duels of (often very witty) verse, and male-only gastronomic societies compete in cooking contests to see who can make the best *marmitako* (tuna stew).

The much-reported Basque independence movement is made up of a small but radical sector of the political spectrum. The underground organization known as ETA, or Euskadi Ta Askatasuna (Basque Homeland and Liberty), has killed more than 700 people in more than 25 years of terrorist activity. While this problem is extremely unlikely to affect the traveler, it will be apparent in the political graffiti—unusually colorful and photogenic—that adorn nearly every free inch of wall space from San Sebastián to Bilbao to Pamplona.

The Basque country also has longtime connections with both Britain and the United States. In particular, Bilbao and its province, Vizcaya, were the source of most of the iron used by the English during the Industrial Revolution. A poor region before industry made it a center of productivity on the peninsula, the Basque country has long sent out waves of immigrants to the New World. Perhaps as a result, the Basques are unusually friendly to both Americans and the British—often friendlier, in fact, than they are to Spaniards from Madrid and points south, who are still widely seen as unwelcome interlopers.

Pleasures and Pastimes

Beaches

Santander has three excellent sandy beaches: Magdalena, nearest to town; El Sardinero, the most elegant and best equipped; and Matalenas, near the Bellavista campground. San Sebastián's best beach, La Concha, curves around the bay directly in front of the city; it's beautiful and clean, but packed wall-to-wall for the entire summer. Ondarreta Beach, at the western end of La Concha, is often less crowded, and the beach on the northern side of the Urumea River, the Playa de Gros, is newer, wilder, and less discovered; surfers gather here for the big breakers. The wide expanse at Zarauz, 22 km (14 mi) west of San Sebastián, is another good choice, as are the smaller beaches at Guetaria (Getaria, in Basque) and Zumaya. The beach at Lequeitio is particularly beautiful.

Dining

If your taste runs toward traditional Spain and the roasts and hearty soups of Castile, concentrate on the rustic taverns and *mesones* (inns) of Burgos, on the edge of the famous Castilian *meseta*. Roast lamb and roast suckling pig are local specialties. Santander is all about mountain cooking—roast kid and lamb or *cocidos* (bean stews)—in the highlands, fresh seafood along the coast. Try the *soropotun*, Santander's stew of bonito, potatoes, and vegetables. Navarra (Navarre) is famous for beef, lamb, and vegetable dishes such as the *menestra de habas* (broad beans cooked with garlic, mint, artichoke hearts, white wine, and thyme). La Rioja is known for meaty stews, in its highlands, and vegetable dishes, in the Ebro basin. The Basque cuisine in and around San Sebastián is generally considered the best in Spain, combining the fresh fish of the Atlantic with a love of sauces that is rare south of the Pyrenees—a result, no doubt, of the region's proximity to France. The now 20-year-old *nueva cocina vasca* (new Basque cooking) movement has introduced exciting new elements. In San Sebastián it's nearly impossible to have anything other than a superlative gastronomical experience no matter where you dine. Don't miss the chance for *besugo al horno* (roast sea bream) or *txuleta de buey* (beef steak). Wines are not a strong point of the northern coast, but the local *txakolí*, a young, white wine made from tart green grapes, is a refreshing accompaniment to both seafood and meats. The Rioja wine-growing region is at the southern edge of the Basque country and provides all the local wine power Basque cuisine needs; Navarre also produces some fine vintages, especially rosés and reds—and in such quantity that churches in Allo, Peralta, and other towns were actually built with a mortar mixed with wine instead of water.

Food is not cheap in Basque country. But for your money, you'll taste some of the most superb creations in Europe, in an ambience that ranges from the traditional hewn beams and stone walls of old farmhouses and Castilian *mesónes* to the most modern and international settings.

CATEGORY	MAJOR CITIES*	OTHER AREAS*
$$$$	over 8,000 ptas.	over 6,000 ptas.
$$$	5,000–8,000 ptas.	4,000–6,000 ptas.
$$	2,500–5,000 ptas.	2,000–4,000 ptas.
$	under 2,500 ptas.	under 2,000 ptas.

per person for a three-course meal, excluding drinks, service, and tax

Fiestas

Pamplona is home to one of Spain's best-known celebrations, the Fiesta de San Fermín (July 6–14), made famous by Ernest Hemingway in *The Sun Also Rises*. The town's population triples for the occasion;

if you want to attend, reserve a room months in advance. In Vizcaya, near Bilbao, the coastal town of Lequeitio is famous for its highly unusual September 1–18 fiestas, in which men dangle for as long as they can from the necks of dead geese strung on a cable above the inlet. In Guipuzcoa province, closer to San Sebastián, the fishing village of Getaria uses the first week of August to celebrate Juan Sebastián Elkano's completion of Magellan's voyage around the world. La Rioja's famous Batalla del Vino (Wine Battle), a free-for-all honoring the local wine tradition, takes place in Haro on June 29.

Hiking and Walking

This multifarious chapter hints at more varieties of hiking and two-footed exploring than you can cover in a lifetime, much less a two-week visit. Well-marked footpaths wend from the Cordillera Cantábrica to the Pyrenees and along the Basque coast, connecting towns, scaling mountains, and ambling from one fishing village to another; the scenery, exercise, and color far exceed anything you'll experience in a car. Try the walks around Zumaya, or the walk over Jaizkibel between San Sebastián and the French border. The GR-11 trans-Pyrenean trail crosses the Pyrenees of Navarre, while the Santiago de Compostela pilgrimage route crosses Navarre and La Rioja on its way west. Local tourist offices can usually suggest routes of your preferred length and intensity.

Lodging

The largely industrial and well-to-do north is a relatively expensive part of Spain, and this is nowhere more apparent than in lodging prices. San Sebastián is particularly pricey, especially in the summer, and Pamplona rates double or triple during the San Fermín fiesta in July. The quality of hotels, service, and connected restaurants is generally quite high; reserve ahead in Bilbao, where the new Guggenheim Museum is filling hotels, and nearly everywhere in summer. Another option is a Basque farmhouse from the Agroturismo lodging network; these are economical, authentic, and beautiful.

CATEGORY	MAJOR CITIES*	OTHER AREAS*
$$$$	over 20,000 ptas.	over 15,000 ptas.
$$$	12,000–20,000 ptas.	9,000–15,000 ptas.
$$	7,500–12,000 ptas.	6,000–9,000 ptas.
$	under 7,500 ptas.	under 6,000 ptas.

All prices are for a standard double room, excluding breakfast and tax.

Monasteries

For a sojourn among the present-day masters of the Gregorian chant, the double-platinum monks of *Chant* and *Chant Noel* fame, stop in the town of Santo Domingo de Silos, 58 km (36 mi) southeast of Burgos. Single men can stay in the monastery for a maximum of 10 days. Guests are expected to be at breakfast, lunch, and dinner but are otherwise left to their own devices. If the monastery is full, as it often is these days, try to drop in for a vespers service. Closer to Burgos (10 km [6 mi]) is the Monastery of San Pedro de Cardeña, which also offers lodging and allows couples and even families as well—possibly as a result of the monastery's importance in the story of El Cid, the medieval Spanish hero who left his wife and children there when sent into exile.

Outdoor Activities and Sports

Basques are known to be most passionate about sports and food. Their athletic tastes run from jai alai to whaleboat regattas to soccer, from horse racing to rural contests such as stone lifting and log chopping. You need not participate to catch the action.

Pelota is the Basque national sport. Most towns have a local *frontón* (arena), where games normally start at 4 or 4:30. Other traditional Basque sports (*herrikirolak*) include the tug-of-war and woodchopping, ram-butting, and scything competitions. The most interesting and potentially bizarre of the local competitions is the *harrijasotazailes* (the raising of huge rocks by stone-lifters). Watch for local postings or ask at the tourist office.

Athletic de Bilbao is the area's traditional soccer giant, with San Sebastián's Real Sociedad just behind; up-and-down first- or second-division teams also compete in Santander, Pamplona, Logroño, and Burgos. Inquire at tourist offices or hotels about schedules and tickets.

Exploring Burgos, Santander, La Rioja, and the Basque Country

The radical geographical and cultural contrasts covered in this chapter are those of Spain itself: the central *meseta*; the Cantabrian Cordillera; the Bay of Biscay; the Pyrenees—habitat for Castilians, Cantabrians, and Basques. Then there is Navarre, part Basque and part Navarrese; and La Rioja, at the periphery of all the others. Each is described and explored below.

Numbers in the text correspond to numbers in the margin and on the Basque Country, Burgos, and Bilbao maps.

Great Itineraries

On the map, this region may not seem like much of a journey compared to the Iberian Peninsula as a whole, but the best roads to explore are also the slowest. Moreover, any one of the four main entities—Burgos, Santander, the Basque Country, Navarre—has enough hills, streams, and villages (not to mention the cities of Burgos, Vitoria, Bilbao, San Sebastián, and Pamplona) to spend a lifetime discovering.

Ten days to two weeks would be a fair time frame for seeing all of this area, although all of that time could be happily spent in the tiniest village or the smallest fishing port. In five days you could cover the high points and come away with an overall impression and some objectives for future visits. Three days is barely more than a drive-through, but it's time at least to lay eyes on some highlights.

IF YOU HAVE 3 DAYS

If three days is all you can manage, make a quick tour of **Burgos** ①–⑦, with its splendid cathedral, and drive through the Picos de Europa to ⊞ **Santander** ⑧ on day one. You might even manage to stop in Santillana del Mar and see the cave paintings at **Altamira** ⑨, or at least the museum and the video (you need to request a permit months in advance to visit the caves themselves). On the second day, follow the Basque coast to **Bilbao** ⑫–⑱ for a morning tour of the Guggenheim; then go on to ⊞ **San Sebastián** ㉗, stopping for lunch in the fishing port of **Guetaria** ㉖. Drive through **Pamplona** ㉚ and Navarre on the third day, approaching either from the north, if you're continuing across Spain, or from the west (and then north) if you're France-bound.

IF YOU HAVE 5 DAYS

If you have five days, start in **Burgos** ①–⑦ and visit the cathedral before driving up into the mountains for lunch on your way to the coast. Stop at **Altamira** ⑨ for a look at the caves, the splendid parador, and the tiny village houses. In ⊞ **Santander** ⑧, get a feel for the beach life along the Playa de la Magdalena and El Sardinero, and browse around the Plaza Porticada. On day two, explore 🖭 **Laredo** ⑩ and **Castro-Urdiales** ⑪, both port towns with lovely old quarters. **Bilbao** ⑫–⑱ could be bypassed as an industrial behemoth, but art buffs should not miss the new Guggenheim Museum (born 1997), designed by American Frank Gehry. Devote the third day to exploring the Basque Coast from Bilbao to San Sebastián; **Bermeo** ㉑, **Elanchove** ㉒, **Lequeitio** ㉓, **Ondárroa** ㉔, **Guetaria** ⑳—each of these fishing ports outdoes the other in activity, color, and cuisine. Day four is for 🖭 **San Sebastián** ㉗ and its delicious (though packed in summer) La Concha beach. **Pasajes** ㉘ (approached by launch from Pasajes de San Pedro, on the San Sebastián side of the straits) is a lovely village for lunch. **Fuenterrabía** ㉙, on the Bidasoa River border with France, is another indispensable visit. The fifth day could be spent at 🖭 **Pamplona** ㉚ and in the province of Navarre, from which you could continue on through southern Navarre and **La Rioja.**

IF YOU HAVE 10 DAYS
If you have 10 days, spend more time in 🖭 **Burgos** ①–⑦. After seeing the cathedral, linger to get the feel of this city's military and clerical austerity. Wander around the Espolón and visit the Casa del Cordón and the Cartuja de Miraflores. See the monastery at 🖭 **Santo Domingo de Silos** or the closer 🖭 **San Pedro de Cardeña.** If you can, spend the night at one of these monasteries, or start toward **Santander** ⑧. Spend a day exploring the mountains between Burgos and Santander. Have a look at the highland town of Reinosa and drive down N611 along the River Saja past semi-abandoned villages such as Cabuerniga Mayor. Plan to spend the night near the **Altamira Caves** ⑨, in the excellent parador at 🖭 **Santillana del Mar.** On the third day, drive to **Santander** ⑧, get settled, and explore the beaches and the Plaza Porticada. If it's summer, see what's going on at the university. The next day, you could investigate the towns of **Laredo** ⑩ and **Castro-Urdiales** ⑪, walking their old quarters and trying one of their excellent taverns, on the way to 🖭 **Bilbao** ⑫–⑱. Settle in for a night in Bilbao, if you're in an urban mood. Visit the new Guggenheim Museum, designed by Frank Gehry, on the morning of the fifth day; then head up the Basque coast for a night in one of the fishing villages between **Bermeo** ㉑ and Zarauz. Take a walk around Zumaya. Walk up the Urola River estuary to the quayside Bedua restaurant for a *tortilla de merluza* (codfish omelet), or have lunch in **Guetaria** ㉖ after walking over from Zumaya through Askizu. Day six can be devoted to 🖭 **San Sebastián** ㉗; explore the three beaches and the Parte Vieja (Old Town). The seventh day is a good chance to visit **Pasajes** ㉘ (Donibane, in Basque). Spend that night in a *caserío,* (Basque farmhouse) such as the Artzu, which overlooks the Atlantic and the town of **Fuenterrabía** ㉙. The eighth day is a chance to see Fuenterrabía (Hondarribia, in Basque). If you're so inspired, take the launch over to Hendaye, in France. Spend the night back at the El Emperador parador before heading up the Bidasoa River into the foothills of the Pyrenees. Explore upper Navarre and 🖭 **Pamplona** ㉚ on the ninth day. If you're here during Pamplona's famous festival of San Fermín, consider trying a smaller and saner version of this legendary fiesta at the village of Lesaka, saving the 10th day for wine tasting in **La Rioja.**

When to Tour Burgos, Santander, La Rioja, and the Basque Country

May–June and September–October are your best opportunities to combine good weather and avoid the tourist crush of summer, which peaks in August. The Basque country is characteristically rainy, especially in winter; summer is fairly temperate, which is why Sebastián first became the favored summer watering hole for Madrid's aristoc-

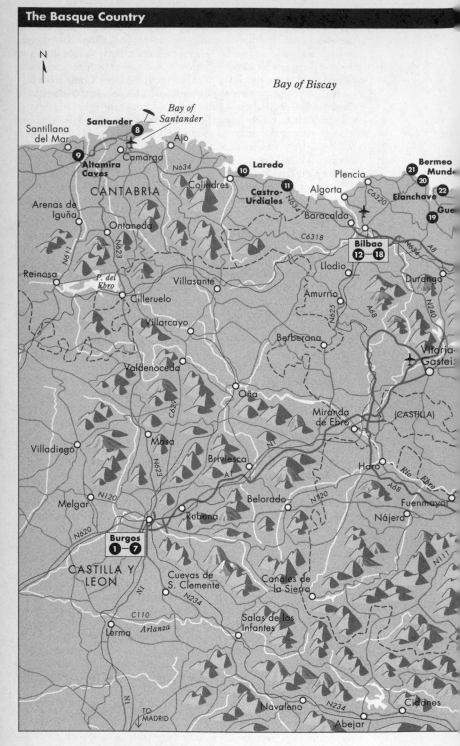

N

Bay of Biscay

Bay of Santander

Santander **8**

Santillana del Mar

Ajo

Altamira Caves **9**

Camargo

N634

Colindres

Laredo

Castro-Urdiales **11**

10

CANTABRIA

Plencia

Bermeo **21** Mund

Algorta

20

Elanchove **22**

19 Gue

Arenas de Iguña

Ontaneda

Baracaldo

N634

C6320

N634

A8

Bilbao **12**—**18**

C6318

N611

N623

Llodio

Durango

N240

Reinosa

P. del Ebro

Cilleruelo

Villasante

Amurrio

Berberana

A68

N625

Villarcayo

Valdenoceda

Oña

Vitoria-Gastei

(CASTILLA)

C629

Miranda de Ebro

Villadiego

Masa

N1

Haro

Río Ebro

A68

Briviesca

N623

A1

Belorado

N120

Fuenmayor

Melgar

N120

Rubena

Nájera

N620

Burgos **1**—**7**

N111

Cuevas de S. Clemente

Cañales de la Sierra

CASTILLA Y LEON

N1

C110

Arlanza

N234

Salas de los Infantes

Lerma

N1

Navaleno

N234

Cidones

TO MADRID

Abejar

racy. June's extended daylight, combined with the absence of crowds and the sweet temperatures, makes June the best time to explore this region.

BURGOS, SANTANDER, LAREDO, AND CASTRO-URDIALES

After a day in Burgos (or just lunch and a look at the cathedral), either take the relatively poor and slow N623 through the Cantabrian Mountains 156 km (97 mi) to Santander or skip Cantabria and head straight for Bilbao, 159 km (99 mi) on the A1 and A68 toll roads.

Burgos

❶ *240 km (150 mi) north of Madrid.*

Set on the banks of the Arlanzón River, Burgos is a small city that packs some of Spain's most outstanding medieval architecture. The first signs of the city, which you can approach by a relatively good road from Madrid, are the spiky twin spires of its magnificent cathedral, rising above the main bridge and gate into the old city center. Burgos's second glory is its heritage as the city of El Cid, the part-historical, part-mythical hero of the Christian Reconquest of Spain.

Burgos has been known for centuries as a center of militarism and religion, and even today you'll see more nuns and military officers on its streets than almost anywhere else in Spain. The city was born as a military camp in 884—a fortress built on the orders of the Christian king Alfonso III, who was having a hard time defending the upper reaches of Old Castile from the constant forays of the Arabs. It quickly became vital in the defense of Christian Spain. The ruins of the castle erected then still overlook Burgos.

Burgos's religious identity as an early outpost of Christianity was consolidated with the founding of the Royal Convent of Las Huelgas, in 1187. The city also became an important station on the Way of St. James, toward Santiago de Compostela, a place where Christian pilgrims stopped for rest and sustenance throughout the Middle Ages.

★ **❷** Start at the **cathedral,** the city's high point, which contains such a wealth of art and other treasures that jealous Burgos residents actually lynched their civil governor on the morning of January 25, 1869, for trying to take an inventory. The proud Burgalese apparently feared that the poor man was preparing to remove the treasures.

Most of the outside of the cathedral is sculpted in Flamboyant Gothic style. The cornerstone was laid in 1221, and the twin 275-ft towers were completed by the middle of the 14th century; the final chapel was not finished until 1731. The interior boasts 13 chapels, the most elaborate of which is the hexagonal Condestable Chapel. You will also find the **tomb of El Cid** (1026–99) and his wife, Ximena, under the transept. El Cid (whose real name was Rodrigo Díaz de Vivar) was a mercenary warrior whose victories over the Moors made him famous; the medieval *Song of My Cid* transformed him into a Spanish national hero.

At the other end of the cathedral, high above the West Door, is the **Papamoscas (Flycatcher) clock,** so named for the sculptured bird that opens its mouth as the mechanism marks each hour. The grilles feature some of the finest wrought-iron work in central Spain, and the choir has 103 delicately carved walnut stalls, no two alike. The 13th-century stained-glass windows that once shed a beautiful, filtered light were destroyed in 1813, yet another cultural casualty of Napoleon's retreating troops.

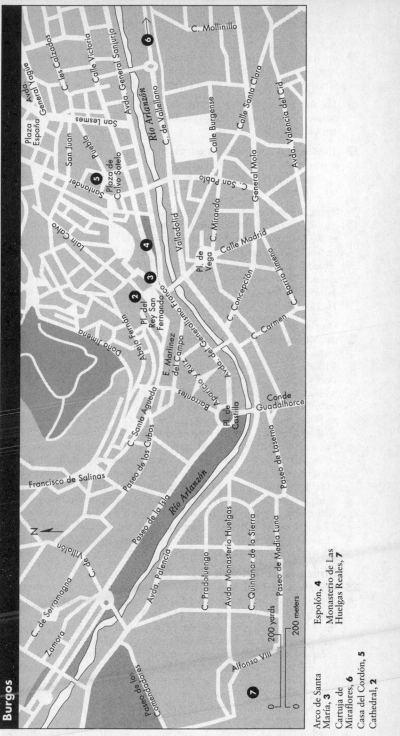

Burgos

C. Mollinillo

C. Calzados
Calle Victoria
Avda. General Sanjurjo
Río Arlanzón
C. de Vallellano
Calle Santa Clara
Avda. General Yagüe
C. les Calzados
Calle Burgense
Calle Valencia del Cid
Plaza
España
Avda.
España
San Lesmes
C. San Pablo
General Mola
Avda.
San Juan
Puebla
Plaza de
Calvo Sotelo
Santander
Valladolid
C. Miranda
Calle Madrid
Laín Calvo
Pl. de
Vega
C. Concepción
C. Barrio Jimeno
C. Carmen
Doña Jimena
Abeja Fernán
Pl. del
Rey San
Fernando
Avda. del Generalísimo Franco
E. Martínez
del Campo
Barrantes
Aparicio y Ruiz
Conde
Guadalhorce
C. Santa Agueda
Paseo de los Cubos
Pl. de
Castilla
Paseo de taserna
Francisco de Salinas
Paseo de la Isla
Río Arlanzón
C. de Villalón
Z
C. de Serramagna
Zamora
Paseo de los
Comendadores
Avda. Palencia
C. Pradoluengo
Avda. Monasterio Huelgas
C. Quintanar de la Sierra
Paseo de Media Luna
Alfonso VIII

200 yards
200 meters

Arco de Santa
Maria, **3**
Cartuja de
Miraflores, **6**
Casa del Cordón, **5**
Cathedral, **2**

Espolón, **4**
Monasterio de Las
Huelgas Reales, **7**

⊠ *Plaza del Rey San Fernando,* ☎ *947/204712.* 🖾 *Cathedral museum and cloister 400 ptas.; in groups, 250 ptas.* ☉ *Daily 9:30–1 and 4–7.*

❸ Across the Plaza del Rey San Fernando from the cathedral is the city's main gate, the **Arco de Santa María.** Walk through it toward the river and look up above the arch—the 16th-century statues depict the first Castilian judges; El Cid; Spain's patron saint James; and King Charles I.

❹ The Arco de Santa María fronts the city's loveliest promenade, the **Espolón.** The walkway follows the riverbank and is shaded with luxuriant black poplars.

❺ The **Casa del Cordón,** a 15th-century palace on the Plaza de Calvo Sotelo, is where the Catholic Monarchs received Columbus after his second voyage to the New World. It's now a bank building and can be viewed only from the outside.

❻ Three kilometers (2 miles) east of town, at the end of a poplar- and elm-lined drive, is the **Cartuja de Miraflores,** which has an unusual link to the Americas. Founded in 1441, this florid Gothic charterhouse has an Isabelline church with an altarpiece by Gil de Siloe, said to be gilded with the first gold brought back from the New World. To get there, follow signs from the city's main gate. 🖾 *Free.* ☉ *Church mass Mon.–Sat. 9 AM, Sun. 7:30 and 10:15 AM; main building Mon.–Sat. 10:15–3 and 4–6, Sun. 11:20–12:30, 1–3, and 4–6.*

❼ On the western edge of town—a long walk if you're not driving—is the **Monasterio de Las Huelgas Reales,** still run by nuns who live in seclusion behind a double iron grille. Founded in 1187 by King Alfonso VIII and his wife, Eleanor (daughter of England's Henry II), this convent for noble ladies was unprecedented for the powers it gave to the women running it. The present building was originally a summer palace for the kings of Castile; in 1988 it underwent renovations for its 800th anniversary. The convent was conceived in the Romanesque style and housed a royal mausoleum, where its founders still lie. All but one of the royal coffins kept here were desecrated by Napoleon's soldiers, but the one that survived intact contained clothes that form the basis of the convent's medieval textile museum. Don't miss the Chapel of St. James, where Castilian noblemen came to be knighted by the articulated (jointed) statue of Spain's patron saint; the figure lowered its sword arm and dubbed the candidates with a tap on the shoulder. ⊠ *1½ km (1 mi) southwest of town, along Paseo de la Isla and left across Malatos Bridge,* ☎ *947/201630.* 🖾 *650 ptas.; free Wed.* ☉ *Tues.–Sat. 10:30–1:15 and 4–5:15, Sun. 10:30–3.*

Dining and Lodging

$$$ ✕🖾 **Mesón del Cid.** In a 15th-century building that once housed one
★   of Spain's first printing presses, this family-run restaurant has been serving up traditional Burgalese food for four generations. The second- and third-floor dining rooms are framed with hand-hewn beams, and many tables have spectacular views of the cathedral. The *pimientos rellenos* (peppers stuffed with meat) are succulent, as are the *pisto Don Diego* (vegetable stew with egg) and the *sopa de Doña Jimena* (a garlic soup with bread and egg). The comfortable hotel next door faces the cathedral's facade, giving it one of the best locations in Burgos if not in all of Spain. The rooms are decorated in traditional Castilian style, and the ample brass beds have porcelain ornamentation. ⊠ *Plaza Santa María 8, 48383,* ☎ *947/205971. Closed Sun. evening. Hotel:* ☎ *947/208715,* 𝐅𝐀𝐗 *947/269460. 27 rooms, 1 suite. Parking. AE, DC, MC, V.*

Shopping

Burgos is famous all over Spain for its wide variety of cheeses. One of the best is known simply as *queso de Burgos* (Burgos cheese), a fresh ricottalike cheese. Pick some up at the **Casa Quintanilla** (✉ C. Paloma 17). Another good buy would be a few bottles of local Ribera de Duero wines, less famous than the neighboring Riojas but widely considered as good as or better, and at considerably lower prices.

Santander

★ ⑧ *390 km (240 mi) north of Madrid, 116 km (72 mi) west of Bilbao.*

Santander is one of the great ports on the Bay of Biscay. The first thing that will strike you, however, is the city's situation on the western edge of the Bay of Santander. A major northern beach resort, especially for Spaniards from the south, Santander is surrounded by beaches that happily lack the package-tour aesthetic of so many other Mediterranean resorts. A fire in 1941 destroyed most of the old town; the city may now be the most modern in Spain. Though traditionally conservative and loyal to the Spanish state, in contrast to its restless Basque neighbors, Santander is a lively place. The province—renamed Cantabria from Santander in 1984, when it became an official autonomous region—is historically part of Old Castile.

The city's origins are obscure, but it was already a busy port in the 11th century and enjoyed a thriving commercial life between the 13th and 16th centuries. The waning of Spain's naval power, however, and a series of deadly plagues during the reign of Felipe II made Santander's fortunes plummet. It came back to life commercially only in the 18th century, when it was finally allowed by Madrid to trade with the Americas. In 1910, a summer residence, the **Palacio de la Magdalena,** was built by popular subscription as a gift to Alfonso XIII and his queen, Victoria Eugenia; the city thus gained status as one of Spain's royal pieds-à-terre, but even this failed to make it thrive like San Sebastián. It still suffers from second-best status among Spain's northern cities.

Apart from having great beaches, Santander benefits from promenades and gardens, most of them facing the bay. Walk east along the Paseo de Pereda, the main boulevard, to the **Puerto Chico,** a small yacht harbor.

Past the Puerto Chico, follow Avenida Reina Victoria and you'll come to the tree-lined park paths above the first of the city's beaches, the Playa de la Magdalena. Walk onto the Península de la Magdalena to the **Magdalena Palace,** today the summer seat of the University of Menéndez y Pelayo, which offers Spanish-language and -culture courses for foreigners. The grounds have dramatic views of the bay.

Beyond the Magdalena Peninsula, wealthy locals have built mansions facing the long stretch of shoreline known as **El Sardinero,** the city's best beach. The heart of the neighborhood is the Belle Epoque **Gran Casino del Sardinero,** an elegant, twin-tower casino and restaurant worth a quick visit even if gaming tables hold no charms for you. A white building fronted with red awnings and set in a small park among sycamores, the casino lies at the center of the vacationer's Santander, surrounded by expensive hotels and some of the finest restaurants in the area. Most of these specialize in the fresh seafood for which Cantabria is famous.

In the old city, the center of life is the **Plaza Porticada,** officially called the Plaza Velarde. This rather unassuming little square is the seat of Santander's star event, the International Festival of Music and Dance, a series of outdoor performances every August. Across Avenida de Calvo Sotelo from the Plaza Porticada is the blockish **Catedral Buen Pastor** (Good Shepherd Cathedral; ✉ Somorrostro s/n), a building marking the transition between Romanesque and Gothic; it was largely rebuilt after serious damage in the 1941 fire. The chief attraction here is the tomb of Marcelino Menéndez y Pelayo (1856–1912), the city's most famous literary figure.

Drop into the **Museo Municipal de Bellas Artes** (Municipal Museum of Fine Arts) for a look at works by Flemish, Italian, and Spanish artists. Noteworthy is Goya's portrait of the absolutist King Fernando VII; the smirking face of the lion at the king's feet clues you into Goya's feelings toward his patron. The same building holds the **Biblioteca Menéndez y Pelayo** (☎ 942/234534), a library with some 50,000 volumes, and the writer's study, kept as it was in his day. Admission to the library is free; hours are weekdays 9–2 and 4–9:30, Saturday 9–1:30. ⊠ *C. Rubio s/n,* ☎ *942/239485.* ☜ *Museum free.* ☼ *Tues.–Fri. 10–1 and 5–8, Sat. 10–1.*

Dining and Lodging

$$ ✕ **Bodega del Riojano.** The paintings on wine-barrel ends that deco-
★   rate this restaurant have given it the sobriquet Museo Redondo (Round Museum). The building dates back to the 16th century, when it was a wine cellar, and this atmosphere lives on in dark-wood beams and tables. The menu changes daily and seasonally, but the fish of the day is always a sure bet on the Cantabrian coast. Desserts are homemade. ⊠ *Río de la Pila 5,* ☎ *942/216750. AE, DC, MC, V. No dinner Sun. in winter.*

$$ ✕ **Zacarías.** This popular spot is great for trying local specialties, whether for tapas or a full dinner. Owner and chef Zacarías Puente-Herboso is a well-known author and an authority on Cantabrian recipes. Try the *maganos encebollados* (calamari and caramelized onion) or the *alubias rojas* (red beans with sausage). ⊠ *General Mola 41,* ☎ *942/212333. AE, DC, MC, V.*

$$–$$$ ⌂ **Las Brisas.** Jesús García and his wife, Teresa, have managed to turn
★   this 75-year-old mansion into a ritzy, cottage-style hotel by the sea. If you like homey atmosphere and a little personality, this is the place for you. Each room is different, from dollhouse alcoves to an odd but attractive two-story family room. The basement bar and breakfast room is especially cozy. You're a short walk from the beach, and many of the rooms have fine views out to sea. ⊠ *Travesía de los Castros 14, 39005,* ☎ *942/270991 or 942/275011. 14 rooms. AE, DC, MC, V.*

$ ⌂ **México.** Don't be put off by the modest exterior. The personal
★   touch still counts in this family-run inn, and the breakfast room is elegant, with Queen Anne chairs, inlaid porcelain rosettes, and oak wainscoting. The rooms are pleasant, with high ceilings and glassed-in balconies. Reserve in advance, as word of this good deal has gotten around. ⊠ *Calderón de la Barca 3, 39002,* ☎ *942/212450,* ℻ *942/229238. 34 rooms. MC, V.*

Nightlife and the Arts

Santander's big event is the **International Music and Dance Festival,** which attracts leading international artists throughout August. Many of the events are in the city's main square, Plaza Porticada; other performances are held in monasteries, palaces, and churches. Collect information at the tourist office and at seasonal box offices in the Plaza Porticada and the Jardines de Pereda park. The city's **Teatro Coliseum** (⊠ Plaza de los Remedios 1, ☎ 942/211460) is normally a movie theater but becomes a theater proper in summer.

Shopping

Santander is known for **ceramics.** There are several touristy retailers on the Calle Arrabal, downtown, but **La Muralla,** at No. 17, is known locally as the best.

Altamira Caves

❾ *29 km (18 mi) west of Santander, 3 km (2 mi) from the medieval town of Santillana del Mar.*

The world-famous Altamira Caves are known as the Sistine Chapel of Rupestrian Art for the beauty of their drawings, believed to be some 13,000 years old. First uncovered in 1875, the caves are a testament not only to early humans' love of beauty but to their skill—especially in the use of rock forms to accentuate perspective. Earlier floods of tourists led to serious deterioration, so visitors must now apply in advance to be among the 25 people allowed in daily. You can visit freely, however, the adjoining museum and another cave with interesting rock formations. To write for permission to see the caves, indicate the number and names of the people in your group, and what date you hope to visit. Plan many months in advance. ✉ *Centro de Investigación de Altamira, 39330 Santillana del Mar, Cantabria,* ☎ *942/818005.*

Dining and Lodging

$$–$$$ ✕⬚ **Parador de Santillana del Mar.** Built in the 16th century, this lovely ★ parador occupies the erstwhile summer home of the Barreda-Bracho family. The rooms are baronial, with rich drapes and curtains and antique furnishings. The dining hall is elegant, if less than intimate, and the fare—as is the rule in paradors—is less splendid than the architecture and decor. ✉ *Plaza Ramón Pelayo 8, 39330,* ☎ *942/818000,* FAX *942/818391. 56 rooms. Restaurant, bar. AE, DC, MC, V.*

Laredo

❿ *N635 southeast and N634 east 49 km (30 mi) from Santander.*

You would hardly know it today, but Laredo was an early home port of the Spanish Armada and remained Spain's chief northern harbor until the French sacked it in the 18th century and Santander became the regional capital. This little town was visited by the most powerful of Spanish royalty, including Isabella the Catholic (as in Ferdinand and Isabella) and Charles I, better known as the Holy Roman Emperor Charles V (Carlos V). When Charles, the most powerful monarch in European history, stopped by in the mid-16th century, he donated two brass choir desks in the shape of eagles; these are now on display in the parish church of **La Asunción** (Church of the Assumption), in the center of the town's tiny **parte antigua** (old quarter). Walk through the old quarter to see ancient mansions with heraldic coats of arms.

Dining and Lodging

$$ ✕⬚ **El Risco.** *Risco* is Spanish for "cliff," an appropriate name for this hotel-restaurant built into the craggy slope overlooking historic Laredo. The food is renowned as an ingenious mixture of classical and nouvelle Cantabrian cuisine. Try the *pimientos rellenos de cangrejo y de buey de mar* (peppers stuffed with crab and fish). Every room has a spectacular view of the town and cove below. ✉ *La Arenosa 2, 39770,* ☎ *942/605030,* FAX *942/605055. 25 rooms. Hotel reservations required July–Aug. Restaurant. AE, DC, MC, V. Restaurant closed Wed. Sept.–June.*

Castro-Urdiales

⓫ *34 km (21 mi) northwest of Bilbao.*

The N634 winds up into the hills behind Laredo, with views of the Bay of Santoña over your shoulder. A short drive, parts of it within sight of the coast, takes you into the fishing village of Castro-Urdiales, believed to be the oldest settlement on the Cantabrian coast. Called

Flaviobriga by the Romans, it became the region's leading whaling port in the 13th and 14th centuries, when it had almost three times today's 13,000 residents. Overlooking the town is the mammoth, rose-colored jumble of roofs and buttresses that is the church of **Santa María,** revered as a Gothic work of art; just behind the church is an ancient **castle,** to which a modern lighthouse has been added. Aside from its arcaded Plaza del Ayuntamiento and the narrow streets of its **old quarter** (much of which burned on May 11, 1813), Castro-Urdiales is famous for seafood.

Dining

$$ ★ **✕ Mesón Marinero.** This pearl of a tavern and restaurant is a gastronomic delight, where local fishermen rub elbows with visiting elites. The array of tapas spread out on the bar will tempt you to forgo the main meal and *tapear* (munch tapas) away your dinner hour; but if you don't succumb, you're in for a treat in the elegant, second-floor dining room overlooking Castro's weathered fishing port. An unbeatable dessert is the *tostada de leche frita* (a milk-based custard concoction). ⊠ *Correría 23,* ☎ *942/860005. AE, DC, MC, V.*

En Route The 45-minute drive on the N634 from Castro-Urdiales to Bilbao takes you through some of the sprawling industrial development that mars much of Vizcaya, the westernmost of the Basque provinces.

Bilbao

⑫ *34 km (21 mi) southeast of Castro-Urdiales, 116 km (72 mi) east of Santander.*

Time in Bilbao (Bilbo, in Euskera) may soon need to be identified as BG or AG (Before Guggenheim, After Guggenheim). Never has a single monument of art and architecture so radically changed a city. Together, Frank Gehry's stunning museum, Norman Foster's subway system, and the glass Santiago Calatrava footbridge, which allows pedestrians to all but walk on water, are just a few ingredients in the urban revolution of Spain's fourth-largest city, the commercial capital of the Basque country. Although the inner city was most recently censed at 367,000, greater Bilbao now encompasses almost 1 million people, nearly half the Basque country's total population. The region's political and social malaise has been nearly eclipsed by the so-called Guggenheiming of Bilbao, which may still escalate when the Euskalduna music and convention center opens here in 1999. Bilbao is now poised to lead the Basque country into the next millennium with optimism and exuberance—it remains to be seen whether life can imitate art.

Founded in 1300 by a Vizcayan noble, Diego López de Haro, Bilbao became an industrial center in the mid-19th century, thanks mainly to the abundance of minerals in the surrounding hills. An affluent industrial class grew up here, as did the working-class suburbs (like Portugalete and Baracaldo) that line the Margen Izquierda (Left Bank) of the Nervión estuary. Many of the wealthy have left in the last 25 years; the fear of kidnapping and the extortion of ETA's so-called revolutionary tax has driven them to Madrid. The Right Bank suburb of Getxo, for instance, is remarkable for its abandoned mansions.

Bilbao's new attractions get more press, but the city's old treasures still perch giddily on the steep hills rising from the Nervión River. The *casco viejo* (old quarter), also known as Siete Calles (Seven Streets), is a charming jumble of bars and restaurants on the river's right bank, near the Arenal Bridge. A number of wide, late-19th-century boulevards, such as Gran Vía (the main shopping artery) and Alameda Mazarredo, are

161

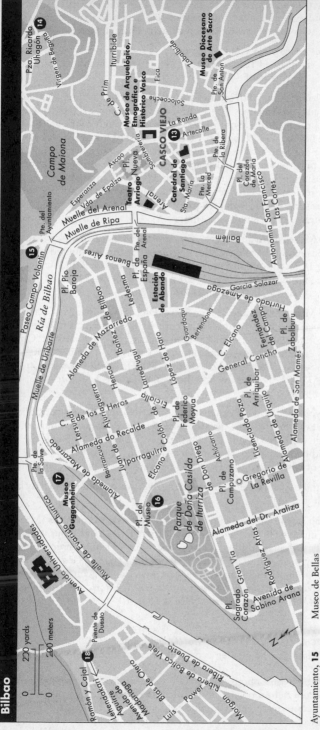

Bilbao

Ayuntamiento, **15**
Basílica de
  Begoña, **14**
Casco viejo, **13**
Guggenheim Museum
  Bilbao, **17**

Museo de Bellas
  Artes, **16**
Puente de Vizcaya, **18**

the city's more formal face. Bilbao is also rich in cultural institutions, including a major (BG) museum of fine arts; and many consider this Vizcayan capital one of the top culinary cities in Spain.

⑬ In the **casco viejo** you can see Bilbao's rust-colored river; the beautifully refurbished **Teatro Arriaga** (built in 1890); and the train that runs along the riverbank.

Walled until the 19th century, the old quarter lies around the **Catedral de Santiago** (St. James's Cathedral; open during mass). This church was a pilgrimage stop on one of the routes to Santiago; work on the structure began in 1379, but fire destroyed most of it in 1571. It has a notable outdoor arcade. Throughout the quarter are ancient mansions and fine ironwork on balconies; the area got a major face-lift after the devastating floods of August 1983 and is now an upscale shopping district replete with bars, restaurants, and happening nightlife. The most interesting square is the 64-arch **Plaza Nueva,** where a street market is pitched every Sunday morning.

The **Museo de Arqueológico, Etnográfico e Histórico Vasco** (Museum of Basque Archaeology, Ethnology, and History) is housed in a stunning 16th-century convent. The collection centers on Basque crafts, fishing, and agriculture. ✉ *C. Cruz 4,* ☎ *94/415–5423.* 🎟 *Free.* ◐ *Tues.–Sat. 10:30–1:30 and 4–7, Sun. 10:30–1.*

The **Museo Diocesano de Arte Sacro** (Diocesan Museum of Sacred Art) opened in 1996, after this 16th-century cloister was carefully restored. The inner patio alone, ancient and intimate, is worth the visit. On display are religious silverwork, liturgical garments, sculptures, and paintings dating back to the 12th century. ✉ *Plaza de la Encarnación 9,* ☎ *94/432–0125.* 🎟 *Free.* ◐ *Tues.–Sat. 10:30–1:30 and 4–7, Sun. 10:30–1.*

⑭ As you head downstream toward the *ayuntamiento,* stop at Calle Esperanza 6 and take the elevator to the **Basílica de Begoña,** a huge church from which you have a stunning view of Bilbao with the Nervión winding through it. The church's Gothic hulk was begun in 1519 on a spot where the Virgin Mary had supposedly appeared long before.

⑮ Near the Ayuntamiento Bridge is the riverside **ayuntamiento** (city hall), built in 1892.

★ ⑯ Don't let the Guggenheim eclipse the **Museo de Bellas Artes** (Museum of Fine Arts) in the Doña Casilda Iturriza Park, a half-hour walk west of the old quarter. It has a large collection of Flemish, French, Italian, and Spanish paintings, including works by El Greco, Goya, Velázquez, Zurbarán, Rivera, Gauguin, Cassatt, Léger, and Bacon as well as modern Basque artists. ✉ *Doña Casilda Iturriza Park,* ☎ *94/441–0154 or 94/441–9536.* 🎟 *Free.* ◐ *Tues.–Sat. 10–1:30 and 4–7:30, Sun. 10–2.*

NEED A BREAK?   The **Café Gran Vía** (✉ Gran Vía 40), in the modern district, a 20-minute walk from the old quarter, is a good place for tapas and a beverage.

★ ⑰ Covered with a photogenic 30,000 sheets of titanium, the **Guggenheim Museum Bilbao** opened in October 1997 and became Bilbao's main attraction overnight. The enormous atrium, more than 150 ft high, is connected to the 19 galleries by a system of curvilinear ramps and glass elevators. With most of the works from New York's Solomon R. Guggenheim Museum, this place is a trip in itself for lovers of contemporary art and architecture. (☞ Close-up: The Guggenheim Museum Bilbao, *below.*) ☎ *94/435–9080.* 🎟 *700 ptas.* ◐ *Tues.–Wed. 11–8, Thurs.–Sat. 11–9, Sun. 11–3. Closed Mon.*

⑱ Down in the Nervión's estuary, the **Puente de Vizcaya,** more commonly called the **Puente Colgante** (Hanging Bridge), is an 85-year-old symbol of Bilbao industry. The bridge, a transporter hung from cables, ferries cars and passengers across the Nervión, uniting two distinct worlds: exclusive, quiet Las Arenas, and Portugalete, a much older, working-class town now filled with jobless steelworkers. (Dolores Ibarruri, the famous Republican orator of the Spanish civil war, known as *La Pasionaria* for her ardor, was born here.) Portugalete is a 15-minute walk from Santurce, where the quayside Hogar del Pescador serves simple and ample fish specialties. *Besugo* (sea bream) is the traditional choice, but the fresh grilled sardines are hard to surpass. To reach the bridge, take the subway to Areeta, or drive across the Puente de Deusto, turn left on Avenida Lehendakari Aguirre, and follow signs for Las Arenas.

Dining and Lodging

$$$ ✕ **Bermeo.** Bermeo is one of Bilbao's top gourmet restaurants, specializing in fresh market cuisine and traditional Basque interpretations of fish, shellfish, and seafood of all kinds. Try the *rodaballo* (turbot) in vinaigrette sauce. ✉ *C. Ercilla 37,* ☎ *94/470–5700. Reservations essential. AE, DC, MC, V. Closed Aug. 1–15. No lunch Sat.*

$$$ ✕ **Goizeko Kabi.** Here you can choose your own crab or crayfish. The dining rooms are of brick and wood set off by Persian rugs and tapestry-upholstered chairs. Chef Fernando Canales's creations include *láminas de bacalao en ensalada con pimientos rojos asados* (sliced cod in green salad with roasted red peppers) and *hojaldre de verdura a la plancha con manito de cordero* (grilled vegetables in puff pastry with leg of lamb). ✉ *Particular de Estraunza 4 y 6,* ☎ *94/442–1129. Reservations essential. AE, DC, MC, V. Closed Sun.*

$$$ ✕ **Zortziko.** This lovely place combines an ultramodern kitchen with an ancient and elegant building that has been declared a historical monument. Try the *langostinos con risotto de perretxicos* (prawns with wild-mushroom risotto) or the guinea hen in truffle sauce. Chef Daniel García is one of the Basque region's culinary stars. ✉ *C. Alameda Mazarredo 17,* ☎ *94/423–9743. Reservations essential. AE, DC, MC, V. Closed Sun. and Aug. 25–Sept. 15.*

$$–$$$ ✕ **Matxinbenta.** Focusing on Basque cooking as well as international cuisine, this cozy spot creates innovative seafood dishes as well as roasts and prepares the most traditional specialties to perfection. Try the *bacalao Matxinbenta con base vizcaina* (cod prepared on a red-pepper base *al pil-pil*—i.e., very slowly, so that the oil makes a popping noise and a white sauce is created by the fish itself). ✉ *Ledesma 26,* ☎ *94/424–8495. Reservations advised. AE, DC, MC, V. Closed Sun.*

$$ ✕ **Aristua.** The upstairs dining room, all wallpaper and dark-wood floor-
★ ing, is homey yet elegant. There's an intriguing and delicious selection of traditional and nouvelle elements: In the former category, try *merluza a la koskera* (hake in a green sauce of clams and asparagus); in the latter, *pastel de verduras* (an aspiclike vegetable delight that looks like a painting and tastes better). One imaginative dessert is *gratinado de frutas* (fruits in a sweet white sauce). ✉ *Somera 1,* ☎ *94/415–9674. AE, DC, MC, V. Closed Sun. and Mon. evenings.*

$$ ✕ **Retolaza.** Bilbao's "in" crowd has been coming to this restaurant
★ since 1906. Operated by the third generation of its founding family, this typical *mesón* has wood beams and low ceilings. Classic Vizcayan fare includes *sopa de aluvias* (red beans and sausage) and *bacalao al pil-pil* (cod fried with garlic and served in a white sauce). ✉ *Tendería 1,* ☎ *94/415–0643. Reservations not accepted. MC, V. Closed Sun.–Mon., July 24–Aug. 23, and Easter wk.*

THE GUGGENHEIM MUSEUM, BILBAO

If Picasso's *Guernica* has been the 20th century's most celebrated and embattled painting, Bilbao's new Guggenheim may be the most anticipated and most spectacular building of all time. Described by Spanish novelist Manuel Vazquez Montalban as a "meteorite," this eruption of light and titanium has reinvented this large city in a dramatic and unprecedented way.

Bilbao has in one master stroke become one of the hot spots in Europe. Perennially chided as the *barrio industrial* (industrial quarter) in contrast to San Sebastián's *barrio jardín* (garden neighborhood), Bilbao has long been perceived as a polluted steel and shipbuilding center sprawled astride the foul-smelling Nervión estuary. Frank Gehry's gleaming brainchild, hailed as "the greatest building of our time" (architect Philip Johnson) is expected to spark a renaissance in the area after more than 60 troubled years. The Spanish civil war (1936–39); Franco's social, political, and cultural repression (1939–75); and separatist terrorism have combined to bring the Basque country to what might be called a turbulent standstill. The launch of the Guggenheim and relaunch of the city are in fact an attempt by the Basque and Bilbao governments to reach past Euskadi's Herri Batasuna separatist party and into the future. The Herri Batasuna party (Popular Unity, the political arm of the IRA-like ETA) controls only 10%–12% of the Basque vote and in no way represents the Basque people. Two days before the museum's official opening, the ETA murdered an Ertzaintza, a Basque Autonomous police agent, while preparing an assassination attempt apparently directed against King Juan Carlos.

The museum itself is even better than all of the advance hoopla suggests. Gehry's quasi-mechanical tour de force provides an ideal context for the postmodern and futuristic artworks it contains. The smoothly rounded, asymmetrical, ship's prow–like amalgam of limestone, glass, and titanium ingeniously recalls Bilbao's steel-manufacturing and shipbuilding past while using transparent and reflective materials to create a shimmering luminosity. The final section of the Nervión's La Salve Bridge is almost part of the structure, rendering the Guggenheim the virtual doorway to Bilbao.

The collection, described by director Thomas Krens as "a daring history of the art of the 20th century," consists of more than 250 works, most of them from New York's Guggenheim. Cubist, expressionist, surrealist, and geometrical abstract works are featured, from masters Kandinsky, Picasso, Ernst, Braque, Miró, Pollock, Calder, and Malevich, to newcomers Nauman, Muñoz, Schnabel, Badiola, Barceló, and Basquiat. The second floor is most identified with the original Guggenheim collection of abstract expressionism, along with European artists of the '50s and '60s: Pollock, Rothko, De Kooning, Chillida, Tàpies, Iglesias, Clemente, and Kiefer. The first floor is dedicated to large-format work, some of which—like Richard Serra's *Serpent*—was created specifically for the space it occupies. Claes Oldenburg's *Knife Ship*, Robert Morris's walk-in *Labyrinth*, and large pieces by Beuys, Boltansky, Long, Holzen, and others round out the heavyweight division in what is now the largest gallery in the world.

$$ ✕ **Victor Montes.** Widely respected as one of Bilbao's hot points for
★ the *tapeo* (daily tapas grazing), with tapas ranging from wild mush-
rooms to sausage or cheese along with splashes of wine, this well-stocked
counter should not be missed. ✉ *Plaza Nueva 8,* ☎ *94/415–7067.
Closed Sun. evening.*

$$$$ ✕⌑ **Hotel Lopez de Haro.** Five minutes from the Guggenheim, Bilbao's
only five-star hotel is becoming quite a scene within the city's new in-
carnation as contemporary-art nexus. The converted 19th-century
building has an English feel and all of the comforts and services your
heart desires. The excellent restaurant, the Club Náutico, serves mod-
ern Basque dishes created by Alberto Vélez—a handy alternative on
one of Bilbao's many rainy evenings. ✉ *Obispo Orueta 2, 48009,* ☎
94/423–5500, ℻ *94/423–4500. 49 rooms, 4 suites. Restaurant, bar,
cafeteria. AE, DC, MC, V.*

$$$ ✕⌑ **Hotel Ercilla.** This modern hot spot fills with the taurine crowd
during Bilbao's *semana grande* in early August, partly because it is close
to the bullring and partly because it has taken over from the Carlton
as the place to see and be seen. Its impeccable rooms, facilities, and
services have also helped its reputation. This might not be the place to
stay if you're looking for a quiet getaway. ✉ *C. Ercilla 3739, 48009,*
☎ *94/410–2020,* ℻ *94/443–9335. 346 rooms. Restaurant, bar, cafeteria. AE, DC, MC, V.*

$$$ ⌑ **Carlton.** The luminaries who have trod the halls of this grand old
hotel include Orson Welles, Ava Gardner, Ernest Hemingway, Lauren
Bacall, and most of Spain's great bullfighters. During the Spanish civil
war it was the seat of the Republican Basque government; later it
housed many nationalist generals. It is still elegant and well attended.
✉ *Federico Moyúa 2, 48009,* ☎ *94/416–2200,* ℻ *94/416–4628.
148 rooms. Restaurant, bar, meeting rooms. AE, DC, MC, V.*

$ ⌑ **Iturriena Ostatua.** This traditional Basque townhouse in Bilbao's old
quarter has heavy wooden beams, stone floors, and all the trappings
of a far more expensive operation. Simple, impeccably clean, and al-
ways eager to please guests, it's a great choice for travelers less than
eager to part with substantial loot in exchange for sleep and comfort.
✉ *Santa María Kalea 14,* ☎ *94/416–1500,* ℻ *94/415–8929. 21
rooms. Breakfast room. AE, DC, MC, V*

Nightlife and the Arts

Bilbao hosts an **August music festival**; inquire at the tourist office, as
venues change. The prized **Teatro Arriaga** (⌑ Plaza Arriaga s/n, ☎ 94/
416–3244), a magnificently restored building on the Nervión River,
consistently draws world-class ballet, theater, concerts, opera, and
zarzuela (comic opera). Opera and *zarzuela* are also performed often
at the **Teatro Coliseo Alvia** (✉ Alameda Urquijo 13, ☎ 94/415–3954);
information on opera is available at Rodríguez Arias 3 (☎ 94/415–
5490).

Bilbao's abundant nightlife breaks neatly down into ages and zones.
Students and anyone else who can pass for being thirtyish and under
are massively present in and around **Calle Pozas** and the **Casco Viejo**,
where serious *poteo* (tippling) continues late into most nights, espe-
cially Thursday to Sunday. Monday through Wednesday is quieter, bar-

ring holidays. Night owls over 30 gather at **Bluesville** and **Flash,** on Calle Telesforo Aranzadi (near the Carlton), for dinner, dancing, and cocktails. **Whiskey Viejo** and **La Ochoa** on Calle Lersundi are other prime watering holes.

Shopping

Basque *txapelas* (berets) are famous worldwide and make fine gifts. They're best when waterproofed and will keep you remarkably warm in rain and mist. Try **Sombreros Gorostiaga** (⊠ C. Victor, ☎ 94/416–1276), in the old quarter, for the most famous line of berets, Eloségui.

En Route   From Bilbao, pick up the A8 toll road and follow signs to the Guernica (Gernika, in Euskera) exit. From there, the Bi 635, a good road through Vizcaya's coastal hills, takes you north to Guernica.

THE BASQUE COAST, FROM GUERNICA TO GUETARIA AND ZARAUZ

This colorful stretch of coast winds along the edges of the Basque hills, dipping into protected fishing villages.

Guernica

⑲ *15 km (9 mi) east of Bilbao.*

On Monday, April 26, 1937, market day, Guernica suffered history's second terror bombing against a civilian population (the first, much less famous, was against neighboring Durango, about a month earlier). The planes of the Nazi Luftwaffe were sent with the blessings of General Franco to experiment with saturation bombing of civilian targets and, in the bargain, to decimate the traditional seat of Basque autonomy. Since the Middle Ages, Spanish sovereigns had sworn under the ancient **oak tree of Guernica** to respect Basque *fueros* (special local rights—just the kind of local autonomy inimical to the centralist *generalísimo* and his centralist movement of Spanish unity). More than a thousand people were killed in the bombing, and today Guernica remains a symbol of independence in the heart of every Basque, known to the world through Picasso's famous painting (now in Madrid's Centro de Arte Reina Sofía; ☞ Chapter 2).

The city was destroyed—though the oak tree miraculously emerged unscathed—and has been rebuilt as a modern, unattractive place. One point of interest, however, is the stump of the sacred oak, which finally died several decades ago, in the courtyard of the **Casa de Juntas** (a new oak has been planted alongside the old one); it is the object of many a pilgrimage. Nearby is the stunning **Ría de Guernica estuary,** a stone's throw from some of the area's most colorful fishing towns.

Dining and Lodging

$$ ✕ **Baserri Maitea.** Here's your chance to see the inside of one of the
★   Basque country's traditional *caseríos* (farmhouses); this one is 300 years old. Strings of red peppers and garlic hang from wooden beams in the cathedral-like interior. Entrées include the *pescado del día* (fish of the day) and *cordero de leche asado al horno de leña* (milk-fed lamb

roasted in a wood-burning oven). The pastries are homemade. ⊠ *Bi 635 road to Bermeo, Km 2,* ☎ *94/625–3408. AE, DC, MC, V. Closed Sun. evening, except in summer.*

$ ⊞ **Boliña.** Not far from the famous oak in downtown Guernica, the
★ Boliña is pleasant, friendly, and modern—a good base for exploring the Vizcayan coast. Rooms are smallish but comfortable. ⊠ *Barrenkale 3, 48300,* ☎ FAX *94/625–0300. 16 rooms. Restaurant, bar. AE, DC, MC, V.*

En Route From Guernica follow signs for Bermeo, but before you get there, stop at the Mirador de Portuondo, a roadside lookout with an excellent view of the estuary (at Km 43 on Bi 635).

Mundaca

⑳ *45 km (28 mi) northeast of Bilbao.*

Mundaca (Mundaka, in Euskera) is a tiny town that draws surfers from all over the world, especially in winter, when the waves are some of the world's longest.

Dining and Lodging

$$ ✕ **Casino José Mari.** Built in 1818 as an auction house for the local fishermen's guild, this building, with wonderful views of Mundaca's beach, is now a local eating club, but the public is welcome. It's a prime lunch stop in summer, when you can sit in the glassed-in, upper-floor porch. Very much a local haunt, the club serves excellent fish caught, more often than not, by members. ⊠ *In park (Atalaya) at center of town,* ☎ *94/687–6005. Reservations not accepted. AE, MC, V.*

$$ ⊞ **Atalaya.** This 1911 landmark is a private house tastefully redone as a hotel. The rooms are charming and comfortable, and those upstairs have balconies with marvelous views. Room No. 12 is the best in the house. The breakfast room is cheerful and light. ⊠ *Itxaropen Kalea 1, Villa María Luisa Esperanza, 48360,* ☎ *94/687–6888,* FAX *94/687–6899. 15 rooms. Bar. AE, DC, MC, V.*

Bermeo

★ ㉑ *3 km (2 mi) west of Mundaca.*

Bermeo, just beyond Mundaca, claims the largest fishing fleet in Spain, 62 long-distance boats of more than 150 tons and 121 smaller craft that specialize in hake. Bermeo was long a whaling port; in the 16th century, local whalers had to donate the tongue of every whale to help raise money for the church. The town still has one of only two wooden-boat shipyards on the northern coast, and the boats that fill its harbor make a cheerful picture. Drive to the top of the town's windswept hill, where a cemetery overlooks the crashing waves below. Townspeople tend family tombs at sunset.

Dining

$$ ✕ **Jokin.** You have a good view of the Puerto Viejo from this cheerful, strategically located restaurant. Jokin's fish comes directly off the boats you see in the harbor below. Try the *rape Jokin* (angler in a clam

and crayfish sauce) or *chipirones en su tinta* (small squid in its own ink) and, for dessert, the *tarta de naranja* (orange cake). ⊠ *Eupeme Duna 13,* ☎ *94/688–4089. AE, DC, MC, V. Closed Sun. evening.*

En Route   From Bermeo you can head back on the Bi 635 past Guernica toward Lequeitio (Lekeitio, in Euskera). For a rewarding side trip, turn left at Muretagana and follow the signs to the road's end in Elanchove (Elantxobe, in Euskera).

Elanchove

㉒   *27 km (17 mi) from Bermeo.*

This tiny fishing village is nestled among huge, steep cliffs, with a small breakwater protecting its fleet from the storms of the Bay of Biscay. The view of the port from the upper village, which is quite unaccustomed to tourists, is breathtaking; if you take the lower fork in the road, you'll drive into the port itself.

NEED A BREAK?   In the upper town, stop into the rustic **Bar Itxasmin,** which has a small restaurant just off the plaza where the road ends.

Dining and Lodging

$ ✕▥ **Arboliz Jatetxea.** Set on a bluff overlooking the coast, about 2 km (1 mi) outside Elanchove on the road to Lequeitio, this rustic inn is isolated yet pleasant. Rooms are simple, modern, and well kept; several have balconies. ⊠ *Arboliz 12, Ibarranguelua 48311,* ☎ *94/627–6283. 9 rooms, 3 with bath. Restaurant. AE, MC, V.*

Lequeitio

㉓   *59 km (37 mi) east of Bilbao, 61 km (38 mi) west of San Sebastián.*

This bright little town is similar to Bermeo but has two wide, sandy beaches right by its harbor. Soaring over the Gothic church of Santa María (open for mass only) is a graceful set of flying buttresses. Lequeitio is famous for its fiestas (September 1–18), which include a gruesome event in which men dangle for as long as they can from the necks of dead geese tied to a cable over the inlet while the cable is whipped in and out of the water by crowds of burly men at either end.

OFF THE BEATEN PATH   **SANTIMAMIÑE CAVERNS –** On the road to Elanchove, the Santimamiñe caverns contain some prehistoric cave paintings (guided visits Tuesday–Sunday at 10:30, noon, 4, and 5:30).

Ondárroa

㉔   *61 km (38 mi) east of Bilbao, 49 km (30 mi) west of San Sebastián.*

Farther east along the coast from Lequeitio, Ondárroa is another gem of a fishing town. Like its neighbors, it has a major fishing fleet painted various combinations of red, green, and white, the colors of the *Ikurriña*, the Basque national flag.

En Route   Continuing along the coastal road through Motrico and Deva, you'll approach some of the prettiest fishing ports and culinary centers in the Basque country. Before these, however, as you come into Zumaya, you'll see the turnoff for Azpeitia and the sanctuary of one of Spain's greatest religious figures, St. Ignatius of Loyola, founder of the Jesuits and spiritual architect of the Catholic Reformation (also known as the Counter Reformation). A half-hour trip up the Gi 631 will bring you to this colossal structure.

Sanctuary of San Ignacio of Loyola

★ ㉕ *Cestona is 34 km (21 mi) southwest of San Sebastián.*

The Santuario de San Ignacio de Loyola (Sanctuary of St. Ignatius of Loyola) was erected in honor of Iñigo Lopez (1491–1556) after he was sainted as Ignacio de Loyola in 1622 for his defense of the Catholic Church against the tides of Luther's Reformation. For many years Iñigo sought earthly glory in the fratricidal struggles that characterized the Basque country at the time; but after being badly wounded at Pamplona and returning to his family's ancestral home to recover, he abandoned war and took up religion. Almost two centuries later, the Roman architect Carlos Fontana designed the basilica that would memorialize the saint, after whom five universities in the United States and Canada and many others worldwide have been named. It's Baroque in style— a severe Baroque that does justice to the austere saint's memory. Inside, however, it's rich with polychrome marble, ornate altarwork, and a huge but delicate dome. The old tower house, a fortresslike structure adjoining the basilica, contains the room where Iñigo gave himself to religion. The massive chest was carved by Indians in Spain's Paraguayan missions.

Back on the coast road is **Zumaya,** a cozy little port and summer resort with the fjordlike estuary of the Urola River flowing (back and forth, according to the tides) through town.

Dining and Lodging

$$ ✕🏨 **Arocena.** One of the European spa hotels so popular around the
★ turn of the century, the Arocena has free bus service to the nearby springs, whose medicinal waters are still used to treat liver-related diseases. The rooms facing away from the road have especially fine views of the mountains. The common rooms, including an elegant restaurant and lobby, faithfully retain the hotel's Belle Epoque flavor. ⌧ *San Juan 12, Cestona, 20740, (10 min from Loyola),* ☎ *943/147040,* 🖷 *943/147978. 109 rooms. Restaurant, bar, pool, tennis court, playground, chapel. AE, DC, MC, V.*

Guetaria

㉖ *22 km (14 mi) from San Sebastián.*

From Zumaya, one of several perfect walking excursions leads to Guetaria, the next town, known as *la cocina de guipúzcoa* (the kitchen of Guipúzcoa province) for its surfeit of restaurants and taverns. Guetaria is the birthplace of Juan Sebastián Elcano (1460–1526), the first circumnavigator of the globe and Spain's most emblematic naval hero— Elcano took command of and completed Magellan's voyage after he was killed in the Philippines in 1521. The town's galleonlike church, with sloping, wooden decks, is a national monument, and the Iribar restaurant (☞ Dining, *below*) across the street is a great place for *besugo* (sea bream) cooked over coals.

Zarauz, the next town after that, is another beauty, with a wide beach and numerous taverns and cafés.

Dining

$$ ✕ **Iribar.** The Iribar has been grilling fish and beef over coals in the street just outside the church for more than half a century (no doubt raising havoc at times with the fasting faithful within). While Kaia and Kai-pe, in the port, are also excellent choices in Guetaria, with views of the fleet of colorful fishing boats in the harbor, the Iribar's warm, family atmosphere makes it the best choice. ⌧ *Kale Nagusia, 38, Guetaria, E-20808,* ☎ *943/140406. MC, V.*

En Route Heading east toward San Sebastián, you have a choice of the toll road or the coastal N634 highway. The former is a quick and scenic 44 km (27 mi), but the latter will take you through the village of Orio past a few more tempting inns and restaurants, not the least of which is the **Sidrería Ugarte,** at Usurbil.

SAN SEBASTIÁN TO FUENTERRABÍA

Relax on the beach or gaze at the beautiful architecture in graceful and elegant San Sebastián. As you head east from here you'll pass through Pasajes, where Lafayette set off to help the colonial forces in the American Revolution. Victor Hugo spent a winter writing here. Before reaching the French border, you'll hit Fuenterrabía (Hondarribia, in Euskera), a quaint and colorful port town.

San Sebastián

★ ㉗ *119 km (74 mi) east of Bilbao.*

San Sebastián is a sophisticated city that arcs around one of the finest urban beaches in the world, **La Concha** (the Shell), so named for its almost perfect resemblance to the shape of a scallop shell.

The best way to see this city, another center of Basque nationalism, is simply to walk around. San Sebastián is full of promenades and pathways, several leading up the hills that surround it; it's a metropolis built for the enjoyment of both eye and spirit.

The first records of San Sebastián date to the 11th century. A backwater for centuries, the city had the good fortune in 1845 to attract Queen Isabella II, who came seeking relief from a skin ailment in the icy Atlantic waters. She was followed by much of the aristocracy of the time, and the city became a favored spot for the wealthy. San Sebastián is laid out in a remarkably modern way, with wide streets on a grid pattern, thanks mainly to the 12 different times it has been all but destroyed by fire. The last conflagration came after the French were expelled in 1813; English-Portuguese forces occupied the city, badly abused the population, and proceeded to torch the place. Today, San Sebastián is a seaside resort in a class with Nice and Monte Carlo. It's probably the most expensive city in Spain in summer, when French vacationers descend in droves.

Smack in the middle of the entrance to the bay, the tiny **Isla de Santa Clara** (St. Claire's Island) protects the city from Bay of Biscay storms, making La Concha one of the calmest beaches on Spain's entire northern coast. A large hill dominates each side of the cove's entrance, and a visit to **Monte Igueldo,** on the southwest side, is a must. (You can drive up for a toll of 125 pesetas per person or take the cable car—funicular—for 170 pesetas round-trip; it's open 10–8 in summer, 11–6 in winter, with departures every 15 minutes.) From the top, you get the remarkable panorama for which San Sebastián is famous: gardens, parks, wide, tree-lined boulevards, Belle Epoque buildings, and, of course, the bay itself.

Every Spaniard will tell you that his or her native town has the best food in Spain; but most will agree that San Sebastián has the second-best. Many of the city's restaurants—along with scores of private, all-male eating societies—are in the **parte vieja** (old quarter) beyond the elegant **Casa Consistorial** (City Hall). This building, next to the formal **Alderdi Eder gardens,** began life as a casino in 1887. After gambling was outlawed early in the 20th century, the town council moved there from the Plaza de la Constitución, the main square in the Old Quarter.

San Sebastián is divided by the **Urumea River,** which is crossed by three bridges inspired by late-19th-century French architecture. At the mouth of the Urumea, the incoming surf smashes the rocks with such force that waves erupt to heights of as much as five stories. Spend some time down here; it's unlike anything else in the world.

Be sure to visit the monumental **Catedral Buen Pastor** (Good Shepherd Cathedral), near the beachfront. The basilica of **Santa María,** the city's first church, is in the Old Quarter.

Dining and Lodging

$$$$ ✕ **Akelarre.** This restaurant is on the slopes of Monte Igueldo, with spectacular views of La Concha Bay and San Sebastián. Chef Pedro Subijana is known for, among other things, his *lubina a la pimienta verde* (sea bass with green pepper) and such Basque classics as squid in a sauce of its own ink. ✉ *Barrio de Igueldo,* ☎ *943/212052 or 943/214086. Reservations essential. AE, DC, MC, V. Closed Sun. evening, Mon., 1st 2 wks of June, and Dec.*

$$$ ✕ **Arzak.** Renowned chef Juan Marí Arzak's restaurant, on the out-
★ skirts of San Sebastián toward Fuenterrabía, is in an intimate cottage—but the place is internationally famous, so reserve well in advance. The entire menu is a wonder, with traditional Basque preparations and more recent creations. The pastries are extremely light and extremely wonderful. Prices are very fair. ✉ *Alto de Miracruz 2,* ☎ *943/285593 or 943/278465. Reservations essential. AE, DC, MC, V. Closed Sun. evening, Mon., last 2 wks in June, and 2 wks in Nov.*

$$$ ✕ **Panier Fleuri.** One of the most select wine lists in Spain complements the food here, which is served in a sober dining room overlooking the crashing surf at the mouth of the Urumea River. Chef Tatus Fombellida is a winner of Spain's national gastronomy prize, no mean feat. Try his *faisán* (pheasant) or the *supremas de lenguado a la florentina* (sole baked with spinach and served with hollandaise sauce), and for dessert the lemon sorbet with champagne. ✉ *Paseo de Salamanca 1,* ☎ *943/424205. Reservations essential. AE, DC, MC, V. Closed Sun. evening, Wed., last 2 wks of Dec., 3 wks in June, Christmas wk.*

$$ ✕ **Salduba.** Javier Arbizu is the cook for the Spanish national soccer team. His restaurant, built of ancient oak beams and heavy wooden furniture, is a bastion of sound cooking and service in the middle of San Sebastián's bustling *parte vieja.* ✉ *C. Pescadería 2,* ☎ *943/425627. AE, DC, MC, V.*

$$ ✕ **Urepel.** Both the cuisine and the interior design balance classical and modern elements in a felicitous way. The *chicharro al escama dorada* (a deboned, skinned mackerel served under a layer of golden-brown sliced potatoes) is a typical Urepel invention. There is no principal chef; the kitchen staff works as a team, in prototypically Basque egalitarian fashion. ✉ *Paseo de Salamanca 3,* ☎ *943/424040. AE, DC, MC, V. Closed Sun. and Tues. evening.*

$ ✕ **Casa Vallés.** Just a two-minute walk from the back of San Sebastián's cathedral, this fine little tapas bar and restaurant displays some 30 to 40 different freshly prepared and irresistible creations at midday and again in the early evening. Beloved by residents, it combines excellent food with great value. ✉ *Reyes Católicos 10,* ☎ *943/452210. AE, DC, MC, V. Closed Wed. and June 15–30.*

$$$$ 🏨 **María Cristina.** The graceful beauty of the Belle Epoque is evoked by San Sebastián's top luxury hotel, which sits like the queen it's named after on the elegant west bank of the Urumea River. The grandeur continues inside, in salons filled with Oriental rugs, potted palms, and Carrara marble columns, and in bedrooms to match. ✉ *Paseo República Argentina s/n, 20004,* ☎ *943/424900,* ℻ *943/423914.*

139 rooms. Restaurant, bar, beauty salon, meeting rooms. AE, DC, MC, V.

$$$ ⌧ **Londres y de Inglaterra.** This stately hotel has a privileged position on the promenade above La Concha Beach. You enter to find a quiet lobby with chandeliers, fine rooms, and attentive, warm service. The bar faces the bay. ⌧ *Zubieta 2, 20007,* ☎ *943/426989,* FAX *943/ 420031. 130 rooms. Restaurant, bar, casino. AE, DC, MC, V.*

$$ ⌧ **Bahía.** A two-minute walk from the beach, this hotel is small but appealing. It has a welcoming lobby, with a friendly minibar and salon, and its rooms are comfortable and modern. ⌧ *San Martín 54 bis, 20007,* ☎ *943/469211,* FAX *943/463914. 60 rooms. MC, V.*

Nightlife and the Arts

San Sebastián's **film festival** takes over in the second half of September, although exact dates vary; ask at the tourist office or read the local press for details and ticket information. The same goes for the **jazz festival,** in late July, an event that draws many of the world's top performers. A varied program of theater, dance, and other events goes on year-round at the beautiful **Teatro Victoria Eugenia** (⌧ Reina Regente s/n, ☎ 943/ 481155 or 943/481160).

At night, look for *copas, potes* (both "drinks"), and general cruising in and around the **parte vieja.** The top disco is **Bataplan,** on La Concha.

Shopping

Ponsol (⌧ C. Narrica 4, ☎ 943/420876) is the best place to buy the Basque berets, called *boinas.* The Leclerq family business has been hatting *donostiarras* (residents of *donosti*—San Sebastián, in Euskera) for three generations. Stop in at **Maitiena** (⌧ Avda. Libertad 32, ☎ 943/ 424721) for a fabulous selection of chocolates.

Pasajes

㉘ *10 km (6 mi) east of San Sebastián.*

The historic port of Pasajes (Pasaia, in Euskera) is where Lafayette set out to aid the rebels of the American Revolution. It's actually three towns in one large bay: **Pasajes Ancho,** an industrial port; **Pasajes de San Pedro,** a large fishing harbor; and **Pasajes de San Juan.** This last is a tiny settlement of 18th- and 19th-century buildings along a single street that fronts the bay's outlet to the sea; it's best reached by driving into Pasajes de San Pedro and catching a launch across the mouth of the harbor (about 100 pesetas depending on the time of day). The town is known for its three fine restaurants: **Txulotxo, Casa Cámara** (☞ Dining, *below*), and **Artzape.**

Dining

$$ ✕ **Casa Cámara.** Four generations ago, Pablo Camara turned this old
★ fishing wharf on Pasajes Bay into a first-class restaurant. The dining room has lovely views and a pit from which lobsters and crayfish are hauled up for inspection by diners. Try *cangrejo del mar* (spider crab with vegetable sauce) or the superb hake in green sauce. ⌧ *Pasajes de San Juan,* ☎ *943/523699 or 943/517874. Reservations essential. V. Closed Sun. evening and Mon.*

Fuenterrabía

㉙ *12 km (8 mi) east of Pasajes.*

Fuenterrabía (Hondarribia, in Euskera) is the final fishing port before you reach the French border. The harbor, lined with fishermen's homes and small fishing boats, is a beautiful but rather touristy spot. If you have a taste for history, follow signs up the hill to the medieval bastion and onetime castle of Charles V, now a parador.

Dining and Lodging

$$$ ✕ **Ramón Roteta.** Set in a beautiful old villa with an informal garden, this restaurant serves excellent food, making it an easy choice for anyone staying at the local parador. Sample the garlic and shrimp pastries or the rice with vegetables and clams. The pastries are all homemade. ⊠ *Villa Ainara, C. Irún 2,* ☎ *943/641693. AE, DC, MC, V. Closed Sun. evening and Thurs., except in summer.*

$ ✕ **La Hermandad de Pescadores.** This centrally located "brotherhood" is owned by the local fishermen's guild and serves simple and hearty fare at reasonable prices. Try the *sopa de pescado* (fish soup) or the *almejas a la marinera* (clams in a thick, garlicky sauce). If you come outside peak hours (2–4 and 9–11), you'll find room at the long communal boards. ⊠ *C. Zuloaga s/n,* ☎ *943/642738. AE, DC, MC, V. Closed Tues. evening and Wed.*

$$$ ▥ **Parador El Emperador.** Replete with suits of armor and other chivalric bric-a-brac, this parador occupies a superb medieval bastion that dates from the 10th century and housed Carlos V in the 16th century. Many rooms have gorgeous views of the Bidasoa River and estuary, which is dotted with colorful fishing boats. Be sure to reserve ahead, and ask for one of the three "special" rooms, with canopied beds and baronial appointments; they're worth the extra $30. ⊠ *Plaza Armas de Castillo, 20005,* ☎ *943/645500,* ℻ *943/642153. 36 rooms. Bar. AE, DC, MC, V.*

$ ▥ **Caserio "Artzu."** This family farmhouse, with its classic low, wide roof-line, has been here in one form or another for some 800 years. Just west of the hermitage of Nuestra Señora de Guadalupe, Artzu offers modernized accommodations overlooking the junction of the Bidasoa estuary and the Atlantic. ⊠ *Barrio Montaña, 20280,* ☎ *943/ 640530. 6 rooms, 1 with bath. Restaurant. No credit cards.*

En Route The fastest route from San Sebastián to Pamplona is the A15 Autovía de Navarra, which cuts through the Leizarán Valley into Navarre and takes about 45 minutes. A somewhat prettier, if slower and more tortuous 134-km (83-mi) drive is via C133, which starts out near the French border (and Fuenterrabía) and follows the Bidasoa River (the border with France) up through Vera de Bidasoa. When C133 meets N121 you can turn left up into the lovely Baztán Valley or right through the Velate pass on to Pamplona, the ancient capital of Navarre.

PAMPLONA, BAZTÁN, AND OLITE

Run with the bulls during Pamplona's annual festival of San Fermín. Should you seek quieter climes, head for the rolling hills of the Baztán Valley or explore a storybook castle in Olite, southeast of Pamplona.

Pamplona

③⓪ *91 km (56 mi) southeast of San Sebastián.*

Pamplona is known the world over for its running of the bulls, made famous by Ernest Hemingway in his 1926 novel *The Sun Also Rises.* The occasion is the festival of San Fermín, July 6–14, when Pamplona's population triples (along with hotel prices) and rooms must be reserved months in advance. Tickets to the bullfights (*corridas*), as opposed to the running (*encierro,* meaning "enclosing"), to which access is free, can be difficult to obtain. Every morning at 7 sharp a skyrocket is shot off, and the bulls kept overnight in the corrals at the edge of town are run through a series of closed-off streets leading to the bullring, a 902-yard dash. Running before them are Spaniards and foreigners feeling festive enough to risk a goring, most wearing the traditional white shirts and trousers with red neckerchiefs and carrying rolled-up newspapers to swat the bulls with. If all goes well—no bulls separated from the pack, no mayhem—the bulls arrive in the ring in just 2½ minutes. The degree of peril in the *encierro* is difficult to gauge. Serious injuries occur nearly every day; deaths are rare but always a very definite possibility. What is undeniable is the sense of danger, the mob hysteria, and the exhilaration.

Pamplona was founded by the Roman emperor Pompey as Pompaelo or Pameiopolis and was successively taken by the Franks, the Goths, and the Moors. The Pamplonans managed to expel the Arabs temporarily in 750, when they put themselves under the protection of Charlemagne. But the foreign commander took advantage of this trust to destroy the city walls, so that when he was driven out once more by the Moors, the Navarrese took their revenge, ambushing and slaughtering the retreating Frankish army as it fled over the Pyrenees through the mountain pass of Roncesvalles in 778. This is the episode depicted in the 11th-century *Song of Roland,* although the French author chose to cast the aggressors as Moors. For centuries after that, Pamplona remained three argumentative towns until they were forcibly incorporated into one city by Carlos III (the Noble, 1387–1425) of Navarre.

Pamplona's **cathedral,** set near the portion of the ancient walls rebuilt in the 17th century, is one of the most important religious buildings in northern Spain thanks to the fragile grace and gabled Gothic arches of its cloister. Inside are the tombs of Charles III and his wife, marked by an alabaster sculpture. The **Museo Diocesano** (Diocesan Museum) houses religious art spanning the period from the Middle Ages to the Renaissance. ☒ *C. Curia s/n.* ☜ *Free.* ☺ *Cathedral: 24 hrs.; museum: Tues–Sat. 9–2, 4–7, Sun. 9–2.*

★ On Calle Santo Domingo, in a 16th-century building that was once used as a hospital for pilgrims on their way to Santiago, is the **Museo de Navarra** (Navarran Museum; ☒ C. Jaranta s/n, ☏ 948/227831), with a collection of regional archaeological artifacts and historical costumes. Admission is 300 pesetas; the museum is open Tuesday–Saturday 9–2 and 5–7, Sunday 9–2. The most remarkable civil architecture in the city is the ornate **ayuntamiento** (city hall), on the Plaza Consistorial; this 18th-century structure is notable for the blackish color it has acquired over the years, set off against its gilded balconies. Stop in for a look at the wood-and-marble interior.

NEED A BREAK?	Pamplona's gentry has been flocking to the ornate, French-style **Café Iruña,** in the central Plaza del Castillo, since 1888. The bar and salons are sumptuously paneled in dark woods. Beyond the stand-up bar is a bingo hall (you must be 18 to play). ☒ *Plaza del Castillo 44.* ☺ *Daily 5 PM–3 AM.*

One of Pamplona's greatest charms is the warren of small streets near the **Plaza del Castillo** (especially Calle San Nicolás), which are filled with restaurants, taverns, and bars. Pamplonans, a hardy sort, are well known for their eagerness and capacity to eat and drink.

The central **Ciudadela,** an ancient fortress, is today a parkland of promenades and pools. Walk through in the late afternoon, the time of the *paseo* (traditional stroll), for a taste of everyday life here.

Dining and Lodging

$$$$ ✕ **Josetxo.** This warm, elegant, family-run place is one of Pamplona's finest restaurants. Its specialties include *hojaldre de marisco* (shellfish pastry), for starters, and *ensalada de langosta* (lobster salad). Try the pigeon stuffed with foie gras and truffles. ⊠ *Príncipe de Viana 1,* ☎ *948/222097. AE, DC, V. Closed Sun. except during San Fermín and Aug.*

$$$ ✕ **Hartza.** Archaic and elegant, this rustic spot serves some of the most creative cuisine in Pamplona without omitting any of the hearty fare Navarre is known for. Try the *oca con jugo de trufa y manzana* (goose with apple and truffles). ⊠ *Juan de Labrit 19,* ☎ *948/224568. AE, DC, MC, V. Closed Sun. night, Mon. July 30–Aug. 24, Dec. 24–Jan. 4.*

$$ ✕ **Erburu.** In the heart of the nightlife district, this dark, wood-beamed ★ restaurant is a true find, frequented by Pamplonans in the know. Come here to dine or just to sample tapas at the bar. Standouts are the *merluza con salsa verde* (hake in green sauce), a Basque classic, or any of a whole range of dishes made with *alcochofas* (artichokes). ⊠ *San Lorenzo 19–21,* ☎ *948/225169. AE, DC, MC, V. Closed Mon. and 2nd half of July.*

$ ✕⌂ **Casa Otano.** This friendly and tumultuous hotel and restaurant is simple and well placed, right in the middle of the tapas and wine circuit and just a few paces from Pamplona's central square. The restaurant downstairs can keep you well fed. The general atmosphere is consistent with the San Fermín madness that will be raging in the street if you come during the fiesta (July 6–14). ⊠ *San Nicolás 5, 31001,* ☎ *948/225095,* FAX *948/212012. 15 rooms. AE, DC, MC, V. Closed (usually) July 16–31.*

$$$$ ⌂ **Los Tres Reyes.** If you must attend the San Fermín blowout (July 6–14) you can arrange to be very comfortable at this wonderful place. Pool, piano bar, restaurant: it's all here, just a step from all the action. Prices double for the duration. ⊠ *C. de la Taconera s/n, 31001,* ☎ *948/ 226600,* FAX *948/222930. 168 rooms. Restaurant, cafeteria, piano bar, pool, beauty salon, car rental. AE, DC, MC, V.*

$$–$$$$ ⌂ **Hotel Yoldi.** This hotel is much frequented by the somewhat snooty foreign *afición*, that is, old-hand bullfight fans. Still, anthropologically they're an interesting lot; the hotel is always teeming with knowledgeable-looking Hemingwayoids debating such taurine esoterica as the placement, angle, intent, and aesthetic of the third sword thrust on the second bull in the fifth *corrida* of the fourth *feria* of the last decade. Who could ask for more? ⊠ *Avda. San Ignacio 11, 31002,* ☎ *948/ 224800,* FAX *948/212045. 50 rooms. Bar, cafeteria. AE, DC, MC, V.*

$$–$$$ ⌂ **La Perla.** Hemingway watched his first running of the bulls here, from his balcony over Calle Estafeta. La Perla is the oldest hotel in town, though far from the best. The founder's son was a bullfighter, and the two bulls he killed before retiring preside over the salon. The timeless decor is simple but charming, straight out of *The Sun Also Rises.* Prices shoot up during San Fermín. ⊠ *Plaza del Castillo 1, 31001,* ☎ *948/227706,* FAX *948/211566. 67 rooms, 45 with bath. AE, DC, MC, V.*

Nightlife and the Arts

Pamplona has a varied summer program of theater, *zarzuela*, ballet, and concerts; contact the **Teatro Gayarre** (⊠ Avda. Carlos III Noble 1, ☎ 948/220139) for information. In August, the **Festivales de Navarra** bring theater and other events.

Shopping

Botas are the wineskins from which Basques typically drink at bullfights or during fiestas. The art lies in drinking a stream of wine while the *bota* is held at arm's length—without spilling a drop, if you want to maintain your honor. You can buy *botas* in any Basque town, but **Anel** (⊠ C. Comedías 7) sells the best ones, made by Las Tres Zetas (The Three Z's; written as ZZZ).

The **neckerchiefs** worn for the running of the bulls are sold in Pamplona shops, as are **gerrikos,** the wide belts worn by Basque sportsmen during contests of strength, to hold in overstressed organs.

For sweets, try **Salcedo** (⊠ C. Estafeta 37), open since 1800, which invented and still sells almond-based *mantecadas* (powder cakes), as well as *coronillas* (a delightful almond-and-cream concoction). **Hijas de C. Lozano** (⊠ C. Zapatería 11) sells the *café y leche* (coffee and milk) toffees that are prized all over Spain.

En Route   From Pamplona, take the N III southwest to Estella and Logroño or the A15 toll road to Olite. Both routes run mainly through wine country, providing a stark contrast to any area yet seen on this itinerary. It's particularly beautiful in spring, with fields full of wildflowers.

Olite

★ ③ *41 km (25 mi) south of Pamplona.*

Much of Olite is ancient and pleasant to walk through. The 11th-century church of **San Pedro** is interesting for its finely worked Romanesque cloisters and portal. The town's parador is part of a **castle** restored by Carlos III in the French style—a fantasy structure of ramparts, crenellated walls, and watchtowers. You can walk the ramparts in the part not occupied by the parador. ☜ *300 ptas.* ☉ *Daily 10–2 and 4–5.*

Dining and Lodging

$$ ✕⚏ **Parador Príncipe de Viana.** This parador is a flight of fancy,
★   named for the grandson of Carlos III, who spent his life here. It's housed in part of Olite's castle complex, and the chivalric atmosphere is well preserved, with grand salons, secret stairways, heraldic tapestries, and the odd suit of armor. ⊠ *Plaza de los Teobaldos 2, 31390,* ☎ *948/ 740000,* ⊠ *948/740201. 43 rooms. Restaurant, bar. AE, DC, MC, V.*

LA RIOJA

Producer of Spain's best wines, this microcosm of highlands, plains, vineyards, and the Ebro River basin is bordered by Navarre and Alava to the north and by Burgos, Soria, and Zaragoza to the south. The area's quarter of a million inhabitants are mainly along the Ebro, in the cities of Logroño, Haro, and Calahorra.

La Rioja's culture and wines both combine Atlantic and Mediterranean influences, as well as Basque tinges and the arid ruggedness of Iberia's central *meseta*. Drained by the Rivers Oja (hence the name, *río oja*), Najerilla, Iruegua, Leza and Cidacos, the La Rioja is composed of the Rioja Alta (Upper Rioja), the moist and mountainous western end, and the Rioja Baja (Lower Rioja), the flatter and dryer eastern end, more Mediterranean in climate. Logroño, the capital, lies between the two. Occupied successively by Gascons, Romans, Moors, Navarrans, and Castilians, La Rioja was part of the Cantabrian duchy from 573 to 711. Asturian kings reconquered the region in 1023, and in 1076 Alfonso VI incorporated the region into the Crown of Castile. In the 15th and 18th centuries, La Rioja was part of Castile and Navarre and was later divided between the provinces of Burgos and Soria. La Rioja's original boundaries continued to be ignored throughout the 19th century, while petitions for *fueros* (special rights), such as those enjoyed by the Basques, were rejected. Finally, in 1980, the region regained the name La Rioja, and in 1982 it became a fully fledged Autonomous Community by decree of King Juan Carlos I.

Logroño

㉜ *92 km southwest of Pamplona on NIII.*

La Rioja's capital is a busy city of 130,000 built over and around the Ebro River. A modern industrial and tourist center, Logroño has a lovely old quarter between its two bridges, bordered by the Ebro and the medieval walls. Breton de los Herreros and Muro Francisco de la Mata are the quarter's most characteristic streets, and La Rioja's four best religious structures are its dominant landmarks.

The 11th-century church the **Imperial de Santa María del Palacio** is known as La Aguja (The Needle) for its pyramid-shaped, 45-yard Romanesque-Gothic tower. The church of **Santiago el Real,** reconstructed in the 16th century, is noted for its equestrian statue of Santiago (St. James, also known as Santiago Matamoros—St. James the Moorslayer) presiding over the main door.

San Bartolomé is a 13th–14th century French-Gothic church with an 11th-century Mudejar tower and an elaborately sculpted 14th-century Gothic doorway.

La Catedral de La Redonda is a landmark for its twin Baroque towers.

Many of Logroño's monuments, such as the elegant **Puente de Piedra** (Stone Bridge), were built as part of the pilgrimage route to Santiago de Compostela. The **Puerta del Revellín,** the **Palacio del Espartero,** and the **medieval walls** are also key sights.

Near Logroño, the **Roman bridge** and the **Mirador** (viewpoint) at **Viguera** are the main sights in the lower Iregua Valley. **Castillo de Clavijo** is where St. James, mounted on a white stallion, is believed to have helped the Christians defeat the Moors. The **Leza (Cañon) del Rio Leza,** not far away, is La Rioja's most dramatic canyon.

Dining and Lodging

$$ ✕ **El Cachetero.** Local dishes based on vegetables are the rule here, with roasts of goat and lamb also featured prominently. The cuisine is simple and homespun, and the raw materials famous for freshness and seasonal relevance. ✉ *C. Laurel 3,* ☏ *941/228463. AE, DC, V. Closed Sun., Wed. evening, and mid-July–mid Aug.*

$$$ ✕▥ **Herencia Rioja.** This modern hotel near the old quarter has bright and comfortable rooms, a healthy buzz about it, and a fine restaurant. ✉ *Marqués de Murrieta 1, 26005,* ☏ *941/210222,* ℻ *941/21020. 81 rooms, 2 suites. Restaurant, bar, cafeteria, exercise room. AE, DC, MC, V.*

La Rioja Alta

La Rioja Alta, the most prosperous part of the region, extends from the Ebro River to the Sierra de la Demanda. La Rioja Alta has the most fertile soil, the best vineyards and agriculture, the most impressive castles and monasteries, a ski resort at Ezcaray, and the economic advantage historically conferred by a location along the Camino de Santiago.

Leave Logroño on route N120 and drive west 12 km (7 mi) to **Navarrete** for a look at its noble houses and the Baroque altarpiece in the Asunción church. **Nájera,** 15 km (9 mi) west, was court of the Kings of Navarre and capital of Navarre and La Rioja until 1076, when La Rioja became part of Castile and the residence of the Castilian royal family.

The monastery of **Santa María la Real** (☎ 941/363650), "pantheon of kings," is highlighted by its 11th-century Claustro de los Caballeros (Cavalier Cloister), a Gothic nobles' cloister with lacy plateresque windows overlooking a grassy patio. The sculpted 12th-century tomb of Doña Blanca de Navarra is the monastery's most famous sarcophagus.

Santo Domingo de la Calzada, 20 km (12 mi) west of Santa María la Real on N120, has always been a key part of the pilgrimage. Santo Domingo was an 11th-century saint who built roads and bridges for pilgrims, including the pilgrims' hospital that is now the town's parador. The cathedral is a Romanesque-Gothic pile containing Santo Domingo's tomb, choir murals, and an elaborate walnut altarpiece carved by Damià Forment in 1541. The live hen and rooster in a chicken coop commemorate a local miracle. The medieval and Gothic quarter is excellent.

Enter the **Sierra de la Demanda** by heading south 14 km (8 ½ mi) on LO-810. Your first stop is the town of **Ezcaray,** with its aristocratic houses emblazoned with family crests, of which the **Palacio del Conde de Torremúzquiz** (Palace of the Count of Torremúzquiz) is the most distinguished. Good excursions from here are the **Valdezcaray** winter sports center; the source of the River Oja at Llano de la Casa; La Rioja's highest point, at the 2,262-yard Pico de San Lorenzo; and the Romanesque church of Tres Fuentes, at Valgañón.

San Millán de la Cogolla is southeast of Santo Domingo de la Calzada. Take LO-809 southeast through Berceo to the Monasterio de Yuso, where a 10th-century manuscript on St. Augustine's *Glosas Emilianenses* is considered the first writing in Castilian Spanish. The nearby Visigothic Monasterio de Suso is where Gonzalo de Berceo, recognized as the first Castilian poet, recited in *roman paladino,* the romance dialect that became the Castilian tongue and ultimately the language of more than 150 million people from the Mediterranean to the South China Sea.

Haro, 49 km (29 mi) west of Logroño, is the wine capital of La Rioja. The town's main monuments are the flamboyant Gothic church of **Santo Tomás,** a single-nave structure built in 1564, and the **Basílica de la Vega,** with a figure of the valley's patron saint, La Virgen de Valvanera (Our Lady of Valvanera). Haro's old quarter and ancient taverns are memorable, as are the cafés in the Plaza Mayor; local wines at local prices flow freely. Haro's winemakers offer guided tours and tasting sessions; sign up at the tourist office. (☞ Close-up: La Rioja: Spain's Wine Country, *below.*) The June 29 **Batalla del Vino** (Wine Battle) is a wet and epic brawl.

Dining and Lodging

$$ ✕ **Terete.** This typical and rustic spot, a favorite with locals, has been roasting lamb in wood ovens since 1877. It has its own wine cellar. ✉ *C. Lucrecia Arana 17,* ☎ *941/310023. AE, DC, V. Closed Mon., July 1–15, Aug. 15–30*

$$$ ✕▣ **Los Agustinos.** Haro's best hotel is built into a 14th-century monastery whose cloister (now a pleasant patio) is considered one of the best in La Rioja. Arches, a great hall, and tapestries complete the medieval look. ✉ *San Agustín 2, 26200,* ☎ *941/311308,* [FAX] *941/303148. 60 rooms. Restaurant, bar, cafeteria. AE, DC, MC, V.*

La Rioja Baja

La Rioja's eastern area is more Mediterranean than Castilian in climate and vegetation, bordering the plains of Navarre, Soria, and Aragon. Its main river, the Cidacos, joins the Ebro at Calahorra (population 20,000), the region's largest city.

La Rioja Baja has a number of key visits, including **Alfaro's medieval houses** and church of San Miguel; Arnedo's **Monasterio de Vico**; Cornago's **castle**, with its four towers (three conical, one rectangular); Igea's **Palacio del Marqués de Casa Torre**; and Enciso's **Parque Jurásico** (Jurassic Park), with foot-long dinosaur tracks 150 million years old. Ten kilometers (6 miles) from Calahorra, there are **castle ruins** at Quel. Autol is the site of **rock formations** known as *El Picuezo y La Picueza* (roughly, Mr. and Mrs. Rockpile) for their resemblance to man and wife.

Calahorra

③ *46 km (27½ mi) southeast of Logroño; 109 km (65½ mi) northwest of Zaragoza.*

Calahorra, birthplace of Roman orator and rhetorician Quintilian (teacher of Tacitus), was founded by the Romans 2,000 years ago. You can explore the town's Roman and medieval remains by following the tour posted near Calahorra's **town hall**—it covers the Quintilian monument, the Jewish quarter, and the medieval quarter along with the churches of San Andrés, Santiago, and San Celedonio. Ask for a map at the *ayuntamiento*.

Calahorra's most important artistic and architectural riches are in the 12th-century **Catedral de Santa María** (St. Mary's Cathedral), on the site of what has been the regional bishopric since the 5th century. The building was restored in 1485 and completed in the 16th century. The choir is decorated with an intricately ornate screen; the Gothic side chapels and their altarpieces are spectacular; and the chapter room has sculpted alabaster saints as well as a Titian and Zurbarán. The sacristy has a 15th-century *custodia* (monstrance) known as El Ciprés (The Cypress), wrought in gold and silver. The **Museo Diocesano** (Diocesan Museum) displays Calahorra's finest art free of charge after the convent masses, until 1:30 PM; paid visits can be arranged by calling the museum's director, Don Angel Ortega (☎ 941/130098).

Dining and Lodging

$$ ✕ **La Taberna de la Cuarta Esquina.** This simple provincial tavern exemplifies what Spain provides best: extraordinarily good and unpretentious food and service. Have a hearty roast or a ragout. ✉ *Cuatro Esquinas 16,* ☎ *941/310023. AE, DC, V. Closed Tues., July 8–31, late Aug.*

$$$ ✕🏨 **Parador de Calahorra.** Calahorra's comfortable, if somewhat routine-bound, parador is definitely the best place to spend a night in La Rioja's second city. The wooden, Castilian-style decor is elegant, and the restaurant serves typical La Rioja home cooking, with a focus on roasts and fresh vegetables. ✉ *Paseo Mercadal, 26500,* ☎ *941/ 130358,* 🆎 *941/135139. 60 rooms. Restaurant, bar, cafeteria. AE, DC, MC, V.*

The Sierra–La Rioja Highlands

La Rioja's highlands have an identity of their own. The rivers forming the seven main valleys of the Ebro basin originate in these moun-

LA RIOJA: SPAIN'S WINE COUNTRY

LA RIOJA'S EBRO RIVER BASIN has been ideal for grapevines since pre-Roman times. Rioja wines were first recognized officially in 1102, and exports to Europe flourished over the centuries. The phylloxera blight that ruined French vineyards in 1863 brought Spain the expertise of Bordeaux vintners and an explosion in the demand for Spanish wine.

With its rich, uneroded soil, Ebro River microclimates, Atlantic moisture, and sun, La Rioja is ideally outfitted to produce high-quality grapes. Shielded from the arid cold of the Iberian *meseta* (plain) by the Sierra de la Demanda and from the bitter Atlantic weather by the Sierra de Cantabria, Spain's wine country covers an area 150 km long and 50 km wide along the banks of the Ebro River. The lighter limestone soils of the Rioja Alta produce the region's finest wines; the vineyards in the Rioja Baja are composed of alluvial and flood-plain clay in a warmer climate, poised to produce great volume.

The main grape of the Rioja Alta is the Tempranillo—so named for its early ripening (*temprano*) in mid-September—a dark, thick-skinned grape known for power, stability, and fragrance. Other varieties include the Mazuelo, used for longevity and tannin; and the Graciano, which lends aroma and freshness and makes high-quality wine. The Garnacha, the principal grape of the Rioja Baja, is an ideal complement to the more acidic Tempranillo.The Viura, the principal white variety, is fresh and fragrant, while Malvasía grapes stabilize wines that will age in oak barrels.

Rioja wines are categorized according to age, from the lowest rank, Garantía de Origen to Crianza and Reserva, to the ultimate Gran Reserva. Rioja wine is distinguished by the fact that most of it ages for a significant amount of time in barrels made of old American oak, as opposed to most French wine, aged for less time in barrels made of new French oak. Thus the average Rioja is deeper and smoother, whereas middle-range French wines are sharper and fruitier. The other difference is economic: a very respectable Rioja (Reserva) can cost under $10.

Wine and ritual overlap everywhere in La Rioja. The first wine of the year is offered to and blessed by the Virgin of Valvanera on September 21, on the riverside of Espolón de Logroño. Haro's famous Batalla del Vino (Wine Battle) is one of the region's most popular celebrations. Everything from the harvest and the trimming of the vines to the digging of fermentation pools and the making of baskets, barrels, and *botas* (wine skins)—even the glassblowing craft—takes on a magical significance in Rioja, where Bacchus reigns supreme.

For a tour of vineyards and wine cellars, start with **Haro,** the Rioja's wine capital. Call the **Carlos Serres** winery (⊠ San Agustín s/n, ☎ 941/311308) for a tour. Other visits in the Upper Rioja could include **Fuenmayor,** an historic winemaking center with a gemlike old quarter; **Cenicero,** with its ancient *bodegas* (wineries); **Ollauri,** home to a lovely cave *bodega,* "the Sistine chapel of the Rioja"; and **Briñas,** with a wine exhibit. At **Sajazarra** you can visit winemakers **Señorío de Líbano** (⊠ Calle del Río s/n, ☎ 941/320066); in Ábalos, call Puelles (⊠ Los Molinos s/n, ☎ 334415).

tains—the Sierra de la Demanda, Sierra de Cameros, and Sierra de Alcarama.

The **upper Najerilla Valley** is La Rioja's mountain sanctuary and wildest corner, an excellent hunting and fishing preserve. The **Monasterio de Valvanera,** off C113 near Anguiano, houses the Virgen de la Valvanera, a 12th-century Romanesque-Byzantine wood carving of La Rioja's favorite icon, the Virgin and child. The **Najerilla River** is a rich, weed-choked chalk stream and one of Spain's best trout rivers. **Anguiano** is renowned for its Danza de los Zancos (Dance of the Stilts), held July 22: Dancers on wooden stilts run downhill into the arms of the crowd in the main square. At the valley's highest point is the Mansilla reservoir and the Romanesque Ermita de San Cristóbal (Hermitage of St. Christopher).

The **upper Iregua valley,** in the **Sierra de Cameros** off N111, has the prehistoric **Gruta de la Paz** caves at Ortigosa. The reservoir at El Rasillo is La Rioja's center for aquatic sports. Villoslada del Cameros is famous for its **artisans,** who make the region's traditional patchwork quilts, *almazuelas.* Climb to **Pico Cebollera** for a superb view of the valley. Work back toward the Ebro along the River Leza, through Laguna de Cameros and San Román de Cameros (known for its basket weavers), to complete a tour of the Sierra del Cameros.

The **upper Cidacos valley** leads to the **Jurassic Park** at Enciso. The upper Alhama valley's main village is **Cervera del Rio Alhama,** a center for handmade *alpargatas* (rope-soled shoes). Jews, Moors, and Christians lived here in harmony as long as 400 years after the Reconquest.

BURGOS, SANTANDER, LA RIOJA, AND THE BASQUE COUNTRY A TO Z

Arriving and Departing

By Boat

Santander is linked year-round to Plymouth, England, by a twice-weekly car ferry. For information, contact **Brittany Ferries** in Santander (⊠ Paseo de Pereda 27, Santander, ☎ 942/220000 or 942/214500), or Plymouth (⊠ Millbay Docks, Plymouth, PL1 3EW, ☎ 0990/360360), or travel agencies in either country. Book at least six weeks in advance in summer, as the 24-hour passages are often sold out. Another option is the twice-weekly ferry between Bilbao and Portsmouth, England; contact **Ferries Golfo de Vizcaya** (⊠ Cosme Etxevarrieta 1, 48009 Bilbao, ☎ 94/423–4477, FAX 94/423–5496).

By Bus

Daily bus service connects all of this region's major cities to Madrid, with several departures a day in some cases. San Sebastián and Bilbao are especially well served. In Madrid, call **Continental Auto bus company** for information (☎ 91/533–0400), or go right to the station at Calle Alenza 20.

By Car

Traveling by car is the best way to see this part of Spain. Even the remotest point is an easy one-day drive from Madrid. From the capital, it's 242 km (150 mi) on the N I (or the A1 toll road) to Burgos, and 396 km (246 mi) if you continue on the N623 to Santander. Driving directly from Madrid to Bilbao will take you 401 km (247 mi); follow the N I or A1 past Burgos to Miranda del Ebro, where you pick up the A68 into Bilbao. From Madrid, San Sebastián is 472 km (293 mi) if you travel the fastest route, via Bilbao, and take the A8 toll road from there. Logroño is 333 km (200 mi) from Madrid via Soria, or 114 km (68.4 mi) east of Burgos on the N120.

By Plane

The major airport in this region is 11 km (7 mi) outside Bilbao; Iberia has regular connections from there to Madrid, Barcelona, France, and England. Smaller, less convenient airports serve Santander, San Sebastián, and Pamplona, with less frequent service to Madrid and Barcelona.

By Train

Burgos, Santander, Bilbao, San Sebastián, and Logroño are all well served by direct trains from Madrid's Chamartín Station, and trains with a change or two from virtually every major city in Spain. If you're leaving from Madrid, call **RENFE** for information (☎ 91/563–0202).

Getting Around

By Bus

Bus service among the main cities and most smaller towns is comprehensive, but few have central bus stations where you can collect information; most have numerous bus companies leaving from different points in town. Ask at travel agencies or local tourist offices. The following do have central bus stations: **Burgos** (✉ C. Miranda 4, ☎ 947/265565), **Santander** (✉ C. Navas de Tolosa s/n, ☎ 942/211995), **Pamplona** (✉ C. Conde Oliveto 8, ☎ 948/223854), **San Sebastián** (✉ C. Sancho el Sabio 33, ☎ 943/463974), and **Logroño** (✉ Avda. España 1, ☎ 941/235983).

By Car

The northern pocket of Spain bounded by Burgos, Logroño, and Pamplona to the south and Santander, Bilbao, and San Sebastián to the north (with Vitoria nearly dead center) is superbly connected by freeways and easily explored by car. Because so many of the attractions are rural landscapes and small towns, a car is the ideal mode of transportation. Some distances within this relatively small area are as follows: Burgos–Bilbao, 159 km (99 mi); Santander–Bilbao, 107 km (66 mi); Bilbao–San Sebastián, 119 km (71 mi); San Sebastián–Pamplona, 91 km (56 mi); Burgos–Logroño 114 km (68½ mi); and Pamplona–Logroño, 92 km (56½ mi).

By Train

Trains are not the ideal way to travel this region, but many cities are connected by rail. The main train stations belong to the RENFE system—these are **Burgos** (✉ End of Avda. Conde de Guadalhorce, ☎ 947/203560; ✉ RENFE agent, C. La Moneda 21, ☎ 947/209131), **Santander** (✉ C. Rodríguez near center of town, ☎ 942/210211; ✉ RENFE office, Paseo de Pereda 25, ✉ 942/212387 or 942/218567), **Bilbao** (✉ Estación del Abando, C. Hurtado de Amezaga, ☎ 94/423–8623 or 94/423–8636), **San Sebastián** (✉ Estación del Norte, Avda. de Francia, ☎ 943/283089 or 943/283599; ✉ RENFE's main office, C. Camino 1, ☎ 943/426430), **Pamplona** (✉ on road to San Sebastián, ☎ 948/130202), and **Logroño** (✉ Plaza de Europa, ☎ 941/240202). In addition, the regional FEVE train company (✉ Estación de FEVE, next to Estación de Abando, Bilbao, ☎ 94/423–2266) runs a delightful narrow-gauge train that winds through stunning landscapes. From San Sebastián, lines west to Bilbao and east to Hendaye depart from the Estación de Amara (✉ Plaza Easo 9, ☎ 943/450131 or 943/471852).

Contacts and Resources

Consulates

Bilbao: Great Britain (✉ C. Alameda Urquijo 2, 8th floor, ☎ 94/415–7600 or 94/415–7722).

Emergencies

Police (☎ 091).

Guided Tours

Travel agencies in the region's major cities will know of tours offered by local firms, usually in summer. Pamplona's tourist office keeps a list of private guides and interpreters for hire.

Jai-Alai

The best local *frontón*, from which the finest players depart for Miami and other U.S. jai alai centers, is **Guernica Jai-Alai.** In **Pamplona,** try Euskal Jai Berri (✉ 6 km [4 mi] out in Huarte, ☎ 948/331159 or 943/331160) or, in **San Sebastián,** Galarreta Jai-Alai (✉ on highway to Hernani, ☎ 943/551023), both of which host games Thursdays and weekends.

Monastery Visits

Contact the **Monasterio de Santo Domingo de Silos** (✉ Santo Domingo de Silos, Burgos, ☎ 947/390068) or the **Monasterio de San Pedro de Cardeña** (✉ Cardeña, Burgos, ☎ 947/290033).

Visitor Information

General information and pamphlets on the Basque provinces (Alava, Vizcaya, and Guipúzcoa) are available in the regional government building in **Vitoria** (✉ Parque de la Florida, Vitoria, ☎ 945/131321) and at the **San Sebastián** tourist office (✉ C. Fueros 1, San Sebastián, ☎ 943/426282).

Bilbao's municipal tourist office is on the ground floor of the Teatro Arriaga, downtown (✉ Plaza Arriaga, 94/416–0022 or 94/416–0288); the regional tourist office (☎ 94/4242277) is at Gran Vía 441 Izquierda. Other municipal tourist offices: **Burgos** (✉ Plaza Alonso Martínez 7, ☎ 947/203125). **Guernica** (✉ Artekale 5, ☎ 94/625–5892). **Haro** (✉ Plaza Monseñor Florentino Rodriguez, ☎ 941/303366). **Logroño** (✉ C. Miguel Villanueva 10, ☎ 941/291260). **Pamplona** (✉ C. Duque de Ahumada 3, ☎ 948/220741). **San Sebastián** (✉ C. Reina Regente s/n, ☎ 943/481166). **Santander** (✉ Estación Marítimo, at ferry landing, ☎ 942/310708). **Vitoria** (✉ Edifício Europa, Avda. Gasteiz, ☎ 945/161261).

6 The Pyrenees

The Pyrenees, snowcapped mountains that have historically sealed off the Iberian Peninsula from the rest of Western Europe, have long been a source of fascination, legend, and superstition. Pyrenean meadows and valleys have protected the last vestiges of several ancient cultures. To explore any one of these valleys thoroughly— flora, fauna, architecture, remote glacial ponds and streams, and the Romanesque art hidden in a thousand chapels and hermitages—could take a lifetime.

By George
Semler

FOR BETTER OR FOR WORSE, the Pyrenees separate the Iberian Peninsula from the rest of Western Europe, making room for a trans-Pyrenean culture distinct from that of neighboring France. Inhabitants of the prehistoric Pyrenees— originally cave dwellers, later shepherds and farmers—saw their first invaders when the Greeks landed at Empúries, in far-northern Catalonia, in the 6th century BC. The seagoing Carthaginians colonized Spain in the 3rd century BC, and their great general Hannibal surprised the Romans by crossing the Oriental (eastern) Pyrenees in 218 BC. After defeating the Carthaginians, the Romans built roads through the mountains: *Vía Augusta* from Le Perthus to Barcelona and Tarragona; *Strata Ceretana* through the Cerdanya valley and La Seu d'Urgell to Lleida; *Summus Pyrenaecus* (or, as the Spanish reflects, *Summus Portus*) at Somport, to Jaca and Zaragoza; and the *Via Lemovicensis* from Bordeaux through Roncesvalles to Pamplona in the western, or Atlantic, Pyrenees.

After the fall of Rome, the Iberian Peninsula was the last of the empire to be overtaken by the Visigoths, who crossed the Pyrenees in AD 409. In the 8th century, the northern tribes faced Moorish invaders from the south. Although Moorish influence was weaker in the Pyrenees than in southern Spain, and only briefly pushed past the mountains into the rest of Europe, the region at the end of the first millennium was a crossroads of Arab, Greek, and European culture. Toulouse was the melting pot of these influences, the medieval artistic and literary center. Christianity survived the Moors' invasion and occupation largely by fleeing to the hills and thus dotting the Pyrenees with Romanesque art and architecture. When Christian crusaders reconquered Spain, the Pyrenees were divided among three feudal kingdoms: Catalonia, Aragon, and Navarre, proud and independent entities with their respective spiritual "cradles" in the Romanesque mountain monasteries of Ripoll, San Juan de la Peña, and San Salvador de Leyre.

Throughout the centuries, the barrier of the Pyrenees remained a force to be reckoned with. Napoleon never completed his conquest of the Iberian Peninsula due mainly to communication and supply problems over the Pyrenees. The German Third Reich decided not to use post–civil war Spain as a base camp for its African campaign. Throughout the Second World War, the Pyrenees were the last stop on the way to freedom for Jews and *résistants* fleeing the Holocaust.

The mountains stretch 435 km (270 mi) along Spain's border with France. There are three main ranges: the Catalan Pyrenees, the central Pyrenees (in Aragon), and the Basque Pyrenees, which fall gently westward through the Basque country to the Bay of Biscay. The highest peaks are in Aragon—Aneto, in the Maladeta ridge; Posets; and Monte Perdido, all of which are about 11,000 ft above sea level. Pica d'Estats (10,372 ft) is Catalonia's highest peak, while Pic D'Orhi (6,656 ft) is the highest in the Basque Pyrenees.

These snowcapped mountains have always been a magical realm, a source of legend and superstition, a breeder of myth and mystical religious significance. Their meadows and valleys have protected the last vestiges of numerous ancient cultures. Each mountain system is drained by rivers, forming some three dozen valleys between the Mediterranean and the Atlantic; these valleys were all but completely isolated until around the 10th century. The local languages range from Castilian Spanish to Euskera (Basque), in upper Navarre; to dialects such as Grausín, Belsetán, Chistavín, Ansotano, Cheso or Patués (Benasqués), in Aragon; to Aranés, a dialect of Gascon French, in the Vall d'Aran; to Catalan, east toward the Mediterranean.

To explore any of these valleys fully—the flora and fauna, the local gastronomy, the peaks and upper meadows, the remote glacial lakes and streams, the Romanesque art hidden in a thousand chapels and hermitages—is a lifetime project. The tours we suggest are introductions to some of Spain's richest and most remote combinations of land and civilization.

Pleasures and Pastimes

Dining

Pyrenean cuisine is characterized by thick soups, stews, roasts and the use of local ingredients prepared differently in every valley, village, and kitchen from the Atlantic to the Mediterranean. The three main culinary schools are those corresponding to the Pyrenees' three main regional and cultural identities—Catalan, Aragonese, and Basque—but within these are further subdivisions: Vall d'Aran, Benasque, Roncal, and Baztán. Game is common throughout. Trout (once supplied by anglers, now often raised in lakes and ponds fed by mountain streams), wild goat, deer, boar, partridge, rabbit, duck, and quail are roasted over coals or cooked in aromatic stews called *civets* in Catalonia and *estofadas* in Aragon and Navarre. Fish and meat are often seared on slabs of slate (*a la llosa* in Catalan, *a la piedra* in Castilian Spanish). Wild mushrooms are another local specialty when in season, as are wild asparagus, leeks, and herbs such as marjoram, sage, thyme, and rosemary.

CATEGORY	COST*
$$$$	over 6,000 ptas.
$$$	4,000–6,000 ptas.
$$	2,500–4,000 ptas.
$	1,000–2,500 ptas.

per person for a three-course meal, including tax, house wine, and service

Fishing

Well populated with trout, Pyrenean streams provide excellent angling from the third Sunday in March to the end of August. Nearly all of the Pyrenees' rivers and streams make fine cold-water fisheries, but the Segre, Aragon, Gállego, Noguera Pallaresa, Arga, and Esca are the most notable. Local ponds and lakes also tend to be rich in trout, providing a good way to combine hiking and angling. Call **Danica** (☎ 908/735376) for horse or helicopter tours with fly-fishing equipment included (for more information, *see* the Pyrenees A to Z, *below*).

Hiking and Walking

Mountain climbing and hiking are fundamental Pyrenean activities in summer. Walking the often grassy crest, with one foot in France and the other in Spain, is an exhilarating experience and well within the reach of the moderately fit. Try walking from Coll de Nuria to Ulldeter over the Sierra Catllar, above Setcases; scaling the Cadí over the Cerdanya; or hiking over the Maladeta glacier to Aneto, the Pyrenees' highest peak. The Iparla Ridge walk, along the Navarre-France border crest, and the Alberes walk from Le Perthus out to the Mediterranean, are two more favorite day hikes. Local *excursionista* clubs, especially the Centro Excursionista de Catalunya in Barcelona (✉ Carrer Paradis 10, ☎ 93/315–2311), can help you get started. Local and trans-Pyrenean paths and trails crisscross the region, offering countless unforgettable views. Wild-mushroom-hunting rambles through the piny, hillside meadows are a way of life for many, combining walking, questing, and cuisine. (Be 100% certain of any wild mushroom you consume; consult with experts.) You can also join equestrian outings, four-wheel-drive excursions to the upper Pyrenees, and horseback fly-fishing tours of the high streams and lakes from Llívia, in the Cerdanya; or just try an autumn hike through the Irati beech forest, in upper Navarre.

Lodging

Hotels in the Pyrenees feel informal and outdoorsy and usually have a large fireplace in one of the public rooms. They often blend with the surrounding mountains and are built of wood and slate, typically with steep roofs. Their comfortable and protected, but not luxurious, atmosphere reflects the tastes of the travelers, who are mostly skiers and hikers. Options include friendly family establishments such as the Güell, in Camprodón, and the Hotel Llívia, in the Spanish enclave at Llívia; grand-luxe places such as Torre del Remei in the Cerdanya Valley; rural accommodations in Basque *caseríos* (farmhouses) like the Iratxeko Berea in Vera de Bidasoa, on the upper reaches of Navarre's Bidasoa River; and town houses such as La Tuca, in Aragon's Canfranc ski station.

CATEGORY	COST*
$$$$	over 15,000 ptas.
$$$	10,000–15,000 ptas.
$$	6,000–10,000 ptas.
$	under 6,000 ptas.

All prices are for a standard double room, including service and tax.

Romanesque Art and Architecture

The treasury of Romanesque chapels, monasteries, hermitages, and cathedrals sprinkled across these mountains is important enough to organize a trip around. Among the best examples of art and architecture are the 10th-century hermitage of Sant Baldiri de Taballera, between Cap de Creus and El Port de la Selva; the tiny chapel at Beget, above Camprodón; the superb rose window and 50 carved capitals of La Seu d'Urgell's cathedral of Santa Maria; the matched set of churches and bell towers of the Noguera de Tor Valley, below the Vall d'Aran; the San Juan de la Peña and Siresa monasteries, west of Jaca; and the village churches of Navarre's Baztán Valley.

Winter Sports

Skiing is the main sport in the Pyrenees, and Baqueira-Beret, in the Vall d'Aran, is the leading resort. Thanks to increasing reliance on artificial snow machines, there is usually fine skiing from December through March at more than 20 resorts—from Vallter 2000 at Setcases, in the Camprodón Valley, west to Isaba and Burguete, Navarre. Although weekend skiing can be crowded in the eastern valleys, Catalonia's western Pyrenees, especially Baqueira-Beret, rank among Spain's best wintersports centers. Cerler-Benasque, Panticosa, Formigal, Astun, and Candanchú are the major ski areas in Huesca. Numerous resorts make room for helicopter skiing and Nordic skiing; Lles, in the Cerdanya; Salardú and Beret, in the Vall d'Aran; and Panticosa, Benasque, and Candanchú, in Aragon are among the leading Nordic areas. Jaca, Puigcerdà, and Vielha have ice-hockey programs, figure-skating classes, and public skating sessions. Spain's daily newspaper *El País* prints complete ski information every Friday in winter (☞ Outdoor Activities and Sports *in* the Pyrenees A to Z, *below*).

Exploring the Pyrenees

Traversing the Pyrenees from the Mediterranean to the Atlantic (or vice versa) is for mountain worshipers a pilgrimage of deep cultural and telluric significance. It's a seven-week hike on foot, but you can make the crossing in 10–14 days by car. The main geographical units are the valleys of Camprodón, Cerdanya, Aran, Benasque, Tena, Canfranc, Roncal, and Baztán.

Numbers in the text correspond to numbers in the margin and on the Catalan Pyrenees and the Central and Western Pyrenees maps.

Great Itineraries

Barcelona is the largest nearby "anchor." A trip through the Oriental Pyrenees would cover an important third of the chain. Five days is enough time to reach the Vall d'Aran and the Noguera de Tor Valley and its Romanesque churches before heading back to Barcelona or farther west; such a trip is probably the most cost-effective in terms of time, terrain, art, and architecture. A 10-day trip grants the satisfaction of a sea-to-sea crossing, but you'll spend the bulk of this time in your car.

IF YOU HAVE 3 DAYS

Begin in Barcelona, the major urban area with the best communication links. On the first day, explore the **Camprodon Valley** and spend a night at the Hotel Güell. Spend the second day in the **Cerdanya,** followed by a night at the Hotel Llívia. On the third day, drive west down the valley through **La Seu d'Urgell** ⑪ and back to Barcelona.

IF YOU HAVE 5 DAYS

If you have five days, starting in Barcelona or from the Costa Brava, go through the **Camprodon Valley** on day one; see the **Cerdanya** on day two; and drive down to **La Seu d'Urgell** ⑪ (with a break to climb **Prat d'Aguiló** ⑩) for the third night. Spend the fourth night in the **Vall d'Aran,** and spend day five driving through the Noguera de Tor Valley and visiting the Romanesque churches. If you have time, go through **Aigüestortes–Sant Maurici National Park** ⑮.

IF YOU HAVE 10 DAYS

If you have 10 days, you can cross the entire range. From Barcelona or from the Costa Brava, begin by wading in the Mediterranean at Cap de Creus (☞ Side Trips *in* Chapter 7), peninsular Spain's easternmost point, just north of Cadaqués, and then cross westward to Fuenterrabía; ☞ Chapter 5) to do the same at the Cabo Higuer lighthouse, in the Bay of Biscay. (Of course, you can also travel in the opposite direction, reversing the order of this chapter.) On the westbound trip, a day's drive up through Figueres and Olot (☞ Side Trips *in* Chapter 7) will bring you to the Camprodon Valley and its unspoiled mountain towns, skiing, and wildlife. The next stop is the Cerdanya, the widest, sunniest valley in the Pyrenees. From there move westward through **La Seu D'Urgell** ⑪ to **Aigüestortes–Sant Maurici National Park** ⑮, **the Vall d'Aran** ⑰, and the winter-sports center Baqueira-Beret. Don't miss the Romanesque churches of the Noguera de Tor Valley. Farther west, explore the remote valleys of Upper Aragon, **Ordesa and Mt. Perdido National Park** ㉘, and **Jaca** ㉚, the region's most important town. Finally, move through western Aragon into the Basque Pyrenees to visit the Irati Forest; go through the tunnel under the Velate Pass (or, more spectacularly, over the pass itself) to explore the **Baztán Valley** ㊲; and then follow the Bidasoa River down to Fuenterrabía (☞ Chapter 5) and the Bay of Biscay.

When to Tour the Pyrenees

For skiing, come between December and April. If you're a hiker, stick to the summer (June through September, with a definite emphasis on July), when the weather is better and there is less chance of a blizzard or a lightning storm at high altitudes. October is nice for enjoying the still-green valleys and hunting wild mushrooms. November brings colorful leaves, the last wild mushrooms, and the first frosts. The green springtime thaw, during which you can still ski on the snowcaps, is another spectacular season here.

THE ORIENTAL PYRENEES

You can reach Catalonia's easternmost Pyrenean valley, the Vall de Camprodón (Camprodon Valley), from Barcelona on N152 through Vic and Ripoll; from the Costa Brava by way of either Figueres or Girona, Besalú, and the new Capsacosta tunnel; or from France through the Col (Pass) d'Ares, which enters the head of the valley at an altitude of 5,280 ft from Prats de Molló. This valley has several exquisite towns and churches; a ski area; and, above all, mountains, such as the Sierra de Catllar, thick with boar, mountain goat, and snow partridge.

Camprodon

❶ *127 km (80 mi) northwest of Barcelona.*

Camprodon, the capital of the *comarca* (county), lies at the junction of the Rivers Ter and Ritort—both excellent trout streams. The rivers flow by, through, and under much of the town, giving it a waterfront character as well as a long history of flooding. The town owes much of its opulence to the summer folks from Barcelona who have built important mansions along the leafy promenade, **Passeig Maristany,** at the town's northern edge. Camprodon's best-known symbol is the elegant **12th-century stone bridge** that broadly spans the River Ter in the center of town. Its wide arch descends at a graceful angle from a central peak. Camprodon is also known for its **sausages** of every imaginable size, shape, and consistency and for its two cookie factories, Birbas and Pujol, locked in eternal competition. (Birbas is better—look for the image of the bridge on the box.)

Lodging

$$ ⊞ **Hotel Güell.** Owned and managed by the charming Güell family, this elegant glass, wood, and stone structure welcomes skiers and general enthusiasts to the Camprodon Valley. Rooms are simple but tasteful, with heavy, Pyrenean wood furniture. ⊠ *Plaça d'Espanya 8, 17867,* ☎ *972/740011,* ⅀ *972/741112. 38 rooms. AE, DC, MC, V.*

Shopping

Don't miss **Cal Xec,** the sausage store at the end of the emblematic Camprodon Bridge. Along with every kind of charcuterie ever conceived, the shop sells Birbas and Pujol cookies.

En Route From Camprodon, take C151 north toward the French border at Col d'Ares and turn east toward Rocabruna, a village of crisp, clean Pyrenean stone at the source of the crystalline River Beget.

Beget

❷ *17 km (11 mi) east of Camprodon.*

The village of Beget, considered Catalonia's *més bufó* (cutest), was completely cut off from motorized transportation until the mid-1960s and was only connected to the rest of the world by asphalt roadway in 1980. Beget's 30 houses are eccentric stone structures with heavy wooden doors and an unusual golden tone peculiar to the Camprodon Valley. Graceful stone bridges span the stream in which protected trout feast. The 11th-century church of **Sant Cristófol** has a diminutive bell tower and a 6-ft Majestat, a polychrome wood carving of Christ in a head-to-

The Catalan Pyrenees

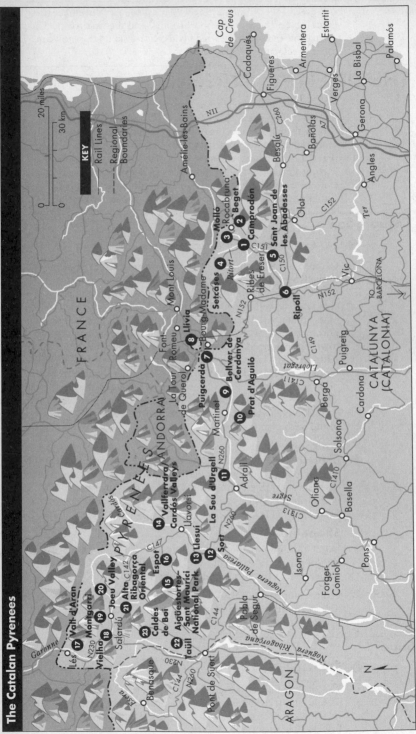

foot tunic, dating from the 12th or early 13th century. The church is usually closed, but townsfolk can direct you to the keeper of the key.

Dining

$$ ✕ **Can Po.** Perched over a deep gulley, Can Po serves first-rate cuisine in an ancient, ivy-covered, stone-and-mortar farmhouse. Specialties are *entrecot amb crema de ceps* (veal in wild mushroom sauce) and *anec amb peras* (duck prepared with stewed pears). ✉ *Carretera de Beget s/n, 17867,* ☎ *972/741045. AE, DC, MC, V. Closed Mon.–Thurs. mid-Sept.–mid-July.*

Molló

❸ *135 km (84 mi) northwest of Barcelona.*

Molló lies on route C151 on the Ritort stream toward Col d'Ares. Here you'll find a **12th-century Romanesque church** of exceptional balance and simplicity, with a delicate, Romanesque bell tower that seems as naturally set into the building and the surrounding countryside as a Pyrenean mushroom.

Setcases

❹ *91 km (57 mi) northwest of Girona, 11 km (7 mi) north of Camprodon.*

This tiny village is nestled at the head of the valley. Although Setcases (literally, "seven houses") is somewhat larger than its name would imply, the town has a distinct mountain spirit and a gravelly roughness, perhaps owing to the torrents flowing through and over its streets en route to the River Ter.

The **Vallter ski area,** above Setcases—built into a glacial cirque reaching a height of 8,216 ft—has a dozen lifts and, on very clear days, views east from the top all the way to the Bay of Roses and Cap de Creus on the Costa Brava.

On the road back down the valley from Setcases, **Llanars,** just short of Camprodon, has a **12th-century church** of an exceptionally rich shade of ocher. The wood-and-iron portal depicts the martyrdom of St. Stephen.

Sant Joan de les Abadesses

❺ *21 km (13 mi) southeast of Setcases, 14 km (9 mi) south of Camprodon.*

South of Camprodon, Sant Joan de les Abadesses—named for the 9th-century abbess Emma, daughter of Guifré el Pilós (Wilfred the Hairy), the founder of the Catalonian nation and medieval hero of the Christian Reconquest of Ripoll—is the site of the important **12th-century church of Sant Joan.** The altarpiece is a 13th-century polychrome wood sculpture of the Descent from the Cross, one of the most expressive and human of that epoch. The town's porticoed main square has a medieval look and feel; the **12th-century bridge** over the Ter is wide and graceful.

Ripoll

❻ *65 km (40 mi) southeast of Puigcerdà.*

Ripoll, one of the first Christian strongholds of the Reconquest and an important center of religious erudition during the Middle Ages, is known as the *bressol* (cradle) of Catalonian nationhood. A dark, mysterious country town built around a **9th-century Benedictine monastery,** Ripoll was a focal point of culture throughout the Roussillon (French

Catalonia and the Pyrenees) from the monastery's founding, in 888, until the mid-19th century.

The 12th-century doorway to the church of **Santa Maria** is one of Catalonia's great works of Romanesque art, designed as a triumphal arch. Its sculptures portray the glory of God and of all his creatures from the creation onward. You can pick up a guide to the figures on the portal (the work of stone masons and sculptors of the Roussillon school) at the church or at the information kiosk nearby. ✉ *Cloister 275 ptas., museum 375 ptas.* ☉ *Tues.–Sun. 10–2 and 3–7.*

North of Ripoll, the **cogwheel train** from Ribes up to Nuria offers one of Catalonia's most unusual excursions. Known as the *cremallera* (zipper), the line was built in 1917 to connect Ribes with the **sanctuary of La Mare de Deu de Nuria** (Mother of God of Nuria). The ride takes 45 minutes and costs 1,500 pesetas round-trip. Nuria, at an altitude of 6,562 ft at the foot of Puigmal, is a **ski area** and was the site of some of Spain's earliest ice-hockey activity, starting in the 1950s.

The legend of Nuria, a Marian religious retreat, is based on the story of Sant Gil of Nîmes, who did penance in the valley of Nuria during the 7th century. The saint left behind a wooden statue of the Virgin Mary, a bell he used to summon shepherds to prayer, and a cooking pot; 300 years later, a pilgrim found these treasures in the sanctuary at Nuria. **The bell and the pot** came to have special importance to barren women, who were enabled to bear as many children as they wished by placing their heads in the pot and ringing the bell, each peal of the bell meaning another child. ✉ *Free.* ☉ *Open daily except during mass.*

En Route   From Ripoll, it's a 63-km (39-mi) drive on N152 through Ribes de Freser and over the Collada de Toses (Tosses Pass) to Puigcerdà. Above Ribes, the road winds to the top of the pass over a sheer drop down to the Freser stream. Here, even during the driest months, emerald-green pastures remain moist in shaded corners—a sharp contrast to the shale and brown peaks above the tree line. In early spring the climate can range from showers, at Ribes, to a blizzard, at Tosses.

This traditional approach to the Cerdanya has been all but replaced by the road through Manresa, Berga, and the Túnel del Cadí (Cadí Tunnel). Tosses was a barrier for centuries, until the railroad connected Puigcerdà to Barcelona in 1924. The 32 km (20 mi) of switchback curves between Ribes and La Molina kept many would-be travelers in Barcelona until the tunnel cut the driving time from three hours to two and all but eliminated the hazardous-driving factor.

LA CERDANYA

The Pyrenees' widest, sunniest valley—said to be in the shape of the handprint of God—is an alpine paradise. High pastureland bordered north and south by snow-covered peaks, La Cerdanya starts in France, at Mont Louis, and ends in the Spanish province of Lleida, at Martinet. Split into two countries and subdivided into two more provinces on each side, the valley is nonetheless an autonomous geographical and cultural unit with an identity of its own.

"Meitat de França, meitat d'Espanya, no hi ha altra terra com la Cerdanya" ("Half France, half Spain, there's no country like the Cerdanya"): La Cerdanya straddles the border, which meanders through the rich valley floor no more purposefully than the River Segre itself. Residents

on both sides of the border speak Catalan, a Romance language derived from early Provençal French, and regard the valley's international division with undisguised hilarity.

Unlike any other valley in the upper Pyrenees, this one runs east–west and thus has a record annual number of hours of sunlight. Two solar stations collect and store energy at Font Romeu, while in Mont Louis, also on the French side of the valley, a solar oven is used for baking ceramics.

Puigcerdà

❼ *65 km (40 mi) northwest of Ripoll.*

Puigcerdà (*puig* means "hill"; *cerdà* derives from "Cerdanya") is the valley's largest town. From the small piece of high ground upon which Puigcerdà stands, the views down across the meadows and up into the Pyrenees give a dizzying sense of simultaneous height and humility. The **Romanesque bell tower** and the **sunny sidewalk café** beside it are among Puigcerdà's prettiest spots, along with the Gothic church of **Santa Maria** and its long square, the **Plaça del Cuartel**. On Sunday, markets sell clothes, cheeses, fruits, vegetables, and wild mushrooms to shoppers from both sides of the border.

The **Plaça Cabrinetty,** with its porticoes and covered walks, has a sunny northeastern corner where farmers in for the Sunday market gather to gab about their lives and times. The square is protected from the wind and ringed by two- and three-story houses of various pastel colors, some with engraved decorative designs and all with balconies. From the lower end of Plaça Cabrinetty, Carrer Font d'en Llanas winds down to the *font* (spring), where **"Voldria . . . "** ("I wish . . . "), a haunting verse by the Cerdanya's greatest poet, Magdalena Masip (1890–1970), is inscribed on a plaque over the fountain: *. . . and I wish that I could have/my house beneath a fir tree/with all the woods for a garden/and all the sky for a roof./And flee from the world around me/it overwhelms me and confuses me/and stay quietly just there/drinking the forest in great gulps/with clods of earth for a pillow/and a bed of golden leaves . . .*

A 300-yard walk west from the *font* around the edge of the town will bring you to the stairs leading up from the train station to the balcony in front of the town hall. From here, an ample view of the Cerdanya Valley stretches all the way past Bellver de Cerdanya down to the rock walls of the Sierra del Cadí, at the end of the valley.

Le petit train jaune (the little yellow train) leaves daily from La Tour de Querol and from Bourg-Madame, a short walk from Puigcerdà, and winds through the Cerdanya to the walled city of Villefranche de Conflent. The *carrilet* (narrow-gauge railway) is the last in the Pyrenees and is used for touring as well as for getting around. The 63-km (39-mi) tour can take most of the day, especially if you stop to browse in Mont Louis or Villefranche. The train looks like an illustration from a Dr. Seuss story and is popular with both adults and children. ⏱ *2,500 ptas. (125 frs.) per person in groups of 10 or more, 3,500 ptas. (175 frs.) singly; boarding at SNCF stations at Bourg-Madame or La Tour de Querol, payable in French frs. only. ⊙ Schedules at Touring travel agency or Turismo office, Puigcerdà; or at RENFE station below Puigcerdà.*

Dining and Lodging

$$–$$$ ✕ **La Tieta.** A nearly 500-year-old restored town house built into the original walls of Puigcerdà, La Tieta is the town's top restaurant. Its garden is an ideal place for a late-night drink in summer. The menu has such mountain specialties as *trinxat de Cerdanya* (a rib-sticking puree of cabbage and potatoes mixed with bits of fried salt pork or bacon) and roasts cooked over coals. ✉ *Carrer de les Ferrers 20,* ☎ *972/880156. AE, DC, MC, V.*

$ ✕ **Madrigal.** This popular bar-restaurant is near Puigcerdà's town hall. The low-ceiling, wood-trim dining room upstairs is filled with tables and benches. Selections include tapas and a meal of assorted specialties, such as *calamares a la romana* (calamari dipped in batter), *codorniz* (quail), *jamon de serrano* (Serrano ham), *albóndigas* (meatballs), *caracoles* (snails), *esqueixada* (raw codfish with peppers and onion), or wild mushrooms in season. Pere Compte, proprietor and host, is always ready with suggestions. The Compte family's new spot, **Tapanyam,** down the same street at No. 45, is a variation on the same theme but is more spacious and has an outdoor terrace. ✉ *Alfons I 1,* ☎ *972/880860. AE, DC, MC, V.*

$$$$ 🏨 **La Torre del Remei.** About 3 km (2 mi) west of Puigcerdà is this splen-
★ did mansion, built in 1910 and brilliantly restored by José María and Loles Boix of Can Boix (☞ Martinet, *below*). Everything about La Torre del Remei, from the Belle Epoque luxury of the manor house to the plush, tastefully redesigned rooms, heated bathroom floors, huge bathtubs, cuisine, and bottle of Moët & Chandon waiting on ice upon your arrival, is superb. Reserve well in advance. ✉ *Camí Reial s/n, Bolvir de Cerdanya, 17463,* ☎ *972/140182,* 𝙁𝘼𝙓 *972/140449. 10 rooms, 1 suite. Restaurant, pool, 18-hole golf course, putting green. AE, DC, MC, V.*

$$ 🏨 **Hotel del Lago.** This comfortable old favorite near Puigcerdà's emblematic lake is a graceful, tastefully appointed and renovated series of buildings built around a central garden. A two-minute walk from the bell tower or the town market, the place feels bucolic but is virtually in the center of town. ✉ *Avda. Doctor Piguillem 7, 17520,* ☎ *972/881000,* 𝙁𝘼𝙓 *972/141511. 13 rooms, 3 suites. Breakfast room, outdoor pool. AE, MC, V.*

Nightlife and the Arts

On weekends and holidays, clubs such as **N'Ho Sé, Transit, Gatzara,** in Puigcerdà, and **De Nit,** 5 km (3 mi) from Puigcerdà (near Caixans, on the road to Alp), are filled until dawn with young French and Spanish night owls.

Shopping

Look for local specialties, such as herbs, goat cheese, wild mushrooms, honey, and basketry, found in the Sunday markets held in most towns. Puigcerdà's **Sunday market** is as social as it is commercial; the long square in front of the church and former military barracks, known as the Plaça del Cuartel, fills with people and produce. In autumn, it's a great chance to learn about wild mushrooms of all kinds. If it's a horse you're shopping for, come to the annual **equine fair** in early November, a nonpareil opportunity to study both horses and horse traders.

Llívia

❽ *6 km (4 mi) northeast of Puigcerdà.*

Llívia is a Spanish enclave in French territory. Marooned by the 1659 Peace of the Pyrenees treaty, which ceded 33 villages to France, Llívia—incorporated as a *vila* (town) by royal decree of Carlos V, who spent a night there in 1528 and was impressed by its beauty and its residents' hospitality—managed to remain Spanish. Llívia's **fortified church** is an acoustic gem; see if anything sonorous is going on. The **ancient pharmacy,** now a museum, was founded in 1415 and is thought to be the oldest in Europe.

Dining and Lodging

$$ ✕ **Can Ventura.** Built into a 17th-century farmhouse, this superb
★ restaurant is the best around Puigcerdà for decor, cuisine, and value. Trout or beef cooked *a la llosa* is one of the house specialties; the *entretenimientos* (a wide selection of hors d'oeuvres) are delicious. ⊠ *Plaça Major 1,* ☎ *972/896178. Reservations essential. MC, V. Closed Tues. No dinner Mon.*

$$ ✕ **La Formatgeria de Llívia.** This new Llívia restaurant was built into a former cheese factory, part of which still functions while you watch. A kilometer (½ mile) east of Llívia on the road to Saillagousse (France), Marta Pous and Juanjo Meya have been a big success with their combination of fine local specialties, panoramic views south to Puigmal, and general charm and good cheer. ⊠ *Pla de Ro, Gorguja,* ☎ *972/ 146279. Reservations essential. MC, V. Closed Thurs.*

$$ ✕⊡ **Hotel Llívia.** Here's an ideal base of operations for anyone skiing or hiking in France, Andorra, *or* Spain. The Llívia is owned and operated by the warm, generous Pous family, the proprietors of Can Ventura (☞ *above*). A spacious place, with large fireplaces and a glass-walled dining room that's nearly as scenic as a picnic in a Pyrenean meadow, the hotel runs spontaneous shuttles to nearby ski resorts and can organize excursions as well as riding, hunting, or trout fishing. ⊠ *Avda. de Catalunya s/n, 17527,* ☎ *972/896000,* ⨳ *972/146000. 68 rooms, 10 apartments. Restaurant, pool, tennis court. DC, MC, V.*

Bellver de Cerdanya

❾ *25 km (13½ mi) west of Puigcerdà on N260.*

Bellver de Cerdanya has conserved its slate-roof and fieldstone Pyrenean architecture more successfully than many of the Cerdanya's larger towns. Perched on a promontory over the **River Segre,** which folds neatly around the town, Bellver is a mountain version of a fishing village—trout fishing, of course. The river is the town's main event; how much water is coming down—and whether it's low or high, muddy or clear, warm or cold—supplants the weather as a topic of conversation. Bellver's **Gothic church** and **porticoed square,** in the upper part of town, are lovely examples of traditional Pyrenean mountain-village design.

Dining

$$ ✕ **Grau de l'Os.** This cozy mountain retreat—whose name translates as "Bear Cave"—has simple, rough-hewn carpentry. The typical Catalan cuisine includes such combinations as roast rabbit with *all i oli* (olive oil and garlic sauce), *civet de jabalí* (wild boar stew) and quail, partridge, trout, and lamb. ⊠ *Jaume II de Mallorca 5,* ☎ *973/510046. AE, DC, MC, V. Closed Tues.*

Martinet

10 km (6 mi) west of Bellver de Cerdanya on N260.

The town of Martinet hasn't much to offer except Can Boix (☞ *below*), one of the top gourmet restaurants in the Pyrenees, and a few cozy watering spots that are hard to pass up in the heat of summer. For a course in trout economy, have a close look over the railing along the river just upstream from the junction of the Llosa and the Segre. Martinet's protected trout are famous in these parts: they dine from 1 to 4, when the sun slants in, cooks off aquatic insect hatches, and illuminates every speckle and spot on these sleek leviathans. For a spectacular excursion, follow the valley of the Riu Llosa up into Andorra. The village of **Lles** is a famous Nordic-skiing resort with miles of cross-country tracks.

Dining

$$$ ✕ **Can Boix.** The modern, Lego-block building doesn't look like much ★ from the outside, but this restaurant in Martinet, 10 km (6 mi) west of Bellver, is one of the Cerdanya's premier establishments. (First prize goes to La Torre del Remei, owned by the same folks; ☞ Puigcerdà, *above*.) José María Boix and his wife, Loles, prepare a mix of Catalan and French cuisine, featuring *setas* (wild mushrooms) in season and such surprises as *canard magret amb mel* (duck breasts with honey) and *trinxat rostit* (chopped potato and cauliflower prepared with bacon). ✉ *Carretera Nacional, Km 204, 25724,* ☎ *973/515050,* 🖷 *973/515268. AE, DC, MC, V.*

Prat d'Aguiló

⑩ *20 km (12 mi) north of Martinet up a dirt road that is rough but navigable by the average automobile.*

The spectacular Prat d'Aguiló (Eagle's Meadow) is one of the highest points in the Cerdanya that you can access without either a four-wheel-drive vehicle or a hike. A relatively short climb (about three hours) to the top of the sheer rock wall of the Sierra del Cadí, directly above the meadow, reaches an altitude of nearly 8,000 ft. On a clear day you can see Puigcerdà and beyond; the River Segre seems no more than a thin, silver ribbon on the valley floor.

La Seu d'Urgell

★ ⑪ *20 km (12 mi) south of Andorra la Vella, 50 km (30 mi) west of Puigcerdà past Bellver and Martinet along the River Segre.*

La Seu d'Urgell is an ancient town tucked under the Sierra del Cadí. Its historical importance as the seat of the regional archbishopric since the Middle Ages (6th century) has left it with a rich legacy of art and architecture. The Pyrenean feel of the streets, dark balconies and porticoes, overhanging galleries, and colonnaded porches makes La Seu d'Urgell medieval, mysterious, and memorable.

★ The 12th-century cathedral of **Santa Maria** is the finest cathedral in the Pyrenees. One of the most moving sights in northern Spain is a show of sunlight gleaming through the rich reds and blues of Santa Maria's southeastern rose window over the transept's deep gloom. The 13th-century cloister is known for the individually carved capitals on its 50 columns. (They were crafted by the same Rousillon school of masons who carved the doorway to Ripoll's church of Santa Maria.) Don't miss the elegant 11th-century chapel of Sant Miquel Chapel. In 1996, archaeologists discovered Roman tombs in the ground beside the cathedral—an astounding find that may change perspectives about La Seu d'Urgell's role in the early history of this region. ▣ *Cathedral, cloister, and museum 375 ptas.* ⊘ *Daily 9–1 and 4–8.*

Dining and Lodging

$$$$ ✕▥ **El Castell.** This wood-and-slate structure is one of the area's finest spots for both dining and lodging. Rooms on the second floor have balconies overlooking the river; those on the third have slanted ceilings and dormer windows. Suites tack on a salon. The restaurant specializes in mountain cuisine, such as *civet de jabalí* (wild-boar stew)

and *llom de cordet amb trinxat* (lamb cooked over coals, served with puree of potatoes and cabbage). You need a reservation to stay overnight. ⊠ *Carretera de Lleida, Km 129, Apdo. 53, 25700,* ☎ *973/350704,* FAX *973/351574. 38 rooms, 4 suites. Restaurant. AE, DC, MC, V.*

$$$ 🏨 **El Parador de la Seu d'Urgell.** For comfortable quarters right in town, don't hesitate to stay at the excellent parador, built into the 12th-century church and convent of Sant Domènec. The interior patio, the cloister of the former convent, is a lush and intimate hideaway. The pool and the dining room have glass ceilings. ⊠ *Carrer Sant Domènec 6, Lleida, 25700,* ☎ *973/352000,* FAX *973/352309. 77 rooms, 1 suite. Restaurant, indoor pool. AE, DC, MC, V.*

WESTERN CATALAN PYRENEES

The main geographical events in this section are the valley of the Noguera Pallaresa River, the Vall d'Aran headwaters of the Atlantic-bound Garonne, and the Noguera Ribagorçana River valley, Catalonia's western limit. The space in the middle of the rhombuslike area delimited by the roads C133, N230, and C144 contains two of the Pyrenees' greatest treasures: Aigüestortes–Sant Maurici National Park, and the Noguera de Tor Valley, with its matched set of gemlike Romanesque churches.

Sort

★ ⑫ *From La Seu d'Urgell, take N260 toward Lleida, head west at Adrall, and drive 53 km (33 mi) over the Cantó Pass to Sort.*

Sort, the capital of the Pallars Sobirà (Upper Pallars Valley), is a center for skiing, fishing, and white-water kayaking. Don't be content with the Sort you see from the main road; one block back, the town is honeycombed with tiny streets and protected corners built against heavy winter weather. Sort is also the origin of the road into the unspoiled **Assua Valley,** a hidden pocket of untouched mountain villages, such as Saurí and Olp.

Llesuí

⑬ *15 km (9 mi) north of Sort.*

At the head of the Upper Pallars Valley, Lesuí's Romanesque **church** of Sant Pere is topped with a bell tower resembling a pointed witch's hat, characteristic of the Vall d'Aran and its environs. The local **ski area** presides over the valley along the slopes of the Altars peak.

Vallferrera/Cardós Valleys

⑭ *From Llavorsí, 14 km (9 mi) on C147 from Sort, at the junction of the Noguera Pallaresa and Cardós rivers, the road up to the valleys of Cardós and Vallferrera branches off to the northeast.*

A trip up the Vallferrera Valley is a good way to penetrate some little-known countryside, explore icy trout streams, or browse through the Romanesque and Visigothic (pre-Romanesque) churches and chapels scattered in and around the village of **Alins** under Catalonia's highest mountain, the Pica d'Estats. In the neighboring Cardós Valley, the svelte, Romanesque bell tower of the church of **Santa Maria** rises amid greens of alfalfa and early wheat and, in May, bright-red splashes of poppies.

Aigüestortes–Sant Maurici National Park

 After Escaló, 12 km (8 mi) from Llavorsí, the road to Espot and the Aigüestortes–Sant Maurici National Park veers west.

This wild domain of meadows and woods in the shadow of the twin peaks of Els Encantats hides more than 150 glacial lakes and lagoons (the beautiful **Sant Maurici** among them) as well as streams, waterfalls, and marshes. Forested by pines, firs, beech, and silver birches, it also has ample pastureland inhabited by Pyrenean chamois, capercaillie, golden eagle, and ptarmigan. The park has strict rules: no camping, no fires, no vehicles beyond certain points, no loose pets. Access to the park is free; shelters equipped with bunks and mattresses provide overnight accommodations. For information and reservations contact the park administration (⊠ Camp de Mart 35, 25004, Lleida, ☎ 973/ 246650).

Lodging

The **Ernest Mallafré Refugio** (shelter) is at the foot of Els Encantats near Lake Sant Maurici (☎ 973/624009); the shelter sleeps 36 and is open February–December. The **L'Estany Llong Refugio** (☎ 973/690284), in the Sant Nicolau Valley, sleeps 57 and is open mid-June–mid-October.

Espot

 Next to the eastern entrance to Aigüestortes–Sant Maurici; 166 km (100 mi) north of Lleida, 15 km (9 mi) northwest of Llavorsí.

Espot, which has a **ski area** (Super-Espot), nestles at the valley floor along a clear, aquamarine stream. **La Capella Bridge,** a perfect, mossy arch over the flow, looks as though it might have grown directly from the Pyrenean slate.

En Route From Esterri d'Aneu, C142 reaches the sanctuary of Mare de Deu de Ares, a hermitage and shelter, at 4,600 ft, and the Bonaigua Pass at 6,798 ft, offering a dizzying look back at the Pallars Mountains and ahead to the Vall d'Aran and the Maladeta massif beyond, shimmering white in the distance.

Vall d'Aran and Environs

 From Esterri d'Aneu, 46 km (27 mi) east to Vielha through the Bonaigua Pass.

The Vall d'Aran is at the western edge of the Catalan Pyrenees and the northwestern corner of Catalonia. North of the main Pyrenean axis, it is the Catalan Pyrenees' only Atlantic valley, opening into the plains of Aquitania and drained by the Garonne, which flows into the Atlantic Ocean north of Bordeaux. The 48 km (30 mi) drive from the Bonaigua Pass to the Pont del Rei border with France follows the riverbed faithfully.

The valley's Atlantic personality shows in its climate—wetter and colder—and its language: the 6,000 inhabitants speak Aranés, a dialect of Gascon French derived from the Occitanian language group. With some difficulty, it can be understood by speakers of Catalan and French. Originally part of the Aquitanian county of Comminges, the Vall d'Aran maintained feudal ties to the Pyrenees of Spanish Aragon and became part of Catalonia-Aragon in the 12th century. In 1389 the valley was assigned to Catalonia.

The Vall d'Aran, neither as wide as the Cerdanya nor as oppressively narrow and vertical as Andorra, has a sense of well-being and order, an architectural consonance unique in Catalonia. The clusters of iron-gray slate roofs, the lush vegetation, the dormer windows (a clear manifestation of French influence)—all make the Vall d'Aran a distinct geographic and cultural pocket that happens to have washed up on the Spanish side of the border. Hiking and climbing opportunities abound here. Guides are available year-round and can be arranged through the tourist office in Vielha (☎ 973/640110).

Vielha

⑱ *79 km (49 mi) northwest of Sort.*

Vielha (Viella, in Castilian Spanish), the capital of the Vall d'Aran, is a lively crossroads vitally involved in the Aranese movement to defend and reconstruct the valley's architectural, institutional, and linguistic heritage. The octagonal, 14th-century bell tower on the Romanesque parish church of **Sant Miquel** is one of the town's trademarks, as is the 15th-century Gothic altar. The partly damaged 12th-century poly-chrome wood carving *Cristo de Mig Aran,* displayed under glass at Sant Miquel, evokes mortality and humanity with a power unusual in medieval sculpture.

From Vielha you can visit **Salardú,** with a porticoed central *plaça* and an especially tall and graceful bell tower.

The village of **Tredós,** home of the church of **Santa Maria de Cap d'Aran**—the symbol of the Aranese independence movement and the meeting place of the valley's governing body, the Consell General until 1827—lies just east of Salardú.

Dining and Lodging

$$ ★ ✕ **Era Mola.** Also known as Restaurante Gustavo y María José, this restored stable with wood beams and whitewashed walls serves Aranese cuisine with a French flair. The *confite de pato* (duck stewed with apple) and *magret de pato* (breast of duck served rare with *carradetas,* wild mushrooms from the valley) are favorites. ⊠ *Carrer Marrech 14,* ☎ *973/642419. Reservations essential. MC, V. No lunch weekdays Dec.–Apr.*

$$$ ✕⌂ **Parador Nacional Valle de Aran.** This modern granite parador has a semicircular salon with huge windows and spectacular views over the Maladeta peaks. Rooms are furnished with traditional carved-wood furniture and floor-to-ceiling curtains. The restaurant serves preponderately Catalan cuisine, such as *espinacas a la catalana* (spinach cooked in olive oil with pine nuts, raisins, and garlic). ⊠ *Carretera del Túnel s/n, 25530,* ☎ *973/640100,* ℻ *973/641100. 135 rooms. Restaurant. AE, MC, V.*

$$ ⌂ **Residencia d'Aran.** On the left side of the road into Vielha, this modern hotel commands some of the best views in town. Rooms are bright and simply furnished. The cozy sitting room and the charming family in charge make a stay here a delight. Book ahead during ski season; you're 15 minutes from the slopes. ⊠ *Ctra. del Túnel s/n, 25530,* ☎ *973/640075,* ℻ *973/642295. 40 rooms. AE, DC, MC, V.*

Montgarri

⑲ *Salardú is 9 km (6 mi) east of Vielha.*

The sanctuary of **Santa Maria de Montgarri** is 12 km (7½) mi northeast of the town of Baguergue, which is just north of Salardú. This partly ruined 11th-century structure was once an important way station on

the route into the Vall d'Aran from France. The beveled, hexagonal
bell tower and the rounded stones, which look like they came from a
brook bottom, give the structure a stippled appearance not unlike that
of a Pyrenean trout. Try to be there for the Romería de Nuestra Señora
de Montgarri (Feast of Our Lady of Montgarri), on July 2, a country
fair with dancing, games, and general carrying-on.

Dining

$ ✕ **Casa Rufus.** Nestled in the tiny, gray-stone village of Gessa, between
Vielha and Salardú, Casa Rufus is cozily furnished with pine and
checked tablecloths. Rufus himself, who also runs the ski school at Baque-
ira, specializes in local country cooking; try the *conejo relleno de tern-
era* (rabbit stuffed with veal). ✉ *Sant Jaume 8,* ☎ *973/645246 or 973/
645872. MC, V. Closed May–July, Sept., Nov., and Sun.*

Outdoor Activities and Sports

Skiing, rafting, horseback riding, and fly fishing are all available
throughout the Vall d'Aran. Check with local tourist offices for the latest specifics.

DOGSLEDDING

La Pirena, the Pyrenean version of the Iditarod, rages through the Vall
d'Aran in early February. The race runs from Panticosa, above Jaca,
to La Molina, near Puigcerdà, February 1–15. For more information
contact the tourist office in Jaca (☎ 974/360098).

HORSE RACES

The Vall d'Aran's most extraordinary winter-sports event is the **Rally
Hipic Internacional Sobre Neu,** a horse race held every February on a
16-km (10-mi) course of packed snow. Contact the tourist office in Vielha
(☎ 973/640979) for information.

Joeu Valley

⓴ *9 km (6 mi) northwest of Vielha.*

The Joeu Valley, above the town of Les Bordes, grants an intriguing
look at Vall d'Aran hydraulics. One of the two main sources of the
Garonne, the Joeu River rises (resurfaces, actually) at Artiga de Lin and
cascades down the Barrancs waterfalls toward the Garonne. Using colored waters, early 20th-century scientists proved that this "spring" was
actually glacier runoff from the Maladeta massif, in the next valley west.
The glacier melt cascades into a massive pothole known as the Aigüal-
luts and reappears 4 km (2½ mi) later at Uelhs deth Joeu (Eyes of Jupiter,
in Aranés), where it flows north toward the Garonne and, eventually,
the Atlantic.

The **Baqueira-Beret Estación de Esquí** (Baqueira-Beret Ski Station),
visited annually by King Juan Carlos I and the royal family, offers Catalonia's most varied and reliable skiing. ✉ *Baqueira-Beret Estación
de Esquí, Salardú 25598,* ☎ *973/644455,* 🖷 *973/644488. Barcelona
office:* ✉ *Passeig de Gràcia 2,* ☎ *93/318–2776,* 🖷 *93/412–2942.*

Alta Ribagorça Oriental

⓴ *From Vall d'Aran take the 6-km (4-mi) Vielha tunnel to the Alta Ri-
bagorça Oriental.*

This valley includes the east bank of the Noguera Ribagorçana River
and the Llevata and Noguera de Tor valleys. The latter has the Pyrenees' richest concentration of medieval art and architecture.

From Vielha, route N230 runs south 33 km (20 mi) to the intersection with N260 (sometimes marked C144), which goes west over the

Fadas Pass to Castejón de Sos. Four kilometers (2½ miles) past this intersection, the road up the Noguera de Tor Valley turns to the northeast, 2 km (1 mi) short of Pont de Suert.

The quality and unity of design apparent in the Romanesque churches along the Noguera de Tor River are the result of the sponsorship of the counts of Erill. The Erill knights, away fighting Moors in distant theaters of the Reconquest, left their women behind to supervise the creation of local houses of worship. The women then brought in the leading masters—architects, masons, sculptors, and painters—to build and decorate the churches. To what extent a single eye and sensibility was responsible for this extraordinarily harmonious and coherent set of churches may never be known, but it's clear that they all share certain distinguishing characteristics: a miniaturistic tightness combined with eccentric or irregular design, and slender rectangular bell towers at once light and forceful, perfectly balanced against the rocky background.

Taüll

㉒ *58 km (36 mi) south of Vielha.*

Taüll, a town of narrow streets and tight mountain design—wooden balconies, steep slate roofs—now has a ski resort, **Boí Taüll,** at the head of the Sant Nicolau Valley.

The three-naved church of **Sant Climent,** at the edge of town, was built in 1123 and has a six-story belfry. The proportions, the Pyrenean stone, the changing hues in the light, and the general intimacy of the place create an exceptional balance and harmony. The church's murals, including the famous *Pantocrator,* the work of the "Master of Taüll," were moved to Barcelona's Museu Nacional d'Art de Catalunya (☞ Chapter 7) in 1922; you can see reproductions here. 🎟 *500 ptas.* ☉ *Daily 9–2 and 4–8.*

Other important churches in Taüll include **Sant Feliu,** at Barruera; **Sant Joan Baptista,** at Boí; **Santa Maria,** at Cardet; **Santa Maria,** at Col; **Santa Eulàlia,** at Erill-la-vall; **La Nativitat de la Mare de Deu** and **Sant Quirze,** at Durro; **Sant Llorenç,** at Sarais; and **Sant Nicolau,** in the Sant Nicolau Valley, at the entrance to the Aigüestortes–Sant Maurici National Park.

Dining

$$ ✕ **La Cabana.** This rustic spot specializes in lamb and goat cooked over coals but also offers a fine *escudella* (sausage, vegetable, and potato stew) and an excellent *crema de carrerres* (cream of meadow mushroom) soup. ✉ *Carretera de Taüll,* ☎ 973/696213. MC, V. Closed Mon. Dec.–Apr., May–June 23, Oct.–Nov.

Caldes de Boí

㉓ *6 km (4 mi) north of Taüll.*

The thermal baths at Caldes de Boí include, between hot and cold sources, 40 springs. The caves inside the bath area are a singular natural phenomenon, with thermal steam seeping through the cracks in the rock. Take advantage of the bath's therapeutic qualities at either the Hotel Caldes or the Hotel Manantial. Services range from a bath, at 1,000–1,500 pesetas, to a 3,000-peseta underwater body massage; arthritic patients are frequent takers. ✉ *Hotel Caldes,* ☎ 973/696230; ✉ *Hotel Manantial,* ☎ 973/690191. ☉ June 24–Sept.

Dining and Lodging

$$ ✕⬚ **Fondevila.** This solid stone structure 3 km (2 mi) from Taüll is warmly decorated inside with wooden trim and simple country furnishings. The rooms are generously proportioned and cozy. The country cuisine features game in season and Catalan specialties. ⬚ *Carrer Única, Boí 25528,* ☎ *973/696011,* 𝙁𝘼𝙓 *973/696011. 46 rooms. AE, DC, MC, V. Closed Oct.–Nov.*

ARAGON AND THE CENTRAL PYRENEES

Alto Aragón (Upper Aragon), the northern part of the province of Huesca, has the Maladeta (11,165 ft), Posets (11,070 ft), and Monte Perdido (11,004 ft) massifs, the highest points in the Pyrenean chain. The north–south valleys were formed by glaciers at their headlands; the still-deeper canyons and gorges were cut by rivers swollen by rainfalls and heavy snow runoff.

Communications here were all but nonexistent until the 19th century. Four-fifths of the region had never seen a motor vehicle of any kind until the early part of the 20th century, and the 150 km (93 mi) of border with France between Portalet de Aneu and Vall d'Aran had never had an international crossing. This combination of high peaks, deep defiles, and lack of communication has produced some of the Iberian Peninsula's most isolated towns and valleys. The residents of much of Upper Aragon speak dialects such as Grausín and Benasqués and have variations on the typical Aragonese folk dance, the *jota*, and different kinds of folkloric costumes. The unspoiled setting is habitat for a wide variety of Pyrenean wildlife, including several strains of mountain goat; deer; and, in Ordesa and Mt. Perdido National Park, the recently reintroduced Pyrenean brown bear.

Benasque

★ ㉔ *79 km (49 mi) southwest of Vielha.*

Benasque, Aragon's easternmost town, has always been an important link between Catalonia and Aragon. This town of just 1,000 people packs a number of notable buildings, including the 13th-century church of **Santa María Mayor** and the ancient, dignified manor houses of the town's old families, such as the **palace of the counts of Ribagorza,** on Calle Mayor, or the **Torre Juste.** Take a walk around and peer into the entryways of these palatial digs; they're left open for this purpose.

Anciles, 2 km (1 mi) south of Benasque, is one of Spain's best-preserved and -restored medieval villages, an excellent collection of farmhouses and *palacetes* (town houses). The summer classical-music series is a superb collision of music and architecture, and the village restaurant, Ansils, combines modern and medieval motifs in both cuisine and design.

The **Cerler** ski area (☎ 974/551012), 6 km (4 mi) from Benasque, covers the slopes of the Cogulla peak, east of town. Built on a shelf over the valley at an altitude of 5,051 ft, Cerler has 26 ski runs, three lifts, and a helicopter service, with guides, to drop you at the highest peaks.

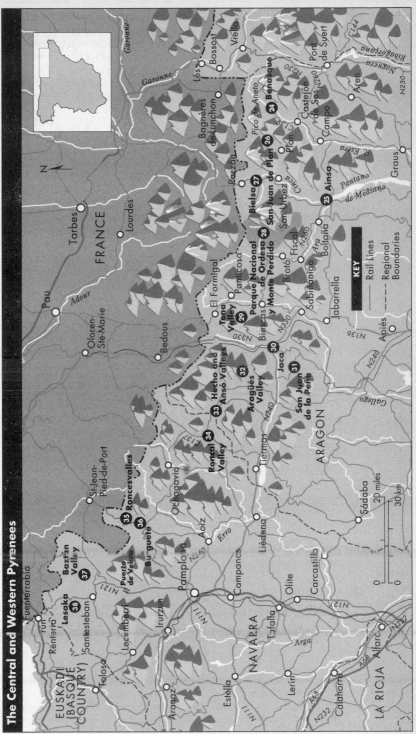

The Central and Western Pyrenees

OFF THE
BEATEN PATH Benasque is the traditional base camp for excursions to Aneto, the high-est peak in the Pyrenees. You can rent crampons and a *piolet* (ice axe) for the two- to three-hour crossing of the Aneto glacier at any sports store in town or at the Refugio de la Renclusa, a way station for moun-taineers; it's an hour's walk above the parking area, which is 17 km (11 mi) north of Benasque. The trek to the summit and back is not dif-ficult, just long—some 20 km (12 mi) round-trip, with a 1,500-yard vertical ascent. Allow a full 12 hours.

Dining and Lodging

$$ ✕ **Asador Ixarso.** Roast goat or lamb cooked over a raised fireplace in the corner of the dining room make this a fine refuge in cold weather. The *revuelto de setas* (eggs scrambled with wild mushrooms) is superb, as are the salads. ⊠ *San Pedro 9, Benasque.* ☎ *974/552057. Closed weekdays Sept. 15–Dec. 8 and Easter–June 29. MC, V.*

$$ ✕ **Restaurante Ansils.** A rustic place ingeniously redesigned in glass, wood, and stone, Ansils specializes in local Benasqués dishes such as *civet de jabalí* (wild boar stew) and *recau* (a thick vegetable broth). They're open for holiday meals on Christmas and Easter. ⊠ *Anciles, Huesca,* ☎ *974/551150. Closed weekdays Oct.–June. AE, DC, MC, V.*

$$–$$$ ✕🏠 **Gran Hotel Benasque.** This spacious new stone hotel is bracketed by the highest crests in the Pyrenees (Aneto and Posets) and serves as an impeccably comfortable base for exploring them. The decor and am-bience are modern yet tasteful. The restaurant's mountain cuisine fea-tures *sopa Benasquesa* (a hearty highland stew) and *crepas Aneto* (crepes with ham, wild mushroom, and béchamel sauce). ⊠ *Carretera de Anciles 3, 22440,* ☎ *974/551011,* ℻ *974/551509. 69 rooms. Restaurant, 2 pools, sauna, exercise room. Closed Nov. AE, MC, V.*

$$ ✕🏠 **Hotel San Marsial.** Filled with antiques, ancient wooden doors, and artifacts, this comfortable spot also has one of Benasque's best restau-rants. Try the lentil soup or the *caldereta de conejo* (rabbit stewed in almonds, olives, and bread crumbs). ⊠ *Carretera de Francia s/n, 22440,* ☎ *974/551616,* ℻ *974/551623. 24 rooms. Restaurant, cafe-teria. AE, DC, MC, V.*

En Route South of Castejón de Sos, down the Esera Valley through the Congosto de Ventamillo—a sheer slice through the rock made by the Esera River—a turn west on N260 cuts over to Aínsa at the junction of the Rivers Cinca and Ara.

Aínsa

㉕ *66 km (41 mi) southwest of Benasque.*

Aínsa's **arcaded central plaza** and **old town** are classic examples of me-dieval village design, with heavy stone archways and tiny windows. The **12th-century Romanesque church** has a quadruple-vaulted door. 🎟 *Free.* ☉ *Daily 9–2 and 4–8.*

OFF THE
BEATEN PATH Añisclo Gorges – On the road north from Aínsa, the Añisclo Canyon is 5 km (3 mi) north of the town of Escalona. A road to the west runs 14 km (8½ mi) along the edge of the sheer rock divide to Urbez. As you drive into Urbez, you'll see the **ancient stone bridge.** On the far bank of the river is the **cave chapel** named for San Urbez, a hermit monk from Bordeaux who lived there in the 8th century.

San Juan de Plan and the Gistaín Valley

㉖ *14 km (8½ mi) east of Salinas.*

San Juan de Plan has become a treasury of local folklore and is well worth a trip. This detour begins with a well-marked road heading east of Salinas, 25 km (15 mi) north of Ainsa. The Cinqueta River drains the Gistaín Valley, flowing by or through the mountain villages of Sin, Señes, Saravillo, Serveta, and Salinas; the town of San Juan de Plan presides at the head of the valley, where an Ethnographical Museum, a weaving workshop, and an early-music and -dance ensemble are the pride of the region. The **Ethnographical Museum** (☉ 9–2 and 4–8; ☒ 500 ptas.) is a fascinating glimpse into the valley's way of life until as recently as 25 years ago. Don't miss a tour of the weaving industry, restored by Amanda Tyson, the town's resident American.

Dining and Lodging

$$ ✕🖭 **Casa la Plaza.** This charming spot has cozy rooms with original antique furniture, and the restaurant serves excellent cuisine. ☒ *Plaza Mayor s/n, 22367,* ☎ *974/506052,* 🖷 *974/506052. 13 rooms. Closed sporadically in winter (Oct.–May); call to confirm. AE, DC, MC, V.*

Bielsa

㉗ *34 km (21 mi) northeast of Aínsa.*

Bielsa, at the confluence of the Cinca and Barrosa rivers, is a busy summer resort with some lovely mountain architecture and an ancient, porticoed town hall.

Northwest of Bielsa the **Mt. Perdido glacier** and the icy **Marbore Lake** drain into the **Pineta Valley** and the Pineta Reservoir. You can take three- or four-hour walks from the parador up to Larri, Munia, or Marbore Lake among remote peaks.

Dining and Lodging

$$ ✕ **El Chinchecle.** This is one of the best restaurants in the Pyrenees for carefully crafted Aragonese cuisine. Don't miss the *migas de pastor* (literally, "shepherd's breadcrumbs"), a delicious concoction of breadcrumbs, garlic, bacon, and olive oil. Try a local Somontano wine, especially a spicy Señorío de Lazán red. For an aperitif, don't miss the nearby bar of the same name (and family), filled with regional folklore, photographs, and music. ☒ *Calle Calvario s/n,* ☎ *974/501182. Closed weekdays mid-Sept.–mid-Dec. and Easter–June. MC, V.*

$$–$$$ ✕🖭 **Parador de Bielsa.** This modern structure of glass, steel, and stone overlooks the national park, the peak of Monte Perdido, and the source of the Cinca River. Rooms are decorated in bright wood, but the best part is its proximity to the park and the views. The restaurant specializes in Aragonese mountain dishes such as *pucherete de Parzán* (a stew with beans, sausage, and an assortment of vegetables). ☒ *Bielsa, 22350,* ☎ *974/501011,* 🖷 *974/501188. 24 rooms. Restaurant. AE, DC, MC, V.*

$$ ✕🖭 **Hotel Valle de Pineta.** This corner castle overlooking the river junction is the most spectacular place in town. The restaurant is excellent, the views without compare. Try for the top corner room, which looks up and down both valleys. ☒ *Baja s/n, 22350,* ☎ *974/501010,* 🖷 *974/501191. 26 rooms. Closed Nov. AE, DC, MC, V.*

En Route You can explore the **Cinca Valley** from the river's source at the head of the valley above Bielsa. From Bielsa, drive back down to Aínsa and turn west on N260 (alternately marked C138) for Broto.

Parque Nacional de Ordesa y Monte Perdido

㉘ *From Aínsa, turn west on N260 for the 53-km (32-mi) drive through Boltaña to Broto, Torla, and the Parque Nacional de Ordesa y Monte Perdido.*

En route to the park, **Broto** is a prototypical Aragonese mountain town with an excellent **16th-century Gothic church.** Nearby villages such as **Oto** have stately manor houses with classic local features: baronial entryways, conical chimneys, and wooden galleries. **Torla** is noteworthy for its mountain architecture and as the entry point to the park; it's a popular base camp for hikers.

The Parque Nacional de Ordesa y Monte Perdido (Ordesa and Mt. Perdido National Park) is one of Spain's great underrated wonders, a domain many consider comparable to North America's Grand Canyon. The entrance lies under the vertical walls of the Mondarruego mountain, source of the Ara River and its tributary, the Arazas, which forms the famous Ordesa Valley. The park was founded by royal decree in 1918 to protect the natural integrity of the Central Pyrenees; it has increased from 4,940 to 56,810 acres as provincial and national authorities have added the Monte Perdido massif, the head of the Pineta Valley, and the Escuain and Añisclo canyons. Defined by the Ara and Arazas rivers, the Ordesa Valley is endowed with pine, fir, larch, beech, and poplar forests; lakes, waterfalls, and high mountain meadows; and protected wildlife, including trout, boar, chamois, and the *Capra Pyrenaica* mountain goat.

Hikes through the park (on well-marked and -maintained mountain trails) lead to waterfalls, caves, and spectacular outlooks. A few spots, while not technically difficult, may seem precarious. You can get information and guidebooks at the booth on the way into the park. The best time to come is from the beginning of May to the middle of November, but check conditions in regional tourist offices before either driving into a blizzard in May or missing out on *el veranillo de San Martín* (Indian summer) in the fall.

En Route After exploring the Ordesa National Park, follow N260 (sometimes marked as C140) west over the Cotefablo Pass from Torla to Biescas.

Tena Valley

㉙ *40 km (25 mi) west of Ordesa.*

The Tena Valley, a north–south hexagon of 400 square km (248 square mi), is formed by the Gállego River and its two tributaries, the Aguaslimpias and the Caldares. A glacial valley surrounded by peaks rising to more than 10,000 ft (such as the 10,900-ft Vignemale), Tena is a busy hiking and winter-sports center. Starting from the top, **Sallent de Gállego,** at the head of the valley, has long been a jumping-off point for excursions to **Aguaslimpias, Piedrafita,** and the meadows of the Gállego headwaters at **El Formigal** (a major ski area) and **Portalet.** The Pyrenean *ibon* (glacial lake) of **Respumoso,** accessible by walking 2½ hours above the old road from Sallent to Formigal, is a peaceful and perfectly horizontal expanse amid all that vertical landscape.

Dining and Lodging

$–$$ ✕🏨 **Morlans.** The rooms here are warm and well equipped with views south over the town of Panticosa's ski area and the mountains beyond.

The lower restaurant specializes in roast lamb, goat, and suckling pig; the upper restaurant serves *civets* of deer, boar, and mountain goat, as well as such Upper Aragonese favorites as *pochas* (bean soup with sausage). ✉ *Calle de San Miguel, Barriada de la Cruz, 22066,* ☎ *974/ 487057,* FAX *974/487386. 25 rooms. 2 restaurants. MC, V.*

Jaca

③⓪ *Down the Tena Valley through Biescas, a westward turn at Sabiñánigo onto N330 leaves a 14-km (9-mi) drive to Jaca.*

Jaca, the most important municipal center in Alto Aragón (with a population of more than 15,000), is anything but a sleepy town. Bursting with ambition and blessed with the natural resources to fuel their relentless drive, Jacetanos are determined to host a Winter Olympics.

Jaca hosts or has hosted a Summer University, the Center for Pyrenean Studies, the biannual Pyrenean Folklore Festival, the Winter Games of the Pyrenees, and the World University Winter Games. Either the National or the World Figure Skating Championships are held here nearly every year, and the national ice-hockey King's Cup is often played on Jaca's **Olympic-size ice rink.** Jaca's ice-hockey program is one of Spain's best, along with San Sebastián's Txuri Urdiñ and Puigcerdà's club.

NEED A BREAK?

One of Jaca's most emblematic restaurants is **La Campanilla** (✉ Escuelas Pías 8, behind the town hall), whose baked potatoes with garlic and olive oil are an institution, unchanged for as long as anyone can remember.

Once the capital of the 11th-century kingdom of Jacetania and an important stop on the pilgrimage to Santiago de Compostela, Jaca has an **11th-century cathedral,** one of Spain's oldest. The **Museo Episcopal** (Bishops' Museum) is filled with excellent Romanesque and Gothic murals (☉ daily 11–1:30, 4:30–6:30, 🎟 350 ptas.). The **Ciutadella** (citadel), in town, is a good example of 17th-century military architecture (☉ Oct.–Mar., daily 11–2 and 4–5; Apr.–Sept., daily 5–6; 🎟 free). The **Rapitán Garrison,** outside town, is also known for its military architecture (☉ July–Aug., Mon.–Sat. 5–8, Sun. 11–1; 🎟 free). The **ayuntamiento door** is a notable Renaissance design.

The ski areas of **Candanchú** and **Astún** are 32 km (20 mi) north on the road to Somport and the French border.

Dining and Lodging

$$ ✕ **La Cocina Aragonesa.** The fresh and innovative cuisine features game specialties in season, including venison, wild boar, partridge, and duck. Try the partridge stuffed with foie gras. ✉ *Cervantes 5,* ☎ *974/ 361050. Closed Wed. AE, DC, MC, V.*

$$–$$$ ✕🏨 **Gran Hotel.** This rambling hotel is central to life and tourism in Jaca. Done up in wood, stone, and glass, it has a garden and a separate dining wing. Rooms are comfortable and are furnished with rich colors and practical wood furniture. ✉ *Paseo de la Constitución I, 22700,* ☎ *974/360900,* FAX *974/364061. 166 rooms. Restaurant, pool, meeting rooms. AE, DC, MC, V.*

Nightlife and the Arts

Discos such as **Dimensión** and **Oroel** are thronged with skiers and hockey players in season (Oct.–Apr.). But the main nocturnal attractions are the so-called *bares musicales* (music bars), somewhat less hard-core, loud, and smoky than the discos. Nearly all of these are in the old part of Jaca, around the Plaza Ramiro I and along Calle Gil Verges and Calle Bellido.

WEST OF JACA, NAVARRE AND THE BASQUE COUNTRY

The Hecho and Ansó valleys, in western Aragon, are among the most pristine enclaves in the Pyrenees. Navarre's Irati Forest, the Baztán Valley, and the route down to the Atlantic along the Bidasoa River are rich in natural, human, and historical resources.

San Juan de la Peña

31 *Reached by driving 16 km (10 mi) south to the town of Bernués, where a right turn leads 12 km (7 mi) to the monastery.*

Before starting west through the Aragonese valleys of Hecho and Ansó, you might want to loop south to visit the **monastery of San Juan de la Peña,** a site connected to the legend of the Holy Grail as well as a symbol of Christian resistance during the Moorish occupation of Spain between the 8th and 15th centuries. It can be traced to the 9th century, when a hermit monk named Juan settled on the *peña* (cliff) on the Pano mountain; a monastery was then founded on that spot in 920. In 1071 Sancho Ramirez, son of King Ramiro I, founded the Benedictine monastery of San Juan de la Peña, making use of the previous monastery, which was built into the mountain's rock wall. The **cloister,** tucked under the cliff, dates from the 12th century and features carved capitals depicting biblical scenes. ☼ *Oct.–Mar., Wed.–Sun. 11–1:30 and 4–6; Apr.–Sept., Tues.–Sun. 10–1:30 and 4–7.*

En Route   The Aragüés, Hecho, and Ansó are the last three valleys in Aragon. From Jaca, head west on N240 and take a hard right at Puente de la Reina (after turning right to cross the bridge) and continue north along the Aragón-Subordán River. The first right after 15 km (9 mi) leads into the Aragüés Valley along the Osia River to Aisa and then Jasa.

Aragüés Valley

32 *Aragüés del Puerto is 2 km (1 mi) from Jasa.*

Above Aragüés del Puerto is the **Bisaurín Peak,** one of the highest in the area at 8,638 ft. **Aragüés del Puerto** is a tidy mountain village with stone houses and diminutive nooks and crannies. The distinctive folk dance in Aragüés is the *Palotiau,* a special variation of the *jota* performed only in this village. At the source of the River Osia, the **Lizara** cross-country ski area is in a flat between the Aragüés and Jasa valleys, where you can find dolmens left from the megalithic period.

Hecho and Ansó Valleys

33 *The Hecho Valley is 49 km (30 mi) west of Jaca. The Ansó Valley is 25 km (15 mi) west of Hecho.*

You can reach the Hecho Valley by returning to the valley of the Aragón-Subordan and turning north again. The **Siresa Monastery,** above the town of Hecho, is the area's most important monument, a 9th-century retreat of which only the 11th-century church remains. The Cheso dialect is still alive in the Hecho Valley and is used by some writers and poets. The **Selva de Oza** (Oza Forest), at the head of the valley, is the natural pièce de résistance, reachable only after passing through the **Boca del Infierno** (Mouth of Hell), a tight draw where the road and the river pass. On the other side of the Selva de Oza is a **Roman road** that was used before the 4th century to reach France through the El Palo Pass and became one of the first routes across the border on the pilgrimage to Santiago de Compostela.

The **Ansó Valley** is Aragon's western limit. Rich in fauna (mountain goats, wild boar, and even a bear or two), the Ansó Valley follows the Veral River up to Zuriza. Above Zuriza are three cross-country ski areas, known as the **Pistas de Linza.** Near Fago is the sanctuary of the **Virgen de Puyeta,** patron saint of the valley. From the town of **Ansó,** head west to Roncal on the difficult but beautiful road through the Sierra de San Miguel.

Lodging

$$ ☒ **Hotel Usón.** If you want to see more of the upper Hecho Valley and explore the Selva de Ozo (Ozo Forest), stay here. This friendly little Pyrenean inn will rent you a bike, get you a trout-fishing permit, or send you off in the right direction for a climb or hike. ☒ *Carretera Selva de Ozo, Km 7, 22720,* ☎ *974/375358. 14 rooms. MC, V.*

En Route   The Basque Pyrenees extend west from Roncal, at the Aragonese border, to Vera de Bidasoa, where the Bidasoa River, the border between France and Spain, flows down through the western Pyrenean foothills to the Bay of Biscay. From the peaks of Anie (8,213 ft) and Ori (6,616 ft) and the plateau of the Tres Reyes (7,984 ft), the mountains descend west to the Pyrenees' last height, Larrún (2,952 ft).

Roncal Valley

③④   *Take N240 from Jaca west along the Aragon River; a right turn north on NA137 follows the Esca River from the head of the Yesa Reservoir up the Roncal Valley.*

The Roncal Valley is famous for its sheep's-milk cheese and as the birthplace of Julián Gayarre (1844–90), the leading tenor of his time. The 34-km (21-mi) drive through the towns of **Burgui** and **Roncal** to the capital at **Isaba** winds through green hillsides and Basque *caseríos* housing farmers and their livestock. Burgui's red-tile roofs backed by rolling pastures contrast with the vertical rock and steep slate roofs of the Aragonese and Catalan Pyrenees; Isaba's wide-arched bridge across the Esca is a reminder of Roman engineering influence on later construction. Try to be in the Roncal Valley for the celebration of the Tribute of the Three Cows, held every July 13 since 1375. The mayors of the valley's villages, dressed in distinctive traditional gowns, gather near the summit of San Martín to receive the symbolic payment of three cows from their French counterparts, in memory of the settlement of ancient border disputes over rights to high pastures and water sources. (Eating, drinking, and celebrating follow.) The road west (NA140) to Ochagavia through the Lazar Pass has views of the peaks of Anie and Ori towering over the French border.

Two kilometers (1 mile) south of Ochagavía, at Escároz, a small secondary roadway winds 22 km (14 mi) over the Abaurrea heights to Aribe, known for its triple-arched medieval bridge and ancient *horreo* (granary). A 15 km (9 mi) detour north through the town of Orbaiceta up to the headwaters of the Irati River, at the Irabia Reservoir, gets you a good look at the **Selva de Irati** (Irati Forest).

The Irati Forest is one of Europe's major beech forests. It is said—if not widely believed—that before the construction of the 16th-century Spanish Armada depleted Spain's forests beyond repair, a squirrel could cross the Iberian Peninsula without touching the ground.

Roncesvalles

★ ㉟ *2.5 km (1.5 mi) north of Burguete, 48 km (30 mi) north of Pamplona.*

Roncesvalles (Orreaga, in Euskera) is the site of the Colegiata, cloister, hospital and 12th-century **chapel of Santiago,** the first church in Navarre on the St. James pilgrimage route. The **Colegiata** (Collegiate Church), built at the orders of King Sancho VII el Fuerte (the Strong), houses the king's tomb, which measures more than 7 ft long. The 3,468-ft Ibañeta Pass, above Roncesvalles, is one of the most beautiful routes into France. A stone **menhir** marks the traditional site of the legendary battle in *The Song of Roland* in which Roland fell after calling for help on his ivory battle horn.

Dining and Lodging

$$ ✕⊡ **La Posada.** This 17th-century building is an ancient way station for pilgrims bound for Santiago de Compostela. The heavy stone entry and simple but comfortable accommodations are a good match for the neighboring Colegiata. ⊠ *Carretera Pamplona–Francia, Km 48, 31650,* ☎ *948/760225,* ℻ *948/760225. 18 rooms. Restaurant. AE, DC, MC, V. Closed Nov.*

Burguete

㊱ *2.5 km (1½ mi) south of Roncesvalles,120 km (75 mi) northwest of Jaca.*

Burguete lies between two mountain streams forming the headwaters of the Urobi River. The town was immortalized when Ernest Hemingway published *The Sun Also Rises,* in 1926, with its evocative description of trout fishing in an ice-cold stream above a moist Navarran village. Visitors to Burguete and to Roncesvalles can feel securely bracketed between 11th-century French and 20th-century American literary classics.

Dining and Lodging

$$ ✕⊡ **Hostal Burguete.** This is the inn where Hemingway's character Jake Barnes spent a few days clearing his head in the cool streams of Navarre before plunging back into the psychodrama of the San Fermín festival and his impossible love with Lady Brett Ashton. It still works for this sort of thing, though there don't seem to be as many trout around these days. Good value and simple Navarran cooking make this a good place to stop for a meal or a night. ⊠ *Calle Única 51, 31540,* ☎ *948/ 760005. 22 rooms. Restaurant. MC, V. Closed Feb.–Mar.*

En Route From Burguete continue 21 km (13 mi) southwest on C135 until you reach a small road on the right to Saigos, Urtason, Iragui, Egozcue, and Olagüe, where it connects with N121 some 20 km (12 mi) north of Pamplona. Turn north and climb over the Puerto de Velate (Velate Pass)—or go through the new tunnel in bad weather or a hurry—to the turn for Elizondo and the Baztán Valley.

Baztán Valley

㊲ *80 km (50 mi) north of Pamplona.*

Tucked neatly over the headwaters of the Bidasoa River and under the peak of the 3,545-ft Garramendi mountain, which looms over the border with France, the Baztán Valley's rounded green hills make an ideal halfway stop between the rocky crags of the central Pyrenees and the flat expanse of the Atlantic Ocean, below. Each village in this enchanted valley seems smaller and simpler than the next, with tiny clusters of red-tile-roofed, whitewashed, stone-and-mortar houses grouped around a central *frontón* (handball court).

Dining and Lodging

$$ ✕ **Galarza.** This stone town house overlooks the Baztán River in the
★ town of Elizondo. The kitchen serves excellent Basque fare, with a Navar-
ran emphasis on vegetables. Try the *txuritabel* (roast lamb in season
with a special stuffing of egg and vegetables) or *txuleta de ternera* (veal
raised in the valley). ⊠ *C. Santiago 1,* ☎ *948/580101. MC, V.*

$ ✕🖃 **Fonda Etxeberria.** This tiny inn in the town of Arizcun, in the Baztán
★ Valley, is an old farmhouse with creaky floorboards and oak doors.
The rooms are small but handsome, and though they share baths, the
baths are palatial. The restaurant serves simple country dishes, such
as bean stew and roast lamb. ⊠ *Next to frontón in Arizcun,* ☎ *948/
453013. 16 rooms. Restaurant. MC, V.*

Lesaka

③⑧ *71 km (43 mi) northwest of Pamplona.*

If you're around for Pamplona's festival of San Fermín (July 6–15),
stop at Lesaka, just 2 km (1 mi) off the N121. Lesaka's patron saint
is also San Fermín, and its *sanfermines txikos* (miniature festival of San
Fermín) may more closely resemble the one described in *The Sun Also
Rises* than today's Pamplonan beer bust does.

OFF THE **CABO HIGUER** – Follow the Bidasoa River down through Vera de Bida-
BEATEN PATH soa to Irún, Fuenterrabía (☞ Chapter 5), and, for its symbolic value as
well as for the view out into the Atlantic, Cabo Higuer. This is the end of
the road, one of two geographical bookends—Cap Creus, on the
Mediterranean, is the other—of a complete trans-Pyrenean trek.

THE PYRENEES A TO Z

Arriving and Departing

By Plane

Barcelona's **El Prat International Airport** is the center for transporta-
tion to and from the Oriental (eastern) Pyrenees. El Prat is a 15-minute
and 2,500-peseta taxi ride from the center of Barcelona, 30 minutes
and considerably cheaper (400 pesetas) by train or bus. Airports at
Zaragoza, Pamplona, and Fuenterrabía also serve the Pyrenees of
Aragon, Navarre, and the Basque country.

To travel from Madrid to a Pyrenean jumping-off point, take the shut-
tle (Puente Aéreo) to Barcelona or go by a scheduled flight to the
Fuenterrabía airport, 20 minutes from San Sebastián.

By Train

The overnight train from Madrid's Chamartín Station to Barcelona or
San Sebastián has a distinct advantage: you leave late (9:15 PM–11 PM)
and arrive early (7:30 AM–8:30 AM), thus losing no daytime activities
at either end.

Getting Around

By Car

The only practical way to tour the Pyrenees, short of hiking, is by car.
The most difficult road into the Oriental Pyrenees is over the Tosses
Pass to Puigcerdà, but it's free and the scenery is spectacular. Safer, faster,
and more expensive but somewhat less scenic (though you will have a
great view of the Montserrat massif) is the approach through the Cadí

Tunnel. The wide, two-lane roads of the Cerdanya are generally new and well paved; as you move west, roads may be more difficult to navigate, but they are rapidly being improved as the Eje Pirenaico (Pyrenean Axis) N260 nears completion. You can rent cars at airports at both ends of the Pyrenees (☞ Chapters 5 and 7).

By Train
Three railheads have been established in the Pyrenees: Puigcerdà, in the Cerdanya; Pobla de Segur, in the Noguera Pallaresa Valley; and Canfranc, north of Jaca, below the ski resorts of Candanchú and Astún.

Contacts and Resources

Emergencies
Barcelona: Red Cross (☎ 93/2051414). **Province of Gerona:** Red Cross (☎ 972/200415); police (☎ 972/201381). **Province of Huesca:** Red Cross (☎ 974/221186); police (☎ 974/244711). **Province of Lleida:** Red Cross (☎ 973/267011); police (☎ 973/245012). **Province of Navarre:** Red Cross (☎ 948/226404); police (☎ 948/237000).

Fishing
Ramón Cosiallf and **Danica** (☎ 908/735376) can take you fly fishing anywhere in the world by horse or helicopter, but the Pyrenees are their home turf. For about $100 a day (depending on equipment), you can be whisked to high Pyrenean lakes and ponds, streams, and rivers and armed with equipment and expertise. You can purchase fishing licenses for each autonomous region (Catalonia, Aragon, Navarre) at local rod-and-gun clubs (Asociaciones de Pesca, Caza).

Golf
Camprodon has a nine-hole course, Club de Golf de Camprodón, (☎ 972/130125). The Cerdanya Valley has three golf courses, two near **Puigcerdà** (Reial Club de Golf de la Cerdanya, ☎ 972/141408; Club de Golf de Fontanals, ☎ 972/144374) and a nine-hole course at **Font Romeu** (Club de Golf de Font Romeu, ☎ 05/68301078), in France. Huesca, Jaca, and Benasque also offer golfing opportunities. Check with local tourist offices for details. Greens fees are generally between 4,000 and 8,000 pesetas.

Guided Tours
The **Touring travel agency** (☎ 972/880602 or 972/881450, FAX 972/881939) in Puigcerdà can help arrange routes, guides, horses, or four-wheel-drive vehicles for treks to upper lakes, peaks, and meadows. Local *excursionista* clubs, and especially the **Centro Excursionista de Catalunya** in Barcelona (✉ Carrer Paradís 10, ☎ 93/3152311), can advise climbers and hikers.

Outdoor Activities and Sports
Jaca (☎ 974/361032), Puigcerdà (☎ 972/880243), and Vielha (☎ 973/642864) have excellent **ice rinks** with hockey programs, figure-skating classes, and public skating sessions.Spain's daily newspaper *El País* prints complete ski information every Friday in season. For up-to-the-minute information in Catalan and Spanish, contact the **hotline** in Barcelona (☎ 93/416–0194). For further information, contact the **Federació Catalana Esports d'Hivern** (Catalan Winter Sports Federation; ✉ Carrer Casp 38, Barcelona, ☎ 93/302–7040).

Visitor Information
The regional tourist offices for the areas covered in this chapter are as follows: **Barcelona** (✉ Palau Robert, Passeig de Gràcia 107 [at Avda. Diagonal], ☎ 93/238–4000); **Girona** (✉ Rambla de la Llibertat 1, ☎ 972/202679); **Lérida** (✉ Plaça de la Paeria 11, ☎ 973/248120); **Huesca**

(✉ Coso Alto 23, Huesca, ☎ 974/225778); **Aragon** (✉ Torreon de la Zuda, Glorieta de Pío XII, Zaragoza, ☎ 976/393537); **Navarre** (✉ Duque de Ahumada 3, Pamplona, ☎ 948/211287).

Local tourist offices in major towns are as follows: **Ainsa** (✉ Avda. Pirenaica 1, Aínsa, Huesca, ☎ 974/500767); **Benasque** (✉ Plaza Mayor 5, Benasque, Huesca, ☎ 974/551289); **Bielsa** (✉ Plaza del Ayuntamiento, ☎ 974/501000); **Camprodon** (✉ Plaça Espanya 1, Camprodon, Gerona, ☎ 972/740010); **Jaca** (✉ Avda. Rgto. Galicia, Jaca, Huesca, ☎ 974/360098); **Puigcerdà** (✉ Carrer Querol 1, Puigcerdà, Gerona, ☎ 972/880542); **Seu d'Urgell** (✉ Avda. Valira s/n, Seu d'Urgell, Lleida, ☎ 973/351511); and **Vielha** (✉ Avda. Castiero 15, Vielha, Lleida, ☎ 973/640979).

7 Barcelona and Northern Catalonia

Barcelona is one of Europe's most dynamic and artistic cities. From the medieval atmosphere of the Gothic Quarter's narrow alleys to the elegance of the Moderniste Eixample or the action-packed modern Olympic Village, Barcelona is on the move. Picasso, Miró, and Dalí have links to this vibrant city with its ever-stronger Catalan identity. After 40 years of repression through post–civil-war Franco dictatorship, Catalan language and culture have flourished since home rule was granted in 1975. Now this ancient romance language is heard in every street and is, along with Castilian Spanish, Barcelona's co-official language.

By George
Semler

THE CAPITAL OF CATALONIA, 2,000-year-old Barcelona has long rivaled, even surpassed, Madrid in industrial muscle and business acumen. Though Madrid has revitalized its role as capital city, Barcelona has relinquished none of its power. After its comprehensive urban refurbishing prior to the 1992 Summer Olympics, Barcelona is coming into its own as one of Europe's most beautiful and modern cities. Few places can rival the narrow alleys of the Gothic Quarter for medieval atmosphere, or the boulevards in the Moderniste Eixample for elegance and distinction.

Barcelona enjoys a frenetically active cultural life and heritage. Perhaps most notably, it was the home of architect Antoni Gaudí (1852–1926), whose buildings are the most startling statements of Modernisme—a Spanish, and mainly Catalan, offshoot of Art Nouveau. Other leading Moderniste architects include Lluís Domènech i Muntaner and Josep Puig i Cadafalch. The painters Joan Miró (1893–1983), Salvador Dalí (1904–89), and Antoni Tàpies (born 1923) are also strongly identified with Catalonia. Pablo Picasso spent his formative years in Barcelona, and one of the city's treasures is a museum devoted to his works. Until recently the city boasted Spain's oldest and finest opera house, the Liceu (which burned down in 1994 and is being restored), and claims native Catalan musicians such as cellist Pablo (Pau, in Catalan) Casals (1876–1973), and opera singers Montserrat Caballé and Josep (José) Carreras. Barcelona's fashion industry is hard on the heels of those of Paris and Milan, and FC (Futbol Club) Barcelona, more a cultural phenomenon than a sports team, is arguably the world's most glamorous soccer club.

In 133 BC the Roman Empire annexed the city built by the Iberian tribe known as the Laietans and founded a colony they called Colonia Favencia Julia Augusta Paterna Barcino. In the 5th century, Barcelona became the Visigothic capital; the Moors invaded in the 8th century; and in 801, the Franks under Charlemagne captured Barcelona and made it their buffer zone at the edge of the Moors' Iberian empire. By 988, the autonomous Catalonian counties had gained independence from the Franks, and in 1137 they were united through marriage with the House of Aragon. In 1474, the marriage of Ferdinand of Aragon and Isabella of Castile brought Aragon and Catalonia into a united Spain. As the capital of Aragon's Mediterranean empire, Barcelona grew in importance between the 12th and the 14th centuries and began to falter only when maritime emphasis shifted to the Atlantic after 1492. Despite the establishment of Madrid as the seat of Spain's government in 1562, Catalonia continued to enjoy autonomous rights and privileges until 1714, when, in reprisal for having backed the Austrian Habsburg pretender to the Spanish throne, all institutions and expressions of Catalonian nationalism were suppressed by the triumphant Felip V of the French Bourbon dynasty. Not until the 19th century would Barcelona's industrial growth bring about a *Renaixença* (Renaissance) of nationalism and a cultural flowering that recalled the city's former opulence.

The tradition of Catalan independence nonetheless survived intact. Catalonia has revolted against Madrid's central authority on numerous occasions, and in particular during the Spanish civil war, when Barcelona was a Republican stronghold and a hotbed of anti-fascist sentiment. As a result, the Catalan identity and language were suppressed during the Franco dictatorship by such means as book burning, the renaming of streets and towns, and the banning of the Catalan language in schools and in the media. This repression had little lasting effect how-

Avda. Diagonal

Avda. de Pedralbes

Passeig de Manuel Girona

Plaça Prat de la Riba

Ronda del General Mitre

C. de les Escoles

C. de Modolell

Via Augusta

Plaça Pius XII

Plaça de la Reina Maria Cristina

C. de Numància

Avda. de Sarrià

C. d'Entença

C. de Calvet

C. de Muntaner

Via de Carles III

Travessera de les Corts

Pl. de Francesc Macià

Avda. de Madrid

Gran

C. del Brasil

C. de Joan Güell

C. del Vallespir

C. de Berlín

Avda. de Josep Tarradellas

C. de París

C. de Villarroel

Avda.

C. de Sants

C. de París

C. de Corsega

C. de Muntaner

C. d'Aribau

Estació Sants

Pl. Països Catalanes

C. del Rossello

C. de Provença

C. de Castanova

C. d'Antoni de Capmany

Avda. de Roma

C. de Calàbria

C. de Viladomat

C. del Comte d'Urgell

C. de Villarroel

C. de

C. de Mallorca

C. de la Creu Coberta

C. de Valencia

Entença

Rocafort

C. d'Arago

C. de

C. de

C. de   la Diputació

Plaça Universitat

Gran Via de les Corts Catalanes

Plaça d'Espanya

C. de Vilamari

Avda. de Mistral

C. de Sepulveda

Avda. Reina M. Cristina

C. de Floridablanca

Plaça de Sant Jordi

Pl. de les Cascades

Avda. del Paral·lel

C. de Tamarit

Joaquin Costa

C. del

Pg. de les Cascades

C. de Lleida

C. de Manso

C. de Hospital

Palau Nacional

C. de Sant Pau

Jardins de Joan Maragall

Rda. de Sant Pau

C. la Unió

C. Nou de la Rambla

Estadi Olímpic

Avda. de Miramar

C. de Blai

C. de Magalhaes

Les Flores

Carretes

Camí dels Tres Pins

KEY

Metro Stations

Railway Lines

Funicular

Telefèric

Parc de Montjuïc

C. dels Mondials

Pg. de Montjuïc

Plaça Portal de la Pau

Jardins de Miramar

Castell de Montjuïc

Moll de Sant Bertrán

TORRE DE JAUME

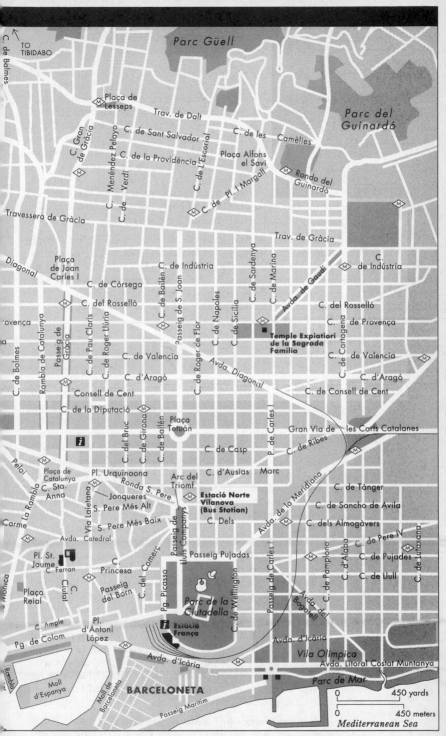

Parc Güell

Parc del Guinardó

C. de Balmes

TO TIBIDABO

Plaça de Lesseps

Trav. de Dalt

C. de Sant Salvador

C. de les   Camèlies

C. Gran de Gràcia

C. Menéndez Pelayo

Verdi

C. de la Providència

C. de L'Escorial

Plaça Alfons el Savi

Ronda del Guinardó

C. de la   Pl. I Margall

Travessera de Gràcia

Trav. de Gràcia

C. de Indústria

Diagonal

Plaça de Joan Carles I

C. de Còrsega

C. de Indústria

C. de Bailén

Passeig de S. Joan

C. de Sardenya

C. de Marina

Avda. de Gaudí

ovença

C. del Rosselló

C. de Pau Claris

C. de Roger Llúria

C. de Nápoles

C. de Sicilia

C. del Rosselló

C. de Provença

C. de Cartagena

a

Rambla de Catalunya

Passeig de Gràcia

C. de Valencia

C. de Roger de Flor

Temple Expiatiori de la Sagrada Família

C. de Valencia

C. de Balmes

C. d'Aragó

Avda. Diagonal

C. d'Aragó

Consell de Cent

C. de la Diputació

C. del Bruc

C. de Girona

C. de Bailén

Plaça Tetuán

C. de Consell de Cent

Pelai

i

Plaça de Catalunya

C. Sta. Anna

Pl. Urquinaona

Ronda S. Pere

C. de Casp

P. de Carles

Gran Via de   les Corts Catalanes

C. de Ribes

Jonqueres

S. Pere Més Alt

S. Pere Més Baix

Arc del Triomf

C. d'Ausias   Marc

Avda. de la Meridiana

C. de Tànger

C. de Sancho de Avila

la Rambla

Carme

Via Laietana

Avda. Catedral

Estació Norte Vilanova (Bus Station)

C. Dels

C. dels Almogàvers

C. de Pere IV

Pl. St. Jaume

C. Ferran

C.

Princesa

Passeig de Lluís Companys

Passeig Pujadas

Passeig de Carles I

Avda. del Bogatell

C. de Pamplona

C. d'Alaba

C. de Pere IV

C. de Pujades

C. de Lutxana

Plaça Reial

C. Ciutat

Passeig del Born

C. del Comerç

Pg. Picasso

C. de Wellington

C. de Llull

Pg. de Colom

C. Ample

Pl. d'Antoni López

Parc de la Ciutadella

Estació França

Avda. d'Icària

Vila Olímpica

Rambla

Moll d'Espanya

Moll de Barceloneta

BARCELONETA

Avda. d'Icària

Avda. Litoral Costat Muntanya

Parc de Mar

Passeig Marítim

450 yards

450 meters

Mediterranean Sea

ever, for the Catalans have jealously guarded their language and culture and generally think of themselves as Catalans first, Spaniards second.

Catalonian home rule was granted after Franco's death, in 1975, and Catalonia's parliament, the ancient Generalitat, was reinstated in 1980. Catalan is now heard on every street and eagerly promoted through free classes funded by the Generalitat. Street names are now in Catalan, and newspapers, radio stations, and a TV channel publish and broadcast in Catalan. The circular Catalan *sardana* is danced regularly all over town. The triumphant culmination of this rebirth was, of course, the staging of the Olympics in 1992—stadiums and pools were renovated, new harborside promenades created, and an entire set of train tracks moved to make way for the Olympic Village. Not content with this onetime project, Barcelona's last two mayors have presided over an urban renewal and the creation of postmodern structures that have made the city an architecture student's paradise.

Today Barcelona is a feast for all of the senses, though perhaps mainly the visual one. The pleasures of the palate, however, are not far behind; music prospers here; the air temperature is almost always about right, and even the fragrance of the Mediterranean occasionally overcomes urban fumes on the beach at Barceloneta or in the port.

Pleasures and Pastimes

Dining

The post-Franco renaissance of Catalan culture brought with it an important renewal of Catalan cuisine. A city where the best policy was once to look for Italian or French food or the odd faux-Castilian roast is now filled with exciting restaurants celebrating local produce from the sea as well as from inland and upland areas. Catalans are great lovers of fish, vegetables, rabbit, duck, lamb, game, and natural ingredients from the Pyrenees or the Mediterranean. The *mar i muntanya* (sea and mountain—that is, surf and turf), a recipe combining seafood with inland or highland products, is a standard specialty on most menus. The influence of nearby France seems to ensure finesse, while Iberian ebullience discourages pretense. The now-fashionable Mediterranean diet featuring "good" (anticholesterol) virgin olive oil, seafood, fibrous vegetables, onions, garlic, and red wine is nowhere better exemplified than in Catalonia. Catalan cuisine is wholesome and served in hearty portions. Spicy sauces are more prevalent here than elsewhere in Spain; you'll find *allioli,* for example—pure garlic and virgin olive oil (nothing else)— beaten to a mayonnaiselike sauce and used to accompany a wide variety of dishes, from rabbit to lamb to potatoes and vegetables. Typical entrées include *habas a la catalana* (a spicy broad-bean stew), *bullabesa* (fish soup-stew similar to the French bouillabaisse), and *espinacas a la catalana* (spinach cooked with oil, garlic, pine nuts, raisins, and bits of bacon). Bread is often doused with olive oil and spread with tomato to make *pa amb tomaquet,* delicious on its own or as an accompaniment to nearly anything. Read Colman Andrews's classic *Catalan Cuisine—Europe's Last Culinary Secret,* which lies on nearly every Catalan gourmet's nightstand, for a more detailed rundown of the products and practices of Catalan chefs.

Catalan wines from the nearby Penedès region, especially the local *méthode champenoise* (sparkling white wine known in Catalonia as *cava*), more than adequately accompany all regional cuisine.

CATEGORY	COST*
$$$$	over 7,000 ptas.
$$$	4,500–7,000 ptas.
$$	2,500–4,500 ptas.
$	under 2,500 ptas.

*per person for a three-course meal, excluding drinks, service, and tax

Lodging

Barcelona's 1992 Olympic Games spawned a massive boom in hotel construction. New hotels shot up, and existing ones were renovated. The most spectacular new hotels are the Hotel Arts and the Hotel Rey Juan Carlos I, which joins (or possibly eclipses) the Princesa Sofía as the Barcelona luxury hotel nearest the airport. Room rates have increased at well above the rate of inflation in recent years, meaning that there are very few real bargains. Don't give up too easily, however, as most receptionists will become flexible about rates if they suspect you might leave based on price. Write or fax ahead asking for a discount; you may be pleasantly surprised.

Generally speaking, hotels in the Gothic Quarter and the Rambla are convenient for sightseeing and have plenty of Old World charm but, with some notable exceptions, are weaker on creature comforts. Those in the Eixample are generally set in late-19th-century to 1950s town houses, often Moderniste in design; all offer a choice of street or court-yard rooms, so be sure to specify when you book. The newest hotels, with the widest range of facilities and the least sense of being in Barcelona (or anywhere in particular), are toward the west, along the Diagonal. In general, reservations are a good idea, if only to make your bid for a good rate, but the Olympic explosion means that you can almost always find lodging with relative ease. Ask about weekend rates, which are often half-price.

CATEGORY	COST*
$$$$	over 20,000 ptas.
$$$	15,000–20,000 ptas.
$$	8,000–15,000 ptas.
$	under 8,000 ptas.

*All prices are for a standard double room, excluding tax.

Modernisme

More than any other city in the world, Barcelona is filled with buildings and other works of the late-19th-century artistic and architectural movement known as Art Nouveau in France, *Jugendstil* in Germany, *sezessionstil* in Austria, *floreale* in Italy, *modernismo* in the rest of Spain, and Modernism in English-speaking countries. This movement was in many ways analogous to the 1960s "greening of America" in that it reflected a disillusionment with the fruits of technology and industry and a return to more natural shapes and aesthetic values. The curved line replaced the straight line; flowers and fruits and wild mushrooms were sculpted into facades. The pragmatic gave way to ornamental excess. Modernisme is everywhere in Barcelona, not only because it tapped into the playfulness of the Catalan artistic impulse (as seen in the works of Gaudí, Picasso, Miró, Dalí, and others) but because it coincided with Barcelona's late-19th-century industrial prosperity and an upsurge of nationalistic sentiment.

Museums

Barcelona's museums are abundant, dynamic, and constantly self-renewing. The Museu Picasso probably is probably the best known, but bear in mind that the city has better permanent collections of art. The best of these is the Romanesque exhibit at the Palau Nacional on

Montjuïc. Other less-discovered gems are the Thyssen-Bornemisza Collection at the Monestir de Pedralbes, above Sarrià, and the Catalan impressionists at the Museu d'Art Modern in the Ciutadella. The Fundació "la Caixa," at Passeig de Sant Joan 108, frequently offers excellent itinerant shows that have ranged from Kandinsky to William Blake. Gaudí's famous Pedrera house, on the Passeig de Gràcia, now has a superb permanent exhibit on the architect's life and work in addition to the frequent shows in Sala Gaudí. The new Centre de Cultura Contemporànea and Museu d'Art Contemporani, in the Raval area west of the Rambla, have shows and events of all kinds. Other museums with excellent displays are the Museu de la Ciencia in upper Barcelona, the Museu d'Història de la Ciutat in the Plaça del Rei, and the Museu d'Història de Catalunya in the Port Vell's Palau de Mar. As of 1997, there's even a Museum of Eroticism.

EXPLORING BARCELONA

Barcelona is made up of two main and contrasting parts. The old city lies between Plaça de Catalunya and the port. Above it is the grid-patterned extension, built after the city's third set of walls were torn down in 1860, known as the Eixample, where most of the Moderniste architecture is concentrated. Farther out are the former outlying towns Gràcia and Sarrià, the Pedralbes zone, and the Collserola hills behind the city. Ask your hotel or the tourist office about the Ruta del Modernisme, a new system of guides that takes you through some 50 Art Nouveau sites(☞ Guided Tours *in* Barcelona A–Z, *below.*)

Numbers in the margin correspond to points of interest on the Barri Gòtic; La Rambla and the Raval; the Moderniste Eixample; Parc Güell, Tibidabo, and Pedralbes; Ciutadella and Barceloneta; and Montjuïc maps.

Great Itineraries

The Rambla, the Gothic Quarter, and all of old Barcelona hold constant surprises, even for longtime residents. Markets such as the Rambla's Boqueria, the Raval's Mercat de Sant Antoni, and the Els Encants flea market are always good browsing grounds, well seeded with cafés, bars, patios, and terraces for mid-itinerary breaks. You'll probably find here that the study of travel objectives is best balanced by the joys of aimless wandering. The air temperature is almost always just right, and occasionally the fragrance of the Mediterranean overcomes urban fumes on the beach at Barceloneta or in the port.

Three days would be sufficient to explore the Rambla and the Gothic Quarter, see the Sagrada Família and the main Moderniste sights, go to one or two of the most important museums, and perhaps take in a concert. Five days would allow a more thorough exploration of the same, as well as more museums and the chance to explore Barceloneta and the Collserola hills. A weeklong stay would give you time to learn the city's authentic rhythms and resources; check the daily papers for gallery openings and concerts; make a side trip to Sitges, Montserrat, or the Costa Brava; and approach a real understanding of what makes this the biggest and busiest city on the Mediterranean.

IF YOU HAVE 3 DAYS

Stroll the Rambla; then cut over to the **Catedral de la Seu** ① and walk around the Mons Taber, the high ground upon which the original Roman settlement was established and enclosed within Barcelona's first set of walls nearly 2,000 years ago. Detour through **Plaça del Rei** ③ before cutting back to **Plaça Sant Jaume** ⑦, where the Catalonian government, the Palau de la Generalitat, stands across the square from the *ajuntament* (city hall). From there it's a 10-minute walk to the **Museu Picasso** ⑤, from which another even shorter stroll leads past the church of **Santa Maria del Mar** ⑥ to Cal Pep, in Plaça de les Olles (for the best tapas in Barcelona), or to Set Portes for lunch or even dinner. Try to catch an evening concert at the **Palau de la Música** ㉛. Day two might be a Gaudí day: spend the morning at the **Temple Expiatori de la Sagrada Família** ㉔, midday at **Parc Güell** ㉖, and late afternoon walking past Casa Vicens, in Gràcia; La Pedrera and Casa Batlló, on Passeig de Gràcia; and the **Palau Güell** ⑪, just off the lower Rambla. On day three, take in the world's best Romanesque art collection at the **Museu Nacional d'Art de Catalunya** ㊸, in the Palau Nacional on Montjuïc, and perhaps wander Montjuïc's other important attractions, such as the **Fundació Miró** ㊷, the **Poble Espanyol** ㊺, and the Olympic facilities, especially Izosaki's superb Palau Sant Jordi and the restored Olympic Stadium. Take the cable car across the port for a late paella in **Barceloneta** ㊳.

IF YOU HAVE 5 DAYS

Walk the Rambla, the Boqueria market, Plaça del Pi, and the Barri Gòtic, including the **Catedral de la Seu** ① on the first day. The next day, take a few hours to see the **Museu Picasso** ⑤ and the church of **Santa Maria del Mar** ⑥. Walk through **Barceloneta** ㊳ and down to the **Olympic port** ㊴, or out onto the *rompeolas* (breakwaters) and back. On the third morning you can explore the Raval, to the west of the Rambla, and visit the new **Museu d'Art Contemporani** (MACB) ⑰ and **Centre de Cultura Contemporània** (CCCB) ⑱, as well as the medieval **Hospital de Sant Pau** ㉕ and Barcelona's oldest church, Sant Pau del Camp. If you have time, have a look at the **Museu Marítim** ⑩, the medieval shipyards, in the Reial Drassanes. In the afternoon you can take a guided tour of the **Palau de la Música** ㉛ and pick up tickets to a concert. The fourth day can be your Gaudí day, with the **Temple Expiatori de la Sagrada Família** ㉔ in the morning and **Parc Güell** ㉖ after lunch. In the late afternoon, walk down through Gràcia and see Gaudí's first house, Casa Vicens; farther down on Passeig de Gràcia you can walk past La Pedrera and Casa Batlló, in the heart of the city's grid-patterned Eixample, and another early Gaudí structure, the **Palau Güell** ⑪, just off the Rambla on Carrer Nou de la Rambla. Day five is a chance to explore Montjuïc: visit the **Museu Nacional d'Art de Catalunya** ㊸, in the Palacio Nacional; the **Fundació Miró** ㊷; the **Poble Espanyol** ㊺; and the Olympic facilities, the Palau Sant Jordi and the Estadio Olímpico. In the afternoon, take the cable car across the port and have an outdoor paella back in **Barceloneta** ㊳.

Barri Gòtic

This walk explores Barcelona's Gothic Quarter, a quiet warren of medieval buildings including the cathedral and the Picasso Museum. Parts of the Barri Gòtic and the Barri Xinès (or Barrio Chino), Barcelona's notorious red-light district, were significantly spruced up in preparation for the Olympic crowds. In the heart of the quarter, you'll come across squares freshly begot by the demolition of whole blocks and the planting of fully grown palms. Bag-snatching is not uncommon in these parts, so it's highly advisable not to carry one.

A Good Walk

A good walk through the Barri Gòtic could begin at **Catedral de la Seu** ① and move through and around the cathedral to the left to the **Museu Frederic Marès** ② (and its little terrace café, surrounded by Roman walls). Next, pass the patio of the Arxi de la Corona d'Aragó (Archives of the House of Aragon); then turn left again and down into **Plaça del Rei** ③.

As you leave Plaça del Rei, the **Museu d'Història de la Ciutat** ④ is on your left. Crossing Via Laetana, pass through the Plaça del Angel and walk down Carrer Princesa; this will take you to Carrer Montcada and a right turn to the **Museu Picasso** ⑤. As you continue down Carrer Montcada you'll pass some of Barcelona's most elegant medieval palaces before emerging into the Passeig del Born. Take a walk down to the Born itself, once one of Barcelona's major produce markets and now scheduled to be converted to a municipal library. Walk back to the church of **Santa Maria del Mar** ⑥, just past the Carrer Montcada end of the Passeig del Born. After spending some time inside, walk around the church's eastern (waterfront) side through the Fossar de les Moreres. A 10-minute walk up Carrer Argenteria and back across Via Laetana to Carrer Ferran will take you to the **Plaça Sant Jaume** ⑦, where the governments of Catalonia and Barcelona face each other in (at the moment) political discord. Try to arrange visits to these buildings, both of which are lavishly endowed with works of art. For a quick tour of Barcelona's *call* (from the Hebrew *qahal*, "meeting"), the medieval Jewish quarter, leave Plaça Sant Jaume on Carrer del Call, turn right on Sant Domènech del Call, and proceed 50 yards to what was once a synagogue on the corner of Carrer Fruita. Now turn left on Carrer Marlet down to the next corner of Arc de Sant Ramón del Call, where a stone plaque in Hebrew marks all that remains of the Jewish community that prospered here until the 1391 pogrom, directed primarily by agrarian revolutionaries. Go left back to Carrer del Call and out to Carrer Ferran via Carrer de la Boqueria and Volta del Remei. Finally, turn right on Carrer Ferran to **Plaça Reial** ⑧, one of Barcelona's few neoclassical squares.

TIMING

This walk covers some 2 km (1 mi) and, depending on stops, should take about three hours (including an hour in the Picasso Museum).

Sights to See

★ ❶ **Catedral de la Seu.** On Saturday afternoon and Sunday morning, Barcelona folk gather in the Plaça de la Seu to dance the *sardana*, a somewhat demure circular dance and a great symbol of Catalan pride. The magnificent Gothic cathedral was built between 1298 and 1450, with the spire and neo-Gothic facade added in 1892. Architects of Catalan Gothic churches strove to make the high altar visible to the entire congregation, hence the unusually wide central nave and slender side columns. Highlights are the beautifully carved choir stalls; Santa Eulàlia's tomb, in the crypt; the battle-scarred crucifix in the Lepanto Chapel; the intimate Santa Llucia chapel, in the front right corner; and the tall cloisters surrounding a tropical garden. ⊠ *Plaça de la Seu,* ☎ *93/315–2213.* ⊙ *Daily 7:45–1:30 and 4–7:45.*

Fossar de les Moreres (Cemetery of the Mulberry Trees). This low, marble monument stands in the open space along the eastern side of Santa Maria del Mar. It honors those defenders of Barcelona who gave their lives in the 1714 siege that ended the War of the Spanish Succession and established Felipe V on the Spanish throne. The inscription (EN EL FOSSAR DE LES MORERES NO S'HI ENTERRA CAP TRAIDOR, or IN THE CEMETERY OF THE MULBERRY TREES NO TRAITOR LIES) refers to the story of the graveyard keeper who refused to bury anyone who fought on the invading side, even when one of them turned out to be his son.

❹ **Museu d'Història de la Ciutat** (City History Museum). Here you can trace the evolution of Barcelona from its first Iberian settlement. Founded by a Carthaginian, Hamilcar Barca, in about 230 BC, the city soon passed into the hands of the Romans during the Punic Wars. It didn't expand much until the Middle Ages, when trading links with

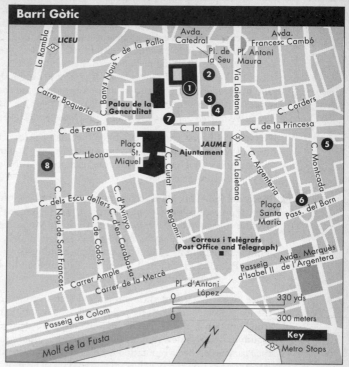

Genoa and Venice began its long and illustrious mercantile tradition. Look for the plans submitted for the 19th-century urban expansion, then called simply the Eixample (from *ensanche*, "widening" in Spanish), to see how different the city might have looked had Antoni Rovira Trias's radial plan not been blocked by cost-conscious bureaucrats in Madrid. Downstairs are some well-lighted Roman excavations. ⊠ *Palau Padellàs, Carrer del Veguer 2,* ☎ *93/315–1111.* 🎟 *600 ptas.* ☉ *Tues.–Sat. 10–2 and 4–8, Sun. 10–2.*

OFF THE
BEATEN PATH

MUSEUM DEL CALÇAT – Hunt down the tiny Shoe Museum, in a hidden corner of the Gothic Quarter between the cathedral and the Bishop's Palace. The collection includes a pair of clown's shoes and a pair worn by Pablo Casals. The tiny square, originally a graveyard, is just as interesting as the museum, with its bullet- and shrapnel-pocked walls and quiet fountain. ⊠ *Plaça de Sant Felip Neri,* ☎ *93/301-4533.* 🎟 *300 ptas.* ☉ *Tues.-Sun. 11-2.*

❷ **Museu Frederic Marès** (Frederic Marès Museum). Here, off the left (north) side of the cathedral, you can browse for hours among the miscellany assembled by sculptor-collector Frederic Marès, which include everything from paintings and polychrome crucifixes to pipes and walking sticks. ⊠ *Plaça Sant Iu 5,* ☎ *93/310–5800.* 🎟 *350 ptas.* ☉ *Tues.–Sun. 10–7:30.*

★ ❺ **Museu Picasso** (Picasso Museum). The Picasso Museum is across Via Laietana, down Carrer de la Princesa—just to the right, on Carrer Montcada, from the Museu Frederic Marès. This narrow street contains some of Barcelona's most elegant medieval palaces, of which the museum occupies two, from the 15th century. Picasso spent many of his formative years in Barcelona, including his Blue and Rose periods (1901–06), and this collection—one of the world's best—is particularly strong on his early work rather than celebrated classics. Still, there is plenty here to warrant a visit, including childhood sketches, pictures from the beautiful Rose and Blue periods, and the famous 1950s Cubist variations on Velázquez's *Las Meninas*. If you're expecting black outlines and tortured lovers, you may be in for a beautiful and educational surprise. ⊠ *Carrer Montcada 15–19.* ☎ *93/319–6310.* ▣ *650 ptas.; ½ price Wed., free 1st Sun. of month.* ☉ *Tues.–Sat. 10–8, Sun. 10–3.*

Passeig del Born. The Passeig, once the site of medieval jousts, is at the end of Carrer Montcada, a long and narrow "square" lined with late-night cocktail bars and miniature restaurants with tiny spiral stairways and intimate corners.

❸ Plaça del Rei. This plaza is generally considered the oldest and most beautiful space in the Gothic Quarter. Upon Columbus's return from his first voyage to the New World, the Catholic Monarchs received him on the stairs fanning out here and in the Saló del Tinell, a magnificent banquet hall built in 1362. Other ancient buildings around the square are the Palau del Lloctinent (Lieutenant's Palace), the 14th-century chapel of Santa Àgata, and the Palau Padellàs.

❽ Plaça Reial. An elegant and symmetrical 19th-century arcaded square, the Plaça Reial is rimmed by yellow houses overlooking the wrought-iron Fountain of the Three Graces and lampposts designed by a young Gaudí in 1879. Sidewalk cafés line the entire square. In recent years the Plaça has earned a reputation for hosting drug pushers and the homeless, who occupy the benches on sunny days. The most colorful time here is Sunday morning, when crowds gather to sell and trade stamps and coins; at night it's a center of downtown nightlife. **Bar Glaciar,** on the uphill corner toward the Rambla, is a booming beer station for young internationals. **Tarantos, Jamboree,** and the **Barcelona Pipa Club** are all hot venues for jazz, flamenco, and rock.

❼ Plaça Sant Jaume. This central square behind the cathedral houses both Catalonia's and Barcelona's governments. The Plaça was built in the 1840s, but the two imposing buildings facing each other across it are much older. The 15th-century **ajuntament** (city hall) to the left has an impressive black-and-burnished-gold mural (1928) by Josep Maria Sert and the famous Saló de Cent, from which the Council of One Hundred ruled Barcelona between 1372 and 1714. You can wander into the courtyard, but to visit the interior you need to make arrangements with the office ahead of time. The **Palau de la Generalitat,** opposite, seat of the autonomous Catalan government, is an elegant 15th-century palace with a lovely courtyard and a second-floor patio with orange trees. The room whose windows you can see at the front is the Saló de Sant Jordi (St. George), named for Catalonia's dragon-slaying patron saint. Normally you can visit the Generalitat only on Día de Sant Jordi (St. George's Day), April 23; check with the *protocolo* (protocol office).

★ ❻ Santa Maria del Mar. Santa Maria del Mar, the most elegant of all Barcelona's churches, is on the Carrer Montcada end of Passeig del Born. Simple and spacious, it's something of an oddity in ornate and complex Moderniste Barcelona. The church was built from 1329 to 1383 in fulfillment of a vow made a century earlier by Jaume I to build a church for the Virgin of the Sailors. Its stark beauty is enhanced by a lovely rose window, soaring columns, and unusually wide vaulting. It's a fashionable place for concerts and weddings; if you happen by on a Saturday afternoon, you're bound to see a couple exchanging vows. ⊠ *Plaça de Santa Maria.* ☉ *Weekdays 9–12:30 and 5–8.*

La Rambla and the Raval

Barcelona's most famous promenade is a constant and colorful flood of humanity past flower stalls, bird vendors, mimes, musicians, newspaper kiosks, and outdoor cafés. Federico García Lorca called this street the only one in the world that he wished would never end; traffic plays second fiddle to the endless *paseo* (stroll) of both locals and visitors alike. The whole avenue is referred to as Las Ramblas (Les Rambles, in Catalan) or La Rambla, but each section has its own name: Rambla Santa Monica is at the southeastern or port end, Rambla de les Flors in the middle, and Rambla dels Estudis at the top leading down from Plaça de Catalunya.

A complete Rambla hike could begin at the Diagonal and continue down Rambla de Catalunya; through the Rambla proper, between Plaça de Catalunya and the Columbus monument; and across the port on the wooden Rambla de Mar boardwalk. El Raval is the area to the west of the Rambla; it was originally a slum stuck outside of Barcelona's second set of walls, which ran down the left side of the Rambla.

A Good Walk

Start on the Rambla opposite Plaça Reial and wander down the Rambla toward the sea, to the **Monument a Colom** ⑨ and the Rambla de Mar. As you move back to the Columbus monument, you may want to investigate the medieval **Drassanes Reiales** shipyards and **Museu Marítim** ⑩ as you start back up the Rambla. Gaudí's **Palau Güell** ⑪, on Carrer Nou de la Rambla, can be the next stop before you pass the **Gran Teatre del Liceu** ⑫ (which will probably still be under reconstruction). At the Miró mosaic at Pla de la Boqueria, cut right to the Plaça del Pi and the church of **Santa Maria del Pi** ⑬. Back on the Rambla, stroll through the **Boqueria** food market ⑭ and the **Palau de la Virreina** ⑮ exhibition center next door; then cut around to the lovely courtyards of the medieval **Antic Hospital de la Santa Creu** ⑯. Next, visit the new **Museu d'Art Contemporani** (MACB) ⑰ and the **Centre de Cultura Contemporànea** (CCCB) ⑱, on Carrer Montalegre, before hooking back into the Rambla. On your return to the Rambla check out the various attractions in the **Port Vell** ⑲, especially the aquarium. Finish your walk along Carrer Tallers, ending up in **Plaça de Catalunya** ⑳.

TIMING

This walk covers about 2 km (1 mi). Allow three hours, including stops and visits.

Sights to See

⑯ **Antic Hospital de la Santa Creu.** Surrounded by a cluster of other 15th-century buildings, this medieval hospital is now home to a number of libraries and cultural and educational institutions. You can approach it from the back door of the Boqueria, or from either Carrer del Carme or Carrer Hospital. Particularly impressive and lovely is the courtyard of the Casa de Convalescència, with its Renaissance columns and scenes of the life of St. Paul portrayed in *azulejos* (ceramic tiles). ⊠ *Carrer Hospital 54 and Carrer del Carme 45.*

Antigua Casa Figueres. This Moderniste grocery and pastry store on the corner of Petxina has a splendid mosaic facade and exquisite Art Nouveau fittings.

Barri Xinès. As you walk south from Plaça Reial toward the sea, Barcelona's notorious red-light district, the Barri Xinès (traditionally called the Barrio Chino in Castilian Spanish) is on your right. The Chinese never had much of a presence here; the name is a generic reference to foreigners of all kinds. The area is ill-famed for prostitutes, drug

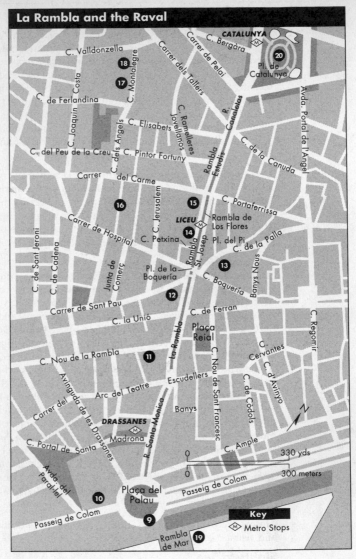

La Rambla and the Raval

pushers, and street thieves, but it's not as dangerous as it looks; in fact, the reinforced police presence here may even make it safer than other parts of the Gothic Quarter.

14 Boqueria. Barcelona's most spectacular food market, also known as the Mercat de Sant Josep, is an explosion of life and color complete with delicious coffee spots and **Pinotxo** (stand number 66–68), a little bar-bistro that has won acclaim as a gourmet sanctuary. Don't miss mushroom supplier and expert Petràs and his mad display of wild 'shrooms, herbs, nuts, and berries ("Fruits del Bosc"—Fruits of the Forest), at stand number 867–870. ⊠ *Rambla 91.*

18 Centre de Cultura Contemporànea de Barcelona (CCCB). This museum, lecture hall, concert hall, and exhibition space is worth checking out no matter what's on the schedule. Housed in the restored and renovated Casa de la Caritat, a former medieval convent and hospital, the CCCB now features a reflecting wall, in which you can see over the rooftops to Montjuïc and beyond. ⊠ *Montalegre 5,* ☎ *93/412–0781.* ⊡ *350 ptas.–650 ptas.* ⊙ *Tues.–Fri. 11–2 and 4–8, Wed. and Sat. 11–8, Sun. 10–3.*

⑫ **Gran Teatre del Liceu.** Barcelona's once and future opera house is one of Europe's oldest and most beautiful. Long one of the city's most cherished cultural landmarks, the Liceu was gutted in early 1994 by a fire whose origins have aroused much speculation. Soprano Montserrat Caballé stood on the Rambla in tears as the beloved venue was consumed. The restoration is scheduled to be completed by early 1999; check for tours of undamaged rooms. ⊠ *Carrer de Sant Pau 13 (at La Rambla).*

⑨ **Monument a Colom** (Columbus Monument). At the foot of the Rambla, take an elevator to the top of the Monument a Colom for a bird's-eye view over the city. (The entrance is on the harbor side.) ⊡ *375 ptas.* ⊙ *June 24–Sept. 24, daily 9–9; Sept. 25–June 23, Tues.–Sat. 10–2 and 4–8, Sun. 10–7.*

⑰ **Museu d'Art Contemporani de Barcelona** (Barcelona Museum of Contemporary Art). This 1992 building was designed by American architect Richard Meier and houses both a permanent collection and traveling exhibits. ⊠ *Plaça dels Àngels,* ☎ *93/412–0810.* ⊡ *Tues. and Thurs.–Sun. 650 ptas.; ½ price Wed.* ⊙ *Tues.–Sat. 10–2 and 4–8, Sun. 10–2.*

⑩ **Museu Marítim** (Maritime Museum). The superb Museu Marítim is housed in the 13th-century **Drassanes Reials** (Royal Shipyards), to the right at the foot of the Rambla. It's full of ships, including a spectacular, life-size reconstructed galley; figureheads; nautical gear; and several early navigational charts. ⊠ *Plaça Portal de la Pau 1.* ⊡ *850 ptas.; ½ price Wed., free 1st Sun. of month.* ⊙ *Tues.–Sat. 10–2 and 4–7, Sun. 10–2.*

⑮ **Palau de la Virreina.** The neoclassical Virreina Palace, built by a viceroy to Peru in 1778, is now a major exhibition center for paintings, photography, and historical items; find out what's on while you're here. The bookstore and municipal tourist office within are also useful stops. ⊠ *Rambla de les Flors 99,* ☎ *93/301–7775.* ⊙ *Tues.–Sat. 10–2 and 4:30–9, Sun. 10–2, Mon. 4:30–9.*

★ ⑪ **Palau Güell.** Antoni Gaudí built this mansion in 1886–89 for his patron, a textile baron named Count Eusebi de Güell, and soon found himself in the international limelight. The prominent Catalan emblem between the parabolic entrance gates attests to the nationalist leanings that Gaudí shared with Güell. The facade is a dramatic foil for the treasure house inside, where spear-shape Art Nouveau columns frame the windows and prop up a series of minutely detailed wood ceilings. Some of Gaudí's early decorative chimneys garnish the roof. ⊠ *Carrer/Nou de la Rambla 9.* ⊡ *500 ptas.; ½ price Wed., free 1st Sun. of month.* ⊙ *Tues.–Sat. 10–2 and 4–7, Sun. 10–2.*

⑳ **Plaça de Catalunya.** The Plaça de Catalunya is Barcelona's banking and transport center. It's at the head of the Rambla, marking the frontier between the new urbanization and the old city, between Plaça de Catalunya and the port.

⑲ **Port.** In the port beyond the Columbus monument—behind the ornate Duana, or former customs building, now headquarters for the Barcelona Port authority—is the **Rambla de Mar,** a sliding boardwalk (with drawbridge) that's taken up at night to allow boats in and out of the inner harbor. The Rambla de Mar extends out to the **Moll d'Espanya,** with its Maremagnum shopping center, IMAX theater, and new aquarium, a loop that can easily take a few hours to explore. Here you can board a Golondrina boat for a tour of the port or, from the Moll de Barcelona on the right, take a cable car to Montjüic or Barceloneta. Trasmediterranea passenger ferries leave for Italy and the Balearic Islands from the Moll de Barcelona. At the end of the quay is Barcelona's World Trade Center.

⑬ **Santa Maria del Pi** (St. Mary of the Pine). The adjoining **Plaça del Pi** and **Plaça de Sant Josep Oriol** are at once two of the Gothic Quarter's most bustling and most tranquil squares. The church of Santa Maria del Pi, like Santa Maria del Mar, is a fine example of Catalan Gothic architecture. Its gigantic rose window, which overlooks the diminutive square, is Barcelona's best.

The Moderniste Eixample

Above Plaça de Catalunya is the elegant checkerboard known as the Eixample. With the dismantling of the city walls in 1860, Barcelona embarked upon a vast expansion scheme fueled both by the return of rich colonials from America and by an influx of provincial aristocrats who had sold their estates after the debilitating second Carlist War (1847–49) (☞ Chronology *in* Chapter 16). The street grid was the work of urban planner Ildefons Cerdà; much of the building here was done at the height of Modernisme. The principal thoroughfares of the Eixample are Rambla de Catalunya and Passeig de Gràcia, where some of the city's most elegant shops and cafés are found.

A Good Walk

Starting in the **Plaça de Catalunya** ⑳, walk up Passeig de Gràcia until you reach the corner of Consell de Cent. Take a deep breath: you are about to enter the Bermuda Triangle of Moderniste architecture, the much-heralded **Manzana de la Discordia** ㉑. This is the "city block" or "apple" of discord (the pun only works in Spanish), where the three great figures of Barcelona's late-19th-century Moderniste (Art Nouveau) movement—Gaudí, Domènech i Muntaner, and Puig i Cadafalch—went hand to hand with three buildings and three very different styles. The Tàpies Foundation, with its rooftop *Chair and Cloud* sculpture by Antoni Tàpies himself, is just west, on Carrer Aragó. Gaudí's Casa Milà, known as La Pedrera, is three blocks farther up Passeig de Gràcia; after seeing it, hike or taxi to Gaudí's emblematic **Temple Expiatori de la Sagrada Família** ㉔. Finally, stroll over to Domènech i Muntaner's **Hospital de Sant Pau** ㉕.

TIMING
Depending on how many taxis you take, this is at least a three-hour walk. Add another two hours for a thorough exploration of the Sagrada Família.

Sights to See

★ ㉓ **Casa Milà.** Gaudí's Casa Milà, nicknamed La Pedrera (The Stone Quarry), has a remarkable, curving-stone facade that undulates around the corner of the block. When the building was unveiled, in 1905, local residents were not enthusiastic about the appearance of these cavelike balconies on their most fashionable street. Gaudí's rooftop chimney park is as spectacular as anything in Barcelona, especially in late afternoon, when the sunlight slants over the city into the Mediterranean. The Espai Gaudí (Gaudí Space), in the attic, has an excellent critical display of Gaudí's works, theories, and techniques. ✉ *Passeig de Gràcia 92,* ☎ *93/484–5995.* 💰 *500 ptas.* ☺ *Guided visits Tues.–Sat. 10, 11, noon, 1, and 4.*

㉒ **Casa Montaner i Simó–Fundació Tàpies.** This former publishing house has been beautifully converted to hold the work of preeminent con-

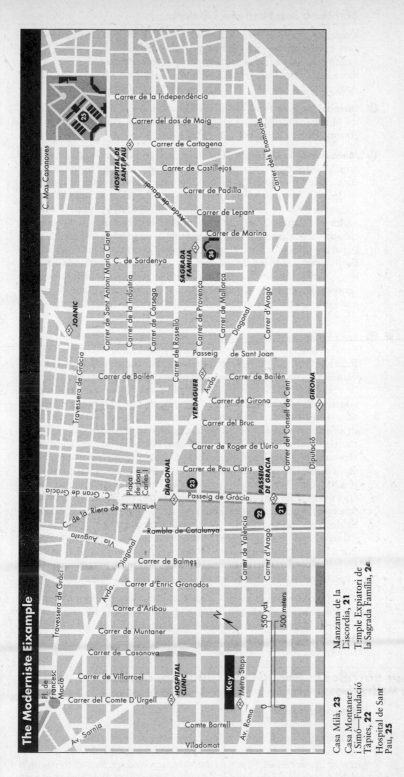

The Moderniste Eixample

Carrer de la Independència

Carrer del dos de Maig

Carrer de Cartagena

Carrer de Castillejos

Carrer de Padilla

Carrer de Lepant

Carrer de Marina

C. Mas Casanoves

HOSPITAL DE SANT PAU

Avda. de Gaudí

SAGRADA FAMILIA

C. de Sardenya

JOANIC

Carrer de Sant Antoni Maria Claret

Carrer de la Indústria

Carrer de Còrsega

Carrer del Rosselló

Carrer de Provença

Carrer de Mallorca

Diagonal

Carrer d'Aragó

Carrer dels Enamorats

Travessera de Gràcia

Passeig de Sant Joan

Carrer de Bailèn

Avda.

Carrer de Bailèn

VERDAGUER

Carrer de Girona

GIRONA

Carrer del Bruc

Carrer de Roger de Llúria

Carrer del Consell de Cent

DIAGONAL

Carrer de Pau Claris

PASSEIG DE GRACIA

Diputació

C. Gran de Gràcia

Plaça de Joan Carles I

Passeig de Gràcia

C. de la Riera de St. Miquel

Rambla de Catalunya

Carrer de València

Carrer d'Aragó

Via Augusta

Carrer de Balmes

Diagonal

Carrer d'Enric Granados

Travessera de Gràcia

Avda.

Carrer d'Aribau

Carrer de Muntaner

Carrer de Casanova

N

Carrer de Villarroel

HOSPITAL CLINIC

Carrer del Comte D'Urgell

Pl. de Francesc Macià

Av. Sarriá

Comte Borrell

Av. Roma

Viladomat

550 yds

500 meters

Key

◇ Metro Stops

0

0

Casa Milà, **23**

Casa Montaner
i Simó—Fundació
Tàpies, **22**

Hospital de Sant
Pau, **25**

Manzana de la
L'iscordia, **21**

Temple Expiatori de
la Sagrada Família, **24**

temporary Catalan painter Antoni Tàpies, as well as frequent temporary exhibits. On top of the building is a tangle of metal entitled *Núvol i cadira* (*Cloud and Chair*). The airy, split-level Fundació Tàpies also has a bookstore that's strong on both Tàpies and Asian art. ⊠ *Carrer Aragó 255,* ☎ *93/487–0315.* ⊠ *600 ptas.* ☉ *Tues.–Sun. 11–8.*

㉕ **Hospital de Sant Pau.** The brick Hospital de Sant Pau is notable for its Mudéjar motifs and wards set among the gardens. ⊠ *Carrer Sant Antoni Maria Claret 167,* ☎ *93/291–9000.*

㉑ **Manzana de la Discòrdia.** The name is a pun on the word *mançana,* which means both "city block" and "apple," alluding to the architectural counterpoint on this block and to the classical myth of the Apple of Discord. The houses here are spectacular. The ornate Casa Lleó Morera (Number 35) was extensively rebuilt (1902–06) by Palau de la Música architect Domènech i Muntaner, and the Eusebi Arnau sculptures on the main floor are excellent. The pseudo-Gothic, pseudo-Flemish Casa Amatller (No. 41) is by Puig i Cadafalch. Next door is Gaudí's Casa Batlló, with a mottled facade that resembles nearly anything you want it to. Nationalist symbolism is at work here: the scaly roof line represents the dragon of evil impaled on St. George's cross, and the skulls and bones on the balconies are the dragon's victims. ⊠ *Passeig de Gràia 35, 41, and 43 (between Consell de Cent and Aragó).*

★ ㉔ **Temple Expiatori de la Sagrada Família** (Expiatory Temple of the Holy Family). Barcelona's most emblematic landmark, Antoni Gaudí's Sagrada Família is still under construction. Unfinished at his death, at age 74—Gaudí was run over by a tram and, unrecognized for several days, died in a pauper's ward in 1926—this striking and surreal creation causes consternation, wonder, howls of protest, shrieks of derision, and cries of rapture. Whatever your feelings, you can't deny that it occupies space in an exceptional and possibly unique manner. Gaudí envisaged three facades: Faith, Hope, and Charity, each with four towers collectively representing the 12 apostles. These, in turn, would be dwarfed by a giant central dome some 500 ft high, still unfinished (in fact, unbegun) today. Construction began again in 1940 but faltered due to confusion over Gaudí's plans; current controversy centers on sculptor Josep Maria Subirach's angular figures on the western facade, condemned by the city's intellectual elite as kitsch and the antithesis of Gaudí's lyrical style, and by religious extremists for depicting Christ in the nude. For 250 pesetas, an elevator can take you to the top of the east towers for a spectacular view, but the stairway, though narrow, steep, and often crowded, is a better way to get a feel for the building.

The crypt has a museum of Gaudí's scale models; photographs showing the progress of construction; and photographs of Gaudí's multitudinous funeral. The architect is buried here. ☎ *93/455–0247.* ⊠ *900 ptas.* ☉ *Nov.–Mar., daily 9–6; Apr.–June and Sept.–Oct., daily 9–7; July–Aug., daily 8 AM–9 PM.*

Upper Barcelona: Parc Güell, Tibidabo, Sarrià, and Pedralbes

A Good Walk

These rambles are spread across Barcelona's upper reaches. It's advisable to hop a cab to Güell Park and then to Güell Park and Sarrià; connecting the two on foot is a one- to two-hour hike from the back entrance of **Parc Güell** ㉖, across the Vallcarca viaduct, and up to Avenida del Tibidabo at Plaça John F. Kennedy. From there, the Passeig de Sant Gervasi leads over to Plaça de la Bonanova, where it becomes Passeig de la Bonanova to Plaça Sarrià. After you wander **Sarrià** ㉘, it's just a 20-minute walk to the **Monestir de Pedralbes** ㉙.

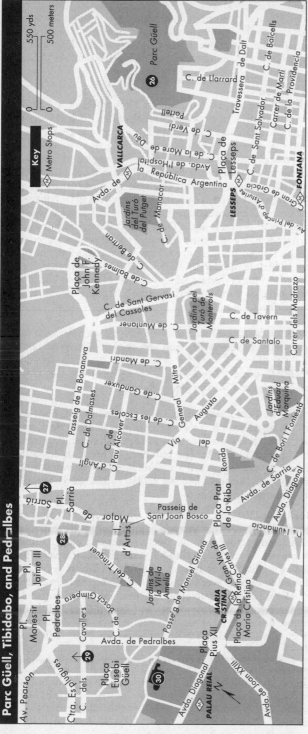

Parc Güell, Tibidabo, and Pedralbes

Key

◇ Metro Stops

0 ——— 550 yds

0 ——— 500 meters

Av. Pearson

Ctra. Esplugues

C. dels

Pl. Monestir

Pl. Jaime III

Pl. Pedralbes

Cavalles

C. de Bosch i Gimpera

Plaça Eusebi Güell

Avda. de Pedralbes

Plaça Pius XII

Avda. Diagonal

PALAU REIAL

Avda. de Joan XXIII

Passeig de Manuel Girona

Jardins de la Vil·la Amèlia

C. del Tinguel

C. d'Anglí

Passeig de la Bonanova

Passeig de Sant Joan Bosco

C. de Dalmases

C. de Pau Alcover

C. de les Escoles

C. de Mandri

C. de Ganduxer

C. de Muntaner

Via Augusta

Via General Mitre

Plaça de John F. Kennedy

C. de Balmes

C. de Berlion

C. de Sant Gervasi del Cassoles

Jardins del Turó de Monterols

C. de Tavern

C. de Santalo

Carrer dels Madrazo

Jardins d'Eduard Morquina

C. de Borí I Fontestà

Avda. de Sarrià

Avda. Diagonal

L'Illumància

Ronda del

Plaça Prat de la Riba

Gran Via de Carles III

Passeig de la Reina Maria-Cristina

Plaça de la Reina Maria-Cristina

MARIA CRISTINA ◇

Pl. Sarrià

Pl. Major de Sarrià

C. d'Artès

C. de Manacor

Jardins del Turó del Putget

Avda. de l'Hospital la República Argentina

Avda. de la Mare de Déu

C. de la Mare de Déu

C. de Verdí

Plaça de Lesseps

LESSEPS ◇

Av. del Príncep d'Astúries

Gran de Gràcia

FONTANA ◇

VALLCARCA ◇

Parc Güell

C. de Llarrard

Travessera de Dalt

C. de Sant Salvador

Carrer de Martí

C. de Balcells

C. de la Providència

C. de Portell

② 27 Sarrià ←

② 28 Jaime III

② 29 ←

③ 30

② 26

Monestir de
Pedralbes and
Thyssen–Bornemisza
Collection, **29**
Palau Reial de
Pedralbes, **30**
Parc Güell, **26**
Sarrià, **28**
Tibidabo, **27**

TIMING

Allowing time for exploring Güell Park, Sarrià, and the Pedralbes Monastery and Thyssen-Bornemisza Collection, this is a five-hour outing that will necessarily end when the monastery closes at 2. Add another two hours if you want to go up to Tibidabo and the Collserola Tower.

Sights to See

㉙ Monestir de Pedralbes. Even without its Thyssen-Bornemisza Collection of Italian masters, this monastery is one of Barcelona's hidden treasures. Founded by Reina Elisenda for Clarist nuns in 1326, the convent has an unusual, three-story Gothic cloister, the finest in Barcelona, and its chapel has a beautiful stained-glass rose window and famous murals painted in 1346 by Ferrer Bassa, a Catalan much influenced by the Italian Renaissance. You can also visit the medieval living quarters. The monastery alone is one of Barcelona's delights, but the new **Thyssen-Bornemisza Collection,** installed in 1989 in what was once the dormitory of the nuns of the Order of St. Clare, sends it over the top. Surrounded by 14th-century windows and pointed arches, these canvases by Tiepolo, Tintoretto, Rubens, and Velázquez should not be missed. ⊠ *Baixada Monestir 9,* ☎ *93/203–9282.* 🎟 *Monastery 350 ptas., Wed. 175 ptas., free 1st Sun. of month; monastery and cloister 350 ptas.; Thyssen-Bornemisza Collection 350 ptas.; combined ticket 650 ptas.* ⊙ *Tues.–Sun. 10–2.*

OFF THE BEATEN PATH   **MUSEUM DE LA CIÈNCIA –** Young scientific minds work overtime in the Science Museum, just below Tibidabo—many of its displays and activities are designed for children ages seven and up. ⊠ *Teodor Roviralta 55,* ☎ *93/212-6050.* 🎟 *550 ptas.* ⊙ *Tues.–Sun. 10-8. Metro: Avinguda de Tibidabo and Tramvía Blau halfway.*

㉚ Palau Reial de Pedralbes (Royal Palace of Pedralbes). Built in the 1920s for King Alfonso XII, this palace is now home to the **Ceramics Museum,** which takes in a wide sweep of Spanish ceramic art from the 14th to the 18th centuries. The influence of Moorish design techniques carefully documented. It's a 20-minute walk downhill from the monastery. ⊠ *Av. Diagonal 686,* ☎ *93/280–5024.* 🎟 *550 ptas.; free 1st Sun. of month.* ⊙ *Daily 10–3.*

㉖ Parc Güell. Güell Park is one of Gaudí's, and Barcelona's, most excellent resources. Whereas the Sagrada Família can be tiring in its massive energy and complexity, Parc Güell is light and playful, uplifting and restorative. Named after Gaudí's main patron, it was originally intended as a hillside garden suburb on the English model, but only two of the houses were ever built. It's an Art Nouveau extravaganza, with a mosaic pagoda, undulating benches, and large, multicolored lizards guarding a Moderniste grotto. ⊠ *Carrer d'Olot 3 (Take metro to Lesseps; then walk 10 minutes uphill or catch Bus 24 to park entrance).* ⊙ *Oct.–Mar., daily 10–6; Apr.–June, daily 10–7; July–Sept., daily 10–9.*

The **Gaudí Museum,** within Güell Park, occupies an Alice-in-Wonderland house in which Gaudí lived from 1906 to 1926. Exhibits include some of his eccentric furniture, decoration, and drawings. ⊠ *Parc Güell (up hill to right of main entrance),* ☎ *93/284–6446.* 🎟 *450 ptas.* ⊙ *Apr.– Oct., daily 10–2 and 4–7; Nov.–Mar., daily 10–2 and 4–6:30.*

OFF THE BEATEN PATH   **"EL BARÇA" –** If you're in Barcelona between September and June, go see FC Barcelona play, preferably against Real Madrid (if you can get in). Games are generally played Saturday night or Sunday afternoon at

5, but there may be cup or international games during the week as well. Ask your hotel concierge how to get tickets, or call the club in advance. The massive Camp Nou stadium seats 130,000 and fills almost to capacity. A museum has an impressive array of trophies and a five-screen video showing memorable goals in the history of one of Europe's most colorful soccer clubs. ⊠ *Arístides Maillol,* ☎ *93/330–9411.* ☒ *Museum 500 ptas.* ◔ *Oct.–Mar., Tues.–Fri. 10–1 and 4–6, weekends 10–1 and 3–6; Apr.–Sept., Mon.–Sat. 10–1 and 3–6.*

㉘ Sarrià. This 1,000-year-old village was once a cluster of farms and country houses overlooking Barcelona from the hills; it's now a quiet enclave surrounded by the roaring metropolis. The main square, Plaça Sarrià, hosts an antiques and crafts market on Tuesday morning, *sardana* dances on Sunday morning, and Christmas fairs in season. The Romanesque church tower, lighted a bright ocher at night, looms overhead. Wander through the brick-and-steel **produce market,** behind and to the right of the church, and the tiny, flower-choked **Plaça Sant Gaietà,** behind the market. Cut through the Placeta del Roser, to the left of the church, to reach the elegant **town hall** in the Plaça de la Vila, noting the buxom bronze sculpture of Pomona, goddess of fruit, by famed Sarrià sculptor Josep Clarà (1878–1958). After peeking in to see the massive ceiling beams (and very reasonable set lunch menu) in the Vell Sarrià restaurant, at the corner of Major de Sarrià, go back and left of the town hall into tiny Carrer dels Paletes and back out to Major de Sarrià. Continue downhill through this (intermittently pedestrian-only) street to the bougainvillea- and honeysuckle-lined **Carrer Canet,** with its diminutive, cottagelike artisans' quarters. Turn right on Carrer Cornet i Mas and walk two blocks down to Carrer Jaime Piquet. A quick probe to the left will take you to No. 30, Barcelona's smallest and most perfect **Moderniste house,** with faux-medieval upper windows, wrought-iron grillwork, floral and fruited ornamentation, and organically curved and carved wooden doors. The next stop down Cornet i Mas is Sarrià's prettiest square, Plaça Sant Vicens, a leafy space ringed by old Sarrià houses and punctuated by a statue of the village patron saint. The café Can Pau is the local hangout, once a haven for authors such as Gabriel García Marquez and Mario Vargas Llosa, who lived in Sarrià in the '70s, on the cusp of their fame. It's a good place for coffee and a slice of tortilla. To get to the Monastir de Pedralbes from Plaça Sant Vicens, walk back up Mayor de Sarrià and through the market to the corner of Sagrat Cor and Ramon Miquel Planas. Turn left and walk straight west for 15 minutes.

Other Sarrià landmarks include the two **Foix** pastry stores, one on Plaça Sarrià 9–10 and the other on Major de Sarrià 57, above Bar Tomás. Both have excellent pastries, artisanal breads, produce, and cold *cava* and stay open until 9 PM on Sundays. The late J. V. Foix, son of the store's founders, was one of the great Catalan poets of the 20th century, a key player in keeping the Catalan language alive during the 40-year Franco regime. ⊠ *Plaça Sarrià (take Bus 22 from the bottom of Avinguda de Tibidabo, or the FFCC train to Reina Elisenda).*

NEED A BREAK? **Bar Tomás,** just out on Major de Sarrià on the corner of Jaume Piquet, is a Barcelona institution, home of the finest potatoes in town. Order the famous *doble mixta* of potatoes with *allioli* and hot sauce. Draft beer (ask for a *caña*) is the de rigueur beverage.

㉗ Tibidabo. Along with Montjuïc, Tibidabo is one of Barcelona's two major promontories. The views from this hill are legendary, really the most panoramic in Catalonia when the wind blows the smog out to sea. The shapes that distinguish Tibidabo from below turn out to be an unprepossessing, commercialized church; a vast radio mast; and the new, 850-ft communications tower, the Torre de Collserola. The exploitation is completed by a noisy amusement park. All in all, there's not much worth seeing here except the vista—particularly from the tower. Clear days are few and far between in fin-de-millennium Barcelona, but if you hit one, this excursion is worth considering. The restaurant **La Venta,** at the base of the funicular, is excellent and a fine place to sit in the sun in cool weather (the establishment traditionally provides straw sun hats). The bar **Mirablau** is also a popular hangout for evening drinks overlooking the lights of Barcelona. *Take the Tibidibo branch off the Sarrià subway; Buses 24 and 22 to Plaza Kennedy; or a taxi. At Avinguda Tibidabo, catch the Tramvía Blau, which connects with the funicular (☞ Getting Around, below) to the summit.*

Torre de Collserola. The Collserola Tower, which dwarfs Mt. Tibidabo, is a creation of Norman Foster, erected for the 1992 Olympics amid controversy over defacement of the traditional mountain skyline. The tower has a splendid panorama of the city when conditions allow. Take the funicular up to Tibidabo; from Plaza Tibidabo there is free transport to the tower. ⊠ *Av. de Vallvidrera,* ☎ *93/406–9354.* ☎ *500 ptas.* ☼ *Wed.–Sun. and holidays 11–2:30, 3:30–8.*

Sant Pere, La Ribera, La Ciutadella and Barceloneta

Barcelona's old textile neighborhood, around the church of Sant Pere, includes the flagship of the city's Moderniste architecture, the extraordinary Palau de la Música. The Barrio de la Ribera (waterfront), the Parc de la Ciutadella, and Barceloneta complete this walk along the periphery of what were once Barcelona's 13th-century walls.

A Good Walk

This neighborhood, or series of neighborhoods, lies generally to the left (north and east) of the Gothic Quarter. The area runs from the medieval Sant Pere textile district to the former waterfront, later silted and filled in to create La Barceloneta. Beginning in **Plaça de Catalunya** ⑳, it's no more than a 10-minute walk to the **Palau de la Música** ㉛, taking your first left off the Rambla. After inspecting the Palau (guided tours can be arranged on weekdays), continue along Carrer Sant Pere Més Alt to the Plaça Sant Pere on your way past the Sant Pere de les Puelles church and out to the **Arc del Triomf** ㉜, on Passeig de Sant Joan. From there, walk through the Parc de la Ciutadella and the Estació de França to the edge of the port, through **Barceloneta** ㊳, and along the beach to the **Port Olímpic** ㊴.

TIMING

Depending on the number of stops, this walk could take half a day. Count on at least three hours of actual walking time.

Sights to See

㉜ **Arc del Triomf.** This imposing, exposed-redbrick arch was built by Josep Vilaseca as the grand entrance for the 1888 Universal Exhibition.

㊳ **Barceloneta.** Once Barcelona's pungent fishing port and waterfront district, Barceloneta retains its colorful ambience. It's a pretty walk through narrow streets with lines of laundry snapping in the breeze overhead. Stop in Plaça de la Barceloneta and have a close look at the Baroque church of Sant Miquel del Port, with its somewhat outsized new sculpture of the saint in the alcove on the facade. Try the tapas bar on the sea side of the square.

Barcelona's beach, a little dusty and often crowded in summer, has improved much in recent years and can actually be used for swimming,

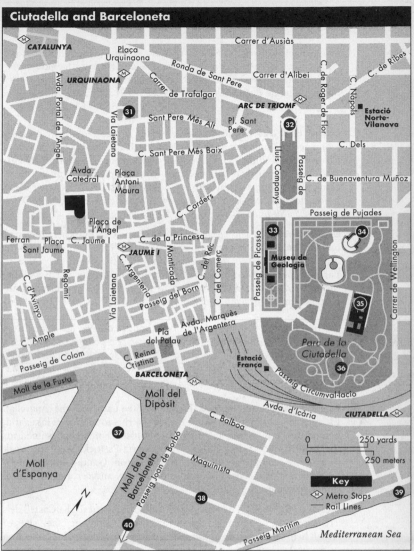

Ciutadella and Barceloneta

CATALUNYA
Plaça Urquinaona
Carrer d'Ausiàs
Ronda de Sant Pere
Carrer d'Alibei
C. de Ribes
URQUINAONA
Carrer de Trafalgar
C. de Roger de Flor
C. Nápols
Estació Norte-Vilanova
Avda. Portal de l'Angel
Via Laietana
Palau de la Música (31)
Sant Pere Més Alt
ARC DE TRIOMF
Pl. Sant Pere
Arc del Triomf (32)
C. Dels
Sant Pere Més Baix
C. Sant Pere Més Baix
Lluís Companys
Passeig de
C. de Buenaventura Muñoz
Avda. Catedral
Plaça Antoni Maura
C. Carders
Passeig de Pujades
Castell dels Tres Dragons (33)
Font de la Senyoreta Paraigua (34)
Plaça de l'Angel
C. de la Princesa
Museu de Geologia
Ferran
Plaça Sant Jaume
C. Jaume I
JAUME I
C. de la Princesa
Monticada
C. del Rec
C. de Comerç
Passeig de Picasso
Palau de la Ciutadella (35)
Regomir
C. d'Avinyo
C. Argenteria
Via Laietana
Passeig del Born
Paro de la Ciutadella
Zoo (36)
C. Ample
Pla del Palau
Avda. Marquès de l'Argentera
Passeig de Colom
C. Reina Cristina
BARCELONETA
Estació França
Passeig Circumval·lacio
Port Vell/Palau de Mar (37)
Moll de la Fusta
Moll del Dipòsit
C. Balboa
Avda. d'Icària
CIUTADELLA
Moll d'Espanya
Moll de la Barceloneta
Passeig Joan de Borbó
Maquinista
Barceloneta (38)
0   250 yards
0   250 meters

Key
Ⓜ Metro Stops
— Rail Lines
Port Olímpic (39)
Teleféric (40)
Passeig Marítim
Mediterranean Sea

provided the winds and currents haven't created a backup of sewage. Take a close look at the water before you dive in.

NEED A
BREAK?

Can Manuel "la Puda," a friendly spot along Passeig Joan de Borbó, is a good choice for tasty and inexpensive paella in the sun. The nickname refers to the fragrance that used to emanate from this fishy district. ⊠ *Passeig Joan de Borbó 60–61,* ☎ *93/221–5013. AE, DC, MC, V. Closed Mon.*

③③ **Castell dels Tres Dragons** (Castle of the Three Dragons). Built by Domènech i Muntaner as the café for the 1888 Universal Exposition, this arresting building greets you as you enter the Ciutadella from Passeig Lluí Companys. It later became a workshop where Moderniste architects met to experiment with traditional crafts and to exchange ideas. It now holds the Museum of Zoology. ⊠ *Passeig Picasso 5,* ☎ *93/319–6912.* 📷 *350 ptas.* ☉ *Tues.–Sun. 10–2.*

Estació de França. The elegantly restored Estació de França, Barcelona's main railroad station until about 1980 and still the stopping point for certain trains to and from France (notably the overnight *Talgo* to Paris), is outside the west gate of the Ciutadella. It's worth walking through to sense the Old World romance of Europe's traditional railroad system. ⊠ *Marquè de l'Argentera s/n,* ☎ *93/319–6416.*

NEED A
BREAK?

You're just a step from Barcelona's best tapas at **Cal Pep** (⊠ Plaça de les Olles 8). Try the *gambitas* (baby shrimp) or *pulpo gallego* (octopus), and don't forget to order *pan de coca* (crunchy toast with oil and fresh tomato paste). Try not to give up if you have to wait for a while; they'll feed you wine in the meantime. It's fun and well worth it.

③④ **Font de la Senyoreta Paraigua** (Fountain of the Lady with the Umbrella). Escape the sights and sounds of the city by this fountain, its lake, and, behind it, the monumental *Cascada,* by Josep Fontserè, designed for the 1888 Universal Exhibition. The waterfall's rocks were the work of a young architecture student named Antoni Gaudí—his first public works, appropriately natural and organic, and certainly a hint of things to come.

Museu de Geologia. The Museum of Geology is next to the Castell dels Tres Dragons, not far from the beautiful Umbracle, the black slats of which help create jungle lighting for the museum's valuable collection of tropical plants. Barcelona's first public museum, it displays rocks, minerals, and fossils along with special exhibits on Catalonia and the rest of Spain. ⊠ *Parc de la Ciutadella,* ☎ *93/319–6895.* 📷 *400 ptas.; free 1st Sun. of month.* ☉ *Tues.–Sun. 10–2.*

③⑤ **Palau de la Ciutadella** (Citadel Palace). This is the only surviving remnant of Felipe V's fortress, now shared by the Catalan parliament and the Museum of Modern Art. The palace's late-19th- and early 20th-century Catalan paintings and sculptures, by such artists as Isidro Nonell, Ramon Casas, and Marià Fortuny, form one of Barcelona's artistic treasures. A stroll through this collection makes it very clear that Catalonia's more famous artists—Gaudí, Picasso, Dalí, Miró—emerged not from nowhere but from an exceptionally rich artistic context. ⊠ *Plaça d'Armes, Parc de la Ciutadella,* ☎ *93/319–5728.* 📷 *500 ptas.* ☉ *Tues.–Sat. 10–7, Sun. 10–2.*

Parc de la Ciutadella (Citadel Park). Once a fortress designed to consolidate Madrid's military occupation of Barcelona, the Ciutadella is now the city's main downtown park. The clearing dates from shortly after the War of the Spanish Succession, when Felipe V demolished some

2,000 houses in what was then the Barrio de la Ribera (waterfront neighborhood) to build a fortress and barracks for his soldiers and fields of fire for his artillery. The fortress walls were pulled down in 1868 and replaced by gardens laid out by Josep Fontserè. Within the park are a cluster of museums, the Catalan parliament, and a zoo.

★ ③ **Palau de la Música.** The Music Palace, on Carrer Amadeus Vives, is a flamboyant tour de force, designed by Domènech i Muntaner in 1908 and considered the flagship of Barcelona's Moderniste architecture. The tiny ticket booths in the richly embellished columns are, sadly, no longer in use. Try to attend a concert here, if only to see the interior, with its inverted, stained-glass cupola (☞ Nightlife and the Arts, *below*); otherwise, you can make an appointment to tour the hall on Tuesday, Thursday, or Saturday. ✉ *Ticket office, Sant Francesc de Paula 2 (just off top of Via Laietana),* ☎ *93/268–1000.*

③ **Port Olímpic.** Choked with yachts, restaurants, and tapas bars of all kinds, the Olympic Port is just a mile up the beach, marked by the mammoth Frank Gehry goldfish sculpture in front of Barcelona's first real skyscraper, the Hotel Arts. The port rages on Friday and Saturday nights, especially in summer, with hundreds of young people of all nationalities circling and grazing until dawn.

③ **Port Vell.** From Pla del Palau, cross to the edge of the port, where the Moll d'Espanya, the Moll de la Fusta, and the Moll de Barceloneta meet. The modern wonders of the new Port Vell complex—the IMAX theater, aquarium, and Maremagnum shopping mall—loom seaward on the Moll d'Espanya. The Palau de Mar, with its five quayside terrace restaurants, stretches down along the Moll de Barceloneta. (Try Llevataps or, on the far corner, the Merendero de la Mari.) Take a stroll through the Museu de Historia de Catalunya (MHC) in the Palau de Mar for a purely Catalonian view of its national history. Along the Passeig Joan de Borbó are a dozen more traditional Barceloneta paella and seafood specialists.

Sant Pere de les Puelles (St. Peter of the Novices). One of the oldest medieval churches in Barcelona, this one has been destroyed and restored so many times that there is little left to see except the beautiful stained-glass window, which illuminates the stark interior. The word *Puelles* is from the Latin *puella* (girl)—the convent here was known for the beauty and nobility of its young women and was the setting for some of medieval Barcelona's most tragic stories of impossible love and romantic agony. ✉ *Lluís El Piadós 1,* ☎ *93/268–0742.* ☉ *Open for mass only.*

④ **Telefèric** (cable car). The cable car at the end of Passeig Joan de Borbócan takes you across to Montjuïc. Alternatively, you can walk to the end of the *rompeolas,* 3 km (1½ mi) out to sea, where you can catch a Golondrinas boat back into the port. ☎ *93/441–1820.* 🎫 *Cable car 850 ptas.* ☉ *Oct.–June 21, weekends 11–2:45 and 4–7:30; June 22– Sept., daily 11:30–9.*

☾ ③ **Zoo.** Barcelona's first-rate zoo—the home of Snowflake, the world's only captive albino gorilla—occupies the whole bottom section of the park. There's a great reptile house, and a full complement of African animals. ✉ *Parc de la Ciutadella,* ☎ *93/221–2506.* 🎫 *1,400 ptas.* ☉ *Oct.–Apr., daily 10–6; May–Oct., daily 9:30–7:30.*

Montjuïc

Montjuïc, the hill to the south of town, is thought to have been named for the Jewish cemetery once located on its slopes, though an alternate explanation has it named for the Roman deity Jove, or Jupiter. The most dramatic approach is by way of the cross-harbor cable car from Barceloneta or from the mid-station in the port; but Montjuïc is normally accessed by taxi or Bus 61 (or on foot) from Plaça Espanya, or by the funicular that operates from the Paral.lel (Paral.lel metro stop on the green line).

A Good Walk

Walking from sight to sight on Montjuïc is possible but not recommended. You'll want fresh feet and backs to appreciate the sights here, especially the Romanesque art collection in the Palau Nacional and the Miró Foundation.

The *teleféric* drops you at the Jardins de Miramar, a 10-minute walk from the Plaça de Dante and the entrance to the amusement park. Rock-and-roll buffs may want to look up Chus Martínez, onetime colleague of Bill Haley and Eddie Cochrane, who runs the Bali restaurant here. Impromptu concerts for his guests are not unheard of. From here, another small cable car takes you up to the **Castell de Montjuïc** ㊶. From the bottom station, the **Fundació Miró** ㊷ is just a few minutes' walk, and beyond it is the Estadi Olímpic (Olympic Stadium). From there, on foot, cut straight down to the Palau Nacional and its **Museu Nacional d'Art de Catalunya** ㊸. From here, a wide stairway leads down toward Plaça de Espanya.

TIMING

With unhurried visits to the Miró Foundation and the Romanesque exhibit in the Palau Nacional, this is a four- to five-hour excursion. Have lunch afterward in the Poble Espanyol.

Sights to See

㊶ Castell de Montjuïc. Built in 1640 by rebels against Felipe IV, the castle has been stormed several times, most famously in 1705, by Lord Peterborough for Archduke Carlos of Austria. In 1808, during the Peninsular War, the castle was seized by the French under General Dufresne. Later, during an 1842 civil disturbance, Barcelona was bombed by a Spanish artillery battery from its heights. The moat has been made into attractive gardens, with one side given over to an archery range. The various terraces have panoramic views over the city and out to sea. The castle now functions as a military museum housing the weapons collection of early-20th-century sculptor Frederic Marès. ⊠ *Carretera de Montjuïc 66,* ☏ *93/329–8613.* ▭ *250 ptas.* ☉ *Oct.–Mar., Tues.–Sat. 10–2 and 4–7, Sun. 10–2; Apr.–Sept., Tues.–Sat. 10–2 and 4–7, Sun. 10–8.*

★ **Estadi Olímpic.** The Olympic Stadium was originally built for the Great Exhibition of 1929, with the idea that Barcelona would then host the 1936 Olympics (ultimately staged in Hitler's Berlin). After failing twice to win the nomination, Barcelona celebrated the attainment of its long-cherished goal by renovating the semiderelict stadium in time for 1992, providing seating for 70,000. Next door and just downhill stands the futuristic Palau Sant Jordi Sports Palace, designed by the Japanese architect Arata Isozaki. The structure has no pillars or beams to obstruct the view and was built from the roof down; that is, the roof was built first and then hydraulically lifted into place. ⊠ *Passeig Olímpic 17–19,* ☏ *93/426–2089.* ☉ *Weekdays 10–2 and 4–7, weekends 10–6.*

★ **㊷ Fundació Miró.** The Miró Foundation was a gift from the artist Joan Miró to his native city and is one of Barcelona's most exciting contemporary-art galleries. The airy, white building was designed by Josep Lluís Sert and opened in 1975; an extension was added by Sert's pupil Jaume Freixa in 1988. Miró's unmistakably playful and colorful style,

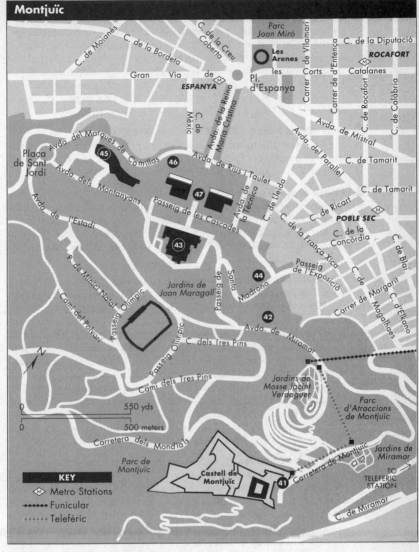

Castell de
Montjuïc, **41**
Fundació Miró, **42**
Mies van der Rohe
Pavilion, **46**
Museu
Arqueològic, **44**

Museu
Nacional d'Art
de Catalunya, **43**
Plaça de les
Cascades, **47**
Poble Espanyol, **45**

filled with Mediterranean light and humor, seems a perfect match for its surroundings, and the exhibits and retrospectives that open here tend to be progressive and provocative, from Moore to Mapplethorpe. Miró himself now rests in the cemetery on Montjuïc's southern slopes. During the Franco regime, which he strongly opposed, Miró first lived in self-imposed exile in Paris and in 1956 moved to Mallorca. When he died in 1983, the Catalans gave him a send-off amounting to a state funeral. ⊠ *Av. Miramar 71,* ☎ *93/329–1908.* ⊡ *650 ptas.* ◷ *Tues.– Wed. and Fri.–Sat. 10–7, Thurs. 10–9:30, Sun. 10–2:30.*

㊻ Mies van der Rohe Pavilion. The reconstructed Mies van der Rohe Pavilion—the German contribution to the 1929 Universal Exhibition—has interlocking planes of white marble, green onyx, and glass. ⊠ *Av. Marquès de Comillas s/n,* ☎ *93/426–3772.* ◷ *Daily 10–6.*

㊹ Museu Arqueològic. Just downhill to the right of the Palau Nacional, the Museum of Archaeology holds important finds from the Greek ruins at Empúries, on the Costa Brava. These are shown alongside fascinating objects from, and explanations of, Megalithic Spain. ⊠ *Passeig Santa Madrona 39–41,* ☎ *93/423–2149.* ⊡ *500 ptas.* ◷ *Tues.–Sat. 9:30– 1 and 4–7, Sun. 9:30–1.*

★ **㊸ Museu Nacional d'Art de Catalunya** (Catalonian National Museum of Art). This museum, housed in the imposing **Palau Nacional,** was built in 1929 and recently renovated by Gae Aulenti, architect of the Musée d'Orsay, in Paris. The Romanesque and Gothic frescoes and altarpieces here are simply staggering. Most were removed from small churches and chapels in the Pyrenees during the 1920s to ward off the threat of export by art dealers. When possible, the works are now being returned to their original homes or are being replicated, as with the famous *Pantocrator* fresco, a copy of which is now back in the church of Sant Climent de Taüll (☞ Chapter 6). The museum also contains works by El Greco, Velázquez, and Zurbarán. ⊠ *Mirador del Palau 6,* ☎ *93/423– 7199.* ⊡ *900 ptas.; 500 ptas. for temporary exhibits only.* ◷ *Tues.– Wed. and Fri.–Sat. 10–7, Thurs. 10–9, Sun. 10–2:30.*

㊼ Plaça de les Cascades. Upon leaving the Mies van der Rohe Pavilion, you'll see the multicolored fountain in the Plaça de les Cascades. Stroll down the wide esplanade past the exhibition halls, used for Barcelona fairs and conventions, to the large and frenetic **Plaça d'Espanya.** Across the square is Les Arenes bullring, now used for theater and political rallies rather than bullfights. From here, you can take the metro or Bus 38 back to Plaça de Catalunya.

☕ **㊺ Poble Espanyol.** The Spanish Village was created for the 1929 Universal Exhibition. A tad too artificial to compete successfully with Montjuïc's other sights, it's a kind of Spain-in-a-bottle, with the local architectural styles of each province faithfully reproduced, enabling you to wander from the walls of Ávila to the wine cellars of Jerez. The liveliest time to come is at night, for a concert or flamenco show. ⊡ *900 ptas.* ◷ *Mon. 9–8, Tues.–Thurs. 9–2, weekends 9–4.*

BARS AND CAFÉS

Barcelona may have more bars and cafés than inhabitants: colorful tapas emporiums; smart, trendy cafés; and a complete range of stylish, chic bars with rubrics ranging from *coctelerias* (cocktail bars) and *whiskerias* (often singles bars with professional escorts) to *xampanyerias* (champagne—actually *cava,* Catalan sparkling wine—bars). We suggest just a few. Most stay open until about 2:30 AM (*see* Nightlife and the Arts, *below,* for spots that close later).

Cafés

Café de l'Opera. Directly across from the Liceu, this high-ceiling Art Nouveau interior played host to opera goers and performers before the 1994 fire destroyed the theater. Central and de rigueur, it's a good bet if you're looking for someone; they're bound to pass through. ⊠ *Rambla 74*, ☎ *93/317–7585*. ⊙ *Daily 10 AM–2 AM.*

Cafe Paris. This popular spot is always a lively place to kill some time. Everyone from Prince Felipe, heir to the Spanish throne, to poet and pundit James Townsend Pi Sunyer can be spotted here in season. The tapas are excellent, the beer is cold, and the place is open 365 days a year from dawn to dawn. ⊠ *Calle Aribau 184, at Carrer Paris*, ☎ *93/209–8530*. ⊙ *Daily 6 AM–3 AM.*

Cafe Viena. The rectangular perimeter of this inside bar is always packed with local and international travellers in a party mood. It's a good place to meet until the reappearance of the traditional Zurich at the head of the Rambla. ⊠ *Rambla dels Estudis 115 ,* ☎ *93/349–9800.* ⊙ *Daily 8 AM–3 AM.*

Cafe Zurich. As this goes to press the Zurich is still out of commission as a result of the reconstruction of the block. However, this classic Rambla meeting point has been so important to Barcelona life that it's sure to reopen successfully. Stay tuned. ⊠ *Plaça Catalunya 1,* ☎ *no phone.* ⊙ *Daily 8 AM–3 AM.*

Els Quatre Gats. This is the café where Picasso staged his first exhibition and met the Modernistes. The restaurant serves respectable cuisine and snacks, such as different variations of *pa torrat* (slabs of country bread with tomato, olive oil, and anything from anchovies to cheese to cured ham or omelets). ⊠ *Montsió 3,* ☎ *93/302–4140.* ⊙ *Daily 8 AM–3 AM.*

Espai Barroc. This unusual "space" (*espai*), filled with Baroque decor and music, is in Carrer Montcada's most beautiful patio, the 15th-century Palau Dalmases, one of the many houses built by powerful Barcelona families between the 13th and 18th centuries. The stairway, decorated with bas-relief of the rape of Europa and Neptune's chariot, leads up to the Omnium Cultural, an institution for the study and exhibition of Catalonian history and culture. ⊠ *Carrer Montcada 20,* ☎ *93/310–0673.* ⊙ *Tues.–Sun. 4 PM–midnight.*

La Bodeguera. If you can find this dive (literally, it's a short drop below the level of the sidewalk), you'll also find a cozy and cluttered space with a dozen small tables, a few places at the marble counter, and lots of happy couples having coffee or beer, and maybe some ham or *tortilla española de patatas* (a typically Spanish, omeletlike potato-and-onion delicacy). ⊠ *Rambla de Catalunya 100,* ☎ *93/215–4894.* ⊙ *Mon.–Sat. 8 AM–2 AM, Sun. 7 PM–2 AM.*

Schilling. Near Plaça Reial, Schilling is always packed with young professionals, to the point where it's hard to get a table. It's a good place for coffee during the day and drinks and tapas at night. ⊠ *Ferran 23,* ☎ *93/317–6787.* ⊙ *Daily 10 AM–2:30 AM.*

Coctelerías

Almirall. This Moderniste bar in the Raval is quiet, dimly lit, and dominated by an Art Nouveau mirror and frame behind the marble bar. It's an evocative spot, romantic and mischievous. ⊠ *Joaquím Costa 33,* ☎ *93/302–4126.* ⊙ *Daily noon–2 AM.*

Boadas. This small, rather formal saloon near the top of the Rambla has become emblematic of the Barcelona *coctelería* concept, which usually entails a mixture of decorum and expensive mixed drinks amid wood and leather surroundings. ⊠ *Tallers 1,* ☎ *93/318–9592.* ☾ *Mon.– Sat. noon–2* AM.

Dry Martini Bar. The eponymous specialty is the best bet here, if only to watch the ritual. This seems to be a popular hangout for mature romantics, husbands, and wives, though not necessarily each other's; it exudes a kind of genteel wickedness. ⊠ *Aribau 162,* ☎ *93/217–5072.* ☾ *Daily noon–2* AM.

El Born. This former codfish emporium is now an intimate little haven for drinks, raclettes, and fondues. The marble cod basins in the entry and the spiral staircase up to the second floor are the quirkiest details, but everything here seems designed to charm and fascinate you in one way or another. ⊠ *Passeig del Born 26,* ☎ *93/319–5333.* ☾ *Daily 7* PM–2:30 AM.

El Copetín. Right on Barcelona's best-known cocktail avenue, this bar has good cocktails and Irish coffee. It's dimly lit, and romantically decorated in a South Seas motif. ⊠ *Passeig del Born 19,* ☎ *93/317–7585.* ☾ *Daily 7* PM–3 AM.

El Paraigua. Behind the *ajuntament,* this rather pricey bar serves cocktails in a stylish setting with classical music. ⊠ *Plaça Sant Miquel,* ☎ *93/217–3028.* ☾ *Daily 7* PM–1 AM.

Miramelindo. The bar has a large selection of herbal liquors, fruit cocktails, pâtés, cheeses, and music, usually jazz. ⊠ *Passeig del Born 15,* ☎ *93/319–5376.* ☾ *Daily 8* PM–3 AM.

Tapas Bars

Cal Pep. This lively hangout has Barcelona's best and freshest selection of tapas, served piping hot in a booming and boisterous ambience. ⊠ *Plaça de les Olles 8,* ☎ *93/319–6183.* ☾ *Mon. 8–midnight, Tues.– Sat. 1–4 and 8–midnight.*

Casa Tejada. The gregarious owner, Mr. Tejada, a former professional soccer player for FC Barcelona, seems to have a photographic memory for everyone who has ever snapped a tapa in his saloon. Though a little out of the way, Casa Tejada is handy to the boiling music-bar scene on nearby Marià Cubí. ⊠ *Tenor Viñas 3,* ☎ *93/200–7341.* ☾ *Daily 6* AM–2 AM.

El Irati. This boisterous Basque bar between Plaça del Pi and the Rambla has only one drawback: it's hard to get into. While this is a clear sign of quality, the narrow shape of the place can be a problem at peak hours. Try to beat the crowds by coming at 1 PM or at 7:30 PM. The excellent tapas can be washed down with *txakolí* (young, white Basque wine). ⊠ *Cardenal Casañas 17,* ☎ *93/302–3084.* ☾ *Tues.–Sun. noon–midnight.*

Euskal Etxea. Euskal Etxea is the best of the three Basque bars in or near the Gothic Quarter. Try a *txakolí.* The tapas and canapés will speak for themselves. A restaurant and a Basque cultural circle round out this social oasis. ⊠ *Placeta de Montcada 13,* ☎ *93/310–2185.* ☾ *Tues.– Sat. 8:30* AM–midnight.

La Palma. Behind the *ajuntament,* toward the post office, is this cozy café reminiscent of a Paris bistro, with marble tables, tapas to graze on, and newspapers to read. ⊠ *Palma Sant Just 7,* ☎ *93/315–0656.* ☾ *Daily 7* AM–3 PM and 7 PM–10 PM.

Xampanyerias

El Xampanyet. Just down the street from the Picasso Museum, hanging *botas* (leather wineskins) announce one of Barcelona's liveliest *xampanyerias*, stuffed to the gills most of the time. The house *cava*, cider, and *pan con tomate* (bread with tomato and olive oil) are served on marble-top tables surrounded by barrels and walls decorated with *azulejos* (tiles) and fading yellow paint. ✉ *Montcada 22,* ☎ *93/319–7003.* ◷ *Tues.–Sun. 8:30–4 and 6:30–midnight.*

La Cava del Palau. Very handy for the Palau de la Música, this champagne bar serves a wide selection of *cavas*, wines, and cocktails, along with cheeses, pâtés, smoked fish, and caviar, on a series of stepped balconies adorned with shiny *azulejos*. ✉ *Verdaguer i Callis 10,* ☎ *93/310–0938.* ◷ *Mon.–Sat. 7 PM–2:30 AM.*

BEACHES

Barcelona beaches have improved and proliferated. Starting at the southern end is the Platja (beach) de Sant Sebastià, recently declared a nudist enclave, followed by the beaches of La Barceloneta, Passeig Marítim, Port Olímpic, Nova Icaria, Bogatell, and, at the northern tip, the Mar Bella. Topless bathing is the rule.

North of the City

North of Barcelona, the first beaches are Montgat, Ocata, Vilasar de Mar, Arenys de Mar, Canet and Sant Pol de Mar, all accessible by train from the RENFE station in Plaça Catalunya. Sant Pol is the pick, with a clean beach, a lovely old town, and Sant Pau, one of Catalonia's top restaurants. The farther north you go, toward the Costa Brava, the better the beaches.

South of the City

Ten kilometers (6 miles) south is the popular day resort Castelldefels, with a series of handy and happening beachside restaurants and bars and a long, sandy beach for sunning and bathing. Sitges, another 25 minutes south, has better sand and clearer water.

DINING

Barcelona restaurants are so many and so exciting that keeping up with them is a lifetime project. Don't be daunted if the selection seems overwhelming. Stick with local produce and local cuisine: roast suckling pig, for example, a Castilian specialty, will nearly always be better in Castile, where the best and freshest piglets prevail. Here, look instead for *mar i muntanya* (surf and turf) specialties such as rabbit and prawns, or dark meat with fruits or sweets, as in duck with pears. *Menús del día* (menus of the day) are good values, though they vary in quality and are generally served only at lunchtime. Restaurants usually serve lunch 1–4 and dinner 9–11. Some places, notably Botafumeiro and Set Portes, serve continuously from 1 PM to 1 AM, a convenience for travelers with jetlag or early flights to catch. Tipping, though common, is not required; 10% is perfectly acceptable.

$$$$ ✕ **Beltxenea.** Long one of Barcelona's top restaurants, Beltxenea retains an atmosphere of privacy in its elegant dining rooms. In summer you can dine outside in the formal garden. Chef Miguel Ezcurra's Basque cuisine is exquisite. A specialty is *merluza con kokotxas y almejas* (hake simmered in stock with clams and barbels). The house wines are excellent. ✉ *Mallorca 275,* ☎ *93/215–3024. Reservations essential. AE, DC, MC, V. Closed Sun. and Aug. No lunch Sat.*

244

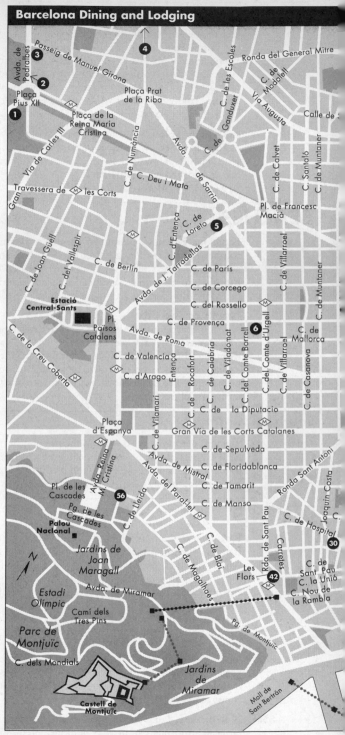

Barcelona Dining and Lodging

245

Lodging

Alexandra, **16**
Avenida Palace, **23**
Calderón, **22**
Colón, **40**
Condes de Barcelona, **17**
Continental, **28**
España, **43**
Fira Palace, **56**
Gallery, **57**
Gran Derby, **5**
Gran Vía, **24**
Hotel Arts, **53**
Hotel Claris, **21**
Hotel Rey Juan Carlos I–Conrad International, **2**
Jardí, **34**
Le Meridien, **33**
Majestic, **20**
Montecarlo, **35**
Nouvel, **36**
Oriente, **44**
Paseo de Gràcia, **14**
Peninsular, **41**
Princesa Sofía, **1**
Regente, **19**
Rialto, **38**
Ritz, **25**
Rivoli Ramblas, **29**
San Agustín, **37**
Suizo, **47**

$$$$ ✕ **Botafumeiro.** Barcelona's finest shellfish restaurant serves continu-
★ ously from 1 PM to 1 AM on Gràcia's main thoroughfare. The mood is
maritime, with white tablecloths and pale varnished-wood paneling,
and the fleet of waiters will impress you with their soldierly white outfits and lightning-fast service. The main culinary attraction is the
mariscos Botafumeiro (myriad plates of shellfish that arrive one after
the other). Costs can mount quickly; try the half-rations at the bar if
you're on a budget. ⊠ *Gran de Gràcia 81,* ☎ *93/218–4230. AE, DC,
MC, V. Closed Mon. No dinner Sun.*

$$$$ ✕ **El Racó de Can Fabes.** Santi Santamaria's master class in Mediter-
★ ranean cuisine is well worth the 45-minute train ride (or 30-minute drive)
north of Barcelona to Sant Celoni. Ranked as one of Spain's top three
gourmet restaurants (along with El Bullí in Roses and Arzak in San
Sebastián), this sumptuous display of good taste and even better tastes
is a must for anyone interested in fine dining. Catch any train bound
for France from the RENFE station on Passeig de Gràcia. ⊠ *Sant Joan
6,* ☎ *93/867–2851. AE, DC, MC, V. Closed Sun. night and Mon. Jan.
27–Feb. 10 and June 23–July 7.*

$$$$ ✕ **Jean Luc Figueras.** Jean Luc Figueras's former restaurants (Eldorado
★ Petit, Azulete) shot instantly to the top of all known gourmet lists, and
this one continued the tradition by earning a Michelin star in its first
year. Charmingly installed in the Gràcia town house that was once
Cristóbal Balenciaga's studio, this exceptional spot makes everyone's
short list of Barcelona's best restaurants. Try the *lubina amb tripes de
bacalao i botifarra* (sea bass with cod tripe and sausage). ⊠ *C. Santa
Teresa 10,* ☎ *93/415–2877. Reservations essential. AE, DC, MC, V.
Closed Sun. No lunch Sat.*

$$$$ ✕ **Neichel.** Hailing from Alsace-Lorraine, chef Jean-Louis Neichel is
not bashful about his reputation as he explains such French delicacies
as the *ensalada de gambas al sésamo con puerros* (shrimp in sesame-
seed sauce with leeks). Prices fluctuate widely depending on your
choice. The setting is the ground floor of a Pedralbes apartment block,
mundane modernity compared with the cooking. ⊠ *C. Bertran i
Rozpide 16 bis, off Av. Pedralbes,* ☎ *93/203–8408. Reservations essential. AE, DC, MC, V. Closed Sun., Jan. 1–6, Holy Week, and Aug.
No lunch Sat.*

$$$$ ✕ **Passadis del Pep.** Hidden away through a tiny passageway off the
Pla del Palau, this lively bistro serves a rapid-fire succession of delicious seafood tapas and wine as soon you appear. Sometime late in the
proceedings you may be asked to make a decision about your main
course, usually a fish of one kind or another. As long as you do not
choose *bogavante* (lobster), criminally expensive in Spain, everything
will be fine. ⊠ *Pla del Palau 2,* ☎ *93/310–1021. AE, DC, MC, V. Closed
Sun. and last 2 wks of Aug.*

$$$$ ✕ **Sant Pau.** Carme Ruscalleda's place in Sant Pol de Mar is a spec-
★ tacular 40-minute train ride along the beach from Plaça Catalunya's
RENFE station (look for the Calella train north), and the train drops
you right at her door. It's one of Barcelona's best gourmet excursions.
Increasingly hailed as one of Catalonia's top culinary artists, Ruscalleda whips up a taster's menu that you won't soon forget—follow
her suggestions and those of her husband, Toni. ⊠ *Nou 10, Sant Pol
de Mar,* ☎ *93/760–0662. AE, DC, MC, V. Closed Mon. April 1–17
and Nov. 3–20. No dinner Sun.*

$$$ ✕ **Can Gaig.** This traditional Barcelona eating house is close to per-
fect in design, decor, *and* dining. Known for its market-fresh ingredi-
ents and traditional yet innovative fare, the menu balances seafood and
upland specialties, game, and domestic raw materials. Try the roast par-
tridge with Iberian bacon. ⊠ *Passeig de Maragall 402,* ☎ *93/429–1017,*

FAX *93/429–7002. Reservations essential . AE, DC, MC, V. Closed Mon., holiday evenings, and Aug.*

$$$ ✕ **Can Isidre.** This small restaurant just inside the Raval from Avinguda del Paral.lel has a longtime following among Barcelona's artistic elite. Pictures and engravings, some original, by Dalí and other prominent artists line the walls. The traditional Catalan cooking draws on the nearby Boqueria's fresh produce and has a slight French accent—the homemade foie gras is superb. Come and go by cab at night; the area between Can Isidre and the Rambla is risky. ⊠ *Les Flors 12,* ☎ *93/441–1139. Reservations essential. AE, MC, V. Closed Sun., Holy Week, and mid-July–mid-Aug.*

$$$ ✕ **Casa Leopoldo.** Hidden away in the dark Raval (literally, "slum"), this excellent *casa* serves some of the finest seafood and Catalan fare in Barcelona. Try to approach by taxi or on foot from Carrer Hospital in order to avoid the dangerous-looking (though not, in fact, very dangerous) Barrio Chino. ⊠ *Sant Rafael 24,* ☎ *93/441–3014. AE, DC, MC, V. Closed Mon.*

$$$ ✕ **El Asador de Aranda.** Few restaurants can compete with this setting—a large, detached redbrick castle above the Avenida Tibidabo metro station. The dining room is large and airy, with a terra-cotta floor and traditional Castilian furnishings. The traditional Castilian cooking has won high praise ever since the restaurant opened in 1988. Try *pimientos de piquillo* (hot spicy peppers) and then *chorizo de la olla* (chorizo stew). ⊠ *Av. Tibidabo 31,* ☎ *93/417–0115. AE, DC, MC, V. No dinner Sun.*

$$$ ✕ **El Racò d'en Freixa.** Chef Ramó Freixa, one of Barcelona's up-and-coming culinary lights, is taking founding father José María's work to another level. His clever reinterpretations of traditional recipes, all made with high-quality raw ingredients, have qualified the younger Freixa's work as *cuina d'autor* (designer cuisine). Try the pig's feet with quail in a garlic-and-parsley gratin. ⊠ *Sant Elíes 22,* ☎ *93/209–7559. AE, DC, MC, V. Closed Sun. dinner, Mon., Holy Week, and Aug.*

$$$ ✕ **El Tragaluz.** *Tragaluz* means skylight—literally, "light swallower"—and is an excellent choice if you're still on a design high from Vinçon, Bd (Barcelona design) (☞ Shopping, *below*), or Gaudí's Pedrera. El Tragaluz is a sensory feast, with a glass roof that opens to the stars and slides back in good weather. The chairs, lamps, and fittings, designed by Javier Mariscal (creator of 1992 Olympic mascot Cobi) all reflect Barcelona's ongoing passion for playful shapes and concepts. ⊠ *Passatge de la Concepció 5,* ☎ *93/487–0196, Reservations advised. AE, DC, MC, V. Closed Jan 5. No lunch Mon.*

$$$ ✕ **Jaume de Provença.** People come here because they've heard about the chef, Jaume Bargués. Dip into his haute-cuisine repertoire for *lenguado relleno de setas* (sole stuffed with mushrooms) or *lubina* (sea bass) soufflé. In the Hospital Clinic part of the Eixample, the restaurant is decorated in modern black and bottle green. ⊠ *Provença 88,* ☎ *93/430–0029. Reservations essential. AE, DC, MC. Closed Mon. and Aug. No dinner Sun.*

$$$ ✕ **La Bona Cuina.** When the Madolell family converted their antiques business into a restaurant, in the late 1960s, it soon gained respect for its neo-Baroque elegance, intimacy, and nouvelle Catalan cuisine. Fresh fish is the house specialty; try the *bacalao à la Cuineta* (cod with spinach, raisins, pine nuts, and white sauce). The location, overlooking the apse of the cathedral, is memorable. ⊠ *Pietat 12,* ☎ *93/268–2394. Reservations not accepted. AE, DC, MC, V. Closed Tues.*

$$$ ✕ **Quo Vadis.** Just off the Rambla, near the Boqueria market, a shiny gray facade camouflages one of Barcelona's most respected restaurants. A succession of small dining rooms decorated in grays and greens provides an atmosphere of sleek intimacy. The much-praised cuisine in-

cludes *higado de ganso con ciruelas* (fried goose liver with prunes). ⊠ *Carme 7*, ☎ *93/317–7447. AE, DC, MC, V. Closed Sun.*

$$$ ✕ **Reial Club Marítim.** For sunset or harbor views, excellent maritime fare, and a sense of remove from the city, try Barcelona's yacht club, El Marítim, just around the harbor through Barceloneta. Make tracks for the shellfish paella, *rodaballo* (turbots), *lubina* (sea bass), or *dorado* (sea bream). Ask for the freshest fish they have and you won't be disappointed. ⊠ *Moll d'Espanya*, ☎ *93/221–7143. Reservations advised. AE, DC, MC, V. Closed Mon.*

$$$ ✕ **Set Portes.** These "Seven Doors" near the waterfront hide a high-
★ ceiling dining room, black-and-white marble floor, and mirrors aplenty. Going strong since 1836, this festive and elegant restaurant serves continuously from 1 PM to 1 AM, seven days a week. The cooking is Catalan, and the portions are enormous. Specialties are paella *de peix* (fish) and *sarsuela Set Portes* (seafood casserole). ⊠ *Passeig Isabel II 14*, ☎ *93/319–3033. AE, DC, MC, V.*

$$$ ✕ **Talaia Mar.** Generally understood as the finest restaurant in the Olympic Port, this bright spot has wonderful views of the Mediterranean and fresh produce from it as well. The taster's menu is a bargain and a good way to see and sample the chef's best work for little more than a regular meal would cost. ⊠ *Marina 16*, ☎ *93/221–9090. Reservations advised. AE, MC, V.*

$$$ ✕ **Tram-Tram.** At the end of the old tram line just uphill from the vil-
★ lage of Sarrià, Isidre Soler and his wife, Reyes, have put together one of Barcelona's finest and most original new culinary opportunities. Try the *menú de gustación* (tasting menu) and you might be lucky enough to get the marinated tuna salad, cod medallions, and the venison filet mignons, among other tasty creations. Perfectly sized portions and the graceful setting—especially in or near the garden out back—keep locals coming back. Reservations are a good idea, but Reyes can almost always invent a table. ⊠ *Major de Sarrià 121*, ☎ *93/204–8518. AE, MC, V. Closed Sun. and Dec. 24–Jan. 6.*

$$–$$$ ✕ **Los Caracoles.** Just below Plaça Reial, a wall of roasting chickens announces one of Barcelona's most famous tourist haunts, a colorful spot with both excellent dining and a cosmopolitan atmosphere. A mere walk through the kitchen into the restaurant is exciting enough to inspire a feeding frenzy. The walls are thickly hung with photos of bullfighters and visiting celebrities, and at night you're likely to be serenaded at your table. House specialties are Castilian roasts, fresh Mediterranean fish dishes, and, of course, *caracoles* (snails). It's open 365 days a year, with continuous service from 1 PM to midnight. ⊠ *Escudellers 14*, ☎ *93/302–3185. AE, DC, MC, V.*

$$ ✕ **Bilbao.** Located at the corner of Venus and Perill, this boisterous
★ bistro is known for top value. Its excellent Catalan menu focuses on simple, popular recipes. The overhanging balcony seems to place all diners on stage, and things get fun and foolish quickly. Early dining is recommended for both lunch and dinner, as it gets crowded later on. ⊠ *Carrer de Perill 33*, ☎ *93/458–9624. No credit cards. Closed Sun.*

$$ ✕ **Brasserie Flo.** Opened in 1982 by a group of Frenchmen, this used to be a textiles factory. You dine in a large, elegantly restored warehouse with arched vaulting, steel columns, and wood paneling all just a block from the Palau de la Música. The menu is an exciting combination of French and Catalan dishes. Try the freshly made foie gras and *choucroute*. ⊠ *Jonqueres 10*, ☎ *93/319–3102. AE, DC, MC, V.*

$$ ✕ **Café de l'Acadèmia.** With wicker chairs and stone walls, this place is sophisticated-rustic, frequented by politicians from the nearby Generalitat. Classical music forms the background, and the excellent cuisine makes it more than a mere café. ⊠ *Lledó 1*, ☎ *93/319–8253.* ☉ *Daily 9–4 and 9–11:30.*

$ ✕ **Agut.** Wood paneling surmounted by white walls, on which hang 1950s
★ canvases, forms the setting for the mostly Catalan crowd in this homey
restaurant in the lower reaches of the Gothic Quarter. Agut was founded
in 1924, and its popularity has never waned—not least because the hearty
Catalan fare offers fantastic value. In season (September–May), try the
pato silvestre agridulce (sweet-and-sour wild duck). There's a good selection of wine, but no frills such as coffee or liqueur. ⊠ *Gignàs 16,* ☎
93/315–1709. AE, MC, V. Closed Mon. and July. No dinner Sun.

$ ✕ **Egipte.** Hidden away behind the Boqueria market, Egipte has be-
come more and more popular over the last few years, especially with
a young set. The traditional Catalan home cooking, featuring such favorites as *favas a la catalana* (broad beans stewed with sausage), em-
anates from an overstretched but resourceful kitchen, and the results
can be uneven. Nonetheless, the many-tiered dining rooms, with marble-
top tables and Egyptian motifs, continue to draw a lively and sophisticated crowd. The best time to come is lunchtime, when the *menú del
día* is a great value. There are sister branches at Jerusalem 3 and Rambla 79. ⊠ *Jerusalem 12,* ☎ *93/317–7480. Reservations not accepted.
AE, DC, MC, V. Closed Sun.*

$ ✕ **El Glop.** Noisy, hectic, and full of jolly diners from all over Barcelona,
El Glop has specials like *calçotades* (giant spring onions baked in a clay
oven) and *asados* (barbecued meats). House wine arrives in a *porró*
(*porrón,* in Spanish; unless you're practiced at pouring wine into your
mouth from some distance, save your blushes—and clothes—by using
the wider opening and a glass). Bright and simply furnished, the restaurant is a few blocks north of Plaça del Sol, in Gràcia. ⊠ *Sant Lluís 24,*
☎ *93/213–7058. MC, V. Closed Mon.*

$ ✕ **La Fonda.** This is one of three Camós-family restaurants that offer
top value for your peseta. The other two locations are in nearby Plaça
Reial: **Les Quinze Nits** (⊠ Plaça Reial 6) and **Hostal de Rita** (⊠ Carrer Arago 279), near the corner of Arago and Pau Claris. Be early (1
for lunch, 8 for dinner); reservations are not accepted, and long lines
tend to form. The food is traditional Catalan, and the decor is a tasteful mixture of modern and rustic design. ⊠ *Escudellers 10,* ☎ *93/301–
7515. AE, DC, MC, V.*

$ ✕ **La Tramoia.** This surprising new place at the corner of Rambla de
Catalunya and Gran Via gives marvelous tastes at low prices in a
lively, boisterous atmosphere. Try the onion soup or the *gambas al ajillo*
(shrimp cooked in garlic and olive oil) and the *allioli. Tramoia* is Catalan for "backstage" as well as for "swindle," or the intrigue behind a
deal, here you see the chef behind glass. ⊠ *Rambla de Catalunya 15,*
☎ *93/412–3634.* ◷ *Daily 1 PM–4:30 PM and 8 PM–1 AM.*

$ ✕ **Sopeta Una.** Dining in this cozy, minuscule restaurant, with old-
fashioned, earthy decor and an intimate ambience, is more like eating
in someone's house. Try the *cors de carxofes* (artichoke hearts), and
for dessert, don't miss the traditional Catalan *música,* if it's on the
menu—a plate of raisins, almonds, and dried fruit served with a glass
of Muscatel. ⊠ *Verdaguer i Callis 6,* ☎ *93/319–6131. AE, V. Closed
Sun. and Aug.*

LODGING

Barcelona's hotel selection is, like the restaurant list, vast. The downtown hotels, such as the Ritz, the Claris, the Condes de Barcelona, and
the Colón, probably best combine comfort with a sense of where you
are, while the sybaritic new palaces, like the Arts, the Rey Juan Carlos I, the Hilton, and the Princesa Sofía, cater more to business travelers seeking familiar surroundings and luxury rather than geography.
Meanwhile, the smaller hotels, such as the Jardí and the España, are

less than half as expensive and more representative of the life of the city.

$$$$ ▥ **Avenida Palace.** At the bottom of the Eixample, between the Rambla de Catalunya and Passeig de Gràcia, this hotel conveys elegance and antiquated style despite dating from only 1952. The lobby is wonderfully ornate, with curving staircases leading off in many directions. Everything is patterned, from the carpets to the plasterwork, a style largely echoed in the bedrooms, although some have been modernized and the wallpaper tamed. If you want contemporary minimalism, stay elsewhere. ⊠ *Gran Via 605–607, 08007,* ☎ *93/301–9600,* 𝔽𝔸𝕏 *93/318–1234. 160 rooms. Restaurant, bar, health club. AE, DC, MC, V.*

$$$$ ▥ **Condes de Barcelona.** This is one of the city's most popular hotels—
★ reserve well in advance. The stunning, pentagonal lobby features a marble floor and the original columns and courtyard from the 1891 building. The most modern rooms have Jacuzzis and terraces overlooking interior gardens. An affiliated fitness club around the corner offers golf, squash, and swimming. ⊠ *Passeig de Gràcia 75, 08008,* ☎ *93/488–2200,* 𝔽𝔸𝕏 *93/487–1442. 183 rooms. Restaurant, bar, parking. AE, DC, MC, V.*

$$$$ ▥ **Fira Palace.** This relatively new hotel (open since the 1992 Olympics) has established itself among Barcelona's finest business and convention havens. Close to Barcelona's Convention Palace, the hotel also offers easy access to Montjuïc and its attractions. Impeccably modern, it's a solid choice for generic creature comfort rather than local color. ⊠ *Av. Rius i Taulet 1, 08004,* ☎ *93/426–2223,* 𝔽𝔸𝕏 *93/424–8679. 260 rooms, 16 suites. Restaurant, piano bar, pool, health club, parking. AE, DC, MC, V.*

$$$$ ▥ **Hotel Arts.** This luxurious Ritz-Carlton monolith overlooks Barcelona from the new Olympic Port, providing unique views of the Mediterranean, the city, and the mountains behind. A short taxi ride from the center of the city, the hotel is virtually a world of its own, with three restaurants (one specializing in Californian cuisine), an outdoor pool, and the beach. ⊠ *C. de la Marina 19–21, 08005,* ☎ *93/221–1000,* 𝔽𝔸𝕏 *93/221–1070. 399 rooms and 56 suites. 3 restaurants, bar, pool, beauty salon, beach, parking. AE, DC, MC, V.*

$$$$ ▥ **Hotel Claris.** Widely considered Barcelona's best hotel, the Claris is a fascinating melange of design and tradition. The rooms come in 60 different layouts, all furnished in classical, 18th-century English style, with lots of wood and marble. On site are a Japanese water garden, a first-rate restaurant, and a rooftop pool, all near the center of Barcelona. ⊠ *Carrer Pau Claris 150,* ☎ *93/487–6262,* 𝔽𝔸𝕏 *93/215–7970. 106 rooms and 18 suites. Restaurant, bar, pool. AE, DC, MC, V.*

$$$$ ▥ **Le Meridien.** The English-owned and -managed Le Meridien vies with the Rivoli Ramblas (☞ *below*) as the premier hotel in the Rambla area. Bedrooms are light, spacious, and decorated in pastels. The hotel hosts such music types as Michael Jackson and is very popular with businesspeople; fax machines and computers in your room are available on request. A room overlooking the Rambla is worth the extra noise. ⊠ *Rambla 111, 08002,* ☎ *93/318–6200,* 𝔽𝔸𝕏 *93/301–7776. 209 rooms. Restaurant, bar, parking. AE, DC, MC, V.*

$$$$ ▥ **Princesa Sofia.** Long considered Barcelona's foremost modern hotel despite its slightly out-of-the-way location on Avinguda Diagonal, this towering high-rise offers a wide range of facilities and everything from shops to three different restaurants, including one of the city's finest, Le Gourmet, and the 19th-floor Top City, with breathtaking views. The modern bedrooms are ultracomfortable and decorated in soft colors. ⊠ *Plaça Pius XII 4, 08028,* ☎ *93/330–7111,* 𝔽𝔸𝕏 *93/411–2106. 505 rooms. 3 restaurants, bar, indoor and outdoor pools, beauty salon, sauna, health club, parking. AE, DC, MC, V.*

$$$$ ⊞ **Rey Juan Carlos I–Conrad International.** This modern skyscraper towering over the western end of Barcelona's Avinguda Diagonal is an exciting commercial complex as well as a luxury hotel. Here you can buy or rent jewelry, furs, art, fashions, flowers, caviar, and even limousines. The lush garden, which includes a pond with swans, has an Olympic-size swimming pool; the green expanses of Barcelona's finest in-town country club, El Polo, spread luxuriantly out beyond. There are two restaurants: Chez Vous serves French cuisine, and Café Polo has a sumptuous buffet as well as an American bar. ⊠ *Av. Diagonal 661–671, 08028,* ☎ *93/448–0808,* 𝔽𝔸𝕏 *93/448–0607. 375 rooms, 40 suites. 2 restaurants (3 in summer), bar, pool, beauty salon, spa, paddle tennis, tennis courts, meeting rooms. AE, DC, MC, V.*

$$$$ ⊞ **Ritz.** Founded in 1919 by Caesar Ritz, this grande dame of Barcelona
★ hotels changed ownership in 1996. Extensive refurbishment has restored it to its former splendor. The imperial entrance lobby is awe-inspiring; the rooms contain Regency furniture, and some have Roman baths and mosaics. As for the price, you can almost double that of the nearest competitor. Service is generally excellent. ⊠ *Gran Via 668, 08010,* ☎ *93/318–5200,* 𝔽𝔸𝕏 *93/318–0148. 158 rooms. Restaurant, bar. AE, DC, MC, V.*

$$$ ⊞ **Alexandra.** Behind a reconstructed Eixample facade, everything here is slick and contemporary. The rooms are spacious and attractively furnished with dark-wood chairs, and those that face inward have thatch screens on the balconies for privacy. From the airy, marble hall up, the Alexandra is perfectly suited to modern martini sippers. ⊠ *Mallorca 251, 08008,* ☎ *93/487–0505,* 𝔽𝔸𝕏 *93/488–0258. 81 rooms. Restaurant, bar, parking. AE, DC, MC, V.*

$$$ ⊞ **Calderón.** Ideally placed on Rambla's chic and leafy Rambla Catalunya, this modern high-rise has a range of facilities normally found only in hotels farther out of town. Public rooms are huge, with cool, white-marble floors, and the bedrooms follow suit. Aim for one of the higher rooms, from which the views from sea to mountains and over the city are breathtaking. ⊠ *Rambla de Catalunya 26, 08007,* ☎ *93/301–0000. 264 rooms. Restaurant, piano bar, indoor and outdoor pools, health club, squash, free parking. AE, DC, MC, V.*

$$$ ⊞ **Colón.** This cozy, old town house has a unique charm and intimacy
★ reminiscent of an English country inn—and it lays claim to the sightseer's ideal location. The rooms are comfortable and tastefully furnished. The ones in the back are, if anything, noisier, as there is no longer any auto traffic on the front side, and the church bells are equally audible all over the neighborhood—so by all means try to get a room with a view of the cathedral. The Colón was a great favorite of Joan Miró, and for comfort, ambience, and location it's very possibly the best place in Barcelona. ⊠ *Av. Catedral 7, 08002,* ☎ *93/301–1404,* 𝔽𝔸𝕏 *93/317–2915. 147 rooms. Restaurant, bar. AE, DC, MC, V.*

$$$ ⊞ **Gallery.** This modern hotel in the upper part of the Eixample, just below the Diagona, offers impeccable comfort and service and a central location for middle and upper Barcelona. In the other direction, it's only 30 minutes' walk from the waterfront. Aptly named, and built primarily of glass and steel, the hotel is near Barcelona's prime art-gallery district, a few blocks away on Consell de Cien. ⊠ *Roselló 249, 08008,* ☎ *93/415–9911,* 𝔽𝔸𝕏 *93/415–9184. 110 rooms, 5 suites. Bar, cafeteria. AE, DC, MC, V.*

$$$ ⊞ **Gran Derby.** Every bedroom in this modern Eixample hotel has its own sitting room, and each is decorated with modern, black-and-white tile floors, plain light-colored walls, and coral bedspreads. Some have an extra bedroom, making them ideal for families. Only the location is less than ideal; for sightseeing purposes, it's a bit out of the way, just below Plaça Francesc Macià. ⊠ *Loreto 28, 08029,* ☎ *93/*

322–3215, FAX 93/419–6820. 44 rooms. Bar, café, parking. AE, DC, MC, V.

$$$ ⊞ **Majestic.** With an unbeatable location on the city's most stylish boulevard and a great rooftop pool, the Majestic is a near-perfect place to stay. The different combinations of wallpaper, pastels, and vintage furniture in the rooms and the mirrors, leather sofas, and marble in the reception area all suit the place well. The building is part Eixample town house and part modern extension, so bear this in mind when booking your room. ⊠ *Passeig de Gràcia 70, 08008,* ☎ *93/488–1717,* FAX *93/488–1880. 335 rooms. Restaurant, bar, pool, health club, free parking. AE, DC, MC, V.*

$$$ ⊞ **Rivoli Ramblas.** Behind the upper-Rambla facade lies imaginative, slick, modern decor with marble floors. Bedrooms are elegant, and the roof-terrace bar has panoramic views. ⊠ *Rambla 128, 08002,* ☎ *93/ 302–6643,* FAX *93/317–5053. 87 rooms. Restaurant, spa, health club. AE, DC, MC, V.*

$$ ⊞ **España.** They've modernized the already-large bedrooms here—the
★ best and quietest overlook the bright, interior patio—and now this erstwhile budget hotel is a winner, even if the stunning public rooms are still the main draw. The highlight is the Moderniste ground floor, designed by Domènech i Muntaner: a superbly sculpted hearth by Eusebi Arnau, elaborate woodwork, and a mermaid-populated Ramón Casas mural in the breakfast room. Try to see this lovely concentration of Art Nouveau, even if you only stop in for a meal. ⊠ *Sant Pau 9–11, 08001,* ☎ *93/318–1758,* FAX *93/317–1134. 76 rooms. Restaurant, breakfast room, cafeteria. AE, DC, MC, V.*

$$ ⊞ **Gran Via.** Architecture is the attraction at this grand 19th-century town house, located near the main tourist office. The original chapel has been preserved, and you can have breakfast in a hall of mirrors, climb an elaborate Moderniste staircase, and make calls from Belle Epoque phone booths. The rooms have plain alcoved walls, bottle-green carpets, and Regency-style furniture; those overlooking Gran Via itself have better views but are quite noisy. ⊠ *Gran Via 642, 08007,* ☎ *93/318–1900,* FAX *93/318–9997. 53 rooms. Breakfast room, parking. AE, DC, MC, V.*

$$ ⊞ **Montecarlo.** The Rambla entrance takes you through an enticing marble hall, and upstairs you come to a sumptuous reception room with a dark-wood Moderniste ceiling. The rooms are modern, bright, and functional; ask for a view of the Rambla if you don't mind a bit of noise. ⊠ *Rambla 124, 08002,* ☎ *93/412–0404,* FAX *93/318–7323. 76 rooms. Bar, cafeteria, parking. AE, DC, MC, V.*

$$ ⊞ **Nouvel.** Centrally located just below Plaça de Catalunya, this hotel blends white marble, etched glass, elaborate plasterwork, and carved, dark woodwork in its handsome Art Nouveau interior. The rooms have pristine marble floors, firm beds, and smart bathrooms. The narrow street is pedestrian-only and therefore quiet, but views are nonexistent. ⊠ *Santa Anna 18–20, 08002,* ☎ *93/301–8274,* FAX *93/301–8370. 74 rooms. Breakfast room. AE, MC, V.*

$$ ⊞ **Oriente.** Down toward the seamier end of the Rambla, Barcelona's oldest hotel has nonetheless retained some style and charm. Ornate public rooms and glowing chandeliers recall a bygone era. The only drawback is the somewhat functional decor of the bedrooms, some of which have an extra bed for families. Located just below the Liceu Opera House, it's popular with businesspeople. ⊠ *Rambla 45–47, 08002,* ☎ *93/302–2558,* FAX *93/412–3819. 142 rooms. Restaurant, bar. AE, DC, MC, V.*

$$ ⊞ **Regente.** The Moderniste decor and copious stained glass lend style and charm to this smallish hotel. The public rooms have been renovated over the last two years and are carpeted in many different patterns. The bedrooms, fortunately, are elegantly restrained; the verdant roof terrace (with a pool) and the prime position on the Rambla de Catalunya seal the positive verdict. ⊠ *Rambla de Catalunya 76, 08008,* ☎ *93/487–5989,* ℻ *93/487–3227. 78 rooms. Restaurant, bar, pool. AE, DC, MC, V.*

$$ ⊡ **Rialto.** This hotel seems to have taken a leaf from the paradors' book with its subdued pine floors, white walls, and walnut doors. The rooms (ask for an interior one if you fancy a quiet night) echo this look, with heavy furniture set against light walls. There's a vaulted bar in the basement and a modern, mirrored *salón* off the lobby. ⊠ *Ferran 42, 08002,* ☎ *93/318–5212,* ℻ *93/310–4081. 140 rooms. Bar, cafeteria. AE, DC, MC, V.*

$$ ⊡ **San Agustín.** Just off the Rambla in the leafy square of the same name, the San Agustín has long been a favorite with musicians performing at the Liceu Opera House. Rooms are small but pleasantly modern, with plenty of fresh wood and clean lines. ⊠ *Plaça de San Agustí 3, 08001,* ☎ *93/318–1708,* ℻ *93/317–2928. 77 rooms. Bar, cafeteria. AE, DC, MC, V.*

$$ ⊡ **Suizo.** The last of the Gargallo hotels lacks the spacious corridors of the Rialto, but its public rooms are preferable, with elegant, modern seating in front, either near the reception area or one floor up, and good views over the noisy square. The bedrooms have bright walls and wood or tile floors. ⊠ *Plaça del Àngel 12, 08002,* ☎ *93/315–0461,* ℻ *93/310–4081. 50 rooms. Restaurant, bar, cafeteria. AE, DC, MC, V.*

$ ⊡ **Continental.** This comfortable hotel, with canopied balconies, stands at the top of the Rambla, just below Plaça de Catalunya. Space is tight, but the rooms manage to accommodate large, firm beds. It's high enough over the Rambla to escape street noise, so ask for a room overlooking Barcelona's most emblematic street. George Orwell stayed here with his wife in 1937 after recovering from a throat wound—so it's a good place to read *Homage to Catalonia.* ⊠ *Rambla 138, 08002,* ☎ *93/301–2508,* ℻ *93/302–7360. 35 rooms. Breakfast room. AE, DC, MC, V.*

$ ⊡ **Jardí.** Perched over the traffic-free and charming Plaça del Pi and Plaça Sant Josep Oriol, this hotel's newly renovated rooms have modern pine furniture, white walls, and small but new bathrooms. Exterior rooms are the prettiest, but they can be noisy in summer. The in-house breakfast is excellent, but the alfresco tables at the Bar del Pi, downstairs, are ideal in summer. All in all, it's a great value. Caveat: the quietest rooms are four flights up, and there is no elevator. ⊠ *Plaça Sant Josep Oriol 1, 08002,* ☎ *93/301–5900,* ℻ *93/318–3664. 40 rooms. Breakfast room. AE, DC, MC, V.*

$ ⊡ **Paseo de Gràcia.** Formerly a hostel, the Paseo de Gràcia has soft-color bedrooms with plain, good-quality carpets and sturdy wooden furniture. Add to this the location, on the handsomest of the Eixample's boulevards, and you have an excellent budget option if you want to stay uptown. Some of the rooms, though not necessarily the newest, have balconies with views west over the city and the Collserola hills beyond. ⊠ *Passeig de Gràcia 102, 08008,* ☎ *93/215–5828,* ℻ *93/215–3724. 33 rooms. Bar, breakfast room. AE, DC, MC, V.*

$ ⊡ **Peninsular.** Built for the 1890 Universal Exposition, this hotel in the
★ Barri Xines features a coral-marble lobby and an appealing interior courtyard painted white and pale green and splashed with hanging plants. The bedrooms have tile floors, good showers, and firm beds. Look at a few before choosing, because each is different—some look onto the street, some into the courtyard. ⊠ *Sant Pau 34, 08001,* ☎ *93/302–3138,* ℻ *93/302–3138. 100 rooms, 80 with bath. Breakfast room. MC, V.*

NIGHTLIFE AND THE ARTS

Barcelona has wide-ranging arts and nightlife scenes that start early and never quite stop. To find out what's on, look in newspapers or the weekly *Guía Del Ocio,* available at newsstands all over town. *Activitats* is a monthly list of cultural events, published by the *ajuntament* and available from its information office in Palau de la Virreina (⊠ Rambla 99).

The Arts

Concerts

Catalans are great music lovers. Barcelona's main concert hall is the **Palau de la Música** (⊠ Sant Francesc de Paula 2, ☎ 93/268–1000), whose ticket office is open weekdays 11–1 and 5–8, Saturday 5–8 only. Sunday-morning concerts, at 11, are a popular tradition. Tickets range from 1,000 to 15,000 pesetas and are best purchased well in advance. Performances run September–June. Check the music listings in *El País,* Spain's daily newspaper, for concerts around town. Watch especially for the *Solistas del OBC,* a series of free performances held in the town hall's opulent Saló de Cent—this is world-class chamber music in an incomparable setting. In June and July, the city's annual summer music festival brings a long series of concerts. In late September, the **International Music Festival** forms part of the feast of Nostra Senyora de la Mercè (Our Lady of Mercy), Barcelona's patron saint.

Dance

L'Espai de Dansa i Música de la Generalitat de Catalunya—generally listed as **L'Espai**, or the Space (⊠ Travessera de Gràcia 63, ☎ 93/414–3133)—was opened by the Catalonian government in February 1992 and is now Barcelona's prime venue for ballet, modern dance, and various musical offerings. **El Mercat de les Flors** (⊠ Lleida 59, ☎ 93/426–1875) near Plaça de Espanya, is the more traditional setting for modern dance and theater.

Film

Though some foreign films are dubbed, more and more movies are shown in their original language. Look for listings marked *v.o.* (*versión original*). The **Icaria Yelmo** (⊠ Salvador Espriu 61, near Carles I metro stop) movie theater complex in the Olympic Port now has the most ample selection of films in English. The **Filmoteca** (⊠ Av. Sarrià 33, ☎ 93/430–5007) shows three films daily in *v.o.,* often English. The **Verdi** (⊠ Verdi 32, Gràcia), **Arkadin** (⊠ Travessera de Gràcia 103, near Gràcia train stop), the **Rex** (⊠ Gran Via 463), **Casablanca** (⊠ Passeig de Gràcia 115), and **Renoir Les Corts** (⊠ Eugeni d'Ors 12) tend to have recent releases in *v. o.*

Flamenco

Barcelona is not richly endowed with flamenco haunts, as Catalans consider flamenco—like bullfighting—a foreign import from Andalusia. **El Patio Andaluz** (⊠ Aribau 242, ☎ 93/209–3378) has flamenco shows twice nightly (10 and midnight) and audience participation in the karaoke section upstairs. **El Cordobés** (⊠ Rambla 35, ☎ 93/317–6653) is the most popular club with tour groups. Other options include **El Tablao de Carmen** (⊠ Poble Espanyol, ☎ 93/325–6895) and **Los Tarantos** (⊠ Plaça Reial 17, ☎ 93/318–3067).

Opera

Barcelona's opulent and beloved **Gran Teatre del Liceu** was gutted by flames in early 1994 and will probably not be restored until early 1999. The box office remains open at San Pau 1 (☎ 93/317–4142); operas and musical events will be staged at the **Palau Sant Jordi** sports hall,

BONUS MILES MAKE GREAT SOUVENIRS.

Earn Miles With Your MCI Card.

Take the MCI Card along on this trip and start earning miles for the next one. You'll earn frequent flyer miles on all your calls and save with the low rates you've come to expect from MCI. Before you know it, you'll be on your way to some other international destination.

Sign up for MCI by calling 1-800-FLY-FREE

Earn Frequent Flyer Miles.

Is this a great time, or what? :-)

Easy To Call Home.

1. To use your MCI Card, just dial the WorldPhone access number of the country you're calling from.
2. Dial or give the operator your MCI Card number.
3. Dial or give the number you're calling.

# Austria (CC) ♦	022-903-012
# Belarus (CC)	
From Brest, Vitebsk, Grodno, Minsk	8-800-103
From Gomel and Mogilev regions	8-10-800-103
# Belgium (CC) ♦	0800-10012
# Bulgaria	00800-0001
# Croatia (CC) ★	0800-22-0112
# Czech Republic (CC) ♦	00-42-000112
# Denmark (CC) ♦	8001-0022
# Finland (CC) ♦	08001-102-80
# France (CC) ♦	0-800-99-0019
# Germany (CC)	0800-888-8000
# Greece (CC) ♦	00-800-1211
# Hungary (CC) ♦	00▼800-01411
# Iceland (CC) ♦	800-9002
# Ireland (CC)	1-800-55-1001
# Italy (CC) ♦	172-1022
# Kazakhstan (CC)	8-800-131-4321
# Liechtenstein (CC) ♦	0800-89-0222
# Luxembourg	0800-0112
# Monaco (CC) ♦	800-90-019
# Netherlands (CC) ♦	0800-022-9122
# Norway (CC) ♦	800-19912
# Poland (CC) ÷	00-800-111-21-22
# Portugal (CC) ÷	05-017-1234
Romania (CC) ÷	01-800-1800
# Russia (CC) ÷ ♦	
To call using ROSTELCOM ■	747-3322
For a Russian-speaking operator	747-3320
To call using SOVINTEL ■	960-2222
# San Marino (CC) ♦	172-1022
# Slovak Republic (CC)	00-421-00112
# Slovenia	080-8808
# Spain (CC)	900-99-0014
# Sweden (CC) ♦	020-795-922
# Switzerland (CC) ♦	0800-89-0222
# Turkey (CC) ♦	00-8001-1177
# Ukraine (CC) ÷	8▼10-013
# United Kingdom (CC)	
To call using BT ■	0800-89-0222
To call using C&W ■	0500-89-0222
# Vatican City (CC)	172-1022

CHASE

Flying to France on Friday? Get Francs from Chase on Thursday. Call Currency To Go at 935-9935 for overnight delivery.

CHASE CURRENCY TO GO 935-9935

Or pounds for London. Or Deutschmarks for Düsseldorf. Or any of 75 foreign currencies. Call **Chase Currency To Go**[SM] **at 935-9935** in area codes 212, 718, 914, 516 and Rochester, N.Y.; all other area codes call 1-800-935-9935. We'll deliver directly to your door.* Overnight. And there are no exchange fees. Let Chase make your trip an easier one.

CHASE. The right relationship is everything.[SM]

on Montjuïc; the **Palacio Nacional,** above Plaza España; and the **Palau de la Música.** Some of the Liceu's most spectacular halls and rooms were unharmed by the fire, and you may be able to tour some of these during the restoration (☞ La Rambla and the Raval *in* Exploring Barcelona, *above*).

Theater

Most plays are performed in Catalan, though some are performed in Spanish. Barcelona is well known for avant-garde theater, and for troupes that specialize in mime and special effects (**La Fura dels Baus, Els Joglars, Els Comediants**). An international mime festival is held most years, as is the **Festival de Titeres** (Puppet Festival).

The best-known modern theaters are the **Teatre Lliure** (⊠ Montseny 47, Gràcia, ☎ 93/218–9251), **Mercat de les Flors** (⊠ Lleida 59, ☎ 93/318–8599), **Teatre Romea** (⊠ Hospital 51, ☎ 93/317–7189), **Teatre Tívoli** (⊠ Casp 10, ☎ 93/412–2063), and **Teatre Poliorama** (⊠ Rambla Estudios 115, ☎ 93/317–7599), all of which stage a dynamic variety of classical, contemporary, and experimental theater.

Many of the older theaters specializing in big musicals are along the Paral.lel. These include **Apolo** (⊠ Paral.lel 56, ☎ 93/241–9007) and **Victòria** (⊠ Paral.lel 6769, ☎ 93/441–3979). In July and August, an open-air summer theater festival brings plays, music, and dance to the **Teatre Grec** (Greek Theater) on Montjuïc (⊠ Rambla 99, ☎ 93/316–2700), as well as other venues.

Nightlife

Cabaret

Drop in at the venerable **Bodega Bohemia** (⊠ Lancaster 2, ☎ 93/302–5061), where a variety of singers perform to an upright piano, or the minuscule **Bar Pastís** (⊠ Santa Mònica 4, ☎ 93/318–7980), where the habitués form the cabaret and a phonograph plays Edith Piaf.

Arnau (⊠ Paral.lel 60, ☎ 93/242–2804) is an old-time music hall that's still going strong. The richly decorated **Belle Epoque** (⊠ Muntaner 246, ☎ 93/209–7711) stages the most sophisticated shows in town.

Casinos

The **Gran Casino de Barcelona** (☎ 93/893–3666), 42 km (26 mi) south in Sant Pere de Ribes, near Sitges, also has a dance hall and some excellent international shows in a 19th-century setting. Rumors of an imminent Gran Casino in the Olympic Port, under the Hotel Arts, persist, so inquire once you get here: you may be a mere elevator ride away from Las Vegas. The only other casinos in Catalonia are in **Lloret del Mar** (☎ 9/2/366512) and **Perelada** (☎ 972/538125), both in Girona province, up the coast from Barcelona.

Jazz Clubs

Try **La Cova del Drac** (⊠ Vallmajor 33, ☎ 93/200–7032) or the Gothic Quarter's **Harlem Jazz Club** (⊠ Comtessa Sobradiel 8, ☎ 93/310–0755), which is small but puts on atmospheric bands. **Barcelona Pipa Club** (⊠ Plaça Reial 3, ☎ 93/302–4732) is another hot jazz club, located above **Glaciar** in the southwest corner of Plaça Reial. **Jamboree-Jazz & Dance-Club** (⊠ Plaça Reial 17, ☎ 93/301–7564) is a center for jazz, rock, and flamenco. **La Boîte** (⊠ Diagonal 477, ☎ 93/419–5950) has an eclectic musical menu, as do **Luz de Gas** (⊠ Muntaner 246, ☎ 93/209–7711) and **Luna Mora** (⊠ Next to the Hotel Arts, in the Olympic Port, ☎ 93–221–6161), offering everything from country blues to soul. The Palau de la Música holds an **international jazz festival** in November, and nearby Terrassa has its own jazz festival in March. The bustling **Blue Note** (☎ 93/225–8003), in the Port Vell's Maremagnum shopping complex, draws a mixture of young and not-so-young nocturnals to musical events and Wednesday-night buffets. Food and drinks are served until dawn, and credit cards are accepted.

Late-Night Bars

Bar musical is Spanish for any bar with music loud enough to drown out conversation. The pick of these are **Universal** (⌧ Marià Cubí 182–184, ☎ 93/200–7470), **Mas i Mas** (⌧ Marià Cubí 199, ☎ 93/209–4502), and **Nick Havanna** (⌧ Rosselló 208, ☎ 93/215–6591). **L'Ovella Negra** (⌧ Sitjàs 5, ☎ 93/317–1087) is the top student tavern. **Glaciar** (⌧ Plaça Reial 13, ☎ 93/302–1163) is *the* spot for young out-of-towners.

For a more laid-back scene, with high ceilings, billiards, tapas, and hundreds of students, visit the popular **Velodrom** (⌧ Muntaner 211–213, ☎ 93/230–6022), just below Diagonal. Two blocks away is the intriguing *barmuseo* (bar-cum-museum) **La Fira** (⌧ Provença 171, ☎ 93/323–7271). Downtown, deep in the Barrio Chino, try the **London Bar** (⌧ Nou de la Rambla 34, ☎ 93/302–3102), an Art Nouveau circus haunt with a trapeze suspended above the bar. Don't miss **Bar Almirall** (⌧ Joaquin Costa 33, ☎ 93/412–1535) or **Bar Muy Buenas** (⌧ Carme 63, ☎ 93/442–5053).

Nightclubs and Discos

Barcelona is currently so hot that it's hard to keep track of the nightspots of the moment. Most clubs have a discretionary cover charge and like to inflict it on foreigners, so dress up and be prepared to talk your way past the bouncer. Any story can work; for example, you own a chain of nightclubs and are on a world tour. Don't expect much to happen until 1:30 or 2.

Tops for some time now is the prisonesque **Otto Zutz** (⌧ Lincoln 15, ☎ 93/238–0722), just off Via Augusta. **Club Fellini** (⌧ Marqués de l'Argentera s/n, ☎ 93/319–5356), in the Estació de França, is a new hot spot, and **Fibra Optica** (⌧ Beethoven 9, ☎ 93/209–5281) and the nearly classic **Up and Down** (⌧ Numancia 179, ☎ 93/280–2922), pronounced "Pen-*dow*," are both anything but calm. **Bikini** (⌧ Deu i Mata 105, at Entença, ☎ 93/322–0005) will present you with a queue on particularly festive Saturday nights. **Oliver y Hardy** (⌧ Diagonal 593, ☎ 93/419–3181), next to the Barcelona Hilton, is more popular with the older set (i.e., you won't stand out if you're over 35); **La Tierra** (⌧ Aribau 230, ☎ 93/200–7346) and **El Otro** (⌧ Valencia 166, ☎ 93/323–6759) also accept postgraduates with open arms. **Zeleste** (⌧ Almogavers 122, ☎ 93/309–1204) is another standard hangout, particularly popular with jazz and rock buffs. **La Boîte** (⌧ Diagonal 477, ☎ 93/419–5950) has live music and a nice balance of civilization and insanity.

For an old-fashioned *sala de baile* (dance hall) with a big band playing tangos, head to **La Paloma** (⌧ Tigre 27, ☎ 93/301–6897); the kitschy 1950s decor creates a peculiar atmosphere that's great fun.

OUTDOOR ACTIVITIES AND SPORTS

Golf

Barcelona is ringed by some excellent golf courses. Call ahead to reserve tee times.

Around Barcelona

Reial Club de Golf El Prat (⌧ El Prat de Llobregat, 08820 , ☎ 93/379–0278), 36 holes. Note: the greens fee at El Prat is 24,000 ptas. **Club de**

Golf de Sant Cugat (⊠ Sant Cugat del Vallès, 08190 , ☎ 93/674–3958), 18 holes. **Club de Golf Vallromanes** (⊠ Vallromanes, 08188, ☎ 93/568–0362), 18 holes. **Club de Golf Terramar** (⊠ Sitges, 08870, ☎ 93/894–0580), 18 holes.

Farther Afield
Club de Golf Costa Brava (⊠ La Masía, Santa Cristina d'Aro, 17246, ☎ 972/837150), 18 holes. **Club de Golf Pals** (⊠ Platja de Pals, Pals, 17256, ☎ 972/637009), 18 holes.

Health Clubs

Catalans are becoming increasingly keen on fitness. You'll see gyms everywhere; for specifics, look in the *Páginas Amarillas/Pàgines Grogues* (*Yellow Pages*) under "Gimnasios/Gimnasis." We can recommend the new and exciting **Crack,** which has a gym, a sauna, a pool, six squash courts, and paddle tennis. ⊠ *Pasaje Domingo 7,* ☎ *93/215–2755.* ⊑ *Day membership 1,750 ptas.; small supplement for courts.*

Hiking

You may not have come to Barcelona with the idea of heading for the hills, but the **Collserola** hills behind the city offer well-marked trails, fresh air, and lovely views. Take the Sabadell or Terrassa FFCC train from Plaça de Catalunya and get off at the Baixador de Vallvidrera. The nearby information center can supply you with maps of this surprising mountain woodland just 20 minutes from downtown.

Swimming

Indoor
Try the **Club Natació Barceloneta** (⊠ Passeig Marítim, ☎ 93/309–3412) or the **Piscines Pau Negre Can Toda** (⊠ Ramiro de Maetzu, ☎ 93/213–4344). Each charges 500 pesetas.

Outdoor
Uphill from Parc Güell is the **Parc de la Creueta del Coll** (⊠ Castell-terçol, ☎ 93/416–2625), which has a huge outdoor swimming pool. The fee is 500 pesetas.

Tennis

The cheapest place to play tennis is the **Complejo Deportivo Can Caralleu** (Can Caralleu Sports Complex), above Pedralbes, a 30-minute walk uphill from the Reina Elisenda subway stop (FFCC de la Generalitat). ☎ *93/203–7874.* ⊑ *Daytime 1,250 ptas. per hr, nighttime 1,450 ptas. per hr.* ☉ *Daily 8 AM–11 PM.*

Alternatively, try the upscale **Club Vall Parc.** ⊠ *Carretera de la Rabassada 79,* ☎ *93/212–6789.* ⊑ *Daytime 2,500 ptas. per hr, nighttime 3,100 ptas. per hr.* ☉ *Daily 8–midnight.*

SHOPPING

Shopping Districts

Barcelona's prime shopping districts are the Passeig de Gràcia, Rambla de Catalunya, and Avinguda Diagonal up to Carrer Ganduxer. Farther out on the Diagonal is shopping colossus **L'Illa,** which includes **FNAC, Marks & Spencer,** and plenty of other consumer temptations. The **Maremagum** mall, in Port Vell, is another shopping option. For small boutiques, try **Carrer Tuset,** north of Diagonal. For more affordable, more old-fashioned, typically Spanish-style shops, prowl the area between the Rambla and Via Laietana, especially around **Carrer Ferran.** The area surrounding **Plaça del Pi,** from the Boqueria to Carrer Portaferrissa and Carrer de la Canuda, has fashionable boutiques and jewelry and gift shops. Most shops are open Monday–Saturday 9–1:30 and 5–8, but some close in the afternoon. Virtually all close on Sunday.

Specialty Stores

Antiques
Carrer de la Palla and Carrer Banys Nous, in the Gothic Quarter, are lined with antiques shops full of maps, books, paintings, and furniture. An **antiques market** is held every Thursday from 10 to 8, in front of the cathedral. The **Centre d'Antiquaris** (⊠ Passeig de Gràcia 57) contains 75 antiques stores. Try **Gothsland** (⊠ Consell de Cent 331) for Moderniste design.

Ceramics
Itaca (⊠ Ferrán 26, ☎ 93/301–3044) has a good selection of ceramic plates, bowls, and inspired objects of all kinds, including pottery from Talavera de la Reina and La Bisbal. **Art Escudellers** (⊠ Calle Escudellers 5, ☎ 93/412–6801) carries ceramics from all over Spain, with more than 140 different artists represented. The big department stores are also worth checking. For Lladró, try **Pla de l'Os** (⊠ Boqueria 3, ☎ 93/301–4088), just off the Rambla.

Art
Many of Barcelona's art galleries are along Carrer Consell de Cent (and around the corner on Rambla de Catalunya) between Passeig de Gràcia and Carrer Balmes, including **Galeria Joan Prats** (Rambla de Catalunya 54), **Sala Dalmau** (Consell de Cent 347), and **Sala Rovira** (Rambla de Catalunya 62). The nearby **Joan Gaspart Gallery** (Plaça Letamendi 1) is another player. Carrer Petritxol, which leads down into Plaça del Pi (☞ La Rambla and the Raval *in* Exploring Barcelona, *above*), is also lined with art galleries, most notably the dean of Barcelona art galleries, **Sala Parès.** Carrer Montcada has **Galeria Maeght** and others, and the Passeig del Born is worth checking out. **Galeria Verena Hofer** is around the corner on Plaça Comercial, across from the Born; and the ticking **Metrònom** is on nearby Carrer Fussina. Near Plaça del Pi, several art galleries command attention along Carrer de la Palla, particularly **Sala d'Art Artur Ramón** (Carrer de la Palla 23). Important spaces for itinerant exhibitions include **Fundació Caixa de Catalunya–La Pedrera** (Provença 261–265), **Fundació La Caixa–Centre Cultural** (Passeig Sant Joan 108), **Sala El Vienès-Casa Fuster** (Passeig de Gràcia 132), and **La Virreina** (Rambla 99).

Boutiques and Fashion
If you are after fashion and jewelry, you've come to the right place. Barcelona makes all the headlines on Spain's booming fashion front. **El Bulevard Rosa** (⊠ Passeig de Gràcia 53–55) is a collection of boutiques that stock the very latest outfits. Others are on Avinguda Diagonal between Passeig de Gràcia and Carrer Ganduxer. **Adolfo Domínguez,** one of Spain's top designers, is at Passeig de Gràcia 35 and Diagonal 570; Toni Miró's two **Groc** shops, with the latest looks for men, women, and children, are at Muntaner 385 and Rambla de Catalunya 100. **David Valls,** at Valencia 235, represents new and young Barcelona fashion design, and **May Day** carries clothing, footwear, and accessories from the cutting edge. **Joaquim Berao,** a top jewelry designer, is at Roselló 277.

Department Stores

The ubiquitous **El Corte Inglés** has four locations: Plaça de Catalunya 14, Porta de l'Angel 19–21, Avinguda Francesc Maciá 58, and Diagonal 617 (Metro: Maria Cristina). **Marks & Spencer** is in the shopping mall L'Illa, at Diagonal 545, along with a full array of stores from **Benetton** to **Zara.**

Design and Interiors

At Passeig de Gràcia 102 is **Gimeno,** whose elegant displays range from unusual suitcases to the latest in furniture design. **Vinçon,** a couple of doors down at No. 96, is equally chic; some 50 years old, it has steadily expanded through a rambling Moderniste house that was once the home of Moderniste poet-artist Santiago Rusiñol and the studio of his colleague, the painter Ramón Casas. It stocks everything from Filofaxes to handsome kitchenware. **Bd** (Barcelona design), at Carrer Mallorca 291–293, is another spectacular design store in another Moderniste gem, Doménech i Muntaner's Casa Thomas.

Food and Flea Markets

The **Boqueria** market, on the Rambla between Carrer del Carme and Carrer de Hospital, is Barcelona's most colorful and bustling food market and the oldest of its kind in Europe. It's open Monday–Saturday and is most active before 3 PM. **Els Encants,** Barcelona's biggest flea market, is held Monday, Wednesday, Friday, and Saturday 8–7, at the end of Dos de Maig, on Plaça de les Glòries (Metro: Glòries, red line). The **Sant Antoni** market, at the end of Ronda Sant Antoni, is an old-fashioned food and clothes market that's best on Sunday. On Thursdays, a natural produce market (honeys, cheeses) fills **Plaça del Pi** with interesting tastes and aromas.

SIDE TRIPS

Numbers in the margin correspond to points of interest on the Side Trips from Barcelona map.

Montserrat

48 *50 km (30 mi) west of Barcelona.*

A nearly obligatory side trip from Barcelona is the shrine of La Moreneta, the Black Virgin of Montserrat, high in the mountains of the Serra de Montserrat. These weird, saw-toothed peaks have given rise to countless legends: here St. Peter left a statue of the Virgin Mary carved by St. Luke, Parsifal found the Holy Grail, and Wagner sought inspiration for his opera. A monastery has stood on this site since the early Middle Ages, though the present 19th-century building replaced the rubble left by Napoleon's troops in 1812. Montserrat is a world-famous shrine and one of Catalonia's spiritual sanctuaries. Honeymooning couples flock here by the thousand seeking La Moreneta's blessing on their marriages, and twice a year, on April 27 and September 8, the diminutive statue of Montserrat's Black Virgin becomes the object of one of Spain's greatest pilgrimages.

Follow the A2/A7 *autopista* on the new upper ring road (Ronda de Dalt) or from the western end of Diagonal as far as Salida (Exit) 25 to Martorell. Bypass this industrial center and follow signs to Montserrat. You can also take a train from the Plaça Espanya metro station to Montserrat, or a guided tour with Pullmantur or Julià.

Only the basilica and museum are regularly open to the public. The **basilica** is dark and ornate, its blackness pierced by the glow of hundreds of votive lamps. Above the high altar stands the famous poly-

Side Trips from Barcelona

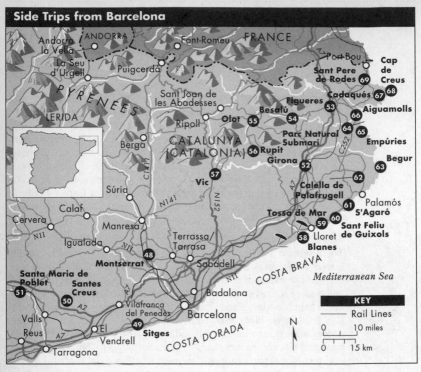

chrome statue of the Virgin and Child to which the faithful can pay their respects by way of a separate door. ☎ *93/835–0251.* ⊙ *Daily 6–10:30 and noon–6:30.*

The monastery's **museum** has two sections: the Secció Antiga (open Tuesday–Saturday 10:30–2) contains Old Masters, among them paintings by El Greco, Correggio, and Caravaggio, and the amassed gifts to the Virgin; the Secció Moderna (open Tuesday–Saturday 3–6) concentrates on recent Catalan painters.

Montserrat is as memorable for its setting as for its religious treasures, so be sure to explore these strange, pink hills. The vast monastic complex is dwarfed by the grandeur of the jagged peaks, and the crests are dotted with hermitages. The hermitage of **Sant Joan** can be reached by funicular. The views over the mountains to the Mediterranean and, on a clear day, to the Pyrenees are breathtaking, and the rugged, boulder-strewn setting makes for dramatic walks and hikes.

Sitges, Santes Creus, and Poblet

This trio of attractions to the south and west of Barcelona can be seen comfortably in a day. Sitges is the prettiest and most popular resort in Barcelona's immediate environs, flaunting an excellent beach, a picturesque old quarter, and some interesting Moderniste bits. It's also one of Europe's premier gay resorts. The Cistercian monasteries west of here are characterized by monolithic Romanesque architecture and beautiful cloisters.

Head southwest along Gran Via or Passeig Colom to the freeway that passes the airport on its way to Castelldefels. From here, the new freeway and tunnels will get you to Sitges in 20–30 minutes. From Sitges, drive inland toward Vilafranca del Penedès and the A7 freeway. The A2 (Lleida) leads to the monasteries.

Regular trains leave Sants and Passeig de Gràcia for Sitges; the ride takes half an hour. From Sitges, trains go to L'Espluga de Francolí, 4 km (2½ mi) from Poblet (Lleida line). For Poblet, stay with the train to Tarragona and catch a bus to the monastery (⊠ Autotransports Perelada, ☎ 973/202058).

Sitges

❹❾ *43 km (27 mi) south of Barcelona.*

Head for the museums here. The most interesting is the **Cau-Ferrat,** founded by the artist Russinyol and containing some of his own paintings together with two El Grecos. Connoisseurs of wrought iron will love the beautiful collection of *cruces terminales,* crosses that once marked town boundaries. ⊠ *Fonollar s/n,* ☎ *93/894–0364.* ☞ *250 ptas.; free Sun.* ☉ *Tues.–Sun. 9:30–2.*

NEED A BREAK?	Linger over excellent seafood in a nonpareil sea-view setting at **Vivero.** ⊠ *Passeig Balmins s/n,* ☎ *93/894-2149. Closed Tues. Dec.–May.*

En Route Upon leaving Sitges, make straight for the A2 *autopista* by way of Vilafranca del Penedès. If you're a wine buff, you may want to stop here to taste the excellent Penedès wine; you can tour and sip at the **Bodega Miguel Torres** (⊠ Comercio 22, ☎ 93/890–0100). There's an interesting **Museu del Vi** (Wine Museum) in the Royal Palace, with descriptions of winemaking history. ☞ *500 ptas.* ☉ *Tues.–Sun. 10–2 and 4–7.*

Santes Creus

❺⓪ *95 km (59 mi) west of Barcelona.*

Santes Creus, founded in 1157, is the first of the monasteries you'll come upon as A2 branches west into the province of Lleida. Three austere aisles and an unusual 14th-century apse combine with the newly restored cloisters and the courtyard of the royal palace. ☎ 977/638329. ☞ *450 ptas.* ☉ *Oct.–Mar., daily 10–1 and 3–6; Apr.–Sept., daily 10–1 and 3–7.*

Montblanc is at Exit 9 off A2, its ancient gates too narrow for cars. A walk through its tiny streets reveals Gothic churches with intricate stained-glass windows, a 16th-century hospital, and medieval mansions.

Santa Maria de Poblet

❺❶ *8 km (5 mi) west of Santes Creus.*

This splendid Cistercian foundation at the foot of the Prades Mountains is one of the great masterpieces of Spanish monastic architecture. The cloister is a stunning combination of lightness and size; on sunny days the shadows on the yellow sandstone are extraordinary. Founded in 1150 by Ramón Berenguer IV in gratitude for the Christian Reconquest, the monastery first housed a dozen Cistercians from Narbonne. Later, the Crown of Aragon used Santa Maria de Poblet for religious retreats and burials. The building was damaged in an 1836 anticlerical revolt, and monks of the reformed Cistercian Order have managed the difficult task of restoration since 1940. Today, monks and novices again pray before the splendid retable over the tombs of Aragonese rulers, restored to their former glory by sculptor Frederic Marés; sleep in the cold, barren dormitory; and eat frugal meals in the stark refectory. You can join them if you'd like; 18 very comfortable rooms are available (for men only). Call Padre Benito (☎ 977/870089) to arrange a stay of up to 15 days within the stones and silence of one of Catalonia's gems. ✉ *600 ptas.* ☉ *Guided tour daily 10–12:30 and 3–6 (until 5:30 Oct.–Mar.).*

Girona and Northern Catalonia

The ancient city of Girona, often ignored by visitors who bolt from its airport to the resorts of the Costa Brava, is an easy and worthwhile day trip from Barcelona. Much of the city's charm comes from its narrow medieval streets—with frequent stairways, as required by the steep terrain. Historic buildings here include the cathedral, which dominates the city from the top of 90 steps; Arab baths; and an antique and charming Jewish quarter.

Northern Catalonia boasts the green rolling hills of the Ampurdan, the Alberes mountain range at the eastern tip of the Pyrenees, and the rugged Costa Brava. Sprinkled across the landscape are charming *masías* (farmhouses) whose austere, grayish or pinkish staggered stone rooftops and ubiquitous square towers make them look like fortresses. Churches dignify the villages, and even the tiniest of these has its own arcaded square and *rambla* where villagers take their evening *paseo.*

Girona

52 *97 km (60 mi) northeast of Barcelona.*

Park in the Plaça Independencia and find your way to the tourist office at Rambla Llibertat 1. Then head to the old quarter, across the River Onyar, past Girona's best-known view: the orange waterfront houses, their windows draped with a colorful array of drying laundry, reflected in the waters of the Onyar. Use the cathedral's huge Baroque facade as a guide up through the labyrinth of streets.

At the base of the 90 steps, go left through the Sobreportes gate to the **Banys Arabs** (Arab Baths). Built by Morisco craftsmen in the late 12th century, long after Girona's Islamic occupation (795–1015) had ended, the baths are both Romanesque and Moorish in design. ✉ *375 ptas.* ☉ *May–Sept., Tues.–Sat. 10–2 and 4–7, Sun. 10–2; Oct.–Apr., Tues.–Sun. 10–1.*

Across the River Galligants is the church of **Sant Pere** (Holy Father), finished in 1131 and notable for its octagonal Romanesque belfry and the finely detailed capitals atop the columns in the cloister. Next door is the **Museu Arqueològic** (Museum of Archaeology), which documents the region's history since Paleolithic times. ✉ *Free.* ☉ *Church and museum daily 10–1 and 4:30–7.*

The stepped Passeig Arquaeològic runs below the walls of the Old City. From there, climb through the Jardins de la Francesa to the highest **ramparts.** From here you have a good view of the 11th-century **Romanesque Tower of Charlemagne,** the oldest part of the cathedral.

To see the inside of Girona's **cathedral,** designed by Guillem Bofill in 1416, complete the loop around it. The cathedral is famous for its immense, uncluttered Gothic nave, which at 75 ft is the widest in the world and the epitome of the spatial goals of Catalan Gothic architects. The **museum** contains the famous *Tapis de la Creació* (*Tapestry of the Creation*) and a 10th-century copy of Beatus's manuscript *Commentary on the Apocalypse.* ✉ *375 ptas.* ☉ *Oct.–June, daily 9:30–1:15 and 3:30–7; July–Sept., daily 9:30–7.*

Next door to the cathedral is **Palau Episcopal** (Bishop's Palace), which houses the **Museu d'Art,** a good mix of Romanesque, Catalan Gothic, and modern art. ✉ *Free with ticket for Arab Baths (☞ above).* ☉ *Tues.–Sat. 10–7, Sun. 10–1.*

Upon leaving Plaça dels Apòstols along Carrer Claveria, turn right down Carrer Lluis Batlle i Prats. Plunge right down the tiny Carrer Sant Llorenç, formerly the cramped and squalid center of the 13th-century *Call,* or Jewish quarter. Halfway down on the left is the small **Bonastruc Ça-porta,** a museum of Jewish history, open Tuesday–Saturday 10–2 and 4–7 and Sunday 10–2, and the **Pati dels Rabís** (Rabbis' Courtyard).

DINING AND LODGING

$$$$ ✕ **Albereda.** Excellent Ampurdan cuisine is served in a bright, if somewhat subdued, setting. Try the *galleta con langostinos glaceada* (zucchini bisque with prawns). ✉ *C. Albereda 7 bis,* ☎ 972/226002. *AE, DC, MC. Closed Sun.*

$$–$$$ ✕ **Cal Ros.** This historic place was once a haunt of Girona intellectuals. *Arroz a la cazuela,* similar to a paella but cooked in a deeper pan, is a specialty, particularly *arroz de perdiz a la cazuela con alcachofas y butifarra negra* (rice and partridge with artichokes and black sausage). ✉ *C. Cort Reial 9,* ☎ 972/217379. *MC, V. Closed Sun. evening, Mon.*

$$–$$$ ✕ **Penyora.** Here you'll find both good local fare and, if you order from the prix-fixe menu, a bargain. ✉ *C. Nou del Teatre 3,* ☎ 972/218948. *AE, DC, MC. Closed Tues.*

$$–$$$ 🏨 **Ultonia.** This central hotel is decorated with attractive wooden tables, paneling, and cupboards. ✉ *Gran Via Jaume I 22, 08002,* ☎ 972/203850, ℻ 972/203334. *45 rooms. Coffee shop. AE, DC, MC, V.*

Figueres

53 *37 km (23 mi) north of Girona.*

Figueres, a bustling country town and the capital of the Alt Empordà (Upper Ampurdan), is 37 km (23 mi) north of Girona on the A7 *autopista.* Walk along the **Figueres Rambla,** scene of the *passeig* (*paseo* in Castilian; the constitutional midday or evening stroll), and visit the **Museu Dalí,** a spectacular homage to a unique artist. The museum is installed in a former theater next to the bizarre, ocher-color Torre Galatea, where Dalí lived until his death in 1989. The remarkable Dalí collection includes a vintage Cadillac with ivy-cloaked passengers whom you can water for 25 pesetas. Dalí himself is entombed beneath the museum. 🎟 *Oct.–May 650 ptas., June–Sept. 1,000 ptas.* ☉ *Oct.–May, Tues.–Sun. 10:30–5:30; June–Sept., Tues.–Sun. 9–7:15.*

OFF THE BEATEN PATH | **AMPURDAN UPLANDS –** For a trip into the Ampurdan uplands, take the N II 10 km (6 mi) north of Figueres and turn west on Gi 502. Work your way 13 km (8 mi) west to the village of Maçanet de Cabrenys. From there, follow signs to the Santuari de les Salines, where you'll find a chapel and a tiny restaurant open in summer. Above Salines is one of the greatest beech forests in the Pyrenees. The new road from Maçanet goes to the village of Tapis and on to Coustouges.

DINING AND LODGING

$$$ ✕ **Ampurdan.** Hailed as the birthplace of modern Catalan cuisine, this restaurant 1½ km (1 mi) north of Figueres on the N II serves hearty portions of superb French, Catalan, and Spanish cooking in a simple setting. Try one of the fish mousses. ✉ *Carretera N II,* ☎ 972/500562. *AE, DC, MC, V.*

$$ ✕🏨 **Hotel Duran.** A well-known hotel and restaurant, the Duran is open every day of the year. Try the *lentilles amb morro de vadella* (lentils with calf snout) or the *mandonguilles amb sepia al estil Anna* (meatballs and cuttlefish), a *mar i muntunya* (surf and turf) specialty of the house. ✉ *C. Lasauca 5, 17600,* ☎ 972/501250. *65 rooms. AE, MC, V.*

Besalú

54 *34 km (21 mi) north of Girona.*

Besalú, once the capital of a feudal county as part of Charlemagne's 8th- and 9th-century Spanish March, is 25 km (15 mi) west of Figueres on C260. This ancient town's most emblematic feature is its **fortified bridge,** with crenellated battlements. Also, main sights are its two **churches,** Sant Vicenç and Sant Pere, and the ruins of the convent of **Santa Maria** on the hill above town. The tourist office is in the arcaded Plaça de la Llibertat and can provide current opening hours for Sant Pere as well as keys to the *migwe,* the unusual **Jewish baths** discovered in the 1960s.

The town of **Castellfollit de la Roca** perches on its prowlike basalt cliff over the Fluvià River 16 km (10 mi) west of Besalu.

Olot

55 *55 km (34 mi) northwest of Girona.*

Olot, the capital of the Garrotxa, is just 5 km (3 mi) from Castellfollit de la Roca. Famous for its 19th-century school of landscape painters, Olot has several excellent Art Nouveau buildings, including one with a facade by Domènech i Muntaner. The **Museu Comarcal de la Garrotxa** (County Museum of La Garrotxa) holds an important assemblage of Moderniste art and design as well as sculptures by Miquel Blai, creator of the long-tressed maidens who support the balconies along Olot's main boulevard. ⊠ *Carrer Hospici 8,* ☎ *972/279130.* ⊒ *450 ptas.* ◷ *Mon. and Wed.–Sat. 10–1 and 4–7, Sun. 10–1:30.*

The villages of **Vall d'En Bas** lie south of Olot off Route A153. A new freeway cuts across this countryside to Vic, but you'll miss a lot by taking it. The twisting old road will lead you through rich farmland past farmhouses characterized by dark wooden balconies bedecked with bright flowers. Turn off for **Sant Privat d'En Bas** and **Els Hostalets d'En Bas.**

DINING AND LODGING

$$$ ✕ **Restaurante Ramón.** Ramón is so exclusive that he adamantly refused to be in this book, so please don't let him see it. Olot's gourmet alcove par excellence, Restaurante Ramón is the opposite of rustic: sleek, modern, international, and refined. Samples of the *cuina de la terra* (home cooking of regional specialties) include *patata de Olot* (potato stuffed with veal) and *cassoleta de judias amb xoriç* (white haricot beans with sausage). ⊠ *Plaça Clarà 10,* ☎ *972/261001. Reservations essential. AE, DC, MC, V. Closed Thurs.*

$ ▦ **Hotel La Perla.** Known for its friendly, family ambience, this hotel is always Olot's first to fill up. On the edge of town toward the Vic Road, it's walking distance from two parks. ⊠ *Avda. Santa Coloma 97, 17800,* ☎ *972/262326,* 𝖥𝖠𝖷 *972/270774. 30 rooms, 30 apartments. Restaurant, bar. MC, V.*

Rupit

56 *97 km (60 mi) north of Barcelona.*

Rupit is a spectacular stop for its medieval houses and its cuisine, the highlight of which is beef-stuffed potatoes. Built into a rocky promontory over a stream in the rugged Collsacabra region, Rupit (about halfway from Olot to Vic) has some of the most aesthetically perfect stone houses in Catalonia, some of which were reproduced for Barcelona's Poble Espanyol.

DINING

$$ ✕ **El Repòs.** Hanging over the river that runs through Rupit, this restaurant serves the best meat-stuffed potatoes around. Ordering a meal is easy: just learn the word *patata.* Other specialties include duck and lamb. ✉ *C. Barbacana 1,* ☎ *93/856–5000. MC, V.*

Vic

57 *66 km (41 mi) north of Barcelona.*

Known for its conservatism and Catalan nationalism, Vic rests on a 1,600-ft plateau at the confluence of two rivers and serves as the area's commercial, industrial, and agricultural hub. Vic's wide **Plaça Major,** surrounded by Gothic arcades and well supplied with bars and cafés, perfectly expresses the city's personality. Vic's religiosity is demonstrated by its 35 churches, of which the largely neoclassical **cathedral** is the foremost. The 11th-century Romanesque tower, El Cloquer, built by the Abbot Oliva, and the powerful modern murals painted twice by Josep Maria Sert (first in 1930 and again after fire damage in 1945) are the cathedral's high points. Next door, the **Museu Episcopal** (Bishop's Museum) houses a fine collection of religious art and relics. ▦ *450 ptas. ⊙ Mon.–Sat. 10–1 and 4–7, Sun. 10–1:30.*

DINING AND LODGING

$$ ✕ **Ca l'U.** Translated as "The One," Ca l'U is in fact *the* place in Vic for hearty local cuisine with a minimum of pretense and expense. Try the *llangostinos i llenguado* (prawns and sole) or the regional standard, *botifarra i mongetas* (sausage and beans). ✉ *Plaça Santa Teresa 4–5,* ☎ *93/886–3504. MC, V. Closed Mon. No dinner Sun.*

$$$ ▦ **Parador de Vic.** This quietly charming parador, also known as the Parador del Bac de Sau, is 14 km (8½ mi) northeast of town off the Roda de Ter road past the village of Tavernoles. The views take in a stunning mountain and nearly lunar landscape over the Sau Reservoir. ✉ *Carretera Vic Roda de Ter, 08500,* ☎ *93/888–7311, 812–2323,* ℻ *93/812–2368. 36 rooms. Coffee shop, pool, tennis court. MC, V.*

Girona and Northern Catalonia Essentials

ARRIVING AND DEPARTING

By Bus: Sarfa (✉ Estació Norte–Vilanova Calle Alí Bei 80, ☎ 93/265–1158) has buses every 1½ hours to Girona, Figueres, and Cadaqués. For Vic try **Segalés** (Fabra i Puig Metro stop, ☎ 93/231–2756), and for Ripoll call **Teisa** (✉ Pau Claris 118, ☎ 93/488–2837).

By Car: Barcelona is now completely surrounded by a new network of *rondas,* or ring roads, with quick access from every corner of the city. Look for signs for these *rondas;* then follow signs to France (Francia), Girona, and the A7 *autopista,* which goes all the way to France. Leave the *autopista* at Salida (Exit) 7 for Girona. The 100-km (62-mi) ride to Girona takes about one hour.

By Train: Trains leave **Sants** and **Passeig de Gràcia** every 1½ hours for Girona, Figueres, and Port Bou. Some trains for northern Catalonia and France also leave from the França Station. For Vic and Ripoll, catch a Puigcerdà train (every hour or two) from Sants or Plaça de Catalunya.

GUIDED TOURS

Trenes Turísticos de RENFE (☎ 93/490–0202) operates guided tours to Girona by train May through September, leaving Sants at 10 AM and returning at 7:30 PM. It also runs train tours to Vic and Ripoll, leaving Sants at 9 AM and returning at 8:40 PM. The cost for each is 1,500 pesetas. Call RENFE to confirm.

The Costa Brava

The Costa Brava (Wild Coast) is a rocky stretch of shoreline that begins at Blanes and continues north through 135 km (84 mi) of coves and beaches to the French border at Port Bou. This tour concentrates on selected pockets—Tossa, Cap de Begur, Cadaqués—where the rocky terrain has discouraged the worst excesses of real-estate speculation. Here, on a good day, the luminous blue of the sea still contrasts with red-brown headlands and cliffs; the distant lights of fishing boats reflect on wine-color waters at dusk; and umbrella pines escort you to the fringes of secluded *calas* (coves) and sandy, white beaches.

Exploring the Costa Brava

⑤⑧ The closest Costa Brava beaches to Barcelona are at **Blanes,** where, between May and October, launches (✉ Crucetours, ☎ 972/314969) can take you to Cala de Sant Francesc or the double beach at Santa Cristina.

⑤⑨ The next stop north from Blanes along the coast road is **Tossa de Mar,** christened "blue paradise" by painter Marc Chagall, who summered here in 1934. The only Chagall painting in Spain is in Tossa's Museu Municipal (Municipal Museum, ☎ 972/340709, ▦ 350 ptas., ☉ Tues.–Sun. 10–1, 5–8). Tossa's walled medieval town and pristine beaches are both among Catalonia's best.

⑥⓪ **Sant Feliu de Guixols** comes next after Tossa de Mar, after 23 km (15 mi) of hairpin curves over hidden inlets. Tiny turnouts or parking spots on this route nearly always lead to intimate coves with stone stairways winding down from the road. Visit Sant Feliu's two fine beaches, church and monastery, Sunday market, and lovely Passeig del Mar.

⑥① **S'Agaró,** one of the Costa Brava's most elegant clusters of villas and seaside mansions, is just 3 km (2 mi) north of Sant Feliu. The 30-minute walk along the sea wall from La Gavina to Sa Conca beach is a delight.

Up the coast from S'Agaró, a road leads east to **Llafranc,** a small port

⑥② with quiet waterfront hotels and restaurants, and forks right to **Calella de Palafrugell,** a pretty fishing village known for its July Habaneras (Catalan-Cuban sea chanties inspired by the Spanish-American War) festival. Just south is the panoramic promontory **Cap Roig,** with views of the barren Formigues (Ants) Isles and a fine botanical garden that you can tour with a guide for 450 ptas. March–December, daily 9–9. The left fork drops down to **Tamariu,** one of the Costa's prettiest inlet towns. A climb over the bluff leads down to the parador at **Aiguablava,** a modern eyesore overlooking magnificent cliffs and crags.

⑥③ From **Begur,** the next town north of Aiguablava, you can go east through the *calas* or take the more inland route past the rose-color stone houses and ramparts of the restored medieval town of **Pals.** Nearby **Peratallada** is another medieval town with fortress, castle, tower, palace, and well-preserved walls. North of Pals there are signs for Ullastret, an Iberian village dating from the 5th century BC. L'Estartit is

⑥④ the jumping-off point for spectacular **Parc Natural Submarí** (Underwater Natural Park), at the Medes Isles, famous for diving and for underwater photography.

⑥⑤ The Greco-Roman ruins at **Empúries** are Catalonia's most important archaeological site. This port, complete with breakwater, is considered one of the most monumental ancient engineering feats on the Iberian Peninsula. As the Greek's original point of arrival in Spain, Empúries was also where the Olympic Flame entered Spain for Barcelona's 1992 Olympic Games.

⑥⑥ The **Aiguamolls** (Marshlands), an important nature reserve filled with migratory waterfowl from all over Europe, lies mainly around **Castelló d'Empúries**, but the main information center is at El Cortalet, on the road in from Sant Pere Pescador. Follow the road from Empúries, crossing the Fluvià River at Sant Pere Pescador, and proceed north through the wetlands to Castelló. From Castelló d'Empúries, a series of roadways and footpaths traverse the marshes, the latter well marked on the maps available at the information center.

⑥⑦ **Cadaqués,** Spain's easternmost town, still has the whitewashed charm that made this fishing village into an international artists' haunt in the early 20th century. The Marítim is the central hangout both day and night; after dark, you might also enjoy the Jardí, across the square. Salvador Dalí's house (now a museum) still stands at Portlligat, a 30-minute walk north of town.

The **Museu Perrot-Moore,** in the old town, has an important collection of graphic arts dating from the 15th to the 20th centuries, including works by Dalí. ⌨ *400 ptas.* ⊘ *June 15–Oct. 15, daily 5–9.*

You can now visit the **Casa Museu Salvador Dalí,** a site long associated with Dalí's summer frolics with everyone from poets such as Federico García Lorca and Paul Eluard (whose wife, Gala, became Dalí's muse and spouse) to filmmaker Luis Buñuel. Filled with bits and pieces of the surrealist's daily life, it's an important point in the "Dalí triangle," completed by the castle at Púbol and the Museu Dalí, in Figueres. ⊠ ⊠ *Port Lligat (3-km walk from town center, along beach,* ☎ *972/ 258063.* ⌨ *1,200 ptas.* ⊘ *Tues.–Sun. 10:30–5:30*

The **Castillo Pubol,** Dalí's former castle-home, is now the resting place of Gala, his perennial model and mate. It's a chance to wander through yet more Dalí-esque landscape: lush gardens, fountains decorated with Wagner (the couple's favorite composer) masks, distinctive elephants with giraffe's legs and clawed feet. Two lions and a giraffe stand guard near Gala's tomb. ⊠ ⊠ *Rte. 255 toward La Bisbal, 15 km (9 mi) east of A7's exit 6,* ☎ *972/511800.* ⌨ *600 ptas.* ⊘ *Daily mid-March–June, 10:30–5:30, July–Sept., 10:30–7:30. Closed Oct.–mid-March.*

⑥⑧ **Cap de Creus,** just north of Cadaqués, Spain's easternmost point, is a fundamental pilgrimage, if only for the symbolic geographical rush. The hike out to the lighthouse—through rosemary, thyme, and the salt air of the Mediterranean—is unforgettable. The Pyrenees officially end (or rise) here. New Year's Day finds mobs of revelers here awaiting the first emergence of the "new" sun from the Mediterranean.

⑥⑨ The monastery of **Sant Pere de Rodes,** 7 km (4.3 mi) by car, plus a 20-minute walk, above the pretty fishing village El Port de la Selva, is the last and one of the most spectacular sites on the Costa Brava. Built in the 10th and early 11th centuries by Benedictine monks—and sacked and plundered repeatedly since—this Romanesque monolith commands a breathtaking panorama of the Pyrenees, the Empordà plain, the sweeping curve of the Bay of Roses, and Cap de Creus. (Topping off the grand trek across the Pyrenees, the Cap de Creus is a 6-hour walk away on the well-marked GR11 trail.)

Dining and Lodging

AIGUABLAVA

$$ ▦ **Parador de la Costa Brava.** This modern parador stands on a promontory overlooking sheer cliffs and surging seas. The service is impeccable. ⊠ *Parador Nacional Aiguablava, 17255, Begur, Girona,* ☎ *972/622162,* ℻ *972/622166. 87 rooms. Restaurant, minibars, pool. AE, DC, MC, V.*

CADAQUÉS

$$$$ ✕ **El Bulli.** This famous restaurant is one of the top three or four in
★   Spain. It's located in Cala Montjoi, near Roses, 7 km (4½ mi) from
Cadaqués by sea or footpath and 22 km (14 mi) by car. Chef Fernando
Adrià will astound and delight your palate with his 12-course taster's
menu. ✉ *Cala Montjoi, Roses, Girona,* ☎ *972/150457. AE, DC, MC,
V. Closed Mon.–Tues.*

$$ ✕ **Can Pelayo.** This tiny, family-run restaurant serves the best fish in
town. It's hidden behind Plaça Port Alguer, a few minutes' walk south
of the town center ✉ *Carrer Nou 11,* ☎ *972/258356. MC, V. Closed
weekdays Oct.–May.*

$$–$$$ ✕⌷ **Hotel Rocamar.** Rocamar has modern rooms with splendid views,
excellent service, and first-rate cuisine with no gourmet pretensions.
✉ *C. Doctor Bartomeus s/n, 17488 Cadaqués, Girona,* ☎ *972/258150,*
FAX *972/258650. 70 rooms. Restaurant, bar, indoor pool, tennis court.
AE, DC, MC, V.*

$$ ⌷ **Hotel LlanéPetit.** This intimate little inn is just below the Rocamar
at beach level. It's charming, slightly less expensive, and has a very
Mediterranean air. ✉ *C. Doctor Bartomeus 37, 17488 Cadaqués,
Girona,* ☎ *972/258050,* FAX *972/258778. 37 rooms. Bar, breakfast room.
AE, DC, MC, V.*

CAP DE CREUS

$$ ✕⌷ **Bar Cap de Creus.** Right next to the Cap de Creus lighthouse, this
restaurant commands spectacular views. The cuisine is simple and
good, and proprietor Chris Little rents three apartments (four beds each)
upstairs. ✉ *Cap de Creus s/n, 17488 Cadaqués, Girona,* ☎ *972/
159271. MC, V. Closed Mon.–Thurs. Oct.–June.*

PALAFRUGELL

$$ ✕ **Cypsele.** This restaurant serves such local fare as *es niu,* an explosive combination of game fowl, fish tripe, pork meatballs, and cuttle-
fish, stewed in a rich sauce. ✉ *C. Ancha 22,* ☎ *972/199005. MC, V.*

PERETALLADA

$$ ✕ **Can Bonay.** The fine local cuisine includes duck with turnips and
pig's feet with snails. The look is rustic, but the quality is first-rate. ✉
Plaça Espanya 4, ☎ *972/634034. MC, V.*

S'AGARÓ

$$$$ ⌷ **El Hostal de la Gavina.** At the eastern corner of Sant Pol beach, this
hotel is a superb display of design and cuisine founded in 1932 by Josep
Ensesa, who invented S'Agaró itself. The Gavina offers complete com-
fort, superb dining, and tennis, golf, and riding nearby. ✉ *Plaça de la
Rosaleda s/n, 17248,* ☎ *972/321100,* FAX *972/321573. Restaurant. AE,
DC, MC, V.*

TAMARIU

$$ ✕ **Royal.** This sunny, beachside spot serves fisherman-style creations
of superb freshness and quality. The *suquet* (fish cooked slowly to create
its own juice, or *suc*) is especially commendable. ✉ *Passeig de Mar 9,*
☎ *972/620041. MC, V.*

TOSSA DE MAR

$$–$$$ ⌷ **Hotel Mar Menuda.** This modern hideaway on the Costa Brava of-
fers as much peace and quiet—*and* as many varieties of water sports—
as you can possibly handle. Equipment and instruction are available
for windsurfing, sailing, swimming, and scuba diving. The hotel terrace overlooks the coast and the town of Tossa de Mar, with a medieval
castle and an old quarter full of cobbled streets. ✉ *Playa Mar Menuda*

s/n, 17320 Tossa de Mar, Girona, ☎ *972/341000,* FAX *972/340087. 40 rooms, 10 suites. Restaurant, pool, tennis court. AE, DC, MC, V. Closed Nov.1–Dec. 27.*

Costa Brava Essentials

ARRIVING AND DEPARTING

By Bus: Buses to Blanes, Lloret, Sant Feliu de Guixols, Platja d'Aro, Palamos, Begur, Roses, and Cadaqués are operated by **Sarfa** (✉ Estació de Norte-Vilanova, C. Ali-Bei 80, ☎ 93/265–1158; Metro Arc de Triomf).

By Car: From Barcelona, the fastest way to the Costa Brava is to start up the A7 *autopista* as if to Girona and take Salida (Exit) 10 for Blanes. Coastal traffic can be slow and frustrating, and the roads tortuous.

By Train: A local train pokes along the coast to Blanes from Sants and Passeig de Gràcia or from Plaça Catalunya.

GUIDED TOURS

Between June 1 and September 31, Julià and Pullmantur run coach and cruise tours to Empúries, L'Estartit, the Medes Isles underwater park, and the medieval town of Pals. The Medes Isles stop includes lunch, swimming, and underwater exploration. Buses leave Barcelona at 9 and return at 6. The price per person is 10,500 pesetas with lunch, 8,250 pesetas without.

BARCELONA A TO Z

Arriving and Departing

By Bus

Barcelona has no central bus station, but most buses to Spanish destinations operate from the **Estació Norte Vilanova** (✉ End of Av. Vilanova, a couple of blocks east of Arc de Triomf, ☎ 93/245–2528). Most international buses arrive at and depart from the **Estació Autobuses de Sants** (✉ Carrer Viriato, next to Sants train station, ☎ 93/490–4000). Scores of independent companies operate from depots dispersed throughout town (☞ Excursions *in* Guided Tours, *below*).

By Car

Don't be intimidated by either driving or parking here. You can usually find a legal and safe parking place on the street, and underground public parking is increasingly plentiful.

By Plane

All international and domestic flights arrive at the spectacular glass, steel, and marble **El Prat de Llobregat** airport, 14 km (8½ mi) south of Barcelona, just off the main highway to Castelldefels and Sitges. For information on arrival and departure times, call Iberia at the airport (☎ 93/401–3131, 93/401–3535, or 93/301–3993; 93/302–7656 for international reservations and confirmations).The only airlines with direct flights from the United States to Barcelona are TWA and Delta.

Check first to see if your hotel provides a free shuttle service; otherwise, you can high-tail it into town via train, bus, taxi, or rental car.

BETWEEN THE AIRPORT AND DOWNTOWN

By Bus. The Aerobus leaves the airport for Plaça de Catalunya every 15 minutes (6 AM–11 PM) on weekdays and every 30 minutes (6:30 AM–10:50 PM) on weekends. From Plaça de Catalunya, it leaves for the airport every 15 minutes (5:30 AM–10:05 PM) on weekdays and every 30 minutes (6:30 AM–10:50 PM) on weekends. The fare is 500 pesetas.

By Car. Follow signs to the Centre Ciutat and you'll enter the city along Gran Via. For the port area, follow signs for the Ronda Litoral. The journey to the center of town can take anywhere from 15 to 45 minutes depending on traffic. Allow 15 minutes before 7:30 in the morning or after 9 at night.

By Taxi. Cab fare from the airport into town is 2,500–3,000 pesetas.

By Train. The train leaves the airport every 30 minutes between 6:12 AM and 10:13 PM. This train stops first at the Sants-Estació, then at Plaça de Catalunya, later at the Arc de Trionf, and finally at Clot. Trains going to the airport begin at 6 AM from the Clot station, stopping at the Arc de Trionf at 6:05 AM, Plaça de Catalunya at 6:08 AM, and Sants at 6:13 AM. The fare is 350 pesetas on weekdays, 375 pesetas on weekends and holidays.

By Train

Almost all long-distance and international trains arrive and depart from the **Sants-Estació** (⊠ Plaça dels Països Catalans s/n, ☏ 93/490–0202). En route to or from Sants, some trains stop at another station on **Passeig de Gràcia** (⊠ At Aragó, ☏ 93/490–0202). The Passeig de Gràcia station is often a good way to avoid the long lines that form at Sants during holidays. The **Estació de França** (⊠ Avda. Marques Argentera s/n, ☏ 93/319–3200), near the port, handles certain long-distance trains within Spain, some international trains, and particularly trains to and from France.

Getting Around

Modern Barcelona, above the Plaça de Catalunya, is built on a grid system, though there's no coordinated numbering system. The old town, from the Plaça de Catalunya to the port, is a labyrinth of narrow streets, and you'll need a good street map to get around it. Most sightseeing can be done on foot—you won't have any choice in the Barri Gòtic—but you'll need to use the metro or buses to link sightseeing areas. The Dia T1 is valid for one day of unlimited travel on all subway, bus, and FFCC lines. For general information on public transport, call 93/412–0000. Maps showing bus and metro routes are available free from booths in Plaça de Catalunya.

By Boat

Golondrinas harbor boats make short trips from the Portal de la Pau, near the Columbus Monument. The fare is 500 pesetas for a 30-minute trip. Departures are spring and summer (Holy Week through Sept.), daily 11–7; fall and winter, weekends and holidays only, 11–5. It's closed December 16–January 2. For information call ☏ 93/442–3106.

By Bus

City buses run daily from 5:30 AM to 11:30 PM. The fare is 145 pesetas (155 pesetas Sunday and holidays); for multiple journeys purchase a Targeta T1, which buys you 10 rides for 800 pesetas (like the metro's T2, plus buses). Route maps are displayed at bus stops. Note that those with a red band always stop at a central square—Catalunya, Universitat, or Urquinaona—and blue indicates a night bus. From June 12 to October 12 the **Bus Turistic** (9:30–7:30 every 30 minutes) runs on a circuit that passes all the important sights. A day's ticket, which you can buy on the bus, costs 1,300 pesetas (850 pesetas half day) and also covers the fare for the Tramvía Blau, funicular, and Montjuïc cable car across the port. The ride starts at Plaça de Catalunya.

By Cable Car and Funicular

The Montjuïc Funicular is a cog railroad that runs from the junction of Avinguda Paral.lel and Nou de la Rambla to the Miramar Amusement Park on Montjuïc (Metro: Paral.lel). It operates weekends and holidays 11 AM–8 PM in winter, and daily 11 AM–9:30 PM in summer; the fare is 145 pesetas. A *telefèric* then takes you from the amusement park up to Montjuïc Castle. In winter the *telefèric* runs weekends and holidays 11–2:45 and 4–7:30; in summer, daily 11:30–9. The fare is 375 pesetas.

A Transbordador Aeri Harbor Cable Car runs between Miramar and Montjuïc across the harbor to Torre de Jaume I on Barcelona's *moll* (quay), and on to Torre de Sant Sebastià, at the end of Passeig Joan de Borbó in Barceloneta. You can board at either stage. The fare is 850 pesetas (1,000 pesetas round-trip), and the car runs October–June, week-days noon–5:45, weekends noon–6:15, and July–September, daily 11–9.

To reach the summit of Tibidabo, take the metro to Avinguda de Tibi-dabo, then the Tramvía Blau (275 pesetas one-way) to Peu del Funicu-lar, and finally the Tibidabo Funicular (375 pesetas one-way) from there to the Tibidabo fairground. It runs every 30 minutes, 7:05 AM–9:35 PM ascending, 7:25 AM–9:55 PM descending.

By Metro
The subway is the fastest, cheapest, and easiest way to get around Barcelona. You pay a flat fare of 135 pesetas no matter how far you travel, but it's more economical to buy a Targeta T2 (valid for metro and FFCC Generalitat trains, Tramvía Blau [blue tram], and the Mon-tjuïc Funicular; ☞ *above*), which costs 700 pesetas for 10 rides. The system runs 5 AM–11 PM (until 1 AM on weekends and holidays).

By Taxi
Taxis are black and yellow and show a green light when available for hire. The meter starts at 325 pesetas (which lasts for six minutes), and there are supplements for luggage, night travel, Sundays and holidays, rides from a station or to the airport, and for going to or from the bull-ring or a football match. There are cab stands all over town, and you can also hail cabs on the street. Make sure the driver turns on the meter. To call a cab, try ☎ 93/387–1000, 93/490–2222, or 93/357–7755, 24 hours a day.

Guided Tours

Excursions
These are run by **Julià Tours** and **Pullmantur** and are booked as out-lined below. The most popular trips are full or half-day tours to Montserrat and day trips to the Costa Brava resorts, including a cruise to the Medes Isles.

Orientation
Urban sightseeing tours are run by **Julià Tours** (✉ Ronda Universitat 5, ☎ 93/317–6454) and **Pullmantur** (✉ Gran Via 635, ☎ 93/318–5195).Tours leave from these offices, but you may be able to arrange a pick up at your hotel. Prices are 4,600 pesetas for a half day and 11,750 pesetas for a full day, including lunch.

Personal Guides
Contact **City Guides Barcelona** (☎ 93/412–0674), the **Barcelona Guide Bureau** (☎ 93/268–2422), or the **Asociación Profesional de Infor-madores Turísticos** (93/319–8416) for a list of English-speaking guides.

Special-Interest and Walking Tours
La Ruta del Modernismo (The Modernism Route), created by Barcelona's *ajuntament* (town hall), connects some 50 key sites in the city's rich endowment of Art Nouveau architecture. Everything from Gaudí's first lamppost to the colossal Sagrada Família to the odd Moderniste phar-

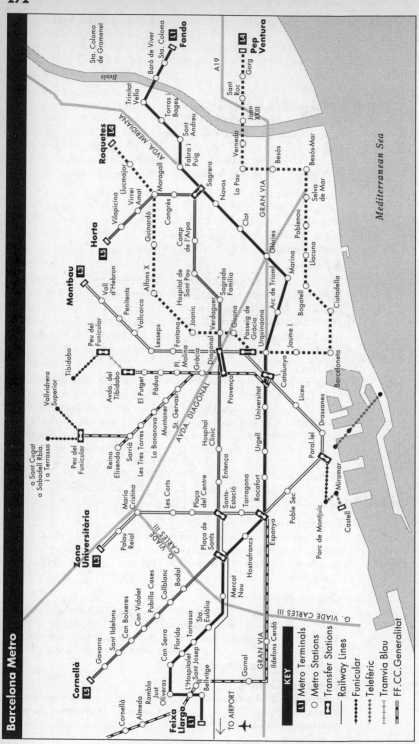

macy or bakery shows up in this comprehensive route, along with guided visits of buildings not open to the general public. Palau Güell (⊠ Carrer Nou de Rambla 3–5, ☎ 93/317–3974) is the tour's "kilometer zero." You can also buy the ticket, which covers admission to all sites on the walk, at the Casa Lleó Morera (⊠ Passeig de Gràcia 35, ☎ 93/488–0139). The price is 1,500 pesetas for adults. Both offices are open Monday–Saturday 10–7.

The bookstore in the Palau de la Virreina (⊠ La Rambla 99) rents cassettes whose walking tours follow footprints painted on sidewalks—different colors for different tours—through Barcelona's most interesting areas. The do-it-yourself method is to pick up the guides produced by the tourist office, *Discovering Romanesque Art* and *Discovering Modernist Art,* which have art itineraries for all of Catalonia.

Contacts and Resources

Bicycle Rental
Try **Bicitram** (⊠ Marquès de l'Argentera 15, ☎ 93/792–2841) and **Los Filicletos** (⊠ Passeig de Picasso 38, ☎ 93/319–7811). **Un Menys**—"One Less," in Catalan, meaning one less car on the streets of Barcelona—organizes increasingly popular outings that tack drinks, dinner, and dancing onto a gentle bike ride for a total price of about 5,000 pesetas. ⊠ *Esparteria 3,* ☎ *93/268–2105,* FAX *93/319–4298 AE, DC, MC, V.*

Car and Motorcycle Rental
Atesa (⊠ Balmes 141, ☎ 93/237–8140), **Avis** (⊠ Casanova 209, ☎ 93/209–9533), **Hertz** (⊠ Tuset 10, ☎ 93/217–3248), and **Vanguard** (cars and motorcycles; ⊠ Londres 31, ☎ 93/439–3880).

Consulates
United States (⊠ Passeig Reina Elisenda 23, ☎ 93/280–2227), **Canada** (⊠ Via Augusta 125, ☎ 93/209–0634), **United Kingdom** (⊠ Diagonal 477, ☎ 93/419–9044).

Emergencies
Tourist Attention, a service provided by the local police department, will provide assistance if you've been the victim of a crime, need medical or psychological help, or need temporary documents in the event of loss of the originals. English interpreters are on hand. ⊠ *Guardia Urbana, Ramblas 43,* ☎ *93/301–9060.*

Other emergency services: **Police** (☎ 091 national police; 092 municipal police; main police station: ⊠ Via Laietana 43, ☎ 93/301–6666). **Ambulance** (Creu Roja, ☎ 93/300–2020). **Hospital** (Hospital Clínic: ⊠ Villarroel 170; ☎ 93/454–6000/7000; Metro Hospital Clinic, blue line). **Emergency doctors** (☎ 061).

English-Language Bookstores
BCN Books (⊠ Aragó 277, ☎ 93/487–3455) is one of Barcelona's top stores for books in English. **El Corte Inglés** (⊠ Plaça de Catalunya 14, ☎ 93/302–1212; ⊠ Diagonal 617, ☎ 93/419–2828) sells English guidebooks and novels, but the selection is limited.For more variety, try the **English Bookshop** (Entença 63, ☎ 93/425–4466), **Jaimes Bookshop** (⊠ Passeig de Gràcia 64, ☎ 93/215–3626), **Laie** (⊠ Pau Claris 85, ☎ 93/318–1357), **Libreria Francesa** (⊠ Passeig de Gràcia 91, ☎ 93/215–1417), **Come In** (⊠ Provença 203, ☎ 93/253–1204), or **Libreria Bosch** (⊠ Ronda Universitat 11, ☎ 93/317–5308; ⊠ Roselló 24, ☎ 93/321–3341). The bookstore at the **Palau de la Virreina** (⊠ La Rambla 99, ☎ 93/301–7775) has good books on art, design, and Barcelona in general.

Late-Night Pharmacies

Look on the door of any pharmacy or in any local newspaper under "Farmacias de Guardia" for the addresses of those open late at night or 24 hours. Alternately, dial 010.

Travel Agencies

American Express (⊠ Roselló 257, at Passeig de Gràcia, ☎ 93/217–0070), **Iberia** (⊠ Diputació 258, at Passeig de Gràcia, ☎ 93/401–3381; ⊠ Plaça de Espanya, ☎ 93/325–7358), **WagonsLits Cook** (⊠ Passeig de Gràcia 8, ☎ 93/317–5500), and **Bestours** (⊠ Diputación 241, ☎ 93/487–8580).

Visitor Information

Tourist offices dealing with primarily with Barcelona are at the **Centre d'Informació Turistic de Barcelona** (⊠ Plaça de Catalunya 17, lower level, ☎ 93/304–3135, ℻ 93/304–3155; ⊙ daily 9–9); **Sants-Estació,** open daily 8–8; **Estació França,** open daily 8–8; **Palau de Congressos** (⊠ Av. María Cristina s/n), open daily 10–8 during trade fairs and congresses only; **ajuntament** (⊠ Plaça Sant Jaume), open June 24–September, weekdays 9–8 and Saturday 8:30–2:30; and **Palau de la Virreina** (⊠ La Rambla 99), open Monday–Saturday 9–9 and Sunday 10–2.

Offices with information about Catalonia and the rest of Spain are at **El Prat Airport** (☎ 93/478–4704), open Monday–Saturday 9:30–8 and Sunday 9:30–3, and **Centre d'Informació Turística** (⊠ Palau Robert, Passeig de Gràcia 107 [at Diagonal], ☎ 93/238–4000), open Monday–Saturday 10–7. For general information and referrals in English, dial 010.

In summer (July 24–September 15), **tourist information aides** patrol the Gothic Quarter and Ramblas area 9 AM–9 PM; they travel in pairs and are recognizable by their uniforms of red shirts, white trousers or skirts, and badges.

8 Southern Catalonia and the Levante

Down the coast of Southern Catalonia's Tarragona province and the Valencia region—known as the Levante because the sun rises (se levanta) out of the Mediterranean here—a landscape of grayish, arid mountains backs a lush coast of sandy beaches, many marred by modern tourist developments. Inland, the rugged landscape is dotted with small fortified towns that were strategically important in medieval times. Tarragona bursts with Roman antiquities, and Valencia, Spain's third-largest city, is rich in art and architecture.

By Philip Eade

Updated by
Katherine
Semler

THIS REGION STRADDLES CATALUNYA (Catalonia) and Valencia, allowing you to sample the differences and similarities between these two feuding Mediterranean cousins. Valencia was part of the House of Aragon, Catalonia's medieval Mediterranean empire, after Jaume I conquered it in the 13th century; staunch Valencian nationalists still regard Catalonia and the Catalan language much as Catalonia regards Madrid and central Spain. Valencia was incorporated, along with Catalonia, into a united Spanish state in the 15th century, but the most energetic cultivators of Valencia's separate cultural and linguistic identity still resent their centuries of Catalan domination. You will notice the subtle differences in the two languages as you move south. Catalan prevails in Tarragona, a city and province of Catalonia, but Valenciano, widely considered (though generally not by Valencianos themselves) a dialect of Catalan, is spoken and written on street signs in the Valencian provinces.

The *huerta* (fertile, irrigated coastal plain) is devoted mainly to citrus and vegetable farming, which lends color to the landscape and fragrance to the air. Grayish, arid mountains provide a stark backdrop to the lush coast. These shores have seen Phoenician, Greek, Carthaginian, and Roman visitors; the Romans stayed several centuries, and there are now archaeological reminders of them all the way down the coast, particularly in Tarragona, the capital of Rome's Spanish empire by 218 BC. Rome's dominion did not go uncontested, however; the most serious challenge came from the Carthaginians of North Africa. The three Punic Wars, fought over this territory between 264 BC and 146 BC, led to the immortalization of the Carthaginian general Hannibal.

The same coastal farmland and beaches that attracted the ancients have called to modern-day tourists, and unfortunately a chain of ugly developments has marred much of the shore. Venturing inland, however, you'll discover a completely different world, where tourism is not the decisive fact of life and where local culture has survived intact. This rugged and often strikingly beautiful territory is dotted with small, fortified towns, several of which bear the name of Spain's 11th-century national hero, El Cid, as proof of the battles he fought here against the Moors 900 years ago. Each has its porticoed Plaza Mayor, whitewashed houses, and countless coats of arms as further reminders of the town's strategic importance in medieval times.

The city of Valencia, founded by the Greeks, was in Moorish hands from 712 to 1238, apart from a brief interlude from 1094 to 1102, when El Cid reconquered the city. The *azulejos* (glazed, patterned tiles) and the bright-blue cupolas on churches reflect Moorish traditions. Spain's golden age left striking souvenirs of the 15th century as well: the Gothic Lonja (Silk Exchange) and mansions, the Primitive paintings of Jacomart and Juan Reixach housed in the Museum of Fine Arts. The flamboyant, 18th-century Palacio de los Dos Aguas embodies the vitality of Churriguerismo, or the early Spanish baroque.

Pleasures and Pastimes

Beaches
If you've just come from the Costa Brava, you'll find the beaches in this area to be quite different, with endless strands of fine-grain sand. Salou has the best beaches at the northern end, along with a lively, palm-lined promenade. More tranquil are the beaches of the Ebro Delta, the best of which is the Playa de los Eucaliptos, reached by a pretty road from Amposta via Montells. Peñíscola's beach seems to go on forever;

the sand is soft, and the old city rises up out of the sea at one end as a scenic bonus. Alcocéber has a series of small, uncrowded, sandy crescents, and just to its north is the sophisticated new marina at Las Fuentes. Benicàssim's long, crescent-shaped beach has the most dramatic setting of all, with mountains rising steeply in the background. Valencia itself has a long beach that's wonderful for sunning and has numerous seaside restaurants, but it's not the best place for swimming; for cleaner water, you need to head south as far as El Saler.

Dining

Romesco (a spicy blend of hazelnuts, peppers, and olive oil) hails from Tarragona and is used as a sauce for fish and seafood, especially in the *calçotada* (spring onion) feasts of February. If you're here during the September Santa Tecla festival, you can try the *espineta amb cargolins* (tuna fish with snails), perhaps accompanied by some excellent wine from the nearby Penedés or Priorato vineyards. The Ebro Delta is renowned for its fresh fish-eels, as well as specialties like *rossejat* (fried rice in a fish broth, dressed with garlic sauce). *Jamones* (hams), *cecinas* (smoked meats), and *carnes a la brasa* (meats cooked over coals) all feature in Maestrazgan (mountain) cooking, together with good *trucha* (trout) and *conejo* (rabbit). You should also try the *trufas* (truffles) that grow here. In Valencia and all along the Mediterranean coast you are in the land of *paella Valenciana* (a rice dish flavored with saffron and embellished with seafood, poultry, meat, peas, and peppers), Spain's most famous dish. Prepared to order in a *caldero* (shallow pan), paella takes a good 20 minutes to cook, so it is not for visitors in a hurry. Good paella is fabulous, but it's often overpriced due to tourist demand, and should never be chosen from a *menú del día*, where it is often tasteless and disappointing. A variant is *arroz a la banda*, in which the fish and rice are cooked separately; the fish is fried in garlic, onion, and tomato, and the rice is boiled in the resulting stock.

CATEGORY	COST*
$$$$	over 6,000 ptas.
$$$	4,000–6,000 ptas.
$$	2,000–4,000 ptas.
$	under 2,000 ptas.

per person for a three-course meal, excluding drinks, service, and tax

Fiestas

Tarragona's most important fiestas are those of St. Magí (August 19) and St. Tecla (September 23), both characterized by colorful processions. In Valencia, Las Fallas fill a week in March and reach their climax on March 19, Día de San José (St. Joseph's Day), when families throughout Spain celebrate Father's Day. This time-honored fiesta grew from the fact that St. Joseph is also the patron saint of carpenters; in medieval times, carpenters' guilds celebrated his feast day by making huge bonfires with their wood shavings. Today Valencia explodes into a weeklong celebration of fireworks, flower-strewn floats, carnival processions, top bullfights, and uncontrolled merrymaking to which Spaniards and tourists both flock. On March 19, huge and often grotesque satirical effigies of popular and not-so-popular figures are ceremoniously burned, creating a surprising sense of nostalgia of the ephemerality of life itself. If you're allergic to firecrackers or large crowds, stay away from this one.

Lodging

Tarragona's hotels are fairly uninspiring, but this problem disappears by the time you reach the Ebro and the Maestrazgo mountains, where antique, one-of-a-kind lodgings are in gratifying abundance. On the coast, lodgings become more mundane, with modern high-rises predominating. We suggest hotels elsewhere on the coast, more because you may wish to stop in these locales than because the hotels are destinations in themselves. Just to the north and south of Valencia, in Puzol and El Saler, are some famous luxury hotels, while in the city itself there is a reasonable range of both old and modern hotels for every budget. If you plan to be in Valencia for the Falla celebrations in mid-March, you'd best book your accommodations months ahead; prices are sure to rise as the festivities approach.

CATEGORY	COST*
$$$$	over 16,500 ptas.
$$$	9,500–16,500 ptas.
$$	6,000–9,500 ptas.
$	under 6,000 ptas.

All prices are for a standard double room, excluding tax.

Exploring Tarragona to Valencia

Numbers in the text correspond to numbers in the margin and on the Southern Catalonia and the Levante and Valencia maps.

Great Itineraries

Mountain villages; wetlands; sweeping beaches; cities filled with art, architecture, and archaeology—there is much to see and do between Tarragona and Valencia. Tarragona is distinguished by its extraordinarily well preserved Roman remains. Next comes the fertile Delta de l'Ebro (Ebro Delta), rich in fauna and flora, followed by the ancient town of Tortosa, where you can enjoy a splendid night in the hilltop parador. A rewarding loop inland explores the wild and remote Beceite and Maestrazgo mountains, including the ancient, contoured town of Morella. The Costa del Azahar (Orange Blossom Coast) down to Valencia is characterized by orange groves against a backdrop of arid hills. Peñíscola, a cluster of white houses on a promontory, is highly picturesque, though it is sadly becoming surrounded by tourist development. Farther south, the Roman town of Sagunto is of architectural note, with its hilltop fortress and amphitheater. Finally, you reach Valencia, a trove of art and architecture whose highlights include the Gothic Lonja (Silk Exchange), the striking, baroque Palacio Marqués de Dos Aguas, and the superb Museum of Fine Arts.

IF YOU HAVE 3 DAYS

If you have three days, see **Tarragona** ① and its Roman ruins before moving on to the **Ebro Delta** ⑤ for a late lunch at the restaurant-museum Estany, near Villafranca del Delta. Next, drive up the Ebro River for a night at the Parador Castillo de la Zuda in 🏨 **Tortosa** ⑥. On the second day, explore the Beceite and Maestrazgo mountains, passing through Miravet, **Gandesa** ⑦, Calaceite, Valderrobres, Beceite, Fredes, and **Morella** ⑩ on the way to coastal Vinaròs and 🏨 **Peñíscola** ⑭, where you can stop for the night. The final day can be devoted to **Valencia** ⑯–㉝.

IF YOU HAVE 5 DAYS

Begin at **Tarragona** ① and spend the night in the 🏨 **Ebro Delta** ⑤. Explore the delta for a day, including a late lunch at the restaurant-museum Estany, near Villafranca del Delta, before driving up to 🏨 **Tortosa** ⑥ for a night at the Parador Castillo de la Zuda. Day three can be devoted to the Beceite Mountains, with visits to Miravet, **Gandesa** ⑦, Calaceite, Valderrobres, Beceite, and Fredes before an overnight rest in 🏨 **Morella** ⑩. On the fourth day, drive through the Maestrazgo mountains for a look at some of the least-visited valleys and villages on the Iberian Peninsula. Take the slow but scenic CS802 up through

Southern Catalonia and the Levante

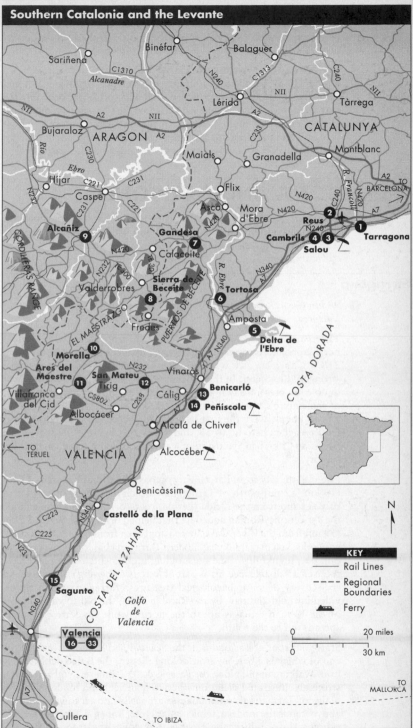

Sariñena

Binéfar

Balaguer

Lérida

Tàrrega

Alcanadre

C1310

N240

C1313

C240

NII

NII

NII

A2

CATALUNYA

Bujaraloz

ARAGON

NII

A2

Montblanc

A2

TO BARCELONA

Río

Maials

Granadella

N420

C233

C240

R. Francolí

N420

Ebro

C230

C231

Flix

N420

N420

Reus

2

A7

Híjar

C221

C231

Asco

N420

Mora d'Ebre

N240

1

Tarragona

C221

Alcañiz

9

Gandesa

7

Calaceite

Cambrils

4 **3**

Salou

CORDILLERA'S RANGE

N232

C300

Sierra de Beceite

R. Ebre

Tortosa

6

N340

A7

Valderrobres

8

PUERTOS DE BECEITE

Amposta

COSTA DORADA

EL MAESTRAZGO

Fredes

Delta de l'Ebre

5

N340

A7

Morella

10

N232

Vinaròs

Ares del Maestre

11

San Mateu

Tirig

12

Cálig

A7

Benicarló

13

Villafranca del Cid

C5802

C238

Peñíscola

14

Albocácer

Alcalá de Chivert

TO TERUEL

VALENCIA

Alcocéber

Benicàssim

Castelló de la Plana

C223

N340

A7

C225

N23

COSTA DEL AZAHAR

KEY

— Rail Lines

--- Regional Boundaries

🚢 Ferry

15

Sagunto

N340

Golfo de Valencia

N

A7

Valencia

16 — **33**

0 ——— 20 miles

0 ——— 30 km

TO MALLORCA

A7

N340

Cullera

TO IBIZA

Iglesuela del Cid and around to Villafranca del Cid before driving through **Ares del Maestre** ⑪, Albocácer, and **San Mateu** ⑫ on your way to ⛱ **Peñíscola** ⑭, where you can spend the night. On the fifth day, travel down through the Costa del Azahar to ⛱ **Valencia** ⑯–㉝.

When to Tour Tarragona and Valencia

It's best to avoid this region in the summer. The weather is hot and arid, and the beaches are crowded. Fall and spring are probably the best times to visit, but anyone who has seen the slanting December light in the delta or the dramatic shadows that the winter sun casts across medieval stone facades might recommend a winter visit just as heartily. Just remember that hours for most sights change with the seasons; many places close as early as 5:30 in winter.

TARRAGONA AND ENVIRONS

Tarragona, less than an hour from Barcelona, offers a bracing melange of fresh provincial capital. An ancient outpost of the Roman Empire, it remains a pungent fishing port, busy shipping harbor, and vibrant cultural center.

Tarragona

❶ *98 km (60 mi) southwest of Barcelona, 251 km (155 mi) northeast of Valencia.*

The name Tarragona promises rich classical remains, and the city does not disappoint. As capital of the Roman province of Tarraconensis (from 218 BC), Tarraco, as it was then called, formed the empire's principal stronghold in Spain. In the 1st century BC, the city's population was double the present-day figure of 110,000, and it was regarded as one of the empire's finest urban creations. Its wine was already famous, and its people were the first in Spain to become Roman citizens. St. Paul preached here in AD 58, and Tarragona became the seat of the Christian Church in Spain until it was superseded by Toledo in the 11th century.

Entering the city from Barcelona, you pass the **triumphal arch of Berà** (19 km [12 mi] north of Tarragona), which dates from the 3rd century BC; and from the Lleida (Lérida) road, or *autopista*, you can see the 1st-century **Roman aqueduct** that helped bring fresh water 32 km (19 mi) from the River Gayo. If you approach from the south, past the gasworks, you may think that modern Tarragona has forsaken her splendor, but, thankfully, some outstanding monuments remain and have received a valuable face-lift as part of the city's ongoing renovation and rediscovery of its archaeological treasures. Tarragona is clearly divided into old and new by the Rambla Vella; the old town and most of the Roman remains are to the north, while modern Tarragona spreads out to the south.

Start your tour of Tarragona at the acacia-lined Rambla Nova, at the end of which is a balcony overlooking the sea, the **Balcó del Mediterràni**. Walking uphill along the Passeig de les Palmeres, you arrive at a strikingly illustrated dichotomy between ancient and modern. The remains of Tarragona's **amphitheater** are visible down toward the sea; above stands the modern, semicircular Hotel Imperial Tarraco, artfully echoing the amphitheater's curve. Go down the steps to the amphitheater to see just how well preserved it is. You're free to wander through the access tunnels and along the seating rows; sitting with your back to the sea, you may understand why Augustus favored Tarragona as a winter resort. In the center of the amphitheater are the remains of two superimposed churches, the earlier of which was a Visigothic basilica built to mark the bloody martyrdom of St. Fructuós and his deacons in AD 259. ✉ *450-pta. pass valid for all of Tarragona's Roman remains and Casa Castellarnau.* ⊙ *June–Sept., weekdays 9–8, weekends 9–3; Oct–Mar., weekdays 10–1:30 and 3:30–5:30, weekends 10–2; Apr.–May, weekdays 10–1:30 and 3:30–6:30, weekends 9–3.*

Across the Rambla Vella from the amphitheater, students have excavated the vaults of the 1st-century AD Roman **Circus Maximus.** The plans just inside the gate show that the vaults you can see were only a small corner of a vast arena (350 yards long), where 23,000 spectators gathered to watch chariot racing. As medieval Tarragona grew, it gradually swamped the Circus. ✉ *450-pta. pass valid for all of Tarragona's Roman remains and Casa Castellarnau.* ⊙ *Summer, weekdays 9–8, weekends 9–3; winter, weekdays 10–1:30 and 4–6:30, weekends 10–2.*

Around the corner from the Circus Maximus, up Passeig Sant Antoni, is the former **Praetorium.** This towering building was Augustus's town house and is reputed to be the birthplace of Pontius Pilate. Its Gothic appearance is the result of extensive alterations in the Middle Ages, when it served as the residence for the kings of Catalonia and Aragon during their visits to Tarragona. It now serves as the city's **Museu d'Història** (History Museum), with plans showing the evolution of the city. The highlight is the **Hippolytus sarcophagus,** with a bas-relief depicting the legend of Hippolytus and Fraeda, on the first floor. ✉ *450-pta. pass valid for all of Tarragona's Roman remains and Casa Castellarnau.* ⊙ *Summer, weekdays 9–8, weekends 9–3; winter, weekdays 10–1:30 and 4–6:30, weekends 10–2.*

★ Next door to the History Museum, in a 1960s neoclassical building, is the **Museu Arqueològic** (Museum of Archaeology), which has a collection of Roman statuary and domestic fittings. Look for keys, bells, and belt buckles on the first floor. The beautiful mosaics include the Head of Medusa, famous for its piercing stare. Don't miss the video on Tarragona's history. ✉ *300 ptas.; free Tues.* ⊙ *June–Sept., Tues.–Sat. 10:30–2 and 4–7, Sun. 10–2; Oct.–May, Tues.–Sat. 10–1:30 and 4–7, Sun. 10–2.*

Follow Passeig de Sant Antoni uphill from the museum, with the city walls on your left, to the ornately sculpted **Portal de Sant Antoni,** and enter the cobbled square. Walk down Carrer d'en Granada, past some lovely arched entryways, to Carrer Sant Bernat, where a right turn will take you into **Plaça del Forum,** once the seat of the provincial Roman authorities. At the far corner of the square you'll see signs for the cathedral; walk down Carrer de la Merceria and under the arcade on the right and you'll soon reach the stairway leading up into the **Pla de la Seu,** the square in front of the **cathedral.** The initial rounded placidity of the Romanesque apse, begun in the 12th century, later gave way to the spiky restlessness of the Gothic; the result is confused. If no mass is in progress, enter the cathedral through the cloister. The cathedral's main attraction is the altarpiece of St. Tecla, a richly detailed depiction of the life of Tarragona's patron saint. Converted by St. Paul and subsequently persecuted by local pagans, St. Tecla was repeatedly saved from demise through divine intervention. ✉ *300 ptas.* ⊙ *Daily 10–1 and 4–7 (10–7 in summer).*

As you continue down the steps from the cathedral into Carrer Major, Carrer Cavallers is the second street to the right. Before turning here, continue down to the Plaça del Font for a look at the 19th-century neoclassical **ajuntament** (town hall) at the far end.

Back up Carrer Major toward the cathedral, Carrer Cavallers will take you down to the **Casa Castellarnau,** a Gothic *palacete,* or town house, built by Tarragona nobility in the 18th century. Now a museum, it features stunning decor from the 18th and 19th centuries. The last member of the Castellarnau family vacated the house in 1954. ☒ *450-pta. pass valid for all Roman remains and Casa Castellarnau.* ☉ *Mon.– Sat. 10–1 and 4–7 (9–8 in summer), Sun. 10–2.*

At the end of Carrer Cavallers is the Plaça Pallol; **Les Voltes,** on the right, a Roman Forum with a Gothic upper story added later, is one of the prettiest corners in Tarragona. Through the **Portal del Roser,** to the right, is the entrance to the **Passeig Arqueològic,** a path skirting the 3rd-century BC Ibero-Roman ramparts, built on even earlier walls of giant rocks. The glacis was added by English military engineers in 1707, during the War of the Spanish Succession. Don't miss the rusted bronze of Romulus and Remus.

Next to the Portal del Roser you can catch Bus 2 to the **Serallo fishing quarter,** where boats create a hive of activity as they unload their catch at the quayside. Sneak a look inside the market, where fish are swiftly auctioned off to fishmongers and restaurateurs. Near the fish market, on the Passeig de la Independencia (also on the Bus 2 route), is the **Necròpolis i Museu Paleocristià** (Tomb and Paleochristian Museum). Both Christian and pagan tombs have been unearthed here. ☒ *Free with ticket to Museum of Archaeology (300 ptas.); free Tues.* ☉ *Summer, Tues.–Sat. 10:30–2 and 4–7, Sun. 10–2; winter, Tues.–Sat. 10–1:30 and 3–5:30, Sun. 10–2.*

Dining and Lodging

$$$ ✕ **Sol Ric.** The flagship of the Tomas family's restaurants remains the classiest in Tarragona. The menu changes constantly as the chef experiments with variants of the regional cuisine. Try the *entremés de marisc* (mixed-seafood hors d'oeuvre) or *romesco* (seafood casserole in a hazelnut, pepper, and olive-oil sauce). The restaurant is 1 km (½ mi) out of town along the old Roman road and has a rustic interior and a leafy terrace. ☒ *Vía Augusta 227,* ☎ *977/232032. Reservations essential on weekends. AE, MC, V. Closed Mon. and Dec. 20–Jan. 20. No dinner Sun.*

$$ ✕ **La Puda.** La Puda's quayside location, opposite the fish auction house, guarantees the freshness of the seafood here. The restaurant is popular with locals, but the menu does appear in several languages. The simple decor includes a tile floor, salmon-colored walls, and white tablecloths. ☒ *Muelle Pescadores 25,* ☎ *977/211511. AE, DC, MC, V. No dinner Sun. Oct.–Mar.*

$$ ✕ **Les Voltes.** Built into the vaults of the Roman amphitheater, this el-
★ egant spot is guaranteed to please all travelers lucky enough to find out about it. The fine cuisine includes Tarragona specialties such as fish dishes, as well as international recipes, with *calçotada* (spring onions) in the winter. ☒ *Carrer Trinquet Vell 12,* ☎ *977/230651. AE, DC, MC, V. Closed Sun. No lunch Mon. July–Aug.*

$$ ✕⊡ **Faristol.** The amiable Agustí Martí and his English wife, Lynne,
★ administer this tiny hotel in the medieval village of Altafulla, 11 km (7 mi) north of Tarragona. The five bedrooms are decorated with period furniture from Agustí's family, and the dining room has murals and a terra-cotta tile floor. Specialties from the kitchen include meats *a la brasa* (cooked over coals). Within striking distance of the city, this is *the* place to stay in Tarragona. ☒ *Carrer Sant Martí 5, Altafulla, 43893 Tarragona,* ☎ *977/650077,* FAX *977/650077. 5 rooms. Restaurant. DC, MC, V.*

$ ⊞ **España.** This modern town house offers comfort at a good price. The bedrooms have white walls, shiny tile floors, and functional 1970s furniture. Each exterior room has a balcony overlooking the Rambla. ⊠ *Rambla Nova 49, 43003 Tarragona,* ☎ *977/232712. 40 rooms. Breakfast room. AE, DC, MC, V.*

$$$ ⊞ **Imperial Tarraco.** This large, white, half-moon hotel has a superb position overlooking the Mediterranean. The public rooms are large, with cool marble floors, black leather furniture, marble-top tables, and Oriental rugs. The bedrooms are plain but comfortable, each with a private balcony; insist on a sea view. ⊠ *Passeig Palmeres, 43003 Tarragona,* ☎ *977/233040,* ℻ *977/216566. 170 rooms. Restaurant, bar, pool, beauty salon, tennis court, meeting rooms. AE, DC, MC, V.*

Nightlife and the Arts

Nightlife in Tarragona comes in two versions: older and quieter in the upper city, younger and more raucous down below. There are some lovely, rustic bars in the Casco Viejo, the upper section of old Tarragona. **Poetes** (⊠ Sant Llorenç 15), near the cathedral, is a music bar set in a bodega-like cellar. Other spots for quiet talking and tippling include **Anticuari, El Mirall,** and **Museum.** In the lower part of town around the train station are some two dozen music bars and clubs, such as **Carpe Diem, Cucudrulus,** and **Toc de Gralla,** where younger denizens rage until dawn on Friday and Saturday nights, holiday eves, and all summer long.

The **Teatro Metropol** (⊠ Rambla Nova 46, ☎ 977/244795) is the center for music, dance, theater, and a variety of cultural events ranging from human castle (*casteller*) formations to folk dancing.

Shopping

You'll have to be careful with the hagglers, but Carrer Major in Tarragona has some exciting antiques stores. They're worth a thorough rummage, as the gems tend to be hidden away. You can also try the shops just in front of the cathedral and in the Pla de la Seu; **Antigüedades Ciria** (⊠ Pla de la Seu 2) has an interesting selection.

SOUTH TOWARD THE MAESTRAZGO

Reus, Salou, Cambrils, the Ebro Delta, Tortosa, Gandesa, Alcañiz, Morella, Ares del Maestre, and San Mateu

This chaotic enumeration truly runs the gamut from the ridiculous, such as the Port Aventura theme park, to the sublime, in the extraordinary natural resources from the Ebro Delta and the Ebro River itself to the Sierra de Beceite and mountain villages such as Morella. This wildly varied route takes you from below sea level, in parts of the delta, to high stone villages in the hills; from wetlands to the arid hinterlands of Tarragona.

Reus

② *13 km (8 mi) inland from Tarragona along the N420 highway.*

Reus is an industrial town with the distinction of having been the birthplace of Antoni Gaudí, as well as the longtime home of his fellow Moderniste architect, Lluís Domènech i Montaner. If Moderniste architecture interests you, Domènech's **Casa Navàs** is well worth the short detour. Following signs to the center of town, you arrive in the Plaça del Mercadal; the Casa Navàs is beside the *ajuntament.* The rich interior decoration includes mosaics, stained glass, tiles with characteristic Moderniste floral motifs, and oddly shaped leather chairs. There are no formal visiting hours, but if you knock on the door during reasonable hours (roughly 9–1 and 4–7), the caretaker will usually let you in. ⊠ *San Juan 27,* ☎ *977/345943.* 🖼 *Free.*

Nightlife and the Arts

The **Teatre Fortuny** (⊠ Plaça Prim 4, ☎ 977/318307) is the region's primary theater and opera showcase.

Salou

❸ *10 km (6 mi) southwest of Tarragona.*

Traveling south from Reus, you may want to stop in Salou, a burgeoning beach resort with a long esplanade of young palms. The old port here is where the conquerors of Mallorca set out in 1229.

ⓒ On the edge of Salou is the macro–theme park **Port Aventura** (⊠ Autovéia Salou/Vila-Seca, Km 2, Apartat 90/43480 Vila-Seca, Tarragona, ☎ 902/202220 or 977/779000), which opened in early 1995. It boldly offers "the adventure of your life" to anyone brave enough to shell out $30–$40 for rides, water slides, steam engines, and boat rides through Mexico, China, Polynesia, the American West, and the Mediterranean.

Cambrils

❹ *7 km (4½ mi) west of Salou, 18 km (11 mi) southwest of Tarragona.*

Cambrils, another coastal town, is a target for gourmets, who come to dine in Fanny Gatell's restaurant (☞ *below*). Less built-up than Salou, it also has a pretty marina.

Dining

$$$ ✕ **Casa Gatell.** Fanny Gatell and her sister used to run two renowned
★   restaurants side by side. Fanny now carries on the tradition of exquisite local meals by herself. Try the *fideos negros amb sepionets* (paella in ink of baby squid) or *lubina al horno con cebolla y patata* (roast sea bass with onion and potato). ⊠ *Miramar 27,* ☎ *977/360057. AE, DC, MC, V. Closed Mon., Oct., Dec. 20–Jan. 30, and Wed. in winter. No dinner Sun. in winter.*

Delta de l'Ebre (Ebro Delta)

❺ *77 km (46 mi) southwest of Tarragona, 60 km (36 mi) south of Cambrils.*

The Ebro Delta, a flat piece of wetland à la the Netherlands, juts into and embraces the Mediterranean. The **Parc Natural del Delta de l'Ebre** (Ebro Delta Natural Park) is a major stopping and breeding place for more than 200,000 birds of more than 300 species. An impressive 60% of Europe's bird species can be found here at some time during the year. To get to the park, take N230 and follow signs to Sant Jaume d'Enveja; at Sant Jaume you can take a ferry to the town of **Deltebre.** The Park Information Office (⊠ Plaça 20 de Maig, ☎ 977/489679) can tell you how to visit the reserve proper, which occupies the delta's northern, eastern, and southern tips (you need a permit).

Lodging

$ ✕🖼 **Hotel Casablanca.** Tucked away in Jesús y María, a quiet residential section of Deltebre, Casablanca features bungalows equipped with kitchenettes, living rooms, and full baths. The staff can arrange for bike rentals, binoculars, babysitters, and more. There is no restaurant, but you can stock your kitchenette with provisions from nearby stores. The price is right. ⊠ *C. Leopoldo Segarra 49, 43780 Deltebre–Jesús y María,* ☏ *977/489291. 3 rooms. Parking (fee). MC, V.*

Tortosa

❻ *80 km (50 mi) southwest of Tarragona.*

The ancient town of Tortosa, which straddles the River Ebro 10 km (6 mi) inland, was successively Roman, Visigothic, Moorish, and Christian. The parador here, set in the ruined hilltop castle of **La Zuda,** is worth visiting even if you don't plan to stay the night; keep to the left bank of the river and follow the signs. Originally a Templar fortress, the citadel (and town) passed, around 713, into the hands of the Moors, who kept it until its reconquest by Ramón Berenguer IV, count of Barcelona, in 1153. Moors, Christians, and Jews then lived peacefully together in the town for more than 300 years. From the castle walls, there are sweeping views across the fertile Ebro Valley to the Beceite Mountains.

Tortosa was the scene of one of the Spanish civil war's bloodiest battles. The Republicans, loyal to the democratically elected government and already in control of Catalonia, crossed the Ebro here in July 1936 to attack the rebel Nationalists' rear guard. They got no farther than Tortosa, however, and were pinned down in trenches until they were forced to retreat with the loss of 150,000 lives. A conspicuously Nationalist monument rises from the Ebro to commemorate the victory of Franco's forces.

Look for the **cathedral,** and follow the warren of streets in its direction. On the way, visit the **Renaissance Colegio Sant Lluís,** which has a pretty arcaded patio, embellished with a frieze depicting the kings of Aragon. The cathedral's main facade is baroque, but if you enter through the cloister, you can see that the facade hides a purely Gothic design. It was common in 18th-century Spain to tack these exuberant stuccos onto Gothic structures; this style is called Churrigueresque, after its first practitioner, José Churriguera. ☉ *Cloister daily; cathedral open for mass only.*

Dining and Lodging

$$ ✕ **San Carlos.** Joan Ros, chef and proprietor of this small restaurant on the northern edge of the old town, excels in seafood and freshwater fish from the Ebro Delta. *Almejas* (marinated clams) are a specialty. ⊠ *Rambla Felip Pedrell 19,* ☏ *977/441018. AE, DC, MC, V.*

$$$ ✕▥ **Parador Castillo de la Zuda.** Few sights around here can equal
★ the superb view from this old Arab castle across the Ebro Valley to the Beceite Mountains. Dark shades of mahogany and plentiful tapestries evoke the past. The bedrooms have heavy wood furniture, terra-cotta floors, rugs, and plain walls. ⊠ *Parador Castillo de la Zuda , Tortosa, 43500 Tarragona,* ☏ *977/444450,* 🆗 *977/444458. 82 rooms. Restaurant, bar, pool, playground, meeting rooms, parking. AE, DC, MC, V.*

Gandesa

❼ *86 km (53 mi) northwest of Amposta, 87 km (54 mi) west of Tarragona.*

Renowned for its strong wine (up to 16% alcohol), Gandesa also contains two architectural landmarks. Out on the Mora road is the extraordinary **Cooperative Agrícola** (Wine Cooperative), designed by the Moderniste architect Cèsar Martinell in 1919. Its white, Islamic-looking facade does little to prepare you for the remarkable vaulting inside, constructed entirely of small bricks ingeniously arranged to allow for expansion and contraction. This is a working building (⊘ open weekdays 9–2 and 4–8), and you can buy some local wine here for a sleepy picnic on the way to Alcañiz or Beceite. You can also visit the parish church in the center of town, **L'Assumpció** (⊘ open daily), where the geometric patterns on the otherwise Romanesque doorway are attributed to Moorish influence.

Dining and Lodging

$ ✕⊞ **Hostal Piqué.** Though uninviting from the outside, this modern roadhouse has a large, smart dining room with a tile floor, pristine white tablecloths, and highly professional service. The restaurant menu ranges from everyday local options to more expensive rarities. Rooms are inexpensive and comfortable. ⊠ *Via Catalunya 68, 43780,* ☎ *977/420068,* ⊠ *977/420329. 48 rooms. Restaurant. MC, V.*

Sierra de Beceite

❽ *15 km (9 mi) west of Gandesa on N420.*

The Sierra de Beceite offers a beautiful excursion as you leave Gandesa, as long as you (and your car) can handle some bumpy roads. Just after you enter the Aragonese province of Teruel, you'll come to **Calaceite** on your right; explore its ancient, labyrinthine streets, which assemble at the arcaded Plaza Porticada. For a closer inspection of the Beceite massif, turn left at the Calaceite crossroads and drive along TE301. Turn right after 18 km (11 mi) at a T-junction to reach **Valderrobres,** with a fortified palace and a Renaissance town hall that served as the model for Barcelona's Poble Espanyol (☞ Chapter 3). Continue to **Beceite** and follow signs to a *panorama* for a bumpy drive along a track culminating in an impressive vista. Depending on the condition of these forest roads, you can drive all the way to **Fredes,** due south of Beceite. Near here, on the Tossal dels Tres Reis (4,450 ft), the kings of Catalonia, Aragon, and Valencia are said to have met to iron out disputes. The best way to explore these hills is either on foot or on horseback; a sign on the way into Beceite points you toward the tourist office, which has trail maps and can arrange horseback rides. From Valderrobres, you can cut back to the Alcañiz road via TE300, which follows the River Matarraña.

Alcañiz

❾ *62 km (37 mi) west of Gandesa, 74 km (46 mi) north of Morella.*

Alcañiz lies on a plain, encircled by the River Guadalope. It is surrounded by ugly, modern apartment blocks, the result of a recent population explosion following the success of the surrounding olive and almond orchards. The highway (N420) enters the town along a modern street that bustles with new construction. For the old town, turn left at the end of this street to the Plaza Mayor. On the right is the **Lonja** (Exchange), with pointed arches defining its Gothic origin; adjoining it on the corner is the Renaissance **ayuntamiento.** The galleries and overhanging eaves on both of these buildings mark them as Aragonese. The **Collegiata** church, with its rhythmic baroque facade, looms over the plaza; the ornate portal is very impressive, but the painted interior is disappointing. Climb to the **hilltop castle,** seat of the Calatrava Knights in the 14th century and now a tiny parador.

Dining and Lodging

$$$ ✕🖬 **Parador de la Concordia.** Installed in the sturdy castle of the Cala-
★ trava Knights, this hotel grandly surveys the surrounding olive-growing
plain and the foothills of the Maestrazgo. Bedrooms have terra-cotta
tile floors, patterned rugs, dark furniture, generous beds, and shutters.
All have good views. The restaurant serves Aragonese specialties, such
as *cordero chilindrón* (lamb in a sauce of tomato, garlic, and pepper).
✉ *Castillo de Calatrava, Alcañiz, 44600 Teruel,* ☎ *978/830400,* FAX
*978/830366. 12 rooms. Restaurant, bar. AE, DC, MC, V. Closed Dec.
18–Feb. 1.*

Morella

★ ⑩ *74 km (46 mi) south of Alcañiz, 64 km (40 mi) northwest of Benicarló.*

The walled town of Morella stands on a towering crag in Castellón,
the northernmost Valencian province. It's not immediately evident if
you approach from the north, but from the south and east the land drops
away sharply, creating a natural fortress—the scene of several bloody
battles. Before you reach the town walls, you pass a well-preserved
14th-century aqueduct. The **castle,** Morella's most prominent feature,
is accessible through the gate on the Plaza de San Francisco, on the
uppermost of the town's contoured streets. Just inside the gate is the
ruined cloister of an old Franciscan monastery. The walk up to the cas-
tle takes a good 15 minutes; the often high winds contribute to its air
of impregnability. In 1088 El Cid scaled these walls and wrought
havoc among the occupying Moors. During the Carlist Wars in the 16th
century, the castle became a stronghold for General Cabrera, who
captured Morella in 1838 for Don Carlos, the pretender to the Span-
ish throne. 🖬 *200 ptas.* ☉ *Oct.–Mar., daily 10:30–6:30; Apr.–Sept.,
daily 10:30–7:30.*

The beautiful church of **Santa María la Mayor,** near the castle on Calle
Hospital, has a blue-tile dome that lends an exotic note to its other-
wise Gothic structure. The larger of its two doorways, depicting the
Apostles, dates from the 14th century. The raised, flat-vaulted choir is
reached by a spiral marble staircase. The sanctuary received the full
baroque treatment, as did the high altar, which would glisten were it
not for the gloomy lighting. The **museum** has a painting by Francisco
Ribalta and some 15th-century Gothic panels. 🖬 *Free.* ☉ *Summer, 11–
2 and 4–7; winter, noon–2 and 4–6.*

Go down the stepped Calle Cuesta de Prades to the arcaded **Calle Don
Blasco de Alagón,** Morella's main thoroughfare. The numerous bars
here are packed on weekends. If you turn right, you'll soon arrive at
the old mansion of **Cardinal Ram,** now a hotel; continuing uphill
brings you into the pretty **Plaza de los Estudios,** whose white houses
are distinguished by attractive wooden balconies.

Dining and Lodging

$ ✕ **Mesón del Pastor.** Housed in a restored, 14th-century stone man-
★ sion on a side street off Calle Don Blasco de Alagón, this rustic *mesón*
combines a family atmosphere with excellent cooking. Chef José Fer-
rer specializes in Maestrazgan dishes; try the *conejo relleno trufado* (rab-
bit and truffles enveloped in ham) or the many dishes featuring wild
and farmed mushrooms in a variety of sauces. Desserts, too, are home-
spun; try the *buñuelos con miel* (fried dumplings with honey) or *mousse
de acerolas* (mousse with wild fruits). The charming restaurant is
scheduled to be joined by a small hotel; 12 guest rooms were sched-
uled to open by late 1998. ✉ *Cuesta Jovaní 5 and 7,* ☎ *964/160249.
MC, V. Closed Wed. No dinner Sat.*

$–$$ ✕🖭 **Cardenal Ram.** Installed in one of Morella's most handsome man-
★   sions, originally Cardinal Ram's 14th-century ancestral home, this
hotel oozes history from its bare, stone walls and ubiquitous coats of
arms. The tall lobby has a huge tapestry depicting the arrival of the
Antipope Papa Luna in Morella in 1414. The bedrooms, all different,
have pine floors; bare, white walls; high- beamed ceilings; and magnificent, heavy furniture. The wide beds are covered with Morellan
striped bedspreads. ✉ *Cuesta Suñer 1, Morella, 12300 Castellón,* ☎
964/173085, 🖸 *964/173218. 19 rooms. Restaurant. MC, V.*

$ 🖭 **Hostal La Muralla.** This hostelry is nothing special, but it's comfortable
and clean, and it sits right on the street that makes up Morella's city
walls. A small living and dining area offers relaxation and breakfast.
✉ *Muralla 12, Morella, 12300 Castellón,* ☎ 🖸 *964/160243. 14
rooms. Cafeteria. MC, V.*

Shopping
The Maestrazgo region produces brightly colored, woven-wool textiles. The best buys are the striped *mantas morellanas* (Morellan bedspreads), available in abundance along Morella's Calles Blasco de
Alagón and Hospital.

Ares del Maestre

⑪ *50 km (31 mi) southwest of Morella on N232, new road to Villafranca
del Cid, and CS802 toward Albocácer .*

Ares del Maestre occupies the most dramatic site of any village in this
area. Like Morella, it rests on a crag, but here the drop is more severe
and the vistas more rewarding. A very steep climb—windy in winter and
scorching in summer—takes you to a ruined **castle.** 🖾 *Free.* ☉ *Daily.*

OFF THE   **TERUEL –** You may want to make the trip (about 110 km [68 mi]) from
BEATEN PATH   Ares del Maestre to Teruel to see the town's famous Mudéjar architecture. Backtrack on CS802 toward Morella. At Villafranca del Cid get on
TE811, which will take you to Teruel via the small towns of La Iglesuela,
Mosqueruela, Linares de Mora, Rubielos de Mora, and Mora de Rubielos. Once in Teruel, visit the **Mudéjar towers,** built between the 12th and
16th centuries in a style more reminiscent of Muslim minarets than Christian belfries. They were once part of Teruel's city walls. The highlight in
the cathedral is the coffered ceiling with 13th-century court and hunting
scenes, visible from the upper gallery. You can spend the night in one of
the spacious rooms of the rustic **Parador de Teruel** (✉ Apdo. 67, ☎
978/601800) and sample local fare at the parador's restaurant.

San Mateu

⑫ *26 km (17 mi) west of Benicarló; CS802 southeast from Ares del
Maestre to Albocácer, then turn left.*

The small town of San Mateu proudly bears the title Capital del Maestrazgo, because it was from here that King Jaume I set out on his decisive reconquering raids in the 13th century, freeing the region finally
from Moorish control. Today, sturdy Gothic mansions near the Plaza
Mayor attest to San Mateu's regal past. Visit the Archpriest's Church
on the corner of the plaza; its nave is a fine example of the Catalan
Gothic style, and the vault covers a wide expanse, dispensing with the
need for columns.

The coast beckons once more. From here, the nearest coastal town is
Benicarló, via Cervera del Maestre and Cálig.

THE COSTA DEL AZAHAR
Benicarló, Peñíscola, and Sagunto

Named for the orange blossom and its all-pervading fragrance along this sweet coastal plain, the Costa del Azahar was hit hard by the tourist-inspired building boom of the '60s and '70s. Castellón de la Plana is the northernmost province of the Levante, a region so named because the sun rises (*se levanta*) out of the Mediterranean on this eastern coast. Phoenician (Syrian) trading ships plied these ports some 2,000 years ago, and it is thought that the Phoenicians, patrolling this stretch of coast and gazing uneasily at the menacing backdrop of mountains, gave the country its name—Spagna, or "hidden land." Benicarló and Peñíscola are, with Vinarós, the northernmost towns on the Costa del Azahar, while Sangunto marks the start of the Costa de Valencia.

Benicarló

⑬ *55 km (34 mi) south of Tortosa.*

The village of Benicarló has become an important tourist center. The harbor is a lively confusion of fishing and pleasure craft, and the beaches are well stocked with northern-European and local visitors most of the year.

Dining and Lodging

$$-$$$ ✕ **Casa Pocho.** Casa Pocho is named after its owner: Paco Puchal is also known as "El Pocho," or "the Tubby One." Wood paneling and maritime motifs set the scene for the restaurant's famously good seafood. *Langostinos* (prawns) are the best choice. ⊠ *San Gregorio 49, Vinaròs,* ☎ *964/451095. AE, DC, MC, V. Closed Mon. No dinner Sun.*

$$$ ✕⌂ **Parador de la Costa del Azahar.** The main attraction of this modern parador, 6½ km (4 mi) north of Peñíscola, is its large, semiformal garden, which runs down to the sea. It's a perfect place to rest up in peace and quiet, away from the most crowded beaches. The decor doesn't match that of the parador's more atmospheric cousins, but the public rooms are huge, bright, and tasteful, with white-wicker furniture and white walls. The guest rooms have shiny tile floors, white walls, and functional furniture; ask for a sea view. People with disabilities are well accommodated here. ⊠ *Avda. Papa Luna 5, Benicarló, 12580 Castellón,* ☎ *964/470100,* ℻ *964/470934. 108 rooms. Restaurant, bar, pool, tennis court. AE, DC, MC, V.*

Peñíscola

⑭ *7 km (4½ mi) south of Benicarló, 60 km (37 mi) northeast of Benicàssim.*

Peñíscola owes its foundation to the Phoenicians. It later became the bridgehead by which the Carthaginian Hamilcar (father of Hannibal) imported his elephants and munitions to wage the first of the three Punic Wars. Carthaginian influence in the peninsula reached its zenith some 20 years later, in 230 BC, but it was eroded by Rome's success in the subsequent campaigns.

★ The **old town** is a cluster of white houses and tiny, narrow streets leading up to the castle, whose setting on a promontory affords perfect surveillance of the coast. You can drive up to the **castle,** but in summer the traffic makes it wiser to leave your car by the town walls and walk. Of chief interest are the chapel and study of the Antipope Papa Luna, to whom the 14th-century castle passed in the 15th century. Hardly any of Papa Luna's effects remain, but while you're in his drafty quarters, try to imagine this 90-year-old Frenchman (formerly Pope Benedict XIII) passing the last six years of his life attending mass and composing schismatic bulls, surrounded all the while by hostile Moorish townsfolk. ▣ *300 ptas.* ☉ *Apr.–Sept., daily 10–8:30; Oct.–Mar., daily 10–1 and 3:15–5:30.*

Dining and Lodging

$$–$$$ 🏨 **Hostería del Mar.** Officially a "semi-parador," this modern, white hotel next to Peñíscola's long beach meets the paradors' high standards. Most of the rooms have balconies overlooking the old town. The rustic, beamed public rooms surround a leafy pool terrace; the bedrooms have white walls, striped bedspreads, tile floors, and Castilian-style dark wood and leather furniture. ⊠ *Avda. Papa Luna 18, Peñíscola, 12598 Castellón,* ☎ *964/480600,* 📠 *964/481363. 86 rooms. Restaurant, bar, pool, tennis court. AE, DC, MC, V.*

Between Peñíscola and Sagunto

Alcalá de Chivert is 49 km (30 mi) north of Castellón de la Plana.

Along the Costa del Azahar, several small towns merit stops on your way from Peñíscola to Sagunto. The route passes through carob and orange plantations. The *autopista* is the fastest road south, but N340 shares the same scenery and grants easier access to places en route. **Alcalá de Chivert** can claim the tallest belfry in the Valencian provinces. The road here is separated from the sea by the Sierra de Hirta, whose rugged outlines contain some ruined castles easily visible from the road. Next down the coast is **Alcocéber,** an expanding but still quiet holiday town with two good beaches. **Benicàssim** (Exit 45 from the *autopista,* or coast road from N340) is appealing for the dramatic shapes in its mountainous background, as well as its long, sandy bathing beach and plenty of nocturnal action. **Castellón de la Plana,** the provincial capital, has little to warrant the struggle through its suburbs unless you're a fan of the Spanish baroque painter Zurbarán, 10 of whose works are in the Convento de las Religiosas Capuchinas on Calle Nuñez de Arce (open for services).

Dining and Lodging

$$ ✕ **Villa del Mar.** An old, country manor house with a verdant terrace for dining, surrounded by palms and pines, forms an elegant and secluded setting. Inside, the decor is modern and the cuisine international as well as regional; try the *arroces Valencianos* (Valencian rice dishes). On summer evenings there is a barbecue in the garden. ⊠ *Paseo Marítimo Pilar Coloma 24, Benicàssim,* ☎ *964/302852. AE, MC, V. Closed Oct. and weekdays in winter.*

$$ 🏨 **Orange.** If it's facilities you're after, look no further than this huge, modern, chalet-style hotel; it has the widest range in town. It's centrally located, 150 yards from the beach, and surrounded by a garden and trees. Loud patterns in browns and oranges set the tone in the public rooms, and the plain bedrooms are no more than functional. Ask for a sea view; rooms over the pool may be noisy. ⊠ *Avda. Gimeno Tomás s/n, Benicàssim, 12560 Castellón,* ☎ *964/394400,* 📠 *964/301541. 415 rooms. Restaurant, bar, cafeteria, 2 pools, beauty salon, miniature golf, tennis court, dance club. AE, DC, MC, V. Closed mid-Nov.–mid-Feb.*

$$ ✕🏨 **Voramar.** At the north end of Benicàssim, right on the beach, this small, white hotel—the closest thing in town to an old-fashioned resort—is encircled by classical balconies. The decor is rather plain and functional, with tile floors, white walls, and 1970s furniture. Ask for a room overlooking the sea; each has a generous balcony. ✉ *Paseo Pilar Coloma 1, Benicàssim, 12560 Castellón,* ☎ *964/300150,* FAX *964/300526. 55 rooms. Restaurant, tennis court. AE, DC, MC, V. Closed mid-Oct.–Easter.*

Nightlife and the Arts

The top club in Benicàssim is **K'asim,** on Avinguda Gimeno Tomás. Things only really get going during summer and Holy Week; at other times the atmosphere is decidedly tame.

Sagunto

⑮ *65 km (40 mi) southwest of Benicàssim, 23 km (20 mi) northeast of Valencia.*

Sagunto will ring a bell if you've read Caesar's history: Saguntum, as the Romans called it, was the sparking point for the Second Punic War. When Hannibal laid siege to the town (at that time a port, from which the sea has since receded), the people heroically held out, faithfully expecting a Roman relief force, and eventually burned the town rather than surrender to the Carthaginians.

Rambling Moorish fortifications dominate the town from the hilltops, and within this citadel earlier **Roman remains** are now being excavated. On the way up, visit the well-restored **amphitheater** (signposted from the town center). More complete than Tarragona's, it went up during the Roman rebuilding five years after Hannibal's siege. Some archaeological finds from this time are displayed in a fascinating and manageable museum just opposite the amphitheater. ✉ *Amphitheater and museum 400 ptas.* ☉ *Tues.–Sat. 10–2 and 4–6, Sun. 10–2.*

Nightlife and the Arts

The first two weeks of August bring **Sagunto a Escena,** a festival of classical Mediterranean drama. Spanish and international theater groups perform a variety of ancient plays in the authentic setting of Sagunto's Roman amphitheater. For information, contact the tourist office there or in Valencia (✉ Barcas 15, ☎ 96/351–0051).

VALENCIA

Valencia, Spain's third-largest city and capital of the Levante, is nearly equidistant from Barcelona and Madrid, the nation's two metropolitan giants. The city's location, on a fertile *huerta,* has been fiercely contested ever since it was founded by the Greeks. El Cid captured the city from the Moors in 1094 and won his strangest victory here in 1099: his corpse was strapped to his saddle and so frightened the waiting Moors as to cause a complete rout. In 1102, his widow, Jimena, was forced to return the city to Moorish rule; Jaume I finally drove them out in 1238.

Valencia is a somewhat confusing place, uneasily poised between old and new. Many of its finer monuments have suffered destruction or damage. The city walls were pulled down late in the 19th century to build a ring road and provide employment for the poor, and the River Turia was later diverted to the south to prevent further flood damage, leaving the city's beautiful *puentes* (bridges) to span a municipal park. Valencia is in a quite different league from Madrid and Barcelona, lacking coherence and overwhelming charm, but it still holds a city's worth of interesting sights.

Valencia is split up here into two sections: Valencia Center and Outer Valencia.

Valencia Center

⑯   *23 km (14 mi) south of Sagunto, 351 km (218 mi) southeast of Madrid, 362 km (224 mi) south of Barcelona.*

A Good Walk

A stroll through Valencia's historical center could begin at the **cathedral** ⑰ in the Plaza de la Reina; inside you can visit the museum and climb the Miguelete Tower for good views of the city. Next, cross the **Plaza de la Virgen** ⑱ and turn right down **Calle Almudín** ⑲ to the Museo de Paleontología. On the left of the Plaza de la Virgen is the Gothic **Palau de la Generalitat** ⑳, which you have to arrange to visit in advance. Continuing down Calle Caballeros, you'll pass Valencia's oldest church, **San Nicolás** ㉑. After spending some time inside, walk to the Plaza del Mercado and the 15th-century **Lonja de la Seda** ㉒. Opposite are the Iglesia de los Santos Juanes, whose interior was destroyed during the civil war, and the Mercado Central. Travel down Avenida María Cristina to the **Plaza del Ayuntamiento** ㉓, one of the city's liveliest areas and the home of the **ayuntamiento** ㉔ itself. After a five-minute walk down Avenida Marqués de Soto, you'll find the Moderniste **Estación** ㉕. Next to the train station is the **Plaza de Toros** ㉖. Back in the center of the city, go to Plaza Patriarca and enter the **Real Colegio del Patriarca** ㉗, with a nice Renaissance patio and a museum featuring works by El Greco, among others. Cross Calle Poeta Quirol to the wedding-cake facade of the **Palacio del Marqués de Dos Aguas** ㉘.

Leave Valencia's historical center and cross the riverbed by Puente de la Trinidad to No. 9, Calle San Pio V. Here is the **Museo de Bellas Artes** ㉙, one of Spain's best galleries, with masterpieces of Velázquez, José Ribera, and the Valencia-born Joaquín Sorolla. The **Jardines del Real** ㉚ adjoin the museum. Walk up Calle San Pio V to the Puente de Serranos. At the other side of the riverbed is the **Torre de Serranos** ㉛, a gate that once served as the entrance to this Mediterranean city. On the right side is the **Casa Museo José Benlliure** ㉜, where you can admire works of this Valencian painter-sculptor. Finally, end your walk with a stroll south down the riverbed park to the modern **Palau de la Música** ㉝.

TIMING
This walk covers some 6 km (4 mi). Depending on stops in museums, it should take about five hours.

⑲   **Almudín.** To the right of the Plaza de la Virgen, down Calle Almudín, stands the 14th-century granary, which houses the **Museo de Paleontología** (Museum of Paleontology), with its impressive collection of bones (including antediluvian skeletons from Argentina) and shells. 🏛 *Free.* ⊙ *Tues.–Sat. 9:15–2 and 4:30–8; Sun. 9:30–2.*

㉔   **Ayuntamiento.** Located just beyond Barrachina, this is the home of the municipal tourist office and a museum of the city's history. 🏛 *Free.* ⊙ *Weekdays 9–2.*

⑰   **Cathedral.** Valencia's historic buildings cluster around the 14th-century cathedral in the Plaza de Zaragoza, a convenient place to begin your visit. The cathedral can be entered by three portals, respectively Romanesque, Gothic, and rococo, the last leading off the Plaza de Zaragoza. Inside, Renaissance and baroque marble was removed in a successful restoration of the original Gothic style, as is now the trend in Spanish churches.

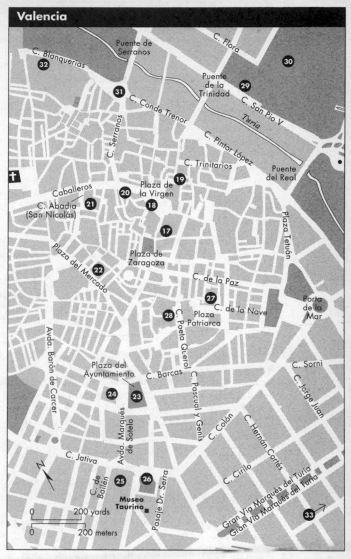

In a side chapel is a purple agate chalice, said to be the Holy Grail (Christ's cup at the Last Supper), which, it is claimed, was brought to Spain in the 4th century. Another highlight of the museum, on display in the treasury, is Goya's famous painting of St. Francis Borgia surrounded by devils eagerly awaiting his demise. ⌨ *Free.* ☉ *Mar.–Oct., daily 10–1 and 4:30–7; Dec.–Feb., daily 10–1.*

Dominating the cathedral to the left of the entrance is the octagonal **Miguelete Tower,** which you can climb for a fine view: it is said that you can see 300 belfries from here. ⌨ *100 ptas.* ☉ *Daily 10–1 and 4:30–7.*

㉕ **Estación** (train station). Down Avenida Marqués de Sotelo from the Ayuntamiento is this splendid Moderniste pile. Designed by Demetrio Ribes Mano in 1917, it is replete with citrus motifs to let travelers know where they've arrived.

★ ㉒ **Lonja de la Seda** (Silk Exchange). Downhill from San Nicolás, on the Plaza del Mercado, the 15th-century Lonja is a product of Valencia's golden age, when arts came under the patronage of Ferdinand I. It is generally regarded as one of Spain's finest Gothic buildings. The perfect Gothic facade, dotted with ghoulish gargoyles, is complemented inside by high vaulting and twisted columns. ▣ *Free.* ⊙ *Tues.–Fri. 9–1:30 and 5–9, weekends 9–1:30.*

★ ㉘ **Palacio del Marqués de Dos Aguas.** After leaving the Plaza Patriarca and crossing Calle Poeta Querol, you'll soon come face-to-face with this building's baroque alabaster facade. The famous Churrigueresque facade around the corner centers on the figures of the *Dos Aguas* (Two Waters), carved by Ignacio Vergara in the 18th century. The palace contains the **Ceramics Museum,** with a magnificent collection of mostly local ware, the highlight being the Valencian kitchen on the second floor.▣ *Palace and museum 350 ptas.* ⊙ *Tues.–Sat. 10–2 and 4–6, Sun. 10–2.*

㉒⓪ **Palau de la Generalitat.** On the left side of the Plaza de la Virgen, fronted by orange trees and box hedges, is the elegant east facade of what was the Gothic home of the Valencia Cortes (Parliament), until its suppression by Felipe V for supporting the wrong (losing) side during the War of the Spanish Succession in the 18th century. The two *salones* (reception rooms) in the older of the two towers have superb woodwork on the ceilings. Call in advance for permission to enter. ☎ *96/386–3461.* ⊙ *Weekdays 9–2.*

㉓ **Plaza del Ayuntamiento.** Down Avenida María Cristina from the market, this plaza is the hub of city life, a fact well conveyed by the massiveness of the baroque facades. Nearby (opposite the Lonja de la Seda) stands the Iglesia de los Santos Juanes, (Church of the Sts. John) whose interior was destroyed during the civil war, and, next door, the Moderniste Mercado Central (central market), built entirely of iron and glass.

⓲ **Plaza de la Virgen.** Leaving the cathedral by the Gothic Apostle Door brings you out into this pedestrian plaza, a lovely place for a refreshing *horchata* (tiger-nut milk) in the late afternoon. Next to its portal, market gardeners from the *huerta* bring their irrigation disputes before the Water Tribunal, which has met every Thursday at noon since 1350. Verdicts are given on the spot, and sentences range from fines to deprivation of water.

㉖ **Plaza de Toros.** Adjacent to the train station stands the bullring, one of Spain's oldest. The best bullfighters are featured on and around July 25 and during the Fallas in March. Just beyond, down Pasaje Dr. Serra, the **Museo Taurino** (Bullfighting Museum) is packed with bullfighting memorabilia, bulls' heads, and matadors' swords from Valencian bullfights. ▣ *Free.* ⊙ *Weekdays 10:30–1:30.*

㉑ **San Nicolás.** Down Calle Caballeros, the main artery of the old part of town (leading out of the Plaza de la Virgen), look for high door knockers—these could be reached without dismounting. Turn left, down the tiny Calle Abadía San Nicolás (just after No. 41), to reach a small plaza containing Valencia's oldest church, once the parish of the Borgia Pope Calixtus III. The first portal you come to, with a tacked-on, rococo bas-relief of the Virgin Mary with cherubs, gives a good hint at what's inside: every inch of the originally Gothic church has been covered with Churrigueresque embellishments.

㉗ **Real Colegio del Patriarca** (Royal College of the Patriarch). Toward the center of town, near the university, is the Plaza Patriarca; this *cole-*

gio is on the far side of the square. Founded by San Juan de Ribera in the 16th century, it has a lovely Renaissance patio and an ornate church, and its museum contains works by Juan de Juanes, Francisco Ribalta, and El Greco. The entrance is off Calle de la Nave. 🎟 *100 ptas.* ☉ *Daily 11–1:30.*

Outer Valencia

③② **Casa Museo José Benlliure.** After you cross the Puente de Serranos, turn right down Calle Blanquerías and stop at No. 23. The elegant house of this modern Valencian painter-sculptor contains many of his works. 🎟 *Free.* ☉ *Tues.–Sat. 9:15–2 and 5:30–9; Sun. 9:30–2.*

③⓪ **Jardines del Real.** These gardens, or *Viveros* (nurseries), contain a pleasant park with fountains, rose gardens, tree-lined avenues, and a small zoo. ☉ *Daily 8–dusk.*

★ ②⑨ **Museo de Bellas Artes** (Museum of Fine Arts). Foremost among the sights outside the city center is this art museum, one of Spain's best. To get there, cross the riverbed by Puente de la Trinidad to No. 9, Calle San Pio V. In the 15th century Valencia was a thriving center of artistic talent, and many of the best works by Jacomart and Juan Reixach—two of several painters known as the Valencian Primitives—hang here. Hieronymus Bosch, or El Bosco, as they call him here, is also represented. Also on the first floor are the murky, 17th-century Tenebrist masterpieces of Francisco Ribalta and his pupil José Ribera, together with a Velázquez self-portrait and a room devoted to Goya. Upstairs, look for Joaquín Sorolla (Gallery 66), the luminous Valencian painter of 19th-century Spanish everyday life. 🎟 *Free.* ☉ *Tues.–Sat. 10–2 and 4–6, Sun. 10–2.*

③③ **Palau de la Música** (Concert Hall). Stroll south down the riverbed park to this modern hall. For concert schedules, check the *Turia* guide, available at newsstands. ✉ *Paseo de la Alameda 30,* ☎ *96/337–5020.*

③① **Torre Serranos.** Cross the Puente de Serranos to this 14th-century fortified gate, which guards the entrance to the old city.

Dining and Lodging

$$$$ ✕ **Civera.** Run by the Civera brothers three blocks northwest of the Museum of Fine Arts, this restaurant enjoys local renown for its fresh fish and seafood, cooked *a la plancha* (grilled), *hervidos* (boiled), or *a la sal* (baked in salt). The decor is marine oriented: white walls, beams, nautical motifs, and sumptuous displays of fish, fruit, and vegetables. ✉ *Lérida 11,* ☎ *96/347–5917. AE, DC, MC, V. Closed Mon. and Aug. No dinner Sun.*

$$$ ✕ **El Timonel.** Decorated to resemble the interior of a yacht, this central restaurant (two blocks east of the bullring) serves outstanding shellfish. The cooking is simple yet benefits from the freshest ingredients. Try the *salmonetes* (whitebait) or *pescado de roca* (rockfish). The clientele ranges from businesspeople at lunch to a fashionable crowd at night. If you flash your Fodor's guidebook, the owner might take special interest in you. ✉ *Félix Pizcueta 13,* ☎ *96/352–6300. AE, DC, MC, V. Closed Mon.*

$$$ ✕ **Eladio.** Some way out of town, this welcoming restaurant is decorated with oak and marble. The many Galician fish dishes are prepared with a mixture of tradition and invention by chef Eladio Rodríguez; try the *mero a la brasa* (charcoal-grilled grouper), and finish up with a mouthwatering Swiss pastry made by Eladio's wife, Violette. ✉ *Chiva 40,* ☎ *96/384–2244. AE, DC, MC, V. Closed Sun. and Aug.*

$$ ✕ **El Plat.** The local press has dubbed this restaurant *el Rey del Arroz* (the King of Paella), because it offers a different variation on Valencia's most celebrated dish each day of the week. The simple decor consists of white, alcoved walls adorned with local ceramics, but the lighting is rather bright. The atmosphere is relaxed, the service is attentive, and the location ideal should you feel like *marcha* (nightlife) after dinner. ⊠ *Ciscar 3,* ☎ *96/374–1254. AE, MC, V. Closed Mon. No dinner Sun.*

$$ ✕ **Gargantua.** The scene is a series of apricot-colored rooms, crowded
★ with pictures, in a 1910 town house. The tone is intimate and chic. The excellent cooking is nouvelle and imaginative, the menu constantly changing. For a regional dish, try the *esgarrat* (grilled cod with green peppers). ⊠ *Navarro Reverter 18,* ☎ *96/334–6849. DC, MC, V. Closed Sat. evening, Sun., and Easter week.*

$$ ✕ **La Riuà.** This fine local secret specializes in Valencian cuisine, served in a colorful setting splashed with ceramic tiles. Order a rice dish, fresh fish prepared with *all i pebre* (garlic and pepper), or the *pato guixado con cebollas i pasas* (stewed duck with onions and raisins). ⊠ *C. del Mar 27,* ☎ *96/391–4571. AE, DC, MC, V. Closed Mon., Easter week, and Aug. No dinner Sun.*

$ ✕ **Patos.** Small, cozy, and very popular, this restored 18th-century town house, just north of Calle de la Paz in the old quarter, is primarily for locals. Terra-cotta tiles, white tablecloths, wood-panel walls, and overhead beams lend it an earthy look, and you can dine outside in summer. The set menu (a real bargain at 1,500 ptas.) often includes *pato* (duck). Get here by 9:30 PM to be sure of a table. ⊠ *C. del Mar 28,* ☎ *96/392–1522. AE, DC, MC, V.*

$$ ✕🖫 **Ad Hoc.** This small, beautifully designed 19th-century town house enjoys the finest location in Valencia, with immediate access to the old quarter and the Turia gardens. The hotel's owner, Luis García Alarcón, is an antiquarian, and the hotel reflects his eye for architectural elegance and ancient design. The small restaurant serves a particularly nice breakfast, but a visit at lunchtime is also worthwhile. ⊠ *Boix 4, 46003,* ☎ *96/391–9140,* 𝔽𝔸𝕏 *96/391–3667. 28 rooms. Breakfast room. AE, DC, MC, V.*

$$$$ 🖫 **Monte Picayo.** If you enjoy the proximity of a casino and don't mind
★ looking at the sea from a distance, consider the Monte Picayo. Set into a hill and draped in greenery, its modern, tiered structure overlooks the *huerta* and offers a rare degree of luxury. The public areas and guest rooms are all spacious and cheerful; each guest room has a balcony; and the service is impeccable. ⊠ *Urbanización Monte Picayo, 46530 Valencia,* ☎ *96/142–0100,* 𝔽𝔸𝕏 *96/142–2168. 83 rooms. Restaurant, 5 bars, 11 pools, beauty salon, sauna, miniature golf, 2 tennis courts, casino, dance club, parking. AE, DC, MC, V.*

$$$$ 🖫 **Sidi Saler.** This stretch of coastline just south of Valencia suffers from being in mid-development, but Sidi Saler's contemporary khaki facade surrounds an oasis of luxury. The guest rooms are modern, bright, and unremarkable; their achievement is to give you the impression that the beach belongs only to you. ⊠ *Playa del Saler, 46012, Valencia,* ☎ *96/ 161–0411,* 𝔽𝔸𝕏 *96/161–0838. 276 rooms. Restaurant, 2 bars, outdoor and indoor pools, beauty salon, massage, sauna. AE, DC, MC, V.*

$$$ 🖫 **Meliá Valencia Palace.** This five-star hotel just steps from the Palau de la Música has become Valencia's ultimate refuge. It's filled with state-of-the-art design and an ample staff of hotel professionals who seem truly excited about making every guest happy. ⊠ *Alameda 32, 46023,* ☎ *96/337–5037,* 𝔽𝔸𝕏 *96/337–5532. 189 rooms, 10 suites. Restaurant, bar, room service, pool, sauna, exercise room. AE, DC, MC, V.*

$$$ 🏨 **Parador de El Saler.** Definitely for golf enthusiasts, this modern parador has a famous course, with the first tee just outside the front door. The hotel has an exposed position on the edge of a pine forest, fronted by sand dunes. The bright and spacious reception rooms have cool marble floors, white walls, and baronial furniture; the guest rooms echo this style. Insist on a sea view. ⊠ *El Saler, 46012, Valencia,* ☎ *96/161–1186,* FAX *96/162–7016. 58 rooms. Restaurant, bar, pool, 18-hole golf course, tennis court. AE, DC, MC, V.*

$$$ 🏨 **Reina Victoria.** The grande dame of Valencia's hotels is an excellent
★ choice for comfort as well as time-worn charm and centrality. The spacious reception rooms have cool marble floors, with rugs to take the chill off; the guest rooms are clothed in green chintz and deep-pile carpets with a subdued pattern. ⊠ *Barcas 4, 46002,* ☎ *96/352–0487,* FAX *96/352–0487. 97 rooms. Restaurant, bar. AE, DC, MC, V.*

$$ 🏨 **Excelsior.** In a centrally located 1930s building, this hotel offers the
★ best value in this price category. From the Art Deco restaurant-cum-bar, a spiral marble staircase leads to a dark, wood-paneled salon with a terrace. The guest rooms have olive-green carpets, the beds have brass headboards, and the white walls have old prints. The general atmosphere is very friendly. ⊠ *Barcelonina 5, 46002,* ☎ *96/351–4612,* FAX *96/352–3478. 67 rooms. Restaurant, bar. AE, DC, MC, V.*

$$ 🏨 **Inglés.** Once the palace of the dukes of Cardona, this hotel is perfectly located for touring the old town, even if the polished wood floors and striped Regency chairs in the public rooms look rather more spartan than they must have in the dukes' day. The guest rooms have a jaded appearance, born of the passé modern decor, but they're perfectly comfortable. All are exterior; ask for one overlooking Hipolito Roviro's alabaster doorway into the palacio next door. ⊠ *Marqués de Dos Aguas 6, 46002,* ☎ *96/351–6426,* FAX *96/394–0251. 62 rooms. Restaurant, bar. AE, DC, MC, V.*

$ 🏨 **Continental.** Filling two floors of a town house just off the Plaza del Ayuntamiento, this friendly establishment is an excellent value for the money if all you need is a clean and comfortable room. It has a small lounge and a breakfast room. ⊠ *Correos 8, 46002,* ☎ *96/351–0926,* FAX *96/351–0926. 46 rooms. Breakfast room. AE, DC, MC, V.*

Nightlife and the Arts

Castellón and Valencia jointly publish *Que y Donde,* the major listings magazine; for Valencia only, there is *Turia,* with events, prices, and reviews.

Throughout July, Valencia hosts a **Feria de Julio** (July Festival) of theater; classical, jazz, and pop music; film; and dance. Contact the *ayuntamiento* (☎ 96/352–0694). If you're homesick, there is the **Instituto Shakespeare** (⊠ Avda. Blasco Ibañez 28, ☎ 96/360–1950), with performances in English and Spanish

Sleep seems to be anathema here. You can experience the nocturnal way of life anytime except summer, when Valencians disappear on vacation. Plaza Canovas del Castillo and the surrounding streets are the liveliest zone, followed closely by Plaza Xuquer, near the university. For a rougher brand of fun, head to the beach. Calle de Eugenia Viñes is lined with numerous loud discotheques and bars; try **Casablanca** (⊠ Eugenia Viñes 152, ☎ 96/371–3366) or the aptly named **Vivir Sin Dormir** (Living Without Sleeping) (⊠ Paseo Neptuno 42, ☎ 96/372–7777).

For a more sophisticated club, try **Belle Epoque** (⊠ Cuba 8, ☎ 96/380–2828) or **Xuquer Palace** (⊠ Plaza Xuquer 8, ☎ 96/361–5811); for *sevillanas* (flamenco), try **Albahaca** (⊠ Almirante Cadarso 30, ☎ 96/

334–1484), **Triana** (✉ Grabador Esteve 11, ☎ 96/374–3001), or **Candela Canovas** (✉ Plaza Canovas del Castillo 6, ☎ 96/373–1882).

Shopping

Try **Salvador Ribes** (✉ Vilaragut 7) for top-quality antiques with correspondingly daunting price tags. A local crafts market is held daily 10–8 in Plaza Alfonso Magnánimo, at the bottom of Calle de la Paz. A flea market is held every Sunday morning in the streets around the cathedral.

Valencia is a good place to buy the famous Lladró porcelain or the slightly cheaper version, Nao; try **Cerámicas Lladró** (✉ Poeta Querol 9). Both brands are made here in town; the tourist office in the *ayuntamiento* can occasionally arrange factory tours. Manises, 9 km (5½ mi) west of Valencia, is another center for Valencian ceramics, known particularly for its *azulejos*.

SOUTHERN CATALONIA AND THE LEVANTE A TO Z

Arriving and Departing

By Boat

Trasmediterránea Ferries (✉ Estación Marítima, ☎ 96/367–6512, FAX 96/367–0614) leave Valencia for Mallorca (Mon.–Sat.) and Ibiza (Mon.–Sat.). They shuttle from Tarragona daily in July and August only (☎ 977/225506).

By Bus

The connection between Barcelona and Tarragona is easy; nine buses daily leave the Estación Vilanova-Norte in Barcelona. **Bacoma, S.A.** (☎ 93/231–3801) also dispatches buses from Tarragona (✉ Plaça Imperial Tarraco s/n, ☎ 977/222072). From Valencia, buses continue down the coast and on to Madrid. The **bus depot** (✉ Avda. Menendez Pidal 13, ☎ 96/349–7222) is across the river; take Bus 8 from the Plaza del Ayuntamiento.

By Car

The A7 *autopista* (motorway) provides excellent road access to the region at both ends. A car is extremely valuable, even necessary, if you want to explore the inland Maestrazgo mountains, where there is some smooth, uncrowded, and scenic driving.

By Plane

The international airport closest to the northern end of this tour is in **Barcelona** (☞ Barcelona A to Z *in* Chapter 7), 100 km (65 mi) from Tarragona. **Valencia** has an international airport (☎ 96/370–9500) with direct flights to London, Paris, Brussels, Frankfurt, and Milan; it is 8 km (5 mi) west of the city center and is best reached by taxi. For **Iberia** flights, call ☎ 96/351–3739.

By Train

Trains bound for Tarragona via Zaragoza leave Barcelona's Passeig de Gràcia and Sants stations every half hour or so (☞ Barcelona A to Z *in* Chapter 7). The **RENFE** station is downhill from the Mediterranean Balcony, south toward the port (☎ 977/240202). Leaving the region from Valencia, you have a choice of train connections to Madrid (via Cuenca) or Alicante (via Játiva). The main station, **Estación del Norte** (☎ 96/352–0202), is on Calle Játiva, next to the bullring; it's very centrally located, only a short walk or cab ride from most hotels.

Getting Around

By Bus

Connections up and down the coast between Tarragona and Valencia are frequent. Transport inland to Morella and Alcañiz can be arranged from Vinaròs, while Castellón and Sagunto have bus lines west to Teruel.

In Valencia buses are the main mode of public transport; central services start from the Plaza del Ayuntamiento. Services for the beaches and outlying suburbs leave from the Plaza Puerta del Mar. The tourist office can supply details of bus routes.

By Car

Roads in this region are generally very good, but the main N340 can get clogged, and you're often much better off paying extra to use the *autopista*. For car rentals in Tarragona, **Avis** is at Viajes Vibus (✉ Pin Soler 10, ☎ 977/219156). In Valencia you can choose from **Avis** (✉ Isabel la Católica 17, ☎ 96/351–0734), **Europcar** (✉ Antiguo Reino de Valencia 7, ☎ 96/374–1512; ✉ airport, ☎ 96/152–1872), and **Hertz** (✉ Segorbe 7, ☎ 96/341–5036; ✉ airport, ☎ 96/152–379).

By Train

Within the region, trains run more or less down the coast: Tarragona–Salou/Cambrils–Tortosa–Vinaròs–Peñíscola–Benicàssim–Castellón–Sagunto–Valencia. A line also goes from Valencia to Zaragoza by way of Sagunto and Teruel, and local lines go around Valencia from the station on Cronista Rivelles (☎ 96/347–4626).

Contacts and Resources

Consulates

British: Tarragona (✉ C. Real 33, ☎ 977/220812), open weekday mornings. **U.S.:** Valencia (✉ C. de la Paz 6, ☎ 96/351–6973), open weekdays 10–1.

Emergencies

Police: ☎ 091.

Ambulance: **Castellón** (Servicio Médico Urgencias, ☎ 964/211253), **Gandesa** (Servei d'Ambulancies, ☎ 977/244728), **Morella** (Cruz Roja, ☎ 964/160380), **Tarragona** (Creu Roja, ☎ 977/222222), and **Valencia** (Cruz Roja, ☎ 96/380–2244).

General medical assistance: **Castellón** (Hospital Provincial, ☎ 964/210522), **Morella** (Ambulatorio, ☎ 964/160962), **Tarragona** (Hospital Joan XXIII, ☎ 977/295800), and **Valencia** (Hospital Clínico, ☎ 96/386–2600).

Guided Tours

For a guided tour of Tarragona's sights, contact the municipal **tourist office** just below the cathedral (✉ Carrer Major 39, ☎ 977/245203). The tour covers all of the important archaeological sites along with the cathedral.

Servei Turistic Parc (✉ Rambla Nova, 118, ☎ 977/702324), in Amposta, runs guided tours of every variety through the Ebro Delta, Amposta, and Tarragona province in general. Among the touring options are vineyards, Templars castles, Cistercian monasteries, and gondola-like *perxar* excursions through the canals and lagoons of the delta. Pop in and talk it over with official Tarragona Diputació guide Josep Valldeperas.

You can book guided tours of Valencia at the municipal **tourist office** (✉ Plaza Ayuntamiento 1, ☎ 96/351–0417). Leaving daily at 10 from the Ayuntamiento, a bilingual guide takes you around the *ayuntamiento* itself, the Lonja, the cathedral, the Ceramics Museum, the bullring, the station, the Museum of Fine Arts, and the Viveros.

In summer, the regional **tourist office** in Valencia (☞ Visitor Information, *below*) organizes tours of the Albufera, the marshlands to the south of Valencia, depending on demand. You tour the port area before continuing south to the Albufera (lagoon), where you can visit a traditional *barraca* (thatched farmhouse). You'll end up in the Devesa Gardens, where you can hire boats to explore the canals through the paddies.

Late-Night Pharmacies

Pharmacies (*farmacias de guardia*) stay open late on a rotating basis: one stays open 24 hours in every sizable town or city. To find out whose turn it is, look on the door of any pharmacy, or in the local press.

Outdoor Activities and Sports

GOLF

This area is well endowed with golf courses, all of them near or on the coast. Call in advance to reserve tee times. Listed geographically, north to south, courses include the following: **Club de Golf Costa Dorada** (✉ Apdo. 43, Calafells, Tarragona, ☎ 977/168032), 9 holes; **Club de Golf Costa de Azahar** (✉ Carretera Grao–Benicàssim, Grao de Castellón, ☎ 964/280979), 9 holes; **Club de Campo del Mediterráneo** (✉ Urbanización La Coma, Borriol, Castellón, ☎ 964/321227), 18 holes; **Club de Campo El Bosque** (✉ Chiva, 31 km [19 mi] west of Valencia, ☎ 96/326–3800), 18 holes; **Club de Golf Escorpión** (✉ Apdo. 1, Betera, Valencia, ☎ 96/160–1211), 18 holes; **Campo de Golf de Manises** (✉ Apdo. 22029, Valencia, ☎ 96/152–3804), 9 holes; **Campo de Golf El Saler** (✉ Apdo. 9034, Valencia, ☎ 96/161–1186), 18 holes.

SAILING

The safe waters off the eastern coast make for good sailing conditions. Ask at local tourist offices about renting boats, or just chance upon rental outfits. Some possibilities are **Club Náutico Tarragona** (✉ Muelle de la Costa, ☎ 977/240360), **Club Náutico Salou** (✉ Espigón del Muelle, ☎ 977/382166), **Club Náutico Castellón** (✉ Port, ☎ 964/280354), and **Club Náutico Valencia** (✉ Camino del Canal 91, ☎ 96/367–9011).

Travel Agencies

Tarragona: **Vibus SA** (✉ Rambla Nova 125, Tarragona, ☎ 977/219278); Valencia: the **Iberia** office (✉ Paz 14, ☎ 96/152–1144), and **Viajes Paz** (✉ Paz 32, ☎ 96/351–8080).

Visitor Information

Three tourist offices have information on the whole region: **Castellón** (✉ Plaza María Agustina 5, ☎ 964/221000). **Tarragona** (✉ Rambla Nova 118, ☎ 977/230312). **Valencia** (✉ Paz 48, ☎ 96/398–6422). Local tourist offices are as follows: **Benicàssim** (✉ Médico Segarra 4, ☎ 964/303851). **Morella** (✉ Torre San Miguel, ☎ 964/173032). **Peñíscola** (✉ Paseo Marítimo, ☎ 964/481729). **Reus** (✉ San Juan 27, ☎ 977/320349). **Sagunto** (✉ Cronista Chabret, ☎ 96/266–2213). **Tarragona** (✉ Major 39, ☎ 977/245203). **Teruel** (✉ Tomás Nogués 1, ☎ 974/602279). **Tortosa** (✉ Plaza España, ☎ 977/442567). **Valencia** (✉ Plaza Ayuntamiento 1, ☎ 96/394–2798; ✉ Estacioán RENFE, Játiva 24, ☎ 96/352–0202).

There are informational phone lines in **Castellón** (☎ 964/221000) and **Valencia** (☎ 96/352–4000); in **Valencia** (✉ Paz 48), a 24-hour machine dispenses information in exchange for 25-pta. coins.

9 The Southeast

Spain's southeastern corner is dominated by a flat, fertile coastal plain, characterized by orange groves, rice paddies, and mountains that give rise to the strange, almost lunar desert landscape of Almería. Most travelers come to the Southeast for its beautiful beaches, but the region's inland vistas are just as attractive. Both the province and the coast are dappled with striking white architecture, a legacy of long Moorish occupation.

By Philip Eade

Updated by
Katherine
Semler

THE SOUTHEASTERN CORNER OF SPAIN is a land of natural contrasts. In the north, the *huerta* (fertile, irrigated coastal plain) produces an orange harvest from late November through April; in spring, you can see fragrant flowers and fruit growing on the same trees. The rice paddies stretching from the Albufera (lagoon) south of Valencia to Gandía give rise to Valencia's culinary specialty, paella. The farther south you go, the drier and more mountainous the country becomes, until you reach the singular desert-lunar landscape of Almería, made famous by spaghetti-western films in the 1960s. The inland province of Albacete, historically part of Murcia, was the scene of Don Quixote's exploits in the Castilian expanses of La Mancha and is worth exploring for its tiny villages and natural treasures.

The striking architecture in most southeastern towns attests to the area's long Moorish occupation. Alicante was in Moorish hands from 718 to 1249; Murcia, from 825 to 1243; and Almería, from 712 to 1489, when it was finally reconquered by Ferdinand and Isabella.

Most visitors come to southeastern Spain for the beaches, from the crowded Costa Blanca to the nearly deserted stretches around Cabo de Gata in Almería, renowned for its scuba diving. Mild temperatures in spring and fall allow you to vacation before and after the thickest crowds.

South of Valencia (☞ Chapter 8), you can drive along a thin strip between the sea and the Albufera before following the coast around the Cabo de la Nao to the Costa Blanca. Just south of Cullera, head inland through the historic towns of Xátiva (also spelled Játiva) and Alcoy en route to Alicante. An exotic and bustling Mediterranean port, Alicante is worth a day of exploration before you move inland toward Murcia, past the palm forest at Elche and the ancient town of Orihuela. The vast inland areas of the Southeast are best placed for travelers approaching Murcia from Madrid; here, readers of Cervantes can explore the setting of *Don Quixote*. Murcia, with its superb cathedral, is an important stop before you behold the Africanesque Almería by way of Lorca, Mojácar, and the stunning, crowd-free coast around Cabo de Gata.

Pleasures and Pastimes

Beaches

Like the region as a whole, the southeastern coastline possesses abundant variety, from the long stretches of sand dunes north of Denia and south of Alicante to the rocky coves and sweeping crescents of the Costa Blanca. The benign climate means you can lounge on the beach most of the year. Major beaches have Cruz Roja (Red Cross) stations with helicopters and flags to warn swimmers of conditions: green for safety, red for danger.

Altea, popular with families, is busy and pebbly, but the old town provides a pretty setting. Benidorm's two white, crescent-shaped beaches extend for more than 5 km (3 mi) and are widely considered the best in Spain. Benidorm takes all prizes for après-beach entertainment; just be warned that in summer you'll be sunbathing head-to-toe. Calblanque is on the road between Los Belones and Cabo de Palos, which takes you down a longish rough track to a succession of nearly deserted beaches frequented by young Murcians. Calpe's beaches have the scenic advantage of the sheer outcrop Peñon de Ifach (Cliff of Ifach), which stands guard over stretches of sand to either side. Denia and Jávea both have family beaches where children paddle in relatively safe waters. Gandía's sandy beach is well kept, and its promenade is lined with bars and restaurants. Although the narrow La Manga del Mar Menor (*Manga* refers to a thin "sleeve" of land), which encloses a huge lagoon, offers some stunning views, it has been ruined by a tasteless sprawl of hotels and condos. Mojácar has a shingly beach backed by bars and good sports facilities, but if you have a car, try some of the deserted beaches to the south. Needless to say, there are no facilities save the odd water tap for campers; and nudity, though illegal, seems generally accepted here, at Calblanque, and just north of Cullera. In Moraira, the best beach is Playa Castillo, just outside the center. Santa Pola and Guardamar del Segura are other good options, with fine, clean sand and pine trees behind the dunes.

Dining

Rice grows better in the Valencian provinces than anywhere else in Spain—which explains why paella originated here. Another rice dish to try is *arroz a la banda* (meat or fish with vegetables and rice, cooked over a wood fire). Remember that paella should be eaten directly after cooking, so don't order it from a *menú del día* (menu of the day) unless you can check its freshness. Alicante and Jijona are famous for their *turrón* (nougat made with almonds and flavored with honey). In Elche you can savor fresh dates. Murcian cooking uses products of the *huerta* and the sea, with a marked Arab influence in the preparation. Traditionally a fisherman's rice dish, *caldero de Mar Menor* is cooked in huge iron pots and has a distinctly oily consistency, flavored by fish cooked in its own juices. Delicious as tapas or a first course are *muchirones* (broad beans in a spicy sauce), similar to the Catalan *habas a la catalana,* and *cocas* (meat pies similar to empanadas). In Almería, the menu features *gazpacho andaluz* (sometimes described as a spicy, liquid salad—and here characterized by the addition of croutons) and *pescaditos fritos* (small fried fish), as well as grapes.

CATEGORY	COST*
$$$$	over 6,500 ptas.
$$$	4,500 ptas.–6,500 ptas.
$$	2,000 ptas.–4,500 ptas.
$	under 2,000 ptas.

*per person for a three-course meal, excluding drinks, service, and tax

Fiestas

Local festivals provide excellent entertainment. Here are some standouts: Almería's lively Festival Internacional de Títeres (Puppet Theater Festival) is held in January. Denia holds a mini Fallas March 16–19. Alcoy's spectacular Moros y Cristianos (Moors and Christians) festival takes place April 21–24 and includes a reenactment of clashes from the Christian Reconquest, the battle to dislodge the Moors at the end of the 15th century. The Semana Santa (Holy Week) processions in Murcia are among Spain's most famous; those in Lorca are particularly known for the opulent costumes of both biblical and Roman participants and for the penitents' solemn robes. Altea's Moros y Cristianos spectacle, held on the third Sunday in May, is a combination of battle reenactment and pageant, complete with elaborate costumes and the town's youngsters dressed up as knights in shining armor. Alicante's main festival is the Hogueras de San Juan (St. John's Day Bonfires), June 21–24. El Misteri (the Mystery Play) is performed in Elche in two parts, August 14–15, preceded by a public dress rehearsal (August 13).

Golf

Spain is one of Europe's top golfing destinations, and the mild southeastern climate makes this region an excellent choice for winter golfing. Golf courses are as follows (north to south): Campo de Golf El Saler, 18 holes (☞ Southern Catalonia and the Levante A to Z *in* Chapter 8); Club de Golf Jávea, 9 holes; Club de Golf Don Cayo, Altea, 9 holes; Campo de Golf Villa Martín, Torrevieja, 18 holes; La Manga Club de Golf, Los Belones, two 18-hole courses; and Golf Almerimar, 18 holes. Reserve tee times in advance, and expect to pay about 8,000 ptas. for 18 holes, 4,000 ptas. for 9.

Lodging

Many hotels on the coast are modern high-rises. If you'd prefer to avoid these, you'll probably have to choose between character and comfort. Paradors have traditionally solved this conundrum, and there are four in the Southeast: Jávea, Puerto Lumbreras (Lorca), Mojácar, and Albacete. The last of these, though likely to be off most people's itineraries, is the most representative of the rustic parador style. The others are tasteful, if modern. Calpe, Alicante, San José, and Almería have older, one-of-a-kind hotels; reserve in advance. Note that some coastal hotels close for the winter.

CATEGORY	COST*
$$$$	over 18,000 ptas.
$$$	11,500 ptas.–18,000 ptas.
$$	7,000 ptas.–11,500 ptas.
$	under 7,000 ptas.

All prices are for a standard double room, excluding tax.

Exploring the Southeast

From Valencia's Albufera, inland to Xátiva and Albacete, and down the Costa Blanca through Alicante and on to Murcia, Cartagena, and Almería, the Southeast is rich in both natural and man-made phenomena. Beaches, salt lagoons, steppes, mountain villages, and Mediterranean port cities provide plenty of attractive diversion.

Numbers in the text correspond to numbers in the margin and on the Southeast map.

Great Itineraries

The Southeast offers three different coastal experiences (the lagoon, the populous beaches of the Costa Blanca, and the deserted strands south of Mojácar), two distinct inland programs (the steppe around Albacete and the mountains near Murcia), and four major cities (Alicante, Albacete, Murcia, and Almería).

In seven days you can see nearly everything—unless, of course, you find the beach or the golf course of your dreams and decide to stay put. Five days will allow a sampling of beaches, inland villages, and the three coastal cities. Three days is enough for a beach or two, an inland village, and at least a look at Alicante, Murcia, and Almería.

IF YOU HAVE 3 DAYS

Start with the Albufera and **El Palmar** ① before continuing through **Cullera** ② and **Denia** ④ to the **Cabo de la Nao** ⑥. Spend the night at the Parador de la Costa Blanca in ⊞ **Jávea** ⑤, or in the village of ⊞ **Moraira** ⑦. Begin the next day with a visit to the fishing village of **Altea** ⑨ before heading for **Alicante** ⑰ for lunch and continuing on through **Elche** ⑱ and **Orihuela** ⑲ to ⊞ **Murcia** ㉒ for the night. On the third day visit **Lorca** ㉕, Aguilas, **Mojácar** ㉖, and the **Cabo de Gata Nature Reserve** ㉗ on the way to ⊞ **Almería** ㉘ for the night.

IF YOU HAVE 5 DAYS

Explore the Albufera and **El Palmar** ① before continuing through **Cullera** ② and **Denia** ④ to the **Cabo de la Nao** ⑥. Spend the night at the Parador de Jávea in ⊞ **Jávea** ⑤, or in the village of ⊞ **Moraira** ⑦. The next day, visit the fishing village of **Altea** ⑨; then hook inland to **Polop** ⑩ and **Alcoy** ⑬ for lunch at the Venta del Pilar. Spend the night in ⊞ **Alicante** ⑰. On day three, see **Elche** ⑱ and **Orihuela** ⑲ before stopping in ⊞ **Murcia** ㉒ for the night. On day four, explore **Cartagena** ㉓ and **La Manga del Mar Menor** ㉔ before heading inland to **Lorca** ㉕ for the night. On the fifth day, explore the coast from **Mojácar** ㉖ to the **Cabo de Gata Nature Reserve** ㉗ on the way to ⊞ **Almería** ㉘ for the night.

When to Tour the Southeast

Mid-autumn to April is the best time to visit this hot corner of the Iberian Peninsula. Summer is usually oppressively hot. Easter is interesting for the often-bizarre holiday pageants and processions, especially in remote towns and villages.

FROM VALENCIA TO THE COSTA BLANCA

This short drive takes you through the Albuferas wetlands and into the northern end of the Costa Blanca, known as La Marina Alta (the High Shore). There are many untouched natural spots to savor on this stretch.

El Palmar

❶ *16 km (10 mi) south of Valencia.*

South of Valencia (☞ Chapter 8), the coastal road runs along a thin strip of land (La Dehesa) that barely separates the sea from the **Albufera,** rimmed with rice fields and shady pine woods. There are large-scale duck shoots here in fall and winter. For a closer look at the Albufera's unique aura, turn right toward El Palmar; here a one-lane road hugs the edge of the lagoon, passing thatched *barracas* (shacks). In El Palmar, you can hire a boat to explore the lagoon.

Cullera

❷ *39 km (24 mi) south of Valencia, 27 km (17 mi) north of Gandía.*

Pass the lighthouse at Cullera; around the rocky point is modern Cullera, a mushrooming resort marked by futuristic high-rises. The climb up to the **Ermita de Nuestra Señora del Castillo** (Hermitage of Our Lady of the Castle) and **castle ruins** culminates in views of the sea, the *huerta,* and the mountains.

Dining

$$$ ✕ **Les Mouettes.** On the road up to the castle, this tiny restaurant has
★ a lovely terrace with stunning sea views. French owner-chef Jacqueline Lagarce prepares secret recipes from home; try the *lenguado con salsa de champiñones* (sole with mushroom sauce) or *pato con salsa de jenjibre* (duck with ginger sauce). ✉ *Carretera subida al Castillo,* ☎ *96/172–0010. AE, DC, MC, V. Closed Dec. 15–Feb. 15. No dinner Sun., no lunch July–Sept.*

Gandía

❸ *30 km (19 mi) northwest of Denia.*

The old town of Gandía lies 4 km (2½) mi inland from the modern beach development. This became the Borgia (Borja, in Spanish) fief after Ferdinand the Catholic granted the duchy to the family in 1485. The

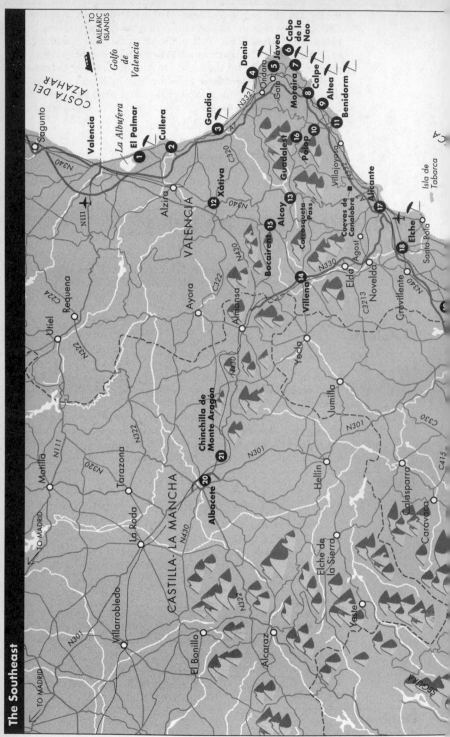

TO
BALEARIC
ISLANDS

TO
VALENCIA

Golfo
de
Valencia

COSTA DEL AZAHAR

Sagunto

N340

N111

Valencia

La Albufera

El Palmar

Cullera

1

2

Gandía

3

A7

N332

Denia

4

Gata

Ondara

5 Jávea

7 Cabo
de la
Nao

6

Moraira

8

Calpe

9 Altea

Benidorm

11

Villajoyosa

N332

Alcira

VALENCIA

Xàtiva

12

N340

C320

C322

Ayora

Almansa

N340

Bocairent

15

Alcoy

13

Cocentaina

16

Guadalest

Polop

10

Cortesqueta
Pass

Cuevas de
Canalobre

Aigüés

Elda

Novelda

Alicante

17

Isla de
Tabarca

Elche

18

Santa Pola

CA

Requena

Utiel

N322

N III

Motilla

N320

Tarazona

Villena

14

N330

C3213

Yecla

N430

Jumilla

N301

Novelda

Crevillente

N340

C330

C415

Calasparra

Caravaca

Villarrobledo

La Roda

N301

El Bonillo

N430

Chinchilla de
Monte Aragón

21

N301

Albacete

20

CASTILLA-LA MANCHA

Alcaraz

Hellín

Elche de
la Sierra

Yeste

SEGURA

TO MADRID

N322

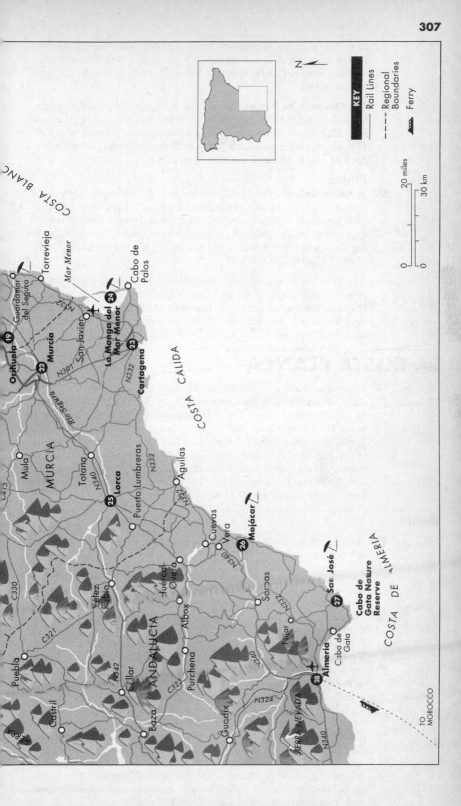

canny Borgia pope Alexander VI was one of the most notorious of all Renaissance prelates, but the family's reputation was later redeemed by the Jesuit St. Francis Borgia (1510–72), born in Gandía and canonized in 1671.

The **Palacio de los Duques** (Ducal Palace), signposted from the city center, was founded by St. Francis in 1546 and still serves as a Jesuit college. Elaborate ceilings and brightly colored *azulejos* (tiles) adorn the 17th-century state rooms. ⌨ *300 ptas.* ☉ *Guided tours summer, weekdays 11 and 6; winter, Tues.–Sat. 11 and 5.*

Dining

$$ ✕ **Mesón Gallego.** This Galician restaurant is a lucky discovery in the port area. The rough and simple decor is a good setting for hearty Galician dishes such as *pulpo* (octopus) or for fish and meat specialties cooked over coals. Ask for Galician *culcas,* shallow, ceramic bowls for drinking the young *ribeiro* wines. ✉ *Levante 37, Grao de Gandía,* ☎ *96/ 284–1892. AE, DC, MC, V.*

En Route As you head south, parchment-colored hills mark the beginning of the province of Alicante. Once past Ondara, which has an unusual stone bullring, you can detour to the **Cueva de las Calaveras** (Skull Cave), near Benidoleig, inhabited by prehistoric humans some 40,000 years ago. ☎ *96/640–4235.* ⌨ *400 ptas.* ☉ *Daily 9–6.*

LA COSTA BLANCA

The popular name for the stretch of coast between Cabo de la Nao and Cabo de Palos is the Costa Blanca, or White Coast. Carnations grow in such abundance here that they even faintly perfume the local wine. The Costa Blanca includes the cities of Alicante and Cartagena as well as numerous beach resorts, which have expanded uncontrollably since the 1960s and early '70s. A drive down this shore grants some quiet and picturesque stops, especially off season. One such spot is the road that branches off N332 at Gata de Gorgos (also known as Gata) to the coastal towns of Denia and Jávea.

Denia

❹ *100 km (62 mi) south of Valencia, 8 km (5 mi) north of Jávea and east of Ondara.*

The northernmost beach resort on the Costa Blanca, Denia is a busy tourist town known for its fleet of fishing boats and for its fiestas and celebrations, culminating in the midsummer St. John's Day bonfires (June 23). Backed by the Montgó massif, rising to more than 2,100 ft to the west, Denia's beaches to the north—Les Marines, Les Bovetes, and Les Deveses—are smooth and sandy, while the coast to the south is rocky, forming *calas* (tiny secluded inlets that recall the Costa Brava, north of Barcelona). Denia's most interesting architectural feature is its **Palau del Governador** (Governor's Palace), overlooking the town, with its 12th-century tower and Renaissance bastion; the latter has a Moorish portal with a lovely horseshoe arch. There are also several interesting churches and convents, such as the **Iglesia de la Asunción** (Church of the Assumption). Known as the gastronomical capital of the Costa Blanca, Denia is a good place to sample fresh Mediterranean seafood. Try a plate of *picaetes de sepia y calamar* (squid and cuttlefish) or *suquet de rape* (stewed hake) at any of the town's fine restaurants. Denia also has the closest **ferry connection to the Balearic islands,** with two companies, Flebasa (☎ 96/578–4200) and Pitra (☎ 96/ 642–3120), sailing the 3½-hour, 80-km (50-mi) crossing to Ibiza and Palma de Mallorca daily (more frequently in summer).

Dining

$$ ✕ **Drassanes.** Built into the original medieval shipyards (for which it's named), Drassanes is a well-known place for fresh, local seafood. The decor is simple and rustic maritime, and both the fare and the people are authentic and good. *Arroz a la banda* (rice cooked with seafood) is the house specialty. ✉ *C. Puerto 15,* ☎ *96/578–1118. AE, DC, MC, V. Closed Mon. and Nov.*

Jávea

⑤ *108 km (67 mi) southeast of Valencia, 92 km (57 mi) northeast of Alicante, 8 km (5 mi) south of Denia.*

A labyrinth of tiny streets and houses with arched portals and Gothic windows, Jávea has an antique aspect contrasted only by its modern church, **Santa María de Loreto.** The church-fortress of **San Bartolomé** is its architectural gem; the **Soler Blasco** ethnological and archaeological museum (open mornings only in winter) is another interesting visit. The **Aduanas del Mar** area around the port is well sprinkled with restaurants serving local dishes, such as *arroz a la marinera* (seafood paella).

Dining

$$$ 🏨 **Parador de Jávea** This modern parador is set in a lush palm grove with terrific views of the white bay below. It's a low structure (four stories), and more tasteful than the high-rise hotels elsewhere on the Costa Blanca. Rooms are airy and pleasant. ✉ *Avenida del Meterráneo 7, Jávea,* ☎ *96/579–0200,* ℻ *96/579–0308. 65 rooms. Restaurant, bar, pool, sauna, exercise room. AE, DC, MC, V.*

Cabo de la Nao

⑥ *10 km (6 mi) southeast of Jávea.*

Cabo de la Nao (Cape Nao) is a great spur of land that juts out into the Mediterranean toward Ibiza, barely 100 km (62 mi) away. As you round the point, you turn from a coast that looks toward Italy to one that mirrors Africa. In the same few kilometers, you pass from an agriculture of oranges and rice to one of olives and palms, from a benign, if variable, climate to tawny aridity.

Moraira

⑦ *12 km (7 mi) northeast of Calpe, 20 km (12 mi) south of Jávea.*

Moraira has managed to preserve an atmosphere of seclusion in the narrow streets leading down to its harbor. The *casco viejo* (old town) has a good selection of bars and restaurants, while the outskirts have been edified with chalets and private residences. The **castle** and **watch tower** overlooking the port were built to protect Moraira from Mediterranean pirates during the Middle Ages.

Dining and Lodging

$$$$ ✕ **El Girasol.** An elegant, ivy-cloaked villa on the Calpe road houses
★ one of the finest restaurants in this region. Owners Joachim and Victoria Koerper preside over a small dining room and terrace. Their cooking is imaginative and outstanding, with the emphasis on French dishes. Highlights on the menu include *ensalada de salmonetes a la vinagretta de naranja* (red mullet salad with orange vinegar) and *solomillo de lechal a la ficele* (veal poached in sherry). ✉ *Carretera Moraira a Calpe,* ☎ *96/574–4373. AE, DC, MC, V. Closed Nov. and Mon. Sept.–June. No lunch Mon.–Sat. July–Aug.*

$$$ 🗷 **Hotel Swiss Moraira.** With a secluded location in a pine forest above Moraira (off the road to Calpe) and well-decorated rooms situated around a creatively shaped swimming pool, this low-rise, luxury hotel is ideal for peace and comfort. During the day, guests leave for the beach and marina, 3 km (2 mi) away. ✉ *C. Haya, 175 Club Moraira, 03724 Alicante,* ☎ *96/574–7104,* ℻ *96/574–7074. 25 rooms. Restaurant, bar, pool, tennis court. AE, DC, MC, V.*

Calpe

★ **8**   *15 km (9 mi) southwest of Jávea, 8 km (5 mi) north of Altea.*

South of Moraira are Calpe and the incredible outcrop known as the **Peñón de Ifach.** Calpe was deserted for nearly 100 years after Barbary pirates killed or enslaved the entire population in the 17th century. The Peñón rises from the sea as a 1,000-ft monolith; the summit is accessible by tunnel. It is said that those who scale these heights at full moon will be hurled to their deaths by goatlike spirits.

Dining and Lodging

$$ ✕ **Al-Zaraq.** Just down the road from the Venta la Chata, Al-Zaraq offers a tasty break from traditional Spanish fare. The Lebanese menu features lamb and many vegetarian delights; highlights are the *cordero en salsa de dátiles* (lamb with date sauce) and *lubina con costra de piñones* (sea bass with a pine-nut crust). ✉ *Carretera de Valencia (N332, Km 172),* ☎ *96/573–1615. MC, V. Closed Mon. and Feb.*

$ ✕🗷 **Venta la Chata.** This pretty hotel represents good value. The downstairs is rustic, as are the wood furnishings and *azulejo* (glazed-tile) floors in the rooms. The premises include terraced gardens with sea views. Ask for a refurbished room with a balcony or terrace. ✉ *Carretera de Valencia (N332, Km 172), 03710 Alicante,* ☎ *96/583–0308. 17 rooms. Bar, tennis court, Ping-Pong. AE, DC, MC, V.*

Altea

9   *10 km (6 mi) south of Calpe, 11 km (7 mi) north of Benidorm.*

Altea is an old fishing village with white houses and blue, ceramic-tiled domes. One of the best-conserved villages on the Costa Blanca, it serves as a foil to the skyscraping tourist towers of Benidorm.

Dining

$$$ ✕ **La Costera.** This restaurant mixes excellent Swiss cooking with bizarre decor and a nightly show. Specialties include the delicious *rostit con carne troceada y champiñon* (chopped meat with mushrooms and potatoes). The place is extremely popular, so reserve in advance if possible. ✉ *Costera del Mestre la Música 8,* ☎ *96/584–0230. DC, MC, V. Closed Wed. and Aug.*

Polop

10   *10 km (6 mi) northwest of Altea.*

In the center of Polop is a collection of taps, each donated by a different town or province, that provide the villagers with mountain water.

En Route   Follow C3318 south to Benidorm.

Benidorm

11   *42 km (26 mi) northeast of Alicante, 11 km (7 mi) south of Altea.*

Benidorm is a hugely overdeveloped resort with a seemingly bottomless capacity for tourists. Its twin, white, crescent-shaped beaches are enhanced by a continual accumulation of sand from other local beaches. For a fantastic view, follow signs to Club Sierra Dorada at the eastern edge of town and climb up to the **Rincón de Loix** (Loix Corner). Hidden among the concrete blocks, the old village still survives.

Dining and Lodging

$$$ ✕ **Tiffany's.** The red and white tones of Tiffany's draw Benidorm's jet set for intimacy and fine international cuisine. Delicacies like *salmón con langostinos* (salmon with shrimp) and *entrecôte al roquefort* (steak with roquefort cheese) are accompanied by piano music. ✉ *Avda. Mediterráneo, Edifício Coblanca 3,* ☎ *96/585–4468. AE, DC, MC, V. Closed Jan. 6–Feb. 6. No lunch.*

$ ✕ **I Fratelli.** The cooking here is Italian, with nouvelle-French and international touches. Neapolitan music complements the stylish Moderniste decor: sleek black chairs, white tablecloths, and exotic potted plants. Try the *pescados a la sal* (fish baked in salt) or a pasta dish. ✉ *Dr. Orts Llorca,* ☎ *96/585–3979. AE, DC, MC, V. Closed Nov.*

$$$ ✕▥ **Gran Delfín.** The Gran Delfín is the most quietly situated hotel in Benidorm—and that's saying something, especially in summer. The salon downstairs is filled with a motley collection of furniture. The bedrooms are Castilian-style, with a smattering of bric-a-brac on the walls. Ask for a room at the front, overlooking the beach. ✉ *Playa de Poniente, 03500 Alicante,* ☎ *96/585–3400,* ℻ *96/585–7154. 96 rooms. Restaurant, bar, pool, tennis court. AE, DC, MC, V. Closed Oct.–Apr. 5.*

Nightlife and the Arts

For a cabaret with Spanish dance and an international musical show, try the **Benidorm Palace**(✉ Carretera de la Diputación, ☎ 965/851661). Dinner starts at 8:30, the show at 10 (both start one hour later in summer). Alternatively, don a crown at the **Nuevo Gran Castillo Conde de Alfaz** (✉ Camino Viejo del Albir, ☎ 96/686–5265) and dine in front of jousting medieval knights. Dinner, drinks, and the show (Friday and Saturday only) cost 3,500 ptas. per person.

Countless bars and discos, with names like Jockey's and Harrods (reflecting Benidorm's popularity with Brits and Germans), line Avenida de Europa and the Ensanche de la Playa de Levante.

INLAND: XÁTIVA AND ALCOY

For a break from sea and sand, cut inland to some of the towns and scenes that deepen the light atmosphere of the Mediterranean coast. Xátiva, Alcoy, Villena, and Bocairent have some of the most rustic villages in the Southeast, where people live much the same traditional, small-town lives that their ancestors lived.

Xátiva

⑫ *42 km (26 mi) southwest of Cullera, 50 km (31 mi) north of Alcoy.*

Xátiva rests on the dry, vine- and cypress-covered slopes of the Sierra de Alcoy and retains a pink **casco antiguo** (old town) dotted with fountains. Under the Moors, Xátiva was famous for paper production; centuries later it became the birthplace of two of the Borgia popes—Calixtus III and his nephew Alexander VI. The latter issued the famous 1493 Papal Bull granting the Indies to Ferdinand and Isabella, though he's more often remembered for his scandalous private life and as the father of Caesar and Lucrezia.

To reach the **castle,** on the slopes of Mount Bernisa, follow signs up a steep path from the Plaza del Españoleto. Halfway up, the 13th-century

Ermita de San Feliú (Hermitage of St. Felix) has a beautiful group of Valencian Primitive paintings. Felipe V destroyed the fortress pretty thoroughly as part of his retribution for Xátiva's opposition in the War of the Spanish Succession, but a partial restoration of the castle and a panoramic view reward your efforts. ⊙ *Tues.–Sun. 10–6 (10–7 in summer).* 🎟 *300 ptas.*

On the Plaza del Seo stands the enormous **Collegiata** (collegiate church), which houses some Borgia Renaissance marble. Opposite the Collegiata is the 16th-century plateresque facade of the **hospital.** Down Calle Corretgeria, the **Museo Municipal** (Municipal Museum) has a small collection of archaeological finds and paintings by Xátiva's other famous son, José de Ribera.

Alcoy

★ ⑬   *55 km (34 mi) north of Alicante, 50 km (31 mi) south of Xátiva.*

Alcoy sits at the confluence of three rivers and is famous for its bridges, which span the deep river gorges. The town owes its size (population 67,000) to its textile, paper, and fruit-canning industries. Alcoy's annual **Moros y Cristianos** (Moors and Christians festival), around the time of Sant Jordi (St. George's Day, April 23), is the most spectacular fiesta of its kind in Spain. Colorful processions and mock battles commemorate the Battle of Alcoy, in 1275, when St. George's intervention helped liberate the city from the besieging forces of Al Azraq, ensuring victory for the Christians.

If you miss this event, walk down Calle Sant Miquel, which leads off the Plaza de España, to **Casal de Sant Jordi** (St. George Civic Center), which houses fiesta paraphernalia including costumes worn by the combatants. ⊠ *Sant Miquel 60,* ☎ *no phone.* 🎟 *200 ptas.* ⊙ *Tues.–Fri. 11–1 and 5–7:30.*

Dining and Lodging

$$ ✕ **Venta Saltera.** A few minutes south of Alcoy, this restaurant serves
★   typical local fare, of which the staff is *muy* proud. Try the *olleta alcoyana* (Alcoy stew, made with white beans and pork). ⊠ *Carretera Nacional 340,* ☎ *96/554–4330. AE, DC, MC, V. Closed Wed. and second half of Aug.*

$$ 🏨 **Reconquista.** There's nothing memorable about the modern, high-
★   rise Reconquista, but it's the most comfortable option for miles around. You can compensate for the plain, dated decor in the bedrooms by requesting a view over the river gorge to old Alcoy. The public rooms have an institutional air, with spotty, gray-tiled floors and functional, plastic furniture. ⊠ *Puente San Jorge 1, 03803 Alcoy,* ☎ *96/533–0900,* 𝖥𝖠𝖷 *96/533–0955. 73 rooms. Restaurant, bar. AE, DC, MC, V.*

Villena

⑭   *40 km (25 mi) west of Alcoy.*

A collection of priceless Bronze Age rings, bracelets, coronets, and bowls of gold was discovered on a dry Villena riverbed in 1963. It is now displayed in the archaeology section of the *ayuntamiento.*

Bocairent

⑮   *27 km (17 mi) northeast of Villena.*

On the N340 from Villena, find time to stop in Bocairent, where the **Museo Parroquial** (Parish Museum) has paintings by Juan de Juanes, who died here in 1579, along with works by Francisco Ribalta and Joaquín Sorolla.

Guadalest

⑯ *36 km (22 mi) east of Alcoy.*

Guadalest is an old town. Perched atop a crag within the walls of a ruined castle, it conquers the steep terrain with tiny, stepped streets. Continue as far as Callosa, turn left toward Tarbena, and brave a dip at the foot of the **Cascada de El Algar** (El Algar falls), icy 12 months a year. Nearby **Tarbena,** a village famed for its sausages, introduces you to spectacular, rocky-mountain scenery.

ALICANTE, ELCHE, AND ORIHUELA

Luminous Alicante seems to shimmer with the kind of light the Mediterranean is famous for, while inland Elche's palm forest shades its ancient treasures from the heat of the summer. Orihuela's twisting back streets tunnel through the town's old Moorish neighborhoods.

Alicante

⑰ *82 km (51 mi) northeast of Murcia, 183 km (113 mi) south of Valencia by the coast road, 42 km (26 mi) south of Benidorm, 55 km (34 mi) south of Alcoy.*

Alicante, at the convergence of inland and coastal roads, has always been known for its luminous skies. The Greeks called it Akra Leuka (White Summit); the Romans named it Lucentum (City of Light). The city is dominated by the **Castillo de Santa Bárbara** set on a rocky peak, but its immediate pride is its grand avenue, the **Explanada,** lined with date palms.

Begin your tour at the tourist office in the arcaded Plaza de Ayuntamiento. It's worth looking inside the Baroque town hall; ask gate officials for permission to explore the ornate halls and rococo chapel on the first floor. Walk through the *ayuntamiento* to the Plaza Santísima Faz, a pedestrian square crowded with sidewalk cafés and restaurants.

From the Plaza Santísima Faz, walk down the busy, pedestrian Calle Mayor and take your first right to reach the cathedral of **San Nicolás de Bari** (open for mass only), built on the site of a former mosque. The cathedral has both an austere Renaissance facade in the style of Herrera (of Escorial fame) and a lavish, Baroque side chapel.

At the far end of Calle Mayor is the **Museo de Arte Siglo XX** (Museum of 20th-century Art), whose collection of abstract art includes works by Picasso, Miró, Braque, Tàpies, Hockney, and Rauschenberg. ✉ *Free.* ☉ *Oct.–Apr., Tues.–Sat. 10–1 and 5–8; May–Sept., Tues.–Sat. 10:30–1:30 and 6–9.*

Across the small plaza from the Museum of 20th-Century Art stands the church of **Santa María,** with a rich Baroque facade. From here, it's a short walk down steps, then left along the back of Playa Postiguet to the foot of Mt. Benacantil (700 ft) and the elevator up to the castle.

★ Originally built as a Carthaginian fortress around 3 BC, the **Castillo de Santa Bárbara** was extensively modified for numerous wars. From here you have a spectacular bird's-eye view of the city. Within the castle walls, a small museum displays objects associated with the annual St. John bonfires on Midsummer Night's Eve. ✉ *Castle 300 ptas., museum free.* ☉ *Castle and elevator Sun.–Fri. 10–7; museum spring–fall 9-7:30.*

Dining and Lodging

$$$ ✕ **Delfin.** Don't let the fantastic view over the palm-lined Explanada and Alicante's yacht culture distract you from Delfin's imaginative food. Opened in 1961, this restaurant remains on the gastronomic front line and is wholly modern, with bright decor and a breezy terrace. The cooking is divided equally between seafood and rice dishes. Try the *tosta de salmon* (toasted salmon). ⊠ *Explanada de España 12,* ☎ *96/521–4911. AE, DC, MC, V.*

$$ ✕ **Quo Vadis.** Just behind the *ayuntamiento,* this most quintessentially
★   Spanish of Alicante's restaurants has a cozy, villagelike atmosphere. The prompt and friendly staff brings you, indoors or out, dishes ranging from local seafood like *dorada a la sal* (sea bream baked in salt) to Castilian favorites like various *carnes flambés* (barbecued meats). Come at any time of day to sample the tapas that line the bar. ⊠ *Plaza Santísima Faz 3,* ☎ *96/521–6660. AE, DC, MC, V. Closed Mon. in winter. No dinner Sun. in winter.*

$$$ ✕▥ **Eurhotel Hesperia.** This modern hotel, 300 yards from Alicante's
★   port, can satisfy all your practical needs. Though the building is insipid, its proximity to the train and bus stations makes it pretty handy. Rates are often reduced by as much as half on weekends. The on-site restaurant, open weekdays, does a thriving business in Mediterranean fish and meat dishes. Try the *rollitos de lenguado de gambas al cava* (sole stuffed with shrimp in champagne) or the *entrecot con mantequilla y albahaca* (steak with butter and basil). ⊠ *C. Pintor Lorenzo Casanova 33, 03003 Alicante,* ☎ *96/513–0440,* 𝕱𝕬𝕏 *96/592–8323. 117 rooms. Restaurant, bar, cafeteria, parking. AE, DC, MC, V.*

$$ ✕▥ **Palas.** Palas is Alicante's oldest hotel, and it has a certain chaotic
★   charm. The rooms, with Regency furniture, lack carpets, but these shouldn't be necessary in any but the coldest months. Ask for a front room if you value a sea view more than tranquility. The restaurant, which has a summer terrace, is popular for rice dishes. ⊠ *Cervantes 15, 03002 Alicante,* ☎ *96/520–9310,* 𝕱𝕬𝕏 *96/514–0120. 39 rooms. Restaurant, bar. AE, DC, MC, V.*

$$$–$$$$ ▥ **Meliá Alicante.** Try the Meliá for both comfort and proximity to the sea. This huge hotel stands on a reclaimed peninsula jutting into the Mediterranean right near the city center. The bedrooms are bright and modern and command sweeping views of the beaches and marina. Downstairs, the lobby is a shrine to postmodernism, with cool marble floors and low, black tables. ⊠ *Playa del Postiguet, 03001 Alicante,* ☎ *96/520–5000,* 𝕱𝕬𝕏 *96/520–5746. 545 rooms. Restaurant, piano bar, pool, car rental. AE, DC, MC, V.*

Nightlife and the Arts

Roughish, lively bars dot the streets behind the *ayuntamiento.* Among the slicker pubs and discos are **Pachá** (⊠ Avda. Aguilera 22) and **Doña Pepa** (⊠ Jorge Juan 18, ☎ no phone). In summer, the liveliest places are along the water, on the Ruta del Puerto and Ruta de la Madera.

Shopping

Local **crafts** include basketwork, embroidery, leatherwork, and weaving, each specific to a single town or village. You'll find all of these crafts for sale in the major resorts, though their prices may be inflated. Often the most satisfying places to shop are local markets, so be sure to inquire about market days while you're in town.

For **ceramics,** go to Agost, 20 km (12 mi) inland from Alicante, where potters make good jugs and pitchers from the local white clay, whose porosity is ideal for keeping liquids cool. At the local **museum,** you can learn how these classic crafts items are made.

Elche

🔞 *24 km (15 mi) southwest of Alicante, 34 km (21 mi) northeast of Orihuela, 58 km (36 mi) northeast of Murcia.*

If Alicante is torrid in summer, Elche is even hotter. Fortunately, the largest palm forest in Europe surrounds this city, allowing occasional escape from the worst of the heat. The Moors first planted the palms for dates, Europe's most reliable crop, and the trees still produce these as well as yellow Palm Sunday fronds. (Throughout Spain, these fronds are blessed and then hung on balconies to ward off evil during the coming year.) Colonized by ancient Rome, Elche was later ruled by the Moors for 500 years. The remarkable stone bust known as *La Dama de Elche,* one of the earliest examples of Iberian sculpture (now in Madrid's Museum of Archaeology), was discovered here in 1897. The Misteri (Mystery Play), performed in the Basilica de Santa María on the Feast of the Assumption, draws many visitors; the performances on August 14 and 15 are particularly spectacular, with a platform bearing the Virgin Mary and guitar-playing angels winched 150 ft up into the dome of the church.

Be sure to visit the **Jardín del Huerto del Cura,** a lush botanical garden and palm grove across from the Hotel Huerto del Cura, where vibrantly colored flowers grow beneath magnificent palms. 🔲 *300 ptas.* ⊙ *Apr.–Sept., daily 9–8; Oct.–Mar., daily 9–6.*

Dining and Lodging

$$$ ✕🔲 **Huerto del Cura.** A subtropical location and a large, private gar-
★ den in Elche's palm grove make this modern hotel-in-the-spirit-of-a-parador perfect for rest and relaxation. The main building houses the excellent Els Capellans restaurant, which serves regional rice and fish dishes. The bedrooms are in bungalow huts, gloomy due to the shady location, but tastefully decorated. The palm-ringed swimming pool resembles something you might hope to find in the Seychelles. ✉ *Porta de la Morera, Elche, 03200 Alicante,* ☎ *96/545–8040,* 🖷 *96/542–1910. 86 rooms. Restaurant, bar, cafeteria, 2 pools, sauna, putting green, exercise room. AE, DC, MC, V.*

Orihuela

🔞 *24 km (15 mi) northeast of Murcia, 34 km (21 mi) southwest of Elche, 29 km (18 mi) inland from the Mediterranean coast at Guardamar del Segura.*

Palm and orange groves dominate the southeastern countryside as far as Orihuela, on the banks of the Segura—another excuse to linger on the N340 south. The town's air of fading grandeur stems from its past life as the capital of Murcia (until the Reconquest). Stroll through Orihuela's winding streets and visit the Gothic cathedral of **El Salvador** to see the rare, spiral vaulting. The adjoining **museum** has paintings by Velázquez and Ribera.

APPROACHING MURCIA VIA ALBACETE AND LA MANCHA

To get the feel of Don Quixote country, drive from Madrid to Murcia through Albacete and the flat and arid La Mancha region. This three- to four-hour drive is punctuated by the Parador Nacional Marqués Villena at Alarcón, the Parador de la Mancha at Albacete, the village promontory of Chinchilla de Monte Aragón, and the Roman town of Cieza.

Albacete

⑳ *172 km (107 mi) northwest of Alicante, 146 km (91 mi) northwest of Murcia, 183 km (114 mi) southwest of Valencia.*

Albacete is an agricultural town known for wine and saffron. Its old quarter, built in the 15th and 16th centuries, sits on the crest of a hill, known as **Alto de la Villa**. The **Ermita de San Antonio** (Hermitage of St. Anthony) is a good example of 17th-century Castellano architecture.

The **Museo Arqueológico** (Museum of Archaeology), in the Parque Abelardo Sánchez, has Roman mosaics, ivory dolls, and objects dating from the Paleolithic era. 🏛 *300 ptas.* ☉ *Tues.–Sat. 10–2 and 4:30–7, Sun. 9–2.*

Dining and Lodging

$$$ **✕🏨 Parador de la Mancha.** Set back from the highway, this low-rise,
★ whitewashed, *manchego*-style parador has a rustic, wood-beamed interior and cozy, comfortable bedrooms. The restaurant serves local cuisine; try the *chuletas de cordero* (lamb chops grilled with garlic). ✉ *Apdo. 384, Carretera N301, 02000 Albacete,* ☎ *967/245321,* 📠 *967/ 243271. 70 rooms. Restaurant, bar, cafeteria, pool, 2 tennis courts. AE, DC, MC, V.*

Chinchilla de Monte Aragón

㉑ *12 km (7 mi) east of Albacete.*

If you detour slightly en route to Alicante, you'll soon see the imposing 15th-century **castle** of Chinchilla de Monte Aragón to your left, and, if the day is clear, the distant Sierra de Alcaraz rising to nearly 6,000 ft to the south. Chinchilla is a fine old pottery town.

En Route Back on the N301, most of the 146 km (91 mi) to Murcia runs adjacent to the uplands of La Mancha, where Don Quixote adventured in Cervantes' famous novel. Across the border into Murcia and through the Roman town of Cieza, dominated by its feudal castle, the road drops some 2,700 ft to farmland before reaching the provincial capital.

MURCIA TO ALMERÍA

Soon after Orihuela, you enter the province of Murcia, where the N340 follows the course of the Segura, though the foothills of the Sierra de Carrascoy often intervene. This is the driest part of Spain, and the least visited. Tawny hills are punctuated by stretches of fertile *huerta,* moistened by life-giving rivers whose waters irrigate three crops in succession a year. Rich metal deposits supply a busy mining industry. The Valenciano language gives way to the Andalusian accent.

Murcia

㉒ *82 km (51 mi) southwest of Alicante, 146 km (91 mi) southeast of Albacete, 219 km (136 mi) northeast of Almería.*

Murcia, capital of the province, was first settled by Romans. Later, in the 8th century, the conquering Moors used Roman bricks to build the city proper; it was eventually reconquered and annexed to the crown of Castile in 1243. The Murcian dialect contains many Arabic words, and many Murcians clearly reveal Moorish ancestry. Modern Murcia is a university city with a population of more than 300,000.

★ The **cathedral** is a masterpiece of eclectic architecture. Begun in the 14th century, it received its magnificent facade—described by the 19th-century English traveler Richard Ford as "rising in compartments, like a drawn out telescope"—as late as 1737. This facade is considered one of Spain's fullest expressions of the Churrigueresque style. The 15th century brought the **Gothic Door of the Apostles** and the splendid chapel of **Isabelline Vélez**, with a beautiful, star-shaped stone vault; carvings by the 18th-century Murcian sculptor Francisco Salzillo were added later. Pop into the **museum**, off the north transept, to see Salzillo's polychrome-wood sculpture of the penitent St. Jerome. Ask the keeper for the keys to climb the monumental, 312-ft bell tower, built between 1521 and 1792. ✎ *Museum and bell tower 250 ptas.* ☉ *Daily 10–noon and 5–8 (winter, 5–7).*

Wander down Calle Trapería, the pedestrian shopping street. You'll soon reach the 19th-century **Casino,** with the style and aura of a British gentlemen's club. The façade is a mixture of classical and modern styles; the inside, inspired by the Alhambra in Granada, features a *patio arabe* (Moorish courtyard) and Mudéjar decor, modeled on the Alhambra in Granada. Despite the name, this has never been a gambling center; Murcians (that is, Murcian men) come to read the newspaper and play billiards.

The **Museo Salzillo,** out by the bus station, has the main collection of Francisco Salzillo's disturbingly realistic, polychrome *pasos* (carvings), carried in the processions every Easter. ✎ *250 ptas.* ☉ *Weekdays 9:30–1 and 4–7; winter, 3–6.*

Dining and Lodging

$$ ✕ **Hispano.** For a typically Spanish brand of rusticity, look no further than the Hispano. A well-known Murcian family of restaurateurs-hoteliers created this restaurant some 20 years ago, and it remains extremely popular for Murcian, traditional, and nouvelle cuisine.✉ *Arquitecto Cerdá 3,* ☎ *968/216152. AE, DC, MC, V.*

✕🏨 **Rincón de Pepe** In the center of the old town, 50 yards from the cathedral's apse, this hotel offers comfort and hospitality. All of the bedrooms have modern, bright, simple decor. The lobby and reception rooms have cool marble floors. The restaurant offers a good selection of *tapeo murciano* (samples of favorite Murcian dishes). Chef Raimundo Frutos doubles as an organic farmer and sticks closely to organic ingredients, with only the freshest supplements, such as the fish from Mar Menor. Highlights on the extensive menu include *ensalada de mariscos y trufas* (shellfish and truffle salad). ✉ *Apóstoles 34, 30000 Murcia,* ☎ *968/212239.* 🖷 *968/221744 151 rooms. Cafeteria, parking (fee). AE, DC, MC, V.*

$ 🏨 **Hispano 1.** The bedrooms at this budget hotel are bright and airy, and the public sitting room is large and tasteful. Ask for an exterior room. The location is central, and the street is pedestrian only. ✉ *Trapería 8 y 10, 30001 Murcia,* ☎ *968/216152,* 🖷 *968/216859. 35 rooms. Breakfast room, parking. AE, DC, MC, V.*

Nightlife and the Arts

Look for the pubs **Latino** and **B12** in the university district.

Cartagena

㉓ *48 km (29 mi) south of Murcia.*

Cartagena, founded in the 3rd century BC by the Carthaginians, is Spain's principal naval base. From here there is easy access to the resort **La Manga del Mar Menor** and the twisty, scenic, 100-km (62-mi) drive along the N332 to the start of the Costa de Almería.

La Manga del Mar Menor

㉔ *45 km (28 mi) southeast of Murcia.*

La Manga del Mar Menor, which forms Europe's largest saltwater lake (170 square km [105 square mi]), is warmer, saltier, and higher in iodine than the Mediterranean and is thus well known as a therapeutic health resort for rheumatism patients. The Manga ("sleeve") itself is a 21-km (13-mi) spit of sand averaging some 990 ft wide and enclosing the Mar Menor (smaller sea), a famously flat, calm expanse of shallow water about 20 ft deep. Four canals, called *golas*, connect the Mar Menor with the Mediterranean. The Manga has 42 km (26 mi) of immense, sandy beaches on both the Mediterranean and the Mar Menor sides, allowing bathers to choose more or less exposed locations and warmer or colder water according to season and weather. La Manga Club-Hotel (☞ *below*) claims to be Europe's most complete sports hotel. The principal towns on and near the Mar Menor are Cartagena and San Javier.

Dining and Lodging

$$$$ 🏨 **La Manga Club-Hotel.** Golf pervades this superbly situated luxury club house–hotel, just above the Mar Menor. Most patrons come here to wallow in the golfy ambience of what has become all but the home course for Sevy Ballesteros. There is also a cricket pitch, which probably accounts for the surfeit of British-registered Range Rovers in the parking lot. You can also rent apartments or villas. ⊠ *La Manga Club, Los Belones, 30385 Murcia,* ☎ *968/137234,* 🖷 *968/137272. 192 rooms. 2 restaurants, bar, 2 pools, hot tub, sauna, 2 golf courses, 17 tennis courts, horseback riding, squash. AE, DC, MC, V.*

Outdoor Activities and Sports

The Mar Menor, notable for the absence of waves of any kind, is a featured venue for sailing. Various schools offer windsurfing, waterskiing, catamaran sailing, and other diversions.

Lorca

★ ㉕ *62 km (39 mi) southwest of Murcia, 158 km (98 mi) northeast of Almería, 37 km (23 mi) inland from the Mediterranean at Águilas.*

Leave the main highway for a glimpse of Lorca, an old market town and scene of some of Spain's most colorful Holy Week celebrations. Your first stop should be the **tourist office** on Lope Gisbert, housed in the beautiful, dilapidated Casa de los Guevara. Head down Alamo to the elegant **Plaza de España,** ringed by a string of rich Baroque buildings, particularly the **ayuntamiento, law courts,** and **Colegiata** (collegiate church). Follow signs from the plaza up to the **castle.**

Dining

$$ ✕ **Cándido.** On the road into town, this rustic, old-fashioned restau-
★ rant has been going strong on its home cooking for more than half a century. The ambience is relaxed, the clientele a happy mix of Lorcans and travelers. The food is locally inspired; try the *trigo con conejo y caracoles* (wheat with rabbit and snails), a typical Lorca offering. ⊠ *Santo Domingo 13,* ☎ *968/466907. No credit cards. Closed Sun. in summer.*

Mojácar

㉖ *93 km (58 mi) northeast of Almería, 73 km (45 mi) southeast of Puerto Lumbreras, 135 km (83 mi) southwest of Murcia.*

A few miles inland, on a hillside overlooking the sea, Mojácar is a cluster of whitewashed cubist houses attesting to the town's Moorish past.

The North African feel and aesthetic have been carefully preserved. In the 1960s, painters and writers gravitated to Mojácar's cliff-dwelling simplicity in search of inspiration, creating a movement that became known as the *Movimiento Indaliano*, named for the *Indalo*, an anthropomorphic protective deity associated with Almerí (and especially with Mojácar) since prehistoric times. Mojácar's beaches and reflective charm make it a top destination in this refreshingly undeveloped corner of Spain. The most attractive part of the Almerían coast lies south of here.

Dining and Lodging

$$ ✕ **El Palacio de Mojácar.** Installed in an old, white Mojácar house with exposed beams and fireplace, this restaurant specializes in, well, good food. The friendly owner-chef doesn't offer a large menu, but what there is tends to be highly inventive. Ask for a local specialty such as *ajo colorao* (red garlic) or *caldo de pescado* (fish broth). ✉ *Plaza del Cano,* ☎ *950/478279. AE, MC, V. Closed Thurs. and Nov.–Feb.*

$$$ ▥ **Parador de Mojácar.** If you prefer to be by the sea rather than in ★ the old town, this rambling, white, modern parador is the best option in Mojácar. The public rooms are some of the most spacious and tasteful you'll find anywhere. Large, open-plan fireplaces add the rustic ingredient. Bedrooms are bright, with Castilian furniture. ✉ *Carretera de Carboneras, 04638 Almería,* ☎ *950/478250,* ℻ *950/478183. 98 rooms. Restaurant, bar, pool, tennis court. AE, DC, MC, V.*

$$ ▥ **El Moresco.** Up in the village itself, this hotel has a stunning position and tasteful, country decor, but it's often beset by large tour groups. ✉ *Avda. D'encamp 15, 04638 Almería,* ☎ *950/478025,* ℻ *950/478262. 147 rooms. Restaurant, pool. AE, DC, MC, V. Closed Nov.–Jan.*

San José and the Cabo de Gata Nature Reserve

㉗ *40 km (25 mi) east of Almería, 86 km (53 mi) south of Mojácar.*

San José is a small, relaxed village, as yet out of developers' clutches and well placed to take advantage of the nearly deserted beaches nearby. It has one tiny hotel, a handful of *hostales* (hostels), and a campsite. Just to the south is the **Parque Natural Marítimo y Terrestre Cabo de Gata Níjar** (Nature Reserve, ✉ road from Almería to Cabo de Gata, Km 6, ☎ 950/160435). Birds are the main attraction here; the park is home to several species proper to Africa, including the *camachuelo trompetero*, which is not found anywhere else outside Africa. The maritime reserve features special kinds of algae. The **Centro Las Amuladeras** has an exhibit and information on the region. For beach action, follow signs south to the **Playa Los Genoveses** and **Playa Monsul**; a dirt track follows the coast around the spectacular cape, eventually linking up with the N332 to Almería.

Dining and Lodging

$$ ▥ **San José.** For access to the beautifully rugged coast toward Cabo ★ de Gata, you couldn't choose a happier spot than this tiny hotel in the laid-back village of San José. Superbly positioned above San José's bay, the medium-size villa has just eight very large bedrooms, all with attractive decor and great sea views, around a large public sitting room with an open fire. It fills quickly, so reserve well in advance. ✉ *C. Correos, 04118 Almería,* ☎ *950/380116,* ℻ *950/380002. 8 rooms. Restaurant, library. MC, V. Closed mid-Jan.–mid-Mar.*

Almería

② *219 km (136 mi) southwest of Murcia, 183 km (114 mi) east of Málaga.*

A capital of the grape industry, Almería has tree-lined boulevards and landscaped squares, and its mild climate in spring and fall makes it especially pleasant then. Its core still consists of distinctly Mudéjar, flat-roofed houses forming a maze of narrow, winding alleys, though now framed by modern apartment blocks. The dazzling white of the older houses gives the city an Andalusian flavor.

Dominating Almería is the city's main sight, the **Alcazaba** (fortress), built by the Caliph Abd ar-Rahman I and provided with a bell tower by Carlos III. From here you have sweeping views of the port and city. Among the ruins of the fortress, damaged by earthquakes in 1522 and 1560, are landscaped gardens of rock flowers and cacti. 🖼 *250 ptas.* ☉ *Apr.–Oct., daily 10–2 and 5:30–8; Nov.–Mar., daily 9–1:30 and 3–6.*

Below the Alcazaba stands the **cathedral,** whose buttressed towers make it look like a castle. The defenses were built to fend off frequent raids by Barbary pirates in the 16th century. The overall design is Gothic, with some classical touches around the doors. ☉ *Daily 10:30–noon and for masses.*

If you're a film devotee and want to see where spaghetti westerns are (and have long been) shot, drive 24 km (15 mi) north on the N340 to **Mini Hollywood,** a film set open to the public when filming is not in progress. ☎ *950/365236.* 🖼 *960 ptas.* ☉ *Tues.–Sun. 9–7 (later in summer).*

Dining and Lodging

$$ ✕ **Valentin.** This centrally located spot serves fine regional specialties. *Cazuela de rape* (anglerfish baked in a sauce of almonds and pine nuts) is a typical entrée. The decor is Andalusian: white walls, wood, and glass. Valentin is popular, so be on the early side (around 9) to get a table. ⊠ *Tenor Iribarne 7,* ☎ *950/264475. AE, MC, V. Closed Sun.*

$$ ✕ **Veracruz.** In Almería's beach barrio, El Zapillo, this popular and excellent seafood restaurant has its own storage tank for oysters, clams, prawns, and lobsters. Its specialty is the *parillada de pescado,* a mixed grill of everything that swims in the Mediterranean. ⊠ *Avda. Cabo de Gata 119, El Zapillo,* ☎ *950/251220. AE, MC, V.*

$ ✕ **Imperial.** White walls and orange tablecloths set the Andalusian scene for local seafood and meat recipes, as well as old-fashioned, semiformal service. The canopied terrace makes for pleasant outdoor meals. Outstanding dishes include the *zarzuela de marisco* (mixed seafood), *solomillo a la pimienta verde* (filet mignon with green peppers), and *gazpacho andaluz.* Spanish families dine at lunchtime. ⊠ *Puerta Purchena 13,* ☎ *950/231740. MC, V. Closed Wed. in winter.*

$$$ 🏨 **Gran Hotel Almería.** These rooms now have brightly painted walls and chintz coverings to complement their fine views over Almería's harbor. The huge, marbled reception rooms evoke the hotel's golden era, when it hosted the film directors who came to make spaghetti westerns in the desert. ⊠ *Avda. Reina Regente 8, 04001 Almería,* ☎ *950/238011,* 🖷 *950/270691. 116 rooms. Bar, breakfast room, pool. AE, DC, MC, V.*

$–$$ 🏨 **Torreluz II.** Value is the overriding attraction of this comfortable and elegant modern hotel. The bedrooms are slick and bright, with the kind of installations you'd expect to pay more for. Also worth trying is the restaurant, which serves satisfying Mediterranean fare. ⊠ *Plaza Flores 1, 04001 Almería,* ☎ FAX *950/234399. 74 rooms. Restaurant, cafeteria, bar. AE, DC, MC, V.*

$ ⊞ **Hostal Andalucía.** If you stay in only one *hostal* during your time in Spain, make it this one. A scruffy facade leads to a large, ornate lobby, off which open an *azulejo* (glazed-tile) restaurant and the bedrooms. Ask for a room with a view; then bask in the old-fashioned atmosphere and savor the great price. The sea air blowing through the non–air-conditioned rooms can make beds slightly damp, so turn them down on arrival. ⊠ *Granada 9, 04003 Almería,* ☎ *950/237733. 77 rooms, 37 with bath. Restaurant. No credit cards.*

Nightlife and the Arts

There is no shortage of discos and flamenco *tablaos* (floor shows) along the Costa Blanca. Most towns have nightspots; inquire at your hotel.

Outdoor Activities and Sports

TENNIS

Most of the coastal hotels have tennis courts, though most of these are for guests only. Some exceptions are **Hotel Eurotennis** (⊠ Villajoyosa, ☎ 96/589–1250), **La Manga Club** (⊠ Los Belones, ☎ 968/137234), and **Club de Tenis V. Alegre** (⊠ Paraje El Olive, Huercal de Almería, ☎ 950/300390).

Shopping

Among the best buys in antiques, if you can find them at about 1,000 ptas. each, are antique *azulejos.* Look for copper and brass, too, especially Art Deco oil lamps. For quality, more expensive antiques, visit **Domínguez Cazorla** in Almería (⊠ Miguel Segura 3).

Biar, Chinchilla, and Níjar (north of Almería) are known for ceramics.

THE SOUTHEAST A TO Z

Arriving and Departing

By Boat

From Denia, **Flebasa Lines** (⊠ Puerto de Denia, ☎ 96/578–4200) sails to Ibiza and Palma de Mallorca at 9 PM daily. From Almería, **Trasmediterránea** (☎ 950/236155) sails to Melilla, a Spanish outpost on the Moroccan coast.

By Bus

Private companies run buses down the coast, and from Madrid to Valencia, Benidorm, Alicante, Murcia, Mar Menor, and Almería (☞ Getting Around, *below*).

By Car

The *autopista* A7 from Barcelona now runs through Valencia and Alicante as far as Murcia. Tolls, though quite high, are often worth it for the time saved, as well as the safe driving conditions. The other main links with the region are the N111 from Madrid to Valencia and the N301 from Madrid to Murcia via Albacete.

By Plane

The Southeast has four major airports: **Valencia** (☞ Chapter 8); **Alicante** (⊠ El Altet, 12 km [7 mi] south, ☎ 96/691–9000); **San Javier** (☎ 968/570073), for Mar Menor and Murcia; and **Almería** (6 km [4 mi] east, ☎ 950/213700). **Iberia** has the most flights (☎ 96/521–4414, 968/285093, or 950/213793).

By Train

For **RENFE** information, contact its offices in **Valencia** (☎ 96/352–0202), **Alicante** (☎ 96/592–0202), **Murcia** (☎ 968/252154), or **Almería** (☎ 950/251135).

Getting Around

By Boat

In summer you can cross from either **Alicante** (☎ 96/521–6396) or **Santa Pola** (☎ 96/541–1113) to the island of Tabarca. Boats leave **Benidorm** hourly for the outcrop Isla de Benidorm; the fare is 750 ptas. round trip.

By Bus

Regular bus service connects the region's towns and cities; the main bus depots are in **Alicante** (✉ Avda. Portugal, ☎ 96/513–0700), **Murcia,** west of town (✉ Plaza San Andrés, ☎ 968/292211), and **Almería** (✉ Plaza Barcelona, ☎ 950/210029).

By Car

Except for short distances, avoid coastal roads in summer. (The road that hugs the Almerían coast can be an exception to this rule.) You can rent a car in any of the provincial capitals and all major resorts, but it costs less if you reserve ahead of time from the United States or the United Kingdom.

By Train

Frequent and comfortable RENFE trains connect the region's chief cities. There's also the locally run FGV line, running along the Costa Blanca from Denia to Alicante.

Alicante has a RENFE station (✉ Avda. Salamanca, ☎ 96/522–6840) and a RENFE office (✉ Explanada de España 1, ☎ 96/521–1303); the FGV station is at the far end of Playa Postiguet (✉ Avda. Villajoyosa, ☎ 96/526–2731), reached by buses C1 and C2 from downtown. Murcia's RENFE station is some way out (✉ Industria, ☎ 968/252154), but there is a RENFE office in town (✉ Barrionuevo, ☎ 968/212842). Almería's station is off Carretera de Ronda (☎ 950/251135).

Contacts and Resources

Consulates

United Kingdom: Alicante (✉ Plaza Calvo Sotelo, ☎ 96/521–6022), open weekday mornings. **United States:** Valencia (✉ C. de la Paz 6, 3rd floor, ☎ 96/351–6973), open weekdays 10–1.

Emergencies

Police: ☎ 091. **Ambulance:** Alicante (☎ 96/511–4676), Murcia (☎ 968/218893). **General medical assistance:** Alicante, **Hospital del SVS** (☎ 96/525–0060); Almería, **Torrecárdenas** (☎ 950/212100), emergencies (☎ 950/141188). Murcia, **Hospital La Arrixaca** (☎ 968/841500), emergencies (☎ 968/222222).

Golf

Club de Golf Don Cayo (✉ Conde de Altea 49, Altea, ☎ 96/584–8046), 9 holes; **Campo de Golf Villa Martín** (✉ Apdo. 35, Torrevieja, ☎ 96/676–5160), 18 holes; **La Manga Club de Golf** (✉ Los Belones, ☎ 968/137234), two 18-hole courses; and **Golf Almerimar** (☎ 950/497454), 18 holes. Be sure to reserve tee times in advance. Expect to pay around 8,000 ptas. for 18 holes, 4,000 ptas. for 9.

Guided Tours

ORIENTATION TOURS

The *ayuntamiento* (town hall; ⊠ Plaza del Ayuntamiento) and travel agencies in Alicante organize tours of the city and bus and train tours to Guadalest, the Algar waterfalls, Benidorm, the Peñón de Ifach (Calpe), and Elche. In Benidorm, large hotels arrange similar excursions. The *ayuntamiento* in Elche (⊠ Plaça de Baix, ☎ 96/545–1000) organizes tours of the city and environs. From Almería, **Viajes Alborán** (⊠ Reina Regente 1, ☎ 950/237477) runs tours of the city and the Almería region. In Melilla, Morocco, **Viajes Cemo** (⊠ Avda. La Gaviota, Urbanización Roquetas de Mar, ☎ 950/333502) is a good resource. In Murcia, contact **Alquibla** (⊠ González Adalid 13, ☎ 968/221219) for tours of the city and region.

SPECIAL-INTEREST TOURS

The *ayuntamiento* in Alicante also runs tours to Jijona, where you can visit one of the famous *turrón* (nougat) factories before seeing the amazing stalactites and stalagmites at the Cuevas de Canalobre (Canalobre Caves). This tour sometimes includes a concert in the cave.

Late-Night Pharmacies

Pharmacies in each town take turns staying open 24 hours. All pharmacies display the address of the *farmacia de guardia,* the one on duty that night.

Travel Agencies

Alicante: Viajes Barceló (⊠ San Telmo 9, ☎ 96/521–0011). **Benidorm:** Viajes Barceló (⊠ Gerona, Edif. Pinos, ☎ 96/585–4750). **La Manga del Marg Menor:** Viajes Hispania (⊠ Urbanización Las Sirenas 3, ☎ 968/564161). **Murcia:** Viajes Internacional Expreso 9 (⊠ Jaime I El Conquistador, ☎ 968/231662).

Visitor Information

Tourist offices with information on the whole region are in **Valencia** (☞ Chapter 8); **Alicante** (⊠ Explanada de España 2, ☎ 96/520–0000); **Almería** (⊠ Parque Nicolas Salmeron, ☎ 950/267233); and **Murcia** (⊠ Alejandro Seiquer 4, ☎ 968/366130). Local tourist-information offices are in **Albacete** (⊠ Virrey Morcillo 1, ☎ 967/580522); **Alicante** (⊠ Avda. Portugal 17, ☎ 96/592–9802); **Benidorm** (⊠ Avda. Martínez Alejos 166, ☎ 96/585–3224); **Calpe** (⊠ Avda. Ejércitos Españoles s/n, ☎ 96/583–1350); **Cartagena** (⊠ Plaza Castellini 5, ☎ 968/596483; ⊠ Ayuntamiento, ☎ 968/506463); **Cullera** (⊠ C. del Riu 56, ☎ 96/172–0974); **Denia** (⊠ Plaza Oculisto Builges 9, ☎ 96/578–0724); **Elche** (⊠ Parque Municipal, ☎ 96/545–3831 or 96/545–2747); **Gandia** (⊠ Marqués de Campo s/n, ☎ 96/287–7788); **Xátiva** (⊠ Moncada, ☎ 96/227–3346); **Jávea** (⊠ Plaza Almirante Basterreche 24, ☎ 96/646–0605); **Lorca** (⊠ López Gisbert, ☎ 968/466157); **Orihuela** (⊠ Francisco Díez 25, ☎ 96/530–2747); **Santa Pola** (⊠ Plaza Diputación, ☎ 96/541–1100); and **Torrevieja** (⊠ Costera del Mar s/n, ☎ 96/571–5936).

10 The Balearic Islands

The Balearics' strategic position—off the eastern coast of Spain, halfway between France and Africa—has historically placed the archipelago in the middle of Mediterranean territorial disputes. While Menorca and Formentera remain largely unspoiled, great stretches of the coasts of Majorca and Ibiza have been marred by developments catering to tourists on package vacations. Still, Majorca's northwestern coast remains nearly as rough and remote as it was when George Sand and Frédéric Chopin spent a winter among its rugged mountains a century and a half ago.

By Sean
Hignett

Updated by
George Semler

THE BALEARIC ISLANDS—Mallorca (Majorca), Menorca (Minorca), Ibiza, and Formentera—lie between 80 and 242 km (50 and 150 mi) from Spain's Mediterranean coast, halfway between France and Africa. Their strategic position made them an important maritime staging post, and they became successive dominions of the Phoenician, the Roman, and the Byzantine empires before receiving a visit from the Moors in 902.

The Moors remained until ousted by Jaume I, of the House of Aragon, in 1229. The islands were part of the independent kingdom of Majorca (which included the Roussillon and the Cerdanya) from 1276 until 1343, when they returned to the Crown of Aragon under Pedro IV. Upon the marriage of Isabella of Castile to Ferdinand of Aragon, in 1469, the Balearics became part of a united Spain. During the War of the Spanish Succession, however, Britain occupied Minorca in 1704 to secure the superb natural harbor of Mahón as a naval base. The British remained for almost a century, interrupted only by an invasion in 1756, which gave the French control for 12 years, and a shorter reoccupation by the Spanish 20 years later. Under the Treaty of Amiens, Great Britain finally returned Minorca to Spain in 1802.

Minorca diverged once more during the Spanish civil war, remaining loyal to the Republican cause while Majorca and Ibiza were taken by the insurgent Franco forces. Majorca became a home base for the Italian fleet supporting the fascist cause. This topic is still broached delicately within the islands; they remain fiercely independent of one another in many ways. Even Mahón and Ciutadella, at opposite ends of Minorca—all of 44 km (27 mi) apart—remain locked in bitter opposition over unresolved differences dating from the war with Great Britain.

The tourist boom, which began during Franco's regime, turned great stretches of Majorca's and Ibiza's coastlines into unplanned strips of high-rise hotels, fast-food restaurants, and discos. Recently, ecology-minded residents have made some headway in lobbying for restrictions on shoreline development.

In 1983 the Balearics became an autonomous province. One result has been the partial replacement of Castilian Spanish by the Catalan language (banned for official use by Franco) in its Mallorquín, Menorquín, and Ibizencan dialects. This is likely to confuse the traveler, because outside the islands the Spanish names for island locations are still used. Within the islands, the problem is compounded by the fact that road signs that have not been officially altered are sometimes obliterated by spray paint. In the sections ahead, we use Catalan or Spanish according to whichever is used locally. *Avinguda* (avenue), *carrer* (street), and *plaça* (square) are Catalan; *avonidu, calle,* and *plaza* are Spanish.

Place names that may cause confusion are (Spanish version first):

Majorca: La Puebla/Sa Pobla; Santa Margarita/Santa Margalida; Colonia San Pedro/Colònia Sant Per; San Juan/Sant Joan.

Minorca: Mahón/Maó; Ciudadela/Ciutadella; San Jaime/Sant Jaume.

Ibiza: Santa Inés/Santa Agnes; San Miguel/Sant Miquel; San Jorge/Sant Jordi; San Antonio Abad/Sant Antoni de Portmany; San José/Sant Josep; San Juan/Sant Joan; Ibiza/Eivissa (Ibiza town is also "Ciutat").

Formentera: San Francisco/Sant Francesc; San Fernando/Sant Ferran.

Pleasures and Pastimes

Beaches

Beaches are a major attraction in the Balearic Islands, even if some of them are far from peaceful and relaxing. Note that *cala* is the local word for "cove" or "inlet."

MAJORCA

The closer a beach is to Palma, the more crowded it is likely to be. West of the city, Palma Nova/Magalluf, with a good, narrow beach, is backed by one of the noisiest resorts on the Mediterranean, while Paguera, with several small beaches, is the only sizable local resort not overshadowed by high-rises. A little farther along, Camp de Mar, with a good beach of fine white sand, is small and relatively undeveloped but can be overrun with day-trippers arriving by bus and boat from other resorts. Sant Telm, at the end of this coast, has a pretty little bay and a tree-shaded parking lot.

East of Palma, a 5-km (3-mi) stretch of sand runs along the main coast road from C'an Pastilla to Arenal, forming an overbuilt package-tour nexus also known collectively as Playa de Palma. The beach is nice enough, but it's crowded.

The only *real* beach on the northwest coast is at Port de Sóller, an attractive bay nearly enclosed by its headlands. Cala St. Vicenç, at the top end of this coast, has fine, soft sand in two narrow bays and is not overdeveloped. At Port de Pollença, on the north coast, sand has been imported, but it's an attractive resort with good water sports. There is frequent water-taxi service from Port de Pollença to Formentor, one of the most attractive beaches on the island. The north coast also has the longest sand beach on the island; gently shelved, and backed in part by pines, it stretches 8 km (5 mi) from Port de Alcúdia to C'an Picafort and beyond.

On the map, the east coast may appear to be peppered with beaches and coves, but few are large. Canyamel, near the Caves of Artà, is one of the least commercial.

A little farther south, Costa d'es Pins is an extensive, expensive urbanization, but it has a good, sandy stretch of beach, backed by a thin line of pines. Tourist buses, decorated to look like train engines, run from here to Cala Millor, which has a long, narrow, sloping beach of soft sand. Much of Cala Millor's beach is accessible by pedestrians only, so it's ideal for children, though very crowded in summer.

Farther south, Cala d'Or is a pleasant resort, and Cala Gran, a short walk away, is even more attractive. Cala Mondrajó, a tiny, sandy bay with little development, is also a good bet; it's most easily reached by boat from Portopetre or Cala Figuera.

On the south coast, the dune-backed beach at Es Trenc, near Colònia de Sant Jordi, is one of Majorca's few undeveloped beaches.

MINORCA

Mesquida, north of Mahón, is popular with the Mahonese; you'll see few tourists here. Another beach, this one development-free, lies on a headland beyond a watchtower.

Farther west, Es Grau, a sandy stretch with dunes behind it, is sometimes a bit littered. Behind Es Grau is the S'Albufera nature reserve. Before the lighthouse at the end of Cap Favàritx are the nudist beaches Cala Presili and Playa Tortuga. Arenal d'en Castell, a sheltered circular bay, and Arenal de Son Saura (also known as Son Parc) are the biggest sandy beaches in the north of the island.

At the junction of the Mahón–Fornells and the Mercadal–Fornells roads, take the small lane leading west and follow signs to Binimellá, an excellent, sandy beach. It's often deserted, and the tiny coves to the west have small caves that give welcome shade in the summer months.

The only reasonable and generally accessible beach to the north of Ciutadella is Cala Morell. Minorcans claim that the inlets and beaches at Cala Algaiarens are the nicest on the island.

Son Saura, Cala en Turqueta, and Macarella, the beaches at the west end of the south coast, are all reached by driving southeast from Ciutadella toward Son Saura. You'll be halted by a gate and a sign prohibiting entry, but no one will bother you if you close the gate behind you. All are classical Minorcan beaches with trees down to the water's edge, horseshoe coves, and white sand. Cala Mitjana, Cala Trebaluger, Cala Fustam, and Cala Escorxada, to the east, are accessible on land only by foot, but you can rent boats with outboard engines to reach them or the Son Saura *calas,* to the west. You can reach the long, straight, sandy stretches of Binigaus, Sant Adeodato, and Santo Tomas from Mercadal, and Son Bou, the island's longest beach (with a nudist section), from Alayor.

Cala 'n Porter is a British enclave. The rectangular cove has a sandy beach sheltered by cliffs.

IBIZA

Immediately southwest of Eivissa is one of Ibiza's longest stretches of sandy beach, Playa d'En Bossa, now almost entirely developed. Farther on, a left turn at Sant Jordi on the way to the airport leads across the salt pans to Cavallet and Mitjorn, two of the best beaches on the island, with little development until recently. All beaches on Ibiza are topless, but Es Cavallet is the official nudist beach. The remaining beaches in this part of the island are all reached from the Eivissa–Sant Josep–Sant Antoni highway, down side roads that often end in rough tracks.

From Sant Antoni north there are no easily accessible beaches until you reach Puerto San Miguel, an almost rectangular cove with relatively restrained development. Next along the north coast, accessible via San Juan, is Portinaitx, a series of small coves with sandy beaches, of which the first and last, Cala Xarraca and Caló d'Es Porcs, are the best.

The beaches on the east coast have been developed, but Santa Eulàlia remains attractive. The resort has a narrow, sloping beach in front of a pedestrian promenade that, despite being entirely lined by hotels and apartment blocks, is not frenetic, like Sant Antoni.

FORMENTERA

Formentera is best for wild and lonely beaches. Playa de Mitjorn is undeveloped and stretches for 7 km (4½ mi) along the south of the island. Trucadors, a long, thin spit at the north, has 2 km (1 mi) of sand on each side, and in summer you can wade to Es Palmador, where you'll find more sandy beaches. Nudity is common on this island.

Dining

MAJORCA

Seafood forms the basis of many local specialties, such as *espinigada* (a pie topped with tiny eels and spinach) and *panades de peix* (fish pies). Lamb, chicken, pork, and their derivatives are also traditional. *Sobrasada* (the bright-red Majorcan sausage paste) is basically pork and red pepper. Even the light-and-fluffy–looking (though cloyingly sweet) *ensaimada*—a powdery spiral pastry that ranges in size from a breakfast snack to a gift-boxed party special a foot in diameter—is based on *saim* (pork fat). Other specialties are *butifarra* and *llonganissa* sausages and *cocas* (pastries filled with meat or a mixture of vegetables). *Frits* (fried sheep's intestines) may be offered as tapas or included in a main course, along with *seisos* (brains), and accompanied by *tumbet* (ratatouille). *Sopa Mallorquina* is a meal of fried vegetables in meat stock, usually served over pieces of thinly sliced bread; *escaldum* is a chicken broth thickened with potatoes and ground almonds. *El tumbet* is a combination of meat or fish stewed with peppers, tomatoes, and potatoes.

MINORCA

Until recently, Minorcan restaurant cuisine consisted almost entirely of seafood and was offered by establishments along the harbors in Mahón, Ciutadella, and the fishing village of Fornells. Fornells is famous for its very expensive *llagosta* (lobster), sold by weight and grilled or served as *caldereta* (soup). Lately, a country cuisine has developed, based on the slow-baked dishes traditionally served in the home.

Mayonnaise—which was invented in Minorca during the French occupation and named after Mahón—is usually freshly prepared. Local tapas include *tornellas* (sheep's intestines stuffed with bread crumbs, garlic, and meat, then braided and cooked).

IBIZA AND FORMENTERA

Because most produce comes to Ibiza and Formentera from the mainland via Palma, the cost of dining here is often high. Sa Penya, the old fisherman's quarter that became famous as a hippie haven in the 1960s, is lined with restaurants of all styles. For a typical local specialty, try a *sofrit pagès*, potatoes and red peppers stewed in olive oil.

CATEGORY	COST*
$$$$	over 7,500 ptas.
$$$	5,500–7,500 ptas.
$$	2,000–5,500 ptas.
$	under 2,000 ptas.

per person for a three-course meal, excluding drinks, service, and tax

Fiestas

MAJORCA

The first fiesta of the year is that of Sant Antoni d'Abat, the traditional blessing of a long processions of animals, on January 17. Sant Joan Pelós (literally, "hairy Saint John") is celebrated on June 24 in Felanitx; a man dresses in sheepskins to represent John the Baptist. The Romería (Pilgrimage) de Sant Marçal, held June 30 in Sa Cabaneta, involves Majorca's typical *siurells*, primitive ceramic whistles.

MINORCA

Minorca's traditional fiestas are essentially celebrations for the townsfolk and villagers and have changed little in deference to tourism. The summer begins with Ciutadella's feast of Sant Joan (June 23–24), when *caixeres* (townspeople representing all classes) take part in a *jaleo*— they dance on horseback to the sound of a band, attempting to keep the horses up on their hind legs while the crowd gathers beneath. From July onward, fiestas follow in quick succession. Sant Lluís, at the end of August, has a fiesta spotlighting equestrian activities; Mahón's Fiestas de Gràcia (Feast of Our Lady of Grace; September 7–8) are the summer's final celebrations.

IBIZA

The feast of Nuestra Señora de las Nieves (Our Lady of the Snows) takes place, somewhat ironically, on August 8. Sant Antoni (January 17) is the annual blessing of the animals, with processions of pets, cavalry, and livestock of all kinds. Sant Josep (March 19) is known for its folk dancing; you can also see folk dancing in Sant Joan every Thursday evening and, on June 24, witness Sant Joan itself (the Feast of St. John the Baptist).

On July 15–16 islanders honor the Virgen del Carmen, the patron saint of sailors, with colorful processions of fishing boats, yachts, and nearly anything else that floats. On July 25, Sant Francesc dances in honor of Sant Jaume (St. James), Spain's male patron saint.

Lodging
MAJORCA
Majorca's newer resorts, concentrated mainly along the southern coast, amount to more than 1,500 hotels, many of which serve the package-tour industry. There are plenty of charming, low-cost spots, however, along the northwest coast and in the central countryside.

MINORCA
Apart from a few hotels and hostels in Mahón and Ciutadella, almost all of Minorca's tourist lodgings are in new beach resorts. As on the other Balearic Islands, many of these are fully reserved by travel operators in the high season, so it's generally more economical to book a package that combines airfare and accommodations.

IBIZA AND FORMENTERA
The greatest concentration of hotels is in the coastal resorts of Sant Antoni and Playa d'En Bossa. Many of these are excellent, but unless you're eager to be part of a mob, Sant Antoni has little to recommend it. Playa d'En Bossa, newer and close to Eivissa, is less brash, but it lies under the flight path into the airport.

CATEGORY	COST*
$$$$	over 20,000 ptas.
$$$	10,000–20,000 ptas.
$$	4,000–10,000 ptas.
$	under 4,000 ptas.

All prices are for a standard double room, including tax.

Exploring the Balearic Islands

Of the four main islands, Majorca and Ibiza are the most overdeveloped; Minorca and Formentera remain less populated and wilder. The north coast of Majorca and parts of Ibiza still have as much rocky coastline and diaphanous water as anyone can use at once, but—on balance—go to Formentera for solitude and intimacy; Ibiza for wilderness with heavy concentrations of humanity; Majorca for the mixture of Palma's urban cosmopolitanism with the wild north coast and interior; and Minorca for what may be the best blend of all of the above.

Numbers in the text correspond to numbers in the margin and on the Majorca, Minorca, and Ibiza and Formentera maps.

Great Itineraries
Visiting one island in an archipelago generally implies going to a single destination and exploring locally. In the Balearics, however, inter-island flights and ferries allow day excursions to neighboring isles, so that if you stay a week or 10 days, you may even have time to sample each of the four.

A three-day trip to the Balearics does require a choice of just one island. Our choice would be Majorca, for Palma's superb art and architecture and excursions to villages of the mountainous north coast and the interior. Five days would still suggest a one-island visit, with time to relax in one spot as well as explore the island more thoroughly. A 10-day trip might allow an ambitious and curious traveler to see it all, or at least to explore Mallorca and Minorca. We suggest a maximum of two islands, with perhaps a day trip to Formentera or Ibiza.

IF YOU HAVE 3 DAYS

Fly to ⚏ **Palma de Mallorca** ① and spend that day and the next morning exploring the historic center of this thick concentration of architectural treasures. On your second day, head for the hills—specifically the Sierra de Tramuntana, on the island's north coast—and see the **Raixa palace** ② on the way to the **Jardins d'Alfàbia** ③, **Sóller** ④, **Deya** ⑤, **Son Marroig** ⑥, and Sa Foradada. Spend the night in ⚏ **Valldemossa** ⑦, where Frédéric Chopin and George Sand spent their best winter together. On your third day, finish exploring the Tramuntana mountains: see Sa Granja, and hike down into the Torrent de Pareis ravine and beach if you have time. Visit the monastery at **Lluc** ⑬ before visiting the town and the port of **Pollença** ⑫. Alcúdia is the last stop before a 40-minute drive back to Palma de Mallorca for your last night.

IF YOU HAVE 5 DAYS

You can either do the Majorca loop from Palma (along the north coast and back through the center) with more time to settle in and explore, or you can devote your trip to Minorca, a good fit for a five-day visit. Start in ⚏ **Mahón** ⑯, and spend a day exploring the town. On the second day, settle into a secluded beach along the southern coast, and perhaps visit the cave dwellings at **Cales Coves.** Spend the night at ⚏ **Son Bou** or ⚏ **Sant Lluís.** On day three, visit the megalithic ruins and remains at Torre d'en Gaumés, Torralba, on your way to Es Mercadal and Minorca's highest point, **Monte Toro.** Have dinner and spend the night at ⚏ **Fornells.** On day four, explore the beaches at Fornells and Cap de Cavalleria before returning through Es Mercadal and Ferreries to ⚏ **Cala Santa Galdana.** Dedicate your fifth day to the remains at Naveta des Tudons, Cala Morell, and ⚏ **Ciutadella** ⑯.

When to Tour the Balearics

Summer is too hot and crowded. May and October are probably ideal, with June and September just behind. Winter, from November through March, is quiet, and while the weather is not always warm enough for the beach, it's fine for hiking, golfing, and general exploring.

MAJORCA

Majorca, more than five times the size of either Minorca or Ibiza, is roughly saddle-shape. The Sierra de Tramuntana, a tough mountain range soaring to nearly 5,000 ft, runs the length of the northwest coast, and a ridge of hills borders the southeast shores; between the two lies a great, flat plain that in early spring becomes a sea of almond blossoms, "the snow of Majorca." Having acquired a reputation as a cheap getaway, especially among the British, Majorca gets more than 5 million visitors per year; but the package-tour industry is confined to a narrow coastal strip. Elsewhere, Majorca has relatively undiscovered charm, particularly in the mountains of the northwest and in the interior. Caves, bird sanctuaries, abandoned monasteries, tiny museums, and village markets provide a good mixture of natural and historic sights.

Palma de Mallorca

❶ *40-min flight from Barcelona.*

If you look north of the cathedral (La Seu, to Majorcans) on a map of the city of Palma, you'll see around the Plaça Santa Eulàlia the jum-

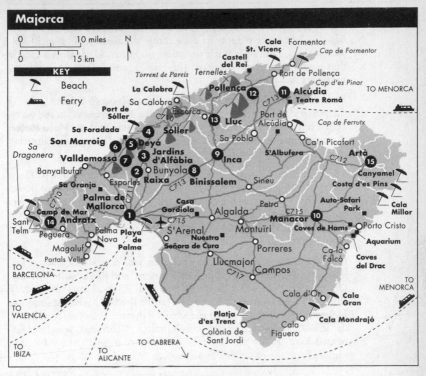

Majorca

KEY

Beach

Ferry

---

ble of tiny streets that made up the early town. Farther out, a circle of wide boulevards, known as the Avenues, zigzags around; these follow the path of the walls built by the Moors to defend the larger city that had grown up by the 12th century. The zigzags mark the bastions that jutted out at regular intervals. By the end of the 19th century the walls were largely torn down; the only place where the massive defenses can still be seen is along the seafront.

Through the middle of the old city ran a stream bed (*torrent*), dry for most of the year but often a raging flood in the rainy season, causing destruction and drowning. In the 17th century it was diverted to the east, along the moat that ran outside the city walls. What was its natural course is now La Rambla and the Passeig d'Es Born, two of Palma's principal shopping streets. The Born is also the place for the traditional evening *paseo* (promenade).

If you come to Palma by car, park in the garage beneath the **Parc de la Mar.** When you emerge, stroll along the park. Beside it run the huge bastions guarding the Almudaina Palace; the cathedral, golden and pinnacled, rises beyond. The park has some **ceramic murals** by the late Catalan artist and Majorca resident Joan Miró, as well as some **modern sculptures.**

From the Parc de la Mer, follow Avinguda Antoni Maura past the steps to the palace. At Plaça de la Reina, the **Born** begins, an avenue with a pedestrian promenade down its center and fashionable shops.

At the top of the Born, turn right into Carrer de la Unió, a few steps down Plaça Santa Catalina Tomàs. On the far side of the square, the ornate facades of the pair of buildings at the entrance to Carrer Santacilia, now an **insurance bank** and a **clothing store,** were designed by Antoni Gaudí.

Past the Palace of Justice, on the right, and just before the steps leading up alongside the Teatro Principal, is the **Forn des Teatre** (Theater Bakery). The tourist literature depicts this landmark as a "typical Majorcan shop," but in fact it's the only shop of its kind, with a facade that recalls a fairground organ. The Forn Teatre is famous for its *ensaimadas* and *cocas*.

From the Forn climb the steps to the Plaça Marqués Palmer (passing the pottery and the tile emporium La Loza Mallorquina on the way); on the left an archway leads to the greater expanse of the **Plaça Major.** A good crafts market is held here on Monday, Friday, and Saturday mornings from 10 until 2.

Make your way down Carrer Colom from the Plaça Major to Plaça Cort, whose south side contains the 17th-century *ajuntament* (town hall). The olive tree in the center of the square is said to be 500 years old. To the west of the *ajuntament,* the Caja de Baleares Sa Nostra, on the corner of Carrer Jaume II and Plaça Cort, occupies a superb Art Nouveau building.

East of the *ajuntament,* follow Carrer Cadena across Plaça Santa Eulàlia to Carrer del Convent de Sant Francesc and Plaça Sant Francesc. On the plaza's north side is the beautiful 13th-century monastery church of **Sant Francesc,** founded by Jaume II when his eldest son took monastic orders and gave up rights to the throne. Fray Junípero Serra, the missionary who founded San Francisco, California, was later educated here. Enter the church and cloisters through the collegiate buildings on the east side. ○ *Mon.–Sat. 9:30–1 and 3:30–7.*

From the church of Sant Francesc, return to Plaça Santa Eulàlia. The eminent 13th-century scholar Ramón Llull is said to have ridden his horse into the church of **Santa Eulàlia** in pursuit of a married lady of whom he was enamored in his wild youth. In 1435, 200 Jews were converted to Christianity in this church when their rabbis were threatened with burning at the stake.

*Just south of the plaza of Santa Eulàlia, off Carrer d'en Morey, is Carrer Almudaina. The **archway** crossing the narrow street was one of the gates to the early Moorish citadel and is now one of the few relics of Moorish occupation remaining on the island, along with the Arab Baths (☞ below).

From the Plaça Santa Eulàlia, continue down Carrer d'en Morey and take the left fork down Carrer Portella. On the left, at No. 5, is the **Museu de Majorca** (Museum of Majorca), with paintings and pottery dating back to Moorish times. ☎ *971/717540.* ▨ *325 ptas.* ○ *Tues.– Sat. 10–2 and 4–7, Sun. 10–2.*

At the bottom of Carrer Portella, turn left onto Carrer Formiguera, a short street that tunnels through the adjoining buildings, then left again (it's the only way you can go). A few yards up Carrer de la Serra, in a small garden, are the 10th-century **Banys Arabs** (Arab Baths). ▨ *150 ptas.* ○ *Daily 9–6.*

The **cathedral,** also known as La Seu, can be approached from the top of Carrer de la Serra, where you turn left and follow the meandering streets west to Plaça Almoina, with its antiques shops and restorers. You enter the cathedral here, through the **museum,** which displays ancient manuscripts, religious paintings, and precious jeweled crucifixes and reliquaries.

Palma's cathedral is an architectural wonder that took more than 300 years to build, between 1230 and 1601. The extraordinarily wide (63-

ft) expanse of the nave is supported on 14 extraordinarily slender, 70-ft columns, which fan out like palm trees at the top. The nave is dominated by an immense rose window (40 ft in diameter) from 1370. Look up into the nave; suspended above the Royal Chapel is the curious **asymmetrical canopy** built by Gaudí, who remodeled the chapel at the beginning of the 20th century. Lights within the canopy come on at regular intervals, permitting photographs.

Take note of the **bell tower** above the cathedral's Plaça Almoina door. It holds nine bells, the largest of which is known as N'Eloi, meaning "praise." N'Eloi was cast in 1389, weighs 4 tons, needs 12 men to ring it, and has been known to shatter stained-glass windows with its sound. Continuing around the cathedral, you'll hit the impressive **west facade,** whose blocked windows are the result of alterations following earthquake damage in 1851. ⊙ *Weekdays 10–12:30 and 4–6:30, Sat. 10–1:30.*

Opposite the cathedral is the **Palau de l'Almudaina** (Almudaina Palace), the residence of the royal house of Majorca during the Middle Ages, and originally an Arab citadel. It is now a military headquarters and can be visited only on guided tours (every half hour). If you have an EU passport, you can get in free on Wednesday. 🕮 *400 ptas.* ⊙ *Weekdays 9:30–1:30 and 4–6:30, Sat. 9:30–1:30.*

If you have some extra time in Palma, consider some other key sights, including **Castell de Bellver** (Bellver Castle), which overlooks the city and the bay from a hillside above the Terreno nightlife area. Built in the 14th century on a circular design, it's a sturdy fortress complete with dry moat and drawbridge. There's a terrific view of Palma and the bay from the ramparts and keep; within the walls is a fascinating historical museum. 🕮 *275 ptas.* ⊙ *Oct.–Mar., Mon.–Sat. 8–6; Apr.–Sept., Mon.–Sat. 8–8.*

The **Llotja** (Exchange), on the seafront a little west of the Born, was built in the 15th century as a commodities exchange. ⊙ *During exhibits, Tues.–Sat. 11–2 and 5–9, Sun. 11–2.*

The **Museu Fundació Pilar y Joan Miró** (Pilar and Joan Miró Foundation Museum) displays numerous works by the Catalan artist, who spent his last years in Mallorca (1979–83). ⊠ *Carrer Joan de Saridakis 29,* ☎ *971/701420.* 🕮 *700 ptas.* ⊙ *Tues.–Sat. 11–6, Sun. 11–3.*

The **Poble Espanyol** (Spanish Village), in the western suburbs of the city, is a kind of Disneyland of reproductions of Spanish buildings and styles, with shops and crafts studios. ⊠ *Carrer Capitán Mesquida Veny 39.* 🕮 *600 ptas.* ⊙ *Village daily 9–8, crafts shops daily 10–6.*

Dining and Lodging

$$$ ✕ **Koldo Royo.** The eponymous owner conjures up Basque specialties,
★ such as lamprey, salt cod, baked hake, tripe, and stuffed quail. The chic, yellow dining room, crowded with modern art, overlooks the marina. Try the *pechuguitas de codorniz rellenas de pétalos de rosas* (quail breasts stuffed with rose petals). ⊠ *Avda. Gabriel Roca 3,* ☎ *971/732435. AE, MC, V. No lunch weekends late Jan. and late June.*

$$$ ✕ **Porto Pi.** Dining in this old Majorcan villa in the Terreno area, 1 km (½ mi) west of Plaza Gomila, is like eating in a private home. Several high-ceiling dining rooms, with round tables and oil paintings, lead off the elegant central hall–cum–drawing room, and you can dine on the terrace in summer. The fine cooking is international. Try the *escalopines de foie gras a la parrilla* (barbecued escallops of foie gras). Alas, the once-excellent bay views have been all but obliterated by ugly, modern apartment blocks. ⊠ *Carrer Garita 23,* ☎ *971/400087. MC, V. Closed Sun.*

$$ ✕ **El Pilón.** Housed in an old vaulted building tucked between the top of the Born and Avinguda Jaume III, El Pilón has the widest range of tapas in town, from cheap clams to expensive eels. You can choose more substantial fish dishes fresh from the tank. ⊠ *Carrer Cifre 1,* ☎ *971/ 726034. AE, DC, MC, V. Closed Sun. and Feb.*

$$ ✕ **Cala Gamba.** Blessed with panoramic views over the bay of Palma, this excellent restaurant specializes in *caldereta de langosta* (a thick lobster soup) and seafood dishes such as *pescado a la sal* (fish cooked in a crust of salt). ⊠ *Passeig de Cala Gamba,* ☎ *971/261045. AE, DC, MC, V. Closed Mon.*

$$ ✕ **Caballito de Mar.** This central spot in the Llotja, at the very center of Palma's port, has views out over the bay and focuses on *caldereta de pescado* (thick fish soup) and other fish concoctions of all kinds. Try the *marmitako de mar,* a hearty fisherman's stew, or the *rodaballo en vino blanco* (turbot cooked in white wine). Best of all, the place never closes—you can drop in 24 hrs a day, 7 days a week. ⊠ *Passeig de Sagrera 5,* ☎ *971/721074. AE, DC, MC, V.*

$$$$ ✕▥ **Son Caliu.** The Son Caliu offers "Grand Hotel" comfort and style within a sleek, modern exterior. It's particularly popular with golfers, who can choose from among five courses within a half-hour drive. Located on a quiet, private beach 15 km (9 mi) west of Palma, the hotel is ideally placed for touring northwestern Majorca. NASA technology ensures virtually chlorine-free swimming in the two attractive pools. ⊠ *Urb. Son Caliu, Costa de Calvia 07016,* ☎ *971/682200,* ℻ *971/ 683720. 230 rooms. Restaurant, bar, indoor and outdoor pools, beauty salon, tennis court, health club, squash. AE, DC, MC, V.*

$$$$ ✕▥ **Son Vida.** This Sheraton contains a 13th-century castle on a hillside outside Palma. The antique furniture of the public rooms contrasts with the futuristic bronze-mirror look of the El Jardín restaurant. Most rooms have panoramic views of Palma Bay, to the south; a few rooms overlook the service area and hillside but, to compensate, are double the size of the others. ⊠ *Castillo Son Vida, 07015,* ☎ *971/ 790000,* ℻ *971/790017. 166 rooms. 2 restaurants, 2 bars, indoor pool, 2 outdoor pools, beauty salon, 4 tennis courts, golf course, health club, library, playground, airport shuttle. AE, DC, MC, V.*

$$$$ ▥ **San Lorenzo.** This tiny place is a gem, if you can get a room. It's
★ built into an elegant and aristocratic Majorcan town house, but the rooms are completely modern, and all comforts are impeccable. The design is classic Majorcan: exposed wood beams; watermarked silks in pastel blues, greens, and yellows; and traditional furniture. Two of the rooms are suites, with terraces and working fireplaces. ⊠ *Carrer San Lorenzo 14, 07012,* ☎ *971/728200,* ℻ *971/711901. 6 rooms. Bar, café, minibars, outdoor pool. AE, DC, MC, V.*

$$ ▥ **Hotel Born.** Right in the middle of a Palma pedestrian street, Born
★ occupies the former mansion of a noble Majorcan family. The bedrooms are in fine condition, but prices remain very reasonable. Romanesque arches surround the central courtyard and reception area. ⊠ *Carrer Sant Jaume 3, 07012,* ☎ *971/712942,* ℻ *971/718618. 29 rooms. AE, DC, MC, V.*

Nightlife and the Arts

The City of Palma Symphony Orchestra performs about twice a month during winter at the **Auditorium** (⊠ Passeig Marítim 18, ☎ 971/ 234735), which also has ballet and drama throughout the year, as does the **Teatre Principal** (⊠ Adjacent to Plaça Major, ☎ 971/784735).

With some 200 discos and music bars scattered throughout the city and across the island, Majorca's nightlife is never difficult to find. In

Palma itself, the **Plaça de la Lonja** is the place to go for *copas* (drinking, tapas sampling, and general carousing).

The most incandescent hot spots are concentrated 6 km (4 mi) west of Palma at **Punta Portals,** in Portals Nous, where King Juan Carlos I moors his yacht along with many of Europe's most beautiful people. **Tristan, Flannigan's,** and **Diablito** are the places to dine, ranging in price and category from Tristan, the best and most expensive, to Diablito, a pizza emporium.

Carrer Apuntadores, on the west side of the Born, is always lively at night. In the cobbled streets of the old town, restaurants and bars jostle each other for room. For stately surroundings and baroque music, try **Abaco** (⊠ Carrer de Sant Joan 1). The section of the Passeig Marìtim known as Avinguda Gabriel Roca is another nucleus of taverns and pubs, with **Pachá, Tito's,** and **Ib's** the top places.

B.C.M., in Magalluf, is the top disco.

Palma's **casino** is on the harbor promenade, Avinguda Gabriel Roca 4. There's a nominal entry charge, and you'll need your passport (and collar and tie) to enter. (☎ 971/454012 or 971/450563). ☉ Daily 3 PM–4 AM.

Outdoor Activities and Sports

GOLF

The island is well stocked with courses: **Canyamel** (⊠ Carretera de las Cuevas, 60 km [37 mi] from Palma, ☎ 971/564457), with 18 holes; **Son Vida** (⊠ Next to Sheraton Son Vida hotel, 5 km [3 mi] from Palma, ☎ 971/791210), with 18 holes; **Poniente** (Magalluf) (⊠ Carretera Cala Figuera, Calvia, ☎ 971/130148), with 18 holes; **Santa Ponça I and II** (⊠ Calvia, ☎ 971/690211), with 18 holes on each course; **Real Golf de Bendinat** (⊠ Carretera Palma–Portals Nous, 5 km [3 mi] from Palma, ☎ 971/405200), with 9 holes; **Pollença** (⊠ Carretera Palma–Pollença, Km 49.3, ☎ 971/533216), with 9 holes; **Vall d'Or** (⊠ Porto Colom–Cala d'Or, Km 7.7, ☎ 971/837068), with 18 holes; **Son Servera** (⊠ Bahía de Los Pinos, ☎ 971/567802), with 9 holes; **Capdepera Golf Club** (⊠ Carretera Palma–Cala Ratjada, Km 71, ☎ 971/565875), with 18 holes; and **Son Antem** (⊠ Carretera Lluchmayor–Palma, 3 km [2 mi] from Lluchmayor [call Balearic Golf Federation, ⊠ Avda. Jaime III 17, Palma, ☎ 971/712753]), with 18 holes.

HORSEBACK RIDING

The **Majorca Riding School** is at Km 12 on the Palma–Sóller road (☎ 971/613157).

SAILING

Call the **Balearic Sailing Federation** (⊠ Avda. Joan Miró s/n, Palma, ☎ 971/402512). The **Club de Mar** (⊠ south end of Passeig Marìtim, Palma, ☎ 971/403611), is famous among yacht sailors. It has its own hotel, bar, disco, and restaurant, and can lead you to other clubs on the island.

SCUBA DIVING

Escuba Palma (⊠ C. Jaume I s/n, ☎ 971/694968) is the primary scuba connection.

TENNIS

Tennis is very popular here; you'll find it at many hotels and at private clubs and tennis schools. For information, call the **Tennis Center** (⊠ Plaça de Santa Ponçay, ☎ 971/690414).

WALKING

Majorca is a walker's paradise, particularly in the Sierra de Tramuntana. You can easily arrange a combination of walking out and taking a boat, bus, or train back. Ask the tourist office for the excellent free booklet "20 Hiking Excursions on the Island of Majorca," which has detailed maps and itineraries. For excellent drawings and maps, track down 12 *Classic Hikes Through Majorca,* by the German author Herbert Heinrich.

WATER SPORTS

Water sports of all varieties are abundant here. You can rent Windsurfers and dinghies at most beach resorts; both skin and scuba diving are excellent; and yacht berths surround the island.

Shopping

Majorca's specialties are leather shoes and clothing; porcelain; souvenirs carved from olive wood; and artificial pearls.

In Palma, big-name fashion stores line Avinguda Jaume III; less expensive shopping strips are Carrer Sindicat and Carrer Sant Miquel—both pedestrian streets running north from Plaça Major—and the jumble of small streets south of Plaça Major. The square itself has an excellent crafts market.

Here's a selection, all central in Palma. **Leather:** Loewe (⊠ Borne 2), Pink (⊠ Plaça Pio XII), Piza (⊠ Carrer Sant Nicolau 20), Don Cocodrilo (⊠ Carrer des Forn del Raco 1). **Pearls:** Perlas Majorica (⊠ Avda. Jaume III 11). **Antiques:** Persepolis (⊠ Avda. Jaume III 22), Casa Belmonte (⊠ La Rambla 8), and shops on Plaça Almoina. **Pottery:** Las Columnas (⊠ Opposite tourist office, C. Sant Domingo 24). **Giftwrapped *ensaimadas*** of all sizes: Forn Teatro (⊠ Plaça de Weyler, at foot of steps leading to Plaça Major).

Raixa

❷ *13 km (8 mi) north of Palma.*

Thirteen kilometers (8 miles) out of Palma, look to the left to see Raixa, an 18th-century palace amid landscaped gardens. It sits at the top of a great flight of steps with statues and fountains on each side.

Dining and Lodging

$–$$ ✕ **C'an Penasso.** The setting at this rustic restaurant, 2 km (1 mi) north of Raixa on the outskirts of the town of Bunyola, is rough stone walls and wooden beams, with an overgrown terrace for outdoor dining. Grilled dishes are cooked on a huge indoor hearth. Specialties include lamb, beef, and fresh fish. ⊠ *Carretera Palma–Soller, Km 14.8,* ☎ *971/ 613212. MC, V. Closed Wed.*

Jardins d'Alfàbia

❸ *4 km (2½ mi) north of Raixa on right.*

Enter the gates to the Jardins d'Alfàbia (Alfàbia Gardens). At the top of the steps is a huge, vaulted cistern, built by a Moorish overlord to irrigate the gardens. A path leads around to a café, then winds through a small, thick wood. What's most remarkable about the gardens is that they're here at all; water is not abundant in this climate. The house is furnished with antiques and lined with painted paneling. ⊠ *Carretera Palma–Soller, Km 17,* ☎ *no phone.* 🖾 *450 ptas.* ☉ *Weekdays 9:30– 5:30, Sat. 9:30–1.*

Dining and Lodging

$$ ✕ **Ses Porxeres.** Former stables at the gardens' edge have been converted into a fine restaurant, airy and high-ceilinged with a charming outside garden. The imaginative menu includes Catalan cuisine and Majorcan specialties, such as pheasant stuffed with tiny plums and rabbit prepared with snails. The wine racks lining the walls are well stocked with excellent selections from the Penedès and La Rioja. ✉ *Carretera Palma–Soller, Km 17,* ☎ *971/613762. MC, V. Closed Aug. and Mon. No dinner Sun.*

Sóller

❹ *17 km (11 mi) north of Raixa, 30 km (19 mi) north of Palma.*

Sóller is a rough but intimate and cozy gray-stone town with both a maritime and a mountain feel. Find your way to the main Plaça Constitució, dominated by the cathedral; arm yourself with a map at the tourist office, in the *ajuntament*; and hop a tram down to the harbor (☞ Getting Around by Train *in* the Balearic Islands A to Z, *below*).

Dining and Lodging

$$ ✕🏠 **Hostal Es Port.** This 15th-century manor house, built around a central courtyard, is the ancestral home of the Montis family, who have added a modern extension and run the place as a hotel. Rooms in the old section have more character. The heavily beamed restaurant is in an old mill, where the olive press makes a striking centerpiece. The hotel's only drawback is its large size, which draws tour groups. ✉ *Carrer Antoni Montis s/n, Port de Sóller 07108,* ☎ *971/631650,* FAX *971/ 631662. 156 rooms, 10 cottages. Restaurant, bar, pool, 3 tennis courts, playground. AE, MC, V.*

$$ ✕🏠 **El Guía.** An elegant old house typical of those built by the mer-
★ chants of this town on the rich rewards of the citrus trade, El Guía is furnished in keeping with its fin-de-siècle style. It's handily located in the center of town, next to the train station. The excellent restaurant serves Majorcan specialties. ✉ *Carrer Castanyer 3, 07100,* ☎ *971/ 630227,* FAX *971/632634. 18 rooms. Restaurant. MC, V. Closed Nov.– Easter.*

Deyá

❺ *9 km (5½ mi) west of Sóller.*

Deyá (Deià, in Catalan) was made famous by the English poet and writer Robert Graves, who lived here from 1929 until his death in 1985. The local bar—up some steps on the left as you enter the village—is still a favorite haunt for writers and artists; on warm afternoons you'll find them gathered in the beach bar in the rocky cove, a 2-km (1-mi) walk down from the village. Walk up the narrow street, lined with titled Stations of the Cross, to the village church; from the small cemetery behind it, you have marvelous views of mountains terraced with olive trees and of the coves below. Graves lies buried in a quiet corner, beneath a simple stone slab.

Dining and Lodging

$$$$ ✕🏠 **La Residencia.** A former 16th-century manor house set in olive
★ and citrus groves above the village, La Residencia is superbly furnished with antiques, modern canvases, and four-poster beds. The arched dining room of the restaurant, Es Molí (The Mill), was once an olive mill. Britain's late Princess Diana was a regular guest. ✉ *Finca Son Canals, 07179,* ☎ *971/639011,* FAX *971/639370. 65 rooms. Restaurant, bar, pool, tennis courts. AE, DC, MC, V.*

$ ⊞ **Costa d'Or.** This attractive villa, a little way north of Deya, is set on the terraced cliffside and has a footpath down to the cove. ⊠ *Llu-calcari, 07179,* ☎ *971/639025,* fAX *971/639347. 42 rooms. Restaurant, pool. Closed Nov.–Apr.*

Son Marroig

❻ *4 km (2½ mi) west of Deyá.*

West of Deyá is Son Marroig, one of the estates of Austrian archduke Luis Salvador (1847–1915), who arrived in Majorca as a young man and fell in love with the place. Speaker of 14 languages and writer of innumerable books on every aspect of Majorca history, wildlife, and folklore, the archduke acquired estates and built great houses, mostly along the northwest coast, which he then furnished with *miradors* (out-looks) at each spectacular viewpoint. Now a museum, Son Marroig remains much as it was in the time of the archduke; it contains his col-lection of Mediterranean pottery and ceramics, old Majorcan furni-ture, and paintings. From late July until early October, the Deyá International Festival holds concerts here. ⊠ *Carretera Deyá–Valldemossa s/n,* ☎ *971/639158.* ⊠ *350 ptas.* ☉ *Apr.–Oct., Mon.–Sat. 9:30–2:30 and 4:30–8; Nov.–Mar., Mon.–Sat. 9:30–2:30 and 3–6.*

From the mirador you can see, nearly 1,000 ft below, **Sa Foradada** (as in "perforated"), a spectacular rock peninsula pierced by a huge arch-way, under which the archduke moored his yacht. A pathway, begin-ning near the café in the parking area, leads down to Sa Foradada (1 hour down, 1½ hours up). Four kilometers (2½ miles) farther, behind the restaurant C'an Costa, on the right, is another of the archduke's miradors, **Ses Pites,** named for the spiky cactus plants that surround it.

En Route   Now the road moves slightly inland. After 2 km (1 mi) more, a left turn will take you into Valldemossa.

Valldemossa

❼ *18 km (11 mi) north of Palma.*

The tourist office, in the plaza next to the church, sells a ticket that gets you into all of the monastery's various attractions. The **Reial Car-tuja** (Royal Carthusian Monastery) was founded in 1339, but when the monks were expelled in 1835, it was privatized, and the cells be-came lodgings for travelers. Later they were leased as summer apart-ments, which they largely remain today. The most famous lodgers were Frédéric Chopin and the French novelist George Sand, who spent three difficult (both the weather and their affair have been always been described as tempestuous) months here in the winter of 1838–39.

The guided tour of the monastery begins in the **church.** Note the fres-coes above the nave—the monk who painted them was Goya's brother-in-law. The next stop, in the cloisters, is perhaps the most interesting: a **pharmacy,** equipped by the monks in 1723 and almost completely preserved. Up a long, wide corridor are the apartments occupied by Chopin and Sand, furnished in period style. Only the piano is origi-nal—transporting it here from France was a monumental effort. Nearby, another set of apartments houses the local **museum,** with mementos of archduke Luis Salvador and a collection of old printing blocks. From here you return to the ornately furnished rooms of what was originally **King Sancho's palace.** A short piano recital of works by Chopin con-cludes the guided tour, except on Mondays and Thursdays, when everything is topped off with typical Majorcan folk dances. ⊠ *1,150* *ptas.* ⊙ *Nov.–Mar., Mon.–Sat. 9:30–1 and 3–5:30; Apr.–Oct., Mon.–Sat. 9:30–1 and 3–6:30.*

Dining and Lodging

$$$–$$$$ ✕🏨 **Vistamar.** This charming, small hotel sits within 250 acres of olive groves overlooking the sea. The building has been faithfully restored; the sitting rooms and bedrooms have exposed beams, heavy furniture, and modern art. The restaurant is popular for its excellent Mediterranean cooking. ⊠ *Carretera Valldemossa–Andratx, Km 2, 07170,* ☎ *971/612300,* 🄵🄰🄷 *971/612583. 18 rooms. Restaurant, bar, pool. AE, MC, V. Hotel closed Nov.–Feb. No lunch Mon.*

Sa Granja

21 km (13 mi) northwest of Palma.

Sa Granja (the Farm) was built by a noble family in the 17th century on what had previously been a farm. Once ensconced, they created pools and gardens. The house is now a historical museum of the Majorcan countryside, including an olive mill and a wide range of ethnographic artifacts. If you come at the right time, you may be able to see some folk dancing. The admission fee entitles you to a sampling of local wines, cheeses, and pastries. ☎ *971/610032.* 🄸 *1,200 ptas.* ⊙ *Daily 10–6 (until 7 in June), folk dancing Wed. and Fri. 3:30–5.*

Binissalem

❽ *18 km (11 mi) northeast of Palma.*

Drive east along the Passeig Marítim from Palma and take the bypass north. Follow it for about 3 km (2 mi) to the Inca turnoff; this becomes a fast *autopista* for 18 km (11 mi), to the outskirts of Binissalem, the home of Majorca's main vineyards and its only D. O. (Denominación de Orígen, i.e., guaranteed-vintage) label.

Dining and Lodging

$$ 🏨 **Scott's.** Here, American George Scott, a former documentary filmmaker, and his English wife have converted a Majorcan mansion into an elegant but snug hotel reminiscent of an English country house. They happily serve a sumptuous breakfast until high noon, and can help you arrange a visit to Binissalem's vineyards. ⊠ *Plaza Iglesia 12, 07350,* ☎ *971/870100,* 🄵🄰🄷 *971/870267. 18 rooms. MC, V.*

Inca

❾ *28 km (17 mi) east of Palma.*

Inca is known for its leather factories and its Thursday market, the island's largest.

Dining and Lodging

$$ ✕ **Celler C'an Ripoll.** A *celler* is a peculiarly Majorcan combination of wine cellar and restaurant, and Inca has no fewer than six. C'an Ripoll is considered the best, and it's certainly the most atmospheric—you'll dine between huge wine vats and beneath heavy oak beams. There's a very pretty garden for warm evenings. ⊠ *Carrer Jaume Armengol 4,* ☎ *971/500024. AE, DC, MC, V. Closed Sun. June–Sept. No lunch Sat. or dinner Sun., Oct.–May.*

Shopping

Along the old Palma–Inca road you'll find **siurells** (brightly colored, ceramic whistles) in Cabaneta, **pottery** in Marratxi, and **ilengos** (a traditional peasant fabric) in Santa María, where the amusingly named Mas Vieja que mi Abuela ("older than my grandmother") shop sells

antiques. Inca has **leather** goods and *galletas* (traditional local biscuits). If you don't find what you want in Inca, browse for traditional crafts, leather, and pottery at the enormous emporium just outside town, on the left side of Alcúdia Road.

Manacor

⑩ *50 km (30 mi) east of Palma.*

Majorca's second-largest town is also an industrial center, thriving on the demand for the island's famous cultured pearls. Manacor is worth a visit and is an ideal center from which to storm the island's southeastern holiday coast. The Romans first settled this site, followed by the Moors, who built a handsome mosque where the Gothic parish church of **Nostra Senyora de les Dolores** (Our Lady of Sorrows) now stands.

Dining and Lodging

$$$$ ✕🖫 **La Reserva Rotana.** This historic, beautifully restored manor house, 3 km (2 mi) north of Manacor, just opened as a luxury hotel in late 1996. Most of the original appointments, including coffered ceilings, ancient woodwork, and Venetian stucco, are still in place. The 500-acre Rotana estate has its own nine-hold golf course, orchards, and kitchen gardens, which supply the excellent restaurant with fresh produce. ⊠ *Apdo. de Correos 69, 07500,* ☏ *971/845685,* ℻ *971/ 555258. 21 rooms. Restaurant, pool, golf, putting green, tennis court. AE, DC, MC, V.*

Alcúdia

⑪ *54 km (34 mi) northeast of Palma.*

Circle the restored remains of Alcúdia's **Moorish city walls**—on Sundays and Tuesdays, there's a market outside. Inside, in a maze of narrow streets, are some fine **17th-century houses** and the excellent **Museu Monogràfic de Pollentia** (Monographical Museum of Pollentia) with Roman and prehistoric items. ⊠ *Carrer Sant Jaume 30,* ☏ *971/ 547004.* 📷 *350 ptas.* ☉ *Apr.–Sept., Tues.–Fri. 10:30–1:30 and 5– 7, weekends 10:30–1; Oct.–Mar., Tues.–Fri. 10–1:30 and 4–6, weekends 10:30–1.*

Just outside Alcúdia, on the port road, a signposted lane leads to the small, 1st-century BC **Teatre Romá** (Roman Amphitheater), which is carved directly from the rock of a hillside (facing south so that audiences could enjoy the evening sunlight). The haunting site was excavated in the 1950s and is always open.

From the Teatre Romá, turn back toward Alcúdia, but at the Inca junction, keep right for **Port de Pollença.** This town is less hectic than many of Majorca's coastal resorts, and the seafront is lined with relaxing cafés and bars.

Outdoor Activities and Sports

BICYCLING

Bicycling is excellent in the flatlands around Port de Pollença; and Alcúdia and C'an Picafort, on the north coast, are ideal. The roads have special bike lanes, and there are rental outlets on every block.

Pollença

⑫ *5 km (3 mi) inland of the port.*

Climb the **Calvari,** a stone staircase with 365 steps. At the top is a tiny chapel with a Gothic wooden crucifix and a fine view that takes in the bays, Alcúdia and Pollença, and Capes Formentor and Pinar. Almost opposite the turnoff to Ternelles is Pollença's **Roman Bridge**, the only one on the island.

OFF THE
BEATEN PATH
CAP DE FORMENTOR – If you enjoy twisty, scenic roads to nowhere, pack a picnic and drive to Cap de Formentor, north of Puerto de Pollença. The road threads its way among huge teeth of rock before reaching a lighthouse at the extreme tip, where the view is spectacular.

Dining and Lodging

$$$$ ✕⚏ **Formentor.** Founded in 1929, this famous hotel is beautifully perched on a cliff at Majorca's northern tip. Terraced gardens descend to an attractive private beach where a barbecue is fired up at lunchtime. The building is long and white, the bedrooms comfortable, if no more than par for hotels of this price; despite the remote site, the place lacks intimacy. Former guests include the Duke of Windsor, Winston Churchill, Charlie Chaplin, Aristotle Onassis, and the Spanish royal family. ⊠ *Playa de Formentor, 07470,* ☎ *971/899100,* ⎚ *971/865155. 127 rooms. Restaurant, 3 bars, grill, beauty salon, miniature golf, 5 tennis courts, horseback riding, beach, windsurfing, boating, waterskiing, playground, airport shuttle. AE, DC, MC, V. Closed Jan. 12–Mar. 8.*

Nightlife and the Arts

Pollença hosts a major international music festival in August and early September, during which concerts are performed in the delightful cloisters of the former monastery of Santo Domingo. For schedules and tickets, contact Pollença's *ajuntament* (⊠ Calvari 2, ☎ 971/534012 or 971/534016).

Lluc

⑬ *20 km (12 mi) west of Port de Pollença.*

The monastery in the remote mountain village of Lluc is widely considered Majorca's spiritual sanctuary. La Moreneta, also known as La Virgen Negra de Lluc (The Black Virgin of Lluc), resides here, in the **17th-century church.** The **museum** has an eclectic collection of ceramics, paintings, clothing, folk costumes, and religious items. A boys' choir sings psalms in the chapel every day at 11:15 AM and 7:30 PM (except June–mid-September). The Christmas Eve performance of El Cant de la Sibila (Song of the Sybil) is a haunting and unforgettable pre-Christian tradition, not to be missed. ☎ *971/517025.* ⎚ *Museum 350 ptas.* ⊙ *Daily 10 5.30.*

Dining and Lodging

$ ✕⚏ **Santuari de Lluc.** The Lluc monastery offers simple, clean, and cheap ★ accommodation, mostly in cells once occupied by monks. Although the vast building has two bars and two Majorcan restaurants, nightlife is restricted, with guests asked to be silent after 11 PM. A big compensation is the spectacular setting, high in the mountains between Sóller and Pollença. ⊠ *Santuari de Lluc, 07315,* ☎ *971/517025,* ⎚ *971/517096. 113 rooms, 97 with bath. 3 restaurants, 2 bars, 2 cafeterias. MC, V.*

Torrent de Pareis

2 km (1 mi) east of Sa Calobra.

From Escorca's church of Sant Pere, you can hike down the Torrent de Pareis, a ravine that drops dramatically to the sea. (Use proper footwear, don't go alone, and don't attempt it if rain is forecast. The *torrent* becomes just that after a downpour, and has been known to cause drownings.)

En Route It's worth taking the turn to Sa Calobra if you want to see the bottom of the Torrent without climbing down. The road descends in a series of sharp loops to the Mediterranean, where the touristy town and beach at its end are a letdown. If you're looking for solitude, take the left turn just before Sa Calobra and continue to isolated Cala Tuent, where the only beach development is a fisherman's hut. Beyond the Sa Calobra junction, C710 passes through tunnels and beside reservoirs, with terrific views. If you have time, take a short detour left through Fornalutx and Biniaraix before you reach Sóller.

Fornalutx/Biniaraix

3 km (2 mi) northeast of Sóller.

Both Fornalutx and Biniraix have been spruced up in recent years by tourist cash, but their cobbled, honey-color plazas and stepped streets are still undeniably charming. Each village has a resident artists' colony.

Banyalbufar

23 km (14 mi) northwest of Palma.

Make a quick stop at this tiny town, which overlooks its tiny harbor from high on a cliff.

Dining and Lodging

$$ ×🖬 **Mar i Vent.** This small, modern, family-run hotel is at the north
★ end of quiet Banyalbufar, where the land was originally terraced by the Romans. Paths lead down to two small, rocky coves for sea bathing. All of the rooms, furnished in traditional style, have mountain and/or ocean views. ⊠ *Carrer Major 49, 07191,* ☎ *971/618000.* ₣₳ˣ *971/ 618201. 23 rooms. Restaurant, bar, pool, tennis courts. MC, V. Hotel closed Dec.–Jan. No lunch weekdays or Sat.*

Andratx

⑭ *23 km (14 mi) southwest of Banyalbufar.*

Andratx is a charming cluster of hillside white and ocher houses, rather like cliff dwellings, watched over by the 3,363-ft Mt. Galatzo. You can take a pleasant walk or drive from here through S'Arracó to the **Castell Sant Elmo** (St. Elmo's Castle) and on to the rocky shore opposite the **Isla Sa Dragonera** (Dragon Cave Isle).

Dining and Lodging

$$$$ ×🖬 **Villa Italia.** This ornate, rose-color villa is one of Majorca's most
★ luxurious and sophisticated hideaways. Built in a Florentine style, with marble floors and faux-classical columns, it has splendid views over the port and, to the west, the Mediterranean. ⊠ *Camino San Carlos 13, Port D'Andratx 07157,* ☎ *971/674011,* ₣₳ˣ *971/673350. 16 rooms. Restaurant, bar, pool. AE, DC, MC, V.*

Santa Ponsa

15 km (9 mi) west of Palma.

Santa Ponsa has a sandy beach on its north side and a small fishing port to the south. A spell on the beach and lunch in the port may beckon before you return by way of the C719 and the *autopista* to Palma.

Side Trips Around Majorca

Artà

⑮ *78 km (48 mi) northeast of Palma.*

The hills of the northeast, beyond Artà, are nearly roadless, thus keeping Artà somewhat off the beaten path. The north side of town is dominated by its **castle** and the church of **San Salvador.** Just below the church, a sign points (somewhat ambiguously; confirm the direction) to the **Ermita de Betlem** (Bethlehem Hermitage), some 9 km (5 mi) farther on. The road soon degenerates into a rocky track that twists hair-raisingly up between dwarf palms and sea holly and then circles down to the isolated hermitage, the home of a small number of hermetic monks. Behind it, a path leads up the hillside to a fine *mirador.*

Randa

26 km (16 mi) southeast of Palma.

For a quick jaunt from Palma, take C715 east from the city to PM501, turn right, and follow signs to Llucmajor until, after about 3 km (2 mi), a left turn leads to Randa. At the center of this tiny village, turn right and follow a twisting road up the Puig de Randa, which has three separate hermitages. Take in the best views from the terrace of the Franciscan monastery of Nuestra Señora de Cura, on the summit; it was founded in the 13th century by philosopher Ramón Llull (☞ Palma, *above*), and its library contains many valuable books that you may be able to see during quiet times. Next to the terrace are a bar and restaurant; the monastery also rents rooms and apartments. ▨ *Monastery 350 ptas.* ☉ *Tues.-Thurs. 10–1 and 4–6, Fri. 10–1.*

MINORCA

Minorca, the northernmost Balearic island, is a cliff-bound, rather knobby plateau with a single central hill—Monte Toro—from whose 1,100-ft summit you can see the whole island. Prehistoric monuments—*taulas* (huge stone T-shapes), *talayots* (spiral stone cones), and *navetes* (stone structures shaped like upturned boats)—left by the first Neolithic settlers are thickly scattered around the countryside. The British controlled Minorca for much of the 18th century and left their legacy in the forms of Georgian architecture (especially in Mahón); a landscape of small, tidy fields bounded by hedgerows and dry-stone walls and grazed by Holsteins; and language—Minorcan speech is sprinkled with English words. Tourism came late to Minorca, partly because it was traditionally more prosperous than its neighbors and thus less needful of visitors; but also because Franco deliberately punished the Republican island by restricting development there. Having sat out the early Balearic boom, Minorca has managed to avoid many of the other islands' teething troubles: there are no high-rise hotels, and the herringbone road system, with a single central highway, means that each resort is small and separate. A lively ecological movement succeeded in having Minorca designated a World Reserve of the Biosphere by UNESCO in 1993.

Mahón (Maó)

⑯ *44 km (27 mi) east of Ciutadella.*

For a good tour of Mahón (Maó, in Catalan), start at the northwest corner of the Plaça de s'Explanada and turn right onto Carrer Comte de Cifuentes. At No. 25 is the **Ateneo,** a cultural and literary society with a display of wildlife, seashells, seaweed, minerals, and stuffed birds. On the staircase are ceramics and old tiles; side rooms hide paintings,

Minorca

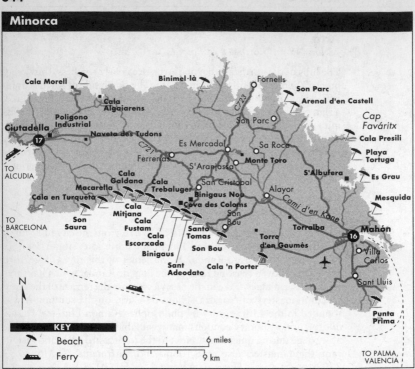

prints, maps, and mementos of Minorcan writers, poets, and musicians. ☎ 971/360553. 🖼 *Free.* 🕓 *Daily 10–2 and 3–10.*

From the Ateneo, follow Carrer Comte de Cifuentes to Carrer Dr. Orfila, a main shopping street, and turn left; then take the second right onto Carrer Bastió (Costa d'en Ga). Where the street curves left you'll see the **Teatre Principal,** built in 1824 as an opera house and now a cinema and theater. You can usually peek inside at the semicircular auditorium, whose columns support tiers of boxes and a gilded ceiling. Continue down Costa d'en Ga onto Plaça Reial. ✉ *C. Bastió.*

S'Arravaleta, a pedestrian street with more attractive shops, leads from Plaça Reial to Plaça del Carme. Up to the right is the church of **Verge del Carme,** with a fine painted and gilded altarpiece. Adjoining the church are the cloisters, now used, surprisingly, as a **public market.** As you wander through the colorful piles of fruit and vegetables, notice the carvings on the church's west and north walls.

From the Verge del Carme Church, return up S'Arravaleta and turn right onto Carrer Nou. At the end is Plaça de la Constitució, dominated by the church of **Santa María,** originally from the 13th century but rebuilt during the British occupation. It was restored after being sacked during the Spanish civil war. The church's pride is its 3,200-pipe Baroque organ, imported from Austria in 1810.

Behind Santa María is **Plaça de la Conquesta,** with a statue of Alfons III of Aragon. At the end of the tiny Carrer Alfons III, which leads off the square, is the best view of Mahón's harbor.

Coming up from the port to the Plaça de la Constitució, you'll find the **ajuntament** on the right. Stroll up Carrer Isabel II, a pleasant street of fine houses. On the corner of Carrer de Rosari, notice the statue of the Virgin up on the wall and the **Palau del Governador** (Governor's Palace) and courtyard on the right.

From the Carrer de Rosari, return to the *ajuntament* and follow Carrer Port de Sant Roc, immediately opposite. Ahead you'll see the 16th-century **San Roque gate,** the only remnant of the city walls built to protect Mahón from the pirate Barbarossa (Redbeard).

Dining and Lodging

$$$ ✕ **La Minerva.** This spectacular quayside restaurant has a floating terrace and a boat, the *Anita,* that serves as an adjoining bar and dining room. Not surprisingly, fish reigns supreme here, but meat roasted over coals doesn't lag far behind. ⊠ *Moll de Llevant 87,* ☎ *971/351995. AE, DC, MC, V.*

$$$ ✕ **Rocamar.** At the extreme end of the twisting, quayside road toward Villa Carlos, Rocamar is an established favorite that serves fresh, simply prepared seafood. You dine four floors up, overlooking the creek and surrounded by dark-wood paneling and maritime lights. The *pimientos rellenos de langostinos* (peppers stuffed with prawns) are superb. ⊠ *Cala Fonduco 32,* ☎ *971/365601. AE, DC, MC, V. Closed Nov.; closed Mon. in winter. No dinner Sun.*

$$ ✕ **Gregal.** This waterside restaurant in Mahón's port specializes in fresh
★   fish. *Pescado a la sal* (fish baked in salt) is excellent here. Whether you sit inside or on the airy terrace, you'll have a fine view of the harbor and its yachts, berthed on the seaward side of the palm-fringed esplanade. ⊠ *Moll de Llevant 306,* ☎ *971/366606. MC, V.*

$$ ✕ **Jágaro.** The feeling here is open air, with lots of greenery in the recently enlarged garden and huge windows overlooking the harbor. Seafood dishes are more inventive here than elsewhere; try the *carpaccio de mero* (halibut). ⊠ *Moll de Llevant 334,* ☎ *971/362390. AE, DC, MC, V. No dinner Sun.*

$$–$$$ ☷ **Port Mahón.** The only high-quality hotel in Mahón itself is magnificently situated, overlooking the harbor from terraced gardens in a quiet residential district. Steps lead directly down to the fashionable bars and restaurants in the port. ⊠ *Avda. Fort de l'Eau 13, 07701,* ☎ *971/362600,* ℻ *971/361050. 82 rooms. Restaurant, bar, piano bar, pool, beauty salon. AE, DC, MC, V.*

$$ ☷ **Hotel del Almirante** (Collingwood House). The 18th-century residence of Nelson's admiral friend Lord Collingwood is located between Mahón and Es Castell and has spectacular views over the creek. The Georgian house became a hotel in 1964, but it retains its original character. Collingwood's ghost reputedly stalks the house (favoring Room 7), so if you're feeling vulnerable, book one of the newer cottages around the secluded swimming pool. ⊠ *Carretera Villacarlos s/n, 07780,* ☎ *971/362700,* ℻ *971/362704. 40 rooms. Restaurant, bar, pool, tennis court, recreation room. AE, DC, MC, V. Closed Nov.–Apr.*

Nightlife and the Arts

The bars opposite the ferry terminal in Mahón's harbor fill with locals late at night. Discos include **Karai,** in a cave at the edge of Mahón, just past the traffic circle on the Es Castell road (⊠ Sá Sinia de's Muret, ☎ 971/366368); **Pachá,** a branch of Ibiza's famous nightspot, on the left at the entrance to San Luis; and **Cova d'en Xoroi,** in a cliffside pirate's cave high above the sea at Cala 'n Porter. Catch live jazz Tuesdays and Thursdays at the **Casino** bar and restaurant in San Clemente (Sant Climent).

Outdoor Activities and Sports

BIRD-WATCHING

S'Albufera, a wetland nature reserve north of Mahón, attracts many species of migratory birds.

DIVING

Equipment and lessons are available at **Cala En Bosc, Son Parc,** and **Cala Tirant.** Compressed air is available at Club Marítimo, in Mahón, and Club Náutico,in Ciutadella. The island's only decompression chamber is at S'Algar.

GOLF

Menorca's only golf course is the nine-hole **Urbanización Son Parc** (☎ 971/188875), 9 km (5½ mi) east of Mercadal.

HORSEBACK RIDING

There are stables on the left of the main road between Alayor and Mercadal, just after the Son Bou turning, as well as between Sant Climent and Cala 'n Porter. Elsewhere on the island, look for the sign *picadero* (riding school). Mahón's **Es Fornás** (⊠ Box 842, ☎ 971/364422) organizes horseback tours of the island for both beginner and advanced riders and tours by horse-drawn carriage.

WALKING

In the south, each cove is approached by a *barranca* (ravine or gully), often from several miles inland, which makes a pleasant and reasonably easy excursion. The head of **Barranca Algendar** is down a small unmarked road immediately on the right of the Ferreries–Cala Galdana road. The *barranca* ends in the beach resort Cala Galdana.

WINDSURFING AND SAILING

Knowledgeable windsurfers and dinghy sailors head for Fornells Bay. Several miles long and a mile wide, but with a narrow entrance to the sea, it gives the beginner a feeling of security and the expert plenty of excitement. **Windsurfing Fornells** (☎ 971/376400) rents boards and gives excellent lessons in English or Spanish.

A little south of Fornells, at Ses Salines on the same bay, **Minorca Sailing Holidays** (call Tim Morris, ☎ 971/376589; in London, ⊠ 58 Kew Rd., Richmond, Surrey, 0181/948–2100) sells a package that includes airfare and accommodations along with various activities.

Shopping

Minorca is known for **gin** and **shoes,** both introduced by the British. The Xoriguer distillery on Mahón quayside, near the ferry terminal, offers a guided tour, free samples, and, of course, bottles for sale. The island is renowned nationwide for its **footwear,** so you'll find high-quality shoes in many Mahón boutiques. Look for **leatherwear** at Marks (⊠ S'Arravaleta 18 and Hanover 38), Patricia (⊠ 31/33 Carrer Dr. Orfila), and Musupta (⊠ S'Arravaleta 26), and **costume jewelry,** another local specialty, at Bali (⊠ Corner of Carrer de Lluna). Up on the Esplanade is a frequent open-air market with cheap clothing and souvenirs.

Ciutadella

⑰ *44 km (27 mi) west of Mahón.*

Before the British came and set up their capital in Mahón, Ciutadella was the capital of Minorca, and its history and architecture are much richer than Mahón's. As you arrive from Mahón by way of the main road across the island, turn left at the traffic lights and circle the old part of the city to the north end of the coniferous **Plaça de**

s'Explanada. Turn left here, down Camí de Sant Nicolau. At the end, near an old watchtower and two rather rusty cannons, is a **monument to David Glasgow Farragut,** the first admiral of the U.S. Navy, whose father emigrated from Ciutadella to the United States.

From the Farragut monument, return up Sant Nicolau and park near the Plaça d'es Born. Next to the *ajuntament,* on the west side of the Born, steps lead up to the **Mirador d'es Port,** from which you can survey the whole length of Ciutadella Creek. The **ajuntament** houses an interesting collection of ancient artifacts and pictures. The local museum, a repository of anything to do with the city—old street signs, keys, shoes, even a record of land grants made by Alfons III after defeating the Moors—is now in an ancient defense tower at the eastern end of the harbor, the **Bastió de Sa Font** (Bastion of the Fountain). ☎ *971/380297.* ▦ *300 ptas.* ☉ *Daily 10–1 and 4–6.*

Circle the Born to the north—you'll find more views of the narrow harbor. The monument in the middle of the plaza commemorates the citizens' resistance of a Moorish invasion in 1588. Continue south along the east side of the Born; the whole of this first block is the **Palau Torresaura.** It's worth going into one of the tiny shops here just to look at the complex pattern of archways and stairwells.

Turn left onto Carrer Major to enter the old city, where you'll see interesting brass and bronze door fixtures. On the left, at No. 8 (yes, even palaces have street numbers), over the doorway of the Palau Torresaura, is a strange carving of a veiled female face. On the right is the **Palau Salort,** its door knockers carved to resemble entwined serpents. This is the only noble home regularly open to the public. The coats of arms on the ceiling are those of the families Salort (a salt pit and a garden: *sal* and *ort,* or *huerta*) and Martorell (a marten). ▦ *400 ptas..* ☉ *Mon.–Sat. 10–2.*

From the Palau Salort, continue up Carrer Major to Plaça de la Catedral (Plaça Píus XII). Inside the Gothic **cathedral** you'll find beautifully carved woodwork and choir stalls. The side chapel has round Moorish arches with intricate carving, remnants of the mosque that was originally on this site.

From the cathedral, turn south from the Plaça de la Catedral onto Carrer Roser, then left onto Carrer Santíssims, where you'll see another **noble home** on the right, one of the Saura palaces. The ground floor houses one of the best antiques shops in the Balearic Islands. Don't miss the coat of arms dated 1718; some primitive naval paintings at the end of the entrance hall; and the carved, domed ceiling.

Turn left onto Carrer del Seminari (Carrer Obispo Vila). On the right is the **Seminari,** the setting for Ciutadella's annual music festival.

Return, keeping north of the cathedral, along Carrer Sant Sebastià. Twisting left and right, you'll reach the steps leading down into the **port.** The waterfront here is lined with seafood restaurants, some of which burrow into caverns far under the Born. Between the restaurants, Carrer Costa del Moll leads left up to the Born again.

Ciutadella is close to many of the archaeological curiosities for which Minorca is famous. Returning around the Avenidas, continue straight at the traffic lights, take the next right (Carrer de Pere Martorell), and follow the signs for **Cala Morell.** Soon you'll be in open countryside, where numerous *talayots* (prehistoric stone towers) dot the fields.

Returning to Ciutadella from Cala Morell, take a shortcut through the Polígono Industrial, on the left, to the Ciutadella–Mahón road. Turn left toward Mahón, and 2 km (1 mi) or so farther on the right are a parking lot and a path leading to the **Naveta des Tudons,** one of the best preserved of Minorca's mysterious prehistoric remains. The name ("Stone Ship") derives from the monument's shape, that of an upturned boat.

Dining and Lodging

$$ ✕ **Casa Manolo.** This well-established paella and seafood restaurant is at the seaward end of the many restaurants that rub shoulders along the east side of the narrow harbor. The maritime dining rooms, with white walls and exposed beams, extend back into the rock face. ⊠ *Marina 117,* ☎ *971/380003. AE, DC, MC, V. Closed Nov.*

$$$ ⊞ **Patricia.** On a quiet boulevard just south of the main plaza, Patricia is close to Ciutadella Creek. The marble hall is light and modern; the bedrooms have pale carpets, pastel wallpaper, and watercolors. ⊠ *Camí Sant Nicolau 90–92, 07760,* ☎ *971/385511,* 𝕱𝕬𝕏 *971/481120. 44 rooms. Restaurant, bar. AE, DC, MC, V.*

$ ⊞ **Hostal Ciutadella.** In the center of town, a block southwest of Plaça Alfonso III, is a pleasant, modern bar with bedrooms upstairs. The latter have white walls, shutters, shiny tiled floors, and comfortable beds. ⊠ *Carrer Sant Eloi 10, 07760,* ☎ *971/383462. 17 rooms. Bar, cafeteria. MC, V.*

Shopping

The industrial estate (*polígono*) on the right as you enter Ciutadella has a number of shoe factories, each with shops. Prices may be the same as in stores, but the selection is greater. Locals head to the Rubrica factory, in Ferreries. In Ciutadella, Azabache (Carrer del Seminari 36) has designer **leatherwear;** Sa Celeria (⊠ 33 Carrer de Santa Clara), a saddler and harness maker, stocks elegant **riding boots.** No. 48 has interesting **pottery.** One of the island's few **antiques** shops is on the ground floor of the 17th-century Can Saura (⊠ Carrer de Santíssim; ☞ *above*).

Side Trips Around Minorca

En route from Mahón to Ciutadella, or on the way to the beach, you can divert yourself with three other pieces of the Minorcan countryside.

Monte Toro
24 km northwest of Mahón.

Follow signs in Es Mercadal (the crossroads at the center of the island) to the peak of Monte Toro, Minorca's highest point. From the monastery on top you can see the whole island and, on a clear day, across the sea to Majorca.

DINING

$$ ✕ **C'an Olga.** It's hard to find, but worth it. Off the Camino de Tra-
★ muntana, in central Mercadal, Olga's is under an archway to the left (or ask for directions). Make for the small patio and try the inventive country cuisine, such as local snails or quail in sherry. ⊠ *Pont Na Macarrana s/n,* ☎ *971/375459. AE, MC, V. Closed Mon.–Tues. Jan.–Feb.*

$$ ✕ **Es Pla.** The modest wooden exterior of this waterside restaurant in Fornells harbor, on the north coast, is misleading. Es Pla is reputedly King Juan Carlos's favorite Minorcan restaurant; the king is said to make regular detours here during Balearic jaunts to sample his pet dish, the Es Pla Caldereta de Langosta (a rich lobster stew). ⊠ *Puerto de Fornells,* ☎ *971/375155. MC, V.*

$$ ✕ **Moli d'es Reco.** The Moli is an old mill sitting high above the main
★ Mahón–Cuitadella highway, just outside Mercadal. In winter or on cold evenings, the ground floor offers snug dining, while the rustic, airy

terrace is an ideal spot on warm summer days. Rabbit dishes are the specialty, but all of the several fish dishes are excellent as well. ⊠ *Carrer Major 53,* ☎ *971/375392. MC, V.*

Torralba
14 km (8½ mi) west of Mahón.

Coming from Mahón, turn south immediately upon entering Alayor toward Cala 'n Porter. Torralba, a megalithic site with a number of stone constructions, is 2 km (1 mi) ahead at a bend in the road, marked by an information kiosk on the left. (As is so often the case in Minorca, you'll be lucky if you find it open.) The massive, T-shape stone *taula* is through an opening to the right. Behind it, from the top of a stone wall, you can see, in a nearby field, the monolith Fus de Sa Geganta.

Torre d'en Gaumés
16 km (9½ mi) west of Mahón.

Turn south toward Son Bou on the west side of Alayor. In about a mile, the first fork left will lead you to Torre d'en Gaumés, a far more complex set of prehistoric ruins with fortifications, monuments, and deep pits of ruined dwellings, huge vertical slabs, and *taulas*.

Cova des Coloms
40 km (24 mi) west of Mahón.

The Cave of Pigeons is the most spectacular cave on Minorca. To reach it, take the Ferreries road at San Cristobal and turn up to the primary school; beyond the school the paved road continues for about 3 km (2 mi) toward Binigaus Nou. At an easily recognized parking area, you'll see wheel marks and possibly cars as well; leave the car. Climb a stile and take a path that follows the right-hand side of the *barranca* (ravine) toward the sea—you'll come to a well-trodden path bearing down into the bottom of the *barranca* and up the other side. The entrance to the cave is around an elbow, camouflaged by a tree. Remember to bring a flashlight.

IBIZA AND FORMENTERA

Settled by the Carthaginians in the 5th century BC, Ibiza (Eivissa, in Majorcan and Catalan) has been transformed by tourism over the 20th century. From a peasant economy, it grew into a wild, anything-goes gathering place for the international jet set and the hippies of the 1960s, only to enter the 1990s with its principal resort, Sant Antoni, regarded as one of the most boorish, noisy, and brash in the Mediterranean. Yet only on Ibiza and on tiny Formentera, just off Ibiza's southern tip, will you still see women in the fields dressed in the simple country costume of long, black skirt and wide-brimmed straw hat, gathering almonds in their aprons or herding errant goats.

Eivissa

⑱ *40-min flight from Barcelona.*

Running along the quay in the town of Eivissa is the area known as **Sa Penya** (the crag, or the cliff). Once a quiet fisherman's quarter, this neighborhood has been a tourist haunt since the '60s, springing into life each evening with lively bars, restaurants, and flea markets.

Enter Sa Penya via Carrer Rimbau, which you'll find at the end of Passeig Vara de Rey—opposite Hotel Montesol, whose fashionable pavement café is a favorite place for people-watching. Carrer Rimbau has some of the exotic boutiques for which Ibiza is renowned, and off it are alleys crammed with stalls, more boutiques, and restaurants.

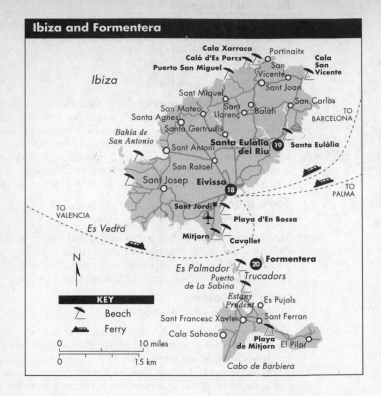

Ibiza and Formentera

Continue on Carrer Major, just east of the church of San Telmo. In this part of Sa Penya none of the streets are quite straight, and the miniature houses appear to have been randomly scattered along the tiny passageways.

From Carrer Major, return to Plaça de la Constitució, just north of San Telmo, where a pretty little building that looks something like a miniature Parthenon houses the local market. Beyond it, a ramp leads up to Las Tablas, the main gate of **Dalt Vila,** the walled upper town. On each side stands a statue, Roman in origin, both now headless: Juno on the right, an armless male on the left.

Inside Dalt Vila, the ramp continues to the right between the outer and inner walls and opens into a long, narrow plaza lined with stalls and pavement cafés. Don't worry about losing your way; aim uphill and you'll arrive at the cathedral, downhill and you'll return to the gate. A little way up Sa Carroza, a sign on the left points back toward the **Museu d'Art Contemporani** (Museum of Contemporary Art), housed in the gateway arch. ⊠ *Ronda Pintor Narcis Putget s/n,* ☎ *971/302723.* ☞ *450 ptas.* ⊙ *Daily 10:30–1 and 6–8:30.*

Uphill from the Museum of Contemporary Art is a sculpture of a priest sitting on one of the stone seats in the gardens. On the left, the wide **Bastió de Santa Lucia** (Bastion of St. Lucia) has a panoramic view.

Wind your way up past the 16th-century church of **Sant Domingo,** its roof an irregular landscape of tiled domes, and turn right in front of the **ajuntament,** housed in the church's former monastery. Then follow any of the streets or steps leading uphill to Carrer Obispo Torres (Carrer Major).

At the top of Carrer Major is the **cathedral** on the site of religious structures from each of the cultures that have ruled Eivissa since the Phoenicians. Built in the 13th and 14th centuries and renovated in the 18th century, the cathedral has a Gothic tower and a Baroque nave. The painted panels above the small vault adjoining the sacristy depict souls in purgatory being consumed by flames and tortured by devils while angels ascend to heaven. The museum, which you enter through the nave, has an interesting collection of religious art, relics, and ecclesiastical treasures. ⊠ *Museum 300 ptas.* ⊘ *Cathedral and museum Sun.–Fri. 10–1 and 4–6:30, Sat. 10–1.*

Across the plaza from the cathedral, the **Museu Dalt Vila** (Museum of Archaeology) has Phoenician, Punic, and Roman artifacts. ⊠ *Plaça Catedral 3,* ☎ *971/301231.* ⊡ *400 ptas.* ⊘ *Mon.–Sat. 10–1.*

A passageway leads from the cathedral to the castle to the **Bastió de Sant Bernardo** (Bastion of St. Bernard). From here there is a panoramic view of the wide bay from Playa d'En Bossa to Figueretas and of the chain of islands that stretches across the sea to Formentera. Steps lead down to a small gate in the bastion, from which you can pick your way along the clifftop to Figueretas and continue along the top of the wall. This trail, by way of the Bastions of Sts. John and James, is called the Route of St. John the Baptist; it ends at the steps to the **Portal Nou** (New Gate).

Go down the dark, curving tunnel of the Portal Nou and up the Vía Romana to reach, on the left, the **Puig des Molins** (Hill of Windmills), so called because it was once covered with them. A major Punic necropolis, with more than 3,000 tombs, has been excavated here, and many of the finds are on display in the new **Museu Puig d'Es Molins** (Punic Archaeological Museum) adjacent to it. ⊠ *Vía Romana 31,* ☎ *971/ 301771.* ⊡ *400 ptas.* ⊘ *Mon.–Sat. 10–1.*

Dining and Lodging

$$$ ★ ✕ **Ca Na Joana.** Joana Biarnés, a well-known journalist in a former life, has put together one of the finest restaurants in the Balearics in this small, 200-year-old country house on a hillside in Sant Josep (10 km [6 mi] from Eivissa). It feels like a private home, and there's an acclimatized wine cellar below. The *estofado de buey* (ragout of beef) is excellent. ⊠ *Carretera Eivissa–Sant Josep, Km 10,* ☎ *971/800158. AE, MC, V. Closed Mon. and Dec. 30–May. No dinner Sun.*

$$–$$$ ✕ **El Porralón.** Just inside and left of the main gate into Dalt Vila, a front terrace announces this intimate French restaurant. One dining room is medieval, with exposed heavy beams, antiques, oils, and coats of arms; another, modern, blends dark orange walls with sleek black furniture. The *pato con salsa de frambuesa* (duck with raspberry sauce) is worth trying. ⊠ *Plaza Desamparados 12,* ☎ *971/303901. AE, DC, MC, V.*

$$–$$$ ✕ **S'Oficina.** The entrance is uninviting, but it leads to an attractive restaurant with a small patio and some of the best Basque cuisine on the island. Marine prints hang on white walls and ships' lanterns from the ceiling. *Lomo de merluza con almejas* (hake with clams) and *kokotxas* (cod cheeks) are house specialties. ⊠ *Avda. d'Espanya 6,* ☎ *971/300016. AE, MC, V. Closed Sun.*

$ ✕ **Comidas San Juan.** This small café at the beginning of Sa Penya has marble topped tables reminiscent of a Paris bistro. The gloss-painted decor is sterile, but the owners are cheerful, the fish dishes usually good, and the value unbeatable. Try the grilled sole. ⊠ *Carrer Montgri 8,* ☎ *971/310766. No credit cards. Closed Sun.*

$$$$ ★ ✕🏠 **Hacienda Na Xamena.** Ibiza's most exclusive hotel is also its most isolated; it's on a rocky headland in Sant Miquel, in the north of the island. Access to the sea is difficult, involving a long hike down

steep steps; but the rooms, arranged around a pretty little patio with a fountain and trees, are elegant. Reserve well in advance. ⊠ *Apdo. 423, Sant Miquel 07080,* ☎ *971/334500,* FAX *971/334514. 63 rooms with bath, 33 with hot tubs. Restaurant, bar, 3 pools, tennis court, fitness center. AE, DC, MC, V. Closed Nov.–Mar.*

$$–$$$ ✕▥ **Los Molinos.** This is the best hotel in town. It's technically in
★   Figueretas, but it's a five-minute walk from the center of Eivissa, at the end of a relatively quiet street. The bedrooms are standard modern; the more expensive ones have balconies facing the bay. ⊠ *Carrer Ramón Muntaner 60, Apdo. 504, Figueretas07800,* ☎ *971/302250 or 302254,* FAX *971/302504. 154 rooms. Restaurant, bar, pool, beauty salon, beach, waterskiing. AE, DC, MC, V.*

$–$$ ▥ **Apartamentos Torre del Canónigo.** These modern apartments, built into a 16th-century tower at the top of the Dalt Vila, 55 yards from the cathedral, have open fireplaces and the flavor of their ancient surroundings. ⊠ *Carrer Major 8, Dalt Vila, 07800,* ☎ *971/301217. 7 apartments. Snack bar. No credit cards. Closed Nov.–Mar.*

Nightlife

If the arts are relatively neglected, nightlife certainly is not. Ibiza's discos are famous throughout Europe. In Eivissa, the trendy place to start the evening is **Keeper** (⊠ Passeig Marítim), where you can sip your drink perched on a carousel horse. There is also a lively, very young scene at **Divino,** another of the music bars on the Passeig Marítim. The "in" place for older nighthawks is the foyer of the former **Teatre Pereira** (⊠ Carrer Comte Rosselló). General favorites are **Pachá** (⊠ Passeig Marítim s/n), **Amnesia San Rafael** (⊠ Sant Antoni road, opposite Km 5 marker), and **Ku** (⊠ Sant Antoni). Hardened discomanes end the night at **Space** (⊠ Far end of Playa d'En Bossa), which doesn't even open until 5 AM.

Ibiza's **casino** is in a Cubist building whose design resembles an Ibizan church, albeit with a pizzeria and piano bar in the side chapels. ⊠ *Passeig Marítim s/n,* ☎ *971/313312.* ⊙ *Weekdays 10 PM–4 AM, weekends 10 PM–5 AM.*

Outdoor Activities and Sports

HORSEBACK RIDING

Club Hípico (⊠ Carretera de Circunvalación, ☎ 971/345198), in Sant Antoni, has horses and equipment.

SPORTS AND FITNESS COMPLEX

Ahmara (⊠ Centro Deportivo, Carretera Sant Josep, Km 2.7, ☎ 971/307762 or 971/307950), on the road to Sant Josep, has tennis courts (and lessons), four squash courts, badminton, indoor football, a gymnasium, an exotic Turkish bath, massage, a sauna, hot tub, a pool, a grill-restaurant, and a bar.

TENNIS

Call **Ibiza Club de Campo** (⊠ Carretera Sant Josep, Km 2, ☎ 971/391458); **Aqualandia** (⊠ Urb. Punta Martinet, Playa Talamanca, ☎ 971/314060); **Port Sant Miquel** (☎ 971/333019), with five public courts; or **Formentera** (⊠ Avda. Port Saler, Sant Francesc).

WALKING

Landscapes of Ibiza (Sunflower Press) outlines 22 different walks, none very strenuous, and six bicycle tours of Formentera.

Shopping

In the late 1960s and '70s, Ibiza built a reputation for extremes of fashion, of which not much survives, though the softer designs of Smilja

Mihailovich (under the **Ad Lib** label) still prosper. While Sa Penya still has a few designer boutiques, much of the area is now a "hippie market" (literally—the locals call it the Mercat dels Hippies) of overpriced tourist ephemera. You'll still find designer leather clothing at **Azara 5** (☎ 971/310671), in front of the Teatro Pereira. **Pink Fly** (✉ Rimbau 4, ☎ 971/310655) and **Modas Olinka** (✉ Pere de Portugal, ☎ 971/311973) are well-known boutiques.

In the newer part of town, **Krystal** (✉ Carrers Canarius and Aragón) specializes in designer glassware. **Casa del Café** (✉ Carrers Bisbe Carrasco and Médico Rapuchin) has an amazing range of coffees, teas, and preserves. **Front Line** (✉ Bartolomé Rosello 1) stocks fashions for both adults and children.

Side Trips Around Ibiza

Head out from Eivissa and explore Santa Eulàlia del Riu, with a Moorish-influenced church, and the fortified village of Balafi.

Santa Eulàlia del Riu

⑲ *15 km (9 mi) northeast of Eivissa.*

At the edge of the town, to the right just below the road, a **Roman bridge** crosses what is claimed to be the only permanent river in the Balearics (hence "del Riu," or "of the river"), though it's usually only damp. Ahead, on the hilltop, are the cubes and domes of the church. Look for a narrow lane to the left, signed Puig de Missa, and follow it to the church. A stoutly arched, cryptlike covered area, clearly of Moorish influence, guards the entrance; inside are a fine gold reredos and blue-tiled Stations of the Cross.

DINING

$$ –$$$ ✕ **Doña Margarita.** This elegant waterfront restaurant has won several awards for its Ibizan seafood preparations. You eat at pine tables, overlooked by the Ibizan landscapes on the white walls. The terrace, next to the crescent beach, is especially pleasant in the evening. ✉ *Passeig Marítim s/n,* ☎ *971/330655. AE, DC, MC, V. Closed Mon. and Dec.*

$$ ✕ **C'as Pagès.** This old farmhouse, with bare stone walls, wood beams,
★ and columns made of olive-press "screws," is not for vegetarians. Try the leg of lamb with baked potato or roast peppers, or the *sofrit pagès* (lamb and chicken stew), topped off with *graixonera* (a mixture of sugar, milk, eggs, and cinnamon). ✉ *Carretera de San Carlos, Km 10 (Pont de S'Argentara),* ☎ *no phone. No credit cards. Closed Tues. and Feb.–Mar.*

$$ ✕ **Su Capella.** It's a 20-minute, 15-km (9-mi) drive west of Eivissa, but
★ this enchanting restaurant in the resort of Sant Antoni is well worth seeking out. It's a former chapel, converted with flair and style into an atmospheric restaurant. Try the roast suckling pig—you won't find better. ✉ *Puig d'en Basora, Sant Antoni,* ☎ *971/340057. MC, V.*

SHOPPING

Broch, on Plaça de Espanya, has leatherwear.

Balafi

10 km (6 mi) northwest of Santa Eulàlia.

To reach the fortified village of Balafi, take the Sant Joan road from Eivissa and, passing the left turn to Sant Llorenç, look for a bar on the right next to a ceramics workshop. Turn right onto Sant Carles—almost opposite, on the left, a rough, narrow track leads to Balafi. You'll see some towers in the distance. These have no entrance on the ground floor; in times of peril, residents climbed a ladder to the second floor and pulled the ladder up after them.

Formentera

⑳ *Ferries leave Eivissa for La Sabina (90 min; 30–40 min by fast boat).*

You can begin this tour from Eivissa, Sant Antoni, or Santa Eulàlia; all have ferries to Formentera. Because Formentera is essentially an island of beach and countryside, you may be inspired to picnic; buy supplies in Ibiza. It's well worth standing on deck during the short passage; you'll have excellent views of the Dalt Vila and the smaller islands en route. Look for Trucadors, the long stretch of sand that almost links Formentera with Es Palmador.

From La Sabina, it's only 3 km (2 mi) to Formentera's tiny capital, **Sant Francesc Xavier,** which is a few yards off the main road. In the small plaza before the church, there's an active hippie market. The interior of the whitewashed church is quite simple, its rough, old wooden door encased in iron and studded with nails. Down a short street directly opposite the church, on the left, is a good antiques and junk shop, complete with a small art gallery featuring paintings and olive-wood carvings.

At the main road, turn right toward **Sant Ferran,** 2 km (1 mi) away. Beyond Sant Ferran the road travels for 7 km (4½ mi) along a narrow isthmus, keeping slightly closer to the rougher, northern side, where waves come crashing over the rocks when a wind is blowing. Just beyond El Pilar you'll see on the right a windmill, still in good order, with all its sails flying.

The plateau on the island's east side ends at the lighthouse **Faro de la Mola.** Nearby is a **monument to Jules Verne,** who set part of his novel *Journey Through the Solar System* in Formentera. Despite being trampled by thousands of tourists, the bare rock around the lighthouse is carpeted with flowers, purple thyme, and sea holly in spring and fall, while hundreds of swallows soar below. At the edge of the cliff you may see turquoise-viridian lizards.

Back on the main road, turn right at Sant Ferran toward Es Pujols. The few hotels here are the closest Formentera comes to beach resorts, even if the beach is not the best. Beyond Es Pujols the road skirts **Estany Pudent,** one of two lagoons that almost enclose La Sabina. Salt was once extracted from Pudent, hence its name, which means "stinking pond," although it no longer does so. The other lagoon, **Estany de Peix** (Fish Pond), was once a fish farm.

At the northern tip of Pudent, a road to the right leads to a footpath that runs the length of **Trucadors,** the narrow sand spit that leads to Es Palmador. The beaches here are excellent.

Dining and Lodging

$$$ ✕ **Le Cyrano.** This family-run restaurant on the Es Pujols waterfront is the best on Formentera. French cuisine—especially foie gras, snails, and pastries—is the main attraction. ⊠ *Paseo Maritimo,* ☎ *971/328386. MC, V.*

$ ✕🖬 **Fonda C'an Rafalet.** This simple inn and restaurant, 12 km (7½ mi) from La Sabina, is known for its fresh seafood and rustic setting—it's just yards from the water at the tiny fishing port of Es Caló. The sound of inboard engines is the most distressing noise you'll hear; the thought that they'll return with raw materials for your lunch is bound to make up for any lost sleep. ⊠ *Apdo. de Correos 225, Es Caló,* ☎ FAX *971/327016. 15 rooms. Restaurant, bar. AE, MC, V. Closed Nov.–Mar.*

$$$ ⊞ **Hotel Club La Mola.** This whitewashed waterfront spa at Playa de Migjorn has a certain cliff-dwelling, Aztec look and as many comforts as you can possibly consume. The Playa, while not as wild as it once was, is still one of the least spoiled beaches on the Mediterranean. ⊠ *Apdo. de Correos 23, Playa de Migjorn,* ☎ *971/327069,* FAX *971/ 328069. 326 rooms. Restaurant, bar, miniature golf, tennis court, conference center, car rental. AE, DC, MC, V.*

Outdoor Activities and Sports

BICYCLING

Cycling is very popular; La Sabina has numerous rental outlets.

THE BALEARIC ISLANDS A TO Z

Arriving and Departing

By Ferry

BETWEEN THE BALEARICS AND THE MAINLAND

Majorca: Trasmediterránea (⊠ Estació Marítima 2, Muelle de Peraires, 07015, ☎ 971/405014, FAX 971/700611) sails daily (and twice on Sundays) between Palma and Barcelona and daily between Palma and Valencia, weekly (Sunday) between Palma and Mahón (Minorca) and Palma and Ibiza. From May to October there is also a daily hydrofoil (Hidrojet) service between Palma and Ibiza: call Naviera Mallorquina (☎ 971/ 710153). From France a service connects Sète and Palma twice a week, June to September. A daily crossing between Alcúdia (Majorca) and Ciutadella (Minorca) is run by Flebasa (represented by all travel agencies on Majorca).

Minorca: Trasmediterránea (☎ 971/366050, FAX 971/369928) sails from Mahón to Barcelona six days a week in summer (mid-June to mid-September) and every Sunday to Palma and Valencia.

Ibiza: Trasmediterránea (☎ 971/315050, FAX 971/312104) sails at least twice a week to Barcelona and Valencia and once a week (Sundays) to Palma. From May until October there is also daily hydrofoil (Hidrojet) service from Palma and Denia, as well as less frequent service from Valencia and Barcelona. A service operates between Sète (France) and Ibiza twice a week, June to September, calling at Palma on the way.

Between Sant Antoni and Denia, on the mainland, Flebasa (⊠ Estació Marítim, Eivissa, ☎ 971/310927; ⊠ Edificio Faro, Sant Antoni, ☎ 971/342871; ⊠ Madrid, ☎ 91/473-1055, ⊠ Denia, ☎ 96/784011) runs both a car ferry and a fast hydrofoil with bus connections to Madrid and Valencia.

INTERISLAND SERVICE

Flebasa (☞ *above*) can **ferry** you and your car from Alcúdia (Majorca) to Ciutadella (Minorca) in three to four hours, depending on the weather. A **hovercraft** makes the journey between Sant Antoni and Benidorm in 2½ hours, daily in the summer months; for information and reservations, contact Coral Travel (⊠ Carrer Mar 11, Sant Antoni, ☎ 971/343711 or 971/343752, FAX 971/344266; ⊠ Carrer Isadora Macabich 14, Santa Eulàlia, ☎ 971/330512 or 971/330561).

Frequent services to Formentera from Ibiza by **ferry, catamaran,** and **hydrofoil** are operated by Transmapi (☎ 971/314513 or 971/310711; ⊠ Formentera, ☎ 971/320703), Marítima de Formentera (☎ 971/ 320157), and Flebasa (☎ 971/310927).

By Plane
MAJORCA

Iberia, Aviaco, Spanair, and **Air Europa** have direct flights daily between Palma (☎ 971/264624) and Barcelona, Madrid, Alicante, Valencia, Minorca, and Ibiza, as well as direct flights two or three times a week to Bilbao and Vitoria. The interisland flights (Ibiza and Minorca) should be booked well in advance in summer. **Iberia** and a large number of charter operators also fly between Palma and major European cities. Bus 17 runs between Palma Airport and the bus station on Plaça d'Espanya, next to the Inca railway terminus. The last bus from town is at 11 PM; the last bus from the airport is at midnight. The fare is 235 pesetas, and the journey takes 30 minutes. Taxi fare from Palma Airport to downtown is about 2,500 pesetas.

MINORCA

Iberia and its subsidiary **Aviaco** fly direct to Mahón from Barcelona and Palma three or four times daily. Most of the Palma services start and end in Madrid. **Air Europa** and **Spanair** also fly to Mahón. Direct charter flights serve Minorca from many European cities in summer. A metered taxi to Mahón costs about 1,100 ptas.

IBIZA

Iberia and its subsidiary **Aviaco** (☎ 971/395377) have several direct, scheduled flights daily to Ibiza from Barcelona, Madrid, Valencia, and Palma. For airport information, call ☎ 971/157000. An hourly bus service runs between Ibiza Airport and Eivissa (Ibiza town) from 7 AM to 10:30 PM (on the hour from town, on the half hour from the airport; fare: 450 pesetas; journey time: 15 minutes). By taxi, the same route costs about 2,500 pesetas.

Getting Around

By Boat
MAJORCA

Boats from Palma, Majorca, to neighboring beach resorts leave from the jetty opposite the Auditorium, on the Passeig Marítim. The tourist office has a timetable.

MINORCA

Excursions to Minorca's remotest beaches—which usually including a paella picnic on the beach—leave daily in summer from the jetty next to the Nuevo Muelle Comercial, in Mahón's harbor.

By Bus
MAJORCA

A good network of bus services fans out from Palma to towns and villages throughout Majorca. Most leave from the city bus station (✉ Estació Central, ☎ 971/752224) next to the Inca railway terminus, on Plaça d'Espanya; a few terminate at other points in the city. Details and timetables are available from the tourist office on Plaça d'Espanya.

MINORCA

Several buses a day run the length of Minorca, between Mahón and Ciutadella, calling at the island's other principal towns (Alayor, Mercadal, and Ferreries) en route. From the smaller villages there are daily buses to Mahón and connections, though often indirect, to Ciutadella. A regular bus service from the west end of Ciutadella's Plaça Explanada ferries travelers between the town and the resorts to the south and west.

IBIZA

In Ibiza, buses run every half hour from Eivissa (✉ Bus terminal, Avinguda Isadora Macabich) to Sant Antoni and Playa d'En Bossa and roughly hourly to Santa Eulàlia. Buses from Eivissa to other parts of the island are less frequent, as is the cross-island bus between Sant Antoni and Santa Eulàlia. The timetable is published in newspapers.

FORMENTERA

A very limited bus service connects Formentera's villages, shrinking to one bus each way between San Francisco and Pilar on Saturdays and disappearing altogether on Sundays and holidays. Ibizan newspapers publish the details.

By Car

MAJORCA

Majorca's main highways are well surfaced, and a fast, 25-km (15-mi) motorway penetrates deep into the center of the island between Palma and Inca. Palma itself is ringed by an efficient beltway (the Vía Cintura). For destinations in the north and west, follow the *Andratx* or *Oeste* signs on the beltway; for the south and east, follow the *Este* signs. Driving in the mountains that run the length of the northwest coast and descend to a cliffside corniche is a different matter; you'll be slowed not only by the winding roads but by the tremendous views and the tourist traffic. A tunnel through the mountains to Sóller, obviating the spectacular but tiring serpentine mountain route, is due to open by 1999.

MINORCA

A car is essential if you want to go beach-hopping in Minorca; few of the island's beaches and *calas* (coves) are served by public transport. However, most of the sights are in Mahón or Ciutadella, both of which have a reasonable bus service from other parts of the island; and once you're in town, everything is within walking distance. You can easily see the island's archaeological remains in a day's drive, so a reasonable compromise might be to rent a car for just part of your visit. The main roads are good; others can be narrow.

IBIZA

Ibiza is best explored by car or motor scooter, as many of the beaches lie at the end of rough, unpaved roads. The main highways are well surfaced and relatively straight, making for fast driving. Several new roads now cross the island in the north.

By Carriage

MAJORCA

In Palma, you can hire a horse-drawn carriage seating four to five passengers at the bottom of the Born; on Avinguda Antonio Maura; in the nearby cathedral square; and on Plaça d'Espanya, at the side farthest from the railway station. A tour of the city costs about 4,000 pesetas.

By Taxi

Taxis in Palma, **Majorca,** have meters. For trips beyond the city, the standard charges are posted at the taxi ranks. In **Minorca,** you can pick up taxis at the airport and in Mahón (✉ Explanada; ☎ 971/367111 radio taxi) and Ciutadella (✉ Carrer Josep Antoni; ☎ 971/381896 radio taxi). In **Ibiza,** taxis are available at the airport (☎ 971/305230) and in Eivissa (✉ Passeig Vara de Rey, ☎ 971/301794; 971/307000 or 971/306602 radio taxi), Figueretas (☎ 971/301676), Santa Eulália (☎ 971/333033), and Sant Antoni (☎ 971/340074 or 971/341721). In **Formentera,** taxis are in La Sabina (☎ 971/322002 or 971/323016) and Es Pujols (☎ 971/328016).

By Train
MAJORCA

Majorca has two separate railway systems.The Palma–Inca line travels to Inca, with stops at about half a dozen villages en route, from the Palma terminus (✉ Ferrocarriles de Majorca, Plaça d'Espanya, ☎ 971/752245). A journey on the privately owned Palma–Sóller railway is a must. Built by the citrus-fruit farmers of Sóller at the beginning of the century, it still uses the carriages of that era. The line trundles across the plain to Bunyola, then winds through tremendous mountain scenery to emerge high above Sóller. An ancient tram connects the Sóller terminus to Port de Sóller, leaving every hour on the hour, 9–7; the Palma terminal (☎ 971/752051) is near the corner of Plaça d'Espanya, on Calle Eusebio Estada, next to the Inca rail station.

Guided Tours

Most hotels in **Majorca** offer a variety of guided tours; ask your porter for information. Typical itineraries are the Caves of Artà or Drac, on the east coast, including the nearby Auto Safari Park and an artificial-pearl factory in Manacor; the Chopin museum in the former monastery at Valldemossa, returning through the writers' and artists' village of Deya; the port of Sóller and the Arab gardens at Alfàbia; the Thursday market and leather factories in Inca; Port de Pollença; Cape Formentor; and northern beaches.

Boat Tours
MAJORCA

Nearly every Majorcan resort runs excursions to neighboring beaches and coves—many of them inaccessible by road—and to the islands of Cabrera and Dragonera. You can also take a morning shopping trip by boat from Magaluf or Palma Nova to Palma; the tourist office has details.

MINORCA

In Minorca, various types of sightseeing trips leave Mahón harbor from the quayside near the Xoriguer gin factory. Several of the boats have glass bottoms for viewing marine life. Fares range from 800 to 1,000 pesetas.

IBIZA/FORMENTERA

Every resort offers trips to neighboring beaches and to islands off the coast. Trips from Ibiza to Formentera include an escorted bus tour. At Sant Antoni, which has little to offer in the way of a beach itself, a whole flotilla advertises trips.

Contacts and Resources

Car Rental

Cars are available through **Avis** and **Betacar** (Palma, Mahón, and Ibiza airports); **Hertz** (Palma and Ibiza airports); **Hiper RentaCar** (✉ Majorca, Son Garcias, Apdo. de Correos 50, C'an Pastilla, ☎ 971/269911 or 971/262223, FAX 971/492000); and **Pitiusas** (Ibiza Airport). Local firms also rent motorbikes, scooters, mopeds, and bicycles (ask for a crash helmet).

Emergencies
Police: (☎ 091 or 092; 971/381095 in Ciutadella; 971/320210 in Formentera). **Medical emergencies:** Clínica Juaneda (✉ Son Espanyolet, ☎ 971/722222).

Consulates:United States (✉ Avda. Jaume III 26, Palma, Majorca, ☎ 971/725051). **United Kingdom** (✉ Plaça Major 3D, Palma, Majorca, ☎ 971/718501).

Pharmacies

Pharmacies are open late by rotation. Schedules are posted on the door of each pharmacy and in local newspapers.

Travel Agencies

Viajes Barcelos (Palma, Majorca: ⊠ Avda. Jaume III 2, ☎ 971/5590874; Mahón, Minorca: ⊠ Avda. Josep María Cuadrado 1, ☎ 971/360250; Ciutadella, Minorca: ⊠ Cami de Maó 5, ☎ 971/380487; Eivissa, Ibiza: ⊠ Avda. d'Espanya s/n, ☎ 971/303250); **Viajes WagonsLits Cook** (Mahón, Minorca: ⊠ Plaça Constitució 9, ☎ 971/364162; Eivissa, Ibiza: ⊠ Passeig Vara de Rey 3, ☎ 971/301503).

Visitor Information

The regional tourist office for the Balearic Islands is the **Consellaria de Turismo de Balear** (⊠ Avda. Jaume III 10, Palma, ☎ 971/712216).

MAJORCA

The **Majorcan Tourist Board** (⊠ Palma Airport, ☎ 971/260803) is supplemented in Majorca by municipal tourist offices in **Alcúdia** (⊠ Carretera Port d'Alcúdia Arta s/n, ☎ 971/548615); **Palma** (⊠ Carrer Sant Domingo 11, ☎ 971/724090; kiosk on northeast side of Plaça d'Espanya, facing rail station, ☎ 971/711527); **Pollença** (⊠ Carrer Miquel Capllonch, Port de Pollença, ☎ 971/534666); **Sóller** (⊠ Plaça de Sa Constitució 1, ☎ 971/630200; ⊠ Carrer Canónigo Oliver, Port de Sóller, ☎ 971/630101); and **Valldemossa** (⊠ ticket office next to monastery, Cartuja de Valldemossa, ☎ 971/612106).

MINORCA

Pick up local tourist information in **Mahón** (⊠ Oficina de Información Turística de Menorca, Plaça Explanada 40, ☎ 971/363790) or **Ciutadella** (mobile office, open irregularly April–September, and at the police station in the *ajuntament*, Plaça d'Es Born). The best map for all purposes is the "Mapa Arqueológico de Menorca," available in bookstores and some hotels.

IBIZA/FORMENTERA

Local tourist offices: **Eivissa** (⊠ Oficina de Información Turística de Ibiza, Passeig Vara de Rey 13, ☎ 971/301900). **Santa Eulàlia** (⊠ Carrer Mariano Riquer Wallis s/n, ☎ 971/330728). **Sant Antoni** (⊠ Passeig de Ses Fonts s/n, ☎ 971/343363). **La Sabina** (⊠ Port de La Sabina, ☎ 971/322057).

11 The Costa del Sol

Most of the Costa del Sol—the central Andalusian coast—is an overdeveloped package-tour magnet for northern European sunseekers and a retirement haven for Britons and Americans. Marbella's luxury hotels attract the most glamorous crowd, Torremolinos the wildest; but just a few miles inland from either are breathtaking scenery and mountain villages, cultural light-years away from the hedonistic carnival raging on the coast. The tiny British colony of Gibraltar has its own English atmosphere.

By Hilary
Bunce

Updated by
Mark Little

TECHNICALLY, THE STRETCH OF ANDALUSIAN SHORE known as the Costa del Sol runs west from the Costa Tropical, near Granada, to the tip of Tarifa, past Gibraltar. For most of the Europeans who have flocked here over the last 40 years, though, the Sun Coast has been largely restricted to the 70-km (43-mi) sprawl of hotels, holiday villas, golf courses, marinas, and nightclubs between Torremolinos, just west of Málaga, and Estepona, 50 km (31 mi) short of Gibraltar. Since the late 1950s this area has mushroomed from a group of impoverished fishing villages afflicted with malaria and near-starvation into an overdeveloped seaside playground and retirement village.

In the 1960s and early '70s, hundreds of high-rises shot up in Torremolinos and Fuengirola, and luxury hotels and leafy villas erupted on the shore of Marbella, pushing this former fishing village to the forefront of upscale European resorts. The late 1980s saw a second boom, which brought new golf courses, luxury marinas, villa developments, and yet more world-class hotels.

This might not be the Spain of the independent traveler's dreams, but it does have its attractions. The Costa averages some 320 days of sunshine a year, and balmy days are not unknown even in January or February. Despite the hubbub, you *can* unwind here, basking or strolling on mile after mile of beaches and enjoying a full range of land and water sports.

Sunseekers from bleaker climes seem crammed into every corner of this region. Choose your resort carefully. Málaga and Ronda, though not strictly resorts, are the most authentically Spanish cities, particularly Ronda. Torremolinos is a budget destination that caters almost exclusively to the mass market; it appeals very much to singles and to those who come purely to soak up the sun and dance the night away. Fuengirola is quieter and geared more toward family vacations; farther west, the Marbella–San Pedro de Alcántara area is more exclusive and, of course, more expensive.

In some places, mountains roll down to the Mediterranean; in others, hillsides of olive groves, cork oaks, and terraced vineyards unfold toward vistas of the sea glinting in the distance. The developed coastal strip contrasts vividly with its hinterland. Just a few miles up in the mountains, you'll find quiet villages where black-shawled women go about their daily routine much as they did a half century ago, and where donkeys and mules are still used for farm work. Steeped in medieval lore, and the scene of many a Reconquest battle, Andalusia's perched, white villages (*pueblos blancos*) are a world apart from the ongoing party on the coast. Gibraltar diverts the anglophile with its English style bobbies, pubs, and regal guardsmen.

Pleasures and Pastimes

Beaches

The beaches of the Costa del Sol range from shingle and pebbles at worst (Almuñecar, Nerja, Málaga) to a fine, gray, gritty sand (from Torremolinos westward). Pebbles and pollution can make swimming in the sea unpleasant. Look for beaches flying the blue EU flag, which indicates that the water conforms to European Union standards. All of the Costa's beaches are packed in July and August, when Spanish families take their annual vacations, and on Sundays from May to October, when they become picnic sites.

All Spanish beaches are free. Changing facilities are usually not available, though you'll find free, cold showers on the major beaches. It's quite acceptable for women to go topless here; if you want to take it *all* off, you'll have to drive to one of the more isolated beaches designated *playa naturista*. The most popular nude beaches are in Maro (near Nerja); between Benalmádena-Costa and Fuengirola; and near Tarifa. Costa Natura, 3 km (2 mi) west of Estepona, is the region's official nudist colony.

The best—and most crowded—beaches are El Bajondillo and La Carihuela, in Torremolinos; the long stretch between Carvajal, Los Boliches, and Fuengirola; and those on both sides of Marbella. You may find the odd secluded beach to the west of Estepona.

Dining

The Costa del Sol is known for fresh seafood exquisitely fried in fine flour. Sardines roasted on skewers at beachside restaurants are another popular and unforgettable treat. Gazpacho shows up in the Andalusian culinary canon as both complement and antidote. Málaga is best for traditional Spanish cooking, with a wealth of bars and seafood restaurants serving *fritura malagueña,* the city's famous fried fish. Torremolinos's Carihuela district is also a paradise for seekers of Spanish seafood. The resorts serve every conceivable foreign cuisine as well, from Thai to the Scandinavian smorgasbord. Marbella has internationally renowned restaurants such as Paul Schiff's La Hacienda. At the other end of the scale, and perhaps even more enjoyable, are the Costa's traditional *chiringuitos* or *merenderos*; strung out along the beaches, these rough-and-ready, summer-only restaurants serve seafood fresh off the boats.

Because of the international clientele, meals on the coast itself are served earlier than elsewhere in Andalusia, with restaurants opening at 1 or 1:30 for lunch and 7 or 8 for dinner. Reservations are advisable for all Marbella restaurants listed as $$$–$$$$, and for the better restaurants in Málaga. Elsewhere, reservations are rarely essential. Expect beach restaurants, such as Málaga's Casa Pedro and all those on Torremolinos's Carihuela seafront, to be packed on Sundays after 3 PM.

CATEGORY	COST*
$$$$	over 6,500 ptas.
$$$	4,000 ptas.–6,500 ptas.
$$	2,500 ptas.–4,000 ptas.
$	under 2,500 ptas.

per person for a three-course meal, including house wine and coffee and excluding tax

Fiestas

JANUARY

Málaga holds a colorful parade on January 5, the eve of the Feast of the Three Kings.

MARCH–APRIL

The Semana Santa (Holy Week) processions in Málaga (March 28–April 4, 1999) are among the most dramatic in Andalusia.

MAY

Nerja and Estepona celebrate San Isidro (May 15) with typically Andalusian *ferias*.

JUNE

Midsummer, or San Juan (June 24), is marked by midnight bonfires on beaches all along the coast.

The Virgen del Carmen is the patron saint of fishermen, and fishing communities all along the coast honor her feast day (July 16) with seaborne processions of fishing boats.

Málaga holds its annual city festival at the beginning of August.

Fuengirola throws one of the Costa's most popular city fairs in the fall, October 6–12.

Golf

Certain hotels cater almost exclusively to golfers, offering guests reduced greens fees: Parador de Golf, near San Pedro de Alcántara; the Hotel Atalaya Park in Estepona; and the El Paraíso, between San Pedro and Estepona. Some other hotels, such as Los Monteros near Marbella, also have their own golf courses.

Indispensable for anyone trying to make independent golfing arrangements is a copy of *Sun Golf,* a free magazine available at hotels and golf clubs. The *Andalucía Golf Guide,* published by Andalusia's regional tourist office, details all of the courses on the Costa del Sol; it's available at any Tourist Office of Spain.

Lodging

Many of the hotels in the Costa del Sol's most highly developed stretch, between Torremolinos and Fuengirola, have gotten much-needed facelifts in recent years. They offer large, functional rooms near the sea at competitive rates. The area's ongoing popularity as a budget destination means that most such hotels are booked in high season by foreign package-tour operators. Finding a room at Easter, in July and August, or around the October 12 holiday weekend can be difficult if you haven't reserved in advance.

Málaga is poorly endowed with hotels for a city of its size. It has an excellent but small parador that can be hard to book, and few other hotels of note. Marbella, conversely, boasts more than its fair share of grand hotels, with five five-star hotels, three of which are classed as "grand deluxe" and rank among Spain's most expensive lodgings. Rooms in Gibraltar's handful of hotels are about 50 percent more expensive than most comparable lodgings in Spain.

CATEGORY	COST*
$$$$	over 23,000 ptas.
$$$	11,000 ptas.–23,000 ptas.
$$	7,000 ptas.–11,000 ptas.
$	under 7,000 ptas.

All prices are for a standard double room, excluding breakfast, tax, and service charge.

Exploring the Costa del Sol

While the coast is generally understood as the area's prime resource, much of it is lined with skyscrapers and crowded with tourists, which may not be what you had in mind when you came to Spain. However, the shore is better endowed with hotels and restaurants than the rest of Andalusia, making it an excellent base for exploring the region. Many of Andalusia's most charming secrets lie inland, and megasights Granada, Córdoba, and Seville are just a few hours away.

Numbers in the text correspond to numbers in the margin and on the Costa del Sol and Gibraltar maps.

Great Itineraries

The best drive takes in the Costa del Sol from east to west along the coastal highway N340. This route starts in the province of Granada, then heads west along the entire coast of Málaga's province, enters the province of Cádiz briefly at Sotogrande and San Roque, and finishes at the Strait of Gibraltar. The main towns on this route are Nerja, Málaga (the region's capital and only major city), Torremolinos, Fuengirola, Marbella, and Estepona; detours inland bring you to mountain villages and the dramatic scenery of the El Chorro gorge. Ronda makes a particularly inspiring excursion, high in the mountains 54 km (34 mi) from the coast.

A week or 10 days would give you time to see nearly all of the major beaches and cities, venture inland, and maybe even hop across to Morocco. Five days is really the minimum if you want to do anything other than drive. Three days gives you a taste of the major sights and a look at the coast.

IF YOU HAVE 3 DAYS

Start with the Costa Tropical (formerly the Costa del Sol Oriental), the eastern end of Sol. See the villages of **Salobreña** ① and **Almuñecar** ② and the town of **Nerja** ③, with its Balcón de Europa over the sea. Have lunch at one of the sea-view restaurants perched near the square. Visit the village of **Frigiliana** ④ before proceeding to 🖫 **Málaga** ⑥ for the night. The next morning, explore Málaga before moving up into the hills for lunch in **Antequera** ⑦. From Antequera, make the 100-km (62-mi) drive over to 🖫 **Ronda** ⑰ for your second night. See Ronda in the early morning and drive to coastal **Marbella** ⑮ for lunch at the beach. From Marbella you can either move west to Sotogrande, **San Roque** ㉖, and **Gibraltar** ㉗–㊴ or back east to tumultuous 🖫 **Torremolinos** ⑪ for a night on the town.

IF YOU HAVE 5 DAYS

Explore Granada's Costa Tropical, including the villages of **Salobreña** ① and **Almuñecar** ② and the town of **Nerja** ③, with its Balcón de Europa over the sea. Have lunch at one of the sea-view restaurants perched near the square. Visit the village of **Frigiliana** ④ before proceeding to 🖫 **Málaga** ⑥ for the night. Your second day can be devoted to exploring Málaga before moving up into the hills for the sunset and a night in the parador at 🖫 **Antequera** ⑦. On the third day, drive from Antequera up to the village of Archidona before working your way back through the Parque Natural de Antequera, **Alora** ⑧, and the Garganta del Chorro to 🖫 **Torremolinos** ⑪, where the Carihuela beach district provides a radical change of scenery. On your fourth day, explore the picturesque village of **Mijas** ⑭ before moving on to 🖫 **Marbella** ⑮ for an afternoon among the glitterati. If this scene is too manicured for your taste, hop up to the village of **Ojén** ⑯ for a complete change of pace. Spend the early evening driving to 🖫 **Ronda** ⑰ for a look at one of Andalusia's most stunning mountain enclaves. Day five is a chance to see more of Ronda before touring **Olvera** ⑱ and the mountain towns of **Setenil de las Bodegas** ⑲, **El Gastor** ⑳, Ronda la Vieja, the Roman settlement of Acinipo, and the village of **Zahara de la Sierra** ㉑. Finish this ambitious day with a look at Sotogrande and **San Roque** ㉖ on your way into 🖫 **Gibraltar** ㉗–㊴.

When to Tour the Costa del Sol

Winter is a good time to be on the Costa del Sol; the temperatures are moderate, and there are fewer tourists. Fall and spring are also prime opportunities. Avoid the summer; it's too hot and crowded. May and June bring the longest days and the fewest travelers. Holy Week offers memorable ceremonies and processions.

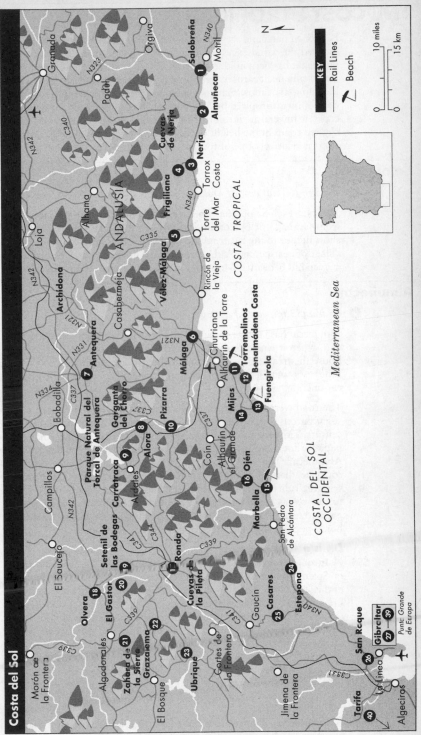

Costa del Sol

THE COSTA TROPICAL

East of Málaga and west of Almería, the so-called Costa Tropical has escaped the worst excesses of the property developers, and its tourist onslaught has been mild. A flourishing farmer center thanks to the year-round climate, it earns its keep not from tourism but from tropical fruit, including avocados, mangoes, papaws, and custard apples. Housing developments inspired by Andalusian village architecture (rather than concrete towers) are the norm. You may find packed beaches and traffic-choked roads at the height of the season, but for most of the year this coast is relatively free of tourists, if not from foreign expatriates.

Salobreña

❶ *102 km (63 mi) east of Málaga.*

You can reach Salobreña either by descending through the mountains from Granada or by continuing west from Almería on the N340. A short detour to the left from the highway brings you to this unspoiled village of near-perpendicular streets and old white houses, slapped onto a steep hill beneath a Moorish fortress. It's a true Andalusian *pueblo.*

Almuñecar

❷ *85 km (53 mi) east of Málaga.*

Almuñecar has been a fishing village since Phoenician times, 3,000 years ago, when it was called Sexi. Later, the Moors built a castle here to house the treasures of Granada's kings. Today Almuñecar is a small-time resort with a shingle beach, popular with Spanish and Belgian vacationers.

The road west from Motril passes through the former empire of the sugar barons who brought prosperity to Málaga's province in the 19th century. The cane fields are now giving way to litchis, limes, mangoes, papaws, and olives; avocado groves line your route as you descend into Almuñecar. The village is actually two, separated by the dramatic rocky headland of Punta de la Mona. To the east is Almuñecar proper, with the ruins of the Moorish castle and a Phoenician burial ground; to the west is La Herradura, a quiet fishing community and a perfect place to relax. Between the two is the pretty Marina del Este yacht harbor, a popular diving center along with La Herradura.

Dining and Lodging

$$$ ✕ **Jacqui-Cotobro.** Acclaimed as one of the finest French restaurants on Spain's southern coast, this small restaurant has new seaside premises at the foot of the Punta de la Mona. The dining area is cozy, with bare brick walls and green wicker chairs, and there's a beachfront terrace in summer. On your plate are imaginative combinations of French and Andalusian cooking. The best bet is the *menú de degustación,* with a selection of three courses plus dessert; it changes weekly but might include such dishes as breast of duck in sweet-and-sour sauce followed by *hojaldre de langostinos con puerros* (shrimp pastry with leeks) and *suprema de rodaballo* (turbot). ⊠ *Eficicio Río, Playa Cotobro,* ☎ *958/ 631802. MC, V. Closed Mon. and late Nov.–early Dec.*

$$$ 🏨 **Los Fenicios.** This relatively new hotel has a good location near the beach in La Herradura, with views of the bay and the cliffs of Punta de Mona to the east, the rocky headland of Cerro Gordo to the west. A gleaming, white entrance with an enormous, Moroccan-style ceiling lamp sets the tone. Each room has a small sitting area with wicker chairs, and all have terraces; ask for a room with a sea view. There's a swimming pool on the roof. ✉ *Paseo de Andrés Segovia, La Herra dura 18697,* ☎ *958/827900,* FAX *958/827910. 42 rooms. Restaurant, cafeteria, pool, meeting rooms. AE, DC, MC, V.*

Nerja

★ ❸   *52 km (32 mi) east of Málaga, 22 km (14 mi) west of Almuñecar.*

The **Cuevas de Nerja** (Nerja Caves) lie between Almuñecar and Nerja on a road surrounded by giant cliffs and dramatic seascapes, the best scenery on this stretch of the coast. Signs point to the cave entrance above the village of Maro, 4 km (2½ mi) before Nerja. These huge caves were discovered in 1959 by children playing on the hillside; they're now floodlit for better views of the spires and turrets created by millennia of dripping water. One suspended pinnacle, 200 ft long, is in fact the world's largest stalactite. The awesome subterranean chambers make an impressive setting for concerts and ballets during July's Nerja Caves Festival. ☎ *95/252–9520.* 🎫 *650 ptas.* ☉ *Sept.–June, daily 10–2:30; July–Aug., daily 10:30–2 and 4–8.*

Nerja—the name comes from the Moorish word *narixa,* meaning "abundant springs"—is a rapidly developing resort. Happily, much of its growth has been confined to *urbanizaciones* ("village" developments) outside the town. The old village of Nerja is clustered on a headland above several small beaches and rocky coves, which offer reasonable bathing despite the gray, gritty sand. In high season, Nerja's beaches are packed with northern Europeans, but the rest of the year it's a pleasure to wander the old town's narrow, whitewashed streets and courtyards. Nerja's highlight is the **Balcón de Europa,** a lookout high above the sea, on a promontory just off the central square.

Dining and Lodging

$$ ✗ **Casa Luque.** One of Nerja's most authentically Spanish restaurants,
★ Casa Luque is in a charming old Andalusian house behind the Balcón de Europa Church. The menu features dishes from northern Spain, often of Basque or Navarrese origin, with an emphasis on meat and game; good fresh fish is also on offer. The lovely patio is a perfect setting in summer. ✉ *Plaza Cavana 2,* ☎ *95/252–1004. AE, DC, MC, V. Closed Mon. and Feb.*

$$$ ✗🏨 **Parador de Nerja.** Surrounded by a leafy garden on the cliff's edge, the rooms in this modern parador have balconies overlooking the garden and, obliquely, the sea; those in the newer, single-story wing open onto their own patios. Some rooms have whirlpool baths. An elevator takes you down to the rocky beach. The restaurant concentrates on local cuisine and is known for its fish dishes; the menu changes daily. It might include *pez espada a la naranja* (swordfish in orange sauce) or giant *langostino* shrimp. ✉ *Almuñecar 8, 29780,* ☎ *95/252–0050,* FAX *95/252–1997. 73 rooms. Restaurant, pool. AE, DC, MC, V.*

$$$ 🏨 **Mónica.** The Mónica is spacious and luxurious, with cool, Moorish-style architecture and lots of marble. All rooms have sea views. Popular with package tours, it's also within easy walking distance of the center of town. ✉ *Playa Torrecilla, 29780,* ☎ *95/252–1100,* FAX *95/ 252–1162. 234 rooms. 2 restaurants, bar, 2 pools, tennis court, nightclub. AE, DC, MC, V.*

Nightlife and the Arts

El Colono (✉ Granada 6, Nerja, ☎ 95/252–1826) is a flamenco club and restaurant in a typical Andalusian house in the town center. Dinner shows begin at 9 PM on Wednesdays in winter, and at 9:30 or 10

PM Wednesdays through Fridays in summer. You can choose from three prix-fixe menus.

Frigiliana

❹ *58 km (36 mi) east of Málaga.*

The village of Frigiliana sits on a mountain ridge overlooking the sea. One of the last battles between the Christians and the Moors was waged here in 1567. The short drive off the main road rewards you with spectacular views and an old quarter full of cobbled streets and ancient houses. You can also take a bus to Frigiliana from Nerja.

Vélez-Málaga

❺ *36 km (22 mi) east of Málaga.*

Vélez-Málaga is the capital of the region of Axarquía. A pleasant agricultural town of white houses, Vélez-Málaga is a center for strawberry fields and vineyards producing the sweet muscatel grapes for which Málaga is famous. Worth quick visits are the **Thursday market,** the ruins of a **Moorish castle,** and the church of **Santa María la Mayor,** built in Mudéjar (Spanish Muslim) style on the site of a mosque destroyed when the town fell to the Christians in 1487.

MÁLAGA AND INLAND

The city of Málaga and the towns and villages of the upland hills and valleys to its north create precisely the kind of sharp contrast that makes traveling through Spain exciting. The Moorish legacy is a unifying visual theme as evidenced throughout the tiny streets honeycombing the steamy depths of Málaga, the rocky cliffs and gorges between Alora and Archidona, the layout of the farms, and the crops themselves (such as oranges).

Málaga

❻ *175 km (109 mi) southeast of Córdoba.*

The city of Málaga, with about 550,000 residents, is technically the capital of the Costa del Sol, though most visitors simply use the airport and bypass the city itself. Approaching the city from the airport, you'll be greeted by an urban sprawl wherein the huge high-rises of the 1970s march determinedly toward Torremolinos. But don't despair, for in its center and its eastern suburbs, Málaga is a pleasant port city, with ancient streets and lovely villas amid exotic foliage. Blessed with a subtropical climate, it's covered in lush vegetation and averages some 324 days of sunshine a year.

A word of warning: Málaga has one of the highest unemployment rates in Spain, and poverty and crime are rife (although drug peddling, once fairly common in the streets, has declined). Numerous muggings have been reported; it's best not to carry a purse or any valuables in the streets or on the way up to Gibralfaro (☞ *below*). If you arrive by car, you'll will have to contend with the pesky *gorrillas,* volunteer parking attendants who demand money to "watch" your car. Stick to areas with parking meters or uniformed parking attendants.

Arriving from Nerja, you'll enter Málaga through the suburbs of El Palo and Pedregalejos, once traditional fishing villages in their own right. Here you can eat wonderfully fresh fish in the numerous crusty *chiringuitos* (fishermen's restaurants) on the beach and stroll Pedregalejos's seafront promenade or the tree-lined streets of El Limonar. At sunset take a walk along the **Paseo Marítimo** and watch the lighthouse start its nightly vigil.

In the city center, the **Plaza de la Marina,** with outdoor cafés and an illuminated fountain overlooking the port, is a pleasant place for a drink. From here, stroll through the shady, palm-lined gardens of the **Paseo del Parque** or browse on Calle Marqués de Larios, the main shopping street.

The narrow streets and alleys on each side of **Calle Marqués de Larios** have charms of their own. Wander the warren of passageways around Pasaje Chinitas, off Plaza de la Constitución, and peep into the dark, vaulted *bodegas* where old men down glasses of *seco añejo* or *Málaga Virgen,* local wines made from Málaga's muscatel grapes. Silversmiths and vendors of religious books and statues ply their trades in shops that have changed little since the turn of the century. Across Larios, in the streets leading to Calle Nueva, you'll find shoe-shine boys, lottery-ticket vendors, carnation-sporting Gypsies, beggars, and a wealth of tapas bars dispensing wine from huge barrels.

NEED A
BREAK?

Antigua Casa de la Guardia (✉ Alameda 18), around the corner from the colorful municipal market, is Málaga's oldest bar, founded in 1840. Andalusian wines flow straight from the barrel, and the floor is ankle-deep in discarded shrimp shells.

After exploring the old town, visit the **cathedral,** built between 1528 and 1782 on the site of the former mosque. Mainly Renaissance in style, Málaga's cathedral is not one of the great cathedrals of Spain, having been left unfinished when the funds ran out. (One story holds that the money allocated was donated instead to the American Revolution.) Because it lacks one of its twin towers, the cathedral has been called *La Manquita* (the one-armed lady). The lovely, enclosed choir, which miraculously survived the burnings of the civil war, is the work of the great 17th-century artist Pedro de Mena, who in places carved the wood wafer-thin to express the fold of a robe or shape of a finger. Next to the cathedral is a museum of religious art and artifacts. ✉ *Calle de Molina Larios,* ☎ *95/221-5917.* 🎫 *Cathedral free, museum 200 ptas.* ⊙ *Mon.–Sat. 10–12:30 and 4–6:30.*

On one side of the square facing the cathedral's main entrance is the **Palacio Episcopal** (Bishop's Palace), now used for art exhibits (☎ 95/260–2722). From here, walk around the cathedral on Calle Cister and check out the oldest part of the building, the Gothic Puerta del Sagrario (a side entrance no longer in use). Then, walk up Calle San Agustín past the **Palacio de Buenavista**—home of the future Picasso Museum, due to open at the end of 1999—and up Calle Granada to the **Plaza de la Merced.** Number 15 was the birthplace and childhood home of Málaga's most famous son, Pablo Picasso; it now houses the Picasso Foundation and a library for art historians (☎ 95/221–5005. ⊙ Daily 11–2 and 5–8 [11–2 only in summer]).

The **Alcazaba,** undoubtedly Málaga's best sight, is a fortress begun in the 8th century, when Málaga was the principal port of the Moorish kingdom. The ruins of the Roman amphitheater at its entrance are now being restored. Major restoration work on the Alcazaba itself continues throughout 1998, so only part of the fortress is open to the public. The inner palace was built between 1057 and 1063, when the Moorish emirs took up residence. Ferdinand and Isabella lived here, too, for a while, after their conquest of Málaga in 1487. The ruins are dappled with orange trees and bougainvillea, and their heights afford great views of the park and port. ✉ *Entrance on Alcazabilla.* 🎫 *200 ptas.* ⊙ *Open Wed.–Mon. 9:30–8.*

★   Magnificent views reward a climb through the Alcazaba gardens to the
    summit of **Gibralfaro.** (Thieves have been said to hover here, so don't
    go alone, and don't carry valuables.) Alternatively, you can drive to
    Gibralfaro by way of Calle Victoria or take a minibus that leaves
    roughly every 1½ hours from Calle Molina Larios (near the cathedral)
    for the parador at the top of Gibralfaro. The fortifications were built
    for Yusuf I in the 14th century, and the Moors called them Jebelfaro,
    meaning "rock of the lighthouse," after a beacon that stood here to
    guide ships into the harbor and warn of invading pirates. The beacon
    has been succeeded by the small parador, a delightful place for a meal
    or drink.

On the far side of the city center, beside the river, is the **Museo de Artes
Populares** (Arts and Crafts Museum), housed in the old Mesón de la
Victoria, a 17th-century inn. On display are horse-drawn carriages and
carts, old agricultural implements, folk costumes, a forge, a bakery, an
ancient grape press, and Malagueño ceramics and sculptures. ⊠ *Pasillo
de Santa Isabel 10,* ☎ *95/221–7137.* ⌷ *200 ptas.* ◷ *Apr.–Oct.,
Tues.–Sat. 10–1:30 and 5–8, Sun. 10–1:30; Nov.–Mar., Tues.–Sat.
10–1:30 and 4–7, Sun. 10–1:30.*

Just off the exit road to Granada—too far to walk, but well worth the
taxi fare from the city center—is the 150-year-old **La Concepción** botanical garden. It was created by the daughter of the British consul, who
married a Spanish shipping magnate; the captains of the Spaniard's fleet
had standing orders to bring back seedlings and cuttings from every
"exotic" country they called at. The garden was abandoned for many
years, the tropical plants left to their own devices; but after careful restoration, La Concepción is a luxuriant green jungle, notable for the variety and size of its palm trees (⊠ Carretera de las Pedrizas, Km 166,
☎ 95/225–2148. ⌷ 400 pesetas. ◷ Tues.–Sun 9:30–sundown). If you
like formal gardens, two other worthwhile visits are **El Retiro** and **La
Cónsula,** both on the Churriana road near the airport. El Retiro, begun
by monks in the 17th century, has an array of exotic birds (☎ 95/262–
1600. ◷ 9–7 in summer, 9–5 in winter. ⌷ 1,250 ptas.). The latter,
surrounding a mansion built by the Prussian consul in 1806, is now
the site of the Málaga hotel school's excellent restaurant (*below*).

Dining and Lodging

$$$ ✕ **Café de París.** The owner of this elegant and intimate Paseo Marí-
★   timo restaurant, with a warm, pink interior, is a former chef at both
     Madrid's Horcher and Marbella's La Hacienda. Sophisticated Span-
     ish diners come from far afield for specialties like *rodaballo sobre es-
     pinacas* (turbot on a bed of spinach) and *hojaldre de langostinos* (giant
     shrimp en croûte). The *menú de degustación* allows you to try a little
     of everything. ⊠ *Vélez Málaga 8,* ☎ *95/222–5043. Reservations es-
     sential. AE, DC, MC, V. Closed Sun.*

$$$ ✕ **Escuela de Hostelería.** For an exquisite lunch, it's well worth going
     out of your way to Málaga's hotel and catering school, housed in a
     19th-century mansion 8 km (5 mi) outside Málaga on the Churriana
     road, near the airport. The dining room itself is a light, airy building
     of striking modern design, adjoining the La Cónsula mansion and its
     luxuriant garden. The seasonal dishes are delicious and exquisitely pre-
     sented. ⊠ *Finca La Cónsula, Churriana,* ☎ *95/262–2562. Reserva-
     tions essential. AE, MC, V. No dinner. Closed weekends.*

$$$ ✕ **Casa Pedro.** It's crowded and noisy, but Malagueños have been flock-
     ing to this no-frills fish restaurant for more than 50 years. Out in El
     Palo, the restaurant has a huge, bare dining room overlooking the ocean.
     If you know a little Spanish, are adventurous and patient, and like local
     color, try joining the families who come for lunch on Sundays. It's qui-

eter at other times. ⊠ *Quitapenas 121, El Palo beach (Bus 11),* ☎ 9͞5͞/ *229–0013. AE, DC, MC, V. No dinner Mon.*

$$ ✗ **El Chinitas.** At one end of Pasaje Chinitas, the most *típico* of Málaga's streets, this dining spot is decorated with colorful Sevillian tiles. The tapas bar is popular, especially for its cured ham. Try the *sopa viña AB* (a fish soup flavored with sherry and thickened with mayonnaise) or fillet steak in Málaga wine sauce. ⊠ *Moreno Monroy 4,* ☎ *95/221– 0972. AE, MC, V.*

$–$$ ✗ **Rincón de Mata.** This is one of the best of the many restaurants in the pedestrian shopping area between Calle Marqués de Larios and Calle Nueva. The menu is more interesting than most, with house specialties such as *tunedor* (calf in sauce). In summer there are tables on the sidewalk. ⊠ *Esparteros 8,* ☎ *95/222–3135. AE, DC, MC, V.*

$ ✗ **La Cancela.** In an alley off Calle Granada, at the top of Molina Larios, this pretty bistro serves standard Spanish fare and is ideal for lunch after a morning of shopping. The two dining rooms (one upstairs, one down) are crowded with curious objects: iron grilles, birdcages, potted plants, plastic flowers. In summer, tables appear on the sidewalk for outdoor lunches on what amounts to a sheltered patio. ⊠ *Denís Belgrano 5,* ☎ *95/222–3125. AE, DC, MC, V.*

$$$ ▥ **Larios.** Málaga's newest hotel opened in 1994 in an elegantly restored 19th-century building on the central Plaza de la Constitución. Black-and-white tiled floors lend subdued elegance to the second-floor lobby; the rooms are furnished with light wood and cream-colored fabrics and polished off with artsy black-and-white photographs. ⊠ *Marqués de Larios 2, 29005,* ☎ *95/222–2200,* ⚏ *95/222–2407. 34 rooms, 6 suites. Restaurant, meeting room. AE, DC, MC, V.*

$$ ✗▥ **Las Vegas.** In a pleasant, if somewhat tumultuous, part of Málaga just east of the center, this conveniently located hotel has a dining room overlooking the Paseo Marítimo; a pool; and a large, leafy garden. The rooms in back enjoy good views of the sea, as does the spacious, panoramic dining room. ⊠ *Paseo de Sancha 22, 29016,* ☎ *95/221–7712,* ⚏ *95/222–4889. 107 rooms. Restaurant, bar, pool. AE, DC, MC, V.*

$$$ ▥ **Don Curro.** Just around the corner from the cathedral, this family classic has been overhauled of late, but an old-fashioned air permeates the wood-paneled common rooms, the fireplace lounge, and the somewhat stodgy, wood-floored guest rooms. The best rooms are in the new wing, at the back of the building. ⊠ *Sancha de Lara 7, 29015,* ☎ *95/222–7200,* ⚏ *95/221–5946. 116 rooms, 4 suites. Restaurant. AE, DC, MC, V.*

$$–$$$ ▥ **Parador de Málaga-Gibralfaro.** Surrounded by pine trees on top of ★ Gibralfaro, 3 km (2 mi) above the city, this cozy, gray-stone parador offers spectacular views of the city and bay. Its typical parador rooms (matching blue curtains and bedspreads, and woven rugs on a bare floor) are the best in Málaga. Reserve far in advance. ⊠ *Monte de Gibralfaro, 29016,* ☎ *95/222–1903,* ⚏ *95/222–1904. 38 rooms. Restaurant, bar, cafeteria, pool, conference rooms. AE, DC, MC, V.*

$ ▥ **Victoria.** This small, renovated hostel offers excellent budget accommodations in a great location. Housed in a 19th-century stone row house whose facade has been painted gleaming white, it's on a side street just off Calle de Molino Larios. ⊠ *Sancha de Lara 3, 29015,* ☎ *95/ 222–4224. 14 rooms. AE, DC, MC, V.*

Nightlife and the Arts

The region's main theater is the **Teatro Cervantes** (⊠ Ramos Marín, Málaga, ☎ 95/222–4100), whose programs include plays (in Spanish), concerts, and flamenco.

The Málaga Symphony Orchestra has a winter season of orchestral concerts and chamber music, with most performances in the Teatro Cervantes. In summer, rock concerts are staged in Málaga's 100-year-old bullring.

The main nightlife districts are along the Paseo Marítimo and out in the eastern suburbs on Avenida Juan Sebastián Elcano and the beachfront at Pedregalejos.

Shopping

In Málaga, the **Corte Inglés** department store provides English interpreters, shipping, VAT refunds, and currency exchange. ⊠ *Avda. de Andalucía 46,* ☎ *95/230–0000.* ⊙ *Mon.–Sat. 10–9.*

Antequera

❼ *64 km (40 mi) northeast of Málaga, 43 km (27 mi) northwest of Pizarra, 108 km (67 mi) northwest of Ronda (via Pizarra).*

Antequera became one of the great strongholds of the Moors following their defeat at Córdoba and Seville in the 13th century. Its fall to the Christians in 1410 paved the way for the reconquest of Granada—the Moors retreated, leaving a **fortress** on the town heights, in whose midst the parador now stands. Of the town's many churches, the collegiate church of **Santa María la Mayor,** a 16th-century sandstone building with a fine ribbed vault (used today as a concert hall and crafts training center), is one of the best; another landmark is the church of **San Sebastián,** with a brick baroque Mudéjar tower.

Antequera's pride and joy is **Efebo,** a beautiful bronze statue of a boy that dates back to Roman times. Standing almost 5 ft high, it's on display in the **Museo Municipal** (Municipal Museum). ⊠ *Palacio de Nájera, Coso Viejo,* ☎ *95/270–4051.* ⊠ *200 ptas.* ⊙ *Tues.–Sat. 10–1:30, Sun. 11–1.*

Just outside Antequera, off the Málaga exit road, are the mysterious prehistoric **dolmens,** megalithic burial chambers built some 4,000 years ago out of massive slabs of stone weighing more than 100 tons each. The best-preserved dolmen is La Menga (⊙ Tues.–Sun 10–1 and 2–6 in winter; 10–1 and 4–8 in summer).

Ten kilometers (6 miles) northwest of Antequera, off the A92 highway to Seville, is **Fuentepiedra,** a shallow saltwater lagoon that serves as Europe's major nesting area for the greater flamingo. In February and March, these birds arrive from Africa by the tens of thousands to spend the summer here. The visitor center has information on local wildlife.

From Antequera, you have several options. To the east of town, along N342, is the dramatic silhouette of the **Peña de los Enamorados** (Lovers' Rock), an Andalusian landmark. Legend has it that a Moorish princess and a Christian shepherd boy eloped here one night and cast themselves to their deaths from the peak the next morning. The rock's outline is often likened to the profile of the Cordoban bullfighter Manolete. Eight kilometers (5 miles) beyond the Peña, the village of Archidona winds its way up a steep mountain slope beneath the ruins of a Moorish castle. This picturesque white cluster is worth a detour for the sake of its contrasting **Plaza Ochavada,** a magnificent 17th-century square resplendent in red and ocher stone.

Ten kilometers (6 miles) south of Antequera on C3310, the **Parque Natural del Torcal de Antequera** (Antequera Cave Region Natural Park) has well-marked walking trails that guide you among eerie pillars o pink limestone sculpted by eons of wind and rain. Wear sturdy shoes, and be careful not to wander from the marked paths, as it's easy to get lost in the maze of rock formations.

Dining and Lodging

$$ ✕ **La Espuela.** To its credit, this restaurant does not rest on its intriguing location (under the grandstand of the Antequera bullring) but puts care into its cuisine, well-prepared Andalusian dishes with some innovative touches. Try the *pimientos rellenos* (peppers stuffed with cuttlefish and shrimp) or the *conejo a la cazadora* (rabbit in a mushroom-and-almond sauce).✉ *Plaza de Toros,* ☎ *95/270–3424. DC, MC, V.*

$$ ✕🏨 **Parador de Antequera.** This modern, white parador is set on a hill overlooking the *vega,* Antequera's fertile valley, with the Peña de los Enamorados in the distance. The public rooms are simple but tasteful, with antique carpets on tile floors and taurine prints on the walls. The comfortable rooms have twin beds, covered with woven rugs, and spacious tile bathrooms. The spacious dining room, with a lofty wood ceiling, serves good local dishes, such as *pio antequerano* (a salad of orange, cod, and olives), or oxtail in a sauce made with the sweet wine from nearby Mollina. ✉ *García del Olmo, 29200,* ☎ *95/284–0261,* 𝔽𝔸𝕏 *95/284–1312. 55 rooms. Restaurant, pool. AE, DC, MC, V.*

Alora

★ ⑧ *37 km (23 mi) southwest of Antequera, 6 km (4 mi) north of Pizarra.*

Taking C337 southwest of Antequera will bring you to the turnoff for Alora. From Alora, follow a small road north to the awe-inspiring **Garganta del Chorro** (Gorge of the Stream). Here, in a deep chasm in the limestone cliff, the Guadalhorce River churns and snakes its way some 600 ft below the road. The railroad track that worms in and out of tunnels in the cleft is, amazingly, the main line heading north from Málaga for Bobadilla junction and, eventually, Madrid. North of the gorge, the Guadalhorce has been dammed to form a series of scenic reservoirs surrounded by pine-clad hills. Informal, open-air restaurants overlook the lakes and a number of picnic spots.

Carratraca

⑨ *17 km (11 mi) northwest of Alora, 54 km (34 mi) northeast of Ronda.*

The old spa town of Carratraca has a Moorish-style **Ayuntamiento** (town hall) and an unusual **polygonal bullring.** It was once a favorite watering hole of both Spanish and foreign aristocracy. Its hotel, the **Hostal del Príncipe,** once sheltered Empress Eugénie, wife of Napoleon III; Lord Byron also came seeking the cure. You can still relax in the sulfur baths of Carratraca's splendid **marble-and-tile bathhouse.**

En Route From Carratraca, return to Alora, from which C337 takes you back to the coast through groves of citrus and olives.

Pizarra

⑩ *6 km (4 mi) south of Alora, 65 km (40 mi) east of Ronda.*

The highlight of Pizarra is the **Museo Municipal de Pizarra,** formerly known as the Hollander Museum. Over the two decades they lived in Pizarra, American artist Gino Hollander and his wife, Barbara, built up this exceptional collection of paintings and objets d'art, furniture, and archaeological finds. One section houses the archaeological displays, including Moorish and Roman objects; the other is devoted to rustic Andalusian furniture and farm implements. ✉ *Cortijo Casablanca*

29, 29560 (1 km [½ mi] south of Pizarra), ☏ *95/248–3237.* ✉ *300 ptas.* ☉ *Tues.–Sun. 10–2 and 4–8 (4–6:30 in winter).*

THE COSTA DEL SOL OCCIDENTAL

After you rejoin N340 11 km (7 mi) to the west of Málaga, the sprawling outskirts of Torremolinos signal that you're leaving the "real" Spain and entering, well, the "real" Costa del Sol. If you're looking for beaches, high-rise hotels, and serious tourist activity, read on; if not, go directly to the next section.

Torremolinos

⑪ *11 km (7 mi) west of Málaga, 16 km (10 mi) northeast of Fuengirola, 43 km (27 mi) east of Marbella.*

Torremolinos is all about fun in the sun. Swarms of northern Europeans—young and not so young—throng its streets in season. Scantily attired and fair in hue, they shop for bargains on Calle San Miguel, down sangría in the bars of La Nogalera, and dance the night away in discotheques. By day, the sunseekers flock to the beaches El Bajondillo and La Carihuela, whose sand is the usual fine, gray grit; in high summer it's hard to find a patch of your own.

Torremolinos has two distinct sections. The first, **Torremolinos** (known to British locals and other expats as "Central T-town"), is built around the Plaza Costa del Sol; Calle San Miguel, the main shopping street; and the brash Nogalera Plaza, full of overpriced bars and "foreign" restaurants. The Pueblo Blanco area, off Calle Casablanca, is more pleasant, and the Cuesta del Tajo, at the far end of San Miguel, winds down a steep slope to the Bajondillo Beach. Here, crumbling walls, bougainvillea-clad patios, and old cottages hint at the quiet fishing village this once was.

The second section of Torremolinos's two major sections is the much nicer district of **La Carihuela.** To reach it, head west out of town on Avenida Carlota Alessandri and turn left by the Hotel La Paloma. Far more authentically Spanish, the Carihuela retains many of its old fishermen's cottages and a large number of excellent fish restaurants. Its traffic-free esplanade makes for an enjoyable stroll, especially on a summer evening or Sunday lunchtime, when it's packed with Spanish families.

The **Aquapark,** off the bypass, near the Palacio de Congresos Convention Center, has water chutes, artificial waves, water mountains, and pools. ☏ *95/238–8888.* ✉ *1,890 ptas.* ☉ *May–Sept., daily 10–7.*

Dining and Lodging

$$$ ✕ **Juan.** This Carihuela hot spot is a good place for seafood in sum-
★   mer, with a sunny outdoor patio facing the sea. House specialties include the great Costa del Sol standbys—*sopa de mariscos* (shellfish soup), *dorada al horno* (oven-roasted giltheads), and *fritura malagueña.* ⊠ *Paseo Marítimo 29, La Carihuela,* ☏ *95/238–5656. AE, DC, MC, V.*

$$ ✕ **Casa Guaquin.** On a seaside patio in La Carihuela, Casa Guaquin is
★   widely known as the best seafood restaurant in the area. Ever-changing daily catches are served alongside such menu stalwarts as *coquinas* (wedge-shell clams) and *boquerones fritos* (fried anchovies). ⊠ *Paseo Marítimo 63,* ☏ *95/238–4530. AE, MC, V. Closed Thurs. and mid-Dec.–mid-Jan.*

$$ ✕ **Europa.** A short walk from the Carihuela, this villa is a very Spanish institution (rare for Torremolinos). It's ensconced in a large garden, so you can dine in leafy surroundings. Local families come en masse

on Sundays for a leisurely lunch. ⊠ *Vía Imperial 32,* ☎ *95/238–8022. AE, DC, MC, V.*

$–$$ ✕ **El Roqueo.** Owned by a former fisherman, this is one of the locals' favorite Carihuela fish restaurants. Ingredients are always fresh, and prices are very reasonable. ⊠ *Carmen 35,* ☎ *95/238–4946. AE, DC, MC, V. Closed Tues. and Nov.*

$$$ 🏨 **Cervantes.** A busy, cosmopolitan hotel—one of Torremolinos's consistently good places to stay in the heart of town—Cervantes is ideal for those who want to be in the center of things. It's not by the beach, but there's a pool, and the rooms are well furnished and comfortable. The service is good, and the panoramic dining room on the top floor is popular with locals. ⊠ *Las Mercedes, 29620,* ☎ *95/238–4033,* 🖷 *95/238–4857. 397 rooms. Dining room, 2 pools, beauty salon, sauna, nightclub. AE, DC, MC, V.*

$$$ 🏨 **Sidi Lago Rojo.** In the heart of old Carihuela, this modern, four-story apartment building is just two blocks back from the seafront. All of the well-maintained rooms have balconies; some overlook the pool and small, tree-filled garden. There's no great view, but prices are moderate, and you're close to the best bars and restaurants in town. ⊠ *Miami 1, 29620,* ☎ *95/238–7666,* 🖷 *95/238–0891. 144 rooms. Pool. AE, DC, MC, V.*

$$$ 🏨 **Tropicana.** On the beach at the far end of the Carihuela, in one of the most pleasant parts of Torremolinos, is this relaxing resort hotel with its own beach club. The tropical theme is carried throughout, from the leafy gardens and kidney-shape pool to the common areas, with their exotic plants, raffia floor mats, and bamboo furniture, to the rooms, with their ceiling fans and marble floors. A range of good restaurants is a five-minute walk away. ⊠ *Trópico 6, 29620,* ☎ *95/238–6600,* 🖷 *95/238–0568. 84 rooms. Pool, beach. AE, DC, MC, V.*

$ 🏨 **Miami.** Set in an old Andalusian villa in a shady garden west of the Carihuela, Miami is something of a find amid the ocean of concrete towers. Staying here is like visiting a private Spanish home; the rooms are individually furnished, and there's a sitting room with a cozy fireplace. It's very popular, so reserve ahead. ⊠ *Aladiño 14, at Miami, 29620,* ☎ *95/238–5255. 26 rooms. Pool. No credit cards.*

Nightlife

Most of the nocturnal action is in the center of town and along the Montemar strip heading west from there. Some bars have occasional live music, but Torremolinos is best known for its discos. Among the most popular are **Atrevete** (⊠ Calle Salvador Allende 10, ☎ 95/237–0899), **Gatsby** (⊠ Avenida Montemar 32, ☎ 95/238–5372), and **Paladium** (⊠ Avenida Palma de Mallorca 36, ☎ 95/238–4289). **Taberna Flamenca Pepe López** (⊠ Plaza de la Gamba Alegre, ☎ 95/238–1284) is the best bet for flamenco.

Benalmádena

⑫ *9 km (5½ mi) west of Torremolinos, 9 km (5½ mi) east of Mijas.*

West of Torremolinos come the similar but more staid resorts of Benalmádena Costa and Fuengirola. Benalmádena Costa is run almost exclusively by package-tour operators and offers little for the independent traveler, though there's a pleasant-enough marina, which draws Málaga's youth at night. It's also home to the **SeaLife** marine center, with aquariums showing varied examples of local fish from local waters, including rays, sharks, and sunfish (⊠ Puerto Marina Benalmádena, ☎ 95/256–0150); the center is open daily 10–6 in winter, 10 AM–midnight in summer, and costs ▨ 975 ptas. Two kilometers (1 mile) inland, at

Arroyo de la Miel, you can visit **Tivoli World,** the Costa del Sol's leading amusement park. Don't expect the sleek perfection of Disneyland, but there's a 4,000-seat, open-air auditorium that often showcases international stars alongside cancan, flamenco, or Spanish ballet performances. The park also has roller coasters, a Ferris wheel, illuminated fountains, a Chinese pagoda, Wild West shows, and 40-odd restaurants and snack bars. ☎ *95/244–2848.* ✉ *600 ptas.* ☉ *Winter, weekends only; summer, daily 4 AM–1 AM.*

Dining

$$$ ✗ **Ventorillo de la Perra.** If you've been searching the coast for something typically Spanish, you may find it in this old inn, which dates to 1785. Outside, there's a leafy patio; inside, a cozy, rustic atmosphere prevails in the dining room and in the bar, with a ham-hung ceiling. Choose between local Malagueño cooking, general Spanish fare, and international favorites. The *ajo blanco* (a cold garlic soup) makes a particularly good appetizer. ✉ *Avda. Constitución, Arroyo de la Miel,* ☎ *95/244–1966. AE, DC, MC, V. Closed Mon.*

$$$ ✗ **Mar de Alborán.** Next to the Benalmádena yacht harbor, this seafood mecca has a bit more class than the usual seaside fish restaurant and has established a solid culinary reputation as one of the best on the coast. The cheerful dining room is illuminated by picture windows at lunchtime. Dishes such as the Basque-inspired *lomo de merluza con kokotxas y almejas* (hake with cheek morsels and clams) are an imaginative switch from the standard Costa fare. ✉ *Avda. de Alay,* ☎ *95/244–6427. AE, MC, V. Closed Mon. No dinner Sun.*

$$ ✗ **Casa Fidel.** This Benalmádena Pueblo restaurant is rustic in flavor, with heavy beams and a large fireplace. The menu, however, is based on expertly cooked international dishes. For starters, you might try *entremeses Casa Fidel,* a tasty selection of hors d'oeuvres. Main courses include old favorites like grilled sole; more exotic options, like *perdiz en salsa de vino de Málaga* (partridge in Málaga wine); and a celebrated house specialty, English-style roast lamb. ✉ *Maestra Ayala 1,* ☎ *95/244–9165. AE, DC, MC, V. Closed Tues. No lunch Wed.*

Nightlife

The **Fortuna Nightclub** of the **Casino Torrequebrada** (✉ Km 220 on N340, Benalmádena Costa, ☎ 95/244–6000) has flamenco and an international dance show with a live orchestra, beginning at 9:30. The gambling casino is open 8 PM–4 AM; passport, jacket, and tie are required.

Fuengirola

⑬ *16 km (10 mi) west of Torremolinos, 27 km (17 mi) east of Marbella.*

Fuengirola is less frenetic than Torremolinos. Many of its waterfront high-rises are holiday apartments catering to budget-minded sunseekers from northern Europe and, in summer, a large contingent from Córdoba and other parts of Spain. The town is also a haven for British retirees (with numerous English and Irish pubs to serve them) and a shopping and business center for the rest of the Costa del Sol. Its Tuesday market is the largest on the coast and a major tourist attraction.

Dining and Lodging

$$ ✗ **El Bote.** This spacious, white restaurant near the eastern end of Fuengirola's Paseo Marítimo is the most popular fish place in town. The terrace and proximity to the beach make the setting ideal. Start with a selection of shellfish or a mixed fish fry; then—if there are at least two of you—share a fish baked in coarse sea salt. ✉ *Paseo Marítimo, Torreblanca del Sol,* ☎ *95/266–0296. AE, MC, V. Closed Wed.*

$$ ✕ **Portofino.** This lively restaurant, one of Fuengirola's best, is camouflaged among the brassy souvenir shops and fast-food joints on the promenade, just east of the port. The menu is international, with a few nods to the owner's Italian origins. The *carpaccio* (thinly sliced raw fillet steak with cheese) is a popular appetizer; for the main course, try the veal scallops in lemon sauce or the roast lamb. Service is fast, friendly, and professional. ⊠ *Paseo Marítimo 29,* ☎ *95/247–0643. AE, DC, MC, V. Closed Mon. No lunch July 1–Sept. 15.*

$$–$$$ ✕ **La Langosta.** This tiny restaurant, two blocks from the water on a side street in Los Boliches, has been a favorite for forty years. Needless to say, the speciality is *langosta* (lobster), prepared in a variety of ways, as well as sole in champagne sauce and mussels in saffron sauce. ⊠ *Francisco Cano 1, Los Boliches,* ☎ *95/247–5049. AE, MC, V. Closed Sun. No lunch.*

$$ 🏨 **Florida.** Almost opposite the port, this simple hotel is set back from the seafront behind a shady, semitropical garden where you can sunbathe and enjoy a drink at the poolside bar. One of Fuengirola's oldest lodgings, it dates back to the years before the land boom and is actually run by its owners. Rooms are basic. ⊠ *Paseo Marítimo s/n, 29640,* ☎ *95/247–6100,* 𝖥𝖠𝖷 *95/258–1529. 116 rooms. Restaurant, bar, pool. AE, DC, MC, V.*

$ 🏨 **Sedeño.** This small, family-run inn makes an ideal base for anyone wanting simple, affordable lodgings. It's in the center of town, one block back from the harbor and just off Jacinto Benavente, the café-lined street that runs down to the water. The rooms have balconies overlooking a tree-filled garden. ⊠ *Don Jacinto 1, 29640,* ☎ *95/247–4788. 30 rooms. No credit cards.*

Nightlife and the Arts

For plays in English, performed by local amateur troupes, try the **Salón de Variétés Theater** (⊠ Emancipación 30, ☎ 95/247–4542).

Mijas

★ ⑭ *8 km (5 mi) north of Fuengirola, 18 km (11 mi) west of Torremolinos.*

The picturesque village of Mijas is in the foothills of the sierra just north of the coast. Buses leave Fuengirola every half hour for the 8-km (5-mi) drive through hills peppered with whitewashed villas. If you have a car and don't mind a mildly hair-raising drive, take the more dramatic approach from Benalmádena Pueblo, a winding mountain road with some great views. Though Mijas was discovered long ago by foreign retirees, and the large, touristy square where you arrive may seem like an extension of the Costa, beyond this are hilly streets of whitewashed houses and a somewhat authentic village atmosphere.

Park in the Plaza Virgen de la Peña, where you can hire a "*burro taxi*" (guided donkey) to explore the village; take a quick look at the Chapel of Mijas's patroness, the Virgen de la Peña. Then pop into the **Carromato de Max,** whose collection of miniature curiosities from all over the world includes a rendition of the Last Supper on a grain of rice, Abraham Lincoln painted on a pinhead, and fleas wearing clothes. 🎟 *500 ptas.* ☉ *Daily 10–7.*

Wander over to the Plaza Constitución, Mijas's old village square, and walk up the slope beside the Mirlo Blanco restaurant to Mijas's tiny **bullring.** It's one of the few square bullrings in Spain. ☎ *95/248–5248.* 🎟 *400 ptas.* ☉ *Daily 10–6.*

Just up the hill from the bullring is the delightful village church of **La Inmaculada Concepción** (the Immaculate Conception). It's impeccably decorated, especially at Easter, and its terrace and spacious gardens afford a splendid panorama.

Meander through any of the **white streets,** heading ultimately up the hill behind the village—the higher you go, the more authentic the atmosphere. Take a peek inside the tiny church at the bottom of Calle San Sebastián; it's filled with flowers and rococo decorations on gleaming white walls.

NEED A
BREAK?   At No. 4 Calle San Sebastián, the **Bar Menguine** (or Casa de los Jamones) has a ceiling strung with row after row of hams, and a few tables set aside for the inexpensive meals served here.

Dining and Lodging

$$$ ✗ **El Padrastro.** Perched on a cliff above the Plaza Virgen de la Peña, this restaurant is accessible via an elevator from the square, or by steps if you're energetic. The views over Fuengirola and the coast are its main drawing card. The menu features international and Spanish dishes such as *lubina flameada al hinojo* (sea bass flambéed in fennel). A terrace and a swimming pool add to the alfresco ambience. ⊠ *Avda. del Compás,* ☎ *95/248–5000, AE, DC, MC, V.*

$$$ ✗ **Valparaíso.** Halfway up the road from Fuengirola to Mijas, this restaurant is all about setting. The sprawling villa stands in its own garden, complete with swimming pool; you can dine on the outdoor terrace in summer and dance the night away afterward to live music. In winter, logs burn in a cozy fireplace. Try the *pato a la naranja* (duck in orange sauce). ⊠ *Carretera de Mijas–Fuengirola, Km 7,* ☎ *95/248–5996. AE, MC, V. Closed Sun. Nov.–May. No lunch.*

$$ ✗ **Mirlo Blanco.** In an old house on the pleasant Plaza de la Constitución, with a terrace for outdoor dining in warm weather, this place is run by the second generation of a Basque family that has been in the Costa del Sol restaurant business for decades. Try Basque specialties on for size, such as *txangurro* (crab) and *merluza a la vasca* (hake with asparagus, eggs, and clam sauce). ⊠ *Plaza de la Constitución 13,* ☎ *95/248–5700. AE, MC, V.*

$$$$ ✗🏨 **Byblos Andaluz.** At the edge of Mijas's golf course, this luxury ★ hotel is the most expensive on the entire Costa del Sol. Set in a huge garden of palms, cypresses, and fountains, it is first and foremost a spa, and is known particularly for its *thalasso* therapy, a skin treatment that uses sea water and seaweed and is applied in a Roman temple of cool, white marble and blue tiles. Both of the outstanding restaurants serve savory regional dishes as well as highly sophisticated international cuisine. ⊠ *Urb. Mijas-Golf, 29640,* ☎ *95/247–3050,* FAX *95/247–6783. 111 rooms, 33 suites. 2 restaurants, indoor and outdoor pools, beauty salon, spa, 18-hole golf course, tennis courts, health club, shops. AE, DC, MC, V.*

$$$ 🏨 **Mijas.** This beautifully situated hotel at the entrance to Mijas has a poolside restaurant and bar; gardens with views of the hillsides stretching down to Fuengirola and the sea; marble floors throughout; wrought-iron window grilles; and Moorish shutters. The lobby is large and airy, and there's a delightful glass-roofed terrace. ⊠ *Urbanización Tamisa, 29650,* ☎ *95/248–5800,* FAX *95/248–5825. 98 rooms, 3 suites. Restaurant, indoor and outdoor pools, spa, tennis court, health club. AE, DC, MC, V.*

Marbella

⑮ *27 km (17 mi) west of Fuengirola, 28 km (17 mi) east of Estepona, 50 km (31 mi) southeast of Ronda.*

Playground of the rich and home of movie stars, rock musicians, and dispossessed royal families, Marbella has attained the top rung on Europe's social ladder. Dip into any Spanish gossip magazine, and chances are the glittering parties that fill its pages are set in Marbella.

Much of this action takes place on the fringes, for grand hotels and luxury restaurants line the waterfront for 20 km (12 mi) on each side of the town center. In the town itself, you may well wonder how Marbella became so famous. The main thoroughfare, Avenida Ricardo Soriano, is singularly lacking in charm, and the Paseo Marítimo, though pleasant enough, with an array of seafood restaurants and pizzerias overlooking an ordinary beach, is far from spectacular.

Marbella's real charm lies in the heart of the **old village,** which remains miraculously intact. Here, a block or two back from the main highway, narrow alleys of whitewashed houses cluster around the central Plaza de los Naranjos, where colorful restaurants vie for space under the orange trees. Climb onto what remains of the old fortifications, and stroll along the quaint Calle Virgen de los Dolores to the Plaza de Santo Cristo. Wander the maze of lanes and enjoy the geranium-speckled windows and splashing fountains.

The **Museo del Grabado Español Contemporáneo,** set in a restored 16th-century building in the old village, has an outstanding collection of modern Spanish etchings (✉ Hospital Bazán, ☎ 95/282–5035, ⊙ Sun. 11–2, Mon. 10–2, Tues.–Fri. 10–2 and 5:30–8:30, 💰 300 pesetas). In a modern building just east of the old quarter is the **Museo de Bonsai,** with a collection of miniature trees (✉ Parque Arroyo de la Repesa, Avda. Dr. Maiz Viñal, ☎ 95/286–2926, ⊙ Daily 11–1:30 and 4–7, 400 pesetas).

NEED A BREAK? Virgen de los Dolores is lined with inviting restaurants with prices more manageable than those in the nearby Plaza de los Naranjos. **Casa Eladio** (✉ No. 6, ☎ 95/277–0083) has a charming indoor patio.

The road to **Puerto Banús** has been called the Golden Mile. Here, a mosque, Arab banks, and the onetime residence of Saudi Arabia's King Fahd illustrate the influence of petro-dollars in this enclave of the rich. Seven kilometers (4½ miles) west of central Marbella (between Km 175 and Km 174), a sign indicates the turnoff leading down to Puerto Banús. Marbella's plush marina, with 915 berths, is a gem of ostentatious wealth, a kind of Spanish answer to St. Tropez. Huge flashy yachts, beautiful people, and countless expensive stores and restaurants make up the glittering parade that continues long into the night. The backdrop is an Andalusian *pueblo*—built in the 1980s in imitation of the fishing villages that once lined this coast.

Dining and Lodging

$$$$ ✕ **La Hacienda.** The menu reflects the late chef-proprietor Paul Schiff's
★ dual influences: his native Belgium and his adopted Andalusia. The *menú de degustación* (about 7,000 pesetas) lets you sample such creations as *tortilla fría de trufas y foie gras* (cold omelet of truffles and foie gras) and *solomillo de pato relleno de aceitunas* (duck breast stuffed with olives). The setting is an elegant hillside villa overlooking the sea. ✉ *Urbanización Las Chapas, N340, Km 193 (12 km [7½ mi] east of Marbella),* ☎ *95/283–1267. AE, DC, MC, V. Closed Mon.–Tues. and mid-Nov.–mid-Dec.*

$$$$ ✕ **La Meridiana.** Favored by the local jet set is La Meridiana, located west of town, behind the mosque. Its striking, modern architecture has a Moorish flavor, and the enclosed terrace allows "outdoor" dining year-round. The cuisine is famous for its quality and the freshness of its ingredients, both of which you can taste in the *menú de degustación*. This is a good place to sample *ajo blanco* (a garlicky local version of gazpacho made with almonds). ✉ *Camino de la Cruz,* ☎ *95/277–6190. AE, DC, MC, V. Closed Jan. No lunch June–Aug., or Mon.–Tues. Sept.–May.*

$$$ ✕ **El Rodeito.** Across the highway from the Marbella Club (☞ *below*), El Rodeito started out as a modest roadside eatery and evolved into a proper restaurant. It must be doing something right, as it never closes: the dining room is open 24 hours a day. Both the decor and the food recall a Castilian tavern, with specialties including *besugo a la espalda* (red bream split and grilled over coals), and roast suckling pig and *lechazo* (lamb). ✉ *Carretera de Cádiz, Km 173,* ☎ *95/281–0861. MC, V.*

$$$ ✕ **In Vino.** This classy restaurant is one of the newest additions to the Marbella dining scene, serving gourmet dishes and Mediterranean cuisine in a rich, wood-beamed dining room or, in summer, on an Andalusian-style terrace. As the name suggests, it has an extensive selection of wines, kept in a state-of-the-art cellar. ✉ *Carretera de Cádiz, Km 176.5, Río Verde,* ☎ *95/277–1211. AE, DC, MC, V. No lunch.*

$$$ ✕ **Santiago.** This busy place is known as the best fish restaurant in Marbella, though the meat dishes are excellent as well. Try the *ensalada de langosta* (lobster salad), followed by *besugo al horno* (baked red bream). ✉ *Paseo Marítimo 5,* ☎ *95/277–0078. AE, DC, MC, V. Closed Nov.*

$$$$ ✕🏨 **Puente Romano.** This spectacular, superdeluxe, modern hotel and
★   apartment complex of low, white-stucco buildings is west of Marbella, between the Marbella Club (☞ *below*) and Puerto Banús. There's a genuine Roman bridge on the beautifully landscaped grounds, which run right down to the beach. A nightclub run by legendary nightlife queen Regine and two outstanding restaurants, El Puente and La Plaza, complete the picture. ✉ *Carretera Cádiz, Km 177, 29600,* ☎ *95/ 282–0900,* 🖷 *95/277–5766. 152 rooms, 77 suites. 2 restaurants, 2 pools, 10 tennis courts, nightclub, meeting rooms. AE, DC, MC, V.*

$$$ ✕🏨 **El Fuerte.** The building is vintage 1950s, but the decor has (finally) been brought up-to-date, making El Fuerte the best all-around choice if you want a central hotel near the old town. All rooms have balconies overlooking the sea. The hotel stands at the end of the Paseo Marítimo, separated from the beach by a pleasant, palm-filled garden with an outdoor pool. ✉ *Avda. El Fuerte, 29600,* ☎ *95/286–1500,* 🖷 *95/ 282–4411. 261 rooms, 2 suites. Restaurant, indoor and outdoor pools, 2 tennis courts, health club, squash. AE, DC, MC, V.*

$$$ ✕🏨 **Los Monteros.** Five kilometers (3 miles) east of Marbella, on the road to Málaga, this exclusive hotel stands surrounded by tropical gardens on the sea side of the highway. The facilities and perks are extensive and include gourmet dining in the famous El Corzo Grill. Just renovated in early 1998, the rooms are formally decorated, and the service is impeccable. ✉ *Urb. Los Monteros, Carretera N340, Km 187, 29600,* ☎ *95/277–1700,* 🖷 *95/282–5846. 158 rooms, 10 suites. 3 restaurants, 1 indoor and 2 outdoor pools, beauty salon, sauna, 18-hole golf course, 10 tennis courts, exercise room, horseback riding, squash, nightclub, conference room. AE, DC, MC, V.*

$$$$ 🏨 **Marbella Club.** This grande dame of Marbella hotels was the creation
★   of Alfonso von Hohenlohe, the man who "founded" Marbella. The

Club has a long-established clientele, as well as local patricians. The bungalow-style rooms, some with private pools, come in various sizes, and the decor varies from regional to modern. The grounds are exquisite; breakfast is served on a patio where songbirds flit through the lush, subtropical vegetation. ⊠ *Carretera de Cádiz, Km 178 (3 km [2 mi] west of Marbella), 29600,* ☎ *95/282–2211,* FAX *95/282–9884. 83 rooms, 36 suites, 10 bungalows. Restaurant, 2 pools, beauty salon, sauna, exercise room, nightclub. AE, DC, MC, V.*

Nightlife and the Arts

Marbella's nightlife is livened by the personal rivalry between **Olivia Valere,** with her Arab fantasy club near the mosque (⊠ Carretera de Istán, Km 0.8), and **Regine,** who runs the club at the stylish Puente Romano hotel (☞ *above*), just across the highway. In the same area is the trendy **La Notte,** an art-deco bar with live music, next to La Meridiana (☞ *above*). Much of the action revolves around the Puerto Banús marina, in bars such as Sinatra's, Joe's Bar, and La Comedia.The **Casino Nueva Andalucía** (⊠ Bajos Hotel Andalucía Plaza, N340, Marbella, ☎ 95/281–4000) is a chic gambling spot in the Hotel Andalucía Plaza, just east of Puerto Banús on the road to Marbella. It's open daily 8 PM–5 AM. Jacket and tie are required for men, passports for all.

Art exhibits are held in private galleries and in several of Marbella's leading hotels, especially the Puente Romano. The tourist office publishes a free monthly calendar of exhibits and other events.

Ojén

⑯ *10 km (6 mi) north of Marbella.*

For a contrast to the glamour of the coast, drive up to Ojén, in the hills above Marbella. This ancient village is another world. Take a look at the beautiful pottery sold here.

Four kilometers (1½ miles) from Ojén is the **Refugio del Juanar,** a former hunting lodge (☞ below) in the heart of the Sierra Blanca, at the southern edge of the Serranía de Ronda, a mountainous wilderness. Not far from the Refugio, you might spot the herd of **wild ibex** that dwell among the rocky crags; the best times to look are dawn and dusk, when they descend from their hiding places. A bumpy trail takes you a mile from the Refugio to the **Mirador** lookout, which offers a sweeping view of the Costa del Sol and the coast of northern Africa.

Dining and Lodging

$$ ✕☰ **Refugio El Juanar.** This secluded hotel and restaurant used to be an aristocratic hunting lodge (King Alfonso XIII was among the guests). Later, it became part of the parador chain, and in 1984 it was sold to its staff for the symbolic sum of one peseta. The hunting theme prevails, both in the common areas—with a roaring log fire in winter and on the restaurant menu, where game dishes get pride of place. The rooms are simply decorated in a rustic style. ⊠ *Sierra Blanca, 29610,* ☎ *95/288–1000,* FAX *95/288–1001. 21 rooms, 2 suites. Restaurant, pool, 2 tennis courts. AE, DC, MC, V.*

RONDA AND THE PUEBLOS BLANCOS

Ronda and the whitewashed villages of the mountains behind the Costa del Sol create one of Spain's most moving and emblematic driving routes. The contrast with Torremolinos could not be more complete. Save time for this region, as it may well leave you with some of your most indelible travel memories.

Ronda

⓱   *61 km (38 mi) northwest of Marbella, 108 km (67 mi) southwest of Antequera (via Pizarra).*

Ronda is one of the oldest towns in Spain and is accordingly moving and picturesque. To get there, take the well-maintained C339 from San Pedro de Alcántara up through the mountains of the Serranía de Ronda. The town of Ronda is 49 km (30 mi) inland, secure in its mountain fastness on a rock high over the River Guadalevín. Once a stronghold for the legendary Andalusian bandits, Ronda is now known for its spectacular position and views. The town's most dramatic feature is its ravine (360 ft deep and 210 ft across), known as **El Tajo,** which divides La Ciudad, the old Moorish town, from El Mercadillo, the "new town," which sprang up after the Christian Reconquest of 1485. Tour buses roll in daily with sightseers from the coast, and on weekends affluent *sevillanos* flock to their second homes here; stay overnight midweek to see this noble town's true colors.

Begin in El Mercadillo, in the Plaza de España, where the tourist office can supply you with a map. Immediately to the south is Ronda's most famous bridge, the **Puente Nuevo** (New Bridge), an architectural marvel built between 1755 and 1793; its lantern-lit parapet offers dizzying views of the river far below. Just how many people have met their ends in this gorge nobody knows, but the architect of the Puente Nuevo fell to his death here while inspecting work on the bridge. During the civil war, hundreds of victims on both sides were hurled from it.

Cross the Puente Nuevo into **La Ciudad,** the old Moorish town, where you can wander through twisting streets of white houses with birdcage balconies, punctuated by stately Renaissance mansions. Turn left down Santo Domingo until you come to the **Casa del Rey Moro.** This so-called House of the Moorish King was, in fact, built in 1709 on the site of an earlier Moorish residence. Despite the name and the *azulejo* plaque depicting a Moor on the facade, it's unlikely that Moorish rulers ever lived here. The garden has a great view of the gorge, and from here a stairway of some 365 steps (known as La Mina) descends to the river. The house is being converted into a luxury hotel and is closed to the public, but you can visit the gardens and La Mina (✉ Cuesta de Santo Domingo 9, ☎ 95/218–7200. ⊡ 500 pesetas. ☉ Daily 10–8 in summer, 10–7 in winter).

Just down the street from the Casa del Rey Moro is the **Palacio del Marqués de Salvatierra,** a Renaissance mansion with wrought-iron balconies and an impressive portal. Note the strange figures carved on the facade. Though the house is still occupied by descendants of the original family, you can tour the interior with a guide. ☎ *95/287–1206.* ⊡ *250 ptas.* ☉ *Sept. 16–July, Fri.–Mon. 11–2 and 4–6.*

Below the Salvatierra palace, a road leads down into the ravine where two more bridges span the river: the Puente Viejo (Old Bridge), built in 1616 on Roman foundations, and the Puente Arabe (Arab Bridge), a much-restored Moorish bridge. Beside the river are the excavated remains of the **Baños Arabes** (Arab Baths), which date from Ronda's tenure as capital of a Moorish *taifa* (kingdom). The star-shape vents in the roof are an inferior imitation of the ceiling of the beautiful bathhouse in Granada's Alhambra (☞ Chapter 12). Gangs of youths have been known to threaten tourists for money here, so be careful. ⊡ *Free.* ☉ *Tues.–Sun. 9–2 and 4–6.*

Climb back up the hill from the river and make your way to the Plaza de la Ciudad. At the end of Marqués de Salvatierra, you'll pass the restored **Minarete Árabe** (Moorish Minaret), all that remains of a mosque destroyed after the Reconquest of 1485. The collegiate church of **Santa María la Mayor,** which serves as Ronda's cathedral, has roots in Moorish times; originally the Great Mosque of Moorish Ronda, it was rebuilt as a Christian church and dedicated to the Virgen de la Encarnación after the Reconquest. Its flamboyant mixture of styles reflects Ronda's heterogeneous past: the naves are late Gothic, the main altar is heavy with Baroque gold leaf, and the Renaissance belfry incorporates part of the original minaret.

Below the cathedral stands the ruined **Alcazaba,** blown up by the French in 1809, and beyond it, the Moorish **Puerta de Almocobar,** through which a triumphant Ferdinand led his troops in 1485.

From the west front of Santa María, the Ronda de Gameros leads to a stone palace with twin Mudéjar towers, known as the **Casa de Mondragón** (Plaza de Mondragón). Appropriated by Ferdinand and Isabella after their victory in 1485, it had probably been the residence of Ronda's Moorish kings. Today you can wander through the patios, with their brick arches and delicate, Mudéjar stucco tracery, and admire the mosaics and *artesonado* (coffered) ceiling. ☎ 95/287–0818. ☉ *Daily 10–6.*

The Plaza Campillo offers good views of the gorge and terraced hillsides. From here, Calle Tenorio leads back up to the Puente Nuevo and into **El Mercadillo,** the commercial heart of Ronda, where the town's hotels, restaurants, bars, banks, and stores are clustered. Most of the action takes place around the Plaza del Socorro and along the Carrera de Espinel, the main shopping street (better known by its nickname, Calle de la Bola).

NEED A
BREAK?

For a drink or snack, try **Don Miguel** (⊠ Calle Villanueva 4, ☎ 95/ 287–1090), a restaurant and café whose terrace has a spectacular view of the gorge and the Puente Nueva.

The main sight in Ronda's commercial center is the **Plaza de Toros,** one of the oldest and most handsome bullrings in Spain. Here, Pedro Romero (1754–1839), the father of modern bullfighting and Ronda's most famous native son, is said to have killed 5,600 bulls during his long career, and in the museum beneath the plaza you can see posters for the very first fights, held here in 1785. The plaza is owned by the famous, now-retired bullfighter Antonio Ordóñez, on whose nearby ranch Orson Welles's ashes were scattered, as directed in his will; indeed, the ring has become a favorite with filmmakers. Every September, the bullring is the scene of Ronda's *corridas goyescas,* named after Goya, whose bullfight sketches (*tauromaquias*) were inspired by the skill and art of Pedro Romero; seats for these fights cost a small fortune and are booked far in advance. Both the participants and the dignitaries in the audience don the costumes of Goya's time for the occasion. Other than that, the plaza is rarely used for fights except during the May festival. ☎ 95/287–4132. ☑ 275 ptas. ☉ *Daily 10–6:30 (10–8 in summer).*

Beyond the bullring, you can relax in the shady **Alameda del Tajo** gardens, one of the loveliest spots in Ronda. At gardens' end, a balcony protrudes from the face of the cliff, offering a vertigo-inducing view of the valley below. Stroll along the clifftop walk to the Old World Reina Victoria hotel (☞ Dining and Lodging, *below*), built by British settlers from Gibraltar at the turn of the century as a fashionable rest stop on their Algeciras–Bobadilla railroad line.

About 30 km (18 mi) west of Ronda are the prehistoric **Cuevas de la Pileta** (Pileta Caves); take C339 toward Algodonales and turn left after a few miles where you see the sign for the caves. The road winds up through the villages of **Montejaque** (worth a stop) and **Benaoján** to peter out at the caves' entrance. A guardian from the farm in the valley below will show you around, but you'll probably have to ask a local where to find him. Armed with lamps, you'll set off on a walk of about 1½ hours that reveals prehistoric wall paintings of bison, deer, and horses outlined in black, red, and ocher. One of the highlights is the Cámara del Pescado (Chamber of the Fish), where a drawing of a huge fish, thought to be 15,000 years old, decorates the chamber wall.

Clinging to the mountainsides of the vast landscape around Ronda are villages of white houses with honey-color tile roofs. These are the remote **pueblos blancos** of the province of Cádiz, on the onetime frontier between Moors and Christians. All are within a day's drive of Ronda; if you've only time for one, make it Grazalema (☞ *below*).

Dining and Lodging

$$ ✕ **Pedro Romero.** Named after the father of modern bullfighting, this restaurant is opposite the bullring and is packed with colorful taurine decor. Sad-eyed bulls peer down at you as you tuck into the *sopa del mesón* (house soup), *rabo de toro* (oxtail stew), *orperdiz a la cazuela* (stewed partridge), and, for dessert, *tocinillo del cielo al coco* (a sweet caramel custard flavored with coconut). ⊠ *Virgen de la Paz 18,* ☎ *95/ 287–1110. AE, DC, MC, V.*

$ ✕ **Mesón Santiago.** Eating at this typical tavern is like taking a meal with an extended Spanish family. Always packed, it feels more like a home than a restaurant; the several dining rooms are decorated with Sevillian tiles and ceramic plates. In summer, you can lunch outdoors on the patio. The cuisine is simple Spanish fare, including tongue, partridge, quail, and the rib-sticking *cocido de la casa*, a savory stew of chard, potatoes, and chickpeas. ⊠ *Marina 3,* ☎ *95/287–1559. MC, V. No dinner.*

$$$ ✕🏠 **Parador de Ronda.** Spain's newest parador—opened in 1994— is an architectural feat. The exterior is the old town hall, standing at the very edge of the Tajo gorge, but only the shell of the building remains—inside, the parador has a daring modern design. The combination of old and new is spectacular, from the moment you step into the glass-enclosed courtyard. The common areas are bright and airy, the staff professional, and the large rooms, in modern cream colors, are comfortable, with enormous bathrooms. The restaurant is justifiably famous: try the gazpacho based on green peppers (the chef's own invention), followed by a regional dish such as *cabrito asado* (roast kid) or *conejo a la rondeña* (rabbit, Ronda-style). ⊠ *Plaza de España, 29400,* ☎ *95/287–7500,* 🖷 *95/287–8188. 62 rooms, 8 suites. Restaurant, pool, conference room. AE, DC, MC, V.*

$$ ✕🏠 **Polo.** Cozy, old-fashioned, homey, and centrally located, the Polo offers comfortably furnished rooms and a good, reasonably priced restaurant. The common areas are spacious, with black and white tiles and huge white settees; in the blue-carpeted rooms, the brand-new beds (as of 1997) are dressed in white bedspreads. ⊠ *Mariano Souvirón 8, 29400,* ☎ *95/287–2447,* 🖷 *95/287–2449. 33 rooms. Restaurant. AE, DC, MC, V.*

$$$ 🏠 **Reina Victoria.** This classic Spanish hotel was built in 1906 by the British in Gibraltar as a weekend retreat for passengers on the new rail line between Algeciras and Bobadilla. It achieved fame in 1912, when the ailing German poet Rainer Maria Rilke came here to convalesce.

(His room has been preserved as a museum.) Today the Reina Victoria maintains a mood of faded decadence and has a somewhat neglected, tumbledown air. It's no longer the only—or even the second-best—place to stay in Ronda, but the views from its garden are still unbeatable. ⊠ *Jerez 25, 29400,* ☎ *95/287–1240,* ℻ *95/287–1075. 89 rooms. Restaurant, pool. AE, DC, MC, V.*

Olvera

⑱ *59 km (37 mi) north of Ronda (via Agodonales), 68 km (42 mi) west of Antequera.*

Two imposing silhouettes dominate the crest of Olvera's hill: the 11th-century **castle of Vallehermoso,** a legacy of the Moors, and the neo-classical church of **La Encarnación,** reconstructed in the 19th century on the foundations of the old Arab mosque.

Setenil de las Bodegas

⑲ *13 km (8 mi) southeast of Olvera.*

Setenil de las Bodegas lies south of the N342, just southeast of Olvera on a small mountain road. The village nestles in a cleft in the rock cut by the River Guadalporcín. Its houses seem to be sculpted from the rock itself; the streets resemble long, narrow caves; and on many houses the roof is formed by a projecting ledge of heavy rock.

El Gastor

⑳ *18 km (11 mi) east from Setenil, 15 km (9 mi) south from Olvera, 30 km (18 mi) northeast from Ronda.*

To the west of Setenil is El Gastor, south of which lie the twin ravines of Alagarines. Nearby are the remains of an ancient dolmen known as **La Sepultura del Gigante** (Giant's Tomb). **Ronda la Vieja,** site of the Roman settlement of Acinipo, is down a track off the Setenil–El Gastor road. (Another track also leads there from C339.) A reconstructed theater is the only vestige of the Roman town.

Zahara de la Sierra

㉑ *35 km (22 mi) northwest of Ronda, 32 km (20 mi) southwest of Olvera.*

West of the C339, a little south of Algodonales, a solitary **watchtower** dominates a crag above the village of Zahara de la Sierra, its outline visible for miles around. The tower is all that remains of a Moorish castle where Alfonso X once fought the emir of Morocco. It remained an important Moorish stronghold until it fell to the Christians in 1470. Along the streets of Zahara you can see door knockers fashioned like the hand of Fatima. The fingers represent the five laws of the Koran and serve to ward off evil.

En Route   The winding mountain road between Zahara and Grazalema, via the Puerto de las Palomas (4,300 ft), is for adventurous drivers. The views from its heights are breathtaking, but unless you have nerves of steel and a head for heights, take a more conventional approach.

Grazalema

㉒ *28 km (17 mi) northwest of Ronda, 23 km (14 mi) northeast of Ubrique.*

Nestled in the Sierra del Endrinal, Grazalema is the prettiest of the *pueblos blancos.* Because it's on a western slope, where rain clouds roll in from the Atlantic, Grazalema has the distinction of being the wettest spot in Spain. Cobbled streets of houses with pink-and-ocher roofs wind up the hillside; red geraniums splash white walls; and black, wrought-iron lanterns and grilles cling to the house fronts.

Grazalema marks the entrance to the Sierra de Grazalema park. Thanks to the park's altitude and prevailing humidity, it's one of the last habitats for the rare fir tree *abies pinsapo* and is home to ibex, vultures, and numerous birds of prey.

Ubrique

㉓ *48 km (30 mi) west of Ronda, 89 km (55 mi) north of San Roque.*

Ubrique, spread on the slopes of the Saltadero Mountains southwest of Ronda and Grazalema on C3331, is known for its leather tanning and embossing industry. Look for the **Convento de los Capuchinos** (Capuchin Convent) and the churches of **San Pedro** and **Nuestra Señora de la O.**

ESTEPONA TO GIBRALTAR

You can still see Estepona's fishing village and Moorish old quarter amid the booming coastal development. Just inland, Casares piles whitewashed houses over the bright-blue Mediterranean below. Sotogrande, with its golf courses and long beach, and old San Roque are the last stops before the British colony at Gibraltar, a bizarre anomaly of Moorish, Spanish, and British influences. Finally, the windy town of Tarifa marks the southernmost tip of mainland Europe.

Estepona

㉔ *17 km (11 mi) west of San Pedro de Alcántara.*

Estepona used to mark the end of the Costa del Sol's urban sprawl, but today, thanks largely to the increasingly important role of Gibraltar's airport, it is fast becoming the biggest boomtown on the coast. Still, the old fishing village hangs on. Its beach, more than 1 km (½ mi) long, is lined with fishing boats, and the promenade is lined with well-kept, aromatic flower gardens. Back from the main Avenida de España, the old Moorish village is surprisingly unspoiled.

Dining and Lodging

$$–$$$ ✕ **Alcaría de Ramos.** José Ramos, winner of the National Gastronomy Prize, opened this restaurant in a restored building outside town and has watched it garner a large and enthusiastic following. Try the *ensalada de lentejas con salmón ahumado* (lentil salad with smoked salmon), followed by *cordero asado* (roast lamb) and Ramos's justly famous fried ice cream. ✉ *Carretera N340, Km 167,* ☎ *95/288–6178. MC, V. Closed Sun. No lunch.*

$ ✕ **Costa del Sol.** This friendly French bistro serves both French and Spanish dishes in an informal setting, tucked away on an unassuming side street next to the Portillo bus station. French favorites include bouillabaisse, onion soup, coq au vin, and duck in orange sauce. The *menú del día* is a steal at less than 1,000 pesetas. ✉ *San Roque s/n,* ☎ *95/280–1101. AE, DC, MC, V. Closed Mon.*

$$$$ ✕🏨 **Las Dunas.** This brand-new (opened in 1997), spectacular hotel rises like a multicolored apparition next to the beach, halfway between Estepona and Marbella. The setting is palatial, with trickling fountains and copious exotic plants; the large rooms are bright and airy, with large easy chairs, hemp carpets, and light-green furniture. The food is first-class, and the health center offers a range of alternative therapies. ✉ *La Boladilla Baja, Carretera de Cádiz, Km 163, 29689,* ☎ *95/279–4345,* FAX *95/279–4825. 36 rooms, 39 suites, 33 apartments. 2 restaurants, pool, massage, sauna, health club. AE, DC, MC, V.*

$$$ 🏨 **Atalaya Park.** Closer to San Pedro de Alcántara than to Estepona itself, this very comfortable resort hotel is set in subtropical gardens beside the sea and has extensive sports facilities. Rooms overlooking the sea cost more than those facing the mountains. ✉ *Carretera N340, Km 163, 29680,* ☎ *95/288–9000,* FAX *95/288–9022. 436 rooms, 32 suites, 10 bungalows. 2 restaurants, 2 bars, indoor pool, 4 outdoor pools, beauty salon, massage, sauna, golf, tennis courts. AE, DC, MC, V.*

$$ 🏨 **Santa Marta.** The Santa Marta is a small, quiet hotel with lodgings in chalet bungalows arranged in a large, peaceful tropical garden. Some of the rooms are a little faded after 30-odd years, but the tranquil setting is a definite plus. In summer, good lunches are served by the pool. ✉ *Carretera N340, Km 166, between Estepona and San Pedro, 29680,* ☎ *95/288–8177,* FAX *95/288–8180. 37 rooms. Restaurant, pool. AE, DC, MC, V. Closed Oct.–Mar.*

Casares

㉕ *20 km (12 mi) northwest of Estepona.*

The mountain village of Casares lies high above Estepona in the Sierra Bermeja. Streets of ancient white houses, piled one on top of the other, perch on the slopes beneath a ruined but impressive Moorish castle. The heights afford stunning views over orchards, olive groves, and cork woods to the Mediterranean sparkling in the distance.

San Roque

㉖ *92 km (57 mi) southwest of Ronda, 64 km (40 mi) west of Marbella.*

San Roque is the point at which you leave the coastal highway and drive the final 8 km (5 mi) to La Línea and Gibraltar along the peninsula that forms the east side of Algeciras Bay. The town of San Roque was founded within sight of Gibraltar by Spaniards who fled the Rock when the British captured it in 1704. Almost 300 years of British occupation have done little to diminish the chauvinism of San Roque's inhabitants, who have protested their displeasure at the prominence Gibraltar is now assuming at this end of the Costa by declaring an official ban on the use of English on local billboards and other advertisements.

Fourteen kilometers (10 miles) east of San Roque is the luxury complex of **Sotogrande**, with sprawling millionaires' villas, a marina yacht harbor, and two golf courses, including the legendary Valderrama, host of the Ryder Cup in 1997.

Dining

$$$$ ✕ **Los Remos.** The dining room inside this gracious colonial villa has peach-colored walls adorned with gilt rococo mirrors, swirling cherubs, friezes of grapes, and crystal lamps. It overlooks a formal, leafy garden full of palms, cedars, and trailing ivy. Entrées include *urta del estrecho en salsa de erizos marinos* (perch from the Straits of Gibraltar in sea-urchin sauce). All of the seafood comes from the Bay of Algeciras area, and the wine cellar boasts some 20,000 bottles. ✉ *Villa Victoria, Campo de Gibraltar between San Roque and Campamento,* ☎ *956/698412. AE, DC, MC, V. Closed Sun.*

$$$-$$$$ 🏨 **Hotel Sotogrande.** This hotel is popular with golfers, as it's right next to Valderrama and has an Irish pub that serves as a 19th hole. The rooms, decorated in light colors, are large and airy, and each has a sitting room—often on a split level—and a large terrace. Some have views of the surrounding cork-oak forest. A new wing, under construction in 1998, will provide 60 more rooms. ⊠ *Carretera N340, Km 131, 11310,* ☎ *965/794387,* 𝔽𝔸𝕏 *956/794333. 44 rooms, 2 suites. Restaurant, bar, pool, tennis. AE, DC, MC, V.*

Gibraltar

㉗   *20 km (12 mi) east of Algeciras, 77 km (48 mi) west of Marbella.*

The tiny British colony of Gibraltar—nicknamed Gib, or simply the Rock—whose impressive silhouette dominates the strait between Spain and Morocco, is actually a rock 6 km (4 mi) long, 1 km (½ mi) wide, and 1,369 ft high. In ancient times it was one of the two Pillars of Hercules, marking the western limits of the known world; across the water, in Morocco, a mountain between the cities of Ceuta and Tangiers formed the other. Gibraltar's position, commanding the narrow entrance to the Mediterranean, led to its seizure by the Moors in 711 as a preliminary to the conquest of Spain. They held it longer than either the Spaniards or the British ever have—a fact to which tribute is paid whenever anyone says its name, for Gibraltar is a corruption of Jebel Tariq (Tariq's Rock), Tariq being the Moorish commander who built the first fort here.

After the Moors had ruled for 750 years, the Spaniards recaptured Tariq's Rock in 1462, on the feast day of St. Bernard (now co-patron of the colony along with Our Lady of Europe, whose shrine stands at the Rock's southernmost tip). The English, heading an Anglo-Dutch fleet in the War of the Spanish Succession, seized the Rock in 1704 after three days of fighting. Following several years of local skirmishing, Gibraltar was finally ceded to Great Britain in 1713 by the Treaty of Utrecht. With the exception of the Great Siege, when a Franco-Spanish force battled at its ramparts for three years (1779–82), Gibraltar has lived a relatively peaceful life ever since. During the two world wars, it served the Allies well as an important naval and air base.

Today, much of Gibraltar looks rather like a faded garrison town. The number of British troops stationed here is being cut back, and millions of dollars are being invested in developing the Rock's tourist potential. The Costa del Sol's 100,000-plus expatriate Britons have given the economy of this tiny colony another boost; many take advantage of Gibraltar's status as an offshore financial center.

There must be few places in the world that you enter by walking or driving across an airport runway, but that's what happens in Gibraltar. First, show your passport; then make your way out onto the narrow strip of land linking Spain's La Linea with Britain's Rock. Here you have a choice: either plunge straight into exploring Gibraltar town or opt for a tour of the Rock's circumference. Unless you have a good reason to take your car—like loading up on cheap gas or duty-free goodies—you're best off leaving it in a guarded parking area in La Linea, the Spanish border town, and relying on buses and taxis in Gibraltar, whose streets are narrow and congested. The Official Rock Tour—conducted either by minibus or, at greater cost, taxi—takes about 90 minutes and includes all the major sights, allowing you to decide which sights you'll want to spend more time at later.

Although the British pound is Gibraltar's official currency, Spanish pesetas are universally accepted. Note that when dialing Gibraltar from

Spain, the area code is 9567; when dialing from other countries, the code is 350.

Numbers in the margin correspond to points of interest on the Gibraltar map.

To begin on the Rock's eastern side, turn left down Devil's Tower Road as you enter Gibraltar. Here, on the eastern shores, you'll find **Catalan Bay,** a fishing village founded by Genoese settlers and now a picturesque resort. On the eastern side you'll see the massive water catchments that once supplied the colony's drinking water. The road beyond here is closed, so head back west through the town of Gibraltar—which you'll explore later—and out to the Rock's southern tip, **Punta Grande de Europa** (Europa Point). Stop here for the view across the strait to Morocco, 23 km (14 mi) away. You are now standing on one of the two ancient Pillars of Hercules. In front of you, the Europa Point lighthouse has dominated the meeting place of the Atlantic and the Mediterranean since 1841; sailors can see its light from a distance of 27 km (17 mi). Near the lighthouse, on **Europa Flats,** is an ancient Moorish cistern, known as the **Nun's Well,** and the **Shrine of Our Lady of Europe,** venerated by seafarers since 1462.

From Europa Flats, follow Europa Road back along the Rock's western slopes, high above **Rosia Bay,** to which Nelson's flagship, HMS *Victory,* was towed after the Battle of Trafalgar in 1805. Aboard were the dead, who were buried in Trafalgar Cemetery, on the southern edge of town—except, of course, for Admiral Nelson, whose body went home to England preserved in a barrel of rum.

From Rosia Bay, continue on Europa Road as far as the Casino, above the Alameda Gardens. Make a sharp right here up Engineer Road to **Jews' Gate,** an unbeatable lookout point over the docks and Bay of Gibraltar to Algeciras. Here you can access the **Upper Nature Preserve,** which includes St. Michael's Cave, the Apes' Den, the Great Siege Tunnel, and the Moorish Castle. £4.50 *(includes all attractions), plus* £2 *per vehicle.* Daily 9:30–sunset.

Queens Road leads to **St. Michael's Cave,** the largest of Gibraltar's 150 caves. A series of underground chambers adorned with stalactites and stalagmites, it provides an incredible setting for concerts, ballet, and drama. Sound-and-light shows are held here most days (at 11 and 4). The skull of a Neanderthal woman (now in the British Museum) was found at nearby Forbes Quarry eight years before the world-famous discovery in Germany's Neander Valley in 1856; nobody paid much attention to it at the time, which is why we call this prehistoric race Neanderthals rather than *homo calpensis* (literally, "Gibraltar Man").

Drive down Old Queens Road from St. Michael's Cave to the **Apes' Den,** near the Wall of Charles V. The famous Barbary Apes are a breed of cinnamon-colored, tailless monkeys native to Morocco's Atlas Mountains; legend holds that as long as the apes remain, the British will keep the Rock. Winston Churchill himself issued orders for their preservation when the ape colony's numbers began to dwindle during World War II; today they are publicly fed twice daily, at 8 and 4. Among their mischievous talents are purse and camera snatching.

At the northern end of the Rock, the **Great Siege Tunnel,** formerly known as the Upper Galleries, was carved out during the Great Siege of 1779–82. Here, in 1878, Governor Lord Napier of Magdala entertained former United States president Ulysses S. Grant at a banquet in St. George's Hall. The Holyland Tunnel leads to a vantage point on the east side of the Rock, high above Catalan Bay.

390

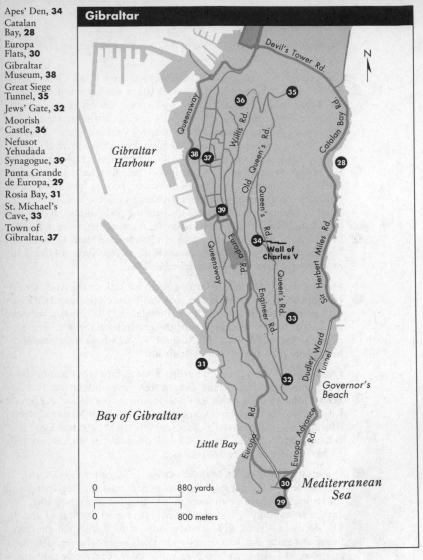

Gibraltar

🅰 The **Moorish Castle,** on Willis Road, was originally built by the descendants of Jebel Tariq, who conquered the Rock in 711. The present Tower of Homage dates from 1333, and its walls bear the scars of sieges, when stones from medieval catapults (and, later, cannonballs) were hurled against it. Admiral Rooke hoisted the British flag from its summit when he captured the Rock in 1704, and it has flown here ever since.

🅱 Willis Road leads steeply down to the colorful, congested town of Gibraltar, where the dignified Regency architecture of Great Britain blends well with the shutters, balconies, and patios of southern Spain. The tourist office is on Cathedral Square. Apart from the shops, restaurants, and pubs that beckon on busy Main Street, you'll want to see the **Governor's Residence,** where the ceremonial Changing of the Guard and Ceremony of the Keys take place, usually about five times a year; the **Law Courts,** where the famous case of the sailing ship *Mary Celeste* was heard in 1872; the Anglican **Cathedral of the Holy Trinity**; and the Catholic **Cathedral of St. Mary the Crowned.**

③⑧ Don't miss the **Gibraltar Museum,** whose exhibits recall the history of the Rock throughout the ages. Its well-presented displays include a beautiful 14th-century Moorish bathhouse, evocations of the Great Siege and of the Battle of Trafalgar, and an 1865 model of the Rock. There's also a reproduction of the "Gibraltar Woman," the Neanderthal skull discovered here in 1848. ⊠ *Bomb House La.,* ☎ *9567/74289.* ☜ *£2.* ⊙ *Weekdays 10–6, Sat. 10–2.*

③⑨ The **Nefusot Yehudada Synagogue,** on Line Wall Road, is worth a look for its inspired architecture. If you're interested in guns, the **Koehler Gun,** in Casemates Square at the northern end of Main Street, is an impressive example of the type of gun developed during the Great Siege.

★ Finally, take a ride on the **cable car** to the top of the Rock. The car, which resembles a ski gondola, isn't especially high off the ground, but the views of Spain and Africa from the rock's pinnacle are superb. It leaves every day except Sunday from the cable-car station on Grand Parade, at the southern end of Main Street. ☜ *£4.90 (includes cable car, Michael's Cave, and Apes' Den).*

Dining and Lodging

$$$ ✕ **La Bayuca.** One of the Rock's oldest restaurants, La Bayuca is renowned for its onion soup and Mediterranean dishes. Prince Charles and Prince Andrew both dined here while on naval service. ⊠ *21 Turnbull's La.,* ☎ *9567/75119. AE, DC, MC, V. Closed Tues. No lunch Sun.*

$–$$ ✕ **Strings.** This popular bistro is heavily decorated with prints, nautical paraphernalia, ensigns, and badges, and there are just six dark, wooden booths clustered around the small bar. Red and orange lamps complete the cozy, cavelike decor. The food is English, with daily specials chalked up on a blackboard. ⊠ *44 Cornwall's La.,* ☎ *9567/78800. AE, MC, V. Closed Sun.*

$$$ ☷ **The Rock.** The Rock, which overlooks Gibraltar, first opened in 1932
★ but has just (1998) undergone a massive refurbishment program. The decor of the rooms and restaurant can compete with those in good "international" hotels anywhere, yet they manage to preserve something of the English colonial style, with ceiling fans and a fine terrace bar. ⊠ *3 Europa Rd.,* ☎ *9567/73000,* ☏ *9567/73513. 102 rooms, 8 suites. Restaurant, bar, pool, beauty salon. AE, DC, MC, V.*

$$$$ ☷ **The Eliott.** This is the most modern of the Rock's hotels, in the center of the town in what used to be the Gibraltar Holiday Inn. The rooms are functional and comfortable. Ask for one at the top of the hotel with a view over the Bay of Gibraltar. ⊠ *2 Governor's Parade,* ☎ *9567/70500,* ☏ *9567/70243. 122 rooms, 8 suites. Pool, sauna. AE, DC, MC, V.*

$$ ☷ **Bristol.** This colonial-style hotel is in the heart of town, with splendid views of the bay and the cathedral. Rooms are spacious but basic. The tropical garden is a real haven, and the wood-panel lounge has two pool tables. ⊠ *10 Cathedral Sq.,* ☎ *9567/76800,* ☏ *9567/77613. 60 rooms. Bar, breakfast room, pool. AE, DC, MC, V.*

Nightlife and the Arts

The **Stakis International Casino** (⊠ 7 Europa Rd., ☎ 9567/76666) is open from 7:30 PM (cocktail bar) and 9 (gaming room) until 4 AM; dress in the gaming room is "smart casual."

Tarifa

④⓪ *35 km (21 mi) west of San Roque.*

Standing on the Strait of Gibraltar at the southernmost tip of mainland Europe, where the Mediterranean and the Atlantic meet and the

Rif mountains of Africa seem so close that you can almost touch them, Tarifa was one of the earliest Moorish settlements in Spain. Its 10th-century castle is famous for its 1292 siege—when the defender Guzmán el Bueno refused to surrender even though the attacking Moors threatened to kill his captive son. In defiance, he flung his own dagger down to them, shouting "Here, use this"—or something to that effect. (According to most versions of the story, the boy was spared.)

Strong prevailing winds kept Tarifa off the tourist maps for years, but they have ultimately proven a source of wealth. Aeolic power is generated on the vast wind farm occupying the surrounding hills, and the wide, white-sand beaches stretching north of the town have become Europe's biggest windsurfing center.

Ten kilometers (6 miles) north of Tarifa on the Atlantic coast are the Roman ruins of **Baelo Claudia.** This settlement was a thriving production center of *garum,* a salty fish paste appreciated in Rome. ۞ *Tues.–Sat. 9–2 and 4–6, Sun. 9–2.*

Lodging

$$$ ⊞ **Hurricane Hotel.** This laid-back, palm-kissed hotel next to the beach is a favorite hangout of the windsurfing set. The atmosphere is fun and informal, the rooms simple but adequate. The staff can organize horseback-riding trips along the beach or inland. ⊠ *Carretera Cádiz-Málaga, 11380,* ☎ *956/684919,* FAX *956/684329. 28 rooms, 5 suites. Restaurant, pool, horseback riding. AE, MC, V.*

THE COSTA DEL SOL A TO Z

Arriving and Departing

By Bus

Long-distance buses serve Málaga from Madrid, Cartagena, Almería, Granada, Ubeda, Córdoba, Seville, and Badajoz. Málaga's main bus station is on Paseo de los (☎ 95/235–0061). Marbella and Algeciras can be reached directly from Madrid or Seville; other connections are between Fuengirola and Seville, and Cádiz and Algeciras. Marbella's bus station is at Avenida Trapiche (☎ 95/276–4400).

By Car

Málaga is 580 km (360 mi) from Madrid by way of the N IV to Córdoba, then N331 to Antequera and N321; 182 km (114 mi) from Córdoba via Antequera; 214 km (134 mi) from Seville; and 129 km (81 mi) from Granada by the shortest route of N342 to Loja, then N321 to Málaga.

By Plane

Gibraltar Airport (☎ 9567/73026) is worth considering if you're arriving from Great Britain, especially if you're heading for the coast west of Marbella. It's right next to the frontier, and once you've crossed into Spain you can catch buses in La Linea for all coastal resorts.

Málaga Airport (☎ 95/204–8804) lies 10 km (6 mi) west of Málaga. Coming from the United States, you'll have to connect in Madrid. Iberia and GB Airways (an affiliate of British Airways) operate several scheduled flights a day from London; numerous British charter companies also link London and Málaga. Most major European cities have direct flights to Málaga on either Iberia or their own national airlines. Iberia and its subsidiary, Aviaco, have up to eight flights a day from Madrid (flight time one hour), three flights a day from Barcelona (1½ hours), and regular flights from other Spanish cities.

Iberia has offices in Málaga (✉ Molina Lario 13, ☎ 95/213–6147) and at the airport (☎ 95/213–6166).

BETWEEN THE AIRPORT AND DOWNTOWN

From Málaga Airport, trains run regularly to nearby cities (☞ Getting Around, *below*), and an Iberia bus leaves every 20 minutes for downtown Málaga (6:30 AM–midnight), with a fare of 150 pesetas. Taxis are plentiful, and official fares to Málaga, Torremolinos, and other resorts are posted inside the terminal. The trip from the airport to Torremolinos will cost about 2,000 pesetas.

By Train

Málaga is the main rail terminus, with eight trains a day from Madrid and one from Barcelona and Valencia. Most Málaga trains leave from Madrid's Atocha station, though some leave from Chamartín. Travel time varies between 4½ and 10 hours; the best and fastest are the daytime *Talgo 200* trains from Atocha. There is also an overnight train, the *Estrella* (9½ hours). All Madrid–Málaga trains stop at Córdoba; there are also direct local trains from Córdoba to Málaga. From both Seville (four hours) and Granada (3–3½ hours), you have to change at Bobadilla for Málaga, making buses a more efficient mode of travel from those cities. In fact, other than the direct Madrid–Córdoba–Málaga line, trains in Andalusia can be slow due to the terrain; you may generally find buses quicker and more convenient.

Málaga Station (✉ Explanada de la Estación, ☎ 95/236–0202) is 15 minutes' walk from the city center, across the river. For tickets and information, the central **RENFE office** is much more convenient. ✉ *Strachan 2, off Calle de Molina Larios, ☎ 95/221–4127. ⊘ Weekdays 9–1:30 and 4:30–7:30.*

Getting Around

By Bus

Buses are the best way of getting around the Costa del Sol (as well as reaching it from Seville or Granada). Málaga's bus station is on the Paseo de los Tilos (☎ 95/235–0061). The **Portillo** bus company, with offices at the Málaga Station (☎ 95/236–0191), serves most of the Costa del Sol. Another company with offices at the station, **Alsina Gräells** (☎ 95/231–8295), has service to Granada, Córdoba, Seville, and Nerja. Málaga's tourist office has details on other bus lines.

By Car

A car will allow you to explore some of the mountain villages for which Andalusia is famous. Mountain driving can be an adventure—hair-raising curves, precipices, and mediocre road services are often the norm—but it's getting more manageable as highways throughout the region are resurfaced and widened and in some cases completely new roadbeds built. To take a car into Gibraltar, drivers need, in theory, an international driver's permit, an insurance certificate, and a logbook; in practice, all you need to show is your passport. Be prepared for parking problems—space is scarce—but beware of phony offers of help from "parking/insurance agents" on the frontier approach.

By Train

A useful suburban train service connects Málaga, Torremolinos, and Fuengirola, calling at the airport and all resorts along the way. It leaves Málaga every half hour between 6 AM and 10:30 PM and Fuengirola every half hour from 6:35 AM to 11:35 PM. Its terminus in Málaga is the **Guadalmedina** Station, near the Corte Inglés department store; it also calls at Málaga RENFE Station. The Fuengirola terminus is just across from the bus station, where you can catch buses for Mijas, Marbella, Estepona, and Algeciras.

Two trains a day run between Málaga and Ronda through the dramatic El Chorro gorge, with a change at Bobadilla. Travel time is around three hours. Between Ronda and Algeciras, three direct trains a day (two hours) travel a spectacular mountain track.

Contacts and Resources

Consulates
United Kingdom (⊠ Duquesa de Parcent 8, Málaga, ☎ 95/221–7571). **Canada** (⊠ Plaza de la Malagueta 3, Málaga, ☎ 95/222–3346). **United States** (⊠ Centro Comercial Las Rampas, Fuengirola, ☎ 95/247–4891).

Guided Tours
Numerous one- and two-day excursions from Costa del Sol resorts are run by **Julia Tours** (⊠ Emilio Esteban 1, Torremolinos, ☎ 95/238–7222), **Pullmantur** (⊠ Avda. Imperial, Torremolinos, ☎ 95/238–4400), and various smaller companies. Most hotels have their leaflets on hand and can book tours, as can any travel agent. Excursions leave from Málaga, Torremolinos, Fuengirola, Marbella, and Estepona. Prices vary slightly according to your departure point; in most cases you can be picked up at your hotel.

Local Tours
Most of the following local tours are half-day: Málaga, Cuevas de Nerja, Mijas, Marbella, and Puerto Banús; Burro safari in Coín; countryside tour of Alhaurín de la Torre, Alhaurín el Grande, Coín, Ojén, and Ronda. Night tours include a barbecue evening, a bullfighting evening with dinner, and a night at the Casino Torrequebrada.

Travel Agencies
The chief international agencies are **American Express** (⊠ Avda. Duque de Ahumada, Marbella, ☎ 95/282–1494) and **Wagons Lits Viajes** (⊠ Strachan 10, Málaga, ☎ 95/221–7695).

Visitor Information
The Costa del Sol's main information office is in **Málaga** (⊠ Pasaje de Chinitas 4, ☎ 95/221–3445). Málaga's municipal tourist office is on ⊠ Avenoda Cervantes 1, Paseo del Parque ☎ (95/260–4410). Local tourist offices serve **Algeciras** (⊠ Juan de la Cierva, ☎ 956/572636), **Antequera** (⊠ Palacio de Najera, Coso Viejo, ☎ 95/284–2180), **Benalmádena Costa** (⊠ Avda. Antonio Machado 14, ☎ 95/244–2494), **Estepona** (⊠ Paseo Marítimo, ☎ 95/280–0913), **Fuengirola** (⊠ Avda. Jesús Santos Rein 6, ☎ 95/246–7457), **Gibraltar** (⊠ 6 Kent House, Cathedral Sq., ☎ 9567/74950), **Málaga Airport** (☎ 95/224–0000), **Marbella** (⊠ Glorieta de la Fontanilla, ☎ 95/282–2818), **Nerja** (⊠ Puerta del Mar 2, ☎ 95/252–1531), **Ronda** (⊠ Plaza de España 1, ☎ 95/287–1272), and **Torremolinos** (⊠ Plaza Pablo Picasso, ☎ 95/237–1159).

12 Granada, Córdoba, and Eastern Andalusia

Eastern Andalusia is a region of lively cities with a deep sense of history; rolling plains whose ordered ranks of olive trees stretch into the distance; mountainous vistas; and whitewashed villages clinging to parched hillsides. Here you'll find two of Spain's most famous monuments, Granada's magical Alhambra palace and Córdoba's great mosque; the Sierra Nevada; and the source of the mighty Guadalquivir River.

Updated by
Mark Little

FROM THE DARK MOUNTAINS of the Sierra Morena down to the mighty, snowcapped peaks of the Sierra Nevada, Andalucía (Andalusia) rings with echoes of the Moors. These North African Muslims dwelled here for almost 800 years, from their first conquest of Spanish soil (Gibraltar) in AD 711 to their final expulsion from Granada in 1492. The name Andalucía comes from the Moors' own name for the land they conquered from the Visigoths: Al-Andalus. Two of Spain's most famous monuments, Córdoba's mosque and Granada's Alhambra, were the inspired creations of Moorish architects and craftsmen. The brilliant, white villages with narrow, shady streets; the thick-walled houses clustered around cool private patios; and the whitewashed facades with modestly grilled windows all stem from centuries of Moorish occupation. The Guadalquivir—the Moors' "Great River"—runs through the whole region; town names like Úbeda and Jaén are derivations of old Arabic names; ruined *alcazares* (fortresses) dot the landscape; and *azahar* (orange blossom) perfumes the patios. It's hard to find a church in Andalusia that wasn't built on the site of an Arab mosque, and high on the southern slopes of the Sierra Nevada, the villages of the Alpujarras, with their cube-shape houses, flat roofs, and chimney stacks, could just as easily be North African.

In the 13th century, King Ferdinand III, one of the champions of the Reconquest, captured Baeza, Úbeda, Córdoba, and Jaén. The defeated Moors fled south to Granada, where they tarried for another 250 years. The next two centuries (14th and 15th) were filled with constant battles and skirmishes between Moors and Christians, until Ferdinand of Aragon and Isabella of Castile, known jointly as the Catholic Monarchs, scored the ultimate victory of the Reconquest in 1492: they entered Granada and accepted the Moors' final surrender. In honor of this victory, Ferdinand and Isabella chose to be buried in Granada.

The Moors left their mark here, but so did the Christian conquerors and their descendants. Andalusia today has Gothic chapels, Renaissance cathedrals, and fanciful Baroque monasteries and churches, and the sturdy, golden-stone mansions of Úbeda and Baeza contrast intriguingly with the humble, whitewashed villages elsewhere in the province.

The landscape, too, is varied and powerful. To the south, the fertile plain of Granada, known as *la vega,* covered with tobacco and poplar groves and lush orchards, stretches up to the mountains of the majestic Sierra Nevada. In this range—snowclad for half the year—you'll find the highest peaks on mainland Spain—the 11,407-ft Mulhacén and the 11,215-ft Veleta. The Guadalquivir River rises to the east in the heights of the Sierra de Cazorla; flowing westward toward Córdoba, it is bounded on the north by the rugged, shrub-covered Sierra Morena and in the south by the rolling olive groves of Jaén. Fruit and almond trees line the river's banks in Córdoba's orchards. Vineyards cover the Córdoban *campiña* (fertile plain south of the Guadalquivir), and white villages cling to hillsides below ruined castles.

Pleasures and Pastimes

Dining

Córdoba has a fair number of gourmet restaurants, whereas Granada's are respectable if mostly undistinguished. Córdoba's specialties are *salmorejo* (a thick, very garlicky version of gazpacho) and *rabo de toro* (bull's-tail or oxtail stew). Many restaurants are now inventing creative dishes based on old Arab recipes from the city's Moorish past. Here, *fino de Montilla,* a dry, sherrylike wine from the province's Montilla-Moriles district, makes a good aperitif or bar drink. Granada's typical dishes are *tortilla al Sacromonte* (an omelet traditionally made of calf's brains, sweetbreads, diced ham, potatoes, and peas), *habas con jamón* (ham stewed with broad beans), *sopa sevillana* (tasty fish and seafood soup made with mayonnaise), and *choto al ajillo* (braised kid with garlic).

Lunch is the main meal here. Restaurants start serving around 2, but most tables don't fill up until at least 3, and most people are still at the table at 5. After such a long, late lunch, few Andalusians dine out in the evening; instead, they do the rounds of the bars, dipping into tapas and plates of ham or cheese. Ham from the Alpujarran village of Trevélez is famous throughout Spain; ask for it in Granada. Reservations are rarely needed (except where specified) if you go for lunch around 2; wait until 3 and you may have trouble finding a table. In the evening, if you dine early (at say, 9 or 10), you shouldn't have problems.

Neat, casual dress is acceptable in all Andalusian restaurants. Shorts and cutoff jeans are best avoided in all but the cheapest restaurants. Spaniards dress more casually for dinner in summer than in winter.

CATEGORY	COST*
$$$$	over 6,000 ptas.
$$$	4,000–6,000 ptas.
$$	2,500–4,000 ptas.
$	under 2,500 ptas.

per person for a three-course meal, including house wine and coffee, and excluding tax and service

Fiestas

JANUARY

Granada celebrates La Toma (the Capture), the 1492 surrender to the Catholic Monarchs, on January 2. On January 5, the eve of the Día de los Reyes (Feast of the Three Kings), there is a procession of the three Wise Men in every city and village.

FEBRUARY

On February 1, Granada holds a pilgrimage to the Monastery of San Cecilio, on Sacromonte; both Granada and Córdoba party hard at Carnival, on the days leading up to Ash Wednesday (February 17 in 1999).

MARCH–APRIL

Granada and Córdoba both celebrate Semana Santa (Holy Week) with dramatic religious processions (March 28–April 4 in 1999). Inquire at local tourist offices about fiestas in the Alpujarras; there are many in the summer months.

MAY

May brings to Córdoba Las Cruces de Mayo (May Days of the Cross), the Fiesta de los Patios (Patio Festival), and the Feria de Nuestra Señora de la Salud (Feast of Our Lady of Health). In Granada Día de la Cruz (Day of the Cross) is celebrated on May 3, San Isidro on May 15, and Mariana Pineda (a 19th-century political heroine) on May 26.

JUNE

In Granada there are two fiestas: Corpus Christi, June 3 in 1999, and San Pedro, June 29. The International Festival of Music and Dance, with some events in the Alhambra, begins late this month and runs into July.

The International Guitar Festival brings major artists to Córdoba.

Córdoba celebrates Nuestra Señora de Fuensanta, and Granada honors Nuestra Señora de las Angustias (Our Lady of Distress), on the last Sunday in September and the Romería de San Miguel (Procession of St. Michael) on September 29.

Hiking and Walking

Thanks to a number of well-run outdoor clubs as well as local interest in preserving natural lands, Andalusia is well endowed with parks for both recreation and camping. The village of Cazorla, in the province of Jaén, leads to the pine-clad slopes of the Cazorla Nature Park. South of Granada, the Sierra Nevada and the Alpujarras have some of the most impressive vistas in all of Spain, terrific skiing in winter, and a gamut of outdoor activities in summer.

Lodging

Andalusia has accommodations for all budgets, from low-key bed-and-breakfasts to luxurious paradors. At the high end, the Parador de San Francisco, nestled beside Granada's Alhambra, is a magnificent way to enjoy both Granada and the storied past of southern Spain. Bed-and-breakfast lodgings, available in many villages, give you better access to the countryside and its rich folk traditions.

Córdoba has some very pleasant hotels set in houses in the old town, close to the mosque. It's usually quite easy to find a room in Córdoba, even if you haven't reserved; just watch out for Holy Week and the May Patio Festival. Granada, on the other hand, can be very difficult; the Alhambra is Spain's most-visited monument. The city has plenty of hotels, but the busy season runs long, from Easter to late October. Hotels on the Alhambra hill need to be reserved long in advance, and those in the city center, around the Puerta Real and Acera del Darro, are unbelievably noisy—ask for rooms at the back. Beware Holy Week and the International Festival of Music and Dance (mid-June–mid-July), when rooms are particularly hard to come by.

CATEGORY	COST*
$$$$	over 20,000 ptas.
$$$	11,500–20,000 ptas.
$$	8,000–11,500 ptas.
$	under 8,000 ptas.

All prices are for a standard double room, excluding tax.

Exploring Andalusia

Numbers in the text correspond to numbers in the margin and on the Andalusia: Granada to Córdoba; Granada; and Córdoba maps.

Great Itineraries

Our itineraries explore three of Andalusia's eight provinces: Granada, Jaén, and Córdoba. If you have limited time, begin in Granada and then make excursions to Santa Fe, Fuentevaqueros, and the Sierra Nevada. Continue on to Baena before winding up your whirlwind tour in Córdoba. The five-day itinerary begins in Córdoba and takes you to Jaén, with historic towns and the Cazorla Nature Park. Explore Granada before heading out to the Sierra Nevada and the charming towns of the Alpujarras. If you have seven days, begin your tour in Córdoba and move on to Úbeda and Baeza, the cave towns of Guadix and Purullena, and Granada; end your journey in the Alpujarras.

IF YOU HAVE 3 DAYS

Begin your tour in ⛫ **Granada** ①–⑯, where you should plan to spend your first night. On day one, visit the mystical Alhambra and wander the Albaicín, the city's extensive ancient Moorish quarter. Have lunch and tea along the Cuesta de Elvira. Spend the afternoon in the alleyways of the Alcaicería, visiting the cathedral and the Capilla Real; then take an evening tour of the Alhambra. On the morning of the second day, head for the village of Baena, in the **Subbética** ㊹ area. Take in the scenery before spending the night in ⛫ **Córdoba** ㉗–㊷. Spend the morning of the third day touring the magical Mezquita before walking about the Judería, the city's old Jewish Quarter. Head out to the River Guadalquivir to view the city and walk across the Puente Romano to the Torre de la Calahorra, which houses a fine museum detailing the region's history.

IF YOU HAVE 5 DAYS

⛫ **Córdoba** ㉗–㊷ makes a good starting point for this medium-size Andalusian tour. On day one, explore the city, giving the Mezquita and the Judería a good, long look. The next morning, head out toward Granada, stopping in the towns of Baena, Rute, and Priego de Córdoba, in the **Subbética** ㊹ region, along the way. Spend the night in ⛫ **Granada** ①–⑯. On day three, tour Granada's Alhambra, the Albaicín, and the alleys of the Alcaicería. The next day, rise early to get on mountain roads toward the **Sierra Nevada** ⑳. Spend the night in the ⛫ **Alpujarras** ㉑; then take a morning walk and return to Granada.

When to Tour Andalusia

Spring and summer are the best times to visit this region. Temperatures can drop to the 30s in winter, and the wind off the Guadalquivir in Córdoba can be as stiff as any in New England. Note that most monuments don't open before 9:30 and are closed for the lunch hour, anywhere between 1:30 and 4.

GRANADA AND ENVIRONS, THE SIERRA NEVADA, AND THE ALPUJARRAS

The city of Granada, the last stronghold of the Moors, is the home of the splendid hilltop Alhambra, replete with fountains, lush gardens, and once-luxurious baths. Alongside the Alhambra, you can relax in the gardens of the Generalife; down in town, visit the tomb of Ferdinand and Isabella and weave your way through the streets of the ancient Albaicín. Outside the city rise the craggy peaks of the Sierra Nevada, seventh heaven for skiers; the picturesque and crafts-rich Alpujarra region; and the cave communities of Guadix and Purullena.

Granada

★ ❶ *430 km (265 mi) south of Madrid, 261 km (162 mi) east of Córdoba.*

Granada rises lightly and majestically from a plain onto three hills, dwarfed—on a clear day—by the mighty snowcapped peaks of the Sierra Nevada. Atop one of these hills perches the pink-gold Alhambra palace, at once splendidly imposing and infinitely delicate. The stunning view from its mount takes in the roofs of the old Moorish quarter, the Albaicín; the caves of the Sacromonte; and, in the distance, the fertile *vega*, rich in orchards, tobacco fields, and poplar groves.

Granada's Moorish Nasrid dynasty, split by internal squabbles, presented Ferdinand of Aragon with the chance he needed in 1491.

Andalusia: Granada to Córdoba

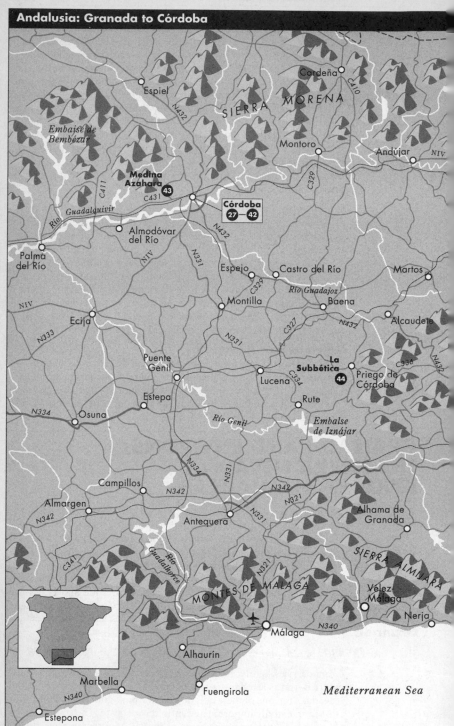

E. del
Jándula

La Carolina

E. del
Rumblar

N322

Bailén

N323

Linares

N322

Baeza 24

25 **Úbeda**

Arquillos

C3210

E. de
Guadalmena

Puente de
Génave

Villacarrillo

Rio Guadalquivir

Embalse del
Tranco

*PARQUE
NATURAL
DE CAZORLA*

Torre de
Vinaigre

C328

C325

C328

C328

Cazorla 26

Huéscar

23
Jaén

Jódar

N323

N324

Pozo
Alcón

Cúllar
Baza

Baza

N342

C223

Fuentevaqueros

18

Viznar

17

Santa Fe

19

N342

Granada 1 — 16

Guadix 22

N324

N340

Solynieve

Pico Veleta

Sierra Nevada

20

Mulhacén

Dúrcal

N323

Alpujarras

Lanjarón

Trevélez

Capileira

21

Órgiva

C333

N331

Almería

Motril

N340

Salobreña

N340

Adra

N340

N
↑

0   40 miles

0   60 km

KEY

— Rail Lines

- - - Regional
Boundaries

Granada

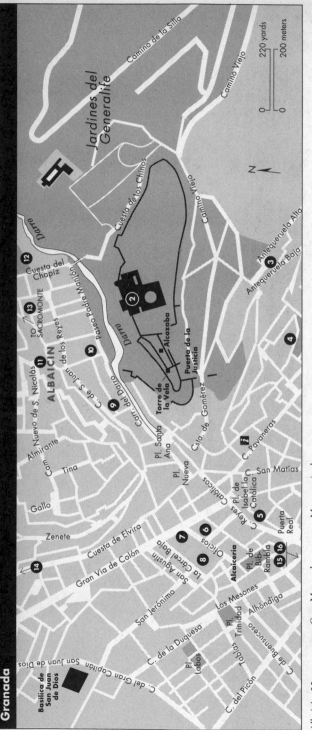

Basílica de
San Juan
de Dios

Jardines del
Generalife

Camino de la Silla

Camino Viejo

Camino Viejo

Cuesta de los Chinos

Antequeruela Alta

Antequeruela Baja

220 yards

200 meters

N

Darro

Cuesta del
Chapiz

Paseo Padre Manjón

TO
SACROMONTE

Darro

ALBAICIN

de los Reyes

Alcazaba

Puerta de la
Justicia

C. de S. Juan

Alc. Nuevo de S. Nicolás

Torre de
la Vela

Carr. del Darro

Almirante

Tina

Gallo

Zenete

Csta. de Gomérez

C. Pavaneras

Pl. Santa
Ana

Pl.
Nueva

San Matías

Camino

Cuesta de Elvira

Gran Vía de Colón

San Agustín

La Cárcel Baja

Oficios

Alcaicería

Pl. de
Reyes
Pl. de
Isabel la
Católica

Puerta
Real

Pl. de
Bib-
Rambla

San Jerónimo

Los Mesones

Alhóndiga

Pl.
Trinidad

C. de Buensuceso

C. del Gran Capitán

San Juan de Dios

C. de la Duquesa

Pl.
Lobos

Tablas

C. del Picón

2 **3** **4** **5** **6** **7** **8** **9** **10** **11** **12** **13** **14** **15** **16**

Albaicín, **11**
Alhambra, **2**
Campo del
Príncipe, **4**
Capilla Real, **7**
Casa de Castril, **10**
Casa del Chapís, **12**

Casa-Museo de
Manuel de Falla, **3**
Cathedral, **8**
Corral del Carbón, **5**
El Bañuelo, **9**
García Lorca
Museum, **16**

Monasterio de
La Cartuja, **14**
Palacio Madraza, **6**
Parque de las
Ciencias, **15**
Sacromonte, **13**

The Alhambra

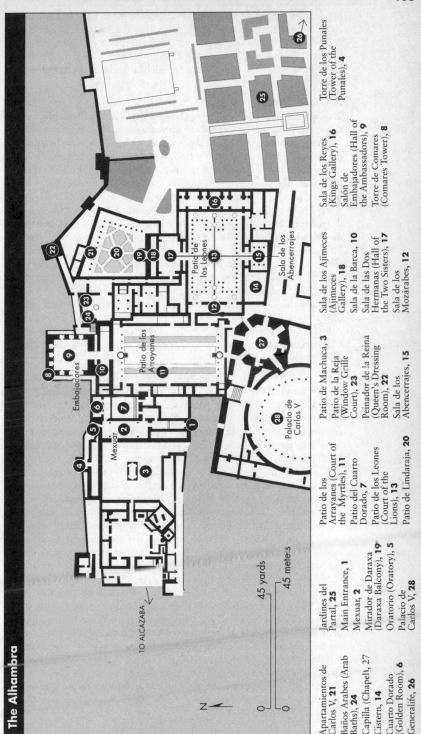

TO ALCAZABA

N

0
0
45 yards
45 meters

Embajadores

Mexuar

Patio de los Arrayanes

Patio de los Leones

Sala de los Abencerrajes

Palacio de Carlos V

Apartamientos de Carlos V, **21**
Baños Arabes (Arab Baths), **24**
Capilla (Chapel), **27**
Cistern, **14**
Cuarto Dorado (Golden Room), **6**
Generalife, **26**

Jardines del Partal, **25**
Main Entrance, **1**
Mexuar, **2**
Mirador de Daraxa (Daraxa Balcony), **19**
Oratorio (Oratory), **5**
Palacio de Carlos V, **28**

Patio de los Arrayanes (Court of the Myrtles), **11**
Patio del Cuarto Dorado, **7**
Patio de los Leones (Court of the Lions), **13**
Patio de Lindaraja, **20**

Patio de Machuca, **3**
Patio de la Reja (Window Grille Court), **23**
Peinador de la Reina (Queen's Dressing Room), **22**
Sala de los Abencerrajes, **15**

Sala de los Ajimeces (Ajimeces Gallery), **18**
Sala de la Barca, **10**
Sala de las Dos Hermanas (Hall of the Two Sisters), **17**
Sala de los Mozárabes, **12**

Sala de los Reyes (Kings Gallery), **16**
Salón de Embajadores (Hall of the Ambassadors), **9**
Torre de Comares (Comares Tower), **8**

Torre de los Punales (Tower of the Punales), **4**

Spurred by Isabella's religious fanaticism, Ferdinand laid siege to the city for seven months. On January 2, 1492, the Rey Chico (Boy King), Boabdil, was forced to surrender the keys of the city to the triumphant Catholic Monarchs. As Boabdil fled the Alhambra by the Puerta de los Siete Suelos (Gate of the Seven Sighs), he asked that the gate be sealed forever.

A Good Walk

This walk covers the nucleus of the city. Begin at the Plaza Nueva, the crossroads for the city's main boulevards; artisans have set up shops in the surrounding area. On the north end of the plaza is the adjacent Plaza Santa Ana, where you'll find the **Iglesia de Santa Ana,** designed by Diego de Siloé. Cross back to the Plaza Nueva and the 16th-century **Real Cancillería,** which now houses the Tribunal Superior de Justicia (High Court). From the Plaza Nueva follow Cuesta de Gomérez up a steep grade to the cool shade of the **Alhambra** ② precincts. In a residential neighborhood just below the Alhambra's walls is the **Casa-Museo de Manuel de Falla** ③. From Antequeruela Alta, follow Antequeruela Baja east and turn right down Carril de San Cecilío, which will take you to the lively **Campo del Príncipe** ④. Leave the square at the western end by way of the Plaza del Realejo, Calle Santa Escolástica, Calle Capitanía, and Calle del Carmen to the **Corral del Carbón** ⑤. Head for the Plaza del Carmen and cross Calle Reyes Católicos to reach the relaxed Plaza Bib-Rambla—a perfect place to grab an ice cream at the colorful Café Bib-Rambla. Nearby is the **Alcaicería,** once the Arabs' silk market and now home to a maze of alleys packed with tourist shops and restaurants.

Head up Calle Oficios to the **Palacio Madraza** ⑥, the old Arab University, and the **Capilla Real** ⑦, next to which is the **cathedral** ⑧. Just outside the cathedral's west front is the 16th-century **Escuela de las Niñas Nobles,** with a plateresque facade. Next to the cathedral, along the Plaza de Alonzo Cano, are the impressive **Curia Eclesiástica,** used as an Imperial College until 1769; the **Palacio del Arzobispo;** and the 18th-century Iglesia de Sagrario, with Corinthian columns. Behind the cathedral is the Gran Vía de Colón, one of Granada's main thoroughfares, named after Columbus. This artery was built in the late 19th century in an effort to modernize cross-town transportation; unfortunately, several wonderful old palaces were destroyed in the process. Head east for the Plaza de Isabel la Católica and check out the statue of Columbus presenting Queen Isabella with his maps of the New World. Continuing north from here will bring you back to your starting point, the Plaza Nueva. Carry on north through the Plaza Santa Ana onto Carrera del Darro and you'll reach the 11th-century Arab bathhouse, **El Bañuelo** ⑨. Just up Carrera del Darro is the 16th-century **Casa de Castril** ⑩. Now take Calles Zafra, Carellos, and San Agustín to the old Moorish quarter, the **Albaicín** ⑪. From the northern edge of the Albaicín, Cuesta del Chapíz leads east to the Morisco **Casa del Chapíz** ⑫. The caves of the **Sacromonte** ⑬, above the Albaicín, require a special expedition by minibus. North of the city, the 16th-century Baroque **Monasterio de La Cartuja** ⑭ stands 2 km (1 mi) from the city center off Calle Real de Cartuja. At the other end of the city are the **Parque de las Ciencias** ⑮, an interactive science museum, and the **Casa-Museo Federico García Lorca** ⑯.

TIMING

This walk covers a small section of the city but a high concentration of sights. Including the Alhambra, it takes a full day.

Sights to See

⑪ Albaicín. Standing on a hill of its own, across the ravine of the Darro from the Alhambra, this old Moorish neighborhood is a fascinating mix of dilapidated white houses and immaculate *carmenes* (private villas in gardens enclosed by high walls). Full of intriguing, cobbled alleyways and secret corners, the area was founded in 1228 by Moors who were expelled from Baeza after its capture by the Saint King Ferdinand. The Albaicín guards its old Moorish atmosphere jealously, though its 30 mosques have long been converted into Baroque churches. A stretch of the Moors' original city wall runs beside the Cuesta de la Alhacaba.

If you're walking, you can enter the Albaicín from either the Cuesta de Elvira or the Plaza Nueva. On Cuesta de Elvira, be sure to try one of the delightful tea shops; thanks to its Moorish background, Granada serves some of the best mint tea in all of Spain. At one of the highest points in the quarter is the **Mirador de San Nicolás,** a small square with a breathtaking view of the Alhambra. (During a visit to Spain in 1997, President Bill Clinton went out of his way to show his wife and daughter the view at sunset from here, which he remembered from an earlier trip to Granada as a student.) On foot or by car (take a taxi, as parking is impossible), begin in the Plaza Santa Ana and follow the Carrera del Darro, Paseo Padre Manjón, and the Cuesta del Chapiz.

★ ② Alhambra. Climb the slopes of green elms planted by the Duke of Wellington to reach the **Puerta de las Granadas** (Pomegranate Gate), a Renaissance gateway built by Charles V (it's topped by three pomegranates—a symbol of Granada) that leads to the **Puerta de la Justicia** (Gate of Justice) and the Alhambra. Yusuf I built the Gate of Justice in 1348; on its two arches are carved a hand and a key, the five fingers representing the five laws of the Koran.

The Alhambra was begun in the 1240s by Ibn el-Ahmar, or Alhamar, the first king of the Nasrids. The great citadel once comprised an entire complex of houses, schools, baths, barracks, and gardens surrounded by defense towers and seemingly impregnable walls. Today, only the Alcazaba fortress and the Royal Palace, built chiefly by Yusuf I (1334–54) and his son Mohammed V (1354–91), remain. The palace is an endless, intricate fantasy of patios, arches, and cupolas fashioned from wood, plaster, and tiles; lavishly colored and adorned with geometric patterns of marquetry and ceramics; and surmounted by delicate, frothy profusions of lacelike stucco and *mocárabes* (ornamental stalactites). Built of perishable materials, it was never intended to last but to be forever replaced and replenished by succeeding generations.

By the early 17th century, ruin and decay had set in, and the Alhambra was abandoned by all but tramps and stray dogs. Napoleon's troops commandeered it in 1812, but their attempts to blow it up were, happily, foiled. In 1814, the Alhambra's fortunes rose with the arrival of the Duke of Wellington, who came here to escape the pressures of the Peninsular War. Soon afterward (1829), Washington Irving arrived to live on the premises and helped revive interest in the crumbling palace, in part through his 1832 book *Tales of the Alhambra.* In 1862, Granada finally launched a complete restoration program that has been carried on ever since.

Buy an entrance ticket and wander over to your left, to the original fortress of the **Alcazaba.** Its ruins are dominated by a tower, the **Torre de la Vela,** whose summit offers superlative views of the city—to the north, the Albaicín; to the northeast, the Sacromonte; and to the west, the cathedral. The tower's great bell was used as an alarm by the

Moors, and later by the Christians, to control the opening and closing of the gates of the Granada *vega*'s irrigation system.

The Renaissance **Palacio de Carlos V** (Palace of Charles V), with a perfectly square exterior but a circular interior courtyard, stands imposing but totally incongruous on the site where the sultans' private
apartments once stood. Begun in 1526 and designed by Pedro Machuca,
a pupil of Michelangelo, the palace was once used for bullfights and
mock tournaments. Today, its perfect acoustics make it a fine setting
for symphony concerts during Granada's annual International Festival of Music and Dance, in June and July. Part of the building houses
the new **Alhambra Museum,** just opened in 1997 and devoted to Islamic art (open Tues.–Sat. 9–2:30).

A wisteria-covered walkway leads to the heart of the Alhambra, the
Casa Real (Royal Palace). Here, delicate apartments, lazy fountains,
and tranquil pools are in vivid contrast to the hulking defense walls
outside. The Royal Palace is divided into three sections. The first is the
mexuar, where business, government, and palace administration were
headquartered. Here are the Oratory and the Cuarto Dorado (Golden
Room); don't miss the views of the Albaicín and Sacromonte from their
windows.

The *serrallo* is a series of state rooms where the sultans held court and
entertained their ambassadors. In the heart of the *serrallo* is the **Patio
de los Arrayanes** (Court of the Myrtles), with a long goldfish pool surrounded by shrubs. At its northern end, in the **Salón de Embajadores**
(Hall of the Ambassadors)—which has a magnificent cedar door—Boabdil signed the terms of surrender, and Isabella received Christopher
Columbus.

The final section is the **harem.** In its time, it was entered only by the
sultan, his family, and their most trusted servants, most of them eu-
nuchs. To reach it, you'll pass through the **Sala de los Mozárabes** (Hall
of the Mozarabs); note the splendid but damaged ceiling, followed
by your first glimpse of stalactite stonework in the arches above. The
postcard-perfect **Patio de los Leones** (Court of the Lions) is the heart
of the harem. From the fountain in the center, 12 lions, which may represent the months or signs of the zodiac, leer out at the tourists. Four
streams flow symbolically to the four corners of the earth and more
literally to the surrounding state apartments.

The **Sala de los Abencerrajes** (Hall of the Moors) lies on the south side
of the palace and may be its most beautiful gallery, with a stalactite
ceiling and a star-shape cupola reflected in the pool below. Here Boabdil's father is alleged to have massacred 16 members of the Abencerrajes family—whose chief was the lover of his own favorite, Zoraya—and
piled their blood-stained heads in this font.

The **Sala de los Reyes** (Kings' Hall) lies on the patio's east side, decorated with ceiling frescoes that may have been painted by Christians
in the last days of the Moors' tenure. To the north, the **Sala de las Dos
Hermanas** (Hall of the Two Sisters) was the abode of the king's favorite.
Its name comes from the two white-marble slabs in its floor, and its
ceiling is resplendent with some of the Alhambra's most superb stucco
work, an intricate pattern of honeycomb cells. Note the symmetrically
placed pomegranates on the walls.

The **Baños Arabes,** the Alhambra's semisubterranean bathhouse, is where
the sultan's favorites luxuriated in baths of brightly tiled mosaic and
performed their ablutions lit by star-shape pinpoints of light in the ceiling above. You'll notice a balcony that looks out over one of the

rooms; from here, the sultan would choose his bed partner for the evening. Relax or stroll in the adjacent gardens.

The **Generalife** was the ancient summer palace of the Nasrid kings. It stands on the Cerro del Sol (Hill of the Sun), and its name comes from the Arabic Gennat Alarif—Garden of the Architect. The terraces and promenades here grant an incomparable view of the city, stretching away to the distant *vega*. During summer's International Festival of Music and Dance, these stately cypresses are the backdrop for evening ballets in the Generalife amphitheater.

The walk to the Alhambra follows a steep road and passes several nice shops in a colorful neighborhood. You can also take the comfortable Alhambra minibus at the Plaza Nueva in the center of town (100 ptas.; buses leave every 15 mins). For a spectacular view, return to town from the opposite side of the Alhambra hill; pass through the elm groves toward the ocher-red Hotel Alhambra Palace. Note well: a limited number people are allowed into the palace every half hour, so to avoid disappointment, call several days in advance to reserve a time. ⊠ *Cuesta de Gomérez,* ☎ *958/221503, 958/220912 for reservations.* ☞ *Alhambra and Generalife 725 ptas.* ☉ *Mar.–Oct., Mon.–Sat. 9–8, Sun. 9–7; floodlit visits Tues., Thurs., and Sat. 10 PM–midnight; Nov.–Feb., daily 9–7; floodlit visits Sat. 8 PM–10 PM. Ticket office opens 30 min before opening time and closes 1 hr before closing time.*

❹ Campo del Príncipe. This is a handsome square surrounded by lively tapas bars and shops. On its northern edge stands a much-venerated crucifix with Cristo de los Faroles (Christ of the Lanterns). Women often come here to pray and offer flowers. Príncipe is a good place to come at lunchtime or early in the evening to sample seafood or *jamón serrano* (mountain-cured ham prized throughout Spain).

★ **❼ Capilla Real (Royal Chapel).** The Capilla Real is a shrine of Granadan history second only to the Alhambra, as it is the burial place of the momentous Catholic Monarchs, Isabella of Castile and Ferdinand of Aragon. The couple originally planned to be buried in Toledo's San Juan de los Reyes, but Isabella changed her mind when they conquered Granada in 1492. When she died, in 1504, her body was at first laid to rest in the Convent of San Francisco (now the parador), on the Alhambra hill. The architect Enrique Egas began work on the Royal Chapel in 1506 and completed it 15 years later; it is a masterpiece of the ornate Gothic style known in Spain as Isabelline. In 1521 Isabella's body was brought to a simple lead coffin in the Royal Chapel crypt, where it was joined by that of her husband, Ferdinand, and later her unfortunate daughter, Juana la Loca (Joan the Mad), and son-in-law, Felipe el Hermoso. Felipe died young, and Juana had his casket borne about the peninsula with her for years, opening the lid each night to kiss her embalmed spouse good night. The elaborate marble tombs in which Ferdinand and Isabella now lie side-by-side were commissioned by their grandson, Charles V, and fashioned by the sculptor Domenico Fancelli. The altarpiece by Felipe Vigarini (1522) shows Boabdil surrendering the keys of the city to its conquerors. In the sacristy are Ferdinand's sword, Isabella's crown and scepter, and a fine collection of Flemish paintings once owned by Isabella. ⊠ *Oficios,* ☎ *958/229239.* ☞ *300 ptas.* ☉ *Mar.–Sept., daily 10:30–1 and 4–7; Oct.–Feb., daily 10:30–1 and 3:30–6:30.*

❿ Casa de Castril. A richly decorated 16th-century palace, this *casa* once belonged to Bernardo Zafra, secretary to Queen Isabella. Before you enter the Castril, notice the exquisite portal, and the facade carved with a phoenix and scallop shells. Inside is the **Museo Arqueológico** (Museum of Archaeology), where you'll find a beautiful Moorish room, with original furnishings; Phoenician burial urns from Almuñécar, on Granada's coast; and artifacts from provincial caves. ⊠ *Carrera del Darro 41,* ☎ *958/225640.* ☎ *250 ptas.* ☉ *Tues.–Sun. 10–2.*

NEED A
BREAK?   The **park at Paseo Padre Manjón,** along the Darro River, is a terrific place for a coffee break. Dappled with fountains and stone walkways, the park affords a stunning view of the Alhambra's backside.

⑫ **Casa del Chapíz.** This fine 16th-century Morisco house has a delightful garden. It houses the School of Arabic Studies and is not generally open to the public, but if you knock, the caretaker may show you around. ⊠ *Cuesta del Chapiz at Camino del Sacromonte.*

③ **Casa-Museo de Manuel de Falla.** The composer Manuel de Falla lived and worked for many years in this house, which is tucked into a charming little hillside lane with stunning views of the Alpujarra mountains. The house is now a small museum. In 1986 Granada finally paid tribute to Spain's musical champion by naming its new concert hall the Manuel de Falla Auditorium. ⊠ *C. Antequeruela Alta 11,* ☎ *958/229421.* ☎ *250 ptas.* ☉ *Apr.–Sept., Tues.–Sat. 9–3; Oct.–Mar., Tues.–Sat. 10–4.*

⑧ **Cathedral.** Granada's cathedral was commissioned in 1521 by Charles V, who considered the Royal Chapel "too small for so much glory" and determined to house his illustrious late grandparents somewhere more worthy. Charles undoubtedly had great designs; the cathedral was created by some of the greatest architects of its time: Enrique Egas, Diego de Siloé, Alonso Cano, and sculptor Juan de Mena. But Charles's ambitions came to little, for the cathedral is a grandiose and gloomy monument, not completed until 1714 and never used as the crypt of his parents and grandparents. ⊠ *Gran Vía s/n,* ☎ *958/222959.* ☎ *300 ptas.* ☉ *Mar.–Sept., Mon.–Sat. 10:30–1 and 4–7, Sun. 4–7; Oct.–Feb., Mon.–Sat. 10:30–1:30 and 3:30–6:30, Sun. 3:30–6.*

⑤ **Corral del Carbón** (Coal House). This building was used to store coal in the 19th century, but its origins are much earlier—it's one of the oldest Moorish buildings in the city. Dating back to the 14th century, when Moorish merchants used it as a lodging house and stored their goods on the upper floor, it's the only Arab inn of its kind in Spain. It was later used by Christians as a theater but has been expertly restored and now displays Spanish furniture and handicrafts. ⊠ *Plaza Mariana Pineda 10, 1 block from Puerta Real,* ☎ *958/225990.* ☎ *Free.* ☉ *Mon.–Sat. 9–7, Sun. 10–2.*

⑨ **El Bañuelo** (Little Bath House). These 11th-century Arab steam baths may be a little dark and dank now, but try to imagine them filled, some 900 years ago, with Moorish beauties, backed by bright ceramic tiles and with hangings on the dull brick walls. Light comes in through star-shape vents in the ceiling, à la the Alhambra bathhouse. ⊠ *Carrera del Darro 31,* ☎ *958/222339.* ☎ *Free.* ☉ *Tues.–Sat. 10–2.*

⑯ **García Lorca Museum.** Granada's most famous native son, the poet Federico García Lorca, gets his due here. In the middle of a new park on the southern fringes of the city, the poet's onetime summer home, **La Huerta de San Vicente,** is now a museum. The living quarters include such artifacts as the poet's beloved grand piano, and temporary exhibits examine specific aspects of Lorca's life. The museum is run by the poet's niece, Laura García Lorca. ⊠ *C. de la Virgen Blanca,* ☎ *958/258466.* ☎ *300 ptas.; free Sun.* ☉ *Oct.–Apr., Tues.–Sun. 10–1 and 4–7; May–Sept., Tues.–Sun. 10–1 and 4–8.*

⑭ **La Cartuja.** This Carthusian monastery in northern Granada (2 km [1 mi] from the center) was begun in 1506 and moved to its present site in 1516, although construction continued for the next 300 years. In time, La Cartuja became one of the most outstanding Baroque buildings in Andalusia. When you enter the church and see its twisted, multicolored marble columns; the profusion of gold, silver, tortoiseshell, and ivory; the intricate stucco; and the extravagant Churrigueresque sacristy, you'll see why Cartuja has been called the Christian answer to the Alhambra. ⊠ *Camino de Alfacar,* ☎ *958/161932.* ☞ *300 ptas.* ◷ *May–Sept., Mon.–Sat. 10–1 and 4–7, Sun. 10–noon; Oct.–Apr., Mon.–Sat. 10–1 and 3:30–6, Sun. 10–noon.*

Palacio de los Córdoba. This palace, at the end of the Paseo Padre Manjón, was a noble house of the 17th century. Today it's used for art exhibits and municipal functions.

❻ **Palacio Madraza.** This building conceals the old Moorish university, built in 1349 by Yusuf I. The Baroque facade is dark and intriguing; inside, an octagonal room is crowned by a dome of Moorish inspiration. The building is now an exhibition and cultural center, open only for special exhibits. ⊠ *Oficios s/n,* ☎ *958/223447.* ☞ *Free.*

⑮ **Parque de las Ciencias** (Science Park). Across from Granada's convention center, on the Avenida del Mediterráneo, this hands-on museum features interactive exhibits, scientific experiments, and a planetarium. ⊠ *Avda. del Mediterráneo,* ☎ *958/131900.* ☞ *350 ptas.* ◷ *Tues.–Sat. 10–7, Sun. 10–3 .*

★ **San Nicolás.** The plaza in front of the church of San Nicolás, called the **Mirador de San Nicolás,** has one of the finest views in all of Granada. On the hill opposite, the turrets and towers of the ocher Alhambra form a dramatic silhouette against the snowy peaks of the Sierra Nevada. The sight is most magical at dawn, dusk, and night, when the Alhambra is floodlit. ⊠ *Plaza San Nicolás.*

⑬ **Sacromonte.** The third of Granada's three hills, the Sacromonte rises behind the Albaicín, dotted with prickly-pear cacti and riddled with caverns. (The name Granada comes from the Arabic word *garnathah,* "mountain cave.") These caves may have sheltered early Christians; 15th-century treasure hunters found a collection of bones inside and assumed they belonged to San Cecilio, the city's patron saint. Thus the hill was sanctified—*sacro monte* (holy mountain)—and a monastery built on its summit.

The Sacromonte is the domain of Granada's Gypsies. Though fewer and fewer of them actually live on the hill today, a good number still earn a healthy living there fleecing the city's tourists. The flamenco shows they stage are generally abysmal, the drinks watered down, and the prices vastly inflated for performances that are not so very *auténtico.* But on another level, the shows are certainly colorful, and they do provide a chance to venture inside the famous *cuevas* (caves). Richly colored rugs and gleaming copper utensils adorn the interiors—as do such modern conveniences as refrigerators and dishwashers. On summer evenings, enterprising Granadinos run minibus tours to the Gypsy caves; your hotel can often put you in touch. Though not cheap, a tour may be the safest way to visit the Sacromonte (and usually includes a drink in the Albaicín first). Only the most adventurous should attempt the trip on their own. Don't bring valuables up here, or more cash than you can afford to lose.

Dining and Lodging

$$$ ✕ **Carmen de San Miguel.** Set on the Alhambra hill in a villa with a glass-enclosed dining room, an Andalusian patio and fountain, and a

terrace, this restaurant commands magnificent views over Granada. The food is less spectacular. Entrées may include the *zarzuela de pescados a la granadina* (the local version of this seafood stew, including almonds and raisins), *lenguado a la naranja* (sole in orange sauce), or grilled meat. ⊠ *Paseo Torres Bermejas 3,* ☎ *958/226723. AE, DC, MC, V. Closed Sun.*

$$$ ✕ **Cunini.** Cunini, just below the cathedral, is Granada's best fish
★ restaurant. Fresh seafood is heaped on the long tapas bar, and the menu presents fish dishes from all over Spain, including some Basque specialties. Both the *pescaditos fritos* (fried) and the *parrillada* (grilled) fish are good choices, or you may prefer *zarzuela* (fish stew). ⊠ *Pescadería 14,* ☎ *958/250777. AE, DC, MC, V. Closed Mon.*

$$$ ✕ **Galatino.** The striking modernistic design—with interesting trompe l'oeil tile decoration—takes center stage at Granada's newest restaurant. The creative cuisine includes such inventions as *espuma de bacalao y gambas* (mousse of codfish and shrimp with roasted peppers) or guinea fowl braised with sage and rosemary. ⊠ *Gran Vía,* ☎ *958/ 800803. AE DC MC V.*

$$$ ✕ **La Alacena.** The sunken dining room in this picturesque place was once the cellar of a 16th-century convent, with vaulted ceilings and whitewashed brick walls. Entrées include *cordero con miel de caña* (leg of lamb with cane molasses). ⊠ *Plaza del Padre Suárez 5,* ☎ *958/221105. AE, MC, V. Closed Sun.*

$$–$$$ ✕ **Ruta del Veleta.** Just over 5 km (3 mi) out of town, in Cenes de la
★ Vega, this typically decorated restaurant offers some of Granada's best cuisine. The many house specialties include *carnes a la brasa* (succulent grilled meats) and fish dishes from Cantabria and the Levante cooked in rock salt, as well as regional dishes like *jabalí estilo mozárabe* (wild boar cooked with apples). Dessert might be pudding *de manzanas en salsa de moras* (apple pudding in blackberry sauce).⊠ *Carretera Sierra Nevada, Km 5.4,* ☎ *958/486134. AE, DC, MC, V. No dinner Sun.*

$$ ✕ **La Mimbre.** Location, location, location: this small, slightly cramped lunch spot is tucked right under the walls of the Alhambra, next to the Generalife garden. Inside, you sit on chairs upholstered with typical Alpujarran fabric; outside, the spacious patio is shady, romantic, and delightful in warm weather. The food is classically Granadino: *habas con jamón* (broad beans and ham), *choto al ajillo* (braised kid with garlic). ⊠ *Avda. del Generalife,* ☎ *958/222276. AE, MC, V. Closed Sat. No dinner.*

$$ ✕ **Los Manueles.** This ancient tavern is usually packed. The food isn't remarkable—*tortilla al Sacromonte,* and other local fare—but the decor, atmosphere, and friendly waiters at this traditional inn off Reyes Católicos make it popular with both Granadinos and travelers. Alpujarran rugs, ceramic plates, and other knickknacks cover the walls, and a ceramic plaque commemorates a visit from Spain's royal family in 1982. Gigantic hams adorn the bar. ⊠ *Zaragoza 2,* ☎ *958/223413. AE, DC, MC, V. Closed 5 PM–7:30 PM.*

$$ ✕ **Sevilla.** This colorful, central restaurant has been going strong since
★ 1930 and has fed the likes of de Falla and García Lorca over the years. There's a superb tapas bar and four picturesque dining rooms; you can also eat on the outdoor terrace overlooking the Royal Chapel. The menu features such Granadino favorites as *sopa sevillana* and *tortilla al Sacromonte* (omelet with kid's brains, ham, and vegetables). ⊠ *Oficios 12,* ☎ *958/221223. AE, DC, MC, V. Closed Mon. No dinner Sun.*

$$$$ ✕▦ **La Bobadilla.** Halfway between Granada and Málaga, this luxu-
★ rious complex, with white walls, tile roofs, patios, fountains, and artificial lake, resembles a Moorish village or a rambling Andalusian *cortijo* (ranch). The buildings center on a 16th-century-style chapel, whose

1,595-pipe organ is used for weekend concerts and weddings. Each room is individually designed and decorated and has its own terrace or garden. The elegant haute-cuisine restaurant, La Finca, cooks with fresh, organic produce from the hotel's garden and meat reared on local farms. A second restaurant, El Cortijo, serves more down-to-earth regional cuisine. ✉ *Finca La Bobadilla, north of Granada–Seville highway between Salinas and Rute, 18300,* ☎ *958/321861,* ☒ *958/321810. 52 rooms, 8 suites. 2 restaurants, indoor and outdoor pools, hot tub, sauna, 2 tennis courts, exercise room, horseback riding, convention center. AE, DC, MC, V.*

$$$–$$$$ ✕☷ **Triunfo.** This comfortable hotel is at the far end of the Gran Vía de Colón. The public rooms have gleaming marble floors, deep sofas, and copious paintings; guest rooms are furnished in traditional style, with dark-wood fittings and apricot curtains and bedspreads. The handsome Puerta Elvira Restaurant serves typical Andalusian dishes. ✉ *Plaza Triunfo 19, 18010,* ☎ *958/207444,* ☒ *958/279017. 37 rooms. Restaurant, cafeteria. AE, DC, MC, V.*

$$$$ ☷ **Alhambra Palace.** A flamboyant, ocher-red, neo-Moorish pile, this
★ hotel was built in 1910 and commands a superb position on leafy grounds at the back of the Alhambra hill. The interior is exotic and Asian, with orange and brown overtones; multicolored tiles; and Moorish arches and pillars. Even the bar is incongruously decorated as a mosque. The rooms overlooking the town have incredible views, as does the terrace, a perfect place to watch the sun set on the Sierra Nevada. ✉ *Peña Partida 2, 18009,* ☎ *958/221468,* ☒ *958/226404. 122 rooms, 12 suites. Restaurant, 2 bars. AE, DC, MC, V.*

$$$$ ☷ **Parador de San Francisco.** Magnificently set within the Alhambra precincts, Spain's most popular parador occupies an old Franciscan convent built by the Catholic Monarchs after their capture of Granada. The rooms in the old section are furnished with antiques, woven curtains, and bedspreads; those in the new wing are simpler. Reserve four to six months in advance. ✉ *Alhambra, 18009,* ☎ *958/221440,* ☒ *958/222264. 36 rooms. Restaurant, bar. AE, DC, MC, V.*

$$$ ☷ **Inglaterra.** Set in a period house just two blocks above the Gran Vía de Colón, in the heart of town, this hotel has Old World charm as opposed to creature comforts, but the accommodations are perfectly adequate. ✉ *Cetti Meriem 4,* ☎ *958/221559,* ☒ *958/227100. 36 rooms. AE, DC, MC, V Cafeteria.*

$$ ☷ **Alixares.** Large and modern but not unattractive, the Alixares has a prime location between the Alhambra and the Generalife. The cream-color rooms are modern and functional; those on the fourth and fifth floors have the best views. The staff is friendly and professional. In summer, there's a barbecue restaurant on the roof in addition to the year-round restaurant indoors. ✉ *Avda. Alixares del Generalife,* ☎ *958/225575,* ☒ *958/224102. 176 rooms. AE, DC, MC, V. Restaurant, cafeteria, meeting rooms, pool.*

$$ ☷ **América.** This simple but charming hotel within the Alhambra precincts is very popular, albeit more for its unbeatable location than for the service; you should book months ahead. It feels like a private home, with simple bedrooms, a sitting room decorated with local handicrafts, and a shady patio where home-cooked meals are served in summer. ✉ *Real de la Alhambra 53, 18009,* ☎ *958/227471,* ☒ *958/227470. 14 rooms. Restaurant. No credit cards. Closed Nov.–Feb.*

$$ ☷ **Juan Miguel.** Here's a reasonably priced option in central Granada, on the busy Acera del Darro. Rooms are on the small side but are pleasingly furnished with light-wood furniture and green curtains and bedspreads. ✉ *Acera del Darro 24,* ☎ *958/521111,* ☒ *958/258916. 66 rooms. AE, MC, V. Restaurant, cafeteria.*

$$ ☒ **Reina Cristina.** In an old house near the lively and central Plaza de la Trinidad, this hotel has been thoroughly modernized. Plants trail from the windowsills of the reception area, a covered patio where a small marble fountain splashes beneath a Moorish lamp. The lively cafeteria is a nice pitstop for afternoon conversation. A marble stairway leads to the bedrooms, which are simply but cheerfully furnished with red curtains and red-and-white-checked bedspreads. ☒ *Tablas 4, 18002,* ☎ *958/253211,* ℻ *958/255728. 43 rooms. Restaurant, bar, cafeteria. AE, DC, MC, V.*

$ ☒ **Britz.** The Britz is at the base of the Alhambra hill, near the downtown attractions. It's a good budget option; rooms are small but comfortable, with modern, charmless decor. ☒ *Plaza Nueva y Gomerez 1, 18009,* ☎ *958/223652. 22 rooms, 9 with bath. MC, V.*

Nightlife and the Arts

Granada's large student population makes for a lively bar scene. Some of the trendiest bars are in converted houses in the Albaicín, on the Paseo de los Tristes (next to the Darro river, between the Alhambra and the Albaicín), and in the modern part of the city, on Pedro Antonio de Alarcon and Martinez de la Rosa. The **Corral del Principe** (☒ Campo del Principe, ☎ 958/228088) has live music, meals, and *sevillanas* dancing into the night. The **Granada 10** (☒ Carcel Baja 10, ☎ 958/224001), in the Albaicín, is a former theater converted into a discotheque.

Get the latest on arts events, including diversions for young people, at the **Area de Bienestar Social Cultura y Juventud** (City Department of Social Welfare, Culture, and Youth), in the Palacio de los Condes de Gabia (☒ Plaza de los Girones 1, ☎ 958/247383). Plays are performed at the **Teatro Alhambra** (☒ Molines 56, ☎ 958/220447). The **Centro Cultural Manuel de Falla** (☎ 958/222188) has information on art exhibits. The **Granada City Orchestra** performs often in the Manuel de Falla Auditorium (☒ Paseo de los Mártires, ☎ 958/220022).

The **Granada International Theater Festival,** organized by Granada's Ayuntamiento (☒ City Hall, ☎ 958/229344), fills 10 days each May. The **Granada International Festival of Music and Dance** (☎ 958/221844) is held annually from mid-June to mid-July; tickets are available at the Corral del Carbón on Mariana Pineda, one block from Reyes Católicos. Contact the tourist office for information about the **November Jazz Festival.**

The flamenco show at **Jardines Neptuno** (☒ C. Arabial, ☎ 958/522533 or 958/251112), though tourist-oriented, can be colorful and often includes a mixture of ballet and folk music. There's a similar show nightly in the somewhat smaller **Reina Mora** (☒ Mirador de San Cristóbal). Many hotels have tickets. Flamenco is also performed at **El Corral del Príncipe** (☒ Campo del Príncipe, ☎ 958/228088) and at the **Corral del Carbón** (☒ Plaza Mariana Pineda, ☎ 958/225990). Never go before 11 PM; the best time is around 1 AM. For *zambra* (singing and dancing) performances by Gypsies in the Sacromonte caves, join an organized tour through a travel agent or your hotel. If you want to go on your own (call ahead for performance times, and be prepared to part with lots of money), try **Cueva los Tarantos** (☒ Camino del Sacromonte 9, ☎ 958/224525).

Shopping

Granada's handicrafts are very much a legacy of the Moors and include brass and copperware, ceramics, marquetry (objects finished with inlaid wood), and woven textiles. The main shopping streets, centering on the Puerta Real, are **Reyes Católicos, Zacatín, Ángel Ganivet,** and the **Gran Vía de Colón.** Most of the antiques stores are on **Cuesta de Elvira.**

Tapas Bars

For the most colorful bars, look around the Albaicín, Campo del Príncipe, Plaza del Carmen–Calle Navas, and Pedro de Alarcón-Martínez de la Rosa. **Bar El Ladrillo** (⊠ Plaza de Fátima) is a tiny but popular tapas bar in the Albaicín with outdoor tables in summer. For a splendid array of regional wines with your tapas, try **La Puerta del Vino** (⊠ Paseo Padre Manjón 5, ☎ 958/210026), a 10-table bar hung with old paintings. **Chikito** (⊠ Plaza del Campillo 9, ☎ 958/223364) is best known for its restaurant's tasty food, but the bar is an excellent spot to nosh tapas. The place is usually packed, even in summer, when additional tables are set up in the plaza. The popular **Bodegas Castañeda** (⊠ Elvira 6) draws many locals. On the Plaza Nueva, **La Gran Taberna** (⊠ Plaza Nueva 12, ☎ 958/228846), a two-tiered bar with wooden gallery upstairs, is famous for its *montaditos,* little open sandwiches made with the ingredients of your choice.

Santa Fe

⑰ *8 km (5 mi) west of Granada just south of the N342.*

The village of Santa Fe was founded in winter 1491 as a campground for Ferdinand and Isabella's 150,000 troops as they prepared for the Siege of Granada. It was in Santa Fe, in April 1492, that Isabella and Columbus signed the agreements that financed his historic trip; the town has thus been called the Cradle of America. Santa Fe was originally laid out in the shape of a cross, with a gate at each of its four ends, inscribed with the initials F Y (for Ferdinand and Isabella's names in Latin). The town has long since transcended its initial boundaries, but the four gates still stand; to see them all at the same time, stand in the square next to the parish at the center of the old town.

Fuentevaqueros

⑱ *10 km (6 mi) west of Santa Fe.*

Federico García Lorca was born in the village of Fuentevaqueros, just beyond Santa Fe, on June 5, 1898, and lived here until the age of six. The **Casa Museo García Lorca,** the poet's childhood home, opened as a museum in 1986, when Spain commemorated the 50th anniversary of Lorca's assassination and celebrated his reinstatement as a national figure after 40 years of nonrecognition during the Franco regime. The house has been restored with original furnishings, while the former granary, barn, and stables have been converted into an exhibition spaces, with temporary art shows and a permanent display of photographs, clippings, and other memorabilia. A two-minute video shows the only existing film footage of the poet. ⊠ *Poeta García Lorca 4,* ☎ *958/ 516453.* 🎫 *200 ptas.* ☉ *July–Sept., Tues.–Sun. 10–1 and 6–8; Oct.– Mar., Tues.–Sun. 10–1 and 4–6; Apr.–June, 10–1 and 5–7.*

The village of Valderrubio, not far from Fuentevaqueros, inspired Lorca's *Libro de Poemas* and one of his best-loved plays, *La Casa de Bernarda Alba.*

Viznar

⑲ *9 km (5½ mi) northeast of Granada (head northeast on N342, then turn left, then left again, when you see signs for Viznar).*

If you're a Lorca devotee, make the short trip to Viznar. The **Federico García Lorca Memorial Park**, 3 km (2 mi) from Viznar up a narrow winding road, marks the spot where Lorca was shot without trial by Nationalists at the beginning of the civil war in August 1936 and where he is probably buried. Lorca, who is now venerated by most Spaniards, was hated by Fascists for his liberal ideas and his homosexuality.

The Sierra Nevada

⑳ *The drive southeast from Granada to Pradollano along C420, by way of Cenes de la Vega, takes about 45 mins. You'd be wise to carry snow chains even as late as April or May.*

Even if you don't have a car, the mountains of the Sierra Nevada make for an easy, worthwhile excursion. From December to May, the Sierra Nevada ski resort—with two stations, Pradollano and the higher Borreguiles—draws crowds, but the same slope is quiet in summer. Buses leave Granada daily at 9, returning at 5:30 in winter, 6:30 in summer (✉ Autocar Bonal, ☎ 958/273100). Buses from Granada depart year-round from the Bar El Ventorillo (where you also buy tickets, for 700 pesetas), next to the Palacio de Congresos. In July and August you can drive right up to the summit of the Veleta on Europe's highest road. It's cold up here, so bring a warm jacket, scarf, and sunglasses, even if the weather in Granada is sizzling hot. The **Veleta**, Spain's third-highest mountain, stands at 11,125 ft, and the view from its summit across the Alpujarra range to the sea, at distant Motril, is stunning. On a very clear day you can even see the coast of North Africa. Away to your left, the mighty Mulhacén, mainland Spain's highest peak, soars to 11,407 ft.

Skiing

The **Sierra Nevada** ski resort is one of Europe's best equipped, having hosted the World Alpine Skiing Championships in 1996. There are 21 lifts, 45 runs, and about 60 km (40 mi) of marked trails, not to mention a snowboarding circuit and two floodlit slopes for night skiing on weekends. A **children's ski school** and rental shop round out the facilities. Contact the Sierra Nevada Information Center (✉ Plaza de Andalucía 4, ☎ 958/249111); you can also call for snow, weather, and road conditions (☎ 958/249119).

The Alpujarras

㉑ *The village of Lanjarón is 46 km (29 mi) south of Granada.*

A trip to the Alpujarras, on the southern slopes of the Sierra Nevada, will take you to one of Andalusia's highest, most remote, and most picturesque areas. The many beautiful villages hide handsome crafts shops where you can buy handwoven textiles and handmade basketware, pottery, and other goods. If you're driving, the road as far as Lanjarón and Orgiva is smooth sailing; after that you should be prepared for steep, twisting mountain roads and few gas stations.

The Alpujarra region was originally populated by Moors fleeing the Reconquest, first from Seville, after its fall in 1248, and later from Granada, after 1492. It was also the last fiefdom of the unfortunate Boabdil, conceded to him by the Catholic Monarchs after his surrender of Granada. In 1568, rebellious Moors made their final stand against the Christians overlords; their revolt was ruthlessly suppressed by Philip II and followed by the forced conversion of all Moors to Christianity.

The villages of the Alpujarras were then repopulated with Christian soldiers from Galicia, who were granted land in return for their service against the Moors. To this day, the Galicians' descendants continue the Moorish custom of weaving rugs and blankets in the traditional Alpujarran colors of red, green, black, and white, and they sell these crafts in many of the villages. The houses here are squat and square; they spill down the mountainside one on top of another, bearing a strong resemblance to the Berber homes in the Rif Mountains, across the sea in Morocco.

En Route A couple of miles east of Granada on N323, the road reaches a spot known as the **Suspiro del Moro** (Moor's Sigh). Pause here a moment and look back at the city, just as Granada's departing boy king, Boabdil, did 500 years ago. As he wept over the city he'd surrendered to the Catholic Monarchs, his scornful mother pronounced her now famous rebuke: "You weep like a boy for the city you could not defend as a man."

Lanjarón, some 46 km (29 mi) from Granada, is a spa town famous for its mineral water, gathered from the melting snows of the Sierra Nevada and drunk throughout Spain. **Orgiva** is the main town of the western Alpujarras, where you leave C333 and follow the signs for Pampaneira and Capileira in the Alpujarra Alta (High Alpujarra).

The villages of the **Poqueira Ravine**—Pampaneira, Bubión, and Capileira—are probably the best known in the Alpujarras. The looms in **Pampaneira's** workshops produce many of the textiles sold nearby. **Capileira,** at the end of the road, is one of the prettiest villages; its Museo Alpujarreño, in the Plaza Mayor, has a colorful display of local crafts. From Capileira, a winding track leads over the mountain peaks to join the road to the Veleta summit; it's passable only in July or August, and then only in a four-wheel-drive vehicle.

If you make it as far as **Trevélez,** which lies on the slopes of the Mulhacén at 4,840 ft above sea level, you will have driven on one of the highest roads in Europe. Reward yourself with a plate of the locally produced *jamón serrano*.

Lodging

$$ ⊞ **Villa Turística de Bubión.** This apartment-hotel puts you up in in
★ dividual whitewashed houses, each with its own sitting room, kitchen, bathroom, and bedrooms that sleep two, four, or six people. The hotel nestles beneath the Veleta and overlooks splendid mountain scenery. ⊠ *Barrio Alto, 18412,* ☎ *958/763111,* FAX *958/763136. 43 units. Restaurant, bar. AE, DC, MC, V.*

Guadix

㉒ *47 km (30 mi) east of Granada on the A92 highway.*

Guadix was an important mining town as far back as 2,000 years ago, and it has its fair share of monuments, including a cathedral (built between 1594 and 1706) and a 9th-century Moorish *alcazaba*. But Guadix and the neighboring village of **Purullena** are best known for their cave communities. There are around 2,000 caves in these parts, carved out of the soft sandstone mountains, and most of them are inhabited. Far from being troglodytic holes in the wall, they are well furnished and comfortable, with a pleasant year-round temperature. There's even a cave hotel (☞ *below*). Follow signs to the **Cueva Museo,** a small cave museum, in the heart of Guadix's cave district. A number of private caves have signs welcoming visitors to inspect the premises; a tip is expected if you do. Purullena, 6 km (4 mi) from Guadix, is also known for ceramics.

Dining and Lodging

$ ✕⊞ **Comercio.** This 1905 building in the center of Guadix is the town's most charming establishment, an enchanting little family-run hotel. Rooms have thick bedspreads in rich red; marble floors; and spanking-new bathrooms. The public areas include an art gallery, a concert room, and the best restaurant in Guadix, serving such local specialties as roast lamb with raisins and pine nuts. ✉ *C. Mira de Amezcua 3,* ☎ *958/ 660500,* FAX *958/665072. 24 rooms. AE, DC, MC, V.*

$$ ⊞ **Cuevas Pedro Antonio de Alarcoín.** There's not much of a view, but what can you expect from a cave hotel? Located not in Guadix's main cave district but in a cave "suburb" outside the town, this unique lodging is installed in 19 different but adjoining caves. There are 18 suites, each with kitchenette, sleeping two to five people. The whitewashed cave walls are decorated with charming Granadino crafts; colorful rugs cover clay-tile floors; and there are handwoven Alpujarran tapestries serve as doors between the rooms. The restaurant, also in a cave, serves regional dishes. ✉ *Barriada San Torcuato,* ☎ *958/664986,* FAX *958/661721. 18 suites. Restaurant. AE, MC, V.*

JAÉN, BAEZA, ÚBEDA, AND CAZORLA

Jaén, north of Granada, has a rich Moorish legacy—Arab baths and a former Alcázar—as well as an ornately decorated cathedral. From Jaén, head northeast along the N321 to the olive-producing towns of Baeza and Úbeda. The typical Andalusian town of Cazorla is the gateway to the Cazorla Nature Park, where you might spot wild boar.

Jaén

㉓ *93 km (58 mi) north of Granada.*

The city of Jaén nestles in the foothills of the Sierra de Jabalcuz, surrounded by towering peaks and rolling, olive-clad hillsides. The Arabs called it Geen (Route of the Caravans) because it formed a crossroad between Castile and Andalusia. Captured from the Moors by the Saint King Ferdinand in 1246, Jaén became a frontier province and for the next 200 years was the site of many a battle and skirmish between the Moors of Granada and Christians from the north and west. Today, the province of Jaén has lead and silver mines and endless olive groves.

★ The **Castillo de Santa Catalina,** perched on a rocky crag 5 km (3 mi) from the center of Jaén, is the city's star monument. The origins of the castle may have been a tower erected by Hannibal; the site was fortified continuously over the centuries. The Nasrid king Alhamar, builder of Granada's Alhambra, constructed an *alcázar* here, but King Ferdinand III captured it from him in 1246 on the feast day of St. Catalina (St. Catherine). St. Catalina consequently became Jaén's patron saint, and when the Christians built a new castle and a chapel on this site, they dedicated them to her. The castle ruins make a dramatic setting for the parador in their midst. ✉ *Castillo de Santa Catalina.* ☎ *Free.* ☉ *Summer Thurs.–Tues. 10:30–1:30, winter Thurs.–Tues. 10–2.*

The Jaén **cathedral** is an imposing hulk that looms above the modest buildings around it. It was begun in 1500 on the site of a former mosque and not finished until the end of the 18th century. Its chief architect was the brilliant Andrés de Vandelvira (1509–75), many more of whose buildings can be seen in Úbeda and Baeza (☞ *below*). The ornate facade was sculpted by Pedro Roldán, and if you look up at the figures on top of the columns, you can see San Fernando (King Ferdinand III) surrounded by the four evangelists. In the **museum,** look for the *Immaculate Conception,* by Alonso Cano; *San Lorenzo,* by Martínez Montañés; and a Calvary scene by Jácobo Florentino. ⊠ *Plaza Santa María.* ▨ *Cathedral free, museum 100 ptas.* ⊘ *Cathedral daily 8:30–1 and 4:30–7, museum weekends 11–1.*

Explore the narrow alleyways of old Jaén as you walk from the cathedral to the **Baños Árabes** (Arab Baths), which once belonged to Ali, a Moorish king of Jaén, and probably date from the 11th century. Four hundred years later, a viceroy of Peru built himself a mansion, the Palacio de Villardompardo, right over them; it took years of painstaking excavation to restore the baths to their original form. ⊠ *Palacio de Villardompardo, Plaza Luisa de Marillac,* ☎ *953/236292.* ▨ *Free.* ⊘ *Tues.–Fri. 9–8, weekends 9:30–2:30.*

The **Museo Provincial** is a delightful little museum in a 1547 mansion. In its patio stands the facade of the Church of San Miguel, another work of Andrés de Vandelvira. A highlight of the fine-arts section is the roomful of Goya lithographs. ⊠ *Paseo de la Estación 29,* ☎ *953/250320.* ▨ *Free.* ⊘ *Tues.–Fri. 10–2 and 4–7:30, weekends 10–2; closed summer afternoons.*

Dining and Lodging

$–$$ ✕ **Casa Vicente.** This popular, family-run restaurant next to the cathedral square is usually packed with locals. You can have drinks and tapas at the colorful mesón-bar, then move on to a cozy dining room. The traditional Jaén dishes—such as game casseroles, Jaén-style spinach, and *cordero Mozábe* (Mozarab-style roast lamb with a sweet-and-sour sauce)—are especially good. ⊠ *Francisco Martín Mora 1,* ☎ *953/232222. AE, MC, V. No dinner Sun.*

$$$ ▣ **Parador de Santa Catalina.** Built on a mountain amid the towers
★ of a medieval Moorish castle, Jaén's parador is one of the showpieces of the parador chain and a reason in itself to visit Jaén. Lofty ceilings, tapestries, baronial shields, and suits of armor add to the castle atmosphere. The comfortable bedrooms, with canopied beds, all have balconies overlooking the mountains. ⊠ *Castillo de Santa Catalina, 23001,* ☎ *953/230000,* 𝔽𝔸𝕏 *953/230930. 45 rooms. Restaurant, pool. AE, DC, MC, V.*

Shopping

The province of Jaén is known for its **pottery** and **ceramics,** and wares woven from **esparto grass**—baskets, mats, and ornaments.

Baeza

★ ㉔ *48 km (30 mi) northeast of Jaén on the N321.*

The delightful town of Baeza is nestled among rolling hills and olive groves. Baeza was founded by the Romans, later housed the Visigoths, and became the capital of a *taifa* (kingdom) under the Moors. The Saint King Ferdinand captured it in 1227, and for the next 200 years Baeza stood on the frontier along with the Moorish kingdom of Granada. In the 16th and 17th centuries, Baeza's nobility gave the city a wealth of splendid Renaissance palaces.

Baeza's **Casa del Pópulo,** in the village's central *paseo*—where the Plaza del Pópulo (or Plaza de los Leones) and Plaza del Mercado Viejo merge to form a delightful cobbled square—is a beautiful plateresque structure from around 1530. The first mass of the Reconquest was reputedly celebrated on its curved balcony. It now houses the town's tourist office.

In the center of Baeza's village square is an ancient Iberian-Roman statue, thought to be of Imilce, wife of Hannibal. The hapless figure is now headless, having been decapitated by an anticlerical crowd, who apparently mistook her for the Virgin, in the 1930s. At the foot of her column is the **Fuente de los Leones** (Fountain of the Lions).

You can find the **university** by following a series of steps on the plaza's south side. The college opened in 1542, closed in 1824, and later became a high school, where the poet Antonio Machado (author of *Tierras de Castilla*) taught French from 1912 to 1919.

The golden-stone **Palacio de Jabalquinto,** on Baeza's Cuesta de San Felipe, was built by Juan Alonso Benavides, second cousin of Ferdinand of Aragon. Its facade is a masterpiece of the late-15th-century Isabelline Gothic.

Baeza's **cathedral** was originally begun by Ferdinand III on the site of a former mosque, but it's undergone many transformations since his day. It was largely rebuilt by Andrés de Vandelvira, architect of Jaén's cathedral, between 1570 and 1593, though the west front has architectural traits from an earlier period. A fine 14th-century rose window crowns the 13th-century Puerta de la Luna (Door of the Moon). Don't miss the Baroque silver monstrance, which is carried in Baeza's Corpus Christi processions; it's kept in a concealed niche behind a painting. To see it in all of its flamboyant splendor, you put a coin in a slot to reveal its hiding place and light it up—it's money well spent. In the cathedral's Gothic cloisters, you can see the remains of the original mosque. ⊙ *Daily 10:30–1 and 5–7.*

The seminary of **San Felipe Neri,** built in 1660, is opposite Baeza's cathedral at the end of Cuesta San Felipe. The ancient student custom of inscribing names and graduation dates in bull's blood (as in Salamanca) is still evident on the walls.

The **Ayuntamiento** (town hall), on Plaza Cardenal Benavides, just north of Plaza del Pópulo, has an ornate plateresque facade. The building was designed by Andrés de Vandelvira. Look up at the facade between the balconies and you'll see the coats of arms of Felipe II, the city of Baeza, and the Magistrate Juan de Borja.

Dining and Lodging

$–$$ ✕▦ **Juanito.** Located on the edge of town (next to a gas station) on the way to Úbeda, this small, unpretentious hotel provides simple, clean, and comfortable rooms. The real drawing card is its well-known restaurant: the proprietor is a champion of the Jaén region's excellent olive oil, and the cuisine reflects his dedication to promoting Andalusian dishes. The chef has done much to revive the art of cooking regional specialties, such as *alcochafas Luisa* (braised artichokes), *ensalada de perdiz* (partridge salad), and *cordero con habas* (lamb and broad beans); desserts are based on old Moorish recipes. ⊠ *Paseo Arca de Agua, 23440,* ☎ *953/740040,* ℻ *953/742324. 36 rooms, 1 suite. Restaurant. MC, V.*

$ ▦ **Fuentenueva Hospedería.** This small, charming, informal hotel was installed in a former women's prison, later the residence of the town judge. The comfortable rooms are attractively decorated in pastels. ⊠ *Paseo Arca del Agua,* ☎ *953/743100,* ℻ *953/743200. 12 rooms. Restaurant, cafeteria, pool. AE, MC, V.*

Úbeda

㉕ *9 km (5½ mi) northeast of Baeza on the N321.*

Úbeda stands in the heart of Jaén's olive groves; olive oil is the main concern here. Although this modern town of 30,000 is relatively dull, the **Casco Antiguo** (Old Town) is a superbly pure example of a Renaissance town and one of the most outstanding enclaves of 16th-century architecture in Spain. Follow the signs to the **Zona Monumental,** where you'll pass countless Renaissance palaces and stately mansions, each with its own distinctive features—an unusual balcony, or a fine sculptured facade. Most of these homes are closed to the public, but you can wander into many of Úbeda's churches.

The **Hospital de Santiago,** on Avenida Cristo Rey, in the modern section, is a short walk from the bus depot and the main drag, Ramón y Cajal. This huge, angular building, often jokingly called the Escorial of Andalusia, is the masterpiece of Andrés de Vandelvira, who was responsible for most of Úbeda's monuments. Its generally plain facade is decorated with ceramic medallions, and over the main entrance is a relief of St. James as a warrior on horseback. Inside are a fine arcaded patio and a grand staircase.

The **Plaza del Ayuntamiento,** in the Old Town, is crowned by the **Palacio de Vela de los Cobos,** built by Vandelvira in the mid-16th century for Úbeda's magistrate, Francisco de Vela de los Cobos. Its special feature is the corner balcony, with a central column of white marble, which you can see echoed in the gallery above.

The Palacio Juan Vázquez de Molina—better known by its nickname, the **Palacio de las Cadenas** (House of Chains)—another Vandelvira work, is so named because iron chains were once affixed to the columns of its main doorway. It currently houses the city government.

The Plaza Vásquez de Molina, in the heart of the Old Town, is home ★ to the **Sacra Capilla del Salvador,** the most elaborate and ornate of Úbeda's churches. Not surprisingly, it is photographed so often that it has become the city's unofficial symbol. The Sacra Capilla was built by Vandelvira, though he based his design on some 1536 plans by Diego de Siloé, architect of Granada's cathedral. It was sacked in the frenzy of church burnings at the outbreak of the civil war but retains its ornate west front and an altarpiece with a rare Berruguete sculpture.

The Plaza del Mercado, by way of the Calle Horno Cantador, leads you to the Ayuntamiento Antiguo (old town hall), begun in the early 16th century but restored as a beautiful arcaded Baroque palace in 1680. From its upper balcony the Town Council watched celebrations and *autos-da-fé* ("acts of faith"—executions of heretics sentenced by the Inquisition) in the square below. On the north side is the 13th-century church of San Pablo, with an Isabelline south portal.

Dining and Lodging

$$$–$$$$ ✕🏨 **Parador Condestable Dávalos.** This splendid parador is in a 16th-
★ century ducal palace on the Plaza Vázquez de Molina, right next to the Capilla del Salvador. A grand stairway, decked with tapestries and suits of armor, leads up to the bedrooms, which have tile floors, lofty wood ceilings, dark Castilian-style furniture, and deliciously large baths. The dining room—complete with waitstaff in traditional dress— serves perhaps the best food in Úbeda, specializing in regional dishes; try one of the *perdiz* (partridge) entrées. Desserts have intriguing names like *suspiros de monja* (nun's sighs). ✉ *Plaza Vázquez de Molina 1, 23400,* ☎ *953/750345,* 📠 *953/751259. 31 rooms. Restaurant. AE, DC, MC, V.*

$$$ 🏨 **Palacio de la Rambla.** This wonderful 16th-century mansion in old Úbeda has been in the same family since it was built, and part of it still hosts the Marquesa de la Rambla when she's in town. Eight of the rooms are open to guests. Each is different, but all are large and furnished with original antiques, tapestries, and works of art, and some have chandeliers. The palace is arranged on two levels around a cool, ivy-covered patio. ✉ *Plaza del Marqués 1, 23400,* ☎ *953/750196,* 🖷 *953/750267. 8 rooms. Breakfast room. AE, MC, V.*

$ 🏨 **La Paz.** This modern, homey hostel on a busy street in modern Úbeda has simply furnished rooms, each with private bath and telephone. ✉ *Andalucía 1, 23400,* ☎ *953/750848,* 🖷 *953/752140. 51 rooms. Breakfast room . AE, MC, V.*

Shopping

Calle Valencia is Úbeda's crafts center. **Antonio Almazara** (✉ Valencia 34, ☎ 953/751200) is a small ceramics shop specializing in Úbeda's green-glazed pottery. **Paco Tito** (✉ Valencia 22, ☎ 953/751496) is a large pottery workshop run by two generations of the same family; there's a showroom above the studio area. All kinds of ceramics are sold at **Alfarería Góngora** (✉ Merced 32, ☎ 953/754605). For handmade *esparto* grassware, such as rugs, mats, and baskets, hit the sprawling **Ana Ubalde Plaza** (✉ Real 47, ☎ 953/750456), supplied by its own factory in Úbeda.

Cazorla

㉖   *48 km (35 mi) southeast of Úbeda.*

The remote and unspoiled Andalusian village of Cazorla, in the far east of the province of Jaén, is a treat for both young and old. The pine-clad slopes and towering peaks of the Sierras of Cazorla and Segura rise above the village, and below it stretch endless miles of olive groves. In spring, purple Judas trees blossom in picturesque plazas.

🔆   The **Parque Natural de Cazorla** (Cazorla Nature Park) is administered by the environmental agency Agencia de Medio Ambiente (AMA). For information on hiking, camping, canoeing, guided Jeep excursions, or horseback-riding tours, contact the park offices in Cazorla or Jaén or the park visitor center (☞ *below*). **AMA, Cazorla** (✉ Tejares Altos, Cazorla, Jaén, ☎ 953/720125), **AMA, Jaén** (✉ Avda. de Andalucía 79, ☎ 953/215000). For fishing and hunting permits, apply well in advance to **IARA** (Jefatura de Jaén; ✉ Avda. de Madrid 25, Jaén, ☎ 953/221150).

Deer, wild boar, and mountain goats roam the slopes of this carefully protected patch of mountain wilderness 80 km (50 mi) long and 30 km (19 mi) wide, and hawks, eagles, and vultures soar over the 6,000-ft peaks. Within the park, at Canada de las Fuentes, is the source of Andalusia's great river, the Guadalquivir. The road through the park follows the course of the river to the shores of **Lago (Lake) Tranco de Beas.** Alpine meadows, pine forests, springs, and waterfalls make the park a perfect place to hike.

At the **visitor center,** at Torre de Vinagre, a short film introduces you to the park's main sights; displays explain the park's plants and geology; and the staff has information on camping, fishing, and hiking trails. Nearby are a **botanical garden** and a **game reserve.** The park has four well-equipped campsites (open June–October).

Dining and Lodging

$$ ✕🏨 **Parador El Adelantado.** Newly refurbished in 1997, this modern, whitewashed parador with a red-tile roof stands isolated on a pine-

covered mountain slope at the edge of Cazorla Nature Park, 26 km (16 mi) above Cazorla village—a quiet spot, popular with hunters and fishers. The restaurant specializes in regional cooking, such as *ajo blanco* (almond soup with garlic), and game dishes in season. ✉ *Sierra de Cazorla, 23470,* ☎ *953/727075,* 𝔽𝔸𝕏 *953/727077. 33 rooms. Restaurant, pool. AE, DC, MC, V.*

$ ⊞ **Sierra de Cazorla.** A low, white two-story hotel nestles in a bend of the road leading up into the mountains 2 km (1 mi) above Cazorla village, at La Iruela. Rooms in the modern section are functional but comfortable. ✉ *Carretera Sierra de Cazorla, Km 2, La Iruela (Jaén)23476,* ☎ *953/720015,* 𝔽𝔸𝕏 *953/720017. 55 rooms, 2 suites. Restaurant, pool. AE, DC, MC, V.*

CÓRDOBA AND ENVIRONS

The city of Córdoba is home to one of Spain's most spectacular monuments, the Mezquita (mosque), which dates from the 8th through 10th centuries. Wander along the narrow alleys past tiled private patios, poke around the old Jewish Quarter, and visit the only synagogue in Andalusia to survive the expulsion of the Jews in 1492. If you have time to move beyond Córdoba, go west to the ruins of Medina Azahara, the site of a once-magnificent palace complex, or south to the Subbética region, a cluster of small towns virtually unknown to travelers.

Córdoba

㉗ *166 km (103 mi) northwest of Granada, 407 km (250 mi) southwest of Madrid.*

On the south bank of the Guadalquivir stands one of Spain's oldest cities. Córdoba is chilly and small, but it contains some of the most striking cultural monuments in the country. Córdoba was both the Roman and the Moorish capital of Spain, and its Old Quarter, clustered around its famous mosque (Mezquita), remains one of Spain's best examples of its Moorish heritage. The Moorish emirs and caliphs of the West held court here from the 8th to the 11th century, and Córdoba's magnificence and opulence became legendary. Chroniclers of the day put the city's population at around a million, making it the largest city in Europe, though historians believe that the real figure was closer to half a million (just 285,000 residents remain today). Under the Moors Córdoba became one of the Western world's greatest centers of art, culture, and learning; one of its libraries had more than 400,000 volumes. Moors, Christians, and Jews lived together in harmony within its walls.

Córdoba remained in Moorish hands until it was conquered by the Saint King Ferdinand in 1236, after which point the Catholic Monarchs used the city as a base from which to plan the conquest of Granada. In Columbus's time, the Guadalquivir was navigable as far upstream as Córdoba, and great galleons sailed its waters. Today, the muddy water and marshy banks of Andalusia's great river evoke little of Córdoba's glorious past, but the impressive bridge, of Roman origin—though much restored by the Arabs and successive generations—and the old Arab waterwheel are vestiges of a far grander era.

A Good Walk

This walk leads you through Córdoba's historic center. How long it takes depends on how much you wander, but it can make for a whole day.

Córdoba

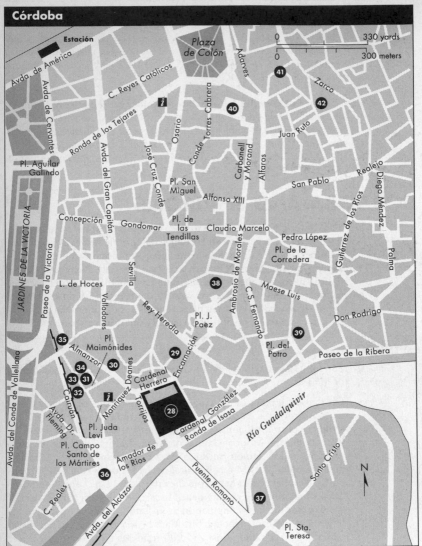

Alcázar de los Reyes
Cristianos, **36**

Callejón de las
Flores, **29**

Judería, **30**

Mezquita, **28**

Museo
Arqueológico, **38**

Museo de Bellas
Artes, **39**

Museo Taurino, **31**

Palacio de los
Marqueses de
Viana, **42**

Plaza de los
Dolores, **40**

Plaza Santa Marina
de las Aguas, **41**

Puerta de
Almodóvar, **35**

Statue of
Maimónides, **32**

Synagogue, **33**

Torre de la
Calahorra, **37**

Zoco, **34**

Begin on Cardenal Herrero at the **Mezquita** ㉘, a truly awesome example of Spanish Muslim architecture. Go up Calle Velázquez Bosco, a narrow alleyway known as **Callejón de las Flores** ㉙, famous for its plethora of ebullient, hanging flower baskets. Come back to Cardenal Herrero, where you can enter the **Judería** ㉚, the old Jewish Quarter. Just around the corner, in the Plaza Maimónides, is the **Museo Taurino** ㉛. Nearby is the Plaza Tiberiades, where the **statue of Maimónides** ㉜, the famous Jewish philosopher, stands. Go up the main street of the Jewish Quarter, Calle Judíos, to find Córdoba's **synagogue** ㉝, the only one in Andalusia to survive the expulsion and inquisition of the Jews in 1492. Across from the synagogue and through an arch you'll enter an inner courtyard called the **Zoco** ㉞, where a former Arab souk hosts flamenco performances on summer evenings. The **Puerta de Almodóvar** ㉟ marks the western limit of the Judería.

Travel down Cairuán to the Plaza Campo Santo de los Mártires to find the **Alcázar de los Reyes Cristianos** ㊱. From Plaza Campo Santo, you have three choices: hire a *coche caballo* (horse and buggy) for a tour of the city—but haggle over the price first (around 4,000 pesetas an hour is enough); wander back to the shops on Deanes and Cardenal Herrero by way of Manríquez and Plaza Juda Levi; or walk back along Amador de los Ríos to the bottom of Torrijos, turn down past the Puerta del Puente (Gate of the Bridge), and cross the **Puente Romano** (Roman Bridge), whose 16 arches span the Guadalquivir. From the bridge you'll have a good view of **La Albolafia,** the huge wheel used to carry water to the gardens of the Alcázar. On the far side of the bridge is the **Torre de la Calahorra** ㊲, now a historical museum.

From whichever option you choose, backtrack to the Mezquita and go up Encarnación to Plaza J. Paez. Pass through the plaza to find the **Museo Arqueológico** ㊳, on the Plaza Jerónimo Paez. Off to the east is the **Museo de Bellas Artes** ㊴. Wind your way southeast from the museum to the Plaza del Potro (Colt Square), named after the Fountain of the Colt, in its center, which is mentioned by Cervantes in *Don Quixote.* Cervantes himself reputedly stayed at the nearby inn, the beautifully restored **Posada del Potro,** now used for displays of local craftwork and painting. The relaxed cafés around the plaza and its fountain are good places for a drink.

Go northwest to the Plaza de la Corredera (some maps call it Plaza Constitución), an intriguing (if sadly dilapidated) arcaded square that dates from around 1690. A market is held here most mornings. To the west of the plaza, along Claudio Marcelo, is Plaza de las Tendillas. Follow Calle Diego Léon from the north side of the Plaza de las Tendillas to the small Plaza San Miguel, whose 13th-century Gothic-Mudéjar church dates from the time of Córdoba's conquest by Saint King Ferdinand. Just north of the Plaza San Miguel is the small, charming **Plaza de los Dolores** ㊵. Around the corner from Dolores is the **Casa de los Fernández de Córdoba,** with a plateresque facade. At the nearby **Plaza Santa Marina de las Aguas** ㊶, on the edge of the **Barrio de los Toreros,** is a statue of the bullfighter Manolete. Southeast of here stands the **Palacio de los Marqueses de Viana** ㊷, an outstanding example of 17th-century residential architecture.

Sights to See

★ ㊱ **Alcázar de los Reyes Cristianos** (Fortress of the Catholic Monarchs). The Alcázar is a Mudéjar-style palace with splendid gardens. (The original Moorish Alcázar stood beside the Mezquita, on the site of the present Bishop's Palace.) It was built by Alfonso XI in 1328, after which the 14th-century Catholic Monarchs held court here and used the palace as a base for their conquest of Granada. Boabdil was imprisoned here for a time in 1483, and for nearly 300 years the Alcázar served as a base for the Inquisition. ✉ *Plaza Campo Santo de los Mártires,* ☎ *957/ 421015.* 🎫 *300 ptas.; free Fri.* ☉ *May–Sept., Tues.–Sat. 10–2 and 6–8, Sun. 9:30–3; Oct.–Apr., Tues.–Sat. 10–2 and 4:30–6:30, Sun. 9:30–3.*

Bodegas San Rafael. Wine lovers should check out the huge wooden wine vats of Bodegas San Rafael, where you can tour through the wine-making process or just buy a bottle right off the company shelf. ✉ *C. R. Sanchez and C. Jesús María, near Plaza Tendillas,* ☎ *957/479324.* ☉ *Oct.–Apr., daily 9–2 and 4–8; May–Sept., daily 8–3.*

㉙ Callejón de las Flores. You'd be hard pressed to find prettier patios than the ones along this street, with their ceramics, lush foliage, and wrought-iron grilles. Patios are very much the key to Córdoba's architecture, at least in the Old Town, where life is lived behind sturdy, outer walls—a legacy of the Moors, who honored both the sanctity of the home and the need to shut out the fierce summer sun. In early May, Córdoba throws a **Patio Festival,** when private patios are filled with flowers and opened to the public.

Córdoba Tourist Office. The tourist office has maps and historical information that will make your tour more enlightening. ✉ *Plaza de Juda Levi s/n,* ☎ *957/200522.* ☉ *Daily 9–2 and 4–8.*

Iglesia San Nicolás de Villa. This classically dark Spanish church, featuring the Mudéjar style of Islamic decoration and art forms, lies at the top of the narrow and colorful Calle San Felipe. Córdoba's well-kept city park, the **Jardínes de la Victoria,** with tiled benches and manicured bushes, lies just a block west of here.

㉚ Judería. The Jewish Quarter is a fascinating labyrinth of narrow streets lined with ancient white houses. It's packed with houses, museums, and monuments that best typify Córdoba's storied past. Alas, the streets around the Mezquita leading up to the Judería have a few too many tourist shops selling the same souvenirs.

NEED A BREAK?   The **Plaza de Juda Levi** is a lively, tree-lined patio great for a snack, particularly an ice cream from the Helados Juda Levi.

★ ㉘ Mezquita (Mosque). Córdoba's mosque, built between the 8th and 10th centuries, is one of the earliest and most breathtakingly beautiful examples of Spanish Muslim architecture. The plain, crenellated walls of the outside do little to prepare you for the sublime beauty of the interior. As you enter through the **Puerta de las Palmas** (Door of the Palms), some 850 columns rise before you in a forest of jasper, marble, granite, and onyx. The pillars are topped by ornate capitals taken from the Visigoth church that was razed to make way for the mosque. Crowning these, an endless array of red-and-white-striped arches curves away into the dim interior. These horseshoe arches in alternating colors are a characteristic feature of Moorish architecture. The ceiling is carved of delicately tinted cedar. The indirect lighting is meant to reproduce the illumination of the mosque as it was in Moorish times.

The Mezquita has served as a Christian cathedral since 1236, but its origins as a mosque are clear. Built in four stages, it was founded in 785 by Abd ar-Rahman I (756–788) on a site he bought from the Visigoth Christians. He pulled down their church and replaced it with a mosque, one-third the size of the present one, into which he incorporated marble pillars from earlier Roman and Visigothic shrines. Under Abd ar-Rahman II (822–852), the Mezquita, which boasted an original copy of the Koran and a bone from the arm of the prophet Mohammed, became a place of Muslim pilgrimage second only to Mecca.

Al Hakam II (961–976) built the beautiful **Mihrab,** the Mezquita's greatest jewel. Make your way over to the **Qiblah,** the south-facing wall in which this sacred prayer niche was hollowed out. (Muslim law decrees that the Mihrab face east, toward Mecca, as it is the point in the mosque toward which worshipers turn to pray. Here, because of an error in calculation, the Mihrab faces more south than east. Al Hakam II spent hours agonizing over a means of correcting such a serious mistake but was persuaded by wise architects to let it be.) In front of the Mihrab is the **Maksoureh,** a kind of anteroom reserved for the caliph and his court; its exquisite mosaics and plasterwork make it a masterpiece of Asian art. The last addition to the mosque as such was completed around 987 by Al Mansur, who more than doubled its size.

After the Reconquest, the Christians left the Mezquita largely undisturbed; they simply dedicated it to the Virgin Mary and set about using it as a place of Christian worship. The clerics did erect a wall closing off the mosque from its courtyard, which helped dim the interior, and thus separate the house of worship from the world outside. In the 13th century, Christians had the **Villaviciosa Chapel** built by Moorish craftsmen, its Mudéjar architecture blending harmoniously with the lines of the mosque. Not so the heavy, incongruous Baroque structure of the **cathedral,** sanctioned in the very heart of the mosque by Charles V in the 1520s. To the emperor's credit, he was supposedly horrified when he came to inspect the new construction, exclaiming to the architects, "To build something ordinary, you have destroyed something that was unique in the world" (though this sentiment didn't stop him from tampering with the Alhambra, to build the Palacio Carlos V, or with Seville's Alcázar).

The **Patio de los Naranjos** (Orange Court), perfumed in springtime by orange blossoms, is a good place to take a break and reflect. The **Puerta del Perdón** (Gate of Forgiveness), along the north wall, serves as the formal entranceway to the mosque. The **Virgen de los Faroles** (Virgin of the Lanterns), a small statue in a niche along the north wall of the mosque, on Cardenal Herrero, stands demurely behind a lantern-hung grille, rather like a lady awaiting a serenade. The painting of the Virgin is by Julio Romero de Torres, an early 20th-century Córdoban artist. The **Torre del Alminar,** the minaret once used to summon the faithful to prayer, has a Baroque belfry. It is now closed to the public. ⊠ *Torrijos and Cardenal Herrero,* ☎ *957/470512.* ⊡ *750 ptas.* ☉ *May–Sept., daily 10–7; Oct.–Apr., daily 10–6.*

㊳ **Museo Arqueológico** (Museum of Archaeology). In the heart of the Old Town (to the north and east of the mosque), this museum displays finds from Córdoba's varied cultural past, including Mudéjar and Renaissance objects. Warning: it's best to avoid exploring this area in the deserted siesta hours, as the narrow streets are prime territory for muggers. Otherwise, the alleys and steps along Altos de Santa Ana make for great wandering. ⊠ *Plaza Jerónimo Paez,* ☎ *957/471076.* ⊡ *250 ptas.* ☉ *June 15–Sept. 15, Tues.–Sat. 10–2 and 6–8, Sun. 10–1:30; Sept. 16–June 14, Tues.–Sat. 10–2 and 5–7, Sun. 10–1:30.*

㊴ **Museo de Bellas Artes** (Museum of Fine Arts). Located in a courtyard just off the Plaza del Potro and faced in deep pink, this museum belongs to a former Hospital de la Caridad (Charity Hospice). It was founded by Ferdinand and Isabella, who twice received Columbus here. The collection includes paintings by Murillo, Valdés Leal, Zurbarán, Goya, and Sorolla. ⊠ *Off Plaza del Potro,* ☎ *957/471314.* ⊡

250 ptas. ⊙ *June 15–Sept. 15, Tues.–Sat. 10–1:30 and 6–8, Sun. 10–1:30; Sept. 16–June 14, Tues.–Sat. 10–1:30 and 5–7, Sun. 10–1:30.*

| NEED A BREAK? | Head for the **Plaza de las Tendillas,** the nexus of modern Córdoba. The outdoor terraces of the **Café Boston** and **Café Siena** are good places to relax with a coffee in warm weather. |

③① Museo Taurino (Museum of Bullfighting). This impressive museum on the Plaza Maimónides (or Plaza de las Bulas) is housed in two adjoining Córdoban mansions. Whatever your thoughts on bullfighting, this museum is worth visiting, as much for the chance to see a restored mansion as for the well-presented posters, Art Nouveau paintings, and memorabilia of famous bullfighters who were native sons of Córdoba. ⊠ *Plaza Maimónides,* ☎ *957/201056.* ☞ *450 ptas.* ⊙ *May–Sept., Tues.–Sat. 9:30–1:30 and 5–8, Sun. 9:30–1; Oct.–Apr., Tues.–Sat. 10–2 and 5–7, Sun. 10–1.*

④② Palacio de los Marqueses de Viana. This 17th-century palace is one of the city's most splendid aristocratic residences. It is known as the Museum of Patios for its 14 patios, each different. Inside are a carriage museum, a library, embossed leather wall hangings, filigree silver, and grand galleries and staircases. The patios and gardens are planted with cypresses, orange trees, and myrtles. ⊠ *Plaza Don Gomé,* ☎ *957/480134.* ☞ *400 ptas.; free Thurs.* ⊙ *June–Sept., Thurs.–Tues. 9–2; Oct.–May, Mon.–Tues. and Thurs.–Sat. 10–1 and 4–6, Sun. 10–2.*

④⓪ Plaza de los Dolores. This small square north of Plaza San Miguel is surrounded by the 17th-century Convento de Capuchinos. It's a secret place, one where you can feel most deeply the city's languid pace. In its center, a statue of **Cristo de los Faroles** (Christ of the Lanterns) stands amid eight lanterns hanging from twisted, wrought-iron brackets.

④① Plaza Santa Marina de las Aguas. At the edge of the **Barrio de los Toreros,** a quarter where many of Córdoba's famous bullfighters were born and lived, stands a statue of the famous bullfighter Manolete. Not far from here, on the Plaza de la Lagunilla, is a bust of Manolete.

③⑤ Puerta de Almodóvar. Outside this old Moorish gate is a **statue of Seneca,** the Córdoban-born philosopher who rose to prominence in Nero's court in Rome and who committed suicide on his emperor's command.

③② Statue of Maimónides. This is a memorial to the famous Jewish philosopher who was born in the Judería in 1135. ⊠ *Plaza de Tiberiades.*

③③ Synagogue. Córdoba's synagogue is the only Jewish temple in Andalusia to survive the expulsion and inquisition of the Jews in 1492 and one of only three ancient synagogues left in Spain (the other two are in Toledo). Though it is no longer in use as a place of worship, it has become a treasured symbol for Spain's modern Jewish communities. The outside is plain, but inside you'll find some exquisite Mudéjar stucco tracery—look for the fine plant motifs and the Hebrew inscription stating that the synagogue was built in 1315. The women's gallery still stands, and in the east wall you can see the arch where the sacred scrolls of the law were kept. ⊠ *C. Judíos,* ☎ *957/202928.* ☞ *50 ptas.* ⊙ *Tues.–Sat. 10–2 and 3:30–5:30, Sun. 10–1:30.*

③⑦ Torre de la Calahorra. The tower on the far side of the Puente Romano (Roman Bridge) was built in 1369 to guard the entrance to Córdoba. It now houses the **Museo Vivo de Al-Andalus** (Museum of Al-Andalus), where films and audiovisual guides (in English) help you learn more of Córdoba's history. The narrative focuses on Córdoba's tricultural past during the time of the Moorish caliphate. Climb the narrow stair case to the top of the tower for the view of the Roman bridge and city on the other side of the Guadalquivir. ⊠ *Avda. de la Confederación,* ☎ 957/293929. ⛃ *Tower 350 ptas., multiscreen show 500 ptas.* ☉ *May–Sept., Mon.–Sat. 10–2 and 5:30–8:30, Sun. 10–2; Oct.–Apr., Mon.–Sat. 10–6, Sun. 10–2.*

㉞ Zoco. This courtyard, near the synagogue, hosts flamenco in summer and local crafts markets throughout the year.

Dining and Lodging

$$$ ✕ El Blasón. Owned by El Caballo Rojo (☞ *below*), this restaurant has earned itself a name for fine food and unbeatable ambience. It's tucked away in an old inn one block west of Avenida Gran Capitán; a Moorish-style entrance bar leads onto a patio enclosed by ivy-covered walls. Upstairs are two elegant dining rooms; blue walls, aquamarine silk curtains, and candelabras evoke early 19th-century luxury. The innovative menu includes *salmón con naranjas de la mezquita* (salmon in oranges from the mosque) and *musclo de oca al vino afrutado* (leg of goose in fruited wine). ⊠ *José Zorrilla 11,* ☎ 957/480625. *AE, DC, MC, V.*

$$$ ✕ El Caballo Rojo. The "Red Horse," on the north side of the mosque,
★ is Córdoba's best restaurant, a winner of the National Gastronomy Prize. The decor resembles a cool, leafy Andalusian patio, and the menu features traditional specialties such as *rabo de toro* (oxtail stew) and *salmorejo* (cold, tomato-based soup), as well as exotic dishes inspired by Córdoba's Moorish and Jewish heritage, such as *alboronía* (a cold salad of stewed vegetables flavored with honey, saffron, and aniseed) or the popular *cordero a la miel* (lamb roasted with honey). ⊠ *Cardenal Herrero 28,* ☎ 957/478001. *AE, DC, MC, V.*

$$ ✕ Casa Pepe de la Judería. This three-floor labyrinth of neat rooms is just around the corner from the mosque, toward the Judería. Flamenco is performed nightly, and during the summer the rooftop opens for a barbecue, serving a full selection of tapas and house specialties such as the *rabo de toro* (oxtail stew). ⊠ *Romero 1, off Deanes,* ☎ *957/200744 or 957/200766. AE, DC, MC, V.*

$$ ✕ El Churrasco. A longstanding Córdoban institution that ranks sec-
★ ond only to El Caballo Rojo (☞ *above*), El Churrasco is in the heart of the Judería, just two minutes' walk from the mosque. The colorful bar is an ideal place for prelunch tapas, and the on-site wine museum and *bodega* specialize in the restaurant's own Montilla-Morilés wine. The kitchen is known for succulent grilled meats, such as *churrasco* (pork in pepper sauce), and an excellent *salmorejo*. ⊠ *Romero 16,* ☎ *957/290819. AE, DC, MC, V. Closed Aug.*

$$ ✕ La Almudaina. This attractive restaurant is in a 15th-century house across the square from the Alcázar gardens, at the entrance to the Judería. The cellar hides an Andalusian patio and a *mesón bodega* (wine cellar). The menu concentrates on fresh market produce and local recipes. You might try pudding *de calabacines* (pumpkin mousse), *lubina al hinojo* (sea bass in fennel), or *jabalí en salsa de romero* (wild boar in rosemary sauce). ⊠ *Campo Santo de los Mártires 1,* ☎ *957/ 474342. AE, DC, MC, V. Closed Sun. in summer. No dinner Sun.*

$ ✕ Federación de Peñas Cordobesa. You'll find this popular budget restaurant on one of the main thoroughfares of the Old Town, halfway between the mosque and the Plaza Tendillas. You can eat inside or at one of several tables around the fountain in the spacious courtyard, surrounded by horseshoe arches. The food is traditional Spanish fare. ⊠ *Conde y Luque 8,* ☎ 957/476698. *MC, V. Closed Wed.*

$ ✕ Mesón El Burladero. This one's off a small patio at the end of an alley near the back entrance to El Caballo Rojo (☞ *above*). There are a few tables outside on the patio; indoors, you'll dine among bullfight posters and an eclectic array of wildlife on the whitewashed walls: stags' heads, stuffed birds, and a boar's head. The *menú Manolete* offers *revuelto de la casa* (scrambled eggs) and *solomillo de cerdo* (pork steak), with bread, wine, and dessert included. ⊠ *Calleja la Hoguera 5, off Deanes*, ☎ *957/472719. AE, DC, MC, V.*

$$$–$$$$ 🏨 **Conquistador.** East of the mosque, this contemporary hotel is built in Andalusian-Moorish style, making good use of ceramic tiles and inlaid marquetry in the bar and public rooms. The reception area overlooks a colonnaded patio, fountain, and small enclosed garden. The rooms are comfortable and elegant; those at the front have small balconies overlooking the walls of the mosque, which are floodlit at night. ⊠ *Magistral González Francés 17, 14003*, ☎ *957/481102 or 957/481411*, 🕿 *957/474677. 100 rooms, 3 suites. Bar, sauna. AE, DC, MC, V.*

$$$ 🏨 **Amistad Córdoba.** This hotel is built around two former 18th-century mansions that looked out upon the Plaza de Maimónides in the heart of the Judería. It features a Mudéjar courtyard (a combination of Islamic and Christian styles), carved-wood ceilings, and a plush lounge area. The rooms are large and comfortable. ⊠ *Plaza de Maimónides 3*, ☎ *957/420335*, 🕿 *957/420365. 69 rooms. Restaurant, bar. AE, DC, MC, V.*

$$$ 🏨 **Parador La Arruzafa.** Five kilometers (3 miles) north of town, this modern parador is set in a peaceful, leafy garden on the slopes of the Sierra de Córdoba. Rooms are traditional, with dark-wood fittings, and many have balconies overlooking the garden or featuring good views toward Córdoba. ⊠ *Avda. de la Arruzafa, 14012*, ☎ *957/275900*, 🕿 *957/280409. 89 rooms, 5 suites. Pool, tennis courts. AE, DC, MC, V.*

$$–$$$ 🏨 **El Califa.** This modern hotel in the Old Town is convenient to both the mosque and the shopping area around Plaza Tendillas. The rooms are fairly spacious and have tile floors. The patio has red and white flagstones and Moorish-style arches. Snacks are served outdoors among the geraniums in summer. ⊠ *Lope de Hoces 14, 14003*, ☎ *957/ 299400. 64 rooms, 2 suites. Bar, cafeteria. AE, MC, V.*

$$ 🏨 **Albucasis.** Tucked away in the heart of the Old Town is the friendly, family-run Albucasis. Its air-conditioned rooms are spotlessly clean, with marble-tile floors, white and green decor, and green-tile bathrooms. Doubles overlook the pretty, ivy-covered patio and have a limited view of the Torre del Alminar. Breakfast and drinks are served in the attractive reception area. ⊠ *Buen Pastor 11, 14003*, ☎ 🕿 *957/478625. 15 rooms. Bar. MC, V.*

$$ 🏨 **González.** This hotel occupies a restored 16th-century palace in the heart of the Judería. The entrance hall, with a white-marble floor and a massive, 18th-century brass lamp, opens off the Plaza Juda Levi. Rooms are simply but comfortably furnished, with tile floors, white walls, twin beds, and air-conditioning. The quietest rooms have black, wrought-iron balconies heaped with flowerpots and overlook the fountain in the central patio. Some readers have noted security problems; think twice about leaving valuables in the hotel safe. ⊠ *Manríquez 3, 14003*, ☎ *957/479819*, 🕿 *957/486187. 16 rooms. Restaurant. MC, V.*

$–$$ 🏨 **Marisa.** The Marisa's facade is an old Andalusian house overlooking the north side of the mosque and the Patio de los Naranjos. Inside, the hotel has been modernized, and the rooms are simple and sparsely furnished. Those in front face the mosque, magnificent when floodlit. (Ask for an inside room if you want to avoid street noise.) Note that not all rooms have baths or showers. Breakfast and drinks are served in the bar area. The staff is friendly and helpful. ⊠ *Cardenal Herrero 6, 14003*, ☎ *957/473142*, 🕿 *957/474144. 28 rooms. AE, DC, MC, V.*

Nightlife and the Arts

Orchestral concerts are performed in the Alcázar's garden on Sundays
in summer. Concerts, ballets, and plays are also performed in the **Gran
Teatro** (⊠ Avda. del Gran Capitán, ☎ 957/480644). In July, the International Guitar Festival attracts top Spanish and international guitarists for over two weeks of great music in July. **Flamenco** is performed
in the Zoco, off Calle Judíos, on summer evenings.One of Córdoba's
favorite flamenco clubs is **Mesón la Bulería** (⊠ Pedro López 3, ☎ 957/
483839), open fall–spring.

Outdoor Activities and Sports

BICYCLING

You can rent bikes by the hour or day at **Quicksilver** (⊠ C. Céspedes
12, near mosque, no phone).

HORSEBACK RIDING

The **Club Hípico (Riding Club)** is at Km 3 on the Carretera de Trassierra.
(☎ 957/271628).

Shopping

The main shopping district is around Avenida Gran Capitán, Ronda
de los Tejares, and Plaza de Colón. **Artesanía Andaluza** (⊠ Tomás
Conde 3), near the Museum of Bullfighting, sells a wide range of
Córdoban handicrafts, including fine embossed leather (a legacy of the
Moors) and filigree silver (from the mines of the Sierra Morena) jewelry. The **Association of Córdoban Artisans** (⊠ C. Judíos opposite synagogue) sells craft wares in the Zoco (many stalls are open
May–September only). **Meryan** (⊠ Callejón de las Flores 2, ☎ 957/
475902) is one of Córdoba's best embossed-leather workshops.

Medina Azahara

43 *8 km (5 mi) west of Córdoba on the C431.*

The ruins and partial reconstruction of the fabulous Muslim palace Medina Azahara are well worth a visit. Begun in 936, Medina Azahara was
built by Abd ar-Rahman III for his favorite concubine, az-Zahra. According to contemporary chroniclers, it took 10,000 men, 2,600 mules,
and 400 camels 25 years to erect this fantasy of 4,300 columns in dazzling pink, green, and white marble and jasper brought from Carthage.
Here, on three terraces, stood a palace, a mosque, luxurious baths, fragrant gardens, fish ponds, even an aviary and a zoo. In 1013 the place
was sacked and destroyed by Berber mercenaries. In 1944 the Royal
Apartments were rediscovered, and there followed a careful reconstruction of the Throne Room; the outline of the mosque has also been
excavated. ⊠ *Off C431; follow signs on way to Almodóvar del Río,*
☎ *957/329130.* 🔲 *250 ptas.* ☉ *May–Sept., Tues.–Sat. 10–2 and 6–
8:30, Sun. 10–2; Oct.–Apr., Tues.–Sat. 10–2 and 4–6:30, Sun. 10–?.*

OFF THE   **ALMODÓVAR DEL RÍO** – If you're driving, continue to Almodóvar del Río,
BEATEN PATH   a further 18 km (11 mi) along C431, where just beyond the town a restored castle towers dramatically over the countryside.

La Subbética

44 *Priego de Córdoba is 103 km (64 mi) southeast of Córdoba.*

In the southeastern corner of Córdoba's province lies a relatively undiscovered cluster of villages and small towns known to locals as the Subbética, and protected as a nature park. For hiking or general information,
contact the **Mancomunidad de la Subbética** (⊠ C. Pilarejo, Carcabuey,
☎ 957/704106) or **Iniciativas Subbéticas** (☎ 957/694545).You'll need

a car to explore this area, and in places you'll find the roads bumpy and rather rough.

Just inside the southern tip of the province, southeast of Lucena, C334 crosses the **Embalse de Iznájar** (reservoir of Iznájar) amid spectacular scenery. Halfway between Lucena and the reservoir on the C334, in **Rute,** you can sample the potent *anís* liqueur for which this small, white town is famous. In **Lucena** you can see the Torre del Moral, where Boabdil was imprisoned in 1483 after launching an unsuccessful attack on the Christians. Today the town makes furniture and brass and copper pots.

The jewel of this area is **Priego de Córdoba,** a town of 14,000 lying at the foot of Mt. Tinosa (from Lucena, head north 9 km [5½ mi] on the C327 to Cabra, where you'll turn right, or east, on the C336; after 32 km [20 mi], you'll reach Priego). Wander down Calle del Río opposite the Ayuntamiento to see fine 18th-century mansions, once the homes of silk merchants. At the end of the street is the Fuente del Rey (Kings' Fountain), with some 130 water jets, built in 1803. Don't miss the lavish Baroque churches of La Asunción and La Aurora, or the Barrio de la Villa, an old Moorish quarter.

Baena, surrounded by chalk fields producing top-quality olive oil, is an old town of narrow white streets, ancient mansions, and churches clustered beneath Moorish battlements. **Zuheros,** at the northern edge of the Subbética, is a jewel of a mountain village. In the rocky mountainface that towers over the town is the **Cueva de los Murciélagos** (Cave of the Bats), which you can explore by appointment (☎ 957/69545). **Castro del Río** has an old Roman bridge; the unfortunate Cervantes was jailed in the town hall here in 1592. At **Espejo,** a majestic castle towers over the countryside. You're now in the Montilla-Moriles vineyards of the Córdoban campiña; every fall, 47,000 acres' worth of Pedro Ximénez grapes are crushed here to produce the region's rich Montillas, fortified wines not unlike sherry. You can visit the *bodegas.*

Dining and Lodging

$$ ⌑ **Villa Turística de Priego.** Near the hamlet of Zagrilla, 6 km (4 mi) from Priego de Córdoba, this gleaming-white holiday complex is in the heart of the Subbética nature park. Each self-catered unit has a kitchenette.✉ *Aldea de Zagrilla, 14816,* ☎ *957/703503,* FAX *957/703573. 52 units. Restaurant, pool. AE, DC, MC, V.*

$ ⌑ **Zuhayra.** This simple but comfortable hotel on a narrow street in picturesque Zuheros makes a good base for exploring the Subbética. ✉ *C. Mirador 10, Zuheros,* ☎ *957/694693,* FAX *957/694702. 18 rooms. Restaurant. AE, DC, MC, V.*

EASTERN ANDALUSIA A TO Z

Arriving and Departing

By Bus

If you're not driving, buses are the best method of transportation in this region. They run to most of the outlying towns and villages, and their connections between major cities are generally faster and more frequent than by train (☞ By Train, *below*). If you're taking public transportation to the villages of the Alpujarras, check bus schedules and accommodations carefully with Granada's tourist office and the Alsina Gräells bus company before you set off.

Buses connect several Spanish cities and **Córdoba.** For bus information, go either to the main tourist office (✉ Torrijos 10) or to the following bus companies: **Alsina Gräells** (⊠ Avda. Medina Azahara 29, ☎ 957/236474) for services to Badajoz, Cádiz, Granada, Seville, and Málaga; **Ureña** (⊠ Avda. Cervantes 22, ☎ 957/472352) for Seville and Jaén; **Priego** (⊠ Paseo de la Victoria 29, ☎ 957/290158 or 957/ 290769) for Madrid (via N IV), Barcelona, and Valencia; **Secorbus** (⊠ Camino de los Sastres 1, Avda. República Argentina, across from Hotel Meliá, ☎ 957/468040) for Madrid and Andújar; and **López** (⊠ Paseo de la Victoria 15, ☎ 957/477551 or 957/474592) for Ciudad Real and Madrid (via Ciudad Real). **Ramírez** (⊠ Avda. de la República Argentina 26, ☎ 957/410100) serves small towns near Córdoba.

Granada's bus station is on the highway to Jaén. The main bus company, **Alsina Gräells** (☎ 958/185010), serves Madrid, Algeciras, Málaga, Córdoba, Seville, Jaén, Motril, and Almería.

By Car
Be prepared for parking problems in the cities of Granada and Córdoba, and, particularly in Granada, for the ever-present threat of break-ins. Most of Córdoba's hotels are located in a labyrinth of narrow streets that can be a nightmare to negotiate, even with a small car. In Córdoba, all sights are within walking distance of one another; in Granada, it's simpler to take a taxi up to the Alhambra or the Albaicín than to negotiate the extremely complicated one-way system and narrow Moorish streets in a rental car.

If you do decide to drive, the route from Granada to Jaén, Baeza, Úbeda, and Cazorla is one of Andalusia's less tourist-packed, though between Granada and Jaén you'll probably encounter the odd tour bus. Still, the roads are smooth, and driving through this region is one of the most pleasant ways to see the countryside.

By Plane
Granada Airport (☎ 958/245200) is 18 km (11 mi) west of Granada. Aviaco has daily flights to and from Madrid and Barcelona and three flights weekly to Valencia.

BETWEEN THE AIRPORT AND DOWNTOWN
J. González buses (☎ 958/131309) run between the airport and city center, leaving Plaza Isabel la Católica about 1¼ hours (less often in winter) before flight departures. Times are listed at the bus stop.

By Train
Services from Córdoba to Granada are poor. There is no train service between Granada and Jaén or between Jaén and Córdoba. Both Córdoba and Jaén have trains to Linares-Baeza, but from there you must take a bus into Baeza or Úbeda.

Contacts and Resources

Car Rental
In Granada: **Autos Fortuna,** (⊠ Camino de Purchil 2, at Camino Ronda, ☎ 958/260254).

Emergencies
Police, emergency telephones: Policía Nacional (☎ 091); Policía Municipal (☎ 092).

Guided Tours
Pullmantur and **Juliá Tours** (☞ Bus Travel *in* the Gold Guide) run numerous tours to this region, which you can book through most travel agents, many hotels, or through the Madrid (☞ Chapter 2) or Costa del Sol (☞ Chapter 11) offices. **Córdoba Vision** offers daytime and nighttime tours, among them trips to Medina Azahara (⊠ Escritor Conde Zamora, ☎ 957/299577, ℻ 957/299968).

Al Andalus is a vintage luxury train (with cars from the 1920s) that makes a weekly trip in season from Madrid to Aranjuez, Úbeda, Córdoba, Seville, Jerez, Málaga, and Granada. For reservations and information contact **Abercrombie & Kent** or **DER** (☞ Tour Operators *in* the Gold Guide).

Horseback-riding tours—some with English guides—are offered in the villages of the Alpujarras and the Sierra Nevada and sometimes elsewhere. Contact tourist offices for information; one agency in the Alpujarras is **Cabalgar** (✉ Bubión, Granada, ☎ 958/763135, FAX 958/763136).

In the **Cazorla Nature Park,** four-wheel-drive or horseback excursions and more specific nature tours, such as bird-watching, can be arranged through Quercus (☎ 953/720115).

WALKING TOURS

In Córdoba, English-speaking guides for the mosque and synagogue can be arranged through the **Asociación Profesional de Informadores Turísticos** (✉ Museo Diocesano, Torrijos 12, Córdoba, ☎ 957486997). In Granada, contact a multilingual guide through the **Asociación Provincial de Guías** (✉ Puerta del Vino, La Alhambra, Granada, ☎ 958/229936). In Jaén and Úbeda, ask at the tourist office.

Visitor Information

The main tourist office for the region is in **Granada** (✉ Plaza Mariana Pineda 10, ☎ 958/225990), with information on both the province and the city. There's a much smaller regional office in **Córdoba** (✉ Plaza de Juda Levi, ☎ 957/200522, FAX 957/200277).

13 Seville and Western Andalusia

The flat expanse of fertile pastures, muddy marshlands, chalky vineyards, and sandy beaches in western Andalusia contrasts vividly with the mountainous provinces to the east. Enjoy the history and romance of Seville, trace the career of Christopher Columbus, sample the famous sherries of Jerez, and visit the region's famous tapas bars.

By Hilary
Bunce

Updated by
Mark Little

WITHIN THE TRIANGLE formed by the cities of Huelva, Seville, and Cádiz lies the estuary of Andalusia's great river, the Guadalquivir. Here the riverbanks are lined with cotton and rice fields, orange groves, stud farms, and bull ranches.

This is a land with a proud seafaring history. History buffs can follow the footsteps of Christopher Columbus from the monastery at La Rábida, whose friars pleaded his cause with Queen Isabella, to Palos, where he set sail on his epic voyage of 1492, and finally to Seville, where he is believed to be buried. The province's shores and rivers echo with the names of other maritime adventurers as well: Ferdinand Magellan, Juan Sebastián de Elcano, Sir Francis Drake, and Pierre de Villeneuve, to name just a few. Spain's trade with the New World centered on Seville for more than 200 years, and treasures from the Americas flowed into her coffers. Later, when this maritime and trading role passed to Cádiz, New World riches funded that city's most impressive buildings.

Many towns of this region are named "de la frontera," including Arcos, Jerez, and Palos, because for 250 years they stood on the frontier between Christian Spain and Muslim Granada.

Pleasures and Pastimes

Bullfighting

Seville is the home of one of Spain's leading bullrings, the Maestranza—few *toreros* (bullfighters) gain nationwide recognition until they have fought in this "cathedral of bullfighting." The season runs from Easter until late October, peaking early on, when Spain's leading *toreros* fight every day during the city's April Fair.

Dining

Western Andalusia is well known in Spain as a gourmand's paradise. Many Spaniards drive for miles to sample the giant shrimp and succulent seafood of Puerto de Santa María or Sanlúcar de Barrameda and to enjoy *fino* (a dry and light sherry) and *manzanilla* (a dry and delicate sherry with a hint of saltiness) from the vineyards of Jerez. Others come just to have tapas in Seville.

The restaurants we suggest in Seville are within walking distance of the center of town. Many restaurants are closed on Sunday evening, and several close for a month's vacation in August.

Restaurants in the $$$ and $$$$ categories tend to be more formal in winter than in summer. Here, jacket and tie are advisable but rarely essential, especially in hot weather. Formal dress is usually required only in restaurants at five-star hotels.

CATEGORY	COST*
$$$$	over 5,000 ptas.
$$$	3,500–5,000 ptas.
$$	2,500–3,500 ptas.
$	under 2,500 ptas.

per person for a three-course meal, excluding drinks, tax, and service

Fiestas

The fame of this region's fiestas has spread far beyond the borders of Spain. Visitors come from far and away to witness the pageant of Seville's Holy Week processions and to join in the fun of its April Fair. Cádiz's carnival is one of the best in the land. Crowds also flock to the revelries of Jerez's May Horse Fair and September Harvest Festival. If you prefer traveling without crowds, be sure to avoid these events.

FEBRUARY
Cádiz celebrates the weeklong Carnival.

MARCH–APRIL
Seville's Semana Santa (Holy Week) processions (March 28–April 4 in 1999) are the most famous in Spain. Jerez and Cádiz also have Semana Santa processions. The Feria de Abril, Seville's annual city fair, is celebrated with top bullfights; horse parades; flamenco costumes; and singing, dancing, and fireworks nightly in the fairground across the river.

MAY
Jerez de la Frontera shows off its Andalusian horses in its Feria del Caballo (Horse Fair).

MAY OR JUNE
Worshipers make the famous Whitsuntide pilgrimage to the shrine of the Virgen del Rocío (Virgin of the Dew) in the village of El Rocío (Huelva). Corpus Christi (the second Thursday after Whitsun) is celebrated with processions in Cádiz, Jerez, and Seville.

AUGUST
The Assumption of the Virgin Mary is celebrated everywhere on the 15th but especially in Seville, where it's the day of the city's patroness, the Virgen de los Reyes (Virgin of the Kings).

SEPTEMBER
All of the wine-producing towns in Cádiz province celebrate the Fiesta de la Vendimia (Grape Harvest Festival). Jerez's Fiesta de Otoño (Autumn Festival) is particularly spectacular.

OCTOBER
Cádiz commemorates its patroness, the Virgen del Rosario (Virgin of the Rosary).

Flamenco

Seville and Jerez are widely acknowledged as Spain's flamenco headquarters, and Jerez now has an institute dedicated to the history of this quintessentially Andalusian art form. In Seville, you can experience the emotion and excitement of flamenco firsthand at some of the finest clubs in Spain (☞ Nightlife and the Arts *in* Seville, *below*).

Horses

Jerez's purebred Carthusian horses are shown off in the annual Feria del Caballo (☞ *above*), in May. These handsome animals also perform every Thursday throughout the year at the Royal Andalusian School of Equestrian Art (☞ Jerez de la Frontera, *below*). Horse races are held on the beach in Sanlúcar de Barrameda on the second and fourth weekends of August, a tradition dating back to 1845 (☞ Sanlúcar de Barrameda, *below*).

Lodging

Western Andalusia has many fine hotels. You'll find four paradors, including converted ancient palaces at Carmona and Arcos de la Frontera; both of these have great views and are worth a special visit. The parador at Mazagón (Huelva) and the parador Atlántico, in Cádiz, are comfortable, modern hotels. You can also stay at a converted monastery (in Puerto de Santa María) or on a private luxury ranch (near Arcos de la Frontera). Seville has grand old hotels like the famous Alfonso XIII and the Colón, both newly renovated, and two former palaces recently converted into sumptuous hostelries. Another fantastic hotel, one of the best in Spain, is the Casa de Carmona, in tiny Carmona, outside Seville.

If you plan to be here during famous festivals, such as Seville's Holy Week or April Fair or Jerez's Horse Fair or Harvest Festival, you *must* book early—four to eight months in advance in Seville. If you want to visit Cádiz during its February Carnival, it's wise to book at least a month or so in advance. All hotel prices in Seville rise steeply, by at least half as much, during Holy Week and the April Fair.

It is possible to sleep cheaply in Seville, but the rooms will be tiny, and you'll have to scour areas far from the city center. Prices fluctuate dramatically with the seasons—much more so than in most other parts of Spain—so you'd be wise to check ahead.

CATEGORY	COST*
$$$$	over 20,000 ptas.
$$$	11,500–20,000 ptas.
$$	8,000–11,500 ptas.
$	under 8,000 ptas.

All prices are for a standard double room, excluding tax.

Exploring Seville and Western Andalusia

This region covers the provinces of Seville and Cádiz and part of Huelva. For touring purposes, it can be divided into three parts, starting with the busy city of Seville. From there, you can go on to visit the Doñana National Park and the villages that played important roles in the voyage of Christopher Columbus. Finally, head for Jerez de la Frontera to taste the sherry, relax in the whitewashed village of Arcos de la Frontera, and feast on seafood in Cádiz.

Numbers in the text correspond to numbers in the margin and on the Western Andalusia: Seville and the Guadalquivir Delta and Seville maps.

Great Itineraries

A week in this region is ideal; it allows time to explore the various landscapes. If time is short, however, a few days will be enough time for sunny Seville to make a lasting impression. Depending on your interests, you may choose to head south and trace the history of the ancient city and province of Cádiz, where you can savor the famous sherry from the *bodegas* in Jerez; or venture farther west to the province of Huelva, where you can take in one of Europe's finest wildlife reserves, Doñana National Park. Your mode of transport will also help determine your itinerary; although the major cities and towns are accessible by train and bus, driving will give you the freedom to explore some smaller, often charming *pueblos*.

IF YOU HAVE 3 DAYS

Base yourself in ⊞ **Seville** ①–㉚. On your first day, visit the cathedral and the Giralda, along with the nearby Moorish-style Alcázar. Later, wander the orange-scented streets of the Barrio de Santa Cruz. On the second day, enjoy the Parque de María Luisa and the colorful Plaza de América. Before leaving the city, stop at the monumental Plaza de España, and head over to the Torre de Oro before enjoying the lively Calle Betis and its many tapas bars. On your final day, visit the ancient town of **Carmona** ㉛, with its Roman necropolis; then head to the Roman ruins at **Itálica** ㉜ before returning to Seville.

IF YOU HAVE 5 DAYS

Follow this tour if you have more time to venture out beyond ⊞ **Seville** ①–㉚. Begin in the city: start with the cathedral and Giralda and spend some time in the Moorish-style Alcázar. Then relax and enjoy a walk through the narrow lanes of the Barrio de Santa Cruz. The ne

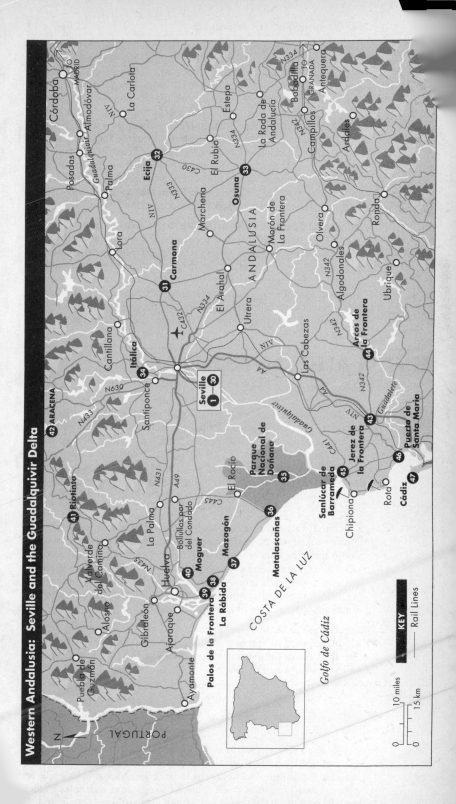

Western Andalusia: Seville and the Guadalquivir Delta

day, take in the impressive collection of art in the Museo de Bellas Artes (Museum of Fine Arts); then head toward the river and walk the Paseo de Colón, where you can see the Maestranza Bullring and visit the Torre de Oro. On your third day, take a walk in the Parque de María Luisa and stop at the Plaza de América and the monumental Plaza de España. On your way back to the center of town, watch for the University of Seville, the former tobacco factory of *Carmen* fame. Next, on day four, head for ☷ **Jerez de la Frontera** ㊸, famous for its sherry. Tour one of the local *bodegas* and taste the world's finest sherry; and if this day falls on a Thursday, watch the spectacular horse show at Jerez's Royal Andalusian School of Equestrian Art. Spend your final night in the small port town of ☷ **Puerto de Santa María** ㊻. On your last day, visit the ancient town of **Cádiz** ㊼ before returning to Seville.

When to Tour Seville and Western Andalusia

If you want to experience the excitement of Spanish fiestas, this is the place to come—just reserve a room far in advance. Aside from the big fiestas, spring and late fall are particularly nice, when the weather is warm but not unpleasantly hot. Winters are mild and uncrowded. If you plan to visit Jerez de la Frontera, try to be there on a Thursday so you can watch the impressive horse show at the Royal Andalusian School of Equestrian Art. Keep in mind that many museums and monuments are closed on Monday.

SEVILLE AND ENVIRONS

Lying on the banks of the Guadalquivir, Seville is Spain's fourth-largest city and the capital of Andalusia. Its whitewashed houses bright with bougainvillea, its ocher-color palaces, and its Baroque facades have long enchanted both *sevillanos* (Sevillians) and travelers. The city's many urban attractions include an opera house, a new riverfront esplanade, an exceptional Museum of Fine Arts, and several dozen other monuments. Seville also benefits from modernized transport, including new train and bus stations, an enlarged and updated airport, new highways in and around the city, seven new bridges, and high-speed rail and four-lane highway links with Madrid.

Of course, this bustling city of almost 800,000 also has a downside: traffic-choked streets, high unemployment, a notorious petty-crime rate, and at times the kind of impersonal treatment you won't find in smaller cities like Granada and Córdoba. But Seville's artistic heritage and its citizens' zest for life more than compensate for its disadvantages. Be warned, however, that hours for the city's monuments and other institutions have a habit of changing almost monthly.

If you want to venture out of Seville on a very quick day trip, head to Carmona, with its stunning Roman necropolis and terrific hotels (either the Casa de Carmona or the parador is perfect for a leisurely lunch), or the ancient town of Itálica.

Seville

❶ *550 km (340 mi) southwest of Madrid, 220 km (140 mi) northwest of Málaga.*

Seville has a long and noble history. Conquered by the Romans in 205 BC, it gave the world two great emperors, Trajan and Hadrian (you can see Hadrian's birthplace at nearby Itálica). The Moors held Seville for more than 500 years and left it one of the greatest examples of the art, the well-loved Giralda tower. Saint King Ferdinand (Ferdinand lies enshrined in glory in the cathedral, one of Seville's greatest m

uments; his rather less saintly descendant, Pedro the Cruel, builde
the splendid Alcázar, is buried here as well.

Seville is justly proud of its literary and artistic associations. Th
painters Diego Rodríguez de Silva Velázquez (1599–1660) and Bartolomé Estéban Murillo (1617–82) were natives of Seville, as were the
poets Gustavo Adolfo Bécquer (1836–70), Antonio Machado (1875–
1939), and Nobel Prize winner Vicente Aleixandre (1898–1984). The
tale of the ingenious knight of La Mancha was begun in a Seville jail,
for Don Quixote's creator, Miguel de Cervantes, twice languished in
a debtors' prison here. Tirso de Molina's character Don Juan carried
on his amorous pursuits in Seville's mansions, later scheming as Don
Giovanni in the Barrio de Santa Cruz. The Barrio was also the setting
for the nuptials of Rossini's barber, Figaro. Nearby, at the old tobacco
factory (now the University of Seville), Bizet's sultry Carmen first met
Don José.

Seville's vivacity and color are most intense during Holy Week, when
lacerated Christs and bejeweled, weeping Virgins from the city's 24
parishes are paraded through the streets on floats borne by barefoot
penitents.

Two weeks later, and this time in flamenco costume, the *sevillanos* celebrate the Feria de Abril (April Fair), the greatest party of the year. This
celebration began as a horse-trading fair, in 1847, and still recalls its
equine origins with midday horse parades featuring men in broad-
brimmed hats and Andalusian riding gear astride prancing steeds, their
women in long, ruffled dresses riding sidesaddle behind them. Bullfights,
fireworks, and all-night singing and dancing in the fairground's *case-
tas* (tents) complete the spectacle.

A Good Walk

Start at the **cathedral** ②, in the Plaza Virgen de los Reyes; then climb
the Giralda, the minaret of the former Moorish mosque. From the top
you can savor a tremendous view over the city. Walk down Avenida
de la Constitución and visit the **Archivo de Indias** ③, in which are the
surviving documents related to the discovery of the New World. Next
door to the archive is the **Museo de Arte Contemporáneo** ④, housed
in a converted mansion, and next to that is the **Alcázar** ⑤, a palace surrounded by high walls, in the typical Moorish style. Backtrack to the
Giralda and the Plaza Virgen de los Reyes, and from there plunge into
the **Barrio de Santa Cruz** ⑥, formerly the district of the Jews. Among its
shady lanes you'll come upon whitewashed buildings, courtyards, and
plenty of flowers. While in the neighborhood, don't miss the **Hospital
de los Venerables** ⑦. On Calle Santa Teresa is the **Casa de Murillo** ⑧,
named for one of Seville's most well-known painters. From there you
can stroll through the **Jardines de Murillo** ⑨, with a statue of Christopher Columbus. At the far end of the gardens is the **University of
Seville** ⑩, once the tobacco factory where the mythical Carmen worked
as a cigar roller. Across the Glorieta de San Diego is the **Parque de María
Luisa** ⑪; at the south end of the park is the **Plaza de América** ⑫; and
at the east end is the **Plaza de España** ⑬, a structure of buildings by
architect Hannibal González. Before leaving the park, visit the **Museo
Arqueológico** ⑭, with marble statues and mosaics from the Roman era.
Opposite is the **Museo de Artes y Costumbres Populares** ⑮.

Head back north along the Paseo de las Delicias toward the old city
center. Near downtown Seville, on Avenida de Roma, stands the
Baroque **Palacio de San Telmo** ⑯, home of the Andalusian regional government. Behind the Palacio is the Mudéjar-style **Hotel Alfonso XIII** ⑰.
On the north side of Puerta de Jerez is **Palacio de Yanduri** ⑱, where
the Nobel Prize–winning Vicente Aleixandre was born.

Walking toward the Guadalquivir River along Calle Almirante Lobo, you'll arrive at the **Torre de Oro** ⑲, which stands on the banks of the river opposite the **Teatro de la Maestranza** ⑳. Behind the theater is the **Hospital de la Caridad** ㉑, with a collection of works by Seville's leading painters. Continuing north along the river, you'll reach the **Plaza de Toros Real Maestranza** ㉒, arguably the most beautiful bullring in Spain.

Now head away from the river toward the Plaza Nueva, in the heart of Seville. Here stands the **ayuntamiento** ㉓. Walk down Calle Sierpes until you reach Plaza del Salvador and the **Iglesia del Salvador** ㉔, a former mosque. A five-minute walk from here, up the narrow Calles del Rosario, Alfalfa, and Aguilas, is the **Casa de Pilatos** ㉕, believed to be modeled on Pilate's house in Jerusalem. If you have the time and energy, explore the sights in northern Seville's Macarena district (if not, head back toward the river and visit the Museo de Bellas Artes, below): first, stop into the Gothic **Convento de Santa Paula** ㉖. From there it's a short walk to the **Basílica de la Macarena** ㉗, where you'll find Seville's most revered image, the Virgen de la Macarena. Walking back south, stop at the church of **San Lorenzo y Jesús del Gran Poder** ㉘ and see the interesting floats used in Seville's Holy Week processions. Continuing south down Cardenal Spinola and San Juan de Ávila, you'll reach Calle Alfonso XII and the **Museo de Bellas Artes** ㉙, with a fine collection of paintings by Zurbarán and El Greco, among others. Your last stop can be **La Cartuja Island** ㉚, with a Carthusian monastery, gardens, and the Isla Mágica theme park.

TIMING

This walk covers about 8 km (5 mi) and is a good six-hour outing. If you end your tour in the Barrio de Santa Cruz, you'll have about a 2-km (1-mi) trek.

Sights to See

★ ❺   **Alcázar** (Reales Alcázares). On the Plaza Triunfo is the entrance to the Mudéjar palace built by Pedro I (1350–69), on the site of the former Moorish *alcázar* (fortress). Don't mistake the Alcázar for a genuine Moorish palace, like Granada's Alhambra—it may look like one and was indeed designed and built by Moorish workers brought in from Granada, but it was commissioned and paid for by a Christian king more than 100 years after the Reconquest of Seville. In its construction, Pedro the Cruel incorporated stones and capitals he pillaged from elsewhere: from Valencia, from Córdoba's Medina Azahara, and from Seville itself. The Alcázar is the finest example of Mudéjar architecture in Spain today, though its purity of style has been much diluted by the alterations and additions of successive Spanish rulers. Today the Alcázar is the official residence in Seville of the king and queen of Spain.

You enter the Alcázar through the Puerta del León and the high, fortified walls of genuine Moorish origin, which belie the exquisite delicacy of the interior. Cross the **Patio de la Montería** to Pedro's Mudéjar palace, arranged around the beautiful **Patio de las Doncellas** (Court of the Damsels), resplendent with the most delicate stucco. Its name probably refers to the annual gift of 100 virgins to the Moorish sultans. Although its Granadan craftsmanship instantly recalls the Alhambra, the upper galleries were added by Carlos V. Opening off this patio, the **Salón de Embajadores** (Hall of the Ambassadors), with its cedar cupola of green, red, and gold, is the most sumptuous hall in the palace. It was here that Carlos V married Isabel of Portugal in 1526—for which occasion he added the wooden balconies.

Seville

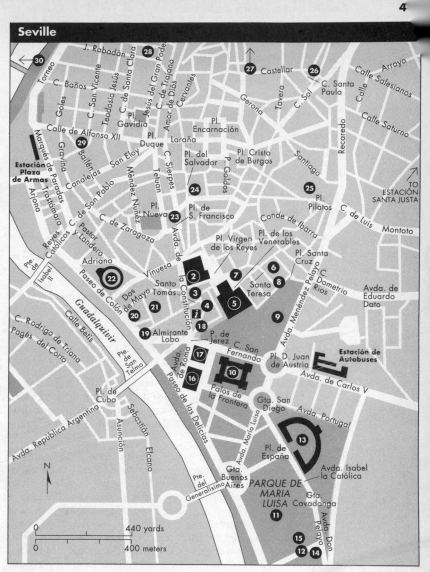

Other royal rooms include Felipe II's dining hall and the three baths of Pedro's wily mistress, María de Padilla. María's hold over her royal lover—and seemingly over his courtiers, too—was so great that they apparently lined up to drink her bathwater. The **Patio de las Muñecas** (Court of the Dolls) takes its name from two tiny faces carved on the inside of one of its arches, no doubt as a joke on the part of its Moorish creators. Here Pedro reputedly had his half brother, Don Fadrique, slain in 1358, and here, too, he murdered guest Abu Said of Granada for his jewels. Pedro presented one of these, a huge, uncut ruby, to the Black Prince (Edward, Prince of Wales [1330–76], eldest son of England's Edward III) in 1367. It now sits among other priceless gems in the Crown of England.

Up a flight of wooden stairs are the **apartments of Carlos V,** built by the emperor at the time of his marriage. The walls hold a rich collection of Flemish tapestries depicting Carlos's victories at Tunis. Look at the tapestry of the map of Spain—it shows the Iberian Peninsula upside-down, as was the custom in Arab mapmaking.

At the end of your visit, pause in the **gardens,** where you can breathe the fragrance of jasmine and myrtle, wander beautiful terraces and ornamental baths, and peer into the well-stocked goldfish pond covered with water lilies. In the midst of this oasis of green is an orange tree said to have been planted in the time of Pedro the Cruel. From the gardens, a passageway leads to the **Patio de las Banderas** (Court of the Flags), which has a classic view of the Giralda. ✉ *Plaza del Triunfo,* ☎ *95/422–7163.* 🎫 *600 ptas.* ⊙ *Tues.–Sat. 9:30–5, Sun. 9:30–1.*

⑰ **Alfonso XIII.** This grand Mudéjar-style building behind San Telmo is Seville's leading hotel and was built—and named—for the king's visit to the 1929 fair. You can admire the inner courtyard or sip a cool martini in the bar and enjoy the hotel's ornate Moorish decor (☞ Dining and Lodging, *below*).

❸ **Archivo de Indias** (Archives of the Indies). Opened in 1785 in the former Lonja (Merchants' Exchange), this dignified Renaissance building was designed by the architect of the Escorial (☞ Chapter 3), Juan de Herrera, in 1572. It holds an impressive collection of documents relating to the discovery of the New World. Maps include Juan de la Cosa's *Mappamundi,* and among the logbooks is one kept by Columbus. There are drawings, trade documents, plans of South American towns, and even the autographs of Columbus, Magellan, and Cortés. Many of the 38,000 documents have yet to be sorted and properly catalogued, so the items on display are constantly being shifted. ✉ *Avda. de la Constitución,* ☎ *95/421–1234.* 🎫 *Free.* ⊙ *Weekdays 10–1 (8–3 for researchers).*

㉓ **Ayuntamiento** (City Hall). In the heart of Seville's commercial center, the Plaza Nueva, is this Diego de Riaño original, built between 1527 and 1564. The facade, which overlooks the plaza, dates from the 19th century, but if you walk around to the other side, on the Plaza de San Francisco, you'll find Riaño's work.

★ ❻ **Barrio de Santa Cruz.** The twisting alleyways, cobbled squares, and whitewashed houses of Seville's old Jewish Quarter were much favored by the city's nobles in the 17th century. Today its houses are beautifully preserved, and some rank among Seville's most expensive properties. The atmosphere is unbeatable: wrought-iron lanterns cast shadows on the white walls, and ocher-framed windows hide behind potbellied grilles. In some places, bars alternate with antiques stores and souvenir shops but most of the quarter is made up of quiet residential streets. The Calle

jón del Agua, beside the wall of the Alcázar's gardens, boasts som_
the quarter's finest mansions and patios.

Pause to enjoy the antiques shops and outdoor café in the **Plaza Alianz**_
A starkly simple crucifix hangs on the dazzling white wall shrouded
in bougainvillea, and blue-and-white tiles bear the square's name. In
the **Plaza de Doña Elvira,** with its fountain and *azulejo* benches, young
sevillanos gather to play guitars. The heart of the Barrio de Santa
Cruz is the colorful **Plaza de los Venerables.**

㉗ Basílica de la Macarena. Here you'll find Seville's most revered image,
the Virgin of Hope—more familiarly known as La Macarena, because
her church adjoins the Puerta de la Macarena (Macarena Gate), a remnant of the old Roman wall. Bedecked with candles and carnations,
her cheeks streaming with glass tears, the Macarena is the focus of the
procession on Holy Thursday, which is the highlight of Seville's Holy
Week pageant. She is the patron of Gypsies and the protector of the
matador; few matadors would dream of entering the ring without saying a prayer to her. So great are her charms that the Sevillian bullfighter
Joselito spent half his personal fortune buying her four emeralds.
When he was killed in the ring at the tender age of 25, in 1920, the
Macarena was dressed in widow's weeds for a full month. ⊠ *Puerta
de la Macarena,* ☎ 95/437–0195. ☞ *Basilica free, treasury 300 ptas.*
⊙ *Basilica daily 9–1 and 5–9, treasury daily 9:30–1 and 5–8.*

Calle Sierpes. On Seville's main shopping street, a plaque and a small
bronze bust of Cervantes mark the spot where the Cárcel Real (Royal
Prison) once stood. Miguel Cervantes began work on *Don Quixote* in
one of its cells.

❽ Casa de Murillo. Calle Santa Teresa 8 houses changing displays of all
kinds; check with the tourist office for current exhibits. The street is
named for Santa Teresa de Ávila (1515–82), who stayed here once and
was so enchanted by Seville that she decreed that anyone who stayed
free from sin in Seville was indeed on the path to God.

㉕ Casa de Pilatos. This palace was built in the first half of the 16th century by the dukes of Tarifa, ancestors of the present owner, the Duke
of Medinaceli. It's known as Pilate's House because of a popular be-
lief that Don Fadrique, first marquis of Tarifa, modeled it on Pilate's
house in Jerusalem, where he went on a pilgrimage in 1518. The palace
has a fine patio and superb *azulejo* decorations and is a beautiful
blend of Spanish Mudéjar and Renaissance architecture. ⊠ *Plaza Pilatos,* ☎ 95/422–5298. ☞ *1,000 ptas.* ⊙ *Daily 9–6; upstairs open
10–1 and 4–6.*

★ ❷ Cathedral. The best place to start your exploration of Seville is in the
Plaza Virgen de los Reyes. From next to the central fountain you can
gaze up at the magnificent Giralda, symbol of Seville, and the east facade of the great Gothic cathedral. After Ferdinand III captured Seville
from the Moors in 1248, the great mosque begun by Yusuf II in 1171
was simply reconsecrated to the Virgin Mary and used as a Christian
cathedral, much as the mosque at Córdoba was. But in 1401 the people of Seville decided to erect a new and glorious cathedral, one more
equal to the status of their great city. They promptly pulled down the
old mosque—all except its minaret and outer court—and set about their
task with a zeal and enthusiasm unparalleled elsewhere. This mighty
building was completed in just over a century—a remarkable feat for
the time. The clergy renounced their incomes for the cause, and a
member of the chapter is said to have proclaimed, "Let us build a church
so big that we shall be held to be insane." This they proceeded to do,
for today Seville's cathedral can be described only in superlatives: it is

the largest and highest cathedral in Spain, the largest Gothic building in the world, and the world's third-largest church, after St. Peter's in Rome and St. Paul's in London.

The exterior, with its rose windows and magnificent flying buttresses, is a monument to pure Gothic beauty. Aside from the well-lit high altar, the dimly illuminated interior can be disappointing, with its five naves and numerous side chapels shrouded in gloom. Gothic purity has been largely submerged in ornate, baroque decoration lit only by flickering candles. Still, there is a great deal worth seeing, even if you have to strain your eyes.

Just south of the visiting entrance, the **Capilla Real** (Royal Chapel) is one area of the cathedral that still shines brightly. At the sides of the chapel stand the tombs of Ferdinand's wife, Beatrix of Swabia, and his son, Alfonso X, called the Wise (died 1284); in a silver urn before the high altar rest the precious relics of Ferdinand III, Seville's liberator (canonized 1671), who was said to have died from excessive fasting. In the vault below (rarely open) lie the tombs of Ferdinand's descendant Pedro the Cruel and Ferdinand's mistress, María de Padilla. Above the entrance grille, you can see Ferdinand III, on horseback, receiving the keys of Seville.

Spend some time peering into the **Capilla Mayor** (Main Chapel), in the central nave, and its intricately carved altarpiece, begun by a Flemish carver in 1482. This magnificent *retablo* is the largest in Christendom (65 ft by 43 ft). It depicts some 36 scenes from the life of Christ; its pillars are carved with more than 200 figures; and the whole work is lavishly adorned with immeasurable quantities of gold leaf.

At the south transept, you can't miss the flamboyant **monument to Christopher Columbus.** The great explorer knew triumph and disgrace and found no repose—he died, bitterly disillusioned, in Valladolid in 1506 and is purported to be buried here. Columbus's coffin is borne aloft by the four kings representing the medieval kingdoms of Spain: Castile, León, Aragon, and Navarre. Columbus's son, Hernando Colón (1488–1539), is also buried here. His tombstone, inscribed with the words A CASTILLA Y A LEÓN, MUNDO NUEVO DIO COLÓN (TO CASTILE AND LEÓN, COLUMBUS GAVE A NEW WORLD), lies between the great west door, the Puerta Mayor, and the central choir.

Between the elder Columbus's tomb and the Capilla Real, the cathedral's **main treasure houses** display a wealth of gold and silver (much of it from the New World), relics, and other works of art. In the dome of the **Sala Capitular** (Chapter House), in the cathedral's southeast corner, is Murillo's *Immaculate Conception,* painted in 1668. Next, in the **Sacristía Mayor** (Main Sacristy), are the keys to the city, which Seville's Moors and Jews presented to their conqueror, Ferdinand. Finally, in the **Sacristía de los Cálices,** look for Martínez Montañés's crucifixion, *Merciful Christ*; Valdés Leal's *St. Peter Freed by an Angel*; Zurbarán's *Virgin and Child*; and Goya's *St. Justa and St. Rufina.*

The **Giralda,** undisputed symbol of Seville, dominates the skyline and can be glimpsed from almost every corner of the city. Built originally as the minaret of Seville's great mosque, from which the faithful were summoned to prayer, it was built between 1184 and 1196, just 50 years before the reconquest of Seville. The Christians could not bring themselves to destroy this tower when they tore down the mosque, so they incorporated it into their new cathedral. In 1565–68 they added a lantern and belfry to the old minaret and installed 24 bells, one for each of Seville's 24 parishes and the 24 Christian knights who fought with Ferdinand III in the Reconquest. They also added the bronze statue of Fa which turned as a weather vane—*el giraldillo,* or "something that turns," thus the name Giralda. In 1997 the statue was removed to give it a rest after 400 years of wear and tear; it may be replaced with a copy.

With its Baroque additions, the slender Giralda now rises 322 ft. In its center, instead of steps, 35 sloping ramps, wide enough for two horsemen to pass abreast, climb to a viewing platform 230 ft up. It is said that Ferdinand III rode his horse to the top to admire the city he had conquered. If you follow in his footsteps, you'll be rewarded with a glorious view of tile roofs and the Guadalquivir shimmering beneath palm-lined banks.

Before you leave the cathedral precincts, take a look inside the **Patio de los Naranjos** (Courtyard of Orange Trees). The old fountain in the center was used for ritual ablutions before entering the mosque. See if you can find the alligator by the Puerta del Largat, in the corner near the Giralda—thought to have been a gift from the emir of Egypt in 1260 as he sought the hand of Alfonso the Wise's daughter—and the ivory elephant tusk found in the ruins of Itálica. Across the courtyard, the Sacristy houses the Columbus Library, a collection of 3,000 volumes bequeathed by the explorer's son, Hernando. ⊠ *Plaza Virgen de los Reyes,* ☎ *95/421–4971 for cathedral, 95/456–3321 for Giralda.* ⌑ *Cathedral and Giralda 600 ptas.* ☉ *Cathedral Mon.–Sat. 10:30–5, Sun. 2–4, also open for mass; Giralda Mon.–Sat. 11–5, Sun. 10–1:30 and 2–4.*

㉖ Convento de Santa Paula. The 15th-century Gothic convent has a fine facade and portico with ceramic decoration by Nicolaso Pisano. The chapel has some beautiful *azulejos* and sculptures by Martínez Montañés. ⊠ *C. Santa Paula,* ☎ *95/442–1307.* ⌑ *Free; donations accepted.* ☉ *Tues.–Sun. 10:30–1 and 4:30–6:30.*

㉑ Hospital de la Caridad. Behind the Maestranza Theater is this almshouse for the sick and elderly, where six paintings by Murillo (1617–82) and two gruesome works by Valdés Leal (1622–90) depicting the Triumph of Death are displayed. The baroque hospital was founded in 1674 by Seville's original Don Juan, Miguel de Mañara (1626–79). A nobleman of licentious character, Mañara was returning one night from a riotous orgy when he had a vision of a funeral procession in which the partly decomposed corpse in the coffin was his own. Accepting the apparition as a sign from God, Mañara renounced his worldly goods and joined the Brotherhood of Charity, whose unsavory task it was to collect the bodies of executed criminals and bury them. He devoted his fortune to building this hospital and is buried before the high altar in the chapel. Artist Murillo was a personal friend of Mañara's, thus La Caridad's chief attractions. ⊠ *C. Temprado 3,* ☎ *95/422–3232.* ⌑ *200 ptas.* ☉ *Mon.–Sat. 9–1:30 and 3:30–6.30, Sun. 9–1.*

❼ Hospital de los Venerables. Once a retirement home for priests, this building has undergone an extensive renovation; don't miss its splendid *azulejo* patio and small museum of floats from the Cruces de Mayo (May crosses) processions. All visits are guided. ⊠ *Plaza de los Venerables,* ☎ *95/456–2696.* ⌑ *500 ptas.* ☉ *Daily 10–2 and 4–8.*

㉔ Iglesia del Salvador (Church of El Salvador). This church (1671–1712), on the Plaza San Salvador, stands on the site of Seville's first great mosque. Inside, look especially for the image of *Jesús de la Pasión,* carved by Martínez Montañés. This statue is borne through the streets on Holy Thursday in one of Holy Week's most moving processions. ⊠ *Plaza San Salvador,* ☎ *95/421–1679.* ⌑ *Free.* ☉ *Daily 9–1 and 6:30–8:30; Sun. 10:30–1:30 and 7–8:30.*

⑨ **Jardines de Murillo** (Murillo Gardens). From the Plaza Santa Cruz you can embark on a stroll through these gardens, where you'll find a statue of Christopher Columbus.

㉚ **La Cartuja.** The year 1992 brought the decennial Universal Exposition to La Cartuja, an island on the Guadalquivir. Seven new bridges were built across the river for this event. Most of the Expo's pavilions were dismantled, but the site remains a public area. The Puerta de Triana, at the western end of the Puente del Cachorro bridge, leads to the **Navigation Pavilion,** which has exhibits, an audiovisual show on the history of ships, and a full-scale reproduction of Juan Sebastián de Elcano's ship, the *Victoria;* the **Omnimax Space Theatre,** which shows panoramic movies on a semispherical screen; and the **Observation Tower,** with a sweeping view of Seville. Next to this area is the original **La Cartuja,** Santa María de las Cuevas, the 14th-century Carthusian monastery for which the island is named. Christopher Columbus, a regular visitor, was buried here for a few years. Between 1841 and 1980 the building housed a ceramics factory, where Seville's famous Cartuja china was made; now fully restored, it is open to the public and regularly hosts art exhibits, which run Tues.–Sun. 11–9 (11–7 in winter) and cost 300 pesetas (☎ 95/448–0611). The eastern shore of the island holds the **Isla Mágica** theme park, with rides, shows, and restaurants. The western part of the island holds an office park and an extension of the University of Seville. *Puerta de Triana,* ☎ *95/446–0089,* ▧ *1,000 ptas.,* ☉ *Tues.–Sun. 8* AM*–midnight; Navigation Pavilion Tues.–Sun. 10:30–12:30 and 3:30–6:30; Omnimax Space Theatre Tues.–Sun. first show 4:30; Observation Tower Tues.–Sun 10:30–1 and 4:30–7. Isla Mágica,* ☎ *95/446–1493,* ▧ *3,100 ptas.,* ☉ *Mar.–Oct., 11–midnight.*

⑭ **Museo Arqueológico** (Museum of Archaeology). Housed in a fine Renaissance building, this museum holds artifacts from Phoenician, Tartessian, Greek, Carthaginian, Iberian, Roman, and medieval times. Some of the best exhibits are marble statues and mosaics from the Roman excavations at Itálica, and the fabulous Carambolo treasure found on a hillside outside Seville in 1958—21 pieces of jewelry, all of 24-karat gold, dating from the 7th and 6th centuries BC. ✉ *Plaza de América,* ☎ *95/423–2401.* ▧ *250 ptas.* ☉ *Tues.–Sat. 9–8.*

④ **Museo de Arte Contemporáneo** (Museum of Contemporary Art). Next door to the Archives of the Indies, this museum is housed in a fine old mansion. Its 20th-century Spanish paintings and sculpture include works by Romero de Torres, Carlos Saura, Antoni Tàpies, Fernando Zobel, and the sculptor Eduardo Chillida. Changing exhibits spotlight contemporary Andalusian artists. ✉ *Santo Tomás 5,* ☎ *95/421–5830.* ▧ *250 ptas.* ☉ *Fall–spring, Tues.–Fri. 10–9, weekends 10–2; summer, Tues.–Fri. 10–2; closed weekends in Aug.*

⑮ **Museo de Artes y Costumbres Populares** (Museum of Folklore). The Mudéjar pavilion opposite the Museum of Archaeology houses this museum of mainly 19th- and 20th-century Spanish folklore. The first floor has re-creations of a forge, a bakery, a wine press, a tanner's shop, and a pottery studio. Upstairs, the exhibits include 18th- and 19th-century court dress, regional folk costumes, carriages, and musical instruments. ✉ *Plaza de América,* ☎ *95/423–2576.* ▧ *250 ptas.* ☉ *Tues.–Sun. 9–2:30.*

㉙ **Museo de Bellas Artes** (Museum of Fine Arts). *Sevillanos* claim that their art museum, housed in a 17th-century convent, is second only to Madrid's Prado in Spanish art. The fine collection features Murillo, Zurbarán, Velázquez, Valdés Leal, and El Greco. ✉ *Plaza del Museo,* ☎ *95/422–0790.* ▧ *250 ptas.* ☉ *Tues. 3–9, Wed.–Sat. 9–8, Sun. 9–3*

⑯ Palacio de San Telmo. This splendid Baroque palace on the Aven⸱ de Roma is largely the work of architect Leonardo de Figueroa. Bu⸱ between 1682 and 1796, it is now the seat of the Presidencia de Junt⸱ de Andalucía, the regional government's chief executive. Look for the exotic main portal, vintage 1734, a superb example of the fanciful Churrigueresque style.

⑱ Palacio de Yanduri. Nobel Prize–winning poet Vicente Aleixandre was born here, on the north side of Puerta de Jerez.

⑪ Parque de María Luisa (María Luisa Park). To see one of the loveliest parks in Spain, make time for this one; the main entrance is at the Glorieta San Diego. Here you'll find a **statue of El Cid** (by Rodrigo Díaz de Vivar, 1043–99, who fought both for and against the Muslim rulers during the Reconquest); and the old **Casino** building of the 1929 Exhibition, now the Teatro Lope de Vega. The park itself, formerly the garden of the Palacio de San Telmo, is a blend of formal design and wild vegetation. In the burst of development that gripped Seville in the 1920s, it was redesigned for the 1929 Hispanic-American Exhibition, and the impressive villas you'll see here today are the fair's remaining pavilions, many of them now consulates or schools.

Plaza Alfaro. Just around the corner from the Hospital de los Venerables, at Callejón del Agua and Jope de Rueda, is where Rossini's Figaro serenaded Rosina on her famous balcony.

⑫ Plaza de América. At the south end of the Parque de María Luisa, past the Isla de los Patos (Island of Ducks), you'll reach this plaza, designed by Aníbal González. It's a blaze of color, with deep-orange sand, flowers, shrubs, ornamental stairways, and fountains of yellow, blue, and ocher tiles. The three impressive buildings that surround the square—in neo-Mudéjar, Gothic, and Renaissance styles—were built by González for the 1929 fair. Two of them now serve as museums.

⑬ Plaza de España. This monumental attraction is just east of the Parque de María Luisa. Designed by architect Aníbal González, the grandiose half-moon was Spain's centerpiece pavilion at the 1929 fair. The brightly colored *azulejo* pictures in its arches represent the 50 provinces of Spain, and the four bridges over the ornamental lake, the medieval kingdoms of the Iberian Peninsula.

㉒ Plaza de Toros Real Maestranza (Royal Maestranza Bullring). Sevillanos have spent many thrilling Sunday afternoons in this bullring, built between 1760 and 1763. The deep ocher–painted stadium is the oldest and, many feel, the most beautiful *plaza de toros* in Spain. ⊠ *Paseo de Colón 12,* ☎ *95/422–4577.* ▨ *Plaza and bullfighting museum 300 pesetas.* ☉ *weekdays 10–1:30 and 4–5:30; weekends 10–1:30.*

Plaza Santa Cruz. A 17th-century, filigree iron cross marks the site of the Santa Cruz church destroyed by Napoleon's General Soult. The painter Murillo was buried here in 1682.

㉘ San Lorenzo y Jesús del Gran Poder. This church has many fine works by such artists as Montañés and Pacheco, but its outstanding piece is Juan de Mesa's *Jesús del Gran Poder* (*Christ Omnipotent*). The *paso* (float), for the Good Friday morning procession of El Gran Poder, is the work of Ruíz Gijón (1690). ⊠ *C. Jesús del Gran Poder,* ☎ *95/438– 5454.* ▨ *Free.* ☉ *Daily 8–1:30 and 6–9.*

⑳ Teatro de la Maestranza (Maestranza Theater). Opposite the Torre de Oro is Seville's opera house, which opened in 1991. Now one of Europe's leading halls, the Maestranza offers opera, classical music, *zarzuela* (Spanish light opera), and jazz. ⊠ *Paseo de Colón,* ☎ *95/422– 6573 or 95/422–3344.*

⑲ Torre de Oro (Tower of Gold). One of Seville's great landmarks, the Tower of Gold stands on the riverside just a short walk from the Puerta de Jerez. A 12-sided tower built by the Moors in 1220 to complete the city's ramparts, it served to close off the harbor when a chain was stretched across the river from its base to another tower on the opposite bank. In 1248 Admiral Ramón de Bonifaz succeeded in breaking through this barrier, thus enabling Ferdinand III to capture the city. Today the Torre del Oro houses a small but well-displayed Naval Museum. ☎ 95/422–2419. 🎫 100 ptas. ☉ Tues.–Fri. 10–2, weekends 11–2.

⑩ University of Seville. At the far end of the Jardines de Murillo, opposite Calle San Fernando, stands what used to be the Real Fábrica de Tabacos (Royal Tobacco Factory); it has only been home to the university since the 1950s. Built between 1750 and 1766, the factory employed some 3,000 *cigarreras* (female cigar makers) less than a century later, including, of course, the heroine of Bizet's opera *Carmen*, who rolled her cigars on her thigh. Today's factory is across the river. ⊠ C. San Fernando, ☎ 95/455–1000. 🎫 Free. ☉ Weekdays 9–8:30.

Bars and Cafés

Because most of the locals eat their main meal at lunchtime, Seville's bars are packed in the evenings with people making a supper of tapas. **El Rinconcillo** (⊠ C. Gerona 40, near the Casa de Pilatos, ☎ 95/422–3183) was founded in 1670 and claims to be the oldest tavern in Seville. Popular **La Alicantina** (⊠ Plaza del Salvador 2, ☎ 95/422–6122) has a tapas bar with pastoral scenes of wine- and beer-making decorating its *azulejo* walls. **Casa Román** (⊠ Plaza de los Venerables, ☎ 95/421–6408), open since 1934, is a classic tapas bar, with wood-paneled walls and ceilings and hanging hams. The **Cervecería Giralda** (⊠ Mateos Gago 9, ☎ 95/422–7435) is a lovely corner bar, set with Moorish-style marble columns and *azulejo* walls and usually thronged with a hip, young crowd. At **El Bacalao** (⊠ Plaza Ponce de León 15, ☎ 95/421–6670) the specialty is, of course, *bacalao* (salt cod), prepared virtually 101 different ways. **Rincón San Eloy** (⊠ San Eloy 24, ☎ 95/421–8079) is popular for tapas among *sevillanos*.

Boating

Paddleboats, canoes, and river cruises make the Guadalquivir prime territory for boating enthusiasts (☞ Boating *in* Seville and Western Andalusia A to Z, *below*).

Bullfighting

The season runs from Easter until late October. Most *corridas* are held on Sundays, except during special fiestas. Fights take place at the **Maestranza Bullring,** on the Paseo de Colón 12 (☎ 95/422–4577). The season highlight is the April Fair, when fights take place each day and feature Spain's leading *toreros*. Tickets for these fights are expensive, and you should buy them in advance from the official *despacho de entradas* (ticket office) on Calle Adriano, beside the Maestranza ring. Other legitimate *despachos* sell tickets on Calle Sierpes, but these are unofficial and charge a 20% commission.

Dining and Lodging

$$$–$$$$ ✕ **Egaña-Oriza.** One of Seville's most acclaimed restaurants, the Egaña-★   Oriza is beautifully situated on the edge of the Murillo Gardens. The decor is modern, with walls painted in deep peach and air-force blue. José Mari Egaña, the owner, is Basque, and the menu reflects his native influence. Try the *lubina al horno* (baked sea bass with a garlic sauce) or *estofado de jabalí con ciruelas y pasas* (casserole of wild boar with plums and raisins). ⊠ San Fernando 41, ☎ 95/422–7211. A DC, MC, V. Closed Sun. and Aug. No lunch Sat.

$$$–$$$$ ✕ **La Albahaca.** One of Seville's prettiest restaurants is in the heart of the Barrio de Santa Cruz. This typical Andalusian house was built by the celebrated architect Juan Talavera as a home for his own family. Inside, three dining rooms are colorfully decorated with ceramic tiles and leafy potted plants. The service is friendly and professional; entrées include *suprema de lubina con almejas negras* (sea bass supreme with venus clams). ⊠ *Plaza Santa Cruz 12,* ☎ *95/422–0714. AE, DC, MC, V. Closed Sun.*

$$$–$$$$ ✕ **La Isla.** Here in the Arenal district, fresh fish is brought in daily from the Cádiz and Huelva coasts. The two attractive dining rooms have cream-color stucco walls above blue-and-white tile decor. *Parrillada de mariscos y pescados* (a fish and seafood grill for two people) is one of the best meals. Simply cooked meat dishes are also on offer. ⊠ *Arfe 25,* ☎ *95/421–5376. AE, DC, MC, V.*

$$$ ✕ **San Marco.** Set in an old neoclassical house in the shopping district, this Italian restaurant has a leafy patio and is furnished with antiques. The menu is a happy combination of Italian, French, and Andalusian cuisines. Count on good pasta dishes, such as ravioli stuffed with sea bass in clam sauce. ⊠ *Cuna 6,* ☎ *95/421–2440. Reservations essential. AE, DC, MC, V. Closed Mon. and Aug.*

$$–$$$
★ ✕ **La Judería.** This bright, modern restaurant gained fast recognition for the quality of its Andalusian and international cuisine and its reasonable prices. Fish dishes from northern Spain and meat from Ávila are specialties. Try *cordero lechal* (roast lamb) or *urta a la roteña* (a fish dish from Rota, on the Cádiz coast). ⊠ *Cano y Cueto 13,* ☎ *95/ 441–2052. Reservations essential. AE, DC, MC, V. Closed Mon. and Aug.*

$$
★ ✕ **Enrique Becerra.** This small, cozy restaurant is a short walk from the cathedral, in a whitewashed house with wrought-iron window grilles. Inside, a lively, crowded bar decorated with ceramic tiles is a meeting place for locals, who appreciate its excellent selection of tapas. The menu concentrates on traditional, home-cooked Andalusian dishes, such as *corvina al amontillado* (meagre, a fish, cooked in dark sherry) and *jarrete de ternera a la cazuela* (veal stew). ⊠ *Gamazo 2,* ☎ *95/ 421–3049. AE, DC, MC, V. Closed Sun.*

$$
★ ✕ **Mesón Don Raimundo.** Tucked into an alleyway off Calle Argote de Molina (which leads up from the cathedral's Plaza Virgen de los Reyes), Don Raimundo is decorated with an odd assortment of blue and white tiles, marble columns, stained-glass windows, iron sculptures, farm implements, a deer's head, and assorted other bric-a-brac. The house specialties are meat dishes, such as Mozarab-style wild duck (braised in sherry) and *solomillo a la castellana* (steak Castilian style), but you'll find fish, too. For starters, try the crunchy *tortillitas de camarones* (batter-fried shrimp pancakes) or stuffed peppers. Portions are generous. ⊠ *Argote de Molina 26,* ☎ *95/422–3355. AE, DC, MC, V. No dinner Sun.*

$–$$ ✕ **Hostería del Laurel.** This restaurant—also a small hotel—is geared to tourists, capitalizing on its location in the Barrio de Santa Cruz. In summer you can dine on the outdoor terrace in the square, surrounded by beautiful white and ocher houses. The two indoor dining rooms are decorated in traditional Castilian style, with wood paneling, white walls, and heavy wooden tables and chairs. There's a menu in English, offering a wide choice of traditional Spanish fare. ⊠ *Plaza de los Venerables 5,* ☎ *95/422–0295. AE, DC, MC, V.*

$–$$ ✕ **La Cueva.** The Cave is a colorful, tourist-oriented *mesón* just off Plaza Doña Elvira. The restaurant has two white-walled dining rooms that face each other from opposite sides of the street. Friendly and helpful service makes the experience enjoyable, and an English menu offers a good choice of traditional Spanish meat and fish dishes. ⊠ *Rodrigo Caro 18,* ☎ *95/421–3143. AE, DC, MC, V.*

$–$$ ✕ **Modesto.** This restaurant, on the edge of the Barrio de Santa Cruz, is popular with *sevillanos,* who come for the excellent value. Downstairs is a lively, crowded tapas bar; upstairs is a restaurant whose stucco walls are decorated with blue and white tiles. A terrace allows outdoor dining in warm weather. The house specialty is a crisp *fritura Modesto* (a selection of small fish fried in top-quality olive oil); another excellent choice is the *Tío Diego* (Uncle Jim—ham, mushrooms, and shrimp). ⊠ *Cano y Cueto 5,* ☎ *95/441–6811. AE, DC, MC, V.*

$ ✕ **Girarda.** You'll find this kitschy but charming restaurant (which doubles as a small hostel) in the heart of the Barrio de Santa Cruz. Half a dozen tables are set in the patio of a private house, where colorful tiles add to the already lively atmosphere. The fare is traditional Spanish. ⊠ *Justino de Neve 8,* ☎ *95/421–5113. AE, MC, V.*

$$$$ ✕⌖ **Alfonso XIII.** Inaugurated by King Alfonso XIII on April 28, 1929,
★ this grand hotel is a splendid, historical Mudéjar Revival palace. Its public rooms are resplendent with marble floors, wood-paneled ceilings, heavy Moorish lamps, stained glass, and ceramic-tile decor in the typical Sevillian colors. The hotel is built around a huge central patio surrounded by ornate, brick arches and filled with potted plants and a fountain. The restaurant, with a painted wood-paneled ceiling, heavy drapes, a huge central table, and an ornate wrought-iron gate, is imposing. ⊠ *San Fernando 2, 41004,* ☎ *95/422–2850,* ⅏ *95/421–6033. 127 rooms, 19 suites. Restaurant, bar, pool, beauty salon, meeting rooms. AE, DC, MC, V.*

$$$$ ✕⌖ **Tryp Colón.** A grand old hotel, the Colón was built for the 1929
★ Exhibition. A white-marble staircase leads up to the central lobby, which has a magnificent stained-glass dome and crystal candelabra. The reception area, La Fuente restaurant, and Bar Majestic open off this circular space. Downstairs is the renowned El Burladero restaurant, with a bullfight theme, and La Tasca tavern. The old-fashioned rooms are elegantly furnished with silk drapes and bedspreads and dark-wood fittings. ⊠ *Canalejas 1, 41001,* ☎ *95/422–2900,* ⅏ *95/422–0938. 204 rooms, 14 suites. 2 restaurants, 2 bars, beauty salon, meeting rooms. AE, DC, MC, V.*

$–$$ ✕⌖ **Giralda.** This modern hotel, in a cul-de-sac off Recaredo, caters largely to the tour-bus crowd, but the service is friendly and professional. Paintings of Spanish scenes, an enormous cage, and Moorish grilles decorate the lobby. The adjoining restaurant has glazed, half-tile walls ornamented with ceramic plates and urns. The spacious, light rooms are furnished in typical Castillian style. ⊠ *Sierra Nevada 3, 41003,* ☎ *95/441–6661,* ⅏ *95/441–9352. 96 rooms, 5 suites. Restaurant, bar, meeting rooms. AE, DC, MC, V.*

$$$$ ⌖ **Casa Imperial.** Opened in 1996, this is Seville's newest hotel and one of its most fascinating. Adjoining the Casa de Pilatos, and at one time connected to it via underground tunnel, this restored 16th-century palace was once the residence of the Marquis of Tarifa's majordomo. Public areas are arranged around four different courtyards. The 24 suites are approached by a stairway adorned with trompe l'oeil tiles. Each suite is different—one even has a private courtyard complete with trickling fountain—but all have kitchenettes. The bathroom fixtures are stylishly old-fashioned, and the curvy bathtubs are made of masonry. Some rooms have king-size beds. ⊠ *Imperial 29, 41003,* ☎ *95/450–0300,* ⅏ *95/450–0330. 24 suites. Restaurant. AE, DC, MC, V.*

$$$ ⌖ **Bécquer.** Well maintained and well located, near the main shoppin district, the Bécquer is one of Seville's best mid-range picks. Marb floors, dark wood, and leather furniture dominate the public areas, which include a small sitting room dedicated to the poet Gustavo Adolfo Bécquer. The guest rooms are traditionally Spanish, with peach-colored walls, floral prints, matching woven bedspreads, and carved-wood headboards. ✉ *Reyes Católicos 4, 41001,* ☎ *95/422–8900,* ⅏ *95/421–4400. 116 rooms, 2 suites. Bar, breakfast room. AE, DC, MC, V.*

$$$ ⚏ **Doña María.** Close to the cathedral, this is one of Seville's most charming hotels. Some rooms are small and plain; others are tastefully furnished with antiques. Room 310 has a four-poster double bed, and 305 has two single four-posters; both have spacious bathrooms. There's also a rooftop pool with a good view of the Giralda, just a stone's throw away. ✉ *Don Remondo 19, 41004,* ☎ *95/422–4990,* ⅏ *95/421–9546. 69 rooms. Pool. AE, DC, MC, V.*

$$$ ⚏ **Inglaterra.** This classic hotel, on the central Plaza Nueva, has long been known for excellent service. It's something of a historic British outpost in Spain, and the room decor might be said to reflect this—furnishings are understated, a bit faded, and sometimes anachronistically floral. The best rooms are on the fifth floor; these have spacious balconies. The second-floor dining room overlooks orange trees and the busy Plaza Nueva. The lobby lounge is comfortable and civilized, and the on-site Irish pub lends a twist. ✉ *Plaza Nueva 7, 41001,* ☎ *95/422–4970,* ⅏ *95/456–1336. 113 rooms, 1 suite. Restaurant, bar, lobby lounge, pub. AE, DC, MC, V.*

$$$ ⚏ **Las Casas de la Judería.** Tucked into a passageway just off the Plaza Santa María, in the heart of the Barrio de Santa Cruz, this labyrinthine hotel occupies three of the quarter's old palaces, each arranged around inner courtyards. Ocher predominates in the suitably palatial common areas; the spacious guest rooms are dressed in tasteful pastels and decorated with prints of Seville. ✉ *Callejón de Dos Hermanas, 41004,* ☎ *95/441–5150,* ⅏ *95/442–2170. 41 rooms, 15 suites. AE, DC, MC, V.*

$$$ ⚏ **Meliá Sevilla.** This vast, modern hotel behind the Plaza de España resembles the best American business hotels. Ask for a room at the front, facing the pool and Plaza de España, which is illuminated on weekends; those in the back have poor views. The best rooms and suites are on the ninth floor. Travelers with disabilities are well accommodated here. ✉ *Dr. Pedro de Castro 1, 41004,* ☎ *95/442–1511,* ⅏ *95/442–1608. 364 rooms, 5 suites. Restaurant, bar, coffee shop, pool, beauty salon, meeting rooms, parking (fee). AE, DC, MC, V.*

$$$ ⚏ **Style Pasarela.** Also behind the Plaza de España, the Pasarela is smaller and cozier than its giant neighbor, the Meliá Sevilla (☞ above). Several ground-floor sitting rooms, some with oil paintings and table lamps, give the place a homey atmosphere. The rooms are large and fully carpeted, with predominantly brown-and-beige modern decor and white bedspreads. ✉ *Avda. de la Borbolla 11, 41004,* ☎ *95/441–5511,* ⅏ *95/442–0727. 77 rooms, 5 suites. Bar, breakfast room, sauna, exercise room, meeting rooms. AE, DC, MC, V.*

$$ ⚏ **La Rábida.** A charming, old Andalusian house in the Arenal district has been converted into a comfortable, modestly priced hotel that retains its Old World atmosphere. Many rooms overlook a leafy patio with oblique views of the Giralda. ✉ *Castelar 24, 41001,* ☎ *95/422–0960,* ⅏ *95/422–4375. 103 rooms. Restaurant, bar. AE, DC, MC, V.*

$$ ⚏ **Murillo.** In the very heart of the Barrio de Santa Cruz, the Murillo can be reached only on foot; take a taxi to the Plaza de Santa Cruz and a porter will collect your luggage. Narrow halls lead to the rooms, which are simple, with bare floors, white walls, and beige bedspreads, and newly (1997) refitted bathrooms. The location, friendly atmosphere, and wonderfully ornate public rooms—with an odd collection of ornaments, including a confessional—are splendid. ✉ *Lope de Rueda 7,*

41004, ☎ 95/421–6095, ⅢXX 95/421–9616. *57 rooms. Bar, breakfast room. AE, DC, MC, V.*

$ Ⅲ **Internacional.** If you seek cheap lodging and can live without the comforts of home, this old Andalusian house near the Casa de Pilatos is for you. Friendly and family-run, the hotel announces itself with a wrought-iron gate that opens into the central patio-reception area. A white-marble staircase leads to the bedrooms, which have twin beds and are very simply furnished. ⊠ *Águilas 17, 41003,* ☎ ⅢXX *95/421–3207. 24 rooms. DC, MC, V.*

$ Ⅲ **Simón.** The Simón is a good choice for inexpensive—if basic—accommodation thanks to its location near the cathedral, in a rambling 19th-century town house. You're greeted by a spacious, airy courtyard. ⊠ *García de Vinuesa 19, 41001,* ☎ *95/422–6660,* ⅢXX *95/456–2241. 29 rooms. AE, DC, MC, V.*

Nightlife and the Arts

To find out what's on in Seville, look in the local newspapers or in *ABC Sevilla, Correo de Andalucía, Sudoeste,* or *Nueva Andalucía.* The free monthly arts leaflet *El Giraldillo* also lists classical concerts, jazz, films (for films in English, look for "v. o."), plays, art exhibits, and dance performances in Seville and all major Andalusian cities. A quarterly leaflet of events at municipal theaters (*Programación Teatros Municipales*) is published by the city of Seville and is available at the tourist office. You can also call a city information line (☎ 010) for up-to-the-minute information on art shows and cultural events; most operators speak English.

FLAMENCO

Seville has three regular flamenco clubs, patronized more by tourists than by locals. Tickets are sold in most hotels; otherwise, make your own reservations (essential for groups, advisable for everyone in high season) by calling the club during the evening.

El Arenal is in the back room of the picturesque Mesón Dos de Mayo. Here you get your own table, rather than having to sit in rows. ⊠ *Rodo 7,* ☎ *95/421–6492.* ▱ *3,900 ptas., excluding dinner.* ☉ *Daily 9:30 and 11:30 (11 in winter).*

El Patio Sevillano caters mainly to tour groups; the show is a mixture of regional Spanish dances (often performed to taped music) and pure flamenco by some outstanding guitarists, singers, and dancers. ⊠ *Paseo de Colón 11,* ☎ *95/421–4120.* ▱ *3,500 ptas.* ☉ *Daily 7:30 and 10.*

Los Gallos is an intimate club in the heart of the Barrio de Santa Cruz. Performances are good and reasonably pure. ⊠ *Plaza Santa Cruz 11,* ☎ *95/421–6981.* ▱ *3,000 ptas.* ☉ *Daily 9 and 11:30.*

MUSIC

Long prominent in the opera world, Seville is particularly proud of its opera house, the **Teatro de la Maestranza** (⊠ Paseo de Colón, ☎ 95/422–3344). Be sure to check out what's on here—it's usually the best show in town. Classical music and ballet are performed at the **Teatro Lope de Vega** (⊠ Avda. María Luisa, ☎ 95/423–4546). You can also catch classical concerts at the **Conservatorio Superior de Música** (⊠ Jesús del Gran Poder), in the cathedral, and in the church of **San Salvador.** The **Teatro Alameda** (⊠ Crédito, ☎ 95/438–8312) stages a variety of productions, including some children's plays.

Shopping

Seville is Western Andalusia's main shopping center and ground zero for souvenirs associated with Andalusia. Most souvenirs are sold in the Barrio de Santa Cruz and on the streets around the cathedral and Giralda, especially Calle Alemanes.

The main shopping area—for *sevillanos,* as opposed to tourists—is the Calle Sierpes, along with its neighboring streets Tetuan, Velázquez, Plaza Magdalena, and Plaza Duque.The **Corte Inglés** (✉ Plaza Duque 7, ☎ 95/422–0931; ✉ Marqués por Luis Montoto, 122–128, ☎ 95/457–1440) is a well-run department store that stays open during siesta hours.

ANTIQUES

For antiques, look along Mateos Gago opposite the Giralda; on Jamerdana, in the Barrio de Santa Cruz; and Rodrigo Caro, between Plazas Alianza and Doña Elvira, in the Barrio de Santa Cruz.

BOOKS

A large assortment of books in English, Spanish, French, and Italian is on sale at the American-owned **Librería Vértice** (✉ San Fernando 30, ☎ 95/421–1654), right near the gates of the university. The **English Bookshop** (✉ Marqués de Nervion 70, ☎ 95/465–5754) also sells English-language books.

CERAMICS

Martian Ceramics (✉ Sierpes 74, ☎ 95/421–3413) has a good range of high-quality plates and dishes, especially the flowers-on-white patterns native to Seville. It's a bit touristy but fairly priced. Try also along Mateos Gago; Romero Murube, between Plaza Triunfo and Plaza Alianza, on the edge of the Barrio; and between Plaza Doña Elvira and Plaza de los Venerables, also in the Barrio.

FANS

Casa Rubio (✉ Sierpes 56, ☎ 95/422–6872) is Seville's premier fan store—no mean distinction. It has everything from traditional to very modern fans.

FLAMENCO DRESSES

Beware: these are prohibitively expensive. You'll find the cheapest ones in **El Corte Inglés,** or, surprisingly, in the souvenir shops on Calle Alemanes. For those interested in serious, and seriously expensive, flamenco dresses and other costumery, **Pardales** (✉ Cuna 23, ☎ 95/421–3709) is the place to go. Esperenza Pardales Acosta makes most of its clothing to order but also sells some off-the-rack pieces.

PORCELAIN

El Corte Inglés (☞ *above*) is your best bet.

STREET MARKETS

The **Plaza del Duque** has a crafts market on Friday and Saturday; the **El Jueves** flea market is on Calle Feria Thursday mornings; the **Alameda de Hercules** crafts market takes place on Sunday mornings; and a coin and stamp market comes to the **Plaza del Cabildo** on Sunday mornings.

WOVEN GOODS

You'll find all kinds of handwoven blankets, shawls, and embroidered tablecloths at **Artesanía Textil** (✉ García de Vinuesa 33, ☎ 95/456–2840), a modern shop on a busy shopping street, supplied by local artisans. **Juan Foronda** (✉ Álvarez Quintero 52, ☎ 95/421–1856) sells handwoven goods as well as Lladro porcelain and souvenirs.

Carmona

③ *32 km (20 mi) east of Seville off N IV.*

Claiming to be one of the oldest inhabited places in Spain (the Phoenicians and the Carthaginians had settlements here), Carmona later became an important town under both the Romans and the Moors. Its incredible Roman necropolis contains about 900 tombs dating from the 2nd century BC. Today, Carmona is a quiet Andalusian town occupying a dramatic position on a steep, fortified hill.

As you wander Carmona's ancient, narrow streets, you'll come upon a wealth of Mudéjar and Renaissance churches, medieval gateways, and simple whitewashed houses of clear Moorish influence, punctuated here and there by a Baroque palace. Pick up a street plan in the parador and set out for a walk.

First, stroll down to the **Puerta de Córdoba** (Córdoba Gate) on the eastern edge of town. This old gateway was first built by the Romans around AD 175, then altered by Moorish and Renaissance additions. One of Carmona's chief attractions is the Moorish **Alcázar de Arriba** (Upper Fortress), built on Roman foundations and later converted by King Pedro the Cruel into a fine Mudéjar palace. Pedro's summer residence was destroyed in 1504 by an earthquake, but the parador (☞ Dining and Lodging, *below*) that now stands amid its ruins commands a breathtaking view.

The Gothic church of **Santa María,** built between 1424 and 1518, stands on the site of Carmona's former Great Mosque. Santa María is a contemporary of Seville's cathedral, and it, too, retains its Moorish courtyard, once used for ritual ablutions. The heart of the old town is the **Plaza San Fernando,** whose 17th-century houses have Moorish overtones.

At the **Puerta de Sevilla** (Seville Gate), the imposing Alcázar de Abajo (Lower Fortress), another Moorish fortification built on Roman foundations, marks the limits of the old town.

On the edge of the "new town," across the road from the **Alcázar de Abajo,** stands the church of **San Pedro,** begun in 1466. Its extraordinary interior is an unbroken mass of sculptures and gilded surfaces, and its **Baroque tower,** erected in 1704, is an unabashed imitation of Seville's Giralda.

At the far end of town lies Carmona's most outstanding monument, the splendid **Roman necropolis.** Here, in huge underground chambers, some 900 family tombs dating from the 2nd century BC to the 4th century AD have been chiseled out of the rock. The walls, decorated with leaf and bird motifs, are punctuated with niches for burial urns. The most spectacular tombs are the **Elephant Vault** and the **Servilia Tomb,** with colonnaded arches and vaulted side galleries. A museum displays artifacts found in the various chambers. ✉ *C. Enmedio,* ☎ *95/414–0811.* 🖼 *250 ptas.* ☉ *Summer, Tues.–Fri. 9–2, Sat. 10–2; winter, Tues.–Fri. 10–2 and 4–6, weekends 10–2.*

㉜ If you have time and a car, venture to the historic neighbor towns of Ecija and Osuna, within easy driving distance of Carmona. **Ecija,** 48 km (30 mi) from Carmona on the N IV to Córdoba, is particularly well endowed with Baroque church towers: it has 11. (It is also known as "the frying pan of Andalusia," as midsummer temperatures often **㉝** reach 100° F.) From Ecija, take C430 south to **Osuna.** In the 16th century, the Dukes of Osuna were among the wealthiest people in Spain, which accounts for the now-sleepy town's impressive Renaissance palaces, Colegiata de Santa María church, and old university. From Osuna, take the A-92 (N 334) back to Seville (64 km [40 mi]).

Dining and Lodging

$$$$ 🏨 **Casa de Carmona.** The Casa de Carmona is one of the most unusual and elegant hotels in Spain, set in the historic Lasso de la Vega ★ Palace. The public rooms are beautifully decorated with antiques, rich fabrics, and museum-quality rugs, and the guest rooms are large and luxuriously furnished. Between jaunts you can relax in the Arabian-style garden, with orange trees and fountain, or swim in the tiled pool. The only reminder that you haven't traveled back in time is the digital key card that lets you into your room. ✉ *Plaza de Lasso, 41410,* ☎ *95/414–3300,* ℻ *95/414–3752. 30 rooms, 3 suites. Restaurant, bar, pool, sauna, health club, library, laundry service, concierge. AE, DC, MC, V.*

$$$ 🏨 **Parador Alcázar del Rey Don Pedro.** This delightful parador has su-
★ perb views from its hilltop position among the ruins of Pedro the Cruel's summer palace. The public rooms open off a central, Moorish-style patio; the vaulted dining hall and adjacent bar open onto an outdoor terrace that overlooks the sloping garden, where even the pool is tiled in Moorish patterns. The rooms are spacious, and those on the top floor have south-facing balconies. At press time, the parador had just reopened after an extensive renovation. ✉ *Alcázar, 41410,* ☎ *95/ 414–1010,* ℻ *95/414–1712. 63 rooms. Restaurant, bar, pool. AE, DC, MC, V.*

Itálica

㉟ *12 km (7 mi) north of Seville, 1 km (½ mi) beyond Santiponce.*

This ancient city was founded by Scipio Africanus in 206 BC as a home for veteran soldiers. By the 2nd century AD, it had grown into one of Roman Iberia's most important cities and had given the Roman world two great emperors, Trajan (52–117) and Hadrian (76–138). Ten thousand people once lived here, in 1,000 dwellings. About 25% of the site has been excavated, and work is still in progress.

The most important monument is the huge, elliptical **amphitheater,** which once held 40,000 spectators. You'll also find traces of city streets, cisterns, and the floor plans of several villas, some with mosaic floors, though all the best mosaics and statues have been removed to Seville's Museum of Archaeology. A small museum contains relics found on the site of a fully excavated Roman theater in Santiponce. Itálica was abandoned and plundered as a quarry by the Visigoths, who preferred Seville. It fell into decay around AD 700. ☎ *95/599–7376 for excavation information.* 💶 *250 ptas.* 🕐 *Tues.–Sat. 9–5:30 (until 6:30 in summer), Sun. 10–4 (9–3 in summer).*

PROVINCE OF HUELVA

Doñana National Park, Matalascañas, Mazagón, La Rábida, Palos de la Frontera, Moguer, Riotinto, and Aracena

Whenever you're ready to bid farewell to the urban bustle of Seville, nature awaits in the province of Huelva. Doñana National Park, one of the largest and richest wildlife refuges in Europe, and pristine beaches on the Costa de la Luz are all about an hour's drive from Seville. This is also a land rich in history; Columbus's voyage to the New World was sparked here, at the monastery of La Rábida and in Palos de la Frontera. From Seville, turn off the Seville–Huelva highway, drive through Almonte and El Rocío—scene of the famous Whitsuntide pilgrimage to the Virgin of the Dew—and you'll come to La Rocina's visitor center.

Parque Nacional de Doñana

③⑤ *100 km (62 mi) southwest of Seville.*

One of Europe's last corners of wilderness, these wetlands beside the Guadalquivir estuary form one of Spain's largest national parks. Doñana covers 188,000 acres (an area 64 km by 14½ km [40 mi by 9 mi]) and is a paradise for nature lovers, especially bird-watchers: the park sits on the migratory route from Africa to Europe and is the winter home and breeding ground for as many as 150 species of rare birds. The park's habitats range from beaches and shifting sand dunes to marshes, dense brushwood, and sandy hillsides of pine and cork oak. Two of Europe's most endangered species, the imperial eagle and the lynx, make their homes here, and kestrels, kites, buzzards, egrets, storks, and spoonbills breed among the cork oaks.

At the **La Rocina Visitor Center** (☎ 959/442340), less than 2 km (1 mi) from El Rocío, you can peer at the many species of birds from a 3½- km (2-mi) footpath. It's open daily 9–2 and 3–sundown. Five kilometers (3 miles)away, an exhibit at the **Acebrón Palace** explains the park's ecosystems; it's open daily 8–3 and 4–sundown (last entrance one hour before closing). Two kilometers (1 mile) before Matalascañas, you'll find the park's main **Reception and Interpretation Center**, at Acebuche (☎ 959/448711), open daily 8–7. Four-wheel-drive tours of the park, which must be reserved in advance (☎ 959/430432), start from here; tours last four hours, cost 2,500 pesetas, and take you on a 70-km (43-mi) route across beaches, sand dunes, marshes, and scrub. Off season (Nov.–Feb.), you can usually book a tour with just a day's notice; at other times, book as far in advance as possible (☞ Guided Tours *in* Seville and Western Andalusia A to Z, *below*).

Matalascañas

③⑥ *3 km (2 mi) south of Acebuche, main reception center at Doñana; 85 km (53 mi) southwest of Seville.*

This town's close proximity to the main reception center (Acebuche) at Doñana makes it a convenient spot for park visitors to spend the night. Otherwise, it's a rather incongruous and ugly sprawl of hotels and vacation homes, very crowded at Easter and in summer and eerily deserted the rest of the year. There are some nice beaches for those who just want to relax in the sun; the ocean waters here are also a haven for windsurfers and other water-sport buffs.

Dining and Lodging

$$ 🏨 **Tierra Mar.** If you want to stay longer to explore the Doñana park, check into this large, beachfront hotel. ⊠ *Matalascañas Parc, 120 Sector M,* ☎ *959/440300,* 📠 *959/440720. 254 rooms. Restaurant, café, pool, sauna. AE, DC, MC, V.*

Mazagón

③⑦ *22 km (14 mi) northwest of Matalascañas.*

True, there isn't much to see or do in this coastal town, but the parador here makes a nice base for touring La Rábida, Palos de la Frontera, and Moguer. The town's beautiful beach is among the nicest in the region.

Dining and Lodging

$$$ ✕🏨 **Parador Cristóbal Colón.** This peaceful, modern parador, 3 km (2 mi) southeast of Mazagón, stands on a cliff surrounded by pine groves and overlooks a sandy beach. The rooms are all well equipped; most have balconies overlooking the garden. The restaurant serves traditional Andalusian dishes and local seafood specialties, like *sopa viña AB* (a fish soup flavored with sherry and thickened with mayonnaise), stuffed baby squid, or hake medallions. ⊠ *Carretera Huelva–Matalascañas, Km 24, 21130,* ☎ *959/536300,* FAX *959/536228. 43 rooms. Restaurant, bar, pool, tennis courts, meeting rooms. AE, DC, MC, V.*

La Rábida

★ ③⑧ *30 km (19 mi) northwest of Doñana, 8 km (5 mi) northwest of Mazagón.*

You may want to extend your Doñana tour to include a visit to the monastery of **Santa María de La Rábida,** "the birthplace of America." In 1485 Columbus came from Portugal with his son Diego to stay in this Mudéjar-style Franciscan monastery. Here, Columbus discussed his theories with friars Antonio de Marchena and Juan Pérez, who interceded on his behalf with Queen Isabella. In the early 15th-century church you'll find a much-venerated 14th-century statue of the **Virgen de los Milagros** (Virgin of Miracles). The **frescoes** in the gatehouse were painted by Daniel Vázquez Díaz in 1930. Next to the monastery is a small, basic, inexpensive hostelry, the Hostería de la Rábida (☎ 959/ 350312). ☎ *959/350411.* 🖾 *Free; donations accepted.* ☉ *Tues.–Sun. 10–1 and 4–6:15 (4–7 in summer).*

Two kilometers (1 mile) from the monastery, on the seashore, is the **Muelle de las Carabelas** (Caravels' Wharf), a reproduction of a 15th-century port. The star exhibits here are the full-size replicas of Columbus's flotilla, the *Niña, Pinta,* and *Santa María,* which were built using the same techniques as in Columbus's day. You can climb aboard each one and learn more (or refresh your memory) about the discovery of America in the adjoining museum. ⊠ *Paraje de le Rabida,* ☎ *959/ 530597.* 🖾 *420 ptas.* ☉ *Winter, Tues.–Sun. 10–7; summer, Tues.– Sun. 10–2 and 5–9.*

Palos de la Frontera

③⑨ *4 km (2½ mi) northeast of La Rábida, 12 km (7 mi) northeast of Mazagón.*

Did you learn *this* in school? On August 2, 1492, Columbus's three caravels, the *Niña,* the *Pinta,* and the *Santa María,* set sail from here. Most of the crew were men from Palos and neighboring Moguer. At the door of the church of **San Jorge** (1473), the royal letter ordering the levy of the ships' crew and equipment was read aloud; and the voyagers took their water supplies from the Fontanilla.

Moguer

④⓪ *12 km (7 mi) northeast of Palos de la Frontera.*

The inhabitants of this old port town now spend more time growing strawberries than they do seafaring, as you'll see from the surrounding fields. Visit the **Convent of Santa Clara,** which dates from 1337. 🖾 *250 ptas.* ☉ *Tues.–Sat. 11–1 and 4:30–6:30.*

While in Moguer, see the **home of Nobel Prize–winning poet Juan Ramón Jiménez,** author of the much-loved *Platero y Yo.* ⊠ *C. Juan Ramón Jiménez,* ☎ *959/372148.* 🖾 *250 ptas.* ☉ *Mon.–Sat. 10–2 and 5–8, Sun. 10–2.*

Riotinto

④ *74 km (46 mi) north of Huelva.*

Heading north from Palos de la Frontera and Huelva along the N435, you'll reach the turnoff to Minas de Riotinto, the mining town near the source of the Riotinto (literally, "red river"). The river's waters are the color of blood due to the minerals leeched from the surrounding mountains; this area contains some of the richest copper deposits in the world, as well as gold and silver. It has been mined since antiquity, as the many Iberian, Tartessian, and Roman artifacts found here attest. In 1873 the mines were taken over by the British Rio Tinto Company Ltd., which started to dig a massive open pit mine and build a 64-km (40-mi) railway to the port of Huelva to transport mineral ore. The British left in 1954, but mining activity continues today, albeit on a smaller scale.

The multicolored landscape, scarred by centuries of intensive mining, makes for an unusual and well-organized tour conducted by the Fundación Riotinto. The tour's first stop, the **Museo Minero** (Museum of Mining) has archaeological finds, exhibits on the area's mining history, and a collection of historical steam engines and railway coaches. Next comes the **Corta Atalaya,** one of the largest open pit mines in the world (4,000 ft across and 1,100 ft deep), and Bellavista, the elegant English quarter where the British mine managers lived. To end the tour, you can take the **Tren Minero** (Miners' Train), which follows the course of the Riotinto more than 24 restored km (15 mi) of the old mining railway. *Fundación Riotinto,* ☎ *959/590025.* ☞ *1,700 ptas. for full tour.* ☉ *Tues.–Sat. 10–2; Miners' Train, July–Aug., daily 2; Apr.–Jun., weekends 5; Sept.–Mar., weekends 4.*

Aracena

④ *105 km (65 mi) north of Huelva.*

Stretching north of the Riotinto mines is the 460,000-acre Sierra de Aracena nature park, an expanse of rolling hills cloaked in cork and holm oak. This region is known for its cured hams, which come from the prized free-ranging Iberian pigs that gorge on acorns in the autumn months prior to slaughter. The hams are buried in salt and then hung in cellars to dry-cure for at least two years. The best hams come from the village of **Jabugo.** The capital of the region is **Aracena,** whose main attraction is the spectacular cave known as the Gruta de las Maravillas (Cave of Marvels). The 12 caverns hide stalactites and stalagmites arranged in wonderful patterns, long corridors, and beautiful underground lakes. ✉ *Plaza Pozo de Nieves, Pozo de Nieves,* ☎ *959/128355.* ☞ *875 ptas.* ☉ *Guided tours daily 10:30, 11:30, 12:30, 1:30, 3, 4, 5, and 6.*

PROVINCE OF CÁDIZ

Jerez de la Frontera, Arcos de la Frontera, Sanlúcar de Barrameda, Puerto de Santa María, and Cádiz

A trip through Cádiz is a trip back in time. Winding roads take you through scenes ranging from flat and barren plains to seemingly endless vineyards. The rolling countryside is carpeted with blindingly white soil known as *albariza,* unique to this area; it's the secret to the grapes used in sherry. Throughout the province, *los pueblos blancos* (white villages) provide striking contrasts with the terrain, especially at Arcos de la Frontera, where the village sits dramatically on a crag overlooking the gorge of the Guadalete River. In Jerez, you can savor the internationally famous sherry or delight in the skills and forms of purebred Carthusian horses. Finally, in the city of Cádiz, absorb about 3,000 years of history—this is one of the oldest continuously inhabited cities in the Western world.

Jerez de la Frontera

43 *97 km (60 mi) south of Seville.*

Jerez, world headquarters for sherry, is surrounded by immense vineyards of chalky soil, whose Palomino grapes have funded a host of churches and noble mansions. An hour's stroll around the center is all you'll need to get a feel for this small city. May and September are the most exciting times to visit Jerez, when spectacular fiestas transform the town. In early May Jerez's Feria del Caballo (Horse Fair) fills the streets with carriages and riders, and purebreds from the School of Equestrian Art compete in races and dressage displays. September brings the Fiesta de Otoño (Autumn Festival), when the grapes are blessed on the steps of the cathedral.

The 12th-century **Alcázar** was once the residence of the caliph of Seville. The Moorish mosque inside was later transformed into a Catholic church by Alfonso the Wise. The terrace of the Alcázar has a nice view of the cathedral. ⊠ *Alameda Vieja.* ☉ *Weekdays 10–2 and 4–6, Sat. 10–2; closed afternoons in summer.*

The **cathedral** has an octagonal cupola and a separate bell tower. ⊠ *Plaza del Arroyo.* ☉ *Weekdays 6–7, Sun. 11–2.*

On the **Plaza de la Asunción,** one of Jerez's most intimate squares, you'll find the Mudéjar church of **San Dionisio** and the ornate **cabildo municipal** (city hall), with a lovely plateresque facade dating from 1575.

Jerez also has an unusual and interesting museum devoted to clocks: the **Museo de los Relojes** (Clock Museum). For the full effect, time your visit for noon, when all of the clocks chime at once. ⊠ *C. Cervantes 3,* ☎ *956/182100.* 💷 *400 ptas.* ☉ *Mon.–Sat. 10–2.*

Names such as González Byass, Domecq, Harvey, and Sandeman are inextricably linked with Jerez. The word *sherry,* first used in Great Britain in 1608, is actually an English corruption of the town's old Moorish name, Xeres. Both sherry and horses are very much the domain of Jerez's Anglo-Spanish aristocracy, whose Catholic ancestors came here from England two or three centuries ago.

★ At any given time, more than a million barrels of sherry are maturing in Jerez's vast aboveground wine cellars. If you visit a **bodega** (winery), the guide will explain the *solera* method of blending old wine with new and the importance of the *flor* (a sort of yeast that forms on the surface of the wine as it ages) in determining the kind of sherry. Most bodegas welcome visitors, but it's always advisable to phone ahead for an appointment, if only to make sure you join a group that speaks your language. Cellars usually charge a token admission fee, rarely more than 400 pesetas. Most wineries close for August. Tours last between 40 minutes and an hour and usually start with an audiovisual program or short film about sherry and the history of that particular winery. You'll then tour the aging cellars, with their endless rows of casks. (You won't see the actual fermenting and bottling, which take place in more modern, less romantic plants outside town.) Finally, you'll be able to sample generous amounts of pale, dry *fino;* nutty *amontillado;* or rich, deep *oloroso,* and, of course, you'll be invited to purchase a few bottles at interesting prices in the winery shop.

Domecq is Jerez's oldest bodega, founded in 1730, and aside from sherry produces the world's best-selling brandy, Fundador (☎ 956/151000). Other wineries worth visiting include **Sandeman** (☎ 956/301100), **Harvey** (☎ 956/151000), and **Wisdom and Warter** (☎ 956/184306). But if you only have time for one, tour the prestigious **González Byass,** home of the famous Tío Pepe (☎ 956/357000); this tour is well organized and includes La Concha, an open-air aging cellar designed by Eiffel.

★ ☙   The **Real Escuela Andaluza del Arte Ecuestre** (Royal Andalusian School of Equestrian Art) operates on the grounds of the Recreo de las Cadenas, a splendid 19th-century palace. This prestigious school was masterminded by Alvaro Domecq in the 1970s. Every Thursday the Cartujana horses—a breed created from a cross between the native Andalusian workhorse and the Arabian—and skilled riders in 18th-century riding costume demonstrate intricate dressage techniques and jumping in the spectacular show "Como Bailan los Caballos Andaluces." ⊠ *Avda. Duque de Abrantes,* ☎ *956/307798.* ⊠ *Numbered seats 2,400 ptas., unnumbered seats 1,500 ptas.* ☉ *Thurs. 11–1 (reservations essential).*

The rest of the week, you can visit the stables and tack room, watch the horses being schooled, and witness **rehearsals** for the show. ⊠ *450 ptas.* ☉ *Mon.–Wed. and Fri. 11–1.*

Bullfighting
Jerez's bullring is on Calle Circo, northeast of the city center. Tickets are sold at the official ticket office on Calle Porvera, though only about five bullfights are held each year, in May and October.

Dining and Lodging
$$$ ✕ **Gaitán.** Within walking distance of the riding school, this restaurant has white walls and brick arches decorated with colorful ceramic plates and photos of famous guests. It's crowded with businesspeople at lunchtime. The menu is Andalusian, with a few Basque dishes thrown in. *Setas* (wild mushrooms) make a delicious starter in season. ⊠ *Gaitán 3,* ☎ *956/345859. AE, DC, MC, V. No dinner Sun.*

$$$ ✕ **La Mesa Redonda.** Chef-owner José Antonio Valdespino has spent years researching the classic recipes once served in aristocratic Jerez homes, and he serves them in this friendly, small restaurant off Avenida Alvaro Domeqc. It feels like a family dining room; the eight tables are surrounded by shelves lined with cookbooks. (The round table at one end of the room gave the restaurant its name.) The menu changes constantly; your best bet is to take the advice of the chef's wife, Margarita— who also has an encyclopedic knowledge of Spanish wines. ⊠ *Manuel de la Quintana 3,* ☎ *956/340069. AE, DC, MC, V. Closed Sun.*

$$–$$$ ✕ **Venta Antonio.** Crowds come to this roadside inn from far and wide to dine on superb, fresh seafood cooked in top-quality olive oil. You enter through the busy bar, where fresh fish bask and lobsters await in a tank. Try the specialties of the Bay of Cádiz, such as *sopa de mariscos* (shellfish soup) followed by *bogavantes de Sanlúcar* (succulent local lobster). ⊠ *Carretera de Jerez-Sanlúcar, Km 5,* ☎ *956/140535. AE, DC, MC, V.*

$$ ✕ **Tendido 6.** This restaurant is near the bullring, opposite Gate 6— hence its name. The tables are set in an enclosed patio decorated with bullfight posters, and draped with bright-red tablecloths. The menu has all of the Spanish standbys: *jamón serrano* (cured ham), *gambas al ajillo* (garlic shrimp), and *tarta de almendra* (almond tart). ⊠ *Circo 10,* ☎ *956/344835. AE, DC, MC, V. Closed Sun.*

$$$ ✕⚐ **Jerez.** This luxury hotel is set in a low, white, three-story building in the residential neighborhood north of town. The bar and elegant El Cartujano restaurant overlook the sun terrace, large pool, and big, leafy garden. Public rooms are light and airy. The best rooms overlook the pool and garden; back rooms face the tennis courts and parking lot. ✉ *Avda. Alvaro Domecq 35, 11405,* ☎ *956/300600,* FAX *956/ 305001. 116 rooms, 4 suites. Restaurant, bar, pool, tennis courts, free parking. AE, DC, MC, V.*

$$$ ⚐ **Royal Sherry Park.** This gleaming, modern hotel is set back from
★ the road in an unusually large, tree-filled garden. It's designed around several patios filled with exotic foliage, and the light, sunny hallways are decorated with modern paintings. The rooms are bright and airy, and most have balconies overlooking the garden. ✉ *Avda. Alvaro Domecq 11, 11405,* ☎ *956/303011,* FAX *956/311300. 173 rooms. Restaurant, bar, coffee shop, pool, meeting rooms. AE, DC, MC, V.*

$$$ ⚐ **Montecastillo Hotel and Golf Resort.** Sprawling and modern, the Montecastillo adjoins a golf course designed by Jack Nicklaus, outside Jerez near the race track. The spacious common areas have marble floors. Rooms are cheerfully decorated, with off-white walls, bright floral bedspreads, and rustic clay tiles. Ask for a room with terrace overlooking the golf course. ✉ *Carretera de Arcos, Km 9,,* ☎ *956/151200,* FAX *956/ 151209. 116 rooms, 5 suites. Restaurant, pool, sauna, 18-hole golf course. AE, DC, MC, V.*

$$$ ⚐ **Avenida Jerez.** Opposite the Royal Sherry Park (☞ above), this modern hotel has light and sunny rooms with hard-wood floors and rich blue decor. All rooms have VCRs. Ask for a room at the back; those at the front are close to the road and can be noisy despite double glazing. ✉ *Avda. Alvaro Domecq 10, 11405,* ☎ *956/347411,* FAX *956/ 337296. 95 rooms. Restaurant, bar, coffee shop, in-room VCRs. AE, DC, MC, V.*

$–$$ ⚐ **Ávila.** This friendly hotel in a side street off Calle Arcos offers affordable central accommodations. A TV lounge and a small bar and breakfast room open off the lobby. The rooms have basic furnishings and tile floors; beds are on the small side. ✉ *Ávila 3, 11401,* ☎ *956/ 334808,* FAX *956/336807. 32 rooms. Bar, breakfast room. AE, DC, MC, V.*

Racing
Formula One Grand Prix car and motorcycle races are held at Jerez's race track, including the Formula One Tío Pepe Grand Prix in late September and early October. For information, call the track (☎ 956/ 151100) or check with the tourist office.

Shopping
In this town famous for its horses, **Duarte** (✉ Larga 15, ☎ 956/ 342751) is the most famous saddle shop, sending beautifully wrought leather all over the world, including to the British royal family. It's worth a visit; you can choose from all kinds of other smaller, but beautifully worked, leather items. You can also find nice wicker and ceramic items along Calle Corredera and Calle Bodegas.

Arcos de la Frontera
★ ㊹ *31 km (19 mi) east of Jerez.*

Perched dramatically on a wild crag crowned by a castle, this white village overlooks the gorge of the Guadalete River. The church of **Santa María**, on the Plaza de España, is a fascinating blend of architectural styles: Romanesque, Gothic, and Mudéjar, with a plateresque doorway, a Renaissance *retablo*, and a 17th-century Baroque choir.

Dining and Lodging

$$ ✕ **El Convento.** The 17th-century Palacio de Valdespina has been decorated with a profusion of Sevillian tiles and converted into a series of dining rooms arranged around a central courtyard. The menu features local specialities such as *abajao* (soup of wild asparagus) and partridge in almond sauce. ⊠ *Marqués de Torresoto 7,* ☎ FAX *956/703222. AE, MC, V.*

$$$ ✕🏨 **Parador Casa del Corregidor.** The terrace has a spectacular view—
★ this parador clings to the cliffside overlooking the rolling valley of the Guadalete River. Charles de Gaulle wrote part of his memoirs while staying here. Public rooms include a bar decorated with tiles and bullfight pictures; a panoramic restaurant that opens onto the terrace; and an enclosed patio. Most rooms are so big that it's hard to watch TV from the bed; they're furnished in traditional parador style, with dark Castilian furniture, *esparto* rugs, and abundant tiles. The best rooms are Nos. 15–18, which overlook the valley. The restaurant's local dishes include *berenjenas arcenses* (spicy eggplant with ham and chorizo); or you can ask for the Gastronomic Menu, featuring 10 different regional specialities. ⊠ *Plaza del Cabildo, 11630,* ☎ *956/ 700500,* FAX *956/701116. 24 rooms. Restaurant, bar. AE, DC, MC, V.*

$$ ✕🏨 **El Convento.** An inexpensive alternative, this tiny hotel is in part of an old convent. Perched on top of the cliff right behind the parador (☞ *above*), it shares the same amazing view but has just eight rooms. The same folks run the nearby El Convento restaurant (☞ *above*). ⊠ *Maldonado 2, 11630,* ☎ FAX *956/702333. 8 rooms. AE, DC, MC, V.*

$$–$$$ 🏨 **Cortijo Faín.** This resort hotel is set in a 17th-century farmhouse on a ranch 3 km (2 mi) southeast of Arcos. The old *cortijo* (farm-estate) is surrounded by olive groves and enclosed in high, white walls covered in bougainvillea. The atmosphere is personal and intimate. Aim for one of the two suites that have their own fireplace. Reservations are essential. ⊠ *Carretera de Algar, Km 3, 11630,* ☎ FAX *956/231396. 2 rooms, 8 suites. Restaurant, pool, horseback riding, library, meeting rooms. AE, MC, V.*

Sanlúcar de Barrameda

❹❺ *24 km (15 mi) west of Jerez.*

Columbus sailed from here on his third voyage to the Americas, in 1498. Twenty years later, Magellan steered his ships out of the same harbor to begin his circumnavigation of the planet. Today this unspoiled fishing town is known primarily for its *langostinos* (giant shrimp) and manzanilla. From the *puerto pesquero* (fishing port), 4 km (2½ mi) north of the town center, there's a fine view of fishing boats and the pine trees of the Doñana on the opposite bank of the Guadalquivir. Sandy beaches extend along Sanlúcar's southern promontory to Chipiona, where the Roman general Scipio Africanus built a beacon tower.

Dining

$$$ ✕ **Bigote.** The Bajo de Guía beach is famous for its seafood, and this colorful, informal fish restaurant sits right on it. The kitchen is known for its fried *acedias* (a type of small sole) and *langostinos* (large shrimp) which come from these very waters—if you want them any fresher, you'll have to catch them yourself. The seafood paella is also good. Reservations are essential in summer. ⊠ *Bajo de Guía,* ☎ *956/362696. AE, DC, MC, V. Closed Sun.*

$$$ ✕ **Mirador de Doñana.** Another Bajo de Guía landmark, the Mirador de Doñana serves superfresh sole, shrimp, and *puntillas* (baby squid). The dining area overlooks the large bar, which is always busy. ⊠ *Bajo de Guía,* ☎ *956/364205. MC, V.*

Puerto de Santa María

★ **46** *12 km (7 mi) southwest of Jerez, 17 km (11 mi) north of Cádiz.*

On the northern shores of the Bay of Cádiz, this attractive, if somewhat dilapidated, little fishing port sports an array of white houses with peeling facades and floor-length green grilles covering the doors and windows. The town is dominated by the Terry and Osborne sherry and brandy *bodegas*. Columbus once lived in a house on the square that bears his name (Cristóbal Colón), and Washington Irving spent the autumn of 1828 at Calle Palacios 57.

Bars

The *marisco* (seafood) bars along the Ribera del Marisco (Seafood Way) are Puerto Santa María's current claim to fame. **Romerijo, Casa Paco,** and neighboring **Bar Salva** are among the most popular.

Dining and Lodging

$$$ ✕ **El Faro de el Puerto** (The Lighthouse in the Port). In a villa just outside town, this restaurant is run by the same family that established the classic El Faro in Cádiz (☞ below). Like its predecessor, it serves excellent fish dishes, but you can also browse in the meat department for such delicacies as veal rolls filled with foie gras in a sweet sherry sauce. ⊠ *Carretera del Puerto-Rota, Km 0,* ☎ *956/858003 or 956/ 870952. AE, DC, MC, V. No dinner Sun.*

$$ ✕ **Casa Flores.** A bit more up-market than most other Ribera del Marisco haunts, Flores serves the same fresh seafood. You approach it through a long bar hung with hams. ⊠ *Ribera del Marisco 9,* ☎ *956/ 543512. AE, MC, V.*

$–$$ ✕ **El Patio.** Hidden a block behind the Ribera del Marisco, this pretty restaurant is built around an 18th-century patio. Colorful ceramic plates and potted plants decorate the dining room. The menu combines local seafood from the Bay of Cádiz with Andalusian dishes like *rabo de toro* (oxtail stew), and the homemade desserts are especially good. ⊠ *Misericordia 1,* ☎ *956/540506. AE, DC, MC, V.*

$$$ 🏨 **Monasterio de San Miguel.** Dating from 1733, this monastery is in
★ the heart of town, a few blocks from the harbor. There's nothing spartan about the former cells; they're now air-conditioned rooms with all of the trappings, though you might need a map just to locate yours along the long corridors. The restaurant is in a large, vaulted hall; the Baroque church is now a concert hall; and the cloister's gardens provide a peaceful refuge. Beamed ceilings, polished marble floors, and huge brass lamps only enhance the 18th-century atmosphere. ⊠ *Larga 27, 11500,* ☎ *956/540440,* FAX *956/542604. 177 rooms. Restaurant, bar, pool, squash. AE, DC, MC, V.*

Nightlife and the Arts

The **Casino Bahía de Cádiz,** on the road between Jerez and Puerto de Santa María, is the only casino in this part of Andalusia. You can play the usual range of games, and there's a restaurant and a disco. You must present your passport to enter. ⊠ *N IV, Km 649,* ☎ *956/871042.* ▦ *500 ptas.* ☉ *Weekdays 7 PM–4 AM, weekends 7 PM–6 AM.*

Sailing

Most towns on and around the Bay of Cádiz have yacht clubs and marinas. Together they host about 50 regattas each year, for all kinds of boats. Inquire at the local tourist office about sailing. The newest marina is **Puerto Sherry** (☎ *956/870203*), on the Bay of Cádiz, near Puerto de Santa María.

Cádiz

★ **④7** *32 km (20 mi) southwest of Jerez, 149 km (93 mi) southwest of Seville.*

Spaniards flock here in February to revel in Cádiz's famous Carnival celebrations, but few foreigners have yet discovered the real charm of this city. Surrounded by the Atlantic Ocean on three sides, Cádiz was founded as Gadir by Phoenician traders in 1100 BC and claims to be the oldest continuously inhabited city in the Western world. Here Hannibal lived for a time and Julius Caesar first held public office.

After centuries of decline during the Middle Ages and under Moorish rule, Cádiz regained its commercial importance after the discovery of America. Columbus set out from here on his second voyage, and Cádiz later became the home base of the Spanish fleet. Its merchants competed fiercely with those of Seville, and when the Guadalquivir silted up in the 18th century, Cádiz monopolized New World trade and became the wealthiest port in Western Europe. Most of its buildings date from this period, including the cathedral, built in part with gold and silver from the New World.

The old city is African in appearance and immensely intriguing—a cluster of narrow streets opening onto charming, small squares. The golden cupola of the cathedral looms above low white houses, and the whole place has a slightly dilapidated air. In an hour's walk around the headlands, you'll visit the entire old town and pass through some enchanting parks with fine views of the bay.

You might begin your explorations in the Plaza de Mina, a large, leafy square with palm trees and plenty of benches. On the square's western flank, the ornamental facade of the College of Architects is especially beautiful.On the east side, you'll find the **Museo de Bellas Artes y Arqueología** (Museum of Fine Arts and Archaeology), well worth visiting for its works by Murillo and Alonso Cano, and the *Four Evangelists* and set of saints by Zurbarán, which have much in common with his masterpieces at Guadalupe, in Extremadura (☞ Chapter 14). ⊠ *Plaza de Mina,* ☎ *956/212281.* 🎟 *250 ptas.* ☉ *Tues.–Sun. 9–2:30.*

A few blocks west of the Plaza de Mina is the **Oratorio de la Santa Cueva,** an oval-shape 18th-century chapel with three frescoes by Goya. ⊠ *C. Rosario,* ☎ *956/287676.* 🎟 *100 ptas.* ☉ *Weekdays 10–1.*

Don't forget to look up while walking the streets around here—the facades are quite splendid. Near the Plaza de San Antonio you'll find the **Oratorio de San Felipe Neri.** Spain's first liberal constitution was declared at this church in 1812, and here the Cortes (Parliament) of Cádiz met when the rest of Spain was subjected to the rule of Napoleon's brother, Joseph Bonaparte (more popularly known as Pepe Botella, for his love of the bottle). On the main altar is an *Immaculate Conception* by Murillo, the great Sevillian artist who in 1682 fell to his death from a scaffold while working on his *Mystic Marriage of St. Catherine* in Cádiz's Chapel of Santa Catalina in Cádiz. ⊠ *Santa Inés,* ☎ *956/ 211612.* 🎟 *Free.* ☉ *Daily 8:30–10 and 7:30–9:20, Sat. 5:30–6:30.*

Next door to the Oratorio de San Felipe Neri, the small but pleasant **Museo Histórico Municipal** (Municipal Historical Museum) has a 19th-century mural depicting the establishment of the Constitution of 1812. Its real showpiece is a fascinating 1779 ivory and mahogany model of the city, which depicts in minute detail all the streets and buildings, much as they are now. ⊠ *Santa Inés,* ☎ *956/221788.* 🎟 *Free* ☉ *Tues.–Fri. 9–1 and 4–7, weekends 9–1.*

Four blocks to the west of Santa Inés is the Plaza Manuel de Falla, overlooked by an amazing neo-Mudéjar redbrick building, the **Gran Teatro Manuel de Falla** (☞ Nightlife and the Arts, *below*). The theater's interior is impressive as well, if you have time to catch a show while you're in town; check with the tourist office about events.

The **cathedral,** with a gold dome and Baroque facade, was begun in 1722, when Cádiz was at the height of its power. The Cádiz-born composer Manuel de Falla, who died in 1946 at the age of 70, is buried in the crypt. The cathedral museum, on Calle Acero, overflows with gold, silver, and precious jewels brought from the New World. One of its most priceless possessions is Enrique de Arfe's processional cross, which is carried in the Corpus Christi parades. ⊠ *Plaza Cathedral,* ☎ *956/286154 for museum.* 🖾 *Cathedral free, museum 400 ptas.* ☉ *Service Sun. noon; museum Tues.–Sat. 10–12.*

The impressive **ayuntamiento** (city hall) overlooks the Plaza San Juan de Diós, one of the city's liveliest hubs. Built in two parts, in 1799 and 1861, the building is attractively illuminated at night.

The **Plaza San Francisco,** near the ayuntamiento, is a pretty square surrounded by white and yellow houses and filled with orange trees and elegant street lamps. It's especially lively during *paseos.*

Dining and Lodging

$$$ ✕ **El Faro.** Gonzalo Córdoba's restaurant in a fishing quarter justly de-
★   serves its fame as the best restaurant in the province. Outside, it's one of many low white houses decorated with bright blue flowerpots; inside, the decor is warm and inviting, with half-tile walls, glass lanterns, oil paintings, and photos of old Cádiz. Fish and seafood dominate the menu, but there are plenty of alternatives, such as *cebón al queso de cabrales* (venison in blue-cheese sauce). ⊠ *San Felix 15,* ☎ *956/ 211068. AE, DC, MC, V.*

$ ✕ **Achuri.** Founded in 1947, this old-fashioned eatery offers excellent value for the money with a menu that combines Andalusian and Basque flavors. Try the Basque specialities, such as *cocochas* (delicate hake morsels) or the Biscay-style hake. ⊠ *Plocia 15,* ☎ *956/253613. MC, V.*

$$$ ▥ **Atlántico.** Cádiz's parador commands a privileged position on the headland overlooking the bay. It's the only hotel in its class in the old part of Cádiz. The spacious indoor public rooms have gleaming marble floors, and tables and chairs surround a fountain on the small outdoor patio. The cheerful, bright-green bar, decorated with ceramic tiles and bullfighting posters, is a popular meeting place for Cádiz society. Most of the rooms have small balconies facing the sea. ⊠ *Duque de Nájera 9, 11002,* ☎ *956/226905,* ☒ *956/214582. 143 rooms, 6 suites. Restaurant, bar, pool. AE, DC, MC, V.*

$$ ▥ **Francia y Paris.** The advantage here is the central location, on a pretty pedestrian square in the heart of the old town. The house has a rather boring, modern interior that includes a vast lobby, a large sitting room, and a small bar and breakfast room. The rooms are simple; some have small balconies facing the square. ⊠ *Plaza San Francisco 2, 11004,* ☎ *956/222348,* ☒ *956/222431. 57 rooms. Bar, breakfast room. AE, DC, MC, V.*

Nightlife and the Arts

Ground zero for cultural events in Cádiz is the **Gran Teatro Manuel de Falla** (⊠ Plaza de Falla, ☎ 956/220828).

Shopping

You'll find all the usual Andalusian handicrafts here, especially ceramics and wicker. **Belle Epoque** (⊠ Antonio Lopez 2, ☎ 956/226810) is one of Cádiz's better—and more reasonably priced—antiques stores, specializing in furniture. **Casa Rodríguez** (⊠ Enrique de las Marinas 1, ☎ 956/213104) displays a wide selection of all kinds of antiques in a large showroom in one of Cádiz's older houses.

SEVILLE AND WESTERN ANDALUSIA A TO Z

Arriving and Departing

By Bus

Long-distance bus services connect Seville with Madrid; with Cáceres, Mérida, and Badajoz in Extremadura; and Córdoba, Granada, Málaga, Ronda, and Huelva in Andalusia. Regional buses take the coastal route from Granada, Málaga, and Marbella to Cádiz. Buses from Ronda run to Arcos, Jerez, and Cádiz. Buses throughout Andalusia, and between Extremadura and Seville, tend to be more frequent and convenient than trains.

By Car

The main road into the region from Madrid is the N IV through Córdoba. This has recently been made into a four-lane *autovía*, but it's one of Spain's busiest roads, and trucks can cause delays. From Granada or Málaga, head for Antequera; then take N334 by way of Osuna to Seville. Several highways in and around Seville were improved and rebuilt for Expo '92, so road trips from Córdoba, Granada, and the Costa del Sol (by way of Ronda) are all reasonably quick and pleasant. From the Costa del Sol, the coastal N340 highway is well paved and rarely very busy west of Algeciras.

By Plane

The region's main airport is Seville's **San Pablo Airport** (☎ 95/444–9000), 12 km (7½ mi) east of the city on N IV to Córdoba. International flights arrive from Amsterdam, Brussels, Frankfurt, London, and Paris, domestic flights from Madrid, Barcelona, Valencia, and other major cities. Seville's **Iberia** office is on Almirante Lobo 2 (☎ 95/422–8901 or 902/400500). There is no bus or train service to the airport; you'll have to take a taxi.

The region's other airport is Jerez de la Frontera's **Aeropuerto de la Parra** (☎ 956/150000), 7 km (4½ mi) from Jerez on the road to Seville. Iberia subsidiary **Aviaco** (✉ Airport, ☎ 956/150010) flies from here to Madrid, Barcelona, Valencia–Palma de Mallorca, and Zaragoza. GB Airways, a British Airways affiliate, flies to London (☎ 956/150093 and 902/111333).

By Train

Seville, Jerez, and Cádiz all lie on the main rail line between Madrid and the southwest corner of Spain. From Madrid, roughly six trains run to Seville daily, via Córdoba; three of these continue on to Jerez and Cádiz. RENFE also operates the high-speed AVE train between Madrid and Seville; it costs more than regular trains, but it makes the journey in 2½ hours and has become the most popular mode of travel between the two cities. From Granada, Málaga, Ronda, and Algeciras, trains go to Seville by way of Bobadilla, where, more often than not, you have to change.

Crime

WARNING: With chronic high unemployment, Seville and Cádiz have built up something of a record in petty crime, such as purse snatching and thefts from parked cars, even the occasional robbery. Drive with your car doors locked; lock all your luggage out of sight in the trunk; *never* leave *anything* in a parked car; and keep a wary eye on scooter riders, who have been known to snatch purses or even smash the windows of moving cars. Take only a small amount of cash and one credit card out with you. Leave your passport, traveler's checks, and other credit cards in the hotel safe, and avoid carrying purses and expensive cameras or wearing valuable jewelry.

Getting Around

By Bus

Buses connect all of the towns and villages in this region. **Cádiz** has two bus depots: **Comes** (✉ Plaza Hispanidad, ☎ 956/224271) runs buses to most destinations in Andalusia; **Los Amarillos** (✉ Diego Fernández Herreras 34, ☎ 956/285852) serves Jerez, Seville, Córdoba, Puerto de Santa María, Sanlúcar de Barrameda, and Chipiona.The Jerez bus station is on the Plaza Madre de Dios, and is served by two companies: **La Valenciana** (☎ 956/341063) and **Los Amarillos** (☎ 956/347844). Seville now has two bus stations. The older one is the **Estación del Prado de San Sebastián** (✉ Prado de San Sebastián, ☎ 95/441–7111), just off the Plaza de San Sebastián between Manuel Vázquez Sagastizabal and José María Osborne; buses from here serve points west and northwest. The second, a glittering, modern terminal on the banks of the Guadalquivir River downtown, is the **Estación Plaza de Armas** (✉ Cristo de la Expiración, next to east end of Cachorro Bridge, ☎ 95/490–8040); it serves central and eastern Spain. The tourist office can confirm which station you need.

By Car

Driving in Western Andalusia is easy—the terrain is mostly flat or gently rolling hills, and the roads are straight. From Seville to Jerez and Cádiz, you can choose between N IV and the slightly faster A4 toll road. The only way to access the Coto Doñana by road is to take the A49 Seville–Huelva highway, exit for Almonte/Bollullos par del Condado, then follow the signs for El Rocío and Matalascañas. Getting into and out of Seville, long a nightmarishly confusing ordeal, has become far easier as a result of a new ring road and several altered accesses, but getting around the city by car is still trying. Try to avoid the 7:15–8:30 PM rush hour in Seville and Cádiz, and by wary of the lunchtime rush hour, around 2–3 PM. Don't try to bring a car to Cádiz at Carnival time (pre-Lent) or to Seville during Holy Week or the April Fair—processions close most of the streets to traffic. *See* Crime, *above,* if you're considering driving and parking in Seville.

By Train

A dozen or more local trains each day connect Cádiz with Puerto de Santa María, Jerez, and Seville. Journey time from Cádiz to Seville is 1½ to 2 hours. There are no trains to the Coto Doñana, Sanlúcar de Barrameda, or Arcos de la Frontera or between Cádiz and the Costa del Sol.

Cádiz's station is on Plaza de Sevilla near the docks; **Jerez's** station is on Plaza de la Estación, off Diego Fernández Herrera, in the east of town. For train information on the entire province of Cádiz, call RENFE in Cádiz (☎ 956/254301). In **Seville,** the sprawling Santa Justa station is on Avenida Kansas City. Contact the downtown RENFE office (✉ Zaragoza 29, ☎ 95/454–0202) for information and reservations.

Contacts and Resources

Boating

Among the many options for boating aficionados on the Guadalquivir are paddleboats and canoes; inquire at the tourist office, or on the riverbank near the Torre del Oro. **Cruceros Turísticos Torre del Oro** (✉ Paseo

Alcalde Marqués de Contadero beside Torre del Oro, ☎ 95/421–1396) runs hourly river cruises at 1,200 pesetas per person.

Consulates

United States (✉ Paseo de las Delicias 7, Seville, ☎ 95/423–1883). **Canada** (✉ Avda. de la Constitución 30, Seville, ☎ 95/422–9413). **United Kingdom** (✉ Plaza Nueva 8, Seville, ☎ 95/422–8874/75).

Emergencies

Police: **Cádiz** (✉ Avda. de Andalucía 28, ☎ 091), **Jerez de la Frontera** (✉ Plaza de Silos, ☎ 091), **Seville** (✉ Plaza de la Concordia 1, ☎ 091). Ambulance: **Seville** (☎ 061).

Guided Tours

In Seville, any of the following organizations can put you in touch with qualified English-speaking guides: **Asociación Provincial de Informadores Turísticos** (✉ Glorieta de Palacio de Congresos, Seville, ☎ 95/425–5957), **Guidetour** (✉ Lope de Rueda 13, ☎ 95/422–2374 or 95/422–2375), and **ITA** (✉ Santa Teresa 1, ☎ 95/422–4641). City tours in open buses are offered by Servirama and Hispalense de Tranvias (✉ stops at Torre del Oro and Plaza de España). For English-speaking local guides in Cádiz or Jerez, contact the tourist office.

DOÑANA NATIONAL PARK

Four-wheel-drive tours of the reserve depart twice daily (Tuesday–Sunday 8:30 and 3) from the park's reception center, 2 km (1 mi) from Matalascañas. Tours (maximum 125 people) should be booked well in advance. Passengers can often be collected from hotels in Matalascañas. Write or call the Parque Nacional de Doñana (✉ Cooperativa Marisma del Rocío, Centro de Recepción, 21760 Matalascañas, Huelva, ☎ 959/448739).

SHERRY BODEGAS

Tours can be arranged from Seville and Cádiz. In Jerez, *bodegas* are open to visitors weekdays except during August. Tours, which include a tasting of brandy and sherry, should be booked in advance; English-speaking guides are usually available. Call the *bodega* and ask for Public Relations. **Domecq** (☎ 956/151500) charges 350 pesetas; **González Byass** (☎ 956/357000) charges 400 pesetas; **Harvey** (☎ 956/151000) charges 300 pesetas; **Sandeman** (☎ 956/301100) charges 250 pesetas, and **Wisdom** (☎ 956/184306) charges 300 pesetas. For schedules, call first or check with the Jerez tourist office.

To visit *bodegas* in Puerto de Santa María, contact **Osborne** (✉ Fernán Caballero 3, ☎ 956/855211) or **Terry** (✉ Santa Trinidad, ☎ 956/483000). In Sanlúcar de Barrameda contact **Barbadillo** (✉ Calle Luis de Eguilaz, ☎ 956/360894). Tours should be booked a day in advance, if possible; otherwise call before noon.

Visitor Information

Arcos de la Frontera (✉ Cuesta de Belén, ☎ 956/702264). **Cádiz** (✉ Calderón de la Barca 1, ☎ 956/211313). **Jerez de la Frontera** (✉ Larga 39, ☎ 956/331150 or 956/331162). **Puerto de Santa María** (✉ Guadalete 1, ☎ 956/542413). **Sanlúcar de Barrameda** (✉ Calzada del Ejército, ☎ 956/366110). **Seville** (✉ Avda. de la Constitución 21, ☎ 95/422–1404 or 95/421–8157, FAX 95/422–9753; Costurero de la Reina ✉ Paseo de las Delicias 9, ☎ 95/423–4465).

14 Extremadura

Extremadura is Spain's Wild West. One of the least explored regions in Spain, Extremadura is a desert wilderness that has quietly inspired several renowned writers (Cervantes, Cela, de Vega). In the villages of Cáceres and Trujillo, medieval quarters and conquistadors' palaces stand perfectly preserved; in Mérida, Roman ruins bake in the sun; and out in the country, a deep blue sky stretches over flora, fauna, lakes, and stark plains. Here you'll find hearty, friendly people, colorful ceramics, and a local cuisine to please any carnivore.

By Michael
Jacobs

Updated by
Annie Ward

THE VERY NAME *EXTREMADURA*—the "land beyond the Duero"—suggests the wild, remote, and isolated character of this haunting region. With its poor soil and minimal industry, Extremadura has experienced extreme poverty. The film director Luis Buñuel established his reputation in the late 1920s with a powerful documentary, *Un Chien Andalou* (An Andalusian Dog), about the mountainous northern-Extremaduran district of Las Hurdes—then virtually unchanged since the Middle Ages, desperately poor, and still accessible only on foot or donkey. The Nobel Prize–winning novelist Camilo José Cela made his own debut with *La Familia de Pascal Duarte* (The Family of Pascual Duarte), a bleakly realistic study set in a southern-Extremaduran village "crouched over a road as long and as flat as a day without bread."

The great artist Francisco de Zurbarán was born in 1601 in Fuente de Cantos, between Andalusia and Extremadura, and a visit to the town is essential to an understanding of his art. The simplified forms, untrammeled colors, and powerful austerity of Zurbarán's works are mirrored in the treeless, undulating ocher expanses that surround his birthplace; it is one of the most abstract landscapes imaginable. After a long period of neglect, Zurbarán's art was hailed in the 19th century as representing all that was profound in the Spanish temperament. Similarly, Extremadura is recognized today as the pure, unsullied essence of Spain—it is a place that has resisted the onslaught of the 20th century, a place where travel remains an adventure.

Despite its strongly provincial character, Extremadura has long been influenced by its diverse neighbors. Officially, Extremadura comprises two provinces: Badajoz to the south, and Cáceres to the north. Badajoz's dazzlingly white villages and sunbaked landscape have much in common with neighboring Andalusia; Cáceres, with its wooded mountain valleys and half-timbered, gray-stone houses, recalls both Castile and northern Spain. And Portugal, which borders both Badajoz and Cáceres, lends its accent as well.

Extremadura has not always been so isolated and impoverished. No other place in Spain has so many Roman monuments as Mérida, the capital of the vast Roman province of Lusitania (the Iberian Peninsula). Economic and artistic decline set in after the Romans left, but the region revived in the 16th century, as the surviving explorers and conquerers of the New World—from Francisco Pizarro and Hernán Cortés to Nuñez de Balboa and Francisco de Orellana, first navigator of the Amazon—returned to their birthplace. These men were responsible for the magnificent palaces that now constitute the glory of towns such as Cáceres and Trujillo, and they turned the remote monastery of Guadalupe—whose miraculous Virgin had inspired their exploits overseas—into one of the great artistic repositories of Spain.

Pleasures and Pastimes

Boating
Extremadura hosts all kinds of water sports in its many artificial lakes, most notably Borbollón and Gabriel y Galán, in northern Cáceres, and Cíjara and García Sola, in northeastern Badajoz.

Camping
Outdoor enthusiasts will find a wealth of opportunity here: hiking in the Gredos and Tormantos ranges; forests of oak, poplar, and cherry; massive gorges; and the winding waterways in the Jerte River valley. Campers have an abundance of campgrounds in incredible natural set-

tings—especially northeast of Cáceres—from which day hikes lead to local attractions. The campground in Yuste is a good base for exploring the Monastario del Yuste, and the one in Mérida works well for the Roman ruins. Cáceres Camping (☎ 927/230403) can direct you to the information office nearest you, where you can pick up maps and brochures.

Dining

Extremaduran food reflects the austerity of the landscape. It is true peasant cuisine, conditioned by poverty but with a strong character and a reliance on fresh produce. Its basis is the pig, of which no part is spared, including the *criadillas* (testicles)—not to be confused with the *criadillas de la tierra* (earth testicles), which are truffles. The dressed meats are outstanding, most notably the sweetish cured hams from Montánchez; chorizo (spiced sausage); and *morcilla* (blood pudding), which is often made here with potatoes.

The lamb stew *caldereta* is particularly tasty. Game is also common, with *perdiz al modo de Alcántara* (partridge cooked with truffles), a famous specialty. Some Extremaduran dishes appall foreigners, as well as other Spaniards—in particular, those involving *ranas* (frogs) and *lagartos* (lizards), the latter usually eaten with an almond sauce. Andalusian specialties show up in the south, such as gazpacho and *ajo blanco* (cold almond-and-garlic soup). A common accompaniment throughout the region is *migas* (bread crumbs soaked in water and fried in olive oil with garlic and pieces of sausage). The excellent local cheeses generally have a crumbly texture and strong flavor; be sure to savor *tortas*, the round, semisoft cheeses of Cáceres. Desserts include the *extremeño* favorite *técula mécula* (an almond-flavored marzipan tart), which combines the flavors of Spain and next-door neighbor Portugal. Extremadura's little-known wines are equally distinctive; try Lar de Lares. Wine production is centered in Almendralejo.

There is little tradition in Extremadura for going to restaurants; you'll find some of the best food in modest bars. Reservations are usually unnecessary.

CATEGORY	COST*
$$$$	over 6,500 ptas
$$$	4,000–6,500 ptas
$$	2,300–4,000 ptas
$	under 2,300 ptas

per person for a three-course meal, excluding drinks, service, and tax

Fiestas

The province of Cáceres has its share of colorful fiestas commemorating past saints and sinners. If you'll be in Extremadura during the Fiesta de San Estéban (Feast of St. Stephen), on January 20, you'll witness interesting folklore in several small towns. In Arcehúche (near Garovillas), *carantonas* ("ugly mugs," men costumed in animal skins and frightening masks) bow before the statue of St. Stephen during his procession through town. In Piornal (near Plasencia), a *jaramplas* (a grotesquely costumed, masked jester) is pursued through the town and pelted with turnips. More savory is November's Celebración del Cerdo y Vino (Pig and Wine Celebration), in Cáceres, during which the area's vast number of sausages and other pork products are prepared the traditional way. If observing the process doesn't ruin your appetite, you can sample free wine and pork after the presentations. Perhaps the most impressive display of all, however, is December's medieval festival La Encamisá, in Torrejoncillo (off the highway between Plasencia and Cáceres), in which white-robed riders brandish torches and thunder through the narrow streets on horseback.

February 3 is the day to toast San Blas (St. Blaise), believed to heal sore throats, with hot cakes bearing his name and various feasts. During February's Carnival, you can see the *Pero Palo,* a large rag-doll figure with a deadpan expression, carried throughout the town of Villanueva de la Vera (near Jarandilla).

Badajoz doesn't have as crowded a fiesta calendar as Cáceres, but most towns and villages do celebrate Carnival with processions. If you'll be in Badajoz in time to say *adios* to winter and *hola* to spring, enjoy the Fiestas de la Primavera and Las Mayos (Spring Festival and Maydays, respectively), usually at the end of April and beginning of May. The most important date is May 3, El Día del Sagrado Cruz (the Exaltation of the Holy Cross), celebrated in the town of Badajoz and the neighboring towns of Corte de Peleas and Feria. A local family is selected a month in advance to prepare a processional cross in its own home, and some of these crosses become magnificent works of art and patience, lovingly created and tended to the point of depleting hard-earned savings. The crowd sings as a stone cross and a statue of the Virgin Mary are paraded through various neighborhoods.

Fishing

Trout fishing is popular in the Vera and Jerte districts, while tench, carp, royal carp, barbel, and pike abound in the Tajo (Tagus) and Guadiana rivers.

Lodging

No other region in Spain has such a remarkable group of paradors as Extremadura. Paradors cover all of the main tourist areas and occupy buildings of great historical and architectural interest. Reservations should be made well in advance for weekend stays. Most of Extremadura's other luxury hotels are in modern buildings with little character; if you prefer character to amenities, you might try the region's modest *fondas* (inns). If you want to establish a base for a series of day trips, consider Cáceres; from there it's a hop, skip, and a jump to Trujillo, Mérida, and Plasencia.

CATEGORY	COST*
$$$$	over 14,000 ptas
$$$	11,000–14,000 ptas
$$	7,000–11,000 ptas
$	under 7,000 ptas

All prices are for a standard double room, excluding tax and service.

Exploring Extremadura

Extremadura is one of the most beautiful and least celebrated of Spain's interior regions. The province is divided by the Toledo Mountains into two sections: upper Extremadura, called Cáceres, and lower Extremadura, called Badajoz. The best way to see Extremadura is by car, as bus and train connections are not ideally suited to roaming this sparsely populated terrain.

Numbers in the text correspond to numbers in the margin and on the Extremadura map.

Great Itineraries

If you seek beautiful landscapes and outdoor activities, include Plasencia, which will also appeal to anyone interested in the life of the emperor Carlos V. If Roman ruins call you, go straight to Mérida. Cáceres and Trujillo are essential if you enjoy good food and are intrigued by medieval surroundings or the parched palaces and trappings of the conquistadors. Guadalupe is worth a trip of its own: it combines a spectacular setting, an appealing village, and one of the most richly endowed and historically important monasteries in Spain.

IF YOU HAVE 1 DAY

You can get a lightning impression of the region in a day's drive between Madrid and Seville. First, take the N V to **Mérida** ⑨, the ancient Roman capital of the Iberian Peninsula and, with its beautiful ruins, one of the country's most popular historic attractions. Stop on the way for an excellent lunch in **Trujillo** ⑦, home of the conquistadors, with its unusually shaped Plaza Mayor. This drive south is infinitely preferable to the usual route through the monotonous plains of La Mancha.

Another one-day exploration could include a drive from Madrid to the monastery of **Guadalupe** ⑧, one of the most revered sites in Spain, nestled in the heart of conquistador country and symbolizing the link between Spain and Spanish America. Christopher Columbus had his two Indian servants baptized in the fountain at the main entrance of the monastery. The sacristy here contains eight paintings by the Spanish master Zurburán. You could return to Madrid the same afternoon or spend the night here, surrounded by mountains.

IF YOU HAVE 3 DAYS

If you have three days to tour from Madrid, take the slow and winding but very beautiful C501 to **Plasencia** ①. Wander through the *casco viejo* (old town) and then drive to the **Monasterio de Yuste** ④, where Roman emperor Carlos V spent his final days. The next day, go south through the provincial capital of **Cáceres** ⑥, with its breathtaking, impeccably preserved old quarter, the Ciudad Monumental. Continue on to ▦ **Mérida** ⑨, with its evocative Roman ruins, and on day three head back north by way of **Trujillo** ⑦ and **Guadalupe** ⑧, where you can either return to Madrid that evening on the well-paved N V or spend the night.

IF YOU HAVE 5 DAYS

Start by heading over to **Plasencia** ① on the N110, enjoying the scenery of the lovely Jerte Valley toward the end. Time permitting, make a slight detour and wander through the ancient *Judería* (Jewish Quarter) of **Hervás** ②, one of Spain's National Heritage Sites. Visit the well-preserved village of **Cabezuela del Valle** ③ to see its half-timbered houses, with their curious doorways built to admit visitors on horseback. Continue on to the town of ▦ **Jarandilla de la Vera** and spend the night at the parador, in the fortified palace where Carlos V lived before moving to his final home, the nearby **Monasterio de Yuste** ④. On day two, start heading south on C524 and pass by the **Parque Natural del Monfragüe** ⑤, a national wildlife preserve and ecological paradise. Spend the night in Trujillo and look for storks' nests on top of the higher buildings. On day three, see Trujillo in the morning, then continue on to **Cáceres** ⑥ in the afternoon, so picturesque that it has served as the setting for several period films. Enjoy lunch there, then continue on to ▦ **Mérida** ⑨, with its splendid Roman monuments. On day four, explore Mérida, then head west to the provincial capital, **Badajoz** ⑩, more renowned for its university nightlife than for any kind of urban ambience. From here, head on to Andalusia. A second option is to head back north on the N V, and turn off to admire breathtaking scenery and the monastery of **Guadalupe** ⑧.

When to Tour Extremadura

Throughout Spain, the most popular festivals take place during the pre-Lenten Carnival (dates vary but generally fall in late February or early March) and Semana Santa (Holy Week). This is not the liveliest region for fiestas, though, and not the place to come if you're looking for running bulls and wild carryings-on. Churches, monasteries, old villages, and towns set the almost fiercely old-fashioned tone.

Summer is a good time to come if you want to hike in natural parks or spend time in the mountains; the lower areas, on the other hand, get brutally hot. Spring and fall may be ideal, since winter can be cold and rainy.

Because Extremadura is still relatively unknown, crowds will not be a problem at any time of year.

UPPER EXTREMADURA

Extremadura stretches from Portugal to Ciudad Real, and from Salamanca to Seville. Crossed from east to west by two important rivers, the Tajo (Tagus) and the Guadiana, the resulting rugged and fertile landscape has for centuries provided food to much of Europe. The Serena reservoir (fed by the Zújar River, which is fed by the Guadiana River) is one of the largest in Europe.

Plasencia

❶ *270 km (169 mi) west of Madrid, 79 km (49 mi) north of Cáceres, 126 km (78 mi) northwest of Trujillo.*

Rising dramatically from the banks of the narrow Jerte River, backed by the peaks of the Sierra de Gredos, Plasencia is the most important town in the far north of Extremadura. Surrounded by brown fields and dominated by an earth-toned cathedral, this dusty community was founded by Alfonso VIII in 1180, just after he captured the whole area from the Moors. The town's motto, *placeat Deo et hominibus* ("It pleases both God and men"), might well have been a ploy on Alfonso's part to attract settlers to this wild and isolated place on the southern border of the former kingdom of León. Badly damaged during the Peninsular War of 1808, Plasencia retains far less of its medieval quarter than do other Extremaduran towns; but it still has extensive fragments of its medieval walls and a scattering of fine old buildings.

Plasencia's **cathedral** was founded in 1189 and rebuilt after 1320 in an austere Gothic style that looks a bit incongruous looming over the red-tile roofs of the town's whitewashed homes. In 1498, the great architect Enrique Egas designed a new structure, intending to compliment or even overshadow the original; but despite the later participation of other notable architects of the time, such as Juan de Alava and Francisco de Colonia, Egas' plans were never fully realized. The entrance to this incomplete, curious, and not wholly satisfactory complex is through the portal on the new cathedral's ornate but somber north facade. The dark interior of the new cathedral is notable for the beauty of its pilasters, which sprout tree-like into the ribs of the vaulting. You enter the old cathedral through the Gothic cloister, off which stands the oldest surviving part of the building, the 13th-century chapter house (now the chapel of San Pablo)—a late-Romanesque structure with an idiosyncratic, Moorish-inspired dome. The **museum** in the truncated nave of the old cathedral has a motley collection of ecclesiastical and archaeological objects. ☎ 927/414852. ▣ *Old cathedral 150 ptas.* ☉ *Daily 9–1 and 4–6.*

Surrounding Plasencia's old and new cathedrals are several austerely elegant Renaissance structures, most notably the **Palacio Episcopal** (Bishop's Palace, closed to the public), the **Hospital de Santa María** (now a cultural center), and the **Casa del Deán** (Dean's House, now a rather run-down police station).

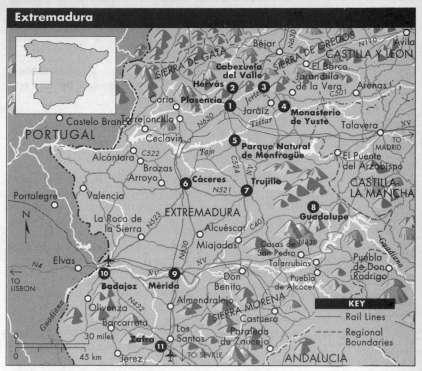

In the center of town you'll find the narrow **Plaza de San Vicente.** Lined with orange trees, this carefully preserved square is dominated on its northern side by the Renaissance **Palacio de Mirabel** (Palace of the Marquis of Mirabel); go through the arch in its middle and you'll come to an alley with a back view of the palace. 🖅 *Tip caretaker.* ⊘ *Usually daily 10–2 and 4–6.*

East of the Plaza de San Vicente, at the other end of the Rúa Zapatería, is the **Plaza Mayor,** a cheerful, arcaded square where a market has been held every Tuesday morning since the 12th century. Farther east is a large section of the town's medieval wall, on the other side of which is a heavily restored Roman aqueduct.

Dining and Lodging

$$ ✕ **Casa Juan.** The proprietor of this small, central, family-run restaurant makes it his business to give you a warm welcome and plates full of home-style food, including everything from simple *pinchos* (tapas) to the specialty of the *jefe de cocina* (head of the kitchen): braised lamb chops with fresh white asparagus. It's more like a comfortable, intimate dinner party than a restaurant; the wine flows freely, and you pay for your intake on the honor system. 🖅 *Calle Arenillas 2, 10600,* ☎ *927/424042. AE, MC, V.*

$$–$$$ ✕🖅 **Alfonso VIII.** The sturdy, gray exterior of this central hotel hides an interior that attempts a French rococo elegance, with gilt plaster and red upholstery. Grand but slightly past its prime, this curious Franco-era relic is strangely agreeable. The restaurant has long been renowned for its food, which has a strong Extremaduran accent; the Parisian-style dining room seems the least likely setting for *lagarto en salsa verde* (lizard in green sauce). The menu changes seasonally; alas,

the lizards are available only in the spring. ✉ *Alfonso VIII 32–34, 10600,* ☎ *927/410250,* 🆇 *927/418042. 57 rooms, 2 suites. Restaurant. AE, DC, MC, V.*

Shopping

If you happen to be in Plasencia on a Tuesday morning, visit the **Plaza Mayor** and do what Extremeños have been doing since the 12th century: scout bargains in the weekly market.

Hervás

②   *63 km (39 mi) northeast of Plasencia, 142 km (88 mi) northeast of Cáceres, 25 km (16 mi) west of Cabezuela del Valle.*

Surrounded by pine and chestnut groves, this picturesque village makes an interesting detour. The town is believed to have become a predominantly Jewish settlement during the Middle Ages, populated by Jews escaping Christian and Muslim persecution in the larger cities. In 1492, however, when the Jews were expelled from Spain, their neighborhood was left intact and their possessions ceded to the local nobility. Stripped of its wealth, the town lost its commercial reputation and faded into the background.

Now, thanks to the recent efforts of the mayors of seven Spanish cities who pledged to create a network (known as *El Camino de Sefarad,* the Journey through Sepharad) of several of the country's most important Jewish settlements, Hervás is recognized as the best-preserved Judería (Jewish quarter) in Spain. Many of the town's residents claim to be descendants of the *conversos,* Jews who converted to Christianity to avoid persecution.

Cabezuela del Valle

③   *34 km (21 mi) northeast of Plasencia. For a scenic route, follow N110 toward Ávila.*

The 150-km (90-mi) route north from Plasencia to Ávila follows the narrow, fast-flowing Jerte River almost to its source, then climbs above it to enter the bleak plateau of Castile. The Greeks supposedly called the **Jerte Valley** "the Valley of Pleasure": its lower slopes are covered with a dense mantle of ash, chestnut, and cherry trees, whose richness contrasts with the granite cliffs of the Sierra de Gredos. Camping is popular in this region, and even the most experienced hikers can find some challenging trails. Full of half-timbered stone houses, Cabezuela del Valle is one of the best preserved of the area's many attractive villages. Like other local settlements, it once had a significant Jewish population.

En Route   The route through the village of Tornavacas is a rough one, passable only on foot or in a strong car. It leads over the Sierra de Gredos and down toward the village of Jarandilla de la Vera, in the Tiétar River valley. (To pick up the track, turn right off the N110, following signs for Jarandilla de la Vera.) The track offers extensive views from its higher points, then descends into a narrow gorge with the dramatic name of La Garganta de los Infiernos (the Gorge of Hell). The Holy Roman Emperor Carlos V took this very path in 1556; the litter he was carried in is on display at the Monastery of Yuste (☞ see below).

Dining and Lodging

$$$$ ✕🏨 **Parador Nacional Carlos V.** Nestled in the town of Jarandilla de la Vera, this important parador is just 17 km (11 mi) southeast of Cabezuela del Valle. (For an easier drive than the N110, take C501 east from Plasencia.) It was built in the early 16th century as a fortified palace and has an arcaded patio with flattened arches; adding to its historical significance is the fact that the emperor Carlos V stayed here for an entire year. The hotel is filled with stylish pseudo-medieval furnishings, and its regal dining room is the perfect place to indulge in royal fantasies. Try the *sopa de gañan* (hearty chicken and vegetable soup) to start; then savor *zancarrón braseado con higos de la Vera* (roast loin of pork with braised figs) as your main dish. ⊠ *García Prieto 1, 10450,* ☎ *927/560117,* 𝗙𝗔𝗫 *927/560088. 53 rooms. Restaurant, bar, pool, tennis court, playground. AE, DC, MC, V.*

Shopping

If you like to cook, pick up a tin or two of *pimentón de la Vera* (paprika), made from the region's famed red peppers. You'll find it in Jarandilla and other towns in the La Vera area.

Monasterio de Yuste

❹ *17 km (11 mi) southeast of Jarandilla de la Vera, 45 km (28 mi) from Plasencia. Turn left off C501 at Curacos. The way is well marked with signs for the monastery.*

The Monasterio de Yuste (Monastery of Yuste) was founded by Hieronymite monks in the early 15th century. It was badly damaged in the Peninsular War and left to decay after the suppression of Spain's monasteries in 1835, but it has since been restored and taken over once more by the Hieronymites. You can visit the Royal Chambers where Carlos V stayed; the bedroom where he died has a view into the church, which enabled the emperor to hear mass from his bed. A ramp, originally meant to be climbed on horseback, leads to a terrace overlooking a fish pond. ☎ *927/172130.* 🈺 *100 ptas.* ☉ *Oct.–May, daily 9:30–12:30 and 3–6; June–Sept., daily 9:30–12:30 and 3:30–6:30.*

OFF THE
BEATEN PATH

GARGANTA LA OLLA – Another town worth finding in the Vera Valley is Garganta La Olla, about 10 km (6 mi) east of Yuste. As you approach the town, the road winds through cherry orchards and eventually dips into the village's narrow, twisting streets. The Museo de la Inquisición (Museum of the Inquisition) displays kitchen utensils from Yuste alongside instruments of torture used by the Inquisitors. You can also visit the Casa de Putas, a brothel used by soldiers of Carlos V's army; it's now a butcher shop, but still painted the traditional "brothel" blue. There are no hotels here, but if you're enchanted with the mountainous isolation and want to relax in the company of the villagers, *el Abuelo Marciano* (Grandfather Marciano, ⊠ Cruce Jaraiz, s/n, ☎ 927/460426) can arrange rustic room-and-board in the countryside.

Parque Natural de Monfragüe

❺ *20 km (12 mi) south of Plasencia, off C524, which connects Plasencia with Trujillo.*

At the confluence of the Rivers Tiétar and Tajo is the Parque Natural de Monfragüe (Monfragüe Nature Park). This beautiful wilderness was turned into a national park in 1979 and is known for its wide range of plant and animal life, including lynx, boar, deer, fox, black storks, imperial eagles, and the world's largest colony of black vultures. If possible, bring binoculars to better enjoy these graceful birds.

Cáceres

★ **❻** *307 km (190 mi) west of Madrid.*

An oasis in Extremadura, Cáceres is a provincial capital and prosperous agricultural town whose vibrant nightlife draws villagers from the surrounding *pueblos* every weekend. Originally a Roman colony, and later heavily disputed between the Moors and Christians, Cáceres also draws tourists who want to escape into the fairy-tale labyrinth of the Ciudad Monumental, the town's startlingly well-preserved old quarter. The bus and rail stations are next to each other, a good half-hour walk from the old quarter, along the uninspiring Avenida de España. Once you reach the Calle San Antón, the look of the town improves considerably, particularly as you reach the intimate Plaza de San Juan, home of one of Extremadura's greatest restaurants, El Figón de Eustaquio (☞ Dining and Lodging, *below*). Beyond this square is the long, inclined, arcaded **Plaza Mayor,** where you'll find several pleasant outdoor cafés, the tourist office, and, on breezy summer nights, nearly everyone in the town, strolling or sitting on the long steps leading up to the Ciudad Monumental. In the middle of the arcade is the entrance to the lively Calle General Ezponda, lined with tapas bars, student hangouts, clubs, and discos that keep the neighborhood awake and moving till dawn.

On high ground on the eastern side of the Plaza Mayor is the beckoning portal through the town's intact (though heavily restored) wall, which surrounds one of the best-preserved old quarters in Spain. Literally packed with treasures (more than 60 sights within a 2-km [1-mi] radius), Cáceres' **casco antiguo** (also called the **Ciudad Monumental**) is a marvel: small, but without a single modern building to distract from its aura. Setting foot in this surreal place is like walking into a time warp and is one of the high points of a visit to Extremadura. With very few shops, restaurants, or bars, the old town is virtually deserted in winter; crammed with somber, gray medieval and Renaissance palaces, at night it looks like a stage set for a tragedy, while the warm glow of the sun makes it look like the mythical city of gold that so moved the conquistadors. In fact, several movies have been shot here, including Ridley Scott's saga of Christopher Columbus.

Enter the old town from the Plaza Mayor, through the gate next to the Torre de la Hierba. Once inside, turn right onto Calle Adarros de Santa Ana, and you'll soon pass the **Palacio de los Golfines de Arriba** on your left, dominated by a soaring tower dating from 1515.

Skirt the town walls until you reach **Plaza de Santa Clara,** on the southern side of the old town, recognizable by its palm trees. Leading from here to the center of the old town is the Calle Ancha, at the beginning of which is the **Casa de Sanchez de Paredes,** a 16th-century palace that now serves as a parador (☞ Dining and Lodging, *below*).

On the Plaza San Mateo, at the northern end of the Calle Ancha, stands **San Mateo,** one of the Cáceres's most important churches. Built mainly in the 14th century, but with a 16th-century choir, it has an impressively austere interior, the main decorative notes being the baroque high altar and some heraldic crests. On the square facing the southern side of San Mateo is the battlemented tower of **Las Cigueñas** (Palace of the Storks), so called because of the storks' nests that adorned it before its restoration.

Farther down the Plaza San Mateo is the **Casa de las Veletas** (House of the Weather Vanes), a magnificent, 12th-century Moorish mansion. The Casa now houses the **Museo de Cáceres.** With an emphasis on local archaeological finds, some dating as far back as the Neolithic era, this collection is an excellent way to acquaint yourself with the many peoples who have inhabited this area. The building itself is partially closed for restoration, but you can visit the eerie but superb Moorish cistern— the *aljibe*—with arches supported by moldy stone pillars. ☎ 927/ 247234. ☞ 200 ptas. ⊙ Tues.–Sat. 9:30–2:30, Sun. 10:15–2:30.

The narrow street that descends from the eastern end of San Mateo to the town's other main church, Santa María, passes first the Jesuit church of **San Francisco Xavier,** then the **Palacio de los Golfines de Abajo.** The latter has the finest exterior of any Cáceres palace; its stony austerity is relieved by Mudéjar and Renaissance decorative motifs.

The Gothic church of **Santa María,** built mainly in the 16th century, is now the town's cathedral and can be visited during mass. Its elegantly carved high altar, from 1551, is just about visible in the gloom. Nearby is the **Palacio de Carvajal** (on the Plaza of Santa María), the only old palace you can tour apart from the Casa de las Veletas. The tourist office can help you arrange a visit.

From Santa María, a 110-yard walk down Calle Tiendas will take you to the town's northern walls. Don't miss the 16th-century **Palacio de los Moctezuma-Toledo** (now a public-record office), built by Juan Cano de Saavedra with his wife's dowry—his wife being the princess daughter of the Aztec ruler Montezuma.

The chief building of interest outside the town walls is the church of **Santiago** (go through the Socorro Gate, then continue north along the Calle de Villalobos). It was rebuilt in the 16th century by Rodrigo Gil de Hontañón, the last great Gothic architect of Spain.

Just up the hill behind the Ciudad Monumental is **El Santuario Virgen de la Montaña** (Sanctuary of the Virgin of the Mountain). Inside you'll find a beautiful 1866 grandfather clock, behind which is a golden baroque altar. The statue of the patroness virgin is paraded through the town in May. Outside, the picturesque view alone is worth the drive up here. ⊠ *Donation.* ☉ *Daily 8:30–2 and 4–8.*

OFF THE BEATEN PATH	**GAROVILLAS** – A possible excursion from Cáceres is Garovillas, 10 km (6 mi) off the main road between Cáceres and Plasencia (turn left, or northwest, onto C522, 25 km [15 mi] north of Cáceres). Now partially deserted, this is a perfectly preserved village from the late 15th century. The walls and pillars appear to be tilting at dangerously uneven angles, but they were built this way to offset the natural slope of the land.

Dining and Lodging

$$$ ✕ **Atrio.** Slickly elegant, this restaurant offers ultrarefined yet adventurous modern cooking in a modern setting. Truffles appear in many of the dishes, including the tastefully presented *perdiz al modo de Alcántara,* a traditional Extremaduran delicacy. ⊠ *Signo 18, 10003,* ☎ 927/242928, ⅨX 927/221111. *DC, MC, V.*

$$$ ✕ **El Figón de Eustaquio.** On the otherwise quiet and pleasant Plaza
★ San Juan, the justly famed Eusaquio is always busy, especially at lunchtime. Its jumble of small, old-fashioned, intimate dining rooms serves mainly regional delicacies, including excellent cured ham from Montánchez, *perdiz al modo de Alcántara* (partridge cooked with truffles), and *merluza a la cacereña* (hake served Cáceres-style). There's also a wide selection of fine Spanish wines. ⊠ *Plaza San Juan 12, 10003,* ☎ 927/244362. *Reservations essential. AE, MC, V.*

$$$$ ✕🏠 **Parador Nacional de Cáceres.** This parador occupies a 16th-century palace right in the heart of the old town. Soft cream tones and wooden beams warm up the plain architecture, and the rooms are cozy and comfortable. Enjoy fine dining on the terrace or in the noble dining room: tasty local game specialties such as *lomo de venado al queso del Casar* (venison with Casar cheese sauce) or *el cabrito asado al romero* (roast kid with rosemary). On Sunday afternoon, the bar, which looks like a wine cellar, hosts wine tasting and serves a tantalizing array of

tapas. ⊠ *Ancha 6, 10003,* ☎ *927/211759,* ℻ *927/211729. 31 rooms, 1 suite. Restaurant, minibars, meeting rooms. AE, DC, MC, V.*

$$$$ 🏨 **Meliá Cáceres.** Equally historic and somewhat more comfortable than
★   the parador, the Meliá Cáceres has its own 16th-century palace, just outside the walls of the old town. It gracefully blends exposed stone, indirect spotlighting, and designer furnishings. Rooms have huge double beds, wall-to-wall carpeting, and ample baths. The street-level bar, with charming wine-bottle lighting, is a popular meeting spot for the town's well-heeled. ⊠ *Plaza San Juan 11–13, 10003,* ☎ *927/215800,* ℻ *927/214070. 86 rooms, 2 junior suites. Restaurant, bar, room service, laundry, meeting rooms. AE, DC, MC, V.*

$$$$ 🏨 **Quinto Centenario.** Opened in 1992 just outside Cáceres on the road to Plasencia, the Quinto Centenario offers remarkable warmth for a modern high-rise. Rooms are large and carpeted, with king-size beds and luxurious baths. The swimming pool and terrace dining make this a good choice on hot summer nights. ⊠ *Manuel Pacheco s/n, 10003,* ☎ *927/232200,* ℻ *927/232202. 138 rooms, 9 junior suites. Restaurant, bar, pool, tennis court. AE, DC, MC, V.*

Nightlife and the Arts

Bars in Cáceres are lively until the wee hours and easy to find, as the crowds spill into the streets. Nightlife centers around the Plaza Mayor, which fills after dinner with families out for a *paseo* as well as students swigging *cuchimollo,* a combination of red wine and Coca-Cola. To escape the college crowd, or to hang in more modern surroundings, try the Calle de Pizarro, on the west side of town. With the best (and priciest) discos, the new town starts hopping when the old one starts dying. Crowds make for **Acuario,** a multilevel dance club (⊠ *Avda. de España 6,* ☎ *927/236423*), at around 3 AM.

Trujillo

★ ❼   *48 km (30 mi) east of Cáceres, 250 km (155 mi) southwest of Madrid; at the junction of N521 and N V.*

No one who comes to the province of Cáceres should fail to visit Trujillo. It is an extreme example of the Extremaduran look: a lonely, nearly deserted place, built of cold and imposing stone, that is nonetheless thrilling to both eye and soul. The stork nests that top several towers in and around the center of the old town—and have become something of a symbol of Trujillo—only add to this strange effect. Unlike Cáceres, Trujillo has none of the hustle and bustle of the new Spain; it seems almost stuck in the time when Extremadura was a symbol of Spanish poverty. Dating back at least to Roman times, when its castle was first constructed, Trujillo was captured from the Moors in 1232 and colonized by a number of leading military families. It was only after Spain's discovery of the Americas in 1492, however, that the town's renown spread. Known today as the Cradle of the Conquistadors, Trujillo spawned some of the leading explorers and conquerors of the New World, men who were later to bring great wealth to their native town, building in the 16th and 17th centuries a splendid series of palaces— radically changing what had been a poverty-stricken provincial town into a showcase of conspicuous consumption. The most famous of these action heroes was Francisco Pizarro, conqueror of Peru, born in Trujillo in 1475. Francisco's educated half brother Hernando, also an adventurer in Peru, built perhaps the most magnificent palace in Trujillo.

Trujillo's economic boom during Spain's golden age led the town to expand well beyond its medieval walls. Then, from the mid-17th century on, building ceased almost entirely, and the town entered a long decline. Today it is possible to wander randomly around its maze of streets and still uncover at every turn poignant memorials of the town's glorious past. Note that it is only practical to see Trujillo on foot, as the streets are mainly cobbled or crudely paved with stone, and rarely flat. The two main roads through Trujillo leave you at the singularly unattractive and unspectacular bottom of the town. Things get progressively older the farther you climb, but even on the lower slopes— where most of the shops are concentrated—you need walk only a few yards to step into what seems like the Middle Ages.

Trujillo's large **Plaza Mayor,** one of the finest in Spain, is a superb Renaissance creation with very few contemporary embellishments, among them—what else?—the tourist office in the center. At the foot of the stepped platform rising on the plaza's north side stands a large, bronze equestrian statue of Francisco Pizarro.

The church behind Pizarro, **San Martín,** is a Gothic structure from the early 16th century, with some fine Renaissance tombs and an old organ. If you visit at dusk, you may be lucky enough to hear the men's choir rehearsing, adding a magical note to eventide.

In the northeastern corner of the Plaza Mayor is the **Palacio de los Duques de San Carlos** (Palace of the Dukes of San Carlos), which has a majestically decorated facade from around 1600. The building is now a convent of Hieronymite nuns, who can occasionally be glimpsed on the balconies in full habit, hanging laundry or watering their flowers. ☎ 927/320058. 💲 *Donation.* ⏱ *June–Oct., daily 9:30–1 and 5–7; Nov.–May, daily 10:30–1 and 4:30–6.*

<table>
<tr><td>NEED A
BREAK?</td><td>If the summer sun has you parched, pop into the newest café on Trujillo's Plaza Mayor. The sparkling-clean Bar Pillete Cafeteria (✉ Plaza Mayor 28, ☎ 927/321449) is a rarity in this area: the menu is an endless variety of fresh-squeezed juices, shakes, and other exotic fruit concoctions.</td></tr>
</table>

The most interesting part of Trujillo extends west of the Plaza Mayor. Your tour of the town could begin near the southwestern corner of the plaza, outside the **Palacio de la Conquista** (Palace of the Conquest), the most dramatic building on the square. Built by Francisco Pizarro's half brother Hernando, the palace is immediately recognizable by its rich covering of exquisite Renaissance ornamentation. Flanking its corner balcony, around which most of the ornamentation is clustered, are lively, imaginative busts of the Pizarro family. Representations of chained Indians are prominent in the coat of arms just above, an interesting reflection of the spirit of the conquests. Parts of the palace's magnificent interior have been opened to the public, including a grandiose staircase, a courtyard, and some 16th-century stables. The palace was closed for renovation at press time but is scheduled to reopen in late 1998; check with the tourist office.

Adjacent to Trujillo's Palacio de la Conquista is the arcaded former town hall, now a court of law. The alley that runs through this building's central arch will take you to the **Palacio de Pizarro de Orellana,** now a school, where Cervantes spent much time writing and where you'll find the most elegant Renaissance courtyard in town. 💲 *Free.*

The oldest part of Trujillo, known as **La Villa,** is entirely surrounded by its original (if much restored) walls. Follow the wall along Calle Almenas, which runs west from the Palace of Pizarro de Orellana, to the **Alcázar de Los Chaves,** a castle-fortress that was turned into a guest lodge in the 15th century and hosted visiting dignitaries, including Ferdinand and Isabella. The building has seen better days and is now a college. Passing the Alcázar, continue west along the wall to the **Puerta de San Andrés,** one of La Villa's four surviving gates (there were originally seven). Once inside, you enter a world inhabited by storks, who, in spring and early summer, hunker down in the many crumbling chimneys and towers of Trujillo's palaces and churches.

The cobbled Calle Palomas leads you up into the Plaza de Santa María, on which stands Trujillo's major artistic monument, the church of **Santa María.** Attached to a Romanesque bell tower, this Gothic structure is occasionally used for masses, but its interior has been virtually untouched since the 16th century. One highlight is the upper choir, with an exquisitely carved balustrade; the coats of arms at each end of this balustrade indicate the seats Ferdinand and Isabella occupied when they attended mass here. The church's chief attraction is its high altar, circa 1480, adorned with great 15th-century Spanish paintings. (To see the altar properly illuminated, place a 100-peseta coin in the box next to the church entrance.) ⌨ *50 ptas.* ☉ *Daily 10–2 and 4:30–6:30 (until 8 in summer).*

Climbing north from Santa María, you'll come almost immediately to the Pizarro family home. This small house has been restored and turned into a museum, the **Casa Museo de Pizarro,** dedicated to the links between Spain and Latin America. ⌨ *250 ptas.* ☉ *Daily 11–2 and 4:30–6 (until 8 in summer).*

Standing in isolation beyond the Casa Museo de Pizarro is the fortress of the large **castle,** built by the Moors on Roman foundations. Climb to the top for spectacular views of the town and its surroundings. From here you can compare modern with medieval: to the south are grain silos, warehouses, and residential neighborhoods. To the north are only green fields and flowers, partitioned by a maze of nearly leveled Roman stone walls. ⌨ *Free.* ☉ *Daily 8–dusk.*

Dining and Lodging

$ ✕ **Mesón La Troya.** Although the food here is not up to the standard of the neighboring Pizarro (☞ *below*), there are few more entertaining places to eat a meal. This raucous restaurant is often filled with carousing soldiers. Don't be daunted by the gamblers playing the slots in the front room; once you pass the bar, littered with dirty napkins from the tapas crowd, you'll enter a pleasant dining room, a vaulted chamber within a beautiful old building. The elderly woman who runs the place is a known eccentric who scolds you if you're unable to finish the enormous helpings. At the beginning of the meal you're served a *tortilla de patatas* (potato omelet) whether you want it or not. ✉ *Plaza Mayor 10,* ☎ *927/321364. MC, V.*

$$ ✕ **Pizarro.** This celebrated restaurant is in a small but quietly elegant
★   upstairs room with a warm and friendly atmosphere. Don't come here if you're in a hurry; it's run by two sweet and slow-moving sisters who lovingly maintain traditional Extremaduran home cooking. A house specialty is *gallina truffada,* an elaborately prepared chicken pâté with truffles, which was once a common Christmas dish but which few today know how to make. ✉ *Plaza Mayor 13,* ☎ *927/320255. MC, V.*

$$$$ ✕▥ **Parador Nacional de Trujillo.** This unusually friendly parador
★   was originally the Convent of St. Clare, and its bedrooms surround a harmonious Renaissance courtyard. As in most paradors, the decor aims for mock-medieval chic, but the atmosphere here is endearingly homey. An entire wall of the dining room is lined with shelves displaying typical regional plates and copperware; you can sup on such local dishes as *criadillas de la tierra en caldereta* (white truffle and meat stew) or

chuleta de novillo retinto con patatas (braised young bull fillet with potatoes). ✉ *Plaza Beatriz de Silva 1, 10200,* ☎ *927/321350,* FAX *927/ 321366. 46 rooms, 1 suite. Restaurant, bar, meeting rooms. AE, DC, MC, V.*

$$ ✕🖭 **Finca Santa Marta.** Surrounded by 60 acres of olive, cherry, and almond trees, this ancient olive-oil and wine farm is now owned by a retired couple and functions as an oh-so-comfortable country refuge. Located 14 km (9 mi) outside Trujillo on the road to Guadalupe, it's a relaxing alternative to staying in town. The restored living quarters have stone floors (rugs keep your feet warm), wood-beam ceilings, and fresh flowers everywhere. Meals are available if requested in advance. ✉ *Pago de San Clemente, Trujillo, 10600,* ☎ FAX *927/319203;* ✉ *Juan Ramón Giménez 12, 8A, 28036 Madrid,* ☎ FAX *91/3502217. 12 rooms, 1 suite. Restaurant, bar, pool, meeting room. MC, V.*

$ ✕🖭 **Mesón La Cadena.** In a rambling 16th-century palace on the Plaza
★ Mayor, this bar and restaurant has some simple but very comfortable upstairs rooms, with wonderful views. Savor the gazpacho *de fiesta extremeña* (with brilliant, yellow-orange tomatoes). ✉ *Plaza Mayor 8, 10200,* ☎ *927/321463. 7 rooms. Restaurant, bar. AE, MC, V.*

Shopping

Trujillo has a wider range of crafts for sale than almost any other place in the region. Near the tourist office on the Plaza Mayor, several shops have enticing selections of regional folk arts and crafts.

Among Extremadura's most attractive crafts are multicolored rugs, blankets, and embroideries. You'll find the best embroidered and woven products at **Maribel Vallar** (✉ Domingo de Ramos 28, ☎ no phone), where they still use a centuries-old loom.

Domingo Pablos Barquillo (✉ Plazuela de San Judas 3, ☎ 927/321066), just 100 yards from the parador, specializes in locally produced wood carvings, basketwork, and furniture.

Guadalupe

★ ❽ *200 km (125 mi) southwest of Madrid, 143 km (88 mi) east of Cáceres, 96 km (60 mi) east of Trujillo, 200 km (125 mi) northeast of Mérida.*

The **Monasterio de Nuestra Señora de Guadalupe** (Monastery of Our Lady of Guadalupe) is one of the most inspiring sights in Extremadura. The approach alone is worth the trip. Whether you come from Madrid, Trujillo, or Cáceres, the last stage of your trip will take you through wild, breathtakingly beautiful mountain scenery. The monastery itself clings to the slopes, forming a magical profile that echoes the gaunt wall of mountains behind it. Pilgrims have been coming here since the 14th century, but only in recent years have they been joined by a growing number of tourists; even so, the monastery's very isolation—it's a good two-hour drive from the nearest town—has saved it from tourism's worst excess.

The story of Guadalupe goes back to around 1300, when a local shepherd uncovered a miraculous statue of the Virgin, supposedly carved by St. Luke. Its fame might have remained local had it not come to the attention of King Alfonso XI, who often hunted here. Alfonso had a church built to house the statue and later vowed to found a monastery should he defeat the Moors at the battle of Salado in 1340. After his victory, he kept his promise. The greatest period in the monastery's history was between the 15th and 18th centuries, when, under the rule of the Hieronymites, it was turned into a pilgrimage center rivaling even Santiago de Compostela in importance. Documents authorizing Columbus's first voyage to America were signed here, and the first Native Americans converted to Christianity were brought here to be baptized. The Virgin of Guadalupe became the patroness of Latin America, honored by the dedications of thousands of churches and towns in the New World. The monastery's decline coincided with Spain's loss of overseas territories in the 19th century. Abandoned for 70 years and left to decay, it was taken over after the civil war by Franciscan brothers, who slowly restored it.

The bus station lies just below the village of Guadalupe, leaving you with a steep climb up to the monastery. On sale everywhere is the copperware that has been made here since the 16th century. In the middle of the tiny, irregularly shaped Plaza Mayor (also known as the Plaza de Santa María de Guadalupe, and transformed during festivals into a bullring) is a 15th-century **fountain,** where Columbus's two Native American servants were baptized in 1496. Looming in the background is the late-Gothic south facade of the **monastery church,** covered in swirling decorative motifs and flanked by battlemented towers.

The entrance to the monastery is to the left of the church. From the large Mudéjar cloister you progress to the **chapter house,** which has a collection of hymnals, illustrated manuscripts, and paintings, including a series of small panels by Zurbarán. The ornate, 17th-century **sacristy** contains the monastery's most important works of art—a series of eight Zurbarán paintings of 1638–47. These powerfully austere works representing monks of the Hieronymite order and scenes from the life of St. Jerome are the artist's only significant paintings still in the setting for which they were intended. The tour concludes with the garish, late-baroque **Camarín,** the chapel where the miraculous Virgin is housed. The focal point is the Virgin of Guadalupe, a dark and mysterious wooden object hiding under a great veil and mantle. Outside, the monastery's gardens have been renovated in the original, geometric Moorish style. ☎ 927/367000. 🎟 300 ptas. ⏱ Daily 9:30–1 and 3:30–6:45.

Dining and Lodging

$ ✗ **Mesón Isabel.** This cozy, family-run restaurant is right next to the monastery and offers a fairly priced, home-cooked meal typical of the region. After pleasing its customers, the family reunites beside the fireplace for a well-deserved meal of its own. Try the *bacalao rebozado* (cod fried in batter) or *caldereta de cordero* (lamb stew). ✉ *Plaza Santa María de Guadalupe s/n, 10140,* ☎ *927/367126.*

$$$–$$$$ ✗🖾 **Parador Nacional Zurbarán.** The first autopsy in Spain was per-
★ formed in this building, a former hospital and pilgrim's hostel dating from the 15th century. The parador has an unusually luxuriant character thanks to its Mudéjar architecture, Moorish-style rooms, and exotic vegetation. In keeping with the spirit of the region, the restaurant serves simple local dishes, such as *bacalao monocal* (cod with spinach and potatoes) and *migas.* ✉ *Marqués de la Romana 12, 10140,* ☎ *927/367075,* ℻ *927/367076. 40 rooms. Restaurant, bar, pool, tennis court, meeting rooms. AE, DC, MC, V.*

$–$$ ✗🖾 **Hospedería del Real Monasterio.** An excellent alternative if the parador is full, this inn was built around the 16th-century Gothic cloister of the monastery. The simple, traditional rooms with wood-beam ceilings are exceptionally quiet. Despite its grand and unforgettable setting in the cloister, the restaurant is a haven of unpretentious charm, specializing in modest local dishes, such as *sopa de tomate* (tomato soup). ✉ *Plaza Juan Carlos I s/n, 10140,* ☎ *927/367000,* ℻ *927/367177. 47 rooms, 1 suite. Restaurant, bar. MC, V. Closed Jan. 15–Feb. 15.*

Shopping

Guadalupe is the place to go for copper and tinware; the local metal-work industry is 400 years old.

LOWER EXTREMADURA

Mérida, Badajoz, and Zafra

The flavors of Extremadura's southern half are sometimes more Andalusian or even Portuguese than classically Spanish. Long stretches of dusty farmland and a dialect tinged with Portuguese make it feel light-years away from Castile. The city of Mérida was established in 25 BC as a settlement for Roman soldiers; then named Augusta Emerita, it soon became the capital of the Roman province of Lusitania, and its many ruins bear witness to its former splendor. Badajoz has also been a settlement since prehistoric times; Paleolithic remains have been found nearby. A mere 7 km (4½ mi) from the Portuguese border, it has historically been considered a gateway to Portugal and is home to many Portuguese as well as Portuguese descendants. Modern and urban relative to the surrounding towns, Badajoz tries (not quite successfully) to make up for its lack of architectural ruins with nighttime energy and the intellectual punch of its university.

Mérida

★ ⊙ *70 km (43 mi) south of Cáceres, 66 km (40 mi) east of Badajoz, 250 km (155 mi) north of Seville.*

Founded by the Romans in 25 BC on the banks of the River Guadiana and strategically situated at the junction of major Roman roads between Salamanca and Seville and Lisbon and Toledo, Mérida today is a rather unattractive, lifeless town—with the exception of its dramatic Roman complex. The city became the capital of the vast Roman province of Lusitania soon after its founding. A bishopric in Visigothic times, Mérida never regained the importance that it had under the Romans; but to this day the town boasts the finest series of Roman monuments in Spain.

The new, glass-and-steel bus station is in a modern district on the other side of the River Guadiana from the town center. It commands a good view of the exceptionally long **Roman bridge,** which spans two forks of this sluggish river.

As you cross the bridge leading into Mérida, you'll see in front of you the sturdy, square **Alcazaba** (fortress), built by the Romans and later strengthened by the Visigoths and Moors. To go inside, follow the fortress walls around to the side farthest from the river. Climb up to the battlements for sweeping river views. ☎ 924/317309. ☞ 600 ptas. (includes admission to Roman theater and amphitheater). ⊙ Daily 9–1:45 and 4–6:15 (5–7:15 in summer).

Mérida's main square, the **Plaza de España,** adjoins the northwestern corner of the fortress and is highly animated both day and night. Its oldest building is the 16th-century palace, which served for many years as the Hotel Emperatriz. Between this former hotel and the town's stylish parador (☞ Dining and Lodging, *below*) stretches Mérida's most charming and best-preserved area, its Andalusian-style white houses shaded by palms.

Off the tiny Plaza de Santa Clara, in the heart of the *casco viejo,* is an abandoned 18th-century church that has been turned into a dusty, old-fashioned **Museo Visigótico** (Visigothic Museum), filled with fragments

of Visigothic stonework. ☎ 924/300106. ⊠ *Free.* ⊙ *July–Sept.,*
Tues.–Sat. 10–2 and 5–7, Sun. 10–2; Oct.–June, Tues.–Sat. 10–2
and 4–6, Sun. 10–2.

From the Plaza de España, head for the Calle Santa Eulalia, a lively
pedestrian shopping street, and continue along the **Rambla Mártir Santa
Eulalia** until you reach the **Basilica de Santa Eulalia** (Basilica of St. Eulalia). This originally Visigothic structure marks both the site of a
Roman temple and the supposed place where the child martyr Eulalia
was roasted alive in AD 304 for spitting in the face of a Roman magistrate. Now, however, it is famous for a somewhat different reason:
in 1990, excavations surrounding the tomb of the famous saint revealed
layer upon layer of Paleolithic, Visigothic, Byzantine, and Roman settlements. Excavation continues, but you can visit the crypt and (from
a distance) watch the archaeologists at work. ⊙ *Daily 10–2 and 4–6.*

Try not to miss a visit to Mérida's superb, modern **Museo Nacional de
Arte Romano** (National Museum of Roman Art), housed in a monumental brick building and containing outstanding mosaics, jewelry, statues, and other Roman works. ⊠ *José Ramón Mélida 2,* ☎ *924/311690.*
⊠ *500 ptas.; 400 ptas. Sun.* ⊙ *June–Sept., Tues.–Sat. 10–1:45 and
5–7, Sun. 10–2; Oct.–May, Tues.–Sat. 10–1:45 and 4–5:45, Sun. 10–2.*

Just past the museum are Mérida's claims to fame—its best-preserved
Roman monuments, the **teatro** (theater) and the **anfiteatro Romano** (amphitheater), arranged in a verdant park. The former, dating from
around 24 BC, is notable for the elegant colonnade on its stage; spectacularly lighted plays are performed here in summer. While the theater has been sensitively restored, the ampitheater was, and remains,
a much cruder construction. At one time 14,000 spectators gathered
on the mammoth stone bleachers for morbidly fascinating duels between gladiators and wild beasts. ☎ *924/312530.* ⊙ *June–Sept., daily
9–1:45 and 5–7:15; Oct.–May, daily 9–1:45 and 4–6.*

OFF THE
BEATEN PATH

EXTREMADURAN SIBERIA – For a taste of truly elemental Spain, drive to
the "Extremaduran Siberia," which lies between Mérida and the La
Mancha town of Ciudad Real (leave N430, which links the two towns,
by following signs for Casas de Don Pedro, and continue south toward
Talarrubias). This poor area of wild, rolling scrubland owes its exotic
name to the 12th duke of Osuna, who came here after 10 years as
Spanish ambassador in Russia and was reminded of the Siberian
steppes. Of the handful of villages, the oldest is Puebla de Alcocer,
which has an arcaded square. More unusual is nearby Peloche, to the
north of Talarrubias, where you can still see women embroidering in the
streets. Many people come to this region solely to enjoy water sports,
such as fishing and windsurfing, on its three reservoirs: Cíjara, García
de Sola, and Orellana.

Dining and Lodging

$$$$
★

✕⬚ **Parador Nacional Via de la Plata.** Built over the remains of what
was first a Roman temple, then a baroque convent, and then a prison,
this spacious, whitewashed building exudes an Andalusian cheerful-
ness, tinged with hints of its Roman and Mudéjar past. The rooms are
bright, with traditional, dark-wood furniture. The brilliant, white interior of the former church has been turned into a particularly restful
lounge. In the dining room, be brave and try the *revuelto de criadillas*
(scrambled eggs with pigs' testicles) or *ranas con aroma de pimentón*
(frogs' legs in paprika sauce). Other traditional offerings include *cabrito
al ajillo* (fried kid with garlic). ⊠ *Plaza Constitución 3, 06800,* ☎ *924/
313800,* FAX *924/319208. 82 rooms. Restaurant, bar, pool. AE, DC,
MC, V.*

Nightlife and the Arts

Surrounding the Plaza España are numerous cafés, tapas bars, and restaurants filled with boisterous crowds late into the evening. As you walk south on Santa Eulalia, the bars get cheaper and the music gets louder. Calle John Lennon, off the northwest corner of the plaza, is your best bet for late-night discos, especially in summer.

The highlight of the cultural calendar is the annual **theater festival,** held in the Roman theater from late June to early August. For information and tickets, contact the tourist office.

Shopping

Antonio Zambrano (⊠ José Ramón Mélida 40, ☎ 924/312818) has a large selection of southern-Extremaduran pottery, which is reddish-brown with delicate engravings (incised into the wet clay with a stone).

Badajoz

⑩ *66 km (40 mi) west of Mérida, 90 km (59 mi) southwest of Cáceres, 85 km (53 mi) northwest of Zafra.*

A sprawling mass of concrete and glass in the midst of desolate terrain, Badajoz looks like a cultural oasis on approach. Hardly an aesthetic haven, however, Badajoz has little to offer the tourist aside from the bustling excitement of a college town. Minutes from Portugal, this "border town" is known mainly as a suitable resting point on your way though Extremadura. Be sure to admire the **Puerta de Palmas,** the 16th-century gateway into the city and the symbol of Badajoz; it consists of two circular, crenellated towers surrounded by decorative cordons (or guardposts) with different motifs on each facade. Badajoz's other noteworthy sight is the **Torre Espantaperros** (literally, Dog-Scarers' Tower—effectively a Christian-scarers' tower), the watchtower of the city's *Alcazaba* (fortress). The practice of building such towers eventually inspired Seville's Giralda.

Dining and Lodging

$$$　✕ **La Toja.** Elegant and expensive for the region, this restaurant specializes in Galician food, and the entrance welcomes you with a familiar sight from the Galician countryside: a *horreo* (small barn raised on stilts). The cuisine attracts a classy crowd; the emphasis is on fish, including such delicacies as *merluza a la Gallega* (hake stewed in onions, potatoes, parsley, and paprika). ⊠ *Sanchez de la Rocha 22,* ☎ *924/273477. AE, DC, MC, V. Closed Sun. No lunch Mon.*

$$$$　🏨 **Gran Hotel Zurbarán.** This large, modern building has a beautiful position near the River Guadiana, overlooking the Castelar park. The decor is brash and slightly dated, but the service is nonetheless impeccable, and few hotels in Extremadura have such a range of amenities ⊠ *Paseo Castelar s/n, 06001,* ☎ *924/223741,* 🖷 *924/220142. 213 rooms, 4 suites. Pool, dance club, meeting rooms. AE, DC, MC, V.*

Nightlife and the Arts

The Plaza España and its side streets to the south are frequented nightly by the local college crowd. More upscale after dark is Avenida República Argentina, with many bars and restaurants.

Zafra

⑪ *62 km (38 mi) south of Mérida, 85 km (53 mi) southeast of Badajoz, 135 km (84 mi) north of Seville.*

Worth a stop on your way north from Andalusia or south to Seville, Zafra is unusual for its Plaza Mayor, which is actually two contiguous squares, the **Plaza Chica** (at one time a marketplace) and the 18th-century **Plaza Grande** (ringed by mansions flaunting their coats of arms), connected by a graceful archway. Both plazas make for enjoyable tapas jaunts.

There are several churches here, the finest being **Nuestra Señora de Candelaría,** near the parador; its *retablo* has nine extraordinary panels by Zurburán.

Dining and Lodging

$$$$ ×☷ **Parador Nacional Hernán Cortés.** The dominant building in this
★   attractive and lively town is the parador, which occupies the 15th-century castle where Cortés stayed before going to Mexico. The building's military exterior conceals an elegant, 16th-century courtyard attributed to Juan de Herrera. The rooms are white and cheerful, some with wood-beam ceilings, others with windows overlooking the marble courtyard. The suite has a superbly elaborate *artesonado* (coffered) ceiling and a Jacuzzi, and the magnificent chapel now serves as the conference room. The dining-room staff will make you feel like an honored explorer home from a daring journey; they'll probably suggest you restore yourself with *caldereta de cordero* (lamb stew). For dessert, try the poached figs with vanilla ice cream or *leche frita* (fried milk custard). ☒ *Plaza María Cristina 7, 06300,* ☎ *924/554540,* ℻ *924/551018. 45 rooms, 1 suite. Restaurant, pool. AE, DC, MC, V.*

EXTREMADURA A TO Z

Arriving and Departing

By Bus

The bus links between Extremadura and the other Spanish provinces are far more plentiful and reliable than the links by train or plane. These include several express buses, which make shorter journeys as well. Regular buses serve Extremadura's main centers from Madrid, Seville, Lisbon, Valladolid, Salamanca, and Barcelona; the main bus company involved is **Auto Res** (☒ Plaza Conde de Casal 6, ☎ 91/551–7200).

By Car

It's best to rent a car outside the region, either in Madrid or Seville, or before you leave for Spain. Traffic moves quickly on the four-lane N V, the main highway from Madrid to Extremadura. The N630, or Vía de la Plata, which crosses Extremadura from north to south, is also effective. The fastest approach from Portugal is along the N IV from Lisbon to Badajoz.

By Plane

The closest international airports to Extremadura are at Madrid and Seville. **Iberia** (☎ 91/329–4353) runs daily flights from both cities to Badajoz. For airlines serving Madrid and Seville, *see* Madrid A to Z *in* Chapter 2 *and* Seville A to Z *in* Chapter 13.

By Train

The principal rail link with Extremadura is the train from Madrid to Seville, which passes through Plasencia, Cáceres, Mérida, and Zafra. The journey from Madrid to Plasencia takes three hours; from Seville to Zafra, 3½ hours. There is also a direct train from Lisbon to Badajoz, which takes five hours. Unfortunately, the trains run infrequently, making them a potentially inconvenient means of travel. Contact the RENFE office in Madrid for more information (☎ 91/328–9020).

Getting Around

By Bus

As in most traditionally poor parts of Europe, buses serve nearly every village. Note, however, that on the lesser routes, buses tend to set off extremely early in the morning; plan carefully to avoid getting stranded.

By Car

If you're in any kind of hurry, driving is the most feasible way to explore Extremadura. The main roads through the province are well surfaced and not too congested. The side roads—particularly those that cross the wilder mountainous districts, such as the Sierra de Guadalupe—can be poorly paved and badly marked.

By Train

Only the main towns can be reached by train, and service is infrequent. The line connecting Plasencia, Cáceres, Mérida, and Zafra, for instance, has just two trains a day, one of which runs at night. Train stations also tend to be some distance from the town centers.

Contacts and Resources

Bus Tours

For specialized art tours accompanied by an expert, contact the English firm **Prospect Art Tours Ltd.** (⊠ 454–458 Chiswick High Rd., London W4 5TT, ☎ 0181/995–2163).

Emergencies

Police: ☎ 091.

Fishing Permits

You can obtain a fishing permit from **Agencia de Media Ambiente** (⊠ Enrique X Canedo, Mérida, ☎ 924/384111) and **ICONA** (⊠ Avda. General Primo de Rivera 2–7, Cáceres, ☎ 927/224666).

Visitor Information

Extremadura's most helpful and best-equipped tourist office is at the entrance to **Mérida**'s Roman theater (⊠ Avda. José Álvarez Saez de Buruaga s/n, ☎ 924/315353). The region's other tourist offices are in **Alcántara** (⊠ Avda. de Mérida 21, ☎ 927/390863), **Badajoz** (⊠ Plaza de la Libertad 3, ☎ 924/222763), **Cáceres** (⊠ Plaza Mayor 33, ☎ 927/246347), **Plasencia** (⊠ C. del Rey 8, ☎ 927/422159), **Trujillo** (⊠ Plaza Mayor s/n, ☎ 927/322677), and **Zafra** (⊠ Plaza de España s/n, ☎ 924/551036). In places without tourist offices, you can usually pick up information and maps at the *ayuntamiento* or the *casa de cultura* (local cultural center).

15 The Canary Islands

Closer to North Africa than to Spain, the ruggedly exotic Canary Islands pack multicultural cities as well as Spanish villages, parched sand dunes as well as seaside resorts. Each of the seven islands in this volcanic archipelago has its own personality. Explore caves once inhabited by ancient tribes; hike to snow-covered peaks; savor a meal grilled over the heat from a volcanic crater. With water sports, wine-tasting, and year-round sun and nightlife, the Canary Islands have long been Europe's favorite winter retreat.

By Deborah
Luhrman

Updated by
Annie Ward

THE CANARY ISLANDS, a volcanic archipelago 1,280 km (800 mi) southwest of mainland Spain and 112 km (70 mi) off the coast of southern Morocco, lie at about the same latitude as central Florida. Each of the seven islands has its own character. Some are fertile and overgrown with exotic tropical vegetation; others are as dry as a bone, with lava caves and desert sand dunes. The Canaries also have Spain's highest peak, Mt. Teide, which is snowcapped for much of the year.

The best thing about the Canaries is their climate, warm in winter and tempered by cool Atlantic breezes in summer. You can swim year-round. The islands' first modern-day tourists arrived from England at the turn of the century to spend the winter at Puerto de la Cruz, in Tenerife; today, huge charter flights from Düsseldorf, Stockholm, Zürich, Manchester, and dozens of other northern European cities unload 6 million sun-starved visitors a year.

The Canary Islands fell one at a time to Spanish conquistadors during Spain's golden age, at the end of the 1400s, and for centuries they lay on the edge of navigators' maps. Columbus resupplied his ships in the Canaries in 1492 before heading west to the New World; he is sometimes called the islands' first tour operator, because he helped establish the archipelago as an important trading port.

Before the arrival of the Spanish, the islands were populated by cave-dwelling people called Guanches. Their ranks were decimated by slave traders by the end of the 16th century; their most significant remains are the Cenobio de Valerón ruins on Gran Canaria.

Pleasures and Pastimes

Beaches

Most visitors come to the Canaries for the sun, and each island has different kinds of beaches on which to enjoy it. The longest and most pristine beaches are the white-sand strands of Fuerteventura. Lanzarote and Gran Canaria offer golden-sand beaches with plenty of tourist amenities, such as lounge chairs and parasailing. Tenerife, despite its fame as a resort, has few natural beaches; the crowded ones that exist are man-made with imported yellow sand.

La Palma, La Gomera, and El Hierro have black-sand beaches, usually in rock-flanked coves. Remember that the Atlantic Ocean can be rough and chilly in winter.

Dining

Canarian cuisine is based on the delicious rockfish that abound near the coast, and its specialties are worth searching out. Prices are lower than in mainland Spain.

A typical meal begins with a hearty stew, such as *potaje canario* (a stew of vegetables, potatoes, and garbanzo beans), *rancho canario* (vegetables and meat), or *potaje de berros* (a watercress soup). Canarians eat *gofio* (similar to mashed potatoes, but made by toasting wheat, corn, or barley flour and then adding milk or broth) with their first course, though it's hard to find in restaurants.

The next course is fresh native fish, the best of which are *vieja, cherne,* and *sama,* all firm-fleshed white rockfish. Accompanying the fish are *papas arrugadas* (literally, wrinkled potatoes), tiny new potatoes boiled in seawater so that salt crystals form on them as they dry. Other specialties include *cabrito* (roast baby goat) and *conejo* (rabbit), both served in *salmorejo,* a slightly spicy paprika sauce.

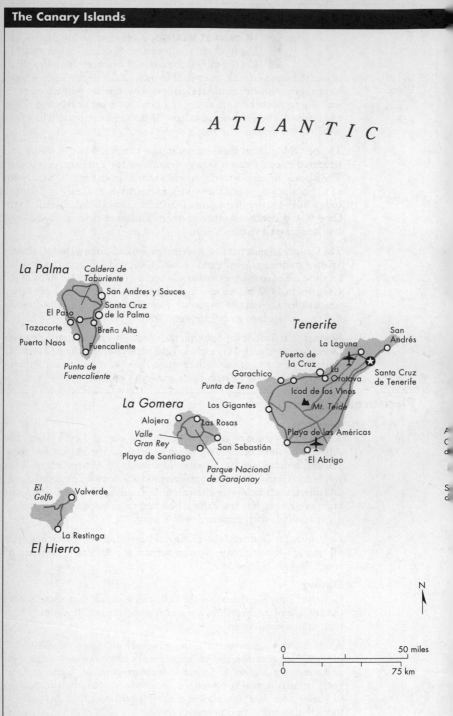

ATLANTIC

La Palma
Caldera de Taburiente
San Andres y Sauces
El Paso
Santa Cruz de la Palma
Tazacorte
Breña Alta
Puerto Naos
Fuencaliente
Punta de Fuencaliente

Tenerife
San Andrés
La Laguna
Puerto de la Cruz
La Orotava
Santa Cruz de Tenerife
Garachico
Punta de Teno
Icod de los Vinos
Mt. Teide
Los Gigantes

La Gomera
Alojera
Las Rosas
Valle Gran Rey
San Sebastián
Playa de Santiago
Parque Nacional de Garajonay

Playa de las Américas
El Abrigo

El Golfo
Valverde
La Restinga
El Hierro

N

0   50 miles

0   75 km

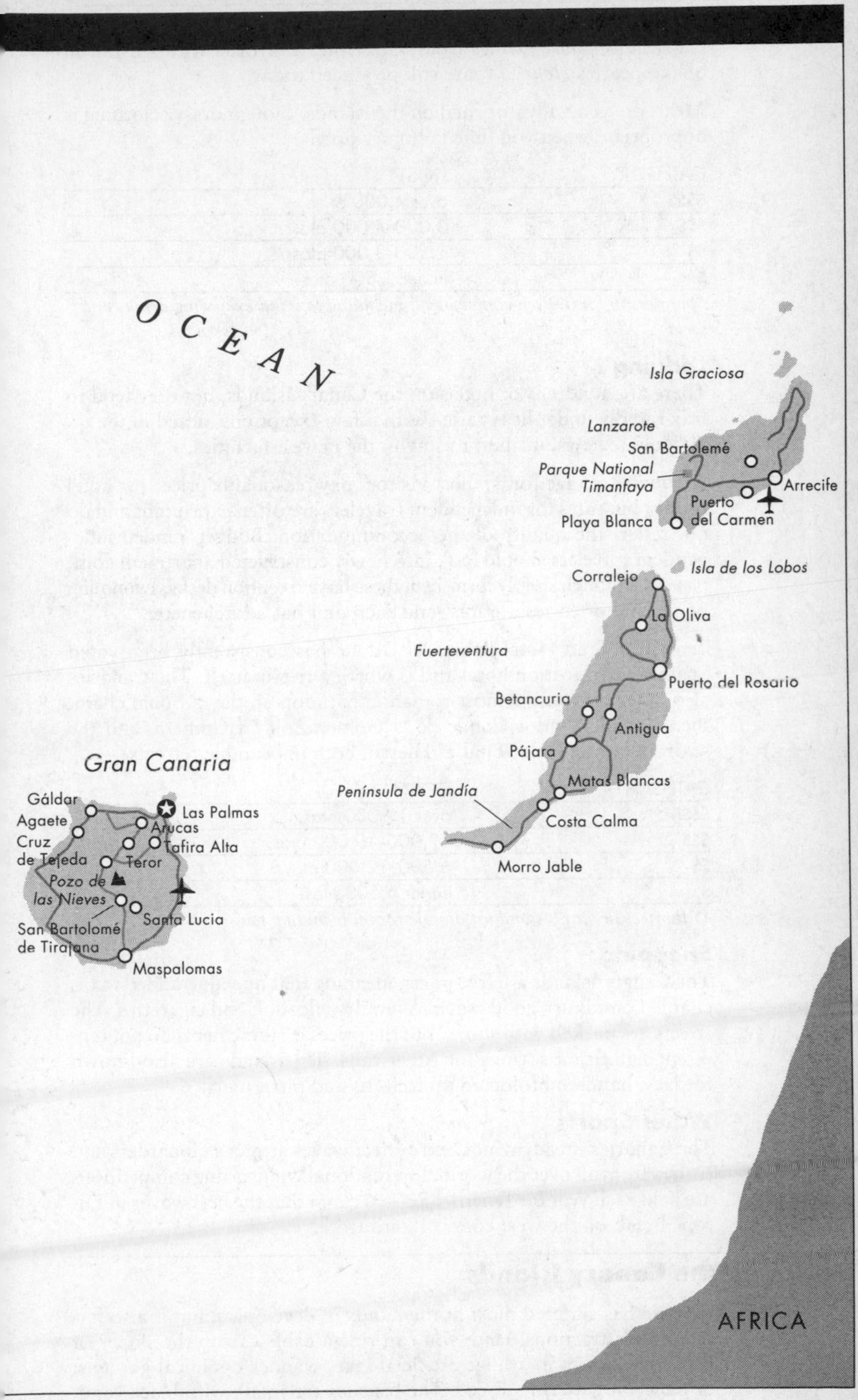

$O C E A N$

Isla Graciosa

Lanzarote

San Bartolemé

Parque National
Timanfaya

Puerto
del Carmen

Playa Blanca

Arrecife

Isla de los Lobos

Corralejo

La Oliva

Fuerteventura

Puerto del Rosario

Betancuria

Antigua

Pájara

Matas Blancas

Península de Jandía

Costa Calma

Morro Jable

Gran Canaria

Gáldar

Agaete

Las Palmas

Arucas

Cruz
de Tejeda

Tafira Alta

Teror

Pozo de
las Nieves

San Bartolomé
de Tirajana

Santa Lucía

Maspalomas

AFRICA

Another island specialty is goat's-milk cheese, made best in La Palma. Canarian malmsey wines from Lanzarote, a favorite with Falstaff in Shakespeare's *Henry IV,* are still produced today.

Meals are generally informal on the islands, though dressy clothing is appropriate when you dine in luxury hotels.

CATEGORY	COST*
$$$$	over 4,000 ptas.
$$$	3,000–4,000 ptas.
$$	1,500–3,000 ptas.
$	under 1,500 ptas.

per person for a three-course meal, including tax and excluding drinks and service

Lodging

There are hundreds of hotels on the Canary Islands, but they tend to fray rapidly under heavy use. With a few exceptions, noted in the individual reviews, it's best to stay in the newest facilities.

Through package tours, most visitors pay reasonable prices for hotel rooms, but rates for independent travelers are often exorbitant and do not reflect the quality of the accommodation. Budget-minded independent travelers should look into newly constructed apartment complexes. Although simply furnished, these have reception desks, swimming pools, and often restaurants, and each unit has a kitchenette.

Tenerife's Gran Hotel Bahía del Duque has consistently been voted Spain's best vacation hotel and is worth a trip in itself. The Canaries also boast two of the most romantic paradors in the national chain, the colonial Parador Conde de la Gomera, on La Gomera, and the seafront Parador Nacional El Hierro, both unbeatable retreats.

CATEGORY	COST*
$$$$	over 19,000 ptas.
$$$	12,000–19,000 ptas.
$$	6,500–12,000 ptas.
$	under 6,500 ptas.

All prices are for a standard double room, including tax.

Shopping

The Canary Islands are free ports, meaning that no value-added tax is charged on luxury goods such as jewelry, alcohol, and cigarettes. The streets are packed with shops, but the prices on these items do not represent significant savings for Americans. The islands are also known for lacy, hand-embroidered tablecloths and place mats.

Water Sports

The Canaries' steady winds and perfect waves attract sailboarders and surfers from all over the world. International windsurfing competitions are held each year on Tenerife. Surfers claim that the best waves in Europe break on the west coast of Lanzarote.

Exploring the Canary Islands

Tenerife has suffered most at the hands of developers, but it also has the most attractions. Here you can ride a cable car up the slopes of Mt. Teide, swim in a huge artificial lake, wander botanical gardens, or dance at glittering discos. The beaches are small, with black sand. The verdant (read: rainy) north coast retains unspoiled villages, while the southern Playa de las Américas is becoming unsightly, with a growing skyline of high-rise hotels.

Gran Canaria was the hot spot of the '60s and is seen as rather passé, but its Maspalomas beach is one of the islands' most beautiful, and some sand dunes behind the beach are being turned into a nature reserve. The capital, Las Palmas, is crawling with sailors, soldiers, and tourists. Though the city is a bit seedy, it does have a sparkling stretch of beach right downtown, with a lantern-lit boardwalk lined with restaurants and bars.

Lanzarote is a desert isle kept beautiful through thoughtful development. It has golden beaches, white villages, caves, and a volcanic national park where heat from an eruption in 1730 is still rising through vents in the earth. Vegetation is scarce, but the grapes grown by farmers in volcanic ash produce a distinctive Canarian wine.

Fuerteventura was ignored until recently, but construction is now racing to keep up with the demands of tourists, who come to windsurf and enjoy the endless white beaches. Luxury hotels now dot the coast, but the island's barren interior is largely the domain of goatherds.

La Palma, called the garden isle, has only recently been "discovered." It has lush foliage, tropical storms, rainbows, and black crescents of beach. The capital, Santa Cruz, is a beautifully preserved example of Spanish colonial architecture, and its people are some of the most genuine and hospitable in all of Spain.

La Gomera is a paradise for backpackers. Ruggedly mountainous, it offers good hiking, and UNESCO protects its forests. The black-sand beaches are usually fringed by banana plantations.

El Hierro is the smallest and least-visited Canary, ideal for those who really want to be alone. It has a few black-sand beaches and a cool, highland pine forest for walking and picnicking.

Many places on the Canary Islands share the same names. Be careful not to confuse the island of La Palma with the city of Las Palmas, which is the capital of Gran Canaria. Equally confusing, the capitals of La Palma and Tenerife are both called Santa Cruz. When writing to an address on one of the islands, note that there are two provinces: the province of Santa Cruz de Tenerife, which includes Tenerife, La Palma, La Gomera, and El Hierro, and the province of Las Palmas, which includes Gran Canaria, Lanzarote, and Fuerteventura.

Numbers in the margin correspond to points of interest on the Tenerife and Gran Canaria maps.

Great Itineraries

The main reasons to go to the Canary Islands are rest and relaxation, but it's worth digging a bit deeper once you're there. Try to combine a visit to the more congested islands—Tenerife, Gran Canaria, or Lanzarote—with side trips to the quieter ones, Fuerteventura, La Palma, La Gomera, or El Hierro.

IF YOU HAVE 3 DAYS

A long weekend in the Canary Islands is a pricey but effective antidote to the stress of city life or fast-paced sightseeing. If you're flying in from mainland Spain, pick one resort, go directly there, and unwind. Tenerife is a good option for first-time visitors—Playa de las Américas in the winter, **Puerto de la Cruz** ② in the summer. On your second day, rent a car and drive up to **Mount Teide** ⑤, stopping at the historic town of Orotava and the Casa de Vino near Los Rodeos Airport. Spend the third day working on your tan.

An indulgent alternative is to fly into Reina Sofía Airport and go to **Playa Los Cristianos** ⑥, where a 35-minute hydrofoil ride will whisk you to tiny La Gomera for three days of swimming and hiking.

One week on the Canary Islands is enough time for a combination trip to two islands. Those who enjoy lots of touring should visit Tenerife and Lanzarote, both with interesting mixtures of lush green and volcanic desert landscapes. Begin your stay in Tenerife with an afternoon at the beach or pool. The second day, rent a car to explore the center of the island, visiting **Mt. Teide** ⑤ and the town of Orotava. On the third day, spend the morning visiting **Santa Cruz** ① and perhaps the nearby town of La Laguna. Stop for lunch or wine-tasting at the Casa de Vino, and in the afternoon explore the north-coast villages of **Icod de los Vinos** ③ and **Garachico** ④. A 30-minute flight will get you to Lanzarote, where you can spend the fifth day exploring the northern part of this island, with stops at the Jameos del Agua and Cuevas Verdes and perhaps a visit to the César Manrique house. On the sixth day, head for Timanfaya National Park for a tour of the volcanic zone. In the afternoon, detour to **Playa Blanca** and Playa Papagayo at the island's southern tip. Save the last day for sunning and swimming.

Most European visitors to the Canaries spend two weeks here. This stretch of time allows you to complete the above itinerary with a few extra days to relax and to see a third island. From Tenerife, La Gomera is a one-hour ferry ride away; from Lanzarote it's a 45-minute ferry ride to Fuerteventura. Either option allows you to keep the same rental car and take advantage of weekly rates. If you choose La Gomera, make an excursion to the **Parque Nacional de Garajonay** and the island's northern coast. You'll need a second day to explore the southern coast with a drive out to **Valle Gran Rey.** Fuerteventura is a better choice for beachcombers or windsurfers; one day here should be sufficient for exploring the island, leaving the rest of the time for loafing or participating in sports.

When to Tour the Canary Islands

As the tourist office loves to point out, the Canary Islands enjoy warm weather in the winter and cool breezes in summer. Christmas and Easter are peak periods for northern Europeans, while Spaniards and Italians tend to come during their August holidays. Reservations are essential at those times. A profusion of wildflowers makes spring the islands' most beautiful season.

Since the Canaries are a year-round destination, prices tend to be about the same no matter when you come. However, you may have some luck negotiating discounts during the slowest months, May and November.

TENERIFE

Tenerife is the largest of the Canary Islands and roughly triangular in shape. It is towered over by the volcanic peak of Mt. Teide, which at 12,198 ft is Spain's highest mountain. The slopes leading up to Teide are forested with pines in the north and covered with barren lava fields in the south.

Tenerife's capital, Santa Cruz de Tenerife, is a giant urban center. Forget whitewashed villas and sleepy streets, and imagine the traffic, activity, and crowds of an important shipping port, as well as the site of Spain's most raucous fiesta (a significant honor), the pre-Lenten Carnival. (Hotels hand out awards to the fiesta's regulars, some of whom have spent 30 consecutive winters here.) In the rainy north, mixed among the tourist attractions, are banana plantations and vineyards.

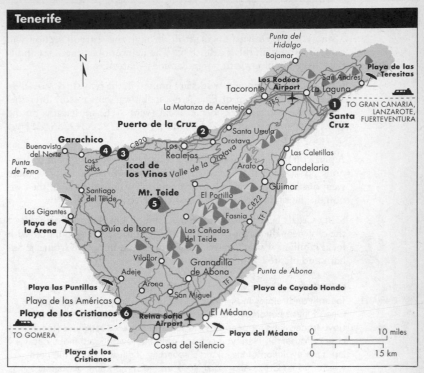

Tenerife

In the dry south, the resort Playa de las Américas has sprung up at the edge of the desert over the past 15 years. It's especially popular with young couples and singles, who appreciate the world-class hotels and swinging nightlife.

Santa Cruz

❶ *10 km (6 mi) southwest of Los Rodeos Airport, 75 km (45 mi) northeast of Playa de las Américas.*

The heart of Santa Cruz de Tenerife is the **Plaza de España.** The cross is a monument to those who died in the Spanish civil war, which was actually launched from Tenerife by General Franco during his exile here. For two weeks before Lent each year, during Carnival, Santa Cruz throbs to a Latin beat emanating from the plaza.

Primitive ceramics and mummies are on display at the **Museo Arqueológico Provincial** (Provincial Museum of Archaeology). The ancient Guanches mummified their dead by rubbing the bodies with pine resin and salt and leaving them in the sun to dry for two weeks. The **tourist office** is just around the corner in the same building. *Palacio Insular,* ⊠ *Bravo Murillo 5, 3rd floor,* ☎ *922/242090.* 🎟 *400 ptas.* ☉ *Tues.–Sun. 10–8.*

The **Iglesia de la Concepción,** or Church of the Conception (⊠ Plaza de la Iglesia), noted for its six-story Moorish bell tower, is expected to remain closed for restoration until the year 2000. It's part of a massive urban-renewal project that has already razed blocks of slums in this area.

The colorful city market **Mercado de Nuestra Señora de Africa,** or Market of Our Lady of Africa (⊠ Avda. de San Sebastián), is part bazaar and part food emporium. Stalls outside sell household goods; inside, stands selling everything from flowers to canaries are arranged around a sunny patio. Downstairs, a stroll through the seafood section will acquaint you with the local fish. ☉ The market opens at 5 AM and is busy from about 6 AM to noon, Monday–Saturday.

Old masters and modern works are housed in the two-story **Museo de Bellas Artes** (Museum of Fine Arts), including canvases by Breughel and Rivera. Many works depict local events. The museum is on the Plaza Príncipe de Asturias. ⊠ *José Murphy 12,* ☎ *922/244358.* 🎫 *Free.* ☉ *Tues.–Fri. 10–7:30.*

A plaza on the northern outskirts of town preserves 18th-century cannons on the site of what was the **Paso Alto Fortress.** In 1794 these weapons held off an attack led by Britain's Admiral Nelson; the cannon on the right fired the shot that cost Nelson his right arm.

Santa Cruz's beach, **Las Teresitas,** is about 7 km (4½ mi) northeast of the city, near the town of San Andrés, and is especially popular with local families. It was created using white sand imported from the Sahara and planted with palms.

OFF THE
BEATEN PATH

LA LAGUNA – The university town of La Laguna was the first capital of Tenerife and retains many colonial buildings along Calle San Agustín. One of these buildings, the 400-year-old colonial home of a former slave trader, was reopened as the **Tenerife Museo de Historia** (Tenerife History Museum). Here you can see antique navigational maps and learn the evolution of the island's economy. It's just 5 km (3 mi) northwest of Santa Cruz. Afterward, soak up the sun and the academic ambience at the coffee shops and bars frequented by local students. ⊠ *C. San Agustín 22,* ☎ *922/630103.* 🎫 *400 ptas.* ☉ *Tues.–Sat. 10–5, Sun. 10–2.*

Dining and Lodging

$$$$ ✕ **El Coto de Antonio.** Considered one of the best restaurants in all of
  ★   the Canaries, this place puts a gourmet spin on local dishes and combines elegant dining with the coziness of a tavern. Dip into a succulent earthenware pot of seafood stew, enhanced with potatoes, yams, blanched *gofio,* and cheese; or order the house specialty, *pejines* (similar to sardines) dried in the sun, soaked in liquor, and served flambé at your table. ⊠ *C. de General Goded 13,* ☎ *922/272105. AE, MC, V. Closed Mon.*

$$ ✕ **Los Troncos.** In a middle-class neighborhood near the bullring is one of the few restaurants in Santa Cruz serving Canarian cuisine. You're greeted by a white Andalusian entryway; inside, steak and spare ribs are grilled to perfection. ⊠ *C. de General Goded 15,* ☎ *922/284152. AE, V.*

$$$$ 🏨 **Hotel Mencey.** "Mencey" was the ancient Guanches' name for their kings, and you may well feel like one at this grandiose, beige stucco-and-marble hotel. Crystal chandeliers and gold-leaf columns ornament the lobby. The rooms are furnished à la Louis XIV. ⊠ *Dr. José Naveiras 38, 38001,* ☎ *922/276700,* FAX *922/280017. 298 rooms. Restaurant, bar, pool, tennis court. AE, DC, V.*

$$ 🏨 **Hotel Taburiente.** Across the street from the city park, this hotel is favored by those who need to catch early-morning flights at Los Rodeos Airport. The white-marble lobby is luxurious, and the rooms are large and comfortable, despite the linoleum floors. Try to get one with a balcony facing the park. ⊠ *Dr. José Naveiras 24A, 38001,* ☎ *922/ 276000,* FAX *922/270562. 116 rooms. Restaurant, pool. AE, MC, V.*

Nightlife and the Arts

The wood- and brass-laden **Andén** (⊠ C. de General Goded 41) attracts a hip young crowd with loud rock music.

Outdoor Activities and Sports

DIVING

Collect information on diving and underwater fishing from the **Club Nautico** (☎ 922/273700).

GOLF

Club de Golf El Peñon (☎ 922/636487) is open to nonmembers on weekdays only. Reservations are essential. The club is near the northern airport, between La Laguna and Tacorante at Guamasa.

HORSEBACK RIDING

The **Club Hípica La Atalaya** (⊠ Camino de San Lazaro s/n, ☎ 922/255739 or 922/251410), on the outskirts of Santa Cruz, can help arrange excursions on horseback.

Puerto de la Cruz

❷ *36 km (22 mi) west of Santa Cruz.*

Puerto de la Cruz is the oldest resort in the Canary Islands. Despite mass tourism, it has retained some Spanish charm and island character. The old sections of town have colonial plazas and *paseos* for evening strolls.

Because Puerto de la Cruz has uninviting black beaches, the town commissioned Lanzarote artist Cesar Manrique in 1965 to build **Lago Martianez,** a forerunner of today's water parks. It's an immense public swimming pool on the waterfront, with landscaped islands, bridges, and fountains that spray sky-high. The complex also includes a restaurant-nightclub and several smaller pools.

Stroll from Lago Martianez along the coastal walkway until you reach the **Plaza de la Iglesia,** beautifully landscaped with flowering plants. Here you can stop at the **tourist office** for a copy of a walking tour that details all of Puerto's architecturally important buildings.

Loro Parque is a subtropical garden with 1,300 parrots, many of which are trained to ride bicycles and perform other tricks. Within the garden is one of Europe's largest aquariums, with an underwater tunnel and a dolphin show, as well as a replica of a village in Thailand. ⊠ *Puerto de la Cruz,* ☎ *922/373841.* 🗌 *2,300 ptas.* ☉ *Daily 8:30–5.*

Filled with thousands of varieties of exotic tropical plants, the **Jardin de Aclimatación de La Orotava** (Orotava Botanical Garden) was founded in 1788, on the orders of King Carlos III, to propagate warm-climate species brought back to Spain from the Americas. ⊠ *Carreterra del Botánico,* ☎ *922/383572.* 🗌 *100 ptas.* ☉ *Oct.–Mar., daily 9–6; Apr.–Sept., daily 9–7.*

Wine lovers should make a point of visiting the **Casa de Vino La Baranda,** located about halfway between Puerto de la Cruz and Los Rodeos Airport, at the El Sauzal exit on the main highway. Opened by the Canary Islands' government in 1996 to promote local vintners, it includes a wine museum, shop, and tasting room, where for a small fee you can sample and learn about some of Tenerife's best wines. The complex also houses a tapas bar and a gourmet restaurant specializing in nouvelle Canarian cuisine. ⊠ *Autopista General del Norte, Km 21,* ☎ *922/572535.* ☉ *Tues.–Sat. 11–8, Sun. 11–6.*

Dining and Lodging

$$$ ✕ **La Magnolia.** Perched near the botanical garden, La Magnolia offers dining in the garden or in the main dining room, where the decor is stalled in the '60s, with a purple ceiling and gold tablecloths. The open kitchen serves huge platters of seafood in garlicky sauces. ☒ *Carretera del Botánico 5*, ☎ *922/385614. AE, MC, V.*

$$$ ✕ **Mi Vaca y Yo.** The name, "My Cow and I," hints at the outdoor summer feast you can put together at this laid-back, plant-filled farmhouse. Few places in the city combine such great food with such a friendly atmosphere. With something for everyone (including finicky kids), the menu presents tasty barbequed beef and a huge variety of fried and grilled fish as well as spaghetti, pizza, chocolate cake, and Canarian meringue cookies. It's popular with local families. ☒ *Cruz Verde 3*, ☎ *922/385247. AE, MC, V.*

$$ ✕ **Casa de Miranda.** Just off the central square, this restored house can trace its history back to 1730. On the ground floor is an inviting tapas bar, strung with gourds and garlands of red peppers, that spills onto a plant-filled patio. Upstairs, the high-ceilinged dining room serves such favorites as filet mignon in pepper sauce and turbot in shrimp sauce. ☒ *Santo Domingo 13*, ☎ *922/373871. AE, DC, MC, V.*

$$ ✕ **El Pescador.** This restaurant claims to be located in the oldest house in town, and you'll believe it when you feel the wood floor shake as the waiters walk by. Slatted green shutters, high ceilings, and salsa music create a tropical air. The specialties include avocado stuffed with shrimp. Ask for *papas arrugadas* (wrinkled potatoes) or you'll get french fries. ☒ *Puerto Viejo 8*, ☎ *922/384088. AE, DC, MC, V.*

$$$$ ✕🏠 **Hotel Botánico.** This luxury hilltop hotel has its subtropical garden, famous in its own right. The lobby now displays a collection of art from Thailand. Rooms have elegant new furnishings, marble baths, minibars, and flowery terraces. Owner Wolfgang Kiessling, who is also an honorary consul of Thailand, has opened Tenerife's first Thai restaurant, the **Oriental**, on the ground floor. The second-floor restaurant, **La Parilla**, specializes in Spanish cuisine and seafood, and the adjacent piano bar has live music every night. ☒ *Avda. Richard J. Yeoward 1, Urb. Botánico, 38400*, ☎ *922/381400*, 📠 *922/381504. 250 rooms. 3 restaurants, bar, minibars, 2 pools, beauty salon, sauna, tennis courts, exercise room, health club. AE, MC, V.*

$$$ 🏠 **San Felipe.** This 19-story hotel has the best location in Puerto de la Cruz—steps from the beach, with million-dollar views of the coast and Mt. Teide. The new Catalan owners are tastefully redecorating the large rooms, which feature balconies and large baths. The room rate includes an elegant champagne-breakfast buffet. ☒ *Avda. de Colón 22, 38400*, ☎ *922/383311*, 📠 *922/373718. 260 rooms. Restaurant, bar, pool, sauna, tennis court. AE, MC, V.*

$$ 🏠 **Hotel Monopol.** One of the town's first inns, the Monopol, built in 1742, has been welcoming travelers for 103 years; before that it was a private home. The small, neatly furnished rooms are arranged on four stories of wooden balconies around a central courtyard. Most overlook the sea or the town's main plaza. ☒ *Quintana 15, 38400*, ☎ *922/384611*, 📠 *922/370310. 100 rooms. Restaurant, 2 bars, pool. AE, MC, V.*

Nightlife and the Arts

The **Casino Taoro** (☒ Carretera del Taoro s/n, ☎ 922/380550) makes room for gambling in a stately former hotel.

Almost all hotels have live music at night. For dancing, try **Victoria,** at the Hotel Tenerife Playa (☒ Avda. de Colón s/n), a favorite with all age groups, or **El Coto** (✉ Avda. Litoral 24), usually jammed with a fast-moving young crowd. The side streets of Avenida Colón are packed with bars and underground clubs; catering mostly to tourists, many offer imported beer, German food, or Irish music. For a more authentic experience, try **Dos Besos** (✉ C. Genovés 12), where you can sip a fruity island drink or sangría to Latin and African rhythms.

Shopping

The largest selection of hand-embroidered tablecloths and place mats is at **Casa Iriarte** (✉ San Juan 17), tucked into the patio of a ramshackle Canarian house.

Icod de los Vinos

❸ *26 km (16 mi) west of Puerto de la Cruz.*

In the quiet town of Icod de los Vinos, attractive plazas rimmed by unspoiled colonial architecture and Canarian pine balconies form the heart of Tenerife's most historic wine district.

A 3,000-year-old **dragon tree** towers 57 ft above the coastal highway, C820. The Guanches worshiped these trees as symbols of fertility and knowledge; the sap, which turns red upon contact with air, was used in healing rituals.

The **Casa Museo del Vino** (✉ Plaza de la Pila 4) is a tasting room where you can sample the sweet local malmsey and other Canary Island wines and cheeses.

Garachico

❹ *5 km (3 mi) west of Icod de los Vinos.*

Garachico is one of the most idyllic and best-preserved towns on the islands. It was the main port of Tenerife until May 5, 1706, when Mt. Teide blew its top, sending twin rivers of lava downhill. One filled Garachico's harbor, and the other destroyed most of the town. Legend has it that the eruption was unleashed by an evil monk.

One of the buildings that withstood the eruption was the **Castillo San Miguel,** a tiny 16th-century fortress on the waterfront. Island crafts, such as embroidery and basketmaking, are demonstrated inside. From the roof you can see the two rivers of lava, now solidified on the mountainside. You can also visit the **Convento de San Francisco,** also unscathed, and the 18th-century parish church of **Santa Ana.**

Mt. Teide

❺ *60 km (36 mi) southwest of Puerto de la Cruz, 63 km (39 mi) north of Playa de las Américas.*

Four roads lead to Mt. Teide from various parts of Tenerife, but the most beautiful approach is the road from Orotava. As you head out of town into the higher altitudes, banana plantations give way to fruit and almond orchards that bloom in January. Higher up is a fragrant pine forest.

Orotava flaunts a row of stately mansions on Calle San Francisco, just north of the baroque church Nuestra Señora de la Concepción. At the **Casa de los Balcones** (✉ C. San Francisco 3), and just across the street at the Casa del Turista (✉ C. San Francisco 2), you can see a variety of island craftspeople at work: basketmakers, cigar rollers, and sand painters. ▨ *Free.* ☉ *Daily 8:30–6:30.*

You enter the **Parque Nacional del Teide** (Teide National Park) at **El Portillo.** Exhibits at the visitor center explain the region's natural history; the center also offers trail maps, video presentations, guided hikes, and bus tours. ☎ *922/290129.* ⊙ *Daily 9–4.*

The park includes the volcano itself and a 6-km (4-mi)-long crater at the foot of the mountain, called the **Cañadas del Teide.** The *cañadas* (glens) are a violent jumble of rocks and minerals, a stark landscape that suggests another planet. About 10 km (6 mi) farther on, in the middle of the crater, the **cable car** to Mt. Teide carries you close to the top. (The final 534 ft require at least half an hour's climb.) On the way up, you'll notice sulfur steam vents. The station has a bar and restaurant. ☎ *922/383711.* ⊡ *1,800 ptas.* ⊙ *Daily 9–5; last trip up at 4.*

The trail to the rim of the volcano is closed when it's snowy, usually about four months a year. You can still get a good view of southern Tenerife and Gran Canaria from the top of the cable-car line, but you'll be confined to the tiny terrace of the bar.

Across from the Parador Nacional Cañadas del Teide are the **Roques de Garcia**—rocks that have eroded into fantastic shapes and provide a good foreground for a photo of Mt. Teide.

Lodging

$$ ▥ **Parador Nacional Cañadas del Teide.** The rooms in this classic mountain retreat overlook the intriguing rock formations of the Las Cañadas plateau, at the foot of Mt. Teide. The large, inviting rooms have wood floors. ⊠ *38300 La Orotava,* ☎ *922/386415. 37 rooms. Restaurant, bar, cafeteria, pool, sauna, tennis courts. AE, DC, MC, V.*

Shopping
Browse for contemporary island crafts and traditional musical instruments at the government-sponsored shop **Casa Torrehermosa** (⊠ Tomás Zerolo 27) in Orotava.

Playa de Los Cristianos

❻ *74 km (44 mi) southwest of Santa Cruz, 10 km (6 mi) west of Reina Sofía Airport.*

This is the newest, largest, and sunniest tourist area on Tenerife, with high-rise hotels built chockablock above the beaches. Sun and nightlife are the attractions here. Playa de Las Américas and Los Cristianos are on the southwest island, about 1 km (½ mi) from each other.

Los Cristianos is a small crescent of gray sand surrounded by apartment houses, while **Playa de las Américas** is a man-made, yellow-sand beach protected by an artificial reef.

Los Gigantes, about 12 km (7 mi) north of Playa de las Américas, is a smallish, gray-sand cove surrounded by rocks and towering cliffs.

☖ **Octopus Aguapark,** a huge water park, has tall slides, meandering streams for inner tubes, and swimming pools. ⊠ *San Eugenio, Playa de las Américas,* ☎ *922/715266.* ⊡ *1,700 ptas.* ⊙ *Daily 10–6.*

Dining and Lodging
$$$ ✕ **El Patio.** This oceanside restaurant has a spectacular location on the grounds of the Jardín Tropical Hotel (☞ *below*). The patio ranks as the south coast's top gourmet restaurant, serving such treats as cold mussel soup with saffron and duck breast in mandarin orange sauce. ⊠ *Jardín Tropical Hotel,* ☎ *922/750100,* ⊞ *922/750100. AE, DC, MC, V. Closed June.*

$$ ✕ **Masia del Mar.** There's no menu here; you simply point to what you
★ want from the vast display of fresh fish and shellfish. Add a salad and
a bottle of white wine to the order, and find a seat on the wide terrace.
✉ *Caleta de Adeje, 5 km (3 mi) west of Playa de las Américas,* ☎ 922/
710241. *MC, V.*

$$$$ 🏨 **Hotel Gran Melia Bahía del Duque.** A cross between a Canarian vil-
★ lage and an Italian hill town, this sprawling hotel is a striking jumble
of pastel houses and palaces, all presided over by a clock tower copied
from the Torre de la Concepción in Santa Cruz. The five-story lobby
is a marvel in itself, with tropical birds, palm-filled bars, and two glass
elevators, and the staff dresses in traditional Canarian costume. Guest
rooms have oversize beds and summery wicker and pine furnishings.
The hotel can arrange sailing and diving expeditions and runs boat trips
to see the whales that cavort just off the coast. ✉ *Adeje 38670,* ☎ 922/
713000, ℻ 922/712616. *362 rooms. 5 restaurants, bars, 4 pools,
beauty salon, sauna, miniature golf, tennis court, exercise room, squash,
dive shop, boating. AE, MC, V.*

$$$$ 🏨 **Jardín Tropical Hotel.** Spread on many levels over several hills, the
Jardín Tropical has white turrets and archways, Moorish tile floors,
and cascading profusions of bright, flowering plants. The rooms are
furnished with carved-pine and wicker furniture and pastel paisley prints;
all have balconies. Baths are decorated with colorful Spanish tile. ✉
Gran Bretaña s/n, 38660 San Eugenio, Adeje, ☎ 922/750100, ℻
922/752844. *376 rooms. Restaurant, bar, 2 pools, beauty salon, sauna,
exercise room. AE, MC, V.*

$$$$ 🏨 **Hotel Marco Antonio Palace.** This decadent hotel is one of five in
the new Mare Nostum Resort complex. Replicas of Greek statues line
the entrance and the vast swimming pool, while the six-story lobby is
a high-tech synthesis of marble, neon, and chrome. Glass elevators glide
up to the rooms, which are filled with black leather and brass. The beds
are oversize, the baths are black marble, and every room has a terrace.
✉ *Avda. de las Américas s/n, 38660 Arona,* ☎ 922/757500, ℻ 922/
793622. *116 rooms. Restaurant, piano bar, pool, beauty salon, sauna,
tennis court, exercise room, squash. AE, DC, MC, V.*

$$ 🏨 **Hotel Atlantic Playa.** This beachfront hotel near the Reina Sofía Airport is a favorite with windsurfers. The lobby is arranged around a
fountain; the rooms have separate sleeping and sitting areas, black modern furniture, and terraces. A breakfast buffet is included, and children
under 12 stay at half price. ✉ *Avda. Europa 2, 38617 El Médano,* ☎
922/176234, ℻ 922/176114 *155 rooms. Restaurant, piano bar, pool,
hot tub, sauna, exercise room, squash, windsurfing. AE, MC, V.*

Nightlife and the Arts

For gambling on the south island, hit the **Casino Playa de las Américas**
(✉ Avda. Marítima s/n, ☎ 922/793758), in the Hotel Gran Tenerife.

Most bars in Playa de las Américas are in a three-building complex
called Veronica's. Here, places like the Kangaroo Pub, Busby's, and
Sgt. Pepper's draw young, rowdy, mostly foreign crowds. The **Banana
Garden** (☎ 922/790365) attracts an older but no less lively crowd with
live salsa music, and the disco **Prismas** (in the Hotel Tenerife Sol) has
become a perennial favorite.

Outdoor Activities and Sports

DIVING
The PADI-licensed school at **Las Palmeras Hotel** (✉ Avda. Marítima,
☎ 922/752948), in Playa de las Américas, has information on diving
and underwater fishing.

GOLF

Near Reina Sofía Airport, **Campo Golf de Sur** (☎ 922/738170) has 27 holes, and not far away there are two 18-hole links at the **Amarilla Golf Club** (☎ 922/730319), in San Miguel.

WINDSURFING

Windsurfing rentals and lessons can be arranged at the **SunWind Windsurf School** (☎ 922/176174), in Playa del Médano.

GRAN CANARIA

The circular island of Gran Canaria has three distinct identities. Its capital, Las Palmas, population 370,000, is a thriving business center and shipping port, while the white-sand beaches of the south coast are tourist magnets. The interior is rural.

Las Palmas, the largest city in the Canary Islands, is a multicultural whirlwind, overrun by sailors, tourists, traffic jams, diesel-spewing buses, and hordes of shoppers. One side of the city is lined with docks for huge container ships, while the other harbors the 7-km (4½-mi) Canteras beach.

The south coast, a boxy 1960s development along wide avenues, is a family resort. At the southern tip of the island, the popular Playa del Ingles gives way to the empty dunes of Maspalomas.

The isle's interior is a steep highland that reaches 6,435 ft at Pozo de las Nieves. Although it's green in winter, Gran Canaria does not have the luxurious tropical foliage of the archipelago's western islands.

Las Palmas

❼ *35 km (21 mi) north of Gran Canaria Airport, 60 km (36 mi) north of Maspalomas.*

Las Palmas is strung out for 10 km (6 mi) along two waterfronts of a peninsula. Though most of the action centers on the peninsula's northern end, the sights are clustered around the city's southern edge. Begin in the old quarter, La Vegueta, at the **Plaza Santa Ana,** with its bronze dog statues. You may be surprised to learn that the Canary Islands were named not for the yellow songbirds but for a breed of dog (*canum* in Latin) found here by ancient explorers. The birds were later named after the islands.

The smog-stained **Catedral Santa Ana** (St. Anne's Cathedral) faces the Plaza Santa Ana. The cathedral took four centuries to complete, so the 19th-century exterior with its neoclassical Roman columns contrasts sharply with the Gothic ceiling vaulting of the interior. Baroque statues in the Andalusian style are displayed in the cathedral's **Museo de Arte Sacro** (Museum of Religious Art), which is arranged around a peaceful cloister. Ask the curator to open the *sala capitular* so you can see the 16th-century Valencian tile floor. The treasury is closed to the public. ⊠ *Espíritu Santo 20,* ☎ *928/314989.* 🎫 *300 ptas.* ☉ *Weekdays 10–4:30, Sat. 9–1:30.*

The **Casa Museo Colón** (Columbus Museum) is housed in a palace where Christopher Columbus may have stayed when he stopped to repair the rudder on the *Pinta*. Nautical instruments, copies of early navigational maps, and models of Columbus's three ships are on display. Two rooms showcase pre-Columbian artifacts. ⊠ *C. Colón 1,* ☎ *928/311255.* 🎫 *Free.* ☉ *Sept.–July, weekdays 9–6, weekends 9–3.*

It's only been open since 1991, but the **Centro Atlántico de Arte Moderno** (Atlantic Center for Modern Art) has already earned a name for

Gran Canaria

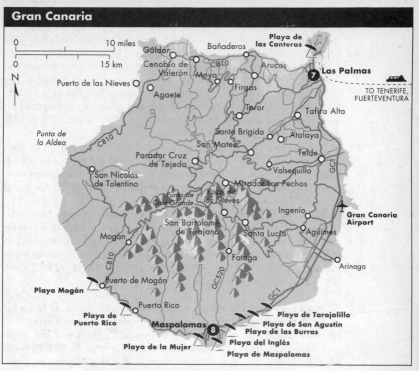

curating some of the best avant-garde shows in Spain. ⊠ *Los Balcones 9 y 11,* ☎ *928/311824.* ⊡ *Free.* ⊘ *Tues.–Sat. 10–9, Sun. 10–2.*

It's quite a walk to the other end of town, so you may want to hop one of the many canary-yellow buses, named the *guaguas* (pronounced "wawas") in honor of the Guanches. Ride to **Parque Santa Catalina,** or get off at the **Parque Doramas** (stops are listed on big yellow signs; the 2, 3, and the 30 generally cover the entire city) to peek at the elegant Santa Catalina Hotel and Casino. Inside the park is the **Pueblo Canario,** a model village with typical Canarian architecture. Regional folk dances are performed here on Thursday (5–7) and Sunday (11:30–1).

NEED A BREAK?	Whether you're sunning or shopping, Las Palmas can be exhausting. Escape to the tranquil, air-conditioned quiet of the **Casa Suecia Salon de Té** (Swiss Tea House) (⊠ Luis Morote 41, near Playa de las Canteras, ☎ 928/271626), with comfortable booths, foreign newspapers, picture windows on the street, delicious pastries and sandwiches, and perhaps the only free coffee refills on the islands.

On a hill north of Parque Santa Catalina, looming over the rather tough port district, is the **Castillo de la Luz,** a fortress built in 1494 (currently closed to the publi). Due west of Parque Santa Catalina are the sparkling white sands of **Las Canteras Beach,** a perfect spot for a swim or a stroll along the *paseo.*

Beaches

The beaches along Gran Canaria's eastern and southern coasts are the island's major tourist attraction. **Las Canteras,** in Las Palmas, is made safe for swimming by an artificial reef. It can be extremely crowded in summer, but the sand is swept clean every night.

Dining and Lodging

$$$ ✕ **Casa Montesdeoca.** In the heart of the historic quarter, this romantic restaurant is housed in a 14th-century mansion built by a Jewish businessman named Montesdeoca. The hallways are stone labyrinths—during the Inquisition, the Montesdeoca family escaped from their pursuers through hidden doors and secret tunnels. The beautiful outdoor patio is draped with bougainvillea; the wine list features the best bottles from each island; and fresh fish is prepared on an outdoor grill just steps from your table. ⊠ *Montesdeoca 10,* ☎ *928/ 333466. AE, MC, DC, V. Closed Sun.*

$$ ✕ **Julio.** In this small dining room, decorated with ropes, portholes,
★   and polished wood, you can tuck into 12 different types of shellfish or local fish, such as *cherne* (sea bass) served in a white-wine clam sauce. A different Canarian soup or stew is prepared each day. ⊠ *La Naval 132,* ☎ *928/460139. AE, V.*

$$ ✕ **Mesón de la Paella.** Green-latticework window trim and lace curtains give this white-stucco *mesón* a homey feel. The kitchen serves up rice dishes from Spain's Mediterranean coast, such as *arroz negro* (black rice) and seafood paella. Look for the big paella-pan sign one block from Plaza España. ⊠ *José María Duran 47,* ☎ *928/271640. AE, V. Closed Sun. No dinner Sat.*

$$$ ▥ **Meliá Las Palmas.** Aimed at business travelers, the Meliá has a superb location and offers large, bright rooms that were newly renovated in 1996. There is a pool on a terrace overlooking the sea. The room rate includes a breakfast buffet. ⊠ *Gomera 6, 35008,* ☎ *928/267600,* FAX *928/268411. 316 rooms. Restaurant, coffee shop, piano bar, pool, dance club. AE, DC, MC, V.*

$$ ▥ **Hotel Imperial Playa.** This business-oriented hotel sits right on Las Canteras beach. The bright rooms have Scandinavian furniture and marble baths, and their small terraces have nice beach views. ⊠ *Ferreras 1, 35008,* ☎ *928/468854,* FAX *928/469442. 142 rooms. Restaurant, snack bar, beach. AE, DC, MC, V.*

$ ▥ **Apartments Brisamar Canteras.** The best-maintained of all the beach apartments, the Brisamar's are a favorite with travelers from Finland. The rooms are merely functional, but they're freshly painted and cheerful. ⊠ *Paseo de las Canteras 49, 35010,* ☎ FAX *928/269400. 52 studio apartments. AE, DC, MC, V.*

Nightlife and the Arts

The **Las Palmas Philharmonic Orchestra** (⊠ Bravo Murillo 2123, ☎ 928/320513), one of Spain's oldest orchestras, offers an ample program between October and May. Its January festival draws leading musicians from around the world. Ticket information is available at the box office at Teatro Pérez Galdós (⊠ Plaza Mercado, ☎ 928/361509).

Gamblers choose the **Gran Casino de Las Palmas** in the Santa Catalina Hotel (⊠ León y Castillo 227, Parque Doramas, ☎ 928/291103). Inside the casino, the elegant and expensive **Restaurant Doramas** (☎ 928/ 233908) will make you feel like a high roller.

Las Palmas has a lively (if sometimes scruffy) nightlife, with most of the bars and discos clustered between Playa de las Canteras and Parque Santa Catalina. **Calle Tómas Miller** is lined with restaurants featuring foods from every corner of the world, and dance music emanates from **Wilson** (⊠ C. Franchy Roca) as well as the nearby **Pacha** (⊠ C. Simón Bolivar 3), which draws beautiful people with cash to burn on the pricey cover and drinks. The discotheque **Coto,** in the **Meliá Las Palmas** (⊠ C. Gomera 6, ☎ 928/268050), is alive with a middle-aged international crowd.

Outdoor Activities and Sports

GOLF

Founded in 1891, the **Royal Golf Club** (☎ 928/350104), on the rim of the Bandama crater roughly 15 minutes outside Las Palmas, is Spain's oldest golf course. Redesigned and relocated in 1956, it now has 18 holes, two putting greens, a sports shop, two tennis courts, a restaurant, and a bar.

HORSEBACK RIDING

To rent horses, contact the **Royal Golf Club** (☎ 928/350104), with 48 stables and five riding rings.

Shopping

Gran Canaria has the best duty-free shops in the islands, and a department store, **El Corte Inglés,** on Avenida Mesa y Lopez in central Las Palmas. For more unusual gift items, try **Antigüedades Linares** or **La Fataga,** in the Pueblo Canario, with a good selection of crafts from all over Spain. The glittering form at the southern edge of the beach is Las Palmas' new glass-and-chrome shopping mall, **Las Arenas** (⊠ C. Pavia 18, ☎ 928/277008), packed with boutiques, restaurants, and cinemas.

Maspalomas

❽ *60 km (36 mi) southwest of Las Palmas, 25 km (15 mi) southwest of Gran Canaria Airport.*

Maspalomas is a built-up beach resort with all the trappings, incongruously backed by empty sand dunes that resemble the Sahara. Despite beachfront overdevelopment in the town, it retains appealing stretches of isolated beach on the outskirts, as well as a bird sanctuary. In recent years, German tour operators, who bring masses of visitors, have helped place a new emphasis on protecting the environment.

☽ **Holiday World** amusement park has roller coasters and a Ferris wheel that children will see from miles away. ⊠ *Carretera General, Campo Internacional Lote 18, Maspalomas,* ☎ *928/767176,* ＦＡＸ *928/767355.* ▥ *1,700 ptas.* ☽ *Daily 6 PM–midnight.*

☽ **Parque Acuático/Ocean Park** is a mammoth new addition to Maspalomas. With dozens of slides, a wave pool, inner tubing, restaurants, and bars, it's a perfect spot for both kids and adults to splash the day away. ⊠ *Exit 47, Hwy. 1,* ☎ *928/764361,* ＦＡＸ *928/765331* ▥ *1,750 ptas.* ☽ *Daily 10–6.*

☽ **Parque de los Palmitos** (Palmitos Park) is part botanical garden and part zoo, with tropical birds and an open-air butterfly house. Trained parrots perform. ⊠ *Carretera Palmitos, 6 km (4 mi) inland from Maspalomas,* ☎ *928/141158.* ▥ *1,800 ptas.* ☽ *Daily 9–6.*

Beaches

Playa de Tarajalillo, with alternating areas of black sand and gravel, is the first beach of the southern resort area and a popular choice with local families. **Playa de San Agustín** is a 1-km (½-mi) strip of black sand fringed with a palm garden; it has rental areas for sailboards, pedal boats, and lounge chairs. **Playa de las Burras** is a gray beach surrounding a crescent-shaped harbor sometimes used by local fishermen.

★ **Playa del Inglés** is Gran Canaria's most famous beach. Its white sands, more than 3 km (2 mi) long, swarm with beach-chair rentals, ice-cream vendors, and fast-food restaurants. West of here are sand dunes and a signposted nude beach.

The **Maspalomas** beach, a 1-km (½-mi) stretch of golden sand, is bordered by endless dunes that provide a sense of isolation and refuge from the chaos of other Canarian resorts. Dozens of varieties of native birds and plants also take refuge in a lagoon alongside the dunes. The western edge of Maspalomas is marked by a lighthouse. **Playa de la Mujer,** a rocky beach around the point from Maspalomas, is a good place to watch the sunset.

Dining and Lodging

$$ ✕ **Loopy's Tavern.** An island tradition that few travelers can resist, Loopy's is styled as an American steak house, with friendly waiters, imaginative cocktails, a western motif, and great meat. Try the shish kebabs, which are served dangling from a metal contraption above your table. ⊠ *Las Retamas, 7 San Agustín,* ☎ *928/762892. V.*

$$ ✕ **Tenderete II.** Canarian cuisine is cherished at Tenderete, one of the
★   few restaurants on the islands where you can order *gofio,* made here with roasted corn flour and fish broth. The first course consists of typical soups and stews, and the main course is always fish, grilled or baked in rock salt. Pick it out from the display hooks in the front window. Wines from Lanzarote, El Hierro, and Tenerife are available. ⊠ *Avda. de Tirajana 5, Edificio Aloe,* ☎ *928/761460. AE, DC, MC, V.*

$$$$ ⊡ **Hotel Don Gregory.** This modern, eight-story, brown-brick hotel sits on the crescent-shaped Las Burras beach, and the atmosphere is appropriately relaxed. The large, carpeted rooms have blond-wood furniture, marble baths, and large terraces; all overlook the beach. ⊠ *Las Talias 11, 35100,* ☎ *928/773877,* FAX *928/769996. 241 rooms. Restaurant, bar, pool, tennis court, beach, dance club. AE, MC, V.*

$$$$ ⊡ **Hotel Palm Beach.** The most sophisticated and luxurious hotel in
★   the Canary Islands, the Palm Beach is on the edge of Maspalomas beach in the middle of a 1,000-year-old palm oasis. The lobby is elegantly striped with black-and-white marble. The tastefully decorated rooms are equipped with huge closets and large, marble baths; terraces overlook the sea or the palms. ⊠ *Avda. del Oasis s/n, 35106,* ☎ *928/140806,* FAX *928/141808. 358 rooms. Restaurant, bar, pool, beauty salon, hot tub, sauna, tennis court, exercise room, beach. AE, DC, V.*

$$$ ⊡ **Hotel Buenaventura.** A veritable Disneyland of color, music, pool parties, and dancing, this resort may be the happiest place on the Playa del Inglés. The rooms are a bright (and appropriate) canary yellow, with flowers and big sliding-glass doors opening onto pool-view balconies. With a thatched-roof poolside bar that energizes sunbathers with thumping music from dawn to dusk, Buenaventura is popular with young couples, singles, and anyone who doesn't mind late-night laughter in the halls. ⊠ *C. Ganigo 6, 35100,* ☎ *928/763450,* FAX *928/760618. 724 rooms. Restaurant, bar, 3 pools, beauty salon, exercise room, dance club, laundry facilities. AE, MC, V.*

$ ⊡ **Duna Flor Azul.** This new complex of two-story, blue-and-white apartment buildings is near the Maspalomas golf course, on a free bus line to the beach. The large pool area is landscaped with bright bougainvillea. The units have twin beds and a small balcony upstairs, a sitting area and kitchen downstairs. ⊠ *Avda. de Neckerman s/n, 35100,* ☎ *928/767675,* FAX *928/769419. 282 units. Restaurant, 2 bars, kitchens, pool, playground. AE, V.*

Nightlife

Gamblers go to the **Casino Gran Canaria** (⊠ La Retama 3, Playa de San Agustín, ☎ 928/762724) in the Hotel Tamarindos, in San Agustín.

Hot nightspots on the south coast include **Spider** (⊠ Avda. Italia s/n, Playa del Inglés), which plays Euro-techno to an international college crowd, and the slightly more sedate **San Agustín Beach Club** (⊠ Playa

Cocoteros s/n), with less-frenetic dancing to the sounds of Euro-pop.
La Bamba (⊠ Avda. Tirajana s/n, Playa del Inglés) is your best bet for
salsa, meringue, and a general Latino ambience.

Outdoor Activities and Sports

GOLF

The 18-hole **Maspalomas Campo de Golf** (☎ 928/762581) is near the
dunes.

HORSEBACK RIDING

To rent horses, contact the **Palmitos Park** (⊠ Carretera Palmitos,
about 6 km ([4 mi]) inland from Maspalomas, ☎ 928/760458).

SAILING

The famous **Escuela de Vela de Puerto Rico** sailing school (☎ 928/
560772), where Spain's 1984 Olympic gold medalists trained and
teach, is at Puerto Rico, about 13 km (8 mi) west of Maspalomas.

WINDSURFING

You can rent windsurfing equipment from the **Club Mistral** at the Hotel
Bahía Feliz (⊠ Playa del Tarajalillo, Carretera del Sur, Km 44, 35479,
☎ 928/764600, FAX 928/764612).

Central Highlands

From Maspalomas on the southern coast, take Route GC520 toward
Fataga for a good drive through the center of the island. This is sage-
brush country, with interesting rock formations and cacti. A **mirador**
(lookout) about 7 km (4½ mi) uphill offers views of the coast and mountains.

San Bartolomé de Tirajana

*23 km (14 mi) north of Maspalomas, 20 km (12 mi) east of Cruz de
San Antonio.*

The administrative center of the south coast, San Bartolomé de Tirajana is an attractive town planted with pink geraniums. Its Sunday-
morning market, in front of the church, is popular with travelers, who
pick up tropical produce and island crafts. Just to the east, the village
of **Santa Lucía** is filled with crafts shops and has a small museum devoted to Guanche artifacts.

En Route Drive up to the Cruz Grande summit on GC520. To the left are several of the island's reservoirs, known as the lakes of Gran Canaria; they're
stocked with trout, and you can fish in them with a permit from the
forest service, ICONA (☎ 928/248735).

Drive along GC520 in the direction of Tejeda, past rural mountain villages. On the right is the spike-shape Roque Nublo, an eroded volcanic
chimney worshiped by the Guanches.

Tejeda

About 7 km (4 ½ mi) southwest of Las Palmas de Gran Canaria.

At the village of Tejeda, the road begins to ascend through a pine forest dotted with picnic spots to the **Parador Cruz de Tejeda**. From the
parador continue uphill about 21 km (13 mi) to the **Mirador Los Pe-
chos,** the highest lookout on the island.

OFF THE   **ARTENARA** – If you want to avoid the throngs of tourists stopping for
BEATEN PATH   lunch at the Parador Cruz de Tejeda, follow the signs to the village of
               Artenara, about 13 km (8 mi) west of the road leading to the parador.
               It's an unspoiled hamlet, with cave houses built right into the side of the
               mountain. The restaurant **Mirador de la Silla** (☎ 928/666108) is in the

entrance to one of these caves, but the cavern opens up to the other side of the mountain, where you can sit in the sun and enjoy a spectacular view. Canarian specialties are served at bargain prices.

$$$ ✕ **Parador Cruz de Tejeda.** Hordes of travelers stop for lunch at this stone-and-stucco parador, and you'll understand why when you feast on its luscious regional dishes. Options range from watercress soup and swordfish to lamb or pork served with Canarian *mojo* sauces. The parador's rooms are closed for renovation until summer 1999. ⊠ *Cruz de Tejeda s/n,* ☎ *928/666050,* FAX *928/666051. AE, DC, MC, V.*

San Mateo
15 km (9 mi) northeast of the parador.

From Tejeda, the road winds down to San Mateo, home to the **Casa Cho Zacarias** museum of rural life and a winery. The museum is open ☉ Monday–Saturday 9–1. Pass **Santa Brigida** and turn right toward the golf club on the rim of the Bandama crater. Continue to the village of **Atalaya,** with cave houses and pottery workshops.

Tafira Alta
7 km (4½ mi) west of Las Palmas.

Along the main road leading into Las Palmas from San Mateo is Tafira Alta, an exclusive enclave of the city's wealthy families.The botanical gardens of the **Jardín Canario Viero y Clavijo** are here, with a respected collection of plants from all the Atlantic islands grouped in their natural habitats. ☉ *Daily 9–6.*

The North Coast

Leaving Las Palmas by the northern road, you pass grim shantytowns before reaching the banana plantations of the coastal route. This is the greenest part of the island and is worth the trip for a seaside lunch in the pleasant village of Agaete.

Arucas
13 km (8 mi) west of Las Palmas.

An agricultural center, Arucas is the island's third-largest town. Its great, gray-stone Gothic church looks wildly out of place among the small white houses.

Teror
10 km (6 mi) south of Arucas.

Amid the most verdant vegetation on Gran Canaria is the village of Teror, an obligatory stop on all island tours. In the 18th-century church of **Nuestra Señora del Pino** (Our Lady of the Pine Tree), Gran Canaria's patron saint is seated on a silver throne above the altar. The statue, said to have been found in a pine tree in the 15th century, is now taken out for special fiestas.

As you head west, you'll see increasingly tropical foliage in the hillside villages of **Firgas** and **Moya.**

Parfumes Oceano, near the church parking lot in the village of Teror, sells perfumes made locally from tropical flowers.

Agaete
8 km (5 mi) southwest of Galdar.

The quiet, leafy town of Agaete is famous for the annual fiesta of the *rama* (branch), on August 4, in which pine branches from the island's upper slopes are carried to the town by dancing crowds. The ritual is a variation on a pre-Christian rain dance that was used by the Guanches in times of drought.

Just beyond Agaete is **Puerto de las Nieves** (Port of the Snows), where painted boats bob in the tiny harbor. The short Avenida de las Poetas leads to an old windmill on the point. Look for the rocky point called the Dedo de Dios (Finger of God).

LANZAROTE

With mostly solidified lava and dark, disconcerting dunes, Lanzarote's interior is right out of a science-fiction film. There are no springs or lakes, and it rarely rains, so all fresh water comes from desalination plants. Despite its surreal and sometimes intimidating volcanic landscape, Lanzarote—the fourth-largest of the Canaries—has turned itself into an inviting resort through good planning, an emphasis on outdoor adventure, and conservation of its natural beauty. No buildings over four stories are allowed, leaving views of the spectacular geology unobstructed.

Lanzarote was named for the Italian explorer Lancelotto Alocello, who arrived in the 14th century. The founder of modern-day Lanzarote, however, was artist and architect César Manrique, the unofficial artistic guru of the Canary Islands. Manrique's aesthetic hand is evident throughout the island; in Lanzarote, he designed most of the tourist attractions and convinced authorities to require all new buildings to be painted white with green trim to suggest coolness and fertility. He also led the fight against overdevelopment.

Arrecife

6 km (4 mi) east of the airport.

Lanzarote's cinderblock capital, Arrecife (named for its many reefs), is the most unattractive part of the island. The well-organized **tourist office,** in the municipal park, can guide you toward the highlights.

The **Castillo San Gabriel** is a double-walled fortress once used to keep pirates at bay. It now houses an archaeology museum, where you can see copies of some of the Guanche cave drawings found on Lanzarote. ⌚ *250 ptas.* ◷ *Weekdays 9–1 and 5–8.*

The old, waterfront fortress Castillo San José was turned into the stunning **Museo de Arte Contemporaneo** (Museum of Contemporary Art) by Manrique, one of whose paintings is on display along with other modern Spanish works. Go down the space-tunnel staircase for a look at the glass-walled, harbor-view restaurant. ⌧ *Avda. de Naos s/n,* ☎ *928/812321.* ⌚ *Free.* ◷ *Museum daily 11–9.*

Dining

$$$ ✕ **Castillo San Jose.** Black-and-white furniture, glass walls, and modern art give this remodeled fortress an elegant feel. In the equally sophisticated restaurant, try the cold avocado soup with caviar, or the salmon steak wrapped in cured ham. ⌧ *C. Puerta de Naos s/n,* ☎ *928/ 812321. AE, V.*

Costa Teguise

7 km (4½ mi) northeast of Arrecife.

Costa Teguise is a tasteful, green-and-white complex of apartments and a few large hotels. Each of the chimneys on the bungalows has different decorative shapes. King Juan Carlos owns a villa here, near the Meliá

Salinas hotel. Costa Teguise has several small beaches; the best is **Las Cucharas.**

The **Jardín de Cactus** (Cactus Garden), just north of Costa Teguise between Guatiza and Mala, was Manrique's last creation for Lanzarote. The giant metal cactus that marks the entrance comes perilously close to tacky, but the gardens artfully display nearly 10,000 cacti. A restored windmill grinds and sells *gofio.* ☎ *928/529397.* ▦ *500 ptas.* ☉ *Daily 10–6.*

Playa de la Garita, not far from the Jardín de Cactus, is a wide bay favored by surfers in winter and snorkelers, for the crystal water, in summer.

★ **Los Jameos del Agua** (water caverns), 15 km (9 mi) north of the Costa Teguise, is a natural wonder created when molten lava streamed through an underground tunnel and hissed into the sea. Eerie music creates a mysterious aura as you explore. Look for the tiny white crabs on the rocks in the underground lake—this species, a blind albino crab, is found nowhere else in the world, and there is talk of closing the *jameos* to save it from extinction. ☎ *928/835010.* ▦ *Days 1,000 ptas., nights 1,200 ptas.* ☉ *Daily 11–6:45, Tues. and Sat. also 7 PM– 3 AM.*

★ ♻ Across the highway from the Jameos del Agua, the **Cuevas Verdes** (Green Caves) are for more adventurous cave explorers. Guided walks take you through a 2-km (1-mi) section of underground volcanic passageway. There is so little humidity that no stalactites have formed, but this gentle spelunk is one of the best tours on the island. ☎ *928/173220.* ▦ *1,000 ptas.* ☉ *Daily 10–6; last tour at 5.*

The little fishing village of **Orzola** is 9 km (5½ mi) north of Jameo del Agua. A small excursion boat leaves here each morning for the neighboring islet of **La Graciosa,** with only 500 residents and plenty of quiet beaches.

♻ **Guinate Tropical Park,** in the northern part of the island, has 1,300 species of exotic birds and animals. ☎ *No phone.* ☉ *Daily 10–5.*

Dining and Lodging

$$$ ✕ **La Jordana.** This unpretentious restaurant, with a beamed ceiling and white walls, is one of Lanzarote's most popular dining spots. The fare is international, with French touches. Try the homemade pâté, veal with apples, or locally caught cherne in orange sauce. ✉ *Los Geranios 10–11,* ☎ *928/590328. AE, V. Closed Sun. and Sept.*

$$ ✕ **El Pescador.** You can't miss this place; local cats will lead you here as they prowl neighboring alleys for tasty scraps. With the sights, sounds, and smells of the marina so close by, you know upon entering that you're getting the freshest of fish. Carved wooden ceilings, fishnets on the walls, and simple benches at long plank tables make El Pescador an authentic haunt for local fishermen. ✉ *Centro Comercial Pueblo Marino,* ☎ *no phone. No credit cards. Closed Mon.*

$$ ✕ **Grill Casa Blanca.** Inside a tiny octagonal house, this restaurant has the atmosphere of an English country cottage, with stained-wood floors and wreaths of dried flowers. You can watch the chef in the open kitchen of the main dining room. Try the avocado-and-shrimp salad, steak with green peppercorns, or local fish dishes. ✉ *Las Olas 4,* ☎ *928/590155. AE, MC, V. No lunch.*

$$$$ ✕▥ **Meliá Salinas.** A stunning hotel built around an interior tropical
★ garden with hanging vines, palms, waterfalls, and songbirds, the Meliá Salinas offers a chance to rub elbows with vacationing European political leaders. The rooms have louvered closets and doors and large,

flower-filled, sea-view terraces. The hotel's gourmet restaurant, La Graciosa, is Lanzarote's swankiest dining spot; savor giant prawns, duck breast in plum sauce, or halibut wrapped in chard. ⊠ *Costa Teguise 35509,* ☎ *928/590040,* FAX *928/590390. 310 rooms. 2 restaurants, 2 bars, pool, beauty salon, sauna, 5-hole golf course, tennis court, archery, basketball, exercise room, squash, beach. AE, DC, MC, V.*

$$$ 🏨 **Teguise Playa.** Don't be put off by this hotel's cold, glass exterior; the six-story lobby is filled with plants, and the staff is friendly. The rooms have white-tile floors and bamboo furniture, and each has a geranium-filled terrace with a sea view over the hotel's private beach. ⊠ *Avda. del Jabillo s/n, Urb. Costa Teguise 35509,* ☎ *928/590654,* FAX *928/590979. 325 rooms. Restaurant, bar, 2 pools, beauty salon, hot tub, sauna, tennis court, exercise room, squash, beach. AE, MC, V.*

$ 🏨 **Apartamentos Las Cucharas.** Housed in attractive, three-story build-
★ ings with decorative chimneys, these new apartments sit right on Las Cucharas beach. They have knotty-pine furniture, terraces, and one or two bedrooms. The pool area is beautifully landscaped. ⊠ *Urb. Costa Teguise 35509,* ☎ *928/590700. 66 units. Restaurant, bar, pool, beach. AE, MC, V.*

Outdoor Activities and Sports

DIVING

The island's only official diving center is at Las Cucharas. **Diving Lanzarote** (☎ 928/590407) is run by a German who speaks perfect English; he rents equipment, leads dives, and offers a certification course.

GOLF

Lanzarote's 18-hole **Campo de Golf Costa Teguise** (☎ 928/590512) is just outside the Costa Teguise development and features unusual sand traps filled with black-lava cinders.

WINDSURFING

You can arrange windsurfing lessons and rent equipment from the **Lanzarote Surf Company** (☎ 928/591974) at Las Cucharas beach.

Shopping

For a good selection of island crafts, drop by the open market in the village of **Teguise** on Sunday between 10 and 2. Some vendors set up stalls in the plaza; others simply lay out a blanket in the street and sell embroidered tablecloths, leather goods, costume jewelry, African masks, and thousands of other items.

Puerto del Carmen

11 km (7 mi) southwest of Arrecife.

Most beach-bound travelers to Lanzarote head to the sandy strands of the Puerto del Carmen area. **Playa Grande,** the main beach, is a long strip of yellow sand where you can rent sailboards, JetSkis, skates, and lounge chairs. It's backed by a 3-km (2-mi) stretch of souvenir shops and restaurants of every national persuasion. **Playa de los Pocillos** is slightly north of Puerto del Carmen and the site of most of the area's development; hotels and apartments are restricted, however, to the other side of the highway, leaving the 2-km (1-mi), yellow-sand beach surprisingly pristine. **Playa Matagorda,** the northern extension of Playa de los Pocillos, has alternating sections of gravel and gray sand; it's favored by surf fishermen.

Dining and Lodging

$$$ ✕ **La Casa Roja.** La Casa Roja is a favorite with visitors because of the beautiful waterfront view overlooking the harbor. The authentically

Canarian food is good, too; specialties include a catch of the day as well as sole covered with a béchamel sauce. ⊠ *Varadero s/n,* ☎ *928/ 513705. AE, DC, MC, V.*

$$ ✕ **El Varadero.** This converted fishermen's warehouse on the tiny harbor has an informal marine atmosphere. The food is typically Canarian, with fresh fish and *papas arrugadas* in ready supply. The tapas bar at the entrance is littered with toothpicks and napkins dropped by a lively crowd enjoying bite-size portions of marinated *calamares* and *pulpo en tinto* (octopus in its own ink). ⊠ *Varadero 34,* ☎ *928/ 513162. AE, V.*

$$$ 🏨 **Apartamentos Sol Lanzarote.** It's no coincidence that this holiday haven has special deals for honeymooners; it's a decadent hideaway on a private stretch of the Matagorda beach, 3 km (2 mi) from the city center. With lush gardens, balcony hammocks, and a gargantuan terrace complex with three pools, four tennis courts, a sand volleyball court, a bar, and an indoor-outdoor disco, it caters to romantics. The minimum stay is two nights, yet no one seems in a hurry to leave. ⊠ *C. Grana 2, Urb. Playa Matagorda, Puerto del Carmen 35510,* ☎ *928/ 514888,* 🖷 *928/512803. 330 rooms. Restaurant, bar, grocery, 3 pools, tennis courts, volleyball, dance club. AE, DC, MC, V.*

$$ 🏨 **Los Fariones.** The granddaddy of Lanzarote's resorts has retained an exclusive, elegant atmosphere as its tropical gardens designed by César Manrique have matured. The rooms are smallish, with rattan furniture and linoleum flooring, but each has a terrace with views of the gardens and sea. ⊠ *Roque del Oeste 1, Puerto del Carmen 35510,* ☎ *928/510175,* 🖷 *928/510202. 237 rooms. Restaurant, bar, pool, sauna, miniature golf, tennis court, exercise room. AE, V.*

$$$$ 🏨 **Los Jameos Playa.** Only a staircase separates the large, atrium-style lobby, with tall palms and huge wooden beams, from the pool. Opened in 1994, this hotel has stylish new rooms and furniture. Most of the rooms have terraces, overlooking the garden, pool, or beach. There's a nude beach on the grounds. ⊠ *Playa de los Pocillos, Puerto del Carmen 35510,* ☎ *928/511717,* 🖷 *928/514219. 530 rooms. Restaurant, bar, pool, beauty salon, sauna, tennis court, exercise room, playground. AE, DC, MC, V.*

Nightlife and the Arts
Most nightlife in Lanzarote centers on the hotel bars, all of which feature live music. For dancing, try **Tiffany's** (⊠ Avda. de Suiza 2, Playa de los Pocillos, ☎ 928/511344), an upscale club for all ages, or the **Big Apple** (⊠ Avda. de las Playas, ☎ no phone), with a good mix of Spaniards and foreigners. The **Casino** (⊠ Avda. de las Playas, ☎ no phone) is a classic spot.

Outdoor Activities and Sports
Mountain biking has become very popular here in the last few years. It's actually a very practical way to tour the island, as Lanzarote is not particularly hilly. You can rent bikes at **Fire Mountain Biking** (☎ 928/ 512267), in Puerto del Carmen.

Tahíche

5 km (3 mi) south of Teguise.

In Tahíche, the unusual former home of artist Manrique has been opened to visitors as the **Fundación César Manrique.** On display are a collection of Manrique's paintings and sculptures, as well as works by other 20th-century artists. But the real attraction is the house itself, designed by Manrique to blend with the volcanic landscape. The lower level is built into a series of caves. ⊠ *Carretera Tahíche–San Bartolomé, 2 km (1 mi) west of Tahíche,* ☎ *928/843078 or 928/843038.* 🎫 *800 ptas.* ⊘ *Mon.–Sat. 10–7, Sun. 10–3.*

Yaiza

13 km (8 mi) west of Puerto del Carmen.

Yaiza is a quiet, whitewashed village with good restaurants. It was largely destroyed by a river of lava in the 1700s and is best known as the gateway to the volcanic national park.

★ The **Parque Nacional Timanfaya** (Timanfaya National Park) popularly known as the fire mountains, takes up much of the southern Lanzarote. As you enter the park from Yaiza, the first thing you'll see is the staging area for the **camel rides.** Many of the Canary Islands offer camel rides, but these are the most famous, and a big tourist attraction. The brief rides are, well, bumpy.

The volcanic landscape inside Timanfaya is a violent jumble of exploded craters, cinder cones, lava formations, and heat fissures. The park is strictly protected, and you can visit it only on a bus tour. Taped commentary in English explains how the parish priest of Yaiza took notes during the 1730 eruption that buried two villages. ☎ *928/840057.* 🎫 *900 ptas.* ⊘ *Daily 9–5.*

Dining

$$ ✕ **El Diablo.** This must be one of the world's most unusual restaurants. Here, in the middle of Timanfaya National Park, chicken, steaks, and spicy sausages are cooked over a volcanic crater using the earth's natural heat. ⊠ *Timanfaya National Park,* ☎ *928/840057. AE, MC, V.*

$–$$ ✕ **La Era.** One of only three buildings to survive the 1730 eruption of Yaiza's volcano, this farmhouse restaurant has simple dining rooms with blue-and-white checkered tablecloths on tables arranged around a center patio. It's is a great place to try regional dishes such as goat stew, cherne in cilantro sauce, and Canarian cheeses. ⊠ *Barranco 3, Yaiza,* ☎ *928/830016. AE, DC, MC, V.*

Playa Blanca

15 km (9 mi) south of Yaiza.

Playa Blanca is Lanzarote's newest resort. The ferry for Fuerteventura leaves from here, but there's not much more to the town. Tourists come for the exquisite white beaches, reached via hard-packed dirt roads on **Punta de Papagayo.** The most popular beach is **Playa Papagayo.** Bring your own picnic; there's just one bar.

Just north of Playa Blanca is Lanzarote's agricultural belt. In **La Geria,** grapes are grown in cinder pits surrounded by a ring of volcanic rock. The rocks provide protection from the wind, and the cinders allow dew to drip down to the roots.

Lodging

$$ 🏨 **Lanzarote Princess.** Near the virgin beaches of Lanzarote's south shore, the Lanzarote Princess is a modern, white, three-story building with an airy, plant-filled lobby. The rooms are a bit small and have linoleum floors; bright floral bedspreads compensate a bit for the somewhat sterile effect. The grounds, on the other hand, are vast, and encompass good sports facilities and a huge pool with a bar in the middle. ⊠ *Playa Blanca, Yaiza 35570,* ☎ *928/517108,* ℻ *928/517011. 439 rooms. Restaurant, bar, beauty salon, miniature golf, tennis court, squash, playground. AE, MC, V.*

Outdoor Activities and Sports

Rent mountain bikes at **Zafari Cycle** (☎ 928/517691).

FUERTEVENTURA

The dry island of Fuerteventura is a beachcomber's dream: it's the second-largest of the Canary Islands, but the least populous, with only 20,000 people.

The two main resort areas are Corralejo, known for its acres of sand dunes, and the Jandia peninsula, with dozens of beaches, including one that's 26 km (16 mi) long. Tourism is relatively new here, and both areas are in the midst of an uncontrolled building craze.

Puerto del Rosario

5 km (3 mi) north of the airport.

Fuerteventura's capital, Puerto del Rosario, has long suffered from an image problem. It used to be called Puerto de Cabra (Goat Port), but the new-and-improved name has not changed the fact that this is a poor city with little of interest.

Corralejo

38 km (23 mi) north of Puerto Rosario.

Towering sand dunes dwarf the beachfront hotels here. These massive hills have blown across the sea from the Sahara, just 96 km (60 mi) away, and it's not hard to imagine this island as a detached piece of Africa.

South 19 km (11 mi) on the inland road is the **Casa de los Coroneles,** the island's main historic building. Military governors built the immense house in the 1700s and ruled the island from it until the turn of the century. It is not open to the public.

Beaches

Playa de Corralejo, about 2 km (1 mi) south of the town, is fringed by mountainous sand dunes and faces Los Lobos Island, across the channel. Nude sunbathing is common at the more remote spots.

Playa el Algibe de la Cueva, on the northwest side of the island, has a castle once used to repel pirates. It's popular with locals.

Lodging

$$$$ ⊞ **Tres Islas.** This luxury resort sits right on the empty white beach near the Corralejo dunes. It's built around a swimming-pool complex decorated with yellow-and-white-striped tents. The bedrooms are more formal, with soft green carpeting, dark-wood furniture, and floral prints. All have terraces. ⊠ *Grandes Playas, 35660 Corralejo,* ☎ *928/535700,* 📠 *928/535858. 365 rooms. Restaurant, piano bar, 2 pools, beauty salon, sauna, tennis courts, exercise room, beach, playground. AE, DC, V.*

$$ ⊞ **Oliva Beach.** The rooms in this boxy, eight-story hotel are fairly small, with linoleum floors and orange drapes, but each has a furnished terrace with views of the endless beach. There is an Olympic-size swimming pool, and the friendly staff runs a miniclub to keep youngsters busy all day. ⊠ *Grandes Playas, 35660,* ☎ *928/866100,* 📠 *928/866154. 410 rooms. Restaurant, bar, pool, beauty salon, tennis court, playground. AE, V.*

Outdoor Activities and Sports

DIVING

The channel between Corralejo and the tiny Isla de Lobos is rich in undersea life and favored by divers as well as sportfishermen.

WINDSURFING

One of Fuerteventura's biggest attractions is **windsurfing.** You can rent boards at most hotels; one of the main schools is **Ventura Surf** (☎ 928/866040).

Betancuria

25 km (15 mi) southwest of Puerto Rosario.

Betancuria was once the capital of Fuerteventura but is now almost a ghost town, with only 150 residents.

The weather-worn colonial church of **Santa María de Betancuria** was meant to be the cathedral of the Canary Islands. The **Museo de la Iglesia** (church museum) contains a replica of the banner carried by the Norman conqueror Juan de Bethancourt when he seized Fuerteventura in the 15th century. Most of the artwork was salvaged from the nearby convent, now in ruins. The museum is open weekdays 9:30–5 and Saturday 9:30–2; admission is 100 pesetas.

The **Museo Arqueológico** (Museum of Archaeology) and a crafts workshop are on the other side of the ravine that cuts through the tiny hamlet.

In **Antigua,** 8 km (5 mi) east, you can visit a restored, white Don Quixote–style windmill that was once used for grinding *gofio*. The modern metal windmills you see throughout the island were imported from the United States and are used to pump water.

Pájara

16 km (10 mi) south of Betancuria.

Pájara is the administrative center of the booming Jandia peninsula and sports a two-block strip of boulevard, pretty wrought-iron street lamps, and a brand-new city hall.

Fuerteventura was once divided into two kingdoms, and a wall was built across the Jandia peninsula to mark the border. Remnants of that wall are still visible today inland from **Matas Blancas** (White Groves), 42 km (26 mi) south of Pájara on Highway GC640.

Costa Calma

7 km (4½ mi) south of Matas Blancas.

As you continue south along the coast from Matas Blancas, the beaches get longer, the sand gets whiter, and the water gets bluer. The famous **Playas de Sotavento** begin near the Costa Calma developments and extend gloriously for 26 km (16 mi). Nude sunning is favored here, except directly in front of hotels.

Dining and Lodging

$ ✕ **La Taberna Costa Calma.** Usually packed with both locals and travelers, La Taberna serves Mexican specialties and typical Canarian dishes in several small dining rooms with stone archways and checked tablecloths. Try the *pescado a la sal* (fish baked in a crust of rock salt, which you chip away before eating); garlic soup; or the islands' famous *queso de majorero*, (very roughly, "fine cheese") served with *mojo* sauce. ✉ *Carretera Jandia s/n,* ☎ *no phone. No credit cards.*

$$$$ ⊡ **Robinson Club Playa Jandia.** People come here to really let go. No cash changes hands; all meals are included; and drinks are paid for with brightly colored chips that make it easy to forget how much you're spending at the flower-strung terrace bar, cozy tavern bar, and romantic cocktail lounge. With nude beaches to the north and south, a thumping nightclub, and lots of tanned European yuppies on holiday, this is Fuerteventura's answer to Club Med. ⊠ *Playa Jandia 35620,* ☎ *928/ 541348,* ⨳ *928/541656. 320 rooms. Restaurant, 3 bars, 2 pools, beauty salon, 4 tennis courts, volleyball, windsurfing, dance club. AE, MC, V.*

$$$ ⊡ **Fuerteventura Playa.** This sophisticated, low-slung hotel, built around a large, kidney-shaped pool and thatched-roof bar, is at the north end of the Sotovento Beach. The rooms have slate-blue carpets and modern white furnishings, including oversize beds. Plant-filled terraces overlook the beach. ⊠ *Urb. Canal del Río Poligono C1, 35627,* ☎ *928/547344,* ⨳ *928/547097. 300 rooms. Restaurant, bar, pool, beauty salon, sauna, tennis court, exercise room, windsurfing. AE, DC, MC, V.*

$$ ⊡ **Barlovento Club Hotel.** The Barlovento is a full-service, all-suite hotel and an excellent value. The three-story building with blue metal railings looks a bit like a ship run aground on Sotovento Beach. The suites include separate bedrooms, sitting areas, terraces, and kitchenettes. ⊠ *Costa Calma, 35627,* ☎ *928/547002,* ⨳ *928/547038. 226 suites. Restaurant, piano bar, kitchenettes, pool, sauna, miniature golf, tennis court, exercise room, squash. AE, V.*

Outdoor Activities and Sports

You can rent windsurfing boards at most beach hotels. For lessons, try **Windsurf Urlaub** (☎ 928/870825) at the Sol Gorriones hotel on Sotavento Beach.

Morro Jable

At the southernmost tip of the island.

At the very southern tip of Fuerteventura is the old fishing port of Morro Jable, well on its way to becoming the next Tenerife. Many more miles of virgin coast stretch beyond here—down a dirt road that eventually leads to the lighthouse—and beaches along the entire windward side of the peninsula remain untouched.

Beaches

Beyond the town of Morro Jable, a dirt road leads to the isolated beaches of Juan Gomez and **Playa de las Pillas.** Following the dirt tracks across the narrow strip of land, you can enjoy the equally empty **Playa de Cofete** and **Playa de Barlovento de Jandia.**

Dining

$$ ✕ **Casa Emilio.** The best of the restaurants blossoming along Morro Jable's harbor, Casa Emilio has a wood-burning grill in the dining room where fresh fish is cooked as you watch. The kitchen also turns out delicious crab cocktail, pepper steak, and paella. ⊠ *1 block uphill from harbor (sign visible from harbor),* ☎ *928/540054. No credit cards.*

Outdoor Activities and Sports

For **scuba diving** and **snorkeling,** head for the rocky outcrops on the windward side of Jandia.

LA PALMA

La Palma is a green and prosperous island that managed quite successfully in the past without tourism. But now that it has been "discovered," La Palma is handling its guests with good taste by emphasizing the island's natural beauty, traditional crafts, and cuisine. The residents, called Palmeros, are especially friendly.

Santa Cruz de la Palma

★ *6 km (4 mi) north of the airport.*

Santa Cruz is the capital of La Palma and was an important port and bustling shipbuilding center in the 16th century. Then, in 1533, a band of buccaneers led by French pirate François le Clerc raided the city and burned it to the ground. La Palma was rebuilt with money from the Spanish king, which is why it now has such a unified colonial appearance.

Walk up the cobblestone main street, Calle O'Daly, which everyone calls Calle Real. Take a peek inside the elegant patio of the **Palacio Salazar,** which contains the tourist office.

The triangular **Plaza de España,** in front of the church of El Salvador, is the focus of La Palma's social life and fills with people in the early evening. The church is the only building that survived the pirate fire; it has a handsome, carved Moorish ceiling. Bring a flashlight if you want to see the religious art on the walls. Note the stone shields on the city hall, across the plaza. One is the coat of arms of Spain's Habsburg kings, and the other is the emblem of La Palma. Walk uphill one block to the corner of Calle de la Puente; then look back at one of the most charming streets in the Canaries.

In the restored cloisters of the church of San Francisco, the **Museo Insular** (Island Museum) traces the navigational and trading history of La Palma and displays Guanche artifacts. ⊠ *Avda. Perez de Brito,* ☎ *922/420558.* 🎫 *200 ptas.* ☉ *Weekdays 9:30–1 and 4–7:30.*

The **Museo de Bellas Artes** (Museum of Fine Arts), next door to the Island Museum, has a good collection of Flemish and Spanish paintings. 🎫 *Free.* ☉ *Weekdays 9:30–1 and 4–7:30.*

You can't miss the life-size cement replica of Columbus's ship *Santa María,* at the end of the Plaza Alameda. There's a tiny **naval museum** below decks. ☎ *922/416550.* 🎫 *150 ptas.* ☉ *Weekdays 9:30–2 and 4–6:30.*

The star-shape **Castillo Real** (Royal Castle), on Calle Mendez Cabezola, is a 16th-century fortress. Nearby, along **Avenida Marítima,** is a much-photographed row of Canarian houses with typical green balconies. Stop in at Tabacos Vargas (⊠ Avda. Marítima 55) to see the famous *palmero* cigars being rolled by hand. The cigar industry is a result of constant migration between the Canary Islands and Cuba. Many with a taste for fine cigars claim that hand-rolled *palmeros* are better than today's Cubans.

The hilltop village of **Las Nieves** (The Snows), 3 km (2 mi) northwest of Santa Cruz, has a beautifully preserved colonial plaza and the opulent church of **Nuestra Señora de las Nieves,** which houses La Palma's patron saint, the Virgin of the Snows. The Virgin, credited with saving many a ship from disaster, sits on a gold altar wearing vestments studded with pearls and emeralds.

Dining and Lodging

$$ ✕ **El Brasero.** Native Palmeros head to this seaside restaurant for a special meal of grilled steak or fish served by especially friendly waiters. ⊠ *Avda. Marítima 54,* ☎ *922/414360. MC, V.*

$$ ✕ **Mesón del Mar.** If you venture to the north part of the island, follow the road down from San Andrés to the tiny fishing harbor at Puerto Pesquero Espindola, and you'll end up at this popular seafood house.

Fish couldn't be any fresher. ⊠ *Puerto Pesquero Espindola,* ☎ *922/450305. AE, MC, V.*

$–$$ ✕ **Restaurant Tamanca.** A sign marks the entrance to this restaurant-in-a-cave, 16 km (10 mi) north of Fuencaliente. Inside are traditional meat and fish dishes with an island flair. ⊠ *Carretera General s/n, Montaña Tamanca, Las Manchas,* ☎ *922/462155. AE, DC, MC, V.*

$ ✕ **Chipi Chipi.** This restaurant is tucked away behind dense tropical
★   gardens—complete with chirping parrots—in the hills above Santa Cruz, 3 km (2 mi) beyond the church in Las Nieves. Each party of diners is seated in a private stone hut. The food is strictly local, and portions are huge. You can start with salad or garbanzo-bean soup, followed by grilled meats washed down with local red wine. ⊠ *Ctra. de las Nieves,* ☎ *922/411024. MC, V. Closed Wed.*

$ ▥ **Castillete Aparthotel.** Right on the ocean but down the street from the heavy traffic, this new hotel is the best choice if you want to stay in the city. Most of the units are studios with separate sleeping and sitting areas and small kitchens. White wood and natural-pine furniture give the rooms a clean, modern look. ⊠ *Avda. Marítima 75, 38700,* ☎ *922/420054,* ℻ *922/420067. 42 apartments. Restaurant, pool, hot tub. AE, MC, V.*

Shopping

La Palma's best crafts and foods are sold at **La Graja Centro de Artesanía,** near the Mirador de la Concepción outside Santa Cruz, where you'll find embroidery, baskets, pottery, cookbooks, bottled *mojo* sauce, cigars, and more. Many local artisans specialize in silk-weaving, so look for great deals on raw silk by the meter in the "garment district," which covers the length of **Avenida del Puerto** as well as the side streets.

Playa de los Cancajos

5 km (3 mi) south of Santa Cruz de la Palma.

La Palma is not known for its beaches, but these black-sand coves are popular with swimmers in the summer. Los Cancajos, 5 km (3 mi) south of the capital, is a small town with a crescent-shaped beach and crystalline water.

Dining and Lodging

$$ ✕ **Tres Chimineas.** An outgoing Palmero and his English wife run this attractive restaurant, just outside Los Cancajos. Three decorative chimneys mark the building; inside you'll find fresh flowers and a sunny, yellow decor. Local fish are the specialty—vieja is the best. ⊠ *Carretera de Los Llanos de Aridane, Km 8,* ☎ *922/429470. AE, V.*

$$$–$$$$ ▥ **Taburiente Playa.** Opened in 1996, this crescent-shaped resort has fantastic sea views from nearly every room. It's designed so that the guest need never leave the premises, with two swimming pools, a gym, activities for kids, and nighttime entertainment. ⊠ *Playa de los Cancajos, 38712,* ☎ *922/181243,* ℻ *922/181285. 293 rooms. Restaurant, 2 pools, wading pool, sauna, exercise room, nightclub, playground. AE, MC, V.*

$$ ▥ **Hacienda San Jorge.** Built to resemble a Canarian village, the San
★   Jorge groups apartment units in pastel bungalows. The apartments have summer-house furniture and separate bedrooms, living rooms, kitchenettes, baths, and terraces. The complex is built on several different levels surrounding a lake-size swimming pool just steps from the black-sand beach. ⊠ *Playa de los Cancajos 22, 38700,* ☎ *922/181066,* ℻ *922/434528. 155 apartments. Restaurant, bar, kitchenettes, pool, hot tub, sauna, exercise room, beach. AE, V.*

Fuencaliente

28 km (17 mi) south of Santa Cruz de la Palma.

Near Fuencaliente, the scenery grows dry as you reach La Palma's volcanic southern tip. Visit the **San Antonio volcano** and the **Teneguía volcano,** the site of the Canaries' most recent eruption. In 1971, Teneguía burst open, sending rivers of lava toward the sea and extending the length of the island by 3 km (2 mi). There are good beaches in the cinders below the volcano, reached via unpaved roads.

Fuencaliente is the heart of La Palma's wine region. While there, visit the modern **Teneguía cooperative winery.** ⊠ *C. Los Canarios s/n,* ☎ *922/444078.*

Tazacorte

28 km (17 mi) northwest of Fuencaliente.

Drive down through the banana plantations to Tazacorte, the old Guanche capital, or explore **Puerto Naos,** 5 km (3 mi) south, where a sunny, black-sand bay created by a 1947 volcanic eruption is now a beach resort.

Beaches
The black-sand bay of **Puerto Naos** is the island's biggest beach and the most popular on the west coast.

Dining and Lodging
$$ ✕ **Restaurant Playa Mont.** Looking like an upscale beach shack, open
★ on one side to the ocean breezes, the Playa Mont serves some of the best seafood in the islands. The secret is in the sauces: traditional *mojos* and a delicious lemon-butter. ⊠ *Puerto de Tazacorte,* ☎ *922/480443. AE, V. Closed Thurs.*

$$ ✕🖬 **Sol La Palma.** Perched at the end of La Palma's best beach, the Sol hotel was the island's first real resort. It has a flashy marble lobby with crystal chandeliers and fountains. The rooms are huge, with understated beige furnishings, gray-tile floors, sun terraces, and enormous baths. The bountiful restaurant buffet features expensive treats (such as fresh shrimp and papaya) not normally found at moderately priced hotels. ⊠ *Puerto Naos 38760,* ☎ *922/408000,* ℻ *922/408014. 308 rooms, 163 apartments. Restaurant, 3 bars, 2 pools, tennis court, ex-ercise room, dance club. AE, V.*

Parque Nacional de La Caldera de Taburiente (Taburiente Crater National Park)

10 km (6 mi) east of Tazacorte.

This striking park fills most of the center of La Palma. The visitor center is 3 km (2 mi) east of El Paso. The park is inside what looks like a huge crater; modern geologists think that the crater was formed by a series of small eruptions that pulled the center of the mountain apart.

A narrow paved road leads through pine forests to the **Mirador Cumbrecita,** a lookout at 6,014 ft, on the crater's rim. It's often raining or snowing up here, and bright rainbows span the canyon. The white dome and tower on the opposite side are the **Observatorio Roque de los Muchachos** (Boys' Castle Observatory), home of Europe's largest telescope. Astronomers say the Canary Island peaks have some of the cleanest air and darkest skies in the world.

Canarian pine trees are especially adapted to fire and volcanic eruptions, taking only four years to regenerate themselves. The park has lots of interesting hiking trails, and you can camp on the valley floor with a permit, obtainable at the visitor center.

LA GOMERA

One of the least developed of the Canary Islands, tiny La Gomera attracts scores of denim-clad backpackers on shoestring budgets, as well as other travelers who care little for the disco beat of the more touristy islands. The mossy, fern-filled central peaks make up the **Garajonay National Park** and include a rare forest of fragrant laurel trees.

The park's mountains fan out into six steep-sided valleys called *barrancos*. Villages in the *barrancos* are dedicated mainly to small-scale banana growing, and you'll see three or four stalks of bananas outside each house in the morning awaiting pickup. The serpentine roads leading in and out of the valleys are so filled with switchbacks that traveling is slow, and villages remain isolated.

Allow plenty of time—two days if possible—for a drive around La Gomera. The distances are short, but they take a long time to cover, and the roads are not for those afraid of heights.

San Sebastián

East of Valle Gran Rey.

La Gomera's scraggly capital makes the most of its historical links with Christopher Columbus—he made his last stop on charted territory at San Sebastián before setting out for the edge of the earth in 1492. The sights east of the capital are all in close proximity.

The **Torre del Conde** (Tower of the Count) was built by the Spanish in 1450 for protection from Guanche tribes. It came in particularly handy in 1487, when the count's wife, Beatriz de Bobadillo, took refuge in the tower after island chieftains killed her husband. The beautiful, black-haired widow is better known for her love affair with Columbus.

The **Pozo de la Aduana** (Customs House Well) at the head of Calle del Medio is the well that Columbus used to resupply his ships with water, which he also used to baptize the New World. ⊠ *Free.* ☾ *Mon.–Sat. 9–1:30 and 3:30–6, Sun. 9–1:30.*

The church of **Nuestra Señora de la Asunción** (Our Lady of the Assumption) was just a tiny chapel when Columbus prayed there. Since then it has been enlarged in a variety of styles. Farther up the street you can visit the **Casa Colón,** the simple Canarian house where the explorer supposedly stayed during his time with Beatriz. It's now devoted to exhibits by local artists. ⊠ *C. Real 56,* ☎ *no phone.* ⊠ *Free.* ☾ *Tues.–Thurs. 4–6.*

The **Degollada de Peraza,** 15 km (9 mi) south of San Sebastián over a winding road, has a lookout with great views. Guanche chiefs pushed Beatriz's cruel husband, Fernan Peraza, to his death from this cliff.

Beaches

A strong current makes La Gomera's northern beaches dangerous for swimming. If you want sun, head for the volcanic sands of the southern shores. **San Sebastián**'s black-sand beach near the ferry dock is clean and popular with local families.

Dining and Lodging

$$ ✕ **Marqués de Oristano.** This is really three restaurants in one. The Canarian patio in the entryway is a tapas bar; in the back is an infor-

mal, open-air grill where you can select your fresh fish or a cut of beef or lamb from a butcher's case. The dining room, upstairs, serves more sophisticated cuisine, such as pork tenderloin in prune sauce, at higher prices. ⊠ *C. del Medio 24,* ☎ *922/141457. AE, V. Closed Sun.*

$$$ ✕⚏ **Parador Conde de la Gomera.** Built in 1970 in the style of an old
★ island manor, the parador has breezeways decorated with Spanish antiques. The large rooms combine bare-wood floors with French-provincial furniture and have louvered shutters that open onto interior patios. The dining room has a barnlike Canarian ceiling, and the kitchen specializes in such local dishes as rabbit in *salmorejo* with *papas arrugadas.* ⊠ *San Sebastián, 38800,* ☎ *922/871100,* 𝖥𝖠𝖷 *922/871116. 42 rooms. Restaurant, bar, pool. AE, V.*

$ ⚏ **Hostal El Pajar.** This small hotel in the center of San Sebastián is aimed at local travelers. Basic guest rooms are arranged around a typical Canarian patio. ⊠ *C. del Medio 23, 38800,* ☎ *922/870207. 16 rooms. Restaurant, bar. No credit cards.*

Shopping
La Gomera has a refreshing lack of shops. If you're looking for typical souvenirs, buy a bottle of palm syrup or a bag of macaroons from the little market on the Plaza de América in San Sebastián. Typical ceramics, made without a potter's wheel, are still made and sold by village women in El Cercado.

Playa de Santiago

34 km (20 mi) southwest of San Sebastián.

Playa de Santiago, complete with fishing port and banana plantations, is at the bottom of a steep canyon. Until very recently, the people who lived on the almost vertical slopes of the island's canyons used a mysterious whistling language called silbo to communicate across the gorges. Although the language is dying out, most of the older generation in the rural areas still understand it, and the gardeners at the parador in San Sebastián sometimes give demonstrations.

Boat excursions leave several times a week from Playa de Santiago to view **Los Organos,** a cliff made up of hundreds of tall basalt columns that resemble organ pipes.

Beaches
Playa de Santiago is a rocky, black-sand beach surrounding a small fishing bay. It has the sunniest weather on the island and is destined to become La Gomera's major resort area.

Dining and Lodging
$$ ✕ **Tagoror.** From the outside, Taragor looks like a small and rather ramshackle pit stop, but through the white archway is a lovely stone patio that smells of burning coals and sizzling island food. In addition to Canarian grilled meats and fish, they serve different paellas and a wonderful seafood pizza of sorts. ⊠ *Tecina 93, Playa de Santiago, 38800,* ☎ *922/895425,* 𝖥𝖠𝖷 *922/895234. AE, MC, V.*

$$$ ⚏ **Hotel Jardines Tecina.** La Gomera's only real resort, the Tecina sprawls luxuriously over a series of terraces high above the sea and provides an elevator down to the beach. The rooms, grouped in hillside bungalows, all have summery-green pine furniture and decor, with big wooden terraces for sunbathing. Baths are decorated with Spanish tile. ⊠ *Playa de Santiago, 38800,* ☎ *922/895050,* 𝖥𝖠𝖷 *922/895188. 434 rooms. Restaurant, pool, bar, sauna, tennis court, exercise room, squash, dance club. AE, MC, V.*

$ ⊞ **Apartamentos Tapahuga.** This attractive building sits right on the fishing harbor, and the apartments' Canarian, carved-pine balconies overlook it. Kitchens and country-style Spanish decor make the apartments homey, and there's a swimming pool on the roof. ✉ *Avda. Marítima, 38800,* ☎ *922/895159,* ℻ *922/895127. 29 apartments. Kitchens, pool. MC, V.*

Parque Nacional de Garajonay

20 km (12 mi) west of San Sebastián.

You drive past fantastic geological formations as you enter Garajonay National Park from the central highway. The road heads into the forest; much of the year this area is in the clouds, and the mossy trees drip with mist. The highest point on the island, the peak of Garajonay (4,832 ft), is to the right.

To learn more about the Park, take the turnoff at Las Rosas for the **Juego de Bolas** Visitor's Center. Exhibits explain the laurel forest, and a garden displays vegetation from various parts of the island. In nearby crafts shops, you can watch artisans at work (*see* Shopping, *below*). *Visitor center,* ☎ *922/800993.* ⊞ *Free.* ☉ *Tues.–Sun. 9:30–4:30.*

Outdoor Activities and Sports
Garajonay National Park provides miles of interesting hikes. You can pick up a trail map at the visitor center or the San Sebastián tourist office.

Shopping
Look before you buy at **Artisans Cooperación Los Organos** (✉ Carretera Las Rosas, Centro de Visitantes del Parque N. Garajonay, ☎ 922/800993), where you'll find local artists making and selling everything from rag rugs and baskets to champagne and Gomeran drums. It's right next to the visitor center in Garajonay National Park.

Valle Gran Rey

72 km (43 mi) west of San Sebastián.

The terraced farms of Valle Gran Rey, planted with bananas and palms, look like something out of a Gauguin painting. The valley boasts two black-sand beaches and is home to a number of German families who have followed the artist's example.

OFF THE **CASA EFIGENIA** – Take your taste buds off the beaten path with a stop at
BEATEN PATH the inexpensive Casa Efigenia, in the hamlet of Las Hayas, about 30 minutes uphill from Valle Gran Rey. The restaurant's plain, whitewashed walls are decorated with a few cobs of dried corn and a dusty case of citations that Doña Efigenia has received for her efforts at preserving traditional Gomeran cookery. It's simple food, prepared and served by Doña Efigenia herself—not gourmet, but certainly authentic. The main course is a vegetable stew, and dessert is a heavy raisin-and-almond cake that you smother in palm-tree syrup. The Casa is open only for lunch.

Beaches
In Valle Gran Rey, **Playa del Inglés** is a sandy black crescent of a beach favored by young people in search of a cheap hideaway, while **Las Vueltas** beach is a favorite with residents.

Dining and Lodging
$ ✕ **Charco del Conde.** This restaurant is named for the *Conde* (Count) of La Gomera, since this is where the Guanche chiefs hatched the plot

to toss him off the cliff. There are good fish, steaks, and chicken with *papas arrugadas* and *mojo* sauce. ⊠ *Carretera Puntilla Vueltas,* ☎ *922/ 805403. AE, V. Closed Wed.*

$$ ⊞ **Apartamentos Charco del Conde.** These low-rise, flower-clad apartments across from Las Vueltas Beach have simple pine furnishings, a kitchen, and a private terrace. ⊠ *Avda. Marítima s/n, 38870,* ☎ *922/ 805597,* 𝖥𝖠𝖷 *922/805502. 50 apartments, 50 studios. Kitchenettes, pool. MC, V.*

Alajero

43 km (26 mi) northwest of San Sebastián.

Alajero and other northern villages on the island are becoming centers of bed-and-breakfast tourism. Contact the tourist office in San Sebastiáan for color brochures of the homes, most with only two to five rooms.

Crowning the northern rim of La Gomera is the town of Alojera (not to be confused with Alajero), with a beautiful little black-sand beach. This area is known for its palm syrup. At night, the syrup trees, which have metal collars around them, produce up to 3 gallons of sap each, which is boiled down into syrup over wood fires the following day.

EL HIERRO

The smallest Canary Island, El Hierro is strictly for those who enjoy nature and solitude. Most residents live in mountain villages that have little in common with the other islands' tropical beach towns. The few travelers who do find their way to El Hierro come for the hiking, the scuba diving, or the complete relaxation.

Valverde

10 km (6 mi) west of the airport.

El Hierro's capital, Valverde, sits on a hillside at 2,000 ft. The town was built inland, in the clouds, to protect it from pirate raids, and its cobblestone streets always seem to be wet with mist. The church, with a balconied bell tower, was once a lookout for pirates.

Driving around El Hierro, you'll pass terraced farms still plowed with mules. The **Mirador de la Peña**, 22 km (13 mi) west of Valverde, stands at 2,200 ft and offers a spectacular view of El Golfo (*see below*), on the island's northeastern corner.

El Golfo (the Bay) is formed by what looks like a half-submerged volcanic crater. The part above water is a fertile, steep-sided valley. At the far end is a health spa with salty medicinal waters, called **Pozo de la Salud**; those who prefer tastier medicine can visit the island's **winery** in the big, beige building near Frontera. The rocky coast along El Golfo is safe for swimming only in summer.

The **Hoya del Morcillo** picnic area is in the fragrant pine forest that covers the center of El Hierro. It has barbecue pits, rest rooms, and a playground. Camping is permitted, and this makes a good starting point for forest hikes.

Dining and Lodging

$$$–$$$$ ✕ **Mirador de la Peña.** Designed by César Manrique, this is surely the island's most elegant dining spot. Glass walls grant a panoramic view of El Golfo, below. ⊠ *Carretera General de Guarazoca 40,* ☎ *922/ 550300. AE, DC, MC, V.*

$$ ✕🏨 **Parador Nacional El Hierro.** The road to the parador takes you around a point jutting into the sea and deposits you at the bottom of a 3,500-ft cliff. Guest rooms are large, with Castilian furniture and heavy, folk-art bedspreads. In the dining room, delicious tidbits of island specialties are laid out as appetizers, but the rest of the menu goes beyond the chef's abilities; it's best to stick to grilled fish and steak. ✉ *38915 Las Playas,* ☎ *922/558036,* FAX *922/558086. 47 rooms. Restaurant, bar, pool. AE, V.*

$ 🏨 **Hotel Boomerang.** Owned by a local islander who once worked in Australia, the Boomerang is right in the middle of town. Rooms are clean and comfortable, with country pine furniture and tile baths. ✉ *Dr. Gost 1, 38900,* ☎ *922/550200. 19 rooms. Restaurant, bar. AE, DC, V.*

La Restinga

54 km (33 mi) south of Valverde.

At the southern tip of La Gomera, La Restinga is a small, rather ugly fishing port surrounded by lava fields. The few travelers who come here tend to be scuba fanatics; some say the diving is the best in the Canaries.

Dining and Lodging

$ ✕ **Casa Juan.** The two plain dining rooms have large tables to accommodate families, who come from all over the island for the delicious seafood soup. The *mojo* sauces, served with *papas arrugadas,* are also outstanding. ✉ *Juan Gutierrez Monteverde 23,* ☎ *922/557102. AE, MC, V.*

$$ 🏨 **Club El Submarino.** Created by and for sports fans, this isolated, ultramodern hotel offers diving, hiking, spelunking, hang-gliding, windsurfing, mountain biking, deep-sea fishing, and a few less adventurous sports. ✉ *Frontera, 38915,* ☎ FAX *922/559202. 10 rooms. Snack bar, pool. AE, V.*

$$ ✕🏨 **Punta Grande.** Built on an old dock that extends into the sea, the four-room Punta Grande was cited in the *Guinness Book of Records* as the world's smallest hotel. The place has personality; rooms have exposed rock walls and nautical decor, with erstwhile porthole windows as nightstands. An old diving suit and ships' lanterns hang in the dining room, which serves piping-hot shellfish soups and stews served with homestyle hunks of bread and goat cheese. Call ahead; rooms fill up in high season. ✉ *38911 Las Puntas, Valle Frontera,* ☎ FAX *922/ 559081. 4 rooms. Restaurant, bar. AE, V.*

$ 🏨 **Apartamentos La Marina.** These tourist apartments occupy a brand-new, three-story building on the harbor. The furnishings are basic but clean, and all units have kitchens and, better still, balconies with unbeatable sunset views. ✉ *Avda. Marítima 10, 38915,* ☎ *922/559016. 12 apartments. Kitchenettes. No credit cards.*

THE CANARY ISLANDS A TO Z

Arriving and Departing

By Boat

Trasmediterranea (✉ Pedro Muñoz Seca 2, Madrid, ☎ 91/431–0700, FAX 91/431–0804) operates a slow, comfortable ferry service between Cádiz and the Canary Islands (Tenerife, 42 hours; Gran Canaria, 48 hours). The boat is equipped with cabins, a tiny pool, restaurants, a recreation room, and a dance club, but it's not a luxury cruise.

By Plane

Iberia and its sister carrier **Aviaco** have several direct flights daily to Tenerife, Gran Canaria, La Palma, and Lanzarote from most cities in mainland Spain (2½ hours from Madrid). **Air Europa** and **Spanair** have flights from Madrid and Barcelona at slightly lower prices. The other three islands are accessible by connecting flights.

From the United States, **Air Europa** (✉ 136 E. 57th St., Suite 1602, New York, NY 10022, ☎ 212/888–7010) flies directly from New York to Tenerife (6 hours) once a week. Package information is available from **Spanish Heritage Tours** (✉ 116–47 Queens Blvd., Forest Hills, NY 11375, ☎ 718/544–2752 or 800/221–2580). You can sometimes buy a seat without the hotel package if space is available.

Getting Around

By Boat

Trasmediterranea operates interisland car ferries. Trips often take all night, so the ferries are equipped with sleeping cabins. Schedules and reservations are available in Tenerife (✉ Maritima Muelle Rivera, Santa Cruz, ☎ 922/277300), Gran Canaria (✉ Muelle Rivera Oeste s/n, Las Palmas, ☎ 928/267766), Lanzarote (✉ Jose Antonio 90, Arrecife, ☎ 928/811188), La Palma (✉ Avda. Perez de Brito 2, Santa Cruz de la Palma, ☎ 922/411121), La Gomera (✉ Estación Marítima del Puerto, San Sebastián, ☎ 922/871324), Fuerteventura (✉ León y Castillo 58, ☎ 928/850877), and El Hierro (✉ Puerto de la Estaca, ☎ 922/550129).

Trasmediterranea also runs passenger-only **hydrofoil** service three times a day between Las Palmas and Tenerife (80 minutes). One hydrofoil daily links Morro Jable, in southern Fuerteventura, with Las Palmas (90 minutes) and Tenerife (3½ hours). La Gomera can be reached by hydrofoil (30 minutes) from Los Cristianos, in southern Tenerife.

The **Ferry Gomera** takes cars and people between Tenerife (✉ Muelle Los Cristianos, ☎ 922/628231) and La Gomera (✉ Avda. Fred Olson, San Sebastián, ☎ 922/871007) three times daily. At night, the same ferry plies between La Gomera and La Palma.

Southern Lanzarote and northern Fuerteventura are linked by two ferry companies. **Linea Fred Olson** (✉ Avda. de Llegada s/n, Playa Blanca, ☎ 928/517266, 𝔽𝔸𝕏 928/517214) makes five round-trips a day from Lanzarote. The Fuerteventura office is in Corralejo (☎ 928/535090). **Lineas Armas** (✉ Main Pier, Playa Blanca, ☎ 928/517266, 𝔽𝔸𝕏 928/517912) also covers the route with a one-hour car ferry.

By Bus

In Tenerife, buses meet all arriving Iberia flights at Reina Sofía Airport and transfer passengers to the bus terminal on the outskirts of Santa Cruz. From there, you can take a taxi or another bus to the northern side of the island. Buses also meet the Gomera hydrofoil and ferry to take passengers on to Santa Cruz.

Each island has its own bus service geared toward residents. Buses generally leave the villages early in the morning for shopping in the capital and depart from its main plaza in the early afternoon. Tourist offices have details.

By Car

Most travelers rent a car or a four-wheel-drive vehicle for at least part of their stay on the Canaries; this is by far the best way to explore the countryside. The roads are generally not good for those with vertigo, as they often curve over high mountain cliffs with nothing but the sea below. Car-rental companies abound on every island, sometimes doubling as bars. You can find good prices with a little shopping around.

Reservations for rentals are necessary only during the Christmas and Easter holidays. **Hertz** and **Avis** have representatives on all the islands, though rates are better at the Spanish company **Cicar** (☎ 928/802790), located at all the airports except El Hierro. The only agency at El Hierro's airport is **Cruz Alta** (☎ 922/550004); at the harbor, try **Rent a Car PAE** (✉ Orilla del Llano 3, ☎ 922/870364).

By Plane
All of the Canary Islands are served by air except La Gomera. Tenerife has two airports: **Reina Sofía** (TFS), near Playa de las Américas in the south, and **Los Rodeos** (TFN), in the north near Puerto de la Cruz. As a general rule, long-distance flights arrive at the southern terminal, and interisland flights use the northern one, but there are exceptions. Try to book a flight that gets you to the part of the island where you'll be staying, and be sure to allow plenty of time to travel between airports for connecting flights. Driving time from one airport to the other is about 1½ hours; taxis charge up to 7,500 pesetas, or you can rent a car for about 4,000 pesetas.

Airport information can be obtained in Tenerife (✉ Reina Sofía, ☎ 922/759200), Gran Canaria (☎ 928/579000), Lanzarote (☎ 928/811450), Fuerteventura (☎ 928/860500), La Palma (☎ 922/411540), and El Hierro (☎ 922/550725).

Interisland flights are handled by **Iberia** and its regional subsidiary, **Binter Airlines**, using small turboprop planes that allow great low-altitude views of the islands. **Binter** has a new coupon that allows the traveler to pay a fixed rate and hop from island to island. Reserve in Tenerife (✉ Avda. de Anaga 23, Santa Cruz, ☎ 922/284951), Gran Canaria (✉ Alcalde Ramirez de Bethancourt 8, Las Palmas, ☎ 928/370877), Lanzarote (✉ Avda. Rafael Gonzalez 2, Arrecife, ☎ 928/810358), Fuerteventura (✉ 23 de Mayo 11, Puerto de Rosario, ☎ 928/852310), La Palma (✉ Apurón 1, ☎ 922/411345), and El Hierro (✉ Dr. Quintero 6, ☎ 922/550854).

Contacts and Resources

Guided Tours
One-day tours of Tenerife, and excursions to other islands with English-speaking guides, can be arranged through **Viajes Insular** (✉ Avda. Generalísimo 20, Puerto de la Cruz, ☎ 922/380262), which has branches on every island except La Gomera and El Hierro. Tours generally last all day and include lunch and/or a folklore presentation.

Visitor Information
Tenerife (✉ Plaza de España 1, Santa Cruz, ☎ 922/605592; ✉ Plaza de la Iglesia, Puerto de la Cruz, ☎ 922/386000) offices are open 8–5:45 and 9–8, respectively. **Gran Canaria** (✉ Parque de Santa Catalina, Las Palmas, ☎ 928/264623) is open 8–2. **Lanzarote** (✉ Parque Municipal, Arrecife, ☎ 928/801517) is open 8–3. **Fuerteventura** (✉ 1 de Mayo 33, Puerto de Rosario, ☎ 928/851024) is open 9–2. **La Palma** (✉ Palacio Salazar, C. Real s/n, Santa Cruz de la Palma, ☎ 922/412106) is open 8–1 and 5–7. **La Gomera** (✉ C. del Medio 20, San Sebastián, ☎ 922/140147) is open 9–2. **El Hierro** (✉ Licinardo Bueno 1, Valverde, ☎ 922/550302) is open 8:30–2:30.

16 Morocco

The ferry ride from Spain to Morocco—just 15 km (9 mi) across the Straits of Gibraltar—may be the longest short trip on the globe. A 90-minute trip from Algeciras to Tangier replaces a Europe on the verge of the 21st century with a timeless and tumultuous North Africa. Islam is the state religion, and Arabic the official language, but Morocco's colorful history means you'll also hear French, Berber, Spanish, and English in the streets.

By George
Semler

MOROCCO'S GEOGRAPHICAL and social diversity are unrivaled this close to Western Europe. Between the Atlantic Ocean's paradigmatic freshness and the Sahara—the world's largest, extending all the way to the Red Sea—are the snowcapped High Atlas Mountains, whose highest peak, Jebel Toubka, soars to 13,751 ft. The road from the Merzouga dunes to Fez goes through the Azrou cedar forest, an alpine enclave with fauna ranging from barbary apes to brook trout. While storytellers still entertain rapt and illiterate Berbers at Djemâa el Fna square, in Marrakesh, the Kairaouine University, in Fez, has been educating the intellectual elite of both the Islamic and non-Islamic world for more than a thousand years, predating Oxford by three centuries. The consummate luxury of Marrakesh's Mamounia Hotel is only minutes from primitive suburbs and under an hour from the stark adobe villages of the High Atlas.

Morocco's striking clarity, brilliant colors, and romantic allure have been irresistible to painters—Eugène Delacroix, Henri Matisse, Mariano Fortuny, contemporary Spain's Claudio Bravo, and countless others have fallen under its spell. Writers and musicians have also fallen hard; Paul Bowles, composer and novelist, has lived in Tangier for 50 years, and Tennessee Williams, William Burroughs, Allen Ginsberg, Jack Kerouac, and Edith Wharton had warm relationships with Morocco. Berber *Gnaoua* music is one of the origins of blues, and the pagan trance music of the *Joujouka* drums has been compared to the modern jazz of John Coltrane.

Morocco's history has been turbulent. The Berbers, Caucasian North African peoples of uncertain origin, were Morocco's first inhabitants and are still the majority of its population of 26 million. Romans and Vandals invaded and colonized the region until the Arabs (and Islam) arrived in the late 7th century. Incessant conflict between Arabs and Berbers fragmented the area until 788, when Morocco became an independent state under the dynasty of Idriss I.

In the early 10th century, the country disintegrated once more into small tribal states until the Almoravids, a dynasty of Muslim Berbers, overran both Morocco and Moorish Spain in 1062. The Almohad and Merinid dynasties succeeded in partially uniting the country through the middle of the 16th century, when the Saadian (or first Sherifian) dynasty took over. From the 17th to the 19th century, Morocco, like the other so-called Barbary States (Tunisia, Tripolitania, and Algeria), was a base for Mediterranean pirates.

In the 19th century, Morocco's strategic importance aroused the interest of the European powers. Imperial rivalries were resolved in 1912 with the establishment of a French protectorate. French Morocco included nine-tenths of the country; Spanish Morocco was based at Tetuán and controlled the Spanish Sahara; and Tangier was declared an international zone.

In 1956, under pressure from the Moroccan national movement (led by the independentist party Istiqlal), France finally relinquished all rights to Morocco. The highly respected Sultan Sidi Muhammad—described as a Moroccan Gandhi—became King Muhammad V and was succeeded by his son Hassan II in 1961. Hassan II has ruled ever since, though not without significant difficulties, including plots, coups, and assassination attempts. As *Al Amir al Muminin* (Commander of the Faithful—both secular and religious leader of the nation), Hassan II initially assumed full executive and legislative control, yielding power only after an abortive 1971 coup d'etat convinced him to embrace a policy of increased democratization. Deftly juggling pressures from religious fundamentalists, nationalists, and militarists, King Hassan has earned respect as a shrewd manager of Morocco's fortunes. Speculation that his heirs will be unable to maintain the delicate balance is generally not taken seriously. If the unanimous celebrations on Morocco's 1998 Throne Day (March 3) were any indication, King Hassan II is in full control, and his *baraka* (divine protection) remains intact.

Pleasures and Pastimes

Beaches
With coasts on both the Mediterranean and the Atlantic, Morocco has hundreds of miles of sandy beaches, many of them lonely strands with little or no development. The best-known resorts are at Tangier, Asilah, Essouira, and Agadir, the best of which is by far Essouira, a lovely fortified town with a fishing port. Agadir could just as easily be on the Riviera or the Costa del Sol, and Tangier is too plagued by hustlers. Asilah is a picturesque fortified village with an important arts festival in late July. Plage des Nations, just north of Rabat, is an excellent beach for swimming and surfing. Beware, though: this Atlantic coast is known for undertow and dangerous currents.

Dining
Like Morocco itself, Moroccan cuisine mixes tastes and ingredients in surprising ways. Sweet-and-salty combinations such as *pastilla de pigeon* (pigeon in a flaky phyllo pastry—a sort of pigeon pot pie) and lemon and olives with *tagine de poulet* (stewed chicken) are common. Moroccan cooking is based on a wide range of spices and vegetables and tends away from thick sauces. For simple, inexpensive street fare, grab a bowl of *harira* (chick-pea, lentil, and meat soup) for about 50¢ in any *souk* (market). *Brochettes* and beef or lamb kebabs may cost as much as 10 dirhams, still under a dollar. Restaurant fare varies widely. The standard Moroccan menu is nearly always composed of varied hors d'oeuvres followed by *pastilla, tagine, couscous,* and, for dessert, another flaky *pastilla* with sweet cream. *Mechoui,* roast lamb, must be ordered before you arrive at the restaurant. After experiencing the traditional menu, order à la carte to try new dishes. The best wines are the red Medaillon, Cuvée du Président, and Ksar and the white Coquillage, all from the Meknes region. Mint tea (known affectionately as Moroccan whiskey, though it's nonalcoholic) is the standard hot beverage.

Fiestas and Moussems
Check with local tourist offices for the exact dates of annual fiestas and *moussems* (celebrations of *marabouts,* or saints). These are spectacular events, including Moroccan music, dance, food, and the famous *fantasias,* mock cavalry charges complete with equestrian acrobatics and musket barrages. Moussem Moulay Abdallah (in El Jadida) and Moussem Moulay Idriss (near Meknes), both in August, are two big attractions. Other festivals include the Rose Festival (Kelaa M'Goun, in the Dadès Valley), in May; Symphonies in the Desert (Ouarzazate), in June; Asilah's arts festival, in August; and the famous Marriage Moussem (Imilchil), in September, when Berber brides are brought to meet and marry their husbands in mass ceremonies.

Lodging
Hotels range from some of the best and most expensive in the world to inexpensive and decent down to dirt-cheap and marginal. Generally speaking, we suggest splurging on first-class lodging if at all possible. In the Moroccan maelstrom, or what can feel like one, it's

comforting to have your car safely off the street. Morocco's top hotels—the Mamounia, in Marrakesh; the Palais Jamai, in Fez; the Gazelle
d'Or, in Tarroudant; the Minzah, in Tangier; the Royal Mansour, in
Casablanca; and the Rabat Hyatt Regency, in Rabat—offer extraordinary comfort and services.

Skiing, Surfing, Golfing, Hiking, Trekking

In a single trip to Morocco, weather permitting, you can swim and surf
in the Atlantic, ski and hike in the High Atlas, and ride a camel out
into the desert. For a breather, you can play on a golf course designed
by Robert Trent Jones.

Shopping

Moroccan crafts are irresistible even to the inveterate nonconsumer.
The souks (markets) are filled with handmade ceramics, handwoven
killims, knotted rugs, marquetry, leather goods, and jewelry. Dyes
have an extraordinarily bright, pure, and natural quality. Spice markets are a great chance to take Morocco's smells and tastes home with
you. Bargaining for any of these wares can be arduous: decide how
much you're willing to pay for an item and quote a third of that price
to start. Better still, resolve to buy nothing and refuse to quote a price;
prices will drop very quickly.

Exploring Morocco

Driving in Morocco is incredibly stimulating. The scenery offers constant surprises, so that the only real difficulty is keeping your eyes on
the road. The light is so sharp and clear that it's crucial to avoid driving into it; travel early when headed west and in late afternoon when
headed east. Early evening is prime driving time, as Moroccan sunsets
are stunning. Women traveling alone or without men will have difficulty; the only solution—which does work—is to wear conservative
clothing, walk fast (as if you know exactly where you are going), and
avoid eye contact completely. Just whiz on by. Women and men alike
can hire guides through any municipal tourist office; they cost $10–
$15 for half a day, are invariably excellent, and help fend off hustlers.

Great Itineraries

IF YOU HAVE 3 DAYS

Find a way to see **Marrakesh** ⑧ and **Fez** ⑬, spending a day and a half
in each, either by plane (to save time) or by train (to save money). Flying directly from Spain to ✈ **Marrakesh** ⑧ saves time and hassle;
otherwise, take the boat to **Tangier** ①, visit the medina and the American Legation Museum, have dinner at the Hotel Minzah, and take the
overnight train to ✈ **Marrakesh** ⑧. On day two, explore this city's souks
and monuments, especially the Djemaa el Fna square around sunset.
Early the next morning, fly to ✈ **Fez** ⑬, and have a guide take you
through the medina, Fez el Bali—the world's largest still-functioning
medieval city.

IF YOU HAVE 5 DAYS

Fly to ✈ **Marrakesh** ⑧ and spend two days. On day three, rent a car
and drive over the High Atlas to **Ouarzazate** ⑨ for lunch at Chez Di-
mitri before driving the spectacular Route of the Kasbahs (fortified houses
and granaries) through the Dadès Valley to ✈ **Erfoud** ⑪ and the Auberge
Derkaouah. Get up in time for the sunrise over the desert rim at the
Merzouga ⑫ dunes before driving north through the Azrou cedar forest en route to ✈ **Fez** ⑬. On day five, spend at least a full morning exploring the medina, Fez el Bali, with a guide.

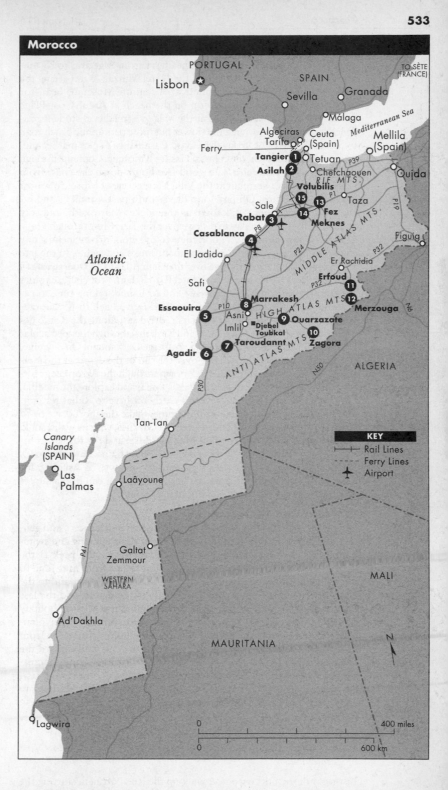

Morocco

PORTUGAL

Lisbon ★

SPAIN

TO SÈTE
(FRANCE)

Sevilla

Granada

Málaga

Mediterranean Sea

Algeciras
Tarifa

Ceuta
(Spain)

Mellila
(Spain)

Ferry

Tangier ❶

Tetuan

P39

Oujda

Asilah ❷

Chefchaouen

RIF MTS.

Volubilis ❶❺

P1

❶❸

Taza

P19

Sale

❶❹

Fez

Rabat ❸

Meknes

MIDDLE ATLAS MTS.

Casablanca ❹

Figuig

El Jadida

P24

Er Rachidia

P32

*Atlantic
Ocean*

Safi

P32

Erfoud

❶❶

Essaouira

P10

Marrakesh

HIGH ATLAS MTS.

❶❷

Merzouga

❺

❽

Asni

Ouarzazate

N10

Imlil

❾

■ Djebel
Toubkal

MTS.

❶⓪

Agadir ❻

❼

Taroudannt

Zagora

ANTI ATLAS MTS.

N50

ALGERIA

P30

Tan-Tan

*Canary
Islands*
(SPAIN)

Laâyoune

❧ Las
Palmas

P41

Galtat
Zemmour

MALI

WESTERN
SAHARA

Ad'Dakhla

MAURITANIA

N

KEY	
┼	Rail Lines
---	Ferry Lines
✈	Airport

Lagwira

0 ———————— 400 miles

0 ———————— 600 km

IF YOU HAVE 10 DAYS

With 10 days, you can just about do it all: beach, cities, mountains, and desert. Take the Trasmediterranea ferry from Algeciras to ⚏ **Tangier** ① and spend the first night in the Hotel Minzah. After seeing the souk, the medina, and the American Legation Museum, head for Rabat, with a possible lunch stop on the beach at **Asilah** ② or Plage des Nations. In ⚏ **Rabat** ③, visit the *medersa* (medieval student residence) in Salé before driving the slower but more panoramic beach road to ⚏ **Casablanca** ④. On day three, visit Casablanca's spice market and, on the way out of town, the colossal Hassan II mosque. Continue through El Jadida to ⚏ **Essaouira** ⑤, a good five hours down the coast from Casablanca; stay overnight at the Villa Maroc, one of Morocco's most charming little inns. On day four, drive south past **Agadir** ⑥ and inland to ⚏ **Taroudannt** ⑦, known as the pocket Marrakesh, and stay at La Gazelle d'Or. On day five, drive over the Tizi n'Test through Ouirgane to ⚏ **Marrakesh** ⑧, a good four- to five-hour drive. Spend a day or two in Marrakesh exploring the main souks and sights. In the late afternoon of the sixth day, drive over the High Atlas to ⚏ **Ouarzazate** ⑨ and establish a base camp at the Hotel Riad Salam. From here, explore the Drâa Valley south to **Zagora** ⑩ and M'hamid, taking time to explore some of the kasbahs along the way. Drive back to ⚏ **Ouarzazate** ⑨ in late afternoon. On day eight, drive east along the Route des Mille Kasbahs (Route of the Thousand Kasbahs) through the spectacular Dadès Valley to ⚏ **Erfoud** ⑪ and the Auberge Derkaouah. On day nine, get up at 5 AM to see the sun rise over the rim of the desert at the **Merzouga** ⑫ dunes before driving back north through the Azrou cedar forest to ⚏ **Fez** ⑬. In Fez, stay at the Palais Jamai and explore the medina, Fez el Bali, on the tenth day. From Fez, fly or drive to Rabat for connections elsewhere. If you have more time, make the short drive to ⚏ **Meknes** ⑭ for the night. On day eleven, see Meknes, with its walls, souk, and *medersa*; the sacred town of **Moulay Idriss**; and the Roman ruins at **Volubilis** ⑮ before making for either **Rabat** ③ or **Casablanca** ④. From here, catch a flight out of the country or up to ⚏ **Asilah** ② for a last night and a morning on the beach. Here you can hop a sunset boat back across the Strait of Gibraltar to Spain.

When to Tour Morocco

Spring (late March–late May) is the high season in Morocco, and generally the best time to come. Early April might allow sunning and swimming in the south, skiing in the Atlas Mountains, and a peek at the desert without extreme temperatures. It's very hot from mid-June to mid-September, though temperatures are fine on the coast and in the High Atlas. Winter can be cold, especially in the desert, and the less expensive hotels may not be heated. Remember the Muslim holiday Ramadan—roughly the same dates as the Christian Lent—when planning a trip to Morocco. This month-long fast requires abstention from food, drink, tobacco, and sex during daylight hours and toward the end of the month tempers can get short. On the other hand, nocturnal festivities heat up. Foreigners are not required to observe the fast, but public consumption of food or drink, and especially smoking, are considered rude and will often result in a rebuke of some kind.

Tangier

❶ *15 km (9 mi) across Straits of Gibraltar, 350 km (220 mi) northeast of Casablanca.*

Just right of the port entrance, walk up the Rue Portugal, skirting the medina. Continue up the hill through a small gate in the medina wall to the **Fondouk Market,** where you'll be surrounded by the same color and vitality—men and women dressed in bright *djellabas* (full-length robes with pointed hoods), bringing produce in from the mountains—that inspired Delacroix, Regnault, Matisse, Fortuny, and so many others to make Morocco a leitmotif. A left on Rue de la Liberté leads up to Place de France and the sumptuous French consulate. Another left on Boulevard Pasteur takes you down past a belvedere to the tourist office.

Walk down through the **Grand Socco** (Great Market) through the pointed archway to the **Petit Socco** (Small Market) and into the heart of Tangier's old quarter and artisan district. Uphill to the left is the **Place de la Kasbah,** where another belvedere has views over the port.

Don't miss the **American Legation Museum** on your way up Rue Portugal. Fifty yards before the first intersection, you'll see a plaque announcing the Legation; steps lead up to the right through a yellow arch into an oasis of peace and quiet (two things you may welcome on your first day in Morocco). An 1821 gift of the Sultan of Morocco to the young American Republic, this museum has a unique history. It was the first property acquired abroad by the United States and served as the consular and diplomatic mission of the United States in Morocco for 140 years. It also is the only U.S. National Historic Landmark on foreign soil. The Legation's two libraries are an important resource for scholars of North Africa—the rooms and the collections of paintings and memorabilia include a letter from George Washington to the Sultan of Morocco, a Kokoschka painting, and a room of Paul Bowles artifacts: letters, documents, traveling cases, and photographs.

Dining and Lodging

$$$$ ✕⌂ **El Minzah.** Ask anyone in Tangier for the finest hotel *or* restau-
★ rant in town, and the immediate answer will be El Minzah. Studded wooden doors, a staff in Ottoman costume, beautiful gardens, an elegant patio, the constant sound of falling water (from a swimming pool—a water music much cherished by Moroccans), and fine views over the Straits of Gibraltar to Spain prove them right. ⊠ *85 rue de la Liberté,* ☎ *2129/935885,* ℻ *2129/934546. 100 rooms. 2 restaurants, piano bar, pool, miniature golf. AE, DC, MC, V.*

$$ ⌂ **Hotel Continental.** Overlooking the port from the edge of the medina, this wonderful Old World palace, vintage 1888, is the best buy in town for aesthetes and romantics—and who else goes to Morocco? Bertolucci stayed in Room 108 while shooting *The Sheltering Sky.* Monsieur Abdessalam is a gracious host. ⊠ *36 rue Dar el Baroud,* ☎ *2129/931024,* ℻ *2129/931143. 15 rooms with bath, 30 rooms share 10 baths. Bar. AE, DC, MC, V.*

$ ⌂ **Hotel Muniria.** William Burroughs wrote *Naked Lunch* in Room 9—now the home of Madame Rabia, the lovely owner. The Tangerinn, underneath, is *the* late-night haunt of the expatriate set, once the stomping ground of Kerouacs and Ginsbergs. Room 8 overlooks the Bay of Tangier. Rue Magellan can be tricky to find; approach from above at night, i.e., from Boulevard Pasteur. ⊠ *2 rue Magellan,* ☎ *2129/935337. 6 rooms with bath, 2 rooms share bath. Bar. No credit cards.*

Asilah

② *46 km (30 mi) southwest of Tangier, 272 km (164 mi) northeast of Rabat.*

Asilah is a lovely fortified beach town less than an hour from Tangier. Known for its summer arts festival, held the second half of July, and its Sunday flea market, Asilah also has an excellent beach and an interesting medina. The Palais Raisuli (currently being restored) was built in 1909 by Er Raisuli, a famous bandit who gained power through a combination of cattle rustling and kidnaping. The best places for lunch are El Espigón, on the beach at the eastern end of the waterfront, and La Alcazaba, which overlooks the Bab (Gate) el Kasaba into the medina.

Dining and Lodging

$$ ✕🖼 **Al Khaima.** Al Khaima is the best hotel in Asilah and would be altogether ideal if it weren't for a merciless combination of mosquitoes and a nearby club that gets going around midnight and thumps until 3 or 4 AM. Bring insect repellent and earplugs. The roar of the surf is constant, and from pillow level you can see the lights of fishing boats working the Atlantic. ⊠ *BP 101/Route de Tanger, Km 1, Asilah,* ☎ *2129/917428,* 🆁🆇 *2129/917566. 90 rooms, 20 apartments. Bar, pool. AE, DC, MC, V.*

$ ✕ **El Espigon.** A great combination of seafood and simple beach atmosphere, El Espigon serves the freshest fish and finest green salads in town. Lines form in summer. ⊠ *Rue Yacob el Mansour,* ☎ *2129/917157. AE, DC, MC, V.*

Rabat

❸ *318 km (191 mi) from Tangier, 91 km (55 mi) from Casablanca.*

Despite being the nation's capital, Rabat seems only mildly Moroccan. Functionaries rush to work at 8:45 AM looking for all the world like European bureaucrats, and the streets are wide and orderly. **Salé,** across the estuary of the Oued (River) Bou Regreg, is more interesting, with its stunning Medersa Bou Inan and its Grande Mosque. Key Rabat monuments include the tower of the Hassan Mosque, the Chellah Necropolis, and the Mohammed V Mausoleum. Bab er Rouah (Gate of the Wind), designed to be the most inspiring approach to the imperial city, is one of the most beautiful gates in Morocco.

Dining and Lodging

$$ ✕ **Koutoubia.** One of Rabat's best traditional Moroccan restaurants, this small place serves the classics: *pastilla de pigeon* (pigeon in phyllo pastry), *harira* (chick-pea, lentil, and meat soup), *tagine* (meat or fish stewed in almonds, plums, and/or vegetables), *mechoui* (roast lamb), and couscous. ⊠ *10 rue Pierre Pavent,* ☎ *2127/760125. AE, DC, MC, V.*

$$$$ ✕🖼 **Rabat Hyatt Regency.** This complex near the Dar es Salam golf
★ course is a world of its own, with four on-site restaurants, one of which is Moroccan. You get complete comfort in an atmosphere that's only remotely—if at all—related to the host country. ⊠ *Aviation Souissi, BP 450,* ☎ *2127/671234,* 🆁🆇 *2127/672492. 218 rooms. 4 restaurants, piano bar, sauna, Turkish bath, tennis courts, exercise room, meeting rooms. AE, DC, MC, V.*

Casablanca

❹ *289 km (180 mi) southwest of Fez, 238 km (148 mi) north of Marrakesh.*

A booming metropolis of 3.5 million, Casablanca is bound to disappoint cineasts and romantics expecting to bump into Ingrid Bergman and Humphrey Bogart at the counterfeit Rick's Bar, in the Hyatt Regency (where waiters take orders in trench coats and fedoras). The **Grande Mosquée Hassan II,** however, will not disappoint. Opened in 1994, the new mosque has room for 25,000 worshipers inside—where the glass floor reveals the ocean below—and 80,000 in the courtyard. The 656-

ft minaret is Morocco's tallest structure, and the mosque is the third-largest in the world after those in Mecca and Medina. The **Corniche** is a pleasant promenade, and the medina's **spice market** is a rich jumble of sights and smells. **Mohamed V Square** is worth a daytime visit for its elegant buildings: the Justice Palace, the Bank of Morocco, the French Consulate, and the Post Office.

Dining and Lodging

$$ ✕ **Al Mounia.** The best restaurant in Casablanca for authenticity and value, Al Mounia serves classic Moroccan fare as well as à la carte selections covering a wide range of both seafood and upland dishes. ✉ *95 rue du Prince Moulay Abdallah,* ☎ *2122/222669. AE, DC, MC, V. Closed Sun.*

$$$$ ✕🛏 **Royal Mansour.** One of Morocco's finest hotels, the Royal Man-
★ sour comes with lots of perks: fabulous food served in a lush garden courtyard, live Cole Porter tunes, and a rooftop *hammam* (Turkish bath). The rooms are complete and luxurious, if not especially memorable.✉ *27 av. des F.A.R.,* ☎ *2122/313011,* 𝔽𝔸𝕏 *2122/312583. 159 rooms, 23 suites. 3 restaurants, piano bar, sauna, Turkish bath, meeting rooms. AE, DC, MC, V.*

$$ 🛏 **Hotel Al Moussafir.** It's new, impeccably clean, well located (near the Casa-Voyageurs train station), and a fraction the price of the Royal Mansour. ✉ *Blvd. Bahmad,* ☎ *2122/401984,* 𝔽𝔸𝕏 *2122/400799. 99 rooms. Restaurant, bar. AE, DC, MC, V.*

Essaouira

❺ *351 km (211 mi) southeast of Casablanca, 172 km (103 mi) north of Agadir, 171 km (102 mi) west of Marrakesh.*

Essaouira's blue-and-white medina is one of Morocco's sweetest retreats, a refuge if you've just come from Casablanca, Tangier, or Marrakesh. An 18th-century fortified port built by French architect Theodore Cornut, who had been captured by Sultan Sidi Mohammed Ben Abdallah, the town is a blend of the Moroccan medina and the French grid plan. Orson Welles found it so compelling that he shot his version of *Othello* here in 1949. Famous for fresh fish grilled in the port, for woodworkers in cedar and thuya, and for the spice markets in its medina, Essaouira is a difficult place to leave. Walk through the Skala de la Ville (the woodworkers' souk) to the North Bastion for marvelous views of the town and the rocky shoreline, or walk around the beach to the village of Diabat, a Jimi Hendrix hangout in the '60s.

Dining and Lodging

$$ ✕ **Chez Sam.** Neatly placed at the farthest edge of the dock, Chez Sam is an institution in Essaouira, the first-choice restaurant and watering hole for foreign travelers, local artists, surfers, and honeymooners alike. The fresh fish and a good Coquillage white wine are more than welcome after the drive down from Casablanca or over from Marrakesh. ✉ *Port, Essaouira,* ☎ *2124/476513. AE, DC, MC, V.*

$$ ✕🛏 **Villa Maroc.** You know you're in the right hotel when you dread checking out. Villa Maroc's charm lies in its simplicity, its good taste, and the easygoing manners of owners Abderrahim Ezzaher and Cornelia Hendry. Each room is different; the nestlike tower room has sea views and continuous surf sounds from pillow level. Dinner, which must be ordered in advance, is excellent Moroccan *cuisine du terroir* (home cooking). ✉ *10 rue Abdellah Ben Yassine, Essaouira,* ☎ *2124/476147,* 𝔽𝔸𝕏 *2124/476758. 26 rooms. Restaurant. AE, DC, MC, V.*

Agadir

6 *173 km (104 mi) south of Essaouira, 303 km (187 mi) southwest of Marrakesh, 85 km (51 mi) west of Taroudannt.*

Agadir's best feature is its airport, from which you can easily travel to Essaouria, Taroudannt, and Marrakesh. Unless you feel the need to leave Morocco and join the world of package tours, you can skip it as a cultural destination. Built in 1505, Agadir became an important port under Mohamed Echeikh el Medhi, founder of the Saadian dynasty, exporting dates, spices, oils, and gold. It was destroyed by an earthquake in 1960 and rebuilt with paradise in mind, but the modern architecture is dull. The beaches, bazaars, and terraces are enjoyable, however, and sports lovers can indulge in tennis, golf, sailing, or scuba diving.

Taroudannt

7 *85 km (51 mi) east of Agadir, 223 km (134 mi) southwest of Marrakesh.*

The ocher walls of Taroudannt against a hazy background of snow-capped High Atlas mountains are one of Morocco's great sights. This Berber market town of some 30,000 people seems largely undiscovered—hence its charm. The ramparts and the souks are the main attractions; the Souk Arab Artisanal specializes in rugs, leather, and jewelry, and the Marché Berbère sells spices, vegetables, clothing, and ceramics. The ramparts were built in the 16th century by the Saadian dynasty, who made Taroudannt their capital. The town is a prime base camp for both trekking the High Atlas and driving the spectacular Tizi n'Test pass to Marrakesh.

Dining and Lodging

$$$$ ✕🏠 **Hôtel Gazelle d'Or.** Long one of Morocco's best hotels, the Gazelle d'Or achieved fame in 1992 when the Duchess of York, then married, turned up here Dukeless. The restaurant is equally renowned and requires jacket and tie. Originally a hunting lodge, built in the 1920s by a French baron, the hotel consists of bungalows surrounding a lush garden. ✉ *Agadir road, Km 2,* ☎ *2128/852039,* ℻ *2128/852537. 30 rooms. Restaurant, pub, tennis courts, horseback riding, Turkish bath. AE, DC, MC, V. Closed Aug.*

$$ ✕🏠 **Salam.** For less wallet strain yet just as palatial, if somewhat more threadbare, surroundings, head straight for the Salam. Housed in a former palace that's built right into the city walls, the hotel has a central patio with luxuriant banana palms. ✉ *Kasbah,* ☎ *2128/ 852312,* ℻ *2128/852654. 75 rooms, 30 suites. 2 restaurants, bar, pool. AE, DC, MC, V.*

Marrakesh

8 *238 km (148 mi) south of Casablanca, 483 km (300 mi) southwest of Fez.*

The tumultuous and panoramic square **Djemâa el Fna** (translated alternately as "Assembly of the Dead" and "Mosque of the Void") is a sensorial feast, the highlight of a visit to Marrakesh. Great clouds of aromatic smoke from the outdoor kitchens in the center combine with Berber musicians and storytellers, snake charmers' flutes, water vendors' bells, the muezzin's call to prayer, scribes and their clients tucked under umbrellas, and tooth pullers surrounded by even rows of molars. The snow-capped Atlas peaks rise behind the 800-year-old Kotoubia minaret, and eventually the warmth of the fires meets a cool evening breeze from the mountains so abruptly that you can feel one on your face and the other on your back.

Essential sights in Marrakesh include the great minaret of the **Koutoubia Mosque,** the **Saadian Tombs,** the **Badi Palace,** the **Bahia Palace,** and, of course, the **souks.** Equidistant from the Atlantic and the High Atlas, Marrakesh was originally a man-made oasis served by underground aqueducts leading in from the mountains. As a result, it's a paradise of gardens, among the finest of which are the **Jardin Agdal,** the **Jardin Majorelle,** and the **Jardin Menara.**

Dining and Lodging

$$$$ ✕ **Yacout.** This graceful space, designed by renowned interiorist Billy Willis, is generally considered the most elegant restaurant in Marrakesh. You're greeted with a drink on the roof or, in colder weather, in front of a fireplace. The cuisine is excellent, the service flawless, and reservations essential. ✉ *79 Sidi Ahmed Soussi,* ☎ *2124/382929,* ℻ *2124/382538. AE, DC, MC, V.*

$$$ ✕ **Dar Marjana.** You'll feel like you've walked into a Delacroix paint-★ ing. Daj Marjana serves excellent cuisine in beautiful surroundings, accented by folk music, belly dancers, and Nubian waiters dressed in rich greens. Honor your reservation punctually, or you might lose your table. ✉ *15 Derb Sidi Ali Tair, Bab Doukkala,* ☎ *2124/445773. Reservations essential. MC, V. Closed Tues. No lunch.*

$$$ ✕ **Stylia.** Not far from Djemâa el Fna, Stylia is housed in an elegant building originally built by a Jewish refugee from Spain in 1492. (Specifically, the dining room is in the former concubinage.) Specializing in Moroccan standards, the menu also spotlights *tangía,* a special *marrakchi* lamb stew. ✉ *34 rue Ksour,* ☎ *2124/445837. AE, DC, MC, V.*

$$$$ ✕▦ **La Mamounia.** Everyone from Winston Churchill to Bryan Ferry ★ has loved this unique oasis within an oasis. One of the most famous hotels in the world despite its queasy mixture of art deco and Moroccan design, La Mamounia is worth every one of the many nickels it costs. The grounds, facilities, and service are all sensational; the staff in particular is impeccably courtly and friendly. You're walking distance from Djemâa el Fna. ✉ *Av. Bab Jdid,* ☎ *2124/448981,* ℻ *2124/ 444940. 171 rooms, 57 suites, 3 villas. 5 restaurants, 5 bars, pool, beauty salon, massage, sauna, Turkish bath, tennis courts, squash, billiards, meeting rooms. AE, DC, MC, V.*

$$$$ ✕▦ **Palmeraie Golf Palace.** This oasis near the Robert Trent Jones golf course has balconies overlooking gardens and—count 'em—eight restaurants, each with a different atmosphere and cuisine. Dining options include Moroccan, Italian, and French. Rooms are simple and faultless, if unremarkable. ✉ *Les Jardins de la Palmeraie,* ☎ *2124/ 301010,* ℻ *2124/305050. 280 rooms, 34 suites. 8 restaurants, 4 bars, 5 pools, 18-hole golf course, 3 tennis courts, bowling. AE, DC, MC, V.*

$$ ✕▦ **Imperial Borj.** In the heart of town, very close to the walls of the city, the Imperial offers bedrooms with both marbled bathrooms and balconies overlooking exotic gardens. The Moroccan restaurant, La Rose de Sables, makes excellent *harira* and couscous. ✉ *Av. Echouhada,* ☎ *2124/447322,* ℻ *2124/446206. 187 rooms, 20 suites. 3 restaurants, cafeteria, piano bar, 3 pools, beauty salon, meeting rooms. AE, DC, MC, V.*

Ouarzazate

❾ *204 km (122 mi) from Marrakesh, 170 km (102 mi) from Zagora, 260 km (156 mi) from M'Hamid, 300 km (180 mi) from Erfoud.*

In late afternoon, the drive to Ouarzazate over the Tizi n'Tichka pass is stunningly spectacular. The oasis of Marrakesh quickly gives way to the rocky soil of the Atlas and the sweeping buffs and browns of these rolling hills. Treeless mountains are sporadically punctuated with adobe villages that seem left over from some remote and primitive past. Boys selling split quartz rush your vehicle (don't be alarmed; they're not dangerous, and it's probably a good buy); bands of colorfully clad children wave as you drive by; Berber women stagger under enormous bundles of firewood. The luxury and chaos of Marrakesh seem a distant memory, the Atlantic freshness of Essaouira a pure fantasy. The turn for the **Alcazaba de Teluet** (Teluet Fortress) cuts off east just after the pass; if you have enough daylight left, take it. The road eventually comes around to Ouarzazate, a good base camp for ventures into the desert.

Dining and Lodging

$$ ✕🖬 **Riad Salam.** This is the place to stay in Ouarzazate: it's simple, friendly, and unpretentious, and the staff tries hard. Berber musicians perform until midnight, often in front of a roaring fire. The manager, Monsieur Benjeddin, is happy to advise you on excursions. ✉ *Av. Mohammed V,* ☎ *2124/883335,* 𝔽𝔸𝕏 *2124/882766. 62 rooms. Restaurant, bar, pool. AE, DC, MC, V.*

$$ ✕ **Chez Dimitri.** Founded in 1928 as the first store, gas pump, post of-
★   fice, telephone booth, dance hall, and restaurant in town, Chez Dimitri may look unimpressive . . . but the food is excellent, and the owners are friendly and helpful. If Ouarzazate is a crossroads of the desert and the southern oasis routes, Chez Dimitri is the heart of it. ✉ *22 av. Mohammed V,* ☎ *2124/882653. MC, V.*

Zagora

  ⑩   *170 km (102 mi) southeast of Ouarzazate.*

The trip to Zagora through the **Drâa Valley** is a spectacular riverside drive, leading to the boundary between the Sahara and what some writers have called "reality." After Zagora, time and distance are measured in camel days: a sign at the end of Zagora's main street reads "TIM-BUKTU 52 DAYS"—as in "52 Days by Camel." The town of M'hamid, 98 km (65 mi) ahead, marks the end of the paved road and the beginning of the Sahara; beware that the road, though paved, may be drifted over with sand. En route to M'hamid are the town of Tamegroute and the village of Tinfou, the latter little more than a few houses and a series of sand dunes (marked simply "Dunes" on some maps). If you have time, stay at the Auberge Repos du Sable de Tinfou (Desert Repose Inn; ✉ BP 6, Tamegroute, Zagora) and experience daybreak in the desert.

En Route   The drive from Ouarzazate through the **Dadès Valley** is one of the great Moroccan adventures, with enough stops and diversions to fill a week. Known as the Route of the Thousand Kasbahs, this river valley is lined with fortified houses and granaries with crenellated battlements. The **Skoura Oasis, Vallée des Roses** (Asif M'Goun), the town of Boumalne and the **Dadès Gorges,** and the town of Tinerhir and the **Todra Gorges** are all spectacular. From Tinejdad, Route 3451 branches right and is paved all the way to Erfoud.

Erfoud

  ⑪   *300 km (180 mi) from Ouarzazate, 446 km (268 mi) from Fez.*

Erfoud is little more than a jumping-off point for the Merzouga dunes. Its best architectural feature is the main door into the medina, designed in the typical Almohad style. Surrounded by one of Morocco's most important oases and more than a million date palms, Erfoud holds a date festival every October.

Dining and Lodging

$$ ✕🖼 **Kasbah Derkaouah.** This extraordinary lodging is at the edge of the desert, 30 minutes' drive from the Merzouga dunes. Michel Auzat and his daughter, Bouchra, serve excellent Moroccan and French cuisine and offer cozy, well-designed accommodations of various kinds: there are nine doubles, two duplexes, two bungalows, one apartment, and two tents. ✉ *24 km (14 mi) southeast of Erfoud (☞ En Route, below). Write c/o Michel Auzat, Erfoud,* ☎ *2125/577140,* FAX *2125/ 5577140. 14 rooms. Restaurant. AE, DC, MC, V.*

En Route To find Kasbah Derkaouah from Erfoud, cross the market square (Place des Far) and follow signs for Dunes Sables d'Or straight out into the desert. Don't be surprised when you find yourself driving across the Oued (River) Ziz—this is not a mirage but a dam and bridge over which, in early spring, the river flows at a depth of an inch or two. Once the pavement ends, follow the green-and-white markers that Michel has provided to guide you in.

Merzouga

⑫ *53 km (32 mi) southeast of Erfoud.*

A sunrise trip to the Merzouga **dunes** (Erg Chebbi) has become something of a classic Moroccan adventure. A series of café-restaurant-hotels overlook the dunes; the Café du Sud runs camels (specifically, one-humped dromedaries) out to the top of the dunes, a 45-minute walk on foot. The Auberge Dunes d'Or, distinguished by a small wooden airplane that appeared in filming Saint-Exupéry's *Le Petit Prince,* has simple rooms and running water. Kasbah Derkaouah (☞ above) is 11 km (7 mi) from the dunes, 25 km (15 mi) from the town of Merzouga; follow the telephone poles to be sure you're on the right track. The nearby seasonal salt lake is a surprising sight and fills in early spring with pink flamingos. The town of Merzouga has little to recommend it other than a few not-too-compelling but livable hotels; if you get as far south as Merzouga, complete the loop through Rissani and the Tafilalt oasis before heading north to Er Rachidia, Midelt, Azrou, and Fez.

En Route The drive from Merzouga to Fez is another astonishing progression: from the desert through the date-palm oases of Tafilalt and the Ziz valley; then, after the town of Er Rachidia, to the Ziz gorges; into the brown-then-green expanses of the High and Middle Atlas; and finally through the Azrou cedar forest, often described as alpine. Nearby Ifrane, a ski resort in winter, is only 63 km (38 mi) south of Fez.

Fez

⑬ *499 km (299 mi) northwest of Merzouga, 483 km (290 mi) northeast of Marrakesh, 60 km (36 mi) east of Meknes, 303 km (182 mi) southeast of Tangier.*

Morocco's Arabic (as opposed to Berber) intellectual and spiritual capital, Fez can at first seem almost too civilized after Marrakesh or the desert. Fez is more refined, more Mediterranean, more Islamic. Divided into three cities—the French-built Ville Nouvelle, Fez el Djedid (New Fez, founded in 1276), and the 9th-century medina, **Fez el Bali** (Old Fez, founded in 808)—the oldest section is a fascinating labyrinth of mosques (no fewer than 360), *medersas* (medieval residential colleges), shops, and artisans. Craftsmen between 14 and 80 years old work on hand- and foot- powered lathes, chisel copper, carve wood, dye skins, bake bread, and peddle spices, ceramics, cloth, antiques, jewelry, and food products of all kinds. The largest functioning and self-sufficient medieval city in the world, the medina limits its traffic to donkeys and pedestrians, with only an occasional motorbike; nothing seems staged for tourists. A large number of travelers pass through, but the life of the medina absorbs them easily. Nowhere else in Morocco is a good guide more indispensable.

The architectural treasures here are many: carving and tilework, the **water clock,** the **Kairaouine Mosque,** and **Kairaouine University**— which, having been founded in the 9th century, predates Bologna by 200 years and Oxford by 300. The medina is hauntingly ancient and aesthetically stunning. Don't miss the foul-smelling **tannery;** the **henna market,** with its plaque commemorating the world's first psychiatric hospital (1286); the 13th-century **fondouks** (inns), or the wood furnaces for heating *hammams* (baths).

Dining and Lodging

$$$ ✕ **La Maison Bleue.** The Abbadi family has renovated the house of a
★ famous Moroccan astrologer into a superb setting for exquisite dining and music. The menu mixes specialties from different regions of Morocco. Monsieur Abaddi graciously shows visitors around the house and the rooftop terrace. ⊠ *2 place de l'Istiqlal Batha,* ☎ *2125/ 741843,* FAX *2125/741843. Reservations essential. AE, DC, MC, V.*

$$ ✕ **Palais de Fes.** Come straight here for a terrace lunch in the center
★ of the medina, overlooking the green rooftops of the Karaouine Mosque. The restored dining rooms downstairs, where crafts are traded, are superbly carved and painted. The food is authentic Moroccan home cooking ranging from *tagines* to a simple green salad. ⊠ *16 Botuille Karaouyne,* ☎ *2125/634707. AE, DC, MC, V. No dinner.*

$$ ✕ **Al Andalus.** This excellent restaurant is a local secret, located off the tourist track on the airport road in the modern part of town. Owner Hilali Fouad's collection of curios and antiques is as enticing as the food, which highlights French and standard Moroccan dishes of high quality. ⊠ *34 rte. d'Immouzzer,* ☎ *2125/603162,* FAX *2125/ 600548. AE, DC, MC, V.*

$$$ ✕ **Al Firdaous.** Dining here is an event. Far more than providing just a Moroccan meal, Al Firdaous is sensory overload: Moroccan art exhibitions, belly dancing, and Berber *gnaoua* music accompany the excellent cuisine and service. The only drawback is the frequent presence of package-tour groups. ⊠ *10 rue Zenjfour,* ☎ *2125/634343,* FAX *2125/634343. AE, DC, MC, V.*

$$$$ ✕▥ **Merinides.** This spectacular hotel is deservedly popular, so reserve well in advance. The views over Fez el Bali from the pool—nicely raised above the fray—are the best in town. ⊠ *Borj Nord,* ☎ *2125/ 646040,* FAX *2125/645225. 79 rooms, 11 suites. 2 restaurants, 2 bars, pool. AE, DC, MC, V.*

$$$$ ✕▥ **Palais Jamai.** The Jamai is simply the best place to stay in Fez. Built 120 years ago, this elegant palace was once the residence of the Vizir Jamai. The rooms, decorated in typical Moroccan brightly painted cedar with geometrical motifs, overlook the gardens and the medina. The two restaurants serve fine Moroccan and international cuisine. ⊠ *Bab Guissa,* ☎ *2125/634331,* FAX *2125/635096. 123 rooms, 14 suites. 2 restaurants, pool, tennis courts, Turkish bath. AE, DC, MC, V.*

Meknes

⑭ *60 km (37 mi) west of Fez, 138 km (85 mi) east of Rabat.*

Known for its 40 km (24 mi) of walls (which enclose the medina, the Imperial City—a stronghold created by Sultan Moulay Ismail within the medina—and, within that, the Royal Palace), Meknes became the capital of Morocca in 1673 under the tyrannical but ambitious Sultan Moulay Ismail (1672–1727). An obsessive builder—he was said to have owned 30,000 slaves, 12,000 horses, and 500 concubines—Moulay Ismail constructed elaborate palaces and mosques that earned Meknes comparisons to Versailles.

The mammoth, horseshoe-arched **Bab-al-Mansour** is one of the most beautiful doors in North Africa. It forms a grand entrance to **Moulay Ismail's mausoleum,** one of four mosques in Morocco open to non-Muslims (the others are Casablanca's Hassan II, Rabat's Mohammed V Mausoleum, and Rissani's Moulay Ali Mausoleum). The **Heri as-Souani** (granary) is one of the most important sights in the Imperial City, once stored barley for the royal cavalry. For an architectural treat, wander the **Bou Inania Medersa,** one of the best in Morocco. The **Dar Jamai** houses the Museum of Moroccan Art, which has superb collections of carpets, jewelry, and needlework. The building itself is exquisite, especially the carved cedar ceilings on the second floor. The souks in Meknes, just behind the Jamai Palace, are known for high-quality workmanship and relatively civilized salesmanship.

Dining and Lodging

$$ ✕▥ **Hotel Transatlantique.** Overlooking Meknes from across the river, the Transatlantique offers poolside comfort, a good Moroccan restaurant, and all of the appropriate amenities. The rooms themselves are not luxurious, but the ones with balconies over the pool and orange trees have a traditional, Old World charm. ⊠ *El-Merinyine,* ☎ *2125/525053,* ℻ *2125/520057. 118 rooms. 2 restaurants, bar, 2 pools, tennis court. AE, DC, MC, V.*

$$ ✕ **Le Dauphin.** This French restaurant in the new part of town, a 15-minute walk from the Hotel Transatlantique, is the best dining option in Meknes and has the added advantage of wine, which restaurants within the medina do not serve. The Dauphin prepares an excellent range of French dishes as well as Moroccan specialties. Seafood features prominently. ⊠ *5 av. Mohammed V,* ☎ *2125/523423. AE, DC, MC, V.*

Volubilis and Moulay Idriss

30 km (18 mi) north of Meknes.

Moulay Idriss is Morocco's sacred town, the site of the tomb of the nation's eponymous religious and secular founder. It is said that five pilgrimages to Moulay Idriss are the spiritual equivalent of one to Mecca; thus its nickname, "the poor man's Mecca." A bird's-eye view of the town is interesting, but Moulay Idriss is routine compared to other Moroccan sights and scenes. Non-Muslims are not allowed inside the tomb.

⑮ Just 4 km (2 mi) from Moulay Idriss is **Volubilis,** a virtual cross-section of a Roman city and one of Morocco's highlights. The rich mosaic floors, baths, brothel, and even bathrooms bring Rome's remotest 1st- to 3rd-century outpost vividly to life. You can engage a guide at the entrance; for 100 dirhams ($10), he'll take you on a two- to three-hour tour of the ruins. His explanations of the different mosaics, the House of Orpheus, the Labors of Hercules, Bacchus discovering Ariadna sleeping, and other historical points are bound to fascinate. ⊠ *Follow signs from Meknes, then from Moulay Idress.* ▧ *20 dh.* ⊘ *Daily, sunrise–sunset.*

MOROCCO A TO Z

You do not need a visa to enter Morocco. Although the water is potable, it's always advisable to stick to bottled spring water. The time is one hour behind Spain.

Arriving and Departing

By Boat

From Algeciras to Tangier, **Trasmediterranea** (✉ Recinto del Puerto s/n, Algeciras, ☎ 956/663850; ✉ Calle Pedro Muñoz Seca 2, Madrid, ☎ 91/436–4164;✉ 31 av. de la Résistance, Tangier, ☎ 2129/935307) has a 90-minute hydrofoil and a two-hour car ferry. The slow boat is larger and more stable and has better views than the hydrofoil.

Having your passport stamped and getting your yellow exit card on the boat itself can save you an hour or more in Tangier. Changing money on board is also a good idea. Tangier's port, whether you're arriving or departing, is the single most daunting and bewildering experience Morocco has to offer. Try not to allow the swarms of hustlers, helpers, and unofficial guides ruin either the trip you're about to have or the one you're finishing up. Despite the confusion that seems to reign unchecked here, things tend to work out in the end.

By Plane

Royal Air Maroc (☎ 91/547–7905; 800/344–6726 in U.S. outside New York City; 212/750–6071 in New York City) and **Iberia** (☎ 902/ 400500, 800/772–4642 in the U.S.) fly to Casablanca from Madrid in 90 minutes. Royal Air Maroc's flight, departing Madrid daily at 9:10 PM, is the most dependable and regular. Connections serve Barcelona and Málaga twice weekly. Royal Air Maroc also flies direct from Paris to Marrakesh, as does Air France, though by no means daily. Royal Air Maroc flies direct from New York–JFK to Casablanca on Tues., Thurs., Sat., and Sun. International connections occasionally serve Tangier, Rabat, Fez, Marrakesh, and Agadir.

Getting Around

By Bus

Buses connect the major cities with Agadir, Asilah, Erfoud, Essaouira, Ouarzazate, Rabat, Taroudannt, and Zagora. For general information, contact **CTM** (Compagnie Transporte Marocaine; ✉ 23 rue Léon l'Africain, Casablanca, ☎ 2124/448127, FAX 2124/317406). Major bus stations include the following: **Casablanca** (✉ 23 rue Léon l'Africain,☎ 2122/268061), **Fez** (✉ Av. Mohammed V, ☎ 2125/ 622041), **Marrakesh** (✉ Bab Doukkala, ☎ 2124/433993), **Tangier** (✉ Av. des F.A.R., ☎ 2129/932415).

By Car

Only by car can Morocco's great panoramas be fully appreciated. Driving in Morocco need not be daunting. Surfaces may be spotty, and freeways are nearly unknown (there's only one, between Larache—soon to be extended to Tangier—and Casablanca), but you'll be fine if you drive slowly and defensively. Some of the roads in the south seem designed for only one-and-a-half cars; one or both approaching vehicles need to give way. Rent with a reputable agency as repair shops and spare parts are few and far between.

Rental agencies in **Casablanca: Budget** (✉ Torres de los Habous, av. des F.A.R., ☎ 2122/313945) and **Hertz** (✉ 25 rue Foucauld, ☎ 2122/ 484710); **Fez: Avis** (✉ 50 blvd. Chefchaouen, ☎ 2125/626746), **Bud-**

get (✉ Bureau Grand Hotel, Av. Chefchaouen, ☎ 2125/620919), and **Hertz** (✉ Hotel de Fez, Av. des F.A.R., ☎ 2125/622812); **Marrakesh: Budget** (✉ 157 av. Mohammed V, ☎ 2124/434604) and **Hertz** (✉ 154 av. Mohammed V, ☎ 2124/434680); **Tangier: Budget** (✉ 79 av. du Prince Moulay Abdallah, ☎ 2129/937994) and **Hertz** (✉ 36 av. Mohammed V, ☎ 2129/933322).

By Plane

Royal Air Maroc (☞ Arriving and Departing, *above*) has comprehensive domestic service; cities served include Agadir, Casablanca, Fez, Marrakesh, Ouarzazate, Rabat, Tangier, and Tetuan.

By Train

For general information, contact **ONCF** (☎ 2127/774747, FAX 2127/774480). The overnight train from Madrid to Algeciras leaves Chamartín Station at 10 PM and arrives at 8:30 AM; you can then buy a boat ticket and change money at the train station before walking to the ferry terminal. The train from **Tangier** to Casablanca leaves at 4 PM and arrives at 10 PM; the overnight train from Tangier to Marrakesh leaves at 10:15 PM and arrives at 8:20 AM. There are two stations in **Casablanca**, the **Gare du Port** (also called Casa-Port, ☎ 2122/223011) and the **Gare des Voyageurs** (also called Casa-Voyageurs, ☎ 2122/243818). The latter serves Marrakesh and the south. There are also ONCF stations in **Asilah** (☎ 2129/917327), **Fez** (☎ 2125/625001), **Marrakesh** (☎ 2124/447768), **Meknes** (☎ 2125/521060), **Rabat** (☎ 2127/767353), and **Tangier** (☎ 2129/931201). ONCF runs buses from Marrakesh to Essaouira, Agadir, and points farther south.

Contacts and Resources

Embassies

United States (✉ Av. de Marrakesh 2, Rabat, ☎ 2127/762265). **Great Britain** (✉ Av. de la Tour Hassan 17, Rabat, ☎ 2127/731403). **Canada** (✉ Rue Jaafar Assadik 13, Rabat, ☎ 2127/672880).

Emergencies

Police (☎ 19). **Fire brigade** (15). **Highway SOS** (177). **Information** (16). **International Directory Assistance** (12).

Golf

Morocco is a boon for traveling golfers, with 14 courses in action and 16 more projected to open by 2000. Greens fees vary from 150 to 600 dirhams ($15–$60). There is even a nine-hole "golf garden" inside the Imperial City of Meknes, illuminated at night. For general information, contact the **Royal Moroccan Golf Federation** (✉ Royal Golf Dar-Es-Salam, Rabat, ☎ 2127/755960, FAX 2127/751026).

Major courses include **Royal Golf of Anfa** (✉ BP 12, Anfa Racetrack, Casablanca, ☎ 2122/365355), 9 holes; **Royal Golf of Fez** (✉ Rte. D'Imouzzer, ☎ 2127/63849), 9 holes; **Royal Golf of Marrakech** (✉ BP 634, Ancienne Rte. de Ouarzazate, ☎ 2124/444341), 18 holes; **Golf de la Palmeraie** (✉ Jardins de la Palmeraie, BP 1488, ☎ 2124/301010), 18 holes; and **Royal Golf of Tangier** (✉ BP 41, Tangier, ☎ 2129/944484), 18 holes.

Horseback Riding

Horseback riding is a superb way to experience the Moroccan countryside. For details, contact the **Royal Moroccan Federation of Equestrian Sports** (✉ Dar Es-Salam, BP 742, Rabat, ☎ 2127/754424, FAX 2127/754738).

Guided Tours

Most Moroccan cities have a swarm of unofficial but very insistent "guides." The best way to get rid of these volunteers—who may falsely tell you that all hotels are full and take you to shops where they get commissions on purchases—is to ignore them and look like you know exactly where you're going. If you do want a guide, hire a cheaper and better one at the local tourist office.

An American tour operator specializing in Morocco is **G.W.T. Inc.** (✉ 190 Moore St., Suite 470, Hackensack, NJ 07601, ☎ 201/343–3929 or 800/868–7498, FAX 201/343–7591). **Globus** (✉ 5301 S. Federal Circle, Littleton, CO 80123, ☎ 303/797–6000 or 800/221–0090, FAX 303/795–0962) has packages that include both Spain and Morocco. The excellent Canadian outfit **Butterfield & Robinson** (✉ 70 Bond St., Toronto, Canada M5B 1X3, ☎ 416/864–1354 or 800/678–1147, FAX 416/864–0541)—"Biking and Walking since 1966"—runs treks and bike trips. For a reliable, multilingual (American, German, Arabic) on-site guide who's able and willing to arrange whatever you have in mind, call Abdie (Abdallah) Aaronson at **Sahara Overland** (✉ BP 153, Tiflet, 15402, ☎ 2127/513925).

If you decide to join a group once you're in Spain, try **A Taste of Morocco** (✉ Apdo. 349, 29680 Estepona, Málaga, ☎ 95/288–6590), which runs tours in autumn and winter, or **Ambassador Tours** (☎ 93/482–7100 in Barcelona, 91/359–5005 in Madrid, 96/374–7855 in Valencia), which is high-end.

Hiking and Trekking

With more than a dozen peaks over 13,200 ft and no fewer than 400 over 9,900 ft, Morocco is a stage set for superb hiking and climbing. A network of mountain huts maintained by the **Club Alpin Français** (✉ BP 6178, Casablanca 01, ☎ 2122/270090, FAX 2122/297292) helps with expeditions from mule-skiing in the High Atlas to hiking through the Azrou cedar forest in the Middle Atlas.

Sailing

For information on sailing, yachting, and chartering boats, contact the **Royal Moroccan Sailing Federation** (☎ 2127/670956) or the **Royal Moroccan Yacht Club** (☎ 2127/720264), both in Rabat. Or try the ocean resort **Mohammedia** (☎ 2123/322331), near Casablanca, a sort of Moroccan Newport.

Surfing and Windsurfing

Atlantic winds and waves make Morocco a favorite of both surfers and windsurfers. Essaouira and Dar Bouazza, near Casablanca, are on the international competition circuits. Contact the **Royal Moroccan Surf Federation** (☎ 2122/259530, FAX 2122/236385).

Visitor Information

United States (✉ 20 E. 46th St., Suite 1201, New York, NY 10017, ☎ 212/557–2520). **United Kingdom** (✉ 205 Regent St., DEW 1R7, London, ☎ 44171/437–0073). **Madrid** (✉ C. Ventura Rodríguez 24, 28008, ☎ 91/542–7431). **Agadir** (✉ Pl. du Prince Héritier Sidi Mohammed, ☎ 2128/846377). **Casablanca** (✉ 55 rue Omar Slaoui, ☎ 2122/271177). **Er Rachidia** (✉ Blvd. Moulay Ali Cherif, ☎ 2125/570944). **Essaouira** (✉ Blvd. La Princesse Lala Amina 54, ☎ 2124/474247). **Fez** (✉ Place de la Résistance, ☎ 2125/623460). **Marrakesh** (✉ 176 blvd. Mohammed V, ☎ 2124/432097; ✉ Pl. Abdel-Moumen Ben Ali, ☎ 2124/436239). **Meknes** (✉ Place Administrative, ☎ 2125/524426). **Ouarzazate** (✉ Av. Mohammed V, BP 297, ☎ 2124/882485). **Rabat** (✉ 22 av. d'Alger, ☎ 2127/730562). **Tangier** (✉ 29 blvd. Pasteur, ☎ 2129/948661).

17 Portraits of Spain

SPAIN AT A GLANCE: A CHRONOLOGY

ca. 12,000 BC Paleolithic (Old Stone Age) settlement; caves of Altamira painted.

ca. 2000 Copper Age culture; stone megaliths built.

ca. 1100 Earliest Phoenician colonies, including Cádiz, Villaricos, Almuñecar, and Málaga. Native peoples include Iberians in south, Basques in Pyrenees, and Celts in northwest.

ca. 650 Greeks begin to colonize east coast.

237 Carthaginians land in Spain; found Cartagena circa 225 BC

206 Romans expel Carthaginians from Spain and gradually conquer peninsula over next two centuries. Spain becomes one of Rome's most important colonies.

AD 74 Roman citizenship extended to all Spaniards.

380 Christianity declared sole religion of Rome and her empire.

409 First Barbarian invasions.

419 Visigothic kingdom established in northern Spain, with capital at Toledo.

Moorish Spain

711–712 Christian Visigothic kingdom destroyed by invading Muslims (Moors) from northern Africa, who create emirate, with capital at Córdoba, of Ummayyad Caliphate at Damascus.

756 Independent dynasty established in Spain under Abd al-Rahman I.

778 Charlemagne establishes rule north of Ebro.

899 Discovery of remains of St. James the Greater; church of Santiago de Compostela, a major pilgrimage site, is built.

912–961 Reign of Abd al-Rahman III: height of Moorish culture, although it flourishes throughout Reconquest.

The Reconquest

1085 Alfonso VI of Castile captures Toledo.

1099 Death of Rodrigo Diaz de Bivar, known as El Cid, who served both Christian and Muslim kings; buried at Burgos Cathedral (completed 1126), first Gothic cathedral.

1137 Aragon unites with Catalonia.

1209 First Spanish university founded at Valencia by Moors.

1212 Victory at Las Navas de Tolosa by united Christian armies: Moorish power crippled.

1236–48 Valencia, Córdoba, and Seville fall to Christians.

1270 End of main period of Reconquest: Portugal, Aragon, and Castile emerge as major powers.

1435 Alfonso V of Aragon and Sicily conquers Naples and southern Italy.

1469 Isabella, princess of Castile, marries Ferdinand, heir to the throne of Aragon.

1478 The Spanish Inquisition is established.

1479–1504 Isabella and Ferdinand jointly rule.

1492 Granada, last Moorish outpost, falls. Christopher Columbus, under the sponsorship of Isabella, discovers America, setting off a wave of Spanish exploration.

1494 Treaty of Tordesillas: Portugal and Spain divide the known world between them.

1499 La Celestina, by Fernando de Rojas, considered the first novel, is published.

1516 Death of Ferdinand. His grandson and heir, Charles I, inaugurates the Habsburg dynasty and Spain's Golden Age.

The Habsburg Dynasty

1519 Charles I is elected Holy Roman Emperor as Charles V. From his father, Philip of Habsburg, he inherits Austria, the Spanish Netherlands, Burgundy, and nearly continuous war with France. Hernán Cortés conquers the Aztec Empire in Mexico.

1519–22 First circumnavigation of the world by Magellan's ships.

ca.1520– ca.1700 Golden Age. Funded by its empire, Spain's culture flourishes. Artists include El Greco (1541–1614), Velázquez (1599–1660), and Murillo (1617–82). In literature, the poet Quevedo (1580–1645), dramatists Lope de Vega (1562–1635) and Calderón (1600–1681), and novelist Miguel de Cervantes (1547–1616) were known throughout Europe. Counter-Reformation Catholicism took its lead from St. Ignatius of Loyola (1491–1556), founder of the Jesuit order (1540), and the mystic St. Teresa of Ávila (1515–82).

1531 Pizarro conquers the Inca empire in Peru.

1554 Charles's heir, Philip, marries Queen Mary of England ("Bloody Mary," circa 1558).

1556 Charles abdicates in favor of his son Philip II, who inherits Spain, Sicily, and the Netherlands; the Holy Roman Empire goes to Charles's brother Ferdinand. Philip II leads cause of Counter-Reformation against Protestant states in Europe.

1561 Capital established at Madrid.

1588 Philip attacks Protestant England with the Spanish Armada, but is defeated.

1598 Death of Philip II.

1609 Moriscos (converted Muslims) expelled and independence of the Netherlands recognized during reign of Philip III.

1618 Beginning of Thirty Years' War; originally a religious dispute, it became a dynastic struggle between Habsburgs and Bourbons.

1621–65 Reign of Philip IV; his minister, Count-Duke Olivares, reforms regime on absolutist model of France.

1640–59 Revolt in Catalonia; republic declared for a time.

1648 End of Thirty Years' War; Spanish Netherlands declared independent.

1659 Treaty of the Pyrenees ends war with France and Spanish ascendancy in Europe.

1665–1700 Reign of Charles II, last of the Spanish Habsburgs.

The Bourbon Dynasty

1701–14 War of the Spanish Succession: Three claimants to the throne are Louis XIV of France, Leopold I of Bavaria, and Philip of Anjou. Philip is recognized as Philip V, first Bourbon king, by the Treaty of Utrecht, 1713. By the Treaty of Rastatt, 1714, Spain loses Flanders, Luxembourg, and Italy to Austrian Habsburgs; it spends much of its energy in the 18th century trying to regain these.

1756–63 Seven Years' War: Spain and France versus Great Britain. 1756: Spain regains Minorca, lost to Great Britain in 1709. 1762: Treaty of Paris: Spain cedes Minorca and Florida to Great Britain and receives Louisiana from France in return.

1779 Spain supports rebels in American War of Independence, regains Florida and Minorca.

1793 Revolutionary France declares war.

1795 By Treaty of Basel, Spain allies with France against Great Britain.

Napoleonic Rule

1808 King Charles IV abdicates in favor of Joseph Bonaparte, Napoleon's brother. Napoleon takes Madrid in December.

The Peninsular War

1809–14 Reconquest of Spain by British under Wellington.

Restoration of the Bourbons

1814 Bourbons restored under Ferdinand VII, son of Charles IV. Like other restored monarchs of the era, he was a reactionary and crushed liberal movements.

1833 Ferdinand deprives brother Don Carlos of succession in favor of his infant daughter, Isabella; her mother, María Cristina, becomes regent.

1834–39 First Carlist War: Don Carlos contests the crown and begins an era of upheaval.

1840 Coup d'état: General Baldomero Espartero becomes dictator, exiles María Cristina, ushers in a series of weak and unpopular regimes.

1843 Espartero ousted; Isabella II restored to throne.

Period of Troubles

1868 Revolution, supported by liberals, topples Isabella II but ushers in the Period of Troubles: Attempts to establish a republic and then to find an alternate monarch fail.

1873 First Spanish Republic declared; Second Carlist War (to 1876).

Restoration of the Bourbons

1874 Alfonso XII, son of Isabella, brought to the throne.

1892 Peasant revolt, inspired by anarchist doctrine; revolt again in 1903.

1895 Revolution in Cuba, one of the few remaining Spanish colonies. Spain moves to suppress it.

1898 Spanish-American War: United States annexes Spanish colonies of Puerto Rico and the Philippines; Cuba is declared independent.

1902–31 Reign of Alfonso XIII: increasing instability and unrest.

1914 Spain declares neutrality in World War I.

1923 Coup d'état of General Manuel Primo de Rivera, who models his government on Italian Fascism.

Republic, Civil War, and Fascism

1930–31 Primo de Rivera is ousted; a republic is declared, and Alfonso XIII is deposed. Liberals attempt to redistribute land and diminish the power of the Church.

1936–39 Spanish Civil War: Electoral victory of Popular Front (a coalition of the left) precipitates rightist military insurrection against the Republic, led by General Francisco Franco. Europe declares neutrality, but Germany and Italy aid Franco, and the USSR and volunteer brigades aid (to a lesser extent) the Republic. More than 600,000 die, including the poet Federico García Lorca. Franco is victorious and rules Spain for the next 35 years.

1939 Fascist Spain declares neutrality in World War II.

1945 Spain is denied membership in the United Nations, but is admitted in 1950.

1953 NATO bases are established in Spain in return for economic and military aid.

1969 Franco names Prince Juan Carlos de Borbón, heir to the vacant throne, his successor.

1970 Basque uprising.

1973 Franco's prime minister, Carrero Blanco, is assassinated by Basque separatists.

Restoration of the Bourbons

1975 Franco dies and is succeeded by Juan Carlos, grandson of Alfonso XIII.

1977 The first democratic elections in 40 years are won by the Center Democratic Union.

1978 A new constitution restores civil liberties and freedom of the press.

1981 An attempted coup by Colonel Antonio Tejero fails.

1982 Spain becomes a full member of NATO. Socialists win a landslide victory in the general election.

1985 The frontier with Gibraltar, closed since 1968, is reopened.

1986 Spain enters European Union. The Socialists win for a second time.

1989 Camilo José Cela is awarded the Nobel Prize for Literature; Socialists lose majority, but continue in office.

1992 The Olympic Games are held in Barcelona. The 1992 Universal Exposition is held in Seville.

1993 The Socialists win their last victory in the general election.

1996 The Popular Party, Spain's conservative party, wins the general election, ending 14 years of Socialist rule.

A TALE OF TWO CITIES

THE ETERNAL RIVALRY between Barcelona, medieval capital of an opulent Mediterranean empire, and Madrid, once the nerve center of one of the greatest global empires ever assembled, may be a driving force behind Spain's current vitality. The two cities debate every national issue from politics to sports to the economy, even as three domestic airlines shuttle thousands of businesspeople daily between the two.

How to get a Catalan to speak Spanish? Misunderstand the price by a peseta. Madrid bureaucrats don't work after lunch? No, that's in the morning; after lunch they don't even show up.

Catalan avarice, Madrid sloth: old standbys in the arsenal of barbs that citizens of Spain's two largest cities routinely toss at each other.

Beneath the humor lies a well-aged and historically rooted bitterness combining elements of the world's great internecine tensions—Québec and the rest of Canada, Milan and Rome, even the United States' North–South divide more than a century after the American Civil War.

Though largely undetectable to a visitor, traces of this rivalry crop up everywhere. Cars with Madrid license plates may encounter extra discourtesies in Catalonia. Madrileños are not known for their patience with the Catalan language and are apt to insist upon being addressed in Castilian Spanish; Catalans, in turn, seem to "forget" their Castilian, or deliberately lapse into bizarre grammatical distortions. A foolproof way to ruin a social gathering in Madrid is to proselytize the Catalan point of view vis à vis Catalonian history and culture. Meanwhile, in Barcelona, the "language of Cervantes" can be a surefire soporific at dinner parties that would crackle with humor and innuendo in Catalan.

This mutual antipathy has been centuries in the making and will not go away anytime soon, even if feelings have cooled considerably since the 1714 siege and conquest of Barcelona by Spain's first Bourbon monarch, Felipe V. Armed conflict between the two is no longer a threat. Catalans are a pragmatic people who have always managed to prosper no matter whose army was manning the cannon over Barcelona; and the cities are now so intertwined and interdependent that a Catalan, Narcis Serra, was a recent Spanish Minister of Defense. Spain's conservative government, elected in 1997, is able to govern only with the support of Catalonian President Jordi Pujol's Catalan nationalist party.

The dramatic changes of the last 25 years—the end of Franco, the establishment of the constitutional monarch—have actually reversed some of the qualities that have traditionally characterized the two cities. Thus, whereas Barcelona was always considered Spain's most European city up to 1975, Catalonia's zealous restoration of its long-suppressed language and culture has made it somewhat self-absorbed and cost it a few points in cosmopolitanism. Madrid, on the other hand, has burst back onto the world stage with a vigor and energy unimaginable when it was the seat of Franco's reactionary and repressive regime. The capital's legendary bureaucratic indolence has been replaced by a frenzy of activity in the arts and business and a powerful international orientation and appeal.

But some things don't change. Madrid remains open; Barcelona, despite its seaport, is less so. Even the topography reinforces this fact: Madrid stands on a promontory at the center of Spain's central steppe, Barcelona nestles in a crease between the hills and the sea. Barcelona is moist, pungent, even fetid, slippery. Madrid is high, arid, brittle. Madrid's streets are broader and seem to embrace the sky, while Barcelona's are predominantly darker and narrower, leafier and more intimate, older: tunnels to the city's medieval past. Barcelona is, after all, 2,000 years old, to Madrid's mere millennium.

Even—maybe especially—the air is different. Barcelona's steamy and passionate Mediterranean breath is a far cry from Madrid's legendary highland air, with its sharp and icy lightness.

Catalans are more private and self-contained, feline, Gallic. Madrileños are a little of everything, coming as they do from all corners of the peninsula and the world, but they are known for a more gregarious, accessible, open, generous spirit. In Madrid they *give* you things—tapas, hot broth, the time of day. In Barcelona, trade is absolutely fundamental to every nuance of social contact.

Catalonia's *fets diferencials,* or "differentiating facts," are based on linguistic and historical realities often dismissed as fantasy by non-Catalans educated during the unity-oriented Franco regime. Barcelona is geographically closer to Marseilles than to Madrid, and medieval Catalonia included much of what is today southern France. The Roussillon, or French Catalonia, stretched as far north as Avignon and Nîmes, where the Catalan language is still spoken. Grammatically closer to Provençal French than to Castilian Spanish, Catalan lacks the fricative phonemes and nearly all of the Arabic-rooted vocabulary that modern Spanish inherited from 700 years of Moorish occupation. Sacked but never colonized by the Moors, Catalonia was the border zone for Charlemagne's Frankish empire, finally gaining independence from the Carolingians in 988, only a few years after Madrid was made a military outpost by the Moorish command defending regional headquarters at Toledo. When Catalonia became, through royal marriage, part of the House of Aragon in 1137, Barcelona's commercial and maritime power made it the kingdom's nerve center and royal court. But in 1469, when Isabella of Castile married Ferdinand of Aragon, Barcelona found itself left dangling on the eastern edge of an Iberian power about to turn its attention west, across the Atlantic.

The "discovery" of the New World and the great enterprise of exploiting its riches definitively sealed Catalonia's fate as a declining power within the new, unified Spain. Legally excluded from participation in Castile's colonization and plunder of the Americas, Catalonia did manage to retain a measure of home rule and cultural identity until 1714, when, as a reprisal for having supported Archduke Carlos of Austria in the War of the Spanish Succession, Felipe V stripped Catalonia of all of its institutions and privileges.

Deprived of the loot pouring in from the colonies, Barcelona developed an industrial power base that led to a resurgence of Catalan nationalism—*la Renaixença*—in the latter half of the 19th century. Limited home rule returned from 1914 to 1924 and, later, during the Second Republic, from 1931 to 1936; but after the Spanish Civil War, 1936–1939, the Franco regime's "National Movement" endeavored to eradicate all traces of the Catalan language and culture, along with any political parties that might threaten the national fabric of church, state, oligarchy, and the army. Officially suppressed but never abandoned, Catalan language and culture have returned more powerfully than ever since Franco's death in 1975.

Madrid's history, shorter but less checkered, took the city from military observation post to provincial town to world capital in just over 500 years. When the previously itinerant royal court was permanently established there in 1561, riches were already pouring in from the Spanish empire's far-flung colonies. Soon Madrid was a teeming boom town, with a burgeoning population and government subsidies promoting architecture, theater, and, especially, painting. Rubens and Velázquez shared a studio; Cervantes and Lope de Vega (the "Spanish Shakespeare") exchanged acerbic sonnets; and the city's literary quarter was a crush of poets, actors, composers, and playwrights. The lavish cultural spending of Spain's Golden Age left a legacy of artistic masterpieces that today fill the Prado and other museums, as well as convents, churches, foundations, and over a hundred art galleries.

Madrid, from the twisting streets of its early Moorish and Jewish quarter, through the stately and austere Habsburg architecture of the 16th and 17th centuries and the broad avenues of the 18th- and 19th-century Bourbon monarchy, has grown into a sprawling industrial and cultural giant of (like Barcelona) more than four million people.

Comparing the pros and cons and respective assets of these two cities—an endless exchange of proposals and rebuttals—may only be valuable as a means of better defining and characterizing each of the two. Certainly, they seem perfectly organized for debate. Madrid's landlocked, highland monochrome, for example, contrasts with Barcelona's vivid and varied palette, a rich mixture of the Pyrenees, the Mediterranean, and metropolitan hues. Madrid offers convenient access to all of the Iberian Peninsula, whereas Barcelona is nearly equidistant from Rome and London, as close to Geneva as it is to Madrid. Madrid is most appealing in winter, when the hearty Castilian cuisine of roasts and thick stews makes the most sense, where Barcelona's sweetest season is springtime, between the lovers' fiesta of Sant Jordi, in late April, and the all-night bonfires of Sant Joan, on Midsummer's Eve. Madrid's treasury of paintings if countered by Barcelona's relentless innovation in art, architecture, and design and by the legacies of Picasso, Miró, Dalí, and Gaudí. Barcelona has delicious markets such as the central Boqueria; Madrid has its Sunday flea market, the Rastro, and bookstall browsing along the Cuesta de Moyanes. Madrid's superb day trips—Toledo, Segovia, El Escorial— are balanced by Barcelona's excellent beaches on the Costa Brava, to the north, and the Delta del Ebro, to the south. Madrid is centered around its peerless and peaceful Plaza Mayor, whereas Barcelona has the meandering Rambla. Madrid has a midtown forest in the stately Retiro, while Gaudí's Güell Park hovers on a hill above Barcelona. Madrid's oldest quarters are a jumble of red, clay-tiled rooftops, while Barcelona's are Roman, Romanesque, and Gothic stone. Ultimately, Barcelona's Mediterranean vitality draws heavily on its rich triangle of mountains, sea, and city life, whereas modern Madrid, brisk and lively, is broader and more universal, the melting pot of the many Spains. Today, both cities are riding a wave of excitement that even terrorism and political scandals can't seem to discourage. Barcelona continues to generate energy in the afterglow of the 1992 Olympic Games, Catalonia's greatest domestic and international triumph since the glory days of its medieval Mediterranean prominence. Madrid, meanwhile, has reassumed an energy and outlook comparable only to that of its own 16th-century Golden Age.

—George Semler

SPANISH FOOD AND WINE

THE CUISINE of Spain is among the most varied and sophisticated in Europe. Favored by a wealth of natural produce almost unrivaled, Spain has traditionally been an agricultural country, famous since ancient times for its extensive wheat fields, vineyards, and olive groves and for pig and cattle raising. A recent medical report has even concluded that the Spaniards eat more healthily than any other Western nation, largely because they insist on fresh produce and avoid canned and convenience foods.

The geographic variety of the peninsula accounts, of course, for the extremely varied nature of Spain's produce. For instance, the snowcapped mountains of the Sierra Nevada have Nordic cultures on their upper slopes, while those lower down yield tropical fruits unique to Europe, such as custard apples. And with both an Atlantic and a Mediterranean coastline, Spain boasts an exceptional range of fish and seafood.

Another major influence on Spanish cuisine has been the 7½ centuries of Moorish presence here. The Moors gave Iberian cooking an exotic quality by using new ingredients, such as saffron, almonds, and peppers; they introduced the art of making sweets and pastries; and they created refreshing dishes such as *ajo blanco* (a cold almond based soup) that are still popular today. One of the world's pioneering gastronomes was Ziryab, an Arab who worked in 10th-century Córdoba and brought to Europe the new Arab fashion for eating a regular sequence of dishes, beginning with soup and ending with dessert.

Whether inherited from the Moors or not, Spaniards' love of food stretches back at least several centuries. A famous poem by the 16th-century Sevillian writer Baltasar del Alcázar expresses this feeling:

There are three things
That hold my heart Love's captive
My fair Inés, cured ham,
And aubergines and cheese

When traveling around their country, Spaniards often seem to prefer hunting down local gastronomic specialties to visiting museums and monuments. They tend to assume that foreigners do not share their passion for food—both because so many tourists are unadventurous in their tastes, and because they refuse to adapt to Spain's idiosyncratic eating times and traditions. You're more likely to find outstanding food in a dirty village bar where olive stones and shrimp heads are spat out onto the floor than in many luxurious urban restaurants; the Spaniards aren't as snobbish about eating as, say, the French are. But if you decide to have lunch before 2 PM or dine before 10, the only restaurants you'll find open are probably those that cater to bland international tastes.

The most Spanish of culinary traditions is undoubtedly that of the tapa (bar snack). Many people who dismiss Spanish food as unimaginative will make an exception of the tapa, without realizing that these snacks are miniature versions of classic dishes served in restaurants or in Spanish homes. The tradition originated in Andalusia, where a combination of heat and poverty made it impractical to sit down to a heavy meal in a restaurant. Today tapas are generally taken as appetizers before lunch or supper, but in the south they are still often regarded as a meal in themselves. Eating tapas allows you to sample the variety of Spanish food and also prevents you from getting too drunk, especially if you decide to go on a *tapeo,* the Spanish equivalent of a bar crawl. In some of the more old-fashioned bars, you are automatically served a tapa of the barman's choice when you order a drink. Having to choose a tapa yourself is not always easy, for the barman often recites at great speed a seemingly interminable list. The timid, baffled tourist usually ends up pointing to some familiar tapa that's standing on the counter.

THE SPANIARDS' predilection for tasting small quantities of many dishes also shows up in restaurants, where they normally share food and order dishes *para picar* (to nibble at).

A selection of *raciones* (larger versions of tapas) makes a popular starter for those dining in a group.

Soups in Spain tend not to be smooth and creamy, as they are in France, but watery, highly spiced, and very garlicky. One of the most common hot soups is a *sopa de ajo* (garlic soup), which consists of water, oil, garlic, paprika, stale bread, and cured ham. This is far more appetizing than it sounds, as is the famous gazpacho, a cold blend of water, bread, garlic, tomatoes, and peppers. Most people today make gazpacho in a blender, but it's best when prepared by hand in a terra-cotta mortar, the ingredients slowly pounded with a pestle. There are several variations on gazpacho, including *salmorejo*, which comes from Córdoba and has a denser texture. Particularly good is the *ajo blanco*, the basis of which is almonds rather than tomatoes; served always with peeled muscatel grapes or slices of honeydew melon, this dish encapsulates the Moorish custom of combining sweet and savory flavors.

The Spanish egg dish best known abroad is the *tortilla* (not the same as the Mexican tortilla—here it's an omelette of onions and potatoes), which is generally eaten cold. *Huevos flamencos* ("Gypsy eggs") is a traditional Sevillian dish now found in all parts of Spain, consisting of eggs fried in a terra-cotta dish with cured ham, tomatoes, and a selection of green vegetables. The exact ingredients vary as much as Gypsy cooking itself, which tends cleverly to incorporate whatever is at hand.

The Spaniards—and the Andalusians and Galicians in particular—are known for consuming vast quantities of fish and seafood. Some of the finest seafood washes up in western Andalusia and in Galicia, the former being renowned for shrimp, prawns, and crayfish, the latter for oysters, lobsters, and crabs, and the much sought-after (if revolting-looking) *percebes* (goose barnacles). Another specialty of the Galician coast is scallops chopped up with breadcrumbs, onions, parsley, and peppers and served in their shells (the same shells that Christian pilgrims wear on their way to Santiago de Compostela). *Changurro*, a stuffed king crab, is a specialty of the Basque country, where you'll also find one of Spain's most interesting fish dishes, *bacalao al pil-pil* (cod fried in garlic and covered in a green sauce made from the gelatin of the fish). A fish dish now common all over Spain is *trucha a la Navarra* (trout wrapped in pieces of bacon). In Andalusia most fish is deep-fried in batter—which is why the place is sometimes disparagingly called the "land of the fried fish" by outsiders. In fact, you need considerable art, as well as spanking-fresh fish, to be able to fry the fish as well as Andalusians do, and to and achieve the requisite texture of crispness on the outside and succulence inside. The *chancetes* (whitebait) and *sardinas* (sardines) are especially good in Málaga, and you should try the *salmonetes* (red mullet) and *acedías* (miniature sole) along the Cádiz coast. *Adobo,* also delicious, is fried fish marinated in wine.

THE COLD MEATS and sausage products of Spain are renowned—in particular, the cured hams of Trevélez and Jabugo, the *chorizo* (spicy paprika sausage), and the *morcilla* (blood sausages) of Granada and Burgos, the latter sometimes incorporating nuts. Meat, when served hot, is usually unaccompanied by a sauce or vegetables and presented rare. The great meat-eating center of Spain is Castile, which is famous for its *cochinillo* (suckling pig), a specialty of Segovia, and *cordero* (lamb), both of which are roasted in wood or clay ovens. The most sophisticated and elaborate poultry dishes in Spain are prepared in the Catalan district of Girona and include chicken with lobster and turkey stuffed with raisins, pine nuts, and *butifarras* (spicy Catalan sausages).

Fish, meat, and seafood come together in *paella,* a saffron-flavored rice dish that many consider the most typical of Spanish dishes. Paella originated in Valencia and, in fact, dates no earlier than the late 19th century. The one Spanish dish that can truly claim to be the most national and traditional is the meat stew referred to by Madrileños as *cocido,* by Andalusians as *potaje*, and by Catalans as *escudella*. Despite the slight regional variations, the three basic ingredients remain the same—meats, legumes, and vegetables. The dish is usually served in three courses, beginning with the broth in which everything is cooked and finishing with the meats, which Spaniards sometimes shred and mix together on their plates to form what they call *pringa*.

The range and quality of Spanish cheeses is impressive, but most of them are little-known and can be bought only in the area where they're made. The hard cheeses of La Mancha are best well matured—a good *Manchego viejo* is almost the equal of an Italian Parmesan. If you can find it, try *Cabrales,* an exquisite sheep's cheese that is rather like a melting Roquefort.

SPANIARDS DO not usually finish a meal with a dessert. They tend to bake the many almond- and honey-based sweets and pastries of Moorish derivation, such as *polvorones,* only around Christmas or Easter. Ever since St. Teresa devised *yemas* (candied egg yolks), Spanish convents have specialized in all kinds of sweet products. The yemas were once distributed free to the poor, but their production has now become a profitable industry for the nuns. The correct procedure for buying anything from a convent is to ring the bell and then address the nun (who is often hidden behind a rotating drum) with the words *Ave María Purísima.* You can then proceed to order your yemas, *bizcochos* (sponge biscuits), *tocinos de cielo* (an excellent variant of crème caramel), or whatever else appears on the list pinned up in the convent's entrance hall.

SPAIN claims to be more extensively covered with vineyards than is any other country in the world. Until recently, foreigners have considered the quality of Spanish wines barely equal to the quantity; Spanish "plonk" was thought suitable only for parties where people would be too drunk to notice. The Spaniards themselves, as unpretentious in their drinking as in their eating habits, did not help matters by washing wine down with *gaseosa* (carbonated lemonade) and buying wine from great barrels simply marked *tinto* (red) or *blanco* (white), along with a figure indicating the alcohol content. Recently, increased tourism has led to the enormous promotion of Spanish wines, which are now very much in fashion. Villages with excellent wine that has yet to be commercialized do still exist.

The cheap variety of Spanish wines comes mainly from Valdepeñas, in the middle of the dreary plains of La Mancha, Spain's largest wine-growing area. On the other end of the scale are the celebrated red wines of La Rioja, which have a full-bodied, woody flavor thanks to having matured for up to eight years in casks made of American oak (the oldest and best of these wines are labeled *Reserva*). This aging technique was introduced by French vintners from Bordeaux and Burgundy, who moved to the Rioja in the 19th century, hoping to escape the phylloxera epidemic that was destroying the vines in their own country. Curiously, however, there are few places today in France where wine is aged as long as it is here. Among the better Riojas are those of Imperial, Marqués de Murrieta, and Marqués de Riscal. Marqués de Riscal, in fact, has recently moved into the nearby Rueda district, where it has marketed one of Spain's most distinguished white wines. Catalonia specializes in sparkling white wines (the most renowned being Codorniu and Freixenet), and produces Spain's greatest variety of wines overall.

THE ONE Spanish wine that has always been popular with foreigners is sherry. The English have dominated the sherry trade in Jerez de la Frontera since the 16th century, and most of the famous labels are foreign (Domecq, Harvey, and Sandeman, for instance). The classic dry sherry is the *fino*; *amontillado* is deeper in color and taste, and *oloroso* is really a sweet dessert wine. Another fortified Andalusian wine is Manzanilla, which is made in the delightful coastal town of Sanlúcar de Barrameda and depends for its production on the cool sea breezes there. This wine, with a faint tang of the sea, does not travel well, and there are even those who believe that it tastes better in the lower part of Sanlúcar than in the upper town. Sherry and Manzanilla are generally thought of as aperitif wines, and indeed they are the ideal accompaniment to tapas; to eat a Sanlúcar prawn with a glass of Manzanilla is many Spaniards' idea of paradise. Spaniards tend also to drink sherry and Manzanilla when sitting down to a meal, a custom that has yet to catch on outside the country. In England, sherry still has the genteel associations of an Oxford college, but the Spaniards have a more robust attitude toward it. You'll probably never think of sherry in the same way again if you attend Seville's *Feria de*

Abril, where more sherry and Manzanilla are reputedly drunk in a week than in the whole of Spain the rest of the year. Incidentally, Manzanilla has a reputation for not creating a hangover, and some make the dubious claim that it is an excellent cure for gout.

Some of Spain's finest brandies, such as Osborne, Terry, Duque de Alba, and Carlos III, also come from Jerez. Málaga has a sweet dessert wine that enjoyed a vogue with the English in the 19th century (look for the label Scholtz). *Aguardientes* (aquavits) are manufactured throughout Spain, with the most famous brands coming from Chinchón, near Madrid. A sweet and popular liquor called Ponche Caballero comes in a silver-coated bottle that looks like an amateur explosive. Sangría, which many tourists enjoy, should consist of fruits, wine, brandy, and Cointreau but is usually served as a watered-down combination of wine and lemonade with the odd piece of orange thrown in. If you *really* want to look like a tourist, try drinking wine from a *porrón,* a glass vessel from which you pour the wine into your mouth from a distance of at least one foot. A raincoat is recommended.

You are truly initiated into Spanish ways after your first night spent drinking until dawn. Ideally, you'll follow this experience by a snack of *churros* (doughnut fritters) dipped into hot chocolate; the more hardened souls will order a morning glass of aguardiente. After a few hours' sleep, you'll have a proper breakfast (around 11 o'clock) consisting of toast rubbed in garlic or covered in *manteca colorada* (spicy pig's fat). Soon it will be time for the midday tapas—and so a typical Spanish day continues.

—Michael Jacobs

BOOKS AND FILMS

A star contributor to this guide, George Semler has authored two guides of his own, which travelers should use for deeper background in Spain's two largest cities. *Barcelonawalks* and *Madridwalks* each take readers on five walking tours full of historical and literary detail. Spain's people and history are explained through the metaphors of their monuments and landscapes in Jan Morris's brilliant series of essays entitled *Spain;* James A. Michener relates sightseeing anecdotes in *Iberia: Spanish Travels and Reflections. Blood of Spain,* by Ronald Frasier, is an oral history of the Spanish Civil War, woven from hundreds of interviews with survivors. Journalist John Hooper examines the post-Franco era in *The Spaniards.*

Ernest Hemingway is the writer most responsible for embellishing the image of Spain. Read *The Sun Also Rises* (published as *Fiesta* in Britain) for a vicarious visit to Pamplona's running of the bulls. *For Whom the Bell Tolls* depicts the physical and psychological horrors of the Spanish Civil War, and *Death in the Afternoon* contains a convincing argument on bullfighting. Larry Collins and Dominique LaPierre's *Or I'll Dress You in Mourning* tells the saga of El Cordobés, one of Spain's most famous matadors.

H. V. Morton (*A Stranger in Spain*), George Orwell (*Homage to Catalonia*), V. S. Pritchett (*The Spanish Temper*), and Washington Irving (the romantic and mystical *Tales of the Alhambra*) have all paid their respects to Spain. *Farewell España,* by James Gerber, is about the Sephardim, Spanish Jews who were forced to flee during the Inquisition.

Among Spanish writers, the story of the errant knight *Don Quixote,* by Miguel de Cervantes, will always be Spain's towering classic. For more modern fare, try translations of the realism-drenched novels of Galician Camilo José Cela, the 1989 recipient of the Nobel Prize for literature; *The Beehive* and *The Family of Pascual Duarte* are his best-known works. *The Story of Spain,* by Mark Williams, is a fascinating account of the role Spain has played in world events throughout the centuries. One of Spain's great 20th-century novels is Mercé Rodoreda's *The Time of the Doves,* the story of a woman buffeted by the misfortunes of the Spanish civil war. Federico García Lorca's play *Blood Wedding* is a disturbing drama of Spain's repressed yet powerful women. Novelist Javier Marías has been hugely successful in several countries; among his best works in English translation are *A Heart So White* and *Tomorrow in the Battle Think on Me.*

The tragic novel of the bullring, *Blood and Sand,* has had three Hollywood adaptations: the first starring Rudolph Valentino; the second, Tyrone Power, the third, Sharon Stone. The last version shows quite a bit of Andalusia.

Carlos Saura has directed several beautifully crafted classics that are mostly dance—*Carmen, Bodas de Sangre* (Blood Wedding) and *El Amor Brujo.* Luis Buñuel's *Un Chien Andalou* is still a hallmark of surrealism, and *Belle de Jour, Tristana,* and *That Obscure Object of Desire* contain fascinating psychological studies. The last has lovely photography of Seville.

One of the current bad-boy darlings of Spanish cinema is Pedro Almodóvar, whose *Women on the Verge of a Nervous Breakdown* (with some nice shots of Madrid), *Tie Me Up! Tie Me Down!,* and *High Heels* were greeted enthusiastically on both sides of the Atlantic.

Belle Epoque is a recent male-fantasy film about a man desired by three beautiful sisters; and *Barcelona,* the story of three American men and three Spanish women living in Barcelona, is by Whit Stillman, an American married to a Catalan.

SPANISH VOCABULARY

Words and Phrases

English	Spanish	Pronunciation
Basics		
Good morning!	¡Buenos días!	**bway**-nohs **dee**-ahs
Good afternoon!	¡Buenas tardes!	**bway**-nahs **tar**-dess
Good evening!	¡Buenas noches!	**bway**-nahs **no**-chess
Goodbye!	¡Adiós!	ah-dee-**ohss**
Yes/no	Sí/no	see/no
Please	Por favor	pohr fah-**vohr**
May I . . . ?	¿Me permite . . . ?	meh pehr-**mee**-teh
Thank you (very much)	(Muchas) gracias	(**moo**-chas) **grah**-see-as
You're welcome	De nada	deh **nah**-dah
Excuse me	Perdón	pehr-**dohn**
Pardon me/ what did you say?	¿Perdón?/Mande?	pehr-**dohn**/ **mahn**-deh
Could you tell me . . . ?	¿Podría decirme . . . ?	po-**dree**-ah deh-**seer**-meh
I'm sorry	Lo siento	lo **syehn**-to
How are you?	¿Cómo está usted?	**ko**-mo es-**tah** oo-**sted**
Very well, thank you.	Muy bien, gracias.	mwee bee-**en**, **grah**-see-as
And you?	¿Y usted?	ee oos-**ted**
Hello (on the telephone)	Diga	**dee**-gah

Numbers

1	un, uno	oon, **oo**-no
2	dos	dohs
3	tres	tress
4	cuatro	**kwah**-tro
5	cinco	**sink**-oh
6	seis	says
7	siete	see-**et**-eh
8	ocho	**o**-cho
9	nueve	**nweh**-veh
10	diez	dee-**es**
11	once	**ohn**-seh
12	doce	**doh**-seh
13	trece	**treh**-seh
14	catorce	ka-**tohr**-seh
15	quince	**keen**-seh
16	dieciséis	dee-**es**-ee-says
17	diecisiete	dee-**es**-ee-see-**et**-eh
18	dieciocho	dee-**es**-ee-**o**-cho
19	diecinueve	dee-**es**-ee-**nweh**-veh
20	veinte	**vain**-teh
30	treinta	**train**-tah

40	cuarenta	kwah-**ren**-tah
50	cincuenta	seen-**kwen**-tah
60	sesenta	sess-**en**-tah
70	setenta	set-**en**-tah
80	ochenta	oh-**chen**-tah
90	noventa	no-**ven**-tah
100	cien	see-**en**
1,000	mil	meel

Days of the Week

Sunday	domingo	doh-**meen**-goh
Monday	lunes	**loo**-ness
Tuesday	martes	**mahr**-tess
Wednesday	miércoles	me-**air**-koh-less
Thursday	jueves	hoo-**ev**-ess
Friday	viernes	vee-**air**-ness
Saturday	sábado	**sah**-bah-doh

Useful Phrases

Do you speak English?	¿Habla usted inglés?	**ah**-blah oos-**ted** in-**glehs**
I don't speak Spanish	No hablo español	no **ah**-bloh es-pahn-**yol**
I don't understand (you)	No entiendo	no en-tee-**en**-doh
I understand (you)	Entiendo	en-tee-**en**-doh
I don't know	No sé	no seh
What's your name?	¿Cómo se llama usted?	**koh**-mo seh **yah**-mah oos-**ted**?
My name is . . .	Me llamo . . .	meh **yah**-moh
What time is it?	¿Qué hora es?	keh **o**-rah es?
It is one, two, three . . . o'clock.	Es la una. . . . Son las dos, tres	es la **oo**-nah/sohn lahs dohs, tress
Yes, please/No, thank you	Sí, por favor/No, gracias	**see** pohr fah-**vor**/ no **grah**-see-ahs
When?	¿Cuándo?	**kwahn**-doh?
Yesterday/today/tomorrow	Ayer/hoy/mañana	ah-**yehr**/oy/ mahn-**yah**-nah
This morning/afternoon	Esta mañana/tarde	**es**-tah mahn-**yah**-nah/**tar**-deh
Tonight	Esta noche	**es**-tah **no**-cheh
How?	¿Cómo?	**koh**-mo?
What?	¿Qué?	keh?
What is it?	¿Qué es esto?	keh es **es**-toh?
Why?	¿Por qué?	por **keh**?
Who?	¿Quién?	kee-**yen**?
Where is . . . ?	¿Dónde está . . . ?	**dohn**-deh es-**tah**
the train station?	la estación del tren?	la es-tah-**syohn** del **train**
the subway station?	la estación del metro?	la es-ta-**syohn** del **meh**-tro
the bus stop?	la parada del autobús?	la pah-**rah**-dah del oh-toh-**boos**

the post office?	la oficina de correos?	la oh-fee-**see**-nah deh-koh-**reh**-os
the bank?	el banco?	el **bahn**-koh
Open/closed	Abierto/cerrado	ah-bee-**er**-toh/ ser-**ah**-doh
Left/right	Izquierda/derecha	iss-key-**er**-dah/ dare-**eh**-chah
Straight ahead	Derecho	dare-**eh**-choh
Is it near/far?	¿Está cerca/lejos?	es-**tah sehr**-kah/ **leh**-hoss
I'd like . . .	Quisiera . . .	kee-see-**ehr**-ah
a room	un cuarto/una habitación	oon **kwahr**-toh/ **oo**-nah ah-bee-tah-see-**on**
the key	la llave	lah **yah**-veh
I'd like to buy . . .	Quisiera comprar . . .	kee-see-**ehr**-ah kohm-**prahr**
a newspaper	un periódico	oon pehr-ee-**oh**-dee-koh
stamps	sellos	**say**-os
How much is it?	¿Cuánto cuesta?	**kwahn**-toh **kwes**-tah
A little/a lot	Un poquito/ mucho . . .	oon poh-**kee**-toh/ **moo**-choh
More/less	Más/menos	mahss/**men**-ohss

Dining Out

A bottle of . . .	Una bottella de . . .	**oo**-nah bo-**teh**-yah deh
A cup of . . .	Una taza de . . .	**oo**-nah **tah**-thah deh
A glass of . . .	Un vaso de . . .	oon **vah**-so deh
Bill/check	La cuenta	lah **kwen**-tah
Bread	El pan	el pahn
Breakfast	El desayuno	el deh-sah-**yoon**-oh
Butter	La mantequilla	lah man-teh-**key**-yah
Cocktail	Un aperitivo	oon ah-pehr-ee-**tee**-voh
Dinner	La cena	lah **seh**-nah
Menu of the day	Menú del día	meh-**noo** del **dee**-ah
Fork	El tenedor	ehl ten-eh-**dor**
Knife	El cuchillo	el koo-**chee**-yo
Large portion of tapas	Una ración	**oo**-nah rah-see-**ohn**
Lunch	La comida	lah koh-**mee**-dah
Menu	La carta, el menú	lah **cart**-ah, el meh-**noo**
Napkin	La servilleta	lah sehr-vee-**yet**-ah
Pepper	La pimienta	lah pee-**myehn**-tah
Salt	La sal	lah sahl
Spoon	Una cuchara	**oo**-nah koo-**chah**-rah
Sugar	El azúcar	el ah-**thu**-kar

INDEX

✕ = *restaurant*, ⊞ = *hotel*

You've read the book. Now book the trip.

For all the best deals on flights, hotels, rental cars, and vacation packages, book them online at www.previewtravel.com. Then click on our Destination Guides featuring content from Fodor's and more. You'll find hotels, restaurants, attractions, and things to do around the globe. There are even interactive maps, videos, and weather forecasts. You'll have everything you need to make your vacation exactly what you want it to be. All it takes is a trip online.

Travel on Your Terms™
www.previewtravel.com
aol keyword: previewtravel

preview travel SM

WHEREVER YOU TRAVEL, *H*ELP IS NEVER FAR AWAY.

From planning your trip to

providing travel assistance along

the way, American Express®

Travel Service Offices are

always there to help

you do more.

American Express Travel Service
Offices are found in central locations
throughout Spain.

Travel